the national experience

third edition

the national

a history of the United States

John M. Blum

Yale University

Edmund S. Morgan

Yale University

Willie Lee Rose

University of Virginia

Arthur M. Schlesinger, Jr.

The City University of New York

Kenneth M. Stampp

University of California, Berkeley

C. Vann Woodward

Yale University

experience

third edition

HARCOURT BRACE JOVANOVICH, INC.

NEW YORK CHICAGO SAN FRANCISCO ATLANTA

Preface

Men and women make history. Their ideas and their hopes, their goals and contrivances for reaching those goals, shape all experience, past and present. The Indians, the first Americans, had to decide, by deliberation or by default, how to use the continent and its extraordinary resources. So have the successors of the Indians and the children of those successors—the early European settlers, the English colonists, the men and women of the new United States, and the generations that have followed them. Each generation has committed the nation to a complex of policies, some the product of thought and debate, others of habit or inadvertence, still others of calculated or undiscerning indifference. As the nation has grown, as its population has diversified, its economy matured, and its responsibilities multiplied, questions of national policy have become more difficult to understand but no more troubling. It took long thought and hard debate to settle the issues of independence, of democratic reform, of expansion, of slavery, of union itself, of control of private economic power, of resistance to totalitarianism across two oceans. All those issues and many more have made up the national experience.

This book endeavors to recount and explain that experience. It examines both the aspirations (often contradictory among themselves) and the achievements (often less grand than the best hopes) of the American people. It examines, too, the ideas, the institutions, and the processes that fed hope and affected achievement. It focuses on the decisions, positive and negative, that reflected national goals and directed national purposes, and consequently it focuses continually on the men and women who made those decisions, on those who made history. The book emphasizes public policy, but the history of public policy perforce demands continuing discussion of the whole culture that influenced it.

The authors of this book believe that a history emphasizing public policy, so conceived, reveals the fabric and experience of the past more completely than does any other kind of history. They believe, too, that an emphasis on questions of public policy provides the most useful introduction to the history of the United States. In the light of those convictions they have agreed on the focus of this book, on its organization, and on the selection and interpretation of the data it contains. The structure of the separate parts and chapters is now chronological, now topical, depending on the form that seemed most suitable for the explanation of the period or the subject under discussion. The increasing complexity of public issues in the recent past, moreover, has persuaded the authors to devote half of this volume to the period since Reconstruction, indeed more than a third to the twentieth century.

The authors have elected, furthermore, to confine their work to one volume so as to permit instructors to make generous supplementary assignments from the abundance of excellent monographs, biographies, and "problems" books now readily and inexpensively available. Just as there are clear interpretations of the past in those books, so are there in this, for the authors without exception find meaning in history and feel obliged to say what they see; the truth cannot lie halfway between right and wrong. The authors also believe that, especially for the beginning student of history, literature is better read than read about. Consequently, in commenting on belles-lettres and the other arts, they have consciously stressed those expressions and aspects of the arts relevant to an understanding of public policy. Finally, they have arranged to choose the illustrations and the boxed selections from contemporary and other sources in order to enhance and supplement not only the text but its particular focus.

This is a collaborative book in which each of the six contributors has ordinarily written about a period in which he or she is a specialist. Yet each has also executed the general purpose of the whole book. Each section of the book has been read and criticized by several of the contributors. This revision has profited from the assistance of many historians who were kind enough to review portions of the book before it was revised. These include: James M. Banner, Jr., Princeton University; Barton J. Bernstein, Stanford University; Stuart Bruchey, Columbia University; Paul Kleppner, Northern Illinois University; Aileen Kraditor, Boston University; Walter LaFeber, Cornell University; Richard P. McCormick, Rutgers University; John J. McCusker, University of Maryland; Earl Pomeroy, University of Oregon; and Robert

H. Wiebe, Northwestern University. As in all previous editions of this text, so in this one, Everett M. Sims has assisted all the authors with his perceptive and gentle criticisms.

Not even a collaboration as easy and agreeable as this one has been can erase the individuality of the collaborators. Each section of this book displays the particular intellectual and literary style of its contributor; each contributor has been permitted, indeed urged, to remain himself. The ultimate as well as the original responsibility for prose, for historical accuracy, and for interpretation remains that of the author (in one case the authors) of each section of this book: Edmund S. Morgan, Chapters 1–6; Kenneth M. Stampp, Chapters 7–12; Willie Lee Rose, Chapters 13–15; C. Vann Woodward, Chapters 16–21; John M. Blum, Chapters 22–26; John M. Blum and Arthur M. Schlesinger, Jr., together, Chapter 27; and Arthur M. Schlesinger, Jr., Chapters 28–33.

JOHN M. BLUM, *Editor*
New Haven, Connecticut

A note

On the suggestions for additional readings

The lists of suggested readings that follow the chapters of this book are obviously and intentionally selective. They are obviously so because a reasonably complete bibliography of American history would fill a volume larger than this one. They are intentionally so because the authors of the various chapters have tried to suggest to students only those stimulating and useful works that they might profitably and enjoyably explore while studying this text. Consequently each list of suggested readings points to a relatively few significant and well-written books, and each list attempts to emphasize, in so far as possible, books available in inexpensive, paperback editions—books whose titles are marked by an asterisk.

Use of the suggested readings, then, permits a student to begin to range through the rich literature of American history, but interested and energetic students will want to go beyond the lists. They will profit from the bibliographies in many of the works described briefly in this text, especially from the excellent bibliographies in volumes of the New American Nation Series (Harper & Row), edited by R. Morris and H. Commager. They should also consult the card catalogs in the libraries of their colleges and the invaluable bibliography in the *Harvard Guide to American History* (Belknap). For critical comments about the titles they find, they should go on, when they can, to the reviews in such learned journals as the *American Historical Review,* the *Journal of American History,* the *Journal of*

Southern History, and the *William and Mary Quarterly.*

Those students who want to acquire libraries of their own and who want also to economize by purchasing paperback editions will find the availability of titles in paperbacks at best uncertain. Every few months new titles are published and other titles go out of print. For the most recent information about paperbacks, students should consult the handy guide, *Paperbound Books in Print* (Bowker), which appears quarterly.

The reading lists refer to very few articles, not because articles are unimportant, but because they are often rather inaccessible to undergraduates. There are, however, many useful collections of important selected articles, often available in inexpensive editions. So, too, students will have no difficulty in finding collections of contemporary historical documents that add depth and excitement to the study of history. A growing number of thoughtful books organize both contemporary and scholarly materials in units designed to facilitate the investigation of historical problems.

The problems books, documents books, and collections of articles will whet the appetite of engaged students for further reading in the fields of their interest. They can serve in their way, then, as can the lists of suggested readings in this volume, as avenues leading to the adventures of the mind and the development of the understanding that American history affords.

Contents

27 The New Deal 629

28 The decay of the peace 654

29 The world in flames 679

30   *The Cold War*   706

31   *Years of repose*   733

Maps

the national experience

third edition

1

Making use of a new world

Exploration

The first Americans. The first American was an immigrant. Although anthropologists disagree about where man first appeared on earth, no one claims the honor for the Western Hemisphere, which had probably never been seen by human eyes until twenty or thirty or at most forty thousand years ago. Presumably the earliest immigrant came by way of the Bering Straits and was followed by hundreds, perhaps thousands, more who trickled slowly southward, spreading out across North America and funneling through Mexico into Central and South America, venturing across the water to the Caribbean islands and perhaps much farther to the South Pacific. The immigration may have gone on for centuries, and it probably included people from various parts of Asia, Africa, and Europe.

For these early arrivals America was no melting pot. The people we lump together as Indians, or Amerinds, were divided into hundreds of tribes, enormously varied in physical appearance, language, and civilization. Those who made their homes south of the present United States were unquestionably the most numerous and the most skillful in exploiting their territory. They were the inventors of Indian corn (maize), as efficient a method of transforming earth into food as man has ever devised. Corn is so civilized a plant, so highly bred, that botanists have only recently been able to track down the wild ancestors from which the Indian plant-breeders developed it. The early inhabitants of Mexico and South America were skilled in other ways too. They built great cities of stone, richly carved and ornamented. They knew enough mathematics and astronomy to construct a calendar that required no leap year and to predict eclipses of the sun. And they knew enough political science to construct strong governments under which they worked out an advanced division of labor. In central Mexico their economy supported a population of several million with a city (Tenochtitlan, now Mexico City) that ranked in size with those of Europe.

By contrast, the Indians who lived north of Mexico were primitive. They made less effective use of the land, and it supported far fewer of them, probably not many more than a million in the present area of the United States. They grew some corn and other vegetables but also relied on nuts and berries, game and fish, and starved when these were unavailable. In parts of the Southeast they organized governments with real authority, the Powhatan Confederacy in Virginia and the Creek Confederacy in the Gulf Plains. But most often they joined together only loosely in tribes or clans under leaders or chiefs whose authority was merely nominal. They had dignity in abundance, self-reliance, and self-control—it was rare for an Indian to show anger or even to raise his voice. Indeed they were so self-reliant, so individualistic, that even in war it was apt to be every man for himself; and in peace they could not achieve the cooperation and organization, the division of labor, needed to make the most of the country's resources or to defend it against strangers better organized than they.

The rise of kings and commerce.

Such strangers began to arrive shortly after 1492. There had been earlier visitors in the eleventh century, when some wandering Norsemen from Iceland, led by Leif Ericsson, spent a winter in what they called Vinland, probably somewhere in New England or Nova Scotia. A few years later other Icelanders attempted to establish a settlement. But the Norsemen had no real need for this vast continent and went home, leaving behind only the ruins of their encampments to show that they had been there.

If Columbus had sailed when the Norsemen did, his voyages would probably have had as little effect as theirs on the course of history. By 1492, however, Europeans were ready for new worlds. During the intervening centuries two important historical developments had prepared them. One was the rise of a large merchant class hungry for foreign trade. Spices, dyestuffs, and textiles from India and the Far East traveled overland by slow, expensive caravan through Asia or partly by sail through the Red Sea or the Persian Gulf, passing from one dealer to another along the way until they finally reached the marketplaces of Europe. The prices people were willing to pay for these exotic imports were enough to send fifteenth-century sailors in search of sea routes to the source of the treasures. A direct sea route would permit importation in greater volume at less expense and would net the importer a huge profit.

Portugal took the lead in maritime exploration with a new type of vessel, the caravel—faster, more maneuverable, more seaworthy than any formerly known. Portuguese explorers, encouraged by their kings and by Prince Henry the Navigator (1394–1460), discovered the Azores and pushed their caravels farther and farther south along the coast of Africa. At first they were probably seeking only new

Lisbon harbor, fifteenth century

trading opportunities in Africa itself, but by the 1480s they were searching for a way around the continent to the greater riches of the Orient. In 1488 Bartholomeu Diaz rounded the Cape of Good Hope. Ten years later Vasco da Gama reached India.

The rise of kings was the second great development that prepared Europeans to use a new world. At the time of Leif Ericsson's voyage Europe was divided into tiny principalities, usually owing nominal allegiance to a king but actually dominated by local magnates who levied tolls on all trade passing through their territories. Even towns and cities tended to be autonomous, bristling with local regulations that discouraged trade with the outside world. The rise of kings meant the reorganization of society into larger units, into national states more wealthy and more powerful than any one of the towns or cities or principalities of which they were composed. A state organized under a king had the power and resources to cut through the strangling web of local trade barriers, to sponsor exploration for new lands to trade with, and even to seize the lands and their riches when the natives were not strong enough to resist.

During most of the fifteenth century Portugal far outran the rest of Europe in pursuit of foreign trade and of new lands to conquer. Other countries were still too troubled by domestic feuds and foreign wars to offer much competition. The first to emerge as a serious rival was Portugal's neighbor, Spain. And, as luck had it, Spain was also first to find America and first to find a use for it.

Columbus and the Spaniards.

Christopher Columbus, the son of a Genoese weaver, was a man with a mission. He wanted to reach the Orient by sailing west, and he was convinced that the distance was no more than three or four thousand miles. Columbus was wrong, and when he tried to sell his idea the experts told him so. The experts had known for centuries that the world was round, and they had a much better notion of its size than Columbus did. The king of Portugal would have none of his scheme, and neither would anyone else until Queen Isabella of Spain, who was not an expert, decided to take a chance. In the very year that the consolidation of the Spanish monarchy was completed by the conquest of Granada from the Moors, she persuaded her husband, Ferdinand II, to pay for an expedition of three ships and to give Columbus authority, under Spain, over any lands he might discover on the way.

Armed with this commission and with a letter to the emperor of China, Columbus made his magnificent mistake. He failed to deliver the letter but found America (so named after his death for a later explorer, Amerigo Vespucci), at the island of San Salvador, on October 12, 1492. From here he threaded his way through the other Bahamas to Cuba and Hispaniola. By March 15, 1493, he was back in Spain. In succeeding years he explored the rest of the Caribbean area, still looking for China and Japan. Though he did not find them, he did find gold; and everyone in Europe knew what to do with that.

But for the gold, Europeans would probably have looked upon America as a mere obstacle on the route to the Orient. Even after Ferdinand Magellan carried out Columbus' original intention by sailing around the tip of South America (1519–22), explorers continued for two centuries to probe hopefully up American rivers in search of the Pacific. But the Spaniards recognized at once that Columbus' substitute for China might have advantages surpassing the original. With approval of Pope Alexander VI they joined the Portuguese in the Treaty of Tordesillas (1494), dividing the world by a line drawn north and south, 370 leagues west of the Cape Verde Islands (between the present forty-sixth and forty-seventh meridians): Spain was authorized to take possession of all the heathen lands she found to the west of the line; Portugal could do the same to the east. Thereafter Spaniards swarmed over the Caribbean islands and onto the mainland of North and South America.

By comparison with the natives the invaders were few in numbers, but they were courageous, unscrupulous, and armed. They wanted gold, and they were ready to take what the natives had and make them dig for more. The Indians were no match for them. In the West Indies the first Spaniards killed or enslaved wherever they went, and slavery was only a slower form of killing. After working the Caribbean natives to death, they brought in black slaves purchased from the Portuguese, the beginning of an involuntary migration that ultimately carried nearly 10 million Africans to the New World. In the Caribbean islands the Africans died, too, but not before they had earned their purchase price many times over. When the supply of gold ran out, the Spaniards turned them to planting sugar, which in the long run proved even more lucrative—and no less deadly— than digging for gold.

On the mainland, where the Indians were more numerous, small armies led by private adventurers, the conquistadors, subdued whole countries. Hernando Cortez with fifteen hundred men conquered Mexico (1519–21), and Francisco Pizarro with still fewer men conquered Peru (1531–35). The extraordinary conquests made by these small forces were possible because Spanish firearms and cavalry seemed irresistible to men who had never seen either guns or horses before—the Indians frequently took a man on horseback to be some superhuman quadruped. But even with this enormous advantage the Spaniards could scarcely have subdued such large and populous areas if the Indians had not been divided among themselves and if most of them had not already been living as subject peoples. To many an Indian the Spaniard was only a more powerful and exacting master than the Aztec or Inca ruler whom he had served before.

The conquistadors were quick to seize the gold and silver with which the native palaces abounded, but the people themselves were the greatest treasure of Spain's new possessions. Spain in the sixteenth century had a population of about 9 million. The native population of Spanish America probably amounted to many more than that, and they all could be put to work for Spain. In the course of the century thousands of Spaniards

Voyages of Columbus

came to the new land, most of them to profit from the immense supply of cheap labor that Columbus and the conquistadors had delivered to them.

The Spanish government passed increasingly elaborate legislation to alleviate the exploitation of its Indian subjects, and the Church sent countless priests, friars, and bishops to look after their souls. Devoted Spanish clerics never ceased to denounce the way in which their countrymen relentlessly overworked the Indians. But everyone agreed that they ought to work, and neither church nor state was able to prevent the new lords of the land from exacting the utmost from every Indian who came within their reach.

Indians who resisted the Spanish advance were enslaved. Others, technically free, were parceled out in *encomiendas,* at first to the conquerors but later to nearly every Spaniard who appeared on the scene. From the Indians of his *encomienda* the *encomendero* could demand labor at token wages and also an annual tribute. When the government finally brought this form of exploitation under control in the middle of the century, the settlers devised other forms of forced labor.

The Spanish colonists made use of the Indians in mining the great deposits of silver ore that were discovered in both Mexico and Peru and in manning huge ranches and farms (haciendas). While the labor supply lasted, many settlers made fortunes, and the Spanish treasury welcomed the silver that poured in from its numerous taxes, which included a fifth of the proceeds of privately owned mines. But within a century the boom had ended, because overwork, despair, and disease destroyed the Spanish empire's basic resource. In the century after the conquest the native population of Mexico declined from several million (some scholars say 25 million) to little more than a million. A comparable decline is thought to have occurred in Peru.

Of the acknowledged causes for this catastrophic loss, probably the most lethal was the unavoidable introduction of European diseases against which the Indians had no natural resistance. Many of those who did survive were of mixed blood, mestizos as they were called. They, together with the creoles (people of European descent born in Spanish America), the Africans, and the few remaining Indians, furnished a base from which Spanish America in succeeding centuries was to recover its population and perpetuate the ad-

vanced civilization that Spain, at whatever cost, had brought to the New World.

North of Mexico the Spaniards at first found little to interest them. Ponce de León cruised along the shores of the Florida peninsula in 1513, and Panfilo de Narváez and Hernando de Soto both explored the western side of the peninsula and the Gulf Plains before the middle of the sixteenth century. But there was no visible gold or silver about and no extensive population to exploit. Both expeditions marched on across the continent to Mexico without finding anything on the way that made them want to stay. In a futile search for seven legendary cities of gold, Francisco Vásquez de Coronado circled through present Arizona, New Mexico, Texas, Oklahoma, and Kansas (1540–42). He too thought the country not worth taking and returned to Mexico.

During the second half of the sixteenth century the Spaniards began to take a more lasting interest in the northern areas. They established a fort at St. Augustine, Florida (1565), and carried on missionary activities as far north as Port Royal (South Carolina) and for a few years even up to Chesapeake Bay. By the end of the century they were settling into present New Mexico and Arizona, planting missions to benefit the peaceable natives and presidios (military outposts) to hold back hostile ones. The mission was an ambitious undertaking, a nucleus from which Spanish civilization might grow in the borderlands of the empire. The mission gathered Indians (often nomadic in this section) into settled communities where, under supervision of the Church, they were taught Christianity along with techniques of farming and handicrafts. During the seventeenth century Spain sowed missions in Texas and during the eighteenth in California. But long before this the force of the Spanish thrust had spent itself, and other countries were ready to make use of the empty and idle North American continent.

The Europeans in North America. Columbus never saw the shores of North America, nor do we know what European was the first to do so. Perhaps other sailors had happened on it just as the Norsemen had. There may even have been fishermen walking the streets of St. Malo or Bristol or Plymouth who could have told Columbus of a distant coast where pines were tall and codfish plentiful. If so, no chronicler set down their discoveries until in 1497 John Cabot, like Columbus a Genoese,

Virginia Indian chief, by John White

Spanish and French explorations of North America

sailed west for the king of England and returned to report a new land. Henry VII gave Cabot £10 and an annuity of £20. Cabot undertook another voyage the next year, but he and other Europeans thought of the new land as a barrier, not an opportunity.

In 1524 the king of France, Francis I, sent a Florentine navigator, Giovanni da Verrazano, along the Atlantic coast from North Carolina to Nova Scotia in search of a passage through the barrier to the Pacific. Ten years later he sent Jacques Cartier on the same errand. Cartier, encouraged by the promisingly large entrance of the St. Lawrence River, sailed inland as far as the first rapids before giving up. He was sufficiently impressed by the surrounding country, however, to attempt a settlement there in 1541. Since Spain had found riches in the southern continent, it seemed reasonable to expect them in the north as well. When Canadian gold proved to be fool's gold, Canadian diamonds quartz, and Canadian winters terrible, the colonists returned home, and France forgot about North America for the rest of the century.

The first people to find a lasting use for the continent were summer people, who liked the fishing there. Every spring in the ports of France, England, Portugal, and Spain fishermen piled aboard their precarious craft and headed for the Grand Banks, where the continental shelf of North America lies submerged at a depth that codfish find congenial. They set up docks and drying stages ashore and assembled knocked-down dories and other small boats carried in the holds of their ships. They killed a few auks or netted some minnows for bait, rowed far out to the deeper waters, and fished all day with hand lines. Each night they brought in their catch to be dried, salted, and packed for sale in the markets of Europe. Caring little for the doings of their remote monarchs, they lived together in little international communities in Newfoundland and Nova Scotia—sleeping aboard their ships or in rough cabins ashore, planting gardens, and visiting one another of an evening—until the approach of winter sent them and the cod to friendlier climates. None of them seems to have contemplated permanent residence.

New Amsterdam, 1653

As the years passed, more and more Europeans sailed west to cruise along the coasts of North America, catching its codfish, prying into bays and rivers, kidnaping an occasional Indian to show off at home. Gradually they became aware that the country had more to offer than fish and pine trees. Behind the coast lay rivers and lakes teeming with beaver, otter, and other fur-bearing animals, which the Indians were adept at trapping. When Indian and European met, the Indian demanded metals, whose superiority to stone he was quick to recognize. The furs he offered in exchange brought a good price in Europe— especially beaver, which was turned into felt for hats.

Early in the seventeenth century the French, the Dutch, and the Swedes all set up permanent fur-trading posts in America. The great French explorer Samuel de Champlain, after reconnoitering the New England coast and the St. Lawrence region, founded Quebec in 1608. Henry Hudson, an Englishman working for a Dutch company, in 1609 sailed up the river he named for himself; the Dutch planted trading posts there in 1624, on the Delaware River in 1623, and on the Connecticut River in 1633. A Swedish company also maintained posts on the Delaware from 1638 until the Dutch seized them in 1655.

The French and the Dutch came to trade with the Indians, not to subjugate them. Neither in New France nor in New Netherland, as their settlements were called, did the Indian become a slave. Instead he lived on in his customary manner, roaming the woods he had roamed before, though trapping beaver in unaccustomed numbers. Contact with the Europeans inevitably meant new things for him: Christianity, comfort, progress, guns, hatchets, deadly drinks, deadlier diseases, sharper rivalry with other tribes, and a weakening of tribal customs. But the continent was still his. In the course of time both the French and the Dutch did try to transform their trading posts into larger settlements of Europeans, who would supplant rather than suppress or exploit the Indian, but this was only after the English had arrived on the continent and begun to fill it with their children.

Tudor England and the New World

Before England could turn her interests to America at all, before her merchants could support expensive and risky overseas expeditions, she had to experience the same political consolidation under a powerful king that Spain and Portugal had undergone a century earlier. Henry VII, who sent John Cabot to America in 1497, began the job; his son Henry VIII and his granddaughter Elizabeth I finished it. In the process they transformed England from a Catholic country into a Protestant one, a fact that would affect profoundly the land that John Cabot had found across the seas.

Dutch map of 1635

Henry VIII and the Reformation. Soon after Martin Luther launched the Reformation, which split the monolithic west-European Church into Protestant and Roman Catholic segments, Luther's teachings reached England. Perhaps no Englishman was less receptive to them than the king, Henry VIII, who demonstrated his devotion to Rome by writing a book against the German heretic. The pope rewarded Henry by conferring on him the title "Defender of the Faith."

Before many years passed Henry found himself, if no friendlier to Luther, a good deal less friendly to the pope. Henry was the most powerful king England had ever known, so powerful that no baron or lesser local potentate could oppose him. Only one set of men in England dared challenge his authority: the priests and bishops, the monks and abbots, who acknowledged a higher power than Henry not only in the heavens but on earth, in Rome. Moreover, the Church owned about one-fourth of England and collected a yearly income of more than £320,000, much of it from the rent of lands owned by monasteries. When Henry needed funds to meet the cost of England's new and growing governmental machinery, the wealth of the monasteries caught his eye. In 1539 he found an opportunity to lay hold of it.

In 1509 Henry had married Catherine of Aragon, daughter of Ferdinand and Isabella, and in twenty years she bore him no son who lived. Henry desperately wanted an heir, and besides he had grown tired of Catherine. In 1529 he asked the pope for a divorce. When the pope refused, Henry defied him, married Anne Boleyn, severed England's ties with Rome, made himself head of the English Church—and in 1539 confiscated the monastic lands.

The results of Henry's break with Rome. Although Henry never showed the slightest interest in the New World, his divorce and his defiance of the pope had enormous consequences for both England and America.

The first and simplest consequence was that his new wife bore him a daughter, Elizabeth, who was to become England's greatest monarch. Elizabeth became queen in 1558 and ruled for forty-four glorious years—years in which Englishmen triumphed on land, at sea, and in the human spirit. Under her direction England became strong enough to begin the building of a North American empire.

Second, by divorcing his Spanish queen Henry touched off over a hundred years of intermittent hostility with Spain. Spain, the spearhead of Catholicism and the headquarters of the Inquisition, gradually became synonymous in Protestant England with the antichrist. Englishmen attacked the Spaniard most successfully at sea not only by outright war but by privateering against Spanish shipping. The English privateers (or sea dogs, as they came to be called) resembled the earlier conquistadors in their daring, toughness, unscrupulousness, and flair for the spectacular and heroic. But the sea dogs operated on water rather than on land, scouring the Atlantic and the Caribbean for Spanish vessels

English explorations of the New World

laden with gold and silver from the New World. Under Queen Elizabeth privateering against Spain reached its height and drew England's attention to the riches of America.

Third, Henry's break with Rome gave impetus to a Protestant movement in England that had been covertly under way for some years. Its adherents interpreted Henry's defiance of the pope as a total repudiation of Roman hierarchy, ritual, and doctrine. Henry himself would have been content to serve as England's pope without substantially altering the internal organization or doctrines of the Church. But he could not wholly control the forces he had unleashed. The ideas of Luther and of the French reformer John Calvin became increasingly popular during the next 125 years; and, as their numbers grew, the extreme Calvinists—the Puritans—became increasingly discontent with the incomplete reformation of the English Church. Many of them

Henry VIII of England

would come to America with a view to completing the Reformation there.

Finally, Henry's confiscation of the monasteries set off a train of unexpected events that indirectly provided still more Englishmen willing to people a new world. Henry, not content with the income from the lands he had confiscated, began to sell them; succeeding monarchs continued the process, selling other royal lands as well. They were led to do so partly by a steady rise in prices during the sixteenth and seventeenth centuries (the so-called Price Revolution) that was induced or accelerated by the flow of Spanish gold and silver from America. Other people felt the pinch, especially landlords whose rents were fixed by custom and unalterable. They too began selling land to make ends meet. The turnover of so much real estate had widespread repercussions: in some places rich men got richer and poor men poorer, while in other places the rich were getting poor and the poor rich. The sale of monastic lands was certainly not wholly responsible for this upheaval, but it was a step in the chain of events that destroyed the social and economic security of large numbers of Englishmen and helped to make the fortunes of others, especially the merchants. Whoever lost from the rise of prices and the sale of lands, it was not they. As the sixteenth century wore on, they accumulated more and more capital, enough to finance overseas expeditions, while men who lost their homes or fortunes began to think of regaining them, perhaps in another part of the world.

Gilbert finds a use for North America.

The historical developments that were set in motion by Henry VIII's break with Rome became significant for America only gradually. After the voyage of John Cabot in 1497, Englishmen showed very little interest in the New World until 1576, when the Cathay Company (Cathay was another name for China) was formed to trade with China by way of North America. The company sent Martin Frobisher to find a way through the continent. He probed the northern waters and found Baffin Land and Frobisher's Bay, where glittering gold-flecked rocks diverted his attention from further search. With the usual captive Indian and a case of ore samples, he hurried back to England. The assayers declared that the ore was indeed gold, and he returned to North America for more. When the twelve hundred tons he brought back turned out to be worthless, the Cathay Company folded. For years thereafter Englishmen with capital to invest were wary of risking it in America.

Although the Cathay Company had planned to establish a small permanent settlement in America, it was intended to serve merely as a supply station for voyages to the Orient. The first Englishman, possibly the first European, to have a glimmering of the northern continent's colonial future was a soldier of fortune named Humphrey Gilbert. Gilbert had served the queen in Ireland, where his skill in exterminating the natives won him a knighthood. While there he concocted a scheme for settling Ireland with Englishmen. But then his interest shifted. North America was a larger Ireland. Englishmen planted there could exploit the natives (the counterpart of the wild Irish), forestall Spanish settlement, catch codfish, and search for a passage to the Pacific

(Gilbert wrote a tract in 1576 to prove that there must be one). When the passage was found, they could supply ships passing through. What was more immediately attractive, an American colony would serve as a base from which sea dogs could raid the Spanish treasure fleets that sailed every year from the Caribbean. In every way America was more attractive than Ireland.

Gilbert, impelled by greed and chauvinism, had vision: he was the first to see America as a place for Englishmen to live. In 1578 he induced Queen Elizabeth to grant him a charter empowering him to discover and take possession of North American lands not claimed by any other Christian monarch. Within six years he was supposed to settle a colony over which he would exercise absolute authority, provided he made no laws contrary to the Christian faith, and provided he gave the queen one-fifth of the gold and silver he mined (a provision generally inserted by subsequent monarchs in such charters).

Gilbert made two attempts to found his colony. The first attempt, in 1578, is a mystery. No one knows where he went or what he found, but there is a strong suspicion that he went not far and found a number of ships not his own—in short, that piracy, for the moment, proved more attractive than colonization.

Gilbert's second attempt, in 1583, was a larger undertaking, for by this time he had managed to sell his idea to other Englishmen: noblemen who felt the pressure of inflated prices and the loss of lands and power their fathers had had; merchants who scented opportunities for trade in the new land; discontented religious minorities, privateers, pirates, paupers, and fools. Drawing men and money from these divergent sources, Gilbert was able to launch an expedition. He got underway in June 1583, with two hundred sixty prospective settlers and five ships, one of which he stole from a pirate just before departing and took along, pirate crew and all. Before reaching America one ship turned back for lack of provisions. The pirate ship had no such trouble: she simply plundered another vessel encountered along the way.

In August the expedition reached Newfoundland, where Gilbert came upon a sizable international community of summer fishermen. He probably did not intend to establish his colony this far north (though it should be remembered that Newfoundland is south of

Elizabeth, the Virgin Queen

England), but he made a great ceremony of taking possession of the settlement. The fishermen humored him and even agreed to pay rent for their fishing stages. They probably calculated, rightly, that no one would come to collect it.

After two weeks in Newfoundland, the men on one of the ships decided they had had enough of America and sailed for home. Gilbert, with the other three, cruised southward, filled with enthusiasm by the splendor of the uninhabited coast. He lost another ship with eighty men on a reef and shortly thereafter was obliged to turn the two remaining ships back to England for supplies. In mid-ocean they ran into an alarmingly heavy sea, but Gilbert demonstrated his nonchalance by sitting on the afterdeck of his small vessel reading a book. At one point he shouted across to a friend in the other ship: "We are as near to heaven by sea as by land." That night, as the others watched, the lights of his vessel went out. No more was ever heard of the man who first envisaged England's American empire.

Raleigh and Roanoke. Although Gilbert's ventures accomplished nothing concrete, he had stirred the imagination of other Englishmen: the kind of men who backed him would back other expeditions to the New World. Before his last voyage, he had enlisted the talents of his younger half-brother, Sir Walter Raleigh. Raleigh equaled Gilbert in daring and exceeded him in polish. He was a favorite with Queen Elizabeth, who gave him nearly everything he asked for. After Gilbert's death, Raleigh asked her for a charter to found a colony in the New World.

Raleigh was as interested as Gilbert in piracy against Spanish treasure fleets, but like Gilbert he wanted his colony to be more than a base of operations. From the beginning he planned it as a permanent settlement, and he enlisted his friend Richard Hakluyt to write propaganda persuading Englishmen to emigrate. Hakluyt was already fascinated by the idea of colonization and developed into England's greatest advocate of overseas expansion.

Raleigh got his charter in 1584 and immediately sent out a reconnoitering force under Philip Amadas and Arthur Barlow. They made their landfall a couple of thousand miles south of Newfoundland—perhaps in order to be closer to the Spaniards—and explored the coast south of Chesapeake Bay. When they returned with glowing descriptions of the region, Raleigh named it Virginia in honor of Elizabeth, the Virgin Queen.

In 1585 Raleigh fitted out an expedition to settle Roanoke Island, near the present boundary between Virginia and North Carolina. The group, under the command of Ralph Lane, included John White, an artist; Thomas Cavendish, who later sailed round the world; and Thomas Hariot, a noted mathematician. White made some excellent drawings of the American Indians, the best executed during the whole colonial period; Hariot took notes from which he later prepared the first detailed description of any part of the present United States. The settlers themselves, instead of digging in, spent their time searching Virginia's rivers unsuccessfully for the Pacific and her shores unsuccessfully for gold. In June 1586, when Sir Francis Drake called to visit them after searching successfully for gold in the Spanish fortresses of the West Indies, the settlers all climbed aboard with him and went home.

Raleigh tried again the next year, 1587, sending one hundred twenty persons under the command of John White. White spent a month getting the new Roanoke settlement started and then returned to England for supplies, leaving his daughter, her husband and their new-born child with the settlers. A supply fleet commanded by Sir Richard Grenville was prepared, but the Spaniards chose this moment for an all-out attack on England (the great Spanish Armada), and Grenville and his ships were pressed into service for defense. Not until 1590 could White sail back to Roanoke, and when he got there his colonists had completely vanished. Someone had carved the name of a neighboring island, CROATOAN, on a post. But no trace of the colonists was ever found there. Presumably, hostile Indians had overwhelmed them, but to this day no real clue to their fate has been found.

The sixteenth century closed without an English colony in North America. Raleigh turned his attention to South America. Richard Hakluyt sang the praises of England's explorers and published accounts of their great voyages in *The Principall Navigations, Voiages, and Discoveries of the English Nation* (1589). But no one else with the vision of a Gilbert or a Raleigh stepped forward to lead Englishmen to new homes.

Actually Gilbert and Raleigh were as wrong,

Sir Walter Raleigh: he sent Englishmen to new homes

Arrival in Virginia (the Roanoke colony)

in their way, as Columbus. He expected to find China and found America. They expected not only to settle North America but to make a profit out of it. They failed, and even if their settlements had succeeded there would almost certainly have been no profit, unless from piracy. But Gilbert and Raleigh were not the last to be mistaken about the New World. In 1606 another group of Englishmen risked their money, and lost it, in an enterprise from which in the fullness of time grew the United States.

The founding of Virginia

While Elizabeth reigned, men of daring in England enjoyed risking their money and their lives for her by attacking Spain. Her successor, James I, was so different from the great queen that he has always suffered by comparison. Elizabeth knew everything about power and kept her own counsel. James knew everything about everything and told everybody. One of the things he knew was that the war with Spain had gone on long enough. In 1604, the year after his accession, he made a peace that lasted twenty years.

James was probably right in ending the war, but Englishmen did not love him for it, especially after he told them that raids on Spanish shipping must cease. During the sixteenth century the line between legitimate privateering and piracy had been left conveniently thin, and hijacked Spanish bullion had

Sir Francis Drake: knighted for his exploits

poured into England. Francis Drake alone picked up $200 million worth of loot from Spanish ships he met during his dramatic voyage around the globe (1577–80). Elizabeth knighted Drake for his exploits and cheerfully collected a share of the profits. But James foreswore such profits for his subjects as well as himself. As a result, men with spare lives and money began to think again about getting gold where the Spaniards got it. Efforts to find it in North America had so far been unsuccessful, but no one had tried very hard. Even if no gold was found, the continent might hold other things of value. After the Roanoke venture of 1586, Thomas Hariot had described some promising native commodities, including sassafras, a root that the Spaniards were selling in Europe at high prices as a cure for syphilis. And piracy itself, now that

Virginia and New England grants

The men who petitioned the king in 1606 were divided into two groups, one from London, the other from Plymouth; and the king gave them a charter incorporating two companies for the colonization of North America: the Virginia Company of Plymouth was to operate in the northern part of the continent, and the Virginia Company of London in the southern part. The companies planned to send out settlers who would agree to relinquish the fruits of their labors to the investors for the first seven years; after that the settlers could enrich themselves. Anyone willing to pay his own passage was free to begin getting rich at once.

Both companies got off to a quick start. The Plymouth group dispatched an exploratory expedition in 1606 and in 1607 founded a colony at the mouth of the Sagadahoc River in Maine. The colony survived only one winter. The Virginia Company of London, in December 1606, sent over its first settlers, a hundred men and four boys crammed aboard three small ships, the *Susan Constant,* the *Godspeed,* and the *Discovery.* In May 1607 they sailed up a river they called the James and landed on a peninsula they called Jamestown. Swampy and forested, the site was well situated for defense but a haven for mosquitoes and microbes. The colonists made almost every possible mistake in their new environment, but they also corrected their mistakes; and they had the vision, the courage, or the foolhardiness to stick it out.

Their first big problem was leadership. In the charter granting authority to settle the colony the king had retained authority to govern the colony himself, and he exercised it through a council sitting in England. This council in turn acted through another sitting in Virginia. The Virginia council consisted of seven men with a president who presided over its meetings but who had no authority to give orders of his own and no power to enforce orders transmitted from the king's council in England. Government by council proved to be no government at all. The members of the council in the colony quarreled with one another, and the colonists, undisciplined and disorganized, neglected the elementary tasks of plowing, planting, and building.

Fortunately one man had the nerve to take command. John Smith, twenty-seven years old, of humble background but no humility, was not popular with the other members of the council, all men of greater age, impor-

the king had pledged his protection to Spanish shipping, might still be carried on from a base out of royal reach on the other side of the Atlantic. And so the tantalizing possibility of riches from America again lured Englishmen to try to plant a colony there.

Jamestown. In 1606 a number of noblemen, gentlemen, and merchants joined to petition the king for authority to establish colonies in America. Merchants had discovered a means of undertaking large and dangerous enterprises without risking financial ruin. Their scheme was the joint-stock company, in which participants profited or suffered in proportion to the number of shares they purchased. By investing modestly in a number of companies a man would gain only modest profits from successful ventures, but he would also avoid heavy losses from unsuccessful ones. In this way, through many small contributions, it was possible to accumulate the large amounts of capital necessary for undertakings that were beyond the range of private fortunes. The joint-stock company became the principal instrument of England's overseas expansion.

tance, and indecision. Smith had spent four years fighting the Turks in Hungary, where he had been captured, sold into slavery, and rescued by fair maidens. In Virginia, by his own account, when the other members of the council proved fools, knaves, or cowards he took control of the colony, explored it, mapped it, overawed the Indians (and was again rescued by a maiden, Pocahontas), and obtained from them the corn that kept the settlers from starving. He stopped the disorganized scramble for gold, built fortifications, planted Indian corn, and cut a cargo of cedar wood to send back to the investors as the first tangible evidence of the colony's worth. He later told about it with such relish for his own role that readers ever since have suspected his veracity. Nevertheless, wherever his account can be checked, it holds up. Moreover, he prepared a surprisingly accurate map of the region—a map that could only have been the product of first-hand observation.

In London, however, the armchair colonizers were not pleased. Smith, they heard, was unkind to the Indians. He had failed to find either gold or the Pacific Ocean. And some of the other members of the Virginia council, returning to the mother country, described his leadership as tyranny. The company did recognize, however, that the colony needed stronger direction. In 1609 it obtained a new royal charter establishing a new governing council (resident in London) composed entirely of company members and empowered to appoint an all-powerful governor or governors in the colony. The council decided on a single governor, who should choose a council of Virginians to advise him. To prevent a repetition of the colony's earlier squabbles over leadership and to ensure that the governor's council understood that its function was limited to advice, the London council specified that the Virginia councilors "shall not have, single nor together, anie bindinge or negative voice or power." The post of governor went not to Smith but to a nobleman, Lord De La Warr.

Under the new charter the company launched an elaborate campaign to sell Virginia to the English public. With the proceeds of stock sold at £12 10s. a share, it fitted out a fleet of nine vessels to carry some six hundred emigrants. Some were servants who had agreed to work for the company for seven years in return for their passage. The rest paid their own way (passage was worth about £6)

C. Smith taketh the King of Pamaunkee prisoner 1608

John Smith had the nerve to take command

and received a share of stock as a bonus. All would work together until 1616, at which time the servants would be freed, the profits would be divided among the shareholders both in England and in America, and every shareholder would receive at least a hundred acres of land.

The expedition set sail from Plymouth in June 1609. Though one of the ships was wrecked at Bermuda, at least four hundred settlers reached Virginia that summer. Unfortunately Lord De La Warr was not among them. His departure from England had been delayed, and his substitute, Sir Thomas Gates, was on the ship lost at Bermuda. John Smith, injured in a gunpowder explosion, returned to England in the fall of 1609, and from then until the arrival of Governor Thomas Dale in 1611 the colony was without effective government and fell into worse disorder than before. Men starved; fortifications fell to ruins; at one point the entire colony had embarked, prepared to abandon the settlement, when a relief ship arrived. After 1611, Governor Dale and Governor Samuel Argall, who succeeded him, imposed rigorous disciplinary laws and re-

I tell thee, gold is more plentiful there than copper is with us; and for as much red copper as I can bring, I'll have thrice the weight in gold. Why, man, all their dripping-pans and their chamber-pots are pure gold; and all the chains with which they chain up their streets are massy gold; all the prisoners they take are fettered in gold; and for rubies and diamonds, they go forth on holidays and gather 'hem by the seashore, to hang on their children's coats, and stick in their caps, as commonly as our children wear saffron-gilt brooches, and groats with holes in 'hem.

From John Marston, *Eastward Ho!*, 1605.

sumed the course set by John Smith. Once again the colonists began to plant corn, erect and repair fortifications, and build houses.

But the men who left England for Virginia wanted more than corn bread and a place to lay their heads. To them survival was a means to an end, and they kept looking for a way to wealth, a way to live better in Virginia than they had in England. Since they had found no gold or silver, they had to find some other commodity of high value that they could produce in sufficient quantity and with sufficient ease to make the long voyage to English or European markets worthwhile. They tried cedar. They tried sassafras. But the market for both was quickly satisfied. The directors of the company had high hopes at different times for wines, silk, iron, tar. But in 1612, though they were not at once aware of it, the Virginians discovered their future—in smoke.

Tobacco was native to America. The Indians had taught the Spaniards to use it, and the Spaniards had taught the rest of Europe. At first it was valued only as a medicine, said to cure any disease afflicting a man from the waist up. But by the end of the sixteenth century people were smoking for the fun of it, much to the distress of those who knew better, including King James, and much to the joy of Spanish tobacco merchants. The Indians of Virginia smoked a native variety, coarse and unpalatable. John Rolfe, who later gained greater fame by marrying Pocahontas, tried planting the West Indian species in 1612, just as other settlers were experimenting with other Spanish products. The West Indian variety grew extraordinarily well in Virginia, but it did not smoke as well as when grown in the tropics and it consequently brought a lower price. It was nevertheless by far the most profitable commodity Virginia had yet been made to yield. The settlers turned enthusiastically to tobacco culture and by 1617

were able to ship twenty thousand pounds to England.

The Virginia Company's great effort. The stockholders of the Virginia Company were pleased to have their faltering confidence in the colony reconfirmed by the promising shipments of tobacco. Hitherto they had received nothing but a few tons of sassafras, cedar, and other trifles in return for an investment of approximately £50,000. In fact, when they sat down to divide up their profits in 1616, they had found nothing to divide except the land itself, and to many of them it hardly seemed worth dividing. Moreover, most of the servants they had sent over to work for the company had served out their time and had become free to work for themselves. To hire more men to produce so little would be to throw good money after bad.

Although the colonists' success with tobacco rekindled the expectations of the investors, they did not suppose that the colony could prosper with that product alone. But if Virginia could grow tobacco there must be other things it could produce too. They must keep the settlers experimenting until the right products were found, and then everyone could sit back and reap the profits of perseverance. While this new burst of enthusiasm was upon them, the members of the Virginia Company decided to revitalize and expand their venture by means of a reform program, which they inaugurated in 1618 under the leadership of Sir Edwin Sandys, a prominent figure in the English House of Commons. The program contained four points designed to entice more adventurers (investors), more planters (settlers), and more servants:

1. By overhauling its land policies the company made both investment and emigration more profitable. Henceforth anyone who paid for the passage of a man to Virginia, himself

People were smoking for fun, to the distress of those who knew better

THE SMOKING AGE
OR
The Life and Death of Tobacco

In those twelve years of Sir Thomas Smythe his government, we aver that the colony for the most part remained in great want and misery under most severe and cruel laws sent over in print, and contrary to the express letter of the king in his most gracious charter, and as mercilessly executed, often times without trial or judgment. The allowance in those times for a man was only eight ounces of meal and half a pint of peas for a day, the one and the other mouldy, rotten, full of cobwebs and maggots, loathsome to man and not fit for beasts, which forced many to flee for relief to the savage enemy, who being taken again were put to sundry deaths as by hanging, shooting and breaking upon the wheel, and others were forced by famine to filch for their bellies, of whom one for stealing 2 or 3 pints of oatmeal had a bodkin thrust through his tongue and was tied with a chain to a tree until he starved.... Many through these extremities, being weary of life, digged holes in the earth and hid themselves till they famished.... So lamentable was our scarcity that we were constrained to eat dogs, cats, rats, snakes, toadstools, horse-hides and what not; one man out of the misery that he endured, killing his wife, powdered her up to eat her, for which he was burned. Many besides fed on the corpses of dead men, and one who had gotten insatiable, out of custom to that food could not be restrained, until such time as he was executed for it.

From "The Tragical Relation of Virginia Assembly," 1624.

Another view of Virginia: maggots and rats

or anyone else, received a "headright" of fifty acres on which he would pay a "quitrent" of a shilling a year to the company. Wealthy investors could thus acquire large tracts (called "particular plantations") simply by sending men to cultivate them on a share-cropping basis. The company in turn, with almost unlimited acreage at its disposal, would gain a perpetual income from quitrents.

2. To make life in Virginia more like life in England the company relaxed the severity of its discipline and assured actual and potential settlers that henceforth the colony would be governed by English law and that the colonists would have the rights of Englishmen.

3. Even more important, the company decided to give the settlers a voice in the management of the colony. The planters were allowed to elect representatives to an assembly, which, along with the governor's appointed council, would have power to make laws for the colony.

4. The final point in the new program called for an all-out effort to diversify the colony's activities. The company itself took responsibility for sending over various craftsmen: vintners, ironworkers, brick-makers, glass-blowers. Somewhere among these skills, it was hoped, would be the right ones to give Virginia a healthy and profitable economy of which tobacco-growing would be only one part.

For five years and more, new settlers streamed into the colony. By the end of 1618 the population, which was only 400 in April of that year, had risen to 1,000. Between 1618 and 1624, about 4,000 more arrived. To judge by the number of ships landing passengers in Virginia, the colony was a success. To judge by the number of graves dug there, it was not. In spite of the heavy immigration the population in 1625 stood at only 1,210 by official count. Some of the settlers had doubtless returned to England, but for most of them the colony had been a death trap. Sandys (who never set foot in Virginia) had sent shipload after shipload of men without supplies. Ill fed, ill clothed, and ill housed, they sickened and died. In 1622 the Indians rose up and killed 347.

Those who survived found themselves subjected to ruthless exploitation, unlike anything known in England. From 1618 until about 1629 Virginia tobacco brought prices ranging from a shilling to three shillings a pound. Since a man could produce 500 to 1000 pounds a year, his labor was worth at least £25 and might be worth over £100 a year. As a result, those who had the nerve, the strength, and the authority (legal or illegal) to

Many went; few survived

control the labor of other men could make small fortunes in a short time. In the scramble for the servants and tenants who arrived each year, the governor and members of his council were among the most successful in laying hold of large numbers. As long as tobacco prices held up, they made handsome profits—but for themselves, not for the company. While they grew rich on the labors of the men the company sent, the company itself was going bankrupt; and rumors reached England that men and boys were sold back and forth in Virginia like horses. In 1624 when James I appointed a commission to investigate, the commissioners reported such shocking treatment of the settlers that the king dissolved the company and resumed control of the colony himself.

Thus ended the Virginia Company of London. At the cost of several thousand lives and perhaps £100,000 it had in the course of eighteen years established only twelve hundred Englishmen in America. But in spite of its wretched beginning, the colony was there to stay.

After the king took over, the population gradually rose as ships that came to carry away the tobacco every year continued to bring new supplies of men and some women. But, because English women were not used for field work, the planters imported many more men than women, giving Virginia a lopsided sex ratio that lasted for most of the century. While the bonanza prices lasted, the newcomers were exploited as ruthlessly as their predecessors. The king's authority at three thousand miles' distance was no greater

obstacle to the local labor barons than the company's had been. But in 1630 tobacco dropped to a penny a pound and then, after a few wild fluctuations, settled for about twenty-five years at a little more than two pence a pound. At that price it still offered reasonable rewards but did not excite the kind of cupidity that had made Virginia in the 1620s a scene of misery, profiteering, and peculation. Men began to settle down and to think of the colony less as a labor camp and more as a home. They built houses, grew more corn, raised more cattle, went to church, and stopped working each other quite so hard. But they kept on growing tobacco.

In the cultivation of tobacco the Virginians had found a way to use America. And, in spite of all efforts to turn them to other occupations, they persisted in growing tobacco. They demonstrated, indeed, a certain headstrongness that England was to find characteristic of Englishmen living in America. In 1619 (before any other permanent English settlement had even been launched) Virginians met in their first representative assembly and passed their first laws. When James I took control of the colony in 1624 he did not provide for the continuance of a representative assembly; nor did his son Charles I, who became king in 1625. Charles was having enough difficulties with his own Parliament in England. But the governors he appointed found it impossible to rule Virginia without the help of Virginians. Though Charles refused them recognition until 1639, annual assemblies of representatives began making laws again in 1629 and have been doing so ever since.

The founding of New England

James I stopped the Virginia Company but not the flow of Englishmen to America. The social, religious, and economic forces that had made their appearance in the time of Henry VIII were still at work, upsetting the lives of an increasing number of people. Prices were still rising; lands were changing hands; and sheep were grazing where men once drove their plows. To make matters worse, a depression settled over the woolens industry in the 1620s and lasted through the next decade. The land seemed "weary of her inhabitants," and the new king made it seem wearier by levying taxes without the consent of Parliament and by repressive measures against religious dis-

senters. The result was the Great Migration, in which perhaps as many as fifty thousand people left for the New World. The exodus lasted until 1640, when Englishmen began to see a more hopeful future for their own country. By that year Virginia's population had risen to eight thousand; Maryland had been founded and peopled; and so had the Bermudas, Barbados, St. Kitts, and other West Indian islands. About twenty thousand of the emigrants came to that northern part of Virginia now called New England.

After the failure of its Sagadahoc settlement in 1608, the Virginia Company of Plymouth had shown only sporadic interest in its territory. The company's most important action was to send Captain John Smith to explore the country in 1614; Smith named the place New England and first described its attractions. But his backers were not sufficiently impressed or not sufficiently affluent to support him in attempts to colonize it, and in 1620 they surrendered their rights to a more distinguished group of forty men who were impressed with New England but not with Smith.

The new group, made up of a duke, two marquises, six earls, a viscount, three barons, nineteen knights, the dean of a cathedral, and seven esquires, had visions of organizing feudal estates on a grand scale. Led by Sir Ferdinando Gorges, a Devonshire man who had also been the leading spirit of the Plymouth group, they gained from the king a charter establishing them as the Council for New England and granting them proprietary and governmental rights over the whole area from the fortieth to the forty-eighth parallels and from the Atlantic to the Pacific. In addition they were to have a monopoly of fishing in the offshore waters.

Cut up forty ways, the region would have provided each member of the council with a huge estate, a whole new England larger than the old. But the future of New England was to be less grand than gritty. In the very month in which the Council for New England was created, a band of humble but determined men and women put ashore below Cape Cod and began to use the country in their own way. Their way was called Puritanism.

Puritanism. Puritanism has come to mean prudishness, cruelty, fanaticism, superstition, Philistinism, and hypocrisy. Actually, the Puritans who settled New England had no greater share of these human qualities than did their contemporaries or their descendants. What they did possess in stronger measure than other men was John Calvin's belief that God is omnipotent and good and that men are evil and helpless, predestined before they are born either to salvation or to eternal torment. Critics of this doctrine of predestination have always charged that it leads to moral indifference: if a man's present behavior does not affect his future salvation, why be good? But the facts belie the criticism: those who accept Calvin's doctrine have always outdone their neighbors in efforts to follow God's commandments as given in the Bible. The Puritan, knowing his

efforts to be futile, nevertheless took a holy joy in them. They made him feel close to God's transcendent purpose. They also helped to ease his agonizing concern over whether he was headed for heaven or hell. Even though good behavior could not alter a man's predestined fate, it was observable that religious conversion (a personal experience by which God let a saved man know he was saved) often befell those who did try to live godly lives. Moreover, conversion manifested itself outwardly in renewed and intensified efforts to obey God's commands. A man's striving might thus be a sign that he was saved.

Not content with his own striving, the Puritan also felt responsible for his fellow men. Indeed he was certain that any society that failed to honor God by punishing infractions of his commands would meet with his sudden wrath, not in the next world but here and now. Governments, he thought, existed for the purpose of enforcing obedience to God.

The Puritan's ideas of what God required were less rigorous than many people have supposed. God did *not* require that men wear drab clothes, live in drab houses, or drink water when something stronger was available. He *did* require that they refrain from drunkenness, theft, murder, adultery, and breaches of the Sabbath. Puritans were vastly uneasy about the English government's indifference to these evils. They were even more concerned because the Church of England—supported by the government—retained corrupt practices inherited from Rome and not sanctioned by God in the Bible. They thought the Church should abolish bishops and ecclesiastical courts and such other relics of Catholicism as kneeling and the use of priestly vestments and altars.

Puritans all agreed on what was wrong with the English Church, but they disagreed on how to make it right. Though they all relied on the Bible for guidance, they extracted different opinions from it about how God wanted his churches to be run. The group that settled New England were Congregationalists, and they differed from the other principal group of Puritans, the Presbyterians, in two beliefs: first, that there should be no general church organization with authority over individual churches; second, that a church should admit to membership only those who gave visible evidence of their Christian beliefs. Persons who openly flouted the laws of God

John Calvin (*as drawn by one of his students*)

Plymouth, England, 1591

should be excluded or expelled. Congregationalists wanted to change the structure and practices of the Church to conform with these beliefs.

Their dissatisfaction with the Church of England led them to the problem of all reformers: whether to remain inside a corrupt institution and try to reform it from within or to separate from it and start a pure new one. In 1583 an early Congregational leader, Robert Browne, advocated the latter course in a pamphlet appropriately titled *Reformation without Tarrying for any.* His followers, known as Separatists, deserted the English Church to meet in little churches of their own—of necessity in secret because the government did not acknowledge or permit any church other than the established one. But most Congregationalists were not Separatists. They preferred to stay within the Church of England and await the opportunity for reform.

The Pilgrims. The men and women who began the settlement of New England at Plymouth in 1620 were Separatists, part of a group that originated in 1607 at the village of Scrooby in Nottinghamshire. The English government did not look with favor on Separatists. Under Elizabeth two had been executed and many more imprisoned for long

periods. Although the members of the Scrooby group were not seriously molested, they were distressed by the hostility of the government and the contempt of their neighbors. In 1608–09 they made their way, not without many hardships, to Holland, where the Dutch were known to be more tolerant. But as the years passed in Leyden they were still unhappy: their children were turning into Dutchmen; the only work they could get was day labor, poorly paid; and the weak among them were being tempted by the other religions that flourished under Dutch tolerance. They thought of Virginia, a place where they might remain Englishmen and work for themselves, a place isolated from contagious heretical religions and far enough from government control so that they could have a church of their own design.

Since they were poor people, without funds to finance their passage, they proposed to set up a ''particular plantation'' in Virginia for a group of English merchants. As in other such ventures, they would work together for seven years as a community, and then the profits would be divided between them and their sponsors. They evidently intended to establish themselves some distance north of the other settlements (the claims of the Virginia Company extended as far north as the present site of New York City) and at one point even considered seeking a grant from the Council for New England, which was then being formed. In the end one hundred two persons boarded the *Mayflower,* bound for Virginia. But after making their landfall at Cape Cod and exploring the coast, they decided to stay. In late December 1620 they began a settlement, which they named Plymouth after the English port from which they had embarked.

These ''Pilgrims'' as Americans have come to call them, were as poorly equipped in everything but courage as any group that ever landed in America. They had guns but knew little about shooting. They planned to become fishermen but knew nothing about fishing. They expected to settle in Virginia but landed in New England without enough supplies to last the winter. Like their predecessors and contemporaries in Virginia, many of them sickened and died. But the living stuck it out and justified their own estimate of themselves: three years earlier they had written to the men they hoped would sponsor their emigration, ''It is not with us as with other men, whom small things can discourage, or small discontentments cause to wish themselves at home again." Since New England was outside the jurisdiction of Virginia's government, the Pilgrims established a government of their own by the *Mayflower* Compact, which forty-one adult males subscribed before going ashore. For governor they elected John Carver; and upon his death in 1621 they chose William Bradford, who recorded the colony's struggles in an eloquent history and was reelected nearly every year from 1621 to his death in 1657. Under his leadership the Pilgrims liquidated their debt to the English merchants (who had failed to send them the supplies they expected) and established for themselves a self-supporting community.

The Pilgrim settlement was important as a demonstration that men could live in New England. It remained, however, a small and humble community, attracting few immigrants. The great Puritan exodus did not begin until ten years after the landing of the Pilgrims. It engulfed, but did not greatly expand, the Plymouth colony.

The Massachusetts Bay Company. While the Pilgrims went their way outside the Church of England first in Holland and then in America, other Puritans, both Congregational and Presbyterian, continued the struggle to reform the Church from within. While James I reigned, the struggle did not seem hopeless. Although James scolded them, and even married his son to a Catholic princess, he did not "harry them out of the land," as he once threatened to do. If he had tried, they would have had enough strength in Parliament to stop him. But when Charles I became king in 1625, he quarreled incessantly with Parliament and finally announced in 1629 that he intended to rule henceforth without it. At the same time he befriended a group of aspiring churchmen who were as eager to suppress Puritanism as the Puritans were to make it prevail. Under the leadership of William Laud, whom Charles made Bishop of London in 1628 and Archbishop of Canterbury in 1633, these friends of the king deprived Puritan ministers of their pulpits and moved the Church of England ever closer to Rome in its ceremonies, vestments, and doctrines.

As the prospects of reform grew dim and the sins of the land grew heavy, the Puritans feared that God was preparing England for some great purging catastrophe. In despair and hope they too turned their thoughts to America, where they might escape God's wrath, worship in purity, and gather strength for future victory.

In 1628 a number of prominent congregational Puritans bought their way into a commercial company that was being organized in London. Called the New England Company, it took over the rights of a defunct group, the Dorchester Adventurers, which in 1623 had tried to plant a farming and fishing settlement at Cape Ann. From the Council for New England, the new company obtained a charter authorizing settlement in the area known as Massachusetts Bay, to the north of Plymouth. A year later, on March 4, 1629, the New England Company reorganized as the Massachusetts Bay Company and had its proprietary and governmental rights confirmed by a new charter obtained directly from the king.

In the shuffle the Puritan stockholders gained control of the company, and they had something more than commerce in mind. The royal charter bestowed on the company full authority to govern its own territory and made no mention of where company meetings were to be held. In 1629 the Puritans simply voted to transfer the company to Massachusetts. This meant that if Puritan company members emigrated, they would have full control of the government under which they would live. Thus in one bold stroke the Puritans won for themselves the opportunity to do in Massachusetts what Puritans for nearly a century had been yearning to do in England.

To act as governor, the company elected a solid Puritan squire, John Winthrop of Groton Manor, Suffolk. He and perhaps a dozen other company members, all Puritans, crossed the ocean in 1630, accompanied by a thousand like-minded men and women, who preferred a wilderness governed by Puritans to a civilized land governed by Charles I. Before the year was over they had planted settlements around Massachusetts Bay at Dorchester, Roxbury, Watertown, Newtown (Cambridge), Charlestown, and Boston. During the next ten years, as Charles ruled without Parliament and Laud grew increasingly powerful, fifteen or twenty thousand more followed and their towns stretched out in all directions.

Winthrop and the handful of other company members had authority from the king's charter to govern this whole body of settlers. But Winthrop and his friends wanted a broader base for their government. And so, shortly after their arrival in New England, they trans-

**Massachusetts:
a contented view**

I prayse God, we haue many occasions of comfort heer, and doe hope, that our dayes of Affliction will soon haue an ende, and that the Lord will doe vs more goode in the ende, then we could haue expected, that will abundantly recompence for all the trouble we haue endured. yet we may not looke at great thinges heer, it is enough that we shall haue heaven, though we should passe through hell to it. we heer enjoye God and Jesus Christ, is not this enough? What would we haue more? I thanke God, I like so well to be heer, as I doe not repent my comminge.... I neuer fared better in my life, neuer slept better, neuer had more contente of minde, which comes meerly of the Lordes good hande, for we haue not the like meanes of these comforts heer which we had in England, but the Lord is allsufficient, blessed be his holy name, if he please, he can still vphold vs in this estate, but if he shall see good to make vs partakers with others in more Affliction, his will be doone, he is our God, and may dispose of vs as he sees good.

From John Winthrop, Letter to His Wife, 1630.

formed the Massachusetts Bay Company from a trading company into a commonwealth. In 1631 they admitted more than a hundred adult males as members, or "freemen," of the company eligible to vote at its meetings. The term "freeman" in seventeenth-century England generally meant a voting member of a business corporation or of an incorporated city or borough. In America the word came to mean a man who had the right to vote for representatives to the assembly in his colony. In Massachusetts, when the company and colony were blended, the freemen of the company became the freemen of the colony. The increase in their numbers did not remove the colony from Puritan control, because most of the new freemen (who must have been a majority of the heads of families then in the colony) were probably Puritans; moreover, it was specified that, in the future, members of Puritan congregational churches (and only such) should be eligible to become freemen.

The charter, which had envisaged only a trading company with limited membership, provided that company members assemble as a General Court four times a year to make laws. Between the meetings of the General Court a governor (or his second in command, a deputy governor) and a council of eighteen "assistants," elected annually, were to manage the company. When Winthrop and his associates opened freemanship to all church members, they foresaw that the number of freemen would soon become too large to as-

semble and work together as a legislature; and they decided to leave lawmaking to the council of assistants, who were still to be elected annually by all the freemen. But in 1634 the freemen insisted that the lawmaking powers assigned to them by the charter be delegated to "deputies" elected from each settlement. Henceforth the General Court consisted of the governor, the deputy governor, the executive council of assistants, and a body of deputies, or representatives. All were elected annually by the freemen. Since the company had power to govern the colony, this General Court was in reality both the legislature and the supreme court of the colony. Here, in truth, was a self-governing commonwealth, a Puritan republic.

Puritan New England. The freedom to do as they pleased posed many new problems to men who had not hitherto wielded the powers of government. Reformers and idealists are notoriously prone to dissipate their energies wrangling with one another. And there were disagreements in New England, though not so numerous or severe as has sometimes been suggested. The New England Puritans agreed on a great deal. They wanted congregational churches. They did not want bishops, church courts, or hierarchy. They wanted a government that would take seriously its obligation to enforce God's commandments and to support pure religion. Accordingly they confined voting to church members and levied taxes to pay ministers' salaries. But, contrary to com-

her cam ouer xxv passeingares and thare cume backe agayn fouer skore and od parsones and as maney more wolld a cume if thay had whare withe all to .bringe them hom.... We may liue if we haue suppleyes euerey yere from ould eingland other weyse we can not subeseiste I maye as I will worck hard sete an ackorne of eindey wheat and if we do not set it withe fishe and that will cost xxs and if we set it witheought fishe they shall haue but a por crope so father I pray consedre of my cause for her will be but a uerey por beinge and no beinge withe ought Louinge father youer helpe withe prouisseyones from ould eingland I had thought to a cam home in theis sheipe for my prouisseyones ware all moste all spente but that I humbley thanck you for youer gret loue and kindnes in sendinge me s[o]me prouis-syones or elles i shold and myne a bine halef famiuyshed but now I will if it plese god that I haue my hellthe I will plant what corne I can and if prouisseyones be no cheper betwein theis and mychellmes and that I do not her from you what I wase beste to do I purpose to c[o]me hom at myckellmes

From John Pond, Letter to His Father, 1631.

---

mon assumption, they did not want their clergy to take any hand in government. For a minister to exercise political authority of any kind seemed to the Puritans a dangerous step toward Roman Catholicism. Compared to the clergy of England and Europe the New England minister, though highly influential, had little authority even within his own church. He taught, prayed, preached, and admonished; he commanded respect—else he lost his job—but he did not rule his church. Admissions to membership, censures, pardons, and excommunications were all decided by vote of the church members.

Neither the leaders of the Massachusetts Bay Colony nor the great majority of settlers were Separatists. Though they organized their own churches in the congregational manner, they took pains to affirm their love and friendship for the churches of England. Some even thought that the churches of Rome were not beyond redemption. But among the thousands who stepped ashore at Boston every year were substantial numbers of Separatists and other extremists, full of zeal and eloquence, full of impatience with anyone who disagreed with them. John Winthrop, whom the freemen elected governor year after year during most of his life, was good at turning away wrath and directing zeal to constructive ends. But during the three years from 1634 to 1637, when lesser men sat in the governor's chair, Massachusetts all but succumbed to the denunciations of a brilliant, saintlike, intractable man and a brilliant, proud, magnetic woman.

Roger Williams, who arrived in 1631, was a Separatist. He wanted everyone to repudiate the wicked churches of England. Moreover, he insisted that the royal charter of Massachusetts contained a lie (in claiming that England first discovered the region) and that the king had had no right to grant the charter or the people to accept it without first purchasing the land from the natives. If word got back to England that the Massachusetts government allowed the expression of such subversive ideas, the king might be prompted to take control of the colony and end the Puritan republic. Williams also tried to persuade people that no government had authority over religious matters, not even the right to punish breaches of the Sabbath. In a community which believed that the prime purpose of government was to enforce God's commandments, his teachings were rank sedition.

Williams was a man whom everyone loved on sight; even John Winthrop became his good friend. But he propagated his inflammatory ideas so insistently, first as assistant to the minister and then as minister of the church at Salem, that the unity of the colony was endangered and the government finally felt obliged to banish him in 1636. He went to Rhode Island, where he was joined by those who believed him. There, while retaining his conviction that the state had no authority over religious matters, he reached the conclusion that in the existing phase of human history God authorized no organized churches at all. In spite of this view, which few of his followers could share, he retained the love and respect of his neighbors and lived out a long and useful life as the leading citizen of the new colony.

Scarcely had Williams been banished when a new threat to the civil and religious security of Massachusetts appeared: Anne Hutchinson, the wife of a merchant whom Winthrop described as "a man of a very mild temper and weak parts, and wholly guided by his wife." An amateur theologian, Mrs. Hutchinson took to elucidating her minister's Sunday sermons in informal gatherings of her neighbors. As the circle of her listeners steadily widened, her discourses became more original, for her keen and imaginative mind could not be contained within the standard doctrines of Puritanism. Starting from the accepted principle that God grants salvation without regard to human merit, she denied (what other Puritans affirmed) that good conduct could be a sign of salvation and affirmed (what other Puritans denied) that the Holy Spirit in the hearts of true believers relieved them of responsibility to obey the laws of God. So, at least, her enemies charged, and she gave substance to their accusation by asserting that all the New England ministers except her favorite, John Cotton, and her brother-in-law, John Wheelwright, were preaching unsound doctrines. By emphasizing morality, she said, they were deluding their congregations into the false assumption that good deeds would get them into heaven. The clergymen hotly denied what was virtually a charge of heresy, and Mrs. Hutchinson herself protested that she had intended no insult. Nevertheless, a host of devoted Bostonians hung on every word she uttered and refused to conceal their contempt for her opponents. The colony split into hostile camps, and finally Mrs. Hutchinson was brought before the authorities. After they had cross-examined her for two days, she made the mistake of claiming that she had received an immediate revelation from God. To Puritan ears, this was blasphemy. So Mrs. Hutchinson too was banished and went to Rhode Island, which thus became the refuge for Puritans with too much originality.

After Charles I was forced to resummon Parliament in 1640, Roger Williams applied to that body (which was overwhelmingly Puritan) for a charter for his colony. The charter, granted in 1644, gave the Rhode Islanders a government much like that of the colony from which they had been expelled: they elected annually a representative assembly, a council of assistants, and a governor (at first called a president), but they did not confine voting to church members or collect taxes to support the clergy. In 1663 the existing government was confirmed by a royal charter that also guaranteed the "liberty in religious concernments" which had been the colony's distinction from the beginning.

Meanwhile another part of New England was filling up with Puritans who differed from those of Massachusetts primarily in their desire for more elbow room. In 1636 Thomas Hooker, the minister of Newtown (Cambridge), led an exodus overland to the fertile Connecticut Valley, where the small garrison of a Dutch trading post at Fort Hope (Hartford) was unable to prevent them from settling. They formed a government by a simple agreement among themselves (called the Fundamental Orders). The model, once again, was Massachusetts (but voting was not confined to church members), and again the existing arrangement was confirmed by royal charter (1662). The charter also joined to Connecticut the colony of New Haven, initiated in 1638 by a group of Londoners who could find no lands in Massachusetts to suit them.

The settlers of New Haven, beginning with a good supply of capital, had been disappointed in their expectations of a thriving commerce; but they had succeeded in establishing a somewhat stricter government than existed elsewhere in New England, and they were not altogether happy about the union with Connecticut.

There was nevertheless no serious difference between New Haven and the rest of New England. In New Haven as in Plymouth, Massachusetts, Rhode Island, and Connecticut, the population was predominantly Puritan. Puritans directed public policy, and the only serious resistance came from other Puritans. Although some of the inhabitants may have been indifferent or hostile to Puritanism, they were never strong enough or discontented enough to challenge Puritan control.

Settlers who wanted nothing more from the New World than an opportunity to make their fortunes or to live more comfortably than in England had little reason to object to Puritan control anyway. The government frowned on private cupidity when it threatened the public welfare, but Puritans saw no virtue in poverty. They had not traveled three thousand miles simply to starve in a holier manner than in

England. They were building a society for all the world to copy, a "city upon a hill," and they meant it to be a success, economically as well as religiously.

So long as the Great Migration lasted, the colonists prospered by selling cattle and provisions to the newcomers each year. When the Migration ended in 1640, New England had its first depression. The leaders looked hard for some native product they could sell to the outside world. Fortunately for them, they found no single product such as the Virginians' tobacco, and they consequently developed a more balanced and more prosperous economy. They caught fish, raised corn and wheat, bred cattle, cut lumber, and built ships. Before many years had passed, New England vessels were prowling the Caribbean and the Mediterranean, peddling their assorted wares, transporting other people's, and bringing home the profits to the city on the hill. By the middle of the seventeenth century New England had laid down its economic as well as its religious foundations.

Proprietary ventures

During the years that Puritans were building their republics in New England, non-Puritans were trying to establish private domains there and elsewhere. Three years after the Pilgrims landed, Sir Ferdinando Gorges, the most active member of the Council for New England, had backed a settlement at Wessagusset (Weymouth) in the Massachusetts Bay region, but it broke up after a year. Its failure discouraged the rest of the council from further efforts, and they apparently raised no serious objections in 1628 when the Earl of Warwick, president of the council, took it upon himself to grant the Puritans permission to settle the Bay area. In 1637 the Council for New England finally dissolved, leaving behind a host of shadowy claims. Only one claim was perfected: that of Ferdinando Gorges to the region north of the Merrimac River. Gorges divided the area with another would-be New England lord, John Mason, and in 1639 obtained a separate royal charter for his own share. He died in 1647, with no feudal retainers in his New World barony except a few hardy fishermen who pledged allegiance to no one. Massachusetts annexed the whole region in 1651.

The king authorized other ambitious gentlemen to colonize Newfoundland, Nova Scotia, and the Carolinas, but to no effect. The first English nobleman to realize the aristocrat's dream of founding a New World domain for his family was George Calvert, Lord Baltimore. A notable figure in the court of James I, Calvert had become interested in America first as a member of the Virginia Company and later as a member of the Council for New England. In 1620 he purchased rights in southeastern Newfoundland from another noble dreamer and started a settlement there. When he visited the place himself, he found that "from the middle of October to the middst of May there is a sadd face of wynter upon all this land." Deciding to leave Newfoundland to the fishermen, he asked the king for a grant farther south. The charter, which was in the making when Calvert died in 1632, was finally issued to his son Cecilius. It conveyed to him 10 million acres on Chesapeake Bay, where the Calvert family was to have complete powers of government. The colony was to be known as Maryland, in honor of the queen of Charles I.

The name was appropriate, for both the queen and the Calverts were Catholics. Maryland was to be a feudal seigniory and at the same time a religious refuge. As a feudal seigniory it came nearer to success than any other attempted in America. Though the Calverts did not live there, they governed the colony (sometimes through a younger son), owned all the public lands, granted small estates or "manors" to their friends, and collected rents from the settlers. Because Virginia, Plymouth, and Massachusetts lent a hand, the settlers of Maryland were spared the early days of starvation that had been suffered by other colonists. Tobacco grew as readily in Maryland as in Virginia, and the two colonies became identical in their economic pursuits and interests.

As a religious refuge Maryland also succeeded. Although official hostility to Catholicism had relaxed in England under Charles, Catholics were still required by law to take oaths and to attend religious services that conflicted with their beliefs. In Maryland they would be free to worship as they chose, and

George Calvert, Lord Baltimore

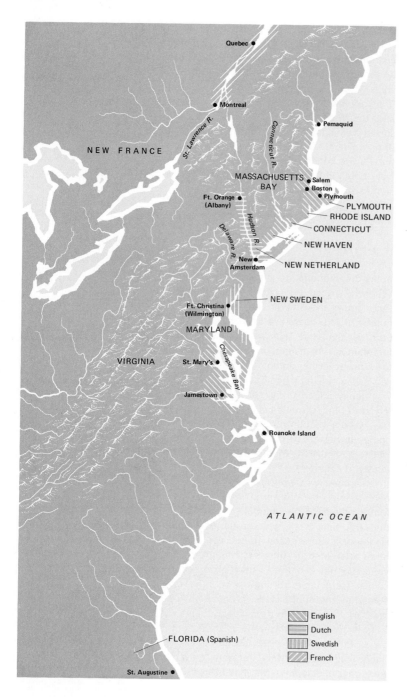

The colonies in 1650

Map labels:

Quebec

Montreal

Pemaquid

St. Lawrence R.

Connecticut R.

NEW FRANCE

MASSACHUSETTS BAY

Salem

Boston

Plymouth

PLYMOUTH

RHODE ISLAND

CONNECTICUT

NEW HAVEN

NEW NETHERLAND

Ft. Orange (Albany)

Hudson R.

Delaware R.

New Amsterdam

NEW SWEDEN

Ft. Christina (Wilmington)

MARYLAND

VIRGINIA

St. Mary's

Chesapeake Bay

Jamestown

Roanoke Island

ATLANTIC OCEAN

English
Dutch
Swedish
French

FLORIDA (Spanish)

St. Augustine

so would other Christians. As it turned out, more Puritans came to the colony than Catholics. The Calverts welcomed both, and from the time of the first settlement in 1634 tried to prevent either group from oppressing the other. When the Jesuits threatened to become too powerful, Baltimore, in 1641, forbade them to hold land in Maryland. The Puritans were harder to handle, especially after 1640, when their friends gained the upper hand in England, but Baltimore did his best to restrain them. By the terms of his charter he was obliged to obtain the consent of the "freemen" (presumably in this case the term meant all adult males not bound as servants) to all legislation. As the population increased, the freemen deputed a few individuals to act for them in this matter, and thus arose a representative assembly similar to those which developed in the other colonies. This assembly in 1649 consented to the famous Maryland Toleration Act, securing freedom of worship for all Christians, whether Protestant or Catholic, who believed in the Trinity. The Calverts upheld the act through successive generations and thus made their colony, like Rhode Island, a model of what the rest of America was one day to become.

By the middle of the seventeenth century England had seeded North America. Many more immigrants were to come, from England and elsewhere, but the future was already visible on the coasts of New England and of Chesapeake Bay. Englishmen had moved in, and whether they favored toleration, as in Maryland and Rhode Island, or intolerance, as in Massachusetts, whether they caught fish or grew tobacco, the continent was effectively theirs.

A good account of the American Indians before the coming of the white man is Kenneth MacGowan and J. A. Hester, Jr., *Early Man in the New World** (1950). Clark Wissler, *Indians of the United States: Four Centuries of Their History and Culture** (1940), is more comprehensive.

Anyone interested in the age of exploration should give his first attention to S. E. Morison's great biography of Columbus, *Admiral of the Ocean Sea* (1942), and to his lively and authoritative *European Discovery of America: The Northern Voyages, 500–1600* (1971). J. H. Parry, *The Age of Reconnaissance* (1963), covers voyages to all the continents. A penetrating and succinct study of Spanish exploits and problems is Charles Gibson, *Spain in America** (1966), which contains a good bibliography of the subject. On the English voyages there is no substitute for Richard Hakluyt's collection of first-hand accounts, *The Principall Navigations, Voiages, and Discoveries of the English Nation* (1589, 1599), reprinted in Everyman's Library, *Hakluyt's Voyages*, 8 vols. Hakluyt's work has been carried on in the voluminous publications of the Hakluyt Society. Among these, see especially the volumes edited by D. B. Quinn, *Voyages and Colonising Enterprises of Sir Humphrey Gilbert*, 2 vols. (1940), and *The Roanoke Voyages, 1584-1590,* 2 vols, (1955).

The English Reformation is ably discussed in F. M. Powicke, *The Reformation in England** (1941). M. M. Knappen, *Tudor Puritanism** (1939), and Patrick Collinson, *The Elizabethan Puritan Movement* (1967), are the best accounts of early Puritanism. Two challenging interpretations are C. H. and Katherine George, *The Protestant Mind of the English Reformation* (1961), and Michael Walzer, *The Revolution of the Saints** (1965). For social conditions in England see Carl Bridenbaugh, *Vexed and Troubled Englishmen, 1590–1642* (1968), and Peter Laslett, *The World We Have Lost** (1965); for economic conditions, Joan Thirsk, ed., *The Agrarian History of England and Wales, 1500–1640* (1967). Mildred Campbell, *The English Yeoman under Elizabeth and the Early Stuarts* (1942), is well matched by Lawrence Stone's monumental *Crisis of the Aristocracy* (1965). The best account of English political and legal institutions is Wallace Notestein, *The English People on the Eve of Colonization, 1603–1630** (1954).

On the first permanent English settlements in America, the most convenient and the most authoritative account is still C. M. Andrews, *The Colonial Period of American History,* Vols. I–III* (1934–37). For the Southern colonies this should be supplemented by W. F. Craven, *The Southern Colonies in the Seventeenth Century* (1949). J. E. Pomfret and F. M. Shumway, *Founding the American Colonies* (1970), incorporates recent research. Captain John Smith tells his own story in *Travels and Works of Captain John Smith,* 2 vols. (1910), ed. by Edward Arber and A. G. Bradley. The fullest modern account is Philip L. Barbour, *The Three Worlds of Captain John Smith* (1964). W. F. Craven, *The Dissolution of the Virginia Company* (1932), is a masterful study of the internal divisions that impaired the company's efforts in America.

The New England Puritans have been subjected to the scrutiny of historians, sympathetic and unsympathetic, from the time the settlers first stepped ashore. William Bradford, governor of the Plymouth Colony, told the story of the Pilgrims in *Of Plymouth Plantation,* an American classic that can best be read in S. E. Morison's edition (1952). The most thorough history by a modern scholar is George Langdon, *Pilgrim Colony: A History of New Plymouth, 1620–1691** (1966). In his *Journal,* Governor John Winthrop did for Massachusetts Bay what Bradford did for Plymouth. The best edition is that of James Savage, 2 vols. (1853), but this is hard to come by. The only edition in print is the modernized and expurgated one of J. K. Hosmer, 2 vols. (1908). For a contrast with Bradford and Winthrop, read Thomas Morton, *New English Canaan* (1637, 1883).

S. E. Morison, *Builders of the Bay Colony** (1930), is by all odds the best modern introduction to the history of New England. Morison continued his study of the Puritans in his works on Harvard, *The Founding of Harvard College* (1935) and *Harvard in the Seventeenth Century,* 2 vols. (1936).

*Available in a paperback edition.

New England Puritanism is also the subject of the most profound study of intellectual history yet written by an American, Perry Miller, *The New England Mind: The Seventeenth Century** (1939) and *The New England Mind: From Colony to Province** (1953). These volumes were preceded by his briefer study, *Orthodoxy in Massachusetts, 1630–1650** (1933), the subject of which falls chronologically between the two. He explores other aspects of New England history in a brilliant collection of essays, *Errand into the Wilderness** (1956). Some of Miller's conclusions are modified in Robert Middlekauff's sensitive study, *The Mathers* (1971), and by David Hall's examination of the New England ministry in *The Faithful Shepherd* (1972). Puritan domestic life and social relations are examined in E. S. Morgan, *The Puritan Family** (1966), and in John Demos, *A Little Commonwealth* (1970). P. J. Greven, *Four Generations* (1969), traces the demographic changes over a century among the families that founded Andover, Massachusetts. Stephen Foster analyzes Puritan social thought in *Their Solitary Way* (1971). The conduct of church affairs is treated in Ola Winslow, *Meetinghouse Hill* (1952); the Puritan conception of the church in E. S. Morgan, *Visible Saints** (1963), and in R. G. Pope, *The Half-Way Covenant* (1969). The best biography of Roger Williams is Ola Winslow, *Master Roger Williams* (1957). E. S. Morgan, *Roger Williams: The Church and the State** (1967), analyzes Williams' ideas. Emery Battis, *Saints and Sectaries* (1962), gives a provocative psychological interpretation of Anne Hutchinson, and Kai Erikson gives a sociological interpretation in *Wayward Puritans** (1966).

A valuable study of early New England economic history is Bernard Bailyn, *The New England Merchants in the Seventeenth Century** (1955). E. S. Morgan has dealt with some of the political problems faced by the founders of Massachusetts in *The Puritan Dilemma: The Story of John Winthrop** (1958). Later Puritan problems as exemplified in the Winthrop family are treated in R. S. Dunn, *Puritans and Yankees: The Winthrop Dynasty of New England* (1962). G. L. Haskins, *Law and Authority in Early Massachusetts* (1960), describes political and social as well as legal institutions, and T. H. Breen, *The Character of the Good Ruler* (1970), treats the development of Puritan political thought during the first century of settlement. E. S. Morgan, *Puritan Political Ideas** (1966), is a collection of source materials.

*Available in a paperback edition.

The pattern of empire

The first settlements in America, which cost Englishmen dearly in lives and money, cost the English government nothing. But in authorizing settlement the government did expect to gain something more than an outlet for disgruntled Puritans, misguided merchants, and adventurous fortune-seekers. Every European government, during the sixteenth, seventeenth, and eighteenth centuries, followed an economic policy that has been known since 1776, when Adam Smith coined the word, as mercantilism.

Mercantilism

Mercantilism meant that the state directed all economic activities within its borders, subordinating private profit to public good. In particular the government sought to increase national wealth by discouraging imports and encouraging exports. The English government let Englishmen go to America because it was persuaded that their presence there would further this end.

Long before the settlement of Jamestown, Richard Hakluyt had explained how the mother country could profit from American colonies: they would furnish England with supplies such as lumber, tar, and hemp, which she was buying from other countries, and they would offer a market for the woolens that were England's principal export. ''It behooves this realm,'' Hakluyt wrote in 1584, ''if it mean . . . not negligently and sleepingly to slide into beggary, to foresee and plant [a colony] at Norumbega [a name for northern North America] or some like place, were it not for anything else but for the hope of the sale of our wool.'' What England wanted from America was what Hakluyt said she would get: a market for her woolen cloth and other manufactures and a source of supply for raw materials that she had to import from other countries.

What England wanted was not incompatible with what the colonists wanted: a ready market for the raw materials they had to sell and a cheap source for the manufactures they had to buy. During the years of settlement, the shortage of labor in North America made manufacturing unfeasible. England, on the other hand, had a surplus of labor and a low wage scale that made for cheap manufactured goods. It was mutually advantageous for the colonies to buy manufactures from the mother country and for the mother country to buy raw materials from the colonies.

The British empire in America was based on this compatibility of interests. But, while the interests were compatible, they required guidance to make them coincide. Left to themselves, the colonies might peddle their produce in France or Holland instead of England

*And in reguard his Majesties Plantations beyond the Seas are en-
habited and peopled by his Subjects of this His Kingdome of England,
For the maintaining a greater correspondence and kindnesse betweene
them and keepeing them in a firmer dependance upon it, and rendring
them yet more beneficiall and advantagious unto it in the farther
Imployment and Encrease of English Shipping and Seamen, vent of
English Woollen and other Manufactures and Commodities rendring
the Navigation to and from the same more safe and cheape, and
makeing this Kingdome a Staple not onely of the Comodities of those
Plantations but alsoe of the Commodities of other Countryes and
Places for the supplying of them, and it being the usage of other
Nations to keepe their Trade to themselves, Be it enacted ... that ...
noe Commoditie of the Growth Production or Manufacture of Europe
shall be imported into any ... Place to His Majestie belonging ... but
what shall be bona fide and without fraud laden and shipped in England
Wales ... and in English built Shipping ... and which shall be carryed
directly thence to the said Lands.*

From The Second Navigation Act, 1663.

and take home French textiles instead of English ones, or they might produce materials not needed in England. In order to make the system work, it was necessary for the mother country to maintain continuous supervision and control over the economic activities of the settlers just as she did over the activities of Englishmen at home. The English government never doubted its right to exercise such control, but it was slow to develop consistent directives or effective machinery for carrying them out.

England's imperial delay. In the early years, before the colonies began to fulfill Hakluyt's glowing predictions, economic regulation probably did not seem urgent. Although the English government in 1621 ordered all Virginia tobacco to be brought to England, the order was not enforced, perhaps because English authorities considered it a mixed blessing for the nation to have its own private supply of smoke. But other regulations, adopted from time to time, also went unenforced. One reason was distance. Three thousand miles of ocean made a formidable barrier in the seventeenth century. Although it was much faster and easier to travel long distances by water than by land, even over water three thousand miles was space enough in which to lose messages, orders, and interest.

A more serious obstacle to English control than either the distance or the seeming unimportance of the colonies was politics. During the seventeenth century, when most of her American colonies were founded, England was torn by a struggle for power between king and Parliament. In the 1630s Charles I ruled without Parliament, but by 1640 he needed it to pay his bills. He called it, dismissed it, called it again, and then found that he could not dismiss it any more. In 1642 the members raised an army to make war on him; in 1649 they cut off his head, and for eleven years England had no king. In his place from 1649 to 1658 stood Oliver Cromwell, the soldier who had defeated him.

When Charles II, son of the old king, was placed on the throne in 1660, the acts passed by Parliament in the preceding eleven years were declared null and void. But Charles had the good sense to realize that English kings henceforth must work with Parliament or not at all. His brother and successor, James II, had no sense, and within three years of his accession in 1685 he had to flee the country. Parliament quietly replaced him with William and Mary in the bloodless Revolution of 1688. After 1688 the king was still no cipher in government, but everyone understood that he was subordinate to Parliament.

All but one (Georgia) of the thirteen colonies that later became the United States were founded before 1688, during the years when the ultimate location of sovereignty in England was uncertain. They were all founded under authority of the king, and their relationship to Parliament remained ambiguous. Parliament sometimes passed legislation affecting them,

*Charles I:
he needed Parliament
to pay his bills*

The use of America: opportunity

but even after 1688 it did not do so regularly. Yet if the king had denied the authority of Parliament in the colonies, Parliament would doubtless have brought him up short.

Distance, indifference, and the uncertain location of authority in England conspired to delay the development of a consistent and continuous colonial policy. From the founding of Virginia in 1607 until the middle of the seventeenth century the colonies interested king and Parliament only as a minor prize in the contest for sovereignty. In 1633, when Charles I was trying to rule without Parlia-ment, he appointed a commission headed by Archbishop Laud to govern the colonies. But the commissioners were too busy in England to do anything about America. During the English civil wars of the 1640s, Parliament and king both claimed authority over the colo-nies, but neither was able to exercise it.

Oliver Cromwell was the first ruler of Eng-land sure enough of his position at home to think seriously about fitting the colonies into a general imperial scheme. In 1650 and 1651 he secured legislation to keep foreign shipping out of the colonies. He also planned a great expansion of the empire in the Caribbean and tried to persuade New Englanders to move to the West Indies, where the cultivation of sugar and other tropical products promised rich re-wards. But his legislation against foreign ship-ping led to war with the uncooperative Dutch;

his large military and naval expedition to the West Indies in 1655 captured only Jamaica; and his powers of persuasion proved insuffi-cient to lure New Englanders from their rocky soil. They suspected, perhaps, that Puritanism would not work well in the tropics.

The Navigation Acts. When Charles II came to the throne in 1660, the colonies, in spite of Cromwell's failures, had grown enough to require attention. Virginia and Maryland were exporting over 7 million pounds of tobacco yearly, much of which never reached England, and New England harbored a group of mer-chants whose ships were already familiar in the markets of the world. English merchants, awakened to the potentialities of colonial trade, pressed the government for measures to prevent the profits from leaking into the pockets of foreign rivals. What they wanted was not merely to exclude foreign shipping from the colonies (as Cromwell had attempted in the acts of 1650 and 1651) but to direct colonial trade into channels profitable to the mother country. King and Parliament, in the first flush of Restoration harmony, agreed on two acts to take care of the matter.

These so-called Navigation Acts (1660 and 1663) were modified from time to time during the ensuing century, but their basic principles remained the same: (1) they forbade all trade with the colonies except in ships owned and

Oliver Cromwell

New Englanders away from home: "Sea Captains at Surinam," by John Greenwood

constructed there or in England and manned by crews of which at least three-quarters were English or colonial; (2) they forbade the transportation *from* the colonies *to* any place except England or another English colony of certain "enumerated commodities," namely sugar, cotton, indigo, dyewoods, ginger, and tobacco; and (3) they forbade the transportation of European goods *to* the colonies *from* any place except England.

Subsequent modification of the Navigation Acts consisted mainly of additions to the list of enumerated commodities (rice in 1704, naval stores in 1705, copper and furs in 1721) or specific limitations on, or encouragement of, colonial products. The act of 1705 that enumerated naval stores (pitch, tar, turpentine, masts, spars) also placed bounties on their production. The Wool Act (1699) forbade export from the colonies of certain textiles manufactured there. The Hat Act (1732) forbade export of colonial-made hats. The Iron Act (1750) removed all duties on English imports of colonial pig and bar iron (thus encouraging their production) but forbade the erection of any new colonial iron mills for manufacturing raw iron into finished products.

The Navigation Acts were ostensibly intended to ensure that the mother country would benefit from the economic activities of the colonies. But, in passing the original acts and in modifying them over the years, Parliament was not immune to the wishes of special groups. Adam Smith, in coining the very name "mercantilism," was charging that English policies were dictated by merchants

at the expense of the rest of the community. And indeed particular acts were often opposed by one group as much as they were favored by another. The Iron Act, for example, represented a victory of English iron-manufacturers over English iron-miners and smelters; and in 1733 the Molasses Act, which placed a heavy duty on foreign molasses imported into North America, was a victory for one group of colonists, the West Indian sugar-planters, over another, the New Englanders who distilled molasses into rum.

Besides serving such private interests, and besides subordinating colonial trade to English trade, the Navigation Acts aimed at increasing the revenue of the English government, at least indirectly. Although the acts of 1660 and 1663 levied no taxes, the government from the beginning had collected duties in England on imports from the colonies. By requiring enumerated commodities to be brought only to England, the government expected to step up the volume of dutiable goods. The expectation was not unrealistic. Revenue obtained from duties on tobacco imports alone amounted in the 1660s to £100,000 annually, or as much as the planters themselves made from the crop.

The Navigation Acts transformed the hopeful predictions of Hakluyt into specific legislation that told the colonists what they could and could not make, where and how they could trade. But the colonies were still three thousand miles from the lawmakers. If England was to receive the full benefit of the acts, they had to be enforced against foreign nations on the

The harbor at New Amsterdam

one hand and against refractory colonists on the other.

The Dutch. The principal foreign threat to England's emerging mercantilist empire in the seventeenth century came from the Dutch. This was their century; they seemed on the way to running the world. After shaking off Spanish domination, they built the largest merchant fleet ever known. Dutch captains nosed out rival vessels everywhere, took over most of the Portuguese empire in the East Indies, opened trade with Japan. Dutch privateers led the pack in raiding Spanish treasure fleets. Dutch merchants controlled the lumber trade from the Baltic and made Amsterdam the sawmill of Europe. Dutch fishermen dominated the North Sea. Dutch textile-workers finished and resold woolen cloth imported raw from England. When England tried to stop the export and save the valuable finishing process for her own workers, the Dutch simply boycotted English cloth, and depression settled over the whole English woolens industry. This was the century of Rembrandt, Vermeer, Hals, Hobbema, DeHooch, the century of Huygens and Spinoza. Man for man, no people has ever matched the seventeenth-century achievement of the Dutch.

In North America the Dutch had not extended themselves with the vigor they showed elsewhere, probably because North America offered fewer prospects of immediate reward. Nevertheless, Dutch ships every year appeared in Virginia's great rivers to carry tobacco to Holland instead of England. Dutch

textiles were sold in the shops of Boston. And the region that the Dutch had chosen for their settlements and trading posts in North America was strategically and economically the most important on the continent. The Hudson River commanded access to the interior by the only water-level route through the Appalachian Mountains. From the Hudson, it was possible to reach the Mississippi Valley along the Mohawk River Valley (or with greater difficulty by Lake George, Lake Champlain, and the St. Lawrence). Economically the Hudson River was the principal outlet of the fur trade south of the St. Lawrence; strategically it was an avenue along which an ambitious nation could strike for control of the inner continent. The Dutch were not that ambitious, but they did find New Netherland a convenient base from which to attack the Spaniards, drain off the continent's fur supply, and collect profit from England's settlements to the north and south. They used their colonies in the West Indies similarly to annex much of the trade of the English sugar planters there.

When Charles II set about enforcing the Navigation Acts, he took care of the Dutch problem in North America in the simplest possible way. He made a gift of the Dutch territories to his brother James, the Duke of York. To the seemingly formidable task of delivering the gift he assigned four commissioners, with four frigates and four hundred men. The commissioners arrived in 1664, a time when the Dutch settlers had been demoralized by arbitrary and incompetent governors. To everyone's surprise, the colony surrendered without resistance, and the commissioners took possession for the duke of the entire region from Maryland to Connecticut.

The Dutch in Holland, already at odds with England, declared war and continued to violate the Navigation Acts wherever willing colonists and the absence of the British navy made it possible. In the long run, the problem of enforcement could be solved not by foreign war but only by effective administrative machinery within the colonies themselves. That problem became at once more difficult and more urgent as a new burst of colonizing activity increased the dimensions of the empire.

The Restoration colonies

The colonies founded in the second half of the seventeenth century were "proprietary," that is, they were founded by proprietors who exercised government over them and initially owned all the land in them. The proprietors, generally friends or relatives of the king, hoped to grow rich from the sale of their lands and from the annual fees, or quitrents (usually a shilling per fifty acres), that they charged the settlers. They kept the quitrents low enough not to deter prospective immigrants but high enough to guarantee themselves a tidy permanent income when the colony should be fully populated.

The new colonies all resembled Maryland in their proprietary origin (see p. 23); they differed from Maryland and the other old colonies in the sources from which they drew their actual settlers: comparatively few came directly from England. Some were on the spot already, like the Dutch and Swedish settlers in New Netherland. More came from Scotland, Ireland, Wales, France, and Germany. Still more came from America itself, men who had grown discontented with the part of the New World they already occupied and wanted to try a new place.

This search for greener pastures was to become one of the abiding characteristics of American life. Once uprooted, a man might wander long before he found a spot where he could remain content. After a few months or years in a new home, one morning he would turn his back on surroundings that had scarcely become familiar and be off to the promised land beyond the horizon. From this restless breed of men the new proprietors hoped to draw tenants for their feudal domains. Tenants less likely to pay feudal rents would have been hard to find, but that fact was not immediately apparent.

New York. The most important of the new colonies was New York, whose settlers and problems the Duke of York had inherited from the Dutch. New Netherland had been primarily a series of riverside trading posts, located at Swaanendael (Lewes), Fort Nassau (Newcastle), and Fort Casimir (in Gloucester County, New Jersey) on the Delaware, and at Fort Orange (Albany) and Esopus (Kingston) on the Hudson. But New Amsterdam (New York City) at the mouth of the Hudson and a few other areas had more advanced settlements. The merchants of New Amsterdam were no longer mere Indian traders, and their flourishing overseas business supported a sizable and diversified community. In the Hudson Valley a number of well-to-do Dutchmen had tried to found agricultural settlements, known as patroonships, of the very kind that English proprietors were hoping to establish. One of these, belonging to Kiliaen van Rensselaer, had approached success. Though Rensselaer himself had gained little profit from it, his tenants still occupied the lands. On Manhattan, on the western end of Long Island, and in the lower Hudson Valley there were a few villages of Dutch farmers; and in eastern Long Island a number of New England Puritans had transplanted themselves and their way of life. The Dutch, finding them difficult to cope with, had left them much to themselves.

The Dutch West India Company had governed these sprawling settlements through a director-general. Of the men who held the post, Wouter van Twiller (1633–38) and Willem Kieft (1638–47) had been disastrously foolish; and Peter Stuyvesant (1647–64), who surrendered the colony to the English, was little better. All had governed without benefit of a popular assembly. English rule brought no immediate changes, except in the quality of the governors. The terms of surrender confirmed the old settlers in their property rights. The Duke of York, by the charter that conveyed the area to him, was given full authority

Peter Stuyvesant

to govern as he saw fit. Since the duke had no fondness for representative assemblies, he appointed a governor to rule in the same manner as the old director-general.

Though the Dutch were not happy about rule by Englishmen, they submitted peacefully to the governors James sent: Richard Nicolls (1664–68), Francis Lovelace (1668–73), Edmund Andros (1674–81), and Thomas Dongan (1683–88). The New Englanders on Long Island were less docile. They showed the familiar unfriendliness of Englishmen toward governments in which the governed had no representation. Governor Nicolls tried to appease them at the outset by compiling a special set of laws for them, drawn in part from the New England laws, which they presumably liked. This code, known as the Duke's Laws, was presented to a meeting of representatives from seventeen towns in 1665, but the meeting was not allowed to alter or add to it. The inhabitants accepted it but not gratefully. During the ensuing years they objected continually to paying taxes without representation and, instead of being happy about their rescue from the Dutch, complained that they were now "inslav'd under an Arbitrary Power."

Perhaps because of the noisy discontent of these New Englanders, New York attracted comparatively few new settlers. There was consequently little profit from rents for the Duke of York. His governors told him of the demand for a representative assembly and hinted that the colony might be easier to govern with one than without. In 1683 he gave way, and on October 17 the first assembly was held at New York with eighteen representatives elected from the various areas of the duke's propriety. One of the assembly's first actions was to pass a Charter of Liberties stating the right of the inhabitants to all the traditional political and civil liberties of Englishmen, such as trial by jury and representative government. Though this charter received the duke's assent, he repudiated it in 1686, after New York had been transformed from a proprietary to a royal colony by his accession (1685) to the throne of England as James II.

New Jersey. New York in 1685 was not as large as New Netherland had been. Three and a half months after receiving his grant of the area, James had transferred the part later called New Jersey to two friends: John, Lord

Routes to the interior of North America

Berkeley, a privy councillor much interested in naval affairs, and Sir George Carteret, Vice-Chamberlain of the Royal Household and Treasurer of the Navy (James himself was Lord High Admiral, in charge of the navy). There followed a comedy of errors that was never entirely straightened out.

James' governor in New York, Richard Nicolls, did not learn of the transfer to Berkeley and Carteret until after he himself granted lands in the New Jersey region to a number of New England Puritans from eastern Long Island. Nicolls, who was anxious to get the land settled and producing revenue, offered the Puritans the right to govern themselves through their own assembly. They in turn agreed to pay quitrents to James. Nicolls actually had no authority to offer such terms, but the Puritans accepted them and moved in.

When Berkeley and Carteret gained possession, they too offered liberal terms to settlers. They too wanted quitrents and promised a representative assembly to make laws. More Puritans, this time from New Haven, accepted the offer and moved in.

James, in transferring New Jersey to Berkeley and Carteret, gave them only property rights over the colony. His own governmental authority was not transferable. Berkeley and Carteret therefore had no authority either to hold a representative assembly or to appoint a governor. Yet they did both, and neither James nor his brother the king objected.

But the cantankerous transplanted New Englanders, who had accepted grants from Nicolls, did object. They held their own assembly and refused to accept the authority of the government established by the proprietors. The vehemence of their protests and their carelessness in paying rents were not diminished by subsequent developments. Berkeley and Carteret divided the province in two in 1674. Berkeley, who had taken the western half, sold it that same year to a Quaker, who resold shares to other Quakers. In 1680, after Carteret died, the eastern half, where both groups of Puritans were located, was sold at auction to another group of Quakers. The fact that the proprietors were now Quakers did not endear proprietary government to the Puritan settlers. They continued to protest until the English government awoke to the fact that the government of New Jersey rested on a false assumption of power by the original proprietors. In 1702 East and West New Jersey were united as a royal colony with a single representative assembly and with the proprietors retaining only their property rights.

The Carolinas. Before Berkeley and Carteret received the grant of New Jersey, they had already become involved with several highly placed friends in a project for another colony in the region directly south of Virginia, known as Carolina. The moving spirit in this enterprise was probably Sir John Colleton, an old royalist soldier. After Charles I lost his head in 1649, Colleton had gone to Barbados. There he found that the Great Migration had deposited thousands of hopeful immigrants, who had carved the island into small farms. After 1640, however, as sugar gradually became the dominant crop, the land was absorbed into ever larger plantations worked by increasing numbers of imported black slaves. Many of the settlers had been squeezed off their farms and were now ready to move to the continent, where land was more plentiful.

When Colleton returned to England in 1660, he realized that this ready-made population for a new colony lay waiting, and he was probably already interested in the Carolina region. In London he met Sir William Berkeley, brother of John and royal governor of Virginia (1641–52 and 1660–77). Berkeley knew that the Virginians had occupied much of their own tidewater land and were ready to expand down the coast into Carolina. Before long, Berkeley and Colleton had assembled a blue-ribbon board of would-be proprietors for the new colony. Besides themselves there were Berkeley's brother John; Sir George Carteret; Anthony Ashley Cooper, later Earl of Shaftesbury; George Monck, Duke of Albemarle (who had engineered Charles II's return to the throne); William, Earl of Craven; and Edward Hyde, Earl of Clarendon. To such men the king could not say no even though they were asking for the whole area extending from the present Atlantic border of the states of North Carolina, South Carolina, and Georgia westward to the Pacific.

The proprietors received the territory by royal charter on March 24, 1663, and they moved at once to fill it with footloose farmers from Virginia, New England, and Barbados. From the beginning they proposed two distinct centers for settlement. The region of Albemarle Sound in the northernmost part of their grant was already sparsely occupied by settlers who had drifted in from Virginia. The proprietors gave them a governor in 1664; a popularly elected assembly met for the first time by June 1665. At the end of the century this colony of North Carolina had a population of four or five thousand. They engaged in subsistence farming and also grew enough tobacco to prompt enterprising New England merchants to go after it every year with shallow draft vessels that could clear the shoals of the area.

Farther south, where the Cape Fear River offered a better harbor than did Albemarle Sound, the proprietors intended to plant a second colony. New Englanders had already tried living here without authorization from England but had pulled out after tacking up a sign at the mouth of the river, warning future settlers that the country was not worth occupying. This may have been an early piece of Yankee shrewdness, for the proprietors found a continuing interest in the region among New Englanders—not enough, however, to induce many Puritans to move there and pay quitrents to absentee proprietors (there were no quitrents in New England). The first authorized colonists were mainly Barbadians, who came in 1665 and dispersed in 1667—to Virginia, to the Albemarle region, to New England, or back to Barbados. A successful settlement, sponsored primarily by

Charles Town grew into a city

Anthony Ashley Cooper, was finally made farther south. Well equipped with provisions, an expedition set out from England in 1669 and picked up reinforcements at Barbados and other islands en route. The settlers located themselves at first on the south bank of the Ashley River about twenty-five miles from the sea. In 1680 they moved to the present site of Charleston (called Charles Town until 1783), where, as later Carolinians would have it, the Ashley and Cooper rivers join to form the Atlantic Ocean.

The proprietors had provided the settlers with a constitution designed to strike a balance between aristocracy and democracy. Drafted presumably by Cooper's secretary, John Locke, the Fundamental Constitutions of Carolina were based more on the political philosophy of James Harrington than on the philosophy for which Locke himself was to become famous (see p. 67). Harrington believed that the structure of government should match the distribution of property among the governed. The proprietors proposed to people three-fifths of their property with ordinary settlers (who would pay an annual quitrent) and to keep the rest in seigneurial and manorial estates for a hereditary nobility. The government was to consist of a governor appointed by the proprietors and a legislature in which the upper house would represent the nobility, the lower the commoners. The upper house was to have the sole right to initiate legislation (another idea of Harrington's).

The settlers of South Carolina, by accretions of Barbadians, French Huguenots, New Englanders, Englishmen, Scots, and black slaves, increased to eight or ten thousand by the end of the century. Having discovered that rice grew well in the area, they cultivated it extensively in plantations around Charles Town. Beyond the plantations, frontiersmen outflanked the Appalachian Mountains, pushed back Spanish missions, and penetrated the interior of the continent to open a brisk trade with the Indians in deerskins and in slaves captured from other tribes. Charles Town grew into a city, the only one in the South. In spite of hurricanes, Indian attacks, and internal quarrels, South Carolina succeeded.

The Fundamental Constitutions did not. As in other colonies, the representative assembly—the lower house of the legislature—was impatient of restrictions: it claimed and took the right to initiate legislation, quarreled with the governor and the upper house, and generally got its way. By 1700 the Fundamental Constitutions were a dead letter, and proprietary rule was faltering. In 1719 a rebellion in Charles Town overthrew the last proprietary governor, and two years later a provisional royal government was organized in the colony. The proprietors finally surrendered their charter in 1729, and royal governments were provided for both North and South Carolina, each with a governor and council appointed by the king and an assembly elected by the landowners.

William Penn's holy experiment. The last English colony to be founded in the seventeenth century was also the private property of a friend of the king. It would be hard to imagine a more unlikely friend for Charles II than William Penn, Quaker, commoner, and enemy of royal prerogative. The association, a tribute to breadth of character in both men, began in the career of Penn's father, who was no Quaker. William Penn the elder started life as an ordinary seaman and by sheer ability worked his way to the rank of admiral. He was in charge of naval operations in Cromwell's grandiose expedition to the West Indies. When the expedition captured nothing but Jamaica, the admiral retired in disgrace to Ireland, where he remained until Charles II took the throne.

Disgrace under Cromwell was no bar to preferment under Charles. Admiral Penn was on hand to see the new king crowned in 1660 and took the occasion to present his son, then aged sixteen. In the ensuing years, while the father headed the navy office under the Duke of York, young Penn did the things that sons of gentlemen were expected to do. It was conventional that he should attend Oxford and almost conventional that he be expelled after two years and sent on the grand tour of the Continent by a worried father. It was conventional too that he should spend some time at the Inns of Court studying law, but without

The Restoration colonies

William Penn on William Penn

From William Penn, Letter to William Popple, October 24, 1688.

---

becoming a barrister. As he reached maturity, Penn had the standard qualifications of a young courtier: high spirits, ready wit, skill as a swordsman. He cut a dashing figure at the court of the king. But he had one quality that was not quite conventional, one that kings, courtiers, and fathers of young gentlemen have often found embarrassing: he took ideas seriously.

What was worse, the ideas he took most seriously were of the most embarrassing kind: radical, lower class, faintly ridiculous. The Quakers (later called Friends) had initially been the lunatic fringe of the Puritan movement. They heard voices; they insulted their betters; they appeared naked in church. One of them, James Nayler, thought he was Jesus Christ and entered the city of Bristol riding on an ass, with his admirers singing holy, holy, holy before him.

The authorities dealt with Nayler: they bored his tongue with a hot iron, cut off his ears, and branded his forehead with the letter *B* for blasphemer—thereby demonstrating what might have happened to Christ if he *had* reappeared. Respectable Englishmen thought that madmen like Nayler were typical of Quakerism. But by the 1660s Quakers had shaken free of these eccentricities and were challenging the world by practicing what they preached.

What they preached was not far different from what other Christians had always preached. What others had variously called conscience, revelation, or saving grace, Quakers called the Inner Light. The Inner Light, they said, glowed in every man. He had only to live by it in order to be saved. Quakers tried to live by it.

All Christians believed that humility is a virtue. But the Quakers studiously, almost fanatically, avoided pride and the institutions that pride erected: they wore conspicuously plain and out-of-date clothes; they refused to honor one another—or anyone else—by bowing or kneeling or taking off their hats, or by using the second person plural when addressing an individual (ultimately they forgot the nominative and used only "thee"). All Christians professed brotherly love; but the Quakers refused to make war. They also refused to give or take oaths, partly because they believed the imposition of an oath implied distrust of one's fellow men.

Ideas of this kind first attacked William Penn as a student at Oxford and may have been responsible for his expulsion. One reason for the grand tour was to get them out of his head and something more fashionable into it. The tour worked, too, but only until Penn encountered a Quaker named Thomas Loe, whom he may have known earlier. In 1667 Samuel Pepys, a diarist who worked in the navy office, recorded the sad fact that Sir William Penn's son was "a Quaker again, or some very melancholy thing."

From this time forward, Penn was Quakerism's most energetic and effective supporter. He knew enough theology to argue with priests, enough law to argue with judges. He was so friendly with the king that no one dared ignore him, and he had such courage

Quakers: an eighteenth-century meeting

Penn saw fit to govern in a manner that he hoped would demonstrate the virtues of Quakerism and of political and religious liberty. Though, like other proprietors, he hoped to profit from his colony by quitrents on land, his primary purpose was to conduct a holy experiment in popular government and Christian living. He served as governor when in the province and appointed a deputy when absent, but neither for himself nor for his deputy did he retain extensive powers. The people, he made plain in a statement issued a month after he received the charter, "would be allowed to shape their own laws." In the Frame of Government that he worked out to embody this principle, Penn placed the legislative power in a council and an assembly, both elected by the freeholders. He probably assumed, however, that the freeholders would choose the more successful and well-to-do among them to the council, while the assembly would be composed of more ordinary men. And Penn, who retained some traditional ideas about the prerogatives of the well-to-do, made the council the more powerful of the two bodies, with the sole right to initiate legislation.

Attracted by the prospect of good land, free government, and religious liberty, English, Irish, Welsh, Dutch, and German Quakers flocked to the colony. It prospered from the start and attracted many non-Quakers as well, partly because Penn advertised its advantages in pamphlets that were circulated widely. Penn himself went to the colony in 1682 but had to return to England in less than two years to defend his southern boundary in a legal dispute with Lord Baltimore. The dispute was not fully settled until the 1760s, when Charles Mason and Jeremiah Dixon surveyed their famous line. Litigation, losses, and revolution kept Penn in England for fifteen years. During that time his friend King Charles died and his friend the Duke of York ascended the throne, only to flee from it in 1688.

that he never allowed his friendship to weaken his arguments against the king's policies. He fought not only for Quakerism but for the right of all Englishmen to worship as they pleased and to run their own government.

The "golden days of good King Charles" were nevertheless hard times for Quakers. The Anglican Church was doing its best to limit and control dissent. Quakers, because they refused to hold their meetings in secret, spent more time in jail than other Dissenters. Penn joined with other Quakers in the purchase of New Jersey, which for a time served as a Quaker refuge. But eastern New Jersey was full of Puritans, always unfriendly to Quakers, and western New Jersey had poor soil. Penn heard that the land across the Delaware was better and that no one was there but wild Indians, who would be easier to live with than English bishops or New Jersey Puritans. The king owed him £16,000, a debt contracted to his father (who died in 1670) for back pay and loans to the royal exchequer. In 1680 Penn asked the king for the land and, after many protests from the king's advisers, got it. Charles named it Pennsylvania after the admiral. In addition, Penn later bought from the Duke of York the region that is now the state of Delaware, which was already populated by a few Dutch and Swedish settlers.

According to the terms of his charter, is-

In Pennsylvania, Quakerism in power fulfilled many but not all of Penn's anticipations. It brought religious peace (other sects found complete freedom), economic prosperity, and political quarrels. Although the council, where power was concentrated, was elected by the same people as elected the assembly, just as the United States Senate and House of Representatives are today, the assemblymen acted as though their lack of the right to initiate legislation was a denial of popular rights. The council and the assembly joined in attacking the governors whom Penn sent over, even though the executive power in Pennsylvania was weaker than in any other colony. It is true that Penn, who could never believe ill of any man, often sent incompetent, or at least inappropriate, governors, such as the old Cromwellian soldier, John Blackwell. Blackwell left the province saying that Quakers prayed for their neighbors on Sundays and preyed on them the other six days of the week.

After the fall of James II, Penn was for a while suspect in England because of their long-standing friendship. His province was temporarily taken from him and, from 1692 to 1694, was under a royal government, which gave the assembly the right to initiate legislation. Upon recovering the colony, Penn recognized that right, but by then the assembly was in pursuit of still larger powers. In 1699 he finally returned to the province and told the members of the assembly, since they did not like his plan of government, to draft one of their own. They did so, eliminating the legislative authority of the council altogether (it retained only the function of advising the governor), and leaving the proprietor with only the ownership of ungranted land and a veto power over legislation, normally exercised through his appointed governor.

The new plan, known as the Charter of Liberties, was established in 1701, with Penn's approval, by an act of the assembly. Pennsylvania thus became the only colony with a unicameral legislature. The same Charter of Liberties gave the counties of Newcastle, Sussex, and Kent (later the state of Delaware) a separate representative assembly, though they retained the same governor as Pennsylvania. In 1701 Penn returned to England, where the brotherly love that had founded Pennsylvania eventually landed him in prison for debts incurred by dishonest agents whom he had trusted. No quitrents arrived from Pennsylvania to extricate him. He died in 1718.

Problems of enforcement

The settlement of Pennsylvania completed English occupation of the Atlantic coast from Spanish Florida to French Canada. All the colonies had been founded under authority of the king, but without his active participation or financial support. The government of each had been uniquely shaped by the varying purposes of the founders and settlers, not by an overall imperial policy. When, with the Navigation Acts, the king and his Parliament proposed to apply an imperial policy to America, they found that most of the machinery of colonial government by which the acts might have been enforced lay beyond their immediate control. Only in Virginia (through the royally appointed governor and council) did England exercise any voice in colonial government.

Even as the Navigation Acts were passed, Charles II was furthering this dispersion of power. In 1663 he gave Rhode Island a royal charter (to replace a similar parliamentary charter of 1644), authorizing the settlers to choose their own governmental officers. In 1662 he had given the same charter privilege to Connecticut (including New Haven, which would have preferred a separate charter). By these charters and by those granted to the Duke of York, the Carolina proprietors, and William Penn, Charles, perhaps thoughtlessly, distributed authority that might have been used to enforce imperial policies.

At the same time he strengthened another element in colonial government that was to make imperial control difficult. In each of his charters, except the one given to the Duke of York, he required the consent of the settlers to local legislation. The requirement was met by popularly elected representative assemblies like those already existing in older colonies. Assemblies had demonstrated their usefulness: to operate effectively, a colonial government had to obtain the advice and cooperation of the actual settlers, especially where they were Englishmen, used to having their laws made by their representatives. But the assem-

*New England:
a royal customs
officer's view*

The day after, I went to visit the governour at his house, and among other discourse I told him I tooke notice of severall ships that were arrived at Boston, some since my being there, from Spain, France, Streights, Canaries and other parts of Europe, contrary to your Majesties lawes for encouraging navigation, and regulating the trade of the plantations. He freely declared to me that the lawes made by your Majestie and your parliament obligeth them in nothing but what consists with the interest of that colony, that the legislative power is and abides in them solely to act and make lawes by virtue of a charter from your Majesties royall father, and that all matters in difference are to be concluded by their finall determination, without any appeal to your Majestie, and that your Majestie ought not to retrench their liberties, but may enlarge them if your Majestie please, and said ... that your Majesty could doe no lesse in reason than let them enjoy their liberties and trade, they having upon their own charge and without any contribution from the crown made so large plantation in the wildernesse ... and that notwithstanding the colony had many enemies, yet they did believe your Majestie to be their very good friend, for that your Majestie had by severall letters expressed your kindnesse to them....

From Edward Randolph, Letter to the King of England, 1676.

---

blies had also demonstrated a truculence, not unlike that of Parliament in England, which promised trouble for policies imposed from above. Nowhere was the threat greater than in New England.

Recalcitrant colonists.

New England, of all the regions in the empire, fitted least well into the mercantilist scheme of supplying needed raw materials to the mother country. She had nothing in quantity that the mother country wanted. Since furs from the interior of the continent came out by way of the Hudson or the St. Lawrence, the New England fur trade lasted only until the local animals had been depleted. Lumber and lumber products, such as pitch and tar, were a minor resource. But mostly New England grew rocks, and even these contained no valuable minerals or ores. Because their resources were limited, New Englanders went into the business of distributing what the rest of the world produced. In trading freely wherever the best price was offered, they competed all too successfully with the merchants of the mother country.

They could still have carried on a successful trade in obedience to the Navigation Acts, but disobedience was more profitable. The merchant who bought French silks and laces in France and carried them directly to Boston could undersell one who bought the same goods in England, because English prices in-

*Boston harbor:
center of
New England trade*

cluded the extra cost of English duties and of transportation from France to England. The same advantage accrued to a merchant or captain who illegally carried enumerated commodities, such as sugar or tobacco, directly from the colonies to Europe.

New Englanders, therefore, had good economic reasons for resisting or evading directions from England. And, as was often the case in New England, economic interest coincided with religious interest. The New Englanders were Puritans, and they had come to New England to live as Puritans. Charles II, whatever else he may have been, was notoriously not a Puritan. New Englanders consequently looked with suspicion on his government and were wary of any move to bring them under its control. Their fathers had struck this defensive attitude almost as soon as they set foot in New England. According to Governor Winthrop, the Puritans had "hastened" their fortifications in 1633 when they heard that Charles I had appointed a commission under Archbishop Laud to govern them. Fortunately the fortifications did not have to be manned against the archbishop. Thereafter New Englanders had easily withstood the halfhearted efforts at control made by Parliament and by Oliver Cromwell. When Charles II came to the throne, they still had the royal charter of Massachusetts intact and did not hesitate to remind the new king of the

As long as Plum Island *shall faithfully keep the commanded Post; Notwithstanding all the hectoring Words, and hard Blows of the proud and boisterous Ocean; As long as any Salmon, or Sturgeon shall swim in the streams of* Merrimack; *or any Perch, or Pickeril, in* Crane-Pond; *As long as the Sea-Fowl shall know the Time of their coming, and not neglect seasonably to visit the Places of their Acquaintance; As long as any Cattel shall be fed with the Grass growing in the Medows, which do humbly bow down themselves before* Turkie-Hill; *As long as any Sheep shall walk upon* Old Town Hills, *and shall from thence pleasantly look down upon the River* Parker, *and the fruitfull Marishes lying beneath; As long as any free and harmless Doves shall find a White Oak, or other Tree within the Township, to perch, or feed, or build a careless Nest upon; and shall voluntarily present themselves to perform the office of Gleaners after Barley-Harvest; As long as Nature shall not grow Old and dote; but shall constantly remember to give the rows of Indian Corn their education, by Pairs: So long shall Christians be born there; and being first made meet, shall from thence be Translated, to be made partakers of the Inheritance of the Saints in Light.*

From Samuel Sewall, *Phaenomena*, 1697.

New England: a New Englander's view

privileges granted by his father (even though they were secretly harboring the men who had passed the death sentence on Charles I).

Charles II knew that New England was full of Puritans, whom he abhorred, and that Massachusetts in particular had passed laws that did not fully satisfy the requirement, stated in her charter (as in other colonial charters), that all laws conform to those of England. In 1662 he sent a letter commanding revisions. The assembly ignored it. And so, in 1664, when Charles sent his commission of four to capture New Netherland from the Dutch, he assigned them the additional task of investigating New England. They were empowered to adjust boundaries, hear appeals from colonial courts, redress grievances against colonial governments, and report to the king on how well New England was obeying the Navigation Acts.

The commissioners, who went to New England fresh from their triumph over the Dutch, made a discovery that was to be repeated often in the history of the British empire: England could govern Dutchmen (and Frenchmen, Spaniards, Egyptians, Indians, and Chinese) more easily than it could govern Englishmen. The commissioners were treated well enough in Rhode Island, Connecticut, and Plymouth, all of which were looking for improvements in their boundaries. Plymouth had no charter and perhaps hoped to get one

by good behavior. But when the commissioners appeared in Boston they met with a reception the coolness of which has seldom been matched even in that city. The officers of government referred them to the charter of 1629 and ostentatiously refused to recognize their authority. A herald appeared before the house where the commissioners were staying and, after a blast from his trumpet, in the name of the king formally forbade anyone to appear before them. Frustrated at every turn, they went back to England to report that the Massachusetts government was making no effort to enforce the Navigation Acts. They also recommended to the king that he revoke the Massachusetts charter, a suggestion echoed by every royal official to visit the colony in the next twenty years.

The king could not revoke the charter at will. It was a contract, binding both grantor and grantee. But the terms required that Massachusetts make no laws contrary to those of England. If it could be shown that Massachusetts had done so, a court of law would declare the charter void, and the king would recover all governmental powers.

After the experience of his commissioners, Charles decided to continue the investigation in England and demanded that Massachusetts send agents to account for its behavior. The General Court (as the Massachusetts assembly was called) sent masts for the king's navy,

The rights of Englishmen: Massachusetts, 1687

Ipswich, Massachusetts. Att a Legall Towne Meeting, August 23, 1687 Assembled by vertue of an Order from John Usher, Esq. Treasurer, for chooseing a Commissioner to joyne with the select men to Assess the Inhabitants according to an Act of his Excellencie the Governor [Edmund Andros] and Councill for Levying of Rates, the Towne considering that the sayd Act doth Infringe their Libertye, as free borne English subjects of his Majesties and Interfering with the statute lawes of the Land; By which it is enacted that noe Taxes shall be levyed on the subjects without consent of an Assembly chosen by the freeholders for Assessing of the same. They doe therefore vote that they are not willing to Choose a Commissioner for such an End without said Priviledges and moreover consent not that the select men doe proceed to lay any such rate untill itt bee appoynted by a generall Assembly Concurring with the Governor and Councill.

From Ipswich Town Records, 1687.

---

money for the sufferers in the great fire of London, provisions for the fleet, but no agents. The leaders of Massachusetts knew that many of their laws did violate England's, especially their laws about religion. It was precisely these laws that they wished to keep, even more than they wished to escape the Navigation Acts. So they tried every means to avoid a showdown, relying heavily on distance to support them in one delaying action after another. For ten years they got away with it and grew ever more prosperous and powerful.

In England the king paid only sporadic attention to them and made no effective move against them. But Parliament, in 1673, passed an act to make smuggling to foreign countries less profitable. It levied export duties, known as "plantations duties," on any enumerated commodity shipped to another colony instead of to England. Now, if a shipper pretended to be taking tobacco from Virginia to Boston but took it instead to Holland, he would already have paid a tax equivalent to that levied in England, and he would be unable to sell his cargo in Holland at a price much lower than that of tobacco reshipped legitimately from England. The act of 1673 made smuggling more difficult but did not stop it. As before, the most persistent evaders were the New Englanders, and the governors of other colonies complained that the example of Massachusetts undermined their own attempts to enforce the Navigation Acts.

The main reason for Charles II's failure to act decisively against Massachusetts during these years was that he had no administrative body devoted primarily to colonial affairs. At

Charles II, King of England

last, in 1675, he appointed a special committee of the Privy Council known as the Lords of Trade, which set about pulling together the strings of empire. The members quickly realized that England could not rely on the colonial governments to enforce her policies. She must have her own means of enforcement in the colonies. The first step, the Lords of Trade decided, was for the king to take a hand in governing them.

The earliest opportunity came in New Hampshire, into which Massachusetts had extended her authority beyond the boundaries set by her charter. Robert Mason, who had inherited a claim to the region from the Council for New England, complained to the king about this encroachment, and in 1679 Charles took New Hampshire away from Massachusetts and gave it a royal government. Massachusetts was in danger of losing Maine as well, after an English court had declared her title to that area invalid. But Massachusetts managed to purchase the title of the counterclaimant, Ferdinando Gorges (who was the heir of the original Ferdinando), before the king could act.

The Lords of Trade took over Charles' fight against the Massachusetts charter by renewing the demand that the colony send agents to London. The General Court finally did so, but it gave them no authority to answer the questions the Lords wanted answered. The Lords insisted that the Massachusetts government enforce the Navigation Acts. The General Court, hardened by thirty years of ignoring and defying orders from England, loftily retorted that it was legally endowed by the king's own charter with full powers to govern

I receaved a wrighting from you by Mr. Shippin wherein you say you have a message from god to deliver to the people of Boston. Well, were it soe indeed, it is meete you should be heard: but for as much as I beleeve the contrary and that it is but a delution or suggestion of satan their is noe reason for me to grant your request for by your behaviour and wrighting you seame to be a professed Quaker and in reason to be thought to be of the same principals and perswations of the cheefe of the Leaders som of whose boocks I have seane and Red and Judg such to be as pernitious hereticks as ever was whose cheaf if not only rule for life and maners is imediate revelation and denying the trew Christian faith and salvation by believing in the Lord Jesus Christ god man and soe no cristians and theirfore that which you call Reasonable I conseave most unreasonable and unsafe and unlawfull as to permit a Jesuit or popish preest to preach or prate to the people and theirfore doe advise and Require you forthwith to depart out of this towne and jurisdiction without giving us any further trouble or disturbance.

From Simon Bradstreet, Governor of Massachusetts, Letter to James Martin, March 27, 1683.

The rights of Quakers: Massachusetts, 1683

---

the province and that therefore Parliament had no authority to pass laws affecting Massachusetts. But, in order to avoid a head-on collision, the General Court formally ordered enforcement of the Navigation Acts. Without waiting to see if Massachusetts would actually carry out the order, the Lords sent an imperial customs officer, Edward Randolph, to do the job; the General Court refused to recognize his commission, set up its own customs office, and imprisoned the deputies appointed by Randolph. The Lords demanded that Massachusetts show cause why its charter should not be revoked; again the General Court sent agents with insufficient powers and inadequate answers. In 1683 legal proceedings were begun, and in 1684 the charter was revoked. In 1685 the Duke of York became King James II.

The Dominion of New England. The accession of James II, which made New York a royal colony, together with the revocation of the Massachusetts charter, cleared the way for a scheme the Lords of Trade had long had in mind: a reconstruction of the American empire from New Jersey northward. The scheme shows that they had identified clearly the immediate sources of trouble; it also shows that they had learned little about political realities in either England or America. They proposed to place New Jersey, New York, Connecticut, Rhode Island, Plymouth, Massa-

chusetts, New Hampshire, and Maine under one governor. And in this whole area, to be called the Dominion of New England, there would be no troublesome representative assembly. The royally appointed governor would be assisted by a council whose members would also be appointed by the king. It apparently did not occur to their lordships that the people, deprived of any share in their own government, might prove more troublesome than the assemblies had been.

When news reached Boston that the Massachusetts charter had been revoked, men talked of resistance, as their fathers had fifty years before when threatened with the rule of Archbishop Laud. But their fathers had never been put to the test and had had less to lose in ships, houses, and money than the Bostonians of 1685. Boston was no longer a mere beachhead on an unsettled coast. It was a prosperous city of some 7,000 people with a fleet rivaling that of any English city except London. Most Bostonians held to the faith of their fathers, but they and other New Englanders were perhaps a little more prosperous than Puritan. They allowed their General Court to be dissolved and submitted reluctantly to the interim government of a council appointed by the king. In 1686, when Sir Edmund Andros arrived to establish the Dominion of New England, he faced hard looks and sullen words but no manned fortifications. Although the charters of Rhode Island and

The Dominion of New England

Connecticut had not been revoked, Andros extended his government over them without difficulty and in 1688 completed his domain by taking over New York and New Jersey, which he ruled thereafter through a lieutenant-governor. In each colony he dissolved the assembly.

Andros was not a happy choice to inaugurate the new system. An administrator of proved ability, he had already served successfully as governor of New York and would, in the years ahead, serve as governor of Virginia. But the present task called for diplomacy and tact as well as administrative skill. A blunt, outspoken man, Andros made decisions more easily than he made friends. He and the Lords of Trade believed, not without reason, that in order to establish imperial authority in New England the grip of the Puritan leaders must be broken and room made for a party of moderation. But it would have required a man of moderate temper and winning ways to organize and lead such a party.

The Lords of Trade, encouraged by the reports of Edward Randolph, supposed that the Puritans were a minority and that the majority of the population was tired of Puritan intolerance toward Quakers, Baptists, Anglicans, and customs officers. Nothing could have been further from the truth. Enemies of the old government were few, and Andros, by following the instructions of his superiors in England, succeeded in alienating what few there were. He levied taxes for the support of government, necessarily without the consent of a representative assembly. And when the in-

habitants objected and pleaded their rights as Englishmen, he told them they had no rights. Massachusetts had parceled out lands to individuals through the agency of incorporated towns; Andros maintained that the Massachusetts Bay Company had no authority to create corporations and that all titles to land granted by towns were therefore invalid. Anyone who wanted to own the land that he or his fathers had carved out of the wilderness had to ask for a new deed from the governor, pay a fee for it, and agree to pay quitrents ever after.

Andros, with the help of customs officers sent from England, enforced the Navigation Acts, and Randolph later claimed that this was the real cause of opposition to him. But the fact was that the Lords of Trade, in their zeal to establish imperial authority, had assigned Andros an impossible task. They required him to violate long-established rights and privileges and, without the support of an army, a police force, or a political party, to rule arbitrarily over a people who for more than fifty years had ruled themselves. Whether Puritan, non-Puritan, or anti-Puritan they could not be expected to like it. As Andros spelled out the dimensions of his immense authority, they began to have second thoughts about the wisdom of their submission.

The Revolution of 1688. Fortunately for New England, the rule of Andros coincided with the reign of James II. Although James could not dispense with Parliament as he had with the New England assemblies, he made it appear that he would have liked to. By exercising his power of pardon he effectively suspended the operation of many parliamentary enactments. He was, besides, a Catholic and made no secret of it. The political patience of Englishmen was as thin in old as in New England. In 1688 they welcomed William of Orange and chased James out of the country.

In Boston the Puritans did not wait for the fall of James to liquidate the Dominion of New England. After they had heard of William's landing in England, but before they had learned of his success in ousting James, they carried out a tidy, bloodless revolution of their own. Spurred by rumors that Andros and James were plotting to hand New England over to the pope, the inhabitants of Boston seized and imprisoned the governor and his council, restored the old government, and waited to hear how William was faring in

England. The colony's most eminent minister, Increase Mather, had gone to London the year before to plead the colony's cause against Andros. Mather did his best to persuade the new monarchs, William and Mary, that the Dominion of New England was part and parcel of James' tyrannical policies in England and that the Glorious Revolution ought to include a glorious restitution of the Massachusetts charter. William gave orders for the recall of Andros and authorized Massachusetts to proceed temporarily under her old government, but he refused to restore the charter until he and his advisers should have time to investigate the situation.

Plymouth, Rhode Island, and Connecticut quietly resumed their old governments, and New Jersey returned to anarchy. But New York had its own revolution, which was not entirely bloodless. Andros' lieutenant-governor there, Francis Nicholson, was left in an anomalous position as the appointee of a deposed officer who was in turn the appointee of a deposed king. Nicholson was, besides, young and headstrong, a professional military officer with an unconcealed scorn for popular rights and liberties. When rumors of popish plots alarmed the population, he did nothing to quiet them.

At the end of May 1689 a party of local militia seized the fort that commanded New York harbor and took control of the government. The party was led by Jacob Leisler, a successful German immigrant who had married into a prominent Dutch family. After Nicholson departed for England in June 1689, a meeting of delegates from different parts of the province chose a committee of safety, which in turn named Leisler as commander in chief of the province. Leisler proclaimed the accession of William, and when ambiguously addressed letters arrived from the new king authorizing a continuation of government, Leisler claimed them.

Basing his authority on the letters, Leisler governed the colony arbitrarily but effectively for nearly two years. New York, thinly settled by people of differing nationalities and religions living in widely differing circumstances, was a long way from political maturity. To maintain order, Leisler had to rely heavily on his followers among the militia. When King William finally got around to appointing a regular governor in 1691, Leisler hesitated before surrendering authority to him and thereby gave the new appointee the pretext for an accusation of treason. Leisler and his

Increase Mather: eminent minister

son-in-law, Jacob Milborne, were convicted and hanged on May 16, 1691. Four years later Parliament reversed the sentence.

The reorganization of 1696. The downfall of the Dominion of New England, together with the revolution in England, brought to a halt the efforts to consolidate the empire. After William mounted the throne, he was kept busy defending England in war against France and trying to shore up what was left of the royal prerogative. The new men he appointed to the Privy Council were unfamiliar with colonial problems, and the Lords of Trade had been turned into a committee of the whole, charged with new and broader functions. Once again nobody in the government devoted himself exclusively to colonial policy. The result was seven years of neglect.

In the colonies merchants and shippers ignored the Navigation Acts, and pirates brazenly pursued their prey in and out of harbors. Edward Randolph, now trying to enforce the acts in Maryland, found himself again thwarted by New Englanders who were buying tobacco from the planters and taking it to Scotland instead of England. Though Scotland had the same king as England, the two countries remained separate until 1707. Under the Navigation Acts, Scotland, like nations on the Continent, was excluded from the benefits of trade with England's colonies.

Scottish competition for the tobacco trade raised such a howl of protest from English merchants that the king and Parliament were driven to act. In 1696, guided by Edward

New England: woodcut, 1677

Randolph, Parliament in one extensive enactment constructed machinery for enforcing the Navigation Acts. Henceforth the governors of all colonies, whether royal, proprietary, or corporate (Rhode Island and Connecticut), were to take an oath to enforce the acts. Failure to do so meant forfeiture of office. In place of the occasional peripatetic customs officer, a regular customs service subject to the English Treasury was established in each colony. The customs officers were authorized to take out "writs of assistance" from local courts entitling them to open buildings by force in search of smuggled goods. The officers were also empowered to prosecute violators of the Navigation Acts in admiralty courts, which the Privy Council ordered to be established in the colonies. Admiralty courts operated without juries, and it was expected that the judges, who held office only as long as they pleased the crown, would give short shrift to colonial offenders.

While Parliament was passing this measure, it also considered, and then rejected, a bill to create a council of trade and plantations to develop and administer colonial policy. The Privy Council, which had already planned a similar body, now swung into action to keep control of colonial policy under the king. In May 1696, by royal order, a new bureau was established to replace the old Lords of Trade. The Lords Commissioners of Trade and Plantations, as it was called, or more simply the

Board of Trade, resembled a national chamber of commerce. It was appointed by the king and was charged to furnish him with information and advice on all colonial matters. Although the board included some members of the Privy Council, ex officio, the eight working members were not councilors and had no authority to issue orders. Their function was purely advisory. But, since they constituted the only body directly concerned with the colonies, their advice was seldom ignored.

Although the king retained control of colonial policy and administration, the circumstances of William's accession affected the kind of control that he and his successors were able to exert in the colonies. After the unhappy experience with James II, Parliament would have looked with suspicion on any move by the king to do away with a representative assembly, even in America. Parliament did not object, however, to the introduction of royal governors in colonies that had not formerly had them. Nor was there serious objection from the settlers, for in almost every case the advent of royal government relieved an intolerable internal situation. Maryland was converted to royal government in 1689, after a local rebellion against the proprietor. (It returned to proprietary government in 1715 after the fourth Lord Baltimore turned Anglican.) As we have seen, New Jersey became a royal colony in 1702 (see p. 34), South Carolina and North Carolina in 1729 (see p.

35). In the new charter that William granted Massachusetts in 1691 (which incorporated Plymouth and Maine as parts of Massachusetts), the king retained power to appoint the governor. Thus most of the colonies reverted eventually to the king.

Wherever a royal government was introduced, the king gained more direct control over his subjects. He appointed the governor, and he appointed the governor's council (except in Massachusetts). Although in each royal colony a representative assembly of freeholders retained legislative authority, the governor's council served as the upper house of the legislature, and its approval was necessary before any act passed by the lower house became law. Even an act passed by both houses was subject to veto by the governor, and even an act approved by the governor might be disallowed by the king. During the eighteenth century, usually on the advice of the Board of Trade, some $5\frac{1}{2}$ percent of the acts passed by colonial assemblies were disallowed by the king, though no act of Parliament was ever vetoed after 1708. Moreover, in the eyes of the mother country the king's instructions to his governors were supposed to bind the assembly as well as the governor. But in spite of royal theories the popularly elected lower house of the assembly remained the most powerful branch of government in every colony. It enjoyed sole authority to levy taxes, and by threatening to withhold them it was often able to get its own way against both king and governor.

The Old Colonial System. Of the three agencies England now had for enforcement of the Navigation Acts, the admiralty courts proved unable to exercise jurisdiction because of ambiguities in the act of 1696; the customs service was ill paid and susceptible to bribes and could not operate effectively without the support of the local government. England's control of her colonies depended most heavily on the success of her royal governors in working with the colonial assemblies. Since every legislative act required the assent of both the governor and the assembly, the needs of neither the mother country nor the colonies could be satisfied if the two parties refused to cooperate.

Thus in the last analysis the Old Colonial System (embodied in the Navigation Acts and in the act of 1696) rested on the harmony of English and colonial interests. Although occasional discord developed, especially at points of contact between royal governors and assemblies, the harmony was real and the system worked. Enriched by her colonies, England grew to be the world's most powerful nation. And, protected by England, the American colonies grew, each in its own style, toward a new way of life.

Suggestions for reading

Eli Heckscher in *Mercantilism,* 2 vols. (1935), sets the economic policies of the seventeenth and eighteenth centuries in historical perspective and thus furnishes the best introduction to an understanding of the Navigation Acts. For the acts themselves and the thinking behind them, the pioneering works of G. L. Beer are still valuable: *The Origins of the British Colonial System* (1908) and *The Old Colonial System,* 2 vols. (1912). On the administration and interpretation of the acts, see L. A. Harper, *The English Navigation Laws* (1939); C. M. Andrews, *The Colonial Period of American History,* Vol. IV* (1938); and T. C. Barrow, *Trade and Empire* (1967). Special aspects of British policy are well treated in Curtis Nettels, *The Money Supply of the American Colonies Before 1720* (1934), and A. C. Bining, *British Regulation of the Colonial Iron Industry* (1933). Michael Kammen, *Empire and Interest** (1970), analyzes the pressure groups that affected policy.

On New Netherland and on the Restoration colonies the fullest general account is again C. M. Andrews, *The Colonial Period of American History,* Vols. II and III*. W. F. Craven, *The Colonies in Transition, 1660–1713** (1968), incorporates more recent research. T. J. Wertenbaker, *The Founding of American Civilization: The Middle Colonies* (1938), stresses social and cultural history. J. E. Pomfret has untangled much of New Jersey's early history in *The Province of West New Jersey, 1609–1702* (1956) and *The Province of East New Jersey, 1609–1702* (1962). The most important works on the Carolinas are Verner Crane, *The Southern Frontier, 1670–1732** (1929), and M. E. Sirmans, *Colonial South Carolina* (1966).

*Available in a paperback edition.

There is no definitive biography of William Penn, but Bonamy Dobrée, *William Penn, Quaker and Pioneer* (1932), is adequate; and F. B. Tolles and E. G. Alderfer have edited a selection of Penn's writings in *The Witness of William Penn* (1957). M. M. Dunn has made a scholarly study of his political ideas and activities in *William Penn: Politics and Conscience* (1967). J. E. Illick, *William Penn the Politician* (1965), treats his relations with the English government. Rufus Jones, *Quakers in the American Colonies** (1911), is a standard work, but see also F. B. Tolles' eloquent essays in *Quakers and the Atlantic Culture* (1960). The early history of Pennsylvania is treated in F. B. Tolles, *James Logan and the Culture of Provincial America* (1957), and G. B. Nash, *Quakers and Politics: Pennsylvania, 1681–1726* (1968).

Efforts of England to enforce the Navigation Acts are dealt with in Michael Hall, *Edward Randolph and the American Colonies, 1676–1703** (1960). Viola Barnes, *The Dominion of New England: A Study in British Colonial Policy* (1923), is the classic account of that episode, exonerating Andros of blame. Kenneth Murdock, *Increase Mather* (1925), treats fully Mather's role in seeking the overthrow of the dominion and in securing a new charter for Massachusetts. The long-range causes and consequences of Leisler's Rebellion are discussed in J. R. Reich, *Leisler's Rebellion* (1953), and in L. H. Leder, *Robert Livingston and the Politics of Colonial New York, 1654–1728* (1961). M. G. Hall, L. H. Leder, and M. G. Kammen, eds., *The Glorious Revolution in America: Documents of the Colonial Crisis of 1689** (1964), is a valuable collection of sources on the revolution in New England, New York, and Maryland.

On the reorganization of colonial administration in 1696, see again C. M. Andrews, *The Colonial Period of American History*, Vol. IV*, and I. K. Steele, *Politics of Colonial Policy: The Board of Trade in Colonial Administration, 1696–1720* (1968). The standard works on the Board of Trade are O. M. Dickerson, *American Colonial Government, 1696–1765* (1912), and A. H. Bayse, *The Lords Commissioners of Trade and Plantations, 1748–1782* (1925). On the activities of the board in securing the disallowance of colonial acts of legislation, see E. B. Russell, *The Review of American Colonial Legislation by the King in Council* (1915). The role of colonial governors in administering British policy is the subject of L. W. Labaree, *Royal Government in America: A Study of the British Colonial System Before 1783* (1930). Finally, Lawrence Gipson, in fifteen volumes, surveys *The British Empire Before the American Revolution* (1936–1970).

*Available in a paperback edition.

3

The first American way of life

Americans moving across their continent have faced three questions again and again: how to live, how to live with one another, how to live with the outside world. They first learned how to live by tobacco, rice, furs, and fish. England told them, in the Navigation Acts, how they must live with the outside world. How did they live with one another?

A few simply did not. When the Puritans explored Boston harbor, they came upon an Englishman at Beacon Hill living alone among the blueberries. William Blackstone was company enough for himself. After the Puritans moved in, he moved out. For nearly three centuries the continent afforded room for men like Blackstone, American hermits who felt crowded when they could see the smoke from their neighbor's campfire.

Patterns of existence

Most Americans have been more gregarious. They have asked *how,* rather than whether, to live together, and they have answered partly from the heritage of ideas and institutions carried from Europe, partly from their own ideas evoked by the opportunities and limitations of their strange new environment. Each generation has solved the problem a little differently from the preceding one, but the first settlers, moving from an old established world to an empty new one, had the biggest problem and made the biggest change. Many of them came to America primarily for a chance to live together in a new and, hopefully, a better way. All of them had to adapt ideas made in Europe to existence in America. The results differed from time to time and from place to place. But before the end of the colonial period most Americans were living together in one of four distinct patterns: the Southern plantation, the New England town, the loose collection of individual farms, or the coastal city.

The plantation. Plantations developed in colonies where the majority of people lived by growing a single crop for export: tobacco in Virginia and Maryland, rice or indigo in South Carolina, sugar in the West Indies. Originally "planter" meant simply a settler, and "plantation" a settlement—Jamestown was the London Company's plantation. Gradually the term plantation came to be attached to individual holdings and then to holdings where substantial numbers of men worked for the owner. Gradually too the term came to imply that the workmen were slaves, the property of the man for whom they worked.

The plantation manned by slaves originated in the West Indies, but within the present United States it developed first in Virginia. It was the most novel way of living that colonial

The tidewater and the piedmont

land during years of the plague. The cause is not clear. Probably it was a combination of malnutrition with malaria and typhoid fever. Between 1625 and 1640 some 15,000 immigrants increased the population of the colony from around 1,300 to only 7,000 or 8,000.

In spite of the heavy death rate, servants were cheap enough to be worth importing even after the price of tobacco dropped to around 20 shillings a hundred pounds (2.4 pence per pound) in the 1640s and 1650s. By then the Virginians' increasing skill with the crop enabled a man to grow from 1,000 to 2,000 pounds of tobacco a year, together with enough corn to feed himself. At that rate his output was still worth between 10 and 20 pounds sterling—while he lived. And beginning somewhere around the middle of the century people in Virginia evidently started living longer. The population rose to about 15,000 by 1653 and about 25,000 by 1660.

Most of those who made up these numbers arrived in the colony as servants. As more and more of them lived to complete their period of service, the added years of labor meant added profits to their masters (who could thus acquire still more servants to operate still larger plantations). And the ex-servants themselves could at long last begin to enjoy the opportunities they had been helping to bring to others. They could start small plantations, grow tobacco for export, and import servants of their own.

For a number of reasons the opportunities diminished sharply after 1660. The increase in population brought an increase in the labor force and a consequent increase in the production of tobacco. Since the rise in production was accompanied by passage of the Navigation Act of 1660, restricting the market for Virginia and Maryland tobacco, the price fell to a penny a pound and sometimes less. At the same time the cost of production went up, especially for beginners, because land was more in demand and hence more valuable. Farsighted planters began acquiring huge tracts and by the 1670s had engrossed most of the best land in the tidewater, the area cut by great rivers and bays along which ocean-going ships could collect tobacco as much as a hundred miles inland. A new freedman looking for a place to plant either had to rent from the big owners or else settle for a location in the interior, cut off from river transportation, or far up one of the rivers, where he would be exposed to Indian attack.

Americans devised for themselves. It was also the most productive, if we may judge by the exports of the thirteen colonies. And it was the most violent and oppressive, a way of living that required the continuous coercion of unwilling and unrewarded labor. In order to understand the role it played in American life, we shall have to look into its beginnings.

The first steps were taken during Virginia's tobacco boom of the 1620s, when everyone was scrambling for labor. A number of successful Virginians at this time were able to gather crews of ten, twenty, even thirty-odd men to grow tobacco for them. The men were mostly Englishmen, who had agreed to serve for up to seven years in return for passage across the ocean to the new land of opportunity. They themselves constituted an opportunity for the planters who bought them, sold them, traded them, and even won or lost them in card games. The planters would buy the labor of any man delivered to them, and Dutch traders delivered a few from Africa bound to serve for a lifetime. But you could buy an Englishman for seven years cheaper than you could buy an African for life; and in early Virginia seven years was more than most immigrants were likely to live anyhow. The death rate was comparable to that reached in Eng-

South Carolina plantation

As a result Virginia and Maryland (where the same conditions prevailed) acquired a growing class of indigent freedmen. They wandered from county to county, living from hand to mouth, dodging the tax collector, renting a bit of land here, squatting there, sometimes working for wages, sometimes trying to live from the land, hunting, stealing hogs, and enticing servants to run away with them. They were mostly young, because planters imported young servants; they were mostly single, because planters imported far more men than women; and they were mostly armed, because guns were a necessity of life in Virginia and Maryland, where dwellings were widely separated and a man had to be ready to shoot it out if attacked by Indians.

The established planters became increasingly uneasy about the band of wild bachelors in their midst. William Berkeley, who had been governor of the colony from 1641 to 1652 and became governor again in 1660, clearly saw danger ahead. When the Dutch made war against England and raided the James River in 1673, Berkeley led the militia against them with considerable trepidation, for he estimated that a large percentage of the men at his back were poverty-stricken freedmen, who ''upon any small advantage the Enemy may gaine upon us, would revolt to them in hopes of bettering their condition by Shareing the Plunder of the Country with them.''

Berkeley's fears were justified. Three years later, sparked by an Indian attack on the frontiers, a band of self-appointed Indian-fighters turned from an unsuccessful pursuit of the elusive enemy to attack their much less elusive rulers. Led by Nathaniel Bacon, a well-to-do sympathizer, the freedmen of the frontier found ready allies in nearly every part of the colony. In the largest popular uprising before the American Revolution they burned the capital settlement at Jamestown and drove the governor and his friends in flight to the Eastern Shore, the only loyal stronghold in the colony. Before it was over, the rebellion had swept up servants as well as freedmen in plundering forays against everyone who offered resistance.

Then, after they had redistributed as much of the wealth as they could lay their hands on, the rebels gave up as quickly as they had risen. Their leader, Bacon, had died of a fever; and he left them with no long-range solution to the problems that faced them, no revolutionary program, not even any revolutionary slogans. Old Governor Berkeley exacted a

A slave ship

savage revenge by hanging the remaining
leaders, though the king had sent a general
pardon. For the rest of the century Virginians
continued to eye one another uneasily, alert
for new Bacons in their midst. Though the
rebellion had subsided, its causes had not.
Servants were still arriving every year to man
the plantations; they were still becoming free
every year in large numbers; and they still
could not afford the land on which to sustain
their freedom. They had crossed the ocean to
a wilderness and sold away seven years of
their lives only to face the prospect of working
out the remainder on another man's plantation. Their continuing discontent posed a real
and present danger to the established planters.

It was under these circumstances that the
traders who had been supplying the West
Indies with slaves began delivering them in
larger numbers to the tobacco colonies. A
slave cost only about twice as much as a
servant, around £20 instead of £10 at the
close of the seventeenth century. With the
decline in Virginia's death rate, slaves became
a more profitable investment than servants,
and for that reason alone the planters bought
all the traders could bring. But the unsought
social benefits to Virginia's big planters were
larger than the economic benefits. Although
every planter worried about taking into his
household men and women who had good
reason to hate him, slaves proved to be less
dangerous than servants who had become
free. No slave rebellion in American history
ever approached the success of Bacon's Rebellion.

Slaves remained permanently under the
control of their masters. They could safely be

denied rights that Englishmen, servant or free,
could legally demand. They could be subjected to harsh punishments without recourse
to the courts. They could be kept unarmed,
unorganized, helpless to resist. And the fact
that they happened to be black announced
their probable status and made escape difficult.

By importing permanent black slaves instead of temporary white servants for their
plantations, Virginians ceased to add to the
band of indigent freedmen, which gradually
diminished. As the competition for land
stopped escalating and the interior became
safer for settlement, a man could once again
get a foothold on the ladder that led up in the
world. Slavery enabled the planters to go on
growing ever larger crops without, on the one
hand, creating a dangerous class of poor and
discontented freedmen or, on the other hand,
reducing those freedmen to some new sort of
bondage that would shackle their discontent.
Bondage was reserved for blacks, who accounted for most of the tobacco and rice produced in the colonies by the middle of the
eighteenth century.

Englishmen recognized slavery as the ultimate degradation to which a man could be
subjected, but they showed surprisingly little
hesitation in imposing that degradation on
men of darker complexion than their own.
Though slavery had no place in English law,
English colonists from the beginning had enslaved Indians who made unsuccessful war on
them. The theory was that the lives of captives
taken in just wars belonged to the captors; but
history records no war acknowledged by the
victors to have been unjust, and Englishmen
had not been in the habit of enslaving pris-

And if any slave resist his master, or owner, or other person, by his or her order, correcting such slave, and shall happen to be killed in such correction, it shall not be accounted felony; but the master, owner, and every such other person so giving correction, shall be free and acquit of all punishment and accusation for the same, as if such accident had never happened: And also, if any negro, mulatto, or Indian, bond or free, shall at any time, lift his or her hand, in opposition against any christian, not being negro, mulatto, or Indian, he or she so offending, shall, for every such offence, proved by the oath of the party, receive on his or her bare back, thirty lashes, well laid on; cognizable by a justice of the peace for that county wherein such offence shall be committed.

From W. W. Hening, *The Statutes at Large; Being a Collection of All the Laws of Virginia,* 1823.

The rights of Africans and Indians: Virginia, 1705

oners taken in their European wars. Making slaves of Indians and later of Africans (allegedly purchased from the victors in righteous tribal wars) was somehow different from making slaves of, say, Frenchmen or Germans.

The difference, of course, was race. Although not all blacks were slaves—from the beginning a substantial minority even in the plantation colonies were free—all slaves were either blacks or Indians. Slavery became the dominant form of relationship between white men and men of other races and was recognized by law in every colony. North of Maryland race relations concerned relatively few people; from Maryland south they concerned most people. Though the plantation had begun with a free or semifree white labor force, it became in the eighteenth century the meeting place of black and white, the primary community in which slaves lived together with free men.

Although the Southern plantation resembled similar establishments in the West Indies and South America, it had distinctive features that were to affect the way Americans of

A community in itself: a tidewater plantation

Riverside settlement in the South

different races lived together after slavery ended. Of first importance was the fact that Southern slave owners, especially in the tobacco colonies, did not make a policy of working their slaves to death. Whether because tobacco required less strenuous labor than sugar, or for other reasons, a slave on a Southern plantation had a longer and less arduous life than a slave on a sugar plantation in the West Indies, where planters counted on replacing a percentage of their worn-out and dying labor force annually by new purchases. The slave women of the West Indies could not or would not raise enough children to match the awful death rate. In the American South, while the planters continued to import slaves throughout the colonial period, the numbers also increased naturally. Though black women, as in the West Indies, worked beside their men in the fields, they were able at the same time to raise children. Southern slaves thus enjoyed a family life, though it was only a semblance of it.

The children, like their mothers and fathers, were the property of the master, and he could break up a family by selling any one of them. But so long as they were together slave families could in some measure—at night, on Sundays, and usually on Saturday afternoons—live lives of their own. The planters' policy of doling out the meagerest of rations

and obliging the slaves to grow what more they wanted in plots adjoining their cabins even encouraged a close family relationship as father, mother, and children worked together, for themselves, in their own garden.

The planters' success in promoting slave families may be judged by the fact that slaves on Southern plantations raised nearly as many children as free Southerners did. And while the colonies that later formed the United States received only $4\frac{1}{2}$ percent of all the slaves imported into the New World, the descendants of that $4\frac{1}{2}$ percent today constitute over 30 percent of the New World's inhabitants with African ancestry. The slave family was not responsible for all of them: the different shades of color among the children in the slave quarters testified to the fact that black women were not reserved for black men. But miscegenation was probably less than in other slave societies and racial prejudice correspondingly stronger.

On the other hand the estrangement of black and white was in some measure limited by the circumscribed environment in which they coexisted. Since the largest effective unit of tobacco production was a thousand acres (including uncleared and exhausted land), few tobacco plantations had as many as a hundred slaves. A smaller area, with no more than thirty slaves, was the most efficient unit for rice.

The plantation often constituted a small community in itself. At the center lay a great house, normally facing a navigable river, and surrounded by trees and shrubs. Arranged symmetrically around it were attendant buildings: laundry, smokehouse, kitchen, and perhaps a schoolhouse, where a hired tutor taught the planter's children—or at least his free children. At some distance lay the barns and the cabins of the slaves.

In addition to field hands, the community included a small army of household slaves and skilled artisans—carpenter, blacksmith, tailor, cobbler—who might be either indentured white servants (bound by a contract to serve a specific number of years) or slaves educated for the purpose. With its own permanent labor force and with ready access to ocean-going ships, the riverside plantation needed little from its neighbors. What could not be made on the premises was imported directly from London.

And yet the planter and his family were not isolated. The river was a highway to the world

New England town: Wethersfield, Connecticut

by which he kept in touch not only with London but with other planters. His children often went to stay for several weeks at other plantations, and his own home was seldom without guests. Sometimes he gave a ball for friends who came from miles around and stayed for three or four days. Or he might attend the representative assembly in Williamsburg or Charles Town and take the family with him.

In the assembly and in the local county court the planter directed the lives of his lesser neighbors, the small farmers who made up the majority of the population even in the plantation colonies. They worked for themselves, but he dominated the society, buying and selling their surplus crops, sometimes renting them their lands, lending them money, selling them manufactures, and perhaps commanding their votes. His command of their votes was by no means automatic, however. The deference his neighbors paid him was the voluntary tribute that success has generally exacted in a free society. It took the votes of free men to place him in the representative assembly, and votes were withheld often enough to remind him that he represented free men.

By officiating in the assembly, the county court, and the vestry of his church, and by managing his plantation, the planter learned to deal with men both free and unfree. And the ships that arrived at his wharf brought him

regular news of the way men were dealing with one another across the water. In their writings he learned that they thought slavery the worst fate that could befall a people. From a closer knowledge than theirs he could agree; and he would, as the years passed, increasingly value and protect his own freedom.

The New England town. Rivers, tobacco, and slavery made the plantation. Puritanism and past experience made the New England town, an institution that also appeared in the parts of New York and New Jersey settled by New Englanders. The past experience of New Englanders (as of other English colonists) included at least three English types of community: the borough, the village, and the parish.

The English borough was a town that normally possessed a charter of incorporation from the king entitling it to send two members to Parliament and to exercise a degree of local governmental independence. The freemen (or burgesses) of the borough, usually a very small proportion of the population, elected the members of Parliament as well as a mayor or a set of aldermen to handle local affairs. In many boroughs the aldermen had become so powerful that they were bypassing the freemen and were filling vacancies in their ranks by themselves.

The English village was not a formal political

institution like the borough. It was simply a cluster of houses inhabited by men and women who cultivated the adjoining lands according to customs prescribed by earlier generations. All the village's arable land was laid out in three or four large fields, and every householder had strips of land scattered through all of them. No man's strips were fenced off from those of his neighbors; and everyone worked together at plowing (and subsequently at sowing, tilling, and harvesting) one field before moving on to the next. Thus every man would get part of his crop early, part of it late. By the time the settlers left England, this open-field system was giving way to individual farms, but it still existed in many places.

Every Englishman, whether he lived in a borough or a village, belonged to a parish. Originally the parish was simply the area served by a single church, but it had gradually taken on, outside the boroughs, many of the functions of local government. In most villages a vestry made up of some ten or twenty of the more substantial inhabitants exercised the powers of the parish or chose two or three churchwardens to do so. The churchwardens or vestrymen not only maintained the church and managed its property but provided for the poor, required fathers to support their children, levied taxes, and sometimes acted as a kind of grand jury.

In creating their towns New Englanders drew something from the parish, the village, and the borough; but they also rejected parts of this institutional heritage because of their Puritan ideas about how men ought to live with one another. Puritans generally "gathered" a church before, or about the same time as, they established a town. The two usually covered the same territory, as was true of the English village and parish. But in New England the church and its officers were entirely distinct from the town and its officers. The church owned no property, not even a church building. People worshiped in a meetinghouse, which was owned by the town and used for any community meeting. It was not regarded as sacred. Nor did the church exercise any temporal, political powers. There was no vestry and no churchwarden. The church might elect ruling elders to reprimand erring members or to report them to the church, but neither elders nor church enjoyed coercive authority. The church was a spiritual association; its severest penalty was excommunication, which could be pronounced only by unanimous vote of the members. Excommunication deprived a man of his church membership but carried no civil or political disabilities. Once a church assumed temporal powers, Puritans believed, it was on the wicked road to Rome. In New England, therefore, they assigned to the town both the duties of local government, performed in the English borough by the mayor and aldermen, and the secular duties exercised in the English parish by church officers.

New England towns and their governments were created under the authority of the colony's General Court (the legislature). A group of men, perhaps already gathered in a church, approached the court and requested a tract of land, usually adjoining some established town. If the court approved, it had the area surveyed and then named the applicants as proprietors of the town of Concord, Sudbury, or whatever name they chose. The proprietors then moved to their new home and laid out the land in a pattern similar to that of an English village. Every man got a house lot in the center of town, where space was also set aside for a meetinghouse, a village green, and perhaps a school. Each man also received one or more parcels of arable land, a parcel of meadow for pasturage, and a parcel of woodland for fuel, all located in different parts of the town. In a few cases there seems to have been an attempt (quickly abandoned) to practice the open-field system. When the land of a town was originally apportioned, most of it was left undivided to meet the anticipated growth in population. The undistributed land, or commons, belonged to the proprietors jointly until they converted it into their private property through subsequent land divisions. A new settler moving into town might buy land from a proprietor's private holdings or might be granted or sold parts of the commons, but he did not necessarily become a proprietor with a share in the ownership of the remaining commons.

The power of the proprietors was limited to control over the commons; government of the town rested in a town meeting, in which they had no greater voice than other inhabitants. The town meeting acted on matters that intimately concerned the inhabitants: repairing roads, building a meetinghouse, hiring a schoolmaster, or deciding whether hogs should be fenced into pens or fenced out of gardens. The meeting also elected representatives to the colonial assembly and town officials of all kinds, including selectmen, who administered the rules made by the meeting. There was some attempt in early Massachusetts to confine voting in town meetings to the freemen, who it will be remembered had to be church members. After 1648, however, and probably before then in many towns, other free adult males, if approved by the freemen, were allowed to vote on all questions except the choice of representatives. Until 1685, representatives continued to be elected only by the freemen.

In the early years of a town's existence there was no conflict of interest between town meeting and proprietors, because all or most of the free adult males were also proprietors. And the inhabitants frequently felt a strong sense of duty to the community, a sense carried over from the religious purposes that guided the settlement. They sought to sustain their brotherhood in the political as well as the spiritual world by talking out any disputes that arose among them and by keeping out any newcomers who appeared likely to disturb their solidarity.

By the opening of the eighteenth century, with the passing of the founders, the waning of the high resolve that had moved them, and the dwindling away of the common lands, the towns began to take on a different character. Fathers could no longer give their sons the amount of land they needed, and the young began to go west in search of greener pastures. Latecomers quarreled with the proprietors over the remaining common lands. Religious dissent began to appear in forms that could not be talked down.

At the same time new towns were being formed by men without the spirit that had moved the first generation. Colonial governments, instead of granting townships gratis to groups of settlers, auctioned them off to groups assembled simply for the purpose of investing in real estate. These proprietors were sometimes not even residents of the towns they founded, and they sold land to settlers with more attention to private profit than to establishing a successful community. The settlers themselves were also less devoted to the community. Instead of living close to the meetinghouse and having their landholdings scattered about the countryside, they scattered their houses and tried to consolidate their land in one piece around the house.

Nevertheless, the New England town remained in the eighteenth century, if not as closely knit as in the seventeenth, remarkably homogeneous and neighborly. Men still rubbed elbows often and tried to work out their differences peaceably. On Sunday everyone gathered in the meetinghouse, where the position of a man's pew indicated his place in the community and whether he must be addressed as "Mister," as "Goodman," or by no title at all. In general, the closer he sat to the pulpit, the higher his social rank. But proximity to God's minister was no sign of proximity to God. Though the law required that everyone attend church, only a minority of the town's inhabitants were "members," and membership in itself carried no social prestige. A slave might belong and a gentleman not. During the eighteenth century church membership became increasingly feminine, with women outnumbering men by more than two to one. But members or not, New Englanders went to church, were taxed for the minister's salary, and had a voice in selecting him.

The men of the town met not only at church and town meeting but on training day when the militia exercised. In frontier settlements, under constant threat of Indian attack, this was a serious business; in the older coastal towns it was likely to require more rum than gunpowder. Rum and hard cider lubricated most community activities in New England, whether marrying or burying, raising a meetinghouse or bringing home a harvest. The tavern, originally intended for the convenience of travelers, became another meeting place, where men of the neighborhood bent an elbow of an evening and where, according to John Adams, "vicious habits, bastards, and legislators" were frequently begotten.

In tavern, school, and church, at town meeting and militia drill, the New Englander measured out the distance between himself and his fellow man. The distance was small, but it was enough to give him an independence of spirit for which he became famous. For those who needed more room, America offered another way of life.

The farm. In the colonies from New England southward, the average American lived a lonely life. He made his living from the land, as his father had done in Europe. But in the great emptiness of the New World, sheer space separated him from his neighbors in a way that few Europeans knew. His farm might run to several hundred acres and might lie miles from any other occupied land, because settlers, whenever they could, chose lands that supported a stand of hardwood. These, they thought, were most fertile.

Hardwood meant hard work in clearing the land, but many farmers simplified the task by girdling trees at the base to kill them, planting crops between the lifeless trunks, and then disposing of the trunks as they rotted away. This technique was probably brought to America by Finnish immigrants who settled along the Delaware River. They had first tried life in the forests of Sweden and had there learned to girdle trees and to build log cabins. The first English settlers, better sawyers than axmen, had built their houses with hand-sawed boards. But succeeding generations copied the Finns. By the eighteenth century an American starting a farm built a log cabin first and put up a frame house only after he had achieved a measure of prosperity.

Though most farmers owned the land they cleared and cultivated, farm tenancy became common in some areas where the soil was fertile enough to support both a landlord and a tenant. In New York's Hudson Valley, for example, landlords exacted high rents and feudal services. In Virginia's tidewater, tenants took farms and even plantations as share-croppers, paying the owner a proportion of the crop as rent. Even in the uncleared back country it was not always easy for a farmer to obtain title to land in the most fertile areas, because speculators often acquired such lands in advance of actual settlers. By the eighteenth century the headright system (practiced earlier in most of the colonies south of New England) had become a mere form. A speculator could obtain title to as much land as he could afford simply by paying a fee (usually 5 shillings per hundred acres) to the colony's secretary or land office. Later he could rent the land to a bona fide settler or else sell it for a good deal more than he had paid. Not all speculators were rich men. Many farmers, tradesmen, and even parsons invested their small earnings in real estate, for everyone knew that land values would rise as population increased, and everyone could see that population was increasing rapidly.

In New England most of the increase came from natural growth of the old stock who, unlike the early Virginia immigrants, arrived primarily in family groups and began multiplying at once. Also unlike Virginians, New Englanders seem to have lived ten or twenty years longer than their contemporaries in England; and they had far more children. Although women married at a later age than is usually supposed (probably at an average of about twenty-three in the seventeenth century and around twenty-one in the eighteenth), they commonly had five or six children. In spite of the heavy toll taken by smallpox, diphtheria, scarlet fever, and childbirth, the population kept growing at rates unheard of in the Old World. In the Southern colonies a shortage of women and a very heavy death rate held down the natural increase during most of the seventeenth century; but the importation of servants, and later of slaves, kept the population growing rapidly nevertheless. After the sex ratio evened out and the mortality rate diminished, natural increase joined with heavy immigration to send the population soaring in the eighteenth century.

The largest ethnic group of immigrants came involuntarily from Africa to man the plantations of Virginia, Maryland, and South Carolina. But the Middle colonies, especially Pennsylvania, welcomed a flood of voluntary immigrants, mainly from northern Ireland and Germany, most of whom became independent farmers. After landing in the New World, usually at Philadelphia, they traveled west to the Appalachian valleys and spilled down into the hinterland of Maryland, Virginia, and the Carolinas. The Scotch-Irish, America's most formidable frontiersmen, led the advance. Germans, in the rear, tidied up the lush valleys into checkerboards of wheat and corn and rye.

At crossroads in the farming areas, storekeepers traded hardware, clothing, and gossip for crops. But there was no real community, no local nucleus of political, social, and religious life. Even the churches responded slowly to the needs of the farmer. In colonies where the Anglican Church was supported by taxation (New York, Maryland, Virginia, and the Carolinas) it organized parishes to keep pace with the westward advance, but they were too large in area to serve the widely scattered farmers, many of whom were not Anglicans anyhow. The parish had been designed for more densely populated areas, where enough people to support a minister lived within Sunday traveling distance of his sermons. By the eighteenth century some denominations, especially Presbyterians and Methodists, were sending itinerant missionaries through the back country. Now the people could hold at least an occasional service, sometimes under a tree, sometimes in a courthouse, sometimes in a church built for the purpose. The circuit-riders, as the missionaries were called, often encountered families whose children had never seen a minister.

In the absence of village or town, colonial farmers relied heavily on a looser and larger community, the county. Every colony was divided into counties, and everywhere the county court was an important arm of government. Even in New England the county judges (appointed as elsewhere by the colonial governments) decided administrative as well as judicial questions, questions as important as where to build new roads. Outside New England, the county court took over the duties of the town and sometimes of the parish. Besides trying cases, both civil and criminal, it might record wills and deeds, take charge of orphans and the poor, register births, marriages, and deaths, collect taxes, license taverns, authorize the establishment of ferries, and pay bounties for wolves' heads. On days when the court was in session, usually once a month, farmers from near and far would gather to sue one another for small sums, to exercise in the militia, to elect a representative to the colony's assembly, or simply to watch the proceedings, learn the news, and share talk and a bottle with distant neighbors.

The thinness of community life put a heavy burden on the family. Everywhere during the colonial period the family fulfilled many more functions than it does today, but among farmers it was everything—factory, church, school, hospital, and tavern. Unless a man held especially rich land and had ready access to a market, his crops went to feed his family, with little left over for sale. He and his wife had to make everything they could not buy, which might be most of their clothing and furniture. Without a school, they had to teach their children to read; without a church, to worship at home; without a tavern, to entertain passing strangers; without a doctor, to care for their sick. Children were plentiful and made more hands to do the endless work. Some might take over the farm as their parents grew old, but most of them would eventually leave to carve new farms out of the empty land. The family with three generations under one roof was exceptional everywhere in America, as it was in England.

The farmer, isolated from his neighbors and living a self-sufficient life within his own family, was the typical eighteenth-century American—even the townsman of western New England resembled him. But as farmers spread out through the interior a significant minority of Americans piled up in five cities and several large towns along the coast.

The city. The colonial farmer riding into a city for the first time left a road that was only a ribbon of stumps and mud and came upon streets of gravel or cobblestones, where a bewildering activity surrounded him. Swine roamed everywhere, feeding on the refuse; drovers herded sheep and cattle to the butchers. Elegant carriages rolled impatiently behind lumbering wagons as great packs of barking dogs worried the horses. Sailors reeled out of taverns, and over the roofs of the houses could be seen the swaying masts and spars of their ships. The farmer had been told that the city was a nursery of vice and prodigality. He now saw that it was so. Every shop had wares to catch his eye: exquisite fabrics, delicate chinaware, silver buckles, looking glasses, and other imported luxuries that never reached the crossroads store. Putting up at the tavern, he found himself drinking too much rum. And there were willing girls, he heard, who had lost their virtue and would be glad to help him lose his. Usually he returned to the farm to warn his children as he had been warned. He seldom understood that the vice of the city, if not its prodigality, was mainly for transients like himself. Permanent residents had work to do.

The key men in the community were the merchants, for colonial cities were built on trade. Merchants bought corn, wheat, cattle, and horses from thousands of farms and fish from hundreds of fishermen and shipped them to the West Indies. The planters there could not waste their valuable sugar lands growing corn, but they needed food for their slaves and horses to turn their sugar mills. Colonial merchants supplied them and brought back molasses, a by-product of sugar-making. Distilleries turned it into rum, much of which the merchants shipped off to exchange for slaves on the coast of Africa or to help fishermen fight back the icy winds of the North Atlantic. The merchants also bought beaver and deerskins from Indian traders and huge pine trunks from lumbermen to send to England for masts. From England they brought back woolens and hardware, which the mother country made better and cheaper than the

Colonial cities were built on trade

ESTIMATED POPULATION OF COLONIAL URBAN CENTERS IN THE 1770s*			
Primary Colonial Cities		**Secondary Colonial Cities**	
Philadelphia	35,000	New Haven	8,000
New York	25,000	Norwich	7,000
Boston	16,000	Norfolk	6,000
Charles Town	12,000	Baltimore	6,000
Newport	11,000	New London	5,000
		Salem, Mass.	5,000
		Lancaster, Pa.	5,000
		Hartford	5,000
		Middletown	5,000
		Portsmouth	5,000
		Marblehead	4,000
		Providence	4,000
		Albany	4,000
		Annapolis	4,000
		Savannah	3,000

*Figures rounded to the nearest thousand.
Figures found in tables on pages 216–17 of *Cities in Revolt* by Carl
Bridenbaugh. Copyright © 1955 by Carl Bridenbaugh. Figure for Philadelphia revised.
Used with permission of Alfred A. Knopf, Inc.

colonists could. Without the merchants there would have been no cities.

Many of the other city-dwellers depended on the merchants for a living. Besides the rum-distillers, there were shipwrights who turned out ships at a lower price than English ones. Workers in ropewalks and sail lofts rigged them. Instrument-makers fitted them with quadrants, telescopes, and clocks. Retail traders helped to distribute the goods imported from abroad. Millers ground wheat and corn into flour, and coopers built barrels to ship it in.

But cities accumulate people by a magic of their own, and many colonists found jobs that had no direct connection with the overseas trade. Schoolmasters were better trained and more plentiful than in the country. Dancing masters taught ladies and gentlemen the newest steps; stay-makers laced them into the newest shapes. Barbers cut their hair; wig-makers put it on again. And dozens of skilled craftsmen offered American-made copies of the latest English fashions in wearing apparel, furniture, and houses.

For all the glamour and excitement of their environment, city-dwellers had problems that other Americans had not yet faced; city opulence bred thieves and vice of all kinds; city filth necessitated sewers and sanitation laws; city traffic required paved streets and lights; and the city's closely packed wooden houses and shops invited fires that might, and repeat-

edly did, destroy vast areas. To cope with these problems citizens relied both on voluntary associations, such as fire companies, and on their city governments. Boston and Newport were governed by selectmen and town meetings, New York (after 1731) by a popularly elected city corporation. In all three, city officials, under direct control of the citizens, were responsive to their needs. In Philadelphia and Charles Town, on the other hand, the citizens had no voice in their local government. Philadelphia was badly governed by a self-perpetuating closed corporation, and Charles Town just as badly by the South Carolina assembly.

By contemporary standards these were all substantial cities. Though small compared with London, by the middle of the eighteenth century they were larger than most English cities. Boston, which reached seventeen thousand in 1740, was at that time the largest, but it had already begun a decline that lasted for the rest of the colonial period. In the seventeenth century it had served as the shipping center for most of the mainland colonies, and it continued to serve as New England's major port. But other New England towns were cutting into its business, most notably Newport, which grew to urban dimensions in the eighteenth century.

New York City was the natural outlet and supply point for farmers in the Hudson Valley and adjoining regions of Connecticut and New Jersey; Philadelphia served not only Pennsylvania and the Delaware Valley and Bay but also the Southern back country. From the Carolinas, Virginia, and Maryland, farmers drove their wagons and cattle north along the great Appalachian valleys to the Philadelphia market. Although Baltimore began to drain off some of this trade after about 1750, Philadelphia continued to grow so rapidly that by the 1770s, with thirty-five thousand people, it ranked after London with Bristol and Liverpool as one of the largest cities in the English-speaking world. South of Baltimore the tobacco-planters dealt directly with London and needed no cities; but in South Carolina the rice- and indigo-planters shipped their produce by way of Charles Town, as did the Indian traders who trekked around the southern limit of the Appalachians and brought deerskins from the lower Mississippi Valley.

Overseas trade gave city-dwellers and plantation-owners communication with the larger world that was denied to most other Americans, and for that matter to most Englishmen and Europeans. Boston and Philadelphia, with hundreds of ships coming and going, were in closer contact with London than many English cities were. The ships carried ideas as well as goods, and colonial cities were as well equipped to distribute one as the other. Every city had at least one newspaper by the middle of the eighteenth century, with every issue devoted largely to news from England and Europe. Through the columns of the newspapers and through the books imported from abroad and sometimes reprinted locally, the city man found his way out of the seventeenth century into the eighteenth. Gradually he learned to make rationality a test of all things, to look upon revealed religion with a degree of skepticism, to cherish tolerance and shun persecution, and to expect from the progress of science (or philosophy, as he called it) what his ancestors had expected only from God. From the city such ideas filtered into the countryside. Although the cities held less than 5 percent of the colonial population, it was the best-informed and most-influential 5 percent.

The emerging American mind

Before the middle of the eighteenth century Americans had little occasion to think of themselves as a distinct people. They had no opportunity at all to act as one. There was no American government, no single political organization in which all the colonies joined to manage their common concerns. There was not even a wish for such an organization except among a few eccentric individuals. America, to the people who lived in it, was still a geographical region, not a frame of mind.

Asked for his nationality, the average American in 1750 would have said English or British. In spite of substantial numbers of Dutch, Germans, and Scotch-Irish, Englishmen and English institutions prevailed in every colony, and most colonists spoke of England as home even though they had never been there. Yet none of their institutions was quite like its English counterpart; the heritage of English ideas that went with the institutions was so rich and varied that Americans were able to select and develop those that best suited their situation and forget others that meanwhile were growing prominent in the mother country. Some of the differences were local: the New England town, for example, and the Puritanism that went with it, set New Englanders off not only from Englishmen but from Virginians. But some ideas, institutions, and attitudes became common in all the colonies and remained uncommon in England. Although American Englishmen were not yet aware that they shared these "Americanisms" with one another or that Englishmen at home did not share them, many of the characteristic ideas and attitudes that later distinguished American nationalism were already present by mid-century.

Responsible representative government. Englishmen brought with them to the New World the political ideas that still give English and American government a close resemblance. But Americans very early developed conceptions of representative government that differed from those prevailing in England during the colonial period. Representative government in England originated in the Middle Ages, when the king called for men to advise him. They were chosen by their neighbors and informed the king of his subjects' wishes. Eventually their advice became so compelling that the king could not reject it, and the representatives of the people, organized as the House of Commons, became the most powerful branch of the English government.

At first the House of Commons consisted of representatives from each county, or shire, and from selected boroughs. Over the centuries many of these boroughs became ghost towns with only a handful of inhabitants, and great towns sprang up where none had existed before. Yet the old boroughs continued to send members to Parliament, and the new towns sent none. Moreover, only a fraction of the English population participated in the election of county representatives. In order to vote, a man had to own property that would, if rented, yield him at least 40 shillings yearly. Few could meet the test. A number of Englishmen thought the situation absurd and said so. But nothing was done to improve it; in fact, a theory was devised to justify it. A member of the House of Commons, it was said, represented not the people who chose him, but the whole country, and he was not responsible to any particular constituency. Not all Englishmen could vote for representatives, but all were "virtually" represented by every member of the Commons.

Colonial assemblies were far more representative than the House of Commons. Although every colony had property qualifications for voting, probably the great majority of adult white males owned enough land to meet them. In apportioning representation, New England colonies gave every town the right to send delegates to the assembly. Outside New England, the unit of representation was usually the county. The political organization of new counties and the extension of representation seldom kept pace with the rapid advance of settlement westward, but nowhere was representation so uneven or irrational as in England.

The American colonist knew nothing of "virtual" representation; to him representation was a means of acquainting the government with his needs and demands and with the amount and method of taxation he could most easily bear. A colonial assemblyman was supposed to be the agent of the people who chose him. In the large counties, of course, it was seldom possible, except on election day, for voters to gather in one place and express their opinions. But elections came every two or three years (annually in New England and Pennsylvania), and a representative was unlikely to stray far from his constituents' wishes in so short a time. In New England, where town meetings could be called any time, people often gathered to tell their delegate how to vote on a particular issue. He was supposed to look after their interests first, those of the colony second.

In America, therefore, representative government meant something different from what it did in England. Government existed to do a job, and it had to be kept responsible to its employers. While "virtual" representatives in Parliament created offices whose only purpose was to enrich the men who filled them, colonial assemblymen, watched closely by their constituents, had comparatively little opportunity to dip into the public purse.

Clergy and laity. Americans looked on their clergymen as they did on their elected representatives. They wanted the clergy to serve, not rule, them. The attitude had its roots in the English Reformation, and most Englishmen were sufficiently Protestant to share it in some degree; English Dissenters shared it wholeheartedly. But the Anglican Church held great powers in England: it was the only church supported by state taxation; during much of the colonial period only its members could hold public office; and its bishops enjoyed an authority that reached far beyond the realm of the spirit. As ex officio members of the House of Lords they voted on every act of Parliament, and as presiding judges in courts with jurisdiction over probate of wills and breaches of morality they could impose sentence of excommunication on offenders. Since excommunication cut a man off from political rights and from intercourse with his neighbors, it could mean economic ruin as well as social ostracism. An offender could get the sentence lifted only by paying a heavy fee.

In the colonies churchmen had no such powers. Except in Rhode Island, Delaware, Pennsylvania, and New Jersey the assemblies did levy taxes in support of churches, favoring the Congregational churches in New England, the Anglican elsewhere. But this was the only connection between church and state that most Americans would tolerate. The Massachusetts rule that only church members could vote had ended with the revocation of the colony's charter in 1684.

In New England the old Puritan hostility to clerical authority persisted into the eighteenth century. Ministers were influential and highly respected; a few were even elected as representatives to colonial assemblies. But no minister enjoyed temporal authority by virtue of being a minister.

The Anglicans in America also kept their clergymen on short leash. Because England never sent a bishop to the colonies (and without a bishop there could be no ecclesiastical court), the Anglican Church lost most of its temporal powers when it was transplanted to America. In the Northern colonies, Anglicans, who were a small minority of the population, repeatedly asked for a bishop—much to the annoyance of Congregationalists and Presbyterians. In the Southern colonies, where the Anglican Church was the established church, its members were cool to the proposal. The Southerners, acting through their vestries, ran their churches and hired and fired their ministers almost as independently as any New England Puritan congregation. The minister, unless he had been formally inducted into office, could be dismissed at any time. With no bishop at hand to insist on induction, a church could simply omit the ceremony.

Probably one reason for the failure of the Anglican Church to send a bishop was the fear of resistance from non-Anglicans, who multiplied rapidly during the eighteenth century. Besides Congregationalists and Presbyterians, there were Baptists, Quakers, Dutch Reformed, Lutherans, Mennonites, and a host of minor sects. This diversity of religious groups, each growing as population grew, made it increasingly difficult for any one of them to dominate the rest and made the extension of religious authority in America ever more unlikely. Even in New England, where the Congregationalists remained a majority, they ceased after the seventeenth century to persecute Quakers and allowed persons of other denominations to support their own ministers through public taxation.

The Great Awakening. In the 1740s the number of religious groups was expanded by a rash of schisms that followed a religious revival. The Great Awakening was touched off in 1741 by a traveling English preacher who combined Calvinism and showmanship. George Whitefield, only twenty-seven at the time, was not a gifted theologian. But he had perfected a technique of preaching that brought remarkable results: he frightened his audience by depicting in vivid detail the pain awaiting sinners in Hell. He dramatized the scene for them, playing all the parts himself. Now he was an angry God booming out fearful judgments, now a damned soul weeping in anguish. He strained to bring his audience to the point of hysterical despair. He wanted them to writhe in agony, for he had found that thorough "conviction"—of their own sinfulness, helplessness, and utter dependence on Christ for salvation—was usually followed by "conversion," the feeling that they actually had been saved. As Whitefield journeyed from the Carolinas to New England, preaching indoors and out, Sundays and weekdays, he wrought conversions by the hundreds, among old and young, rich and poor, educated and ignorant.

His technique, requiring only a flair for the dramatic, was not hard to imitate. In his wake other self-appointed messengers of Christ traveled about the country, outdoing him in the sound and fury of their preaching. Gilbert Tennent, a Pennsylvania Presbyterian, made a specialty of laughing loud and long at sinners in the throes of conviction. James Davenport, an itinerant Congregationalist, was at his best at night, when smoking torches revealed him half naked, jumping up and down to stamp on the devil.

In spite of these excesses, the Awakening brought religious experiences to thousands of people in every rank of society. One of its staunchest defenders was Jonathan Edwards, minister of Northampton, Massachusetts, who had himself inspired a local revival in 1735. Edwards was the most talented theologian America ever produced. He preached a stricter Calvinism than New England had ever heard, and he recast Calvinist doctrines to give a primary place to the emotions. Although his own manner in the pulpit was an austere contrast to Whitefield's, his doctrines emphasized the emotional impact of an omnipotent God on impotent man. Both conviction and conversion, Edwards insisted, were such overwhelming emotional experiences that the human frame could scarcely contain them. If occasionally a man fell to the ground or cried out in the grip of such powerful experiences, this was no reason to doubt that the spirit of God was the moving cause. Edwards' theology commanded respect in Europe as well as America and furnished the Awakening with an intellectual foundation that Whitefield could not have provided.

But not everyone agreed with Edwards. Many ministers thought that the new method of preaching provoked more hysteria than holiness. They were shocked by the sight of masses of people wallowing in terror or ecstasy on the cue of an ignorant man screaming damnation. They were offended when itinerants entered their churches unbidden and wrung from a hitherto sane congregation a chorus of shrieks and groans and hallelujahs. After listening to an itinerant preacher, people sometimes decided their own minister was worthless, and the most enthusiastic followers of the Awakening deserted their old churches to form new ones with more rigorous doctrines and standards of admission.

Once the shrieking had subsided, it became apparent that the Awakening had seriously undermined the position of the clergy. In every denomination, but especially in the Calvinist ones, ministers had been forced to take sides in favor of the revival (New Light) or against it (Old Light). And those who

Jonathan Edwards: the most talented theologian America ever produced

The Great Awakening: New Light conviction

George Whitefield: the Great Awakener

Now it pleased God to send Mr. Whitefield into this land ... I longed to see and hear him, and wished he would come this way ... then on a Sudden, in the morning about 8 or 9 of the Clock there came a messenger and said Mr. Whitefield preached at Hartford and Weathersfield yesterday and is to preach at Middletown this morning at ten of the Clock, I was in my field at Work, I ... ran home to my wife telling her to make ready quickly to go and hear Mr. Whitefield preach at Middletown, then run to my pasture for my horse with all my might.... when we came within about half a mile or a mile of the Road that comes down from Hartford Weathersfield and Stepney to Middletown; on high land I saw before me a Cloud or fogg rising; I first thought it came from the great River, but as I came nearer the Road, I heard a noise something like a low rumbling thunder and presently found it was the noise of Horses feet coming down the Road and this Cloud was a Cloud of dust made by the Horses feet; it arose some Rods into the air over the tops of Hills and trees and when I came within about 20 rods of the Road, I could see men and horses Sliping along in the Cloud like shadows and as I drew nearer it seemed like a steady Stream of horses and their riders, scarcely a horse more than his length behind another, all of a Lather and foam with sweat, their breath rolling out of their nostrils every Jump; every horse seemed to go with all his might to carry his rider to hear news from heaven for the saving of Souls, it made me tremble to see the Sight, how the world was in a Struggle ... and when we got to Middletown old meeting house there was a great Multitude it was said to be 3 or 4000 of people Assembled together.... When I saw Mr. Whitefield come upon the Scaffold he lookt almost Angelical; a young, Slim, slender youth before some thousands of people with a bold undaunted Countenance, and my hearing how God was with him every where as he came along it Solemnized my mind; and put me into a trembling fear before he began to preach; for he looked as if he was Cloathed with Authority from the Great God; and a sweet sollome solemnity sat upon his brow And my hearing him preach, gave me a heart wound; By Gods blessing: my old Foundation was broken up, and I saw that my righteousness would not save me.

From Nathan Cole, "Spiritual Travels," October 23, 1740.

opposed it were not reconciled by the less exuberant expressions of piety that followed the initial madness. "Nay han't it been common," asked the Boston minister Charles Chauncy, "in some Parts of the Land, and among some Sorts of People, to express their religious Joy, by singing through the Streets, and in Ferry Boats?" The Old Lights, having set themselves against emotional "enthusiasm," prided themselves on a cool rationality. In this mood they reexamined Calvinist dogma and found it wanting. It was absurd, Chauncy decided, that men should suffer eternally by divine predestination: a rational God would allow some merit in human effort. The Old Lights took the road that led ultimately to Unitarianism, Universalism, and deism, to a world in which there was little need either for Christ or for clergymen. Not many Americans went the whole length of that road in the eighteenth century, but many of the best educated traveled it for some distance.

The New Lights undermined the position of the clergy in a more direct manner by teaching congregations to be bold in judging ministers. Itinerant preachers often pronounced local ministers unregenerate and made much of the idea that a minister could not be God's instrument in bringing salvation to others unless he himself was saved. With this principle in mind, the New Lights in a church did not hesitate to interrogate the minister and then

The Question is, whether it be'nt a plain, stubborn Fact, that the Passions have, generally, in these Times, been apply'd to, as though the main Thing in Religion was to throw them into Disturbance? Can it be denied, that the Preachers, who have been the Instruments of the Commotions in the Land, have endeavoured, by all Manner of Arts, and in all Manner of Ways, to raise the Passions of their Hearers to such a Height, as really to unfit them, for the present, for the Exercise of their reasonable Powers? Nay, in order to alarm Men's Fears, has it not been common, among some Sort of Preachers, to speak and act after such a wild Manner, as is adapted to affrighten People out of their Wits, rather than possess their Minds of such a Conviction of Truth, as is proper to Men, who are endow'd with Reason and Understanding? And under the Notion of speaking to the Affections, were the Things of God and another World ever preached with more Confusion of Thought; with greater Incoherence; with the undue Mixture of more rash, crude, unguarded Expressions; or with Conceit to a higher Degree, appearing in fulsome Self-Applauses, as well as unheard of Contempt of others? These are Things of too publick a Nature to be denied: They have been too often practised, and in Places of too great Concourse, to admit of Debate.

From Charles Chauncy, *Seasonable Thoughts on the State of Religion in New England,* 1743.

---

declare him saved or damned. The minister's learning, which had once won him respect, suddenly became a handicap, for many itinerants, uneducated and uneducable, dismissed religious erudition as an impediment to saving grace.

Ironically, in the decades that followed the Great Awakening, the New Light clergy of New England involved themselves so deeply in learned pursuit of Edwards' Calvinist theology that they in turn alienated their congregations. Edwards was not easily understood at best, but his disciples drew out his doctrines in subtle elaborations that scarcely anyone understood but themselves. The New Divinity it was called, and among many bright young men of the day it became the prevailing intellectual fashion. Entering the ministry, they uttered its complexities in sermons addressed more to one another than to their audience. The passionate preaching of the Awakening was forgotten, and the New Divinity grew into a recondite game for clergymen.

Congregations reacted with the boldness they had been taught by deserting the preachers who seemed to have deserted them. By the third quarter of the eighteenth century the diversity of denominations allowed a man to shop around for a preacher and a religion that suited him. An American minister was expected to serve his people. When they thought he was failing to do so, they dismissed him or left him.

Education. If the American colonist stood in no awe of his ministers and government officials, it was because the workings of state and church held no mysteries for him. He understood them better than the average European, not only because he had a large share in operating them but because he was better educated. Europeans were fond of picturing Americans as children of nature who learned wisdom from the trees and flowers but not from books. Actually, in spite of their wilderness life, or perhaps because of it, colonial Americans were a bookish lot.

Most of them were Protestants, and Protestants believed that religious truth was incomprehensible to the man who did not read the Scriptures for himself. They wanted to read; they wanted their children to read. And their desire was sharpened by the sight of the real children of nature, the Indians, naked, savage, and ignorant. In Massachusetts the law directed every town of fifty families to maintain a schoolmaster, and other New England colonies had similar requirements. The laws were not always enforced, but the rate of literacy (compared to that of England or the rest of Europe) was high throughout the colonies and especially high in New England.

Yale College

By the middle of the eighteenth century nearly every colony had at least one printing press, and the printer usually produced a weekly newspaper, devoted mainly to news from abroad and from other colonies—everybody knew the local news—and to literary and political essays and verse, much of which was culled from English newspapers. The printers also turned out broadsides, almanacs, pamphlets, and books. Though the clergy were the most prolific colonial authors and sermons the most popular reading matter, local political issues were often discussed in print. There were even some efforts at verse. The best of these, the meditative poems of Edward Taylor, minister of Westfield, Massachusetts, were not published until the present century, but colonial readers bought another minister's versified account of the Last Judgment (*The Day of Doom* by Michael Wigglesworth) in such numbers that it went through five editions between 1662 and 1701.

The colonists made early provision for higher education. In 1636, only six years after the Puritans came to Massachusetts, they founded the college that later took the name of its first benefactor, John Harvard. Although the founders' purpose was to furnish the colony with a learned ministry, Harvard was no mere theological seminary. From the be-

ginning its students followed the traditional curriculum of the liberal arts taught in European universities: they studied grammar (Latin, Greek, and Hebrew), rhetoric, logic, mathematics, astronomy, physics, metaphysics, and moral philosophy. Only once a week, on Saturdays, did they turn to theology. Those who intended to become ministers received their professional training after they graduated, not before. But many Harvard graduates, the majority after the seventeenth century, went into professions other than the ministry.

The same was true of most other colonial colleges: William and Mary, chartered in 1693, remained for some years little more than a grammar school, but Yale (1701) offered a program similar to Harvard's, and so did Princeton (1746), Rutgers (1766), Pennsylvania (1755), Columbia (1754), and Brown (1764). It was not simply the children of the well-to-do who attended these colleges. Tuition rates were low, and every class contained boys fresh from the farm. Education even at the college level was widely diffused by comparison with that of England.

The fact that New Englanders fell victim to hysteria over witchcraft has often been cited as evidence of the shallowness of their education. How could educated people be so superstitious? The answer is that educated people everywhere believed in witchcraft. In 1692 twenty persons were hanged as witches in Massachusetts, and hundreds more had been accused when the ministers' objections to the unfairness of the trials induced the government to stop them. No subsequent execution for witchcraft is recorded in America, but in Europe thousands were executed in the seventeenth century, and the executions continued into the eighteenth.

The Enlightenment. The ideas that conquered man's belief in witchcraft were originated, not by Americans, but by a succession of Europeans who had the imagination and daring to take the measure of God's world for themselves. During the sixteenth and seventeenth centuries Copernicus, Galileo, and Kepler had studied the motions of the planets and accumulated evidence to show that they rotated around the sun. Sir Isaac Newton, building on their work, discovered the laws of motion, the "natural laws" by which God governed the movement of the planets. He also studied light and learned to break it into its different colors and to bend it with mirrors and lenses. Newton's success convinced his contemporaries that human reason was capable of exploring the universe and of ascertaining by observation and experiment the principles by which God governed it. Men who had been taught that reason was a feeble instrument, all but destroyed by Adam's original sin, now turned inquiring eyes on the world around them. They wanted to measure everything, to see how the world worked.

In looking so closely at God's world, men formed a new image of God himself. Where he had formerly been an arbitrary monarch, who glorified himself in the damnation of sinners and the salvation of saints, he now became a divine craftsman whose glory lay in his craftsmanship, a celestial watchmaker whose intricate and orderly handiwork lay everywhere visible to the eyes that reason directed toward it. The new God appeared more reasonable than the old, but also more remote and indifferent, a watchmaker who wound up his universe and then left it to run itself. He seemed, in fact, so reasonable that some men decided he was reason itself, or at least that reason was an adequate substitute for him.

Though few went this far, the eighteenth century earned the title of the Age of Reason. And the English philosopher John Locke furnished the century with a theory about reason that gradually won acceptance and further encouraged the pursuit of experiment and observation. In *An Essay concerning Human Understanding* (1690) Locke concluded that the human mind at birth was not the repository of any innate ideas placed there by the Creator. Rather, it was a complete blank and only gradually accumulated knowledge from the experiences of the five senses attached to it. He who would grow in knowledge, therefore, must devote himself not simply to books, perhaps not even to the Bible, nor to abstract contemplation, but to seeing, hearing, feeling, tasting—in a word, to observation and experiment.

Man himself was a fair subject for scrutiny, and Locke turned his attention to the relations of men to one another. He decided that God had provided natural laws to make the human world run as smoothly as the physical world; but the enforcement of these natural laws of society God had left to men. In two treatises on civil government (published in 1689 and 1690 but written earlier) Locke explained that men had voluntarily left the free state of nature (in which they were born and originally lived) and had, by mutual agreement, instituted civil government for the purpose of enforcing natural laws. The most important natural law was that no man should take away the life, liberty, or property of another (these were "natural rights" of man). A government that failed to protect life, liberty, and property lost its reason for existence and deserved to be altered or overthrown by the people it governed.

Reason led Locke to condemn absolute government, whether in church or state. It led others to advocate free trade, free speech, free thought. Together, Locke and Newton gave men confidence that all the world's evils as well as its mysteries would yield to the persistent application of human reason.

This confidence in reason, which animated the European philosophers of the eighteenth century, came to be known as the Enlightenment. Although the Enlightenment originated in Europe, its doctrines penetrated society more widely in America. Students in American colleges learned Newton's physics and Locke's psychology. Ministers, whether Old Light or New, adapted their theology to the new ideas and welcomed the discoveries of reason as an aid to revelation, a means to improve their understanding of God's creation. Politicians cited Locke to support their arguments. Gentlemen formed clubs to discuss philosophy. Men awakened to the newness of the New World and turned amateur scientists; they described American plants and animals and made astronomical observations of the American skies to swell the growing body of scientific information that might provide answers to the limitless questions reason could now ask. In Boston the Reverend Cotton Mather and Dr. Zabdiel Boylston demonstrated by experiment the efficacy of inoculation against smallpox. In Philadelphia David Rittenhouse built the first American orrery, a mechanical model that reproduced the motions of the solar system.

Even the common man, who never himself read Locke or Newton, was receptive to their philosophy. To the European peasant, following the footsteps of his ancestors, unable to read or write, with no voice in church or state, the Enlightenment meant little. But the ordinary American colonist had constantly to apply his reason to new situations, whether

Cotton Mather: he welcomed the discoveries of reason

Printers are educated in the Belief, that when Men differ in Opinion, both Sides ought equally to have the Advantage of being heard by the Publick; and that when Truth and Error have fair Play, the former is always an overmatch for the latter: Hence they chearfully serve all contending Writers that pay them well, without regarding on which side they are of the Question in Dispute....

That it is unreasonable to imagine Printers approve of every thing they print, and to censure them on any particular thing accordingly; since in the way of their Business they print such great variety of things opposite and contradictory. It is likewise as unreasonable what some assert, "That Printers ought not to print any Thing but what they approve;" since if all of that Business should make such a Resolution, and abide by it, an End would thereby be put to Free Writing, and the World would afterwards have nothing to read but what happen'd to be the Opinions of Printers.

From Benjamin Franklin, "Apology for Printers," 1731.

---

in field or forest, church or state. The Enlightenment made a virtue of his necessity and encouraged him to lift his voice against unreasonableness wherever he met it.

It is perhaps no accident that the man who best exemplified the Enlightenment both to his countrymen and to foreigners was not only an American but an American who came from the ranks of common men and never lost touch with them. Benjamin Franklin (1706–90) was born in Boston, made his fortune in Philadelphia, and then spent much of the remainder of his life in England and France on political missions for the American people. His genius brought him success in everything he tried, whether it was running a Philadelphia newspaper in his youth or wooing the ladies of Paris in his old age. The Enlightenment sang the praises of intellectual freedom; Franklin as a printer defended his right to publish what he pleased. The Enlightenment called for freedom of trade; Franklin worked as a diplomat to achieve that freedom. The Enlightenment encouraged scientific experiment. Franklin made significant observations on a wide variety of scientific subjects (from ocean currents to the theory of heat); he was a prolific inventor (a stove, a clock, a musical instrument); and, as one of the first experimenters with electricity, he made important contributions to both the theory of the subject (positive and negative current) and to its application (lightning rods).

As a son of the Enlightenment, Franklin was at home anywhere in the world, yet everywhere men recognized him as a typical American. Even without the fur cap he wore to emphasize it, no one could miss his American style, his down-to-earth insistence on doing things his own way and finding out for himself. Franklin's insistence on results in everything he undertook accorded with his countrymen's insistence that their governments and churches perform what was expected of them.

Social structure. In describing America for Europeans, Franklin advised no one to go there unless he had more to recommend him than high birth, for Americans, he said, "do not inquire concerning a Stranger, *What is he?* but, *What can he do?*" Franklin wrote these words after the period we are considering—probably in 1782. But by mid-century it had already become clear that high birth meant less in America than in Europe.

Europeans learned at an early age that God made men unequal. To some he gave riches beyond measure, to others nothing. Riches brought dignity. It might take more than one generation for a wealthy family to climb to the top of the social ladder, but once there its members enjoyed the security of a title—count, duke, earl, marquis—that passed in perpetuity from father to son. In Europe, men of title generally had a voice in government. In England, even though the House of Commons became the dominant branch of Parliament, its members were drawn from the higher ranks of English society, and they could still pass no law without the consent of the highest ranks, assembled in the House of Lords.

Although the eighteenth-century American was taught that God assigned men to different ranks in society, the idea did not have quite the same meaning as in Europe. The American could see plainly that merchants and planters had more wealth and dignity than other men. And in the older settlements, by the middle of the eighteenth century, a larger share of the wealth was concentrated in the hands of a few than had been the case in the seventeenth century. But America was still the land of opportunity; with hard work and luck a humble man could better himself. The top of the social ladder was lower than in Europe and easier to reach but at the same time more difficult to hang on to. Mobility, not nobility, determined the ranks of American aristocrats, who had no titles and no place of their own in the government. They were always having to make room at the top for new arrivals; and, if they wanted to gain and keep the power that came naturally to their European counterparts, they had continually to please other people. American voters commonly recognized the socially and economically successful by electing them to representative assemblies, and governors commonly selected the most successful for seats on the council. But the voters would drop a man who did not suit them as quickly as the governor would. No one could claim a place in the government simply by virtue of his birth or social position.

If the highest born had fewer rights in America than in England, so did the lowest born. No Englishman was born a slave. And though the slave born on a tobacco plantation might have the kind of security enjoyed by a fine horse, though he might live longer than the slave on a sugar plantation in the West Indies, he had virtually none of the rights that Englishmen had attained for themselves over the centuries. By the end of the colonial period 20 percent of the colonial population was in this position. Slaves probably constituted a majority of the labor force, of persons, that is, who worked for another man rather than for themselves. And they had no hope of becoming anything else. Nobody asked either "What are they?" or "What can they do?" Everybody knew.

With so much of the labor force enslaved, the remainder of the American population was far better off than the bulk of the English or European population. A small proportion, perhaps 6 or 7 percent of the total adult males, were artisans or laborers of one sort or another who spent their lives working for other men. Most worked for themselves on land of their own. The average American, neither slave nor slave owner, enjoyed the economic and political independence that everyone in the eighteenth century associated with the ownership of land. If there was not enough land where he was born and raised, a man could find more a little farther west. Standing on his own ground, raising his own food, he could bid defiance to landlords, merchants, and politicians alike. Moreover, he was likely to have in hand an instrument of defiance with which few European peasants were familiar—a gun. It was not safe to push him very hard.

In a number of ways, then, the eighteenth-century American differed from the Englishman or the European. Unless he was a slave, he was better educated and therefore less in awe of his superiors, who were in any case not far above him. He had more control over his government and over his clergymen. He had a greater opportunity to mold his own life. He used whatever tools might serve him to do it, whether ax, plow, musket, or vote; and he got results, from governments as well as from forest and field. He did not yet know it, but he was becoming a new kind of man.

The contest for the continent

America was the spearhead of European growth. The European population did not begin its own spectacular growth until after the middle of the eighteenth century. Meanwhile Europe grew in America, where population doubled every twenty-five years.

American ways of living together had been designed for growth: the plantation with its reserve of unused and uncleared land, the New England town with its undivided commons, the farm surrounded by forest. But population rapidly outgrew existing communities, and Americans thrust steadily westward until they came up against other peoples who were uninterested in sharing American ways of living together. Indians, Frenchmen, and Spaniards preferred their own ways, and the contest with these rivals for the continent was one of the persistent facts of life for colonial Americans.

UNITED STATES POPULATION GROWTH, 1620–1860*			
1620	2,000	1750	1,171,000
1630	5,000	1760	1,594,000
1640	27,000	1770	2,148,000
1650	50,000	1780	2,780,000
1660	75,000	1790	3,929,000
1670	112,000	1800	5,297,000
1680	152,000	1810	7,224,000
1690	210,000	1820	9,618,000
1700	251,000	1830	12,901,000
1710	332,000	1840	17,120,000
1720	466,000	1850	23,261,000
1730	629,000	1860	31,513,000
1740	906,000		

*Figures rounded to the nearest thousand.
From *Historical Statistics of the United States: Colonial Times to 1957,* Series A 1–3, Z 1–19.

Indian warfare. The Indians of eastern North America were slow to perceive that their way of life was incompatible with that of the English. They often sold their land or gave it away without realizing that it would no longer be theirs too. They used the land mainly for hunting and were willing to let the English hunt on it with them. But Englishmen taking possession cut the trees, drove out the game, and evicted the Indians. Before the Indians realized what was happening, they were outnumbered.

They could probably have done nothing to stem the English advance anyhow. They were many peoples, not one, and they made war on one another as often as they did on the white invaders. Indeed they often welcomed the white man for the assistance they hoped he would offer in quarrels with their neighbors. But, except when directed and organized by the French or Spanish, they were not formidable military opponents for the English. Superior woodsmanship gave them some advantage, especially when they were armed with the white man's weapons, and they posed a constant threat to the isolated frontier farmer. But they were too independent, too incorrigibly individualistic, to submit for long to military discipline. They might gather for a surprise assault, but they could not stick together long enough to take advantage of their success.

The colonists, if not more warlike, were better armed, better organized, and more systematic about killing. Indians of the Powhatan Confederacy in Virginia massacred 347 set-tlers in a surprise attack in 1622 (Indian victories in American history are generally known as massacres), but from that time on the Virginians pursued a policy of extermination that gradually eliminated the Indian menace in the tidewater area. In 1637 the Puritans, acting in support of a group of tribes, broke the power of the one most dangerous New England tribe, the Pequots. An army led by John Mason surprised their main village at night, set fire to it, and shot men, women, and children as they ran to escape the flames. Thereafter New England suffered no serious Indian attack until 1676, when the Wampanoag chieftain Philip undertook a war that lasted longer than usual but ended with the usual result.

Rivalry with France and Spain. After 1676 the surviving Indians east of the Appalachians were too few in number to menace the English settlers. But those farther west, led by the French, stood ready to halt English

The extension of settlement, 1660–1760

expansion at the mountains. Frenchmen in Canada, from the time of Champlain's founding of Quebec in 1608, had taken an acquisitive interest in the interior of North America. Missionaries in search of souls and *coureurs de bois* in search of furs traveled up and down the Mississippi and through the wilderness of its eastern tributaries. The *coureurs* were as good woodsmen as the Indians and as casual with their lives as the old English sea dogs. One of them, Louis Jolliet, together with the Jesuit Father Marquette, descended the Mississippi to the Arkansas as early as 1673. Robert Cavelier, Sieur de la Salle, reached the mouth of the Mississippi in 1682, and seventeen years later the French took possession of Louisiana by planting a settlement at Biloxi. In 1702 they started another one at Mobile. They also set up forts and trading posts in the Illinois country at Kaskaskia, Cahokia, and Vincennes, way stations between the St. Lawrence and the Mississippi, the two main arteries into the heart of North America.

In the competition for Indian furs, the French worked under a handicap, because French craftsmen could not supply as cheaply as the English did the textiles and hardware that the Indians demanded in exchange. But, in spite of the better bargains offered by the English, the Frenchman did a better job of winning the Indians' friendship. Instead of evicting them from their land, he lived in their wigwams, married their daughters, and taught them to like Catholicism and hate the English.

The French government during the seventeenth century did not appreciate the exploits of its wandering subjects. In 1663 the king had taken New France from a French trading company, and thereafter the colony was governed by royal decrees (executed through a governor and an intendant, with no representative assembly). The king consistently discouraged the activities of the *coureurs*. He rejected, for example, the scheme of two *coureurs,* Pierre Radisson and Médart Chouart, Sieur de Groseilliers, who proposed a trading company to reach the northern fur supply by sea instead of by land; as a result, in 1672 they formed the Hudson's Bay Company in England instead of France.

Louis XIV was not interested in the wastes of Hudson Bay. Guided by his great minister Colbert, he wanted New France to be populated with hard-working, docile farmers. He sent women to entice the wild *coureurs* into a more settled life; he placed a bounty on

large families. He forbade all but a few privileged individuals to engage in the fur trade. He even enlisted the Church in the cause: men who left their farms without permission were liable to excommunication. But all Louis' efforts produced only a meager scattering of agricultural settlements in Nova Scotia, along the St. Lawrence River, and later in Louisiana and in the Illinois country. Immigrants were few, and the total population remained small, no more than fifty or sixty thousand by the middle of the eighteenth century.

Fifty thousand Frenchmen proved formidable to a million and a half Englishmen only because Louis' governors in Canada had not enforced his decrees. Count Frontenac (who governed during most of the period from 1672 to 1698), perceived the strategic importance of what the *coureurs* were doing and disregarded instructions to halt them. When-

Major Indian tribes in the East

French penetration of North America

ever France went to war with England, the *coureurs* led their Indian friends in raids on outlying English settlements in New England and New York. The English protected themselves by an uneasy alliance with the Iroquois. The Iroquois controlled the Mohawk Valley, which, in combination with the Hudson Valley, Lake George, and Lake Champlain, was the only easy invasion route through the mountains that stretched from New England to the Carolinas.

From 1689 to 1713 warfare between England and France was almost continuous, in the War of the League of Augsburg (1689–97) and the War of the Spanish Succession (1702–13), known in the colonies as King William's War and Queen Anne's War. At this time neither France nor England considered America worth the expenditure of royal troops. But the settlers, aware of how much was at stake, carried on their own warfare. The French sent their Indians to raid Schenectady and Deerfield and the thinly populated villages in Maine. The New Englanders in turn captured Port Royal in Nova Scotia in 1690, saw it returned to France at the Peace of Ryswick in 1697, and recaptured it in 1710. The Treaty of Utrecht in 1713, besides recognizing England's claim to Hudson Bay, gave her Nova Scotia with its population of more than a thousand French farmers; it left Cape Breton Island, unpopulated but strategically located at the mouth of the St. Lawrence, to the French.

In the South, where the Appalachian barrier ended, both sides had carried on their warfare largely through Indians. South Carolina furtraders rivaled the French in their skillful handling of Indian tribes. Ranging as far as the Mississippi in search of deerskins, they gradually gained the allegiance of the Yamasee and of most of the tribes forming the great Creek Confederacy of the Southeast. With Indian assistance they pushed back the Spaniards in Florida and threatened the French in Louisiana. Two years after Queen Anne's War ended, however, the Creeks and Yamasee turned and attacked their English allies. But for the loyalty of the Cherokee, South Carolina might have suffered disaster.

After their assault failed, the Creeks moved westward and the Yamasee southward. Spain had always claimed the area they vacated and now threatened to recover it. When England's countermove, the planting of Fort King George on the Altamaha River in 1721, proved

Savannah, Georgia, 1734

ineffective, she turned to a more familiar method of holding the territory. Forts and missions and Indian diplomacy were a Spanish and French specialty. The English way of occupying America had always been to live in it. English settlers had striven not so much to exploit the Indian as to displace him entirely. And in 1732 Englishmen prepared to move their homes into the area deserted by the Creeks and Yamasee.

The founding of Georgia.

During the quarter-century of peace following the Treaty of Utrecht, the population of the English colonies passed the million mark. The expansion took place east of the mountains, within the bounds of the old colonies. But one new colony, Georgia, was organized in the exposed region of South Carolina.

Like most of the original colonies, Georgia was founded for two purposes, one worldly and realistic, the other altruistic and hopeful. In order to defend her southern flank in America, England needed settlers. At the same time, an English gentleman with military experience and philanthropic motives wanted to do something for the poor. General James Oglethorpe, while serving on a parliamentary

The trustees of Georgia and American visitors

committee, had looked into the appalling condition of English debtors and paupers who frequently wound up in jail through no fault of their own.

General Oglethorpe organized other philanthropic gentlemen to seek a charter for a colony in which the unfortunate but deserving poor might rehabilitate themselves. The English government was glad to get people out of trouble at home and into the firing line on the southern frontier of the Carolinas, but it did not propose to let them get out of hand. In 1732 the government gave Oglethorpe and his friends a charter granting them authority as trustees for twenty-one years, after which the colony would revert to the king.

The trustees collected enough capital to get the enterprise off to a strong start. The area had been pictured in English tracts as a paradise compared to which the Garden of Eden was ''at most but equal,'' and settlers eager to pay their own way appeared from Scotland, Germany, and New England as well as from England. The trustees gave them their blessing and rounded up deserving paupers to go with them. In Georgia, Oglethorpe himself saw that each man got fifty acres of land (those who paid their own way might get up to five hundred acres), tools to work it with, and enough supplies for the first year.

The trustees did their best to bar sin and temptation from the new paradise. To keep the rehabilitated colonist sober they forbade rum. To keep him industrious they forbade slavery. To ensure his livelihood they forbade land sales without their permission. But the zeal was only on the part of the trustees. Georgia proved after all to be somewhat less attractive than paradise, and the Georgians thought they deserved at least the compensation of sinning like other men. In 1751 the trustees conceded defeat, allowed slavery and rum, and in 1752, a year before their charter expired, turned their fallen colony over to the king.

The colony's more worldly purpose was better realized, for Georgia had begun to serve as a very effective buffer. When England and Spain fought the War of Jenkins' Ear (1739–42) over English infiltration and Spanish atrocities in the Caribbean, Oglethorpe led the Georgians in campaigns against Florida and held off a Spanish invasion.

After the European conflict broadened into the War of the Austrian Succession (1740–48), known in the colonies as King George's War, the action shifted to the Northern colonies. There New Englanders got up an expedition under William Pepperell, a merchant from Maine, to attack the French fortress of Louisburg on Cape Breton Island. The colonists' capture of Louisburg was England's only real success on any front during the war. Although the Treaty of Aix-la-Chapelle (1748) restored the status quo and thus gave Louisburg back to France, its capture had focused the attention of both countries on the increasing strength and importance of England's American subjects.

They were a million and a half now and growing steadily. The advance guard of settlement—speculators, fur-traders, and explorers—were already probing the mountain passes and eyeing the rich bottom lands of the Ohio. France had no settlers to occupy those lands, but she did have men to fight for them. If the English grew any further, she was prepared to make it hurt as never before. The English grew.

Suggestions for reading

In many ways the most challenging problem of American history has been to discover in colonial America those institutions, attitudes, and events that found fruition in the later American way of life. George Bancroft first made the attempt on a large scale in his *History of the United States*, 10 vols.* (1834–74), in which he saw divine providence guiding the colonists toward independence. F. J. Turner searched for the answer along the frontier in *The Frontier in American History** (1920), and V. L. Parrington traced a conflict between the common man and the would-be aristocrat in *Main Currents in American Thought, Vol. I: The Colonial Mind** (1927). These men were giants, and their works are too lightly dismissed today. More recent attempts to discern the abiding meaning of the colonial past are Max Savelle, *Seeds of Liberty** (1948); Clinton Rossiter, *Seedtime of the Republic* (Part I: *The First American Revolution**) (1953); and D. J. Boorstin, *The Americans: The Colonial Experience** (1958).

The origins of the plantation system in Virginia are traced in T. J. Wertenbaker, *The Planters of Colonial Virginia* (1922), which argues that the seventeenth century was the heyday of the yeoman farmer. The servants who supplied the colonial labor force, both North and South, before the rise of slavery are the subject of A. E. Smith, *Colonists in Bondage* (1947). The origins of slavery are discussed in two thoughtful works: W. D. Jordan, *White over Black** (1968), and D. B. Davis, *The Problem of Slavery in Western Culture** (1966).

The best overall account of plantation agriculture is L. C. Gray, *History of Agriculture in the Southern United States to 1860,* 2 vols. (1933). On the Virginia plantation in the mid-eighteenth century, Louis Morton, *Robert Carter of Nomini Hall** (1941), offers a close-up view. L. B. Wright, *The First Gentlemen of Virginia** (1940), does the same for a number of earlier planters. On domestic life in the South see E. S. Morgan, *Virginians at Home** (1952), and Julia Spruill, *Women's Life and Work in the Southern Colonies* (1938). Carl Bridenbaugh, *Myths and Realities: Societies of the Colonial South** (1952), challenges many conventional ideas about Southern society.

The New England town has recently become a subject of lively interest among social historians. An important case study of a single town (Sudbury) and its English origins is Sumner Powell, *Puritan Village** (1963). Darrett Rutman has analyzed social changes in *Winthrop's Boston: Portrait of a Puritan Town, 1630–1649** (1965). K. A. Lockridge, *A New England Town** (1970), traces social and cultural forces in Dedham's first century. Michael Zuckerman, *Peaceable Kingdoms* (1970), stresses the forces making for consensus in eighteenth-century towns. Charles Grant describes a single eighteenth-century town in *Democracy in the Connecticut Frontier Town of Kent* (1961). Much valuable information about town affairs is contained in Ola Winslow, *Meetinghouse Hill* (1952).

There is no good study of the American farm in the colonial period, but the anonymous *American Husbandry,* H. J. Carman, ed. (1775, reprinted 1939), offers a wealth of information.

On the colonial cities the works of Carl Bridenbaugh are unique and outstanding: *Cities in the Wilderness, 1625–1742** (1938); *Cities in Revolt, 1743–1776** (1955); *The Colonial Craftsman** (1950); and, with Jessica Bridenbaugh, *Rebels and Gentlemen** (1942). The last is a study of Philadelphia in the age of Franklin. An outstanding history of a colonial merchant firm is J. B.

*Available in a paperback edition.

Hedges, *The Browns of Providence Plantation: Vol. I, Colonial Years* (1952). Stuart Bruchey in *The Colonial Merchant** (1966) offers a well-selected collection of source materials.

The rise of American representative government is dealt with in L. W. Labaree, *Royal Government in America* (1930), and in J. R. Pole, *Political Representation in England and the Origins of the American Republic* (1966). Jack P. Greene, *The Quest for Power* (1963), traces the rising power of the lower houses of assembly in the Southern colonies. Chilton Williamson, *American Suffrage: From Property to Democracy, 1760–1860** (1960), shows that the right to vote was enjoyed by the majority of adult males in all the colonies. A sophisticated approach to the distribution of political power is found in Robert Zemsky's analysis of Massachusetts politics, *Merchants, Farmers, and River Gods* (1971), and in Bernard Bailyn, *The Origins of American Politics** (1968). A sensitive study of social change is Richard Bushman, *From Puritan to Yankee: Character and Social Order in Connecticut, 1690–1765** (1967).

The best general survey of colonial social and intellectual history before the Revolution is L. B. Wright, *The Cultural Life of the American Colonies: 1607–1763** (1957).

W. W. Sweet, *Religion in Colonial America* (1942), is more concerned with church history than with religion itself. On the Great Awakening, see E. S. Gaustad, *The Great Awakening in New England** (1957), and L. J. Trinterud, *The Forming of an American Tradition* (1949). Ola Winslow, *Jonathan Edwards, 1703–1758** (1940), is the best biography; Perry Miller, *Jonathan Edwards** (1949), is a brilliant interpretation of Edwards' thought. Joseph Haroutunian, *Piety Versus Moralism: The Passing of New England Theology** (1932), traces the development of Edwards' theology in the New Divinity, while Conrad Wright, *The Beginnings of Unitarianism in America** (1955), shows how a liberal theology developed among the opponents of the Awakening. W. G. McLoughlin, *New England Dissent, 1630–1833*, 2 vols. (1971), is authoritative on the role of the Baptists. Brooke Hindle, *The Pursuit of Science in Revolutionary America, 1735–1798** (1956), concentrates on the organization of scientific investigation in this period. Benjamin Franklin's contributions to science are ably treated in I. B. Cohen, *Benjamin Franklin's Experiments* (1941) and *Franklin and Newton* (1956). The best biographies of Franklin are Carl Van Doren, *Benjamin Franklin** (1941), and V. W. Crane, *Benjamin Franklin and a Rising People** (1954). E. S. Morgan, *The Gentle Puritan: A Life of Ezra Stiles, 1727–1795* (1962), shows how the various intellectual forces discussed in this chapter influenced a learned New Englander.

In *American Education: The Colonial Experience* (1970), L. A. Cremin has written a broadly conceived and brilliantly executed treatment of the subject. The history of Harvard College through the seventeenth century has been written by a master in S. E. Morison, *The Founding of Harvard College* (1935) and *Harvard College in the Seventeenth Century*, 2 vols. (1936). Robert Middlekauff, *Ancients and Axioms* (1963), is an excellent study of secondary education in New England.

Francis Parkman made a study of the conflict between England and France in North America his life work, and all his writings are worth careful reading. More recently, George Hunt, *The Wars of the Iroquois** (1940), challenges some of Parkman's views; and A. W. Trelease, *Indian Affairs in Colonial New York: The Seventeenth Century* (1960), offers still another interpretation. Wilcomb Washburn, *The Governor and the Rebel** (1957), sees Bacon's Rebellion as the result of frontiersmen's desire for Indian lands. Alden Vaughan defends the Puritans' treatment of the Indians in *New England Frontier: Puritans and Indians, 1620–1675** (1965). Later New England relations with the Indians are treated in Douglas Leach, *Flintlock and Tomahawk: New England in King Philip's War** (1958) and *The Northern Colonial Frontier, 1607–1763* (1966). A valuable study of French institutions in the Mississippi Valley is C. E. O'Neill, *Church and State in French Colonial Louisiana* (1966).

*Available in a paperback edition.

4   *The second discovery of America*

England had joined the War of the Austrian Succession in order to prevent France from gobbling up the Austrian empire and thus destroying the European balance of power. The Peace of Aix-la-Chapelle, which ended the war in 1748, was recognized everywhere in Europe as more a truce than a treaty. It restored the status quo, returned Louisburg to France, took away her conquests in the Austrian Netherlands, but left her power unbroken. She set about at once to ensure that her position in America would be stronger in the next war. Not only did she refortify Louisburg, but in a more ominous move she sent her agents along the western slope of the Appalachians to build forts, to cement alliances with the Indians, to claim the region for the king of France.

Contest for empire

The Albany Congress. The English Board of Trade and the Privy Council, in order to bolster the loyalty of their own allies, called on the colonies from Virginia northward to send representatives to a meeting with the Iroquois at Albany. Virginia and New Jersey ignored the summons; but in June 1754 nineteen delegates from New Hampshire, Massachusetts, Connecticut, Rhode Island, Pennsylvania, and Maryland, together with the lieutenant-governor of New York and four gentlemen of his council, rode into Albany to confer with Iroquois chieftains who had slipped down the Mohawk Valley in response to a similar summons. As the Iroquois listened, the white men went through the formalities that Indians demanded in all negotiations: the grandiloquent declarations of esteem, the ceremonial presentation of gifts—scarlet coats, silver buttons, axes, scissors, guns. But the Iroquois had just been watching the French at work on fortifications in the interior, and they found

English talk and English gifts less impressive than French action. They departed with the gifts but without offering the hoped-for assurance that they would help when the fighting began.

While in Albany the twenty-three colonial delegates discussed a scheme that had been talked of before: the formation of a permanent intercolonial union to conduct Indian relations. Benjamin Franklin, as he rode north from Philadelphia, had thought out a plan, which he presented at the beginning of the congress. By the time the congress ended, the delegates had agreed to propose to the colonial assemblies a grand council with authority over matters of defense, westward expansion, and Indian relations. The council would handle purchases of land from friendly Indians and the planting of new settlements. It would raise armies and build forts and warships. And it would pay its own expenses by levying taxes. Its presiding officer, appointed by the

The Ohio country

king, would have veto power over all its actions.

When the plan reached the assemblies, their reaction was cool—some rejected it, others ignored it. Experience had shown them that the power to tax was father to every other governmental power. They often used it to get their own way in legislative conflicts with royal governors, and they did not propose to share it with any intercolonial council. Nor did they wish to be deprived of the chance to beat their neighbors in the race for Indian lands.

The assemblies' rejection of the Albany plan spared the English government the embarrassment of having to veto it. England wanted a unified direction of Indian affairs, not a permanent colonial union that might prove more difficult to deal with than the separate assemblies. Failure of the plan suggested that she need not worry about a union: the assemblies were apparently more uncooperative in dealing with one another than with England. No one stopped to think that Indian relations and Western policy had always been the most divisive issues in colonial politics. How to use the unsettled land in the West and how to deal with its Indian inhabitants were questions that divided coast from interior, farmer from fur-trader, merchant from landowner, colony from colony. On other questions the colonists were more united than either they or England knew.

English defeats. As the gentlemen at Albany were conducting their elaborate and unsuccessful courtship of the Iroquois, a younger gentleman was already firing on the French in the Ohio country. Virginia, instead of sending delegates to Albany, had sent a twenty-two-year-old colonel of the militia, George Washington, to help construct a fort at the forks of the Ohio (where the Monongahela and Allegheny rivers join). When Washington arrived in the Ohio country, the French were already in possession of the forks and hard at work on their own Fort Duquesne. He built a crude stockade, which he called Fort Necessity, at Great Meadows, fifty miles south, but was obliged to surrender it to a superior French force on July 3, 1754. Then the French let Washington march his men home to report that the land over the mountains belonged to France.

Washington's defeat was bad news to his fellow Virginians, for many reasons: as Englishmen they disliked Frenchmen; as Protestants they disliked Catholics; as Virginians they disliked anybody who invaded their empire. On the basis of their 1609 charter Virginians claimed all land to the west and northwest of their colony, and they were jealous of encroachments on their territory. Reluctance to admit that other colonies should have any voice in dealing with the great Virginian West may have been behind Virginia's absence from the Albany Congress.

One group of Virginians in particular regarded the Ohio country as private property. In 1747 a number of prominent planters, including George Washington's brothers, Lawrence and Augustine, had organized the Ohio Company to trade with the Western Indians and to speculate in Western lands. In 1749, with the approval of the Privy Council, the government of Virginia gave the company 200,000 acres between the Monongahela and the Great Kanawha rivers, and followed this by other grants of Western lands to other speculators. By 1751, when Robert Dinwiddie became governor, many Virginians were looking to the lands of the trans-Appalachian West to make their fortunes, and Dinwiddie himself became a member of the Ohio Company.

Dinwiddie had arranged Washington's expedition in order to hold the Ohio Valley for England, for Virginia, and for the Ohio Company. Upon Washington's return, it was apparent that the job was too big for either the Ohio Company or Virginia, and Dinwiddie signaled for help from England. Although officially England and France remained at peace, the home government recognized that the new

Cartoon by Benjamin Franklin, 1754

The war in the north, 1758–60

war was beginning, and it dispatched General Edward Braddock with two regiments.

Braddock, arriving in Virginia early in 1755, expected to increase his force by a large number of colonists and Indians and then to march on Fort Duquesne and teach the French that the Ohio Valley belonged to England. But Virginia had no wilderness diplomats to furnish the general with Indian braves. South Carolina could have delivered them, but Virginians were wary of letting Carolinians into the affairs of the Ohio country. Some Pennsylvania fur-traders showed up with their own Indian friends, who executed an impressive war dance for the general but disappeared when it came time to march. In the end, Braddock set off with only 8 Indians and about 1,200 colonial militia to supplement his 1,500 regulars. He took them successfully over the mountains, along with enough cannon to pound Fort Duquesne to dust. But as they were approaching the fort on July 9 the French surprised them and turned the march into a disastrous rout. Braddock himself was fatally wounded, and 976 of his men were killed or wounded.

The Indians of the area concluded that the English were finished, and for the next two years it looked as though they were. The colonists, despite their numerical strength, seemed more interested in scoring against one another than in defeating the French; and the English government was occupied with its European involvements. England gave Gover-

nor William Shirley of Massachusetts the title of commander in chief but left him to collect most of his men and money from the colonists. Shirley was an able man, the most popular of the royal governors, but his abilities were no match for the jealous intrigues of the other governors, the recalcitrance of the colonial assemblies, or the firepower of the French. While the assemblies dallied over raising troops, Shirley's ill-supported expeditions in 1755 against Fort Niagara and Crown Point both failed, but he did manage to build Fort William Henry at the southern end of Lake George.

Fear that France might try to regain Nova Scotia (or Acadia) led the British government in 1755 to deport several thousand French inhabitants from the province. The Acadians had lived under English rule since 1713, but they had never lost their affection for France and conscientiously passed it on to their children. Governor Shirley, recognizing that in case of a French invasion they were likely to side with the enemy, had suggested their deportation as early as 1747. In 1755 the British dispersed them through the other English colonies instead of sending them off to Canada, where they would have augmented the French forces. The circumstances of the deportations and the treatment of the refugees by the English colonists were unnecessarily cruel. But Nova Scotia was made more secure.

In 1756, after gaining the support of Prussia, England finally resolved on a full-scale conflict and declared war. It lasted for seven more years and so earned in Europe the title of the Seven Years' War. In America it was the French and Indian War. The formal declaration of war did nothing to break England's losing streak, for immediately the French defeated the English fleet in the Mediterranean and captured Minorca. In America a new commander in chief, Lord Loudoun, was given military authority over the colonial governors in order to unite the colonies in their own defense. But the colonial assemblies, holding fast the purse strings, regarded Loudoun's authority with suspicion and complied only casually with his requests for men and supplies. Nor did he achieve success with the troops, regular or colonial, that he did get. Shortly after he assumed command, the French captured Fort Oswego; in the following year they took the new Fort William Henry.

Victory under Pitt. In 1757 the English at last found a statesman to bring their real strength into play. William Pitt had never doubted England's need for him. "I am sure," he said, "that I can save the country, and that no one else can." Pitt's assurance rested on a view of the war and of England's imperial future unlike that of earlier leaders. Hitherto the war in America had been regarded as an incidental part of a traditional European war. The fighting, it was hoped, would facilitate the continued expansion of colonial population, but English statesmen weighed American victories and defeats on a European scale, for their effect on the balance of power. When Pitt took office, English policy underwent a radical change. Pitt's object was not simply to reduce French power in the European balance or to facilitate colonial expansion. He proposed instead to make England master of all North America and perhaps of the rest of the world too.

In Pitt's vision of empire Europe loomed less large than America and India. Accordingly he paid Frederick of Prussia to wage the European war and threw England's weight into a campaign of violent aggression abroad. Territory was his object, and he dipped into the national treasury with a lavish hand to pay the men who would seize it for him. Rather than waste time bickering with colonial assemblies over the cost, he promised them reimbursement for all their expenses in raising troops. The national debt went soaring, but so did colonial enlistments.

The death of General Wolfe

To drive France from the New World, Pitt needed not only men and money but military talent. He got it, as statesmen frequently have, by jumping young men over the heads of their elders. His greatest find was a gangly, hollow-chested boy of thirty, with a receding chin and a vile temper. James Wolfe was a prig and a martinet, but Pitt sensed his talent. Pitt also promoted Lieutenant Colonel Jeffrey Amherst, who at the age of forty had been in the army twenty-two years without ever holding an independent command, to the rank of major general and put him in charge of a large-scale expedition against Louisburg. With Wolfe supervising the landing operations, Amherst took the fortress on July 26, 1758, giving England her first great victory of the war.

The capture of Louisburg destroyed French power at the mouth of the St. Lawrence and jeopardized communications between New and old France. A month later Lieutenant Colonel John Bradstreet captured Fort Frontenac, which guarded the other end of the St. Lawrence on the shores of Lake Ontario. Now the French in Canada were cut off from the Mississippi Valley and had to give up Fort Duquesne, which the British renamed Fort Pitt (later Pittsburgh).

At last Pitt was ready for his grand strategy, a pincers move on Quebec and Montreal, with troops approaching from the north by the St. Lawrence and from the south by the Hudson River, Lake George, and Lake Champlain. Amherst was to operate from the south, Wolfe from the north. Wolfe sailed up the St. Lawrence with nine thousand men and on September 12, 1759, made a surprise night attack up one of the steep gullies in the cliffs that protect Quebec. In the battle that then took place on the Plains of Abraham the British were victorious, but both Wolfe and the able French commander, the Marquis de Montcalm, received fatal wounds.

With the capture of Quebec, English victory in North America was only a matter of time. The French immediately laid siege to the city, but, when spring opened the ice-choked river and a British fleet appeared, the French withdrew. During the late summer, the expected troops from the south and a force from Quebec converged on Montreal for the final campaign. On September 8, 1760, the French gave up the city and all Canada with it. The war did not end until 1763, but in its final phases the action shifted from North America

Quebec, 1759

to the Caribbean, India, and the Philippines, as England plucked the overseas empires of her European rivals.

George III. Six weeks after the fall of Montreal, King George II died. Between them, George II and his father, George I, had ruled England since 1714, when the latter had been summoned to the throne from the quiet German principality of Hanover. Neither was distinguished in intelligence or character, but George II was the more energetic and enjoyed leading the army, which knew him affectionately as the Little Captain. Though George II took an active part in selecting his ministers, the English government during his reign and his father's fell more and more into the hands of a powerful group of private families. They called themselves Whigs, in memory of the Revolution of 1688, from which they liked to date their ascendancy. Though they made an occasional bow to the principles of liberty, there was nothing revolutionary about them. Comfortable and wealthy, they entered politics to get wealthier and organized small groups or factions to juggle the spoils of office.

George II outlived his eldest son Frederick (who died in 1751 of a blow from a tennis ball); George III, who ascended the throne in 1760, was the old king's grandson. At twenty-two George III had a mind, such as it was, of his own and no intention of letting the great Whig families run *his* government.

Under the tutelage of a Scottish peer, the Earl of Bute, he had learned to dislike vice, to distrust talent, and to love patriotism, barley water, and the Earl of Bute. As a Scot, Bute had no seat in the House of Lords, and as a lord he was disqualified from the House of Commons. But the new king gave him at once a place in the inner "Cabinet Council," which was taking the place of the larger Privy Council in conducting the executive branch of government. Together, George and the Earl of Bute set about reforming the wicked ways of English politics.

The politicians shared neither the king's aversion to vice nor his fondness for Bute, and they were not interested in reform. Lacking any party organization, they could not present a united front against the king, but he and they both knew that he could not run the government without their help, and they made him pay dearly for it. For ten years George appointed and dismissed members of the council at a bewildering rate. Ministers responsible for colonial affairs came and went and came again as the king sparred with politicians over issues that usually had nothing to do with the colonies. Consequently, English colonial policy in this crucial decade was inconsistent and incoherent, not to say capricious.

When George took the throne, Pitt was running the war and the government. Trouble broke out almost immediately. Tormented by gout, hobbling about on crutches, Pitt

*George III,
King of England,
1760–1820*

North America in 1763

The Peace of Paris. With Pitt's resignation in 1761, the king's "dearest friend" became the leading figure in the council and the most unpopular man in England. Bute did not enjoy either role and retired from politics in 1763, but not until he had presided at Paris over the treaty that ended England's most successful war. The momentum of victory generated under Pitt carried the country through the final year of war without him. As he had foreseen, England ultimately had to add Spain to her list of enemies, but after crushing defeats at Manila and Havana, Spain was ready to call a halt. When Bute made peace in 1763, he took the whole of North America east of the Mississippi (Florida from Spain, Canada from France), and also took back Minorca, carved up the French possessions in India, and extricated England from her commitments in Germany. But Bute was schooled in the traditional diplomacy of balancing European powers against one another, and he was unmoved by Pitt's imperial ambitions. He gave Cuba and the Philippines back to Spain and let France give Louisiana to Spain. He returned Guadeloupe and Martinique to France and allowed her to keep the two tiny islands of St. Pierre and Miquelon as fishing bases.

Pitt was outraged by Bute's liberality toward France and Spain, and some of the colonists shared his view. But most Englishmen, both in England itself and in the colonies, welcomed the treaty even while they denounced its maker and glorified Pitt. For the colonists it meant the end of a threat that had been hanging over them for as long as anyone could remember. Now, as their children grew up and went looking for new homes, they could trek over the mountains into the lush Ohio Valley, into bluegrass lands they would name Kentucky and Tennessee, into the prairies of the Illinois country. The Indians, without the French to organize and direct them, could offer no serious obstacle to the settlement of the interior by Englishmen.

snapped at everyone who disagreed with him and did not gladly suffer the many fools he had to deal with. The politicians liked him as little as they liked Bute. With the fall of Canada and the subsequent British successes in the rest of the world, they were ready to make peace with France and rid themselves of the tyranny of this ailing genius.

Pitt was ready for peace too, provided he could strip France of all her overseas possessions. France, however, though defeated abroad, was still a formidable power in Europe and was courting the support of Spain. Pitt, hearing of the negotiations, stopped talking peace and demanded instead that England declare war at once against Spain—Pitt always preferred to attack. No one had dared oppose Pitt while England was underdog in the war with France. But he had made England strong enough to do without him, and now his colleagues would not agree to take on a new enemy. When he could not have his way, Pitt resigned the ministry.

A new empire and new ideas

In England men looked with pride at their new territories. America was still the spearhead of European growth, and the conquest of New France conjured up the vision of a Mississippi Valley filled with men who spoke English and talked fondly of a small island across the ocean as "home." Englishmen had been the first to think of North America as a place to live. Now their perception was rewarded with an empire that promised to cover the continent.

The question of imperial authority. With the coming of peace a few men sensed that the government of the empire again needed overhauling, for it was clearly inadequate for a population of 2 million about to advance into the immense interior of North America. Several colonial governors, who had seen America at first hand, wrote urgently on the subject. From Massachusetts, for example, Francis Bernard warned his superiors in England that this was "the proper and critical time to reform the American governments upon a general, constitutional, firm, and durable plan; and if it is not done now, it will probably every day grow more difficult, till at last it becomes impracticable."

Bernard's sense of urgency was justified. Most of the colonies had been founded before the supremacy of Parliament in England had been firmly established. Even after the question of supremacy was settled Parliament concerned itself little with them. But now that America had grown important to England, Parliament would be giving it more attention. That attention (as Bernard foresaw) might not be welcomed by the colonies; for, since the time of their founding, they had regularly dealt with the mother country through the king, his councils, his governors. Before Parliament began making laws for them or levying taxes on them it needed to establish its own authority over them by reorganizing their governments.

Bernard thought that all the colonial governments should be given identical constitutions by act of Parliament, with governors appointed by the king. He recognized that the colonists, like other Englishmen, expected a share in their government, and he suggested that they be represented in Parliament. He did not think that they had any right to such representation, but he felt that it would be good politics to give them a voice in the decisions that Parliament would doubtless be making about them.

Francis Bernard was an ambitious man, and his superiors probably smiled at his advice. They realized that the empire needed repair, but Bernard's far-reaching plans seemed grandiloquent and prompted as much by a desire for promotion as by the actual needs of the situation. At the moment more immediate and pressing problems demanded their attention. For the next thirteen years a succession of shortsighted politicians and an industriously dull king kept their minds on a succession of immediate and pressing problems. By so doing, they inadvertently and unintentionally taught the colonists that Americans had more in common with one another than with Englishmen.

Trouble in the West. After the war England decided to station several thousand troops permanently in America. So much blood and money had been spent winning the continent that it seemed only proper to guard it, and the presence of troops would also help to restrain any possible insubordination on the part of the colonists and discourage France from trying to regain her losses. Almost at once the troops were called into action, not against France but against her former allies, the Indians, for whom the coming of peace presaged another westward surge of English colonists. The Indians of all tribes had been restive ever since the fall of New France, and the contemptuous and shortsighted policies of General Amherst toward them gave them a foretaste of what English rule of the continent would mean. When the Ottawas, led by their chieftain Pontiac, attacked Detroit in the spring of 1763, other tribes, following his lead, fell upon the English forts and settlements from the Great Lakes to the back country of Pennsylvania, Maryland, and Virginia. Since the British troops were not well located to protect the frontiers, the outlying settlers suffered heavily before the attacks could be stopped.

Pontiac's Rebellion had the divisive effect that Western problems usually produced among Americans. Easterners were reluctant to take it seriously. Westerners blamed the Easterners for the loss of farms and the death of wives, husbands, children, and friends. In western Pennsylvania a group of outraged pioneers known as the Paxton boys fell upon a village of peaceful Indians, massacred them, and marched on Philadelphia to get some action out of the government. They were halted by the Philadelphians, who evidently feared other Pennsylvanians more than Indians.

English statesmen could easily conclude that the Americans were a hopelessly uncooperative and cowardly lot, unwilling to help one another and unable to protect themselves against savages. During the preceding French and Indian War British officers had sent back disparaging reports of colonial troops. General Wolfe himself had characterized his four companies of American rangers at Quebec as "the worst soldiers in the

Universe." Now, once again, it seemed, the colonists had demonstrated their weakness—and England proceeded to demonstrate hers.

When Bute took the Mississippi Valley from France and returned the islands of Guadeloupe and Martinique, the decision was widely justified on the grounds that the valley was potentially more valuable than the West Indies. But if its potential was to be realized, the area would have to be settled and exploited by Englishmen, not kept as a giant game preserve. British politicians recognized this fact, but most of them saw no need to hurry settlers into the great emptiness beyond the mountains, where they would be less accessible to British control. Moreover, westward expansion would aggravate the most pressing colonial problem—the Indian resistance. While their troops crushed Pontiac's warriors, the politicians drafted a solution to the problem of Indian warfare: keep the colonists out of Indian territory. They had the king issue a proclamation forbidding settlement beyond the crest of the Appalachian Mountains and advising settlers in search of homes to go to Nova Scotia or Florida, for which England now provided governments.

The proclamation had little effect on American westward expansion, for the colonists took little notice of it. But it showed that the British were incapable of grasping the desperate speed of American growth. They thought they could take their time about developing the West, that they could deflect the expanding population by issuing a proclamation.

George Grenville: he stunned the colonists

George Grenville's search for revenue.

While the king was erecting his paper fence along the crest of the Appalachians, one of his ministers was occupied with a matter closer to home, the enormous national debt that England had piled up in acquiring Canada and the Mississippi Valley. George Grenville, First Lord of the Treasury, knew his pounds, shillings, and pence. With the end of the French and Indian War and the retirement of Bute, the king turned to him as the man best qualified to put England's finances in order. Grenville was not impressed with a continent full of naked savages, impecunious Frenchmen, and wild beaver; he was impressed with a national debt that had doubled since 1754; and he was still more impressed with the cost of keeping troops under arms to protect England's new possessions. He did not question

the need for the troops. That was beyond his concern. But he had to find the money to pay them, as well as the money to pay the interest on the national debt.

Soon after he took office in April 1763 Grenville came upon a remarkable fact: the American customs service was costing the government nearly £8,000 a year in salaries but was collecting less than £2,000 in duties. Everyone knew that the colonists were importing large quantities of molasses from the French West Indies, on which the Molasses Act of 1733 required them to pay a duty of sixpence a gallon. Obviously they were evading the duty. In October 1763 Grenville issued a sharp directive for its collection and ordered the British navy to patrol American waters for smugglers.

Grenville had another grievance against the colonists: they alleviated their perpetual currency shortage (resulting from their unfavorable balance of trade with the mother country) by issuing paper money. Although the money served an essential purpose and showed little depreciation in most colonies, its value was less than that of English sterling coin. English creditors feared that the colonists might manipulate the rate of exchange between their currency and sterling and try to pay their English debts at an artificially low rate. As a result of complaints by creditors, the New England colonies had been forbidden in 1751 to make their paper money legal tender. By the Currency Act of April 1764, Grenville extended the prohibition to all the colonies.

In the same month Grenville directed through Parliament an act (later known as the Sugar Act) revising American customs duties and regulations. With good reason he reduced the duty on foreign molasses from sixpence a gallon to threepence. The purpose of the original levy had been to induce the colonists to buy their molasses from the British West Indies, where they could get it duty free (though higher priced). But colonial rum-distillers balked at paying premium prices for British molasses or the sixpence duty for French. To have done so, they claimed, would have raised the price of their rum to the point where it could not be sold in competition with other spirits. So the colonial importers simply bribed the customs officials (from a halfpenny to a penny and a half per gallon) not to collect the duty. Grenville accepted the fact that the sixpence duty was too high, but he believed that if the merchants could afford to pay bribes, they could afford, instead, a three-pence duty.

The Sugar Act also imposed new duties on colonial imports of sugar, indigo, coffee, pimento, wine, and textiles. To discourage smuggling, it required that elaborate official papers be filed for every ship entering or leaving a colonial port. Finally, it provided that violators of the customs regulations could be tried in admiralty courts, which operated under royally appointed judges acting without juries (in the common-law courts juries made up of local residents were inclined to sympathize with offenders). The colonists had been subject to such an enactment since 1696, but ambiguities in it had often enabled smugglers to avoid admiralty jurisdiction.

The stated purpose of the Sugar Act was to help defray the expenses England would incur in protecting her new American possessions. Grenville did not expect to raise the whole amount from the colonists, but he did expect more than the new duties were likely to yield; and in introducing the bill for the Sugar Act to Parliament he announced that he might levy a stamp tax on the colonies.

There was nothing novel in the idea of stamp taxes. Englishmen at home had been paying them ever since the reign of King William, and there had already been suggestions that Parliament impose such taxes on the colonies. Massachusetts had even tried a stamp tax of her own in 1755. By February 1765 Grenville had completed his study of taxable items being used in the colonies and was ready to introduce his Stamp Act to Parliament. It called for taxes on every type of legal document and on newspapers, almanacs, playing cards, and dice (all of which had to bear a stamp, signifying that the tax was paid). As in the case of the Sugar Act, violators would be prosecuted in admiralty courts. A few members of Parliament raised objections to taxing the colonists. Colonel Isaac Barré, who had served under Wolfe in North America, warned that the Americans would resist. But the act passed both houses and was signed by the king on March 22, 1765, to take effect November 1.

In May 1765 Grenville put through a third measure, the Quartering Act, to help support English troops in America. This act provided that any colony in which troops were stationed must furnish them with living quarters and with fire, candles, vinegar, salt, bedding, and beer, cider, or rum.

Colonial suspicions. The colonists were stunned by Grenville's actions. In 1763 colonial merchants felt sure that his order calling for the strict collection of molasses duties would ruin the rum trade and the whole New England economy with it. Nor did they welcome the reduction in duties provided by the Sugar Act, for they believed that even a three-pence duty would drive their rum out of the market. Moreover, the act established customs procedures so strict and complicated that all kinds of trade would be hampered. The currency restriction made matters still worse. With silver in short supply and with paper money no longer legal tender, merchants had no medium of exchange and were sometimes reduced to barter. When economic depression followed the acts, Americans blamed Grenville.

But the most shocking aspect of Grenville's measures was that they seemed to embody a new policy—a deliberate aim to disinherit the colonists by denying them the rights of Englishmen. The Americans believed that it was their right as Englishmen not to be taxed except by their own elected representatives; but Parliament had taxed them directly in the Stamp Act, indirectly in the Sugar Act and the Quartering Act. They believed that it was their right as Englishmen to be tried by juries of their peers; but Parliament had made infringement of the Sugar and Stamp acts punishable in admiralty courts. These courts were objectionable not only because they violated the right to trial by jury but because they put the burden of proof on the defendant, assuming that he was guilty until he proved himself innocent. Furthermore, in England admiralty courts tried only cases arising on the high seas. By giving the courts a wider jurisdiction in the colonies, the Sugar and Stamp acts suggested that England thought Americans not entitled to rights long recognized in the mother country.

Further evidence of some sinister design seemed apparent in the announced purpose of the acts: to support troops in America. Why, the colonists wondered, did England want to keep armed soldiers in their midst? The troops had helped, to be sure, in crushing Pontiac's Rebellion, which the rash actions of their commander, General Amherst, had actually helped to bring on. But protection against Indians was patently not the purpose of keeping troops in America. Before 1754, while the French were sending their Indian allies to attack the colonists from Maine to Carolina, England had maintained scarcely any military garrison in America. Now, with the danger gone, with the French crushed and the Spaniards pushed beyond the Mississippi, she insisted on keeping several thousand men on hand. Why? Perhaps, it was whispered, England intended to use the army not to protect but to suppress the colonists. There is evidence in British documents that such an intention did in fact exist, but the evidence was not known to the colonists. Grenville's acts, however, were sufficient in themselves to prompt suspicions.

Colonial convictions. The British statesmen who started Americans talking of standing armies, taxation without representation, and trials without juries would have done well to consider the origin and history of the colonies. New England and many other parts of America had been founded by Puritans who carried to America the ideas that shortly led to Oliver Cromwell's commonwealth in England. After that commonwealth ended with the restoration of the monarchy in 1660, many more Dissenters joined the exodus to America, and their descendants could talk of Hampden and Pym and other heroes of the struggle against Charles I with a familiarity that might have struck some Englishmen as quaint. Though loyal to the House of Hanover, the colonists admired much in the writings of James Harrington, the advocate of republican government, of Algernon Sidney, and of John Locke.

Locke no Englishman found quaint. In affirming the natural right of a people to alter their government (see p. 67), he had provided his countrymen with an intellectual justification for their long contest to gain ascendancy over their kings. All Englishmen believed that the course of their history had been a struggle to achieve a government that would protect their lives, liberty, and property. They believed that they had at last achieved such a government with the overthrow of James II in 1688 and the establishment of the House of Hanover in 1714. The colonists shared this belief, and they were proud to be members of the nation whose government stood foremost in the world in protecting the natural rights of its subjects.

Like other Englishmen the colonists regarded the representative nature of English government as the most important guarantee of continued protection. They rejoiced in Parliament's supremacy in England and in the supremacy of their own assemblies in America. In each the elected representatives of the people guarded the rights of Englishmen, and the most precious right they guarded was the right of property, without which neither life nor liberty could be secure. Since the power to tax was a power to take away property, no man could call himself free if he was taxed without his own consent, given either personally or by his representative. The right to be taxed in this way, and in no other, was a hard-won principle of the British constitution. In England only the representative branch of Parliament, the House of Commons, could initiate tax bills; and in the colonies the representative assemblies claimed the same exclusive privilege. It therefore seemed monstrous to Americans that, in the Sugar Act and the Stamp Act, Parliament, a body in which they had no representative, had presumed to tax them. If Parliament could levy these taxes it could levy others. Once the precedent was set, the colonists would be as badly off as England had been before the rise of Parliament. They would, ironically, be oppressed by the very body that had rescued England from the same kind of tyranny.

As the colonists measured acts of Parliament against their own ideas of right, they faced the question that Governor Bernard had wished to settle earlier, the question of Parliament's authority in America. Their decision was different from Bernard's. Parliament, they believed, had some right to legislate for them; but it had no right to tax them. It was the central legislative body for matters of common concern to the entire empire, and as such it could regulate their commerce, even by imposing duties to discourage certain kinds of trade that it believed prejudicial to the good of the empire as a whole. But it had no right to levy duties to raise money; such duties were taxes, and Parliament had no right to tax the colonies in any manner. Its members could not grant the property of people whom they did not represent.

The American colonists in 1764 and 1765 were remarkably unanimous in adopting this distinction between taxation and legislation. They began to affirm it in pamphlets and newspaper articles as soon as the Sugar Act was passed. New York and Virginia expressed it officially in petitions to Parliament. By the time the Stamp Act was passed, people in every colony were discussing the limits of Parliament's authority, and during the summer and fall of 1765 colonial assemblies passed resolutions setting forth those limits.

The Stamp Act crisis. The Stamp Act was to go into effect on November 1. In the May session of the Virginia assembly, Patrick Henry, a young lawyer, presented a series of resolutions declaring that only the House of Burgesses had the right to tax Virginians. The Burgesses adopted the resolutions but rejected some additional ones calling for outright resistance if England should try to collect the stamp tax. The other colonial assemblies rapidly followed Virginia's example, modeling their own resolutions on hers. Although the newspapers had printed Henry's rejected resolutions as though they had actually been passed, thus creating the impression that Virginia had acted more radically than was the case, nevertheless most of the other assemblies stopped where Virginia did, with a simple denial of Parliament's right to tax the colonies.

In addition to the resolutions of their individual assemblies, the colonies prepared a joint statement of their position. In June, before the colonial consensus had become apparent, Massachusetts proposed that all the colonies send delegates to a general meeting for the purpose of concerting their opposition to parliamentary taxes. Nine assemblies complied: in October 1765 the Stamp Act Congress met at New York. After avowing "all due subordination" to Parliament, the delegates resolved that colonial subordination did not include acceptance of parliamentary taxation

or of admiralty courts operating beyond their traditional limits. They also sent petitions to king and Parliament demanding repeal of the Sugar and Stamp acts.

In objecting to taxation by Parliament, the colonists believed that they had common sense, natural law, and the British constitution all on their side. It was common sense that they already contributed to the wealth of the mother country by submitting to the Navigation Acts. If a more direct contribution was required, it ought to be made by the colonists' own representatives, who alone could know, as the Virginia resolves said, "what Taxes the People are able to bear, or the easiest Method of raising them, and must themselves be affected by every Tax laid on the People." If the members of Parliament could establish their authority to tax the colonies, they would have an all but irresistible motive to shift their own burdens and those of their constituents to America. Every penny collected in the colonies would be a penny less to take from English pockets. It was common sense that such a situation spelled tyranny.

It was also a violation of the British constitution and of the laws of nature by which every free people should be governed. The people's right to be taxed only by their own representatives was "the grand Principle of every free State . . . the natural Right of Mankind," proclaimed the members of the New York assembly. The Massachusetts assembly, in the same vein, announced that "there are certain essential Rights of the British Constitution of Government, which are founded in the Law of God and Nature, and are the common Rights of Mankind." Among those rights was "That no man can justly take the Property of another without his Consent."

Besides informing Parliament and posterity of what was right, the colonists took practical steps to see that right prevailed. Merchants in New York, Philadelphia, and Boston agreed to stop importing British goods, hoping by economic pressure to enlist British merchants and manufacturers against the Stamp Act. Other Americans, too impatient to wait for repeal, were determined to prevent the Stamp Act from taking effect. On the night of August 14, a Boston mob stormed the house of Andrew Oliver, the local stamp-distributor. They broke the doors and windows and roamed through the house calling for the owner's head. Oliver resigned his office the next day. Stamp-distributors in other colonies

"Stamp Master Hanged in Effigy"

THE REPEAL. — or the Funeral Procession, of MISS AMERIC-STAMP.

hastened to follow Oliver's example. Mobs helped those who hesitated to make up their minds. On November 1, when the act was scheduled to go into effect, there was no one to distribute the stamps.

In every colony the violence that forced the resignation of the distributors had been carefully engineered by a group of conspirators. These men now organized under the name of Sons of Liberty and prepared to resist ''to the last extremity'' any efforts to enforce the Stamp Act. They had learned from John Locke that a people could alter or overthrow a government that exceeded its authority; and they repeated Locke's precepts to their countrymen in resolves, like those adopted at New London on December 10, 1765, declaring that ''the People have a Right to reassume the exercise of that Authority which by Nature they had, before they delegated it to Individuals.''

The total overthrow of government did not prove necessary. For a few weeks after November 1, people in most colonies simply refrained from doing any business that required stamps. Then newspapers began to appear without them. By threatening mob action, the Sons of Liberty soon persuaded judges to try cases and customs officers to clear ships with unstamped bonds and clearance papers. In less than three months the Stamp Act had been effectively nullified.

English response to colonial defiance was not what it might have been had Grenville remained in power. George III, for reasons that had nothing to do with the colonies, dis-

missed Grenville in July 1765 and in his place named the Marquis of Rockingham as first minister. Rockingham and the men he brought into the administration with him had opposed the Stamp Act in the first place and wanted nothing more than to escape the embarrassment of trying to enforce it. English merchants, stung by the American boycott, reinforced Rockingham's determination to wipe the act off the books, and he enthusiastically favored a repeal bill in Parliament.

But the spate of resolutions and riots in the colonies made repeal difficult. Most members of Parliament were reluctant to back down, especially after William Pitt, with his usual tactlessness, publicly rejoiced at American resistance and endorsed the colonists' definition of the limits of Parliament's authority. Taxation, he said, was ''no part of the governing or legislative power.'' Other members were baffled by the distinction between taxation and legislation. Grenville declared it absurd. But in March 1766 Parliament repealed the act after first passing a Declaratory Act, which deliberately skirted the distinction and simply affirmed the authority of Parliament to ''make laws and statutes of sufficient force and validity to bind the colonies and people of America . . . in all cases whatsoever.'' Precisely what that meant Americans were to find out later. For the moment they rejoiced in the end of the contest that had led them to the brink of war with the mother country. Repeal of the Stamp Act seemed to signal a return to the Old Colonial System under which England and her colonies had alike enjoyed freedom, prosperity, and harmony. Now they might take up once again the position of leadership in world trade that they had won together.

Colonial discoveries. Nevertheless, as the colonists joined their English friends in celebrating repeal, they could reflect on their discoveries of the preceding two years. They had already found out more than England could have wished. A decade earlier, when the Albany Congress proposed a union against a danger in the west, they had unanimously declined. This time, when the danger came from the east, they had spontaneously joined to boycott British goods, to prevent the distribution of stamps, to define the limits of Parliament's authority. Indian tomahawks and French guns had revealed nothing but discord; the threat of tyranny had revealed fundamental agreement. The definition of Parliament's authority that the Stamp Act Congress had formulated was no compromise measure reluctantly agreed to under the pressure of circumstance. The congress merely reiterated principles already familiar in newspapers and pamphlets, principles that the colonial assemblies themselves had embodied in their resolutions. It nevertheless surprised the Americans to find themselves agreeing so readily. "The Colonies until now were ever at variance and foolishly jealous of each other," Joseph Warren of Massachusetts wrote to a friend, "they are now . . . united . . . nor will they soon forget the weight which this close union gives them."

In defending their rights the colonists also discovered that the ideas which united them and which they thought inherent in the British constitution were not shared by most Englishmen. Men in England had denied not only the colonists' distinction between taxation and legislation but also their conception of representation. At the outset of the tax controversy Grenville and his backers, admitting that Englishmen had a right to representation in the body that governed them, had claimed that the colonists *were* represented—not actually but virtually. A member of Parliament, Grenville maintained, represented not only the men who elected him, but the whole empire. The concept of virtual representation was widely accepted in England, but it was nonsense to Americans, who thought that a representative should be directly responsible to his constituents. By Grenville's reasoning, they said,

Parliament could equally well claim an authority to tax the whole world.

Although a few suggestions had been made, like Governor Bernard's, that England should allow the colonies to send representatives to Parliament, the colonists did not take to the idea. It would be impractical, they thought, because of the great distance. Colonial representatives in London would lose contact with their constituents; it would cost too much to send them back and forth and to pay for their keep; they would be corrupted by the metropolis. But most important, there would be too few of them to have any real effect on the decisions of empire, yet their presence could be used to justify Parliamentary taxation of America.

These objections were serious, but not insuperable had either England or the colonies wanted to resolve them. But the plain fact was that the colonists did not want representation in Parliament. Perhaps they were unconsciously influenced by a new attitude that had been taking shape in the colonial mind but that few men yet recognized. England, by treating the colonists differently from Englishmen at home, was teaching them what she should have done her best to conceal: that they actually *were* different, and perhaps even wanted to be.

Though England had no way of knowing it, the men in whom this attitude first took hold included several of extraordinary ability. In Massachusetts three emerged as leaders of the opposition to Parliamentary taxation: James Otis, Samuel Adams, and John Adams. Otis, a lawyer, was volatile, unpredictable, and unbalanced, but powerful in argument and very influential among the people of Boston. Samuel Adams, a failure at everything else he tried, was a brilliant politician, gifted in organizing popular support for any measure. In the years to come, as Otis became more erratic and finally went insane, Adams would become the virtual dictator of Boston, against whom royal governors would write home in helpless expostulation. John Adams, whose gifts were more those of a statesman than of a politician, was as ardent as his cousin Samuel in hostility to Parliament. He despised everyone who sought political office by royal appointment, and he searched out opportunities to advance the interests of America and Americans.

In Virginia the Stamp Act had alerted another trio of men whose names would likewise

Samuel Adams: a brilliant politician

The Fact is, that the Inhabitants of the Colonies are represented in Parliament: they do not indeed chuse the Members of that Assembly; neither are Nine Tenths of the People of Britain Electors; for the Right of Election is annexed to certain Species of Property, to peculiar Franchises, and to Inhabitancy in some particular Places; but these Descriptions comprehend only a very small Part of the Land, the Property, and the People of this Island....

The Colonies are in exactly the same Situation: All British Subjects are really in the same; none are actually, all are virtually represented in Parliament; for every Member of Parliament sits in the House, not as Representative of his own Constituents, but as one of that august Assembly by which all the Commons of Great Britain are represented. Their Rights and their Interests, however his own Borough may be affected by general Dispositions, ought to be the great Objects of his Attention, and the only Rules for his Conduct; and to sacrifice these to a partial Advantage in favour of the Place where he was chosen, would be a Departure from his Duty; if it were otherwise, Old Sarum would enjoy Privileges essential to Liberty, which are denied to Birmingham and to Manchester; but as it is, they and the Colonies and all British Subjects whatever, have an equal Share in the general Representation of the Commons of Great Britain, and are bound by the Consent of the Majority of that House, whether their own particular Representatives consented to or opposed the Measures there taken, or whether they had or had not particular Representatives there.

From Thomas Whately, *The Regulations Lately Made...*, 1765.

Patrick Henry: eloquent and erratic

become unpleasantly familiar to Englishmen. Patrick Henry, as eloquent and almost as erratic as James Otis, gained instant fame by sponsoring Virginia's resolutions against the Stamp Act. George Washington, known to at least a few outside Virginia for his service in the late war, was more given to actions than to resolutions. He was at the House of Burgesses and may have voted for Henry's resolutions, but his thoughts went more toward home manufactures and new crops as a means of shaking off America's economic dependence on Great Britain. Thomas Jefferson, a twenty-two-year-old law student, was too young for politics in 1765. But he stood at the door of the House of Burgesses and listened to Henry's "torrents of sublime eloquence." Later Jefferson would show a certain eloquence himself.

Townshend's folly. The repeal of the Stamp Act set the bells ringing in England and America. But the Marquis of Rockingham, who had engineered the happy event, found himself unable to please either king or Parliament. In July 1766 he went the way of Grenville, and George III gave the government once again to William Pitt, now Earl of Chatham. Unfor-

tunately, bad health made Pitt a mere figurehead, and the new government fell under the influence of the headstrong and irresponsible Chancellor of the Exchequer, Charles Townshend.

In taking up the search for revenue, Townshend, like Grenville, looked to the colonies. Fastening on their reviving trade as the likeliest source of new income, he persuaded Parliament in 1767 to pass an ill-considered act levying duties on colonial imports of lead, paint, paper, glass, and tea. Since these items could be legally imported only from England, the new taxes would actually discourage purchases from the mother country and encourage the manufacture of taxable goods in the colonies, thus violating every principle that British economic policy had hitherto supported. The taxes also violated the colonists' expressed views on the limits of Parliament's authority.

The colonial assemblies were at this time registering their unabated disapproval of Parliamentary taxes by resisting Grenville's Quartering Act, which they regarded as a form of taxation. To demonstrate their own superior authority, they voted to supply only part of the provisions that the act specified.

Representative government: an American view

From the Providence *Gazette,* May 11, 1765.

Townshend nevertheless believed that the colonists were becoming more amenable to taxation, especially to taxes on trade, because they were paying the duty on molasses. In 1766 the duty had been reduced to a penny a gallon, which approximated the cost of a bribe; it had also been extended to include molasses of British production. This new duty was clearly a tax and not a regulation of trade. Encouraged by the colonists' seeming compliance, Townshend decided that, if he but acted boldly, he could now settle the question of Parliament's authority in America for good and all.

To cow the assemblies into obeying the Quartering Act, he made an example of New York, one of the principal offenders: in 1767, at his bidding, Parliament declared all acts of the New York assembly to be void until the colony furnished full supplies for the troops quartered there. To ensure collection of his new taxes on trade and of older regulatory duties as well, Townshend directed a reorganization of the American customs service. Hitherto customs officers throughout the empire had been under the administration of a board of commissioners located in England. From now on a special board of commissioners for America would reside in Boston, the center alike of colonial smuggling and of open resistance to taxation.

Americans did greet the Townshend Acts less violently than they had the Stamp Act, but they soon made it clear that they were just as determined as ever to rid themselves of Parliamentary taxation. The New York assembly was hailed everywhere for its resistance to the Quartering Act. Once again newspapers and pamphlets cited the British constitution and the laws of nature. Once again the representative assemblies, stiffened by a circular letter from Massachusetts, denied the authority of Parliament to tax the colonies. Once again merchants joined in nonimportation agreements, and violators received visits from the Sons of Liberty.

The new customs commissioners were as unpopular as the new duties. They were regarded as superfluous bureaucrats sent by a corrupt ministry to fatten on the toil of Americans. And, it was feared, they were only the first of many to come; soon the colonist would have to support as many functionless office-holders as the taxpayer in England did.

The commissioners lost no time in exceeding everyone's worst expectations. The procedures prescribed by the Sugar Act were immensely complicated, and it was easy for a merchant to make an unintentional mistake in carrying them out. By insisting on technicalities, an unscrupulous commissioner could usually find a pretext for seizing a ship and its cargo of goods. Rather than take the risk, most merchants were willing to grease the commissioners' palms. Anyone who refused to play the game was likely to have his ship condemned in an admiralty court: unless he could prove that he had fulfilled every provision of the law, the court would order his ship and cargo sold. One-third of the proceeds went to the English Treasury, one-third to the governor of the colony, and one-third to the customs officers prosecuting the case.

The officers had nothing to lose—except perhaps their lives. Even that danger was reduced when the commissioners persuaded the authorities in England to provide special protection against the hazards of their occupation. In September 1768 two companies of troops were sent to Boston.

England's readiness to send the troops indicated how far her relations with the colonies had deteriorated and what caliber of men had taken over the empire. In 1768 Lord Hillsborough had just been made Secretary of State for the Colonies, a post created to handle the increasingly complex colonial business. His decision to send the troops to Boston may have sprung from ignorance of the situation there, but it was one of a series of blunders that prompted Benjamin Franklin to characterize his conduct in office as "perverse and senseless."

The Boston Massacre

The English troops landed in Boston without trouble. Samuel Adams had called for resistance. But the Massachusetts assembly was under suspension for refusing to rescind its circular letter against the Townshend Acts, and the extralegal convention that Adams organized in its place was unwilling to act on his radical demand.

The presence of the soldiers in Boston nevertheless spelled tyranny to Americans everywhere and showed again that England regarded Americans as not quite Englishmen. The soldiers themselves contributed to the impression by their arrogance. Even during the French and Indian War, when British and colonial troops were fighting side by side, the regulars had never disguised their contempt for the Americans. Now the feeling was returned with interest.

For a year and a half the soldiers lived in Boston, suffering icy stares, open taunts, and all the subtle harassments the citizens could devise. Hostility was steadily aggravated by the inflammatory speeches and publications of the indefatigable Samuel Adams on the one side and by the rapacity of the customs commissioners on the other. But there was no real violence until March 5, 1770. On that day a crowd looking for trouble found it in front of the Boston customhouse. They jeered the ten soldiers who stood guard before it, pelted them with oyster shells, snowballs, and sticks of wood, dared them to fire. The soldiers did fire, and so, it was later charged, did some of the customs men from the windows of the building. Eleven of the unarmed rioters were hit, five of them fatally. The massacre, as the Bostonians called it, roused such hostility to the troops that Lieutenant-Governor Thomas Hutchinson ordered them to Castle Island in the harbor. There they sat for the next four years.

Meanwhile a movement to repeal Charles Townshend's taxes was growing in England. Townshend died shortly after his acts were passed, and almost at once Englishmen began to realize that the Townshend duties were a mistake. Even without the pressure of colonial nonimportation agreements, English merchants would have protested against taxes that encouraged colonial manufacturing. Many members of the king's council favored outright repeal of the duties, but once again the government was reluctant to back down in the face of colonial defiance. The new Chancellor of the Exchequer, Lord North, who took office January 31, 1770, suggested that all the duties that encouraged colonial manufactures be repealed and that only the duty on tea, which could not be grown in America, be retained. Since Americans were inordinately fond of tea, they were importing substantial quantities of it in spite of the duty. By keeping the duty in force, England would preserve an annual revenue of ten or twelve thousand pounds and would also sustain her authority.

Parliament adopted North's solution, and the king was pleased. North was the kind of politician George had been looking for—a plodding, dogged, industrious man, neither a fool nor a genius, much like the king himself. For the next twelve years, despite the opposition of abler men, he remained at the head of the government.

Toward independence

North's repeal of all the Townshend duties except the one on tea was well calculated. In England it mollified both the merchants and the Parliamentary critics of the administration. In America it brought a wave of good feeling for the mother country, comparable to that following repeal of the Stamp Act. The Sons of Liberty met defeat when they demanded perseverance in the boycott of British goods until the tax on tea should be repealed. Merchants began importing, and trade boomed. Royal governors reported that only a factious few continued to object to British policies.

Discord and concord. As good will toward the mother country rose, the recent harmony among the colonists themselves gave way to new quarrels, from which England concluded, too hastily, that American unity was a fiction. Anglicans in the Northern colonies petitioned for the appointment of an American bishop; most Anglicans in the Southern colonies opposed such an appointment; Congregationalists and Presbyterians everywhere were horrified at the prospect but were unable to cement an effective union amongst themselves to work against it.

The West was also causing trouble again. In both North and South Carolina settlers in the back country complained that the assembly was dominated by Easterners, that its taxes were too high, that its officials were corrupt, that it had failed to extend county organization in the West. In 1771 a large force of Westerners calling themselves Regulators rose against the tax collectors of North Carolina. An army of Easterners defeated them easily at the Battle of Alamance, but the clash left the back-country men with an enduring hatred of the East.

In other colonies disputes arose over the control of western lands. Connecticut claimed land on the Susquehanna River in northeastern Pennsylvania and even organized a county there. In England Connecticut agents pressed for official recognition of their claim and Pennsylvania agents for its rejection. Meanwhile Pennsylvanians and Virginians were squabbling over lands in the Ohio Valley.

England still adhered to the land policy outlined in the Proclamation of 1763 —namely, that a boundary line should be maintained between settlers and Indians. But now, instead of following the crest of the Appalachians, the line was set farther west by treaties with various Indian tribes (with the Iroquois at Fort Stanwix in 1768, with the Cherokee at Hard Labor in 1768 and at Lochaber in 1770). Americans, however, were still competing vigorously for land beyond the line. A group of speculators from the Middle colonies kept agents in England lobbying for the creation of a colony, to be known as Vandalia, south of the Ohio River. The site of the proposed colony was in territory claimed by Virginia, and the speculators of the Ohio Company angrily protested the scheme. The company was also quarreling with other Virginia speculators. Hillsborough refused to authorize the new colony.

To British politicians all these disagreements seemed more serious than they were, and colonial good will toward England seemed stronger than it was. The good will, though real, rested on the hope that Parliament was retreating from its new policies. American hostility to those policies was by no means extinguished, nor was it likely to be, so long as customs commissioners sat in Boston, the British navy patrolled American waters, and admiralty courts condemned American vessels without jury trial. Men like Samuel Adams were able to keep the colonists talking about

The West: Indian treaties and speculative claims

colonial rights and Parliamentary tyranny by seeing to it that every new affront committed by the British was given wide publicity in the newspapers. And then, in 1772, at Adams' instigation the towns of Massachusetts appointed committees to formulate statements of American rights and grievances and to correspond with one another on the subject. From Massachusetts the idea spread through the rest of New England; and in 1773, as a result of the *Gaspee* affair, it was taken up on an intercolonial basis.

The *Gaspee* was a British naval vessel, which, in 1772, patrolled Narragansett Bay and inflicted daily outrages upon the inhabitants: her commander seized small boats engaged in local traffic; her sailors cut orchards for firewood and helped themselves to livestock. When the *Gaspee* ran aground on one of her missions, the people of Providence came out after dark and burned her. It was a daring action and not the first of its kind. England decided to make an example of the colony. Suspecting that Rhode Island courts would make no serious effort to uncover the culprits, she appointed a special commission to investigate the incident. But Rhode Islanders would give no helpful testimony, and the commissioners never discovered the guilty parties.

The *Gaspee* commission attracted attention throughout America. Because it bypassed the Rhode Island courts, the colonists regarded it as an infringement of common-law procedures and consequently of the rights of Englishmen. In Virginia the assembly felt incited to establish a committee of correspondence for the whole colony (Patrick Henry was a member) and to propose that each of the other colonies appoint a committee of its own. When the proposal was accepted, Americans gained the machinery for coordinating their views and actions on any question affecting their common interests.

"The Bostonians paying the excise man"

The Intolerable Acts.

The Intolerable Acts. While men like Adams and Henry were laying the foundations of American union, Lord North was worrying over another immediate and pressing problem. England had left the administration of her empire in the East largely in the hands of a giant trading corporation, the East India Company; and the company was in serious financial trouble. After bringing it under more direct supervision of the British government, Lord North secured legislation to increase the company's profits from tea-drinking Americans.

The Tea Act of May 1773 relieved the company of various taxes in England and empowered it to export tea directly from its English warehouses to America, where it would be distributed by company agents. Hitherto the company had been required to sell its tea only by auction to English wholesale merchants, who sold it to American merchants, who in turn sold it to retailers. By eliminating the middlemen's profits and the company's taxes, North hoped to lower tea prices in America so sharply that the colonists would step up their purchases and put the East India Company back on its feet. The Americans would still have to pay the tax imposed by the Townshend Act, but even so they would be able to buy tea cheaper than ever before.

North, it soon became apparent, had misjudged the colonists. By the Tea Act he lost whatever ground he had won in America by repealing the other Townshend duties. Merchants who had been importing tea themselves resented being shut out of the competitive market by a powerful, privileged company. Even the consumers, who would have benefited by the act, were hostile to it. Political leaders warned that the scheme was a trap to make Americans accept Parliamentary taxation. When the first shipments from London arrived in colonial ports, angry citizens forced the ships to return without unloading or stored the tea in warehouses from which no East India man dared remove it. In Boston, where Governor Hutchinson ruled that the ships could not depart without unloading their cargoes, a well-organized mob boarded the ships and pitched the tea into the harbor.

Lord North, who had had enough trouble with Boston, decided to punish the town with another demonstration of authority. Assisted by a new Secretary of State for the Colonies, Lord Dartmouth (Hillsborough had resigned in August 1772), he drafted the Boston Port Act, which ordered the port closed to shipping until the town made restitution for the tea. Parliament readily passed the act. North and Dartmouth might have been willing to stop there, but their fellow ministers insisted on proving Parliament's authority with three more acts (1774).

The Massachusetts Government Act altered the old constitution established by the charter of 1691 (see p. 47): henceforth the governor's council would be appointed by the king (rather than elected by the assembly) and town meetings would be held only once a year except by express permission of the governor. The Administration of Justice Act provided that any government or customs officer indicted for murder could be tried in England, beyond the control of local juries. A new Quartering Act authorized the quartering of troops within a town (instead of in the barracks provided by a colony) whenever their commanding officer thought it desirable. To underline the meaning of this act the British troops, with heavy reinforcements, were brought back into Boston from the fort in the harbor; and General Thomas Gage, the commander in chief of all the North American troops, was sent to act also as governor of the colony.

The colonists promptly dubbed these new measures the Intolerable Acts. They were followed by the Quebec Act, which had no punitive intention but which the colonists thought as outrageous as the others. Canada, since its acquisition in 1763, had been provisionally in the hands of a military governor; the Quebec Act gave the province a permanent government with no representative assembly, established French civil law, and offered special protection to the Catholic Church. Although Canada as a French colony had never had a representative assembly, Americans thought it ominous that Parliament had failed to establish one now that it was an English colony. It disturbed them even more that the act ignored colonial territorial claims by annexing the whole region west of the Appalachians and north of the Ohio to the province of Quebec. Now when settlers moved west they would have to live under Canada's autocratic government.

The Quebec Act and the Intolerable Acts were not the result of hasty or capricious decisions. The Quebec Act had been drafted only after lengthy discussions with officials who had been in Canada, and the Intolerable Acts incorporated certain changes that had often been recommended by royal governors and customs officers. The redesigning of the Massachusetts government in particular was a long-awaited assertion of Parliament's authority over colonial governments. It came, however, as Governor Bernard had feared it would, too late. By subjecting Massachusetts to direct Parliamentary control and by backing up that control with an army, Lord North and his colleagues thought they could teach

The Quebec Act, 1774

Americans to respect the supremacy of Parliament. But the lesson the colonists learned was that the supremacy of Parliament meant an end to the power of their own representative assemblies and courts, an end to the right to trial by jury, an end to every political principle they held dear.

The committees of correspondence went into action immediately. Boston had once been known, and not loved, throughout the colonies for the hard bargaining of its merchants and the riotous behavior of its inhabitants. Now the town received universal admiration and sympathy. It was deluged with gifts of rice from the Carolinas, flour from Pennsylvania, and pledges of support from everywhere. To help carry out the pledges and to coordinate action against the Intolerable Acts, the committees of correspondence arranged for an intercolonial congress to meet in September.

The First Continental Congress. Fifty-five delegates from twelve colonies (Canada, Florida, and Georgia sent none) assembled at Philadelphia in September 1774. As soon as the sessions began, it became apparent that the Southerners and the New Englanders had more radical ideas about what should be done than did the moderates from Pennsylvania and New York. Samuel Adams of Boston presented a set of resolutions that had just been passed by a convention in Suffolk County, Massachusetts, recommending outright resistance to the Intolerable Acts. The congress adopted these Suffolk Resolves and went on to adopt a nonimportation, nonexportation, and nonconsumption agreement, called "The Association," against trade of any kind with Great Britain, Ireland, and the West Indies.

Joseph Galloway of Pennsylvania, speaking

Colonial government: a royal governor's view

I know of no line that can be drawn between the supreme authority of Parliament and the total independence of the colonies: it is impossible there should be two independent Legislatures in one and the same state; for, although there may be but one head, the King, yet the two Legislative bodies will make two governments as distinct as the kingdoms of England and Scotland before the union. If we might be suffered to be altogether independent of Great Britain, could we have any claim to the protection of that government, of which we are no longer a part? Without this protection, should we not become the prey of one or the other powers of Europe, such as should first seize upon us? Is there anything which we have more reason to dread than independence? I hope it never will be our misfortune to know, by experience, the difference between the liberties of an English colonist, and those of the Spanish, French, or Dutch.

From Governor Thomas Hutchinson, Speech to the Council and House of Representatives of Massachusetts, 1773.

for the moderates, countered with a plan for imperial reorganization, which he wanted the congress to present to the king and Parliament. Galloway's plan called for a grand council of the colonies along the lines projected at the Albany Congress (see p. 77). Enactments of the council would be subject to Parliamentary review and veto; acts of Parliament affecting the colonies would likewise have to receive the approval of the grand council. But Galloway could not quite persuade the delegates to subordinate their union to Parliament. In the years since the Stamp Act crisis they had had time and provocation to think further about their relationship to that body.

In 1765 the colonists had categorically denied that Parliament had the authority to tax them; and they had acquiesced in its general legislative authority over the whole empire, mentioning specifically only trade regulation and amendment of the common law as examples of what kind of legislation they thought acceptable. Apart from an unexplained stipulation in some of their resolutions that Parliament should not alter their "internal polity" (as it finally did in the Massachusetts Government Act of 1774), they had not defined the limits of Parliament's legislative authority over them.

Since 1765 many of them had decided that Parliament had no more right to make laws concerning them than it did to tax them. This idea had few adherents until the punishment of the New York assembly, the *Gaspee* commission, and the Intolerable Acts clearly demonstrated that Parliament could destroy men's

rights as readily by legislation as by taxation. Thereafter the idea spread rapidly. Benjamin Franklin adopted it privately as early as 1766, and Samuel Adams led the Massachusetts assembly in affirming it to Governor Hutchinson in 1773. In the summer of 1774 prospective members of the coming congress could read powerful demonstrations of it in two pamphlets. In *Considerations on the . . . Authority of the British Parliament,* James Wilson, a Pennsylvania lawyer, pointed out that all the familiar arguments against Parliamentary taxation applied equally well against Parliamentary legislation. Jefferson took the same position in *A Summary View of the Rights of British America.*

Neither Jefferson nor Wilson was present at the First Continental Congress, but enough of the delegates agreed with them to defeat Galloway's plan by one vote. The radicals were unable, however, to bring this block to repudiate all colonial ties with Parliament. Of those who were no longer willing to admit that Parliament had any authority in the colonies, some still believed that it should be allowed to regulate colonial trade as a just compensation for the British navy's protection of colonial shipping. When the delegates came to framing a statement of colonial rights and grievances, John Adams finally got them to compromise on a series of resolutions that denied that Parliament had any authority over the colonies but agreed—as a matter of fairness and expediency—to submit to its acts for regulation of trade.

The congress was inviting Parliament to return to the same supervisory role it had

Your Excellency adds, "for although there may be but one head, the King, yet the two Legislative bodies will make two governments as distinct as the kingdoms of England and Scotland, before the union." Very true, may it please your Excellency; and if they interfere not with each other, what hinders, but that being united in one head and common Sovereign, they may live happily in that connection, and mutually support and protect each other? Notwithstanding all the terrors which your Excellency has pictured to us as the effects of a total independence, there is more reason to dread the consequences of absolute uncontroled power, whether of a nation or a monarch, than those of a total independence. It would be a misfortune "to know by experience, the difference between the liberties of an English colonist and those of the Spanish, French, and Dutch:" and since the British Parliament has passed an act, which is executed with rigor, though not voluntarily submitted to, for raising a revenue, and appropriating the same, without the consent of the people who pay it, and have claimed a power of making such laws as they please, to order and govern us, your Excellency will excuse us in asking, whether you do not think we already experience too much of such a difference, and have not reason to fear we shall soon be reduced to a worse situation than that of the colonies of France, Spain, or Holland?

From the Answer of the Massachusetts House of Representatives to Governor Hutchinson, 1773.

exercised in the colonies before 1763. Had Parliament been willing to do so, the breach, instead of widening, might have closed. The Earl of Chatham (William Pitt) and Edmund Burke both recognized the opportunity, but neither could muster more than a few votes for proposals to repeal the Intolerable Acts and renounce American taxation. Lord North, however, did secure passage in February 1775 of what he regarded as a conciliatory measure proposing to withhold Parliamentary taxation of any colony whose inhabitants taxed themselves "for contributing their proportion to the common defence." The proposal gave no indication of how much each colony's "proportion" might be or how large a total contribution would be required, and it was silent on the other issues raised by the Intolerable Acts and by the declarations of the Continental Congress. To Americans it appeared to be only an insidious attempt by the ministry to draw away individual colonies from the new union.

But English statesmen were in no mood for softer measures. Most of them were convinced that Samuel Adams and his tribe were leading the colonists toward independence and that the march could be halted only by more forceful demonstrations of Parliamentary supremacy. The session that passed Lord North's conciliatory resolve also passed an act excluding New Englanders from the Newfoundland fisheries and prohibiting them from all trade except with the mother country and the British West Indies. At the same time the ministry took steps to prevent exportation of arms and ammunition to the colonies. Even the king expected the worst. "The New England Governments are in a State of Rebellion," he had told Lord North in November 1774. "Blows," he added, "must decide whether they are to be subject to this Country or Independent."

England clearly anticipated war, but her leaders had no conception of the size of the enemy. In spite of the increasingly obvious signs of colonial unity, Lord North and his colleagues persisted in regarding the enemy as Massachusetts alone. General Gage, sitting uneasily in the governor's chair in Massachusetts, did his best to disillusion them. The Americans, he reported, were as ready for blows as the English; to enforce Parliament's authority he would need twenty thousand men. Until England was prepared to send that many, he said, it would be well to suspend the Intolerable Acts.

George III thought Gage's dispatches absurd; Lord North turned from them to ask Parliament for a reduction in the size of Britain's armed forces. Gage was allowed about thirty-five hundred.

*The English
anticipated war*

Lexington and Concord, April 19, 1775

From Lexington to Bunker Hill.

The general knew from his informers that the colonial militia were assembling arms and ammunition at strategic points. In Portsmouth, New Hampshire, they carried off a hundred barrels of powder belonging to the crown. Gage did not dare detach any part of his small force to recover the royal gunpowder, but occasionally he marched sizable columns for a few miles into the country around Boston, hoping by this show of strength to overawe incipient rebels. On April 14 he received instructions from Lord Dartmouth to take the offensive against the rebellious colonists, and on April 19 he sent seven hundred men to Concord to seize a supply of arms reportedly stored there.

Although the force got started in the dark of early morning, the tolling of alarm bells and the firing of signal guns showed that its errand was no secret. Anticipating trouble, the commanding officer sent back for reinforcements but ordered six companies under Major John Pitcairn to proceed. At Lexington, Pitcairn found colonial militia drawn up on the village green. At his command, they began to disperse. Then suddenly a shot rang out. Whether British or American, musket or pistol, accidental or deliberate, was not apparent; but when they heard the shot, the British soldiers fired a volley into the departing militiamen, killing eight of them and wounding ten.

This episode delayed the troops for only fifteen minutes, and by eight o'clock they were entering Concord. The Americans had already removed most of the military stores they had assembled there, but the British burned a few gun carriages and repulsed a group of militiamen who tried to drive them off. Two colonials and three British were killed in the skirmish. By noon the ''battles'' of Lexington and Concord were over and the British troops started back to Boston.

Now a real battle began, a battle unlike any the troops had ever seen. Colonial militiamen for miles around had been alerted by a system of riders organized for just such an emergency, and the seven hundred British regulars were obliged to run a gauntlet of fire from three or four thousand Americans. At Lexington the returning troops were joined by nine hundred reinforcements, but still the Americans fired from rock and tree at the massed target of moving redcoats.

The total casualties on both sides were not

Retreat from Concord

large: the British lost 73 killed, 174 wounded, and 26 missing; the Americans, 49 killed and 39 wounded. But Gage's worst fears had been justified: his offensive had turned into a rout. That night, as haggard British soldiers dragged themselves into Boston, watch fires dotted the landscape around the city: militia were beginning to move in from all over New England. Boston was already under siege by a people who had no proper army, no system of command, no regular government.

On June 17, less than two months later, Gage found how tightly he was held. Reinforced by sea with 1,100 troops and 3 major generals (William Howe, John Burgoyne, and Henry Clinton), he decided to roll back the siege. On the night of June 16, the Americans, forewarned of his plans, marched 1,200 men to Breed's Hill (just south of Bunker Hill, from which the ensuing action, for no good reason, received its name), overlooking Boston from the north. By morning, when 400 more joined them, they had dug a formidable redoubt.

That afternoon General Howe set out with 2,200 men to displace the rebels from their position. Since Breed's Hill was on a peninsula, Howe could have cut the Americans off by landing a force at their rear. Instead, he bombarded nearby Charlestown at the end of the peninsula and launched a frontal assault. The Americans inside the redoubt held their fire as the enemy, firing regularly and harmlessly, marched coolly up the hill. When the

Boston and Charlestown, June 17, 1775

Americans returned the fire, the British went down in rows.

Howe regrouped his forces and tried again, with the same result. But now the Americans were low on ammunition, and the British regulars, reinforced by 600 men, finally forced the redoubt with bayonets. The Americans, clubbing their muskets, retreated slowly, leaving 140 of their men dead, 271 wounded, and 30 captured. Howe's victory had cost him 226 killed and 828 wounded. Another such victory, wrote Clinton ruefully, "would have ruined us." It had now been demonstrated

The battle at Charlestown

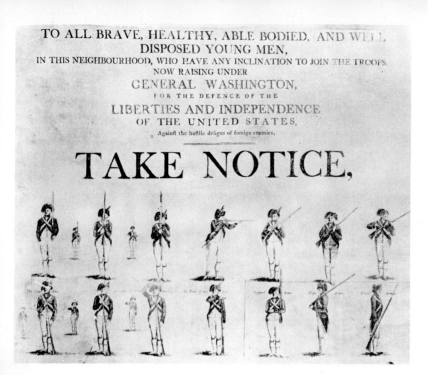

TO ALL BRAVE, HEALTHY, ABLE BODIED, AND WELL
DISPOSED YOUNG MEN,
IN THIS NEIGHBOURHOOD, WHO HAVE ANY INCLINATION TO JOIN THE TROOPS
NOW RAISING UNDER
GENERAL WASHINGTON,
FOR THE DEFENCE OF THE
LIBERTIES AND INDEPENDENCE
OF THE UNITED STATES,
Against the hostile designs of foreign enemies,

TAKE NOTICE,

beyond dispute that Americans with guns were dangerous men. The British never again underestimated the men they were fighting.

One people. While 16,000 colonial militia pinned down the British forces in Boston, other Americans were taking the necessary steps to support the war. Royal governors everywhere watched their authority collapse, as surely as Gage's had collapsed outside Boston. A few tried to organize loyalist support to combat the rebellion, but sooner or later they all gave up and fled to the safety of British warships. The colonial assemblies, which had hitherto met under royal authorization, now gathered as extralegal provincial congresses and began to act as independent governments, raising troops and issuing forbidden paper money to pay them. The transition in government presented no serious difficulty, because the representatives to the provincial congresses were for the most part former assemblymen and they simply carried on with their usual business.

A more extraordinary task faced the delegates who, in May 1775, assembled at Philadelphia for the Second Continental Congress (which had been arranged by the First Congress). Previous intercolonial meetings, the Albany Congress, the Stamp Act Congress, and the First Continental Congress, had de-

voted themselves to hammering out agreements of principle. But by the time the Second Congress met, the colonists were already deeply committed to common principles and a common cause. Fighting had just begun, and the delegates, instead of conducting another debating council, found themselves conducting America's first central government: they assumed responsibility for the provincial militia besieging Boston, ordered their transformation into a Continental Army, named George Washington as commander, issued paper money to support the troops, and appointed a committee to negotiate with foreign countries.

Although in taking these actions the Congress assumed many of the powers of an independent government, the members still did not intend to establish an independent nation. Repudiation of Parliament was not repudiation of England, and they did not see why Englishmen in America and in England should not retain their brotherhood in loyalty to a common king. In July they laid their cause at the feet of the king with a petition asking him personally to promote repeal of the oppressive measures. Significantly they placed the blame for those measures on the ministry—"those artful and cruel enemies who abuse your royal confidence and authority for the purpose of effecting our destruction." They issued at the same time a "Declaration of the causes and necessity for taking up arms," in which they explained that they were "reduced to the alternative of choosing an unconditional submission to the tyranny of irritated ministers, or resistance by force." In choosing resistance, they said, they had no "ambitious designs of separating from Great Britain, and establishing independent states." As soon as England acknowledged their rights, they would lay down their arms.

Although some Americans had already begun to think of independence, the declarations of the Congress were made in good faith. Even at this date the repeal of the Intolerable Acts and the restriction of Parliamentary legislation to the regulation of trade might have kept the colonists in the empire. They still thought of their rights as the rights of Englishmen and of their union as a means of protecting those rights. But George III and Lord North were bent on subjecting the colonists to a Parliament in which they elected no representative. The king did not answer their petition; Parliament did, however, answer their "declaration"—by voting to send twenty-five thousand more troops against them. The addition would bring British military strength in America to forty thousand. In August the king issued a proclamation declaring the colonies in a state of rebellion, and in December Parliament passed an act outlawing all their trade and subjecting their ships and goods to confiscation.

Each British action weakened the colonists' emotional attachment to England. The principal ingredient in their national feeling had been admiration for the British form of government, which better than any other guaranteed the human rights of its subjects. When their admiration for Parliament crumbled, they had fastened the last shreds of their loyalty on the king alone. But he had enthusiastically supported Parliament against them. If the whole English government was determined to destroy the rights of its subjects, then it was a dubious privilege to be an Englishman.

In January 1776 the new image of George III as a tyrant was presented to the colonists with biting eloquence in a publication called simply *Common Sense.* The author, Thomas Paine, an Englishman who had arrived in America only in 1774, argued that it was foolish for Americans to stake their lives and fortunes simply to obtain a repeal of Parliamentary laws. "The object contended for," he said, "ought always to bear some just proportion to the expence. . . . Dearly, dearly, do we pay for the repeal of the acts, if that is all we fight for." Common sense forbade that Americans should remain loyal to a king who sanctioned the spilling of their blood. In fact monarchy itself was an absurdity, a form of government that had laid the world in blood and ashes. "Of more worth," declared Paine, "is one honest man to society and in the sight of God, than all the crowned ruffians that ever lived." Here Paine struck a responsive chord. Since the days of Cromwell republican government had never ceased to have its devotees both in Great Britain and in America, and the old distrust of kings had never entirely died out. The colonists' very devotion to the House of Hanover was in part an expression of this distrust, an oblique way of denouncing the House of Stuart (which the Hanovers had replaced) and of affirming the right of a people to change kings. By calling on Americans to cast off kings altogether, Thomas Paine kindled a latent enthusiasm for republican government.

In the six months that followed the publication of *Common Sense,* sentiment in favor of independence and republicanism grew rapidly. Many who hoped that George III would save American liberty had been convinced by Paine that no king could help them. Many who had considered independence impossible to attain now began to change their minds. Ever since Lexington, American forces throughout the colonies had been fighting the British with heartening success in one engagement after another. And, as men thought beyond the mere repeal of Parliamentary laws, they began to cut their ties with England and England's king. The provincial congress of South Carolina established a republican constitution in March, and in May the Rhode Island congress repealed the law requiring allegiance to the king. North Carolina in April and Virginia in May instructed their delegates in the Continental Congress to vote for independence.

The Continental Congress, with representatives from thirteen colonies (delegates from Georgia had arrived in September, 1775), was itself behaving more and more like an independent national government. In March it authorized privateering against British ships. In April it forbade the further importation of slaves and declared other trade open to all the world except Great Britain. In May, urged by John Adams, it even recommended that any member colonies who had not already done so should suppress all vestiges of royal authority within their borders and establish governments resting on popular consent.

By this time Adams and many other delegates from New England and the Southern colonies were prepared to make an outright declaration of independence. They were restrained only by the reluctant rebels of the Middle colonies. Although virtually the whole Congress had by now concluded that Parliament had no constitutional authority at all in America, some Americans still felt bound to England by a lingering loyalty to the king and a sentimental attachment to the English people. By the end of June both feelings had worn too thin to sustain the weight of continuing war. On July 2, the Congress finally agreed to a motion that had been introduced by Richard Henry Lee of Virginia nearly a month before: "That these United Colonies are, and of right ought to be free and independent states." Thomas Jefferson, assisted

Richard Henry Lee of Virginia

Signing the Declaration of Independence

by Franklin and John Adams, expanded the resolution into the famous declaration that was adopted on July 4.

Jefferson's declaration was an eloquent application of the ideas made familiar by John Locke and by a century and a half of American experience. It affirmed the origin of government in the consent of the governed, its obligation to protect natural rights, and the duty of a people to alter or abolish a government that failed to fulfill its obligation. That the British government had failed was demonstrated by a long list of misdeeds. These were attributed not to Parliament, whose authority the colonists had already denied, but to the king, the only remaining link between the colonies and England. Every grievance suffered by Americans since 1763 was laid at his door. The indictment was not altogether realistic, but it effectively expressed the American rejection not only of George III but of monarchy itself. Embedded in the preamble was evidence that the colonists had learned the lesson England had taught: "When in the course of human events, it becomes necessary for one people to dissolve the political bands which have connected them with another. . . ." Englishmen were "another" people; and the colonists, who twenty-two years before had rejected the union proposed at Albany, now spoke of themselves as "one people."

Suggestions for reading

The period covered by this chapter was first treated in the grand manner by George Bancroft in Vols. IV–VII of his *History of the United States,* 10 vols. (1834–74); Bancroft is still grand reading. Although subsequent historians have been able to correct him on many points, few if any have matched him in literary gifts or in comprehensive knowledge of the sources. Where Bancroft saw events with the future of the United States always in mind, G. L. Beer, in *British Colonial Policy, 1754–1765* (1907), viewed the French and Indian War from a British point of view. L. H. Gipson sees events in America in relation to Britain's imperial problems throughout the world in *The British Empire Before the American Revolution,* 15 vols. (1936–70). Vols. V–VIII deal with the French and Indian War, which Professor Gipson has renamed "The Great War for the Empire." Vols. IX–XII cover the years from 1763 to 1776. The first two volumes of Douglas Freeman, *George Washington,* 7 vols. (1948–57), cover Washington's role in the war.

The understanding of British politics in the 1760s and 1770s has been considerably altered since Bancroft's time. The older views were well expressed in G. O. Trevelyan's magnificently written *The American Revolution,* 4 vols. (1898–1907, reprinted 1964). L. B. Namier, in *The Structure of Politics at the Accession of George III,* 2 vols.* (1929), and *England in the Age of the American Revolution** (1930), has since shown that the party system assumed by Trevelyan did not yet exist and that George III was a better monarch than anyone had supposed. Bernard Donoughue, *British Politics and the American Revolution: The Path to War, 1773–75* (1965), spells out the implications of Namier's views. On the other hand, Herbert Butterfield, *George III and the Historians* (1959), argues that the older views were not quite so mistaken as Namier and his followers thought them to be. A valuable study of the radical political tradition in England is Caroline Robbins, *The Eighteenth-Century Commonwealthman* (1959).

Clarence Alvord, *The Mississippi Valley in British Politics,* 2 vols. (1916), is a classic study of British policy toward the American West. This should be supplemented by T. P. Abernethy, *Western Lands and the American Revolution* (1937), and J. M. Sosin, *Whitehall and the Wilderness: The Middle West in British Colonial Policy, 1760–1775* (1961).

Perhaps the best introduction to the multitude of books on the origins of the Revolution is C. M. Andrews, *The Colonial Background of the American Revolution** (1924, rev. ed., 1931). A good one-volume account of the events from 1763 to 1783 is J. R. Alden, *A History of the American Revolution* (1969). A fuller account of the years 1763–76, stressing political history, is Merrill Jensen, *The Founding of a Nation* (1968). E. S. Morgan, *The Birth of the Republic** (1956), is a brief account of the period 1763–89. O. M. Dickerson, *The Navigation Acts and*

*Available in a paperback edition.

the *American Revolution* (1951), argues that the Navigation Acts were not a cause of the Revolution. A. M. Schlesinger, *The Colonial Merchants and the American Revolution, 1763–1776* (1917), shows how the merchants initially took the lead in opposition to England but became wary as popular feeling seemed to threaten their own position. John Shy, *Toward Lexington* (1965), traces the role of the British troops in bringing on the Revolution. B. W. Labaree, *The Boston Tea Party* (1964), shows how this event precipitated the crisis. H. B. Zobel, *The Boston Massacre* (1970), emphasizes the provocations that led the British to fire. A contemporary Tory view of the coming of the Revolution, pungently expressed, is Peter Oliver, *Origin and Progress of the American Rebellion*, Douglas Adair and John Schutz, eds. (1961).

Several books discuss the political and constitutional principles developed by the colonists before 1776. E. S. and H. M. Morgan, *The Stamp Act Crisis: Prologue to Revolution* (1953), describes the events and ideas of the years 1764–66; and E. S. Morgan, *Prologue to Revolution: Sources and Documents on The Stamp Act Crisis, 1764–1766* (1959), reprints many of the resolutions, petitions, newspaper articles, and pamphlets in which the colonists expressed their views. Later development of colonial opinion is treated in Carl Becker, *The Declaration of Independence* (1922), and R. G. Adams, *The Political Ideas of the American Revolution* (1922). Bernard Bailyn, ed., *The Pamphlets of the American Revolution, 1750–1776* (1965), reprints the most important tracts on the American side, with an important introduction analyzing the arguments, printed separately as *The Ideological Origins of the American Revolution* (1967). Richard Merritt employs techniques of modern political science to trace the rise of American nationalism in *Symbols of American Community, 1735–1775* (1966). Pauline Maier, *From Resistance to Revolution: Colonial Radicals and the Development of American Opposition to Britain, 1765–1766* (1972), traces the evolution of popular hostility to England.

A number of able books describe the internal developments within different colonies in the years preceding independence. R. E. Brown, *Middle-Class Democracy and the Revolution in Massachusetts, 1691–1780* (1955), stresses the absence of internal class conflict, but R. J. Taylor finds more evidence of such conflict in the West in *Western Massachusetts in the Revolution* (1954). A good close-up of Boston is found in G. B. Warden, *Boston, 1689–1776* (1970). David Lovejoy, *Rhode Island Politics and the American Revolution, 1760–1776* (1958), traces political divisions and shows that all sides in Rhode Island were united against the British. Carl Becker, *The History of Political Parties in the Province of New York, 1760–1776* (1909), shows that in New York the Revolution was a contest not only about home rule but also about "who should rule at home." Becker's views are modified in P. U. Bonomi, *A Factious People* (1971). Similar studies for other states are Theodore Thayer, *Pennsylvania Politics and the Growth of Democracy, 1740–1776* (1953); C. A. Barker, *The Background of the Revolution in Maryland* (1940); R. E. and B. K. Brown, *Virginia 1705–1786: Democracy or Aristocracy* (1964); C. S. Sydnor, *Gentlemen Freeholders* (1952); Carl Bridenbaugh, *Seat of Empire: The Political Role of Eighteenth Century Williamsburg* (1950); and Oscar Zeichner, *Connecticut's Years of Controversy, 1750–1776* (1950).

*Available in a paperback edition.

An American people

5

Although the colonists had moved slowly and reluctantly toward declaring independence, once the deed was done most of them had no regrets. There were, of course, loyalists, many of whom left for Canada. Of those who remained, some were ready to fight their countrymen for their king—some, but never enough to win. There were also men indifferent to who ruled them and willing to sell supplies to either side, depending on the price offered. But in every colony that joined in the Declaration of Independence, the patriots were sufficiently numerous, vociferous, and aggressive to outweigh the loyalists and the indifferent. Once the royal governments collapsed, it proved impossible to revive British authority except in the immediate vicinity of British guns.

The winning of independence

The rebel army. Perhaps because they could overawe the loyalists, the patriots counted too easily on doing the same to the British armies. After the rout on April 19 and the slaughter on June 17 (see pp. 98 and 99), they were inclined to believe that their militia could handle any force the British sent against them. George Washington knew better; the men encamped around Boston did have spirit, courage, and marksmanship, but they were not an army. To make them into one was Washington's first concern after taking command at Cambridge on July 3, 1775.

It was not simply a matter of instruction and training in the art of war. Militia units had to be reorganized under a corps of officers appointed from above. In the process, many of the old officers lost rank and stalked off in a huff. Furthermore, the militia who had come to besiege Boston were used to electing their own officers and were touchy about taking orders from higher up. They were also used to short terms of service (for a local emergency or a particular campaign) and eager to get home to their crops. Wherever the enemy appeared, Americans from miles around would turn out to fight him; but they did not want to join the army. To join the army was to desert one's family for danger, discomfort, and disease hundreds of miles from home. The pay was low, and no pension system existed to compensate a man or his family for the loss of life or limb. It therefore took all of Washington's diplomacy and tact to persuade ten thousand militiamen to enlist until the end of 1776 as regular soldiers in the Continental Army. In addition the provincial governments supplied him with about seven thousand short-term militiamen.

The total was much smaller than Washington had hoped for. Throughout the war Congress was able to provide him with an ample army of men on paper. But men with arms, legs, heads, and guns remained in short sup-

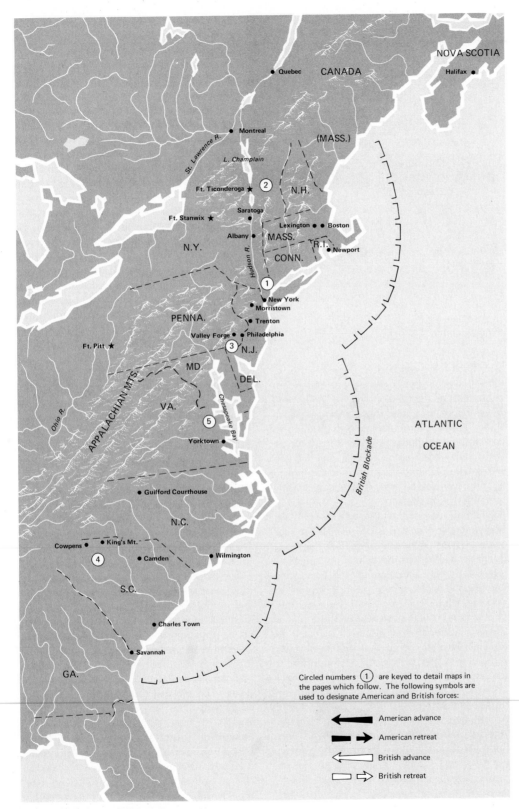

Quebec

CANADA

NOVA SCOTIA

Halifax

Montreal

St. Lawrence R.

L. Champlain

(MASS.)

Ft. Ticonderoga ★ ②

N.H.

Saratoga

Ft. Stanwix ★

Lexington ● Boston

Albany ●

MASS.

R.I.

N.Y.

CONN.

Newport

Hudson R.

①

New York

Morristown

PENNA.

Trenton

Ft. Pitt ★

Valley Forge ● ● Philadelphia

③ N.J.

MD.

DEL.

Ohio R.

VA.

⑤

Chesapeake Bay

ATLANTIC

OCEAN

Yorktown ●

APPALACHIAN MTS.

British Blockade

Guilford Courthouse ●

N.C.

Cowpens ● ● King's Mt.

④ ● Camden

● Wilmington

S.C.

● Charles Town

● Savannah

GA.

Circled numbers ① are keyed to detail maps in the pages which follow. The following symbols are used to designate American and British forces:

American advance

American retreat

British advance

British retreat

Major campaigns of the Revolutionary War

① *Washington's moves in New York and New Jersey, 1776–77*

"The American Rifle Men"

ply. Since Congress had no power either to raise money or to draft men, it was dependent on requisitions to the states for both; and when the states lagged in supplying their assigned quotas, Congress could do nothing to coerce them. Supplies were as hard to come by as men; Washington had to spend much of his time pleading for both, and he had to fight the war with an army that was constantly in danger of dissolution.

The new army's first venture away from Boston began while Boston was still under siege, before independence was declared. Congress had invited the people of Canada to join their union, and, though the Canadians had failed to respond, some reports suggested that they would welcome an invading army. In any case, it was desirable to strike at the British in Quebec and Montreal in order to forestall an attack from that direction. After a grueling winter march, the effective forces that converged on Quebec amounted to only a thousand men, and the Canadians showed no disposition to help them. Colonel Benedict Arnold and General Richard Montgomery, who had already taken Montreal on his way north, besieged the city through the winter; but smallpox, hunger, cold, and an unsuccessful assault so thinned their ranks that in the spring they retreated to Ticonderoga. The colonists made no further military effort to draw Canada into their union.

In the South the Americans fared better. In June 1776, when Generals Henry Clinton and Charles, Lord Cornwallis, and Admiral Sir Peter Parker arrived at Charles Town, South Carolina, with fifty ships and an army of three thousand men, they were met by deadly fire from a seemingly impregnable fort constructed of palmetto logs and dirt. After a ten-hour duel the British withdrew and left Charles Town alone for the next four years.

In Massachusetts, Washington had meanwhile built a force strong enough to close in on Boston. He began by occupying and fortifying Dorchester Heights, which overlooked the city on the south as Breed's Hill did on the north. This time the British did not try to storm the hills. Instead, on March 17, 1776, they departed by sea for Halifax, Nova Scotia, taking over a thousand loyalists with them.

A few months after the British evacuation of Boston, when Americans declared their independence, they appeared to be in a strong position. Although they were challenging the world's greatest military and naval power and had failed to win Canada to their cause, they had overpowered the British army in the march from Concord, withstood its assaults at Breed's Hill, forced its withdrawal from Boston, and fought off the British navy at Charles Town. But the British war machine, always a slow starter, was now grinding into action. Parliament had authorized an army of 55,000, and, when recruitment lagged in England, the government hired 30,000 German mercenaries, 17,000 of them from Hesse-Cassel (hence the name Hessians). General William Howe and his brother, Admiral Richard Howe, were given command.

The Howes were authorized to end the war as soon as the colonists submitted. Hoping to end it before they began, they addressed a conciliatory letter to "George Washington, Esq." (thus ignoring his military status). But General Washington was not receiving letters for George Washington, Esq., letters that denied American independence even in the address. The Howes therefore proceeded according to plan. On August 12, 1776, they arrived in New York harbor with 32,000 troops and 10,000 seamen (the city's normal population was 25,000) aboard 400 transports and 30 warships. Ten days later 20,000 of the troops landed on Long Island near Brooklyn.

Washington had 23,000 men in the New York area, but most of them were inexperi-

Battle of Princeton, January 3, 1777

enced local militia. When Howe, with plenty of men to spare, launched both frontal and flank attacks, Washington was forced to withdraw to Manhattan with heavy losses. Thinking that this taste of British power might have chastened the Americans, Howe offered to confer about a settlement before any more blows were struck. Congress sent Franklin, John Adams, and Edward Rutledge to deal with him, but the resulting conference broke off when it turned out, as Washington had suspected, that Howe was empowered to negotiate only with submissive colonists, not with the proud representatives of an independent nation. In September the British drove Washington off Manhattan Island; and by November the Continental Army, depleted by captures and desertions, was in full retreat across New Jersey.

Washington crossed the Delaware River into Pennsylvania on December 7. Now, with the river between him and the enemy, he planned his next move. The outlook was bleak. While pursuing him across New Jersey, the British had been able simultaneously to send a large force to Rhode Island, where on December 8 they occupied Newport. Washington's force was down to fewer than 8,000 effective fighting men, all of them dispirited, exhausted, ready to quit. By the end of the month all but 1,500 would have completed their term of enlistment, and with winter coming on they would sling their packs, head for home, and let someone else fight the war. While he still

had them, Washington attacked. On the night of December 25, 1776, in high, freezing winds, he shuttled his men back across the river, marched them nine miles to Trenton, and caught the enemy asleep and befuddled. With a loss of only 4 men he took 900 prisoners. A few days later at Princeton he dealt the British another smashing blow, and they pulled back to New Brunswick for the winter. The brilliant reversal so cheered the troops that Washington was able to persuade many of them to reenlist. With spirits high again, the army moved into winter quarters at Morristown.

General Howe, contemplating the reverses that Washington had dealt him, had difficulty making up his mind about what to do when spring should come. After changing plans several times he finally decided to storm the rebel capital of Philadelphia, which, like New York, contained a large loyalist population. In July he took 15,000 men by sea from New York to the head of Chesapeake Bay. From there they marched north toward Philadelphia, the Hessians helping themselves to food, furniture, and women along the way. Washington intercepted them at Brandywine Creek; but, as on Long Island, Howe won the pitched battle and entered Philadelphia on September 26, 1777. When Washington challenged him a week later at Germantown, where most of the British troops were quartered, Howe again was victorious.

These defeats discouraged the colonists, but

② *The war in the North, 1775–79*

would have signified little in a military sense; his surrender did not seriously reduce the British margin of superiority in troops and equipment. Saratoga had its great effect, not in New York or Philadelphia, but in London and Paris.

In London a complacent Parliament began to sense the possibility that England might lose the war. Better make peace, the ministry decided, and it authorized a commission headed by Lord Carlisle to offer the Americans virtually everything they had previously demanded: renunciation of Parliamentary taxation, repeal of the Intolerable Acts, and suspension of every other objectionable act passed since 1763. Two years earlier such concessions would probably have kept the colonies within the empire. But by now the rebels found independence exhilarating. England's eagerness to have them back merely furnished them with the final weapon they needed to make their independence last: the recognition and assistance of France.

From the outset the Americans had been hoping for help from England's traditional enemy, and on November 29, 1775, Congress had appointed a secret committee to seek foreign aid. Louis XVI, delighted by the rebellion of England's colonies, had sent Achard de Bonvouloir to observe the situation in America. With Bonvouloir's encouragement the committee dispatched Silas Deane, a shrewd and sophisticated Yankee, to negotiate with France. Deane arrived in Paris on July 7, 1776, to find that the French foreign minister, the Comte de Vergennes, had already persuaded the king to help the American rebellion with a million livres' worth of munitions and supplies. Furthermore, Spain had matched the amount. The goods were to be dispensed secretly through a fake trading company run by Pierre Beaumarchais (author of *The Barber of Seville*). They were Deane's for the asking, though whether as a gift or as a loan remained uncertain.

Deane's negotiations took place before news of the Declaration of Independence reached France, when secret assistance was all the Americans dared ask for. Once the declaration had been announced, they hoped that France would recognize their independence and offer open assistance. To help Deane push these more ambitious requests, Congress sent Arthur Lee, a Virginian who had been serving the American cause in London, and Benjamin Franklin, who arrived from

actually Howe's success was hollow. Though he had captured America's largest cities and repeatedly defeated her generals, he had captured no armies and controlled only a small portion of American territory. And to the north of him disaster was brewing. General John Burgoyne had been authorized by the high command in England to mount an expedition for a march south from Canada by the Lake Champlain route. He set out from Fort St. John's in June with 4,000 British, 3,000 Germans, 1,400 Indians, and a pleasing mistress to cheer him along. Everything went swimmingly for a time. But American forces, under Horatio Gates and Benedict Arnold, gathered ever stronger before him, and each time they clashed Burgoyne lost several hundred men. On October 17, 1777, he finally surrendered at Saratoga.

The French alliance. Saratoga was one of the turning points of history, but not because it turned back any threat to the American armies. Burgoyne's march, if successful,

Philadelphia in December 1776. The three men constituted a commission with power to make treaties of amity and commerce.

The French at this time envisaged America as an Arcadia peopled by noble savages and almost equally noble farmers, rich in nature's wisdom; Franklin, seeing what was expected, donned his fur cap and played the role to the hilt. Completely enchanted, the Parisians showered the arch-American with favors, but Vergennes and his royal master remained cautious. Besides furnishing supplies to the colonists they sometimes allowed American privateers the use of French harbors. They hesitated, however, to join in open war on England when the British armies, with the capture of New York, appeared to be winning.

As American military fortunes declined, Congress instructed the commissioners to go beyond their request for French assistance and to seek the deeper commitment of an alliance. All Franklin's charm was insufficient to win it. Vergennes wanted Spain by his side before he took on the British lion, and Spain was unwilling. Spain feared even to give open assistance to the Americans lest she encourage her own colonies to revolt.

When news of Saratoga reached Paris on December 3, 1777, Vergennes perceived at once that the American victory might produce a conciliatory temper in England, and the last thing he wanted was to see the rebellious colonies reconciled to the mother country. Franklin played on his fears, and Vergennes sent frantic messages to Spain. When Spain remained immovable, he finally told the commissioners that France was ready to enter into a treaty of commerce and amity and a treaty of alliance with the Americans. He indeed required an alliance before entering the war, in order to prevent the United States from making peace before England was humbled.

The terms of the alliance, signed on February 6, 1778, were all that the United States could have wished for. The stated purpose of both parties was to maintain the independence of the United States. In case of war between France and England (which the signing of the treaty made inevitable), neither France nor the United States was to make peace without the consent of the other. France renounced all future claims to English territory on the continent of North America and agreed that any such territory captured in the war would go to the United States. These generous terms were less the result of American

"The Surrender of General Burgoyne," by John Trumbull

diplomatic skill than of French determination to weaken England and French distaste for further colonizing in the New World.

Even before the alliance the Americans had depended heavily on aid from France. The victory at Saratoga, for example, would have been impossible without French supplies. And French financial support helped to bolster American credit at a time when Congress, with no authority to tax, was financing the war with money begged from the states or manufactured by the printing presses. With the signing of the alliance the hopes of the Americans soared, for France was the first nation to recognize them as "one people," and she had the military and naval power to make that recognition meaningful.

From Saratoga to Yorktown. After the battle of Saratoga the British fought a cautious war, their dreams of easy victory gone. Howe, snug in Philadelphia during the winter of 1777–78, did not even try to attack Washington's wretched forces, who were starving and

Central campaigns, 1777–79

The unsinkable John Paul Jones

Monmouth Courthouse on June 28) was badly bungled by General Charles Lee, and the main body of Clinton's troops arrived safely in New York.

While the British and American armies were marching across New Jersey, the first French forces arrived in America—Vice Admiral the Comte d'Estaing with seventeen ships and four thousand troops. Washington proposed to use them in recovering Newport. But in August, just before the American-French assault was to begin, a storm scattered and damaged the French fleet, and the unsupported land forces withdrew when British reinforcements arrived. D'Estaing took his ships to Boston to refit and, in November 1778, sailed south to protect the French West Indies.

The departure of D'Estaing was a serious disappointment to Washington, for the Americans had no means of their own to combat the British navy. It offered deadly support to British land troops along the coast, and it regularly sent raiding parties to devastate towns far from any army. Though the Americans commissioned hundreds of privateers (probably over two thousand in all), which rendered invaluable service in disrupting the merchant shipping, communications, and supply lines of the enemy, the privateers were no more a navy than the militia were an army; they were simply not up to engaging British warships in a sustained action.

The Congress had tried to create a navy, but it could scrape together the money for only a few ships, which were no match for the Royal Navy. Nevertheless, one of them, commanded by the unpopular but unsinkable John Paul Jones, carried the war to the British Isles, raiding coastal towns and seizing British ships. Unfortunately there were not enough Joneses to divert the British navy from North America; and Clinton kept most of his troops near the coast within reach of naval assistance. Without naval assistance of his own Washington dared not risk an all-out assault on the British army, and after following it from New Jersey to New York he had camped outside the city at White Plains and waited for the French fleet to return or to draw the British ships to other waters. For a year and a half he waited while the fighting was carried on mostly by small forces remote from New York, the strategic center. In the fall of 1779 all prospect of French naval support disappeared when D'Estaing took his fleet from the West Indies back to France.

freezing in their winter quarters at nearby Valley Forge. In the spring Howe was replaced by Sir Henry Clinton, who was to prove somewhat less languid though no bolder. The spring of 1778 also brought France's entry into the war and American refusal of the Carlisle Commission's peace overtures (see p. 108). Uncertain of where France would throw her weight, the British high command decided to play safe and ordered Clinton to withdraw from Philadelphia to New York. There he should plan a major campaign in the South, where—according to the strategists—loyalists would lend a decisive hand.

At Valley Forge, as mild weather came on, Washington's forces thawed out and were drilled with Prussian precision by Baron Friedrich von Steuben, an idealist from the Old World who had come to help usher in the independence of the New. By June he and a good supply of provisions had turned the haggard men into a hard and maneuverable army. When Clinton pulled out of Philadelphia to march across New Jersey to New York, Washington kept pace with him on a parallel route and watched for a chance to strike. But the only opportunity that came (the Battle of

Meanwhile a British expeditionary force had occupied Georgia, and Clinton prepared to go ahead with the Southern campaign he had been ordered to conduct. Leaving an army equal to Washington's to hold New York, he pulled his troops out of Newport (thus freeing New England of all British troops) and, in December 1779, sailed with an expeditionary force of over eight thousand for Charles Town, South Carolina. He took it on May 12, 1780, along with its defending general, Benjamin Lincoln, and his entire force of fifty-five hundred men. The Carolinas now lay open to a British sweep. On June 8 Clinton sailed for New York, leaving Cornwallis in command with instructions to secure the British hold on South Carolina and then to recover North Carolina. Cornwallis was at first successful. On August 16, 1780, near Camden, he intercepted and routed over three thousand men under General Horatio Gates who were coming to the defense of South Carolina. Washington sent General Nathanael Greene, his ablest commander, to pick up the pieces.

With the assistance of Daniel Morgan, a Virginia rifleman, Greene built a mobile fighting unit, which owed much to the Southern militiamen who appeared whenever a fight was in the offing. A group of these tough campaigners had already demonstrated their worth before Greene arrived by capturing a British force atop King's Mountain in North Carolina (October 7, 1780). Greene and Morgan lured Cornwallis into trap after trap, chewing off a bit of his force here and a bit there (notably at Hannah's Cowpens on the Broad River, January 17, 1781, and at Guilford Courthouse, March 15).

In April 1781 the two generals turned their backs on each other: Greene headed south to pick off more British outposts in South Carolina and Georgia, while Cornwallis, having failed in the Carolinas, set out to conquer Virginia. By July, after a few inconclusive engagements, he had settled at Portsmouth, from which he later moved to Yorktown. Portsmouth and Yorktown both lay on the seacoast, the only safe place for a British army in America; but the coast would remain safe only so long as the British navy commanded the sea. Without naval support Cornwallis could be cut off from his own forces in Charles Town and Savannah and from Clinton's forces in the North.

In New York Clinton still looked out at Washington's waiting army, and Washington

④ Southern campaigns, 1778–81

still waited for the French navy. The French had sent five thousand land troops under the Comte de Rochambeau to occupy Newport in July 1780, but the eleven warships that accompanied them under the Comte de Barras had been promptly bottled up inside the harbor by a superior British fleet.

In August 1781 Washington's patience was finally rewarded by news that Admiral de Grasse with twenty warships was heading for the Chesapeake but would be able to stay only a short time. Washington immediately decided to dash south for a try at Cornwallis. Leaving behind a part of his New York troops to fool Clinton, he marched the rest to the head of

⑤ The convergence of troops on Yorktown, 1781

Washington and his generals at Yorktown

Chesapeake Bay and placed them aboard transports for the last leg of the journey. Additional forces under Anthony Wayne and the French volunteer, Lafayette, were already within marching distance of the target. Barras meanwhile had managed to slip out of Newport and was sailing south loaded with siege guns. When the British naval squadrons discovered what was going on, they hurried to the Chesapeake to drive off Barras and de Grasse but found themselves hopelessly outnumbered and outgunned. French naval power was at last decisive. Back went the British fleet to New York for repairs and reinforcements, and Washington with 5,700 Continentals, 3,100 militia, and 7,000 French began to close in on Yorktown. On October 19, when a relief expedition was already under way from New York, Cornwallis gave up. With the bands playing "The World Turned Upside Down," 7,000 British troops marched out of Yorktown and stacked their arms in surrender.

Peace. Yorktown was as much a French as an American victory. And because the war too was a French war, it could not end at Yorktown. France was ready for peace but encumbered by a commitment to Spain. Vergennes, upon concluding the treaty of alliance with the United States on February 6, 1778, had continued his efforts to bring Spain into the war; he finally succeeded after agreeing not to stop fighting until Spain had won Gibraltar from England. Since the United States had agreed not to make peace without French consent,

Americans were indirectly bound to await the capture of Gibraltar also. Spain, on the other hand, refused to recognize the independence of the United States, and after entering the war on June 21, 1779, accorded only a devious and frosty tolerance to the American cause. Once she had seized the thinly held territory of West Florida (a former Spanish possession) from the British, she confined herself mainly to blockading Gibraltar.

After the defeat at Yorktown, most Englishmen were ready to give up the struggle for the colonies even though George III was bent on continuing it. On March 20, 1782, Lord North was forced from office, and the king was obliged to accept a ministry favorable to peace, which immediately sent agents to get in touch with the American commissioners in France.

Congress had first formulated American war aims in August 1779, when it optimistically sent John Adams to France as minister plenipotentiary. Adams was then forbidden to enter into any peace negotiations with Great Britain unless she first recognized the United States as a sovereign, free, and independent state. After that recognition had been granted, he was to insist on certain boundaries for the new nation: the Mississippi on the west, the thirty-first parallel and the Flint and St. Mary's rivers on the south, and roughly the present boundary on the north.

In June 1781 the French ambassador to the United States, the Chevalier de la Luzerne, persuaded Congress to revise its arrangements for making peace. John Adams was replaced as sole negotiator by a five-man commission consisting of himself, John Jay (minister to Spain), Franklin (minister to France), Henry Laurens (designated as minister to the Netherlands but captured by the British en route and held in the Tower of London), and Thomas Jefferson (who was unable to go and was dropped from the commission). The commissioners' instructions were weak: they were still to insist on British recognition of American independence before undertaking peace negotiations, but they were free to accept any settlement "as circumstances may direct and as the state of the belligerent and the disposition of the mediating powers may direct." What was worse, they must do nothing without the knowledge and concurrence of the French and, indeed, must be governed by their advice and opinion.

These instructions put the commissioners

under the direction of Vergennes, a position none of them relished. When secret information reached them that he would not support the American demand for prior recognition of independence, and that his secretary, Rayneval, had secretly encouraged the British to think of a boundary well to the east of the Mississippi, with Spain and England dividing up the territory between, they decided they would do better to negotiate with the British separately rather than to sit down at the peace table under French direction. Violating their instructions, they negotiated with British representatives without insisting on advance recognition of independence, and they did not keep Vergennes informed of what they were doing.

By playing on British desires to destroy the American alliance with France, the commissioners were able to secure both recognition of independence and the boundaries prescribed in John Adams' original instructions. In preliminary articles signed on November 30, 1782, they presented this diplomatic triumph to Vergennes as an accomplished fact. Actually there had been no violation of the alliance, for the treaty based on the articles was not to go into effect until France and England had concluded a treaty of their own. The commissioners' coup enabled Vergennes to exert pressure on Spain to give up the fight for Gibraltar, and in the end she settled for East and West Florida and Minorca. The final treaties were signed at Paris on September 3, 1783, and the last British troops left New York on November 25. The Declaration of Independence was at last a statement of fact, not a wish.

The Experimental Period

At Lexington, Concord, and Bunker Hill Americans had fought against Parliamentary taxation. After July 2, 1776, they had fought for independence, though in the beginning probably few of them had any clear idea of what independence would mean besides the end of British tyranny. Between 1776 and 1789 they explored the possibilities of their new freedom. These thirteen years may be considered the Experimental Period in American history, the time when Americans were trying their wings, discovering their nationality. They formulated ideas and ideals that had been only half articulate before, and they found ways and means to put their ideas and ideals into practice. During this period the Americanisms discussed earlier (see Chapter 3) underwent further development, and some of them were transformed from characteristic attitudes into national principles.

The fruition of Americanisms. American ideas about the separation of church and state and about education advanced less rapidly during the Experimental Period than did political and social concepts. But the assumption that widespread education was desirable did show itself in a revival of schooling, which had lapsed during the war, and in the proliferation of new educational institutions, most of them private. Many academies were founded (especially in New England) to furnish instruction at the secondary level, and sometimes beyond, to both boys and girls. And the number of colleges in the United States doubled: in 1776 there were nine; by 1789 as many more had been opened or chartered; and every state but Delaware had at least one in operation or being organized. Writers in newspapers and pamphlets argued about what kind of education was best suited to Americans. Many demanded that it be made more practical, and new textbooks reoriented traditional subjects like arithmetic and grammar in this direction.

The colonists' wariness of allowing their clergy a hand in government gave rise to a greater separation of church and state. Though most states continued to levy taxes in support of the Protestant religion, the Anglican Church lost the exclusive claims to that support which it had enjoyed in the Southern colonies. Under all the state constitutions a man could at least specify which Protestant church his taxes should support. And in Virginia the principle of complete separation of church and state received its finest expression in an act drafted by Thomas Jefferson and adopted by the Virginia legislature in 1786. Beginning with the assertion that "Almighty God hath created the mind free," the act provided that "no man shall be compelled to frequent or support any religious worship, place, or ministry whatsoever."

Jefferson was also author of the phrase that translated social mobility into an American principle. By declaring on July 4, 1776, that "all men are created equal," the United States committed itself to a doctrine that was to prove the world's most powerful lever for social and political change. The declaration was intended simply to justify the colonists' withdrawal from the mother country, which had refused to treat them as the equals of Englishmen. But no great imagination was required to discern wider implications in Jefferson's axiomatic statement of human equality.

Its relevance to black slavery was inescapable. As soon as Americans complained that British taxation would reduce them to slavery, they began to feel uneasy about their own enslavement of Africans; they even foreswore the slave trade in their nonimportation agreements. In the Experimental Period most of the states, Southern as well as Northern, forbade the further importation of slaves, and the Northern states passed laws for the eventual liberation of those already within their borders. Massachusetts seems to have rid herself of the institution by judicial decision: her constitution, echoing the Declaration of Independence, stated that "all men are born free and equal," and her courts interpreted the phrase literally. Many Southerners also freed their slaves voluntarily at this time. But Americans were not yet ready to face up to the racial meaning of their egalitarian creed. Black slavery was not abolished in any Southern state; Jefferson himself continued to hold slaves throughout his lifetime; and slaves continued to do the work that accounted for the major

exports of the United States. Eventually Americans would have to pay for their failure. Meanwhile the contradiction between the creed of equality and the practice of slavery was heightened as white Americans gradually turned their written commitment into an active force to better their own lives.

The principle of equality was as hostile to aristocracy as to slavery. Having got along without a titled nobility for a century and a half, Americans were determined to continue without one and looked suspiciously at anything that smacked of special privilege. States forbade their citizens to accept titles from foreign nations. And when officers of the Continental Army formed the Society of the Cincinnati in 1783, they met with a storm of protest from critics who feared that the association might become the nucleus of an aristocracy. In Connecticut even a medical society, seeking to raise the standards of the profession by licensing practitioners, was at first denied a charter because its members were to be chosen for life and might thus become a privileged order.

The Revolutionary War itself had an equalizing effect on property: wealthy merchants had lost heavily from the British blockade of commerce, while many a poor farmer had prospered in selling his produce to the armies. Wartime finance, with its reliance on steadily inflating paper currency, favored debtors (who were most often farmers) at the expense of creditors. The confiscation and sale of loyalists' lands and the abolition of primogeniture (the inheritance of a man's entire estate by his eldest son) by the state governments likewise contributed to a more equal distribution of property by breaking up some of the larger concentrations of wealth. Although in many cases the initial purchasers of loyalist lands were large-scale speculators, the overall effect of the confiscations was probably to increase the number of landowners. By the time the war ended many Americans regarded equality of property as a goal in itself. When economic depression struck in the 1780s, legislators in some states sponsored bills favoring debtors, on the grounds that republican government required a general equality of property.

The emerging doctrine of equality can also be detected in the reform of voting laws. Property qualifications had disfranchised only a small minority in most colonies (because most Americans owned property) and there had been few complaints. But every state except Massachusetts reduced the amount of property required for voting. There remained, nevertheless, a strong belief that political rights should be confined to property-holders. Only two states, Georgia and Pennsylvania, opened the franchise to all taxpayers. And in most states there were higher property qualifications for holding office than for voting. In the eighteenth century it was assumed that a man without property had no reason to participate in government either by voting or by holding office. According to Locke the purpose of government was to protect property, so a man without any was thought to have little stake in society. Moreover, only property could free a man from the control of employers or landlords. Without property that would support him a man was not a free agent and could not be trusted with authority or even with a voice in the selection of those who were to wield it. Hence the concern already noted for the maintenance of a wide distribution of property. If America were to become like Europe, with a mass of propertyless workers and peasants, liberty would fall with equality; and authority, concentrated in the hands of a few, would turn into tyranny.

Authority in the hands of the many, of the people, was the essential characteristic of a republic; and with independence colonial insistence on responsible representative government turned into a conscious pursuit of republicanism. Although nothing in the Declaration of Independence had precluded the possibility of monarchy, Americans took it for granted that the new states would be republics. After severing their ties with England, Connecticut and Rhode Island, which in effect were republics already, simply continued the governments defined by their old charters. In other colonies the provincial congress, which replaced the representative assembly (often with the same membership), acted without formal authority until independence was declared. Then, sooner or later, it drafted a written constitution establishing and defining a new government, usually similar in structure to the old one but more responsible to the people.

Since the colonial representative assembly (or lower house) had always been the branch of government most directly dependent on the people, the state constitutions gave the greatest powers to the lower houses of the new legislatures. In some states the lower house chose both the upper house and the governor.

North America in 1783

Only Pennsylvania, which had had a unicameral legislature since 1701, actually did without an upper house. In other states there was a marked change in the composition of this body: the members were not as ''upper'' in wealth or social position as their colonial counterparts. They sat, not as the favorites of a governor, but as representatives of the whole people, indistinguishable in this respect from the lower house.

Determination that the government should be the servant of the people and not their master also prompted the inclusion of bills of rights in most of the state constitutions. The Virginia Bill of Rights began by asserting that ''all men are by nature equally free and independent, and have certain inherent rights, of which, when they enter into a state of society, they cannot by any compact deprive or divest their posterity.'' It then enumerated the rights that lay beyond the reach of government, such as freedom of religion and of the press and the right to trial by jury.

In most states, after the provincial congress had drafted and approved a constitution, it went into effect without being submitted to a popular vote. But Massachusetts (the last state to adopt a constitution) elected a special convention to draft hers and submitted its work to direct vote by the people. Once it had been ratified in 1780, it could be changed only by another popularly elected convention called for that specific purpose. This was a step that other states had groped for but never quite reached. The purpose of writing out a

Crèvecœur on the American

I wish I could be acquainted with the feelings and thoughts which must agitate the heart and present themselves to the mind of an enlightened Englishman, when he first lands on this continent.... If he travels through our rural districts he views not the hostile castle, and the haughty mansion, contrasted with the clay-built hut and miserable cabin, where cattle and men help to keep each other warm, and dwell in meanness, smoke, and indigence. A pleasing uniformity of decent competence appears throughout our habitations. The meanest of our log-houses is a dry and comfortable habitation. Lawyer or merchant are the fairest titles our towns afford; that of a farmer is the only appellation of the rural inhabitants of our country. It must take some time ere he can reconcile himself to our dictionary, which is but short in words of dignity, and names of honour.... We have no princes, for whom we toil, starve, and bleed: we are the most perfect society now existing in the world.

From Michel Guillaume Jean de Crèvecœur, "What Is an American?" *Letters from an American Farmer,* 1782.

constitution was to set limits to government by a fundamental law embodying the will of the people. British jurists had often maintained that the unwritten British constitution, consisting of traditions and customs, was superior to government, but custom and tradition had failed to protect the colonists from what they regarded as tyranny by the British government. They wanted something in black and white by which to measure any departure by their own governments from the proper limits of authority. They began to get what they wanted when their provincial congresses wrote and adopted state constitutions. But keen minds soon noted a flaw in this procedure: as the town of Concord pointed out in 1776, a constitution adopted by a legislative body could be altered or abolished by the same body and thus would constitute no protection against legislative tyranny. The device of a special convention and popular ratification elevated the constitution above the legislature and made it easier for the other branches of government to nullify unconstitutional legislation. The courts, for example, could and would refuse to enforce any law that violated the constitution. The Massachusetts invention of the constitutional convention was so widely admired by other Americans that subsequent constitution-making in America followed the Massachusetts method.

Building a national government.

The same passion for responsible government that resulted in written constitutions and constitutional conventions prevented for a long time the creation of an effective national government. Americans, like other men of the eighteenth century, believed that republican government was not adaptable to large areas. In a large republic the central legislature must inevitably sit so remote from most of its constituents that it would eventually escape their control and thus cease to be republican. On the other hand, a small republic could never survive in a world of aggressive large nations. There was only one way, it was thought, to overcome these difficulties: a number of small republics might join in a federation and exert their united power for specific purposes.

Americans had formed such a federation in 1774 in the Continental Congress, and after independence the Congress had continued to exercise governmental powers for the whole nation. It was composed of delegates (usually several from each state) appointed annually by the state legislatures. Each state had one vote, which was determined by the majority of its delegates (if they were evenly divided the state's vote was lost).

In the absence of a more effective central organization, Congress served a useful purpose. But it existed only by common consent, and from the beginning the members felt the need for a more binding union. As Americans joined against a common enemy and became aware of their shared principles and beliefs, their feeling of nationality grew stronger. Something more than an unstable succession of congresses was necessary to embody this

It cannot be worth any Man's while, who has a means of Living at home, to expatriate himself, in hopes of obtaining a profitable civil office in America; and, as to military Offices, they are at an end with the War, the Armies being disbanded. Much less is it adviseable for a Person to go thither, who has no other quality to recommend him but his Birth. In Europe it has indeed its Value; but it is a Commodity that cannot be carried to a worse Market than that of America, where people do not inquire concerning a Stranger, What is he? *but,* What can he do? *If he has any useful Art, he is welcome; and if he exercises it, and behaves well, he will be respected by all that know him; but a mere Man of Quality, who, on that Account, wants to live upon the Public, by some Office or Salary, will be despis'd and disregarded. The Husbandman is in honor there, and even the Mechanic, because their Employments are useful. The People have a saying, that God Almighty is himself a Mechanic, the greatest in the Universe; and he is respected and admired more for the Variety, Ingenuity, and Utility of his Handyworks, than for the Antiquity of his Family.*

Franklin on the American

From Benjamin Franklin, *Information to Those Who Would Remove to America,* 1782.

sentiment and to demonstrate to other nations that the United States too was a nation and not merely a diplomatic alliance of thirteen small republics. Congress accordingly, in the intervals between dealing with the everyday problems of the war, often discussed the formation of a permanent national government. As early as July 12, 1776, a committee had brought in the draft of a constitution, but acceptance had foundered on how expenses and voting power should be apportioned among the states and on the old question of Western policy.

On November 17, 1777, Congress finally agreed on a constitution to be presented to the state legislatures for approval or rejection. The Articles of Confederation provided for a congress like the existing one. Each state, whatever its size, was still to have only one vote, to be cast, as before, by delegates appointed by the state legislatures; each state (by taxing itself) was to contribute to the common expenses according to the value of its lands; none was to be deprived of its Western lands for the benefit of the United States; and each was to retain its "sovereignty, freedom and independence, and every power, jurisdiction, and right" not expressly delegated to Congress. Congress was permitted to decide on war or peace, appoint military and naval officers, requisition the states for men and money, send and receive ambassadors, enter into treaties and alliances, establish a post office, coin money, borrow money or issue paper money on the credit of the United

States, fix weights and measures, regulate Indian affairs, and settle disputes between states.

Although the states found much to object to in the Articles of Confederation, the need to give permanent form to the union moved all but Maryland to accept it by 1779. Maryland's refusal, though probably prompted by narrow, partisan, and pecuniary motives, forced the settlement of a problem that might have wrecked the union—the problem of Western lands.

The West had always been a divisive force, as Bacon's Rebellion, the failure of the Albany Congress, and the Regulator movement all testified. Even more serious trouble lay ahead. Colonial assemblies from Pennsylvania southward had failed to extend full representation to their Western regions as population increased there. Pennsylvania remedied the inequality in her state constitution, but Virginia and the Carolinas did not, and the result was Western resentment against the Eastern-dominated state governments.

Concurrent with these internal disputes the state governments quarreled with one another about the West. The Revolution had dissolved their ties to England but not their territorial boundaries, which had been fixed by royal charters. By their charters, Georgia, the Carolinas, Virginia, Connecticut, and Massachusetts extended to the Pacific Ocean, while Maryland, Delaware, Pennsylvania, New Jersey, and Rhode Island were limited to a few hundred miles on the seacoast. The "land-

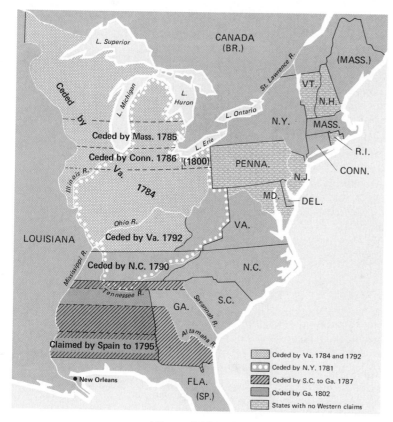

Western lands ceded by the states, 1781–1802

less'' states wanted Congress to take control of unoccupied Western lands and restrict the western boundaries of the ''landed'' states. The landed states resisted any such proposal and squabbled with one another over their conflicting charters. Virginia, whose charter was the oldest, could claim most of the West all to herself. The people of every state, when they looked west, found reason for jealousy or distrust of their neighbors.

The problem was aggravated by land speculation. Before the war, speculators from Pennsylvania, Maryland, and New Jersey (all landless states) had purchased land from the Indians and sought authorization from the king to establish a new colony (Vandalia) in the Ohio Valley. Though bitterly opposed by Virginia's Ohio Company, they had been on the verge of success when the Revolution upset their plans. Now they argued that Congress had inherited the king's authority over all unoccupied lands; and, supported by their state governments, they pressed Congress to recognize their claims. The landed states had fought them off by including in the Articles of Confederation a guarantee that no state

should be deprived of territory for the benefit of the United States. But Maryland stubbornly refused to approve the articles as long as the proposed union lacked control over Western lands. Without her the union was stalled, for it was not to go into effect until unanimously approved.

Maryland could produce better arguments than the mere greed of her land-speculators. The landed states, she pointed out, would be able to command such an abundant source of revenue by selling their Western lands that their citizens would pay few or no taxes. People from the landless states would consequently move to the landed ones. Maryland, next door to the leviathan Virginia, would be depopulated.

In Virginia the sentiment for union was strong, and some patriots wanted to give up the state's Western territory, which they thought was too large for a single republican government anyhow. Rather than jeopardize republicanism in Virginia, they preferred to see new states formed in the West and joined to the old ones by the Articles of Confederation. Thomas Jefferson accordingly led Virginia (on January 2, 1781) to offer Congress her claims to all lands north of the Ohio. The transfer was contingent on a number of conditions that in effect canceled speculative claims to the region and required that the land be divided into ''distinct republican States,'' which should ultimately be admitted to the union on equal terms with the old ones. When Virginia's cession was made known, Maryland capitulated (though the speculators still tried to block her) and approved the Articles of Confederation in February 1781. New York had already ceded her shadowy Western claims, and the other landed states eventually followed the example that she and Virginia had set (Georgia held out until 1802).

Congress under the Confederation. In the Articles of Confederation the American people got what most of them at that time wanted. Having just suffered from the power of a distant British government, they were wary of allowing much authority to their own central government. They charged Congress with the responsibility for making decisions about a multitude of their common concerns, but they neglected to give it the powers to carry its decisions into effect. It could pass resolutions, make recommendations, enact ordinances; but it had no courts, no way of enforcing its orders either on individuals or on states. It could not even levy taxes to pay its own expenses but had to rely on the several states to furnish its funds. In fact Congress was allowed less authority than the colonists had once acknowledged in Parliament: Congress did not even have the right to regulate trade. The disadvantages of such a powerless central government soon became apparent.

After the coming of peace diminished the urgency of united action, the states became increasingly enamored of their own power and increasingly casual, even contemptuous, in their relations with Congress, ignoring its resolutions, refusing to fill its requisitions for funds, sending inferior men to represent them or sometimes none at all. Congress was unable to cope with the situation because the Articles of Confederation had provided it with no means to enforce obedience. The weakness of the national government made the years from 1783 to 1789, in the phrase of one historian, the "Critical Period" of American history.

A man elected to Congress during these years might arrive at the meeting place on the appointed day and find a dozen or more delegates like himself eager to proceed to business. But the Articles of Confederation required that each state be represented by at least two delegates and that the representatives of at least seven states be present to make a quorum. Unless more than seven states were represented, every decision had to be unanimous; and the assent of nine states was necessary in most matters having to do with war and peace (including treaties) and with appropriating money. Because the states were often slow about appointing delegates and the delegates themselves slow in taking up their duties, the first arrivals at a session sometimes had to wait several weeks before enough members were present to transact business. Even after a session was organized, it led a precarious existence; for if one or two delegates fell sick, the rest might have to twiddle their thumbs until more arrived or the sick got well.

Each delegate was elected for a one-year term and was prohibited from serving for more than three years in six. As a result, the membership of Congress was constantly shifting. The government was further handicapped by the failure of the Articles of Confederation to provide a regular executive department. Congress exercised executive powers through special commissions and committees and achieved a degree of continuity by appointing three secretaries to manage crucial executive matters (Benjamin Lincoln, followed by Henry Knox, as Secretary of War; Robert Morris as Superintendent of Finance; and Robert Livingston, followed by John Jay, as Secretary for Foreign Affairs).

These officers struggled to give the United States the appearance of a government. But Congress, pursuing its intermittent existence, belied the appearance. Even when it could scrape together a quorum it had no permanent headquarters or capitol. A mutiny in the Philadelphia barracks frightened it out of that city in 1783, and thereafter the delegates wandered from Princeton to Annapolis to Trenton to New York—talking endlessly about where they should settle permanently. Shortly after they began their travels, Oliver Ellsworth, a congressman from Connecticut, observed dryly, "It will soon be of very little consequence where Congress go, if they are not made respectable as well as responsible, which can never be done without giving them a power to perform engagements as well as make them." Congress, in short, had responsibility without power. It could recommend endlessly but no one either inside or outside the United States paid much attention to what it recommended.

The impotence of Congress made the United States a beggar in the eyes of the world. During the Revolution, Congress had boldly capitalized on popular enthusiasm for the cause of independence by printing paper money, but the money had become worthless before the war's end. Congress had also begged money and supplies from France, but after the peace France preferred to keep her ally poor and humble. Dutch bankers, with more vision than many Americans, did continue to lend. But when Congress turned to the states for funds or for the power to levy a 5 percent tariff on imports, the states turned the beggar down. The power to levy tariffs would have required the unanimous approval of the states, and each time it was proposed (in 1781 and again in 1783) at least one state refused; and the others insisted on conditions that would have made the power meaningless anyhow.

The one area in which the United States enjoyed at least the appearance of power was the wilderness north of the Ohio River, a region thinly populated by squatters, Indians,

A western township = 36 sq. miles
One section = 1 sq. mile (640 acres)

6	5	4	3	2	1
7	Income reserved for school support				12
18	17	16	15	14	13
19	20	21	22	23	24
30	29	28	27	26	25
31	32	33	34	35	36

Half section (320 acres)

Quarter section (160 acres)

Half-quarter section (80 acres)

Quarter-quarter sections (40 acres each)

Numbering system adopted 1796

1 mile

--- Present state boundaries
★ British posts after 1783

CANADA

L. Superior

Ft. Michilimackinac ★

L. Huron

L. Michigan

NORTHWEST

St. Lawrence R.

Dutchman's Point

Pointe-au-Fer ★ ★

Oswegatchie ★

CANADA (Br.)

L. Ontario

Oswego ★

Ft. Niagara ★

N.Y.

Detroit ★

L. Erie

LOUISIANA (Sp.)

Mississippi R.

TERRITORY

Scioto Co. Option

PENNA.

N.J.

MD. DEL.

Ohio Co. Grant

VA.

Ohio R.

The Old Northwest

and French. When Virginia offered to cede the area in 1781, Congress had been prevented from taking any formal action to accept it because of pressure from speculators who objected to the terms attached to the cession. Early in 1784, when Virginia renewed the offer, Congress was stalled for lack of a quorum. But by March 1 enough members were present to act favorably, and the United States gained formal authority over the Northwest.

Now Congress might begin to raise the funds it needed by selling land in the newly acquired territory. On April 23 the delegates passed an ordinance, drafted by Thomas Jefferson, that fulfilled the terms of Virginia's cession. It divided the territory into states, each of which was to be admitted into the Union on equal terms with the existing states as soon as its free population equaled any of theirs. Until then the inhabitants could govern themselves according to the constitution and laws of any of the existing states.

To prepare for the sale of lands to individuals, Congress passed an ordinance in 1785 providing that the Northwest be surveyed into townships six miles square along lines running east-west and north-south. Each township was

divided into thirty-six lots one mile square (640 acres). A lot (later called a section) was the smallest unit that could be purchased, and neither a township nor a lot was to be sold for less than a dollar an acre in specie. To speed up the transformation of the national domain into hard cash, land offices were to be established in all the states.

Surveying and the settlement of Indian claims proceeded slowly. Before the lands were ready for public sale, a group of ambitious and not very scrupulous speculators from New England came to Congress with a proposition. Calling themselves, like an earlier group, the Ohio Company, they offered to buy a million and a half acres, for which they would pay in currency so badly depreciated that the price amounted to less than 10 cents an acre in specie. Presumptuous as the offer was, the United States needed the money desperately, and Congress decided to accept it. The Ohio Company also agreed to take an option on 5 million additional acres, to be turned over to a subsidiary company known as the Scioto Company. By no coincidence, this company included several congressmen.

To oblige the Ohio Company, Congress passed a new ordinance for governing the Northwest. Jefferson's ordinance of 1784 had never gone into operation, because the area as yet contained no authorized settlers. It did, however, contain many squatters who had helped themselves to public lands and stoutly resisted eviction. Because of the difficulty anticipated in establishing property rights against squatters, and because of the frontier's reputation for violence and disorder, many Easterners believed that congressional rule would be more appropriate than self-government during the initial years of settlement. Accordingly, the Northwest Ordinance of 1787 provided for a period during which a governor, a secretary, and a court of three judges, all appointed by Congress, would hold full powers. Once the population had reached five thousand free adult males, a representative legislature would be established, but none of its actions would be valid without the approval of the governor, who would still be appointed by Congress. The legislature could send a representative to Congress, but he would have no vote. The whole area was to be divided into not fewer than three or more than five territories, each of which would be admitted to the Union on equal terms with the existing states when it attained a population of sixty thousand. Slavery was forbidden throughout the area; no person was to be "molested" for his religious beliefs or mode of worship; and "schools and the means of education" were to be encouraged. Though the ordinance did not say how the encouragement was to be effected, the Land Ordinance of 1785 had already reserved one lot in each township "for the maintenance of public schools."

The Northwest Ordinance, if less liberal than the one drafted by Jefferson, nevertheless established for the United States a Western policy that embodied the most cherished American principles. Though the ordinance applied to only a part of the West, it set a precedent that guided the territorial expansion of the nation until the end of the nineteenth century.

National humiliation. One serious obstacle stood in the way of Congress' noble aspirations for the American West: the United States held only a tenuous grip on the area. England had never completely evacuated the Northwest, nor had Spain recognized American possession of any territory south of the Ohio. As the weakness and poverty of the new nation grew more apparent, European statesmen intrigued to push its western boundary back to the Appalachians.

When England made peace in 1783, she was not fully persuaded—nor was the rest of Europe—that the United States would last. While the king officially proclaimed the treaty and commanded his subjects to comply with it, his ministers sent secret orders to the governor-general of Canada to retain Britain's trading posts and military garrisons in the Northwest. The United States, with its own armies disbanded and the French forces gone, was in no position to compel the British to withdraw. To excuse their continued occupation of the posts, the British charged that the Americans had violated the treaty.

Again the weakness of the national government was to blame. The treaty required that neither side make laws impeding the collection of private debts contracted before the war, and it required that Congress "earnestly recommend" to the states the restoration of confiscated loyalist property. Congress did recommend the restitution, and the fact that the states did not follow the recommendation was not technically a violation of the treaty. But when some states passed laws impeding the collection of British debts, they violated the treaty as surely as England did in keeping troops on American territory. Congress was as helpless to prevent one violation as the other. It sent John Adams to England as American minister; and he protested the British garrisons with characteristic Adams vigor, but in vain, for England knew that no American troops stood behind him.

England showed her contempt for the government of her former colonies by failing to establish a legation in the United States to match the American legation in London. More ominously she dickered with the influential Allen brothers, Ethan and Levi, for help in acquiring Vermont. Claimed by both New Hampshire and New York, Vermont had asserted its independence of both and applied for statehood. Congress was reluctant to antagonize either claimant by admitting Vermont into the Union, and there was danger that the Vermonters might attach themselves to Canada (Vermont was not admitted until 1791).

In the Southwest, Spain was grasping for the area that later became the states of Kentucky and Tennessee. Americans were moving into it at such a rate that by 1790 it contained more than a hundred thousand of them, but their presence was hardly a guarantee of permanent American possession. Barred by the mountains from trade with the East, the settlers relied on the Mississippi River to float their produce to market at New Orleans. New Orleans belonged to Spain, and so did the lower Mississippi. The Spaniards had gained Louisiana in 1763, the Floridas in 1783; and they maintained forts on the west bank of the Mississippi as far north as St. Louis, on the east bank as far as the present site of Memphis. Anyone who wanted to use the river had to do business with Spain.

Although commercial exports from the Southwest were still meager, everyone in the region was expecting future prosperity through the Mississippi trade. Spain was well aware of that expectation. In 1784 she closed the river to navigation by Americans and waited for the settlers to abandon their feeble Congress for the solid commercial advantage of Spanish citizenship. For a time it seemed that the settlers might do just that, for they were far from pleased with the way Eastern Americans were treating them. In 1772, by the Watauga Compact, pioneers in the Tennessee area had formed a government of their own, which lasted until 1776, when North Carolina organized them into Washington County. In 1784, after her land-speculators had established claims to the most valuable land, North Carolina ceded the region to Congress in order to avoid the expense of protecting it from the Indians. When she changed her mind the next year and tried to regain possession, many settlers grew disgusted and began to look favorably toward Spain. In Kentucky, the Western region of Virginia, a similar secessionist movement and a similar flirtation with Spain threatened to disrupt the Union.

As the Southwest began to draw away from the United States, Spain in 1785 sent Don Diego de Gardoqui to wring from Congress a formal recognition of her exclusive control over the Mississippi. Congress instructed its Secretary of Foreign Affairs, John Jay, to insist in his negotiations with Gardoqui on the right of Americans to navigate the Mississippi through Spanish territory to its mouth. This was a subject about which the two men had tilted inconclusively once before, during the Revolution, when Jay had gone to Spain in search of assistance in the war against England. Jay now found Gardoqui as adamant as ever about refusing to recognize an American right of navigation but willing to make other concessions. The Spaniards would agree to recognize American territorial rights as far south as the old border of British West Florida and as far west as the Mississippi and to give American merchants a few trading privileges in Spain. In return, he asked only that the United States agree to give up navigation of the Mississippi for twenty-five years. The offer was attractive to Easterners. Jay was ready to accept, and so were a majority in Congress. But ratification of a treaty required the approval of nine states, and the five Southern states would not agree to it. Now Gardoqui's shrewdness became apparent; for though the treaty failed, Spain still gained an advantage: the willingness of the Northern states to give up the Mississippi further weakened the Southwest's attachment to the Union.

While Gardoqui led Jay into alienating the Westerners, the Spanish governor of Louisiana, Esteban Rodríguez Miró, was wooing them with bribes and privileges. General James Wilkinson, a veteran of the Revolutionary War and a consummate double-dealer, took a trip to New Orleans in 1787. While there, he took a secret oath of allegiance to

Spain in return for trading concessions. The following year he accepted a Spanish pension, with the understanding that he would lead his neighbors in the Tennessee region to repudiate the United States. Wilkinson was not the only Southwestern traitor. Daniel Boone, James Robertson, and John Sevier all accepted Spanish gold. Instead of doing what they were paid to do, however, they cheerfully deceived both sides while they waited to see what was going to happen. If, as seemed likely, the United States should break up, they were ready to learn Spanish.

The United States had troubles even in the Mediterranean. For years European countries had been protecting their Mediterranean shipping from pirates by paying an annual tribute to the rulers of Morocco, Algiers, Tripoli, and Tunis. As long as American ships carried the British flag, they were safe; but after 1776, when they began to fly the Stars and Stripes, pirates swarmed out upon them. The captured American captains and crews were put on the auction block and sold as slaves. Congress bought protection from Morocco in 1787 but had neither money nor guns to stop the other African pirates.

Nor were pirates the only difficulty to beset American trade. The whole American economy was in a precarious position. With the coming of peace, American merchants had sensed a huge demand for the British dry goods and hardware to which American consumers had been accustomed before the war. The merchants placed their orders, and warehouses and stores were soon bulging, with the British extending liberal credits. The American merchants in turn extended credit to retailers and consumers, and the country indulged itself in a buying spree. Only when it came time to pay the bills did the Americans discover their situation.

The colonial economy had been a complex one, in which Americans paid for British imports by carrying their own and other people's goods to market in various ports throughout the world, but mostly within the empire. Now they were no longer a part of the empire, and Britain closed her West Indian ports to American vessels. Prices of American produce dropped, merchants found themselves cut off from usual channels of trade, and depression settled over the land—while British merchants called for payment.

Americans blamed themselves and their merchants. Having won their political independence, they had promptly mortgaged it by extravagant purchases from their old masters. It seemed that the British, by craftily extending liberal credits and closing their ports to Americans, had rewon economically the position of dominance that they had lost politically. Congress instructed John Adams to ask England for a commercial treaty, but he was no more successful in this than in pressing for the evacuation of British garrisons in the Northwest.

There were loud demands for retaliation against the British restrictions on American trade, and some states passed laws to discourage imports. But such partial legislation by single states only added to the difficulties by injuring the economies of sister states. As John Sullivan confessed concerning the New Hampshire law, "It was a blow aimed at Britain but wounds us and our friends." What was needed was an overall national regulation of commerce, not simply to discourage unnecessary imports, but to create a balanced economy in which manufacturing, agriculture, and commerce would all find their place. Only in this way could the United States become economically as well as politically independent and insure herself against domination by Britain or any other nation. But the American Congress, with no power to regulate commerce, could not even begin to direct the economy toward such a goal.

The crisis of American nationality

Many Americans found the impotence of the national government intolerable. The Revolution had widened their vision beyond the affairs of town or county or colony and had taught them to think, as Alexander Hamilton put it, "continentally." They knew that the only way to solve the difficulties of the United States was to strengthen the national government—they had known it before the ink was dry on the Articles of Confederation. Now, as the weakness of the government became more and more embarrassing, they spoke out ever more loudly.

Thinking continentally. The Americans had had plenty of practice in making and breaking governments. Their usual method had been to call an extralegal convention—like the Stamp Act Congress or the Continental Congress or the provincial congresses that replaced the royal governments. Conventions were also summoned whenever the people of a state or region wanted to achieve a public purpose for which their regular government had proved inadequate. Several interstate conventions had met during the war in an effort to regulate prices. Connecticut held a convention in 1783 to protest the founding of the Society of the Cincinnati and the granting of extra pay to army officers. And, as we have seen, Massachusetts called a convention to draft a state constitution.

It was only natural, then, for men who had begun to think "continentally" to turn to a convention for the purpose of strengthening the continental government. As early as 1784 they had talked of it, but at that time public sentiment was overwhelmingly against it. The opposition did not arise from a deficiency of national patriotism or from too much local patriotism. Nationalism, which has proved the most lively—and deadly—force in the modern world, attached itself in America to the Union rather than to the states. Thomas Paine, in his first publication after the peace, wrote: "I ever feel myself hurt when I hear the Union, the great palladium of our liberty and safety, the least irreverently spoken of. . . . Our citizenship in the United States is our national character. Our citizenship in any particular state is only our local distinction."

This sentiment was echoed by statesmen, poets, painters, and schoolmasters. George Washington, the nation's hero, was a great Virginian but a greater American. "We are known by no other character among nations," he declared in 1783, "than as the United States." Connecticut during the 1780s produced a host of brilliant young men who celebrated in literature and art not their own state but America. John Trumbull depicted the great events of the American Revolution in a series of historical paintings. Joel Barlow attempted an American epic in *The Vision of Columbus*. Noah Webster wrote schoolbooks designed to teach American English. Jedidiah Morse published an *American Geography*. And Ezra Stiles, the president of Yale, preached of *The United States Elevated to Glory and Honor*. Some authors, to be sure, wrote the history of their own states (Jefferson, for example, published his *Notes on the State of*

John Trumbull: he celebrated America

Virginia in 1785), but the local pride they exhibited was different in kind from the national pride that was evident throughout the Union.

Yet however proud of their country's past and confident of its future, Americans needed leadership and a government capable of elevating the United States to the glory and honor they wanted for it. National policy was drifting, and continental-minded men warned that the nation faced collapse or conquest if its government was not strengthened. But their appeals met resistance from people who feared that a stronger government might become aristocratic or tyrannical; it might threaten the principles that had brought the Union into being—the principles of equality and of responsible, republican government. In 1785, for example, when the legislature of Massachusetts proposed a general convention to strengthen the national government, her delegates in Congress objected. Would-be aristocrats, they argued, would use such a convention to establish a government based on special privilege, loaded with lucrative positions for themselves, and bolstered by a standing army.

Because of such sentiments on the part of honest and patriotic men, a national constitutional convention, though often talked of, had failed to materialize. By 1786, however, Americans had become so impatient with British trade restrictions, conflicting state commercial laws, and national economic helplessness that they arranged for an interstate meeting at Annapolis, Maryland, to consider the extension of national authority to the regulation of commerce. The first delegates to arrive at Annapolis told one another that the contemplated revision of the national government was insufficient; those from New Jersey had even been instructed to ask for a general overhaul of the Articles of Confederation. When representatives from five states had convened, though more were on the way, they drew up a proposal to Congress and the several states and dissolved the convention. What they proposed was another convention the next year at Philadelphia for the larger purpose of making "the constitution of the Federal Government adequate to the exigencies of the Union."

The message reached the states along with some alarming news from Massachusetts. In the summer of 1786 the citizens in the economically depressed western part of the state, laboring under a heavy burden of debt, had called a number of local conventions to demand changes in the state government: they objected to the state senate (the upper house of the legislature) as a needless expense and an aristocratic influence; they objected to the heavy taxation of land; and they objected to the high fees charged by lawyers and county courts. After the conventions had voiced their protests and adjourned, mobs prevented the county courts from sitting and thus put an end to the collection of debts. Then, during the winter of 1786–87, some two thousand Western farmers rose in armed rebellion under the leadership of Daniel Shays, a veteran of the Revolutionary War.

Though Shays' Rebellion was easily quelled by the loyal militia of Massachusetts, it alarmed Americans in every part of the United States. By threatening law and order, the rebellion threatened property: the closing of the courts in western Massachusetts had halted mortgage foreclosures and deprived creditors of property owed to them. Other states too had depressed areas and discontented debtors who, it was feared, might imitate the Shaysites. Property was also endangered from other directions. In several states, the coming of peace had brought no end to the flood of paper money that inflated values and defrauded creditors. Rhode Island made it illegal for a man to refuse the state's worthless paper money as payment for debts owed him.

Even before Shays' Rebellion people had realized that something must be done about this undermining of property rights. It would be a mockery of the national purpose if Americans who had undertaken a revolution to defend property, should themselves destroy property through irresponsible government. After the shock of Shays' Rebellion every state but Rhode Island agreed to send delegates to Philadelphia to revise the Articles of Confederation.

The great convention. The United States in the Revolutionary period produced six men of indisputable greatness: Franklin, Washington, Jefferson, Madison, Hamilton, and John Adams. Four of them—Franklin, Washington, Madison, and Hamilton—were among the fifty-five delegates sent by the state governments to the convention that met in Philadelphia from May 25 to September 17, 1787. Jefferson and Adams would doubtless have

I rejoice most exceedingly that there is an end to our warfare, and that such a field is opening to our view as will, with wisdom to direct the cultivation of it, make us a great, a respectable, and happy People; but it must be improved by other means than State politics, and unreasonable jealousies and prejudices; or (it requires not the second sight to see that) we shall be instruments in the hands of our Enemies, and those European powers who may be jealous of our greatness in Union.... No man in the United States is, or can be more deeply impressed with the necessity of a reform in our present Confederation than myself. No man perhaps has felt the bad efects of it more sensibly, for to the defects thereof, and want of Powers in Congress may justly be ascribed the prolongation of the War, and consequently the Expences occasioned by it. More than half the perplexities I have experienced in the course of my command, and almost the whole of the difficulties and distress of the Army, have there origin here....

From George Washington, Letter to Alexander Hamilton, March 31, 1783.

Thinking continentally: George Washington

I find also the pride of independance taking deep and dangerous hold on the hearts of individual states. I know no danger so dreadful and so probable as that of internal contests. And I know no remedy so likely to prevent it as the strengthening the band that connects us. We have substituted a Congress of deputies from every state to perform this task: but we have done nothing which would enable them to enforce their decisions. What will be the case? They will not be enforced. The states will go to war with each other in defiance of Congress; one will call in France to her assistance; another Great Britain, and so we shall have all the wars of Europe brought to our own doors.... I feel great comfort on the prospect of getting yourself and two or three others into the legislature. My humble and earnest prayer to Almighty god will be that you may bring into fashion principles suited to the form of government we have adopted, and not of that we have rejected, that you will first lay your shoulders to strengthening the band of our confederacy and averting those cruel evils to which it's present weakness will expose us, and that you will see the necessity of doing this instantly before we forget the advantages of union, or acquire a degree of ill-temper against each other which will daily increase the obstacles to that good work.

From Thomas Jefferson, Letter to Edmund Randolph, February 15, 1783.

Thinking continentally: Thomas Jefferson

We have now happily concluded the great work of independence, but much remains to be done to reach the fruits of it. Our prospects are not flattering. Every day proves the inefficacy of the present confederation, yet the common danger being removed, we are receding instead of advancing in a disposition to amend its defects. The road to popularity in each state is to inspire jealousies of the power of Congress, though nothing can be more apparent than that they have no power; and that for the want of it, the resources of the country during the war could not be drawn out, and we at this moment experience all the mischiefs of a bankrupt and ruined credit. It is to be hoped that when prejudice and folly have run themselves out of breath we may return to reason and correct our errors.

From Alexander Hamilton, Letter to John Jay, July 25, 1783.

Thinking continentally: Alexander Hamilton

been there too if they had not been representing the United States in Europe, for the convention was an extraordinary assemblage of talent. The delegates had a wealth of experience and tradition to draw upon: the heritage of British political and constitutional ideas stretching back to Magna Carta and beyond; the experience of five generations of colonists in representative assemblies, town meetings, and county courts; the searching debates about authority that preceded the Declaration of Independence; the drafting of state constitutions; the running of state governments and of a rudimentary national government. In no period of American history could a group have been gathered with more sophistication in political thought or with more practical experience in the construction and reconstruction of governments.

Almost without exception the delegates were men who thought continentally; and they were eager for a central government that would preserve and embody the national feeling that had grown out of the Revolution, a government that would be respected at home and abroad. The only way to achieve that end, they believed, was to give the central government more authority than Congress had been allowed. It had to be able to levy taxes so that it could support itself and not be starved into impotence, so that it could raise the armies and build the navy that might one day be needed to defend the independence so dearly won. It had to be able to regulate commerce so as to bargain effectively with foreign nations. It had to offer better protection to private property than the existing national or state governments did. And it had to have coercive powers to enforce its decrees.

The delegates, while agreeing on these objectives, realized that two obstacles stood in the way of attaining them. The first was the fear of the American people that a national government, if given enough power to do its job, would quickly seize more than enough, that it would fall into the hands of a select group of wealthy and clever men who would use it to their own advantage and to the disadvantage of ordinary men. The American people would not accept an effective central government unless they could be sure of controlling it.

The second obstacle was rivalry among the states. Each state feared that a strong national government might give unfair advantage to the others. For example, it might levy taxes

that would injure one state and benefit another. Fortunately quarrels over the West were momentarily at a minimum because of Virginia's renunciation of claims to the Northwest and because the status of future states in the territory was determined by Congress (in the Northwest Ordinance) while the convention was sitting. The convention itself, after preliminary debates, skirted the knotty question of whether new states should be equal to old and decided simply that "New States may be admitted by the Congress into this Union."

But another form of state rivalry could not be bypassed and threatened to deadlock the convention: in a national government composed of states, how was representation to be apportioned? Under the Articles of Confederation, each state, no matter what its size, had one vote in Congress (this manner of voting was also followed in the convention). Such an arrangement gave undue advantage to the citizens of small states: 68,000 Rhode Islanders had the same influence on decisions as 747,000 Virginians. The large states would not be satisfied with any national government in which their influence was not at least approximately commensurate with their size. But the small states believed that unless they retained an equal vote the large states would be able to advance their own interests at the expense of the small states.

The rivalry between small and large states masked a more serious rivalry between North and South, which had already appeared in voting alignments in the Continental Congress. The Southern states, where slave labor produced crops for export, were wary of subjecting their labor or its produce to a government dominated by the more numerous Northern states where free labor, diversified farming, and large commercial interests prevailed.

When the convention opened, Edmund Randolph of Virginia presented a plan, drafted by his colleague James Madison, that was designed to overcome both the fears of the people and the fears of the states. Madison, who at thirty-six was the most astute political thinker of his day, proposed to rest the government of the United States on the people rather than on the state governments and to apportion representation not by states but by population. The population of the Southern states (including slaves) equaled that of the Northern states and was expected to grow more rapidly in the future. In a government where representation was proportioned according to population the South would be safe.

Nor would small states be endangered by large ones. Their fears, Madison perceived, were partly an illusion: the people of a small state did not necessarily have different interests from the people of a large state. The people of Delaware, for example, probably had more in common with their neighbors in Pennsylvania than with distant Rhode Islanders.

To keep the government from seizing more power than it was assigned, Madison proposed to divide it into different branches that would check and balance one another: a two-house legislature, an independent executive, and an independent judiciary. Each would have specific functions and would see to it that the others did not overstep their bounds. Thus the most distant constituent in America would have guardians within the government itself watching to make sure that it did not get out of hand. The Americans had already endorsed the principle of separation of powers in their state governments, but their discussions of national government had usually revolved around the granting of further powers to the existing unicameral Congress. Only a few, like Jefferson and John Jay, had seen the need for separation of powers in the national government itself; but as soon as Madison made the proposal, its advantages were obvious, and many of the fears about the government's escaping control were dispelled. Pierce Butler, a delegate for South Carolina, said that "he had opposed the grant of powers to Congress heretofore, because the whole power was vested in one body. The proposed distribution of the powers into different bodies changed the case, and would induce him to go great lengths."

The delegates spent two weeks revising Madison's plan and working out its details, without altering its basic structure. Then on June 15 William Paterson of New Jersey suddenly came up with a new plan calling for a continuation of the existing unicameral Congress with increased powers, but with each state retaining its equal vote. Paterson and his supporters would allow Congress the power to tax, to regulate trade, and to enforce its own decrees, but they wanted the national government to remain what it had been, an assembly of the states, not of the people, its members chosen by the state governments, not by popular election. Paterson's plan was

rejected, but the small-state delegations had rallied to it and finally threatened to bolt the convention unless each state was given an equal vote in at least one house of the national legislature. To pacify them, the other members of the convention agreed on July 16 that all the states would have equal representation in the upper house; but to this concession they attached several provisions, designed mainly to protect the interests of the South: representation in the lower house and direct taxation would be apportioned according to population, with five slaves to be considered the equivalent of three free men; all bills for raising or spending money would originate in the lower house; a census would be taken every ten years.

These conditions in effect gave the voters of slaveholding states a larger representation in the lower house than the voters of non-slaveholding states. And if Southern population grew as rapidly as expected, the representation would be increased. On the other hand, the voters of small states (mostly Northern) would have a far larger share of power in the upper house than their numbers would entitle them to.

Once they had made this Great Compromise there was no longer any serious danger that the delegates would fail in their attempt to strengthen the national government. They had started out in substantial agreement about what needed to be done, and they had overcome, in large measure at least, both the rivalry of the states and the fear of tyranny. They still argued about details; but within three and a half months of assembling, they had finished their job.

Their proposed Constitution provided for a national government with authority to collect taxes, make treaties with foreign countries, maintain an army and a navy, coin and borrow money, regulate commerce among the states and with foreign nations, and make any laws necessary to carry its powers into execution. The United States Constitution and all the treaties and laws made under it were to be the supreme law of the land, superior to state laws and binding on state courts. Moreover, the federal government would have its own executive and its own courts to enforce its treaties, Constitution, and laws, and to settle disputes between states. As a last resort it could call on the militia for help.

The national legislature, or Congress, was to consist of an upper house, or Senate, and a House of Representatives. Each state was to have two senators, both appointed by the state legislature for six-year terms, and one representative for every thirty thousand persons, to be popularly elected for a two-year term by the same persons who were qualified to vote for members of "the most numerous Branch of the State Legislature." The executive, known as the President, was to be elected every four years by an electoral "college" to which each state might appoint (in any way its legislature prescribed) as many members as the total of its representatives and senators in Congress. It was intended, of course, that the members of this body should exercise their own discretion in selecting the best man in the country. The man who received the second largest number of votes became the Vice President, who was to preside over the Senate.

The Constitution hedged both the federal and the state governments with specific prohibitions. To protect private property, it forbade the state governments to pass laws impairing the obligation of contracts, or to coin money, issue paper money, or make anything but gold and silver legal tender in payment of debts. To prevent the states from encroaching on the sphere of the federal government, it forbade them to make treaties, levy import or export duties, or engage in war unless actually invaded. Conversely the states were protected by clauses prohibiting the federal government from levying direct taxes except in proportion to population, from levying export taxes at all (a protection for the tobacco- and rice-exporters of the South), and from restricting immigration "or Importation of such Persons as any of the States now existing shall think proper to admit" before the year 1808 (a protection for the slave trade until that time). Republicanism and individual rights were protected by clauses forbidding either the states or the federal government to grant titles of nobility, or to pass bills of attainder or ex post facto laws. And the federal government could not make any religious test a qualification for public office or suspend the writ of habeas corpus "unless when in Cases of Rebellion or Invasion the public Safety may require it."

Apart from these prohibitions, the Constitution did not contain any guarantee of individual rights such as freedom of speech or religion or trial by jury. In the last days of the convention Elbridge Gerry of Massachusetts and George Mason of Virginia proposed that this omission be corrected, but their colleagues rejected the suggestion as unnecessary on the grounds that the Constitution defined and limited the powers of the national government to specified actions and that the state constitutions already contained bills of rights. But in case experience should prove this or any other of their decisions to be unwise, the convention provided a means of correction: the Constitution could be amended if two-thirds of both houses of Congress and three-fourths of the state legislatures agreed. The convention adjourned on September 17, after sending a copy of its work to Congress for transmission to the states.

Ratification. The constitution drafted at Philadelphia was the greatest creative triumph of the Experimental Period, and it showed how much its authors had learned during those experimental years. After the war the initial reaction against monarchy and aristocracy had led Americans to create state governments with feeble executives and ineffective upper houses; the new Constitution proposed a powerful executive and a Senate equal in power to the House of Representatives. The Articles of Confederation had created a national government controlled by the state governments and having no direct relation to the individual citizen; the new Constitution proposed a national government independent of the state governments, with a House of Representatives elected directly by the people of the United States and with federal courts acting directly on them. The Articles of Confederation had placed the national government in the hands of a single congress of delegates and had provided it with little authority; the new Constitution split up the national government to prevent abuses and gave it real authority.

The members of the Philadelphia Convention had been empowered only to revise the Articles of Confederation. Actually, they had drawn up a completely new government to take the place of the debating society that Congress had become. Knowing that their ambitious plan would meet opposition, and unwilling to have it defeated by the stubbornness of a few states, the delegates boldly proposed that as soon as nine states had accepted the new Constitution it should go into effect among those nine (revisions of the Articles of Confederation required unanimous approval). The convention also proposed the revolutionary technique of bypassing the state legislatures, where power-hungry state politicians and pressure groups might exert an influence as pernicious as the speculators had exerted against ratification of the Articles of Confederation. In each state the people would elect a special convention to judge the new constitution. The state government would issue the call for the ratifying convention but would have no part in accepting or rejecting the Constitution. The new national government, if adopted, would thus be authorized directly by the people; its power would derive from them.

The prestige of its authors, especially Washington and Franklin, as well as its intrinsic merits assured the Constitution a hearing. But its adoption was not at all certain. Several members of the convention, including the influential Edmund Randolph, had refused to sign the completed document. When it reached Congress, Richard Henry Lee took an immediate dislike to it. Why, he asked, should Congress approve its own dissolution? Why should nine states be allowed to withdraw from the Confederation to form a new and dangerously powerful government? Before transmitting the document to the states, Lee proposed at least the insertion of a bill of rights.

Lee's proposal was defeated by what he termed "a coalition of monarchy men, military men, aristocrats and drones whose noise, impudence and zeal exceeds all belief." When the Constitution reached the American people, many reacted as Lee had. But in every state the legislature eventually, if sometimes reluctantly, issued the necessary call for a popular ratifying convention.

The opponents of the Constitution were moved less by a desire to perpetuate the superiority of the state governments than by the old fear that a strong national government would escape from popular control and become oppressive. The system of checks and balances, they felt, was not adequate insurance against tyranny. The House of Representatives was too small to represent so many people and would be filled with the rich and well-born. The failure to include a bill of rights seemed an ominous indication of the direction the national government would take. Madison had argued at the convention, and now wrote in the newspapers, to persuade people that there were no grounds for the long-accepted notion that a large republic would fall into tyranny. In a large republic there would be so many different groups with such varied and opposing interests that they would be unable to submerge their differences and combine into a tyrannical majority. The danger of a tyrannical coalition was far greater in a small republic, Madison pointed out, because of the fewer divergent interests and the greater ease of communication.

The supporters of the Constitution were generally more aggressive than their opponents, and sometimes their tactics were unworthy of their cause. In Pennsylvania they pushed through the call for a convention after the legislature had voted to adjourn; they rounded up a quorum only by forcibly detaining two members. Everywhere they campaigned with a vigor and invective born of urgency. This, they felt, was the crisis of American nationality. If the Constitution failed to be adopted, the Union might be doomed.

Opposition to the Constitution was generally weakest in the small states, which would have more than their share of power in the new government. But the Federalists, as the supporters of the Constitution called themselves, knew that it was imperative to win over the four largest states: Massachusetts, Pennsylvania, New York, and Virginia. For any one of them to abstain would imperil the success of the new government. Pennsylvania, in spite of determined opposition, fell in line first, on December 12, 1787. Massachusetts ratified on February 6, 1788, by a narrow majority, which included several anti-Federalist delegates. They had been persuaded after John Hancock proposed that a recommendation for a bill of rights accompany ratification.

In Virginia the opposition, led by Patrick Henry, was weakened when Edmund Randolph swung back in favor of adoption. The state accepted the Constitution by a vote of eighty-nine to seventy-nine on June 26. Meanwhile every other state but New York, North Carolina, and Rhode Island had voted for ratification. Several had, like Massachusetts, included recommendations for amendments. In New York Alexander Hamilton, John Jay, and James Madison had campaigned for the Constitution in an impressive series of newspaper articles, known as *The Federalist*. Though these were perhaps the most searching discussion of the Constitution ever written, they did not prevent the election of a hostile ratifying convention. Only after news of Vir-

John Hancock, by John S. Copley

ginia's decision reached New York did the state fall into line on July 26. North Carolina did not ratify until November 21, 1789; and Rhode Island withheld its approval until May 29, 1790. But the rest of the country did not wait for them. As soon as the four big states had given their assent, Congress arranged for its own demise by ordering national elections to be held in January 1789.

The United States was at last to have a government that would embody on a national scale the American principle of responsible representative government. The world had said that republican government was impossible for a country the size of the United States, that only a federation of republics or a powerful monarchy or aristocracy could extend so wide. But here was a new kind of republic, a federation that would be more than a federation, a government that would remain responsible to the people though its territory and population expanded tenfold, a union in which the people would be joined not as citizens of rival states but as a nation of equals.

Suggestions for reading

Two good introductions to the military history of the Revolution are Howard Peckham, *The War for Independence** (1958) and Willard Wallace, *Appeal to Arms** (1951). The standard account of naval operations is G. W. Allen, *Naval History of the American Revolution,* 2 vols. (1913), but for the exploits of John Paul Jones see S. E. Morison, *John Paul Jones: A Sailor's Biography** (1959). T. G. Frothingham, *Washington, Commander in Chief* (1930), assesses the general's military genius, but a more complete, day-by-day account is D. S. Freeman, *George Washington,* 7 vols. (1948–57).

The classic account of the diplomacy of the Revolution is S. F. Bemis, *The Diplomacy of the American Revolution** (1935). Richard B. Morris gives a lively and detailed narrative of the peace negotiations in *The Peacemakers* (1965). On the loyalists, C. H. Van Tyne, *The Loyalists in the American Revolution* (1902), should be supplemented by W. H. Nelson, *The American Tory** (1962), Wallace Brown, *The King's Friends* (1965), and L. W. Labaree, *Conservatism in Early American History** (1948). Clarence Ver Steeg, *Robert Morris* (1954), deals largely with the financing of the Revolution. A more extensive study is E. J. Ferguson, *The Power of the Purse: A History of American Public Finance, 1776–1790* (1961).

Since 1909, when Carl Becker offered his opinion that the Revolution, in New York at least, was a contest about who should rule at home, many historians have addressed themselves to the effect of the Revolution on social conflicts within the participating states. J. F. Jameson, *The American Revolution Considered as a Social Movement** (1926), argued that the Revolution acted as a leveling movement in the direction of greater democracy and accelerated social change. Not all of the studies of individual states in the period from 1776 to 1789 bear out this contention. For example, Richard McCormick, *Experiment in Independence: New Jersey in the Critical Period, 1781–1789* (1950), finds little evidence of class conflict, but E. W. Spaulding, *New York in the Critical Period, 1783–1789* (1932), finds a good deal, as does Staughton Lynd, *Class Conflict, Slavery and the United States Constitution* (1968). Robert Brown, *Middle-Class Democracy and the Revolution in Massachusetts, 1691–1780** (1955), argues that there was little democratizing of Massachusetts during the Revolution, because Massachusetts already had democratic government, with the vast majority of adult males enjoying the right to vote. Chilton Williamson, *American Suffrage from Property to Democracy, 1760–1860* (1960), finds that the majority of males in most colonies had the right to vote but that the majority became larger during the Revolution as a result of reductions in property qualifications. E. S. Morgan, *The Birth of the Republic** (1956), emphasizes the growth of common principles rather than conflicts among Americans of the period 1763–89. J. T. Main, *The Social Structure of Revolutionary America** (1965), contains valuable statistical information about the distribution of property, and his *Upper House in Revolutionary America, 1763–1788* (1967) shows the democratizing effect of the Revolution on this legislative branch.

*Available in a paperback edition.

John Fiske, *The Critical Period of American History, 1783–1789* (1883), painted a black picture of the United States under the Articles of Confederation and told of the nation's rescue by the Constitution of 1787. Merrill Jensen, *The Articles of Confederation** (1940, 2nd ed., 1959), and *The New Nation** (1950), sought to redeem the reputation of the Articles, which he saw as a true embodiment of the principles of the Declaration of Independence. Irving Brant, *James Madison the Nationalist, 1780–1787* (1948), gives a view of the period through the eyes of one of America's most perceptive statesmen. Gordon Wood, *The Creation of the American Republic, 1776–1787* (1969), traces the development of popular influences in government during the period.

Most modern accounts of the Constitutional Convention take their point of departure from Charles Beard, whose *Economic Interpretation of the Constitution of the United States** (1913) exercised a powerful influence. Beard maintained that the authors of the Constitution had invested heavily in public securities and sought to bolster the national government in order to gain protection for the economic interests of their own class. Beard's thesis has been attacked and all but demolished by Robert Brown, *Charles Beard and the Constitution** (1956), and Forrest McDonald, *We the People: The Economic Origins of the Constitution** (1958). In *E Pluribus Unum* (1965), McDonald gives his own view of the economic and political maneuvering that brought about the Philadelphia convention, while J. T. Main, in *The Antifederalists** (1961), examines the forces of opposition. Max Farrand, *The Framing of the Constitution of the United States** (1913), is still a good account of the convention itself, but there is no substitute for the records of the convention and the debates in it, which are published in Max Farrand, ed., *Records of the Federal Convention of 1787,* 4 vols.* (1911–37), and C. C. Tansill, ed., *Documents Illustrative of the Formation of the Union of the United States* (1927). Jacob E. Cooke, ed., *The Federalist* (1961), is the definitive edition of these papers, which are also available in a reliable paperback edition by Clinton Rossiter (1961).

For the reader who wishes to approach this period through the original sources, a wealth of material, besides *The Federalist* and the *Records* of the convention, is readily available in complete modern editions, now in process of publication, of the *Papers* of the period's great men. These editions, besides printing everything that a man wrote, include letters and communications written to him. Among the men whose *Papers* are thus being published are Thomas Jefferson (Julian P. Boyd, ed.), John Adams (Lyman Butterfield, ed.), Benjamin Franklin (L. W. Labaree and W. B. Wilcox, eds.), Alexander Hamilton (H. C. Syrett and J. E. Cooke, eds.), and James Madison (W. T. Hutchinson, W. M. E. Rachal, and R. A. Rutland, eds.).

*Available in a paperback edition.

The establishment of national institutions

6

In adopting the Constitution, Americans gave the United States a permanent and effective government with powers that would enable it to shape the future of the nation. But the men who drafted the Constitution were well aware that they had left many details undecided and that the first officers of the new government would have a greater opportunity than their successors to determine what the United States should be and become.

Launching the new government

Fortunately many of the leaders of the Philadelphia convention were eager to finish the job they had begun. Franklin was too old now to do more than give his blessing, but most of the nation's other great men repaired to New York in 1789 to launch the new government and help shape its institutions. There had never been any question about the candidate for President: Washington's election was unanimous and unopposed. His progress from Mount Vernon to New York was marked by a succession of triumphal arches, cheering spectators, and pretty girls strewing his path with flowers and offering him crowns of laurel. He bore it all with his usual dignity. Though he would rather have stayed at home, he was excited by the opportunity to give stature to the nation he had done so much to create.

The Vice President, John Adams, who had just returned from England, was a more complicated man, vain enough to invite laughter, but so quick, so keen, so talented in every way that no one dared laugh. Benjamin Franklin had once said of him that he was "always an honest man, often a wise one, but sometimes, and in some things, absolutely out of his senses." Adams soon found that the Vice Presidency carried little prestige or power, and an Adams could not be comfortable without a good deal of both. During Washington's Administration the Vice President set the pattern for future holders of the office by keeping himself in the background.

More influential in the first years of the new government was James Madison, the young Virginian who had played so large a role at Philadelphia. Madison's old political opponent, Patrick Henry—a powerful figure in the Virginia legislature—had succeeded in preventing his election to the Senate, but his neighbors had elected him to the House of Representatives. There, in spite of his lack of humor, his small frame and unimposing appearance, he quickly became the dominant figure. In the early months he was also Washington's principal adviser.

Madison, like many Americans who had lived through the Revolution, was passionately interested in the art of government. So were his two friends, Thomas Jefferson and Alexander Hamilton, both of whom Washington also called on for advice and assistance.

Hamilton, the younger of the two, had a brilliant analytical mind and great talents as an administrator. He also had large ambitions, both for the United States and for himself. Thomas Jefferson was as intensely devoted to the new nation as Hamilton but had a greater range of interests and loyalties. Jefferson was interested in government because he was interested in human beings, of whom he thought well. The new government, he believed, was going to be a good thing for them, but he remained less committed to it than to them.

A strong executive. In this galaxy of leaders, Washington was the most limited and at the same time the strongest. His strength came, not only from the fact that he had earned the unbounded confidence of the people, but from his simplicity of mind. As commanding general of the Revolutionary armies, he had devoted himself wholly to winning the war. As President of the United States he devoted himself with equal singleness of purpose, equal detachment, and equal success to making the new government respected at home and abroad.

The biggest part of the job, Washington felt, was to establish respect for his own office. In the first flush of republican revulsion from England, Americans had identified executive power with hereditary, irresponsible monarchy, and they had accordingly neglected or suppressed it in their new governments. Most of the state constitutions, while affirming the need for a separation of powers, had actually made the executive the creature of the legislature; the Articles of Confederation had provided for no real executive. The Constitutional Convention had rectified that error by creating the office of President and assigning extensive powers to it: command of the army and navy, responsibility for foreign negotiations, and authority to appoint other governmental officers. Some of the powers were to be shared with the Senate, but the line of demarcation between the executive and legislative branches was not clear. It was up to him, Washington believed, to establish the extent of executive power and to organize the office so that future Presidents would be able to keep it strong.

Simply by taking office Washington went a long way toward achieving this end, for his own immense prestige could not fail to lend weight to any position he accepted. But he took pains to surround himself with more of the trappings of honor than he allowed himself at Mount Vernon. When he rode abroad it was on a white horse, with a leopard-skin saddle-cloth edged in gold, or in an elegant coach pulled by six cream-colored horses. He rented one of the most sumptuous mansions in New York and stationed powdered lackeys at the door. He held "levees" in the manner of European monarchs, passing among the dignitaries to give each a moment of the presidential presence.

Some of Washington's associates thought this was going too far; others could not get enough of it. After the President's inauguration on April 30, 1789, his admirers in Congress had brought on a heated debate by proposing to address a formal congratulatory message to "His Highness the President of the United States and Protector of their Liberties." John Adams and Richard Henry Lee argued strenuously that some such title was needed to testify to the President's eminence, especially for the edification of the foreigners for whom he would personify the United States. The idea horrified ardent republicans, and James Madison carried the majority with him by proposing that the message be addressed simply to "George Washington, President of the United States."

By eliminating ostentatious titles Madison had no intention of minimizing the executive office. He had written most of the President's inaugural address as well as the congressional

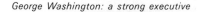

George Washington: a strong executive

reply to it. In the first crucial months of the new government his was the hand that guided President and Congress alike in the legislation that organized the executive office and gave it the strength the President sought.

Though the Constitutional Convention had not directly provided for any executive departments except the Treasury, it clearly envisaged them in stating that the President should have power to call for the opinions of the principal officer in each such department. One of the first acts of the new government was to pass laws establishing the departments of the Treasury, State, and War, which, together with the offices of Attorney General and Postmaster General, were the only executive departments under Washington.

Had Washington and Madison been less insistent on executive independence, these departments might have formed the nucleus of a "cabinet" responsible to the legislative branch, as in the emerging British system. Such a development was prevented when Madison persuaded the House of Representatives, against considerable opposition, that the heads of departments, though appointed by the President with the consent of the Senate, should be subject to removal by the President alone.

Washington's first appointments to the new offices included Jefferson at State and Hamilton at the Treasury. His other choices were less distinguished: Henry Knox as Secretary of War and Edmund Randolph as Attorney General. Washington did not regard his secretaries as a team or cabinet that must act collectively. Rather, he thought of them as assistants, and in the first years they held no regular meetings. The President might refer decisions to them when he was absent from the seat of government, and he expected them to take the initiative in developing plans within their own fields of responsibility. But he kept the reins in his own hands. Executive decisions were his decisions.

Legislative decisions were not. Washington made only very general suggestions for legislation and scrupulously refrained from disclosing his views on specific measures being considered by Congress. He was extremely reluctant to use his veto power and did so only twice during his Presidency. It was his business, he believed, to administer the laws, not to make them. Consequently, while he established the authority and independence of executive action within the range allowed by the Constitution, he took no active part in the formation of public policy by legislation.

In the absence of presidential initiative three men guided Congress: Madison, Hamilton, and Jefferson. For the first five months Madison had the job to himself, for no other member of Congress combined the requisite political talents with the imagination that the new situation demanded. Hamilton acquired a position of leadership by his appointment to the Treasury on September 11, 1789, because in creating that department Congress had provided for a close connection between the Secretary and the legislature. At Madison's insistence, Congress had authorized the Secretary to prepare plans for collecting revenue and sustaining public credit and to present them to the House of Representatives, which under the Constitution had the sole right to initiate money bills. Washington approved Hamilton's active participation in the affairs of the House for, though he refrained from legislative matters himself, he did not think it necessary or desirable that his department heads should do so.

Jefferson did not accept the Secretaryship of State until January 1790 and did not arrive in New York until two months later. His office was less closely connected with legislative affairs than Hamilton's. Moreover, while Hamilton ran the Treasury pretty much by himself, Washington took an active part in the management of foreign affairs and frequently overruled his Secretary of State. Nevertheless, Jefferson's close friendship and alliance with Madison gave him considerable influence in Congress.

The Bill of Rights. In ratifying the Constitution, six states had suggested amendments to specify the popular rights that the government must never invade. Many of the legislators who had been elected to the first Congress under the new Constitution arrived in New York prepared to carry out the suggestions. Although Madison had opposed a bill of rights both before and during ratification, when it became clear to him that the people of the United States were determined to have one he decided to draft it himself.

Madison had initially opposed a bill of rights, for two reasons. First, he thought that declarations of popular rights, while useful against a monarch, would be ineffective against a republican government, in which the people themselves were ultimately the law-givers. Second, he feared that any explicit statement of rights would prove too narrow and might be used to limit freedom instead of limiting authority: a wayward government might construe the specified rights as the only rights of the people. The debates over ratification had introduced another ground for fear: many advocates of amendment, including some members of Congress, wanted to reduce the authority of the federal government in relation to that of the state governments. In order to forestall amendments that might weaken the new government or ones that might undermine American freedom, Madison wanted to frame the bill of rights himself.

From the proposals he first presented to Congress in June 1789 there emerged the first ten amendments to the Constitution, which were ratified by the necessary number of states in December 1791. Known as the Bill of Rights, the amendments protected freedom of religion, of speech, and of the press, and the rights to assemble, to petition the government, to bear arms, to be tried by a jury, and to enjoy other procedural safeguards of the law (see Appendix). They forbade general warrants, excessive bail, cruel or unusual punishments, and the quartering of troops in private houses.

To prevent the government from ever claiming that the people had no rights except those specifically listed, the Ninth Amendment provided that "The enumeration in the Constitution of certain rights shall not be construed to deny or disparage others retained by the people." The Tenth Amendment reassured the state governments about their relationship to the federal government by affirming, "The powers not delegated to the United States by the Constitution, nor prohibited by it to the States, are reserved to the States respectively, or to the people."

Madison fought hard for his amendments, because in preparing them he had convinced himself that a bill of rights might be more effective than he had originally supposed. If a republican legislature proved hard to control, specific prohibitions would at least form a rallying point around which popular resistance could gather. The amendments would also assist the executive and judiciary branches in checking the legislature, for the amendments would be part of the Constitution, which every officer of government must swear to uphold. Even the state governments might be brought into action to resist encroachments, a thought that recurred some years later to Madison and Jefferson alike (see p. 153).

While Madison guided the Bill of Rights through Congress, the Senate passed a judiciary bill establishing the Supreme Court and thirteen inferior district courts. When the bill came to the House of Representatives, some members wanted to eliminate the provision for district courts and leave the everyday enforcement of federal laws to the state courts. But Madison persuaded the majority that the states could not be trusted in the matter. The Judiciary Act of 1789 as finally passed established thirteen district courts and three circuit courts with both concurrent and appellate jurisdiction. It also explicitly provided that the Supreme Court should review decisions of state courts and nullify state laws that violated the United States Constitution or the laws and treaties made under it.

The shaping of domestic policy

By adopting the Bill of Rights and by establishing federal courts to uphold the Constitution, Americans completed the work of the Constitutional Convention and made secure the inheritance that the preceding generation had won for them. The next pressing problem was to recover the nation's economic credit.

National credit and national debt. At the Constitutional Convention it had been understood that the new government would levy taxes to pay not only its own expenses but the debts of the old government. The debts were the debts of the nation, regardless of which government contracted them. On July 4, 1789, Congress established customs duties on all imports and two weeks later placed a tonnage duty on all shipping, with high rates for foreign vessels, low ones for American. When Alexander Hamilton took office at the Treasury, it became his task to apply the income from these duties to the national debt.

Hamilton found that the United States owed $54,124,464.56, including interest. It was widely assumed that the amount would be scaled down, at least the amount owed to creditors who were themselves citizens of the United States. Much of the domestic debt was in the form of certificates that had been either issued as pay to soldiers during the Revolution or bought by patriotic citizens to further the war effort. But by now most of the certificates were held by speculators or merchants who had bought them at much less than face value when the credit of the government fell and hard times forced the owners to sell. The restoration of national credit, it seemed to many Americans, did not require payment at face value to men who had themselves discounted that value. Hamilton thought otherwise. In his Report on Public Credit, presented to Congress on January 14, 1790, he proposed to fund—that is, to pay—the entire national debt, both foreign and domestic, at its face value. Existing certificates of indebtedness would be redeemed by interest-bearing government bonds worth the original value plus the unpaid interest, calculated at 4 percent.

The very boldness of the proposal won acclaim, and there was no real opposition to the full payment of the nation's obligations. The only question—and a large one—was who should be paid. On this question Madison and Hamilton came to a parting of the ways.

Hamilton insisted that payments be made to whoever held the certificates. Many of his associates had known that his report would contain such a recommendation and had begun buying up certificates wherever they could be found. Madison, shocked by the scramble, rose in the House of Representatives to offer an alternative to Hamilton's scheme. Madison proposed to pay the face value of the certificates only to original holders who still possessed them. To subsequent purchasers he would have paid the highest market value that the certificates had formerly commanded (fifty cents on the dollar). He would have paid the difference between this amount and the face value to the soldiers and citizens who had supported the Revolution and who had then been obliged to part with their certificates at less than face value because of the government's inability to maintain its credit.

Madison's plan would not have reduced the amount paid by the government. It would simply have prevented speculators from making large profits at the expense of the government's original creditors. Unhappily for Madison, and not by accident, the speculators

included many members of Congress, who did not hesitate to wrap their own shady transactions in the national honor. Men who had agents combing the country for certificates stood on the floors of Congress and denounced Madison's proposal as an attempt to make the government evade its just obligations. Madison, hitherto the master of Congress, now saw his motion defeated in the House of Representatives by a vote of thirteen to thirty-six.

Madison's proposal was defeated not by greed alone. If accepted, it would have jeopardized the basic purpose of funding the debt: to restore national credit. The credit of the government had to be sustained without regard to the motives or merits of its creditors, because when the government had need for more money than it could obtain by current taxation (and every government has such a need in national emergencies), it would have to rely on bankers and speculators, men with money to lend. Their confidence had to be purchased in advance.

Before bringing Hamilton's funding scheme to a vote, Congress took up an even more controversial matter, which Hamilton had also recommended in his report—the assumption by the national government of debts owed by the state governments. Such a move was not necessary to sustain national credit, and many supporters of the funding measure failed to see the point of it. Gouverneur Morris, a staunch conservative, was in London when he heard of the scheme and wrote back in puzzlement: "To assume the payment of what the States owe, merely because they owe it, seems to my capacity not more rational, than to assume the debts of corporations, or of individuals." Senator Robert Morris of Pennsylvania, to whom the letter was written, had other views. "By God," he said, "it must be done."

The crucial difference between Gouverneur Morris and Robert Morris was that one was in England and the other in America. Robert, like other speculators in America, had an opportunity to take advantage of assumption before it became a fact. During the Revolutionary War the states, like the national government, had borrowed money by issuing securities. Many of these state securities had since depreciated even more than national ones. Speculators, including congressmen, now rushed to buy them. And with the prospect of making fortunes they lined up behind the assumption of state debts as they did behind the funding of the national debt.

But there was more opposition to assumption than to funding because Hamilton's proposition contained no allowance for states that had already paid a large proportion of their debt. These states included Virginia, Maryland, North Carolina, and Georgia. The largest debts were owed by Massachusetts and South Carolina. As a result, Virginians, for instance, having been taxed by the state government to pay its debt, would be taxed again by the federal government to help pay the debts of Massachusetts and South Carolina.

The inequity of the scheme enabled Madison to muster a small majority against it on a test vote in the House. But he did not dare to push his advantage, because the speculative interests threatened to vote against funding unless they got assumption as well. Much as he disliked Hamilton's funding plan, Madison knew that the rejection of funding altogether would mean the total destruction of national credit and possibly of the national government itself.

In July 1790, after Hamilton and his friends agreed to a partial allowance for states that had already paid a large part of their debts, Madison and his friends agreed to a bill providing for both funding and assumption. The fact that the two sides had been able to reach a compromise was heartening, but the line of division was ominous: Hamilton spoke for the merchants and creditors of the North, who would benefit enormously from funding and assumption, because they had accumulated most of the government's certificates of indebtedness; Madison and Jefferson spoke for the planters and farmers of the South, whose taxes would flow steadily north to pay the debt. The same division was evident in a simultaneous dispute about the location of the national capital, settled by a 13–12 vote in the Senate for a site on the Potomac River. The differing interests of North and South, which Madison had already perceived in 1787, were beginning to affect national politics.

The Hamiltonian program.

Hamilton's victory, for it amounted to that, was not simply a successful swindle. The speculative frenzy set off by his measures was a calculated part of one of the boldest programs ever envisaged for the development of the nation and the nation's economy. Hamilton believed that the future of the United States depended on a large-scale expansion of industry and commerce. The suspension of imports from England during the war had forced the growth of manufacturing in America; and the production of hardware and textiles had continued in some measure afterward. To effect the kind of growth that Hamilton wanted the primary need was capital, capital in large quantities concentrated in the hands of men willing to risk investing it. By means of funding and assumption Hamilton created just such a group of wealthy investors, or, to use a less attractive word, profiteers. Hamilton was no profiteer himself—he was too interested in power to give much attention to his own finances. But he was well satisfied with the huge speculative profits that others reaped from his measures, for those profits meant capital for business investment. Moreover, funding and assumption, by restoring national credit, would make investment in American enterprises more attractive to foreign capital.

Hamilton's measures were prompted not merely by economic considerations but by his consistent determination to strengthen the national government and to overcome the centrifugal force of the state governments. He anticipated that all the capitalists created by funding and assumption would be eager to maintain the national credit and the national government, if only to protect their investments. By the same token, the assumption of state debts would deprive the state governments of such support. The national government, working hand in glove with powerful investors, would grow strong as industry and commerce grew.

Hamilton's scheme generated its own support. The opportunity to get rich easily and by methods not strictly illegal was more than congressmen could resist. Washington was disturbed by the rumor that "The funding of the debt has furnished effectual means of corrupting such a portion of the Legislature as turns the balance between the honest voters whichever way it is directed." Hamilton, who was doing the directing, assured the President that "there is not a member of the Legislature who can properly be called a stock-jobber or a paper-dealer. . . . As to improper speculations on measures depending before Congress, I believe never was any body of men freer from them." Washington believed him.

Hamilton's next objective was a national

Alexander Hamilton: architect of the national economy

It is now proper ... to enumerate the principal circumstances from which it may be inferred that manufacturing establishments not only occasion a positive augmentation of the produce and revenue of the society, but that they contribute essentially to rendering them greater than they could possibly be without such establishments. These circumstances are:

1. *The division of labor.*
2. *An extension of the use of machinery.*
3. *Additional employment to classes of the community not ordinarily engaged in the business.*
4. *The promoting of emigration from foreign countries.*
5. *The furnishing greater scope for the diversity of talents and dispositions, which discriminate men from each other.*
6. *The affording a more ample and various field for enterprise.*
7. *The creating, in some instances, a new, and securing, in all, a more certain and steady demand for the surplus produce of the soil.*

Each of these circumstances has a considerable influence upon the total mass of industrious effort in a community; together, they add to it a degree of energy and effect which are not easily conceived.

From Alexander Hamilton, Report on Manufactures, 1791.

bank with capital supplied partly by the government and partly by private investors. But since the investors would be permitted to pay in government bonds for three-fourths of the bank stock they purchased, the bank's notes would rest very largely on the national debt. With the government furnishing most of the capital and assuming most of the risk, the bank could offer an irresistible invitation to wealthy men to invest their money. Furthermore, the national debt, if utilized for a bank, could be a national advantage. In arguing for funding and assumption, Hamilton had emphasized the fact that where a national debt "is properly funded, and an object of established confidence, it answers most of the purposes of money." He intended to make it serve this purpose through the bank: notes issued by the bank would serve as a much needed medium of exchange (specie being scarce) and would greatly facilitate business and the financing of new commercial and industrial enterprise. Besides acting as a central exchange, the bank would handle government finances; and it would expedite borrowing both by the government and by individuals. Through this government-sponsored expansion of credit, the bond between private capital and the national government would be tightened.

When the bill to charter the bank came before the House early in February 1791,

Madison attacked it with arguments he would not have used two years earlier. Before the adoption of the Constitution, he had argued strenuously that Congress should assume all the powers it needed to do its job. Under the new government he had hitherto taken a generous view of the extent of congressional authority. By now, however, he was thoroughly worried over the emerging shape of Hamilton's program and intent on stopping it. He argued that because the Constitution did not specifically empower Congress to issue charters of incorporation it had no right to do so. Hamilton answered that the Constitution empowered the government to do anything "necessary and proper" to carry out its assigned functions.

This was the first great debate over strict, as opposed to loose, interpretation of the Constitution. Congress readily accepted Hamilton's loose construction and passed the bill. Washington weighed the question more seriously, listening carefully to Madison and Jefferson as well as to Hamilton. Though he remained doubtful to the end, at the last minute, on February 25, 1791, he signed the bill. Hamilton's program moved ahead another step.

Having provided capital and credit Hamilton was now ready to direct the expansion of manufacturing. In December he presented to Congress his Report on Manufactures, a

Those who labour in the earth are the chosen people of God, if ever he had a chosen people, whose breasts he has made His peculiar deposit for substantial and genuine virtue. It is the focus in which he keeps alive that sacred fire, which otherwise might escape from the face of the earth. Corruption of morals in the mass of cultivators is a phenomenon of which no age nor nation has furnished an example. It is the mark set on those, who not looking up to heaven, to their own soil and industry, as does the husbandman, for their subsistance, depend for it on the casualties and caprice of customers. Dependance begets subservience and venality, suffocates the germ of virtue, and prepares fit tools for the designs of ambition. This, the natural progress and consequence of the arts, has sometimes perhaps been retarded by accidental circumstances; but, generally speaking, the proportion which the aggregate of the other classes of citizens bears in any State to that of its husbandmen, is the proportion of its unsound to its healthy parts.... While we have land to labour then, let us never wish to see our citizens occupied at a workbench, or twirling a distaff ... for the general operations of manufacture, let our workshops remain in Europe.

From Thomas Jefferson, *Notes on the State of Virginia,* 1787.

Jefferson's view of the good society

scheme to make investment in industry attractive by means of protective tariffs and bounties. It was Hamilton's aim to direct the nation toward a balanced economy that would include manufacturing as well as agriculture and commerce. Only through such a balance could the United States make the most of its resources, reduce its foreign debt and its reliance on foreign nations, and attain true independence. But Hamilton was not allowed to add this capstone to his economic edifice. Farmers and merchants, fearing that protective tariffs would prompt retaliatory action by other countries against American agricultural exports, preferred free competition to keep down the price of manufactures. And almost everyone wondered whether the United States could afford a measure that would discourage importation, since the government's principal income came from import duties. To raise them to protective levels might reduce the volume of imports so drastically as to endanger the national credit. Moved by these considerations, Congress dealt Hamilton his first defeat by shelving his report.

Madison and Jefferson, who engineered the defeat, were both alarmed by the apparent intent of Hamilton's program. No one had done more than Madison to resuscitate and strengthen the central government a few years earlier at the Constitutional Convention, but in the Hamiltonian system he saw the beginnings of a national government so strong that it would endanger the individual liberties he had been trying to protect in the Bill of Rights. Jefferson, even more than Madison, was wary of governmental power.

To this distrust of government, Jefferson joined a dislike of cities and of the merchants and manufacturers who thrived in them. Farmers, he believed, enjoyed a greater virtue and a closer contact with their Maker than did the inhabitants of cities. From Paris he had written to Madison in 1787, "I think our governments will remain virtuous for many centuries; as long as they are chiefly agricultural. . . . When they get piled upon one another in large cities, as in Europe, they shall become corrupt as in Europe." Jefferson and Madison were both convinced that the federal government would have all the strength it needed and would be less likely to exceed its authority if it depended not on an alliance with powerful creditors but on the support of the producing classes, especially the farmers, who formed the bulk of the population. Opponents of the Constitution had feared that a strong central government would be manipulated to bring power and wealth to a few. Hamilton seemed bent on justifying their fears, which he and Madison had earlier joined to combat in *The Federalist.* Moreover, Hamilton's program was driving a wedge between the North, where capital and credit were accumulating, and the South, whose farmers and planters feared that the accumulation was at their expense. Almost all the stock in Hamilton's United States Bank was purchased by Northern and European creditors; and Hamilton made it plain that the bank was intended to assist the expansion of commerce and industry, not agriculture, which in his view needed no encouragement. He dismissed out of hand a proposal that the bank lend money to Southern planters on the security of tobacco warehouse receipts.

Thus within three years of the inauguration of the national government its leaders had reached a fundamental disagreement over its scope and policy. The disagreement was perhaps less dangerous than it seemed at the time, because both sides were still determined to make the new government work and because slavery, the issue in which Southerners most feared interference, had gone unchallenged. In 1793 when they introduced a bill in Congress requiring all courts, state and federal, to assist slave owners in recovering fugitive slaves, Northern congressmen readily supplied the votes to pass it, in spite of the fact that its terms were so vague as to imperil the rights of every free black.

Nevertheless, the gap between the views of Hamilton on the one hand and of Jefferson and Madison on the other was about as wide as constitutional government could stand. Each side thought the other was betraying the republican ideals of the Revolution. Each now aimed more at defeating and suppressing the other than at bargaining. Fortunately Washington stood above the quarrel, and both sides could still join in persuading him to accept another term when the national elections were held in 1792. But during his second term the dissension spread from domestic to foreign affairs, increasingly open, increasingly bitter, and accompanied by a public rhetoric that grew increasingly violent.

Foreign affairs under Washington

The Constitution assigned to the President the conduct of relations with Europeans and Indians, and Washington undertook the task himself. While he gave Hamilton a free hand in developing financial policy and refused to meddle in congressional enactments of that policy, he gave Jefferson no such freedom as Secretary of State. He turned to Jefferson for advice, but he sought advice from other department heads as well. As foreign affairs assumed greater and greater complexity, he began the practice of calling together the Attorney General and the Secretaries of State, War, and the Treasury to discuss policy. During these meetings, from which grew the Cabinet as an institution, Jefferson and Hamilton again revealed their differing conceptions of the national welfare.

Jeffersonian neutrality. The discord in foreign affairs first showed itself in 1790, when a threatened war between Spain and England offered the United States an opportunity to press American claims against both countries. Spain had seized three British vessels trading in Nootka Sound, Vancouver Island, which had been Spanish territory ever since its discovery. England demanded the return of the ships, reparation for damages, and recognition of British trading rights in the area. It seemed likely that Spain would fight rather than submit.

Washington's advisers all agreed that the United States should remain neutral in case of war, but they did not agree on what the United States should do if England decided to march troops through American territory in the Mississippi Valley in order to attack the Spaniards in Florida and Louisiana. Since Hamilton had just tied his funding program to duties on British trade, he was reluctant to do anything that might offend England and was ready to declare American neutrality at once. Jefferson, on the other hand, had just come from five years as the United States Ambassador to France, where he had seized every opportunity to bargain for national advantages. He wanted to bargain now, to keep both Spain and England guessing about America's intentions and to make them bid high for her neutrality.

As it happened, Spain gave in to the British ultimatum, and no war occurred. But another European war was clearly in the making, and mounting tensions in Europe generated a notable increase in the cordiality of European countries toward the United States. In 1791 England sent a minister plenipotentiary, George Hammond, to reside in Philadelphia; the United States in turn sent Thomas Pinckney to London. Full diplomatic relations had thus been established between England and the United States when war finally did break out in 1793 between England and France— and something close to war between Hamilton and Jefferson.

Thomas Jefferson, as American minister to France during the 1780s, had learned to admire French civilization and French people. Just before returning to the United States late in 1789, he had witnessed the beginnings of their revolution. At first he was skeptical that a people who had lived so long under absolute monarchy could successfully undertake republican government. But as the Revolution progressed, he became increasingly enthusiastic. When he took up his post as Washington's Secretary of State, he brought with him a warm sympathy for the French and their cause, a sympathy that was not destroyed by the execution of Louis XVI in 1793 or by the reign of terror that followed.

Hamilton, by contrast, watched with horror as the French Revolution overturned the foundations of society, destroying monarchy and aristocracy, exalting democracy and demagogues. His horror mounted when the French Revolutionists launched the "war of all peoples against all kings," with England and Spain as primary targets. England, even under King George III, seemed to Hamilton a safer friend for Americans than mob-wracked republican France. Hamilton was moved not simply by his repugnance for the French Revolution but by the belief that, if the United States had to choose sides, England was more to be feared than France, because England had the stronger navy. American commerce was more vulnerable to English sailors than to French soldiers.

Hamilton agreed with Washington's other advisers that the United States should stay out of the war, but he wanted to use the crisis as an opportunity to scrap the French alliance. The treaties of 1778, he argued, had been made with the French monarchy and were no longer binding now that the monarchy had been overthrown. The United States should therefore declare its neutrality and refuse to receive the minister, Edmond Genêt, sent by the new French republic early in 1793.

Jefferson argued that the treaties had been made with the French nation and were still binding. He was as certain as Hamilton that the United States should stay out of the war but wanted the country to do so without pub-

licly announcing its intention. A declaration of neutrality would affront the French and would destroy the possibility of bargaining with the British, who still had troops stationed in the American Northwest and still withheld trading privileges in the empire. Washington decided the matter on April 22, 1793, by issuing a proclamation of neutrality addressed to American citizens only and not actually mentioning the word "neutrality." The treaties with France were not repudiated, and Citizen Genêt was accorded formal recognition. But the bargaining power that Jefferson valued was gone. Shortly afterward he announced that he would retire at the end of the year.

Genêt was a fool. From the moment of his arrival he assumed powers that no independent country could permit a foreign envoy: he commissioned American ships to sail as privateers under the French flag; he set up courts to condemn the ships they captured; he arranged an expedition of Western frontiersmen to attack Spanish New Orleans. Jefferson tried hard to like him but gave up in disgust. Finally Washington demanded Genêt's recall.

While Genêt was losing friends for France, the British government was losing them for England. Under the slogan "free ships make free goods," Americans claimed the right as neutrals to carry noncontraband goods (including naval stores) to and from the ports of belligerents. France had lifted some of her mercantilist restrictions regulating trade with her West Indian islands, and American ships were swarming there to take advantage of the new opportunity. But England adhered to her rule of 1756 that trade closed in peacetime could not be opened to neutrals in wartime. In December 1793, without warning, her naval vessels began seizing American ships trading with the French West Indies.

The seizures combined with an Indian episode in the Northwest to bring the United States, in spite of Hamilton, to the brink of war with England. The record of Washington's government in dealing with hostile Indians had not been good. He had arranged a treaty with Alexander McGillivray, the half-breed chieftain of the Creeks, but the Creeks had broken it as soon as it was made. He had sent General Josiah Harmar to crush the Miamis in Ohio, but they had crushed him. He had sent Arthur St. Clair with a much larger force in 1791, but St. Clair, like Braddock in 1755, had been surprised just short of his objective

The Treaty of Greenville, 1795

and completely routed. In February 1794, as General Anthony Wayne gathered a force to try again, the governor-general of Canada, Lord Dorchester, made a speech to the Indians in which he in effect exhorted them to do their worst. Reports of the speech reached Congress along with news of the Caribbean seizures.

The House of Representatives was then debating whether restrictions against British commerce (suggested by Jefferson shortly before his resignation) might lead England to reduce her own restrictions against American commerce. News of the seizures precipitated an overwhelming demand for much stronger anti-British measures, to which Hamilton felt sure England would react by declaring war on the United States—if indeed the United States did not declare war first. The country was swept by war hysteria; volunteer defense companies sprang up. Mobs mistreated English seamen and tarred and feathered pro-British Americans. To prevent a plunge into actual warfare, Hamilton urged Washington to send a special mission to England. Hamilton seems to have thought of heading it himself, but Washington gave the job to Hamilton's alter ego, John Jay.

John Jay: Hamilton's alter ego

A Hamiltonian treaty. Although Jay had had abundant experience as a diplomat, in the eyes of most Americans it had been unsuccessful experience. As envoy to Spain during the Revolution, he had failed to gain either alliance or recognition of American independence. As Secretary for Foreign Affairs under the Articles of Confederation, he had

conducted the nearly disastrous negotiations with Gardoqui. In both cases failure arose less from lack of skill on his part than from the fact that the other side held all the cards. This time, with England engaged in a major European war, Jay was in a strong position to play the game that Jefferson had recommended all along: namely, to convince England that unless she made concessions she could not count on continued American neutrality. Edmund Randolph, the new Secretary of State, agreed with the Jeffersonian strategy. He instructed Jay to consult with Russia, Sweden, and Denmark about the possibility of an armed-neutrality agreement in order to bring pressure on England to stop seizures of neutral shipping.

Once again, however, Jay found himself on the losing side through no fault of his own. Denmark and Sweden, which shared the American view of the rights of neutral ships, took the initiative, and just after Jay's departure for Europe the United States received an invitation from them to join in forming an alliance of neutrals. Randolph wanted to accept, for he felt that such backing would strengthen Jay's hand. But Hamilton persuaded Washington to decline, on the grounds that the alliance would jeopardize Jay's mission by antagonizing the British. Not content with rejecting the assistance of other neutrals, and eager to create a friendly climate of opinion in England, Hamilton weakened Jay's position still further by informing George Hammond, the British minister in America, of Washington's decision.

With this information to guide him, Lord Grenville, the British foreign minister, felt safe in conceding little. He promised again to surrender the Northwest posts—provided the United States permitted the continuation of the English fur trade with the Indians in the area; he promised recompense for the American ships that had been seized without warning in December 1793 in the Caribbean—provided the United States compensated British creditors for prerevolutionary debts whose collection had been impeded by state governments. He refused to compensate American slave owners for slaves kidnaped or liberated by the British during the Revolution, and he refused to give any guarantee against the British navy's practice of stopping American vessels to impress alleged British subjects as seamen. Instead of stopping the seizure of neutral ships he required the United States to give up her own view of neutral shipping rights for the duration of England's war with France and for two years thereafter. He consented to reciprocal trading rights between England and America but restricted American trade with the British West Indies to vessels of no more than seventy tons, and even these he allowed only in return for an American promise to ship no molasses, sugar, coffee, cocoa, or cotton from the islands or from the United States to any other part of the world. The only generosity he showed was at the expense of the Spanish: it was agreed that both British subjects and Americans should have the right to navigate the Mississippi through Spanish territory to the sea.

When the treaty containing these terms reached Washington on March 7, 1795, Hamilton was no longer at the Treasury. He had resigned at the end of January, a little more than a year after Jefferson, but he retained as much influence over the President out of office as in. His replacement, Oliver Wolcott, Jr., had been his assistant and continued to consult him on every important matter. Hamilton thought that the treaty was satisfactory and that failure to ratify it would mean war. Washington reluctantly agreed, but he could see that other Americans might not. To avoid a premature hardening of opposition, he tried to keep the terms secret until he could present the treaty for ratification at a special session of the Senate called for June 8. It was impossible. By the time the Senate met, rumors of the contents had produced wide public hostility, which increased as the details became known. Nevertheless, the senators, after striking out the clause regarding trade with the West Indies, accepted the treaty by the exact two-thirds majority required.

As the treaty came before Washington for his signature, the press was denouncing Jay, the treaty, the Senate, and even the President. Popular meetings in Boston, Philadelphia, New York, and other cities urged Washington to reject it. In the Cabinet everyone but Randolph urged him to sign. Dismayed by the public antagonism, Washington hesitated. In the meantime, the British minister handed to Oliver Wolcott some intercepted dispatches written by the French minister, Jean Fauchet. In them Fauchet, referring to some transactions with Randolph, seemed to imply that Randolph had turned over state secrets to him for money. Although the dispatches had nothing to do with the treaty, they discredited the

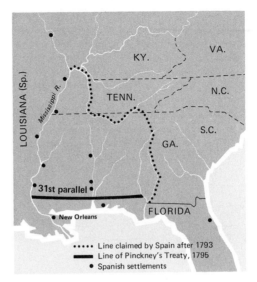

Pinckney's Treaty, 1795

only Cabinet member who opposed it. Washington signed the treaty, and, after confronting Randolph with the dispatches, refused his explanations and accepted his resignation.

The winning of the West. Jay's Treaty was the low-water mark of foreign affairs under Washington. General Wayne had defeated the Indians of the Northwest at the Battle of Fallen Timbers (August 20, 1794) and had gone on to devastate their settlements. At the Treaty of Greenville (August 3, 1795) they gave up most of the territory that was to become the state of Ohio. In the next year the British at last honored their agreement to evacuate their posts in the Northwest.

Meanwhile, Spain had become fearful that the United States would throw her small weight on the British side in the precarious European balance. The clause about the Mississippi in Jay's Treaty suggested that England and the United States might be contemplating joint action against Louisiana. Taking advantage of this fear, the American envoy, Thomas Pinckney, who was sent to negotiate a treaty, won for the United States everything she had been seeking from Spain: free navigation of the Mississippi, permission for American traders to deposit goods for shipment at the mouth of the river, acknowledgment of the American southern boundary at the thirty-first parallel and the western boundary at the Mississippi, and an agreement by each country to prevent Indians

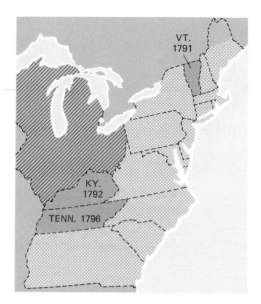

New states, 1791–96

within its territory from making incursions into the territory of the other.

The Senate accepted Pinckney's Treaty unanimously on March 3, 1796. With it the danger of secession in Kentucky and Tennessee (admitted to the Union in 1792 and 1796) disappeared; with the Mississippi open to trade, any attachment to Spain lost its charm for the Americans of the Southwest. Although Washington's foreign policy had produced some vastly unpopular concessions to Britain, it must be credited with the restoration of reciprocal trading rights and with achieving at last recognition by both Spain and Britain of United States sovereignty over the area first won from Britain in 1783.

Federalists versus Republicans

Alexander Hamilton, by dictating domestic policy to Congress and foreign policy to the President, gave the national government its initial direction. Although Madison and Jefferson managed to modify some of his measures, in all essentials Hamilton prevailed. But in their efforts to defeat him, Madison and Jefferson set a pattern of political action that in ten years' time gave them control of the government and thereafter became the only way of gaining or keeping control. They started a political party.

The Republican challenge. The framers of the Constitution, Madison included, had not thought well of parties. "Faction" was the word generally used for party in the eighteenth century, and a faction meant, by Madison's own definition, a group of men organized to procure selfish advantages at the expense of the community. Denunciation of factions or parties was a standard ingredient in every discussion of politics in the eighteenth century, as safe and as platitudinous as denunciation of corruption and praise of honesty.

The parties of the time deserved denunciation. In the British House of Commons, and to some degree in the colonial assemblies, politicians had joined forces from time to time in order to make legal raids on the public purse. Because neither Madison nor Jefferson had any such end in view, they did not at first think of their opposition to Hamilton as con-

stituting a party. Madison, to be sure, had a following in the House of Representatives and was an old hand at collecting votes in support of his measures. But in lining up opposition to indiscriminate funding and wholesale assumption, neither Jefferson nor Madison anticipated a continuing, organized opposition.

It was only as the full dimensions of Hamilton's program revealed themselves that the two men deliberately set out to gather and consolidate their strength against him inside the government and out. Jefferson was aware that Washington consulted Hamilton on every kind of measure, including matters that seemed to belong properly in the Department of State; in response, he tried to extend his own influence within the executive departments. Washington liked Jefferson, as did most of the other members of the presidential entourage. And yet Jefferson made little headway in his campaign. Though he succeeded in having the Mint established under the State Department instead of the Treasury, his attempts to get the Post Office transferred to the State Department failed, and so did his efforts to get his friend Tench Coxe appointed as Comptroller and Thomas Paine as Postmaster General.

Madison was more successful. In the House of Representatives he was often defeated, but every defeat strengthened the loyalty of his followers. Though he lacked Jefferson's personal charm and was not eloquent in debate, he knew how to work in the corridors; and on the floor his colleague from Virginia, William Branch Giles, was an able spokesman of his views. John Beckley, the perennial Clerk of the House, who seemed to know everybody's secrets, turned over valuable information to him. As the Madison forces hardened, they began to call themselves the "republican interest," and by 1792 they even dared to say the "republican party"—a phrase that gradually acquired capital letters.

Their opponents, not considering themselves a party, appropriated the name of Federalists, which had been used earlier by the advocates of the Constitution of 1787. This maneuver identified the Republicans with the anti-Federalists of that period. Actually there was no connection. The leaders of the Republican party had supported the Constitution in 1787 and still did; the Federalists of the early 1790s were distinguished, not by any special reverence for that document, but by a conception of the national welfare that included a permanent national debt, a national bank, and dependence on England.

Madison and Jefferson believed that the source of Federalist strength, apart from Washington's support of Hamilton, was typical of faction or party in the traditional sense: it lay in the corruption of congressmen through the speculative opportunities that accompanied funding and assumption. Their own strength, they believed, lay with the people at large. Perhaps because they assumed that the people were on their side, they did not at first organize their party except within the government itself; they did, however, take steps to let the people know, through the press, what their side was.

Before 1791 the *Gazette of the United States* was the only newspaper that gave full coverage to national politics, and its editor, John Fenno, was an ardent Hamiltonian. Madison and Jefferson persuaded the poet Philip Freneau, whom they knew to be Republican in sentiment, to establish a newspaper that would report national issues from their point of view. On October 31, 1791, the first issue of the *National Gazette* was published, and the Republicans gained a medium for spreading attacks on the Hamiltonian program (some of them written by Madison) throughout the country.

At the same time spontaneous popular societies that might have furnished the basis for Republican party organization at the local level

Whiskey Rebellion: no rebel fired a shot

began to form. Admiration for the French Revolution and discontent with the government's evident bias in favor of England prompted the formation of these "Democratic Clubs," first in Pennsylvania and then all over the country. The clubs, which were imitations of the Jacobin societies in France, felt that they were continuing the tradition of the Sons of Liberty of the 1760s and 1770s. They sympathized with the French Revolution and passed resolutions against the government's pro-British foreign policy; they supported the Republicans in Congress and in elections for Congress. But before Madison and his friends could capitalize on their support, the Federalists found an opportunity to discredit the clubs and capture a wide popular following for themselves.

The Federalist response. The Federalist opportunity arose from a tax on whiskey passed by Congress in 1791 to help pay the expenses of funding and assumption. Excise taxes, especially on alcoholic beverages, were unpopular in the eighteenth century. A cider tax nearly caused rebellion in England in 1763, and so did a rum tax in Massachusetts in 1754. By 1794 the federal excise tax on liquor did cause rebellion, or what looked like it, in Pennsylvania. Farmers in the western part of the state generally turned their surplus grain into whiskey. This could be transported over the mountains more easily than wheat or corn, and it brought a better price in the Eastern markets. But the profit was small even without

Washington: President and General

the excise, and hence there was much evasion of the tax. In July 1794 the United States marshal, summoning offenders to court, met with mass resistance.

The governor of the state, Thomas Mifflin, thought that the courts could handle the situation. But Washington, urged on by Hamilton, decided that the challenge to national authority called for military action, and in October the President marched fifteen thousand militiamen to western Pennsylvania. No rebel fired a shot against him, and Washington returned to Philadelphia, leaving Hamilton to complete the arrest of the ringleaders.

When Congress assembled shortly after his return, Washington delivered an address that made clear his contempt for all organized opposition to the policies of the national government, whether from whiskey rebels, Democratic Clubs, or Republicans. Although there is no evidence that the clubs had anything to do with the rebellion, Washington had somehow got the notion that they had. In spite of the fact that the Constitution guaranteed the right to assemble, he rebuked the clubs as "self-created societies." Dismayed by his disapproval, many of them dissolved at once, and the rest expired within a year or two.

Washington's personal popularity was thus revealed as the strongest weapon in the Federalist arsenal. The Republicans were not fully aware of how strong it was or of how it could be used against them. Nor was Washington

aware. He continued to regard himself as standing above party and seems never to have realized that as he came more and more to rely on Hamilton he was choosing sides in a party conflict. Hamilton did realize it and used Washington's prestige to turn popular opinion against the Republicans.

When the President signed Jay's Treaty, in spite of popular meetings that urged him not to, the Republicans, instead of conceding defeat, carried the battle to the House of Representatives. Although the Constitution gave only the Senate the authority to approve or reject treaties, the House, under Madison's leadership, asserted its right to examine treaties before appropriating funds to implement them. On this basis, the House demanded copies of the papers that had passed to and from Jay during the negotiations. Washington, defending the integrity of the executive department, indignantly refused; Hamilton, by decrying the demand of the House as an insult to the President and a step toward war, soon had Congress flooded with petitions supporting the President. Republican efforts to secure counterpetitions were less successful, and Madison saw his majority dwindle to a minority. The House in the end supported the treaty.

The election of 1796. When the Republicans attacked the treaty in the House of Representatives, they had an eye on the presidential election that was to take place later in the year. In the elections of 1788 and 1792 there had been no serious contest for the Presidency. In 1796 it was probable, though not certain, that Washington would retire. If he did, the Republicans would have a chance to challenge Hamilton at the polls. But the Republican hope of unseating the Federalists received a strong setback when Madison's attack on the treaty foundered against Washington's popularity.

As the election approached, Washington gave the Federalists another advantage by delaying his decision to withdraw. The Republicans were wary of advancing any candidate of their own unless the still insuperable national hero was out of the race. It was understood that if Washington chose not to run, Adams would be the Federalist candidate; for Hamilton, though influential among politicians, did not have a wide enough popular following to assure election. For the same reason the Republicans had settled on Jefferson rather than Madison. In September Washington finally announced his retirement and delivered a farewell address written by Hamilton. The address contained a strong warning against partiality for foreign countries (meaning France) and against political parties (meaning Republicans). Washington still refused to think of the Federalists as a party.

Having secured Washington's support for a Federalist successor, Hamilton set about substituting a more pliable candidate for the prickly, independent Adams. Because of Adams' popular following, Hamilton could not renounce him publicly, but he hoped to achieve his purpose by manipulating the electoral vote.

The maneuver was made possible by the peculiar constitutional provisions for electing the President. Each state could select its members for the Electoral College in any manner it saw fit. Six did it by popular vote, nine by vote of the state legislature, and one, Massachusetts, by a combination of the two. Most candidates for the college announced beforehand for whom they would vote; but this practice was not universal, and the college as an institution retained some small measure of choice. Each elector cast two ballots, without specifying which man he preferred for President; the candidate who received the largest vote became President, and the candidate with the second largest vote became Vice President. Since this was a system designed for a partyless government, complica-

tions arose when political parties appeared. If all the electors who favored the strongest party voted for both its candidates, a tie vote would result. In order to elect the party's preferred presidential candidate some electors had to divert their second vote from the party's vice-presidential candidate to some other candidate. This could be dangerous: if too many votes were diverted from the party's vice-presidential candidate he might be left with fewer than the presidential candidate of the opposing party, who would then become Vice President instead. There was also the possibility that if both parties wanted the same man for Vice President, he might receive more votes than either presidential candidate and thus become President.

It was this latter possibility that led Hamilton to arrange for Adams' running mate on the Federalist ticket to be Thomas Pinckney of South Carolina. Pinckney, who had just returned in triumph from his Spanish mission, enjoyed great popularity in the South, where the Republicans were strongest. Southerners would certainly give most of their votes to Jefferson, but they might be persuaded to designate Pinckney as second choice. If a substantial number of electors did so, the combined Federalist-Republican vote might be large enough to put Pinckney into the Presidency.

But Hamilton was not the only one who knew the deficiencies of the electoral system. When the votes of the Electoral College were cast, it appeared that his advocacy of Pinckney had failed. Adams' friends in Connecticut and New Hampshire, refusing to endanger his success, had all scattered their second votes, and the Southern Republicans had actually given Pinckney nothing. Even so, he had fifty-nine votes; but Adams with seventy-one became President and Jefferson with sixty-eight became Vice President. Jefferson's running mate, Aaron Burr of New York, had only thirty.

Had the Federalist electors of Connecticut and New Hampshire given Pinckney their second votes, Hamilton's strategy could have succeeded. Pinckney would have tied Adams' vote, and tied presidential elections, according to the Constitution, were to be decided in the House of Representatives. There, with Jefferson out of the contest, Southern Republicans might have joined with Hamilton's forces to make Pinckney President. For Adams it was a bitter thing to have come so close to losing and to know that Hamilton was to blame.

The Presidency of John Adams

The new President was a man of conflicting emotions, ideas, and loyalties. Round of face and frame, he looked like an English country squire and often behaved like one, lashing out at those who crossed him as though he were lord of the manor. Yet he was sometimes remarkably patient when there was real cause for anger. Like Washington and Jefferson and George III, he loved the land and found high office uncongenial and inconvenient. Yet no man wanted the Presidency more or would have found defeat more humiliating.

Adams had had a distinguished career during the Revolution, both in the Continental Congress and in negotiating the peace treaty. His political experience and his study of history had given him strong ideas about the proper form of government: liberty, he believed, could be preserved only where a strong executive presided over a legislature divided into two houses, the upper representing the wealthy and well-born, the lower representing the people at large. This idea, expounded at length in his *Defence of the Constitutions of the United States* (1787), had influenced the Philadelphia convention and had helped produce the strong executive office that Adams inherited from Washington. As President, Adams continued to think that the executive must stand above the other branches of government and mitigate differences between them.

The President and the politicians. Adams, like his contemporaries, spoke of political parties only to condemn them. Though he had been elected in a contest between parties, the circumstances were not such as to endear either side to him. The Republicans had branded him a monarchist because of his openly avowed advocacy of a strong executive, while the Federalists had almost betrayed him for Thomas Pinckney.

In his inaugural address Adams did his best to minimize party differences. Answering for the first time the accusations that had been made against him during the campaign, he assured the Republicans that he did not want a monarchical or aristocratic or indeed any but a republican government. Lest anyone think him an enemy of the French alliance, so dear to Jefferson, he affirmed his personal esteem for the French nation, "formed in a residence of seven years, chiefly among them"; and his

"sincere desire to preserve the friendship which has been so much for the honor and interest of both nations."

The Republicans were delighted. Newspaper editors who had been warning of the approach of tyranny suddenly discovered the President's "incorruptible integrity," his intelligence, his patriotism. Jefferson had always liked Adams. The two had become estranged in 1791 when one of Jefferson's friends published a private letter from him criticizing Adams' political writings. Before the inauguration they made it up and took rooms in the same Philadelphia boardinghouse. In assuming office as Vice President, Jefferson hailed the man "whose talents and integrity have been known and revered by me through a long course of years."

The political backers of both men were suspicious of the new harmony and uneasy about the effect it might have on the party organizations they had been building. Before coming to Philadelphia, Jefferson had drafted an open and generous letter to Adams, declaring his pleasure in the outcome of the election. He had always served as a junior to Adams and would be glad to continue doing so. He sent the letter to Madison to deliver at his discretion. Madison thought it best not to: if made public, it might alienate Jefferson's supporters and embarrass him in a future contest. Jefferson himself avoided getting too close to the Administration: the separation of powers, he decided, should prevent his sitting in the President's Cabinet.

Federalist leaders, equally cautious, were worried about Adams' charity toward the Republicans and blocked him when he proposed appointing Madison as special envoy to France. Adams, who had already told Jefferson of his intention, with some embarrassment withdrew the nomination when Oliver Wolcott, Jr., the Secretary of the Treasury, threatened to resign in protest. Thereafter relations between the President and the Vice President cooled off, for Adams' behavior seemed to indicate that in spite of his good beginning he would not stand very far above party.

It might, in the end, have been better for Adams if he had used his famous temper on Wolcott. Since there was as yet no tradition requiring Cabinet officers to submit their resignations when a new President took office,

Adams inherited the Cabinet that Washington left behind. And a sorry lot they were. Besides Wolcott at the Treasury, there was James McHenry in the War Department and Timothy Pickering at State. Hamilton, in suggesting McHenry's appointment to Washington, had said that "he would give no strength to the administration, but he would not disgrace the office." Three years later, Hamilton had to admit that "my friend McHenry is wholly insufficient for his place." Timothy Pickering had originally served as Postmaster, a position that strained his talents to their limits. When Randolph resigned, Washington gave Pickering the State Department temporarily but was unable to persuade a more competent man to take the job.

Apart from their palpable mediocrity, the only thing that Wolcott, McHenry, and Pickering had in common was that they all took orders from Hamilton. Adams was too keen a man not to perceive the quality of their minds, but he did not realize that the advice they gave him came by mail from New York. Even had he known, he might have hesitated to drop them. They had been appointed by the great Washington, and it would have been brash for a President who had barely won the office to cashier the advisers whom the national hero had thought adequate. Even if Adams had let them go, he might have had difficulty replacing them. Cabinet officers received a salary of only $3,000 a year, and a man of talent who could earn much more in private business might be reluctant or unable to make the financial sacrifice, especially since there was as yet little prestige in any appointive office. Washington had kept second-rate men simply because he could not get first-rate ones.

Surrounded by incompetent advisers who remained loyal to a politician who had betrayed him, Adams could have preserved the strength of the executive department only by showing a resolute determination to make his own decisions. Instead, he spent much of his time at home in Quincy, Massachusetts, leaving the members of his Cabinet to deliberate by themselves. Consequently his Administration drifted into policies with which he did not fully agree and from which he finally extricated it only at the expense of his political career.

The end of the French alliance. In the opening months of his Administration Adams' cordiality for France, as for Jefferson, cooled rapidly. During Washington's Presidency the French government had become increasingly angered by the apparent partiality of its American ally for England. Although the commercial treaty of 1778 stated that the United States would give no nation greater trading privileges than it gave to France, Congress had never given France anything more than equality with other nations—and that only on paper. In operation, the laws that Congress passed consistently favored England. Jay's Treaty had outraged France, and the French minister to America, Pierre Adet, had warned that his country would henceforth treat American ships "in the same manner as they suffer the English to treat them." Actually the French had already intercepted several American vessels bound for England and had impounded them in French harbors. Now France announced that she would no longer recognize the treaty principle that free ships made free goods and that she would treat American sailors serving on British ships as pirates. She went even further: she refused to have anything to do with the American minister, Charles Cotesworth Pinckney (brother of Thomas).

President Adams proposed to meet the crisis diplomatically by sending a three-man mission to France, the mission for which he had considered Madison. The members of his Cabinet were at first opposed not only to Madison but to any mission. Only after Hamilton cautioned them not to get too far ahead of public opinion did they fall in with Adams' plan. The commissioners appointed were the Virginia Federalist lawyer, John Marshall; the rejected minister to France, C. C. Pinckney; and an astute but unpredictable Massachusetts politician, Elbridge Gerry. To announce the mission the President called a special session of Congress in May and delivered a message that the Cabinet, speaking for Hamilton, had thought the only proper accompaniment to negotiations. It called for strengthening coastal defenses, arming merchant vessels, completing three frigates begun in 1794, and establishing a provisional army.

The message put an end to Republican sympathy for the President. Jefferson, the former advocate of bargaining from strength, now thought that the recommendations would be offensive to France and would make the mission's task impossible. As it turned out, neither American nor French belligerence but

John Adams:
a man of
conflicting emotions

French corruption prevented the mission's success. The French minister of foreign affairs, Talleyrand, after keeping the envoys waiting for several weeks, informed them through three unaccredited go-betweens, known only as X, Y, and Z, that the price of negotiating would be $250,000 for himself. The price of a treaty would be several million dollars for France. "Not a sixpence," said Pinckney, as he and Marshall departed, leaving Gerry to continue the futile conversations until he was ordered home.

When Adams reported the XYZ Affair, incredulous Republicans in Congress demanded to see the commission's papers. Adams did not follow Washington's example in the case of the Jay's Treaty papers, probably because he knew that the record would fully sustain him. He turned the papers over, and Congress supported the President in retaliating against France by actions just short of war. The treaties of 1778 were repudiated. Commercial intercourse was suspended. American ships were authorized to seize French armed vessels, and for the next two years French and American ships fought an undeclared war on the seas.

It would have been foolhardy to go to such lengths without preparing for full-scale war. But the President and his advisers could not agree on the kind of preparation to make. The most ardent Federalists saw in the crisis an opportunity to strengthen themselves as well as the government at the expense of the Republicans. They wanted a large standing army, not merely to repel a French invasion but to overawe and if necessary to suppress their political opponents. Hamilton also dreamed of leading an army of conquest into Florida and Louisiana. Adams, while denouncing the French and their American friends, had a more realistic and more comprehensive view of the national interest. He thought it wise to keep a small army in readiness, but he discounted the possibility of a French invasion, and he had no ambition to rule by military force or to conquer territories peopled by Frenchmen and Spaniards. What the country really needed, he believed, was a navy to defend its commercial interests in the shifting tides of European conflict. To concentrate on an army would leave the United States no choice but to side always with the country whose navy dominated the seas, in other words, with England. Though Adams' own sympathies lay with England, he thought

Elbridge Gerry: astute but unpredictable

it was bad policy to let the safety of American commerce depend on the good will of any foreign country. Accordingly, in May 1798 he persuaded Congress to establish a Department of the Navy, with Benjamin Stoddert, a Maryland merchant, as Secretary. In Stoddert, Adams gained his first loyal adviser in the Cabinet.

While Adams and Stoddert proceeded with the construction and commissioning of warships, the High Federalists, as the more extreme branch of the party came to be called, continued their buildup of the army, dragging the reluctant President with them, and levying heavy taxes to pay for it. Washington was persuaded to accept command again, and Hamilton was eager to join him. Adams agreed to make Hamilton a general but refused at first to rank him above Henry Knox, Daniel Morgan, and Benjamin Lincoln, Hamilton's seniors in the Revolutionary army. Hamilton, perhaps with more than military ends in view, declined to play second fiddle to anyone but Washington and made his refusal a test of strength. When Washington, still willing to play Hamilton's game, joined with the Cabinet in demanding that Hamilton be his second in command, Adams was forced to back down.

After this victory, the High Federalists pressed hard for a declaration of war against France. The harder they pressed, the more apparent it became that their aims were domestic rather than foreign. England's depredations against American shipping had continued unabated, while France, according to reports from Elbridge Gerry, had become far more conciliatory in response to the violent American reaction to the XYZ Affair. Gerry was denounced by the Federalists upon his return in 1798, but he was courted by the Republicans and heeded by the President. George Logan, an ex-Quaker from Philadelphia who had conducted an unauthorized peace mission of his own, confirmed Gerry's view of the shift in France's attitude. Adams objected to private citizens meddling in the country's foreign relations and got the Logan Act passed to prevent it in the future, but he was impressed by what Logan told him. Similar reports were arriving from the President's son, John Quincy Adams, also in Europe, and from Rufus King, the American minister in London, and from William Vans Murray at The Hague. In January the President received from Murray a letter sent by Talleyrand to the French chargé at The Hague, specifically stating that an American envoy to France would "undoubtedly be received with the respect due to the representative of a free, independent and powerful nation."

Adams did not assume that Talleyrand's character had improved, but he suspected that American firmness had worked a change in French policy. To declare war now would be to lose all the advantages of neutrality, to sacrifice the national interest to party politics. To make a gesture toward peace, on the other hand, would still leave the United States a free hand and would reduce party tensions at home. Such a reduction would not please the High Federalists, who had visions of a Republican rebellion that the new army commanded by old heroes would crush. That way, Adams believed, lay disaster for the Union, and he decided for once to be President. In February 1799, without consulting his Cabinet further, he sent to the Senate the nomination of William Vans Murray as minister to negotiate a new agreement with France.

Having done so, Adams went off to Quincy, leaving the High Federalists furious and frustrated and the Republicans delighted. With party tensions eased, Adams was not in any hurry to get his mission under way. He was by no means sure that it would succeed, and he wanted to have his new naval vessels ready in case it should fail. By October, three squadrons were fit for duty, and Adams gave orders for Murray's departure. Murray was accompanied now by Oliver Ellsworth (Chief Justice of the United States) and William R. Davie (former governor of North Carolina). When the three-man commission arrived in France, they found Bonaparte in control. He was eager to line up a coalition of neutral nations against England and ready to renew Franco-American relations on terms advantageous to the United States. France was willing to declare the old treaties of 1778 void, thus formally freeing the United States of its only permanent alliance. France was also willing to accept again the principle of free-ships–free-goods and, on September 30, 1800, the negotiators signed a convention that put an end to French spoliation of American commerce. The President's declaration of independence from his Cabinet had thus saved his country from a needless war and gained it greater freedom on the seas.

The Alien and Sedition laws. In sending the mission to France, John Adams had risen above party, as he believed a President should. But he never fully admitted, even to himself, how much he had been and still remained a member of the Federalist party. After his initial *rapprochement* with Jefferson had faded, his very devotion to the national interest and to the dignity of his office betrayed him, as it had Washington, into regarding himself and his supporters as impartial patriots and the Republican opposition as a criminal conspiracy.

After the disclosure of the XYZ Affair, Adams had been deluged by addresses from groups of patriotic citizens declaring their readiness to fight the French. In his public replies he commended his correspondents and deplored the "few degraded or . . . deluded characters" who viewed the crisis differently. "These lovers of themselves," he announced, "who withdraw their confidence from their own Legislative Government, and place it on a foreign nation, or Domestic Faction, or both in alliance, deserve all our contempt and abhorrence." The references to Republicans were oblique but unmistakable. Even Hamilton thought the President might be pushing anti-Republican sentiment a little too far. But other Federalist leaders (without specific encouragement from either Adams or Hamilton) persuaded Congress to pass legislation designed to harass, if not destroy, the Republican opposition.

The Alien Acts, three in number, were passed in June and July 1798. One, the Alien Enemies Act, was a nonpartisan measure that simply provided for the restraint of enemy aliens in time of war. Since war was never declared against France, the act did not operate during Adams' Presidency. The other two were partisan measures aimed against immigrants, who were widely suspected of being Republican in politics. The Naturalization Act required that an alien seeking citizenship must have resided for fourteen years in the United States, five of them in the state where naturalization was sought. The Alien Friends Act, which was to run for two years only, gave the President power to deport any alien whom he considered dangerous to the welfare of the country.

The Sedition Act, which was passed in July 1798, was one of the most repressive measures ever directed against political activity in the United States. It provided fines and imprisonment for persons unlawfully combining or conspiring "with intent to oppose any

Lyon and Griswold: "congressional pugilists"

measure or measures of the government of the United States," or counseling or advising such opposition, or writing, printing, uttering, or publishing "any false, scandalous, and malicious writing or writings against the government of the United States, or the President of the United States, with intent to defame . . . or to bring them or either of them, into contempt or disrepute." The blatant political purpose of the act was admitted in the date it was to expire: March 3, 1801, when the next President would be inaugurated. The act would last long enough to gag Republican criticism of the Administration until the next election was safely over; it would expire soon enough to permit Federalist criticism in case the election brought in a Republican administration.

The first victim of the Sedition Act was Matthew Lyon, Republican representative from Vermont. On the floor of the House, Lyon and the Connecticut Federalist Roger Griswold had already engaged each other with canes, fire tongs, and spit. In the autumn following the passage of the Sedition Act, Lyon, who was up for reelection, directed his campaign against the Federalist party's conduct of the government. Although his attacks were returned measure for measure by his opponent, Lyon was indicted, convicted, and sentenced (by a Federalist judge) to four months in jail

and a $1,000 fine. He was reelected while serving his jail sentence.

The Republicans were alarmed—and rightly so. The Alien and Sedition Acts demonstrated that the Federalists were prepared to abandon the principles of the Enlightenment, of the Revolution, and of the Constitution. When Madison sponsored the first amendments to the Constitution, he had recognized that they might one day have to be defended against an ambitious executive or legislature. He had suggested that the federal courts might protect them, but thus far the courts had shown a disposition to restrain the states more than the national government. They had declared a few state laws unconstitutional, and in the case of *Chisholm* v. *Georgia* (1793) the Supreme Court had awarded judgment against the state of Georgia in a suit brought by citizens of South Carolina. This affront to state sovereignty caused so many protests that an eleventh amendment to the Constitution was adopted to deny federal jurisdiction in suits brought against a state by foreigners or by citizens of another state.

The Eleventh Amendment, which was ratified in January 1798, was a direct blow at the federal courts, whose prestige was already at a low ebb. Men of high talents refused to serve on them. John Jay had resigned as

Chief Justice of the United States in 1795 in order to run for the governorship of New York. The judges who remained and who presided at sedition trials had no more scruples about the constitutionality of the Alien and Sedition Acts than John Adams had had when he signed them.

Since there seemed to be no other way of protecting the Constitution from the Federalists, Madison and Jefferson turned to the state governments. With the election of Adams, Madison had retired temporarily from Congress and returned to Virginia. In the Virginia legislature, he now secured passage (December 24, 1798) of a series of resolutions affirming the authority of the states to judge the constitutionality of federal legislation and declaring the Alien and Sedition Acts unconstitutional.

Madison's resolutions did not go beyond the statement of unconstitutionality. But Vice President Jefferson had framed another set, for the state of Kentucky (November 16, 1798), which declared the acts to be "void and of no force." When the other states declined to support Virginia and Kentucky, Kentucky reaffirmed in another set of resolutions (November 22, 1799) that "nullification" by the states was the proper remedy for unconstitutional actions by the federal government. But the other states still refused to follow suit and allowed the Alien and Sedition Acts to expire under their own terms. Though the resolutions of Kentucky and Virginia failed in their immediate object, they posed a question that would trouble the nation for many years to come. The Philadelphia convention had not decided which was sovereign, state governments or national government, and the resolutions were a reminder that the question was still open.

The election of 1800. The steadily declining fortunes of the Republicans convinced them that in order to survive they would have to build a national organization. As a result of the XYZ Affair they had lost congressional seats in the elections of 1798; even Virginia, the Republican stronghold, had returned five "certain Federalists" and three moderates who leaned toward Federalism. With Jefferson directing party strategy, the Republicans resolved to do better in the next election. Following regional patterns of local government, they appointed county committees in the South and township committees in the

ELECTORAL VOTE

Jefferson (Dem.-Rep.) 73
Burr (Dem.-Rep.) 73
Adams (Fed.) 65
Pinckney (Fed.) 64*

*One R.I. elector cast one of his ballots for Jay.

Tie resolved by House of Representatives. Jefferson elected.

VT. 4 — N.H. 6
MASS. 16
N.Y. 12
R.I. 4
CONN. 9
PENNA. 8 — 7
N.J. 7
DEL. 3
VA. 21
MD. 5 votes to each party
KY. 4
N.C. 8 — 4
TENN. 3
S.C. 8
GA. 4

Note: For all election maps in this book, the electoral vote will be given within each state. When a state's electoral vote is split, as were the votes of Pennsylvania, Maryland, and North Carolina in this election, the split will be shown with the number of electoral votes going to each candidate. The graphic presentation in such cases is not intended to indicate the geographic distribution of votes within the state.

The election of 1800

North to instruct the voters about the vices of Federalists and the virtues of Republicans. The local committees were supervised by state committees, which in turn took their direction from a caucus of Republican congressmen in Philadelphia. By now there were Republican newspapers scattered throughout the country, the most prominent of which was Philadelphia's *Aurora.* The editors, defying the Sedition Act, charged the government with aristocratic and monarchical pretensions and with levying heavy taxes to support an expensive navy, a standing army, and a corrupt funding system.

The charges struck home, for they were substantially correct. Armies and navies are always expensive, and in 1798 the Adams Administration had levied an extremely unpopular direct tax on houses, lands, and slaves to pay the rising costs. What was worse, in 1799 the army had been ordered into action to enforce collection of the tax, after a mob led by one John Fries released two tax-evaders from prison in Northampton County, Pennsylvania. Although the army, as in the case of the Whiskey Rebellion, could find no one to fight, the use of it lent support to Republican accusations of tyranny.

Federalist newspapers replied by calling Republicans the tools of the godless French. Federalist attorneys and judges made full use

Federalist rhetoric, 1800

The fate of Frenchmen will be the fate of Americans. The French boasted that they were the most civilized and humane people in the world. We can say no more of ourselves. Their Jacobins were wicked, cruel, profligate, atheistical—ours are the same. Their pretence ever was, to consult the good of the people—ours make the same. The people in that country have been robbed, enslaved, and butchered—we shall be served in the same manner, unless we arouse instantly, and rescue our government from the fangs of those who are tearing it in pieces. The struggle will be great, but, if successful on our part, it will also be glorious. Look at your houses, your parents, your wives, and your children. Are you prepared to see your dwellings in flames, hoary hairs bathed in blood, female chastity violated, or children writhing on the pike and the halberd? If not, prepare for the task of protecting your Government. Look at every leading Jacobin as at a ravening wolf, preparing to enter your peaceful fold, and glut his deadly appetite on the vitals of your country. Already do their hearts leap at the prospect. Having long brooded over these scenes of death and despair, they now wake as from a Trance, and in imagination seizing the dagger and the musket, prepare for the work of slaughter. GREAT GOD OF COMPASSION AND JUSTICE, SHEILD MY COUNTRY FROM DESTRUCTION.

From *The Connecticut Courant*, September 29, 1800. Signed "Burleigh."

Republican rhetoric, 1800

It is not so well known, as it should be, that this federal gem [John Adams], this apostle of the parsons of Connecticut, is not only a repulsive pedant, a gross hypocrite, and an unprincipled oppressor, but that he is, in private life, one of the most egregious fools upon the continent. When some future Clarendon shall illustrate and dignify the annals of the present age, he will assuredly express his surprise at the abrupt and absurd elevation of this despicable attorney. He will enquire by what species of madness, America submitted to accept, as her president, a person without abilities, and without virtues; a being alike incapable of attracting either tenderness, or esteem. The historian will search for those occult causes that induced her to exalt an individual, who has neither that innocence of sensibility, which incites us to love, nor that omnipotence of intellect which commands us to admire. He will ask why the United States degraded themselves to the choice of a wretch, whose soul came blasted from the hand of nature; of a wretch, that has neither the science of a magistrate, the politeness of a courtier, nor the courage of a man.

From James T. Callender, *The Prospect before Us*, 1800.

---

of the Sedition Act to silence Republican editors, but the wheels of the law did not turn rapidly enough to make more than a few martyrs. The Federalists also caucused at Philadelphia and tried to organize support at the local level. But their efforts were hampered by their own divisions. The rank and file of the party approved John Adams' peace mission to France and would have been outraged by a proposal to support any other candidate for the Presidency. The High Federalists, however, considered Adams a traitor. Pickering thought that the mission to France would "subvert the present administration and with them the government itself." Hamilton declared he would never again support Adams and even wrote a pamphlet attacking him.

In spite of the defection in his own camp, Adams made a strong bid for reelection. By the spring of 1800 it had become probable that he would take New England and New Jersey, that Jefferson (the natural Republican candidate) would win most of the South, and that a deadlock would neutralize Pennsylvania. New York and South Carolina, both uncertain, held the balance. In New York the legislature chose the presidential electors, and the state was so divided that the thirteen representatives from New York City held the balance of power in the legislature. In 1800 Aaron Burr, perhaps the Republican's best working politician on the local level, was able to offer the city a slate of thirteen extremely influential and popular candidates for representative. They took the city by five hundred votes, thus assuring Republican control of the state legislature and of New York's electoral votes in the coming national contest.

New York City had hitherto been the private preserve of Alexander Hamilton, and the significance of his defeat was not lost on John Adams. The President knew that he had been right about the peace mission, regardless of party considerations; but he knew now that he was also right politically and that the High Federalists were wrong. After putting up with their insolence for three years, he had had enough. On May 6 he asked for and received McHenry's resignation from the War Department. On May 10 he asked for Pickering's; when Pickering refused, Adams simply discharged him.

While Adams was cutting loose from the High Federalists, the Republicans had decided that Aaron Burr would again make the best running mate for Jefferson. The Federalists' vice-presidential candidate was Charles Cotesworth Pinckney. Hamilton, who had been responsible for the choice, used the same strategy as in 1796: to throw support to a vice-presidential candidate in the hope that he would overtake both presidential candidates.

The outcome of the election was in doubt for some time, for electors were still chosen at different times and in different ways; but when the ballots were finally counted, Adams had sixty-five electoral votes, and Pinckney sixty-four. The Republican machine, working a little too well, had given Jefferson and Burr each seventy-three. It had been understood that Burr was the vice-presidential candidate, but no Republican elector had diverted one of his two ballots to preclude a tie. To prevent this situation from recurring, the Twelfth Amendment to the Constitution, adopted in 1804, required the Electoral College to vote separately for President and for Vice President. But in February 1801, as directed by the Constitution, the choice between Jefferson and Burr was thrown into the House of Representatives, with each state allowed only one vote. Voting went on for a week through thirty-five ballots without the necessary nine-state majority being reached. Finally Hamilton, who considered Jefferson a lesser evil than Burr, persuaded some of the latter's supporters to cast blank ballots. Jefferson was declared elected.

Since Republican candidates for Congress were also victorious, the election of 1800 brought to an end Federalist control of the national government. Nevertheless, the Federalists could look forward to a continuing influence: the United States judiciary, manned by Federalist appointees, enjoyed a lifetime tenure. The last acts of the Adams Administration made the most of this fact. A new judiciary act of February 27, 1801, created sixteen circuit courts; and Adams, instead of leaving the appointment of the new circuit judges to his successor, filled the offices with loyal Federalists. Even more significantly Adams in January 1801 appointed as Chief Justice of the United States John Marshall of Virginia, an ardent Federalist. Under Marshall the Court was to rise to new heights of prestige and power, to the considerable annoyance of Marshall's fellow Virginian in the White House.

Jefferson liked to think of his election as the "Revolution of 1800." But the election had been no landslide. John Adams had only eight votes fewer than the winners. If he had taken either New York or South Carolina, he would have won; and he might have taken them had he parted sooner from the High Federalists. Actually John Adams' capture of the Federalist party marked as great a political change as Jefferson's triumph at the polls, a change possibly more crucial to the preservation of national unity. Hamiltonian policies, tied to urban business interests at home and to Great Britain abroad, had repeatedly threatened to divide the nation. By sending the mission to France and by repudiating Hamilton, Adams reduced the gap between Federalist and Republican views of the national interest. His action came too late to win an electoral majority for himself or his party, but it did ensure peace, not only between the United States and France, but between two groups of Americans who had drifted dangerously far apart.

Aaron Burr: working politician

Suggestions for reading

The period covered by this chapter is surveyed by J. C. Miller, *The Federalist Era** (1960). L. D. White, *The Federalists** (1948), assesses the achievements of the Washington and Adams Administrations in establishing the bureaucratic machinery of national government. The political foundations of Federalist power are analyzed in Manning Dauer, *The Adams Federalists** (1953). In *The Economic Origins of Jeffersonian Democracy** (1915), Charles Beard saw the rise of the Republican party as a continuation of the small-farmer hostility to the Constitution, which he had described in his *Economic Interpretation of the Constitution of the United States** (1913). Joseph Charles, *The Origins of the American Party System** (1956), denies that there was any such continuity.

A. F. Young, *The Democratic Republicans of New York: The Origins, 1763–1797* (1967), finds some elements of continuity in that state. But Paul Goodman finds none in *The Democratic-Republicans of Massachusetts* (1964). In *The Partisan Spirit* (1972), Patricia Watlington discloses a complex relationship between state and national politics in Kentucky. Noble Cunningham, *The Jeffersonian Republicans* (1957), describes the political organizing activities of the Republicans and is particularly good on the election of 1800. A good general account of the first parties is W. N. Chambers, *Political Parties in a New Nation** (1963). Richard Hofstadter, *The Idea of a Party System** (1969), stresses the absence of such a system in the 1790s.

Two aspects of political discontent during the 1790s are treated in E. P. Link, *Democratic-Republican Societies, 1790–1800* (1942), and L. D. Baldwin, *The Whiskey Rebels** (1939). R. A. Rutland, *The Birth of the Bill of Rights, 1776–1791* (1955), discusses the origins of the first ten amendments. Irving Brant, *The Bill of Rights** (1965), is more comprehensive and deals with the later interpretations of the amendments. L. W. Levy, *Legacy of Suppression** (1960), shows that the First Amendment offered less firm protection for freedom of speech and the press than has generally been supposed. J. M. Smith, *Freedom's Fetters** (1956), is the most complete account of the Alien and Sedition Acts. J. M. Banner, *To the Hartford Convention* (1970), emphasizes the Federalists' adherence to republican principles of government.

S. F. Bemis, *Jay's Treaty** (1923, rev. ed., 1962) and *Pinckney's Treaty** (1926, rev. ed., 1960), definitively treats two important episodes in foreign relations in the Federalist decade. Felix Gilbert, *To the Farewell Address** (1961), discusses the origins of attitudes classically expressed in Washington's warning against alliances. Alexander De Conde, *Entangling Alliance* (1958) and *The Quasi-War** (1966); L. M. Sears, *George Washington and the French Revolution* (1960); Charles Hazen, *Contemporary American Opinion of the French Revolution* (1897, reprinted 1964); and L. S. Kaplan, *Jefferson and France* (1967), discuss relations with France. In *Number 7* (1964), Julian Boyd gives evidence of Hamilton's efforts in the Nootka Sound crisis to turn American policy in favor of the British.

So many men of large stature shared in the making of public policy during the 1790s that much of the history of the period has been written in the form of biography. D. S. Freeman, *George Washington,* 7 vols. (1948–57), is the most complete account; Vol. VII was written after Freeman's death by J. A. Carroll and M. W. Ashworth. J. C. Miller, *Alexander Hamilton: Portrait in Paradox** (1959), is the best biography of Hamilton. Hamilton's great reports are conveniently gathered in J. E. Cooke, ed., *The Reports of Alexander Hamilton** (1964). Irving Brant, *James Madison: Father of the Constitution, 1787–1800* (1950), the third volume of a six-volume study of Madison, contains a wealth of information about the formation of the Republican party. Gilbert Chinard, *Honest John Adams** (1933), is good, but C. P. Smith, *John Adams* (1962), is more definitive. J. R. Howe, *The Changing Political Thought of John Adams** (1966), is a sensitive interpretation. Stephen Kurtz, *The Presidency of John Adams** (1957), is very good on the election of 1796; Zoltan Haraszti, *John Adams and the Prophets of Progress** (1952), is a charming account of Adams' notes in the margins of his books. Dumas Malone, *Jefferson and His Time,* 3 vols. (1948, 1951, 1962), covers Jefferson's career up to his election as President. A stimulating interpretation of Jefferson's thought is D. J. Boorstin, *The Lost World of Thomas Jefferson** (1948). Merrill Peterson, *Thomas Jefferson and the New Nation* (1970), is an excellent one-volume biography.

*Available in a paperback edition.

7 *Jeffersonian Republicanism*

The peaceful inauguration of Thomas Jefferson as President, on March 4, 1801, was an event of uncommon significance, for it marked the first occasion under the new Constitution when executive power passed quietly from one political party to another. Only a short time before, Federalist partisans had attacked "mad Tom" Jefferson as a "Jacobin" and an atheist, and many of them had believed the Republican party to be a treasonable organization against whose activities the Sedition Act was a justifiable defense. The Jeffersonians, in turn, had denounced the Federalists as a "faction" with "aristocratical tendencies," ready even to conspire "with the enemies of their country."

Moreover, as we have seen, few Republican or Federalist leaders had accepted the idea of political parties as legitimate organizations essential to a republican electoral process. In the view of most, parties were evil and corrupt; they promoted selfish interests, appealed to the passions of men, and prevented public leaders from deliberating together in search of the common good. Republicans had suspected that Federalists planned to subvert the Constitution and establish a monarchy. An organization with such designs could never be legitimate; and Jefferson, neither before nor after his election, ever really acknowledged Federalist legitimacy. He had viewed his own party as a temporary expedient aimed at uniting the people against a threat to republican institutions. Meanwhile, Federalists had accused the Republican "faction" of seeking

to usurp functions that belonged to the government itself.

Yet, in spite of deep anxieties, Federalists acquiesced in their loss of control of both Congress and the executive department. Actually, the election gave them little choice, unless they were prepared to set it aside and rule by military force; and for this, fortunately, they had no taste. Since the Federalists still controlled the New England states, which formed a powerful base for future political activity, and since they believed that the Republicans were incompetent, they could comfort themselves with hopes of an early return to power. Besides, Jefferson may have reassured certain Federalist leaders privately on various matters that concerned them—especially that no Jacobin reign of terror would follow the "Revolution of 1800." Hamilton found solace in his rather unflattering view of Jefferson as a man inclined "to temporize; to calculate what will be likely to promote his own reputation and advantage." This trait, he thought, would cause Jefferson to accept financial policies, "which being once established, could not be overturned without danger to the person who did it." Hence the heated rhetoric of the campaign had no violent aftermath; and the two-party system, whatever theoretical objections men may have had, won a more secure footing and a kind of practical legitimacy that it had never enjoyed before.

After a decade of protest against Federalist policies, Jefferson was now obliged to spell

Thomas Jefferson on the American political experiment

I know, indeed, that some honest men fear that a Republican govern-ment can not be strong, that this Government is not strong enough; but would the honest patriot, in the full tide of successful experiment, abandon a government which has so far kept us free and firm on the theoretic and visionary fear that this Government, the world's best hope, may by possibility want energy to preserve itself? I trust not. I believe this, on the contrary, the strongest Government on earth. I believe it the only one where every man, at the call of the law, would fly to the standard of the law, and would meet invasions of the public order as his own personal concern. Sometimes it is said that man can not be trusted with the government of himself. Can he, then, be trusted with the government of others? Or have we found angels in the forms of kings to govern him? Let history answer this question.

From Thomas Jefferson, First Inaugural Address, 1801.

---

out policies of his own. This, in broad outline, he accomplished in a brilliant inaugural ad-dress (the first to be delivered in the new capital on the banks of the Potomac) that affirmed his liberal democratic philosophy and his faith in the wisdom of the people. Once again he soothed the Federalists by inviting them to join Republicans ''in common efforts for the common good.'' He cautioned Repub-licans that though the will of the majority must prevail, ''the minority possess their equal rights, which equal law must protect.'' He reminded members of both parties that in spite of the acrimonious campaign just past

every difference of opinion is not a differ-ence of principle. We have called by different names brethren of the same principle. We are all Republicans, we are all Federalists. If there be any among us who would wish to dissolve this Union or to change its Republican form, let them stand undisturbed as monuments of the

safety with which error of opinion may be tolerated where reason is left free to combat it.

These conciliatory words reveal Jefferson's basic strategy in dealing with the Federalists. Though still opposed to parties and convinced that good citizens would spurn them, his method was not harsh repression but gentle absorption. He would destroy the party system by winning the support of all reasonable Fed-eralists (''the honest part''), leaving the re-mainder of irreconcilables not a party but a small and harmless faction. ''Nothing shall be spared on my part,'' he wrote privately, ''to obliterate the traces of party and consolidate the nation, if it can be done without the aban-donment of principle.'' It is ironic that a party leader as skilled as Jefferson should never have understood how indispensable and inev-itable the party system was, or have esteemed the role he played so well.

Economy and simplicity

Thomas Jefferson: ''We are all Republicans, we are all Federalists''

The new regime. The rustic simplicity and democratic manners that Jefferson thought proper for the leaders of an agrarian republic seemed appropriate in a crude, half-built capi-tal city that lacked the social and cultural opportunities of Philadelphia. Though the President was a cultivated gentleman to the manner born, his plain informality was natural and uncontrived. Unlike his predecessors, he sent his annual messages to Congress to be read by a clerk, lest reading them in person should suggest that he was imitating the Brit-ish monarch delivering his speech from the

throne. Jefferson abandoned the elegant weekly presidential levees that had previously been such a delight to the capital's aristoc-racy. At his infrequent state dinners and re-ceptions and in his dealings with the diplo-matic corps he avoided anything that smacked of the pomp and pretentiousness of European courts. In the White House he lived simply and made himself accessible to countrymen who claimed to have business with him.

Although Jefferson believed in the sover-eignty of the people and tended to romanticize the independent farmer, he did not assume

I agree with you that there is a natural aristocracy among men. The grounds of this are virtue and talents.... There is also an artificial aristocracy founded on wealth and birth, without either virtue or talents; for with these it would belong to the first class. The natural aristocracy I consider as the most precious gift of nature for the instruction, the trusts, and government of society. And indeed it would have been inconsistent in creation to have formed man for the social state, and not to have provided virtue and wisdom enough to manage the concerns of the society. May we not even say that that form of government is the best which provides the most effectually for a pure selection of these natural aristoi into the offices of government? The artificial aristocracy is a mischievous ingredient in government, and provision should be made to prevent its ascendancy....

I think the best remedy is ... to leave to the citizens the free election and separation of the aristoi from the pseudo-aristoi, of the wheat from the chaff. In general they will elect the real good and wise. In some instances, wealth may corrupt, and birth blind them; but not in sufficient degree to endanger the society.

Thomas Jefferson on aristocracy

From Thomas Jefferson, Letter to John Adams, October 28, 1813.

---

that untrained men could handle the responsibilities of important administrative posts. He rejected the theory of government by a political élite, and yet the men in the key posts of his Administration were educated, talented, and experienced upper-class Republicans of as high a caliber as their Federalist predecessors. James Madison, Jefferson's close friend and political collaborator, a Virginia aristocrat who had led the political fight against the Federalists, joined the new Administration as Secretary of State. Albert Gallatin of Pennsylvania, a gifted and devoted Jeffersonian, accepted the crucial office of Secretary of the Treasury and served with such distinction that he won the respect of even the Federalists.

In spite of his doubts about the wisdom of political parties, Jefferson, far more than his predecessors, played the dual role of President and party-leader. As party-leader he was concerned about the weakness of the Republicans in the Northern states, where Federalists had identified them with the interests of the South. In order to strengthen his party in the chief bastion of Federalism, Jefferson appointed three New Englanders to major offices: Levi Lincoln of Massachusetts as Attorney General, Henry Dearborn of Massachusetts as Secretary of War, and Gideon Granger of Connecticut as Postmaster General. He also made skillful political use of the patronage. Though permitting many Federalists to remain in non-policymaking offices, he was determined that Republicans should have their fair share—

two-thirds or three-fourths of them, he once suggested. Jefferson removed Federalists whom Adams had appointed after the election of the preceding year, those who were guilty of "malversation," and those who had shown "open, active and virulent" partisanship. As a wise politician he showed some restraint, but party advantage—his desire to destroy the Federalists—clearly governed his policy; nearly all his appointees were Republicans.

Republican policies. Jefferson repudiated most of Hamilton's mercantilist theories in favor of a general policy of laissez faire. The success of his Administration, therefore, cannot be measured in terms of positive legislation or innovative action. His ideal was "a wise and frugal Government, which shall restrain men from injuring one another ... [and] leave them otherwise free to regulate their own pursuits of industry and improvement." The principal responsibilities of such a government, Jefferson explained, would be to honor the Bill of Rights, seek equal justice for all men, respect the rights of the states ("the surest bulwarks against antirepublican tendencies"), and practice strict economy, "that labor may be lightly burthened."

But the Jefferson Administration soon discovered—as would future administrations when political supremacy passed from one party to another—that it could reverse the actions and repudiate the commitments of its predecessor only at the risk of serious confu-

Albert Gallatin: gifted and devoted Jeffersonian

sion. "Some things," wrote the essentially cautious Jefferson, "may perhaps be left undone from motives of compromise for a time, and not to alarm by too sudden a reformation." Republicans, therefore, thought it best not to tamper with some of Hamilton's economic measures. The Bank of the United States, for example, continued its operations undisturbed until 1811, when its charter expired. By then many Republicans, including Madison and Gallatin, favored granting the Bank a new charter, a proposal that failed in each house of Congress by a single vote. Nor did the Republicans reverse Federalist measures for refunding the national debt, or for federal assumption of the Revolutionary debts of the states, or for encouraging American shipping. "What is practicable," Jefferson confessed, "must often control what is pure theory."

Indeed, in his quest for national unity, Jefferson even sought to win the support of at least a portion of the banking, commercial, and manufacturing interests for his party, and in this he had much success. In Providence, Rhode Island, he saw to it that federal funds were transferred from a Federalist-controlled to a Republican-controlled state bank. "I am decidedly in favor of making all the banks Republican," he wrote, "by sharing deposits among them in proportion to the disposition they show." To justify this sort of fiscal politics, he explained that it was important "to detach the mercantile interest" from the enemies of republicanism "and incorporate them into the body of its friends."

Without changing his opinion about the primacy of agriculture, Jefferson as President developed a greater respect for other economic pursuits. In his first message to Congress he referred to manufacturing, commerce, and navigation, along with agriculture, as "the four pillars of our prosperity"; and he even suggested, though somewhat vaguely, that "within the limits of our constitutional powers" their protection from "casual embarrassments" might be "seasonably interposed."

The "Revolution of 1800" did not, however, lack substance, for the Republicans lost no time in disposing of some of the Federalists' pet measures. They refused, of course, to renew the Alien Act when it expired in 1801. They reduced the residence requirement for naturalization from fourteen years to five; once again America became, in Jeffer-

son's words, an "asylum" for "oppressed humanity." The Sedition Act also expired in 1801, and Jefferson saw to it that those who had been imprisoned for violating it were freed and that all fines were refunded. The Republican Congress repealed the Judiciary Act of 1801 and abolished, as a needless extravagance, the sixteen new circuit judgeships that act had created. Thus, defeated ("lame duck") Federalists to whom Adams had given "midnight appointments" in the judicial branch lost their jobs; and the courts, as one Republican explained, ceased to be a "hospital for decayed politicians." The House of Representatives then turned on the Supreme Court and, in 1804, impeached Associate Justice Samuel Chase, an arch-Federalist who had used the bench as a political stump. But the Senate did not interpret Chase's offense as a misdemeanor within the meaning of the Constitution and refused to remove him. Henceforth, the Republicans relied on new appointments in their efforts to reform the courts.

The Jeffersonian revolution also wrought a significant change in fiscal policy. There is a tendency for governments, the new President said, "to multiply offices . . . and to increase expense"—to leave to labor only a small portion of its earnings and to "consume the whole residue of what it was instituted to guard." Unlike Hamilton, Jefferson regarded a public debt and the accompanying interest charges as beneficial only to a small class of investors and felt that it was a "mortal canker" on the rest of the community. With the able support of Secretary of the Treasury Gallatin, he strove to retire the whole public debt, which had grown to $83 million, at the earliest possible date—in sixteen years, according to the original plan. Since the excise tax had been repealed, the only way to retire the debt was through revenues from import duties and the sale of public lands and through the most rigid government economy. To cut costs in the executive department Jefferson reduced the number of officers in the diplomatic corps and revenue service. He urged Congress to abolish other public offices, to replace wasteful general appropriations with grants of "specific sums to every specific purpose," and to hold the Treasury Department responsible for all funds spent.

Jefferson was convinced, too, that military and naval expenditures could be cut without jeopardizing national defense. America, he said, was fortunately "separated by nature and a wide ocean from the exterminating havoc" of the Old World and consequently needed no large standing army. For defense against invasion, the country should rely on "the body of neighboring citizens as formed into a militia." Accordingly, the regular army was reduced from four thousand to twenty-five hundred officers and men. Jefferson realized, however, that the state militia systems needed to be improved, and in 1808 the federal government began to take a hand in reorganizing them and in defraying part of the cost of arms and equipment. Moreover, in 1802 Jefferson was instrumental in establishing the U.S. Military Academy at West Point.

Turning to the navy, the new Administration proceeded to sell some ocean-going vessels, lay up others, and halt construction on still others; it discharged many Navy Department employees, reduced the number of officers and enlisted men, and abandoned the improvement of navy yards and dry docks. Shore defense was to be maintained by coastal fortifications and by a fleet of small, inexpensive gunboats serving as a kind of naval militia. This policy was designed, Jefferson explained, "merely for defensive operations," not to protect commerce or to establish the United States as a sea power. The quarreling European states would thus be kept "at a distance" and at little cost.

Here, in short, was Jefferson's formula for an agrarian utopia: simplicity, frugality, and "a government founded not on the fears and follies of man, but on his reason"—a government whose authority the ordinary citizen would scarcely feel. For a time all worked according to plan, and in his second annual message Jefferson congratulated Congress for the "pleasing circumstances . . . under which we meet." The United States had become a nation of peaceful, prosperous citizens "managing their own affairs in their own way and for their own use, unembarrassed by too much regulation, unoppressed by fiscal exactions."

Jefferson's cheerful view of the state of the Union was valid enough for most white Americans, but not for those Americans (approximately 19 percent of the population) who were Negroes or of mixed white and Negro ancestry. In 1800 nearly 90 percent of these people (894,000) were still slaves, and the rest were everywhere more or less the victims of a deep and pervasive racial prejudice. Though the federal government had no constitutional power to interfere with slavery in the states, the institution had already provoked several sharp congressional debates during the decade of Federalist ascendancy. In earlier years Jefferson, though himself a large slaveholder, had professed, usually privately, antislavery sentiments; but during the eight years of his Presidency, like every other chief executive before the Civil War, he carefully avoided the subject. The "Revolution of 1800" brought no change in the condition of black Americans, and Jefferson seems always to have assessed the state of the Union without giving them a thought.

In his annual message of December 2, 1806, however, Jefferson did remind Congress that the time was approaching when it could constitutionally stop citizens of the United States from participating in the African slave trade—a trade that every state except South Carolina had already made illegal. Congress responded with a law prohibiting the trade after January 1, 1808, and punishing violators with fines and imprisonment. But it was a poor law with no machinery for enforcement, and many thousands of African slaves were imported after its adoption. In 1820 Congress passed another law defining participation in the slave trade as piracy; but, significantly, not until 1862 was anyone convicted under its terms.

Ferment in the West

The westward movement. In his vision of America as the ideal republic, Jefferson projected upon the nation at large an image of the stable, mellow society of Virginia's rural gentry. This image, however, did not fit much of the rest of the country—not even the trans-Appalachian West in whose future Jefferson placed such confident hopes. In 1800 nearly a million settlers were living in the vast area between the Appalachians and the Mississippi River; a new land act that year encouraged others to come by offering land for sale in individual tracts of 320 acres and by permitting four-year credits with a down payment of 25 percent. A revision of this law in 1804 reduced the minimum tract to 160 acres; thus,

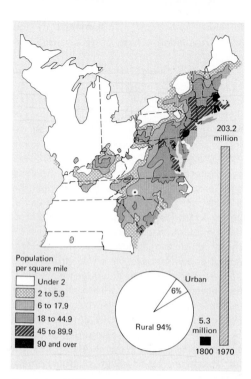

Population per square mile

- Under 2
- 2 to 5.9
- 6 to 17.9
- 18 to 44.9
- 45 to 89.9
- 90 and over

Urban 6%

Rural 94%

5.3 million 1800

203.2 million 1970

Population 1800

with public land selling at a minimum price of $2 an acre, a buyer could obtain a farm for an initial payment of $80. This generous federal policy brought a steady tide of immigrants into the West, whose rich lands Jefferson thought would afford "room enough for our descendants to the thousandth and thousandth generation." As the forests were cleared and farms and villages dotted the land, new states were created from time to time—Kentucky in 1792, Tennessee in 1796, and Ohio in 1803.

Most of the Westerners liked Jefferson's politics and found much in his philosophy that pleased them, but they had mixed feelings about his economics and scarcely understood his agrarian dream—in fact, they did much to destroy it. Jefferson's ideal of a stable, self-sufficient yeomanry free of the corrupting influences of commercialism was hardly the ideal of the traders and speculators who infested the West—or, for that matter, of many of the farmers. Soon after they arrived, most Westerners began to dream not of self-sufficiency but of cash crops, of outlets to markets, and of the comforts and luxuries of the East.

The problem of transportation. Between the Western settlers and their ambitions stood two major obstacles: the mountains, which cut them off from the East, and the French, who were taking over from Spain possession of New Orleans and the mouth of the Mississippi. Before Jefferson left office, he was to find solutions to both these problems—solutions that in the long run helped to undermine his original goal of a simple agrarian society. In 1806 Congress authorized the building of a road from Cumberland, Maryland, across the mountains to Wheeling, Virginia, as a government-financed "internal improvement." Jefferson approved the measure, even though, without the constitutional amendment he had urged, it required a stretching of federal power to do so. Construction on the National Road, as it was called, began in 1811 and was completed in 1818. In subsequent years the road was extended westward to Vandalia, Illinois.

The second problem—navigation of the Mississippi River—forced Jefferson to take vigorous action that compromised not only his constitutional scruples but his fiscal policy, his foreign policy, and perhaps even his principles of public ethics. Since 1763 the mouth of the Mississippi and the immense territory of Louisiana, stretching westward to the Rockies, had been held by a declining and enfeebled Spain; and Spain, in Pinckney's Treaty of 1795, had opened the Mississippi to American navigation and granted Western flatboatmen the right to deposit their cargoes at New Orleans for shipment abroad. This arrangement satisfied the Westerners, who saw in Spain no serious threat. But they were bound to react violently if Louisiana were to fall into the hands of a stronger power or if their river outlet were cut off. As Madison explained: "The Mississippi is to them every thing. It is the Hudson, the Delaware, the Potomac, and all the navigable rivers of the Atlantic states, formed into one stream."

The Louisiana Purchase. Soon after Jefferson became President two events shocked and angered the Western settlers. The first was the revelation that Napoleon, in the secret Treaty of San Ildefonso (1800), had negotiated the transfer of Louisiana from Spain to France (though formal possession by France was long delayed). The second was a proclamation by the Spanish intendant at New Orleans, on October 16, 1802, that the right of deposit was to be suspended. Taking this as a foretaste of Napoleon's future policy, indignant Westerners looked to Jefferson for support.

The Louisiana Purchase and explorations of the Far West

Alarmed, Jefferson feared for a time that Napoleon might force him to reconsider his basic foreign policy, perhaps even to abandon temporarily his opposition to "entangling alliances." The United States, he told Robert R. Livingston, the American minister in Paris, has always looked upon France as her "natural friend"; but there was

> on the globe one single spot, the possessor of which is our natural and habitual enemy. It is New Orleans, through which the produce of three-eighths of our territory must pass to market. . . . France placing herself in that door, assumes to us the attitude of defiance. The day that France takes possession of New Orleans

> . . . [we will be forced to] marry ourselves to the British fleet and nation.

To Congress he spoke of "the danger to which our peace would be perpetually exposed whilst so important a key to the commerce of the Western country remained under foreign power."

But before taking any drastic steps, Jefferson tried to negotiate peacefully with France. He instructed Livingston to offer to purchase New Orleans and West Florida; he obtained from Congress an appropriation of $2 million for vaguely defined expenses; and he sent James Monroe, who had the confidence of Westerners, as a special envoy to assist Livingston. Monroe arrived in Paris on April 12, 1803, two days after Talleyrand, negotiating for France, had startled Livingston by asking whether the United States would like to buy the whole of Louisiana! The two American diplomats, whose instructions were essentially to buy a city, hesitated, though only momentarily, before agreeing to buy an empire that would double the size of their country.

There were several reasons for Napoleon's sudden decision to abandon his imperial ambitions in America and to concentrate on Europe. First, he suffered a major disaster when his troops failed to crush a slave insurrection, led by Toussaint L'Ouverture, in the French colony of Santo Domingo. Second, the Peace of Amiens of 1802 had really settled nothing, and a renewal of war between France and Great Britain seemed all but inevitable. Third, Napoleon needed money, and it was obviously wise to sell a province that the British navy could prevent France from occupying in any case. Finally, selling Louisiana to the United States would remove a source of friction and avoid an Anglo-American *rapprochement.* Accordingly, on April 11 Napoleon told one of his ministers: "I renounce Louisiana. It is not only New Orleans that I will cede, it is the whole colony without any reservation."

Livingston and Monroe soon decided that this was a poor time to quibble over the letter of their instructions. On April 30, 1803, after some higgling over price, they made the purchase for $15 million and a promise (written into the purchase treaty) to give citizenship and religious freedom to the Catholics residing in Louisiana. The boundaries of Louisiana were then only vaguely defined, and the treaty merely stated that they were to be the same as they had been when Spain possessed it. "You have made a noble bargain for yourselves," said the realistic Talleyrand, "and I suppose you will make the most of it." In later years the United States did precisely that.

Westerners were delighted with the terms of the treaty, and their devotion to Jefferson and confidence in the federal government grew correspondingly stronger. But New England Federalists, viewing the West as enemy territory, criticized Jefferson severely for accepting a treaty that was tainted with duplicity. In making the sale, they pointed out, Napoleon had violated the French constitution and a promise to Spain not to cede Louisiana to another power. Yet Jefferson approved the

transaction knowing this to be the case— knowing, too, that the Constitution did not explicitly authorize the acquisition of new territory. Federalists also complained that the purchase of these worthless lands was a wasteful expenditure and meant a staggering addition to the public debt.

Jefferson was sensitive to such criticism, especially to the charge that he was exceeding the limits of the Constitution strictly construed. His first impulse was to urge an amendment to the Constitution expressly granting the power to acquire territory; but the amending process was painfully slow, and Livingston warned that Napoleon might have a change of heart. Moreover, some Republicans argued that the power to acquire territory might be *implied* from the power to make treaties. Such an argument could hardly have satisfied Jefferson, but he concluded that Congress would be wise to cast aside "metaphysical subtleties." Trusting that "the good sense of our country will correct the evil of [constitutional] construction when it shall produce evil effects," Jefferson submitted the treaty to the Senate.

During the debate Federalists and Republicans reversed their former positions on questions of constitutional interpretation—a few extreme Federalists even spoke of dissolving the Union. But the treaty was ratified by a vote of twenty-four to seven, and the House appropriated the money required to fulfill its terms. Thus the United States acquired the whole of the Mississippi River and its tributaries, some 828,000 square miles of territory, millions of acres of rich farmland, and a vast store of natural resources. Moreover, the purchase of Louisiana removed a major source of American concern about the internal politics of Europe; and, in the long run, it produced a basic shift in the national balance of political power. After the treaty was ratified, Jefferson seemed to forget quickly his anxieties about it—except to regret that Spanish West Florida had not been part of the bargain. Though for the present neither threats nor money—he tried both—could pry the Floridas loose from Spain, Jefferson was confident that it was America's destiny to obtain them, too, "and all in good time."

Western exploration. On December 20, 1803, just a few weeks after France had taken formal possession of Louisiana from Spain, the French prefect at New Orleans turned the

Meriwether Lewis: successful explorer

lower part of the territory over to the United States. The transfer of the upper part was delayed until the spring of 1804, when, at St. Louis, Meriwether Lewis, Jefferson's private secretary, accepted it in behalf of the United States. But Lewis was not there for that specific purpose; in fact, his presence was the result of presidential plans that antedated the Louisiana Purchase.

In January 1803 Congress had secretly appropriated money for an expedition to explore the upper reaches of the Missouri River and from there westward to the Pacific—though none of this territory at the time belonged to the United States. The expedition, which Jefferson had been trying to promote for many years, had several purposes. The President assured the Spanish minister that it would ''have no other view than the advancement of geography''; and, to be sure, his scientific curiosity about the great unexplored interior was genuine. Lewis and his fellow explorer, William Clark (a brother of George Rogers Clark), were instructed to make astronomical observations, to study the flora and fauna, and to compile the fullest possible records. But they were to be alert to more practical matters, too, especially trading opportunities and mineral deposits. Moreover, Jefferson was fully aware that explorations had diplomatic value when nations laid claims to unsettled lands.

The Lewis and Clark expedition, which took more than two years to complete, was a remarkable success. The party of forty-five men ascended the Missouri River to the Great Falls, crossed the Rockies, and descended the Snake and Columbia rivers to the Pacific. The explorers brought back with them an enormously expanded factual knowledge of Western North America (first made available to the public when their journals were published in 1814), a large botanical collection, information of value to American fur-traders, and a strengthened foundation for an American claim to the Oregon country. This was only one of several Western explorations that Jefferson promoted. Two others were led by Zebulon Pike: one in 1805 up the Mississippi River in search of its source, and a second in 1806 up the Arkansas River to the Rockies in what is now Colorado. All of them combined the scientific and practical interests that Jefferson himself personified.

From the journal of William Clark

Political complications

Even though Jefferson accommodated his political and economic principles to some of the realities of American life, and even though he converted many rank-and-file Federalists to Republicanism, he never managed to appease his more ardent opponents or to bring party politics to an end. Organizations of disgruntled old Federalists, such as the Essex Junto around Boston, deplored the growth of democratic ''licentiousness'' and the decline of public virtue. The new Administration, said Hamilton, seems ''to imagine that to govern well, is to amuse the wondering multitude with sagacious aphorisms and oracular sayings.'' Senator Timothy Pickering of Massachusetts described Jefferson as a ''cowardly wretch,'' a ''Parisian revolutionary monster,'' who debased the public morals by his ''corrupt and corrupting system. . . . Men are tempted to become apostates, not to Federalism merely, but to virtue and to religion, and to good government.'' Seeing the Republicans growing stronger even in New England, Pickering and a handful of Northern Federalists in Congress privately urged a dissolution of the Union before it was too late; but their radical schemes won little support.

It was not this old guard, however, but a younger generation of Federalists, more flexible and less embittered, who kept the party alive and a significant force in national politics. Aware of the failures that had caused their defeat, they worked to build party organizations, to imitate Republican electioneering techniques, to alter their pro-British, antidemocratic image, and to find popular issues that would broaden their appeal. ''We must court popular favor,'' advised Fisher Ames of Massachusetts. ''We must study popular opinion and accommodate measures to what it is.'' The young Federalists never won a national election, for the intransigence of the old guard and the élitist image that the Jeffersonians had fixed on them were more than they could overcome. Yet they made an important contribution to the development of two-party politics, contributed to a dramatic increase in voting, and helped to reconcile men who had once scorned popular electioneering to the politics of a new age.

In addition to the Federalist threat, Jefferson was troubled with factionalism in his own party. Personal rivalries and patronage disputes in New York and Pennsylvania produced for a time local third-party movements, some of whose leaders assumed the label of "Tertium Quids." More distressing to Jefferson was the criticism he received from the uncompromising state righters of Virginia, who felt that he had moved too far toward Federalism. His good friend, John Taylor, observed with dismay that "Federalism . . . has gained a new footing, by being taken into partnership with republicanism." Jefferson's most persistent Virginia critic was the brilliant but erratic Congressman John Randolph of Roanoke, who would tolerate not the slightest deviation from the principles of the Kentucky Resolutions of 1798 (see p. 153). "Asking one of the states to surrender part of her sovereignty," he said, "is like asking a lady to surrender part of her chastity."

Randolph grumbled about several Administration-sponsored measures, even more about Jefferson's repeated and highly successful efforts to intervene in the affairs of Congress. He bitterly opposed a proposal to use federal funds to settle the claims of certain land-speculators organized into the so-called Yazoo Land Companies. These speculators had corruptly obtained a large grant from the Georgia legislature before the state, in 1802, ceded its Western lands to the federal government. Jefferson's desire to facilitate the transfer by compensating the Yazoo claimants, even though many of them were Northern speculators and their claims were tainted with fraud, drove Randolph and a small faction of Republicans into open rebellion. Randolph's break with Jefferson was completed in 1806, when he announced his willingness to support "*quidism*," that is, a third-party movement. He and his Virginia friends blocked the settlement of the Yazoo claims for many years and tormented Jefferson with accusations of apostasy. However, neither the Quid movements in New York and Pennsylvania nor the Randolph defection in Virginia ever reached the proportions of a national third party; and eventually Randolph himself simply lost his influence in Congress.

Meanwhile, Vice President Aaron Burr, whom Jefferson had deprived of patronage and excluded from party councils after the disputed election of 1800 (see p. 155), seemed ready for almost any reckless maneuver that might improve his political fortunes. By 1804 he was willing to accept the support of the Federalists and dissident Republicans in a campaign for the governorship of New York. The handful of Federalists who had been toying with a scheme to unite New York and New England in an independent Northern Confederacy now hoped to enlist the services of Burr. But Hamilton exposed and denounced the plot and played a major role in Burr's defeat. The enraged Burr then challenged his old New York rival to a duel, in which Hamilton, on July 11, 1804, was mortally wounded. In the presidential election of that year, Jefferson replaced Burr with George Clinton of New York as his running mate; together they crushed the discredited Federalists. Charles Cotesworth Pinckney, the Federalist candidate, carried only Connecticut and Delaware.

The talented Burr had wrecked a promising political career by overreaching himself; having been indicted for murder in both New York and New Jersey, he now courted final disaster by involving himself in a quixotic intrigue whose exact nature was obscured in a maze of conflicting reports. The British minister had heard that for a half-million dollars Burr would separate the Western part of the United States from the East; the Spanish minister had heard that he planned to establish a buffer state between Louisiana and Mexico; others had heard that he planned to conquer Mexico and establish an empire. Whatever his scheme was, Burr won the support of two confederates: General James Wilkinson, who commanded the American troops in Louisiana and had as great a taste for conspiracy as Burr; and Harman Blennerhassett, a wealthy Irish exile who lived on an island in the upper Ohio River. In the summer of 1806 Burr and some sixty men on thirteen flatboats departed from Blennerhassett's Island and floated down the Ohio and Mississippi for some unknown purpose to some nameless glory.

The enterprise collapsed when General Wilkinson shifted sides and sent Jefferson a report that Burr was plotting treason. On Jefferson's orders the fleeing Burr was caught and taken to Richmond, where, in 1807, he was indicted for treason and conspiracy. In the curious trial that followed, Jefferson seemed determined to get a conviction whether or not the evidence warranted it; and the presiding judge, John Marshall, a Federalist, seemed as interested in discrediting Jefferson as in giving Burr justice. In the end Burr was acquitted,

John Randolph: he lost his influence

for the case against him did not fulfill the terms of the Constitution's definition of treason. According to the Constitution, treason consists in "levying war" against the United States or in "adhering to their enemies, giving them aid and comfort." A conviction for treason requires "the testimony of two witnesses to the same overt act." In his charge to the jury, Marshall insisted that the witnesses must have directly implicated Burr in a specific "overt act" of treason, not merely in planning treason or just loosely in organizing "a military assemblage." Since the witnesses had failed to fulfill this constitutional requirement, Marshall's charge prepared the way for Burr's acquittal. It also set an important precedent that made convictions for treason extremely difficult and indictments rare.

Trouble on the high seas

War and American trade. When Jefferson became President in 1801, he was determined that the United States pursue its destiny free from "entangling alliances" and from the wars and diplomatic duplicity of the Old World. Yet he found himself entangled in world affairs throughout most of his second Administration, and he left office with the country fast approaching total involvement. The abrogation of the French alliance in 1800, it appeared, did not mean that America had closed the door on Europe. Since she exported foodstuffs and raw materials, imported foreign manufactured goods, and sent merchant ships to distant ports, America was bound to be affected by the course of international politics and by the state of the world economy.

Even during Jefferson's first Administration the Barbary pirates, operating from bases on the coast of North Africa, had provoked the pacifistic President into surprisingly vigorous action. For many years these corsairs had been harrying American vessels and forcing the federal government, like the governments of Europe, to buy immunity by paying tribute to the rulers of Morocco, Algiers, Tunis, and Tripoli. To Jefferson this costly and humiliating practice was intolerable, and in 1801 he dispatched a naval squadron to the Mediterranean. For several years the United States was engaged in virtual war with Tripoli, until the Pasha, in 1805, was obliged to make a satisfactory peace. Tribute payments to other Barbary states, however, did not cease altogether until 1816.

The Tripolitan War, though a minor affair, had forced Jefferson to modify his naval policy. 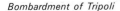 But the resumption of hostilities between

Bombardment of Tripoli

Great Britain and France in 1803—a conflict that raged without interruption for the next eleven years—provided a far more strenuous test of the President's pacifism. In a larger sense, it was a test of how much the American people were ready to endure and sacrifice to remain at peace, for peace has its price as well as war. As Jefferson warned Congress, with ''the flames of war lighted up again in Europe . . . the nations pursuing peace will not be exempt from all evil.'' To him the price was not too great, and he thanked ''that kind Providence which . . . guarded us from hastily entering into the sanguinary contest and left us only to look on and to pity its ravages.'' America's sole interest and desire, he said, would be ''to cultivate the friendship of the belligerent nations by every act of justice and of innocent kindness.'' Of them he would ask only respect for the rights to which American vessels and citizens were entitled as neutrals under international law. Since American friendship and trade were useful to them, Jefferson was certain that ''it can not be the interest of any to assail us, nor ours to disturb them.''

While Jefferson professed confidence in his country's capacity to bring ''collisions of interest to the umpirage of reason rather than force,'' the European belligerents were locked in a conflict whose stakes seemed to justify any means that promised ultimate victory. In 1805 Napoleon's smashing victory over the armies of Austria and Russia at Austerlitz made him for the time master of much of the European continent, while Lord Nelson's decisive defeat of the French and Spanish fleets at the Battle of Trafalgar gave Britain control of the high seas. Thereafter, in a savage war of attrition, neither antagonist showed much concern for the rights of neutrals or the punctilios of international law. Both rained blows on American shipping interests and insults on sensitive patriots.

Trouble began in 1805, when a British court ruled that goods from the French West Indies bound for Europe on American vessels, even though shipped by way of the United States, were subject to seizure. When the commercial provisions of Jay's Treaty of 1794 expired in 1807 and American diplomats were unable to negotiate a new agreement satisfactory to Jefferson, British interference with American shipping increased. Meanwhile Napoleon had developed a program of economic warfare; his so-called Continental System, elaborated in

Building the frigate ''Philadelphia''

his Berlin Decree of 1806 and Milan Decree of 1807, closed the European ports under his control to British goods and stated that neutral ships complying with British trade regulations would be confiscated. The British government retaliated with a series of Orders in Council, the most important of which proclaimed a blockade of the ports of France and of the nations under her control. Thereafter American ships bound for western Europe risked seizure by one or the other of the belligerents, depending on whose rules they flouted. In the three years prior to 1807 the British seized at least a thousand American merchantmen and the French half that many.

To Americans the most grievous British wrong was the revival and vigorous application of the centuries-old system of impressment, by which the Royal Navy procured its manpower. In times of crisis British law permitted the commander of a warship, when he needed men, to draft able-bodied subjects of the king wherever they could be found. In enforcing the system British warships stopped American merchantmen on the high seas to search for deserters; they took off British-born sailors who had become Americans by naturalization; and in the process they heedlessly impressed an unknown number of native-born Americans as well. The issue reached a crisis in June 1807, when the British frigate *Leopard* overhauled the United States frigate *Chesapeake* within sight of the Virginia coast and demanded the right to search her for deserters. When the commander of the unprepared *Chesapeake* refused, the *Leopard* fired three broadsides that killed three Americans and wounded eighteen others. The crippled *Chesapeake* submitted to the seizure of four deserters and then returned to Norfolk. This humiliation of an American frigate infuriated both Federalists and Republicans. ''Never, since the battle of Lexington,'' wrote Jefferson, ''have I seen this country in such a state of exasperation as at present.'' Judging from the tone of the press and the speeches of politicians, the country seemed ready to unite behind a war policy. But Jefferson asked for less: he ordered British warships out of American waters and demanded reparations and an apology.

The embargo. Jefferson asked something of Americans, too. He called for a supreme effort, not to win a war, but to achieve what he considered the nobler goal of keeping the country at peace. He believed that denying the belligerents the benefits of American trade would cause them so much distress that they would abandon their encroachments on American neutral rights. For this purpose, and to avoid further provocative incidents, Jefferson proposed a policy that he had long cherished as an alternative to war, a policy he described as "peaceable coercion." On December 22, 1807, in response to his urgent plea, Congress passed the Embargo Act, which stopped the export of American goods and prohibited all ships from clearing American ports for foreign ports. This act, in effect, required shipowners to abandon their risky but extremely profitable wartime trade and obliged planters and farmers to give up their rich European export market.

Jefferson asked for a greater sacrifice than most Americans seemed ready to make. Angry New England merchants, preferring risks and insults to commercial stagnation, denounced the embargo as a ruthless attempt to enlarge the federal government's constitutional power to regulate foreign commerce into an unconstitutional power to prohibit it altogether. Many of them defiantly engaged in an illicit trade that severe enforcement measures, some of dubious legality, could not entirely suppress. The Federalists had at last found a popular issue and, in consequence, enjoyed a modest revival. Some again hinted at secession. Timothy Pickering described Jefferson as capable of almost any "nefarious act" and called on the states to resist "the usurpations of the general government." The agricultural interest was equally distressed when farm commodities began to accumulate at the ports and prices declined. John Randolph's assaults on the Administration matched those of the Federalists. The embargo, he complained, had furnished "rogues with an opportunity of getting rich at the expense of honest men."

"Ograbme [Embargo], or the American Snapping-turtle"

Eventually Congress yielded to overwhelming pressure and passed an act repealing the embargo. On March 1, 1809, a disappointed Jefferson, his prestige somewhat diminished, signed it. Still, "peaceable coercion," though it had failed to win public support, had kept the country at peace; moreover, there is reason to believe that, given time, the embargo might even have wrung concessions from the British.

"Nature intended me for the more tranquil pursuits of science by rendering them my supreme delight," wrote the weary Jefferson at the close of his second Administration. Retirement was a welcome relief not only from the vicissitudes of domestic politics, in which he counted more successes than failures, but from the trials of international affairs, in which he suffered his greatest defeat.

The decision for war

By declining to run for reelection in 1808, Jefferson helped to establish the two-term tradition. His favorite, Secretary of State James Madison, easily won the nomination of the Republican caucus over James Monroe, the candidate of the Randolph faction. Though the Federalists, who again nominated Charles Cotesworth Pinckney, regained control of New England and increased their strength in the new Congress, Madison won the Presidency by a decisive majority of 122 to 47 in the Electoral College. His inaugural address reflected the changing conditions of the preceding eight years, especially in its concern for the promotion of commerce and industry; but in spirit it was still a thoroughly Jeffersonian document, which endorsed the domestic and foreign policies of his predecessor.

Few Presidents have brought to the White House such rich experience in public life as did Madison; none, save John Adams, was so profound a student of political philosophy. Yet, though Madison had contributed much to the formulation of Republican doctrine and had never been Jefferson's mere pliant tool, the scholarly Virginian lacked Jefferson's political acumen and administrative skill.

The failure of diplomacy.

The overshadowing problem confronting the new President and Congress was the continuing European holocaust, which still created difficult situations for neutrals. Although the embargo had been repealed, the policy of "peaceable coercion" persisted in less drastic forms. The Madison Administration blundered badly in applying it, however. The first substitute for the embargo was a Nonintercourse Act, passed in 1809, which reestablished trade with all nations except Great Britain and France so long as the latter continued to enforce their obnoxious orders and decrees. This act encouraged the British government to try negotiation. David Erskine, the friendly and sympathetic British minister, concluded an agreement that was highly satisfactory to the United States, though he violated his instructions in doing so. On June 10, 1809, the delighted President renewed trade with Great Britain without waiting for the agreement to be approved in London, and hundreds of American ships cleared their home ports for the first time in many months. Unfortunately the British government repudiated the Erskine "treaty" as soon as it arrived and recalled its too-generous minister. Madison, embarrassed and humiliated, then proclaimed the restoration of nonintercourse, and Anglo-American relations worsened.

On May 1, 1810, nonintercourse gave way to a new policy incorporated in a curious measure called Macon's Bill Number 2. This bill restored trade with both Great Britain and France but threatened to resume nonintercourse with either of them whenever the other agreed to respect America's neutral rights. Now it was Napoleon's turn to try some shifty diplomacy. Proclaiming his love for Americans and his concern for their prosperity, he announced that on November 1, 1810, the French commercial restrictions would be repealed—but he attached conditions that made his promise almost meaningless. Madison fell into Napoleon's trap and on February

James Madison: a greater man than President

2, 1811, reestablished nonintercourse with Britain, though, in fact, the French continued to seize American ships. Unable to get Britain to repeal her Orders in Council, Madison recalled the American minister, William Pinkney, and thus virtually severed diplomatic relations.

Ironically, a few months later the policy of "peaceable coercion" won a striking victory. On June 23, 1812, beset by an economic crisis at home, the British foreign secretary announced the immediate suspension of the Orders in Council (but not impressment). The announcement came too late. On June 1, Madison had asked for a declaration of war against Great Britain, and Congress soon complied: the House on June 4 by a vote of 79 to 49, the Senate on June 18 by a vote of 19 to 13. The division in both houses was largely political, for all Federalists voted against war, while the Republicans voted for it 98 to 22.

The motives of the prowar Republicans.

Though foreign policy had become a party issue, the geographical distribution of the vote for and against war nevertheless raises some difficult questions about its causes. In the House, Pennsylvania and the Southern and frontier states, including Vermont, voted 65 to 15 for war; New York, New Jersey, and the New England maritime states voted 14 to 34 against. The Federalist commercial interests were directly affected by British impressment and interference with American shipping on the high seas, but they considered war with Great Britain the ultimate folly. War would be more devastating to their trade than the Orders in Council had been—and the blow would be dealt by their own government. Moreover, to them Britain was not only a profitable market but the defender of conservatism, stability, and order against the obscenities of Napoleonic France. Sharing these views with the Federalists were a handful of Republicans representing Southern coastal districts and about a third of those representing the Northeast. John Randolph, a severe critic of the war policy, urged Republicans to live up to their principles of economy and retrenchment and not to become "infatuated with standing armies, loans, taxes, navies, and war."

An able and highly articulate group opposed the declaration of war, but the majority seemed to support it. Although the center of this majority was in the agricultural South and West, rather than in New England, neutral rights and impressment were issues of major importance in the decision to go to war. The grievances Madison stressed in his war message were "the injuries and indignities which have been heaped upon our country"—the British actions "hostile to the United States as an independent and neutral nation." Patriotic Southerners and Westerners felt these insults keenly and resented the implicit unwillingness of the British to concede the reality of American independence. According to one Kentuckian, "we must now oppose the farther encroachments of Great Britain by war, or formally annul the Declaration of Independence, and acknowledge ourselves her devoted colonies." The vindication of national honor, many Republicans believed, would also be a vindication of republican institutions against their foreign and domestic enemies. This notion of an American mission to defend republicanism was widespread; according to Jefferson, "The last hope of human liberty in this world rests on us."

Neutral rights involved economic interests, too; as Madison explained, British policy struck not only at commerce but at agriculture as well. By closing European markets to American staples, the British threatened the prosperity of farmers and planters who lived hundreds of miles from the sea and might never have seen an ocean-going vessel. "The interests of agriculture and commerce are inseparable," said Representative Langdon Cheves of South Carolina.

The Congress that voted for war contained a remarkable little band of youthful Republicans from the Southern and Western states. Some of them had taken their seats for the first time in November 1811 and had at once begun to badger the President and harangue their colleagues with truculent anti-British speeches. They managed to elect Henry Clay of Kentucky Speaker of the House; Clay in turn gave important committee assignments to aggressive young Republicans such as Richard M. Johnson of Kentucky, Felix Grundy of Tennessee, and John C. Calhoun of South Carolina. These second-generation Republicans—the Federalists called them "War Hawks"—were critical of the pacifistic measures of Jefferson and Madison, indifferent to the state-rights political tradition embodied in the Resolutions of 1798, nationalistic to a degree exceeding the Federalists in

their prime, and eager for geographic expansion and economic growth, with none of the anxieties that Jefferson sometimes seemed to feel. To them, after diplomacy had failed, war was necessary to demonstrate America's power and to redress intolerable wrongs too long endured: impressment, violations of America's neutral rights, disregard for her dignity as a sovereign power. Eventually these so-called War Hawks also viewed the war as an opportunity to capitalize on Europe's strife for the purpose of acquiring additional territory.

The insatiable Southern and Western demand for land was indirectly a source of the crisis that culminated in war. The American frontier was not advancing in a slow, orderly manner, with contiguous tracts of the public domain successively opened for sale and then compactly settled. Rather, farmers and speculators rushed into new areas, often before Indian claims were cleared and surveys completed, and sought out the most fertile parcels. With such an abundance of good land, few buyers were interested in land of second- and third-rate quality. Hence, the government was under constant pressure to open additional tracts even before those already open had been fully settled.

The government seldom raised a restraining hand. Even Jefferson, in spite of a professed concern for the welfare of the Indians, as President had been more often a party to the land grabs than a protector of Indian rights. "Our system," he told William Henry Harrison, governor of Indiana Territory, "is to live in perpetual peace with the Indians," to protect them from injustice, to introduce among them "the implements and the practice of husbandry and of the household arts," and to persuade them to "incorporate with us as citizens of the U.S." When they became farmers they would no longer need their extensive forests and would trade land "for necessaries for their farms and families." But Jefferson also suggested means of speeding the process of land acquisition. At the government trading houses "the good and influential" Indians might be encouraged to run into debt, thus forcing them eventually to make a settlement "by a cession of land." If any tribe should be "foolhardy enough to take up the hatchet . . . the seizing [of] the whole country of that tribe and driving them across the Mississippi" would be justified. Finally, Jefferson advised Governor Harrison on ways

A statement of war aims

Before we relinquish the conflict, I wish to see Great Britain renounce the piratical system of paper blockade; to liberate our captured seamen on board her ships of war; relinquish the practice of impressment on board our merchant vessels; to repeal her Orders in Council; and cease, in every other respect, to violate our neutral rights; to treat us as an independent people. The gentleman from Virginia (Mr. Randolph) has objected to the destination of this auxiliary force—the occupation of the Canadas, and the other British possessions upon our borders where our laws are violated, the Indians stimulated to murder our citizens, and where there is a British monopoly of the peltry and fur trade. I should not wish to extend the boundary of the United States by war if Great Britain would leave us to the quiet enjoyment of independence; but, considering her deadly and implacable enmity, and her continued hostility, I shall never die contented until I see her expulsion from North America, and her territories incorporated with the United States.... This deep rooted enmity to Great Britain arises from her insidious policy, the offspring of her perfidious conduct toward the United States. Her disposition is unfriendly; her enmity is implacable; she sickens at our prosperity and happiness.

From Richard M. Johnson of Kentucky, Speech in the House of Representatives, December 11, 1811.

to cajole the various tribes into making land cessions.

An unfortunate consequence of both the planless expansion and the cajolery was that Western Indians were repeatedly induced to make treaties whose terms they rarely comprehended, treaties by which they surrendered more and more of their hunting grounds. In the Ohio Valley alone, during the first decade of the nineteenth century, the Indians had been obliged to cede more than a hundred million acres of land. In 1809, in Indiana Territory, Governor Harrison negotiated the last of a series of cessions under particularly dubious circumstances, bargaining with the demoralized remnants of several tribes for nearly three million acres in the lower Wabash Valley. The Indians realized that if they were ever to make a stand east of the Mississippi, it would have to be now.

At this crucial time two Shawnees of uncommon ability, Tecumseh and his brother Tenskwatawa ("the Prophet"), managed to unite the tribes east of the Mississippi for resistance against further white encroachments. Tecumseh supplied political leadership, while the Prophet provided spiritual inspiration and a call for moral regeneration. Together they organized an efficient Indian confederation supported by braves determined to preserve their lands and uncorrupted by the white man's proffered gifts of liquor.

Terror spread along the frontier. In the summer of 1811, when Tecumseh went south to bid for the support of the Creeks, Governor Harrison decided to take advantage of his absence. He advanced with a force of a thousand men to the outskirts of Prophetstown, the chief Indian settlement, on the Wabash River near the mouth of Tippecanoe Creek. There, on November 7, after repelling an Indian attack, his men destroyed the town. The Battle of Tippecanoe marked the beginning of a long and savage Indian war and was directly related to the American declaration of war on Great Britain.

In his war message Madison expressed an opinion held by the majority of Westerners: that the Indians had been receiving arms and encouragement from the British in Canada. Some of the young militants, though lacking evidence, were certain of it. "I can have no doubt of the influence of British agents in keeping up Indian hostility" and of encouraging them "to murder our citizens," cried Richard M. Johnson of Kentucky. Felix Grundy of Tennessee agreed, adding, moreover, that there would be no peace on the frontier until the British were driven out of Canada. "We shall drive the British from our continent," Grundy affirmed; "they will no longer have an opportunity of intriguing with our Indian neighbors. . . . That nation will lose her Canadian trade, and, by having no

Tecumseh: Shawnee chief

resting place in this country, her means of annoying us will be diminished.'' To Westerners, the rich lands of Upper Canada were not the least of the prizes to be won in a successful war with the British. To Southerners the conquest of East and West Florida, still in the possession of Spain, Great Britain's ally, might well be another reward of a war policy. The Floridas contained fertile cotton lands, and through them flowed the navigable rivers of the Mississippi Territory. As early as 1810, Madison, in collusion with American settlers, had seized a portion of West Florida; but nothing short of the whole of the Floridas would now satisfy the expansionists. This ''agrarian cupidity,'' as John Randolph called it, was not in itself a sufficient force to precipitate a conflict with Great Britain, but it was a common characteristic among those who voted for war.

In a letter summarizing the causes of the war, Andrew Jackson mentioned neutral rights, impressment, national vindication, Indian pacification, and the desire for territorial conquest. He then condensed all these motives into two phrases: ''to seek some indemnity for past injuries, some security against future aggression.'' Jackson seems to have reflected the sentiment of the majority in the Southern and Western states, and in the presidential election of 1812 they, along with Pennsylvania and Vermont, endorsed the war policy by giving their electoral votes to Madison. De Witt Clinton of New York, the candidate of the Federalists and Peace Republicans, carried the rest of the New England and Middle Atlantic states.

Madison's rather narrow margin in the Electoral College (128 to 89—the shift of one state, Pennsylvania, could have changed the result), together with the bitter resentment of the commerical centers, meant that the country went to war dangerously divided. No patriot, wrote a Boston editor, ''conceives it his duty to shed his blood for Bonaparte, for Madison or Jefferson, and that Host of Ruffians in Congress.'' The revitalized New England Federalists wanted no part of ''Mr. Madison's war.''

The War of 1812

National unpreparedness. The prowar Republicans were convinced that the war could be won with little effort and a minimum of sacrifice. Henry Clay announced that ''the militia of Kentucky alone are competent to place Montreal and Upper Canada at your feet.'' His friends in Congress must have believed him, for they led into war a country that was not only internally divided but hopelessly unprepared. As war approached, the Madison Administration loyally adhered to Jefferson's policy of relying on small gunboats and continued to neglect the regular navy; even in his message to Congress of November 1811 Madison made no recommendation for naval expansion. The following January two-thirds of the representatives who were to vote for war five months later helped to defeat a modest proposal to add ten frigates to the navy. During the debate on this measure, Richard M. Johnson of Kentucky, one of the young militants, vowed that he would not vote a penny for a naval force ''destined to entail upon this happy Government perpetual taxes and a perpetually increasing public debt.''

Congress made no effort to increase American naval power until months after the outbreak of war, and the new forty-four-gun frigates and seventy-four-gun ships of the line then provided for were not ready for action until the war had ended. Indeed the United States had an ocean-going navy of only sixteen vessels fit for service with which to challenge the world's foremost sea power, whose warships numbered in the hundreds. The American navy had the advantage of a talented, well-trained group of officers but suffered from a serious shortage of experienced seamen. It had no real fleet organization, each ship operating more or less as an independent unit. Moreover, since most of the ships were expected to function as commerce-raiders, the question of naval strategy seemed superfluous.

But the Republican majority, after all, was thinking primarily of a land war, not of challenging Britain's naval supremacy. With Florida weakly defended, with fewer than 5,000 British troops in Canada, and with war raging in Europe, the odds seemed to favor the Americans. Had the United States trained, equipped, and put in the field an army of only 50,000 men—no serious strain on the country's resources—it might have conquered Canada and Florida with relative ease. Congressional action seemed adequate enough: it

The War of 1812: Northern campaigns,
1812–14

authorized an expansion of the small regular army by the recruitment of 25,000 five-year volunteers; provided for the raising of an additional 50,000 one-year volunteers; and made repeated calls on the state militias, which numbered, on paper, some 700,000 men.

Even in the regions most enthusiastic for war, however, Americans were reluctant to abandon their civilian pursuits; neither coercion nor persuasion, such as offers of cash bounties and land grants, had much effect. Never during the war did the army number more than 35,000 men, and even this small force was poorly trained and unimaginatively commanded by over-age veterans of the Revolution and incompetent militia officers. Militiamen, moreover, generally felt that their duty was limited to state defense, and some refused to leave their states for operations across the frontier.

Congress, including those who had voted for war, hesitated to adopt the fiscal measures demanded by a war policy. Eventually Congress doubled tariff rates and levied a new excise tax, a stamp tax, and a direct tax on the states, but these unpopular measures brought the government little revenue until near the end of the war. It authorized loans, but the Treasury Department managed to market the bulk of about $80 million in securities only at a discount and at high interest rates. Since most New England capitalists opposed the war, and since the Bank of the United States had been abolished in 1811, Secretary of the Treasury Gallatin had to rely

on state banks, which were poorly equipped to handle business of this sort. In short, the whole configuration of Republican policy over the past decade had been designed for a simple agricultural nation at peace with the world; now Republicans, in effect, attempted to apply Jeffersonian means to a non-Jeffersonian end. In so doing, they barely escaped national disaster.

The military campaigns. Plans for the conquest of Canada (which Southern Republicans, incidentally, had never viewed with much enthusiasm) ended in a complete fiasco. Effective strategy called for a concentration of forces in an attack on Montreal, whose fall would have cut British communications along the St. Lawrence and the Great Lakes and made the British position in Upper Canada untenable. But, in response to the Western demand for protection from Tecumseh's Indian confederation, the nation's forces were diffused. As a result, the military campaign of 1812 was a feeble, poorly planned, uncoordinated attempt to invade Canada at three separate points. General William Hull marched an army from Detroit toward the British garrison at Malden. But, doubting the wisdom of an invasion before winning control of Lake Erie, and hearing that Tecumseh and his warriors had joined the British, Hull soon lost his nerve and returned to Detroit. There, on August 6, a brilliant British commander, General Isaac Brock, surrounded Hull's army and forced him to surrender without firing a shot. A second invasion across the Niagara River culminated in defeat and surrender when New York militiamen refused to enter Canada to reinforce their countrymen. Finally, General Henry Dearborn led an advance along Lake Champlain toward Montreal. When he reached the Canadian border he found that his militiamen would not cross it and was obliged to march back to Plattsburg. So ended the land campaigns of 1812. If they had made no conquests and won no glory, at least they had cost few lives.

Things went little better the next year. Canadians astonished their would-be "liberators" by vigorously supporting British efforts to drive the invaders out. Two events, however, enabled the Americans to recover lost ground on the Northwest frontier and all but eliminate the danger of another British offensive there. The first was Captain Oliver Hazard Perry's notable victory at Put-in-Bay on Lake

"We have met the enemy": battle on Lake Erie, 1813

Erie, September 10, 1813. When Perry reported, "We have met the enemy and they are ours," he gave the Americans control of the Great Lakes and made the British position at Detroit hopeless. The second event was General Harrison's victory over the retreating British at the Battle of the Thames, October 5, 1813. Here the great Indian leader Tecumseh was killed; with his death the Indian confederacy collapsed, and the Northwest frontier was secure. But the conquest of Canada was as remote as ever.

By 1814 the Americans were striving desperately to prevent the British from invading their land and, perhaps, taking a slice of it. With the defeat of Napoleon and his exile to Elba, the British were able for the first time to give their undivided attention to the American war and to send some of their best troops across the Atlantic. Their plan was to harass the cities on the Atlantic coast with amphibious operations while launching invasions at three points: Niagara, Lake Champlain, and New Orleans.

The most ambitious coastal attack was a thrust up Chesapeake Bay culminating in the capture of Washington on August 24. As the President and other Administration officials fled, the British burned the Capitol, the White House, and other public buildings. Having avenged an earlier American raid on York (Toronto) with this crowning humiliation, and failing in an attempt to capture Baltimore, the British withdrew. The military significance of the raid was negligible, but it underscored the utter failure of the Administration's war policy.

The British invasion plans, however, seriously miscarried, for by 1814 the Americans had found some vigorous young officers and no longer had to rely on untrained, undisciplined militia units. The projected British offensive at Niagara was thwarted by the aggressive operations of General Jacob Brown and his able young subordinate, Winfield Scott. The Battle of Lundy's Lane, near Niagara Falls, on July 25, was itself indecisive, but it ended the British invasion threat from that position. In August a powerful force of British veterans commanded by Sir George Prevost advanced toward Lake Champlain with the apparent purpose of cutting off the New England states from the rest of the Union. Early in September Prevost paused before the strong American fortifications at Plattsburg to await the outcome of a bitter duel between British and American flotillas on Lake Champlain. On September 11 Captain Thomas Macdonough's American fleet won a decisive victory, forcing Prevost to abandon his campaign and retire to Canada. Clearly, the war on the Canadian frontier had reached a stalemate.

The final campaign took place in the Southwest. Here Andrew Jackson of Tennessee, an authentic self-trained military genius, somehow managed to make soldiers out of militiamen and to furnish them with supplies. Jackson had already smashed the military power of the Southwestern Indians by defeating the Creeks at the Battle of Horseshoe Bend, on March 27, 1814, and had also forced them to cede some of their richest

Andrew Jackson:
"Hero of New Orleans"

Victory at New Orleans: occasion for capital rejoicing

lands in Mississippi Territory. Next he captured and destroyed Pensacola in Spanish Florida to prevent the British from using it as a base and then marched his army to New Orleans to meet the invaders. Placing his men behind earthworks and bales of cotton, he awaited the attack of eight thousand seasoned British troops commanded by Sir Edward Pakenham. Contemptuous of Jackson's motley army of militiamen, sailors, and pirates, Pakenham, on January 8, 1815, led his men in tight formation in a rash frontal assault. American rifles and artillery raked the

The War of 1812: Southwestern campaigns, 1813–15

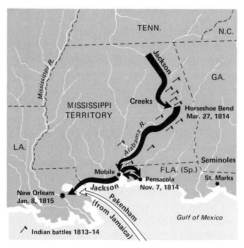

British columns with a deadly fire. Before the British withdrew, the Americans had killed the British commander and inflicted more than two thousand casualties, while suffering little more than a dozen of their own. The Battle of New Orleans was the last engagement of the war—in fact, it was fought two weeks after a treaty of peace had been signed. But it helped sweeten the bitter taste of the defeats and disappointments of the previous two and a half years, and it launched Andrew Jackson, the Hero of New Orleans, on his dazzling career.

On the high seas in the early months of the war the tiny American navy won a series of stunning victories in single-ship engagements, bolstering public morale during the disasters on the Canadian frontier. The most spectacular of these victories were those of the American frigate *Constitution* (Old Ironsides) over the British frigates *Guerrière* and *Java*, and of the *United States* over the *Macedonian.* These successes shocked the British public, which had heard the American navy described as a "few fir-built frigates, manned by a handful of bastards and outlaws"; but they constituted no real challenge to British naval supremacy, nor did they have any great strategic significance.

By 1813 most of the American men-of-war were bottled up in their home ports by an effective British blockade, and by the end of

I would ask, sir, whether the supporters of these measures have well weighed the difficulties of their undertaking. Have they considered whether it will be found easy to execute laws which bear such marks of despotism on their front, and which will be so productive of every sort and degree of misery in their execution? For one, sir, I hesitate not to say that they cannot be executed.... The operation of measures thus unconstitutional and illegal ought to be prevented by a resort to other measures which are both constitutional and legal. It will be the solemn duty of the State Governments to protect their own authority over their own militia, and to interpose between their citizens and arbitrary power. These are among the objects for which the State Governments exist; and their highest obligations bind them to the preservation of their own rights and the liberties of their people....

In my opinion, sir, the sentiments of the free population of this country are greatly mistaken here. The nation is not yet in a temper to submit to conscription. The people have too fresh and strong a feeling of the blessings of civil liberty to be willing thus to surrender it. You may talk to them as much as you please, of the victory and glory to be obtained in the enemy's provinces; they will hold those objects in light estimation if the means be a forced military service.

From Daniel Webster, Speech in the House of Representatives, December 9, 1814.

Daniel Webster on conscription and federal tyranny

---

the war only the *Constitution* and a few smaller vessels were still at sea. American cruisers and privateers continued to prey on British commerce and altogether captured more than a thousand merchantmen. These commerce-raiders were a costly annoyance to the British but fell far short of seriously crippling her overseas trade or disrupting her economy. The decisive fact of the naval war was the British blockade of the American coast, which dealt an almost mortal blow to the American carrying trade. In 1814 exports and imports fell to less than 10 percent of what they had been in the peak year of 1807. Flour exports declined from 1,443,000 barrels in 1812 to 193,000 barrels in 1814. The blockade was equally disastrous to American interstate commerce, most of which still moved along coastal waterways. Francis Wayland described the devastating impact of the blockade on the whole economy: "Our harbors were blockaded; communications coastwise between our ports were cut off; our ships were rotting in every creek and cove where they could find a place of security; our immense annual products were mouldering in our warehouses; the sources of profitable labor were dried up." If the land war was a stalemate, the war on the high seas culminated in a British victory that was well-nigh complete. Floating in the wreckage was Jefferson's gunboat policy.

Disaffection in New England. These disasters were what antiwar Federalists in the Northeast had anticipated—what Josiah Quincy of Massachusetts had in mind when he said, "This war, the measures which preceded it, and the mode of carrying it on, are all undeniably southern and western policy, not the policy of the commercial states." Feeling betrayed by their own government, convinced that the Madison Administration had deliberately set about to destroy their political and economic power, New England Federalists throughout the war regarded the Republican politicians in Washington, not the British, as their mortal enemies. And, having regained political control of all the New England states, they were in a position to translate their angry polemics into defiant deeds.

Federalist governors contested federal calls on the state militias, insisting that their proper function was to repel invasion, not to invade foreign territory. Federalists discouraged voluntary enlistments; and when Congress debated a militia draft they defended state sovereignty against national tyranny. "Where is it written in the Constitution," asked Daniel Webster, a young Federalist congressman from New Hampshire, "that you may take children from their parents, and parents from their children, and compel them to fight the battles of any war in which the folly or the wickedness of government may engage it?"

Josiah Quincy: he felt betrayed

THE WAR OF 1812   **177**

The Hartford Convention or *LEAP NO LEAP.*

Federalists resisted tax measures and boycotted government loans. According to a Boston editor, "any man who lends money to the government at the present time will forfeit all claim to common honesty." Meanwhile, New Englanders defiantly continued to trade with Canada and even furnished supplies to the British fleet. The more extreme dissenters, especially the ardent Federalists of the Connecticut River Valley, favored either a separate peace and the withdrawal of New England from the war or else secession from the Union.

In 1814 British depredations along the New England coast and the belief that the federal government would do nothing to check them precipitated a serious political crisis. In October the Massachusetts legislature called for a convention of the New England states to prepare an adequate defense against invasion and to consider amendments to the federal Constitution. The call asserted that in the existing Union the "Eastern sections" had not obtained "those equal rights and benefits which are the greatest objects of its formation." Twenty-six delegates—twelve from Massachusetts, seven from Connecticut, four from Rhode Island, and three from Vermont—assembled in Hartford on December 15 and deliberated secretly for nearly three weeks. Federalist extremists, such as Timothy Pickering, were not among the delegates; the moderates, led by Harrison Gray Otis of Massachusetts, gained control and adopted a final report that was relatively mild.

The report, much of which dealt with the problem of defending the New England coast, began with a gloomy account of the evils the country had endured under the "withering influence" of the Republicans. The Jeffersonians, it claimed, had debauched the civil service; destroyed "the balance of power which existed among the original states" by creating new Western states; and entertained a "visionary and superficial theory in regard to commerce, accompanied by a real hatred but a feigned regard to its interests." As a remedy for these grievances the Hartford report demanded a series of constitutional amendments abolishing the three-fifths compromise, requiring a two-thirds vote of both houses of Congress to declare war and to admit new states, prohibiting embargoes lasting for more than sixty days, excluding the foreign born from federal offices, limiting the President to one term, and prohibiting the election of two successive Presidents from the same state. If these demands were ignored and the war continued, the report recommended that another convention be called and given "such powers and instructions as the exigency of a crisis so momentous may require."

When representatives from the Hartford Convention arrived in Washington with their ultimatum, they found the capital rejoicing over Jackson's victory at New Orleans and over the signing of a treaty of peace. Under the circumstances their complaints seemed pointless, and their demands were ignored. But the Hartford Convention was remembered; to nationalists it symbolized the disloyalty, the narrow, selfish provincialism, of the Federalists. Consequently, the Federalist party, though for a time retaining strength in several New England states, was itself one of the casualties of the War of 1812.

Oddly enough, New England, in spite of her political disaffection, was the only region that profited materially from the war. Since the British blockade was not enforced along her coast until 1814, she received the bulk of foreign imports. Gold from the rest of the country flowed to her banks, which were thus able to maintain specie payments while other banks were forced to suspend payments. Above all, the war gave a strong impetus to New England manufacturing; between 1810 and 1814 the number of cotton spindles in the area increased sixfold. A war that was launched in part to acquire more land for the farmers and planters of the Northwest and South ended without an acre of new territory but with many thousands of spindles whirling in New England factories.

Peace negotiations

The Treaty of Ghent. Almost from the start of this curious conflict there had been talk of peace. As early as September 1812 the czar of Russia, anxious that the British give their full attention to Napoleon, offered to act as mediator. President Madison responded favorably and, early in 1813, sent Albert Gallatin and James A. Bayard to work with John Quincy Adams, the American ambassador in St. Petersburg. The British declined the Russian offer—Russia could not be trusted to support the British position on neutral rights—but soon indicated a willingness to negotiate directly with the Americans. This, too, was acceptable to Madison, though he did not hear of the suggestion until January 1814. He then appointed Henry Clay and Jonathan Russell to join the three commissioners already in Europe, and in August negotiations began in the city of Ghent.

The British diplomats, an unimpressive group, were under the strict control of the Foreign Office in London. The Americans, superior in talent, had received from their government broader powers and greater freedom to negotiate. But they found it difficult to agree among themselves on matters of policy, and during the tedious months of negotiation their personal relations sometimes became tense. Adams' colleagues found him an irritating companion, and Adams, in turn, took a dim view of them, especially of Clay with his taste for cards and late hours. "They sit after dinner and drink bad wine and smoke cigars, which neither suits my habits nor my health, and absorbs time which I cannot spare," wrote the austere new Englander. Gallatin turned out to be the chief peacemaker in dealings not only with the British but with his own colleagues.

Had the two delegations adhered to their initial instructions, the negotiations would have been brief and the result complete failure. The Americans were to insist that the British abandon impressment, agree to respect international law in setting up blockades, and pay indemnity for their illegal seizure of American ships. The British, anticipating decisive military victories in the campaigns of 1814, presented a list of terms that would have jeopardized the sovereignty and future growth of the United States. They demanded territorial cessions in northern New York and Maine, the surrender of American control of the Great Lakes, the creation of an autonomous Indian buffer state south of the Great Lakes, the right to navigate the Mississippi River, and the relinquishment of American fishing rights off the coasts of Newfoundland and Labrador. The Americans made it clear that if the British insisted on these terms the war would continue. "Our negotiations may be considered at an end," wrote Gallatin to his government.

But the British did not insist. News of Macdonough's victory on Lake Champlain and Prevost's retreat from Plattsburg drastically changed the military picture, and the Duke of Wellington, when consulted by the British ministry, argued that failure to gain control of the Great Lakes made the British demands unreasonable. "I confess," he said, "that I think you have no right, from the state of the war, to demand any concession of territory from America." British merchants and manufacturers, eager to resume trade with the United States, favored an end to hostilities. The tax-burdened British public, too, had had enough of war.

As negotiations proceeded, the diplomats dropped one demand after another and eventually agreed to a peace treaty that settled nothing but simply restored the status quo antebellum. The Treaty of Ghent, signed on December 24, 1814, was silent on impressment and neutral rights, boundaries and fisheries, trade and indemnities—although it referred some of these questions to joint commissions for future settlement. In submitting the treaty to the Senate for ratification, Madison claimed no victory. "The late war," he said with more than a little ambiguity, "has been waged with a success which is the natural result of the wisdom of the legislative councils, of the patriotism of the people, of the public spirit of the militia, and of the valor of the military and naval forces of the country." As Adams described the document, "Nothing was adjusted, nothing was settled—nothing in substance but an indefinite suspension of hostilities was agreed to." Clay, though he signed it, described it as a "damned bad treaty."

Nevertheless, Americans looked back on the war with pride and satisfaction. They ignored the fact that the British had yielded nothing on neutral rights or impressment, because these issues lost their significance when the war ended in Europe. In the selective memo-

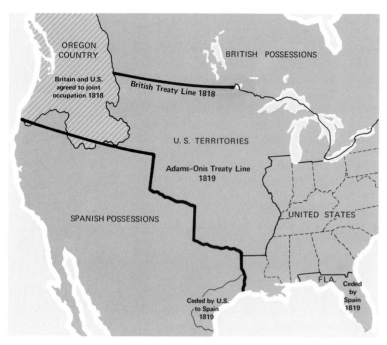

Boundary treaties, 1818–19

ries of patriots the military defeats, the bungling of the Canadian campaigns, and British supremacy on the high seas faded into insignificance; the early exploits of American frigates and privateers, Perry's victory on Lake Erie, and, best of all, Jackson's victory at New Orleans were remembered vividly as the crucial events of the war. The very fact that no territory had been lost—that the British had abandoned their extreme demands—contributed to this myth of military success. Moreover, the death of Tecumseh, the collapse of the Indian confederation, and the destruction of Indian military power east of the Mississippi meant that at least one purpose of the war had been fully achieved. Finally, the rise of manufacturing made the country more self-sufficient, and the preservation of their threatened independence gave the Americans a greater feeling of national identity than ever before. As Gallatin observed: "The war has renewed and reinstated the national feelings and character which the Revolution had given. . . . The people now have more general objects of attachment. . . . They are more Americans; they feel and act more as a nation."

Postwar settlements. Though memories of the war were to keep alive an undercurrent

of Anglo-American hostility for many years, several specific issues that might have caused trouble were resolved soon after the stalemate at Ghent. In 1815 a commercial treaty removed most of the restrictions on Anglo-American trade (except with the British West Indies). An agreement of 1817, signed by Richard Rush, the acting Secretary of State, and Charles Bagot, the British minister, provided for naval disarmament on the Great Lakes. Though either side could terminate it on six months' notice, the Rush-Bagot Agreement became a permanent policy and eventually was applied to the land frontier as well. Another agreement the following year reopened the coasts of Newfoundland and Labrador to American fishermen, established the forty-ninth parallel as the northern boundary of the Louisiana Purchase from the Lake of the Woods to the Rocky Mountains, and provided for a joint occupation of Oregon for the next ten years. Neither the British nor the Americans could have guessed it then, but these postwar negotiations, rather than the War of 1812, were to set the pattern for subsequent Anglo-American relations.

Another long-standing source of diplomatic friction was removed when Spain finally agreed to give up the Floridas. Internally weak and rapidly losing her once great empire in South and Central America, Spain maintained only a tenuous hold on the Floridas. Her feeble garrison was unable to control the Seminole Indians or to prevent white outlaws and runaway slaves from using the region as a sanctuary. In 1818 Andrew Jackson, giving the broadest possible interpretation to vague instructions from his government, led a military force into the Floridas to punish the Seminoles for depredations along the American frontier. In the process he seized St. Marks and Pensacola, deposed the Spanish governor, and raised the American flag; he also arrested two British subjects for inciting the Indians, tried them by court-martial, and executed them. At home Jackson's highhanded conduct added to his popularity, but it immensely complicated matters for Secretary of State John Quincy Adams, who had been negotiating with the Spanish minister, Luis de Onís.

Making the best of a bad situation, Adams brazened his way through. He not only refused to apologize for Jackson's behavior but threw responsibility on the Spanish for failing to preserve order in the Floridas. Spain, he insisted, must either govern the provinces efficiently or cede them to the United States, for they had become "a derelict, open to the occupancy of every enemy, civilized or savage, of the United States, and serving no other earthly purpose than as a post of annoyance to them." This was a challenge that the Spanish were in no position to accept, and in 1819 the Adams-Onís Treaty arranged for the transfer of the Floridas to the United States. In exchange, the American government agreed to assume payment of $5 million worth of claims that American citizens held against the Spanish government. The treaty also drew a boundary between the Louisiana Territory and Spanish possessions in the Southwest. The line followed the Sabine, Red, and Arkansas rivers to the Rocky Mountains, then the forty-second parallel west to the Pa-

cific. Thus the United States gave up her claim to Texas (as part of the Louisiana Purchase) and Spain her claim to territory in the Pacific Northwest. Ratification of the treaty was delayed for two years, but in 1821, Jackson triumphantly reentered the Florida Territory as the first American governor.

Those who had moral sensibilities about the rough tactics of Jackson and Adams soothed their consciences with the argument that since the Floridas were contiguous to American territory, Providence intended that America should have them. A later generation would call this argument "Manifest Destiny." Even so, the age of the Jeffersonians, who believed in man's reason and disliked the cynicism of the Old World, was closing on a slightly sour note.

JEFFERSON IN POWER

Suggestions for reading

Jefferson's political philosophy has had an enduring influence on American thought; it is analyzed sympathetically in C. M. Wiltse, *The Jeffersonian Tradition in American Democracy** (1935), and Adrienne Koch, *The Philosophy of Thomas Jefferson** (1943). How it has been interpreted and used by subsequent generations is explained in Merrill Peterson, *The Jefferson Image in the American Mind** (1960). The best completed biographies of Jefferson are Nathan Schachner, *Thomas Jefferson: A Biography,* 2 vols. (1951), and Merrill Peterson, *Thomas Jefferson and the New Nation: A Biography* (1970). Dumas Malone, *Jefferson the President: First Term, 1801–1805* (1970), is part of an authoritative multivolume biography not yet completed. The contributions of Jefferson's two ablest lieutenants can be studied in three works of genuine distinction: Adrienne Koch, *Jefferson and Madison: The Great Collaboration** (1950), Irving Brant, *James Madison: Secretary of State, 1800–1809* (1953), and Raymond Walters, Jr., *Albert Gallatin: Jeffersonian Financier and Diplomat** (1957). Ralph Ketcham, *James Madison* (1971), is a good sympathetic one-volume biography.

The best and most comprehensive survey of the Republican era is Marshall Smelser, *The Democratic Republic, 1801–1815** (1968). Three brief, well-written surveys are also useful: Marcus Cunliffe, *The Nation Takes Shape, 1789–1837** (1959), C. M. Wiltse, *The New Nation, 1800–1845** (1961), and Morton Borden, *Parties and Politics in the Early Republic, 1789–1815** (1967). An older analysis that is a classic, in spite of its hostility to Jefferson and Madison, is Henry Adams, *History of the United States of America During the Administrations of Jefferson and Madison,* 9 vols.* (1889–91). Two excellent accounts of the party battles and Republican party organization are W. N. Chambers, *Political Parties in a New Nation, 1776–1809** (1963), and Noble Cunningham, *The Jeffersonian Republicans in Power: Party Operations, 1801–1809* (1963). Richard Hofstadter, *The Idea of a Party System* (1969), is a lucid essay on the beginnings of two-party politics in America. The role of the Federalist opposition is traced in D. H. Fischer, *The Revolution of American Conservatism: The Federalist Party in the Era of Jeffersonian Democracy** (1965). L. K. Kerber, *Federalist in Dissent: Imagery and Ideology in Jeffersonian America* (1970), is a study of Federalist political and social thought. L. D. White, *The Jeffersonians: A Study in Administrative History, 1801–1829** (1951), is an expert analysis of Republican administrative organization. J. S. Young, *The Washington Community, 1800–1828* (1966), stresses the failure of the Jeffersonians, because of certain negative attitudes, to develop an effective federal government. Alexander Balinky, *Albert Gallatin: Fiscal Theories and Policy* (1958), is a sharply critical evaluation of Jeffersonian finance.

*Available in a paperback edition.

John Randolph and other conservative Republicans are studied in N. K. Risjord, *The Old Republicans: Southern Conservatism in the Age of Jefferson* (1965). The case for Aaron Burr is presented in Nathan Schachner, *Aaron Burr: A Biography** (1937); the case against him, in T. P. Abernethy, *The Burr Conspiracy* (1954).

FOREIGN POLICY AND THE WAR OF 1812

Two useful works on the Louisiana Purchase are E. W. Lyon, *Louisiana in French Diplomacy, 1759–1804* (1934), and A. P. Whitaker, *The Mississippi Question* (1934). The best account of the conflict with the Barbary pirates is R. W. Irwin, *Diplomatic Relations of the United States and the Barbary Powers* (1931).

Several excellent works are available on the problems of American neutrality. A good place to begin is with Irving Brant's study of Madison as Secretary of State, mentioned above, and with the same author's *James Madison: The President, 1809–1812* (1956). Brant's multivolume biography of Madison is now available in a one-volume abridged edition, *The Fourth President: A Life of James Madison* (1970). Outstanding monographs include W. W. Jennings, *The American Embargo* (1921); J. F. Zimmerman, *Impressment of American Seamen* (1925); L. M. Sears, *Jefferson and the Embargo* (1927); Harry Bernstein, *Origins of Inter-American Interest, 1700–1812* (1945); and Bradford Perkins, *First Rapprochement: England and the United States, 1795–1805* (1955).

Reginald Horsman, *Expansion and American Indian Policy, 1783–1812* (1967), is a fair account of a sordid chapter of American history. The same author's *The Frontier in the Formative Years, 1783–1815** (1970), an excellent work of synthesis, is especially valuable for conditions on the frontier in the years before the War of 1812.

The view that the War of 1812 was caused by Western and Southern expansionism and fear of the Indians is developed in J. W. Pratt, *Expansionists of 1812* (1925). The case for impressment and neutral rights as the fundamental causes of the war is presented, with varying emphases, in A. L. Burt, *The United States, Great Britain, and British North America from the Revolution to the Peace after the War of 1812* (1940); Bradford Perkins, *Prologue to War: England and the United States, 1805–1812** (1961); and Reginald Horsman, *The Causes of the War of 1812** (1962). R. H. Brown, *The Republic in Peril: 1812* (1964), stresses the desire of Jeffersonians to defend Republican institutions as a force leading to war. The careers of two militant young Republicans can be studied in Bernard Mayo, *Henry Clay, Spokesman of the New West* (1937), and C. M. Wiltse, *John C. Calhoun: Nationalist, 1782–1828* (1944).

Irving Brant, *James Madison: Commander in Chief, 1812–1836* (1961), strongly defends the President's wartime leadership. The best general account of the war is F. F. Beirne, *The War of 1812* (1949). Two good brief surveys are H. L. Coles, *The War of 1812** (1965), and Reginald Horsman, *The War of 1812* (1969). Marquis James, *Andrew Jackson, Vol. I: The Border Captain** (1933), gives an absorbing account of the campaigns in the Southwest. Federalist disaffection is treated perceptively in George Dangerfield, *The Era of Good Feelings** (1952); James M. Banner, *To the Hartford Convention* (1970); and S. E. Morison, *Harrison Gray Otis, 1765–1848: The Urbane Federalist* (1969). An excellent analysis of the peace negotiations is in S. F. Bemis, *John Quincy Adams and the Foundations of American Foreign Policy* (1949).

*Available in a paperback edition.

8

Nationalism and economic expansion

One might have expected the prowar Republicans to be discredited by their failure to capture Canada and their general mishandling of military affairs. But at the end of the War of 1812 the Republican party was still firmly in power. Though the record of Madison's wartime Administration was less than brilliant, the country was still intact, and the people were prospering. Southern planters were regaining their European markets, and a growing number of Western farmers were taking advantage of cheaper transportation to send their agricultural surpluses to markets in the South, the Northeast, and overseas. Farm-commodity prices were good, and land values were rising. Settlers were swarming into the West, and within a few years after the Treaty of Ghent five new states—Indiana (1816), Mississippi (1817), Illinois (1818), Alabama (1819), and Missouri (1821)—entered the Union. A new economic interest, manufacturing, was growing in importance and striving to expand at the rate it had achieved during the wartime dearth of British goods. Shipping, though it would never again dominate the economy of the Northeastern maritime states as it once had, was gradually recovering from blows the embargo and the war had dealt.

This vast land, with its burgeoning economy and its optimistic, nationalistic people ($9\frac{1}{2}$ million of them by 1820), was no longer the plain, uncomplicated republic that Jefferson, in theory at least, had once so much admired. Jefferson's party was changing with the country and now counted manufacturers, factory workers, and other urban groups, as well as farmers and planters, among those it had to serve. Henry Clay, John C. Calhoun, and John Quincy Adams were impatient with the old-fashioned Virginia Republicans' emphasis on constitutionalism, state rights, and agrarianism. They had a vision of national growth, economic expansion, and social progress that required a more dynamic federal government pursuing more positive and imaginative policies than had been contemplated in traditional Republican philosophy. In fighting their political battles, postwar Republicans still used Jeffersonian rhetoric, but the old creed had lost much of its substance. In 1801 Jefferson's remark that ''We are all Republicans, we are all Federalists'' was only a loose figure of speech; in 1816 it was almost a fact.

New states, 1812–21

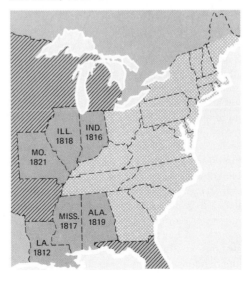

The triumph of neo-Federalism

The American System. Circumstances had forced Madison, like Jefferson, time after time to compromise traditional Republicanism. In his seventh annual message to Congress, December 5, 1815, Madison's surrender to the nationalists was well-nigh complete; Hamilton himself could hardly have composed a message that embraced orthodox Federalist doctrine more fully. In the name of national defense, Madison urged an expansion of the navy, a reorganization of the militia, and an enlargement of the Military Academy at West Point. Without a blush he recommended federal assumption of certain state debts incurred for militia expenses during the recent war. To establish a uniform national currency, he suggested that "a national bank will merit consideration." A federal tariff should provide industry with the protection that "is due to the enterprising citizens whose intersts are now at stake." Finally, Madison urged Congress to finance such internal improvements as required "a national jurisdiction and national means," thus "binding more closely together the various parts of our extended confederacy."

Congressional leaders had few qualms about this program of neo-Federalism, and Henry Clay soon labeled it the "American System." The prewar economy, Clay and his supporters thought, had depended too much on the exchange of American raw materials for European manufactured goods, a dependence that exposed it to the whims of other powers and made it the victim of every international crisis. "Dame Commerce," said Clay, "is a flirting, flippant, noisy Jade and if we are governed by her fantasies, we shall never put off the muslins of India and the cloths of Europe." Hence the foundation of Clay's American System was a protective tariff to stimulate domestic manufacturing and to create an enlarged domestic market for the agricultural products of the South and West. Internal improvements, financed with tariff revenues, would encourage interstate commerce; and a national bank would provide banknote currency of uniform value to facilitate an expanding volume of business transactions, as well as the short-term credits required for economic growth. This nationalistic program, Clay believed, would bring to all sections of the country both prosperity and independence from the outside world.

". . . put off the muslins of India and the cloths of Europe"

The Tariff of 1816. The first postwar Congress, one of the most fruitful of the nineteenth century, took long strides toward Clay's goal of an American System. By 1816 the Republican party numbered in its ranks a large cluster of interest groups, both urban and rural, clamoring for protective duties on certain foreign goods entering the American market. Leading the protectionists were those who had invested in New England textile mills and Pennsylvania iron-smelters when the embargo and war had choked off European supplies. Seconding them were the hemp-growers of Kentucky, the wool-growers of Ohio and Vermont, and an assortment of Southerners and Westerners who hoped either to promote industry or to expand their domestic market behind a tariff wall.

The cries of the protectionists increased when British exporters, seeking to dispose of surpluses accumulated during the war and to drive competing American manufacturers out of business, flooded the American market with low-priced goods. A member of Parliament suggested that British goods might even be sold at a loss for a time, in order "to stifle in the cradle, those rising manufactures in the United States, which war has forced into existence, contrary to the natural course of things." In the critical years immediately following the war, British competition forced many small, less efficient American manufacturers to close their doors. Protectionists claimed that the British were plotting to wreck the American economy and asserted that a higher tariff was essential for national economic survival. America's "infant industries" were fragile things, they said, requiring the tender care of the federal government while they matured.

Congress responded with the Tariff of 1816, an act that raised duties to an average of 20 percent to meet the need for increased revenues and the demand for greater protection. In the House the Western and Middle Atlantic states gave the bill overwhelming support; New England divided seventeen to ten for it, the South twenty-three to thirty-four against. Webster and other Federalists, speaking for the shipping interests, opposed higher duties as an obstacle to foreign trade; John Randolph, like most Southerners, vowed that he would not "agree to lay a duty on the cultivator of the soil to encourage exotic manufactures.'' On the other hand, Calhoun, the South Carolina nationalist, hoped that the manufacturing interest would ''at all times, and under every policy . . . be protected with due care.'' In 1816 a considerable minority in the South shared Calhoun's point of view; within a few years, as conditions and expectations changed, Southern support for the tariff—and for the American System in general—almost vanished.

The second Bank of the United States.

Republican leaders, chastened by their fiscal experiences during the war, made their most dramatic surrender to Federalism when they revived both Hamilton's plan and his arguments for a national bank. When the first Bank of the United States perished in 1811, its business had fallen to the state-chartered banks; within five years the number of these banks had increased from 88 to 246, their issues of bank notes from $28 million to $68 million. Since most state-chartered banks did not maintain adequate specie reserves (gold and silver), their notes usually circulated at a discount. The bewildering variety of notes, their fluctuating value, and an epidemic of counterfeiting brought the country to the edge of fiscal chaos. The final blow came when the state banks, except those in New England, suspended specie payments altogether during the war—and showed no disposition to resume specie payments with the restoration of peace.

Meanwhile, the federal government lacked a safe depository for its funds, a reliable agency to transfer them from place to place, and adequate machinery to market securities when it needed to borrow. The absence of a uniform paper currency was a severe handicap to businessmen engaged in interstate commerce. Even some of the old Republican agrarians, though they opposed all banks that issued paper currency, favored chartering a new national bank as the lesser of two evils. Madison discarded his constitutional doubts and decided that the question had been settled ''by repeated recognitions . . . of the validity of such an institution, in acts of the legislative, executive, and judicial branches of the government, accompanied by . . . a concurrence of the general will of the nation.'' Changed circumstances, he concluded, required measures ''which may be as proper now as they were premature and suspicious when urged by the champions of federalism.''

Calhoun, taking a thoroughly nationalistic position, attacked the state banks for usurping the federal government's exclusive power to issue and regulate the country's currency. Clay, who had opposed rechartering the first Bank, confessed that he had not anticipated the evils its demise had caused.

In 1816 a bill to grant a twenty-year charter to a second Bank of the United States, with headquarters in Philadelphia, passed both houses of Congress over the opposition of state banking interests, Federalist partisans, and Virginia agrarians. The functions and structure of the second Bank were essentially the same as those of the first, except that its capital was increased from $10 million to $35 million and the number of its branches from eight to twenty-five. The federal government again held one-fifth of the stock, and the President appointed five of the twenty-five directors. Its liabilities were not to exceed its capital, one-fifth of which must be in specie; and it was to report annually to the Treasury Department and open its books for periodic inspection.

This powerful banking corporation could serve a number of useful purposes: it could assist the government in its fiscal business by helping to market federal securities and by providing a depository for federal funds; it could regulate the banknote currency of the state banks; and it could encourage business enterprise by providing a sound paper currency in national-bank notes and by making available short-term credits, principally to merchants. But as the largest capitalistic institution in the country, exercising immense power over the supply of money and credit, depending as it did upon the government for special favors, it was essential that the Bank be responsibly directed and that its operations be subjected to adequate federal control. Lacking these, it was bound to find itself in political trouble, for it would then loom as a threat to democracy and an instrument of economic tyranny. Indeed, even under the best of circumstances, the Bank, because of its size and strength, was always a tempting political target.

Internal improvements.

The War of 1812, by disrupting coastal shipping, had demonstrated the inadequacy of the country's internal transportation system for both interstate commerce and national defense. The West, where high transportation costs still deprived

Henry Clay: nationalist

Along the National Road

many farmers of outside markets and tied them to an economy of pioneer self-sufficiency, was the most persistent solicitor of federal funds for internal improvements. New England, suffering a loss of population and a decline of political strength, was the center of opposition. President Madison, stretching his constitutional scruples to support projects that were national in scope, approved appropriations for the continued building of the National Road to Wheeling, which had been started during Jefferson's Administration. But he doubted that Congress had the power to subsidize local roads and canals without an appropriate amendment to the Constitution. In 1817 Congress ignored his doubts and passed a bill to distribute among the states for local internal improvements a $1,500,000 bonus that the Bank of the United States had paid the government for its charter. For Madison this was going too far, and in one of his last presidential acts he vetoed the so-called Bonus Bill. Calhoun, disgusted with this narrow view of things, grumbled that the Constitution "was not intended as a thesis for the logician to exercise his ingenuity on . . . it ought to be construed with plain good sense." But Madison's veto stalled this crucial phase of the American System. Local internal improvements remained, for the time being, the responsibility of the individual states and private enterprise.

The Era of Good Feelings.
Nearing the end of his second term, Madison supported another Virginian, his Secretary of State, James Monroe, to succeed him to the Presidency. The Randolph Republicans preferred William H. Crawford of Georgia, and some Northern Republicans fretted about the long domination of their party by the "Virginia Dynasty." But Madison had his way, and Monroe won an easy victory over his Federalist opponent, Rufus King of New York. Four years later, with the Federalists too feeble even to run a candidate, Monroe was reelected without opposition.* After a few more years of activity in scattered localities, the Federalist party was extinct. The party's war record, the failure of its older leaders to adjust to new conditions, its narrow particularism, and the Republican pirating of its program all contributed to its death. Thus the eighteenth-century ideal of a republic without political "factions" seemed to have been achieved at last. "Surely our government may go on and prosper without the existence of parties," wrote Monroe, who shared Jefferson's views of both the Federalists and the party system. "I have always considered their existence the curse of the country." In his first inaugural address, Monroe told his countrymen that they could rejoice when they reflected "how close our Government has approached to perfection; that in respect to it we have no essential improvement to make. . . ."

James Monroe, a representative of the small-planter class of the Virginia piedmont, reached the Presidency at the age of sixty-one after many years of devoted, though not bril-

*One elector from New Hampshire voted for John Quincy Adams.

liant, public service. Once the favorite of John Randolph and other Virginia state righters, Monroe continued to interpret the Constitution more narrowly than the nationalists in his party. He accepted the tariff and the banking legislation passed during Madison's last year in office, as well as the use of federal funds for internal improvements national in scope, but while he was President the American System made only limited progress. Though he was less talented than his distinguished predecessors, Monroe's contemporaries found something solid and reassuring in this member of the Revolutionary generation. In Monroe, with his wig, his cocked hat, and his knee-length pantaloons, the postwar generation had a last nostalgic look at the eighteenth century.

The year of Monroe's inauguration, 1817, found the country in a complaisant mood. On a good-will tour that ultimately carried him into once-hostile New England, the new President saw everywhere abundant signs of national unity. His warm reception in Boston caused the *Columbian Centinel,* a Federalist paper, to speak of an "Era of Good Feelings," thus giving a popular label to Monroe's Administrations. Political factionalism was at a low ebb, and there was relative harmony among the sections. Above all, as Monroe observed in his first message to Congress, the country was in a "prosperous and happy condition. . . . The abundant fruits of the earth have filled it with plenty." The "Era of Good Feelings" lasted, however, only about two years—until the middle of Monroe's first Administration—when political strife and sectional bitterness suddenly revived, and the national prosperity came to an abrupt and shocking end.

James Monroe: a last nostalgic look

John Marshall and the Supreme Court

Marshall's role. In these postwar years still another Virginian played a key role in the formulation of public policy and in the molding of the American political structure. This was John Marshall, Chief Justice of the United States Supreme Court from 1801 to 1835, who gave the judicial branch of the government the prestige it had previously lacked and who, unlike most of his fellow Virginians, supported a relatively broad interpretation of federal power in the interest of national supremacy. Born in 1755, Marshall saw military service during the Revolution and then went home to become one of the most successful lawyers before the Richmond bar. In 1792 Jefferson, already suspicious of Marshall's politics, suggested to Madison that Marshall ought to be appointed a judge to keep him out of mischief. As it turned out, Jefferson understood his man—Marshall became a Federalist—but he could scarcely have been more mistaken about how to render him harmless. After a term in Congress and brief service as John Adams' Secretary of State, Marshall received his appointment as Chief Justice shortly before the last Federalist President left office. The Supreme Court, at least, would remain in Federalist hands!

In personal appearance and social intercourse Marshall impressed one as a plain, homespun democrat, for he was the most unpretentious of men, an amiable lover of sports and other simple pleasures. But underneath he was a resolute Federalist, suspicious of popular government and contemptuous of what he considered Jefferson's sentimental trust in the people. Marshall was in no sense a scholar or philosopher of the law; he lacked the patience for intensive study and the imagination for metaphysical speculation. But he had a keen intelligence and a tough mind that readily discovered the logic of a case and swiftly drove to its core. According to Joseph Story, whom Madison made an Associate Justice in 1811, Marshall "examines the intricacies of a subject with calm and persevering circumspection and unravels its mysteries with irresistible acuteness." His personal magnetism and intellectual powers gave him enormous influence over his colleagues on the bench, including those appointed by Republicans. Marshall's domination of the Court is evident from the fact that during his thirty-four years as Chief Justice he wrote almost half the decisions and dissented from the majority opinion only eight times. Caring little for precedents, avoiding legal jargon, using crisp prose and careful reasoning, Marshall delivered a series of the most momentous decisions in American judicial history.

Judicial review. Soon after assuming his new office, Marshall found an opportunity to pronounce a vigorous and, in the long run, decisive opinion on a matter of prime importance to a federal system based on a written constitution. While the Federalists were in power there had been a persistent but inconclusive debate over who was to decide when Congress had exceeded its delegated powers or encroached upon the rights of the states. Since the Constitution is not explicit on this point, the answer had to be found by inference rather than from the plain language of the document. Probably the majority of delegates to the Constitutional Convention had expected the Supreme Court to pass on the constitutionality of the acts of Congress, and Hamilton, in one of the articles in *The Federalist,* had upheld the principle of judicial review. Jeffersonian Republicans, however, were later to argue that the federal government was the agent of the sovereign states and that those who had created it must define its powers. The individual states, said Jefferson in the Kentucky Resolutions of 1798, would decide when the Constitution had been violated, as well as "the mode and measure of redress."

This is where things stood when, in 1803, Marshall gave the Court's decision in the case of *Marbury* v. *Madison.* Intrinsically of minor importance, this case related to a section of the Judiciary Act of 1789 that, according to Marshall, expanded the Court's original jurisdiction beyond what the Constitution intended it to be. "The question whether an act repugnant to the constitution can become the law of the land, is a question deeply interesting to the United States," Marshall wrote. His answer to the question was clear: The wording of the Constitution establishes the principle "that a law repugnant to the constitution is void; and that courts, as well as other departments, are bound by that instrument." Moreover, "It is emphatically the province and duty of the judicial department to say what the law is. Those who apply the rule to particular cases must of necessity expound and interpret that rule."

Marbury v. *Madison* thus established a precedent for the Supreme Court to determine the constitutionality of congressional legislation and to act as the final authority on the meaning of the Constitution. This doctrine of judicial review has been challenged many times, but it has weathered all the storms and survives to this day. Having established the precedent, Marshall never again disallowed an act of Congress—more than a half-century passed before the Supreme Court exercised

this power again. But Marshall subsequently applied the positive side of judicial review—that is, he reviewed and *approved* congressional legislation as constitutional.

National supremacy. As a nationalist Marshall was inclined to give the powers of Congress a broad interpretation and to assert the federal government's supremacy over the states. For example, in two important cases, *Martin* v. *Hunter's Lessee* (1816) and *Cohens* v. *Virginia* (1821), the Marshall Court affirmed its right to review and reverse decisions of state courts when they concerned issues arising under the federal Constitution. On thirteen occasions it voided state laws as violations of "the supreme law of the land." One of the most significant of these cases, *Gibbons* v. *Ogden* (1824), involved a New York law giving a steamboat company a monopoly of the business of carrying passengers on the Hudson River to New York City. In rejecting the law Marshall gave the term "commerce" an extremely broad definition and came close to saying that the power of Congress over interstate commerce is absolute. This power, he ruled, "is complete in itself, may be exercised to its utmost extent, and acknowledges no limitations other than are prescribed in the constitution."

The Chief Justice expounded the nationalist doctrine most fully in the case of *McCulloch* v. *Maryland* (1819), which tested the constitutionality of the second Bank of the United States. Conceding that the Constitution does not explicitly grant Congress authority to charter a bank, Marshall insisted that Congress must have some discretion in exercising the powers it does possess. Surely the authority could be implied from the "necessary and proper" clause. Then Marshall made a classic statement of the doctrine of "loose construction": "Let the end be legitimate, let it be within the scope of the Constitution, and all means which are appropriate, which are plainly adapted to that end, which are not prohibited, but consist with the letter and spirit of the constitution, are constitutional." After this decision the nationalist advocates of the American System had no reason to anticipate any judicial obstacles to the development of their program.

Sanctity of contracts. As a conservative defender of property rights and a believer in laissez faire, Marshall also sought to make the

*[The Constitution] contains an enumeration of powers expressly
granted by the people to their government. It has been said that these
powers ought to be construed strictly. But why ought they to be so
construed? Is there one sentence in the constitution which gives
countenance to this rule? In the last of the enumerated powers, that
which grants, expressly, the means for carrying all others into execution, congress is authorized ''to make all laws which shall be necessary
and proper'' for the purpose.... What do gentlemen mean by a strict
construction? If they contend only against that enlarged construction
which would extend words beyond their natural and obvious import,
we ... should not controvert the principle. If they contend for that
narrow construction which, in support of some theory not to be found
in the constitution, would deny to the government those powers which
the words of the grant, as usually understood, import, and which are
consistent with the general views and objects of the instrument; for
that narrow construction, which would cripple the government, and
render it unequal to the objects for which it is declared to be instituted,
and to which the powers given, as fairly understood, render it competent; then we cannot perceive the propriety of this strict construction,
nor adopt it as the rule by which the constitution is to be expounded.*

From Gibbons v. Ogden, 9 Wheat. 1, 1824.

*If any one proposition could command the universal assent of mankind,
we might expect it would be this: that the government of the Union,
though limited in its powers, is supreme within its sphere of action.
This would seem to result necessarily from its nature. It is the government of all; its powers are delegated by all; it represents all, and acts
for all.... The nation, on those subjects on which it can act, must
necessarily bind its component parts. But this question is not left to
mere reason: the people have, in express terms, decided it, by saying,
''this constitution, and the laws of the United States, which shall be
made in pursuance thereof,'' ''shall be the supreme law of the land,''
and by requiring that the members of the State legislatures, and the
officers of the executive and judicial departments of the States, shall
take the oath of fidelity to it.*

*The government of the United States, then, though limited in its
powers, is supreme; and its laws, when made in pursuance of the
constitution, form the supreme law of the land, ''anything in the
constitution or laws of any State, to the contrary, notwithstanding.''*

From McCulloch v. Maryland, 4 Wheat. 316, 1819.

federal courts a sanctuary of the propertied
classes whenever they were harassed by unfriendly state legislatures. He sympathized
with creditors and entrepreneurs who considered contracts sacred and inviolable, and he
admired the clause in the Constitution that
prohibited states from ''impairing the obligation of contracts.'' In the case of *Fletcher* v.
Peck (1810), Marshall gave evidence of the
extremes to which he would go to defend this
principle. As we have seen (p. 166), the
Georgia legislature, in 1795, had granted a

large tract of Western land to the Yazoo Land
Companies. The following year a new legislature, discovering bribery and fraud, repudiated the grant and thus provoked litigation
that ultimately reached the Supreme Court. To
Marshall the case was perfectly clear: the
grant of land was a binding contract, and the
circumstances under which it was negotiated
did not concern the Court. The withdrawal of
the grant, therefore, was an unconstitutional
violation of the obligation of contract.

Another case, *Dartmouth College* v. *Wood-*

ward (1819), enabled Marshall to make an equally extreme application of the contract clause. The case originated in an attempt of the New Hampshire legislature to revise Dartmouth's charter, which dated back to colonial days, and to transform the college into a state institution. The trustees went to court and employed Daniel Webster, a Dartmouth alumnus, to represent them. Webster's sentimental plea in behalf of his alma mater brought tears to the eyes of the unsentimental Chief Justice, who ruled that a charter was a contract and could not be violated. Thereafter, to escape this restriction, the states usually wrote reserve clauses into corporation charters permitting subsequent amendment of the charters' terms.

Some old-line Republicans believed that Marshall's decisions had dealt "a deadly blow to the sovereignty of the states." Judge Spencer Roane of Virginia sent angry dissenting opinions to the newspapers, and John Taylor waged a pamphlet war against the Supreme Court. To Jefferson the federal justices were a "corps of sappers and miners" steadily undercutting the powers of the states. "The Constitution," he wrote, "is a mere thing of wax in the hands of the judiciary, which they may twist and shape into any form they please." Yet, except for Marshall's interpretation of the contract clause (which later courts have modified), there was little in these decisions that the dominant element in the postwar Republican party really cared to criticize. Giving his blessing to the nationalistic trend of Republican legislation, Marshall used the Constitution as a flexible instrument adaptable to conditions that the Founding Fathers could never have anticipated. If judicial review was a usurpation, no majority in Congress ever agreed on any alternative to it. As for Marshall's defense of property rights, the Republicans could hardly have been called enemies of property.

The Monroe Doctrine

Revolutions in Latin America. One of the most striking expressions of postwar American nationalism was in the field of foreign policy. While Spain was preoccupied with France during the Napoleonic wars, her South and Central American colonies had had a pleasant taste of freedom from her strict political and commercial control. Their appetite whetted, the colonies revolted and soon expelled the Portuguese from Brazil and the Spanish from all their American possessions save Cuba and Puerto Rico. When, in 1820, revolutions broke out in Spain and Portugal, all hope of recovering the lost colonies perished—unless other European powers could be induced to intervene.

To the people of the United States this was 1776 all over again. Henry Clay, a warm admirer of the Latin American patriots, rejoiced at "the glorious spectacle of eighteen millions of people, struggling to burst their chains and to be free." When a modest commerce developed with South America, Clay, optimistic about its further expansion, incorporated Pan-American trade into his American System. Both justice and self-interest, thought Clay, required quick recognition of the revolutionary governments.

After 1815 the State Department had pursued a policy of neutrality that recognized the revolutionists as belligerents and permitted them to purchase supplies in the United States; but a Neutrality Act of 1818 prohibited American citizens from serving in the rebel armies. Impatient with Secretary of State Adams' coolness toward the rebel cause, Clay introduced a resolution in the House giving the *de facto* governments of Latin America immediate recognition. The resolution alarmed Monroe and Adams, who feared that it would end the negotiations then in progress for the purchase of Florida or even lead to war. After the President and Secretary of State exerted their influence against the resolution, the House finally voted it down. Recognition came in 1822, after the Florida negotiations had been completed and after the new governments in South America had shown themselves capable of maintaining their independence. To Clay this recognition was disgracefully late, but the United States was nevertheless the first nation to grant it.

The fear of foreign intervention. Granting recognition at that time was in fact a bold step. Thus far the British had refrained from establishing diplomatic relations with Latin America and had even indicated a willingness to see Spain reestablish her authority there. Moreover, the reactionary governments of

Russia, Prussia, Austria, and France had formed an alliance pledged not only to preserve the status quo and to suppress liberalism but to intervene in the internal affairs of any country that threatened the peace and security of Europe. Under this mandate Austria had invaded Italy and France had invaded Spain to liquidate revolutionary movements for which many Americans felt a deep sympathy. Perhaps the alliance would now apply its policy to the New World and assist Spain in the reconquest of her colonies. France, it was rumored, had an eye on Cuba as a reward for intervening in Spain; and Russia seemed intent on spreading her influence southward from Alaska along the Pacific coast. Actually there was not much danger that any European power would intervene in Latin America without British support, and, when Adams warned Russia that the Western Hemisphere was closed to further colonization, the two countries soon negotiated a satisfactory agreement. Nevertheless, the time seemed appropriate for formulating some kind of policy that would cover all contingencies.

By 1823 Great Britain, too, was ready to take a stronger stand. Her liberals resented the reactionary schemes of the continental alliance, and her merchants and manufacturers were determined to maintain the profitable markets they had established in Latin America. Accordingly, the British foreign minister, George Canning, approached the American minister in London, Richard Rush, with a proposal that their governments make a joint statement of policy. Canning told Rush that his government was now convinced that Spain could not recover her colonies and that recognition of their independence was only a matter of time. Great Britain had no designs on any of them, nor would she permit any portion of them to be transferred to another power. If the American government shared these feelings, Canning asked, "why should we hesitate mutually to confide them to each other; and to declare them in the face of the world?"

In October 1823 President Monroe had the British proposal before him and turned to the Republican elder statesmen for advice. Jefferson and Madison both supported his own inclination to accept it. An exception to the policy of nonentanglement in European politics was justified in order, as Jefferson explained, to bring British power into the scale of free government and to "emancipate a continent at one stroke." Oddly enough, it was a statesman from New England, the traditional center of pro-British sentiment, who objected most strenuously to accepting British leadership in the Western Hemisphere. Secretary of State Adams opposed any agreement by which the United States would, in effect, commit itself not to annex additional territory. With an eye on Texas and Cuba, Adams argued that "we should at least keep ourselves free to act as emergencies may arise." Moreover, he disliked a joint statement that would make the United States appear "to come in as a cockboat in the wake of the British man-of-war." After long discussion in the Cabinet, Adams noted with satisfaction that his position "was acquiesced in on all sides." The President, it was agreed, would make a statement of *American* policy emphasizing the separateness of the Old World and the New.

The American response. Monroe incorporated his famous doctrine rather unsystematically in his annual message to Congress on December 2, 1823, a message that dealt with many other topics as well. With some rearranging, the relevant passages run substantially as follows: First, wherever American sympathies may lie, it does not comport with American policy to intervene in the "internal concerns" or the wars of European powers when they involve matters only "relating to themselves." Second, the United States will not interfere with "existing colonies or dependencies" in the Western Hemisphere. Third, with the Latin American governments "whose independence we have . . . acknowledged, we could not view any interposition for the purpose of oppressing them, or controlling in any other manner their destiny, by any European power in any other light than as the manifestation of an unfriendly disposition toward the United States." Fourth, "the American continents, by the free and independent condition which they have assumed and maintain, are henceforth not to be considered as subjects for future colonization by any European powers." Finally, Monroe warned the autocrats of Europe that "we should consider any attempt on their part to extend their [political] system to any portion of this hemisphere as dangerous to our peace and safety." In brief, the essence of this nationalistic pronouncement was the concept of two worlds, each of which was to refrain from intervening in the internal affairs of the other.

Monroe and Adams, of course, were responsible for the precise phrasing of these principles, but they owed much to earlier Presidents and Secretaries of State. They had brought together the elements of an American foreign policy that had been gradually evolving since the Revolution. To European diplomats, the promulgation of a policy that the young republic lacked the power to enforce was a piece of presumptuous impertinence. Canning, who knew that British diplomacy and the British navy had been decisive in preventing continental powers from meddling in America, was particularly annoyed. He was aware that Monroe's unilateral statement could be invoked against Great Britain as well as against other nations. Yet, though the response of the American people was overwhelmingly favorable, within a few years the President's dramatic message had been nearly forgotten. A generation later it would be rediscovered and identified as the Monroe Doctrine; and for many years thereafter it would be accepted as the authoritative and almost definitive statement of American foreign policy.

The westward movement

These displays of nationalism in domestic politics and foreign policy reflected the underlying optimism of the American people—their confidence in the destiny a kind Providence had planned for them. To be sure, their nationalistic creed also embraced an awareness of their past: they had their nostalgic and sentimental side; they gloried in their traditions each Fourth of July; and they were deeply stirred when a Webster waxed eloquent upon the Constitution and the Founding Fathers. But most Americans would have agreed with Jefferson's affirmation that he liked "the dreams of the future better than the history of the past," for there existed among them a widespread feeling of emancipation from history. According to one editor, "Our national birth was the beginning of a new history . . . which separates us from the past and connects us with the future only." America was still primarily a promise: as Ralph Waldo Emerson rejoiced, it was "a country of beginnings, of projects, of designs, of expectations."

The general confidence and optimism of the American people were rooted both in a popular belief that man's potentialities were unlimited when he was free to develop them and in the practical social and economic realities of nineteenth-century America. One of the

A center of Western power: Cincinnati, 1848

most important of these realities was the virgin land—the seemingly unlimited space and inexhaustible resources that promised a life of greater dignity and abundance than Europe's common people had ever dreamed of. The West—the untapped wealth of the great interior stretching from the Appalachians to the Rockies—helped to give the future its rosy hue; and the West became one of the central interests of the American people in the decades after the Treaty of Ghent.

Advance of the agricultural frontier.

The story of the westward movement of population is, in the main, the story of the expansion of American agriculture—of the development of new areas for the raising of livestock and the cultivation of wheat, corn, tobacco, cotton, and wool. After 1815 improved transportation drew more and more Western farmers out of a self-sufficient way of life and into a national market economy. Farmers involved in this kind of commercial agriculture specialized in a ''money crop''—one produced for sale in distant markets—and used the proceeds to buy consumer goods manufactured in the Northeast or in Europe. During periods when commodity prices were high, the rate of westward migration, the sale of public lands, and eventually the supply of Western staples increased spectacularly.

''Old America seems to be breaking up and moving westward,'' observed an English visitor in 1817, during the first great wave of postwar migration. After falling off for a few years during the depression following the Panic of 1819 (see p. 208), the number of emigrants increased again and reached a peak in the 1830s. Whereas in 1810 only a seventh of the American people lived west of the Appalachians, by 1840 more than a third lived there. Below is a table showing population growth in the new Western states between 1810 and 1840:

	1810	1840
Ohio (1803)	230,760	1,519,467
Louisiana (1812)	76,556	352,411
Indiana (1816)	24,520	685,866
Mississippi (1817)	40,352	375,651
Illinois (1818)	12,282	476,183
Alabama (1819)		590,756
Missouri (1821)	20,845	383,702
Arkansas (1836)	1,062	97,574
Michigan (1837)	4,762	212,267

Some of the people who settled the great Mississippi Valley were recent immigrants from Europe, but most of them came from the older states. Kentuckians and Tennesseeans moved to the new cotton lands of the Southwest or crossed the Ohio River into the Northwest; migrants from New England and the Middle Atlantic states generally settled in the Great Lakes region; and people from the South Atlantic states (the largest group of all) invaded southern Ohio, Indiana, and Illinois, as well as the Southwest. By and large those who moved west came from the lower middle classes and traveled with their few worldly possessions loaded on wagons or flatboats—or even on pack horses or pushcarts.

Factors encouraging migration.

Why were these hundreds of thousands of settlers—most of them farmers, some of them artisans—drawn away from the cleared fields and established cities and villages of the East? Apart from the fact that the West happened to be an inviting land of opportunity, certain characteristics of American society help to explain this remarkable migration. The European ancestors of the American people had lived century after century rooted to the same village or the same piece of land until some religious or political or economic crisis uprooted them and drove them across the Atlantic. Many of those who experienced this sharp and devastating break thereafter lacked the ties that had bound them and their ancestors to a single place. Moreover, in the relatively stratified European society men inherited the occupations and social status of their fathers, but in American society there was a less rigid class structure. Men changed occupations easily and believed that it was not only possible but almost a moral duty to improve their social and economic position. As a result, Americans were, as many European visitors observed, an inveterately restless, rootless, and ambitious people.

The Frenchman Alexis de Tocqueville, who published a remarkably penetrating study of American society after a tour in the early 1830s, was impressed with these traits.

> In the United States, a man builds a house in which to spend his old age, and he sells it before the roof is on . . . he brings a field into tillage and leaves other men to gather the crops . . . he settles in a place, which he soon afterwards leaves to carry his changeable longings

Westering

Transportation to the West, about 1840

elsewhere . . . the tie that unites one generation to another is relaxed or broken . . . every man there loses all trace of the ideas of his forefathers or takes no heed of them.

The reasons for this "strange unrest," Tocqueville believed, were, first, the American "taste for physical gratifications"; second, a social condition "in which neither laws nor customs retain any person in his place"; and, third, a pervasive belief that "all professions are open to all, and a man's own energies may place him at the top of any one of them." These social traits helped to produce the nomadic and daring frontiersmen who kept pushing westward beyond the fringes of settlement, as well as the less adventurous immigrants who followed them across the mountains in search of new homes, material success, and a better life.

The West had plenty of attractions for a people conditioned to appreciate them. The alluvial river bottoms, the fecund soils of the rolling forest lands, and the black loams of the prairies were tempting to New England farmers working their rocky, sterile acres and to Southeastern farmers plagued with soil exhaustion. The Indian menace east of the Mississippi was now substantially reduced; after 1815 the helpless tribes made a succession of treaties ceding lands, which the government surveyed and put up for sale. In 1820 a new

land law ended the credit system but reduced the minimum tract for individual sales to eighty acres and the minimum price to $1.25.* Now it was possible for a man to buy a farm for $100, and the continued proliferation of state banks made it relatively easy for those without cash to negotiate loans in paper money. Western farmers borrowed with the confident expectation that the expanding economy would keep farm prices high, thus making it easy to repay loans when they fell due.

Transportation was becoming less of a problem for those who wished to move west and for those who had farm surpluses to send to market. Prior to 1815 Western farmers who did not live on waterways were connected with the outside world only by dirt roads and mountain trails. High-value products, such as whiskey and furs, might be carried profitably on pack horses or by wagon across the mountains, but the cost of transporting bulky grains in this fashion was several times greater than their value in Eastern markets. Goods could be shipped across the Atlantic for less than the cost of transportation from western New York or western Pennsylvania to cities along the seaboard.

The first step toward an improvement of Western transportation was the construction

*New lands, however, were first put up at auction, and the best sold for a good deal more than the minimum price.

Fulton's "Paragon": steamboat on the Hudson

of graded and paved turnpikes. Built by private corporations that charged tolls, most of the turnpikes were designed to connect Eastern cities, but a few served the tramontane West. By the 1820s migrants could follow the Baltimore Turnpike to Cumberland, Maryland, and then the National Road to Wheeling (ultimately, to Vandalia, Illinois); the Lancaster Turnpike and Forbes Road to Pittsburgh; or the Mohawk and Genesee Turnpike to Lake Erie. These roads made possible a substantial reduction in transportation costs and thus stimulated the commercialization of agriculture along their routes.

Two developments brought an end to the era of turnpikes and started a transportation revolution that resulted in increased regional specialization and the growth of a national market economy. First came the steamboat. In 1811, four years after Robert Fulton's *Clermont* made its celebrated voyage up the Hudson River, Nicholas J. Roosevelt launched the steam-powered *New Orleans* at Pittsburgh and sent it on a successful voyage down the Ohio and Mississippi. A witness found it an awesome spectacle: "a boat moving without appearance of sail, oar, pole, or any manual labor—moving within the secrets of her own mechanism and propelled by power undiscoverable." Within twenty years some two hundred shallow-draft sternwheelers were plying the Western waters and had superseded

all other craft in the carrying of passengers and freight. Steamboats were not only faster but transported upriver freight for about one-tenth of what it previously had cost on hand-propelled keelboats.

Next came the Erie Canal, which spanned the three hundred fifty miles between Buffalo on Lake Erie and Albany on the Hudson River. With the support of Governor De Witt Clinton and funds from the New York legislature, construction began in 1817 and was completed in 1825. After the Erie Canal went into operation, the cost per mile of transporting a ton of freight between Buffalo and New York City declined from nearly 20 cents to less than 1 cent. Until the 1840s the canal was used primarily by the farmers of western New York, but eventually the Western states diverted much of their produce from the rivers to this shorter route to Eastern markets.

The Erie Canal's immediate success (tolls enabled the state to recover the cost within seven years) launched the country into the Canal Age. New York's rivals, such as Philadelphia and Baltimore, strove to tap the West with their own canal systems, but with less success; Ohio and Indiana built canals to connect the Ohio River with the Great Lakes. Between 1815 and 1840 (after which construction declined), various states invested about $125 million in three thousand miles of canals. By the 1830s the country had a

Lockport on the Erie Canal, 1836

complete water route from New York City to New Orleans. By then, however, a new marvel, the railroad, promised an even more dazzling answer to the West's transportation needs (see p. 295).

In all phases of this transportation revolution government provided a large proportion of the needed funds. State and local governments sometimes helped finance the turnpike companies by subscribing to their stocks; the states built all the important canals; federal and state governments paid for all river and harbor improvements; and in later years federal, state, and local governments aided the Western railroads with various forms of subsidies. Thus even in the years of alleged laissez faire the states had begun to play a modest role in the nation's economic life, supplementing the dynamic federal role urged by Henry Clay in his American System.

Life on the frontier. Only the hope of a better future could make bearable the hardships of a farmer getting his start on the Western frontier. The propaganda literature of the land-speculators abounds in descriptions of the salubrious climate, the health-giving waters, the ease with which one could make the land bloom, and the increasing comforts of civilization. The realities, for some years at least, were quite different. Clearing a piece of land for cultivation—girdling the trees to kill them, cutting the branches and rolling the logs into great piles to burn, grubbing out the stumps, and breaking the root-infested ground with primitive plows—meant backbreaking labor for pioneer families. Disease and death hung over the Western settlements; trained doctors were scarce, and the only resort was

to home remedies or the patent-medicine panaceas of itinerant quacks. Malaria, dysentery, pneumonia, smallpox, yellow fever, cholera, and dietary deficiencies took a heavy toll; travelers often commented on the pale and sickly appearance of Westerners. Living in primitive lean-tos or floorless cabins, surviving on a diet mainly of corn and salt pork, making their own clothing from homespun and deerskin, enduring the almost unmitigated bleakness of frontier life, these pioneers would have been hard put to discover the Arcadian quality that some romanticists see in their isolated, self-sufficient agrarian society. A prospective migrant to Illinois warned his family: "What awaits you in this region, which, as of now, is not much better than a wilderness, is a life full of hardships, want and toil. By this choice we shall close ourselves off from the rest of the world for many years."

But the settlers looked beyond the ordeal of these early years, and eventually better times did come. Life softened for them as schools and churches were built, as neighbors became less remote, as transportation improved and Eastern manufactured goods became cheaper and more plentiful, and as the growing villages and county seats acquired printing presses and newspapers, developed small local industries, and offered social diversions to the surrounding countryfolk. These cultural amenities, the modest comforts earned from operating a family-size farm, and the feeling of independence derived from landownership, were the ultimate rewards of many who made their homes in the Western wilderness.

For many others, however, this was not enough. The more ambitious Westerners, if they came to farm, thought of agriculture as a business enterprise and of themselves as small capitalists producing for the market. Moreover, to those who invaded the West in search of wealth, farming was only one way —and perhaps the slowest—to gain their end. Along with the yeomen came the frontier boomers, the speculators in real estate to whom land was simply a commodity to be bought and sold for a profit. Indeed, many of the yeomen themselves were as much interested in land speculation as in agriculture. The greatest rewards in the West were not always earned by industrious and thrifty farmers; they were often won by shrewd operators who knew how to exploit the vagaries of federal land policy or to buy favors at the local land offices. A long chapter in the history of the West belongs to the land companies—one of the earliest forms of large-scale American business enterprise—whose agents spied out the best tracts, bought them at public auction, and then sold them at higher prices to authentic settlers.

Other Westerners engaged in the fascinating business of promoting towns at strategic trading sites. Many of these wilderness metropolises never materialized, and often the giddy purchasers of unseen town plots wound up with a ''business block'' knee-deep in swamp water. But important urban centers, such as Cincinnati, Cleveland, Detroit, Indianapolis, St. Louis, and Chicago, did grow with amazing speed. To them came not only promoters and speculators but men with capital to invest in banking, commerce, and manufacturing. Surprisingly early these cities became the centers of Western political and economic power, and of Western culture when it pushed out its first tender shoots.

The significance of the frontier.

What impact did the New West make on American society? Not much in the way of political innovation, for state and local government in the West was for the most part modeled after the East. Apparently the forces generating the trend toward increased political democracy in these years were as much Eastern as they were Western. Socially and culturally the West was dependent on the East and again showed a greater tendency to copy than to innovate. This was natural enough, for those who moved west were less often critical of the fundamental structure of Eastern society than dissatisfied with their position in it.

Realities sent some back

But the impact of the New West was not insignificant. Because of its lack of local traditions, its interior position, and its need for protection and improved transportation, the West was usually the most nationalistic section of the country. Certainly the problems that settlers faced on a raw frontier encouraged them to develop to a high degree such qualities as individualism and resourcefulness. By stripping Eastern and European civilization down to its fundamentals, Westerners exposed some of its shams and discarded some of its superficialities. Though the West did not produce a society of social and economic equals, it did give emphasis to the notion that all artificial barriers to advancement must be removed—that all must have an equal chance to make their way in the world. Moreover, Westerners showed great respect for the man who, starting with little, achieved success in the competitive struggle.

Above all, the New West was America's treasure house of unused land and untapped resources. It was a major, though not exclusive, factor in producing the economic expansion and steadily rising standard of living from which all white Americans profited more or less. When the historian Frederick Jackson Turner, near the end of the nineteenth century, called his colleagues' attention to the significance of the frontier in American history, he doubtless claimed too much, as recent critics have shown. But there is some truth in his assertion that ''this expansion westward with its new opportunities'' accounted for the ''fluidity of American life.'' These Western wilds, Turner wrote, ''constituted the richest free gift that was ever spread out before civilized man.''

Slavery and the Cotton Kingdom

Southern expansion. The migration into Alabama, Mississippi, and Louisiana was, as we have seen, a part of the westward movement; and the great majority of the early settlers were pioneer farmers, mostly from Virginia and the Carolinas, who endured the same hardships and cherished the same ambitions as those who settled north of the Ohio River. They engaged in subsistence farming to begin with, and many of them never managed to produce more than occasional small surpluses for the market. But enterprising farmers in the Southwest knew that cotton-planters in the South Carolina and Georgia piedmonts had been making fortunes ever since Eli Whitney, in 1793, invented a gin that efficiently separated seeds from the lint of "upland," or short-staple, cotton. Before Whitney solved this technological problem, most of the cotton used in European textile mills had come from Egypt and Asia. Southerners had grown small amounts of high-quality "sea-island" cotton on the coast of South Carolina and Georgia, but this variety could not be grown inland. In 1793 the South produced only about 10,000 bales of cotton; but by the 1820s, with the Cotton Kingdom spreading westward, the South's annual production rose to a half-million bales.

Since cotton prices before 1837 seldom fell below 15 cents a pound and often rose much higher, those who obtained suitable land soon devoted at least part of their time to cotton cultivation, usually with the labor of Negro slaves. Eventually a fortunate few—some beginning as small farmers, others bringing slaves with them from the Southeast—established large plantations on the rich, silt-loamed prairies of the Alabama-Mississippi Black Belt, or on the alluvial bottom lands of the Mississippi and Yazoo delta. These great cotton-planters, together with the rice-planters of coastal South Carolina and Georgia and the sugar-planters of Louisiana, developed agriculture to the highest levels of efficiency, complexity, and commercialization to be found anywhere in nineteenth-century America.

After 1815 the economy of the South was tied to the cultivation of cotton, for investments in new cotton lands brought higher returns than any of the possible alternatives. Indeed, during the next few decades cotton was a crucial factor in the whole developing national market economy and in the economic growth of all regions. It accounted for more than half the country's exports and thus paid for most of its imports. The cotton plantations provided a substantial market for manufactured goods from the Northeast, and the marketing of Southern cotton gave the Northeastern commercial interests their most profitable trade.

Within two decades after the War of 1812 the booming Gulf states were ceasing to be part of the New West and were becoming increasingly identified with the Old South, even though they differed socially from Virginia and the Carolinas in many significant ways. Their identification with the South Atlantic states came at a time when Southerners were becoming more, rather than less, conscious of their special sectional problems and interests.

The survival of slavery. What was it that gave the Old South its special identity? Not physical isolation, for it lacked natural frontiers separating it from the rest of the country; nor geographic and climatic uniformity, for it had great diversity of soils, topography, mean temperatures, growing seasons, and average rainfalls. Not a difference in population origins, for the South, like the North, was originally settled by middle- and lower-class people; nor contrasts in religion or political philosophy, for here, too, the similarities outweighed the differences. Not even the economies of North and South were altogether dissimilar, for, although there were important differences, the majority of the white people of both sections were independent yeomen farmers who worked their own lands. In contrast to the Western farmers, however, few Southern farmers benefited from improved transportation and became part of the national market economy. Wealth was less evenly distributed in the South than in the West; less money was invested in education; and the rate of illiteracy was higher. Fewer towns and less local industry developed, with the result that much of the income of the cotton-planters flowed out of the region to pay for goods and services provided by the West and Northeast. In short, the Old South remained more rural and economically less diversified than the North, and a larger proportion of its small farmers lived a life of pioneer self-sufficiency.

The Peculiar Institution, Virginia, 1830

Nat has survived all his followers, and the gallows will speedily close his career. His own account of the conspiracy ... reads an awful, and it is hoped, a useful lesson, as to the operations of a mind like his, endeavoring to grapple with things beyond his reach.... [The conspiracy] was not instigated by motives of revenge or sudden anger, but the result of long deliberation, and a settled purpose of mind....

... It has been said he was ignorant and cowardly ... [but] for natural intelligence and quickness of apprehension, [he] is surpassed by few men I have ever seen.... He is a complete fanatic, or plays his part most admirably. On other subjects he possesses an uncommon share of intelligence, with a mind capable of attaining any thing; but warped and perverted by the influence of early impressions.... I shall not attempt to describe the effect of his narrative, as told and commented on by himself, in the condemned hole of the prison. The calm, deliberate composure with which he spoke of his late deeds and intentions, the expression of his fiend-like face when excited by enthusiasm, still bearing the blood of helpless innocence about him; clothed with rags and covered with chains; yet daring to raise his manacled hands to heaven, with a spirit soaring above the attributes of man; I looked on him and my blood curdled in my veins.

From Thomas R. Gray, *The Confessions of Nat Turner*, 1831.

A white Virginian's impression of the captured Nat Turner

Turner's Rebellion

But all these differences between North and South were of secondary importance. By far the most significant difference was the presence and survival in the South of Negro slavery, which Southerners themselves called their "peculiar institution." More than anything else, it was slavery, with all its ramifications, that eventually gave the Old South its identity and white Southerners their feeling of separateness from the rest of the Union.

In the eighteenth century, of course, Southern slavery had not been a peculiar institution, for it existed in the Northern colonies and throughout the Western Hemisphere. During or soon after the Revolution, however, the Northern states abolished it; and in the first half of the nineteenth century slaves gained their freedom in most of Central and South America. Some Southerners of Washington's and Jefferson's generation, moved by anxieties about social dangers as well as by the ideals of the American Revolution, were cautiously and rather abstractly critical of slavery. As late as the 1820s a scattering of emancipation societies in the Upper South, supported mostly by Quakers, carried on a discreet campaign for gradual emancipation and the colonization of free blacks outside the boundaries of the United States.

In Virginia, in the late eighteenth and early nineteenth centuries, a prolonged agricultural depression resulting from low tobacco prices and soil exhaustion led some to believe, or hope, that slavery would soon die. In August 1831, Southampton County, Virginia, was the scene of the South's bloodiest slave insurrection, led by a bondsman named Nat Turner, in which sixty whites and scores of blacks (including Turner) lost their lives. The Turner rebellion, which caused profound alarm throughout the South, precipitated an earnest debate in the Virginia legislature the following January, during which various legislators denounced slavery as a social canker and an economic blight. The antislavery legislators, showing clearly that their concern was not for blacks but for the safety and welfare of whites, demanded a program of gradual emancipation and colonization. But the Virginia emancipationists, like those in other states of the Upper South, were defeated; and soon after 1832 Southern critics were either silenced or were driven into exile.

Southern slavery, then, did not die of natural causes; it did not even decline. Instead, with the rise of the Cotton Kingdom and the eventual improvement of agriculture in the seaboard states, it flourished and seemed to have the vitality to survive indefinitely. Since the federal Constitution recognized slavery as a local institution within the jurisdiction of individual states, Southerners saw nothing to prevent them from introducing it into the Southwest. Some moved there with their

Slavery auction: the demand was heavy

slaves, while others stayed behind and operated new plantations as absentee owners. Still others took advantage of high slave prices resulting from the labor shortage in the Southwest and sold a portion of their slaves to professional traders who took them to the busy markets in New Orleans and Natchez. There at the slave auctions the self-made men of the Cotton Kingdom, some of whom had started with no slaves at all, purchased "prime field hands" to work their growing estates.

Negro slaves thus became an important element in the migration to the Southwest and played a major role in clearing the land for cultivation. By 1840 almost half the population of Alabama and Louisiana and more than half the population of Mississippi (by then the leading cotton-producing state) consisted of Negro slaves. Yet at all times nearly three-fourths of the white families in the South as a whole held no slaves and depended on their own labor alone. Moreover, the great majority of slaveholders owned just a few slaves; as late as 1860 only ten thousand Southern families belonged to the planter aristocracy operating large estates with slave gangs numbering more than fifty.

Why did Southern slavery survive far into the nineteenth century? Not because Negroes were natural slaves; nor because white labor could not adjust to the Southern climate and successfully cultivate the Southern crops; nor because the Negroes' health was not adversely affected by living in the malarial swamps, where the sugar and rice plantations and many of the cotton plantations were located. The reasons the South clung so te-

naciously to slavery are to be found in the fears, ambitions, and aspirations of Southern white men.

By the nineteenth century the South's peculiar institution was two hundred years old, and to abolish it would have brought painful changes in long-established habits and attitudes. Those who would destroy slavery, warned a Georgian, "would have to wade knee-deep in blood"; indeed, slavery is "so intimately . . . mingled with our social conditions that it would be impossible to eradicate it." Most white Southerners—indeed, most white Americans—believed that blacks were innately shiftless, untrustworthy, and sexually promiscuous. Slavery, therefore, was a means of controlling an inferior race, of preventing it from becoming a burden on society, and of maintaining the purity and supremacy of the white race. To nonslaveholders slavery symbolized their link with the privileged caste of white men and the blacks' social and legal subordination. "Now suppose they was free," explained a poor Southern farmer to a Northern visitor, "you see they'd all think themselves as good as we." To the master class the possession of slaves brought great prestige, for in the South the ownership of a plantation worked by slave labor was the sign of success and high social position.

But, above all, slavery survived because it was a viable and profitable labor system and because it represented an enormous investment of Southern capital. Slavery, of course, did not make every master a rich man, nor did every master strive to wring the last ounce of profit from his toiling bondsmen. Nevertheless, most slaveholders earned good returns on their investments—and this accounts for the generally heavy demand for slaves and for their high price in the market. The system, moreover, was highly adaptable. Slaves were employed, not only in agriculture and as domestics, but as skilled artisans, as laborers in construction gangs, and as workers in iron foundries, textile mills, and tobacco factories. In short, the master class had no compelling economic reason for wanting to abolish slavery; as late as 1860 it was still a vigorous and viable social institution.

The nature of slavery. In governing their bondsmen most masters were neither inordinately cruel nor remarkably indulgent; they simply dealt with their human property in the manner they deemed necessary to make the

[Slaves] would compose and sing as they went along, consulting neither time nor tune. The thought that came up came out—if not in the word, in the sound;—and as frequently in the one as in the other.... [They] would sing, as a chorus, to words which to many would seem unmeaning jargon, but which, nevertheless were full of meaning to themselves.... Every tone was a testimony against slavery, and a prayer to God for deliverance from chains. The hearing of those wild notes always depressed my spirit and filled me with ineffable sadness. I have frequently found myself in tears while hearing them....

I have often been utterly astonished, since I came to the north, to find persons who could speak of the singing among slaves, as evidence of their contentment and happiness. It is impossible to conceive of a greater mistake. Slaves sing most when they are most unhappy. The songs of the slave represent the sorrows of his heart.... The singing of a man cast away upon a desolate island might be as appropriately considered as evidence of contentment and happiness, as the singing of a slave....

An escaped slave's observations on slave music

From *Narrative of the Life of Frederick Douglass, An American Slave,* 1845.

---

system work. They bought and sold slaves, used them as security for loans, and divided them among heirs. In these transactions husbands were often separated from their wives and children from their mothers, for state laws gave slave marriages no recognition. Except for the deliberate killing or maiming of a slave, the master's power to administer physical punishment was virtually unlimited, and planters could delegate this power to white overseers employed to manage their estates. Most slaveholders used the whip for "moderate correction" only when they believed it essential to maintain discipline; but an element of cruelty was inseparable from slavery, as even many of its defenders recognized. Some slaves fell into the hands of brutal masters, or of men who were corrupted by the power the institution conferred upon them. Since a black was unable to give testimony against a white man, the justice he received in court was, at best, very eccentric.

The average slave's standard of living was near the subsistence level. He lived on a diet mainly of corn and pork, adequate in bulk but unbalanced and monotonous; he wore coarse, skimpy clothing made from some variety of cheap "Negro cloth"; and he lived in a cabin that was too often drafty, cramped, and scantily furnished. His labor routine kept him at work from dawn to dusk. By nineteenth-century standards, he was not often worked excessively, but a long day of hard toil was usually exacted from him. The slave was

most in danger of being overworked to the detriment of his health on the large cotton and sugar plantations managed by overseers.

One cannot pretend to know all that being a slave meant to the Negroes, for slaves were seldom able to express their feelings and most of the evidence comes from white sources. One certainly must be cautious about assuming that they accepted slavery as their natural lot and cheerfully submitted to their white masters. No doubt they made certain psychological adaptations to their condition; no doubt they enjoyed the occasional holidays and simple pleasures that most masters permitted them; no doubt their untrained intellects seldom dwelt on freedom as a philosophical abstraction. But to conclude from this that they had no idea of the meaning of freedom, no comprehension of its practical advantages, no desire to obtain it, would be quite unwarranted. The evidence of their submission and obeisance suggests not so much contentment as the superior power of the white caste and the effectiveness of its elaborate techniques of control. Moreover, there is much evidence indicating that most plantation slaves consciously played the role of a docile, cheerful Sambo as a protective device in their relationships with whites. Consequently, slaveholders often knew less about the true character of their slaves than they thought. "The most general defect in the character of the Negro," complained one planter, "is hypocrisy . . . and if the master treats him as a fool, he will be sure to act the fool's part." The swift and ruthless suppression of Nat Turner's followers drove home to the slaves the futility of organized rebellion. But it did not deter some of the bolder ones from less spectacular forms of protest. Of these protests, running away was one of the most common—and certainly the most irksome to the master class.

White men paid a high price for slavery: artisans and yeoman farmers suffered from the competition of cheap slave labor; most white slaveholders were more or less distressed by the obvious paradox of slavery in a republic whose moral commitment was to individual freedom and natural rights; and all were bedeviled by a nagging fear of slave rebellions, a fear that occasionally reached the proportions of mass hysteria. But the black, not the white, was the chief victim of the system. Slavery exposed him not only to its cruelties and meager rewards but to its strong dehumanizing tendencies and its powerful pressures toward emasculated personalities. It destroyed most of the cultural tradition that Negroes had brought with them from Africa and for long left them, in many respects, a culturally rootless people; it made the Negro family unstable, encouraged sexual promiscuity, and exposed black women to the lust of white men; and it encouraged infantile, irresponsible behavior and put a premium on docility. Above all, slavery deprived a whole race of the opportunity to develop its potentialities and of the freedom that white men treasured so much.

Yet, in spite of the damage done to them, Southern slaves found ways to maintain a degree of psychic balance and to avoid total dehumanization and infantilization. Though slave marriages had no legal support and slave fathers could not be the authority figures traditional in nineteenth-century families, slaves nevertheless customarily lived in family groups. In the plantation slave quarters they were not under the constant scrutiny of their masters; and there, in their relationships with each other, they could play roles other than Sambo and develop a community life of their own. They found opportunities for self-expression in their religious services, in their music and folklore, and in other social activities. In later years these experiences of slave community life, which blended a modified white culture with fragments of African cultural survivals, would provide the ingredients from which a semiautonomous Afro-American subculture would grow.

Missouri and the issue of slavery expansion.

Eventually the South's peculiar institution was to have a tragic impact upon the whole nation, and a few intimations of the ultimate tragedy were evident even in the early years. Slavery was a topic of debate at the Constitutional Convention of 1787, and just what would happen to it under the new Constitution was a subject of inquiry at Southern ratifying conventions. The compromise by which Southerners obtained congressional representation for three-fifths of their slaves (see p. 127) provoked repeated complaints, especially from New England. Antislavery Northerners frequently resisted enforcement of the Fugitive Slave Act of 1793, which enabled Southern masters to recover runaways in the free states. In the Deep South some doubted the wisdom of the federal law closing the African slave trade, and, as we have seen, the law was often flagrantly violated.

But these were minor irritants compared to the succession of crises generated by the steady march of slavery into the Southwest. Before 1820 five additional slave states (Kentucky, Tennessee, Louisiana, Mississippi, and Alabama) had been admitted to the Union; these increased the total number to eleven, which, as it happened, were balanced by eleven free states. The resulting political equilibrium in the Senate was threatened, however, when the territory of Missouri, settled mostly by proslavery Kentuckians and Tennesseeans, petitioned for admission as a slave state. In February 1819, a House committee reported an enabling act; but Representative James Tallmadge, Jr., a Republican from New York, proposed an amendment to prohibit the introduction of additional slaves into Missouri and to provide gradual emancipation for those already there. The Tallmadge Amendment passed the House on a sectional vote but was defeated in the Senate. When neither chamber would yield, slavery's critics and defenders plunged into an ill-tempered debate that showed the existence of a deep sectional cleavage.

Much of the Missouri debate revolved around constitutional issues. Southerners, especially Virginians, insisting that new states had the same sovereign rights as the old, denied that Congress could make the abolition of slavery a condition of admission. Northerners claimed that the Founding Fathers had thought of slavery as a temporary institution and had not intended that it should spread into the Western territories. In the heat of the debate angry Southerners accused Federalists of deliberately fomenting a crisis in order to win popular support in the North and revive their dying party. Jefferson, who strongly opposed the Tallmadge Amendment, was convinced that the Federalist leader Rufus King was "ready to risk the Union for any chance of restoring his party to power and wriggling himself to the head of it." Northern opposition to slavery expansion, wrote Charles Pinckney of South Carolina, "sprang from the love of power, and the never ceasing wish to regain the honors and offices of the government."

No doubt political advantage and sectional power—the North already had a substantial majority in the House—were basic ingredients of the Missouri controversy. But the crisis might have looked less portentous had this been all there was to it. Tallmadge himself appeared to have no crass political motive; rather, he seems to have acted from a conviction that slavery was a moral evil that should not be permitted to spread. So did many others whose humanitarian impulses were aroused by the apparent vitality of Southern slavery. In urging his colleagues to prevent its further spread, Representative Arthur Livermore, of New Hampshire, stressed the importance of the decision they were about to make:

> An opportunity is now presented, if not to diminish, at least to prevent the growth of a sin which sits heavy on the soul of every one of us. By embracing this opportunity, we may retrieve the national character and, in some degree, our own. But if we suffer it to pass unimproved, let us at least be consistent, and declare that our Constitution was made to impose slavery, and not to establish liberty.

Never before had the peculiar institution been so severely attacked—and so vigorously defended—on moral grounds as it was during the Missouri debate.

The basic issue was not resolved on this occasion; it was simply postponed by a compromise that passed largely through Henry Clay's efforts. In 1820 Congress finally agreed to admit Missouri as a slave state, but it preserved the balance by admitting Maine as a free state. It divided the remaining territory acquired in the Louisiana Purchase along the

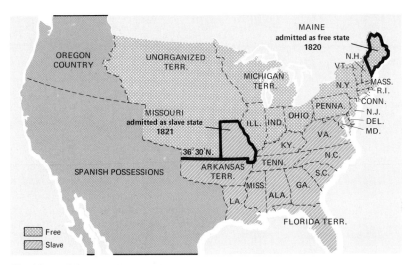

The Missouri Compromise, 1820

line 36°30' north latitude. North of that line, except for Missouri, slavery was "forever prohibited."

The Missouri crisis made some Americans apprehensive about the future of the federal Union. John Quincy Adams foresaw the possibility of a realignment of political parties along sectional lines, hastening the "emancipation of all . . . [Southern] slaves, threatening in its immediate effect that Southern domination which has swayed the Union for the last twenty years." Tallmadge, said a Georgia congressman, had "kindled a fire which all the waters of the ocean can not put out, which seas of blood can only extinguish." And Jefferson, showing hardly a glimmer of his earlier antislavery sentiments, poured his indignation on Northerners for opening this sensitive issue. "All, I fear, do not see the speck on our horizon which is to burst on us as a tornado, sooner or later. The line of division lately marked out between different portions of our confederacy is such as will never, I fear, be obliterated." Writing thus in 1821, Jefferson had, in effect, formulated the doctrine of an "irrepressible conflict" between North and South.

Even in an era of nationalism and expansion, then, slavery disturbed the politics and threatened the survival of the young republic. And in the South the conflict between slavery, which Southerners would not abolish, and the American liberal tradition, which they claimed as their birthright, created tensions that were ultimately to become unbearable.

Another frontier: industry and technology

Beginnings of the factory system. The western edge of settlement was not the only frontier that attracted Americans and promised a future of increased abundance. Since the War of 1812 growing numbers had been drawn to the thriving towns and cities of the New England and Middle Atlantic states. Here lived the pioneers of the American Industrial Revolution—the men who devoted their lives to the promotion of business enterprises and to the application of science and technology to the twin goals of lightening the burdens of labor and multiplying the comforts of human life. Their efforts gradually rendered obsolete the system of domestic manufacturing that had been almost universal in colonial days. Under this system farmers outside the market economy had made their own clothes and household necessities, while village artisans had produced items such as cloth, shoes, hats, and tools for sale to consumers in local markets. The independent artisan survived longer in some crafts than in others, and household manufacturing was always a part of life on the isolated agricultural frontier; but after 1830 both were clearly doomed by the factory and the spreading market economy.

In a sense the Industrial Revolution, in America as in Europe, was merely an acceleration of technological changes that had no clear beginning and as yet have no foreseeable end. It involved the development and increasing use of power-driven machines in industrial production; the location of these machines in factories that tended to grow in size and complexity; and, with the decline of transportation costs, the distribution of their products in ever widening mass markets. As the domestic market expanded, manufacturing enterprises became increasingly specialized. The early textile mills, for example, marketed their own products and constructed their own machinery; but eventually they concentrated on spinning and weaving, selling their products to wholesalers, and buying their machinery from independent machine shops. The essential features of the Industrial Revolution, then, were mechanization, specialization, and a trend from local to regional and national distribution.

American industrial technology was in part copied from England and in part an indigenous outgrowth of the genius of American scientists, inventors, skilled mechanics, and

To supply the domestic market

entrepreneurs. Manufacturers found an impelling incentive for mechanization in the high cost of domestic labor, whose wages in the early nineteenth century were from 30 to 50 percent higher than wages in Great Britain. The dearness of labor was the direct result of the high productivity of American agriculture, which forced industry to pay wages comparable to what could be earned on the land. Another incentive was the presence of cheap waterpower to which machinery could easily be harnessed. Moreover, the optimistic American entrepreneurs, anticipating continued technological advances, usually built machines that wore out quickly, thus making it relatively inexpensive to retool. Nowhere in Europe did environmental conditions provide so many inducements for mechanical innovation; nowhere was there a society so free from the sort of hampering traditions that impede technological change. "Everything new is quickly introduced here," wrote a European visitor in the 1820s. "There is no clinging to old ways; the moment an American hears the word 'invention' he pricks up his ears."

The Northeastern states, for a variety of reasons, were the first to industrialize to a significant degree. In the years before the embargo and War of 1812, their profitable foreign trade had enabled them to accumulate the necessary capital and to build the banks and other commercial facilities that were now useful to industry. Their substantial urban centers provided large local markets, coastal waterways opened regional markets, and turnpikes gave them early access to the hinterland. In addition, the Northeast had superior entrepreneurial talent, a relatively abundant and well-educated labor supply, easy access to Southern cotton, and rich resources in the waterpower of New England and the iron and coal of Pennsylvania. In the years after 1815 manufacturing gradually superseded commerce as this region's primary economic concern.

What the pioneers in technology accomplished lacks the romance and drama of the Western frontiersman's elemental struggle for survival. Yet their work was equally vital to national growth and expansion, and its long-run social and economic consequences were, if anything, greater. In the field of transportation, for example, the builders of turnpikes experimented with various kinds of road-surfacing and with truss-type and suspension bridges; engineers on the Erie Canal designed new excavating equipment and developed a special cement for use in its eighty-eight locks; and Henry M. Shreve, among others, built flat-hulled steamboats of shallow draft especially adapted to service on the Western rivers. Meanwhile, a patent act adopted by Congress in 1790 (revised in 1793) encouraged numerous men to pursue fame and fortune through the improvement or invention of devices useful to mankind. As Hamilton claimed in his Report on Manufactures, there did seem to exist "in the genius of the people of this country, a peculiar aptitude for mechanical improvements."

The factory system in the United States had its beginnings during the Presidency of Washington. In 1790 Samuel Slater, an English immigrant who knew the secrets of English textile machinery, built a cotton-spinning mill at Pawtucket, Rhode Island, for the merchant Moses Brown. This first successful American factory contained seventy-two spindles tended by nine children, and its machinery was soon harnessed to waterpower. After years of slow and faltering growth, Jefferson's embargo and the War of 1812 gave the American cotton-textile industry a chance to become a significant part of the national economy. By the end of the war cotton factories were counted in the hundreds, most of them in New England, and the number of spindles in operation approximated 130,000. Immediately after the war many of these mills failed because of renewed British competition; but others survived, and by 1840 the number of spindles in operation exceeded 2 million.

In the years of expansion constant improvements were made in the machinery for carding the raw cotton and for spinning it into yarn and thread. But the weaving long continued to be done in the homes of small craftsmen, who sold the cloth in their own shops or who worked for wages for merchant capitalists. After 1814, however, the introduction of the power loom soon brought weaving as well as spinning into the factory. Many American mills specialized in the manufacture of a coarse white cloth called "sheeting," which was in wide demand and could be mass produced. American manufacturers of sheeting could compete successfully with the British in the domestic market, and by the 1830s they were even selling in foreign markets.

From cotton textiles the factory spread to other industries. In 1793, at Byfield, Massachusetts, John and Arthur Schofield, who came to the United States from Yorkshire, England, built the first factory to manufacture woolens. War in Europe, a series of improvements in carding, napping, and shearing machines, and the introduction of waterpower soon placed the American woolens industry on a secure foundation. Meanwhile, merchant capitalists were taking the manufacture of shoes out of the cobblers' shops and into the homes of semiskilled workers who specialized in making a single part of the finished product. Eventually, when the shoe industry began to be mechanized, the workers were brought into factories where their role changed from that of craftsmen to that of tenders of machines. Similarly, in the iron industry Pennsylvania's furnaces and rolling mills were fast supplanting small local forges and blacksmith shops.

In 1804 Oliver Evans of Philadelphia, one of the most remarkable pioneers of American technology, developed a high-pressure steam engine that was adaptable to a great variety of industrial purposes. Within a few years it was being used not only in steam navigation but to run sawmills, flour mills, and printing presses—and, in 1828, steam power replaced waterpower at the Slater cotton mills. Evans also experimented with the techniques of mass production and built the first completely mechanized flour mill. Eli Whitney and Simeon North, a Connecticut clockmaker, applied these techniques to the manufacture of guns and conceived the idea of interchangeable parts. Whitney taught his workers to make identical parts from metal molds, or "gigs"; after the perfection of this system, guns could be assembled in a fraction of the time required by a skilled gunsmith. North then introduced his system in the clock industry, and Connecticut manufacturers were soon mass-producing inexpensive clocks for a national market.

To build a factory equipped with expensive machinery run by steam or waterpower required more capital than the average individual entrepreneur or even partnership could obtain. While these older forms of business organization predominated as late as the 1850s, the ultimate answer to this financial problem was the corporation. Chartered under state laws, corporations could accumulate capital from numerous small investors; and the stockholders enjoyed "limited liability"—that is, they were financially responsible for the corporation's debts only to the extent of their investment. Used first by bankers and the builders of turnpikes, bridges, and other internal improvements, the corporate form slowly spread to manufacturing, especially textiles, after the War of 1812. In 1813 a group of wealthy merchants known as the Boston Associates, including Francis Cabot Lowell, Nathan Appleton, and Patrick Tracy Jackson, formed the Boston Manufacturing Company in Waltham, Massachusetts. With capital exceeding a half-million dollars and an efficient managerial staff, these men built the first integrated textile factory that performed every operation from the carding of raw cotton to the weaving of cloth with power looms. A decade later the Boston Associates shifted the center of their activities to Lowell, "the Manchester of America," where they chartered the Merrimack Manufacturing Company. During the 1820s and 1830s they chartered additional companies in Massachusetts and New Hampshire, until, by the 1850s, they and their imitators had made the manufacturing corporation an entrenched economic institution.

In other areas, too, the American economy began to show the effects of advancing technology. Eastern merchants used improved transportation and marketing techniques to compete for the trade of the hinterland, with New York merchants rapidly outstripping their rivals. The New York group siphoned much of the Western trade through the Great Lakes and the Erie Canal and captured a large share of the cotton trade between the South and Europe. The skill of Yankee shipbuilders and the initiative of New York merchants combined to improve transatlantic service for passengers and cargo. The New York packet lines, beginning with the Black Ball Line in 1818, were the first to post sailing dates and observe them, whether or not a full cargo was on board. The sleek vessels in this service were built for speed and maximum cargo; they were, said an English reporter, "probably the finest and fastest sailing vessels in the world . . . beautifully modeled and of the best workmanship." The whaling industry, concentrated at New Bedford and Nantucket Island, Massachusetts, was also more highly organized after the War of 1812 than before, because the depletion of the Atlantic supply necessitated long, expensive voyages to the Pacific. Still another sign of the new era was John Jacob Astor's American Fur Company, a million-dollar corporation chartered in New

York in 1808. Until the 1830s, when the fur supply of the Northwest began to near exhaustion, Astor used efficient organization and ruthless methods to destroy his weaker competitors and lay the foundation for the first great American fortune.

As mechanical devices played an increasingly important part in the lives of the American people, applied science began to invade the precincts of American education. A network of mechanics' institutes, beginning with one in Boston in 1795, spread through American cities to train men in the mechanical arts. When President Madison, like his predecessors, urged the founding of a national university, he stressed its potential value as a "temple of science" to diffuse "useful knowledge." Nothing came of this, but several private colleges soon added applied science to their curricula. At Harvard, in 1814, Dr. Jacob Bigelow began to lecture on "The Elements of Technology" and tried to awaken his students to the possibilities of this exciting frontier. At Yale, Benjamin Silliman brought a similar message not only to his students but to a wider audience through his *American Journal of Science,* founded in 1818, and through his enormously popular public lectures. In 1825 Rensselaer Polytechnic Institute, the first of its genre, opened its doors at Troy, New York, "for the purpose of instructing persons who may choose to apply themselves in the application of science to the common purposes of life."

If newspapers and periodicals accurately reflected public opinion, the American people were proud of their technological achievements and fascinated by the many useful products of applied science. The promise of a rising standard of living encouraged them to rationalize agriculture, to build great internal improvements, to mechanize industry, and to widen commercial horizons. Looking back at the half-century of economic growth following independence, Tocqueville concluded that "no people in the world had made such rapid progress in trade and manufactures as the Americans; they constitute at the present day the second maritime nation in the world"; their manufacturing makes "great and daily advances"; "the greatest undertakings and speculations are executed without difficulty. . . . The Americans arrived but as yesterday on the territory which they inhabit, and they have already changed the whole order of nature for their own advantage."

Lowell: "the Manchester of America"

Capital and labor. Yet, while they found the promises of the Industrial Revolution irresistible, many Americans were at the same time a little uneasy about what had been happening to their society since industry got a foothold. Carrying with them into the new age the assumptions of a simple agrarian society, they watched apprehensively the growth of cities, the "paper-money speculations" of urban businessmen, and the movement of young people from the land to the factory. They wondered whether the American tradition was somehow being betrayed, whether the craving for material success was undermining their morals and compromising their virtue. To be sure, these fears were still rather vague and sporadic, for in the 1820s and 1830s the cities and the factories were not very large, and the urban industrial population was a small fraction of the whole. But the trend was clear.

One consequence of the factories and machines was the gradual emergence of two new social classes. The first were the industrial capitalists, whom the agrarian gentry regarded as vulgarly ambitious and dangerously powerful. With their wealth they gained considerable political power and, as James Fenimore Cooper complained, substituted their "fluctuating expedients for the high principles of natural justice." Industrialists operated in mysterious ways, some through corporations, those cold, impersonal institutions "having neither a body to be kicked nor a soul to be damned." The second new social class were the factory workers, the hirelings who tended machines for a weekly wage and, in the larger establishments, had no personal contact with either owners or ultimate consumers. They were recruited from the farms and, increasingly by the 1830s, from among newly arrived immigrants.

Thanks to a chronic labor shortage, workingmen's living conditions were far better in America than in Europe. Visitors to Lowell often commented on the attention that the Boston Associates gave to the welfare of the young women who worked in their mills. The "Lowell girls" lived in comfortable boardinghouses built by the company; their morals were strictly supervised; and they were provided with recreational facilities, educational opportunities, and religious instruction. They published their own monthly magazine, the *Lowell Offering,* "as a repository of original articles, written by females employed in the

mills." After a visit to Lowell, Charles Dickens reported that he had seen "no face that bore an unhealthy or an unhappy look." According to Anthony Trollope, Lowell was "the realization of a commercial utopia," where the women were "taken in, as it were, to a philanthropical manufacturing college."

But industrial paternalism soon declined in the Lowell mills as professional managers fought competitors by cutting costs and making increased use of immigrant labor. Even in the 1830s the working day at Lowell was thirteen hours in summer and from sunrise to sunset in winter. Another visitor had a less happy report about conditions among the women employees: "The great mass wear out their health, spirits, and morals without becoming one whit better off than when they commenced labor." Children under sixteen, who constituted two-fifths of the labor force in New England textile mills, worked twelve or more hours a day. Real wages declined; in 1830 it was estimated that some twenty thousand of the lowest paid women in Eastern cities worked sixteen hours a day for $1.25 a week. The callousness of the factory system in a laissez-faire economy began to be reflected, too, in the crowded dwellings of drab factory towns.

Such conditions ultimately produced disturbing social fissures and a greater awareness of class interests and class identity than had been the case before the rise of the factory. When workingmen tried to improve their status through united action, unprecedented tensions developed in the relations between labor and capital. In the 1790s carpenters, printers, and cordwainers had begun to organize in several cities; in the early nineteenth century other skilled trades followed their example. The next step was the formation of city federations of craft unions, six of which united, in 1834, to form the short-lived National Trades' Union. Strikes for higher wages usually failed, first, because labor organizations were still weak and inexperienced and, second, because state courts usually treated them as criminal conspiracies under common law.* Turning briefly to political action in the 1820s, work-

*The common law, introduced to America from England in colonial days, consists of a body of judicial decisions based on custom and precedent. It became the basis of the legal system in all the states except Louisiana. In the early nineteenth century, state courts repeatedly used common-law precedents to find guilty of criminal conspiracies the combinations of workmen attempting to force employers to bargain with them over wages and working conditions.

Most wore out their health

ingmen's parties, especially in New York and Philadelphia, agitated for free public education, shorter working hours, and other social reforms to aid the laboring class. Distressed by such novel phenomena as trade unions and workingmen's parties, some conservatives might well have recalled Jefferson's pessimistic predictions about the evil consequences of industrialization.

Economic crisis. The Panic of 1819 introduced the United States to still another hazard of a commercial-industrial economy: the depression phase of the modern business cycle. When Americans first began to experience the rhythmic rotation of booms, panics, and depressions, they were so mystified that many of them turned to the supernatural for an explanation. An angry deity, they said, periodically brought hard times to punish man for his moral delinquencies—extravagance, speculation, and greed. This first modern panic followed several years of postwar prosperity. In the boom years, when cotton sold for more than 30 cents a pound and wheat for $2 a bushel, land speculation financed by the state banks became a national disease. Soon the Bank of the United States caught the spirit of the times; rather than acting as a stabilizing force, it extended credit generously to speculators and business-promoters in both the East and the West. Public land sales rose sharply; and between 1814 and 1819, under the impetus of high prices, cotton production doubled.

At length an accumulation of adverse economic forces brought these flush times to a sudden end. First came a decline in the European demand for American agricultural products, especially cotton, then a shrinking of the market for textiles. Early in 1819 the Bank of the United States, now under new and more conservative management, began to call in its loans and to exert pressure on the state banks to redeem their notes with specie. The Bank's attempt to save itself from its own recent follies was the immediate cause of a financial panic that forced many state banks to close their doors. In the subsequent depression prices fell disastrously—in 1823 cotton sold for less than 10 cents a pound—and public land sales nearly ceased. Thousands of farmers and planters saw their lands sold at public auction to satisfy the claims of creditors; numerous speculators and business-promoters forfeited property to the Bank of the United States for failing to repay their loans. In the Eastern cities a half-million workers lost their jobs when factories closed down or curtailed their operations.

Those suffering from economic distress turned to government for relief. Manufacturers demanded higher tariff protection, and after a long battle Congress came to their aid with the Tariff of 1824. To help Western farmers who had bought public land on credit, Congress permitted them to delay payments or to keep as much of the land as they had paid for. Several Southern and Western states passed "stay laws" postponing the time when creditors could foreclose on the property of debtors. The demand for "stay laws" and other measures of debtor relief became bitter issues in the politics of various states, especially Kentucky and Tennessee.

By the mid-twenties prosperity had returned, but not before the panic and depression had created angry feelings that were reflected in national politics. Many accused the Bank of the United States of coldly sacrificing thousands of innocent victims to protect the interests of its stockholders. Thereafter much of the anxiety about the new economic order was focused on the monopolistic Bank, the most powerful of the "soulless" corporations. Senator Thomas Hart Benton of Missouri pictured the Bank as a ruthless "money power" to which the Western cities were enslaved: "They may be devoured by it at any moment. They are in the jaws of the monster! A lump of butter in the mouth of a dog! One gulp, one swallow, and all is gone!"

The ground had been prepared for the growth of the Jacksonian movement, which, in a strange way, benefited from both the acquisitive impulses that the new order had aroused in the American people and the lingering doubts they felt about its results.

POSTWAR NATIONALISM

George Dangerfield has written two superb books on the period from the War of 1812 to the election of Andrew Jackson as President: *The Era of Good Feelings** (1952) and *The Awakening of American Nationalism, 1815–1828** (1965). P. C. Nagel, *One Nation Indivisible: The Union in American Thought, 1776–1861* (1964), is a study of the intellectual roots of American nationalism. An excellent study of the postwar decline of the Federalists is Shaw Livermore, Jr., *The Twilight of Federalism* (1962). The period may also be studied through several good biographies of Republican leaders: Harry Ammon, *James Monroe: The Quest for National Identity* (1971); C. M. Wiltse, *John C. Calhoun: Nationalist, 1782–1828* (1944); G. G. Van Deusen, *The Life of Henry Clay** (1937); and Clement Eaton, *Henry Clay and the Art of American Politics** (1957). Bray Hammond, *Banks and Politics in America from the Revolution to the Civil War** (1957), provides a sympathetic account of the chartering of the second Bank of the United States and its role in the American economy.

The role of the Supreme Court in the Marshall era is treated fully in A. J. Beveridge's distinguished biography of the great Chief Justice, *The Life of John Marshall,* 4 vols. (1916–19). Some of the best of the briefer studies are E. S. Corwin, *John Marshall and the Constitution* (1919); C. G. Haines, *The Role of the Supreme Court in American Government and Politics, 1789–1835* (1944); and R. E. Ellis, *The Jeffersonian Crisis: Courts and Politics in the Young Republic* (1971). R. K. Faulkner, *The Jurisprudence of John Marshall* (1968), provides a comprehensive analysis of Marshall's thought. A. M. Bickel, *Justice Joseph Storey and the Rise of the Supreme Court* (1971), is a satisfactory biography of a distinguished nineteenth-century jurist.

Several excellent monographs on the Monroe Doctrine are available: Dexter Perkins, *The Monroe Doctrine, Vol. I, 1823–1826* (1927); E. H. Tatum, Jr., *The United States and Europe, 1815–1823* (1936); C. C. Griffin, *The United States and the Disruption of the Spanish Empire* (1937); and A. P. Whitaker, *The United States and the Independence of Latin America, 1800–1830** (1941). Two fine biographies should also be consulted: J. H. Powell, *Richard Rush: Republican Diplomat, 1780–1859* (1942), and S. F. Bemis, *John Quincy Adams and the Foundations of American Foreign Policy* (1949). Frank Thistlethwaite, *The Anglo-American Connection in the Early Nineteenth Century** (1959), describes the economic and intellectual ties of the United States and Great Britain.

THE WESTWARD MOVEMENT

Two good syntheses of the westward movement in this period are Dale Van Every, *The Final Challenge: The American Frontier, 1804–1845* (1964), and F. S. Philbrick, *The Rise of the West, 1754–1830** (1965). The classic statement of the importance of the West to the whole of American society is F. J. Turner, *The Frontier in American History** (1920). R. A. Billington, *America's Frontier Heritage** (1967), is a sympathetic appraisal of the Turner thesis in the light of modern scholarship. The best studies of public land policy in the West are R. M. Robbins, *Our Landed Heritage: The Public Domain** (1942), and M. J. Rohrbough, *The Land Office Business: The Settlement and Administration of American Public Lands, 1789–1837* (1968). P. W. Gates, *The Farmer's Age: Agriculture, 1815–1860** (1960), is a comprehensive study of Southern and Western agricultural development. The importance of urban development in the West, long neglected, is stressed in R. C. Wade, *The Urban Frontier** (1959). R. C. Buley, *The Old Northwest: Pioneer Period, 1815–1840,* 2 vols. (1950), provides an exhaustive study of social conditions in the West.

G. R. Taylor, *The Transportation Revolution, 1815–1860** (1951), a general study, has much detail on efforts to deal with this problem in the West. L. C. Hunter, *Steamboats on the Western Rivers* (1949), is a classic. Other valuable studies are P. D. Jordan, *The National Road* (1948); L. D. Baldwin, *The Keelboat Age on Western Waters* (1941); Carter Goodrich, *Government Promotion of American Canals and Railroads, 1800–1890* (1960); Carter Goodrich, *et al., Canals and American Economic Development* (1961); R. E. Shaw, *Erie Water West: A History of the Erie*

*Available in a paperback edition.

Canal, 1792–1854 (1966); and H. N. Scheiber, *Ohio Canal Era: A Case Study of Government and the Economy, 1820–1861* (1969).

THE OLD SOUTH AND SLAVERY

The best surveys of the Old South are Clement Eaton, *A History of the Old South* (2nd ed., 1966), and Monroe Billington, *The American South* (1971). There is a brilliant essay on the Old South in the first section of W. J. Cash, *The Mind of the South** (1941). Clement Eaton, *The Growth of Southern Civilization** (1961), is a perceptive study of the social and cultural life of the Old South. W. R. Taylor, *Cavalier and Yankee: The Old South and American National Character** (1961), is a study of the evolution of the Southern legend. U. B. Phillips, *Life and Labor in the Old South** (1929), is a somewhat sentimental description of life on the plantations. F. L. Owsley, *Plain Folk of the Old South** (1949), deals, almost as sentimentally, with the life of the nonslaveholders, whom Phillips almost ignored. E. D. Genovese, *The World the Slaveholders Made* (1969), attempts to apply a Marxian class interpretation to the social structure of the Old South. An indispensable book, based on extensive travels in the South in the 1850s, is F. L. Olmsted, *The Cotton Kingdom* (1861). A new edition of Olmsted, edited by A. M. Schlesinger, was published in 1953.

Slavery may be studied from several perspectives in U. B. Phillips, *American Negro Slavery** (1919); K. M. Stampp, *The Peculiar Institution** (1956); and Stanley Elkins, *Slavery: A Problem in American Institutional and Intellectual Life** (1959, 2nd ed., 1968). Among the best books on special aspects of slavery are Frederic Bancroft, *Slave Trading in the Old South** (1931); R. C. Wade, *Slavery in the Cities* (1964); W. K. Scarborough, *The Overseer: Plantation Management in the Old South* (1966); and R. S. Starobin, *Industrial Slavery in the Old South* (1970). C. N. Degler, *Neither Black Nor White: Slavery and Race Relations in Brazil and the United States** (1971), is an excellent comparative study. D. L. Robinson, *Slavery in the Structure of American Politics, 1765–1820* (1971), traces the issue through a series of crises in the early national period. The best study of the Missouri Compromise is Glover Moore, *The Missouri Controversy** (1953).

INDUSTRY AND TECHNOLOGY

Useful surveys of the beginnings of industrialization are V. S. Clark, *History of Manufactures in the United States,* 3 vols. (1928), and J. W. Oliver, *History of American Technology* (1956). Books especially valuable for their interpretations are Roger Burlingame, *The March of the Iron Men** (1938); T. C. Cochran and William Miller, *The Age of Enterprise** (1942); D. C. North, *The Economic Growth of the United States, 1790–1860** (1961); D. C. North, *Growth and Welfare in the American Past** (1966); and Stuart Bruchey, *The Roots of American Economic Growth** (1965). H. J. Habakkuk, *American and British Technology in the Nineteenth Century** (1962), is a penetrating analysis of the relationship between high labor costs and mechanization. Numerous essays in R. W. Fogel and S. L. Engerman, eds., *The Reinterpretation of American Economic History* (1971), are relevant to the problems discussed in this chapter.

Three outstanding studies of the early textile industry are A. H. Cole, *The American Wool Manufacture,* 2 vols. (1926); C. F. Ware, *The Early New England Cotton Manufacture* (1931); and P. F. McGouldrick, *New England Textiles in the Nineteenth Century: Profits and Investment* (1968). C. W. Pursell, Jr., *Early Stationary Steam Engines in America: A Study in the Migration of Technology* (1969), stresses the importance of steam power in American industry before the Civil War. The beginnings of the corporation can be studied in E. M. Dodd, *American Business Corporations until 1860* (1954). The best treatments of the early labor movement are in J. R. Commons, *et al.,* Vol. I of *History of Labour in the United States,* 4 vols. (1918–35), and Edward Pessen, *Most Uncommon Jacksonians: The Radical Leaders of the Early Labor Movement** (1967). The best work available on the Panic of 1819 is M. N. Rothbard, *The Panic of 1819: Reactions and Policies* (1962).

*Available in a paperback edition.

9

Politics for the Common Man

The rapid economic growth and social change that followed the War of 1812 had a profound effect on the nation's political life. During the 1820s the death of the Federalists (see p. 186) and the subsequent fragmentation of the Republicans brought the first American party system to an end. But in the sixteen years between the presidential elections of 1824 and 1840 a new party system took shape—one that differed from the first in many crucial ways, most notably in the willingness of its leaders to abandon the eighteenth-century ideal of social harmony and to accept parties and political conflict as both inevitable and constructive. As vigorous two-party politics developed in all sections of the country—it had never before existed in the South and West—a growing number of voters turned out in national elections, and control of public affairs became less exclusively the business of prudent gentlemen from old and distinguished families than it had been before. The Democratic party, under the leadership of Andrew Jackson and Martin Van Buren, made skillful and dramatic appeals to the fears and aspirations of the common man; but the National Republicans (renamed the Whigs in the 1830s), under the leadership of Clay and Webster, also made an effective bid for mass support and became equally adept in the use of the new political tactics. The politics of the Jacksonian era was enlivened by bitterly fought presidential contests—they were the lifeblood of the second American party system—by disputes over who were the friends and who were the enemies of the people, by ill-tempered conflicts between nationalists and state righters, and by a heightened sectionalism. Party battles were waged with intense fervor and with an unprecedented amount of demagoguery and political flimflam, each party predicting that the victory of its rival would bring disaster to the nation. Yet, though the heated rhetoric of political partisans should not be taken at face value, though party leaders were far more pragmatic and less ideological than they sometimes sounded, and though the parties tried to mute divisive national issues, these political wars often did involve important questions of public policy.

The new democracy

The celebration of the Common Man. The Jacksonian era, it was once claimed, marked the "rise of the common man," a concept whose meaning is vague and whose validity is doubtful. It is true that in the 1820s and 1830s an ambitious and energetic young white man (most black men, of course, remained in slavery) could easily find tempting opportunities in his thriving and relatively fluid society to achieve material success. With economic affluence he or his children would, more than likely, soon gain both political influence and social prestige. This was the road followed by numerous men who began with

211

modest means—in effect, they emerged from the ranks of common men and pushed their way into the ranks of the élite, as Jackson himself did.

However, if this is what was meant by the rise of the common man, there was nothing remarkable about the Jacksonian era. For in this sense a limited number of common men had been rising ever since the colonial period. We have seen that the people who came to the English colonies seldom carried much in the way of worldly possessions or social prestige; hence, the fact that America, by the end of the eighteenth century, had an upper class of wealthy merchants and landowners indicates that success had already rewarded the enterprise of some. In the years of prosperity and expansion after the War of 1812, other common men flourished and rose by engaging in manufacturing in New England and the Middle Atlantic States, or by speculating in Western lands, or by growing cotton with slave labor in Alabama and Mississippi. And long after the Jackson era had closed some of the American élite continued to be recruited from the ranks of common men.

But the great majority of common men, in this era as in those that preceded and followed it, neither grew rich nor rose to high social position. Instead they managed only to make a more or less comfortable living and continued to be common men—small farmers, village mechanics, city laborers. The social mobility of Jackson's America was neither new nor remarkably great—it may even have been less than in earlier years—and the lines between social classes were as clearly drawn at the end of the era as at the start. To be sure, a major goal of the Jacksonians was to remove obstacles to success and to provide equal opportunities for all to prosper materially. Nevertheless, the striking feature of the period had nothing to do with social fluidity; it was the emergence of a new party system combined with certain changes in political procedures that broadened the base of American democracy and increased the influence of the common man while he *remained* a common man. More than ever before politicians were obliged to square their goals with the desires and adapt their tactics to the tastes of a mass of ordinary voters. In consequence, the Jacksonian era was notable less for the rise than for the celebration of the Common Man—for its rhetorical equalitarianism, which honored the average voter's moral virtue and common-sense wisdom. "Never for a moment believe," said Jackson, "that the great body of the citizens . . . can deliberately intend to do wrong."

Democratic reforms. This was not the beginning of American democracy, only its expansion; nor was the expansion initiated by President Jackson, for the trend had been evident long before. The impulse came in part from the newly settled West, where conditions of life encouraged a spirit of equalitarianism; but it also came from the cities of the East, where middle-class reformers, small businessmen, and spokesmen for urban artisans demanded that government be not only *for* the people but *of* and *by* the people as well. Armed with the Declaration of Independence and the doctrine of natural rights, they argued that they were seeking no radical innovations but merely harmonizing political practices with the principles on which the nation was founded. Restrictions on the popular will, insisted one reformer, "arose from British precedents." Moreover, America was safe for political democracy, because there were no sharp class lines, no mass poverty, and no need for ambitious men to remake society before they could advance in it. Indeed, conservative property-holders could yield, if sometimes grudgingly, to the democratic upsurge and to the new form of mass politics without fearing that they were paving the way to their own destruction.

When, for example, political reformers urged the removal of property restrictions on the suffrage, they invariably stressed the argument that no one would be hurt. A delegate to the New York constitutional convention of 1821 agreed that if manhood suffrage would in fact impair the rights of property "this would be a fatal objection." But this was not the case: "Will not our laws continue the same? Will not the administration of justice continue the same? And if so, how is private property to suffer?" Unlike Europeans, said another delegate, "We have no different estates, having different interests, necessary to be guarded from encroachments. . . . We are all of the same estate—all commoners."

The best-remembered protest against manhood suffrage was that of Chancellor James Kent, a New York Federalist. Though Kent warned of the "tendency in the poor to covet and to share the plunder of the rich," he did not advocate the rule of a small aristocracy of large property-holders. Rather, he accepted the election of the governor and the lower house of the state legislature by manhood suffrage and asked only that the upper house be chosen by owners of freehold estates worth at least $250. In defending his position he sounded more like a Jeffersonian than a champion of a capitalist plutocracy, for he spoke of the "freeholders of moderate possessions" as the "safest guardians of property and the laws." Like Jefferson, Kent feared "the crowds of dependents connected with great manufacturing and commercial establishments, and the motley and undefinable population of crowded ports." In large cities like New York, "one master capitalist with his one hundred apprentices, and journeymen, and agents, and dependents will bear down at the polls an equal number of farmers of small estates who cannot safely unite for their common defense." Another New York conservative professed "great veneration for the opinions of Mr. Jefferson," quoted his view that cities are "ulcers on the body politic," and expressed fear that manhood suffrage "would occasion political demoralization, and ultimately overthrow our government." But these conservatives frightened few and went down to overwhelming defeat.

Indeed, it is remarkable how easily the reformers carried the day—how feeble the resistance of the conservatives proved to be. The constitutions of the new Western states provided for white manhood suffrage—or at least enfranchised all taxpayers, which was almost the same thing. The Eastern states had originally restricted the suffrage to property-holders, but one by one they gave way, until, in the 1850s, the last of them, Virginia and North Carolina, adopted manhood suffrage. Only in Rhode Island did the movement for reform result in violence—in the so-called Dorr Rebellion—but even there, by 1843, the conservatives had surrendered.

Manhood suffrage alone, however, had only a minor impact on American politics until the mass of qualified voters began to take a personal interest in it. Since the Revolution, a large proportion of the voters had been apathetic; save for an occasional state election, they turned out in limited numbers and seemed willing to accept the leadership of a small political élite. To the mass of village artisans and self-sufficient farmers, both federal and state governments seemed remote, and in an age of laissez faire neither visibly affected their daily lives. Politics was the business of wealthy men who had things at stake and had the experience necessary for the management of public affairs. State governments, therefore, were often controlled by a few great families, who ruled through factional alliances and only occasionally faced the challenge of an aroused electorate.

But when ordinary voters became involved in the money economy as small entrepreneurs, industrial wage-earners, or farmers producing for the market, they developed a greater personal interest in questions of public policy such as the tariff, internal improvements, and banking. The shock of the Panic of 1819 and the depression that followed intensified their political concerns and shook their confidence in the old political leadership. The Virginia Dynasty came to an end in 1825; and the subsequent growth of a second American party system, which began at the state level, soon gave politics an unprecedented vitality. Eventually the new system brought two-party politics to every state, and the close political contests that occurred in most of them caused public interest to increase dramatically. Inexpensive party newspapers appeared in every town to arouse and educate the people; and the new breed of politician, skilled in the art of popular appeal, developed the business of electioneering into a unique cultural phenomenon, second only to religious revivalism in its emotional charge. These new, pragmatic political leaders came less often from the well-established American élite; they viewed politics as a profession and loyalty to party as a supreme virtue. Focusing as they did on efficient organization for the presidential campaigns, the parties were like corporations that made bids every four years for the job of administering the federal government.

It was in this new political environment that attendance at the polls began to rise. When Jackson was elected President in 1828, 56 percent of the adult white males voted, which was more than double the percentage of 1824; and in 1840, 78 percent of them voted. Since no state yet had the secret ballot, ordinary voters were still subject to the influence of powerful neighbors. Nevertheless, an increasing number paid less deference to the gentry and became more independent in exercising their political rights. To be sure, voting behavior in the new party system was significantly affected by religious and ethnic affiliations and by irrational influences such as local traditions, appeals to party loyalty, spectacular electioneering tactics, and pure demagoguery, but local and national issues were seldom irrelevant to the decisions voters made.

Another democratic reform supposedly gave the common man a more direct role in the selection of presidential candidates. From the time of Jefferson, Federalists and Republicans had named their candidates in secret congressional caucuses. This system was used for the last time in 1824; by 1832 ''King Caucus'' had given way to the national nominating convention, which in theory gave the party rank and file a voice in the nominations. Meanwhile, one state after another transferred the election of presidential electors from the legislature to the voters, and by 1832 only South Carolina adhered to the old system. The states also made an increasing number of state offices elective rather than appointive.

Finally, the idea of a trained—and therefore, presumably, aristocratic—civil service was repudiated so that common men could aspire to state and federal offices as a reward for faithful party service. Party leaders ''claim as a matter of right, the advantages of success,'' said William L. Marcy, a leader of the New York Jacksonians. ''They see nothing wrong in the rule, that to the victor belong the spoils of the enemy.'' In its day the ''spoils system'' appeared to be another step toward the democratization of American politics. The anti-Jacksonians were critical of this debasing of the civil service, but when they came to power they found the system irresistible and used it with equal enthusiasm.

John Quincy Adams and National Republicanism

The election of 1824. As the end of his second term approached, President Monroe hoped that his successor would be William H. Crawford, his Secretary of the Treasury, a Virginian by birth though a resident of Georgia, and a state-rights representative of the planter class. A sparsely attended congressional caucus nominated Crawford as the official Republican candidate. But this time there were other ambitious politicians in the field—all professed Republicans—whose supporters repudiated the caucus system as undemocratic and won endorsements for their candidates from state legislatures and mass meetings. Crawford's competitors included John Quincy Adams, the talented Secretary of State, a nationalist, and the favorite of New England; Henry Clay, Speaker of the House, champion of the American System, and a man of captivating charm; and Andrew Jackson, a military hero with wide popular appeal but, at the time, rather vague political views. With four competing candidates, each attracting somewhat different sections and interests, the Republican party quickly disintegrated as a national political organization.

In the election Jackson won a plurality of the popular vote and ninety-nine electoral votes; he had substantial support everywhere except in New England. Adams' eighty-four electoral votes came chiefly from New York and New England, Crawford's forty-one from the Southeast, and Clay's thirty-seven from the Northwest.* Since none of the four polled a majority in the Electoral College, the choice had to be made by the House of Representatives from among the three leading candidates, with the congressional delegation from each state casting one vote. Clay, who had come in fourth, was thus eliminated from the competition, and a serious illness had put Crawford out of the running. The choice was between Adams and Jackson.

Clay, because of his power in the House and his control over the three states he had carried, could swing the election either way.

*Calhoun easily won election as Vice President.

The election of 1824

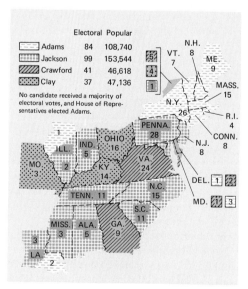

Electoral Popular

	Electoral	Popular
Adams	84	108,740
Jackson	99	153,544
Crawford	41	46,618
Clay	37	47,136

No candidate received a majority of electoral votes, and House of Representatives elected Adams.

Jackson's friends approached Clay and argued that their man had the stronger claim, because he had polled the largest popular vote; and the Kentucky legislature instructed Clay to support the Hero of New Orleans. But Clay not only feared Jackson as a formidable competitor in Western politics but doubted that he was qualified to be President—doubted, too, that he would support the American System. Adams, meanwhile, was tortured by a conflict between his ambition to be President and his distaste for the political higgling that was required to win the prize. Eventually his ambition triumphed: he made the necessary promises and had an interview with Clay that seemed to satisfy the President-maker and win his support. Adams and Clay were as different as two men could be, and their personal relations had been far from cordial; but Adams was still the logical man for Clay to favor, because he shared Clay's views on public policy. Accordingly, when the House voted on February 9, 1825, Adams, with Clay's backing, won a clear majority on the first ballot (Adams thirteen, Jackson seven, Crawford four).

When President Adams appointed Clay Secretary of State, the disappointed Jacksonians immediately detected a shocking case of political jobbery. Adams, they claimed, had purchased Clay's support by giving him the post from which he could best hope to succeed to the Presidency. It was, said John Randolph, an alliance "of the puritan and the black-leg." The nation's political virtue, wrote an angry Jacksonian editor, had died "of poison administered by the assassin hands of John Quincy Adams, the usurper, and Henry Clay." For the next three years the enemies of the Adams Administration charged that "bargain and corruption" had betrayed the plain will of the people. Though Adams doubtless had reached a political understanding with Clay, he had in fact made no corrupt bargain. But neither man ever successfully refuted the accusation. Jackson resigned his seat in the Senate, the Tennessee legislature again nominated him for the Presidency, and the political campaign of 1828 was under way almost as soon as Adams was settled in the White House.

The Adams Administration. Adams' term as President was a tragic episode in an otherwise brilliant public career, which included service as a diplomat, as Secretary of State,

and in later years as a congressman from Massachusetts. Unfortunately the superb talents of this son of John Adams did not include a sensitivity to trends in public opinion or the adroitness, tact, and personal warmth essential to presidential leadership. As a result he met with a series of political disasters. This was all the more unfortunate because Adams represented a point of view on the federal government's role in the national economy, and on its responsibilities to the states and the people, that deserved to be considered on its own merits.

The new President was an enthusiastic champion of national economic growth, especially of commercial and manufacturing expansion, and he looked benevolently upon the new capitalistic enterprises that were spawned by the Industrial Revolution. He was, moreover, as he made clear in his first annual message, a nationalist who believed that the Constitution gave the federal government ample power to direct and encourage this growth and to undertake numerous projects "for the common good." Adams spoke in support of the American System with as much fervor as Clay, especially when he urged the use of federal funds for internal improvements. Citing the National Road as a precedent, he asked: "To how many thousands of our countrymen has it proved a benefit? To what single individual has it ever proved an injury?" After the retirement of the public debt he would use the proceeds from the sale of public lands for roads and canals to facilitate communication "between distant regions and multitudes of men." More, he would build a great national university at Washington for "moral, political, and intellectual improvement," finance explorations of the interior and of the Northwest coast, and establish an astronomical observatory. Adams believed that Congress might even pass laws designed to promote "the elegant arts, the advancement of literature, and the progress of the sciences." Congress would, in fact, betray a sacred trust by not doing so; nor should it use as an excuse for inaction "that we are palsied by the will of our constituents." The time was ripe for action, said Adams confidently, for "the spirit of improvement is abroad upon this earth."

But these very sentiments prompted his critics to assail him as a tyrant and an aristocrat. Crawford found them "replete with doctrines which I hold to be unconstitutional."

John Quincy Adams: scrupulous nationalist

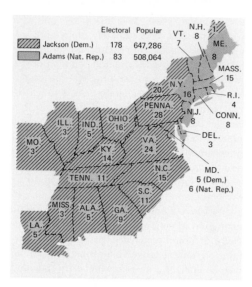

	Electoral	Popular
Jackson (Dem.)	178	647,286
Adams (Nat. Rep.)	83	508,064

The election of 1828

Jefferson accused Adams of seeking to establish "a single and splendid government of an aristocracy . . . riding and ruling over the plundered ploughman and beggared yeomanry." Congress responded to the President's proposals with little enthusiasm—even his friends thought he had gone too far—and after the congressional election of 1826 his enemies had full control of the Senate and the House. Appropriations for internal improvements far surpassed those provided during previous administrations but fell short by a great deal of Adams' grand design. A new tariff, enacted in 1828, sponsored by both Administration and anti-Administration congressmen from the Middle and Western states, was not the judicious measure he had called for. The bill was poorly drawn, and because of its concessions to the extreme protectionists the Southern cotton interest called it the "tariff of abominations." Yet Adams signed it.

Somehow his good intentions always seemed to lead him to personal disaster. He conscientiously repudiated a fraudulent Indian treaty, by which the Creeks were to be shorn of all their lands in Georgia, and ordered the negotiation of a new one. But his scrupulous concern for the rights of Indians irritated both Southerners and Westerners. Worse, when the governor of Georgia defied the federal government and threatened to take jurisdiction over the disputed lands, Adams flouted the principle of state rights: he warned that it was the President's duty to vindicate federal authority "by all the force committed for that purpose to his charge." Even in foreign affairs, in spite of Adams' rich experience, the Administration failed to achieve its goals. In 1826, chiefly for partisan reasons, Congress obstructed Clay's attempt to strengthen ties with Latin America by sending delegates to a conference at Panama. Adams also failed to persuade the British to open their West Indian islands to American trade.

At home, while his foes continued their unmerciful attack, Adams further weakened his position by spurning the role of party leader and refusing to use the patronage weapon in his own defense. Many hostile politicians continued to hold office in his Administration—among them Postmaster General John McLean, whose appointment policy seemed to be to reward the President's enemies and punish his friends. Adams was, in fact, the last of the Presidents to look upon parties as an evil and to cling to the eighteenth-century ideal of a national consensus with himself as its spokesman.

The triumph of the Jacksonians. Adams realized that his chances for reelection in 1828 were slim; "the base and profligate combination" of his critics, he wrote bitterly, would probably succeed in defeating him. During the preceding three years the anti-Administration forces had rallied around the charismatic figure of Andrew Jackson. Joining the original Jacksonians was a heterogeneous group that included most of the previous supporters of Crawford and Calhoun and others who disliked the nationalistic American System or had been alienated by the President's inept handling of public affairs and public relations. Though political divisions did not follow class or occupational lines, the Jacksonians seemed to win a majority of the planters and farmers in the South and West, many small entrepreneurs in all parts of the country, and a substantial number of artisans and factory workers in the towns and cities. What strength remained to Adams and the National Republicans was concentrated in the Northeast, mostly in New England.

Thinking it proper to remain aloof from electioneering, the President gave little help to those who ran his campaign. He would not "exhibit himself" to the public or in any other way actively seek a second presidential term. "If my country wants my services, she must ask for them," was his naive but altogether sincere response to those who urged more vigorous action. But his lieutenants were no match, in any case, for the Jackson organization and its able, hard-hitting leaders, among whom were three senators: Martin Van Buren of New York, Thomas Hart Benton of Missouri, and John H. Eaton of Tennessee; and three newspapermen: Amos Kendall and Francis Preston Blair of Kentucky and Isaac Hill of New Hampshire. These men and their associates skillfully exploited the fears and prejudices as well as the ideals of the mass electorate.

In the background of the campaign were a number of specific public-policy issues: the tariff, internal improvements, banking, land policy, and at the local level the question of bankruptcy laws and debtor-relief laws. But the politicians and party editors were usually vague on these issues, first, because they feared to divide their friends and hoped to win over the doubtful and, second, because they found other appeals that seemed better calculated to win votes. In a campaign that revolved largely around personalities, few political leaders showed much respect for the intelligence of the American electorate.

Jacksonians described the election as a contest between democracy and aristocracy. Old Hickory, they said, was a man of the people who had their interests at heart. Adams was a monarchist, an enemy of the people, a parasite who had lived off the taxpayers all his life, the head of a band of rascally officeholders, an extravagant waster of public funds for his own pleasure, and the darling of the old Federalists. (Actually, many one-time Fed-

eralists supported Jackson.) Voters were also reminded of the "corrupt bargain" of 1825 and of the need to vindicate the will of the people. Friends of Adams retaliated by describing Jackson as an inexperienced, hot-tempered incompetent—a demagogue having no program and totally unfitted for the responsibilities of the Presidency. At a still lower level campaign leaders, resorting to mud-slinging and character assassination, exchanged charges of pandering, adultery, and murder.

The outcome of such a campaign cannot be explained apart from its substantial element of irrationality. Moreover, sectional feelings doubtless accounted for much of Jackson's Southern and Western support. Even so, many of those who voted for Jackson evidently had come to the conclusion that he would better protect the interests of the people against special privilege. Though scarcely more than half the adult males went to the polls, they gave Jackson a substantial popular majority: 647,286 to 508,064. The electoral vote was 178 to 83, with Adams carrying only New England, New Jersey, Maryland, and Delaware. Observing the boisterous celebration in Washington on the day of Jackson's inauguration, men with different perspectives came to different conclusions. Some saw the start of the reign of King Mob, others the triumph of the common man. Webster observed dryly, "People have come five hundred miles to see General Jackson, and they really seem to think that the country has been rescued from some dreadful danger."

Jacksonian democracy

The new President. Andrew Jackson was a controversial figure in his own day and has been one ever since. This may be explained in part by the complexity of the man, in part by the divergent expectations of those who supported him, and in part by the fact that he soon became not only a man but an abstraction—a symbol and a myth. Jackson's original appeal was not as an experienced statesman with a clear-cut program but as a nationally popular figure who embodied numerous American virtues and towered above the ranks of "mere" politicians. To some his election represented a victory for the nationalistic West, to others a victory for the state-rights South, and to still others a victory for

those everywhere who would dislodge entrenched privilege from positions of power.

Above all, Jackson's victory was interpreted as a vindication of the common man. Born in poverty to Scotch-Irish immigrant parents in the Carolina back country, lacking formal schooling, he had moved to Tennessee and made his own way as a lawyer, land-speculator, soldier, politician, and planter. He was the first President who did not come from a well-established American family in comfortable circumstances. Jackson was, in fact, the first President to embody the American success story in its most romantic form: from a log cabin to the White House. This does not mean, however, that he was at the time of his

Andrew Jackson: commanding Democrat

election still a crude and simple frontiersman, as his political enemies described him. For he had already held several public offices; he had accumulated lands and more than a hundred slaves and lived in a mansion, "The Hermitage," near Nashville; and he had been allied with affluent speculators and creditors in Tennessee politics. In fact, Jackson had entered the ranks of the gentry of the Southwest and with advancing years had become increasingly mellow and perhaps a little pompous. A visitor who met him after his inauguration reported that he had seen dukes and princes and kings, "but none of such elegance and courtliness of manners, and of so commanding presence, as were possessed by General Jackson."

Nevertheless, Jackson was closer to the people than any of his predecessors had been, and his view of himself as their special defender was not a mere demagogic pose. As the one officer of the federal government chosen in a truly national election, he felt that he was in a position of peculiar responsibility. He was not intimidated by congressmen, whose acts, he felt, were too often controlled by small, selfish groups of powerful constituents, and he used his veto power more freely than had any previous President. Nor would Jackson agree that the Supreme Court had the final word on matters of constitutional interpretation, for he believed that the President's oath bound him to support the Constitution "as he understands it, and not as it is understood by others." The decisions of the Court were entitled "to have only such influence as the force of their reasoning may deserve." Beyond being governed by the dictates of his own judgment, Jackson professed to know of no tribunal to which a public man "can appeal with greater advantage or more propriety than the judgment of the people."

In his dual role as party leader and guardian of the people's interests, Jackson promised to use his appointive power to "reform" the civil service and to make it more responsive to the public will. He would discharge all "unfaithful or incompetent" officeholders who had acquired a "habit of looking with indifference upon the public interest" or who had come to regard their offices "as a species of property" and "a means of promoting individual interests." Long tenure in the civil service, he said, was corrupting; a rotation of civil servants every four years would force them to "go back to making a living as other people do." Jackson saw little to be gained from long incumbency, for in general the duties were "so plain and simple that men of intelligence may readily qualify themselves for their performance; and I can not but believe that more is lost by the long continuance of men in office than is generally to be gained by their experience."

Jackson thus elevated the spoils system to a democratic principle, though its practical purpose was to reward loyal party workers with public offices. His rejection of an experienced civil service was not a major disaster in an age when the functions of government were relatively few and uncomplicated; but it did nothing to encourage efficiency or to increase the devotion of officeholders to the public interest. One Democrat observed with dismay that "office-seeking and office-getting was becoming a regular business, where impudence triumphed over worth." Clay indignantly described the "lank, lean, famished" Jacksonians who descended on Washington in 1829 with the cry: "Give us bread! Give us treasury pap! Give us our reward!" But Clay and other critics exaggerated the thoroughness with which Jackson applied his principle. In practice he left 80 percent of the officeholders undisturbed during his eight years as President, and at least a few of the removals were not for political reasons but for dereliction of duty. Though Jackson used the spoils system more freely than his predecessors, subsequent administrations, as the new party system developed, used it with far less restraint than he.

In selecting heads of departments Jackson drew on the various regions and factions that had elected him. But save for Van Buren, who became Secretary of State, the men he appointed were an undistinguished lot, and he never consulted them as an organized group of Cabinet advisers. Instead he counseled informally with a shifting group of men in whom he had confidence, among them the shrewd, talented, ambitious Van Buren; the Second Auditor of the Treasury, Major William B. Lewis of Tennessee, who lived with Jackson in the White House; Francis Preston Blair of Kentucky, who came to Washington to edit the Washington *Globe* as an Administration organ; Isaac Hill, editor of the New Hampshire *Patriot*; Roger B. Taney of Maryland, who later became Attorney General, Secretary of the Treasury, and Chief Justice of the United States; and the Fourth Auditor of the Treasury, Amos Kendall, a man of great influence, who helped Jackson prepare many of his state papers. This so-called Kitchen Cabinet, which was not a Cabinet in any formal sense, played an important role in the development of Administration policies and ideas.

The Jacksonian philosophy. To speak of a Jacksonian philosophy may be to dignify too much the ideas of its pragmatic leaders. The Jacksonians, of course, were never of one mind; nor were their differences with the Whigs always sharp and clear, for the two parties were not ideological opposites. In fact, they were often divided more over means than ends. Nevertheless, there was a Jacksonian way of looking at things, and much of its ideology can be found scattered unsystematically in the President's inaugural addresses, annual messages to Congress, and veto messages.

The Jacksonians lived in a more complex society than had Jefferson, and they generally favored the advances in political democracy that individual states had recently achieved. Yet they were strikingly traditional and conservative on most questions of public policy at the federal level. In a sense, John Quincy Adams had endorsed a more radical program for national economic growth and social progress with the aid of a vigorous federal government. Adams' call for government action was in sharp contrast to Jackson's warning: "To suppose that because our government has been instituted for the benefit of the people it must therefore have the power to do whatever may seem to conduce to the public good is an error into which even honest minds are

too apt to fall." Jackson repeatedly emphasized that the federal government was one of limited powers and cautioned against "overstrained constructions" of the Constitution. He would guard against "all encroachments upon the legitimate sphere of State sovereignty."

Federal intervention in the affairs of the people, Jackson believed, usually came in the form of special favors to influential minorities or of encouragement to monopolistic corporations. There would always be distinctions in society, he conceded, as a result of "superior industry, economy, and virtue . . . but when the laws undertake to add to these natural and just advantages artificial distinctions, to grant titles, gratuities, and exclusive privileges, to make the rich richer and the potent more powerful, the humble members of society—the farmers, mechanics, the laborers—who have neither the time nor the means of securing like favors to themselves, have a right to complain of the injustice of their Government."

As an exponent of federal lasssez faire, Jackson promised to reduce the government "to that simple machine which the Constitution created." Experience had vindicated the Founding Fathers in their decision to withhold "the power to regulate the great mass of the business and concerns of the people" and to leave them to "free enterprise . . . aided by the State sovereignties." The people would find happiness not in a "splendid government . . . but in a plain system, void of pomp, protecting all and granting favors to none, dispensing its blessings, like the dews of Heaven, unseen and unfelt save in the freshness and beauty they contribute to produce."

Some Jacksonians favored this formula of state sovereignty, strict construction, and federal laissez faire because they hoped for a return to old-fashioned, agrarian-oriented Jeffersonianism. On numerous occasions Jackson, unlike Adams with his enthusiasm for economic and social progress, looked back wistfully to the simpler, and presumably purer, young republic of Jefferson's day. He praised "the examples of public virtue left by my illustrious predecessors"; he suggested that it was "time to pause in our career to review our principles"; and, disillusioned by his own earlier speculations and resulting bankruptcy, he expressed a desire "to revive and perpetuate those habits of economy and simplicity which are so congenial to the character of republicans.'' Like Jefferson, Jackson idealized an agrarian society. he described the agricultural interest as ''superior in importance'' to all others and the cultivators of the soil as the ''best part'' of the population. ''Independent farmers are everywhere the basis of society and true friends of liberty.''

But the agrarian ideal was already hopelessly out of date. Reducing the government's role in the economy made it harder for favored groups to win special privileges, but it also gave free rein to irresponsible entrepreneurs in a period of frantic economic activity. At best, Jackson's followers had mixed feelings about his conception of the ideal society. Many of them doubtless shared his nostalgia, but few could resist the temptations of their age. Indeed, more often than not they liked Jackson because, in one way or another, they expected him to help them get ahead in the world—and it was not Jefferson's world that interested them.

Internal improvements and public lands

After his inauguration in 1829, Jackson faced a problem that every American President has faced: that of holding together the disparate groups that had elected him. Typical of the second American party system, the national Democratic party of Jackson's day was essentially a federation of state parties—an unstable coalition of men from many regions with differing needs and interests. Insofar as voters had favored Jackson over Adams for rational reasons, they preferred what they believed would be his stand on most, but seldom all, of the issues that concerned them. Moreover, since the Democrats were loosely organized at the national level, party discipline tended to be lax. Not even the Democratic majority in Congress shared Jackson's view on every issue, and it seldom voted as a unit. Those who differed with the President on questions of secondary importance might rebel momentarily but still remain in the party and continue their general support of the Administration. But those who differed with him on a crucial issue might break away entirely and join the opposition party. This is what actually happened to many of the men who had supported Jackson in 1828, while some of his original opponents turned to him because of his stand on one or another major issue.

The Maysville veto. On one issue, internal improvements, Jackson was bound to antagonize either his friends in the West who favored federal support or his friends in the South and in New York and Pennsylvania who opposed it. He gave a full statement of his position in 1830 when he vetoed a bill to subsidize the construction of a sixty-mile road from Maysville on the Ohio River to Lexington, Kentucky.

In this veto message as well as in other state papers, apparently in part because of Van Buren's influence, he opposed in principle federal spending for internal improvements of any kind. But, like Madison and Monroe, Jackson insisted that if such appropriations were to be made without a constitutional amendment, they must be for projects that were national and not local in character. The Maysville Road, he protested, had ''no connection with any established system of improvements; is exclusively within the limits of a State . . . and even as far as the State is interested . . . [it gives] partial instead of general advantage.''

Federal appropriations for such purposes, Jackson feared, would bring logrolling, wasteful spending, and corruption; they would lead to a consolidated government with powers so vast as to endanger the liberties of the people. It would be far better for the government, after the public debt was retired, to distribute its surplus revenues among the states and permit them to manage their own internal improvements. (At the state level the Jacksonians were anything but consistent proponents of laissez faire.) Yet, in spite of these views, Jackson did not veto all the internal-improvement bills that Congress passed, not even all that were for local projects. At most it can be said that his Maysville veto checked the acceleration of such appropriations and diminished the role of the federal government relative to that of the states. Jackson even saw to it that the completed portions of the National Road were turned over to the four states that contained them, thus enabling the federal government to escape the burden of maintenance costs. This general policy gave the National Republicans an issue which they exploited in those parts of the West where the need for improved transportation determined the political affiliations of many voters.

Land policy. On the question of public land policy Jackson redeemed himself somewhat in the West. In general, Westerners wanted the government to encourage the rapid settlement of unoccupied lands by offering generous terms rather than to seek maximum revenue for the federal treasury. With this in mind, Senator Thomas Hart Benton of Missouri advocated a gradual reduction of the minimum price of public lands of inferior quality from $1.25 to 50 cents an acre, after which any lands still unsold might be given free to actual settlers. Another favorite scheme of Westerners was to permit "squatters"—that is, men who had settled on the public domain before the land was surveyed and offered for sale—to purchase at the minimum price the land they had improved. Neither the first of these schemes (called "graduation") nor the second (called "preemption") was enacted into law during Jackson's Administration, but the President clearly shared the Western point of view. In his message to Congress in 1832 he urged that "the public lands shall cease as soon as practicable to be a source of revenue." To give everyone a chance to obtain a freehold, land should be sold to settlers in small tracts at a price barely sufficient to cover the cost of surveys and clearing Indian titles. More, Jackson recommended that each new state be given that portion of the public domain that lay within its boundaries.

Easterners, especially the manufacturers, hoped to slow down the westward movement and the resulting depletion of the labor supply. They strongly opposed both graduation and preemption and even looked with favor on a proposal to stop temporarily the survey and sale of new Western lands. Henry Clay, seeking a plan that would satisfy all sections, suggested that rather than giving public lands to individual Western states the proceeds from the sale of the lands should be distributed among all the states, to be used as each saw fit. In 1833 Congress passed such a bill, but the President vetoed it. Land policy thus remained an unsettled issue when Jackson left office.

Thomas H. Benton.

Religious and ethnic minorities

Although President Jackson repeatedly professed his devotion to and trust in "the people" and claimed to speak for them, he never really had in mind all the people who lived within the boundaries of the United States. Of the country's three largest religious and racial minorities—Negroes, Indians, and Irish Catholics (the last of whom came in increasing numbers during the 1830s and 1840s)—most Jacksonian leaders showed concern only for the Irish. Because of the tendency for antiforeign, especially anti-Catholic, sentiment to be centered in the Whig party, recent immigrants in general and Irish Catholics in particular voted overwhelmingly Democratic. Indeed, their votes were vital to the Jacksonian organizations in the cities of the Northeast.

In the case of the American Negroes, however, Democratic leaders were at best indifferent to their condition. Jackson was not only one of the largest slaveholders in the Southwest; he was a good deal less troubled about the morality of the institution than Jefferson had been. (On one occasion he advertised for a runaway slave and offered the captor a double reward if he would punish the runaway with one hundred lashes.) The Jackson Administration tried to keep the divisive issue of slavery out of national politics, but the President and Postmaster General Amos Kendall showed their hostility to antislavery organizations by refusing to protect their right to use the mails to distribute their literature in the Southern states. Though race prejudice was rampant in all sections and among members of both political parties, it is still true that in the Northern states the Democrats were more aggressively anti-Negro and more prone to make demagogic, racist appeals than the Whigs. In New York State the small Negro vote was almost solidly anti-Democratic.

Indian removals. Since Indians could not vote, neither party cared very much about them, and Indian policy caused President Jackson relatively little political trouble. Criticism of his policy was limited to a handful of humanitarians concentrated in the Northeast, most of them already affiliated with the anti-Jackson party. Jackson, to the delight of land-hungry Southerners and Westerners, vigorously enforced a plan, favored by both

The Seminole Rebellion

Monroe and Adams and approved by Congress, to remove all the Indian tribes to lands west of the Mississippi. Removal would be better for the Indians themselves, said Jackson, because they were not only unhappy living among the whites but threatened with extinction. "Doubtless it will be painful to leave the graves of their fathers," he conceded, but we need only "open the eyes of those children of the forest to their true condition" to make them appreciate the "humanity and justice" of removal. "Rightly considered," Jackson concluded, "the policy of the General Government toward the red man is not only liberal, but generous." Federal Indian policy, President Van Buren told Congress a few years later, had been "just and friendly throughout . . . its watchfulness in protecting them from individual frauds unremitting."

These unctuous words covered a policy that was callous in its conception and often brutal in its execution. Most of the tribes were more or less coerced into signing removal treaties; usually the lands they received in the West were inferior to those they gave up; the migrations themselves were poorly planned and caused much suffering; and in some cases the Indians were literally driven from their old

homes by military force. Only a few tribes put up organized resistance. In 1832 about a thousand Sac and Fox Indians, led by Chief Black Hawk, defiantly returned to Illinois, but militiamen and army regulars easily drove them back across the Mississippi. This so-called Black Hawk War was hardly more than a skirmish, but the resistance of the Seminoles in Florida was a good deal more formidable. In 1835 many of them, led by Chief Osceola and supported by scores of runaway slaves, rose in rebellion and thus began a costly war that dragged on into the 1840s. The highly civilized Cherokees of Georgia, on the other hand, tried resistance through legal action. When the government of Georgia refused to recognize their autonomy and threatened to seize their lands, the Cherokees took their case to the Supreme Court and won a favorable decision. Marshall's opinion for the Court majority was that Georgia had no jurisdiction over the Cherokees and no claim to their lands. But Georgia officials simply ignored the decision, and the President refused to enforce it. At length the Cherokees had to leave, too, and when Jackson retired from office he counted the near-completion of Indian removals as one of his major achievements.

The tariff and nullification

Disaffection in South Carolina. Jackson favored a fiscal policy that, in its broad outlines, was consistent with old-fashioned Republican principles: he promised rigid economy and a swift reduction of the public debt in order to "counteract that tendency to public and private profligacy" encouraged by large federal expenditures. But on one critical issue, the tariff, he wavered. Some of his early statements gave aid and comfort to the protectionists—for example, in his first inaugural address he endorsed protective duties on all products "that may be found essential to our

national independence." As Southern opposition increased, however, Jackson's position began to change. By 1832 he advocated a tariff designed primarily to provide the government with revenue, one that would give only "temporary and, generally, incidental protection"; and he warned manufacturers not to expect the people to "continue permanently to pay high taxes for their benefit." This shift in favor of tariff reduction antagonized the Northern protectionists. Subsequently, however, when South Carolina resorted to direct action to force a reduction of duties,

Jackson firmly denounced her and thereby alienated many Southerners who believed in free trade and extreme state rights.

Though the tariff was never a clear-cut sectional issue, protectionist sentiment was concentrated in the North and free-trade sentiment in the South. By the 1820s most Southerners, especially the cotton-growers, were convinced that the protective tariff was a discriminatory tax—designed, according to a public meeting in Charleston, to elevate the manufacturing interest "to an undue influence and importance" and thus to benefit "one class of citizens at the expense of every other class." Clay's American System, Southerners believed, gave no advantage to the South, because the South had built few factories and because it exported two-thirds of its cotton crop to European markets. Southern exports paid for most of the country's imports, and the federal government supported itself chiefly by taxing this exchange. Hence Southerners complained that they were paying more than their share of federal taxes; and, to make matters worse, much of the income from the tariff was spent on internal improvements, mostly in the North. In short, the tariff was a peculiar tax on Southern farmers and planters, one that raised the price of everything they consumed and the cost of everything they produced. Such an arrangement, many Southerners soon concluded, was unconstitutional. They agreed that the Constitution had empowered Congress to levy moderate duties on imports, but the purpose was to provide the government with revenue, not to protect industry.

These were the opinions of cotton-growers everywhere, but nowhere were they so strongly held as in South Carolina. Here a combination of economic disaster and social anxiety caused a reaction not only against the tariff but against nationalism generally. Looming large in the background was the fear—widespread in this state, whose black population outnumbered the white by a considerable margin—that federal power might somehow be used to weaken or destroy slavery. The Missouri debate had increased the concern of white South Carolinians; and in 1822 rumors (which had some basis in fact) of a formidable slave conspiracy, led by Denmark Vesey, a Charleston free Negro, created a veritable frenzy. Throughout the 1820s white South Carolinians were inordinately sensitive to the slightest criticism of this peculiar institution from any source. The tariff, many said, was only the first dangerous manifestation of federal usurpation; the same arguments that justified protection might subsequently justify congressional emancipation.

More immediately, however, South Carolina was in the midst of a severe economic crisis. Prior to 1819 the state had flourished, and its proud and aristocratic planters had made fortunes from the cultivation of rice and cotton. But the Panic of 1819 and the subsequent depression were cruel blows, for they brought a sharp decline in cotton prices—a decline that hit South Carolina planters with exceptional force. Facing the competition of the new cotton states in the Southwest, South Carolinians found production costs on their long-used lands relatively high and their crop yield per acre and profit margin correspondingly low. Charleston's commercial interest was languishing, and the state's population had almost stopped growing as farmers moved west in search of better land. Economic adversity, along with worries about slavery, caused political unrest and a swing to extreme state rights.

The majority of white South Carolinians had a simple explanation for their plight. Not soil exhaustion, not the competition of the Southwest, but the high tariff and other federal encroachments on the rights of the states, they said, were to blame. They looked suspiciously at their leading politician, John C. Calhoun, who had supported the Tariff of 1816 (see p. 185) and still in the early 1820s gave evidence of being a nationalist and protectionist. To have a political future in his state Calhoun had no choice but to revise his views; to advance his ambitions in national politics he had to find some remedy that would satisfy the South without alienating all his friends in the North and West. He faced this challenge while he was still Vice President under Adams, and he faced it even more after the passage of the high Tariff of 1828 while he was seeking reelection with Jackson.

Calhoun and state interposition. By then Calhoun had changed his mind and adopted the Southern position that the protective tariff was not only discriminatory but unconstitutional. Now, in 1828, he proposed a remedy in an essay entitled *The South Carolina Exposition and Protest*, which the state legislature published without revealing the name of its

Picking cotton

The great and leading principle is, that the General Government ema-nated from the people of the United States, forming distinct political communities, and acting in their separate and sovereign capacity, and not from all of the people forming one aggregate political community; that the Constitution of the United States is, in fact, a compact, to which each State is a party, in the character already described; and that the several States, or parties, have a right to judge of its infrac-tions; and in case of a deliberate, palpable, and dangerous exercise of power not delegated, they have the right, in the last resort, to use the language of the Virginia Resolutions, ''to interpose for arresting the progress of the evil, and for maintaining, within their respective limits, the authorities, rights, and liberties appertaining to them.'' This right of interposition ... be it called what it may—State-right, veto, nullification, or by any other name—I conceive to be the fundamental principle of our system, resting on facts historically as certain as our revolution itself, and deductions as simple and demonstrative as that of any political or moral truth whatever; and I firmly believe that on its recognition depend that stability and safety of our political institu-tions.

From John C. Calhoun, Fort Hill Address, July 26, 1831.

author. This document indicated that Calhoun had abandoned much of his earlier national-ism and that he had become a conservative spokesman for the Southern planter class. From his new state-rights position he found the way by which a numerical minority, such as the South, could protect itself from obnox-ious legislation adopted by the majority. His solution was the doctrine of nullification, or state ''interposition,'' which he offered as a procedure less drastic than the dissolution of the Union. It was his hope that this remedy would find approval in other sections and thus enable him to protect the interests of the South while continuing his pursuit of the Presidency.

Calhoun was an able student of political theory and a skillful logician. The premises on which he based his doctrine of nullification, however, were not altogether original, for he borrowed much from Madison's and Jeffer-son's Virginia and Kentucky Resolutions of 1798 (see p. 153). As they had, Calhoun argued that before 1787 the states had been completely sovereign and that in framing and ratifying the new Constitution they had not given up their sovereignty. Rather, they had merely formed a ''compact'' and created the federal government as their ''agent'' to exe-cute it. This agent had only limited powers, and the sovereign states, not the Supreme Court, were the judges of what powers had been delegated to it.

From these premises Calhoun concluded that if Congress exceeded its delegated powers by enacting, say, a protective tariff, any one of the states might interpose state authority to block enforcement of the law. To accomplish this the people of a state would elect delegates to a state convention; if the convention decided that the act in question was unconstitutional, it would declare the act null and void within the state's boundaries. Congress might then choose between ac-quiescing in nullification or proposing a con-stitutional amendment specifically granting to the government the desired power. Thus whenever a single state challenged the consti-tutionality of an act of Congress, the cumber-some amending process, requiring ratification by three-fourths of the states, would be the government's only recourse. This system, thought Calhoun, would provide a sufficient safeguard for the interests of the minority South. True democracy, he said, was not the rule of an absolute, or numerical, majority, for such a majority could ride roughshod over the rights of minorities. Instead, he proposed rule by the ''concurrent'' majority, with the people of each state having a veto over federal legis-lation. Minority rights would thereby be pro-tected, and only legislation beneficial to all sections would be enacted.

Calhoun's ingenious system had a full re-view in the United States Senate early in 1830 during a debate that began over public land

The ordinance is founded ... on the strange position that any one State may not only declare an act of Congress void, but prohibit its execution; that the true construction of that instrument permits a State to retain its place in the Union and yet be bound by no other of its laws than those it may choose to consider as constitutional.... But reasoning on this subject is superfluous when our social compact, in express terms, declares that the laws of the United States, its Constitution, and treaties made under it are the supreme law of the land, and, for greater caution, adds "that the judges in every State shall be bound thereby, anything in the constitution or laws of any State to the contrary notwithstanding." And it may be asserted without fear of refutation that no federative government could exist without a similar provision....

If the doctrine of a State veto upon the laws of the Union carries with it internal evidence of its impractical absurdity, our constitutional history will also afford abundant proof that it would have been repudiated with indignation had it been proposed to form a feature in our Government....

I consider, then, the power to annul a law of the United States, assumed by one State, incompatible with the existence of the Union, contradicted expressly by the letter of the Constitution, unauthorized by its spirit, inconsistent with every principle on which it was founded, and destructive of the great object for which it was formed.

Andrew Jackson on nullification

From Andrew Jackson, Proclamation to the People of South Carolina, December 10, 1832.

policy but soon centered on the nature of the federal Union. Robert Y. Hayne of South Carolina and Daniel Webster of Massachusetts, both brilliant orators, were the chief contestants, while Vice President Calhoun listened carefully as presiding officer of the Senate. Hayne explained and defended the doctrine of nullification, enumerated his section's grievances, appealed to the West to join the South in resisting the avarice of the Northeast, and reminded New Englanders that they themselves had toyed with both nullification and secession during the War of 1812. Webster, now an intense nationalist, denied that the Constitution was a mere compact to be interpreted as individual states might please. The people, not the states, had created it, and the Supreme Court was the proper authority to settle disputes over its meaning. Nor was the federal government simply an agent of the states; in exercising its powers it was sovereign and acted directly on the people. "It is," he said, "the people's Constitution, the people's government, made for the people, made by the people, and answerable to the people." The Union was not a voluntary federation of sovereign states; it was intended to be perpetual, and any attempt to dismember it would be treasonable and would lead

to civil war. There may have been flaws in Webster's logic and in his history, but he understood better than Hayne the direction of events and the views of the majority. The South sympathized with Hayne's expression of its grievances, but outside South Carolina few Southerners showed much sympathy for his remedy.

The cold response of Congress to the doctrine of nullification disappointed Calhoun, but the response of President Jackson produced a major crisis in Calhoun's political career. Jackson had a deep respect for the rights of the states, and he was now convinced that Southerners had reason to complain about the existing tariff; but to talk of nullification or secession, as South Carolinians did, was another matter. Soon after the Webster-Hayne debate, at a public banquet, Jackson rose, looked squarely at Calhoun, and proposed his famous toast: "Our *Federal* Union—*It must be preserved.*" This incident was only one of numerous signs of a growing rift between the President and the Vice President, a rift that Secretary of State Van Buren encouraged in his effort to supersede Calhoun as Jackson's successor to the Presidency. Even a petty social tiff among Administration wives contributed to Calhoun's downfall. Mrs. Calhoun,

Daniel Webster: for a perpetual union

a South Carolina aristocrat, snubbed the wife of the Secretary of War, Peggy Eaton, the attractive daughter of a Washington tavern-keeper. Jackson had no patience with this kind of snobbery, and Van Buren, a widower, made it clear that he shared the irritated President's admiration for Mrs. Eaton. Meanwhile, Calhoun's enemies let Jackson know that back in 1818, Calhoun, as Secretary of War, had denounced Jackson for his high-handed invasion of Florida. Explanations were offered and rejected. In 1831 there was a Cabinet reorganization, and Calhoun's friends were forced out of the Administration. Van Buren was now Jackson's candidate to succeed him, and Calhoun found himself pushed more and more out of his role of national leadership into the position of chief defender of the South.

The nullification crisis. The doctrine of nullification was put to the test in 1832, when Congress passed a new tariff bill that conceded little to the Southern demand for lower duties. After Jackson signed the bill, South Carolina's congressmen sent an address to their constituents stating that "all hope for relief from Congress is irrecoverably gone," and Calhoun now openly announced his support of nullification. The nullifiers won control of the South Carolina legislature, and when it met in October it ordered the election of delegates to a state convention. On November 24, 1832, the convention, by an overwhelming majority, adopted an ordinance that pronounced the tariffs of 1828 and 1832 "unauthorized by the Constitution" and therefore "null, void, and no law, nor binding upon this State, its officers or citizens." The ordinance prohibited state or federal officers from enforcing the tariff laws after February 1, 1833, forbade appeals to federal courts, and warned that any federal attempt to coerce the state would force South Carolina to secede from the Union. At this juncture Hayne resigned from the Senate to become governor of South Carolina, and Calhoun resigned as Vice President to take Hayne's place and lead the fight on the Senate floor. The tariff issue had precipitated a serious national crisis.

But South Carolina's position was an uncomfortable one, for no other Southern state was prepared at that time to approve of her radical action. And the angry President reacted vigorously: he threatened to hang Calhoun, he sent a warship and revenue cutters to Charleston harbor, and he announced his readiness to take the field personally in case of a clash of arms. In a proclamation to the people of South Carolina, Jackson endorsed Webster's position on the nature of the Union and warned them of the serious consequences of their action. As President he had no choice but to see that the laws of the United States were executed.

Tension increased when the legislature of South Carolina defiantly replied that Jackson's views were "erroneous and dangerous" and that the state would "repel force by force . . . and maintain its liberty at all hazards." It increased further when Congress considered a "force bill" authorizing the President, if necessary, to use the army and navy to enforce the laws. Yet Jackson hoped to avoid violence except as a last resort, and South Carolina politicians, feeling their isolation, were eager to find a way to escape from their predicament without losing face. At length Henry Clay came forward with a compromise tariff, the details of which he worked out in consultation with Calhoun. It provided that tariff schedules would be gradually reduced over a period of nine years, until by 1842 no duty would exceed 20 percent. On March 1, 1833, Congress passed both the compromise tariff and the force bill, and Jackson signed them. On March 15, the South Carolina convention accepted the compromise and withdrew its nullification of the tariff; but, yielding nothing in principle, it solemnly declared the force bill null and void. Since the crisis had passed, Jackson had the good sense to overlook this final petulant gesture.

Though Jackson irritated both the uncompromising protectionists and the state-rights followers of Calhoun, nationalists in subsequent sectional crises remembered him fondly for his bold action against the nullifiers. At the same time, even though most Southerners rejected nullification, the fight over the tariff made them more conscious than ever before of their minority position. Looking back at the tariff crisis, Chancellor Harper of South Carolina was pessimistic about the future:

> It is useless and impracticable to disguise the fact that the South is a permanent minority, and that there is a *sectional* majority against it—a majority of different views and interests and little common sympathy. . . . We are divided into slave-holding and non-slave-holding states; and . . . this is the broad and marked distinction that must separate us at last.

The Bank war

Criticism of the Bank. Before the controversy over the tariff and nullification had been resolved, Congress and the Administration were engaged in an equally bitter dispute over whether the charter of the Bank of the United States should be renewed when it expired in 1836. Jackson had been hostile to the Bank long before he became President, criticized it repeatedly during his first term in office, made it a basic issue in his campaign for a second term, and gave it so much attention after his reelection that he seemed almost obsessed with a desire to destroy it. To many agrarian-oriented Jacksonians the Bank was by far the most crucial problem, for it went to the very heart of their philosophy; and Jackson himself doubtless counted his ultimate victory over "the Monster" his greatest single accomplishment. To his critics, however, the destruction of the Bank was a major blunder in public policy, a singularly irresponsible exercise of presidential power that did incalculable harm to the country. The merits of the two positions remain a subject of historical debate.

After a shaky start this powerful financial institution had settled down to become, in the decade after the Panic of 1819, a conservative, prosperous, and reasonably responsible business enterprise. Since 1823, the president of the Bank had been Nicholas Biddle, an aristocratic, cultivated, and talented Philadelphian, whose acumen as a banker was unfortunately matched by his ineptitude in dealing with politicians. Many of his admiring contemporaries credited him with developing the Bank and its twenty-nine branches into an effective regulator of the expanding American economy. The Bank marketed government bonds and served as a reliable depository for government funds; it was an important source of credit for the business community; its bank notes provided the country with a sound paper currency; it exerted a restraining influence on the state banks by forcing them to back their notes with adequate specie reserves; and it thus helped to create confidence in the entire banking system of the United States. The source of its power was its control of one-fifth of the bank notes and one-third of the bank deposits and specie of the country.

But it was in part the Bank's possession of this vast economic power that made it so vulnerable politically. Many Jacksonians had not forgotten its seemingly selfish behavior during the Panic of 1819 (see p. 208), and they believed that democracy was in peril when so much power was concentrated in a single corporation. During the 1820s Biddle ran the Bank with considerable restraint, but he tactlessly admitted to a congressional committee that most state banks might have been "destroyed by an exertion of the powers of the [United States] Bank." Moreover, its control over the supply of short-term credit was not subjected to sufficient government regulation. Its charter did not assign to it the public responsibilities of a central bank, as did the legislation creating the Federal Reserve System a century later. This Bank was responsible primarily to its own investors, and its chief function was to earn dividends for them. Many state bankers resented it not only because it forced them to maintain adequate specie reserves but because its federal charter gave it a considerable competitive advantage.

Senator Benton complained that it was to this privileged monopoly that "the Federal Government, the State Governments, and great cities, must, of necessity, apply, for every loan which their exigencies may demand." Biddle's enemies also accused him of corrupting the nation's political life, because many influential politicians and editors were indebted to the Bank for loans. Webster was not only a heavy borrower but was on the Bank's payroll as a legal counsel. "I believe my retainer has not been renewed or *refreshed* as usual," he once wrote to Biddle. "If it be wished that my relation to the Bank should be continued, it may be well to send me the usual retainer."

Thus, by the time Jackson became President the Bank had incurred the hatred of numerous groups for either practical or ideological reasons. Curiously, it antagonized both those who favored "soft money" (more state-bank notes) and those who favored "hard money" (only gold and silver coins). The former included some state banking interests, land-speculators, and small entrepreneurs who felt that their needs were best served by an abundant paper currency. The latter included Eastern workingmen who resented receiving their wages in paper of uncertain value, and agrarian-oriented Southerners and Westerners, such as Senator Benton, who considered any currency other than gold and silver dishonest. The hard-money men were

Nicholas Biddle: aristocratic banker

Defense of the Bank The national bank, though not properly a political *institution, is one of the most important and valuable instruments that are used in the practical administration of the government....* As the fiscal agent of the executive, it has exhibited a remarkable intelligence, efficiency, energy, and above all, INDEPENDENCE. This ... has been its real crime. As the regulator of the currency, it has furnished the country with a safe, convenient and copious circulating medium, and prevented the mischiefs that would otherwise result from the insecurity of the local banks. As a mere institution for loaning money, it has been ... the Providence of the less wealthy sections of the Union.... Through its dealings in exchange at home and abroad, the bank has materially facilitated the operations of our foreign and domestic trade. The important advantages which have thus been derived from this institution have been unattended by any countervailing evil. As its term advanced, and its officers acquired additional experience, it has been constantly gaining on the public favor.

From the Boston *Daily Advertiser,* September 1832.

Death of the Bank The Bank of the United States ... enjoys ... a monopoly of ... favor and support, and, as a necessary consequence, almost a monopoly of the foreign and domestic exchange. The powers, privileges, and favors bestowed upon it in the original charter, by increasing the value of the stock far above its par value, operated as a gratuity of many millions to the stockholders....

The modifications of the existing charter proposed by this act are not such, in my view, as make it consistent with the rights of the States or the liberties of the people.... All the objectionable principles of the existing corporation, and most of its odious features, are retained without alleviation.... Already is almost a third of the stock in foreign hands and not represented in elections. It is constantly passing out of the country, and this act will accelerate its departure. The entire control of the institution would necessarily fall into the hands of a few citizen stockholders....

If we can not at once ... make our Government what it ought to be, we can at least take a stand against all new grants of monopolies and exclusive privileges, against any prostitution of our Government to the advancement of the few at the expense of the many, and in favor of compromise and gradual reform in our code of laws and system of political economy.

From Andrew Jackson, Veto of the Bank Bill, July 1832.

hostile to banks of any kind, state or national, that issued bank notes; they tended to look upon banking as a parasitic enterprise. Among them was Jackson, who once told Biddle, "I do not dislike your Bank any more than all banks." By using gold and silver in ordinary business transactions, he told Congress, the country would avoid "those fluctuations in the standard of value which render uncertain the reward of labor."

Veto of the Bank bill. Jackson's first two messages to Congress left little doubt that he would veto any bill to recharter the Bank. In his first message, in December 1829, he affirmed that "both the constitutionality and the expediency of the law creating this bank are well questioned by a large portion of our fellow-citizens." A year later he again pointed to the dangers posed by the Bank as it was then organized. If a national bank was needed, he suggested that it be established as a branch of the Treasury Department, to act simply as a bank of deposit without power to issue notes, make loans, or acquire property. Such a bank, "having no stockholders, debtors, or property," would raise no constitutional objections. To be sure, the Supreme Court had already affirmed the constitutionality of the present Bank, but to Jackson this was irrelevant. "I have read the opinion of John Marshall," he said, "and could not agree with him."

Biddle, in his campaign to save the Bank, could not avoid getting deeply involved in national politics. He had started as a Jeffersonian Republican and had tried to appease Jackson by appointing some of his supporters to directorships of the branch banks. But Jackson's hostility drove Biddle into the camp of the opposition, and Biddle's loans to congressmen and newspaper editors became increasingly motivated by politics. At length, in 1832, he took the advice of Clay and Webster and applied for a new charter, though the old one would not expire for four more years. Clay assured Biddle that Congress would pass the bill, and he was ready to make a presidential veto an issue in the coming campaign. The bill to recharter the Bank, amended to meet some of Jackson's objections, easily passed both houses of Congress with the support of a substantial minority of the Democrats. Jackson accepted the challenge. "The Bank," he told Van Buren, "is trying to kill me, but I will kill it."

Jackson's veto message, a powerful political document, maintained that the Bank was unconstitutional in spite of the changes in its charter and described the dangers of "such a concentration of power in the hands of a few men irresponsible to the people." Much of the stock was held by foreigners, "and the residue is held by a few hundred of our own citizens, chiefly of the richest class." Their demands for "grants of monopolies and special privileges" had "arrayed section against section, interest against interest, and man against man, in a fearful commotion which threatens to shake the foundations of the Union." Webster bitterly denounced the President for executive usurpation and for seeking "to inflame the poor against the rich," but the veto stood and became a central issue in the presidential election of 1832. Indeed, Clay, Biddle, and the National Republicans helped to make it so by giving the veto message wide circulation, mistakenly thinking that it would serve to discredit Jackson. Whatever the weaknesses of its reasoning, however it may have exposed Jackson's limitations as a student of money and banking, the election showed that Jackson knew how to reach the ordinary voter better than they.

Jackson vindicated. The campaign of 1832 was notable not only for its vindication of Jackson but for two political innovations: the appearance of the first national third party, the Anti-Masonic party, and the holding of the first national nominating conventions. The new party, like so many third parties, focused on a single issue: opposition to secret societies, especially the Society of Freemasons. The party's strength was concentrated in the rural districts of New England and the Middle Atlantic states, where its supporters objected to the secrecy, exclusiveness, and allegedly undemocratic character of these societies. In 1826 William Morgan of Batavia, New York, a former Mason who was about to publish an exposure of the secrets of Freemasonry, suddenly vanished, and rumors spread that members of the society had murdered him. The resulting popular indignation eventually took the form of a political movement designed to drive the "grand kings" of Freemasonry out of public office. In September 1831 the Anti-Masonic party held a national convention at Baltimore and nominated William Wirt of Maryland for President, the first candidate to be selected in this fashion. The new party, in spite of its democratic assaults on a presumably privileged group, was essentially anti-Jacksonian—Jackson was himself a Mason—and in a short time most of its leaders joined the National Republicans.

Wirt hoped to win the nomination of the National Republicans, too, but in December 1831 this party held its own convention in Baltimore and nominated Henry Clay for President and John Sargeant of Pennsylvania for Vice President. The Democrats also met in Baltimore, in May 1832, but Jackson had already been renominated by numerous local conventions, and a party platform seemed superfluous. All that remained was to nominate a candidate for Vice President, and Jackson saw to it that his choice, Van Buren, was selected.

National Republicans attacked Jackson for abusing the patronage and the veto power, endorsed Clay's American System, and boldly demanded the rechartering of the Bank, but to no avail. Jackson was then at the peak of his popularity, and with Wirt taking votes away from Clay the outcome of the campaign

Martin Van Buren:
"the Little Magician"

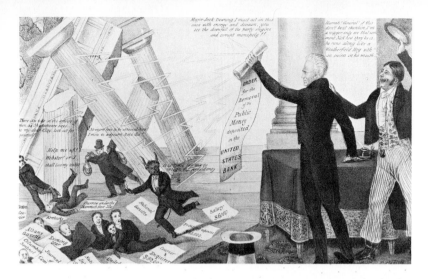

was never in doubt. Jackson won by a comfortable majority in the popular vote, and in the Electoral College he polled 219 votes to Clay's 49. Wirt carried only Vermont, while the disaffected leaders of South Carolina gave their state to John Floyd of Virginia. To Jackson the significance of the election was clear: he had been given a mandate to press his war against the Bank of the United States until this "Hydra of corruption" had been destroyed.

The Bank destroyed. Nicholas Biddle was not yet ready to surrender. "This worthy President," he said, "thinks that because he has scalped Indians and imprisoned judges, he is to have his way with the Bank. His is mistaken." So the battle went on, and in its final phase the friends and enemies of the Bank fought so recklessly that they impaired the stability of the entire American economy.

Jackson refused to wait for the Bank's charter to expire, for he feared that Biddle might still use its political and economic power to buy a new charter from Congress. Soon after the election Jackson decided to deprive the Bank of federal support for its financial operations by ceasing to use it as a depository for government funds. He justified his decision on the grounds of the Bank's "misconduct"—its attempt to influence the outcome of the election by playing on "the distress of some and the fear of others." Jackson had to get rid of two uncooperative Secretaries of the Treasury before he found a man in complete sympathy with his scheme: Roger B. Taney, the former Attorney General. The gradual removal of federal funds from the Bank was accomplished simply by paying government expenses from the existing deposits and by refusing to place current revenues in its vaults. These revenues

BORN TO COMMAND.

OF VETO MEMORY.

HAD I BEEN CONSULTED.

KING ANDREW THE FIRST.

were now distributed among numerous state banks—eventually, eighty-nine of them—which critics called "pet banks." The use of state banks of varying degrees of soundness was, as Jackson himself admitted, an unsatisfactory expedient subject to strong political pressures.

Jackson's enemies struck back hard. In the Senate Clay mustered a majority in 1834 to pass a resolution censuring the President for removing the deposits and thus assuming power "not conferred by the constitution and the laws." Not until 1837 were indignant Jacksonians able to get this partisan resolution expunged from the Senate record. Meanwhile, as federal deposits diminished, Biddle began calling in the Bank's loans and contracting credit, in part to protect himself and in part as a deliberate means of creating economic distress in order to force the government to return the deposits and renew the charter. The resulting credit shortage caused unemployment and business failures and brought delegations of businessmen to Washington to petition for relief. But the angry President told them to "go to Biddle." "I never will restore the deposits," he vowed, "I never will recharter the United States Bank, or sign a charter for any other bank, so long as my name is Andrew Jackson." At length the businessmen turned against Biddle and forced him to relax his credit policy, but not before he had managed to increase his unpopularity and thus to destroy even the faint hope that a drastically revised federal charter could be obtained. In 1836 Biddle received a charter from the state of Pennsylvania, which enabled the Bank to continue in business until 1841, when, because of the economic depression and unwise speculations, it was finally forced to close its doors.

The Bank war was over, and Jackson's victory was complete. The anti-Jacksonians fumed at his highhanded tactics; they spoke indignantly of the "reign of King Andrew I"; They renamed themselves the "Whigs" in imitation of the British party that, in the eighteenth century, had sought to reduce the power of the monarch; and they formed a loose coalition of those who opposed the Administration. In 1836, in their extremity, they held no national convention and drew up no platform; still lacking effective national party leadership, they ran not one but three presidential candidates: Webster to appeal to New England, Hugh Lawson White of Tennessee to appeal to the South, and General William Henry Harrison of Ohio to appeal to the West. The Whigs hoped thus to throw the election into the House of Representatives, where they might unite behind a single candidate. The Democrats held a convention at Baltimore, dutifully nominated Van Buren, and presented him on Jackson's record without a formal platform. In the election Van Buren won by a slim majority in the popular vote and by 170 electoral votes to 124 for his several opponents.

Panic and depression

Economic crisis. Jackson remained in Washington to witness Van Buren's inauguration, and Benton observed dryly that "the rising was eclipsed by the setting sun." It was not easy to follow the dynamic Jackson into the Presidency, not even for Van Buren, whose political adroitness had earned him the title of "the Little Magician." Like Jackson, this New Yorker of Dutch descent was a self-made man from a rural family of modest means. After a successful law career that gave him financial independence, Van Buren turned to state politics and soon became the leader of an efficient Republican machine called the Albany Regency. A career politician who relished the give-and-take of political life, he was a founder of the second American party system and a defender of parties as "inseparable from free governments" and "highly useful to the country." Following the presidential campaign of 1824, he linked his political fortunes with Jackson's and rose with him as a faithful advocate of his principles. But Van Buren was a pale copy of his chief: he lacked Jackson's forcefulness and popular appeal and had to rely on his tact and his skill in the management of men. Unfortunately neither these talents nor the Jacksonian philosophy enabled him to cope with the serious economic problems that beset the nation while he was President. Jackson was fortunate to have left office when he did, for within two months the country plunged into a panic and depression. Van Buren thus had the misfortune of being remembered as a "depression President."

During Jackson's two Administrations, except for the brief "Biddle panic" of 1833–34, the country enjoyed a period of glorious prosperity and unprecedented economic expansion. Southerners found seemingly limitless markets for their cotton at good prices, and planters and slaves poured into the states of the Southwest to open up vast new cotton lands. Between 1831 and 1836, because of rising prices and expanded production, the value of cotton exports trebled. In the West farmers, also finding ample markets and enjoying high prices, continued to be drawn into the spreading money economy. Western cities experienced a phenomenal growth as they developed commercial facilities and manufacturing enterprises to serve local needs. In the Northeast merchants prospered from the flourishing cotton trade, and manufacturers expanded to supply their growing Southern and Western markets. Land prices shot up as speculation once again became a national mania; between 1834 and 1836 the speculators were responsible for a fivefold increase in government land sales. Meanwhile, the states and private entrepreneurs undertook ambitious canal and railroad projects. In the years between 1830 and 1838 state debts increased by nearly $150 million, two-thirds of which were spent for internal improvements.

Funds for all this economic activity came from British capitalists, who assumed that investments in state bonds were as safe as investments in federal bonds, and from the multiplying state banks and other domestic investors. Between 1829 and 1837 the number of state banks more than doubled, their note issues trebled, and their loans quadrupled. In an economically "underdeveloped" country with a rapidly growing population, much of this business activity was healthy. But some of it was reckless and speculative—and the economy now lacked even the modest control that the Bank of the United States had exercised.

Before Van Buren took office, the Jackson Administration, besides trying to divorce the government from business, had adopted fiscal policies that probably intensified the crisis when it came. First, as Jackson himself observed, the deposit of federal funds in numerous "pet banks" tended to multiply state-chartered banks and "had a great agency in producing a spirit of wild speculation." Though most state banks maintained adequate specie reserves, some indulged in "wildcat financiering" by recklessly expanding their note issues and by making loans without demanding adequate collateral. Speculators borrowed paper of dubious value from these institutions and gave it to the government land offices for new lands; the government in turn deposited the paper in the "pet banks," which made the money available again for further speculation. This was a happy situation for those who favored soft money, but it distressed the hard-money men who, as Benton said, had not joined "in putting down the paper currency of a national bank in order to put up a paper currency of a thousand local banks." Jackson shared this point of view and, in July 1836, suddenly intervened with his so-called Specie Circular. In the future, he ordered, federal land offices would accept only gold and silver in payment for public lands. This was a severe blow to the speculators, and for a time land sales almost ceased and inflated land prices dropped precipitously.

Next, the Congress, with Jackson's approval, gave an enormous stimulus to costly internal-improvement projects launched by the states. In 1836, with the federal government out of debt and with a surplus of almost $40 million, an act provided that beginning on January 1, 1837, the surplus above $5 million was to be distributed among the states in proportion to population in four quarterly installments. Many states, assuming that they would receive a similar subsidy each year and ignoring the fact that the federal funds were intended to be only a loan, immediately designed ambitious projects that exceeded the limits of their own resources. At the same time, the act deprived the "pet banks" of the bulk of their federal deposits and, in consequence, obliged them to call in their loans from private borrowers.

But the economic crisis had causes more fundamental than federal fiscal policy. For example, most of the inflation that preceded it was caused not by the expansion of state bank notes but by a substantial increase in specie imports, some of it from Great Britain and France but most of it from Mexico; by a decline of specie exports to the Far East; and by British credits that permitted the purchase of British goods at high prices without the loss of specie. Under these circumstances, in a period of prosperity and free spending, the country sustained a considerable international balance-of-payments deficit. When, eventually, Great Britain suffered from hard times, British investors began to withdraw their support of American economic expansion; and the British demand for American cotton began to decline just as the opening of new Western lands caused a sharp increase in the supply. Business conditions in the United States had been deteriorating for some months, but the real panic began in May 1837, when New York banks, soon followed by banks in the rest of the country, suspended specie payments. It was at this point that the Bank of the United States was missed, for its destruction reduced confidence in the whole banking system, thus stimulating runs on state banks, which, in turn, forced these banks to curtail loans in an effort to increase their specie reserves.

The Panic of 1837 was followed by a brief period of economic recovery, but in 1839 the collapse of cotton and other agricultural prices and the decline of foreign investments brought on one of the most severe depressions in American history. Banks and business houses failed by the hundreds, factories closed and unemployment mounted, cotton sold for as low as 6 cents a pound, internal-improvement projects were abandoned, and some states, their credit exhausted, either stopped payments on their debts or repudiated them outright. The most feverish economic activity was among lawyers and auctioneers who arranged the foreclosure sales of farms, plantations, and urban business properties. Recovery did not come until the middle of the 1840s.

The Independent Treasury. Understanding of the causes of business cycles had advanced very little since the depression following the Panic of 1819—President Van Buren attributed the present crisis to "overbanking" and "overtrading." The idea that government might give assistance to distressed farmers, workers, and businessmen was not yet seriously considered. In so far as the government did react to the crisis, it adopted fiscal policies that served to deepen the depression and heighten economic distress. Distribution of funds to the states for internal improvements was stopped, federal spending was curtailed, and the President concentrated on getting the government out of debt. Van Buren also rejected pleas for the withdrawal of the Specie Circular and continued the hard-money policy of his predecessor; he scorned the argument that the crisis justified the chartering of a new national bank. He thus identified himself with the radical, or Locofoco,* wing of his party— the extreme hard-money, antibank, antimonopoly faction that was especially strong among workingmen and reformers in his own state of New York.

The chief aim of the Locofocos was to divorce the federal government from banking altogether by denying all private banks the use of federal deposits. Van Buren urged such a step repeatedly, and finally, in 1840, Congress passed the Independent Treasury Act. This act authorized the establishment of subtreasuries in various cities where government funds could be placed in vaults for safekeeping. Although this system insured the government from loss, it made economic recovery more difficult, because it deprived the banks of funds that otherwise could have been used for private loans.

Banking was now entirely in the hands of the states. A few, notably New York and the New England states, managed to establish reasonably satisfactory and responsible state banking systems; a couple of Western states adopted the Locofoco philosophy and for a time abolished banking altogether. In many states the Jacksonians established "free banking" systems, which enabled promoters to secure a bank charter without a special act of the legislature. Free banking and so-called general incorporation laws were important aspects of Jacksonian Democracy at the state level. By eliminating the need for small entrepreneurs to have political influence in order to obtain state charters, these laws were expected to provide equal opportunities for all.

The election of 1840. As the presidential campaign of 1840 approached, the country was still deep in economic depression; the Democrats were bound to lose the support of many voters who would express their discontent by turning against the party in power. The Democratic national convention at Baltimore was a gloomy affair. The delegates renominated Van Buren unanimously, but with restrained enthusiasm, and adopted a platform reaffirming the party position on state rights, banking, internal improvements, and the In-

*"Locofoco" was a popular name for the newly invented friction matches. Radical New York Democrats once carried candles and "locofocos" to a party meeting, because they feared that the conservatives would try to break it up by turning off the gaslights. This incident explains how the Locofocos got their name.

	Electoral	Popular
Harrison (Whig)	234	1,275,000
Van Buren (Dem.)	60	1,128,000

The election of 1840

dependent Treasury. The Democrats were on the defensive throughout the campaign.

The Whigs, however, were in an optimistic mood when their convention assembled at Harrisburg, Pennsylvania. Having been branded the enemies of the common man, a party of aristocrats and monopolists, having endured a succession of humiliating defeats, they now looked forward to giving the Democrats some of their own medicine. They had already attributed the depression to Democratic fiscal measures, charged that the Independent Treasury scheme was a callous attempt of the government to protect itself without regard for the welfare of the country, and accused Van Buren of indifference to the suffering of the people. Now, with a far more efficient party organization, having learned much from the tactics of their enemies and from their own mistakes, they prepared to out-Jackson the Jacksonians in a bid for popular support. The Whigs passed over Clay in favor of a military hero: William Henry Harrison of Ohio, who had defeated the Indians at the Battle of Tippecanoe and the British at the Battle of the Thames. With an eye on the South, they nominated John Tyler of Virginia, a conservative, state-rights Whig, for the Vice Presidency. They adopted no platform, for the campaign they planned was to have little relevance to concrete issues.

The Democrats were guilty of much low-level electioneering, but their campaign seemed almost dignified compared to the antics of the Whigs. Though Harrison was descended from an aristocratic Virginia family and lived as an Ohio country gentleman in a sixteen-room mansion, the Whigs transformed ''Old Tippecanoe'' into a simple frontier farmer and man of the people. When a blundering Democratic editor sneered that Harrison would be satisfied to retire to a log cabin with a barrel of hard cider, the Whigs happily accepted the statement as true. They praised his simple tastes, made log cabins and cider barrels their party symbols, and boasted of their own log-cabin backgrounds. (Webster apologized for not having been born in one.) The Whigs described Van Buren as a squanderer of public funds on lavish entertainment, a man of expensive aristocratic tastes who fancied fine wines, ate from gold plates, and effeminately scented his whiskers with cologne. They dazzled the voters with boisterous mass meetings, barbecues, and torchlight processions; they nicknamed Van Buren ''Martin Van Ruin'' and ''Sweet Sandy Whiskers''; they promised to cleanse the civil service of corruption and to restore prosperity; and they chanted their campaign slogans: ''Tippecanoe and Tyler too'' and ''Van, Van is a used-up man.'' If this was the way to win democratic elections, the Whigs proved that they had mastered the technique as well as their opponents.

The voters responded by turning out in larger numbers than in any previous presidential election—even Jackson had not attracted so large a proportion to the polls. Harrison's popular majority was small, but he won overwhelmingly in the Electoral College: 234 votes to 60 for Van Buren. After twelve years of Democratic supremacy, the Whigs were to have their turn. Equally important, the presidential election of 1840 marked the final emergence of a fully developed second American party system, with vigorous two-party politics in every section and in all the states.

The Supreme Court under Taney. But the Democrats, like the Federalists in 1801, re-

tained a firm hold on the third branch of the federal government: the judiciary. While he was President, Jackson had appointed six new Associate Justices to the Supreme Court, all of them staunch Democrats; and when Chief Justice Marshall died in 1835, Jackson had selected Roger B. Taney, a one-time Federalist but now a state-rights agrarian, to replace him. Jacksonians thus controlled seven of the nine positions on the Court, and conservatives such as Webster feared an irresponsible and radical new departure from the constitutional doctrines laid down by Marshall. Actually, though the Taney Court modified Marshall's opinions on the rights of corporations and the sanctity of contracts, the main corpus of his decisions remained almost intact. Even the doctrine of judicial review went unchallenged; in several important cases the Court threw out state and (on one occasion) federal legislation that it found to be unconstitutional.

The chief departure from the extreme nationalism of Marshall was the new Court's tendency to give the states greater power to regulate corporations. This change is best illustrated in the case of *Charles River Bridge* v. *Warren Bridge* (1837). The issue was whether the state of Massachusetts, having earlier given a charter to the Charles River Bridge Company to build and operate a toll bridge, could now grant a charter to a second company to build and operate another and competing bridge. The first company contended that this would constitute a breach of contract, but the Court disagreed and held that the rights of corporations are subordinate to the interests of the community—''that the community also have rights, and that the happiness and well-being of every citizen depends on their faithful preservation.'' The Court thus provided an admirable statement of several of the basic goals of Jacksonian Democracy: encouragement to new entrepreneurs, an attack on special privilege and entrenched ''monopoly,'' and the promotion of the happiness and welfare of all the people.

Tyler and paralysis

The Whig disaster. As the Whigs organized their first administration, they looked forward to a period of progress along the lines of Whig principles. Harrison, who appeared to favor the goals of the American System, seemed ready to accept guidance from Webster and

Clay, for he made Webster Secretary of State and gave most of the other Cabinet posts to followers of Clay. Then disaster struck. Only a month after his inauguration the sixty-eight-year-old President died of pneumonia, and for the first time the Vice President rose to the Presidency. Unfortunately for the Whigs, their new President, John Tyler, a Virginia aristocrat, sympathized with the Southern planters who opposed nearly everything the Whig majority hoped to accomplish. As a result, within less than a year, the Whig party was so torn by factionalism that it accomplished little, and the country had to suffer through a period of almost complete political stalemate.

Tyler had once been a Democrat but had broken with Jackson over nullification and the removal of federal deposits from Biddle's Bank. He drifted over to the Whigs because in his state they were dominated by affluent men of high social status and because he opposed the radical, Locofoco tendencies of the Democrats under Jackson and Van Buren. Tyler was thought to be a political friend of Clay, but he made it clear that the imperious Kentuckian was not going to run his Administration; none of his messages showed any sympathy for Clay's views on banking, tariffs, or internal improvements.

Clay, however, confidently planned a legislative program that would at last put his American System into full operation. In 1841 he introduced a bill to distribute the proceeds from the sale of public lands among the states to finance internal improvements. In a bid for Western support, this bill also contained a provision for preemption by which squatters on the public domain could purchase 160 acres of the land they had improved at the minimum price of $1.25 an acre when the land was put up for sale. To get his bill adopted, Clay had to agree that the distribution of proceeds from land sales would cease if tariff schedules were increased. A year later, in 1842, the Whigs tried to raise the tariff without repealing distribution. But a presidential veto forced them to give up distribution in order to get the increase in duties for which manufacturers were clamoring. Tyler then reluctantly approved the Tariff of 1842 to solve the government's need for more revenue, though it restored the level of duties provided in the Tariff of 1832. The new tariff was virtually the only Whig achievement—Tyler not only forced the abandonment of distribution but vetoed internal-improvement bills with essentially the same arguments Jackson had used.

The final disappointment came when Clay and the majority of Whigs attempted to establish a third Bank of the United States. Tyler approved the repeal of the Independent Treasury Act, but it was well known that he would not accept a new system of national banking in its place. Hence the Whigs tried to disguise their purpose by using other names. First they provided for the creation of a "Fiscal Bank," but Tyler was not deceived and vetoed the bill; then they proposed the chartering of a "Fiscal Corporation," only to be thwarted by another presidential veto. With that, national banking ceased to be a serious issue in national politics for two decades. The angry Whigs in Congress formally read Tyler out of the party, the Cabinet resigned (except Webster, who was involved in diplomatic negotiations with the British), and Clay gave up his seat in the Senate to try again for the Presidency. After making a fiasco of the Whig victory, Tyler and his Southern allies began to drift back to the Democratic party, where in subsequent years they would challenge the Jacksonians for control.

Foreign affairs under Tyler. The political paralysis at home did not prevent the Tyler Administration from solving several problems in the country's foreign relations. Jackson, in spite of his blunt tactics, had already disposed of two issues that had survived the negotiations following the War of 1812: he managed to persuade the British to permit American merchants to trade with their West Indian islands; and he made a satisfactory settlement of claims against France for damages inflicted on American shipping during the Napoleonic wars. But new sources of friction in Anglo-American relations had begun to appear during the 1830s and had reached serious proportions by the time Tyler became President. The traditional undercurrent of hostility, heightened by British travelers who made disparaging comments on American culture and by local politicians bidding for the Irish vote, made it dangerous to permit disagreements to go unsettled.

Trouble began in 1837, when an insurrection broke out in the eastern provinces of Canada. Though many Americans hoped the uprising might ultimately lead to annexation, the British suppressed it with relative ease. But while it was in progress Americans along the frontier aided the rebels and afterward gave the defeated rebel leaders refuge. When raids across the border continued from American bases on the Niagara River, Canadian officials

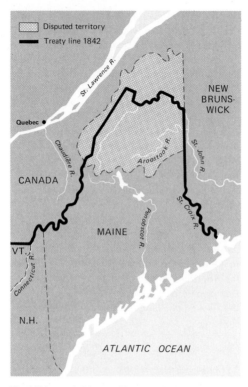

The Webster-Ashburton Treaty, 1842

one night impetuously crossed the river, killed one American, and burned an American steamer, the *Caroline,* which had been carrying supplies to the rebels. In spite of growing tension, the British government ignored the American demand for reparations and an apology. Then, in 1840, a Canadian named Alexander McLeod was arrested in New York on suspicion of being a member of the party that had attacked the *Caroline;* he was brought to trial for murder and arson. The British government responded with a vigorous protest: it assumed responsibility for the attack on the *Caroline* and warned that McLeod's conviction would have serious consequences. Fortunately McLeod established an alibi and was acquitted, much to the relief of the State Department.

Meanwhile, a long-standing controversy over the Maine boundary flared up when, in 1838, American and Canadian lumberjacks battled for possession of part of a disputed area along the Aroostook River. Another dispute grew out of a British request that its naval patrols along the west coast of Africa be permitted to stop and search ships flying the American flag to determine whether they were engaging in the slave trade. This request re-

vived memories of British practices during the Napoleonic wars, and the American government would not agree to it. Finally, in 1841, a group of slaves being transported from Virginia to New Orleans on the American brig *Creole* mutinied and sailed to Nassau, where British officials freed them. Prodded by angry Southerners, Secretary of State Webster demanded that the slaves be returned, but the British refused.

At this point a new British government decided that the time had come for negotiations and sent Lord Ashburton to Washington as a special envoy. Ashburton was a happy choice, for he was friendly to the United States and a man of infinite tact; moreover, he had met Webster in England, and the two men liked each other. Neither was an experienced professional diplomat, but both were in a conciliatory mood, and their patient and highly informal negotiations culminated in the important Webster-Ashburton Treaty of 1842.

Except for Oregon, which remained under joint occupation, the treaty settled all border controversies by awarding seven-twelfths of the disputed territory along the Maine boundary to the Unites States and by making minor adjustments around Lake Champlain and between Lake Superior and the Lake of the Woods. The treaty also included an agreement for the mutual extradition of fugitives accused of any of seven major crimes. As for the slave trade, the United States did not agree to British search of her vessels but did agree to maintain a squadron off the African coast to apprehend slavers flying the American flag. Neither the *Caroline* nor the *Creole* affair was dealt with in the treaty, but Ashburton disposed of them through an exchange of notes that Webster chose to accept as satisfactory. With regard to the *Caroline* affair, Ashburton simply expressed regret ''that some explanation and apology for this occurrence was not immediately made.'' In the case of the *Creole,* the slaves were not to be returned, but he promised that in the future there would be no ''officious interference'' with American vessels forced to enter British ports by ''violence or accident.''

Webster, after concluding these negotiations and seeing the treaty ratified by both governments, followed the example of the other Whigs and resigned from Tyler's Cabinet. Thereafter the Tyler Administration, disrupted and lacking congressional support, looked rather futile in the face of increasing sectional conflict. The resulting tensions would have a shattering effect on both national parties and, eventually, on the federal Union itself. In the critical years ahead, disheartened patriots would remember the strength and firmness of Andrew Jackson with growing admiration. As the country moved from crisis to crisis, the cry that would be heard more and more frequently was "Oh, for an hour of Old Hickory."

Suggestions
for
reading

THE ADVANCE OF DEMOCRACY

The most perceptive contemporary analysis of the workings of American democracy in the Jacksonian era is Alexis de Tocqueville, *Democracy in America,* 2 vols.* (1945). Moisie Ostrogorski, *Democracy and the Organization of Political Parties,* 2 vols.* (1902), though dated, is still a useful general work on the democratization of American politics. Chilton Williamson, *American Suffrage from Property to Democracy, 1760–1860** (1960), supersedes all other works on the extension of the suffrage. The advance of democracy in two important states can be studied in A. B. Darling, *Political Changes in Massachusetts, 1824–1848* (1925), and D. R. Fox, *The Decline of Aristocracy in the Politics of New York** (1919). The latter book, however, should be compared with D. T. Miller, *Jacksonian Aristocracy: Class and Democracy in New York, 1830–1860* (1967), an important revisionist study that stresses social stratification, a decline in class mobility, and growing class antagonisms.

The disputed election of 1824, as well as the goals and misfortunes of the Adams Administration, are described with rich detail in George Dangerfield's two books: *The Era of Good Feelings** (1952), and *The Awakening of American Nationalism, 1815–1828** (1965). Two biographies are essential for an understanding of these years: G. G. Van Deusen, *The Life of Henry Clay** (1937), and S. F. Bemis, *John Quincy Adams and the Union* (1956). A fascinating personal record of Adams' Presidency can be found in C. F. Adams, ed., *The Memoirs of John Quincy Adams,* 12 vols. (1874–77). R. V. Remini, *The Election of Andrew Jackson** (1963), is the best study of the election of 1828.

THE AGE OF JACKSON

Three recent surveys, based on modern scholarship, deal critically with Jacksonian Democracy: G. G. Van Deusen, *The Jacksonian Era** (1959), C. M. Wiltse, *The New Nation, 1800–1845** (1961), and Edward Pessen, *Jacksonian America** (1969). The latter is the most interesting and the most decidedly anti-Jackson. Marquis James, *Andrew Jackson, Vol. 2: Portrait of a President** (1937), is a sympathetic and lucid biography of the presidential years. R. V. Remini, *Andrew Jackson** (1966), brief and breezy, portrays Jackson sympathetically as a skilled politician. Two of Jackson's strongest supporters in Congress are the subjects of distinguished biographies: C. G. Sellers, Jr., *James K. Polk: Jacksonian, 1795–1843* (1957), and W. N. Chambers, *Old Bullion Benton: Senator from the New West* (1956). There are also excellent biographies of two key figures in the Jackson Administration: C. B. Swisher, *Roger B. Taney* (1936), and W. B. Hatcher, *Edward Livingston: Jeffersonian Republican and Jacksonian Democrat* (1940). An authoritative study of administrative organization is L. D. White, *The Jacksonians: A Study in Administrative History, 1829–1861** (1954). R. P. McCormick, *The Second American Party System: Party Formation in the Jacksonian Era** (1966), is a revisionist study of major importance.

The meaning of Jacksonian Democracy is still the subject of animated controversy. In addition to the study by Edward Pessen, cited above, the following books, each notable for its distinctive interpretation, provide a sample of the various ways in which Jacksonian Democracy can be viewed: A. M. Schlesinger, Jr., *The Age of Jackson** (1945); Richard Hofstadter, *The American Political Tradition** (1948); J. W. Ward, *Andrew Jackson: Symbol for an Age** (1955); Joseph Dorfman, *The Economic Mind in American Civilization,* 5 vols. (1946–49); Marvin Meyers, *The Jacksonian Persuasion** (1957); and Lee Benson, *The Concept of Jacksonian Democracy: New York as a Test Case** (1961).

*Available in a paperback edition.

All the above books deal with Jackson's views on banking and are important to a study of the controversy over the second Bank of the United States. But the key work on this topic is Bray Hammond, *Banks and Politics in America from the Revolution to the Civil War** (1957). R. V. Remini, *Andrew Jackson and the Bank War** (1967), is a brief, balanced study stressing the political side of the Bank war. Two other works merit consultation: R. C. H. Catterall, *The Second Bank of the United States* (1903), and W. B. Smith, *Economic Aspects of the Second Bank of the United States* (1953). The best possible case for Nicholas Biddle is presented in T. P. Govan, *Nicholas Biddle: Nationalist and Public Banker* (1959). J. A. Wilburn, *Biddle's Bank: The Crucial Years* (1967), is a study of sources of public support for the Bank before the election of 1832. J. R. Sharp, *The Jacksonians versus the Banks* (1970), traces Jacksonian banking policy at the state level after the Panic of 1837.

The tragedy of Indian removals is the subject of Angie Debo, *The Road to Disappearance: A History of the Creek Indians* (1941); A. H. DeRosier, Jr., *The Removal of the Choctaw Indians* (1970); and Grant Foreman, *Indian Removal: The Emigration of the Five Civilized Tribes of Indians* (1932). J. K. Mahon, *History of the Second Seminole War, 1835–1842* (1967), is a vivid account of Seminole resistance. F. P. Prucha, *American Indian Policy in the Formative Years** (1962), is a history of federal legislation. Land policy in the Jacksonian era is treated fully in R. G. Wellington, *The Political and Sectional Influence of the Public Lands, 1828–1842* (1942), and R. M. Robbins, *Our Landed Heritage: The Public Domain** (1942).

THE NULLIFICATION CONTROVERSY

C. S. Sydnor, *The Development of Southern Sectionalism, 1819–1848** (1948), analyzes the nullification crisis in the broad setting of Southern history. The best study of nullification is W. W. Freehling, *Prelude to Civil War** (1966). Calhoun's ideas can be studied in a collection of his writings edited by R. K. Crallé: *Works of J. C. Calhoun,* 6 vols. (1851–55). Sympathetic analyses are provided in A. O. Spain, *The Political Theory of John C. Calhoun* (1951); C. M. Wiltse, *John C. Calhoun, Nullifier, 1829–1839* (1949); and M. L. Coit, *John C. Calhoun: American Portrait** (1950). More critical appraisals appear in Richard Hofstadter, *The American Political Tradition** (1948); G. M. Capers, *John C. Calhoun, Opportunist* (1960); and R. N. Current, *John C. Calhoun** (1966).

DEPRESSION AND THE WHIG INTERLUDE

The best available biographical studies of Van Buren are Holmes Alexander, *The American Talleyrand* (1935), and R. V. Remini, *Martin Van Buren and the Making of the Democratic Party** (1959). These should be supplemented by Van Buren's relatively candid account of his own life: *The Autobiography of Martin Van Buren,* edited by J. C. Fitzpatrick (1920). The Van Buren Administration is analyzed in J. C. Curtis, *The Fox at Bay: Martin Van Buren and the Presidency, 1837–1841* (1970). In a challenging new interpretation of the panic and depression, Peter Temin, *The Jacksonian Economy** (1969), absolves the Jacksonians from major responsibility for the inflation and the subsequent collapse. Earlier studies of the economic crisis are R. C. McGrane, *The Panic of 1837** (1924), and W. B. Smith and A. H. Cole, *Fluctuations in American Business, 1790–1860* (1935).

R. P. McCormick, *The Second American Party System,* and G. G. Van Deusen, *The Jacksonian Era,* both cited above, are the best introductions to a study of the origin and growth of the Whig party. Three biographies of Whig leaders also need to be consulted: the biography of Clay by Van Deusen, cited above; C. M. Fuess, *Daniel Webster,* 2 vols. (1930, 2nd ed., 1968); and R. N. Current, *Daniel Webster and the Rise of National Conservatism** (1955). R. G. Gunderson, *The Log-Cabin Campaign* (1957), is a brisk account of the election of 1840. The Tyler Administration is treated competently in O. D. Lambert, *Presidential Politics in the United States, 1841–1844* (1936), and O. P. Chitwood, *John Tyler: Champion of the Old South* (1939). A. B. Corey, *The Crisis of 1830–1842 in Canadian-American Relations* (1941), and J. B. Brebner, *North Atlantic Triangle* (1945), are good monographs on foreign policy under Tyler.

*Available in a paperback edition.

10

An era of reform

Many nineteenth-century Americans believed that the destiny of their country concerned not only themselves but all mankind. In America's congenial environment man would reveal his capacity to govern himself, to live in harmony with the laws of God's universe, and to eradicate social injustice; he would build an ideal society led by righteous men motivated by disinterested benevolence. In achieving these noble goals America would serve as a model for the rest of the world. To fail would be to betray a sacred trust.

This belief in a divine mission, together with a nagging awareness of their shortcomings, made Americans inordinately sensitive to criticism from European visitors. Tocqueville noted that their "irritable patriotism" caused them to take offense at any comment that was even mildly unfavorable. Outsiders could not speak freely, without risking resentment, "of anything at all except, perhaps, the climate and the soil; and even then Americans will be found ready to defend both as if they had cooperated in producing them."

But if Americans regarded criticism by outsiders as impertinent, they periodically displayed an ample capacity for self-criticism. For they knew that their society had not yet achieved that state of near-perfection toward which so many of them hopefully aimed. Though they cherished an optimistic belief that a benign providence made progress inevitable, improvements did not always come fast enough to satisfy them, and they sometimes tried to give providence a helping hand. "We could not retard the great forward movement of Humanity if we would," wrote Horace Greeley, editor of the New York *Tribune,* "but each of us may decide for himself whether to share in the glory of promoting it or incur the shame of having looked coldly and indifferently on."

In the 1820s movements for moral uplift and social reform began to attract people who were unwilling to compromise with evil and were impatient with the slow pace of progress. The causes they championed were by no means peculiarly American—British reformers influenced reformers across the Atlantic—but there was a millennial quality about the American crusades that was unique. Theodore Parker, a distinguished Boston clergyman, described the aims of the reformers who kept the country in a turmoil for a whole generation: They looked to a society

> full of industry and abundance, full of wisdom, virtue, and the poetry of life; a state with unity among all, with freedom for each; a church without tyranny, a society without ignorance, want, or crime, a state without oppression; yes, a world with no war among the nations to consume the work of their hands, and no restrictive policy to hinder the welfare of mankind.

The goals of this perfectionist program, the reformers believed, not only were attainable but could be achieved with relative speed and without violent upheaval. There existed in America, one of them explained, "abundant elements for progress, and a field of action comparatively free from those obstacles which so impede reform elsewhere." Other countries might have to resort to violence in order to overthrow tyranny, but here "the better course of effecting reform by moral and intellectual means is more trustingly expected."

The proper agencies of reform were the churches and benevolent societies, rather than revolutionary movements or even political parties. To be sure, some clergymen frowned on the crusaders and refused to become involved in secular affairs, but many of them thought it their proper function to help realize the promise of American life by advancing the cause of reform.

The religious background

The decline of orthodox Calvinism. Tocqueville believed that there was "no country in the world where the Christian religion retains a greater influence over the souls of men than in America." Certainly the Americans of the first half of the nineteenth century were still deeply religious, and the church was still a powerful force in their lives. But the various Protestant sects, especially those that had been based on Calvinist theology, had gone through some critical times during the century since the Great Awakening and Jonathan Edwards' stout defense of orthodoxy. By the start of the nineteenth century many of the Puritan dogmas—predestination, infant damnation, and the total depravity of man—had already been rejected, or at least qualified, by a more liberal theology that replaced Calvin's God of wrath with a benevolent God of love. The conservatives fought back: they admonished the faithful to "guard against the insidious encroachments of innovation—that evil and beguiling spirit which is now stalking to and fro in the earth, seeking whom it may devour." But this was no more than a rear-guard action.

Even in the eighteenth century a number of heresies, some of them actually quite old, had begun to trouble the minds of a few New England clergymen: Arminianism, which raised doubts about certain tenets of Calvinism, especially predestination, and eventually became the theology of the Methodists; Arianism, which questioned the divinity of Christ; and Socinianism, which rejected both the Trinity and predestination. These early challenges were fortified by the rationalism of the Enlightenment and the more optimistic view of human nature expressed by the philosophers of the American and French revolutions. Respect for the dignity of the individual, confidence in man's capacity to improve himself, and belief in the idea of progress led to

a decline in otherworldliness and a growing interest in temporal affairs. Life on earth, according to this new view, was not a mere preparation for the hereafter, at best a kind of winnowing of the saved from the damned; rather, it had its own beauty and value.

These intellectual trends caused orthodox Calvinism to give way to a theology that was at once more rational and more humanistic. Many leaders of the Revolutionary generation, such as Jefferson and Franklin, withdrew from the established churches and became deists. Deism, which originated in Europe in the early eighteenth century, rejected the Trinity, the divinity of Christ, the idea of original sin, and the Bible as divine revelation. It held that God had created the universe but had then withdrawn to let it run by natural laws. The humanistic implications of deism were evident in Thomas Paine's *The Age of Reason:* "I believe in the equality of man, and I believe that religious duties consist in doing justice, loving mercy, and endeavoring to make our fellow creatures happy." Paine accepted the creed of no church; indeed, he described the established churches as "human inventions set up to terrify and enslave mankind and monopolize power and profit." But few intellectuals were prepared to carry rationalism this far, and most church leaders saw no difference between deism and atheism.

Unitarianism. In the long run those who worked for a liberalized theology within the churches had a broader influence than the freethinkers who deserted organized Christianity entirely. These liberalizers rebelled especially against the deterministic Calvinist doctrine of salvation only for the elect in favor of the more hopeful doctrine of free will and salvation open to all. The revolt against traditional Calvinism produced several new sects, such as the Universalists, and a division of the

Presbyterians into Old and New schools. But the largest and most influential of the organized religious groups produced by eighteenth-century rationalism and humanism was the Unitarian Church. An offshoot of Congregationalism, it appealed chiefly to the better-educated and more affluent descendants of the New England Puritans. It showed its greatest vitality and grew most vigorously in the early decades of the nineteenth century. Unitarians, as their name indicates, did not believe in the Trinity—Jesus was mortal, the founder of a great religion but not the son of God. They denied that man was conceived in sin or that he was totally depraved; rather, he was capable of goodness and virtue through the development of a Christian character. Moreover, according to this comfortable theology, Christians received their reward on earth as well as in the hereafter, for they "enjoy the world more than other men [and] find more satisfaction in it." God was a merciful and loving Father, not a vindictive and arbitrary deity who predestined the mass of mankind to damnation. Unitarians were skeptical of fine-spun theological systems and urged each individual to search the Scriptures for truth. And once he had found it, he must not pervert it into dogma to be imposed on others. Instead, Unitarians preached tolerance of differences among sincerely devout men.

William Ellery Channing (1780–1842), pastor of the Federal Street Church in Boston, was the most eminent Unitarian clergyman of the early nineteenth century. Channing stressed the primary responsibility of man to his own conscience and helped to link the liberal Unitarian creed with humanitarianism. To him "God is infinitely good, kind, benevolent," and the essence of religion is "the adoration of goodness." Belief in predestination and the God of Calvinism tends "to form a gloomy, forbidding, and servile religion, and to lead men to substitute censoriousness, bitterness, and persecution, for a tender and impartial charity." Since Channing believed in man's capacity for virtue and denied original sin, he found the doctrine of atonement preposterous—it was as if "the Creator, in order to pardon his own children, had erected a gallows in the centre of the universe, and had publicly executed upon it . . . an Infinite Being, the partaker of his own Supreme Divinity." Channing supported humanitarian reform, "because I have learned the essential equality of men before the common Father . . . because I see in him a great nature, the divine image, and vast capacities." In Channing, Unitarianism found its ideal leader, for he balanced its rationalism and tolerance with a humanistic warmth and with an active concern for the welfare of mankind.

The transcendentalists. In the course of time, however, Unitarianism began to crystallize into a new orthodoxy. The Church's well-fed members, though more reasonable and tolerant than their Puritan ancestors, became at least as smug; though given to philanthropy, they were free to pursue individual gain with far less restraint. Unitarianism struck a growing number of New England intellectuals as distressingly cold, formal, and passionless and its communicants as more concerned with material than with spiritual well-being. "Nothing quieted doubt so completely as the mental calm of the Unitarian clergy," wrote Henry Adams. "For them, difficulties might be ignored; doubts were waste of thought; nothing exacted solution. Boston had solved the universe."

Moreover, eighteenth-century rationalism, the foundation of Unitarianism, was succumbing to a romantic movement that was associated with the German philosophers Immanuel Kant and Georg Wilhelm Friedrich Hegel and with the British men of letters Samuel Coleridge, Thomas Carlyle, and William Wordsworth. The romanticists rejected experience and pure reason as the keys to truth and substituted for them intuition, or spiritual insight, which they believed gave man knowledge that he could not derive through his senses. They idealized the natural, spontaneous man rather than the educated, sophisticated man. In a sense, Jacksonian Democracy, with its faith in the good judgment of the common man, was the political manifestation of romanticism in America.

During the 1830s, a small group of intellectuals living in and around Concord, Massachusetts, met at the home of the former Unitarian minister, Ralph Waldo Emerson, to exchange ideas about philosophy and theology. In addition to Emerson, this distinguished group included, at one time or another, clergymen such as Theodore Parker, George Ripley, and James Freeman Clark; literary figures such as Henry Thoreau, Amos Bronson Alcott, Nathaniel Hawthorne, and Orestes Brownson; and talented women such as Margaret Fuller and Elizabeth Peabody. The

Ralph Waldo Emerson

Nathaniel Hawthorne

Orestes A. Brownson

Margaret Fuller

*The intuition of the moral sentiment is an insight of the perfection
of the laws of the soul. These laws execute themselves. They are out
of time, out of space, and not subject to circumstance. Thus in the
soul of man there is a justice whose retributions are instant and entire.
He who does a noble deed is instantly ennobled. He who does a mean
deed is by the action itself contracted. He who puts off impurity,
thereby puts on purity. If a man is at heart just, then in so far is he
God; the safety of God, the immortality of God, the majesty of God
do enter into that man with justice.... Good is positive. Evil is merely
privative, not absolute: it is like cold, which is the privation of heat.
All evil is so much death or nonentity. Benevolence is absolute and
real. So much benevolence as a man hath, so much life hath he. For
all things proceed out of this same spirit, which is differently named
love, justice, temperance, in its different applications.... Whilst a man
seeks good ends, he is strong by the whole strength of nature. In
so far as he roves from these ends, he bereaves himself of power,
or auxiliaries; his being shrinks out of all remote channels, he becomes
less and less, a mote, a point, until absolute badness is absolute death.*

From Ralph Waldo Emerson, "Divinity School Address," 1838.

Concord neighbors of this little band of idealists, in good-natured amusement, began to refer to them as the Transcendental Club. The members of the club were appalled by the crass materialism of a country preoccupied with economic development and were concerned that spiritual progress was not keeping pace. They were too individualistic and too hostile to institutional restraints to start a church of their own, but the philosophy of transcendentalism was shot through with theological implications. It was clearly an outgrowth of Puritanism and Unitarianism (with a touch of Quakerism and oriental mysticism) as well as of romanticism.

The transcendentalists, like the Unitarians, rejected Calvinist dogma and hopefully believed in man's essential goodness and in a God of love. But their idealism was warm and affirmative, not the bland concoction of "pale negations" that Emerson found so unsatisfying in Unitarianism. As Theodore Parker explained, transcendentalists held that man has "faculties which give him ideas and intuitions which transcend sensational experience; ideas whose origin is not from sensation, nor their proof from sensation." The mind of man "is not a smooth tablet on which sensation writes its experience, but is a living principle which of itself originates ideas." Moreover, God dwells in every man, and human nature, therefore, is not simply excellent but divine. Since the transcendentalists discovered no evil in the mind of man and had faith in his intuitive knowledge of right and justice, they urged everyone to follow his conscience even if he was thus driven to defy church or state. "To know what is right," said Parker, "I need not ask what is the current practice, what say the Revised Statutes, what said holy men of old, but what says conscience? what, God?" Thoreau, in his famous *Essay on Civil Disobedience*, asked: "Must the citizen ever for a moment, or in the least degree, resign his conscience to the legislator? Why has every man a conscience, then?" Carrying an old Jeffersonian slogan to what he thought was its logical conclusion, he argued: "That government is best which governs not at all."

The transcendental belief that God, or the Oversoul, permeated both matter and spirit, that man had in him a spark of divinity, and that his potentialities were limitless had several consequences. It led to a celebration of individualism and self-reliance and to an admiration of men who had the strength and confidence to strike out on their own. In this spirit Thoreau, in 1845, built a cabin on Walden Pond near Concord, where he lived for two years to illustrate that man can rely on himself and live a full life apart from society. Transcendentalism also produced a rather naive faith that in the long run everything would turn out well. As Emerson wrote: "An eternal beneficent necessity is always bringing things right. . . . The league between virtue and nature engages all things to assume a hostile front to vice."

But although the transcendentalists were optimists, they did not ignore the shortcomings of American society or wait complacently for an inevitable progress to produce the remedies. Instead, they were severe critics of governments, laws, social institutions, and debasing commercialism—whatever prevented man from realizing his full potential. "Their quarrel with every man they meet," said Emerson, "is not with his kind, but with his degree." Hence the transcendentalists, though they were not given to organizing or joining reform societies, nonetheless contributed to the country's intellectual climate of reform. Emerson asked,

> What is man born for but to be a Reformer, a Re-maker of what man has made; a renouncer of lies; a restorer of truth and good, imitating that great Nature which embosoms us all, and which sleeps no moment on an old past, but every hour repairs herself, yielding to us every morning a new day, and with every pulsation a new life? •

The Protestant sects and revivalism.
If Unitarianism was too cold, transcendentalism was too intellectual (and perhaps too cheerful) to attract a large following. Most Americans remained in the Congregational, Presbyterian, Baptist, and Methodist churches or joined one of the numerous evangelical sects that proliferated in the nineteenth century. Even at the popular level, however, the hard tenets of orthodox Calvinism began to soften. Devout Protestants continued to believe in man's sinful condition, but they accepted the doctrine of a benevolent God who offered all men the chance of salvation through the experience of spiritual conversion and through faith. Moreover, the material opportunities that lay before Americans in a growing and flourishing society discouraged otherworldliness and tempted them to expect virtue to be rewarded on earth as well as in heaven.

Even so, much of orthodoxy still survived in the religion of the common man. In his cosmology, the Copernican revolution in astronomy notwithstanding, the earth was still the center of the universe; and God continued to be actively and intimately involved in the affairs of man. The ordinary churchgoer still believed in the Trinity, in the Bible as divine revelation, and in a literal heaven and hell. He might doubt man's total depravity, but he could never accept the transcendentalist's extreme optimism about human nature. For the reality of evil in the world was too manifest, human frailty in the face of temptation too obvious. The continued prevalence of endemic and epidemic diseases, and the resulting short life expectancy and high infant mortality, made the average man acutely conscious, sometimes almost obsessed, with the imminence of death. This awareness helps explain the persistence of a measure of gloom and pessimism in his outlook on life; it intensified his religious fervor and turned him to the church for strength and solace.

With few exceptions, notably the Quakers, the various Protestant denominations actively proselytized those who were seeking comfort and salvation. Some had greater success than others. After the Revolution the Protestant Episcopal Church, formerly the Anglican Church, was discredited by the fact that much of its clergy had been Loyalist; it grew only slowly, appealing mostly to well-to-do Eastern conservatives. The Congregationalists of New England lost members to the Unitarians. In the newly settled regions of the West they joined with the Presbyterians in 1801 to adopt a Plan of Union, by which they agreed to establish united churches that might select either Congregational or Presbyterian ministers. In the long run the Plan of Union benefited the Presbyterians, because most of the united churches entered their fold. Although the Presbyterians thus experienced a considerable growth, they were far surpassed by two other Protestant denominations. One of these, the Baptists, had phenomenal success with their system of autonomous congregations and with an untrained, uneducated clergy that spoke the language of the common man. Their ministers brought a primitive but passionate message of hellfire for sinners and redemption for those who experienced conversion and admitted God into their souls. The second, and most successful of all, were the Methodists, each of whose itinerant ministers rode a circuit of several congregations in the scattered settlements of the West and preached an equally simple Christianity.

After the Great Awakening of the mid-eighteenth century, revivalism became a periodic phenomenon. During these interludes of religious enthusiasm Presbyterians, Baptists, and Methodists won new converts by the thousands. In the course of the Second Awakening, which began around 1800, the religious frenzy spread with increasing intensity

Methodist camp meeting: new converts by the thousands

from east to west. An innovation of this revival was the camp meeting, which brought crowds together for several days of uninterrupted preaching and prayers. Under the emotional influence of exhorters who called for repentance, many experienced conversion. Since the battle with Satan was often violent, a familiar spectacle was the jumping, shouting, and moaning of tortured souls. When the battle had been won and Satan put to rout, as one witness observed, "hundreds were prostrate upon the earth before the Lord."

The intensity of religious feeling and the relative autonomy of many individual congregations often led to disputes over questions of doctrine, church organization, and ritual, and these in turn caused schisms and the formation of numerous small fundamentalist denominations. For example, the quest of a group of Methodists in western New York for holiness and perfect love led them ultimately to separate from the Methodist Episcopal Church and to form the Free Methodist Church. The divisions among Baptists produced the Hard-Shells, Soft-Shells, Primitives, and Free Willers, as well as new denominations such as the Campbellites (Disciples of Christ). Among the new sects, one of the most important was the Mormon Church, founded in the 1820s by Joseph Smith in western New York. The Church of Jesus Christ of Latter-Day Saints, as it was officially called, was based on miraculous revelations that Smith claimed to have received from God and that he incorporated in the Book of Mormon. Still another sect, the Adventists, believed in the imminence of the Bible's prophesied second coming of Christ. Early in the 1840s, William Miller, a Vermont Baptist preacher, after a series of elaborate calculations, predicted the start of the millennium, first in 1843, then in 1844. The disappointment that Miller's Adventist followers eventually experienced led most of them to desert him, but for a few years they numbered hundreds of thousands.

During another period of revivalism in the 1820s many of its leaders, for the first time, combined a desire to save souls with an active interest in social reform. The greatest preacher of this revival was the Reverend Charles G. Finney, who gathered his first harvest of converts from the fertile soil of upstate New York, a land of transplanted New Englanders. Finney preached not only salvation through faith but the importance of good works and the obligation of the churches to take "right

Joseph Smith: Latter-Day Saint

ground . . . on all the subjects of practical morality which come up for decision from time to time." To him original sin was a "deep-seated but voluntary . . . self-interest. . . . All sin consists in selfishness; and all holiness or virtue, in disinterested benevolence." Salvation was not the end but the beginning of life—a life of useful work and benevolent activity. Since Finney's doctrine, as one contemporary observed, encouraged mankind "to *work* as well as to *believe*," Finney became a powerful influence for social reform. In addition to winning the support of many established preachers, he sent out a remarkable group of young converts to advance his work, notably Theodore Dwight Weld, who went into the West to preach and to advance the cause of moral reform.

In 1830 Finney brought his revival to New York City, which he regarded as carrying the Gospel into the precincts of hell itself. Here he met two remarkable brothers, Arthur and Lewis Tappan, wealthy merchants and pious men who were already devoting most of their energy and fortunes to philanthropy. The Tappans welcomed Finney and organized an Association of Gentlemen to give financial support to both his religious and his reform work. Lewis Tappan, once a Unitarian, had become dissatisfied with that faith and had moved not toward transcendentalism but back to evangelical Protestantism. He had concluded, he explained, that the Unitarians "did not, in an equal degree, consider themselves as stewards, and their property as consecrated to the cause of Christianity; and that they were deficient in a devotional frame of mind."

Religion thus encouraged reform in two different but parallel trends. First, the transcendentalists celebrated the divinity of man and called on him to trust his conscience in his quest for right and justice. Thoreau wrote: "It is not desirable to cultivate a respect for the law, so much as for the right. The only obligation which I have a right to assume is to do at any time what I think right." Second, the evangelical Protestantism of the revivalists made good works a manifestation of holiness and of the experience of conversion, and reform a vital function of the churches. "And what is to reform mankind but the truth?" asked Finney. "And who shall present the truth if not the church and the ministry? Away with the idea that Christians can remain neutral and keep still, and yet enjoy the approbation and blessing of God."

The movement for reform

The nature of the movement. William Ellery Channing observed that one of the remarkable circumstances of his age was "the energy with which the principle of combination, or of action by joint forces, by associated numbers, is manifesting itself. It may be said, without much exaggeration, that everything is done now by Societies. . . . You can scarcely name an object for which some institution has not been formed." Though the benevolent societies were numerous, there was a considerable overlapping of both leaders and members. Active reformers tended to be attracted to several causes, and the same names appeared repeatedly among the directors of the various reform organizations.

The reformers, for a variety of reasons, were severely criticized by their conservative contemporaries and have been treated unsympathetically by some historians as well. In the first place, as a leading reformer himself noted, there is a "tendency of every reform to surround itself with a fringe of the unreasonable and half-cracked"; and the reformers had within their ranks a full quota of cranks whose bizarre crusades exposed the whole movement to ridicule. Some devoted their energies to stopping the wearing of corsets; others to food fads, such as the eating of whole-wheat bread; and still others to the "science" of phrenology. A surprising number of them developed an interest in Spiritualism, especially in the ideas of the Swedish philosopher, Emanuel Swedenborg, who described a spirit world where all were received and were able to strive for perfection. Reformers were accused, too, of being more concerned with denouncing evil than with advancing constructive remedies. Their movement, it has been said, was a vehicle for righteous men to assert their righteousness—for teetotalers to deplore the use of alcohol, and for the virtuous to denounce immorality. Moreover, as Emerson complained, many of them were "narrow, self-pleasing, conceited men" given to petty bickering and "personal and party heats." They often exhibited an uncompromising inflexibility that made them unattractive as human beings and ineffective in striving toward their own goals.

From the perspective of the twentieth century, these reformers have also been criticized for their naive optimism about human nature and for their confidence that social problems could be solved simply by exposing them and by appealing to the innate goodness in man. In addition, most of them were blind to the problems of the growing class of urban factory workers. Reform leaders usually came from the old middle-class families of rural and small-town New England; their social backgrounds and economic assumptions made them singularly insensitive to conditions in the industrial centers—or prone to blame the plight of the workingman on his use of liquor and tobacco. Indeed, it has been suggested that in a sense they were themselves victims of the Industrial Revolution. Belonging to families that in the past had been accustomed to social recognition and leadership in public affairs, they were now losing status and being displaced by the rising merchants and manufacturers. Presumably the discontent provoked by their loss of prestige found an outlet in movements for reform.

This psychological interpretation of the reform movement, which stresses the subjective needs of the reformers themselves, can be neither proved nor disproved; but in any case, it is hardly a sufficient explanation of their crusade. Though their shortcomings and personal problems were real enough, the movement they launched cannot be written off as an enterprise of impractical, shortsighted cranks and neurotics. There were in the ranks of reform many dedicated men and women who demonstrated a keen understanding of, and sensitivity to, at least some of the social problems of their day. They reacted to objective conditions, not merely to their own internal need for self-expression. The severe dislocations of a period of rapid economic growth and unsettling social change, which produced both a widespread feeling that traditional values were being lost and a cluster of new or sharply intensified social problems, undoubtedly contributed to the reform impulse. No doubt, too, the existing political structure and party system discouraged a resort to political action and explains in part the reliance on voluntary nonpolitical societies. But the dislocations of growth and change were not new phenomena in America, nor were the social problems all of recent vintage. The crucial ingredient that acted as the catalyst in producing a reform movement seems to have been the changes in secular and religious

William Ellery Channing: "...everything is done now by Societies"

thought noted above. These changes best explain why the reformers were sensitive to certain social problems, why certain organizational methods appealed to them, and why they resorted to the tactics they used in fighting their foes.

The accomplishments of the reformers were far from negligible. If they were a trial to their friends, it was in part because their work, by its very nature, forced them to "disregard the peace and proprieties of the social world." Each reformer seemed to bear a burden of personal guilt for the evils in his society and felt driven to do something to eliminate them. This sense of individual responsibility, which can easily be lost in a mass society, was in itself a thing of inestimable value.

Treatment of criminals and the insane.

Humane and sensitive men and women who investigated the care of paupers, criminals, and the insane in their own communities found an ample field for reform. These social derelicts, the victims of public ignorance or indifference, were treated almost as they had been in the Middle Ages. In atrocious jails and dungeons young offenders were thrown together with hardened criminals and the violently insane; in neglected almshouses idiots and the destitute were left to the mercy of low-paid, untrained attendants. Humanitarians managed at least to start the painfully slow process of providing prisons with better physical accommodations. With their more enlightened approach to penology, they urged, with some success, that the community concentrate on reforming, rather than punishing, criminals. Meanwhile, the states, one by one, responded to the new spirit by abolishing several vestiges of primitive justice: the imprisonment of debtors, public floggings, and public executions.

Since little was known about the causes of insanity, or about therapy, society provided almost no mental hospitals; the insane were either cared for by relatives or committed to jails and almshouses. Among those who took an interest in the treatment of the insane, Dorothea Dix, a Boston schoolmistress, was the most active advocate of state-supported mental hospitals and of experiments in therapy. In 1841 she launched her crusade by investigating the condition of the insane in her own state. Two years later, she presented the legislature with an eloquent but factual memorial that described "the present state of

Dorothea Dix: sincerity and sensitivity

insane persons confined in this Commonwealth, in cages, closets, cellars, stalls, pens! Chained, naked, beaten with rods, and lashed into obedience." Until her death in 1887 she worked with tireless patience to arouse public officials throughout the country, and her sincerity and command of the facts won her considerable success.

Temperance. Concern for criminals, paupers, and the insane was intimately related to another goal of the reform movement: temperance. It was commonly believed that excessive drinking was a basic cause of the condition of these unfortunates, as well as of the poverty that plagued city workers. Temperance, therefore, would not merely redeem the individual sinner but would advance the whole program of social reform. There can be no doubt that drunkenness was a genuine problem, for this was an age of heavy drinking in which the per capita consumption of whiskey, hard cider, and rum was staggering. The temperance movement began with the formation of numerous local societies, which, in 1826, combined to form a national organization, the American Society for the Promotion of Temperance. Some leaders merely preached moderation in the use of liquor, but others sought converts who would pledge total abstinence. Some relied on the voluntary decisions of individuals; others urged the use of the coercive power of state governments. In 1846 Maine passed the first prohibition law; within the next decade a dozen other Northern and Western states followed Maine's example, but most of these laws remained in force for only a few years. At its height the temperance movement resembled a religious revival; its flavor is suggested by a stanza from one of its popular songs, "One Glass More":

> Stay, mortal, stay! nor heedless thus
>   Thy sure destruction seal;
> Within that cup there lurks a curse,
>   Which all who drink shall feel.
> Disease and death forever nigh,
>   Stand ready at the door,
> And eager wait to hear the cry—
>   "O give me one glass more!"

Women's rights. Women took a special interest in temperance, but when they tried to participate actively in this or other reform movements they confronted a wall of prejudice and the rebuff that a woman's place was in the home. American men characteristically

The history of mankind is a history of repeated injuries and usurpations on the part of man toward woman, having in direct object the establishment of an absolute tyranny over her. To prove this, let facts be submitted to a candid world.

He has never permitted her to exercise her inalienable right to the elective franchise.

He has compelled her to submit to laws, in the formation of which she had no voice....

He has made her, if married, in the eyes of the law civilly dead.

He has taken from her all right in property, even to the wages she earns....

He has monopolized nearly all the profitable employments, and from those she is permitted to follow, she receives but a scanty remuneration.

He closes against her all the avenues to wealth and distinction, which he considers most honorable to himself....

He has denied her the facilities for obtaining a thorough education—all colleges being closed against her....

He has created a false public sentiment, by giving to the world a different code of morals for men and women, by which moral delinquencies which exclude women from society, are not only tolerated but deemed of little account in man....

He has endeavored, in every way that he could, to destroy her confidence in her own powers, to lessen her self-respect, and to make her willing to lead a dependent and abject life.

From the Seneca Falls, New York, "Declaration of Sentiments and Resolutions," 1848.

The grievances of American women

treated women with deference but would not accept them as equals. They upheld a double standard of morality; they idealized the pure, submissive wife and mother who devoted her life to domestic chores; and, according to one European visitor, they guarded them with "a sevenfold shield of insignificance." Woman's inferiority was sanctioned by laws, which treated unmarried women as minors, and which recognized the husband as the dominant figure in the family and even gave him control over the property his wife brought to the marriage.

Except for female seminaries where the daughters of the well-to-do could learn the social graces, schools were closed to girls. Women were excluded from the professions. They could neither vote nor hold public office. Indeed, it was considered unfeminine for them even to speak in public places or to offer prayers in church. In 1840 a group of American women, including Elizabeth Cady Stanton and Lucretia Mott, went as delegates to a World Antislavery Convention in London, but they were denied the right to participate. This and similar experiences provoked a women's rights movement that became at once an in-

tegral part of the general reform crusade and a divisive issue among male reformers, some of whom favored and some of whom opposed permitting women to join their organizations.

In 1848 the first Women's Rights Convention was held at Seneca Falls, New York. Here the delegates adopted a statement that paraphrased the Declaration of Independence and proclaimed that "all men and women are created equal." After listing women's specific grievances, the statement demanded that women "have immediate admission to all the rights and privileges which belong to them as citizens of the United States." They had, it concluded, "too long rested satisfied in the circumscribed limits which corrupt customs and a perverted application of the Scriptures" had marked out for them.

In the years before the Civil War, the women of the United States did make some limited gains. A few states gave married women control over their own property, and everywhere one profession, elementary education, was opened to them. They secured admission to a few high schools and normal schools, and in 1837 Oberlin College became the first coeducational college. Also in 1837 the first women's college, Mount Holyoke, opened its doors. But most important was the example set by a courageous group of women who defied prejudice and played an active and constructive role in public affairs. Dorothea Dix, as we have seen, contributed to improved treatment of the insane; Dr. Elizabeth Blackwell won distinction as a physician; Margaret Fuller for a time edited the transcendentalist journal, *The Dial,* and then served as literary editor of the New York *Tribune;* Emma Willard campaigned for educational reform; Lucy Stone was a popular lecturer as well as a crusader for equal suffrage; and a small host of women, notably Frances Wright, Elizabeth Cady Stanton, Lucretia Mott, and Sarah and Angelina Grimké, worked to abolish slavery. Most men (and more than a few women) sneered at these ''unsexed'' women, citing Mrs. Amelia Bloomer's wearing of pantalettes as evidence of where it would all end. But the feminists had effectively challenged the myth that women were physically and intellectually unfitted for any useful activity outside the home.

Education. The reform movement revealed its debt to Jacksonian Democracy, and the reformers their concern for the welfare of the common man, in the crusade for free, tax-supported public education. In the early nineteenth century, except in Massachusetts, the children of the poor obtained their elementary education at home or in church or charity schools, and the children of the rich in private schools or from tutors. The lack of public support, together with the fact that most teaching was done by low-paid, untrained young men who regarded it as a temporary occupation, left a mass of people, both urban and rural, in a state of semiliteracy. In the two decades after 1830 the crucial battle to establish public responsibility for elementary education was fought and won, though in many states it took much longer for the idea to be translated into reality.

Opposition came from those who considered education a private concern, from taxpayers who objected to paying for the education of other people's children, and from religious groups that maintained their own schools. Support came from practical men in an increasingly commercial society, where more and more occupations required the ability to read, write, and cipher. It came, too, from those who believed that mass education

Mount Holyoke Seminary, 1839

was essential to a political system based on manhood suffrage. Further support came from those who viewed public education as a means of providing the common man with better opportunities to advance. They hoped thus to achieve a more general diffusion of property ownership and a softening of class lines. In 1848, Horace Mann, in one of his celebrated reports as secretary of the Massachusetts Board of Education, noted the alarming contrasts of wealth and poverty in his state; he maintained that ''nothing but Universal Education can counterwork this tendency to the domination of capital and the servility of labor.'' Educate the workingman, and he will improve his position and acquire property, for ''such a thing never did happen, and never can happen, as that an intelligent and practical body of men should be permanently poor.'' Education, Mann concluded, ''is the great equalizer of the conditions of men— the balance wheel of the social machinery. . . . It does better than to disarm the poor of their hostility toward the rich; it prevents being poor.'' The city workers themselves made state-supported education one of their prime demands. A resolution adopted by the mechanics of Philadelphia in 1830 declared ''that there can be no real liberty without a wide diffusion of real intelligence . . . [and] that until means of equal instruction shall be equally secured to all, liberty is but an unmeaning word, and equality an empty shadow.''

By the 1850s the states were committed to making tax-supported public education available to all without the stigma of charity. Some of the states had already passed laws requiring local communities to establish elementary schools, and most of the others had at least required that when schools were established they must admit all children, not just those able to pay tuition. One of the decisive battles was fought in Pennsylvania, where in 1834 a state school law was passed. But opposition to the law was so formidable that the legislature seemed ready to repeal it in favor of one providing free education only for the poor. After a bitter struggle, the law was saved largely through the efforts of a young Whig legislator, Thaddeus Stevens, whose brilliant defense of free education carried the day. Similar battles were fought and won in other states. As a result, outside the South, where the movement was impeded by rural conditions and the indifference of the planter class, a steadily growing number of children found free public schools available to them.

But this was only the beginning, for compulsory-attendance laws had not yet been passed, school terms were short, the curriculum was thin, and teaching methods were still based on rote memorization and corporal punishment. Massachusetts led the way in remedying these conditions in 1837 by establishing a state Board of Education, with Horace Mann as secretary. Mann had devoted many years to teaching and the study of education, and during his eleven years as secretary his annual reports made him the most influential man in the public-school movement. In Massachusetts he did much to improve the curriculum and teaching methods, lengthen the school year, raise teachers' salaries, establish the first state-supported normal school for teacher-training, and organize a state association of teachers. Other states appointed their own boards or superintendents of education, who tried, with varying degrees of success, to achieve similar reforms.

For most American children formal education ceased after a few years in an elementary school. Secondary education was limited to those who could afford to pay the tuition to a private academy, where, in preparation for college, they took courses in mathematics, rhetoric, and the classics. In 1827 Massachusetts passed a law requiring every town of five hundred or more families to set up a public high school, and the other New England states soon followed suit. But as late as 1860 there were only slightly more than three hundred public high schools in the United States, with almost a third of them in Massachusetts and only a scattering in the South and West.

In higher education, which was less influenced by reform, the most notable development was the proliferation of private denominational colleges throughout the country. In the two decades between 1830 and 1850 about eighty of these colleges were founded. Most of them had meager endowments, small student bodies, and incompetent faculties; but every village seemed determined to have a college, and every religious sect wanted a network of colleges to train its clergy and indoctrinate its youth. The idea of state-supported institutions of higher learning was an old one, and four states (Vermont, North Carolina, Georgia, and Tennessee) chartered them in the late eighteenth century. The first one actually to win academic distinction, however, was the University of Virginia, founded in 1819. By the 1850s numerous state universities, most of them in the South and West, had been founded, but few were in reality more than small colleges limping along on slender budgets.

Both state and private colleges offered a traditional liberal-arts curriculum, which stressed Latin, Greek, science, mathematics, moral philosophy, and political economy. True universities in the modern sense, with professional schools, graduate teaching, and emphasis on scholarly research, did not emerge until after the Civil War. Too many colleges were founded during these years, and few of them had the libraries and scholars they needed to become centers of creative intellectual life. The idea of academic freedom, moreover, had few defenders, and countless instructors fell victim to the political and sectarian controversies of the age.

Since the colleges served only a tiny fraction of the population, the mass of adults with a thirst for learning searched for other and more accessible avenues to cultural advancement. The "penny press," which began in 1833 when the New York *Sun* went on sale at a penny a copy, put newspapers within the reach of everyone and served up a mixed fare of sensationalism, news, and essays on practical and scientific subjects. Hundreds of magazines catered to all tastes, but the best of them offered essays, poetry, and fiction by the most distinguished European and American writers. This was an era of organized efforts for self-improvement, and most communities had their debating societies, literary societies, and library associations. The lyceum movement, a nationally organized program of adult education initiated in 1826 by a New Englander, Josiah Holbrook, was the most ambitious of these enterprises. The original plan was to encourage local lyceums to assemble libraries, study scientific subjects, and form discussion groups, but most of them soon concentrated on lecture courses. Though many a fraud and charlatan managed to get on the lyceum lecture circuit, men of letters such as Emerson and Charles Dickens, scientists such as Harvard's Louis Agassiz, and a host of reformers made the program a useful instrument of mass education.

The peace movement. Reformers not content with the piecemeal alleviation of domestic social ills turned to more ambitious projects,

New Harmony, 1832

such as the cause of world peace. Remembering the dreadful suffering and waste of the Napoleonic wars, some reformers were attracted to the pacifist principles of the Quakers or at least hoped to find nonviolent ways of settling international disputes. Local peace societies, which had begun to appear soon after the War of 1812, united in 1828 to form the American Peace Society. William Ladd, the Maine merchant who founded the national organization, proposed the formation of a Congress of Nations to interpret international law and a Court of Nations to apply it. Most peace men, however, distinguished between the use of force for aggressive and for defensive purposes and condemned only the former. In 1838 the peace movement split when the "ultraists," headed by Henry Clark Wright and William Lloyd Garrison, formed a Non-Resistance Society committed to oppose violence even in self-defense. Their constitution denounced military service, forceful resistance to tyranny, capital punishment, and actions at law for civil damages. This millennial program was designed to put Christian precepts into immediate action—to prepare the way "for the full manifestation of the reign of Christ on earth." It would secure "the reconciliation and salvation of a warring and lost world."

The Shakers: holiness through Christian communism

Communitarianism.
Other perfectionists worked for the complete regeneration of society by building model communities that they hoped would form the nuclei of a better social order. Early communitarian projects had been undertaken by several small religious sects, such as the Shakers, with the goal of achieving holiness through a form of Christian communism. In 1825 Robert Owen, a Scottish textile-manufacturer and philanthropist, established the first significant nonreligious communitarian enterprise at New Harmony, Indiana. Owen hoped to abolish poverty and crime through cooperative labor and the collective ownership of property, but within two years New Harmony proved an economic failure. Communitarianism reached its peak during the 1840s, when the ideas of the French reformer Charles Fourier were embraced by many transcendentalists and popularized by his chief American champion, Albert Brisbane. The transcendentalists were attracted by Fourier's optimistic view of human nature, his goal of social harmony, and his plan of voluntary associations, or "phalanxes," free of governmental intervention. Association, explained the idealistic Brisbane, offered "the means of effecting peaceably and in the interest of all classes, a complete transformation in the social condition of the world." The successful establishment of only one association, he believed, would inspire men to form others. At last the movement would become universal, and there would emerge "a true Social and Political Order in the place of the old and false one." Of the many phalanxes that briefly put Fourier's ideas into practice, the best remembered was Brook Farm near Boston, founded in 1841 by George Ripley. Until its abandonment in 1847 a number of transcendentalists repaired to it, as Ripley explained, "to prepare

a society of liberal, intelligent, and cultivated persons'' who could lead ''a more simple and wholesome life, than can be led amidst the pressures of our competitive institutions.''

Young Nathaniel Hawthorne was one of the transcendentalists who went to Brook Farm, but he left with doubts about the divinity of man and a conviction that the reformers did not understand the true source of evil in the world. ''The heart, the heart,'' he wrote,

''there was the little yet boundless sphere wherein existed the original wrong of which the crime and misery of this outward world were merely types.'' His caution to the perfectionists is perhaps more understandable to our generation than it was to his: ''The progress of the world, at every step, leaves some evil or wrong on the path behind it, which the unrest of mankind, or their own set purpose, could never have found the way to rectify.''

The crusade against slavery

The beginnings of abolitionism. In Boston on January 1, 1831, William Lloyd Garrison began publishing a weekly newspaper, *The Liberator,* dedicated to the immediate abolition of Southern slavery without compensation to the masters. This event, though an important turning point, did not mark the beginning of the crusade against slavery, for organized activity, especially among the Quakers, dated back to the eighteenth century. Pressure from antislavery groups had already achieved the abolition of slavery in the Northern states, and in the 1820s a small manumission movement in the Upper South had called for gradual, compensated emancipation with colonization of the free Negroes in Africa. Benjamin Lundy, a New Jersey Quaker, organized local societies in Kentucky, Tennessee, North Carolina, and Virginia and at the same time edited an antislavery newspaper, *The Genius of Universal Emancipation,* in Baltimore. Garrison got his start writing for Lundy's paper, but he was a man of different temperament who brought a new stridency and militancy to the attack. He set the tone for his crusade in the prospectus printed in the first issue of *The Liberator:*

> I *will* be as harsh as truth, and as uncompromising as justice. On this subject, I do not wish to think, or speak, or write with moderation. . . . I am in earnest—I will not equivocate—I will not excuse—I will not retreat a single inch—AND I WILL BE HEARD.

In 1832 Garrison organized the New England Anti-Slavery Society and a year later helped to establish a national organization, the American Anti-Slavery Society. During the next few years abolitionist agents were busy establishing local societies, until by 1840 a network of some two thousand of them with nearly two hundred thousand members stretched across the North. To many, Garrison was the embodiment of abolitionism, and the angry response of the South to his harsh words kept him in the public eye. But he was more an editor and publicist than an effective leader and tactician, and the movement soon grew too large for him to control. Other abolitionists also played significant roles: Wendell Phillips in New England, Gerrit Smith and the Tappans in New York, and Theodore Dwight Weld in the West. Weld, a product of the Finney revival in upstate New York, was perhaps the most successful of the abolitionist organizers. In 1834, at the Lane Theological Seminary in Cincinnati, Weld persuaded the students to engage in a prolonged debate on the subject of slavery. In the course of the debate many students became converts to abolitionism, and in subsequent years they joined Weld as agents and organizers for the American Anti-Slavery Society. Using the techniques of the revivalists, these men had notable success in New York, Pennsylvania, and the Old Northwest; they won thousands of converts and sometimes managed to abolitionize entire communities.

At length, in 1840, resentment against Garrison, disagreement over his effort to admit women to full participation, and differences over tactics caused a split in abolitionist ranks and led to the withdrawal of the anti-Garrisonians from the American Anti-Slavery Society to form a society of their own. Thereafter abolitionism was only loosely organized at the national level, and the real force of the crusade came from the state and local groups.

By the end of the 1830s, for several reasons, abolitionism had become the most popular cause of the whole reform movement. Most of the reformers had come to agree that slavery was the greatest social evil in the way

William Lloyd Garrison: harsh as truth

THE NORTH STAR.

VOL. I. NO. 1.   ROCHESTER, N. Y. FRIDAY, DECEMBER 3, 1847.   WHOLE

Frederick Douglass' newspaper

of the nation's moral regeneration. In this romantic age they found particularly obnoxious a system that denied the individual control over his own destiny. To prove its wickedness, the abolitionists dwelt on the cruelties of slavery, for they were always less interested in presenting a balanced picture than in winning converts. Slavery provided them with plenty of illustrations of cruelty. In 1839 Weld published a powerful abolitionist tract, *Slavery As It Is,* which was simply a documented compilation of incidents reported in Southern newspapers and court records. The Southern states made themselves especially vulnerable to criticism by refusing to eliminate the system's worst abuses: its physical cruelty, its failure to give legal recognition to slave marriages, the separation of children from their parents, the callous practices of the interstate slave-traders, and the denial to Negroes of opportunities for self-improvement.

Abolitionism also attracted Northern reformers because the Southern manumission societies had failed to accomplish their purpose; slavery, it appeared, would never be destroyed without intervention by the North. It no longer seemed to be a weak and declining institution that could be left to die a natural death; instead it was flourishing and spreading westward into new territories and states. The reformers were shocked by the Southerners' growing tendency to regard slavery as a desirable and permanent institution and by their increasingly harsh treatment of even native Southern critics. One reformer expressed his dismay at ''the sentiments openly expressed by the southern newspapers, that slavery is not an evil . . . [and] that it is criminal toward the South . . . to indulge even a hope that the chains of the captive may some day or other, no matter how remote the time, be broken.'' Moreover, the reformers were acutely conscious of the hypocrisy of America's posing as a model of liberal institutions while remaining one of the last countries in the Western world to tolerate human bondage. Finally, the success of British abolitionists

Sojourner Truth

in securing emancipation in the British West Indies (1833) stimulated the reformers to undertake a similar crusade in America.

One small group of Americans, the free blacks, needed no prodding from white reformers to support abolitionism, and in the North they made a significant contribution to the movement. Northern free Negroes always constituted the majority of subscribers to Garrison's *Liberator,* and after the organization of the American Anti-Slavery Society three Negroes always served on its executive committee. Among the most prominent Negro abolitionist agents and orators were Samuel Ringgold Ward, who escaped from slavery in Maryland; Lunsford Lane, who was born a slave in North Carolina and bought his own freedom; Sojourner Truth, who was born a slave in New York and was freed by the state emancipation act; Charles Lenox Remond, a well-educated Massachusetts Negro who lectured in Great Britain as well as in the United States; and Frederick Douglass, who escaped from slavery in Maryland to become editor of an anti-slavery newspaper, one of the greatest of all antislavery orators, and the preeminent American Negro leader of the nineteenth century. Though most black abolitionists accepted the peaceful tactics of their white brethren, a few helped to build a tradition of militant activism. In Boston, in 1829, David Walker, a free Negro born in North Carolina, published an angry *Appeal to the Colored Citizens of the World,* justifying violence to destroy slavery and warning white masters of the consequences of holding blacks in bondage. In 1843, Henry H. Garnet, in an address before a Negro convention in Buffalo, urged slaves to strike for their liberties: ''Let your motto be resistance! . . . No oppressed people have ever secured their liberty without resistance.'' Many free Negroes guided fugitives to freedom over the so-called underground railroad. Among them was Harriet Tubman, who escaped from slavery in Maryland but returned nineteen times to help several hundred slaves flee from their bondage.

Abolitionist tactics. The tactics of the abolitionists were determined by their optimistic assumptions about human nature, by their belief in the power of truth, by their belief that slavery was essentially a moral issue, and by the restrictive political structure within which they had to operate. They were confronted with the problem that Congress, unlike the British Parliament, had no constitutional power to interfere with slavery. At the same time, the pacifism of most abolitionists discouraged the use of force. In its statement of principles, the New England Anti-Slavery society affirmed that "we will not operate on the existing relations of society by other than peaceful and lawful means, and that we will give no countenance to violence or insurrection." Abolitionists, therefore, relied on "moral suasion." Their first goal was to persuade slaveholders that slavery was both a sin and a denial of the "unalienable rights" with which, according to the Declaration of Independence, all men are endowed. Though abolitionists believed in immediate emancipation—slaveholding, being a sin, moral men could not advocate abandoning it gradually—they were practical enough to understand that the actual implementation of emancipation might take a little time. In an era of revivalism they might hope for mass conversions of slaveholders, but they could hardly hope that all slaveholders would give up the institution in a single year. Moreover, they understood that there would probably have to be a period of transition while the Negroes were prepared for their new status as freedmen. Hence they usually qualified their "immediatism" by defining it, in one way or another, as a program of emancipation "promptly commenced" but "gradually accomplished." Thus Garrison, while demanding immediate abolition, agreed privately that "it will, alas, be gradual abolition in the end. We have never said that slavery would be overthrown by a single blow: that it ought to be, we shall always contend." But the theoretical immediatism to which abolitionists were committed strengthened the conviction of indignant Southerners that abolitionists were reckless incendiaries seeking to bring ruin upon the South.

When the abolitionists failed to move the slaveholders to action, when they found it nearly impossible to carry their message into the South, they turned to building up antislavery opinion in the North. Their propaganda hammered relentlessly at their central argument: every person of full age and sane mind has a right to freedom unless convicted of a crime; "mere difference of complexion is no reason why any man should be deprived of any of his natural rights"; "man cannot, consistently with reason, religion, and the eternal and immutable principles of justice, be the property of man"; "whoever retains his fellow-man in bondage is guilty of a grievous wrong." Abolitionists sometimes spoke of the alleged economic waste of slavery, but their indictment was chiefly moral and religious.

Whether moral suasion might be supplemented by some form of political action was a question on which abolitionists differed. Garrison's nonresistance principles turned him against government as an instrument of force and therefore against involvement in politics. Moreover, he viewed the political parties as tools of the slaveholders, the Union as their protector, and the Constitution as a proslavery document (in his words, "a covenant with death and an agreement with hell"). Most abolitionists, however, though recognizing that Congress could not touch slavery in the states, believed that some things might be accomplished through political action—for example, the abolition of slavery in the District of Columbia, the outlawing of the interstate slave trade, and the exclusion of slavery from federal territories. Hence they took an active part in politics and put pressure on congressional candidates to take antislavery positions. In 1840 a group of political abolitionists organized the Liberty party and nominated James G. Birney for the Presidency, but the small vote the party attracted in this and subsequent elections indicated that most abolitionists preferred to operate through existing parties. With the growth of political abolitionism there was a notable decline in pacifist sentiment, and the sectional conflict of the 1850s prepared many abolitionists to turn from moral suasion to force as the ultimate remedy.

In the early years of the movement most Northerners shared the opinion of Southerners that abolitionists were irresponsible fanatics, and antislavery meetings were frequently broken up by violence. In 1834 a mob invaded Lewis Tappan's house and destroyed the furnishings; in 1835 a Boston mob treated Garrison so roughly that authorities took him to jail for his own protection; and in 1837 a mob in Alton, Illinois, murdered Elijah Lovejoy, an abolitionist editor. After being mobbed on

Harriet Tubman

CANNIBALS ALL!

OR,

SLAVES WITHOUT MASTERS.

BY

GEORGE FITZHUGH,

OF PORT ROYAL, CAROLINE, VA.

"He hand will be against every man, and every man's hand against him."—Gen. xvi. 11.
"Physician, heal thyself."—Luke iv. 23.

RICHMOND, VA.
A. MORRIS, PUBLISHER.
1857.

The negro slaves of the South are the happiest, and, in some sense, the freest people in the world. The children and the aged and infirm work not at all, and yet have all the comforts and necessaries of life provided for them. They enjoy liberty, because they are oppressed neither by care nor labor. The women do little hard work, and are protected from the despotism of their husbands by their masters. The negro men and stout boys work, on the average, in good weather, not more than nine hours a day.... Besides, they have their Sabbaths and holidays. White men, with so much of license and liberty, would die of ennui; but negroes luxuriate in corporeal and mental repose. With their faces upturned to the sun, they can sleep at any hour; and quiet sleep is the greatest of human enjoyments.... The free laborer must work or starve. He is more of a slave than the negro, because he works longer and harder for less allowance than the slave, and has no holiday, because the cares of life with him begin when its labors end. He has no liberty, and not a single right.

From George Fitzhugh, *Cannibals All!*, 1857.

---

several occasions, Weld warned fellow abolitionists that each would have to decide "whether he can lie upon the rack," or "if cloven down, fall and die a martyr."

Northern businessmen, viewing antislavery agitation as a threat to their profitable trade with the South, more than once joined or encouraged the mobs. Nationalists opposed the abolitionists, because their crusade endangered the federal Union; conservative churchmen feared that attacks on slavery might divide the churches along sectional lines. However, race prejudice, which was nearly as intense in the North as in the South, was always the fundamental cause of the hostility to abolitionism. The prevailing prejudice exposed Northern free Negroes to many forms of discrimination. They were prohibited from entering most trades and professions and forced into menial occupations; they were excluded from the public schools or sent to segregated schools; they were assigned segregated seats in white churches and on public transportation; they were barred from office-holding and jury duty; they were denied the ballot except in five New England states and in New York (where they had to meet a property qualification not required of whites); and they were prohibited from settling in several Western states. Indeed, it is safe to say that if Southern slaves had been white rather than black, Northerners would have been far less prone to advance practical arguments against antislavery agitation. Even some of the abolitionists were unable to free themselves entirely from the prevailing prejudice and shrank from personal contacts with Negroes, but as a group their racial attitudes were so liberal that their contemporaries often denounced them as "nigger-lovers." There is much evidence that the efforts of abolitionists to eliminate discrimination and segregation in the North, which was a second goal of many of them, greatly intensified Northern hostility toward them.

A broadening appeal. Though abolitionists had only limited success in reducing Northern prejudice against Negroes, the growing sectional tension of the 1840s and 1850s caused Northerners to listen more sympathetically to what they had to say about the evils of slavery. Eventually abolitionist agitation helped to persuade large numbers of Northerners that even black slavery was morally wrong and therefore could not be accepted as a permanent institution. This agitation also produced an image of slaveholders as undemocratic, arrogant, immoral, and cruel. The slaveholders and their political henchmen, said the abolitionists, formed a sinister "Slave Power" that ruled the South and conspired to rule the entire Union in order to destroy freedom. Theodore Parker described the Slave Power as

the blight of this nation, the curse of the North and the curse of the South. . . . It confounds your politics. It has silenced your ablest men. It has muzzled the pulpit, and stifled the press. It has robbed

The slave is held simply for the use of his master, *to whose behests his life, liberty, and happiness are devoted, and by whom he may be bartered, leased, mortgaged, bequeathed, invoiced, shipped as cargo, stored as goods, sold on execution, [and] knocked off at public auction ... all according to law. Nor is there anything, within the limit of life, inflicted on a beast, which may not be inflicted on the slave. He may be marked like a hog, branded like a mule, yoked like an ox, hobbled like a horse, driven like an ass, sheared like a sheep, maimed like a cur, and constantly beaten like a brute,—all according to law. And should life itself be taken, what is the remedy? The Law of Slavery ... openly pronounces the incompetency of the whole African race, whether bond or free, to testify against a white man in any case, and thus, after surrendering the slave to all possible outrage, crowns its tyranny by excluding the very testimony through which the bloody cruelty of the Slave-Master might be exposed....*

... Unhappily, there is Barbarism elsewhere in the world; but American Slavery, as defined by existing law, stands forth as the greatest organized Barbarism on which the sun now looks.

From Charles Sumner, Speech in the United States Senate, June 4, 1860.

Slavery: an abolitionist's view

three million men of what is dearer than life; it has kept back the welfare of seventeen million more.

Meanwhile, as the abolitionists braved mobs to defend freedom of assembly and of the press, they began to win admiration as champions of civil liberties not only for black but for white men. They aroused sympathy when Southern mobs broke into post offices to seize and destroy packages of antislavery pamphlets, for now the right of minority groups to disseminate their ideas through the mails seemed to be at stake. In 1836, when the abolitionists deluged Congress with petitions urging the abolition of slavery in the District of Columbia, Southerners forced through the House a so-called gag rule, which provided that petitions relating to slavery were to be laid on the table without being printed, referred to committee, or debated. Until the repeal of the gag rule in 1844, abolitionists stood as defenders of another sacred liberty: the right of petition.

Most Northerners also sympathized with the more or less systematic efforts of abolitionists to assist fugitive slaves to freedom along the routes of the underground railroad. Few could help feeling compassion for the pathetic fugitive seeking his own liberty, and even a Negrophobe might resent the activities of the professional slave-catchers who roamed the free states. In 1842 an important case (*Prigg v. Pennsylvania*) involving the constitutionality of the Fugitive Slave Act of 1793 came before

the Supreme Court. Though the Court ruled that the act was constitutional, it conceded that a state might prohibit its own officers from helping to enforce it. Thereafter a number of states, under pressure from the abolitionists, adopted "personal-liberty laws" that withheld assistance in the capture of fugitives.

On one issue—whether slavery should be introduced into new territories and states— the abolitionists eventually gained overwhelming Northern support. Northerners continued to agree that the Constitution prevented federal interference with slavery in the Southern states, but by the 1850s they felt strongly that slavery ought to be confined to its present limits. Often this sentiment sprang less from sympathy for the black than from a determination of free white farmers to keep slaveholders out of the territories they coveted. But the abolitionist indictment of slavery proved a handy weapon for them to use against Southern expansionists.

In one fundamental respect the abolitionist crusade was a failure. Since it did not convert the slaveholders, it never achieved its original goal: peaceful abolition through the triumph of Truth over Evil. Abolitionists who hoped to eliminate prejudice and discrimination in the Northern states, of course, suffered a second defeat. But in another and unexpected way the crusade was a success. Though it was launched by pacifists, by 1861 abolitionism, which had itself grown increasingly militant, had helped to arm the Northern population morally for the terrible struggle that lay ahead.

The proslavery argument

Slavery a positive good. In January 1837 Senator John C. Calhoun boldly took a position toward which many Southerners had been drifting:

> I hold that in the present state of civilization, where two races of different origin, and distinguished by color and other physical differences, as well as intellectual, are brought together, the relation now existing in the slaveholding states between the two is, instead of an evil, a good—a positive good.

There would be no more apologies—no concessions that slavery was at best a necessary evil—as Southern dialecticians spun out the arguments affirming the benign qualities of their peculiar institution. Never before had the justification of human bondage been presented with so much moral fervor and in such elaborate detail as in the antebellum South. Indeed the proslavery argument was one of the most impressive products of its intellectual life. Southern poets, theologians, moral philosophers, social theorists, jurists, and scientists combined their talents to uphold slavery and denounce heresy and radicalism.

This body of proslavery literature is significant not only because it was one of the principal contributions of Southern men of letters but because it was a rare expression in nineteenth-century America of deep pessimism about human nature, of doubt about the liberal tradition, and of skepticism about progress. One Southerner wrote with sarcasm:

> No word in the English language is so much used as the dissyllable *progress*. In America we use it so much, that we have made a verb of it. This is an age of progress—a country of progress—a people of progress. Progress is synonymous with enlightenment, and he who falls into the rear rank, is considered recreant to the cause of civilization.

And yet, insisted another Southerner, "it cannot be denied that we must still look to antiquity for the noblest deeds and grandest thoughts that illustrate the race of men." Romanticism, which found expression in the North in the reform movement and in a remarkable burst of literary productivity, found expression in the South in a cult of chivalry and in the identification of the planter class with traditional aristocratic values.

The nature of the defense. Since the average slaveholder was highly religious, a theological defense of slavery was fully developed and almost invariably incorporated in the numerous treatises on the subject. Out of the mass of Scriptural arguments, three were of crucial importance. The first identified the Negroes as the descendants of Canaan, the son of Ham, of whom Noah said, "Cursed be Canaan; a servant of servants shall he be unto his brethren." The second pointed to Mosaic law, which authorized the Jews to make bondsmen "of the heathen that are round about you." The third noted that neither the prophets of the Old Testament nor Christ and his apostles ever condemned slavery. Rather, they repeatedly admonished servants to obey their masters and to submit to their earthly lot. The proper role of the church, therefore, was not to attack slavery but to bring spiritual salvation to the slaves and to urge benevolence on their masters.

Turning to history, the defenders argued that slavery had always existed in some form and that it had been the foundation of all the great civilizations of antiquity. Aristotle, whose thought permeates the proslavery argument, taught that in every organized society the men of superior talents would become masters over those of inferior talents. Slavery thus enabled a class to emerge that could devote its genius to art, literature, and other intellectual pursuits. "It is a common remark," wrote George Fitzhugh of Virginia, "that the grand and lasting architectural structures of antiquity were the results of slavery."

Yet, in spite of such generalizations, few Southerners were prepared to defend their own slave system on a class basis—that is, as a desirable condition for certain classes of men of all races. Rather, their defense was essentially a defense of *black* slavery—of the subordination of the black race to the white. Since all Southern slaves had at least some African ancestors, evidence that Africans were innately inferior to whites was crucial to the Southern justification of the peculiar institution. By a curious combination of comparative anatomy and the pseudoscience of phrenology Southern ethnologists attributed to blacks certain distinct physical and psychic traits that suggested their inferiority to the whites. In the Negro, claimed a Georgia doctor, "the animal parts of the brain preponderate over the moral and intellectual,'' which explains why he is ''deficient in reason, judgment and forecast . . . thoughtless of the future, and contented and happy in the enjoyment of the mere animal pleasures of the present moment.'' The inevitable conclusion was that ''nothing but arbitrary power can restrain the excesses of his animal nature: for he has not the power within himself.'' These and other alleged racial diversities established the master-slave relationship between whites and blacks as a natural condition, its abolition a profound disaster to both.

Belief in the Negro's inferiority led also to the conclusion that the affirmations of the Declaration of Independence, the provisions of state bills of rights, and the benefits of citizenship did not and were not intended to apply to him. Society must have a class ''to perform the drudgery of life,'' affirmed James H. Hammond of South Carolina, a class ''requiring but a low order of intellect,'' a class that ''constitutes the very mud-sill of society.'' Black slavery provided this class and, by freeing the whites from menial tasks, elevated all members of the privileged caste to a condition of perfect equality.

The South had found in slavery, argued its defenders, a way to avoid the dangers to order and property posed by the laboring classes in free society. Slavery served as a conservative bulwark against all the radical ''isms'' that threatened the North with revolution. ''There are two kinds of labor, hireling labor and slave labor,'' explained a writer in the Charleston *Courier*. ''The task of each is the same— continued hard work. The promised reward of each is the same also—subsistence.'' In the North and in Europe the hirelings were discontented; they clamored for change, for ''communism, socialism, the organization of labor.'' In the South the slaves were ''orderly and efficient,'' and society had within it no element of disharmony. ''It is the only condition of society in which labor and capital are associated on a large scale in which their interests are combined and not in conflict. Every plantation is an organized community . . . where *all work,* where *each member gets subsistence and a home.*'' Slavery, in short, was a practical form of socialism.

In every respect, said Southern apologists, the slaves were better off than so-called free laborers. They were happy and contented, because they were well treated, well fed, well housed, and well clothed; they were cared for

Calhoun on slavery

"Sun of Intellectual light & liberty stand ye still, in masterly inactivity, that the Nation of Carolina may continue to hold Negroes & plant Cotton till the day of Judgment!"

in childhood, in old age, and in times of sickness. The free-labor system, which left the worker to shift for himself, was far more cruel and heartless. ''I may say with truth,'' said Calhoun, ''that in few countries so much is left to the share of the laborer, and so little exacted from him.'' Indeed, wrote a Virginian, ''a merrier being does not exist on the face of the globe, than the Negro slave of the United States.''

The endorsement of such ideas in the South at a time when a great reform movement was agitating the North produced an ideological conflict between the sections that threatened the survival of the Union. Slavery was no longer open to discussion in the South, and slaveholders intensely resented its denunciation on moral grounds in the North. Not even the two largest Protestant churches were able to bear the strain, and the slavery issue led to sectional splits—the Methodists in 1844, the Baptists in 1845. Eventually the national political parties would also disintegrate, and thus another major institutional tie would be broken. Abolitionists and proslavery polemicists had raised a moral issue—the right and wrong of slavery—that stubbornly resisted resolution by the best efforts of a generation of able politicians and statesmen.

Suggestions for reading

RELIGION

All the surveys of American cultural and intellectual history devote much space to religion in the first half of the nineteenth century. The best on this subject are R. H. Gabriel, *The Course of American Democratic Thought* (rev. ed., 1956), and Perry Miller, *The Life of the Mind in America: From the Revolution to the Civil War,* Vol. I (1966). I. H. Bartlett, *The American Mind in the Mid-Nineteenth Century** (1967), is brief and readable. Several useful general studies of American religion should also be consulted: W. W. Sweet, *The Story of Religion in America* (1920, rev. ed., 1950); W. L. Sperry, *Religion in America** (1946); E. S. Gaustad, *A Religious History of America* (1966); M. E. Marty, *Righteous Empire: The Protestant Experience in America* (1970); and J. W. Smith and A. L. Jamison, eds., *Religion in American Life,* 4 vols. (1961). Alexis de Tocqueville, *Democracy in America,* 2 vols.* (1945), makes some interesting comments about religion and the American people.

The revolt against orthodox Calvinism can be traced in H. M. Morais, *Deism in Eighteenth Century America* (1934); Albert Post, *Popular Free Thought in America* (1943); Conrad Wright, *The Beginnings of Unitarianism in America** (1955); R. L. Patterson, *The Philosophy of William Ellery Channing* (1952); D. P. Edgell, *William Ellery Channing* (1955); and M. H. Rice, *Federal Street Pastor: The Life of William Ellery Channing* (1961). D. W. Howe, *The Unitarian Conscience: Harvard Moral Philosophy, 1805–1861* (1970), is a lucid, comprehensive analysis of Unitarian thought. Transcendentalism is examined in all the surveys of American intellectual history and in two distinguished works on American literature covering the period: V. W. Brooks, *The Flowering of New England, 1815–1865** (1936), and F. O. Matthiessen, *American Renaissance** (1941). Three other books worth consulting are: O. B. Frothingham, *Transcendentalism in New England** (1876); H. C. Goddard, *New England Transcendentalism* (1908); and H. W. Schneider, *History of American Philosophy** (1946). There are good biographies of several transcendentalist leaders: H. S. Commager, *Theodore Parker: Yankee Crusader** (1936); A. M. Schlesinger, Jr., *Orestes A. Brownson: A Pilgrim's Progress** (1939); J. W. Krutch, *Henry David Thoreau** (1948); and R. L. Lusk, *The Life of Ralph Waldo Emerson* (1949). Perry Miller, ed., *The Transcendentalists** (1950), is an excellent collection of transcendentalist writings.

A good survey of Protestant revivalism is W. W. Sweet, *Revivalism in America** (1944). Much valuable detail is added in W. R. Cross, *The Burned-Over District** (1950); C. A. Johnson, *The Frontier Camp Meeting* (1955); B. A. Weisberger, *They Gathered at the River** (1958); and W. G. McLoughlin, Jr., *Modern Revivalism: Charles Grandison Finney to Billy Graham* (1959). Two important books tie revivalism to the reform movement: C. C. Cole, Jr., *The Social Ideas of the Northern Evangelists, 1826–1860* (1954), and T. L. Smith, *Revivalism and Social Reform in Mid-Nineteenth Century America** (1957). F. M. Brodie, *No Man Knows My History: The Life of Joseph Smith* (1945), is an outstanding biography of the founder of Mormonism.

REFORM

A. A. Ekirch, *The Idea of Progress in America, 1815–1860* (1944), is a critical analysis of one of the reformers' basic assumptions. A. M. Schlesinger, *The American as Reformer* (1950), is a perceptive introduction to the reform movement. The most comprehensive general treatment is A. F. Tyler, *Freedom's Ferment: Phases of American Social History to 1860** (1944). C. S. Griffin, *The Ferment of Reform, 1830–1860** (1967), is an excellent brief, interpretive, and historiographical essay. Other useful books are Meade Minnigerode, *The Fabulous Forties, 1840–1850* (1924); E. D. Branch, *The Sentimental Years, 1836–1860** (1934): R. E. Riegel, *Young America, 1830–1840* (1949); and C. S. Griffin, *Their Brothers' Keepers: Moral Stewardship in the United States, 1800–1865* (1960).

In the vast literature on specific reforms, the following are among the best: Blake McKelvey, *American Prisons: A Study in American Social History Prior to 1915* (1936); H. E. Marshall, *Dorothea Dix: Forgotten Samaritan* (1937); F. L. Byrne, *Prophet of Prohibition: Neal Dow and His Crusade* (1961); R. E. Riegel, *American Feminists* (1963); A. S. Kraditor, ed., *Up from the*

*Available in a paperback edition.

Pedestal: Selected Writings in the History of American Feminism (1968); W. L. O'Neill, *Everyone Was Brave: The Rise and Fall of Feminism in America* (1970); Page Smith, *Daughters of the Promised Land** (1970); Paul Monroe, *The Founding of the American Public School System* (1940); L. H. Tharp, *Until Victory: Horace Mann and Mary Peabody* (1953); Carl Bode, *The American Lyceum** (1956); Peter Brock, *Pacifism in the United States: From the Colonial Era to the First World War* (1968); A. E. Bestor, Jr., *Backwoods Utopias: The Sectarian and Owenite Phases of Communitarian Socialism in America, 1663–1829* (1950); and Charles Crowe, *George Ripley: Transcendentalist and Utopian Socialist* (1967).

ABOLITION AND PROSLAVERY

The best available surveys of the abolitionist movement are Louis Filler, *The Crusade Against Slavery** (1960), and D. L. Dumond, *Antislavery** (1961), which is marred by its polemical style. G. H. Barnes, *The Antislavery Impulse, 1830–1844** (1933), now dated but a pioneer work, stresses the role of Theodore Dwight Weld at the expense of Garrison. It should be compared with a provocative new study: A. S. Kraditor, *Means and Ends in American Abolitionism: Garrison and His Critics on Strategy and Tactics, 1834–1850** (1967). D. G. Mathews, *Slavery and Methodism* (1965), traces the conflict in one of the largest Protestant demoninations. Two important facets of abolitionism are examined in R. B. Nye, *Fettered Freedom: Civil Liberties and the Slavery Controversy, 1830–1860** (1949, rev. ed., 1963), and Carleton Mabee, *Black Freedom: The Nonviolent Abolitionists from 1830 through the Civil War* (1970). Benjamin Quarles, *Black Abolitionists** (1969), describes the role of the Negro in the antislavery movement. Arthur Zilversmit, *The First Emancipation* (1967), traces the abolition of slavery in the Northern states. D. B. Davis, *The Problem of Slavery in Western Culture** (1966), is a brilliant study of the intellectual origins of the American antislavery movement.

Among the best biographies of abolitionist leaders are B. P. Thomas, *Theodore Weld: Crusader for Freedom* (1950); Betty Fladeland, *James Gillespie Birney: Slaveholder to Abolitionist* (1955); I. H. Bartlett, *Wendell Phillips: Brahmin Radical* (1962); J. L. Thomas, *The Liberator: William Lloyd Garrison* (1963); M. L. Dillon, *Benjamin Lundy and the Struggle for Negro Freedom* (1966); Gerda Lerner, *The Grimké Sisters from South Carolina: Rebels Against Slavery* (1967); T. G. Edelstein, *Strange Enthusiasm: A Life of Thomas Wentworth Higginson** (1968); and Bertram Wyatt-Brown, *Lewis Tappan and the Evangelical War Against Slavery* (1969).

Racism, one of the chief obstacles the abolitionists confronted, is analyzed in William Stanton, *The Leopard's Spots: Scientific Attitudes Toward Race in America, 1815–1859** (1960); Lorman Ratner, *Powder Keg: Northern Opposition to the Antislavery Movement, 1831–1840* (1968); and G. M. Fredrickson, *The Black Image in the White Mind: The Debate on Afro-American Character and Destiny, 1817–1914* (1971). L. F. Litwack, *North of Slavery: The Negro in the Free States, 1790–1860** (1961), is an excellent empirical study of race prejudice in the North. Violence against abolitionists is analyzed in L. L. Richards, *Gentlemen of Property and Standing: Anti-Abolition Mobs in Jacksonian America** (1970).

W. S. Jenkins, *Pro-Slavery Thought in the Old South* (1935), is a comprehensive analysis of the proslavery argument. Harvey Wish, *George Fitzhugh: Propagandist of the Old South* (1943), is an excellent biography of a leading defender of slavery. A special aspect of proslavery thought is analyzed by Richard Hofstadter in his essay on Calhoun in *The American Political Tradition** (1948).

*Available in a paperback edition.

Expansion and sectional crisis

11

The acquisition of Louisiana and Florida in the early nineteenth century temporarily quieted the American urge for geographic expansion. Feeling secure from foreign intervention, and satisfied that there was ample space for a growing population, most Americans who moved west in the 1820s and 1830s were content to take up the vacant lands in their already immense country. They occupied the unsettled regions of Mississippi, Missouri, and Illinois and poured into new territories that soon would become states: Arkansas (1836), Michigan (1837), Florida (1845), Iowa (1846), and Wisconsin (1848). The vast area beyond Missouri and Arkansas, stretching out to the Rocky Mountains, was then of no interest to the westward-moving settlers. Because explorers reported that the land was too arid for farming, cartographers labeled it the "Great American Desert," and white Americans presented it as a "permanent" gift to the Indians. The donors felt there was room enough and plenty for white men to the east of this "Indian Country."

Or so it seemed until the 1840s, when the impulse to expand suddenly stirred anew. Actually, few Americans had ever assumed that the boundaries of the United States would stand forever unchanged, though it is surprising that the desire for more territory revived so soon. Some Americans pressed expansion more aggressively than others, but few challenged the idea that providence had destined their country to continued growth. Expansion in itself was not an issue that seriously divided the electorate. But it had a vexatious consequence: it raised the touchy question of whether slavery should be permitted to spread into the territories that were acquired. Much of the controversy recently generated by proslavery and antislavery propagandists began to center on this problem, and by the end of the 1840s it had precipitated a national crisis. In 1850, after months of bitter debate, a compromise was painfully constructed—a makeshift arrangement that settled nothing yet somehow served to hold the Union together for another decade.

Westward to the Pacific

Manifest Destiny. The reasons for the revived interest in territorial expansion were several. The first and most obvious was that the American people, with their sense of mission, were sorely tempted by the boundless

tracts of unsettled or sparsely settled land lying just beyond the borders of their country. All through the 1820s and 1830s American fur-trappers, in their search for beaver streams, had been blazing trails, searching out

Texas has been absorbed into the Union in the inevitable fulfilment of the general law which is rolling our population westward.... It was disintegrated from Mexico in the natural course of events, by a process perfectly legitimate on its own part, blameless on ours.... [Its] incorporation into the Union was not only inevitable, but the most natural, right and proper thing in the world....

California will, probably, next fall away from ... Mexico.... Imbecile and distracted, Mexico never can exert any real governmental authority over such a country.... The Anglo-Saxon foot is already on its borders. Already the advance guard of the irresistible army of Anglo-Saxon emigration has begun to pour down upon it, armed with the plough and the rifle, and marking its trail with schools and colleges, courts and representative halls, mills and meeting houses. A population will soon be in actual occupation of California, over which it will be idle for Mexico to dream of dominion.... All this without agency of our government, without responsibility of our people—in the natural flow of events, the spontaneous working of principles, and the adaptation of the tendencies and wants of the human race to the elemental circumstances in the midst of which they find themselves placed.

From the *Democratic Review,* July 1845.

---

passes through the mountains, and ranging over the fertile valleys of the Far West. The publicity they gave to the region beyond the Great American Desert at once strengthened the myth of the West as a land of romance and adventure and aroused interest in its agricultural possibilities. A second reason was a growing desire to develop trade with the Far East and the belief, as one expansionist politician expressed it, that along the valley of the Columbia River "lies the North American road to India." Many Eastern businessmen began to look covetously at the three best natural harbors on the Pacific coast, at San Diego, San Francisco, and Puget Sound. A third reason—and the one that probably explains the rebirth of expansionism at this precise time—was renewed fear that the security of the United States might be impaired by foreign intervention in areas along her borders, especially by British activity in Texas, California, and Oregon. Once again freedom and republican institutions in North America seemed threatened by the aggressive meddling of Europeans.

The expansionist drive was further strengthened by a mystical and romantic concept that, though hardly new, now received an attractive label. In 1845 a New York editor wrote exuberantly that it was America's "manifest destiny to overspread and to possess the whole of the continent which Providence has given us for the development of the great experiment of liberty and federated self-government entrusted to us." This doctrine of Manifest Destiny, quickly taken up by the press and politicians, was in part the kind of rationalization that expansionists everywhere have used to justify territorial aggrandizement. They invariably celebrate the superiority of their own culture and insist that their conquests are merely the fulfillment of a divine mission impelled by forces beyond human control. So did Americans when they spoke of their Manifest Destiny, and editors and stump-speakers often advocated expansion in terms so extravagant as to make the United States sound like a nation of swashbucklers. "Make way, I say, for the young American Buffalo," shouted a New Jersey politician, "he has not yet got land enough."

But running through the boasts and the threats was a thread of idealism that tied expansion to America's supposed mission to serve as a model of political democracy. Expansion in these terms was simply a means of "extending the area of freedom," to quote a popular phrase of the day. America's destiny was not merely to teach by precept but to bring more land and more people under the nation's jurisdiction—in short, to spread its democratic institutions over the entire North American continent. Thus, as one politician explained, America would become "a vast theatre on which to work out the grand experiment of Republican government."

Unfortunately, along with the thread of democratic idealism, there was also a thread of racism in the arguments used to justify the conquest of Indians and Latin Americans and their subordination to the authority of the North American republic. The "grand experiment," politicians and publicists often noted, was to be carried out "under the auspices of the Anglo-Saxon race." American expansionists, when they spoke of "extending the area of freedom," commonly assumed a racial explanation for the political instability and the weakness of democracy in the countries south of the United States. Thus the same racial attitudes that justified the enslavement of blacks in the South and discrimination against them in the North helped to make manifest America's "destiny" to expand.

Texas. The first area outside the United States to which settlers moved in substantial numbers was Texas. Many Westerners had been disappointed when the national government, in the Florida-purchase treaty of 1819, accepted the Sabine River as a southwestern boundary, thereby surrendering whatever vague claim the government might have had to Texas, as part of the Louisiana Purchase. Mexico, after winning her independence from Spain in 1822, twice rejected American offers to buy this sparsely settled province; but during the 1820s she welcomed Americans who would submit to her jurisdiction and abide by her laws. Among the promoters of settlement, the first and most successful was Stephen F. Austin, who obtained a huge land grant from Mexico and planted a flourishing colony on the banks of the Brazos River. Most of the immigrants were Southern yeoman farmers and small slaveholders who were attracted by the rich lands suitable for cotton culture and avilable for a few cents an acre. By 1830 eastern Texas had been occupied by nearly twenty thousand whites and a thousand Negro slaves from the United States.

The Mexican government soon had cause to regret its hospitality, for the American settlers had no intention of giving their allegiance to a nation whose culture was so different from their own. Among numerous sources of friction, one of the most irritating was the fact that Texas did not have its own state government but remained a part of the state of Coahuila, whose legislature the Mexicans controlled. Moreover, the Americans were suspicious of Mexican land titles, which were

Santa Anna and aide-de-camp

unlike those they had been used to in the United States. In 1830 the mounting tension had prompted the Mexican government to make a drastic switch in policy: it prohibited further immigration from the United States, stopped the importation of slaves, placed heavy duties on American goods, and dispatched troops to the frontier to see that these laws were enforced. The final blow came when General Santa Anna, who had seized political power in Mexico, not only repudiated his promise to give Texas separate statehood but nearly abolished the nation's federal system.

To the Texans the parallel between British oppression under George III and Mexican oppression under Santa Anna was clear, and revolution was the obvious and justifiable remedy. For a short time they claimed to be fighting in defense of the old Mexican constitution, but on March, 2, 1836, they declared their independence. The struggle was brief. Santa Anna moved into Texas with a large army and won a few minor skirmishes, the most notable being the extermination of a small garrison of Texans at the Alamo mission in San Antonio. But on April 21, 1836, at the Battle of San Jacinto, an army commanded by General Sam Houston decisively defeated the Mexicans and took Santa Anna prisoner. Santa Anna was forced to sign a treaty recognizing Texan independence; and though Mexico later denounced the treaty as having been signed under duress, she made no further attempt to reestablish her authority. The new Republic of Texas then framed a constitution, but in September 1836, when the voters ratified it, they also indicated overwhelming support for annexation to the United States. President Houston forthwith began negotiations with the government at Washington, first for recognition and then for annexation.

American volunteers and supplies had contributed to the Texans' victory over Santa Anna, and proannexation sentiment was strong, especially in the South and West. But opposition to the admission of another slave state began to grow among Whigs and abolitionists in the Northeast. Some practical Whig politicians feared that annexation would lead to war with Mexico and objected that it would increase the South's power to block legislation favorable to Northern economic interests. Abolitionists charged that the settlement of Texas, the revolution, and the movement for annexation were all parts of a slaveholders' plot to enlarge their empire and open new markets for the vendors of human flesh. Texas thus became an issue between the critics and the defenders of slavery.

President Jackson was an ardent annexationist, but he acted cautiously lest he impair Van Buren's chances of winning the presidential election of 1836. Jackson even delayed recognition of Texan independence until the eve of his retirement from office, and Van Buren refused to recommend annexation during his term as President. Rebuffed by the United States, Texas in 1838 turned to Europe for recognition and aid; her leaders began to talk boldly of creating a nation that would expand to the Pacific and rival the United States in size and strength. This was a pleasing prospect to the British, who saw in Texas a buffer to American expansion, a threat to the American cotton monopoly, and a promising new market. Moreover, British abolitionists hoped to persuade the Texans to abolish slavery and prove that cotton could be produced with free labor. As Texan leaders doubtless expected, British interest in their affairs alarmed the United States government, and the talk of abolition angered the slaveholders of the South.

These developments spurred President Tyler to reopen negotiations with Texas, and he worked vigorously to get a treaty of annexation before his term expired. By April 1844 Tyler's new Secretary of State, John C. Calhoun, had secured the desired treaty, and it was submitted to the Senate for approval. Unfortunately Calhoun also sent a note to the British government concerning its interest in Texas, in which he defended slavery as a positive good and thus strengthened the abolitionist claim that annexation would be the culmination of a proslavery plot. This, along with the continued anxiety about war with Mexico, doomed the treaty; only sixteen senators voted for it, while thirty-five voted against. Annexation was again delayed, and Texas became an issue in the approaching presidential election.

The Santa Fe trade. Meanwhile, a resourceful group of small entrepreneurs had aroused American interest in another of Mexico's remote provinces: New Mexico. Santa Fe and other smaller Spanish outposts on the upper Rio Grande, planted in the seventeenth century, were hundreds of miles from the nearest Mexican settlements, and

Spain's rigid trade restrictions had long deprived them of supplies from the United States. In the 1820s, however, the independent Mexican government had opened the Santa Fe trade to Americans. Every spring for the next two decades petty merchants assembled their wagons at Independence, Missouri, for the long journey along the Santa Fe Trail. Only a few merchants engaged in the trade—usually not many more than a hundred—but they always found a highly profitable market for their goods. In 1844, to the dismay of the traders, bad feeling generated by the Texas question caused Santa Anna again to exclude Americans from Santa Fe. By then, however, the trade had enlarged the American vision of Manifest Destiny to encompass New Mexico. Though few of the traders had actually settled in Santa Fe, they had opened a route into the Far West, demonstrated that heavily laden wagons could cross the plains, and developed a system of organized caravans for protection against the Indians. Another sparsely settled territory seemed ripe for American plucking.

Oregon. Far to the northwest, in the Oregon country, during the 1830s and early 1840s, merchants, fur-trappers, and missionaries were awakening Americans to the potentialities of still another area, one to which the United States had a solid, though not exclusive, claim. That claim was based on the voyages of Boston merchants to the Oregon coast to buy furs from the Indians in the late eighteenth century; on Captain Robert Gray's discovery of the mouth of the Columbia River in 1792; on the explorations of the Lewis and Clark expedition between 1804 and 1806; and on the founding of Astoria on the Columbia River in 1811 by John Jacob Astor's Pacific Fur Company. In addition, the United States had acquired the French claim to Oregon in the Louisiana Purchase treaty of 1803 and the Spanish claim in the Florida-purchase treaty of 1819. But the British claim was at least as good as the American. Sir Francis Drake, the British insisted, had discovered the Oregon coast in 1579; Captain James Cook and Captain George Vancouver had visited it again in the eighteenth century; and Alexander Mackenzie had made the first overland trip to Oregon in 1793 as an agent of British fur-trading interests. In short, both the Americans and the British could make strong claims to a huge territory bounded on the south by the

Spanish church at the Santa Fe mission

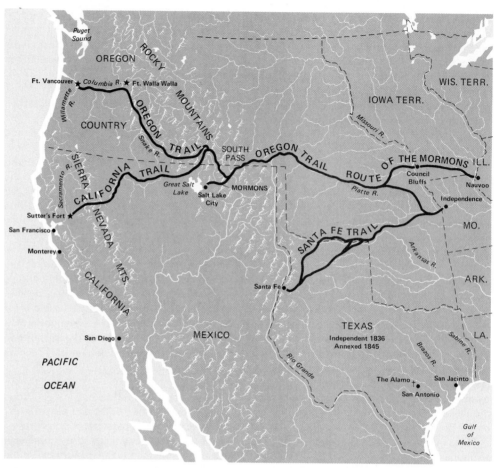

Trails to the Far West

A native Californian

forty-second parallel, on the north by the line of 54° 40' (the southern boundary of Russian Alaska), on the east by the Rocky Mountains, and on the west by the Pacific Ocean.

In the early nineteenth century, though neither the British nor the Americans claimed the whole of Oregon, they were unable to agree on a line of division. On several occasions the United States proposed an extension of the forty-ninth parallel to the Pacific, while the British suggested that the line follow the Columbia River from the forty-ninth parallel to its mouth. In 1818 the two countries postponed the settlement of this question and agreed to leave Oregon "free and open" to the citizens of both for a period of ten years. In 1827 they extended the agreement indefinitely, with the proviso that either country could terminate it on a year's notice. There the matter rested until the 1840s.

For many years Americans showed little interest in Oregon, and British fur-traders had the area largely to themselves. After 1821 the

Hudson's Bay Company monopolized the fur trade, establishing its headquarters at Fort Vancouver on the north bank of the Columbia and sending Dr. John McLoughlin there to serve as its chief factor. For more than twenty years McLoughlin gave Oregon the only government it had; he was scrupulously fair in dealing with the Indians, and under his efficient direction the company flourished. In the 1830s, however, agents of the Hudson's Bay Company operating in the Rockies began to encounter fierce and ruthless competitors: the intrepid Mountain Men, who hunted beaver skins for the Rocky Mountain Fur Company, directed by Thomas Fitzpatrick, James Bridger, and Milton Sublette. The Mountain Men, along with the agents of Astor's American Fur Company, were the advance guard of American overland penetration of Oregon.

Efforts by several Eastern promoters to stimulate American migration to Oregon in the 1820s and 1830s ended in failure. But the impulse for settlement soon came from another source. In 1833 an Eastern religious periodical published a report that the Indians of the Oregon country were eager for instruction in the Christian faith. In response to this report (which had little substance to it) the Methodists sent the Reverend Jason Lee, who established a mission in the fertile Willamette Valley; the Presbyterians and Congregationalists sent Dr. Marcus Whitman, who was active farther east, near Fort Walla Walla; and the Catholics sent Father Pierre Jean de Smet, a Jesuit priest from St. Louis, who worked among the Indians in the Rockies. Dr. McLoughlin gave the missionaries a cordial welcome and much assistance, but the Indians showed little interest in the Gospel. Indeed, the religious work of the missions proved to be less important than the publicity they gave to Oregon. Scores of missionary letters and reports filled with reference to Oregon's fecund soil and salubrious climate found their way into the Eastern press.

As word spread that the Willamette Valley was a new Garden of Eden, the people of the Mississippi Valley began to catch the "Oregon fever." In the late 1830s and early 1840s a trickle of emigrants began to follow the Oregon Trail in quest of free virgin land; in 1843 the first substantial caravans of covered wagons made the two-thousand-mile journey; and soon after the movement to Oregon was taking on the dimensions of a mass migration. The Oregon Trail began at Independence, Missouri, ran northwest to the Platte River, followed the Platte and its north fork into southern Wyoming, made an easy crossing of the Rockies at South Pass, followed the Snake River to a cutoff that led to the Columbia River, and then followed the Columbia to the Willamette Valley. By 1845 at least five thousand Americans had reached Oregon along this route; they had already formed a provisional government and were now demanding that the United States establish exclusive jurisdiction over them. Joint occupation with the British was no longer a satisfactory formula, and a final settlement could not be delayed much longer.

California. South of Oregon lay California, another of Mexico's remote provinces and the fourth area in the Far West where Manifest Destiny seemed to beckon Americans. In the eighteenth century the Spanish, in order to strengthen their control over California and to convert the Indians to Christianity, had encouraged Franciscan friars to build a chain of missions along the coast from San Diego to San Francisco. The missions were highly successful both in their religious work and as large-scale agricultural enterprises; but in 1834 the Mexican government began to deprive them of their lands, and the mission system soon fell apart. Under a succession of weak, inefficient, and often corrupt secular administrators, California sank into political chaos. But the sparse Mexican population, which, in 1846, numbered approximately seven thousand settlers, still managed to live in easygoing comfort, most of them on cattle ranches.

The first American contacts with California were made by merchant ships putting in along the coast for modest trading, and by whaleboats stopping for supplies. Now and then an American sailor deserted his ship and settled down; an occasional party of Mountain Men found its way to California on a trapping expedition; and by the 1830s a few merchants had come to trade with the Indians and Mexicans. Among the merchants was Thomas O. Larkin, who arrived at Monterey in 1832, built a flourishing trade, and worked tirelessly to promote American immigration to California. In the 1840s a few emigrants began to leave the Oregon Trail near the Snake River to follow the California Trail across the Nevada desert and the Sierra Nevada to the Sacramento River Valley. Invariably their goal was Sutter's Fort, the center of a private empire ruled by John A. Sutter, a German-born immigrant who had acquired Mexican citizenship and was a law unto himself. Sutter welcomed the Americans, furnished them with supplies, and helped them find land. By 1845 California was the home of about seven hundred Americans, almost none of whom expected to give up their American citizenship or to remain beyond the jurisdiction of their government very long.

The "California fever" had become almost as virulent as the "Oregon fever." Emigrants were attracted by the abundance of fertile, unoccupied land and by extravagant descriptions of California as "the richest, the most beautiful, and the healthiest country in the world." Eastern businessmen became increasingly interested in the commercial opportunities, and the American government coveted the harbors at San Diego and San Francisco—the latter was described as "ca-

A California miner

Salt Lake City, 1853

peace, they first moved from New York to Kirtland, Ohio, then to Missouri, then (in 1839) to Nauvoo, Illinois, where their numbers soon grew to fifteen thousand. In 1843, after five prosperous years, a new crisis developed when Smith received another revelation, this one justifying polygamy. The result was a schism in the Church, a rash of violence, and Smith's arrest and imprisonment. On June 27, 1844, an anti-Mormon mob took him from jail and murdered him. Once more the Mormons were obliged to abandon their homes and renew their wanderings.

Leadership now passed to Brigham Young, a brilliant, strong-willed man, who organized the most remarkable migration and settlement in the annals of the American West. In 1846 Young led almost the whole Mormon community across Iowa to the Council Bluffs on the Missouri River; the next year he sent the first band to the Salt Lake basin, which he had selected for the new Zion. No place could have appeared less promising; the first to arrive saw only ''a broad and barren plain . . . a seemingly interminable waste of sagebrush . . . the paradise of the lizard, the cricket and the rattlesnake.'' But within a decade the Mormons, under the stern leadership of Young and the theocratic control of the Church, had transformed the landscape. Substituting cooperative labor for the individual effort of the typical pioneer, they built a thriving city and an efficient irrigation system with which they made the desert bloom. In the critical early years their economy benefited from the sale of supplies to emigrants passing through on their way to California. When their lands were annexed to the United States soon after they arrived, the Mormons tried first to organize their own state of ''Deseret.'' Failing, they acquiesced when Congress created the Territory of Utah. Even then, however, the Mormon Church continued to be the dominant political as well as religious force in the land of the Saints.

pacious enough to receive the navies of all the world.'' Reports of British designs on California, though inaccurate, gave the matter a special urgency. In 1842 Commodore Thomas ap Catesby Jones, commander of the United States Pacific squadron, somehow got the impression that his country had gone to war with Mexico and that British warships were moving toward California. Accordingly, he sailed into Monterey Bay, seized the city, ran up the American flag, and proclaimed the annexation of California to the United States. The embarrassed State Department disavowed Jones' act and made apologies to the Mexican government, but the incident was a clear sign of what the expansionists had in mind.

The Mormon migration. One group of emigrants to the Far West had no interest in Manifest Destiny—indeed, they sought to escape the jurisdiction of the United States. These were the Mormons (see p. 244), who in 1847 after many years of persecution, crossed into Mexican territory and established a settlement in the isolated Great Salt Lake basin. From the beginning the Mormon Saints had annoyed the ''gentiles'' about them with their close-knit communitarian social pattern, their thriving economic life, and their contempt for other religious sects. In their search for a Zion where they could escape this hostility and live in

Brigham Young: brilliant and strong-willed

Polk and the triumph of Manifest Destiny

The election of Polk. The presidential election of 1844 exposed a variety of tensions that had been growing in American society in recent years. First, the long depression following the Panic of 1837 had kept alive issues of national policy concerning money, banking, and public lands, issues that sometimes di-

vided labor and capital, sometimes farm and city. Second, the entrance of the abolitionist crusade into politics had given sectional differences a moral dimension that made compromise increasingly difficult to achieve. Third, the doctrine of Manifest Destiny was reaching the height of its influence, and the drive for expansion to the Pacific was becoming an irresistible force. The complexity of these issues, all of which were more or less interrelated, sorely tried the national party system and led ultimately to a fragmentation of the Whig and Democratic organizations.

In 1844 Henry Clay and Martin Van Buren expected to receive the presidential nominations of their respective parties. They found the unsettled Texas question a source of embarrassment, because it had become involved in the slavery controversy. Hence they tried to eliminate it as a campaign issue by making separate but very similar statements (apparently after private consultation) opposing the annexation of Texas at that time without the consent of Mexico. The Whig convention unanimously nominated Clay and adopted a platform that avoided taking a stand either on Texas or on most other national issues. But the Democratic convention, where expansionist sentiment was stronger, denied Van Buren the nomination he coveted. Instead, on the ninth ballot, after a bitter conflict on the convention floor, the delegates chose James K. Polk of Tennessee, whose commitment to territorial expansion (including the immediate annexation of Texas) was clear and unqualified. To avoid the accusation of sectional favoritism, the Democratic platform cleverly united a demand for the admission of Texas with the dubious assertion that "our title to the whole of the Territory of Oregon is clear and unquestionable; that no portion of the same ought to be ceded to England or any other power." It followed, therefore, "that the re-occupation of Oregon and the re-annexation of Texas at the earliest practicable period are great American measures, which this convention recommends to the cordial support of the Democracy of the Union."

By combining the expansionist desires of South and West, the Democrats had found a winning formula. Throughout the campaign Manifest Destiny transcended all other issues, so much so that Clay began to shift his position on Texas. He would favor annexation after all if it could be accomplished without war and upon "just and fair terms." But this commitment still sounded halfhearted when compared with the spread-eagle oratory and aggressive slogans of the Democrats. Clay converted few of the expansionists but lost some antislavery votes to the Liberty party (see p. 253), especially in New York. In the election Polk won by a small plurality of 38,000 in the popular vote and by a margin of 170 to 105 in the Electoral College.

Though Polk is remembered as the first "dark-horse" presidential candidate, the term is valid only in the sense that he had not been considered for the nomination before the Democratic convention. He was far from a political unknown in 1844. Born in North Carolina, he had moved to Tennessee as a young man and soon became a successful lawyer and planter. He entered politics as a Jacksonian Democrat and served seven terms in the House of Representatives (two as Speaker) and one term as governor of Tennessee. As President, Polk displayed neither extraordinary talent nor a striking personality, but by hard work and stubborn determination he had remarkable success in redeeming the pledges his party had made during the campaign. His inaugural address was unimaginative—a mere reiteration of the old-fashioned republican principles with which Jefferson and Jackson had been identified. Polk, showing little understanding of the new problems of his age, promised a passive domestic role for government "by abstaining from the exercise of doubtful or unauthorized implied powers."

Polk's Administration reflected both the continuing influence of Jacksonian principles on the Democratic party and the growing power of the South within the party. As a planter and slaveholder Polk shared the Southern hostility toward abolitionists; if they achieved their goal, he warned, "the dissolution of the Union . . . must speedily follow." He favored a low revenue tariff, and in 1846 his Secretary of the Treasury, Robert J. Walker of Mississippi, helped to frame such a measure, which Congress passed. The Walker Tariff delighted the South, but it angered Northern protectionists and increased their hostility to further strengthening the antiprotectionists by the admission of any more slave states. Polk shared Jackson's views on national banking and persuaded Congress to reestablish the Independent Treasury system, which it had abolished during the Tyler Administration. On two occasions, to the intense annoyance of Westerners in the Great Lakes region, he vetoed internal-improvements bills. In short, Polk blocked every effort to revive the American System of Henry Clay and John Quincy Adams, and in his last message to Congress he devoted much space to attacking that system and celebrating its demise.

James Knox Polk: agent of Manifest Destiny

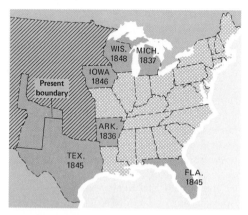

New states, 1836–48

The acquisition of Texas and Oregon.

Important as these domestic policies were, the Polk Administration's primary concern was with geographic expansion. The Texas question was the first to be disposed of, for Congress had virtually settled the matter shortly before Polk's inauguration. After the presidential election Tyler assured Congress that the verdict of the voters had been in favor of annexation, and he proposed now that the two houses accomplish it by a joint resolution. Annexation would thus require only a simple majority, rather than the two-thirds majority needed in the Senate to approve a treaty. The introduction of a resolution for this purpose provoked a heated debate between proslavery and antislavery congressmen, but it finally passed the House by a vote of 120 to 98 and the Senate by a vote of 27 to 25. President Tyler signed the joint resolution on March 1,

The Oregon controversy, 1818–46

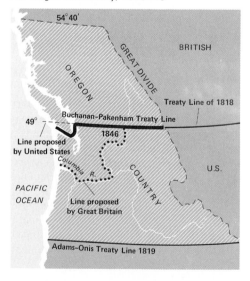

1845. Polk approved of this action, and within a few months Texas had accepted the terms of annexation. In December 1845 Texas was admitted to statehood.

The problem of Oregon was not so easily resolved, for the Americans and British still had not agreed on a line of division. Indeed, the restless settlers in Oregon and the expansionists in the East were growing increasingly belligerent in their demand that the government make no division at all but, as the Democratic platform of 1844 had insisted, take the whole territory to its northern limits. "Where shall we find room for all our people, unless we have Oregon?" asked Representative Andrew Kennedy of Indiana. "What shall we do with all those little white-headed boys and girls—God bless them!—that cover the Mississippi valley, as the flowers cover the western prairies?" America claimed Oregon for a noble purpose, explained John Quincy Adams: "To make the wilderness blossom as the rose, to establish laws, to increase, multiply, and subdue the earth, which we are commanded to do by the first behest of God Almighty." In January 1845 the British government, realizing that continued joint occupation was impossible, proposed arbitration, but the State Department rejected the offer.

In referring to the Oregon question in his inaugural address, Polk seemed to stand firmly on his party's platform; it would be his duty, he said, "to assert and maintain by all constitutional means the right of the United States to that portion of our territory which lies beyond the Rocky Mountains. Our title to the country of the Oregon is 'clear and unquestionable,' and . . . those rights we are fully prepared to maintain." Meanwhile, there was a good deal of irresponsible saber-rattling on both sides of the Atlantic, and the situation threatened to get out of hand. "We want thirty thousand rifles in the valley of the Oregon," cried Senator Benton of Missouri. "They will make all quiet there . . . and protect the American interests."

But Polk did not want war with England at a time when there was danger of war with Mexico; accordingly, he soon decided to abandon the Democratic platform and try for a compromise. In July 1845 he notified the British minister in Washington, Richard Pakenham, that the United States was willing to renew its offer to divide Oregon along the forty-ninth parallel. Pakenham, without even consulting his government, rejected the offer and held firm to the earlier British demand for a division at the Columbia River. The indignant President then withdrew his offer, concluded that "the only way to treat John Bull was to look him straight in the eye," and decided to pursue "a bold and firm course." In his message to Congress that December, Polk recommended that the British government be given the year's notice required to end joint occupation. He also invoked the almost forgotten Monroe Doctrine to fortify his case: "it should be distinctly announced to the world as our settled policy that no future European colony or dominion shall with our consent be planted or established on any part of the North American continent." Meanwhile, truculent American expansionists, apparently ready for another war with the British, repeated the slogans "All of Oregon or none," and "Fifty-four forty or fight." Once Congress had approved the termination of joint occupation of Oregon, the only remaining hope for a peaceful settlement seemed to be an offer of concessions on the part of the British.

Fortunately the British Foreign Office disapproved of Pakenham's blunt rejection of Polk's offer to compromise, for it did not believe that the disputed segment of Oregon between the Columbia River and the forty-ninth parallel was worth a war. Indeed, the flood of American settlers and the depletion of the fur resources had already prompted the Hudson's Bay Company to transfer its headquarters from Fort Vancouver on the Columbia northward to Fort Victoria on Vancouver Island. In June 1846 Secretary of State James Buchanan received from Pakenham the draft of a proposal to divide Oregon at the forty-ninth parallel but to retain for the British all of Vancouver Island and the right to navigate the Columbia River. Polk was at first inclined to reject the proposal, but he decided to submit it to the Senate and let that body assume responsibility for the decision.

After an angry debate the Senate advised acceptance; the treaty was signed on June 15, and the Senate approved it by a vote of 41 to 14. Most of the opposition came from Western Democrats who bitterly criticized Polk for backing down on the demand for the whole of Oregon. But most of the country was satisfied with the settlement, for the British, rather than the Americans, had given up their original claim. Eastern business interests had no taste for a war to secure the area north of the forty-ninth parallel; nor did the Southerners, whose interest in Oregon waned once Texas had been safely annexed. Besides, the United States was already at war with Mexico and had a richer prize in view.

War with Mexico

The background. Among the causes of the war with Mexico were the inability of United States citizens to obtain compensation for claims against the Mexican government, the anger of Mexican patriots over American annexation of Texas, a dispute over the southern and western boundaries of Texas, and the instability of the Mexican government, which made negotiation with it difficult and irritating. But even more important was the determination of Polk (and of the expansionists generally) to obtain the provinces of New Mexico and California—with money if possible, by force if necessary. Though Mexico was far from blameless for the war that came—indeed, welcomed it—the central cause was nevertheless the readiness of the Polk Administration to resort to arms to achieve its expansionist goals.

As soon as the United States annexed Texas, Mexico broke off diplomatic relations, thus closing the normal channels of negotiation. Yet there was need for negotiation, because Texas was not satisfied with its traditional southern boundary, which in Spanish days had been the Nueces River, but claimed instead the Rio Grande. Polk, convinced that the Texas claim was justified, ordered General Zachary Taylor to take fifteen hundred troops into the disputed area. By the summer of 1845, Taylor's small army was encamped at Corpus Christi on the Nueces River; in March of the following year it obeyed Polk's command and advanced to the Rio Grande. To Mexican patriots this act, following soon after what they considered the illegal seizure of Texas, was a further aggressive invasion of their territory, and the war spirit grew among them.

There was now little hope that Polk could persuade Mexico to give up California and New Mexico peacefully, but he decided to try

Mr. Polk's war

The responsibility of the President and his administration in permitting the country to become involved in a war which could and should have been avoided, is fearfully great. Among a virtuous and wise people, this condemnation alone should be enough to overwhelm those who have been guilty of so great a crime....

... The Constitution constitutes Congress the war-making power of this government; but in this case ... the President made the war. The Constitution contemplates that before deliberate hostilities shall be undertaken in any case, a declaration of war shall be made; but in this case, a hostile aggressive movement was made under the personal orders of the President....

*... The President thought to glorify his reign by pushing the limits of the Progressive Republic in one direction or another, far beyond any serious dream of any Anglo-American land-robber of preceding times. He first tried his hand with England, by protesting that he would have the whole of Oregon, every minute of it, up to "fifty-four forty"....
Disappointed in not being able to carry the nominal line of our national jurisdiction quite as far ... as his unmeaning ambition had prompted him to desire, he turned his regards to the opposite quarter of North America, and there ... he saw New Mexico and the Californias.... It is to the influence of this motive on his mind, that we attribute the daring resolution which he took originally to precipitate this war. He counted on a weak enemy, an easy conquest, and a speedy accomplishment of his purpose.*

From *The American Review*, October 1847.

---

nonetheless. In the fall of 1845 he explored the possibility of resuming diplomatic relations. When he learned that Mexico would receive an American commissioner to settle the Texas dispute, he appointed John Slidell of Louisiana as envoy extraordinary and minister plenipotentiary with authority to discuss not only Texas but California and New Mexico as well. Slidell was instructed to offer (1) the assumption by the United States of all claims of its citizens against Mexico if Mexico would accept the Rio Grande boundary; (2) $5 million for the rest of New Mexico west of the Rio Grande; and (3) as much as $25 million for California. Since the Mexican government needed money and since its hold on these distant territories was weak, to Polk it seemed the course of wisdom for Mexico to sell.

When Slidell reached Mexico City on December 6, 1845, news about his purpose had already leaked out, and Mexican nationalists were furious at this brazen attempt to dismember their country. The existing government was collapsing, in part because of its alleged lack of firmness in dealing with the United States, and a new revolutionary government came to power pledged to uphold the national dignity. Neither the old nor the new

government would receive Slidell. Mexico, he was reminded, had agreed only to receive a commissioner to negotiate on Texas, and until that question was settled there could be no regular diplomatic relations. The Slidell mission had failed. "Be assured," the angry diplomat wrote Polk, "that nothing is to be done with these people until they shall have been chastised."

Polk apparently agreed. On May 9, 1846, he told his Cabinet that the unpaid claims and the snubbing of Slidell would justify a declaration of war, and he began at once to prepare a war message to Congress. That evening news arrived that on April 25 Mexican troops had crossed the Rio Grande and engaged in a skirmish in which sixteen American soldiers were killed or wounded. Polk hastily revised his war message and sent it to Congress on May 11. After reviewing recent relations between Mexico and the United States, his message concluded: "The cup of forbearance had been exhausted even before the recent information from the frontier. . . . But now, after reiterated menaces, Mexico has passed the boundary of the United States, has invaded our territory and shed American blood on the American soil." Therefore, "war exists, and, notwithstanding all our efforts to avoid it, exists by the act of Mexico herself." Two days later Congress passed a resolution declaring that "by the act of the Republic of Mexico, a state of war exists between that government and the United States," the Senate by a vote of 40 to 2, the House by a vote of 174 to 14. It then appropriated $10 million for war purposes and authorized the recruitment of an army of fifty thousand volunteers.

The country went to war somewhat less united than these votes in Congress indicated. Though most Whig politicians felt they had no choice but to support the military measures, they showed less enthusiasm for the conflict than the Democrats. War sentiment was strong in the Southwest, but it diminished to the east and north. Abolitionists and antislavery Whigs (who called themselves Conscience Whigs) denied that Polk had tried to avoid war and insisted that American blood had been shed not on American soil but on disputed soil that American troops should never have occupied. Senator Tom Corwin of Ohio accused Polk of involving the country in a war of aggression, and added bitterly: "If I were a Mexican, I would tell you, 'Have you not room in your own country to bury your dead men? If you come into mine, we will greet you with bloody hands and welcome you to hospitable graves.'" Another Whig, though seeing no alternative to supporting the war, was distressed to think "that when we pray 'God defend the right' our prayers are not for our own country." Abolitionists viewed the war as another attempt of the Slave Power to enhance its strength. In 1847 the Massachusetts legislature resolved that the war was "unconstitutionally commenced by the order of the President" and that it was being waged for the "dismemberment of Mexico" with "the triple object of extending slavery, of strengthening the slave power, and of obtaining the control of the free states." A new sectional crisis thus began to take shape almost as soon as the war commenced.

The military campaigns. In all probability the Mexicans entered the war with greater unity and enthusiasm than the Americans. They had concluded that war was the only way to check Yankee aggression, and they were confident that their regular army, vastly superior in numbers to the American, could easily defeat the invaders. But the Mexicans were sadly deluded, for they did not take into account their outdated weapons, their limited supplies and inferior resources, and their oversupply of incompetent generals. The United States War Department was inefficient enough, but the Mexican was even more so. Though the United States had a regular army of fewer than eight thousand officers and men, it was able quickly to raise a force of sixty thousand volunteers. With this manpower, with superior equipment, and with at least one gifted military commander, General Winfield Scott, the Americans won the war with relative ease.

Polk, who planned the military operations himself, hoped that a few quick victories would persuade Mexico to make the desired territorial cessions. According to Senator Benton, Polk "wanted a small war, just large enough to require a treaty of peace." In the first of three major campaigns, General Taylor crossed the Rio Grande, captured Matamoros, and pushed on to Monterrey. There, in a severe battle (September 21–23, 1846), Taylor defeated the Mexican garrison but permitted it to withdraw rather than surrender. Because of these early victories, Old Rough and Ready, as Taylor's men affectionately called him, became a national hero, but he had betrayed limitations as a tactician and a tendency to be overcautious—serious flaws in a commanding officer. As a result, Polk lost confidence in him, took away half his army for a new offensive at Vera Cruz, and would have been content to let him remain idle for the rest of the war. But Santa Anna, who had regained power in Mexico, moved north to attack Taylor's weakened forces. At the Battle of Buena Vista (February 22–23, 1847) Taylor added to his national popularity by defeating Santa Anna and forcing him to return to Mexico City. This action ended the war in northern Mexico, but the decisive victories were still to be won elsewhere.

The second offensive was designed to bring the coveted Mexican provinces under American occupation before a peace treaty was negotiated. In the summer of 1846 a force of seventeen hundred men, commanded by Colonel Stephen W. Kearny, marched from Fort Leavenworth to Santa Fe and, on August 18, captured it without firing a shot. After proclaiming the annexation of New Mexico to the United States, Kearny sent part of his troops to join Taylor, left a small garrison at Santa Fe, and took the rest to California. There some of the American settlers, in the "Bear

The Mexican War, 1846–48

THE MEXICAN EAGLE BEFORE THE WAR!

THE MEXICAN EAGLE AFTER THE WAR!

Flag Revolt,'' had already declared the independence of California; and Captain John C. Frémont, who had arrived earlier at the head of an exploring expedition, was in command of the rebels. Meanwhile, naval forces had landed at Monterey and raised the American flag. Hence, when Kearny arrived late in 1846 the only remaining task was to subdue scattered resistance to American authority in southern California. By January 1847 the United States had virtually undisputed possession of both New Mexico and California.

It took a third American campaign to force Mexico to accept these realities. In March 1847 an army commanded by General Scott landed near Vera Cruz, forced that city to surrender after an eighteen-day siege, and then began a slow and difficult advance toward Mexico City. Scott won a decisive victory over Santa Anna at Cerro Gordo (April 17–18, 1847), and by August he was on the high plateau before the Mexican capital. On Sep-

tember 14 American troops forced their way into the city, and soon after Mexico surrendered.

The Treaty of Guadalupe Hidalgo. A new Mexican government was now ready to sign a treaty of peace. In anticipation of this outcome, Polk had sent Nicholas P. Trist, chief clerk in the State Department, along with Scott's army ''to take advantage of circumstances, as they might arise to negotiate a peace.'' Trist was instructed to offer essentially the same terms that Slidell had offered. In November 1847, after a long and irritating delay, negotiations were about to begin when Trist received orders from the impatient President to return to Washington. But Trist, convinced that he was on the verge of getting all he had been sent for, decided to ignore his orders and enter into negotiations. On February 2, 1848, he signed the Treaty of Guadalupe Hidalgo, by which the United States obtained California, New Mexico, and the Rio Grande boundary for $15 million and the assumption of the claims of United States citizens against Mexico. Trist then hurried back to Washington, but he got no thanks from the President. Instead, Polk denounced him as an "impudent and unqualified scoundrel" for disobeying orders and dismissed him from his job.

But Polk could find no fault with the treaty and, notwithstanding "the exceptional conduct of Mr. Trist," decided to submit it to the Senate. By then some of the more rabid expansionists were asking why the United States should settle for only California and New Mexico. Why not take the whole of Mexico? As one partisan of Manifest Destiny asked, why "resign this beautiful country to the custody of the ignorant cowards and profligate ruffians who have ruled it for the last twenty-five years?" But after a volley of bombastic oratory, the Senate, on March 10, 1848, approved the treaty by a vote of 38 to 14. Thus, as one disgruntled Whig observed, the Mexican War ended with a peace "negotiated by an unauthorized agent, with an unacknowledged government, submitted by an accidental President to a dissatisfied Senate." Through it the United States gained possession of more than a half-million square miles of territory.

Crisis and compromise

The issue of slavery expansion. On August 8, 1846, shortly after the outbreak of the Mexican War, the House of Representatives had under consideration a request from the President for passage of a bill appropriating $2 million to facilitate the purchase of territory from Mexico when a peace treaty was negotiated. The bill immediately provoked several Northern congressmen to announce their opposition to the spread of slavery into whatever territory might be acquired. One of them, David Wilmot, a Pennsylvania Democrat with close ties to the Van Buren wing of the party, finally rose and moved an amendment making it "an express and fundamental condition to the acquisition of any territory" that "neither slavery nor involuntary servitude shall ever exist in any part of said territory." The Wilmot Proviso, as the amendment was called, twice passed the House but each time failed in the Senate, and on several other occasions it was reintroduced and bitterly debated. During the next fifteen years the issue of slavery expansion, which had been a latent source of trouble ever since the Missouri controversy, was to drive a wedge ever deeper between North and South.

Support for the proviso came from resentful Northern Whigs who felt that Polk had been less than candid with Congress in explaining the background of the Mexican War. It also came from Northern Democrats who were discontented with the Walker Tariff, with Polk's veto of internal-improvements bills, with the Oregon compromise, with the rejection of Van Buren in 1844, or, more generally, with what they regarded as the unduly pro-Southern stance of the Administration. What personal motives Wilmot may have had for introducing his proviso is of no great historical importance, because other Northern congressmen were prepared to offer similar proposals had Wilmot not acted first.

More important is the question whether the long and angry controversy over slavery expansion involved a genuine problem or was simply a flight from reality. Polk was the first of many contemporaries to denounce the Wilmot Proviso as "mischievous and foolish" and to accuse "Southern agitators and Northern fanatics" of raising a false issue merely for political advancement. He and other conservatives held that, since none of the territory acquired from Mexico was geographically suitable for plantation agriculture with slave labor, any legislation to exclude slavery from it would be unnecessarily provocative, because it would needlessly reenact a "law of nature." From this, presumably, it followed that irresponsible demagogues were creating a great national crisis and endangering the Union over a mere abstraction.

By the end of the 1840s the Southern plantation system may well have reached its natural geographic limits within the existing boundaries of the United States, but it does not necessarily follow that the debate over slavery expansion was therefore meaningless. Though the politicians who had to deal with the problem may not have handled it well, many of them were convinced that the problem had substance to it. In the first place, not all Northerners and Southerners were sure that geography alone would keep slavery out of California and New Mexico. Some believed that even if the familiar plantation system could not be developed in these areas, slavery might still be introduced there in other forms of agriculture, as well as in industry and mining. Slaves, after all, were employed in many occupations in the South. In the second place, few Americans thought that their country's growth would stop with the territory acquired in the Treaty of Guadalupe Hidalgo. There was a widespread conviction that at least Cuba would one day become part of the United States, and perhaps other Caribbean islands and Central America as well. In these tropical lands slavery would certainly not be merely an academic question. Indeed, much of the controversy over slavery expansion was waged with an eye on future annexations and with the understanding that laws excluding slavery from existing territories would provide significant precedents.

Finally, and perhaps most important, the issue had meaning in terms of the moral positions of proslavery and antislavery interests in the two sections. The debate over slavery expansion was in part an extension of the debate over slavery where it already existed. When Northerners with antislavery sentiments argued that it would be morally wrong to legalize slavery in New Mexico, they were by implication arguing that it was also morally wrong to tolerate it in Virginia. Constitutional limitations on federal power prevented them from doing anything about slavery in the Southern states; hence their efforts to prohibit it in the territories, where they believed Congress had authority to act, had symbolic as well as practical significance. Southerners understood this perfectly well, which explains in part why they so vigorously opposed all exclusion proposals, such as the Wilmot Proviso, even when applied to territories where they might have doubted that slavery would ever be introduced. For example, Southern congressmen delayed for two years (until 1848) the passage of a bill creating Oregon Territory, because the bill contained a clause excluding slavery. Representative James R. Seddon of Virginia protested that territorial exclusion was a ''direct attack on the institutions'' of the Southern states, an ''insult and injury, outrage and wrong, on them and theirs.''

Support for the Wilmot Proviso, however, did not arise exclusively from hostility toward slavery or concern for the Negro. Many opponents of slavery expansion, because of sectional tensions over other questions of public policy, seemed to be more anti-Southern than antislavery. Many more betrayed essentially racist motives—that is, a determination to keep Negroes, whether slave or free, out of the territories. Wilmot himself assured his colleagues that he felt no ''squeamish sensitiveness upon the subject of slavery, nor morbid sympathy for the slave. I plead the cause of the rights of white freemen. I would preserve for free white labor a fair country, a rich inheritance, where the sons of toil, of my own race and own color, can live without the disgrace which association with negro slavery brings upon free labor.'' An Ohio congressman confessed that he was selfish enough ''greatly to prefer the welfare of my own race to that of any other,'' and vindictive enough ''to wish . . . to keep [in] the South the burden which they themselves created.'' In short, Northern support for the Wilmot Proviso arose from three sources: from ideological antislavery feelings, from sectional anti-Southern feelings, and from racist anti-Negro feelings.

Much of the debate over the Wilmot Proviso centered on the question of how much power the Constitution had given Congress to govern the territories. Supporters of Wilmot cited the clause authorizing Congress to ''make all needful rules and regulations respecting the Territory or other Property belonging to the United States.'' Until the 1840s, as Henry Clay observed, this clause had been accepted as giving Congress power over slavery in the territories ''by the uniform interpretation and action of every department of our government, legislative, executive, and judicial.'' Moreover, the power had repeatedly been used. The First Congress had reenacted the Ordinance of 1787, which prohibited slavery in the Northwest Territory; a later Congress had applied the same restriction to the Illinois and Michigan territories when they were created; and overwhelming majorities in the House and Senate had voted in 1820 to prohibit slavery in that portion of the Louisiana Purchase north of the line 36° 30'. After the Mexican War, when President Polk and many other Southern moderates suggested extending the Missouri compromise line to the Pacific, they were again, in effect, agreeing that Congress did have the authority to regulate slavery in the territories.

Calhoun, however, led proslavery Southerners toward an extreme state-rights position similar to the stand that some Virginians had taken during the Missouri debates. In 1847 he introduced a series of resolutions in the Senate asserting that the territories were the common property of all the states; that Congress had no power to deprive the citizens of any state of their right to migrate to the territories with their property, including slaves; and that only when a territory was ready for statehood could it constitutionally prohibit slavery. Calhoun's position, therefore, was that *all* the territories must be open to slavery—which made even the Missouri Compromise unconstitutional. Some of his supporters went a step further and insisted that it was the duty of Congress to *protect* slavery in the territories if necessary. This being the case, the Wilmot Proviso was, in the words of one Southern congressman, "treason to the Constitution," and its adoption would justify the secession of the South.

Between these uncompromising antislavery and proslavery doctrines, a third doctrine, called "popular sovereignty," began to win the support of moderates in all sections but especially in the Old Northwest. With two Democratic senators, Lewis Cass of Michigan and Stephen A. Douglas of Illinois, its chief advocates, popular sovereignty was designed in part to remove the explosive territorial question from the halls of Congress. Why not respect the American tradition of local self-government, these moderates asked, and permit the people who actually settled in a territory to decide the question of slavery for themselves? Congress could then organize new territories without reference to slavery. Southerners would escape the humiliation of congressional prohibition, while Northwestern farmers might hope that their numerical superiority over Southern slaveholders would enable them to win the territories for freedom.

The election of 1848. Meanwhile, as the debate over the territorial question dragged on, California and New Mexico were left without government, and the issue was injected into the presidential campaign of 1848. President Polk had failed to unite the Democrats behind his Administration, and as the election approached the party was torn by factionalism. Calhoun led a group of Southern-rights men unwilling to accept anything less than his extreme position on slavery expansion. Martin Van Buren commanded a faction of disaffected

New York Democrats, called the "Barnburners" (presumably because they would burn the barn to get rid of the rats), who had thirsted for revenge ever since Polk defeated Van Buren for the presidential nomination in 1844. Throughout the North, especially in the Northeast, groups of free-soil Democrats endorsed the Wilmot Proviso. When the Democratic convention met in Baltimore, the party leaders, having decided that a Northern candidate was essential, threw the nomination to Lewis Cass of Michigan, a colorless old party wheel horse whose opposition to the Wilmot Proviso and support of popular sovereignty would appease the Southern moderates. The platform praised Polk for his territorial acquisitions and domestic policies but was silent on the slavery question. As a result, the Barnburners and pro-Wilmot delegates left the convention prepared for revolt.

The Whigs, meeting in Philadelphia, again staked their chances on a military hero, General Zachary Taylor. Born in Virginia and now a Louisiana slaveholder, Taylor was expected to reassure Southern Whigs who had grown uneasy about the antislavery sentiments of Northern Whigs. Old Rough and Ready had spent his whole career in the regular army; he had neither political principles nor political experience—and, indeed, had discovered only recently that he was a Whig ("but not an ultra Whig"). After nominating Taylor on the fourth ballot, the convention tried to avoid controversy by writing no platform at all. But this surrender to expediency was more than the Northern Conscience Whigs could bear. Many of them decided that rather than support a slaveholder whose views were unknown and who was uncommitted to a platform they would bolt their party.

Antislavery leaders saw in the disgruntled Van Buren Barnburners, free-soil Democrats, Conscience Whigs, and political abolitionists the elements of a powerful third party, one that would take a firm stand on the territorial question and make a broader appeal than the Liberty party had made in the two preceding elections. In August 1848 delegates representing all these groups met in Buffalo, organized the Free-Soil party, and nominated Van Buren for President and Charles Francis Adams (a Conscience Whig, the son of John Quincy Adams) for Vice President. The platform bluntly demanded that slavery be excluded from the territories and opposed any additional concessions to the Slave Power. It

Taylor:
"Old Rough and Ready"

Sacramento, 1849

A few struck it rich

supported federal appropriations for internal improvements and the passage of a homestead act giving actual settlers free farms from the public domain. In a concluding statement the platform summarized the principles of the new party as "Free Soil, Free Speech, Free Labor, and Free Men." Among the Free-Soilers were numerous self-seeking politicians and an abundance of Negrophobes, but the organization also reflected much of the idealism of the antislavery crusade.

In spite of the intensity of feeling about the territorial question, the campaign itself was unexciting, the voters apathetic. Taylor defeated Cass by a small plurality in the popular vote (1,360,967 to 1,222,342) and by a majority of 36 in the Electoral College (163 to 127). The Free-Soil party failed to carry a single state, but its popular vote of 291,263 was impressive for a party organized less than three months before the election. A dozen Free-Soilers were elected to Congress, among them Ohio's new senator, Salmon P. Chase.

Taylor and the crisis. President Taylor was a man of honesty, integrity, and determination; he was capable of quick action, and he had a store of plain common sense. But these virtues were not sufficient to offset his limitations as chief executive in a time of cri-

sis: his lack of training in politics and civil administration, his ignorance of public affairs—above all, his tendency to oversimplify complex problems. In a brief and vacuous inaugural address, he promised to devote his Administration "to the welfare of the whole country, and not to the support of any particular section or merely local interest." This pledge he tried conscientiously to fulfill; though he was a Southerner, he was a nationalist with no strong sectional loyalties.

When Taylor came into office, California and New Mexico, still lacking civil government, were being ruled by army officers directly responsible to the President. The settlers found this situation annoying under the best of circumstances, but it became intolerable soon after the discovery of gold in California. James Marshall had made the discovery in January 1848, along the American River about forty miles from Sutter's Fort; within six months San Francisco and other coastal towns were all but deserted as men rushed headlong into the "diggings" in the Sierra. By the end of 1848 the news had spread to the East, and during the next year some eighty thousand "forty-niners" came to California from the Mississippi Valley, from the Atlantic coast, and from Europe, Asia, and Australia. Most of them followed the overland trails across the continent, others took the easier but more expensive route by ship around Cape Horn, and still others risked death by taking a shortcut through the jungles of Panama. The miners dreamed of fortunes in gold as they worked the beds of streams with picks, shovels, and wash-pans; a few struck it rich, but most of them gained only modest returns from their backbreaking labor and their months of discomfort in primitive mining camps. Much of the gold ultimately found its way into the pockets of merchants in San Francisco and Sacramento, who in effect mined the miners by selling them supplies at exorbitant prices.

By the end of 1849 California's population had grown to one hundred thousand, and in the absence of civil government crime and violence were endemic in the cities and mining camps. With military authorities unable to restore law and order, with Congress seemingly paralyzed by the slavery issue, President Taylor decided to take matters into his own hands. As he saw it, there was a simple solution to the problem that had bedeviled Congress ever since the introduction of the Wil-

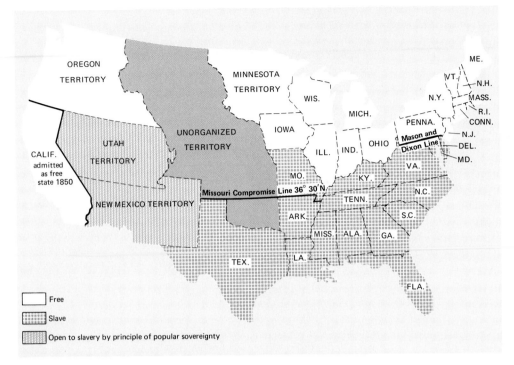

Free

Slave

Open to slavery by principle of popular sovereignty

The Compromise of 1850

mot Proviso. He proposed to avoid the territorial issue by encouraging the people of California and New Mexico to frame constitutions and apply for immediate admission to the Union as states. Californians wasted no time in taking Taylor's advice; by October 1849 a convention had drafted a constitution prohibiting slavery, and in November the voters ratified it and elected state officers to whom the military gladly yielded its political authority. The people of New Mexico took more time, but by May 1850 they too had adopted a free-state constitution. Thus, when Congress met in December 1849, Taylor congratulated the country on the fact that the problem had been solved. All that remained was for Congress to admit California as a free state at once, and New Mexico as soon as it was ready.

The Compromise of 1850. Taylor had miscalculated. Rather than settling the matter, he helped precipitate one of the most bitter sectional debates in American history, one that carried the country dangerously close to disunion and civil war. Southerners denounced Taylor as an apostate and a tool of the abolitionists, while the followers of Calhoun vowed that they would break up the Union rather

than see slavery excluded from California and New Mexico. Several other issues intensified the crisis: Texans and New Mexicans were on the verge of a private war over their common boundary; abolitionists were gaining Northern support for their demand that slavery be abolished in the District of Columbia; and Southerners were clamoring for a more effective fugitive-slave law. Legislatures and mass meetings in both the North and the South adopted fiery resolutions, and violence threatened to break out in the halls of Congress. A Massachusetts convention of Democrats and Free-Soilers resolved that "we are opposed to slavery in every form and color, and in favor of freedom and free soil wherever man lives." Mississippi contributed to the atmosphere of crisis by issuing a call for a convention of the Southern states to meet at Nashville in June 1850. Many feared that the friends of Calhoun would use the convention to expedite Southern secession.

Moderates in both sections were convinced that nothing short of a comprehensive settlement of all outstanding issues could save the Union. And it was to Henry Clay, then in his seventy-third year and near the end of his long career, that lovers of the Union looked almost instinctively for a just and durable compromise. On January 29, 1850, Clay offered the

The Union cannot ... be saved by eulogies on the Union, however splendid or numerous. The cry of "Union, Union, the glorious Union!" can no more prevent disunion than the cry of "Health, health, glorious health!" on the part of the physician, can save a patient lying dangerously ill....

How can the Union be saved? There is but one way by which it can with any certainty; and that is, by a full and final settlement, on the principle of justice of all the questions at issue between the two sections....

But can this be done? Yes, easily; not by the weaker party, for it can of itself do nothing—not even protect itself—but by the stronger. The North has only to will it to accomplish it—to do justice by conceding to the South an equal right in the acquired territory, and to do her duty by causing the stipulations relative to fugitive slaves to be faithfully fulfilled—to cease the agitation of the slave question, and to provide for the insertion of a provision in the Constitution, by an amendment, which will restore to the South, in substance, the power she possessed of protecting herself before the equilibrium between the sections was destroyed by the action of this Government....

If you, who represent the stronger portion, cannot agree to settle them on the broad principle of justice and duty, say so; and let the States we both represent agree to separate and part in peace. If you are unwilling we should part in peace, tell us so; and we shall know what to do, when you reduce the question to submission or resistance.

From John C. Calhoun, Speech in the Senate, March 4, 1850.

Senate a series of resolutions proposing (1) that California be admitted as a free state; (2) that territorial governments be provided for the rest of the Mexican cession without any restriction on slavery; (3) that Texas abandon its claim to the eastern portion of New Mexico; (4) that the federal government compensate Texas by assuming the public debt Texas had contracted before annexation; (5) that the use of the District of Columbia as a depot in the interstate slave trade be prohibited; (6) that slavery in the District of Columbia be abolished only with the consent of its residents and of the state of Maryland and with compensation to the slaveholders; (7) that a new and more rigorous fugitive-slave act be adopted; and (8) that Congress declare that it had no power to interfere with the interstate slave trade. Among the many moderates who labored long and hard to secure the adoption of these compromise proposals, Stephen A. Douglas of Illinois was second only to Clay.

Congress debated the proposals for more than seven months, with the moderates under constant attack from both proslavery and antislavery opponents of compromise. Clay opened the memorable debate in February. For two days he spoke in defense of his meas-

ures and urged mutual concessions for the sake of the Union. He asked Northerners why they insisted on the Wilmot Proviso when they had a stronger force working for them: "You have got nature itself on your side." He warned Southerners that they would gain nothing and lose a great deal by secession—that secession was certain to lead to civil war, "furious, bloody, implacable, exterminating." On March 4, John C. Calhoun, ill and close to death, listened to a colleague read his last address to the Senate. The present crisis, Calhoun insisted, was due to a breakdown of the old sectional equilibrium, to Northern aggression against the South, and to the destruction of the rights of the states and the creation of a consolidated government. Nothing could save the Union but an end of antislavery agitation, a faithful enforcement of the Fugitive Slave Law, equal rights for the South in the territories, and a constitutional amendment restoring the balance between the two sections. If these points were not conceded, if the South were forced to choose between "submission or resistance," it would know how to act.

On March 7, three days after Calhoun had sounded his grim protest against Clay's com-

I wish to speak to-day, not as a Massachusetts man, nor as a northern man, but as an American, and a member of the Senate of the United States.... I speak to-day for the preservation of the Union. "Hear me for my cause"....

In the excited times in which we live, there is found to exist a state of crimination and recrimination between the North and South. There are lists of grievances produced by each....

I should much prefer to have heard, from every member of this floor, declarations of opinion that this Union could never be dissolved, than the declaration of opinion that in any case, under the pressure of circumstances, such a dissolution was possible. I hear with pain, and anguish, and distress, the word secession....

Instead of speaking of the possibility or utility of secession, instead of dwelling in these caverns of darkness ... let us come out into the light of day.... Let us cherish those hopes which belong to us.... Let us make our generation one of the strongest, and brightest links in that golden chain which is destined, I fully believe, to grapple the people of all the States to this Constitution, for ages to come.

From Daniel Webster, Seventh of March Speech, 1850.

---

promise, Daniel Webster delivered the last great oration of his career. To the dismay of his antislavery constituents, he repudiated his free-soil sentiments and announced that he would speak "not as a Massachusetts man, nor as a northern man, but as an American." Though Webster refuted Calhoun's charges against the North, his speech was clearly an attempt to make the compromise palatable to his own section. He denounced antislavery agitation, urged Northerners not to insist on the Wilmot Proviso when slavery would not expand into the new territories in any case, called for an end to resistance to the Fugitive Slave Act, and concluded with a tearful plea for the Union. Webster's speech immensely strengthened the forces of compromise, but for the remaining two years of his life anti-slavery men vilified him for his apostasy. Most of the Northern Conscience Whigs stood firm. Senator William H. Seward of New York spoke for them when he denounced compromise as "radically wrong and essentially vicious." There was only one way to end antislavery agitation, he said, and that was by "yielding to the progress of emancipation." In reply to Calhoun's constitutional defense of the right to carry slaves into the territories, Seward appealed to "a higher law than the Constitution," a divine law that intended these rich lands to be enjoyed by free men.

As the debate wore on and the House and Senate considered numerous variations of Clay's proposals, it became increasingly evi-dent that opinion in favor of a compromise of some kind was steadily building up in both North and South. Northern businessmen, frightened by the talk of secession, favored a compromise in order to protect their Southern trade and investments. The country had recovered from the depression of the 1840s, and practical men longed for political peace so that they could make the most of a new era of prosperity and economic growth. Those who were indifferent to the moral issue of slavery saw no point in permitting continued antislavery agitation to endanger the Union. The compromisers were further strengthened when the moderates won control of the Southern convention at Nashville and indicated that they were ready to accept a fair settlement. Now the most formidable obstacle to compromise was President Taylor, who bitterly resented Clay's rejection of the Administration's recommendations on New Mexico and California in favor of proposals of his own. The possibility of a presidential veto loomed until Taylor's sudden death on July 9 after an attack of gastroenteritis. His successor, Vice President Millard Fillmore, though a New York Whig of free-soil proclivities, immediately allied himself with Webster and Clay and used his influence in favor of compromise.

Even then, the adoption of a compromise was not easy. When Clay's major proposals had been combined in an "omnibus bill," they were threatened with defeat by a combi-

Millard Fillmore: influence for compromise

nation of Free-Soilers, antislavery Whigs, and Southern-rights men. But the moderates discovered that each of the measures might be enacted separately, for the moderates could then combine with those who opposed the compromise as a whole but favored individual parts of it. In the final weeks of the battle, Senator Douglas replaced the exhausted Clay as leader of the compromisers, and by September 1850 all the measures had been passed and signed by President Fillmore. The Compromise of 1850 as it was finally adopted was essentially like the one Clay had proposed the January before: California was admitted as a free state; the territories of New Mexico and Utah were created from the rest of the Mexican cession, with no restriction on slavery; the Texas boundary was fixed as it exists today; Texas was paid $10 million from the federal treasury as compensation for yielding to New Mexico in their boundary dispute; slave-trading was prohibited in the District of Columbia; and a more severe fugitive-slave act replaced the old one of 1793.

The aftermath

Public reaction to the compromise. Few Northerners or Southerners were altogether satisfied with the Compromise of 1850, and some in each section spurned it as an unclean thing. Abolitionists and Free-Soilers refused to be bound by its terms and denounced as unprincipled tools of the Slave Power the Northern congressmen who had voted for it. Emerson publicly declared that no man could obey the new Fugitive Slave Law "without loss of self-respect and forfeiture of the name of a gentleman." In 1851 the Massachusetts legislature delivered a stern rebuke to Webster (who had joined Fillmore's Cabinet as Secretary of State) by electing Charles Sumner, a radical Free-Soiler and enemy of the compromise, to the United States Senate.

In the South, "fire-eaters" like Robert Barnwell Rhett of South Carolina and William L. Yancey of Alabama termed the compromise a fatal defeat for their section and called for drastic action. The position of the South in the Union was now hopeless, they said, and the proper remedy was immediate secession. In South Carolina the secessionists were defeated with the greatest difficulty, and then only because the "moderates" insisted that action be delayed until other Southern states were ready for independence. A state convention in Georgia adopted a series of resolutions, known as the Georgia Platform, that were probably an accurate expression of public opinion in the Deep South. These resolutions accepted the Compromise of 1850 but warned that Georgia would resist, "even (as a last resort) to a disruption of every tie which binds her to the Union," any congressional act abolishing slavery in the District of Columbia, refusing to admit a slave state, excluding slavery from the territories, or repealing the Fugitive Slave Law.

But most Americans in both sections, though doubting the wisdom of some provisions of the compromise, accepted it with great relief and hoped for a respite from sectional agitation. Mass meetings throughout the country celebrated its passage, and the merchants of New York City formed a Union Safety Committee to mobilize public opinion in its defense. Stephen A. Douglas announced that he had resolved "never to make another speech on the slavery question. . . . Let us cease agitating, stop the debate, and drop the subject." In his annual message of December 1850 President Fillmore told Congress that he regarded the compromise measures as "a final settlement of the dangerous and exciting subjects which they embraced." And forty-four congressmen of both parties signed a pledge to respect the terms of the compromise and never to support a candidate for public office who threatened to disturb it.

Franklin Pierce. The presidential election of 1852 gave further evidence of the widespread hope that the Compromise of 1850 would in fact be a "final settlement." The Democrats adopted a platform that endorsed the compromise without qualification and promised to resist "agitation of the slavery question, under whatever shape or color the attempt may be made." After many futile ballots the convention dropped the leading candidates—Douglas, Cass, and James Buchanan of Pennsylvania—and nominated another "dark horse," Franklin Pierce of New Hampshire. The Whig party, with its Northern and Southern wings now almost hopelessly divided,

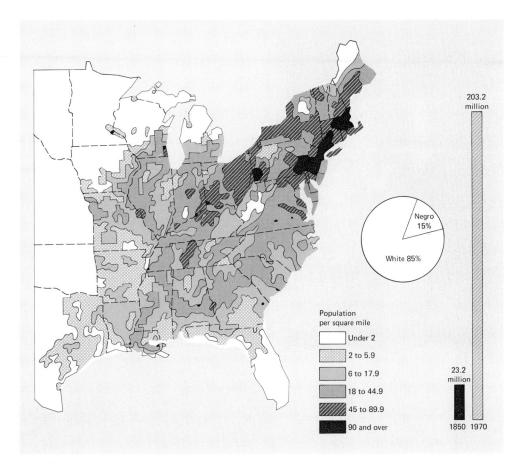

203.2 million

Negro 15%

White 85%

Population per square mile

☐	Under 2
▨	2 to 5.9
▨	6 to 17.9
▨	18 to 44.9
▨	45 to 89.9
■	90 and over

23.2 million

1850   1970

Population 1850

wrangled over a platform that unenthusiastically "acquiesced in" the compromise and therefore pleased almost no one. The convention rejected Fillmore and turned to another military hero, General Winfield Scott of Virginia, whose friendship with Seward and whose failure to endorse the compromise made him suspect in the South. In the election, though Pierce's popular majority was not overwhelming, he carried twenty-seven states with 254 electoral votes, while Scott carried only four states with 42 electoral votes. The Barnburners had returned to the Democratic fold, and the Free-Soil party, with John P. Hale of New Hampshire as its candidate, polled only about half as many votes as it had four years earlier.

Pierce was a Jacksonian Democrat of amiable disposition, modest talent, and almost no capacity for executive leadership. His close ties with Southern Democrats, especially with his Secretary of War, Jefferson Davis, and his sympathy for their views on questions of public policy caused antislavery leaders to damn

him as a "doughface"—"a northern man with southern principles." But his promise in his inaugural address that the provisions of the Compromise of 1850 would be "unhesitatingly carried into effect" suited the popular mood. In his first message to Congress, in December 1853, Pierce rejoiced that the recent compromise had "given renewed vigor to our institutions and restored a sense of repose and security to the public mind." With the country prospering, with the hope that sectional issues had been disposed of, some optimists went so far as to predict a new era of good feelings.

Surviving sources of friction. But very soon there were abundant signs that the truce would be short. The disintegration of the Whig party after its defeat in 1852 snapped another of the ties holding the Union together. The admission of California had upset the sectional balance in the Senate—prior to 1850 there had been fifteen slave and fifteen free states—and the admission of several more

THE AFTERMATH   281

Harriet Beecher Stowe:
"I will write something"

UNCLE TOM'S CABIN;

OR,

LIFE AMONG THE LOWLY.

BY

HARRIET BEECHER STOWE.

VOL. I.

BOSTON:
JOHN P. JEWETT & COMPANY.
CLEVELAND, OHIO:
JEWETT, PROCTOR & WORTHINGTON.
1852.

with kidnapers who sought to sell free Negroes into slavery. In the Northern strongholds of antislavery sentiment the new law simply could not be enforced; during the 1850s abolitionists executed a series of dramatic rescues of fugitives and sent them on to Canada and freedom. Moreover, various Northern states passed personal-liberty laws that nullified the Fugitive Slave Act or at least interfered with its enforcement. This was an assertion of state rights and a form of nullification that Southerners scarcely appreciated.

Above all, the Compromise of 1850 could not stop the pens or quiet the voices of the abolitionists. Less than two years after the compromise was passed the most eloquent and influential appeal in behalf of the slave ever to be written appeared in Harriet Beecher Stowe's justly celebrated novel, *Uncle Tom's Cabin.* Mrs. Stowe was the daughter of a New England clergyman, sister of seven others, and wife of still another. Her anger over the Fugitive Slave Act prompted her to declare: "I will write something. I will if I live." First published serially in an antislavery weekly, her novel appeared in book form in March 1852. By the end of the year, three hundred thousand copies had been sold. Thereafter the novel, together with its various adaptations for the stage, won thousands of converts to the antislavery cause. *Uncle Tom's Cabin* has more than a few flaws as a piece of literature: its situations are contrived; its dialogue is unreal; its slaves are romanticized. Mrs. Stowe knew almost nothing of slavery firsthand, but she understood clearly its tragic aspects; moreover, she had the wisdom to direct her moral indictment against the institution itself rather than against the Southern men and women who were caught in its toils. Indeed, the chief villain of her plot, the cruel overseer Simon Legree, was Northern born. But these subtleties made the book no more attractive to Southern slaveholders than the cruder forms of abolitionist propaganda.

Slavery, then, still threatened the nation's peace and unity. On the eve of the Civil War Abraham Lincoln wrote to Alexander H. Stephens of Georgia: "You think slavery is right and ought to be extended, while we think it is *wrong* and ought to be restricted. That I suppose is the rub."

free states could not be long delayed. The immigrants who poured into the United States during the 1840s and 1850s (see p. 292) shunned the South and thus further increased the North's numerical majority, and railroad-building and industrial expansion gave the North an accelerating economic supremacy. Now secessionists could argue that the rights and interests of the minority South were at the mercy of a hostile and overbearing North.

To Southern-rights men the controversy that began at once over the enforcement of the new Fugitive Slave Act proved their point. This provision of the Compromise of 1850 was the one Southerners regarded as their principal gain and the one Northerners found most difficult to accept. It was a harsh measure that subjected alleged fugitives to summary hearings before federal commissioners without trial by jury or the right to testify in their own behalf. Since a commissioner received a fee of $10 if he ruled that a black prisoner was a slave but only $5 if he ruled that the Negro was free, abolitionists charged that the commissioners were being bribed to collaborate

WESTWARD TO THE PACIFIC

Among the surveys of the westward movement, R. A. Billington, *Westward Expansion* (3rd ed., 1967), is especially good on American penetration of the Far West. General coverage of the diplomacy of expansion is provided in S. F. Bemis, *A Diplomatic History of the United States* (5th ed., 1965); T. A. Bailey, *A Diplomatic History of the American People* (8th ed., 1969); J. W. Pratt, *A History of United States Foreign Policy* (1955, rev. ed., 1965); R. H. Ferrell, *American Diplomacy: A History* (1959, rev. ed., 1969); and Alexander De Conde, *A History of American Foreign Policy* (1963, rev. ed., 1971). The best book dealing comprehensively with expansion in this period is R. A. Billington, *The Far Western Frontier, 1830–1860** (1956). N. A. Graebner, *Empire on the Pacific* (1955), stresses the desire for Pacific ports as a motive for expansion. A. K. Weinberg, *Manifest Destiny** (1935), is an excellent analysis of the ideology of expansionism. Frederick Merk has written two important books on the motivation and rationalization of expansionism: *Manifest Destiny and Mission in American History: A Reinterpretation** (1963), and *The Monroe Doctrine and American Expansionism, 1843–1849* (1966). H. N. Smith, *Virgin Land** (1950), brilliantly analyzes the place of the West in American literature and thought.

The two basic works on the American occupation of Texas are E. C. Barker, *Mexico and Texas, 1821–1835* (1928), and W. C. Binkley, *The Texas Revolution* (1952). A good popular account of the Santa Fe trade is R. L. Duffus, *The Santa Fe Trail* (1930). The best introductions to the fur trade of the Far West are H. M. Chittenden, *The American Fur Trade of the Far West,* 3 vols. (rev. ed., 1935); R. G. Cleland, *This Reckless Breed of Men: The Trappers and Fur Traders of the Southwest* (1950); D. L. Morgan, *Jedediah Smith and the Opening of the West** (1953); P. C. Phillips, *The Fur Trade,* 2 vols. (1961); and G. G. Cline, *Exploring the Great Basin* (1963). Missionary activity in Oregon can be studied in two competent biographies: C. J. Brosnan, *Jason Lee: Prophet of the New Oregon* (1932), and C. M. Drury, *Marcus Whitman, M.D., Pioneer and Martyr* (1937). Two books on the overland trails, reliable and well written, are W. J. Ghent, *The Road to Oregon* (1929), and Jay Monaghan, *The Overland Trail* (1937). A superb contemporary account, Francis Parkman, *The California and Oregon Trail* (1849), is available in several modern editions under the title *The Oregon Trail**. The American occupation of Oregon is treated adequately in O. O. Winther, *The Great Northwest* (2nd ed., 1950), and D. O. Johansen and C. M. Gates, *Empire on the Columbia* (2nd ed., 1967). Early American interest in California is covered in two general histories: A. F. Rolle, *California: A History* (1963, rev. ed., 1969), and W. E. Bean, *California: An Interpretive History* (1968). Wallace Stegner, *The Gathering of Zion: The Story of the Mormon Trail* (1964), is an excellent account of the Mormon migration. The Mormon settlement in the Salt Lake basin is viewed from several perspectives in Nels Anderson, *Desert Saints: The Mormon Frontier in Utah** (1942); R. B. West, Jr., *Kingdom of the Saints* (1957); T. F. O'Dea, *The Mormons** (1957); and L. J. Arrington, *Great Basin Kingdom** (1958). Preston Nibley, *Brigham Young: The Man and His Works* (1936), is warmly sympathetic. S. P. Hirshson, *The Lion of the Lord: A Biography of Brigham Young* (1969), is more critical.

POLK AND THE TRIUMPH OF MANIFEST DESTINY

The authoritative study of the election of 1844 and the first two years of the Polk Administration is Charles Sellers, *James K. Polk: Continentalist, 1843–1846* (1966). Polk's presidential years can also be studied in E. I. McCormac, *James K. Polk* (1922), and in Allan Nevins, ed., *Polk: The Diary of a President, 1845–1849* (1952). A lively and readable introduction to the expansionism of the Polk era is Bernard De Voto, *The Year of Decision, 1846** (1943). Two books deal with negotiations for the annexation of Texas: J. H. Smith, *The Annexation of Texas* (1911), and J. W. Schmitz, *Texan Statecraft, 1836–1845* (1945). M. C. Jacobs, *Winning Oregon* (1938), is a good summary of the Oregon dispute and its settlement. F. W. Merk, *The Oregon Question* (1967), is a collection of excellent interpretive essays. The standard works on the background of the Mexican War are J. S. Reeves, *American Diplomacy under Tyler and Polk* (1907), and G. L. Rives, *The United States and Mexico: 1821–1848,* 2 vols. (1913).

*Available in a paperback edition.

Though dated and marred by its biases, the fullest and most authoritative work on the Mexican War is J. H. Smith, *The War with Mexico,* 2 vols. (1919). Three later books contribute few fresh interpretations but are brief and readable: A. H. Bill, *Rehearsal for Conflict: The War with Mexico, 1846–1848* (1947); R. S. Henry, *The Story of the Mexican War* (1950); and O. A. Singletary, *The Mexican War** (1960). The military campaigns are traced in two excellent biographies: C. W. Elliott, *Winfield Scott* (1937), and Holman Hamilton, *Zachary Taylor: Soldier of the Republic* (1941).

CRISIS AND COMPROMISE

Allan Nevins, *Ordeal of the Union,* 2 vols. (1947), contains a full, incisive, and well-written account of the issue of slavery expansion and of the Compromise of 1850. Among the most useful books for the politics of slavery expansion are T. C. Smith, *The Liberty and Free-Soil Parties in the Northwest* (1897); R. H. Shryock, *Georgia and the Union in 1850* (1926); J. T. Carpenter, *The South as a Conscious Minority* (1930); A. O. Craven, *The Growth of Southern Nationalism, 1848–1861* (1953); K. J. Brauer, *Cotton Versus Conscience: Massachusetts Whig Politics and Southern Expansion, 1843–1848* (1967); and C. W. Morrison, *Democratic Politics and Sectionalism: The Wilmot Proviso Controversy* (1967). Negrophobia as a motive for opposition to slavery expansion is stressed in E. H. Berwanger, *The Frontier Against Slavery: Western Anti-Negro Prejudice and the Slavery Extension Controversy* (1967). J. G. Rayback, *Free Soil: The Election of 1848* (1970), is both scholarly and readable. The Taylor Administration is treated thoroughly in two good biographies: Brainerd Dyer, *Zachery Taylor* (1946), and Holman Hamilton, *Zachary Taylor: Soldier in the White House* (1951).

Of the many books on the California gold rush, the following are among the best: R. W. Paul, *California Gold: The Beginning of Mining in the Far West** (1947); R. W. Paul, *Mining Frontiers of the Far West, 1848–1880** (1963); J. W. Caughey, *Gold Is the Cornerstone* (1949); O. C. Coy, *The Great Trek* (1931); A. B. Hulbert, *Forty-Niners* (1931); and J. H. Jackson, *Anybody's Gold: The Story of California's Mining Towns* (1941).

The best study of the Compromise of 1850 is Holman Hamilton, *Prologue to Conflict: The Crisis and Compromise of 1850** (1964). The crisis and compromise can also be studied through the numerous biographies of national political leaders. Among the most useful are: C. B. Going, *David Wilmot, Free-Soiler* (1924); W. Y. Thompson, *Robert Toombs of Georgia* (1966); G. G. Van Deusen, *William Henry Seward* (1967); F. B. Woodward, *Lewis Cass: The Last Jeffersonian* (1950); G. F. Milton, *Eve of Conflict: Stephen A. Douglas and the Needless War* (1934); G. M. Capers, *Stephen A. Douglas: Defender of the Union* (1959); C. M. Fuess, *Daniel Webster,* 2 vols. (1930, 2nd ed., 1968); R. N. Current, *Daniel Webster and the Rise of National Conservatism** (1955); G. G. Van Deusen, *The Life of Henry Clay** (1937); G. G. Van Deusen, *Thurlow Weed: Wizard of the Lobby* (1947); J. H. Parks, *John Bell of Tennessee* (1950); Rudolph Von Abele, *Alexander H. Stephens: A Biography* (1946); and C. M. Wiltse, *John C. Calhoun: Sectionalist, 1840–1850* (1951).

*Available in a paperback edition.

12 America at mid-century

From the Mexican War to the Civil War the major themes of American political history were sectional conflict and the gradual disintegration of the national party system. Outside the realm of politics, however, this period was notable for its positive achievements—its industrial growth, railroad construction, agricultural expansion, and technological innovations. In spite of the mounting political crisis Americans in general were concerned most of the time with other affairs, for there was much work to be done. They were occupied with ships and railroads and machines and farm implements, with the settlement and development of the West, and with geographic expansion and Manifest Destiny. Stephen A. Douglas, energetic and tough-minded, idol of a bumptious element in the Democratic party that called itself Young America, cared little for the moral issue of slavery and was impatient with those who did. In the early 1850s Douglas struck a popular note when he urged his countrymen to forget the sectional quarrel and turn to the main business of building a prosperous and powerful nation. Young America was, to be sure, concerned about its soul, but it was concerned even more about getting things done.

The emergence of an American literature

The 1850s were also one of the most distinguished and productive periods in the history of American literature. The decade was preceded, however, by many years of literary dependence on Europe. As late as the 1820s American readers were buying more than twice as many books by British as by American authors.

The first writers to win more than local recognition—Washington Irving (1783–1859) and James Fenimore Cooper (1789–1851)—had exploited American themes, but they had spent much of their lives abroad and had observed the conventions of Europe's men of letters. Irving, after writing an amusing and popular *History of New York* (1809) and *The Sketch Book* (1819–20), which depicts village life in rural New York through characters such as Ichabod Crane and Rip Van Winkle, went off to Europe hoping to exchange "the commonplace realities of the present" for "the shadowy grandeur of the past." Cooper used the American frontier as the setting for his five *Leatherstocking Tales* (1823–41), but it is a romantic, unrealistic frontier where the hero, Natty Bumppo, embodies the courage, nobility, innocence, and naturalness supposedly characteristic of men who live in the wilderness. Though defending American democracy to Europeans, Cooper had little confidence in the future of literature in his native land. "There is scarcely an ore which contributes to the wealth of the author, that is found, here, in veins as rich as in

The American genius: Whitman

The genius of the United States is not best or most in its executives or legislatures, nor in its ambassadors or authors or colleges or churches or parlors, nor even in its newspapers or inventors ... but always most in the common people. Their manners, speech, dress, friendships—the freshness and candor of their physiognomy—the picturesque looseness of their carriage ... their deathless attachment to freedom—their aversion to anything indecorous or soft or mean—the practical acknowledgment of the citizens of one state by the citizens of all other states—the fierceness of their roused resentment—their curiosity and welcome of novelty—their self-esteem and wonderful sympathy—their susceptibility to a slight—the air they have of persons who never knew how it felt to stand in the presence of superiors—the fluency of their speech—their delight in music, the sure symptom of manly tenderness and native elegance of soul ... their good temper and openhandedness—the terrible significance of their elections—the President's taking off his hat to them not they to him—these too are unrhymed poetry. It awaits the gigantic and generous treatment worthy of it.

From Walt Whitman, Preface to *Leaves of Grass*, 1855.

Europe,'' he complained. ''There are no annals for the historian; no follies . . . for the satirist; no manners for the dramatist; no obscure fictions for the writers of romance . . . nor any of the rich artificial auxiliaries of poetry.'' A third writer of extraordinary talent, Edgar Allan Poe (1809–49), born in Boston but a Virginian by adoption, was too exotic a figure, too much lost in a weird world of his own creation, too alienated from his optimistic, democratic countrymen, to be the founder or precursor of an American literature.

Yet the call for a national literature as an essential part of a genuine American independence was heard soon after the Revolution and grew stronger with the passing years. In 1815 a group of Boston intellectuals began publishing a literary magazine, the *North American Review,* but rather than breaking new ground it soon became the chief spokesman for a conservative, European-oriented, genteel literary tradition. It often spoke in terms of a cultural nationalism, but it did little in these early years to disturb the local literary establishment. In 1830 William Ellery Channing, in his ''Remarks on National Literature,'' criticized these traditionalists, many of them his Unitarian coreligionists, by urging Americans to encourage their own scholars and cease depending ''for intellectual excitement and enjoyment on foreign minds.'' The true rulers of a country, he said, ''are those who

Herman Melville

determine its mind, its tastes, its principles, and we cannot consent to lodge this sovereignty in the hands of strangers.''

Eventually several transcendentalist writers made the first successful break with the traditionalists. One of the milestones in this revolt was Emerson's Phi Beta Kappa address at Harvard in 1837, entitled ''The American Scholar.'' Calling for a literature of democracy, Emerson advised American writers to stop imitating the ''courtly muses of Europe'' and to produce a distinctive literature of their own. ''Our day of dependence, our long apprenticeship to the learning of other lands draws to a close,'' he exulted. ''The millions that around us are rushing into life cannot always be fed on the sere remains of foreign harvests. Events, actions arise, that must be sung, that will sing themselves.'' The writer should look to the life of the common man, who, Emerson believed, was the finest product of this new nation. He should turn away from ''the great, the remote, the romantic'' and ''sit at the feet of the familiar, the low. . . . What would we really know the meaning of? The meal in the firkin; the milk in the pan; the ballad in the street; the news of the boat; the glance of the eye; the form and gait of the body.''

In the 1840s and 1850s American writers began to heed Emerson's advice. Emerson's own essays, as well as those of Thoreau, marked a turning away from Europe, a trend

The authority of government ... must have the sanction and consent of the governed. It can have no pure right over my person and property but what I concede to it. The progress from an absolute to a limited monarchy, from a limited monarchy to a democracy, is a progress toward a true respect for the individual. Is a democracy, such as we know it, the last improvement possible in government? Is it not possible to take a step further towards recognizing and organizing the rights of man? There will never be a really free and enlightened State, until the State comes to recognize the individual as a higher and independent power, from which all its own power and authority are derived, and treats him accordingly. I please myself with imagining a State at last which can afford to be just to all men, and to treat the individual with respect as a neighbor; which even would not think it inconsistent with its own repose, if a few were to live aloof from it, not meddling with it, nor embraced by it, who fulfilled all the duties of neighbors and fellow-men. A State which bore this kind of fruit, and suffered it to drop off as fast as it ripened, would prepare the way for a still more perfect and glorious State, which also I have imagined, but not anywhere seen.

From Henry David Thoreau, *Essay on Civil Disobedience*, 1849.

---

still more apparent in the novels of Nathaniel Hawthorne (1804–64) and Herman Melville (1819–91) and in the poetry of Walt Whitman (1819–92). These writers gave this age of distinguished American literature its finest expression. Their masterpieces—Hawthorne's *The Scarlet Letter* (1850), Melville's *Moby Dick* (1851), which many critics call the greatest American novel, Thoreau's *Walden* (1854), and the first edition of Whitman's *Leaves of Grass* (1855)—conveyed the spirit of America at mid-century to a limited but appreciative audience of educated men and women. Both Hawthorne, fascinated with the Puritan tradition and with New England's history and legends, and Melville, drawing on his adventures on the high seas, were tormented by deep philosophical questions: the nature of man and the source of the evil that they saw as a powerful force in the world.

Whitman, far more a buoyant transcendentalist than either Hawthorne or Melville, responded most heartily to Emerson's call. His poetry—sensuous, exuberant, unorthodox, paying no attention to rhyme or meter—was denounced by some as crude, vulgar, even immoral. When *Leaves of Grass* first appeared, Emerson found it a little shocking, because some of the poems dwelt on "the form and gait of the body" somewhat more than he had bargained for; nevertheless, he greeted Whitman "at the beginning of a great career." Drawing his themes from nature and the common people, Whitman called *Leaves of Grass* "the great psalm of the republic." In his preface he expressed the humane, democratic idealism that underlies his poetry: "Love the earth and sun and the animals, despise riches, give alms to everyone that asks . . . hate tyrants, argue not concerning God, have patience and indulgence toward the people, take off your hat to nothing known or to any man or number of men." In effect, Whitman took the ideas of the transcendentalists out of the study and gave them joyous, uninhibited life.

Intimations of imperialism

During the 1850s America's politicians doubtless understood the spirit of the people at least as well as her poets, and they were listened to more attentively. As in the 1840s, politicians found widespread support for proposals for national geographic expansion. In his inaugural address President Pierce served notice that the acquisition of Oregon, California, and New Mexico was not the complete fulfillment of his country's Manifest Destiny. There were other areas that circumstances might force the United States to acquire, and Pierce announced that his Administration would not shrink from further expansion because of "any timid forebodings of evil." In part he was expressing the continuing belief that eventually all or part of Canda and the rest of Mexico would be annexed to share the blessings of American democracy. But by mid-century some expansionists were looking beyond these adjacent territories to Cuba, Central America, and Hawaii, where commercial and strategic considerations fortified the hunger for land. This was a sign that Manifest Destiny might easily be converted into a doctrine of imperialism.

Cuba. The Spanish colony of Cuba, a land of slaves and plantations, interested Southerners who hoped to acquire it in order to increase their political and economic power. Cuba also attracted certain Northern commercial interests, especially a small but active group of business-speculators in New York. Moreover, its proximity to Florida and its commanding position at the mouth of the Caribbean Sea and the Gulf of Mexico gave it great strategic importance. The United States had always been apprehensive about the possibility that Cuba might pass from Spain to a stronger power. As early as 1810 President Madison had warned that his country "could not be a satisfied spectator" if Cuba were to fall to some European government "which might make a fulcrum of that position against the security and commerce of the United States."

Until the 1840s the chief aim of American diplomacy had been merely to keep Cuba out of the hands of Britain and France. After the Mexican War, however, proannexation sentiment became so strong that the government changed its policy. In 1848 James Buchanan, Polk's Secretary of State, instructed the American minister at Madrid to offer as much as $100 million for Cuba. The Spanish government responded with a cold refusal; indeed, the foreign minister vowed that he would sooner see the island sunk in the ocean than sold.

Failing to gain Cuba by diplomacy, some expansionists (mostly Southerners) were ready to try force. In 1848 General Narciso López, a Venezuelan adventurer, appeared in New Orleans to find arms and recruits for a filibustering expedition against Cuba. The next year, in spite of federal attempts to stop him, López invaded the island with two hundred

Franklin Pierce of New Hampshire

fifty volunteers, mostly Mexican War veterans, but Spanish troops quickly repulsed them. In 1851 López tried again with a force of four hundred men, but once more he was defeated; this time Spanish authorities executed him and fifty other captives as pirates. Disappointed sympathizers in New Orleans retaliated by destroying the Spanish consulate, and the American and Spanish governments exchanged angry notes. Eventually the United States paid an indemnity for the damage committed by the New Orleans mob, and Spain pardoned the rest of the captured filibusters. But the government did not disavow its interest in Cuba; indeed, it rejected a British and French proposal for a tripartite agreement designed to assure the island's continued possession by Spain.

The Pierce Administration made the acquisition of Cuba one of its chief goals. It sent Pierre Soulé of Louisiana, a flamboyant French exile and ardent expansionist, as minister to Spain, and it gave him cause to believe that his mission was to acquire the island regardless of methods. Secretary of State William L. Marcy authorized Soulé to renew the attempt to purchase Cuba, this time for $130 million; failing in this, he might try to "detach" it from Spain by intrigue. Lacking the most elementary qualifications of a diplomat, the impetuous minister soon engaged in a bitter dispute with the Spanish government. In February 1854 an American merchant vessel, the *Black Warrior,* was seized at Havana for a technical violation of Spanish customs laws. Soulé promptly demanded a disavowal of the act and an indemnity; when he received no immediate reply, he renewed his demands in the form of a virtual ultimatum. The Spanish foreign minister simply ignored Soulé and negotiated a settlement directly with Washington and with the owners of the *Black Warrior.*

At this point Soulé might well have been replaced by a more skillful minister. Instead, Marcy showed no outward sign of disapproval and gave him an even more delicate assignment. Soulé was to confer with John Y. Mason, minister to France, and James Buchanan, minister to Great Britain, about methods of acquiring Cuba and of dealing with possible British and French opposition. In October 1854 the three ministers met for a few days at Ostend and then for a week at Aix-la-Chapelle. They sent their recommendations to the Secretary of State in a confidential memorandum, but its contents were soon known to the public—and the document itself was quite inaccurately named the Ostend Manifesto. Largely the work of Soulé, the memorandum declared that the United States would benefit from the possession of Cuba, while Spain would be better off without it. Accordingly, it proposed that another effort be made to purchase the island. If Spain again refused to sell, the United States would have to consider whether Cuba was a threat to her internal peace. If it was found to be such a threat, "then by every law human and divine, we shall be justified in wresting it from Spain, if we possess the power."

The Ostend Manifesto delighted Southern expansionists and the Young America element in the Democratic party, and it played no small part in Buchanan's presidential nomination two years later. But the criticism from abroad and the indignation of antislavery Northerners forced the Pierce Administration to repudiate it. Marcy sent a strong rebuke to Soulé, and the shocked and humiliated minister resigned. But Cuba was not forgotten; the Democratic platform of 1856 favored annexation, and in three of his annual messages to Congress President Buchanan urged another attempt to purchase it. Cuba, however, had become a sectional issue, and any further action was impossible.

Central America. For centuries men had dreamed of joining the Atlantic and Pacific by cutting a canal through Panama or Nicaragua, but the United States did not become seriously interested in the idea until after the Mexican War and the acquisition of California. In 1848 the need for faster communication between the East and the Far West led to the signing of a treaty with New Granada (Colombia), which gave the United States transit rights through Panama in exchange for a guarantee of New Granada's sovereignty over this isthmian province. By 1855 a group of American promoters had built a railroad across Panama; until the completion of the first transcontinental railroad in 1869, this was the easiest route to the Pacific coast.

Meanwhile, American diplomats, speculators, and adventurers had become deeply involved in the affairs of the small and politically unstable Republic of Nicaragua, which seemed as promising a site for a canal as Panama. Here, however, the Americans met

a formidable competitor in Great Britain, whose worldwide trade, large navy, and extensive colonial possessions gave her a keen interest in an isthmian canal. Indeed, because of the enormous cost of such a project, many assumed that when a canal was built, British capitalists would finance and control it. The British government, watching American movements suspiciously, established a foothold at the mouth of the San Juan River (the probable eastern terminus of a Nicaraguan canal) and claimed a protectorate over the Mosquito Indians on the eastern coast of Nicaragua. This action alarmed the American government, and in the resulting diplomatic exchanges each country warned that it would not permit the other to have exclusive control over an isthmian canal. In 1850 the dispute was settled when Sir Henry Lytton Bulwer, the British minister to the United States, and John M. Clayton, President Taylor's Secretary of State, agreed to the terms of a treaty. It provided, first, that any canal built through Panama or Nicaragua was to be unfortified, neutral in time of war, and open to the ships of all countries on equal terms; second, that neither country was to colonize or establish dominion over any part of Central America.

The Clayton-Bulwer Treaty was approved by the Senate and remained in force for the next half-century, but it was unpopular from the start. Expansionists disliked the commitment not to acquire territory in Central America which meant, they said, that the United States had voluntarily applied the Monroe Doctrine against itself. This concession, together with the implicit recognition that Britain had equal interests in Central America, provoked critics to accuse Clayton of having been outwitted by Bulwer—Buchanan suggested that Clayton ought to be rewarded with elevation to the British peerage. Resentment increased when the British government maintained that the treaty applied only to the future and was not an obligation to abandon its existing protectorate over the eastern coast of Nicaragua. Impulsive Southern expansionists applauded when, in 1855, William Walker, a Tennesseean by birth, led a filibustering expedition into Nicaragua and seized control of her government. Walker was soon driven out, and when he tried to return in 1860 he was captured and executed.

In spite of the criticism, the Clayton-Bulwer Treaty was not a bad bargain for the United States, given the circumstances of the time.

1850 English cartoon: "Master Jonathan tries to smoke a Cuba, but it doesn't agree with him!"

The British government removed one cause of complaint when in 1859 it voluntarily gave up its protectorate over the Mosquito Indians. Then and later the treaty avoided a race between the two countries for possessions in Central America. Above all, it assured the United States equal access to an isthmian canal at a time when she was in no position to ask for more.

Hawaii. Even before the acquisition of Oregon and California made the United States a Pacific power, some Americans had developed an interest in Hawaii. Merchantmen engaged in trade with the Far East, and whaling ships, had stopped there for supplies; by the 1830s missionaries had begun to arrive; other Americans had come in search of land or commercial opportunities. In these early years there was little talk of annexation, but the government was uneasy about the intentions of the British and the French. In 1849, when France seemed ready to seize the islands, Secretary of State Clayton, though denying that the United States desired to establish her sovereignty over them, warned that she "could never with indifference allow them to pass under the dominion or exclusive control of any other power." The Pierce Administration, however, pursued a more aggressive policy;

in 1854 Secretary of State Marcy negotiated a treaty of annexation with the Hawaiian government. But British protests and Senate opposition caused Pierce to drop the matter. Thereafter, until the 1880s, the United States seemed content merely to keep Hawaii free from foreign control.

The Gadsden Purchase. The only tangible result of the various expansionist schemes of the 1850s was the purchase from Mexico of another slice of land in the Southwest. In 1853 the War Department made a survey of possible routes for a transcontinental railroad. The survey revealed that if a line were to be built westward from a Southern city it would probably have to enter Mexican territory south of the Gila River. Realizing that this would be an effective argument for a Northern route, Secretary of War Jefferson Davis persuaded President Pierce to send James Gadsden, a Southern railroad-promoter, to negotiate with Mexico. When Gadsden arrived in Mexico City, he found Santa Anna back in power and in need of money. In 1853 they signed a treaty giving the United States a forty-five-thousand-square-mile strip of desert land below the Gila for $10 million. Except for Alaska, the Gadsden Purchase rounded out the continental frontiers of the United States.

International trade

Europe. American merchants and shipowners recovered only slowly from the disasters they had suffered during the War of 1812, and they were severely hurt again by the long depression following the Panic of 1837. By the mid-1840s however, economic recovery and several other favorable developments combined to encourage a revival of foreign trade. The repeal of the British Corn Laws in 1846 opened a large market for American wheat; the passage of the low Walker Tariff the same year (followed by a still lower tariff in 1857) encouraged the flow of European manufactured goods to the United States; and a spectacular rise in immigration kept American ships filled to capacity on the homeward voyage. As a result, the combined value of American exports and imports increased from $222 million in 1840 to $318 million in 1850; during the next decade they more than doubled, to reach $687 million in 1860.

More than two-thirds of this commerce was

with Europe, and the most valuable part of it was the exchange of American cotton, wheat, and flour for the products of British factories. In 1860 finished manufactured goods constituted only 10 percent of United States exports but nearly half of her imports. As is typical of an agricultural country, the value of imports usually exceeded the value of exports—by $29 million in 1850. This unfavorable trade balance forced the United States to send a large part of the gold mined in California to Europe. Nevertheless, foreign trade was vital to the whole national economy. Though Americans still concentrated on their own internal development, they were bound to the outside world by important commercial ties.

China. As late as 1860 scarcely more than 5 percent of American trade was with Asia. Ever since the late eighteenth century, however, many New York and New England merchants had been dazzled by the profits they anticipated from the penetration of Far Eastern markets. As we have seen, their hope of developing this trade was related to the desire for ports on the Pacific coast. By the early nineteenth century, American merchant ships were stopping in the Philippines, Java, and India, and in 1833 the United States signed a trade treaty with Siam. But the center of activity was at Canton, the one Chinese port open to foreigners, where furs were traded for tea, spices, and nankeens.

Though the United States government never took the initiative in wringing commercial concessions from China, it always capitalized on opportunities afforded by the encroachments of others. When Britain, after the Opium War of 1839–42, forced open several additional Chinese ports and gained various other advantages, American merchants demanded that their government intervene in their behalf. President Tyler responded by sending Caleb Cushing of Massachusetts, a man of rare diplomatic talent, to negotiate with China. In the Treaty of Wanghia (1844) Cushing won access to the ports that had been opened to the British; he established the right of extraterritoriality, which enabled resident Americans accused of crimes to be tried in American rather than Chinese courts; and he obtained a promise of "most favored nation" treatment for the United States, whereby privileges granted to other powers would also be granted to her. In subsequent years, as the British and French forced China to make further concessions, American merchants were thus able to claim similar rights. Since the United States merely asked to be given what others had seized by force, however, relations with China remained friendly.

Japan. From the sixteenth century to the middle of the nineteenth century Japan's only contact with the outside world had been a limited trade with the Dutch East India Company through the port of Nagasaki. The military Shoguns, who dominated the weak emperors, had excluded foreign merchants, missionaries, and diplomats in order to preserve a feudal society. But during the 1840s some Americans began to take an interest in Japan. The Pacific whaling industry needed a treaty to assure proper treatment of shipwrecked sailors cast upon Japanese shores; merchants engaged in the China trade hoped to make Japan a port of call; and textile-

manufacturers were eager to exploit the Japanese market.

In 1852 pressure from these groups caused President Fillmore to send Commodore Matthew C. Perry to Japan with an imposing fleet of steam warships. Perry bore a letter and gifts to the emperor and an array of gadgets illustrating the wonders of Western civilization. In July 1853 he arrived at Yedo Bay, insisted that his letter be delivered to the emperor, and promised to return in the spring. Perry made his second visit early in 1854 and found Japanese officials conciliatory and ready to negotiate. By combining vague threats of war with skillful diplomacy, he secured a treaty of friendship that opened two small ports to American trade, permitted the establishment of a consulate at one of them, guaranteed the safety of shipwrecked sailors, and gave the United States "most favored nation" treatment. Other Western powers soon negotiated their own treaties and forced Japan to open other ports and make additional concessions.

The State Department sent Townsend Harris, a brilliant diplomat, to Japan as the first American consul. Pointing to the fate of China under foreign domination, Harris assured Japan that the United States had no territorial ambitions and urged her to protect herself by modernizing and Westernizing under American guidance. "If you accept my proposals," he predicted, "Japan will become the England of the Orient." His case was persuasive, and in 1858 he signed another treaty greatly enlarging the concessions that Perry had won. Ministers were now to be exchanged; American consuls could reside at the six ports then open to foreigners; American citizens could buy property and enjoy freedom of religion at the so-called treaty ports; and Japan could buy warships and merchantmen from the United States. In 1860 the first Japanese diplomatic delegation visited Washington, and soon thereafter Japan began to make rapid strides toward catching up with the modern world.

The clipper ships. The recovery of American foreign trade was immensely aided by a series of dramatic changes in the design of the old three-masted packet ships (see p. 206), changes that produced a fleet of the swiftest and most beautiful sailing vessels ever to engage in ocean commerce. In 1845 the *Rainbow*, a seven-hundred-fifty-ton ship designed

Perry at Yokohama, 1854

The clipper "Flying Cloud": triumph of American practical art

record. The *Sovereign of the Seas* soon surpassed that with 495 miles in a day's run. Another clipper, the *Lightning,* set a record of thirteen and a half days for a voyage from New York to Liverpool; still another, the *Oriental,* set a record of eighty-one days for a voyage from New York to Hong Kong.

From the mid-1840's to the mid-1850s the clippers gave the United States a larger share of the world's peacetime carrying trade than ever before, a share that briefly promised to surpass the British. The new ships and their masters took a commanding position in the commerce of both Europe and the Far East. But the most spectacular role of the clippers came in the early 1850s in the growing trade between the Atlantic coast and California. The older sailing vessels had taken more than five months to make the voyage around the Horn, whereas the clippers made it in three.

by John Griffith, a naval architect, was completed; it had a long, sleek hull with a concave bow, convex sides, and a rounded stern, and tall masts with an enormous spread of canvas. The launching of the *Rainbow,* a ship that incorporated the advances of several decades, marked the beginning of the era of the famed clipper ships.

Among the builders of clippers, Donald McKay, of Newburyport, Massachusetts, was the most successful; his yards produced scores of vessels, including the 1,783-ton *Flying Cloud,* the 2,421-ton *Sovereign of the Seas,* and the 4,000-ton *Great Republic.* Commanded by daring, hard-driving captains, these ships broke all records for speed. In 1851, on her maiden voyage, the *Flying Cloud* covered 374 miles in a day; then, on a voyage from New York to San Francisco, she made a run of 433 miles in a day to break her own

The era of the clipper ships, however, soon ended, for by the mid-1850s advances in technology were making them obsolete. The opening of the Panama Railroad in 1855 deprived them of the California trade, because cargoes could reach San Francisco along the shorter route in five weeks. Meanwhile the clippers were losing out in the competition with British ironclad steam vessels, which were less beautiful in design but superior in speed and cargo space. American steamship companies had only indifferent success in their rivalry with the British, who now recaptured much of the ocean commerce they had lost to the clippers. Not until the First World War would the United States again hold the position in the carrying trade that she enjoyed for a decade in the mid-nineteenth century.

Immigration

One of millions

The role of the immigrant. Between 1830 and 1860 the population of the United States increased from 12,866,000 to 31,443,000. But in spite of this remarkable growth the country was still sparsely settled and short of manpower. The factories needed more and more hands to tend the machines. Revived programs of internal improvements following the depression of the early 1840s created another heavy demand for workers. Above all, the supply of arable land still seemed to be inexhaustible, and the Western states and territories eagerly welcomed new settlers. Depression created temporary unemployment in the Eastern industrial centers, but most of the

time before the Civil War there were not enough men and women to meet the labor requirements of cities and farms.

The manpower problem would have been even more acute had it not been for a sharp increase in European immigration to the United States beginning in the mid-1840s. Until then immigrants had been arriving at a slowly accelerating annual rate—8,385 in 1820; 23,322 in 1830; and 84,066 in 1840—but in the decade before 1840 fewer than 600,000 had crossed the Atlantic. In the following decade, however, immigration increased to 1,713,000, and during the 1850s to 2,598,000. Each year between 1850 and

1854 the number of immigrants exceeded 300,000, reaching a peak of 428,000 in 1854—a figure that would not be surpassed until the 1870s.

The overwhelming majority of immigrants still came from northern and western Europe. During the 1850s slightly more than 300,000 migrated from Great Britain, about 25,000 from the Scandinavian countries. But Germany and southern Ireland had now become the two principal sources. In addition to the usual incentives—technological unemployment in Europe, the lure of cheap land in America, and the vision of the United States as a country of opportunity, freedom, and social equality—several special conditions helped to bring in a tide of Irish and Germans. In Ireland the failure of the potato crop of 1845 began a succession of famine years that caused widespread misery and actual starvation. As a result, in the fifteen years after 1845 approximately a million and a half Irishmen, most of them in extreme poverty, crossed the Atlantic. In Germany the suppression of the liberal Revolution of 1848 brought many political refugees along with those who came in search of improved economic conditions. Between 1850 and 1860 nearly a million Germans arrived.

In the main these immigrants were not systematically recruited, and they were seldom subsidized by organized groups. The Mormon Church helped its converts, and an Irish Pioneer Emigration Fund, supported by British, Irish, and American leaders, paid the passage of a few. In addition, some immigrants helped friends or relatives to join them. But most came on their own. A minority of them were fairly well-to-do middle-class people whose motive for coming, according to one report, was "not want or oppression, but . . . a rage for speculation, or a desire to acquire wealth more rapidly." Usually, however, the immigrants were poor people who could afford to pay their way only because competing merchant ships, needing return cargoes, reduced fares to as low as $30. Immigrants were crowded into steerage quarters, where they suffered from poor food, inadequate sanitary facilities, and the ravages of smallpox, dysentery, and "ship fever."

Much of this immigrant stream poured into the country through New York, some of it through Boston, Philadelphia, Baltimore, and New Orleans. Since there was no public program to help these strangers find homes and

Landing in New York

jobs or to ease the difficult adjustment to a new environment, many of them at first had unhappy experiences. Until the state of New York, in 1855, gave immigrants some protection by establishing Castle Garden as a controlled landing place, they often fell victim to swindlers who cheated them with exorbitant charges for lodgings or transportation or with false promises of employment. Because the Irish seldom had the means to become farmers, they congregated in the slums of New York and Boston and in the factory towns of New England. A much larger proportion of the Germans arrived with enough money to move to the Middle West, where they acquired farms or established business enterprises in cities such as Cincinnati, St. Louis, Chicago, and Milwaukee. Immigrants rarely settled in the South. Most of them debarked at Northern ports, but even those who arrived at New Orleans often took steamboats up the Mississippi to the free states. They were drawn north by their preference for the cooler climate, by their unwillingness to compete with slave labor, and, in the case of many Germans, by their opposition to slavery itself.

Though few immigrants found it easy to settle in a new land, though far too many lived in abject poverty in the cities of the East, in the long run most of them did manage to improve their economic lot, and their contributions to the American society and economy were incalculable. From the ranks of the immigrants in subsequent years came many of the country's distinguished leaders in politics, the professions, journalism, the fine arts, banking, industry, and transportation. The English and Germans augmented the short supply of skilled craftsmen; the Welsh and Cornish worked the coal mines of Pennsylvania and the lead mines of Missouri and Wisconsin; the Irish tended the machines in New England factories, built railroads, and dug canals; men and women from all the immigrant groups brought millions of acres of Western land under cultivation. Not the least of the immigrants' contributions was the richness and variety they gave to American society through the customs and amenities they brought with them from their old homes.

Nativism. Notwithstanding the value of the immigrants to a thinly settled country, their growing numbers began to alarm some Americans. By the 1850s aliens constituted half the population of New York City and outnumbered the native-born Americans in Chicago, Milwaukee, and St. Louis. Such conditions helped to produce the first significant nativist, or antiforeign, movement in American history, a movement that briefly exerted considerable influence in both state and national politics.

The causes of nativism were several. A few racists feared that the Celts from southern Ireland would pollute the old American stock, and that the United States would cease to be predominantly an Anglo-Saxon nation. Some criticized the Irish and Germans for their clannishness and for their tendency to preserve Old World customs and habits of dress. Others were distressed by the prevalence of crime and pauperism in the immigrant slums, resented the burden that alien indigents put on public funds and private charity, and accused European governments of deliberately exporting their "undesirables" to the United States. Native workingmen disliked the immigrants as economic competitors whose low standard of living threatened to depress wages. Southerners were unhappy to find them adding to the North's majorities in population and congressional representation. Conservatives were concerned about the immigrants' political power, for many states permitted them to vote before they became naturalized citizens. Most immigrants supported the Democratic party as the party of the common man, and in the Eastern cities Democratic bosses used them to build political machines.

Though all these anxieties contributed to the nativist movement, the strongest force behind it was anti-Catholicism. In the early nineteenth century Roman Catholics were a small fraction of the population, but in the 1840s and 1850s nearly all of the Irish and many of the German

"Mexicans shall rule America": bigotry in Baltimore

immigrants were adherents of this faith. With the growth of the Catholic population, there was a corresponding increase in the number of Catholic priests and bishops, convents and monasteries, schools and colleges. Anti-Catholic sentiment among American Protestants was old and deep rooted, having grown from a combination of bigotry and genuine disagreement over Christian doctrine. Frightened nativists viewed every Catholic immigrant as an agent of the pope sent to seize the government and destroy Protestantism. They believed the Church to be the ally of tyranny and reaction in Europe, the enemy of freedom and democracy in America. And their prejudices were confirmed by lurid accounts of immorality in the convents and among the priesthood.

Nativist agitation started in the 1830s. In New York the Reverend George Bourne edited an anti-Catholic weekly, *The Protestant,* while other clergymen organized a Protestant Association "to promote the principles of the Reformation" and to "unfold the true character of Popery." In 1834 Samuel F. B. Morse, portrait-painter and promoter of the telegraph, published an influential anti-Catholic book, *A Foreign Conspiracy Against the Liberties of the United States,* that went through numerous editions. Urging Protestants to unite against the Catholic menace, Morse advocated stricter immigration laws to "stop this leak in the ship through which the muddy waters from without threaten to sink us." Nativists incited anti-Catholic riots, stoned Catholic institutions, and, in 1834, burned the Ursuline Convent School in Charlestown, Massachusetts.

During the 1840s, when Catholic immigrants began to arrive in large numbers, a bewildering array of secret nativist societies sprang up: the Sons of '76, the Sons of America, the Druids, the Order of United Americans, and many others. Early in the 1850s most of these groups united to form a powerful national organization, the Order of the Star Spangled Banner. Because members were sworn to secrecy and refused to answer questions about their aims and activities, they were usually called the Know-Nothings. It soon became evident, however, that their purposes were to defend Protestantism against Catholicism, to make immigration laws more restrictive, to increase the number of years required for naturalization, and to deprive aliens of the ballot.

Meanwhile, nativism had entered politics and had begun to score successes in local elections. After the presidential election of 1852, many former Whigs joined the movement as their own party disintegrated. Political nativism reached its peak in 1854 and 1855, when the Know-Nothings captured several state legislatures, elected numerous governors, and claimed the allegiance of at least seventy-five congressmen. Their most spectacular victory came in Massachusetts, where they controlled every state office and had an overwhelming majority in the legislature. In 1856 the nativists formed the American party, nominated Millard Fillmore for President, and polled about 25 percent of the popular vote.

Thereafter, nativism rapidly declined. In Massachusetts most of the Know-Nothing legislators proved to be incompetent, and they were able to write almost none of their demands into laws. Nationally the nativists soon lost their appeal as the country became increasingly absorbed in the conflict over slavery expansion—indeed, the American party itself split over this issue. Moreover, the religious bigotry and xenophobia of the Know-Nothings failed to destroy certain traditional American attitudes that soon began to reassert themselves: the belief in religious toleration, the idea of America as a refuge for the oppressed of the Old World, and a confidence that the United States could in time assimilate as many immigrants as came to her shores. Besides, nativism betrayed the Christian ideal of the brotherhood of man—as one critic observed, it "judges men by the accidents of their condition, instead of striving to find a common lot for all, with a common access to the blessings of life." Finally, nativist racism was refuted by a popular argument which held that the mixing of various nationalities was producing a new man, the American, superior to the old by the very fact of the mixing. As Herman Melville observed, "We are the heirs of all time, and with all nations we divide our inheritance."

Nativism in politics

Economic development

Domestic commerce. The flourishing American foreign trade of the mid-nineteenth century required the movement of huge quantities of bulky raw materials and foodstuffs to the seaports on the Atlantic and Gulf coasts as well as the distribution of finished European goods to the markets of the interior. At the same time, internal trade expanded as the population grew and as the economies of the various regions became increasingly interdependent and somewhat more specialized. Much of this commerce continued to move along the country's excellent waterways. Coastal vessels carried cotton from Southern ports to New York and New England, while the glamorous Mississippi River steamboats, in spite of canal and railroad competition, carried more freight and passengers in the 1850s than ever before.

The paths of inland water transportation were rapidly changing, however, for the canals were diverting a growing amount of business from the rivers to the Great Lakes. The Miami and Erie Canal through Ohio, and the Wabash and Erie Canal through Indiana, both connected the Ohio River with Lake Erie at Toledo, while the Illinois and Michigan Canal united the Mississippi and Illinois rivers with Lake Michigan at Chicago. As trade shifted to the Great Lakes and the Erie Canal, New York replaced New Orleans as the chief outlet for Western commodities destined for European markets, and young cities on the lakes outgrew the older cities on the rivers. In the 1830s Chicago had been a small village; by 1860 it had a population of 109,000.

Meanwhile, all forms of water transportation were beginning to face serious competition from the railroads. The principle of running cars on wooden or iron rails had long been in use in the British mining districts for hauling coal, but until the early nineteenth century men or animals had always provided the power. Experiments with steam engines began soon after 1800, and in 1820 John Stevens of New Jersey demonstrated a steam locomotive that successfully pulled a train of cars over a short piece of track. Five years later a small British line, the Stockton and Darlington, became the first commercial railroad to utilize steam power.

This development was enough to stimulate feverish activity in the cities of the Eastern United States, where merchants had been seeking a way to compete with New York for the trade of the interior. In 1828 construction began on the Baltimore and Ohio, and by 1830 a thirteen-mile segment was open for

The growth of the railroad network, 1850–60

business. A year later the Mohawk and Hudson established service over sixteen miles of track between Albany and Schenectady. In 1833 South Carolina's 136-mile Charleston and Hamburg line was completed and became for a time the longest railroad in the world. Philadelphia soon had a rail connection with the coal fields of central Pennsylvania, Boston with Worcester and other interior New England cities. By 1840 these and other lines had a combined trackage of 2,818 miles; by 1850 the trackage had grown to 9,021 miles and by 1860 to 30,627 miles.

Emerson once observed that "the Americans take to this little contrivance, the railroad, as if it were the cradle in which they were born." They took to it (after first showing considerable hostility) in spite of such early inconveniences as irregular schedules, frequent breakdowns, and the likelihood of being showered with sparks from the wood-burning locomotives. A major annoyance was the lack of a standard-gauge track—as late as 1860 there were still a dozen gauges in use—which made it impossible for the rolling stock of one railroad to use the tracks of another. Worse than the inconveniences were the disastrous wrecks resulting from soft roadbeds, broken rails, and collapsed bridges.

Construction engineers gradually increased the safety and efficiency of the railroads. They built solid roadbeds using crushed rock for ballast, substituted cast-iron "T" rails for the old wooden rails covered with iron straps,

learned how to make curves and negotiate grades, erected sturdier bridges, and improved the design of locomotives and cars. By the 1850s, though accidents still occurred with painful frequency, technological advances had reduced the risks of travel by railroad to a point where they were not much greater than by steamboat. The speed of the railroads (twenty to thirty miles an hour by 1860), their ability to get through the roughest terrain and to tap the remotest markets, their serviceability in winter when the canals froze, made them the ideal solution to the country's transportation needs.

During the 1850s, in addition to an enormous expansion of railroad mileage, considerable progress was made toward the consolidation of small, independent lines to form trunk lines. In the South, although both Norfolk and Charleston had established rail connections with the Mississippi River at Memphis, most lines continued to be short and to serve merely as feeders for river transportation. The railroad network that had emerged by 1860 was largely a system that united the Northwest with the Northeast. The Baltimore and Ohio had now reached the Ohio River at Wheeling, the Pennsylvania Railroad had connected Philadelphia and Pittsburgh, and several lines had given Boston access to the Erie Canal and the Great Lakes. Meanwhile, the Hudson River Railroad from New York to Albany, together with the New York Central, formed by the consolidation of seven lines between Albany and Buffalo, had given New York a through route to the West. A second railroad, the Erie, had been built across southern New York State from Jersey City to Buffalo. Powerful corporations, controlled by railroad capitalists like Erastus Corning of Albany and John Murray Forbes of Boston, directed the construction and consolidation that produced the trunk lines. Most of the funds came from American and British investors, a little from state and local government subsidies.

In the West, where most of the railroad construction of the 1850s took place, various lines in Ohio, Indiana, and Illinois linked the Ohio and Mississippi rivers with the Great Lakes. The most important of these north-south lines was the Illinois Central, which by 1858 had given Chicago a connection with the rivers at Cairo. Other railroads ran eastward from Chicago, now the transportation hub of the West, to meet the Eastern trunk lines. By 1860 both the Erie and the New York Central either controlled or had agreements with a series of lines that gave them access to Chicago. Railroad bridges now spanned the Mississippi River, and new lines had penetrated as far west as Burlington, Iowa, and St. Joseph, Missouri.

Railroad-builders in the West depended on public support more than those in the East. State and local governments aided them with loans, subsidies, and stock subscriptions, and in 1850 Congress passed a momentous bill providing the first of many railroad land grants. This act, whose chief sponsor was Senator Stephen A. Douglas, was for the benefit of the Illinois Central; it gave the state of Illinois three square miles of land in alternate sections on both sides of the proposed line (six square miles for each mile of track), with the understanding that the land would be turned over to the company as the railroad was built. Southern support was obtained by making a similar grant for a line from the Ohio River to Mobile. By 1860 approximately 28 million acres from the public domain had been granted to various states for railroad construction.

After 1850 there was much talk of a transcontinental railroad to be built with a federal subsidy, but sectional disagreement over the location of the route delayed action until after the start of the Civil War. Meanwhile, in 1855 the firm of Russell, Majors & Waddell, aided by a government subsidy, established regular

West from Boston: a locomotive of the fifties on the Fitchburg line

overland freight service by wagon train between Kansas and California. Three years later the Butterfield Overland Mail Company began to run subsidized semiweekly stagecoaches between St. Louis and San Francisco. In the spring of 1860 Russell, Majors & Waddell introduced the pony express, which carried mail from St. Joseph, Missouri, to Sacramento in ten days. But in less than a year and a half the pony express was put out of business by a device that was revolutionizing communication: the electric telegraph. In 1844 Samuel F. B. Morse had demonstrated its practicality, and by 1860 the country had been tied together with fifty thousand miles of telegraph wire. In October 1861, when the Pacific Telegraph Company completed its line to San Francisco, communication between the Atlantic and Pacific coasts became a matter of minutes.

Agriculture. The revolution in transportation, the rapid growth of industry, and advances in agricultural technology profoundly affected the life of the American farmer. In New England the rural population declined as many families moved west in search of better land, or to the cities to find employment in factories. Even so, in the 1850s a large proportion of the country's raw wool came from New England, while much wheat and corn were grown in New York and Pennsylvania. But farmers in the Northeast were rapidly turning from these crops to the production of fruits, vegetables, and milk for the growing cities nearby. Railroads enabled the owners of orchards, truck gardens, and dairy herds to make daily shipments to city markets from considerable distances. In this highly specialized and commercialized form, Eastern agriculture found new life and became a rewarding enterprise.

In the South the 1850s were prosperous years for the producers of the great staples (tobacco, rice, sugar, and cotton) with slave labor. By then the heart of the Cotton Kingdom had shifted from the Southeast to the Alabama-Mississippi Black Belt, the Mississippi Delta, the valleys of the Arkansas and Red rivers, and the prairies of eastern Texas. With cotton selling for 10 to 12 cents a pound, production rose from 2,469,000 bales in 1849 to 5,387,000 bales in 1859, and the South came near to monopolizing world markets. Able-bodied young slaves sold for $1,500 in the New Orleans market. In eastern Virginia, where a generation earlier soil exhaustion had produced agricultural stagnation, conditions had greatly improved. The slave-plantation system gained new vitality from the introduction of fertilizers, improved methods of cultivation, and systems of crop rotation, but the sale of surplus slaves in the markets of the Southwest continued to be vital to the economy of the older plantation districts. Throughout the South the plantations, though highly commercialized agricultural enterprises, were less affected by technological changes than the farms of the Northeast and Northwest. Planters continued to cultivate the staples with gangs of unskilled slaves using simple hoes and plows. As for the mass of nonslaveholding yeoman farmers, they often planted a few acres in cotton or tobacco, but in the main they raised corn and hogs for their own subsistence and remained outside the market economy.

By 1860 the Old Northwest had become the center of wheat, corn, beef, and pork production. Responding to the growing demands of the East and of Europe, native-born farmers and German and Scandinavian immigrants had opened up the virgin lands of northern Illinois and Indiana, southern Michigan and Wisconsin, and eastern Iowa and Minnesota. With their help the corn crop had increased from 592 million bushels in 1849 to 839 million bushels in 1859, the wheat crop from 100 million bushels to 173 million bushels. Illinois and Indiana now led in hog production,

On virgin land

Illinois in corn production, and Illinois, Indiana, and Wisconsin in wheat production.

Widening markets, the high cost of labor, and the abandonment of self-sufficient agriculture for specialized crops stimulated the improvement of farm implements and mechanization. To cut through the tough prairie sod, Western farmers needed plows that were more efficient than the old ones made of wood or cast iron and drawn by slow-moving oxen. In 1847 John Deere began to supply this need when he opened a factory at Moline, Illinois, to manufacture light steel plows that cut deeper furrows and could be drawn by horses. The fifties also saw the substitution of grain drills for hand planting and the introduction of mowers to harvest the hay crop. Most important for the wheat farmers was the invention of mechanical reapers to replace hand sickles and cradles. In 1831 Cyrus Hall McCormick, a Virginian, built a successful reaper, and in 1847 he moved to Chicago to begin manufacturing them on a large scale. Mechanization advanced another step when threshing machines began to outmode the old method of flailing wheat by hand.

Having entered the market economy, a growing number of Western farmers thought of agriculture as a business enterprise rather than, in Jefferson's terms, as a way of life. Technological advances enabled them to cultivate more acres but also forced them to make heavier investments in implements and machinery. The railroads opened new markets to them but increased their dependence on the middlemen who financed, transported, stored, and marketed their crops. Specialization made them more efficient but increased their dependence on Eastern manufacturers for things they had once made for themselves. In short, the farmers were being caught up in the capitalist world of merchants, manufacturers, bankers, and railroad-operators, and by 1860 some of them were showing signs of dissatisfaction with their place in this world. Out of their discontent would grow the farmers' movements of the post-Civil War years.

Industry. In 1851, at London's Crystal Palace Exhibition, the products of American industry and technology were shown to the world. More than a hundred of them won prize medals, including the McCormick reaper, which attracted by far the greatest admiration. The success of the American exhibits was an indication of the rapid progress the country

Economic progress in young America

Wealth and poverty in young America

had made in manufacturing since the founding of the first textile mills in the early nineteenth century.

The industrial growth of the 1850s far surpassed that of any previous decade. The capital investment of a half-billion dollars in 1849 had nearly doubled by 1859, the number of manufacturing establishments had increased from 123,000 to 140,000, and the annual value of their products had grown from $1,019 million to $1,886 million. Manufacturing was concentrated in the New England and Middle Atlantic states. The market was almost entirely a domestic one, with the Northeast exchanging its industrial surpluses for the foodstuffs and raw materials of the agricultural South and West.

Yet industry in the 1850s had certain characteristics indicating that the United States was still in the early stages of the Industrial Revolution. First, most of the manufacturing involved the processing of the products of American farms and forests. In 1860 the leading industry was the milling of flour and meal, whose value was about one-eighth of the total value of manufactures. Other important industries included lumber-milling, distilling, brewing, leather-tanning, and meatpacking. A second indication of industrial immaturity was the smallness of the typical manufacturing enterprises; on the average they employed fewer than ten workers and had a capital value of less than $7,500. Finally, as we have seen, the United States was still a large consumer of foreign manufactured goods and primarily an exporter of agricultural products.

Nevertheless, by 1860 the direction of American economic development was clear. Textile-manufacturing had already become the core of New England's economy: the investment in mills and machinery was more than $100 million, and the number of cotton spindles in operation had grown to 5,236,000—a 100 percent increase since 1840. In 1844 Charles Goodyear had patented a method of "vulcanizing" raw rubber to make it resist heat and cold, and a new rubber-goods industry was soon manufacturing hundreds of products. In 1846 Elias Howe had patented a sewing machine, and five years later Isaac Singer had begun to manufacture and market an improved model. During the 1850s these machines were used in hundreds of factories making shoes and ready-made clothing. The iron industry had expanded to supply the needs of the producers of farm machinery and at least some of the needs of the railroads. Between 1840 and 1860 pig-iron production rose from 321,000 tons to 920,000 tons a year. Originally the locomotives for American railroads had to be imported, but by the 1840s Pennsylvania iron-manufacturers were able to meet the domestic demand. Their rolling mills were still unable to turn out heavy rails, however, and the railroads continued to import them from Great Britain.

During the years of rapid industrial growth in the 1840s and 1850s, the chronic shortage of skilled workers and the relatively high cost of labor kept alive the American manufacturer's keen interest in increased efficiency and technological advances. As a result, by the 1850s the United States had outstripped all other industrial countries in turning out products whose manufacture involved the use of precision instruments. A few industries began to apply the methods of modern mass production. The manufacturers of guns, clocks, sewing machines, and farm implements introduced assembly lines on which

New England mill, 1850

New York ironworks in the 1840s

unskilled workers, performing standardized tasks, made the finished product from interchangeable parts. During the 1850s, two British commissions visited the United States to study manufacturing techniques, especially the remarkable progress of American technology. The British visitors were struck by the inventiveness of American artisans and by the fact that they seemed to be as fascinated by mechanical improvements as their employers.

Meanwhile, in America's growing industries the corporate form of business organization spread rapidly—during the 1850s the number of manufacturing corporations nearly doubled. Industry and the building and organizing of railroads were rivaling commerce as the road to wealth and economic power. Thus Amos and Abbot Lawrence of Boston, Phelps, Dodge & Company of New York, and many others, got their start in mercantile enterprises but transferred their capital to manufacturing, railroads, and mining. The industrial entrepreneur had already become an important figure in the country's economic life.

By 1860 American factories were employing 1,311,000 workers, the mines and transportation a half-million more. Although skilled labor was still in great demand, each craft felt severely threatened by the steady encroachments of the machines and of mass production. Already the factories had made nearly obsolete several old and honorable crafts, notably those of the cordwainers, coopers, and ironsmiths. As the factories grew in size and the ranks of the unskilled were filled with recent immigrants, the relations of labor and capital became increasingly impersonal. Employers began to think of their workers less as human beings than as commodities to be bought at the lowest price. They paid their employees $6 a week or less for a working day of twelve to fifteen hours. They often ignored feeble state laws fixing maximum hours or regulating the labor of children. And they viewed with indifference the poor sanitary conditions and the high rate of industrial accidents in their factories. Conditions such as these touched the lives of only a small fraction of the population, but by the 1850s there had emerged in the factory slums of Eastern cities an unskilled, propertyless proletariat. The Industrial Revolution thus introduced the United States for the first time to the problem of poverty in an affluent society.

Middle-class reformers who took an interest in the plight of the laboring population usually urged low-paid workers to form their own cooperative workshops or to go west and become farmers. They seldom approved of direct economic action through trade unions. This, however, was the means by which factory workers eventually improved their condition. The promising labor movement of the 1830s (see p. 207) had been destroyed by the depression following the Panic of 1837, and it took many years for another movement to get started. A legal barrier was partially removed when the Massachusetts Supreme Court, in the case of *Commonwealth* v. *Hunt* (1842), ruled that trade unions were not in themselves conspiracies in restraint of trade, a rule that courts in other states soon accepted. But when workers resorted to strikes or boycotts they still ran into trouble with the courts, which continued to interpret such activities as violations of the old common-law doctrine of conspiracy. Trade unions were also handicapped by a hostile press, by generally unfavorable public opinion, and by the ability of employers to recruit strikebreakers.

In the 1850s, though conditions showed little improvement, only a few American workingmen belonged to trade unions. In 1852 the International Typographical Union was formed, and by the end of the decade the stonecutters, hat-finishers, iron-molders, and machinists had also established national organizations. The other skilled crafts were organized only locally, while the mass of unskilled workers had no unions at all. Strikes for higher wages or shorter hours occurred in the shoe and textile industries and on the railroads, but they usually failed. Though trade unionism had made a new beginning, a formidable labor movement would not emerge until after the Civil War.

Economic discontent in the South

The colonial South. On the surface the economic conditions of the 1850s would seem to have given no cause for sectional conflict. The South was prospering, and its economy appeared to be neatly complementary to that of the North—each section needed the products of the other. And yet, throughout the decade, there was in the South an undercurrent of economic discontent.

After the Panic of 1837 Southern cotton no longer played so dynamic a role in the economic development of the country as it had before. Industry now played the role that cotton once played, and Northeastern business interests were less dependent on the Southern market. In short, the South, though still flourishing, was not keeping pace with the other sections.

Far more than that of the Northeast, even more than that of the Northwest, the economy of the South was based on agriculture. In 1860 the eleven states that were to form the Southern Confederacy produced less than one-tenth of the country's manufactured goods; they contained about half as many manufacturing establishments as the Western states. Moreover, Northern ships carried Southern staples to European markets, and most Southern imports came indirectly via New York City. An Alabama editor complained,

> With us every branch and pursuit of life, every trade, profession, and occupation, is dependent upon the North. . . . In Northern vessels [the Southerner's] products are carried to market, his cotton is ginned with Northern gins, his sugar is crushed and preserved by Northern machinery; his rivers are navigated by Northern steamboats . . . his land is cleared with a Northern axe, and a Yankee clock sits upon his mantel-piece; his floor is swept by a Northern broom, and is covered with a Northern carpet; and his wife dresses herself in a Northern looking-glass.

Southerners resented this dependency and searched for ways to strengthen their economy. As early as 1837 a group of Georgians had sponsored a convention at Augusta "to attempt a new organization of our commercial relations with Europe." During the 1840s and 1850s a series of commercial conventions urged the establishment of direct trade between Southern and European ports. While some Southerners planned steamship lines, others favored the building of railroads to divert Western trade to Southern cities. Neither goal was achieved.

For a time there seemed to be a better prospect of improving the South's industrial position. During the depression years of the 1840s, when the price of raw cotton was low, interest in manufacturing increased in the older states of the Southeast, and a number of factories were built. William Gregg of South Carolina, a vigorous propagandist for industrialization, demonstrated its profitability at his highly successful cotton factory in Graniteville. In the 1850s, however, the revival of agricultural prosperity once again made it clear that the South's comparative advantage was in the production of staples, and Southern industry therefore found it difficult to compete for capital. Moreover, the Northern manufacturer was usually able to undersell his Southern competitor and to provide a superior product. As a result, the South's economy remained agricultural.

Rumors of a Northern conspiracy.

The failure of these various efforts toward economic diversification was one of several factors, among which Negro slavery was the most important, producing a state of mind in the South that contributed to sectionalism and ultimately to disunion. Agriculture, Jefferson had taught and Southerners believed, was the most productive pursuit of man, and the man who worked the soil was the chief repository of human virtue. Yet the North had surpassed the South in wealth and population and, according to this widely held though highly inaccurate analysis, had reduced her to a colonial status. This, said angry Southern sectionalists, was an evil and unnatural condition. Many of them seemed to think it was the result of a sinister conspiracy planned by a close-knit body of Northern bankers, merchants, and manufacturers. The chief haunts of the conspirators were New York and Washington; their distinguishing characteristics were their essential unproductiveness and their skill in amassing wealth from the labor of others. Their special field of operation was the South, from which they extracted a major portion of their profits.

Northern businessmen, according to this conspiracy theory, took advantage of the plain, homespun Southerner, who was no match for the artful Yankee in the techniques of chicanery. They were accused of exacting exorbitant middlemen's charges, of rigging prices, of manipulating the money market, and of keeping much of the wealth produced in the South flowing steadily into their coffers. The price of Southern property, wrote an indignant Virginian, "is dependent upon the speculative pleasure of the Merchants, Bankers, and Brokers of New York. And why? Because Wall Street can depress the money

market when it pleases." The South, said a Mississippian, had permitted itself to fall into a condition of "serfdom" and to become "the sport and laughing stock of Wall Street." A Southern editor described New York as "a mighty queen of commerce . . . waving an undisputed commercial scepter over the South." With an "avidity rarely equalled," she "grasps our gains and transfers them to herself."

But, according to this sectional indictment, Northern capitalists did not make their profits solely from their adroit maneuvers in a free economy. Rather, in advancing their conspiracy they had enlisted the support of the federal government. In November 1860 Senator Robert Toombs, in a speech before the Georgia legislature, described the political side of the alleged Northern conspiracy to prostrate the South. No sooner had the government been organized, he claimed, than "the Northern States evinced a general desire and purpose to use it for their own benefit, and to pervert its powers for sectional advantage, and they have steadily pursued that policy to this day." They demanded, and received, a monopoly of the shipbuilding business; they demanded, and received, a monopoly of the trade between American ports. The New England fishing industry obtained an annual bounty from the public treasury; manufacturers obtained a protective tariff. Through its policy of subsidizing "every interest and every pursuit in the North," the federal treasury had become "a perpetual fertilizing stream to them and their industry, and a suction-pump to drain away our substance and parch up our lands."

By the 1850s the notion that Northern profits were largely a form of expropriation of Southern wealth, that the South was "the very best colony to the North any people ever possessed," was having a powerful effect on Southern opinion. Much of this analysis of the antebellum economic relationship between North and South has been effectively challenged by modern economic historians. But what is important historically is not the inaccuracy of this economic analysis but the fact that most Southerners apparently believed it to be true. The attitudes they shared were characteristic of those held by nineteenth-century farmers and planters concerning the "middlemen" who financed, transported, and marketed agricultural commodities. Since they regarded the activities of middlemen as nonproductive and parasitic, they were bound to consider marketing costs exorbitant. Sectional leaders exacerbated the existing resentment by using the concept of Northern exploitation as a rhetorical device to unify the South. Southerners had convinced themselves, remarked a Northerner, "that in some way or other, either through the fiscal regulations of the Government, or through the legerdemain of trade, the North has been built up at the expense of the South." Not even agricultural prosperity could banish this thought from the Southern mind.

When the sectional conflict was reopened in 1854, slavery transcended all other issues. Yet there is evidence that Northern attacks on slavery were sometimes intensified by sectional conflicts over federal economic policy, while Southern expressions of economic grievances may well have concealed deeper anxieties about the institution of slavery. As the historian Charles A. Beard once observed, it was not always easy to tell "where slavery as an ethical question left off, and economics—the struggle over the distribution of wealth—began."

AMERICAN LITERATURE

Suggestions for reading

The surveys of American intellectual history listed in the suggested readings for Chapter 10 all deal with American writers of the pre-Civil War years. The best special study is F. O. Matthiessen, *American Renaissance** (1941). Edmund Wilson, ed., *The Shock of Recognition: The Development of Literature in the United States Recorded by the Men Who Made It** (1943), is an excellent anthology. The biographies of individual writers should also be consulted: J. W. Krutch, *Henry David Thoreau** (1948); R. L. Rusk, *The Life of Ralph Waldo Emerson* (1949); Mark Van Doren, *Nathaniel Hawthorne** (1949); Newton Arvin, *Herman Melville** (1950); and G. W. Allen, *The Solitary Singer: A Critical Biography of Walt Whitman** (1955).

EXPANSIONISM AND FOREIGN TRADE

American interests in Cuba, Central America, and the Far East are treated adequately in four general surveys of American foreign policy: S. F. Bemis, *A Diplomatic History of the United States* (5th ed., 1965); T. A. Bailey, *A Diplomatic History of the American People* (8th ed., 1969); J. W. Pratt, *A History of United States Foreign Policy*, (1955, rev. ed., 1965); and Alexander De Conde, *A History of American Foreign Policy* (1963, rev. ed., 1971). Several excellent monographs may also be consulted: M. W. Williams, *Anglo-American Isthmian Diplomacy, 1815–1915* (1916); Dexter Perkins, *The Monroe Doctrine, 1826–1867* (1933); and Basil Rauch, *American Interests in Cuba, 1848–1855* (1948). E. S. Wallace, *Destiny and Glory* (1957), is a vivid account of filibustering.

The most useful special studies of American-Far Eastern relations that deal with this period are: Tyler Dennett, *Americans in Eastern Asia* (1941); A. W. Griswold, *The Far Eastern Policy of the United States** (1938); P. J. Treat, *Diplomatic Relations Between the United States and Japan, 1853–1905,* 3 vols. (1932–38); F. R. Dulles, *China and America: The Story of Their Relations Since 1784* (1946); and L. H. Battistini, *The Rise of American Influence in Asia and the Pacific* (1960). Arthur Walworth, *Black Ships off Japan* (1946), is a readable account of the Perry mission to Japan. H. W. Bradley, *The American Frontier in Hawaii: The Pioneers, 1789–1843* (1942), is the best study of early American interest in Hawaii.

The standard works on the growth of American foreign trade are E. R. Johnson, *et al., History of Domestic and Foreign Commerce of the United States,* 2 vols. (1915), and J. H. Frederick, *The Development of American Commerce* (1932). The commerce of New England and New York City are the subjects of two distinguished books: S. E. Morison, *Maritime History of Massachusetts: 1783–1860** (1921), and R. G. Albion, *The Rise of New York Port, 1815–1860* (1939). The best books on the clipper ships are A. H. Clark, *The Clipper Ship Era* (1910); C. C. Cutler, *Greyhounds of the Sea* (1930); and Robert Carse, *The Moonrakers* (1961).

IMMIGRATION AND NATIVISM

Several excellent surveys of immigration to the United States are valuable for this period: Carl

*Available in a paperback edition.

Wittke, *We Who Built America** (1939, rev. ed., 1964); M. L. Hansen, *The Atlantic Migration, 1607–1860** (1940); and M. A. Jones, *American Immigration** (1960). Oscar Handlin, *The Uprooted** (1951), is a sensitive study of the immigrant's problems. Four specific immigrant groups are the subjects of individual volumes: T. C. Blegen, *Norwegian Migration to America,* 2 vols. (1931–40); R. T. Berthoff, *British Immigrants in Industrial America, 1790–1950* (1953); Carl Wittke, *Refugees of Revolution: The German Forty-Eighters in America* (1952); and by the same author, *The Irish in America** (1956). The immigrant populations of two large Eastern cities are studied in Oscar Handlin, *Boston's Immigrants** (1941), and Robert Ernst, *Immigrant Life in New York City, 1825–1863* (1949).

A perceptive account of mid-nineteenth-century nativism is in Allan Nevins, *Ordeal of the Union,* 2 vols. (1947). R. A. Billington, *The Protestant Crusade, 1800–1860** (1938), emphasizes the anti-Catholic aspect of the movement. Two special studies are also useful: Sister M. E. Thomas, *Nativism in the Old Northwest, 1850–1860* (1936), and W. D. Overdyke, *The Know-Nothing Party in the South* (1950).

ECONOMIC DEVELOPMENT
All of the books on agriculture, industry, transportation, and technology listed in the suggested readings for Chapter 8 are useful for this period. There are also several good chapters on the American economy at mid-century in Nevins, *Ordeal of the Union,* cited above.

A good introduction to the history of the railroads is J. F. Stover, *The Life and Decline of the American Railroad* (1970). Problems of railroad promotion and finance can be studied in F. A. Cleveland and F. W. Powell, *Railroad Promotion and Capitalization in the United States* (1909); A. M. Johnson and B. E. Supple, *Boston Capitalists and Western Railroads: A Study in the Nineteenth Century Railroad Investment Process* (1967); L. H. Haney, *A Congressional History of Railways in the United States to 1850* (1908); and by the same author, *A Congressional History of Railways in the United States, 1850–1877* (1910). An outstanding history of the New England railroads is E. C. Kirkland, *Men, Cities and Transportation,* 2 vols. (1948). Railroad promotion in the Southeast is described in U. B. Phillips, *A History of Transportation in the Eastern Cotton Belt to 1860* (1908). T. C. Cochran, *Railroad Leaders, 1845–1890* (1953), contains important material on early railroad-promoters and their social attitudes. The following histories of individual railroads are useful: F. W. Stevens, *The Beginnings of the New York Central Railroad* (1926); P. W. Gates, *The Illinois Central Railroad and Its Colonization Work* (1934); Edward Hungerford, *The Story of the Baltimore and Ohio Railroad, 1827–1927,* 2 vols. (1928); and by the same author, *Men of Erie* (1946); and R. C. Overton, *Burlington West* (1941). Two books deal with the impact of the railroads on the American economy: R. W. Fogel, *Railroads and American Economic Growth* (1964), and Albert Fishlow, *American Railroads and the Transformation of the Ante-Bellum Economy* (1965).

In addition to the listings in the suggested readings for Chapter 8, the following books on industry and technology are worth consulting for this period: G. S. Gibb, *The Saco-Lowell Shops: Textile Machinery Building in New England* (1950); Waldemar Kaempffert, ed., *A Popular History of American Invention,* 2 vols. (1924); Allan Nevins, *Abram S. Hewitt: With Some Account of Peter Cooper* (1935); J. A. Kouwenhoven, *Made in America** (1948); D. J. Struik, *Yankee Science in the Making** (1948); and Mitchell Wilson, *American Science and Invention: A Pictorial History* (1954). The best book on labor in this period is N. J. Ware, *The Industrial Worker, 1840–1860** (1924). Hannah Josephson, *The Golden Threads* (1949), is excellent on the women textile-workers of New England. Two good general treatments are J. G. Rayback, *History of American Labor** (1959), and H. M. Pelling, *American Labor** (1960). R. H. Bremner, *From the Depths** (1956), deals with the emergence of the problem of poverty in America.

The causes of economic discontent in the South can be studied in R. R. Russel, *Economic Aspects of Southern Sectionalism, 1840–1861* (1924); J. G. Van Deusen, *The Ante-Bellum Southern Commercial Conventions* (1926); Herbert Wender, *Southern Commercial Conventions, 1837–1860** (1930); and Clement Eaton, *The Growth of Southern Civilization, 1790–1860** (1961).
*Available in a paperback edition.

13   *A decade of crisis*

Between the Compromise of 1850 and the outbreak of civil war lay ten years of mounting tension punctuated by outbursts of hostility between North and South. Each crisis hinged on the question of slavery and its role in the expansion of the nation, and each brought the nation closer to war. By 1860 many Southerners believed that the North was bent not only on the containment of slavery where it then existed but on its ultimate extinction. Many Northerners, on the other hand, fearing the "slave power conspiracy," believed that the South would not rest until federal law protected slave property everywhere in the Union.

Those fears reflected valid concerns. Having lost equality in the Senate as a result of the compromise measures of 1850, the South soon insisted on an interpretation of the Constitution that would guarantee the survival of slavery, not only as the economic basis of society but as the only conceivable solution to the emotional question of race relations in the South. By 1860 Jefferson Davis, a United States senator who was soon to become president of the Confederacy, was demanding a slave code to govern and protect slave property in the territories. Believing that expansion was essential to the survival of slavery, William Lowndes Yancey of Alabama and a few extremists from each Southern state backed Davis' demand. These so-called fire-eaters met passionate resistance from the free farmers of the North, who were bent on carrying their own way of life into the new federal territories. The South's idea that the states retained their sovereignty under the Constitution and that the federal government must enforce Southern state laws on slavery in the federal territories was unacceptable to the large majority of Northerners, whether Democrats or Whigs.

At bottom, then, the Civil War resulted from the conflict over slavery, even though few Northerners hated it enough in 1860 to go to war for emancipation. The successive crises of the 1850s strained the bonds of union ever more sharply until the end of the decade, when at last both North and South saw the sectional problem as a moral issue. By then a breach was unavoidable.

The divisive issue

The Kansas-Nebraska bill. The peace that followed the Compromise of 1850 was illusory. Although the Democrats had won the Presidency for Franklin Pierce, who campaigned for the acceptance of the compromise as final, they also urged national expansion. And national expansion was incompatible with sectional harmony on the issue of slavery in the territories.

Early in January 1854 Senator Stephen A. Douglas, chairman of the Committee on the Territories, abruptly shattered the sectional

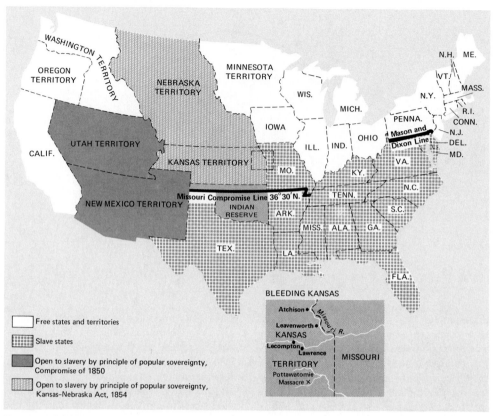

The Kansas-Nebraska Act, 1854

truce by introducing a bill for the organization of the Kansas and Nebraska territories for statehood on the principle of "popular sovereignty." That principle had already been applied to New Mexico and Utah in the Compromise of 1850. Letting the people of a territory decide on the question of slavery seemed eminently reasonable to men like Douglas, the cocksure little senator from Illinois, whose motives for reopening the territorial question were unclear. Douglas certainly had presidential aspirations, and his critics promptly charged him with trying to appease Southern Democrats whose backing he needed for the nomination. Yet the presidential contest was still two years away, and few Southern senators were enthusiastic about organizing new territories ill adapted to slavery.

Probably the "Little Giant" from Illinois was acting primarily as a regional booster. "The tide of immigration and civilization must be permitted to roll onward," he declared. The country needed "a continuous line of settlements, with civil, political and religious institutions all under the protection of the law. . . ." Douglas was thinking of the eastern terminus of the projected transcontinental railway. If the "continuous line of settlements" should lead out from Chicago, it would benefit not only Illinois but all the Midwestern states. The South hoped for a terminus at New Orleans. Even while Douglas was readying his bill for action, Jefferson Davis of Mississippi, Pierce's Secretary of War, was concluding the Gadsden Purchase, which was essential to the southern route challenging Chicago's aspirations.

Douglas knew there was danger of reopening the slavery question whenever new territories were organized. He realized too that that question had potentialities for dividing the Democratic party. He took those risks because of his interest in the Chicago terminus and because of intense pressure from a group of senators led by tough-minded David Atchison of Missouri, whose interest in organizing Kansas was even stronger than that of Douglas. Further, Atchison had the power, as president of the Senate, to remove Douglas from his cherished chairmanship of the Committee on Territories. Atchison bragged later about having persuaded the senator from Illinois to accept amendments to the bill that were anathema to the free-soil Democrats.

What Douglas failed to assess accurately was the extent to which slavery had become a moral issue. Opponents of slavery in the territories would not be satisfied with the mere probability that slavery would be turned down on the Kansas plains: they would take no chances. Free-soilers had an excellent argument. Because Kansas and Nebraska were north of the 36°30' parallel, passing Douglas' bill would endanger the rule of 1820, adopted in the Missouri Compromise, which prohibited slavery above that line in all lands secured by the Louisiana Purchase. Free-soil leaders therefore introduced an amendment explicitly reaffirming the Missouri prohibition. Quickly countering this move, Southern senators secured instead a specific repeal of the Missouri prohibition. The final version of the Kansas-Nebraska bill included that inflammatory feature and called for the Platte River country to be divided into two territories, each to be organized immediately on the basis of popular sovereignty. Because the northern territory, Nebraska, was west of Iowa, a free state, few feared the development of slavery there. Kansas, to the south and immediately west of Missouri, a slave state, was another matter. Missouri seemed to think of Kansas as her own backyard. In final form the bill appalled the free-soil wing of the Democratic party as well as Northern antislavery Whigs, because it repealed the Missouri Compromise. With stunning perversity, Southerners abandoned their initial coolness to the Kansas-Nebraska bill and endorsed it as a measure "reasonable in its operation and effect" and fair to the South.

A new political party. The outcry was loud and immediate. "The Appeal of the Independent Democrats," a pamphlet written by Salmon P. Chase of Ohio, voiced the outrage of free-soilers, but they could not dissuade President Pierce from endorsing the Kansas-Nebraska bill. On March 3 the Senate passed the controversial measure. After nearly three months, and after a heated and lengthy debate, the House did the same. On May 30, by a narrow margin of three votes and as a result of active pressure on the part of the President, the Kansas-Nebraska bill became law. New England and the Northwest exploded in angry demonstrations as "anti-Nebraska" people came together across party lines to denounce Douglas and his bill. Douglas declared that he could travel from Washington to Chicago in the light of his own burning effigies. Some of the strongest opponents of the act were Northern Democrats, who had divided evenly on the issue in the House of Representatives. The territorial issue had already demolished the Whigs. Now it threatened to divide the Democrats as well.

As early as February, in Ripon, Wisconsin, a gathering of anti-Nebraska Whigs and Democrats united to form a new party, and similar meetings took place elsewhere. Two weeks after President Pierce signed the Kansas-Nebraska bill one of these fusionist groups met at Jackson, Michigan, and adopted the name "Republican." This party was composed entirely of members from one section and was devoted to the containment of slavery within the states where it was already established. The new party stressed most its belief in the dignity of free labor; it held that the spread of slavery endangered not only the agrarian way of life idealized by Americans since Jefferson's day but the way of life of artisans and mechanics as well. Ever since the election of 1852, the Whig party had been in disarray. Now the "conscience" Whigs began joining the new party, where they were met by numbers of Northern Democrats alienated by the Kansas-Nebraska Act.

By 1854 the Whig party was all but defunct, but whether the Republicans would take their place as the chief party to oppose the Democrats was still uncertain. Democrats sustained heavy losses in the congressional elections that year, but it was hard to tell whether they lost to combinations of the various opponents of the Kansas-Nebraska Act or to the American party (see p. 294). That party was winning votes on the distrust of Catholics and foreign-born citizens so strong in urban areas, along the Middle Atlantic area, and in the entire border-state region. There was such hearty cooperation between the anti-Nebraska forces and the members of the American party, called "Know-Nothings," that distinguishing the head from the tail of the victorious combination was not easy. But as the Pierce Administration began organizing the Kansas Territory, the attention of the country was riveted by a chaotic contest that worked to the benefit of the Republicans.

The test in Kansas. Critics of "popular sovereignty" preferred to call it "squatter sover-

Salmon P. Chase: outraged pamphleteer

eignty." Once the policy had gone into effect in Kansas, its shortcomings seemed to merit that comtemptuous phrase. Nobody expected trouble in Nebraska, and there was none. But in Kansas there was general and sustained disorder that discredited popular sovereignty as a workable solution to the question of slavery in the territories. The customary lawlessness of the frontier was heightened by special causes of dispute. The government had permitted speculators to make claims in Kansas before legal titles had been acquired from the Indians, and early purchasers were making claims where they supposed towns would spring up and along the line of the anticipated transcontinental railroad. They were greedy, not for homesites, but for a rise in values. Speculators came from everywhere, but Missourians, on the scene early, apparently regarded Kansas as their rightful territory, their natural place to expand. Senator Atchison blustered that he preferred to see the new territory "sink in hell" rather than to have it organized as a free state.

Preparing to fight matters out on a popular-sovereignty basis, since that was now the law, free-soil forces determined to make themselves the more numerous party in Kansas. In Massachusetts an Emigrant Aid Society was formed under the leadership of Eli Thayer, a wealthy cotton-manufacturer, to give financial help to those willing to undertake the westward trek. Thayer's views on free soil were tainted by racism, for he believed in excluding blacks from the territories, whether free or slave. But that bias went unnoticed as Northerners idealized the emigrants. To John Greenleaf Whittier, the poet of antislavery, the emigrants were crusaders, rearing "a wall of men . . . on freedom's southern line." All told, only 1,240 settlers came to Kansas under Thayer's auspices, and efforts to promote Kansas in the Southern states inspired even fewer emigrants. Most of the Kansas settlers came, as they usually did when new territories were opened, from neighboring states. Many were from Missouri, and though the slaveholders among them were few, even the non-slaveholders abhorred abolitionism.

When Andrew C. Reeder, the Pennsylvanian chosen by Pierce to be the first territorial governor of Kansas, arrived there in the fall of 1854, he found several thousand settlers ahead of him. The first elections called by Reeder set the pattern for many Kansas elections to follow. The proslavery forces won overwhelmingly, electing a territorial delegate to Congress in the fall of 1854 and a proslavery legislature the following spring. Both elections were riddled with fraud. Encouraged by Senator Atchison to believe that their own security depended on getting a government set up in Kansas that would protect slave property, Missourians living in the counties adjacent to the border crossed the state line to cast illegal ballots. Governor Reeder threw out the most blatantly fraudulent returns but permitted the main result to stand. President Pierce, who should have called a new election, vacillated and then did nothing. The new Kansas legislature drew up a territorial slave code so severe that it set the death penalty for anyone aiding a fugitive slave.

The free-soil forces denounced the actions of the "bogus" legislature, as they called it, and organized their own "shadow" government. They drew up the so-called Topeka constitution, which provided for the end of slavery by 1857; less admirably, it also excluded free blacks from entry into Kansas. The free-soilers announced new elections for a state legislature and established a capital at Lawrence. Now two governments, complete with capitals, governors, and legislatures, confronted each other: one was the product of fraud; the other lacked legal foundation.

For three weeks in late November armed bands of "border ruffians" from Missouri roamed the countryside. They claimed to be helping the legal government of Kansas restore order, but their real intent was to terrify the free-soil settlers. The free-state men met the invaders with "Beecher's Bibles," named for Henry Ward Beecher, a famous preacher who in an indiscreet moment had declared Sharps rifles a better force than Bibles for morality in Kansas. Finally the free-state "governor," Charles Robinson, struck a truce with Governor William Shannon, whom Pierce had sent out to replace Reeder. Shannon denied that he had sent for the Missourians, and Robinson explained that the free-state men had no intention of disobeying territorial laws.

The winter of 1855–56 was exceptionally severe in Kansas, and the settlers had all they could do to keep from freezing. With the spring thaw, trouble broke out again. In Leavenworth violence at a free-state election resulted in death and injury to several persons, including one particularly brutal murder of a free-state militia captain. A newspaper war followed, with the Missouri papers excusing atrocities against "abolitionists," as they wrongly labeled the free-soilers, and with the Eastern papers, particularly the New York *Tribune,* freely exaggerating the number of victims. Free-staters were justifiably indignant when President Pierce attributed the violence in Kansas to the emigrant aid societies and placed no blame on the raiders from Missouri. Pierce rejected the Topeka, or free-state, constitution as illegal, thus almost inviting an attack on the free-state capital at Lawrence. In May the attack occurred. A roving band of Missourians broke up the free-state printing press at Lawrence, burned out a hotel, intimidated the inhabitants, and rode off after this assault unscathed.

"Bleeding Kansas." One grim free-stater undertook a savage retaliation. The roving survivor of many failed enterprises, John Brown had come to Kansas in the fall of 1855 to settle down with his large tribe of sons and their families in support of the free-state cause. An early advocate of armed resistance, Brown was outraged that nothing had been done to punish the border ruffians; after the Lawrence episode, he resolved to even the score himself. Leading a small band of his sons and followers in a midnight attack on the sleeping community of Pottawatomie Creek, Brown ordered them to kill five of the settlers with broadswords he had deliberately sharpened for the purpose and then made off with the victims' horses. Brown thought of himself as God's instrument of revenge. Although his victims were associated with the proslavery party, not one was a slaveholder, and none had done special services for the Missourians. The seemingly random character of those murders lent a special terror to the episode. Within days the whole of southeast Kansas was at war. John Brown went into hiding with his men, but the Missourians took revenge by burning the free-state town of Osawatomie and killing one of Brown's sons while seeking Brown himself.

A summer of guerrilla war followed. The death toll for the first year of settlement under popular sovereignty rose to over two hundred; property losses in barn-burnings, theft, and general destruction reached nearly $2 million. Pierce removed Shannon and sent yet another governor to replace him. In September 1856 Governor John Geary brought order to the territory with federal troops. Though he per-

suaded the Missourians to abandon hostilities, nobody believed that the question of slavery in the territories was settled.

Tempers in Congress soon matched those on the frontier. An ugly event on the floor of the Senate contributed to the fierce climate of politics. Just as the Missourians were burning the hotel in Lawrence, Senator Charles Sumner of Massachusetts, a famous antislavery orator, gave a ringing denunciation of the "Crime Against Kansas." In the course of a two-day speech during which he urged the admission of Kansas as a state under the Topeka constitution, he lashed the Administration for its alleged partiality to the proslavery settlers and defined the "crime" as the "rape of a virgin territory, compelling it to the hateful embrace of slavery. . . ." Pursuing his sexual metaphors, Sumner even insinuated that the aging Senator Andrew Butler of South Carolina had taken "slavery" as his mistress; then he referred to the "loose expectoration" of Butler's speech. That cruel reference to a partial paralysis caused by a stroke prompted the senator's young cousin, Congressman Preston Brooks, to walk into the Senate a few days later and cane Sumner into unconsciousness. Because of his injuries Sumner was not in the Senate again for several years, and his empty seat became a focus of antislavery sympathy. To Northern supporters the senator from Massachusetts was a martyr to Southern barbarism; but to Southerners he was a hyprocrite, and "Bully" Brooks' admirers sent Brooks complimentary walking canes. The polarization of sympathies in the Sumner-Brooks affair symbolized the hardening of attitudes on every issue touching on slavery in the territories.

The election of 1856. The Pierce Administration had promised to reconcile the sections, but in the gamble to organize Kansas for statehood it had forced the slavery issue into open conflict. Now the country and the Democratic party drifted rudderless toward a crucial presidential election. Only the Republicans faced the future with confidence, for they had made important gains since the congressional elections two years earlier. Through the skillful political management of Senator William H. Seward and his able political adviser Thurlow Weed, the great Whig party of New York State had come over to the Republicans en masse. In Ohio, Salmon P. Chase, elected governor in 1855, announced his departure from the

"The Great Presidential Sweepstakes of 1856"

Democrats. He joined the Republicans at the same time his old Whig antagonist Benjamin Wade did. The two men disliked each other, but they disliked slavery even more. Other important public figures, including Abraham Lincoln, were cooperating with the Republicans while retaining their old party labels. By 1856 most state governments in the North were under the control of political leaders sympathetic to the Republicans. They reflected a growing popular conviction that only the new party could halt the aggressions of the "slave power conspiracy."

Even the Know-Nothing threat to Republican ascendancy disappeared in February before the presidential elections. At the American party convention one wing withdrew because it was unable to get an anti-slavery plank included in the platform. It too prepared to endorse the Republican candidates.

In June the Republicans met in Philadelphia and adopted a strong free-soil platform. Denouncing the repeal of the Missouri Compromise, they asserted that Congress had the duty to prohibit slavery—"a relic of barbarism"—in the territories. Free-soil but not abolitionist, the platform did not condemn Kansas, or indeed the Midwestern states, for their policy of excluding free blacks. Many Republicans tacitly accepted the view that blacks could not be citizens. They aimed specifically to contain slavery where it already existed. Further, they made no effort to attract Southern votes, and they condemned the Ostend Manifesto as an imperialist design of

the Administration to expand slave territory into the Caribbean (see p. 289). Former Whigs in the party applauded the call for internal improvements, particularly for federal aid to the construction of a Pacific railroad.

The old Whigs' preference for popular but otherwise weak presidential candidates was also reflected in the choice of John C. Frémont. Though thoroughly antislavery, the "Pathfinder of the West" had had no more political experience than such successful Whig candidates of the past as William Henry Harrison and Zachary Taylor. Frémont added to a soldier's glory the fame of an explorer, and he knew how to dramatize himself. Flamboyant and self-assured, he was married to Jesse Benton, the daughter of Thomas Hart Benton, who shared the personality traits of her husband; Frémont and his wife were an exceptionally "available" political couple. One of Frémont's detractors said of him that he had every qualification of genius except talent.

The Democrats nominated James Buchanan, one of the architects of the Ostend Manifesto. An amiable but mediocre Pennsylvanian, he enjoyed the inestimable advantage of having been minister to the Court of St. James while troubles in Kansas were ruining the chances of abler men. Recognizing the destructive potential of the slavery question, the Democratic platform denied the authority of Congress to legislate on slavery in the territories and avoided the question of whether the population of a territory could exclude slavery before achieving statehood. The Democrats might well have lost to the Republicans had they been more explicit on this latter point, which raised the fine question of just when the people would become sovereign under the Democratic formula of popular sovereignty. That was what the fighting was about in Kansas. The platform also endorsed the Ostend Manifesto, which voiced a continuing belief that expansion would shore up the declining representation of the slave states in Congress.

Buchanan won the election handily with 174 electoral votes against 114 for Frémont;

Millard Fillmore, the candidate of the marginal Whigs and Know-Nothings, got only the 8 votes of Maryland. In the popular vote, however, Buchanan had only 45 percent of the total. Without the South he would have lost the election, for Frémont carried all but five of the free states. Without even a single vote from the South, Frémont could have won had he been able to carry Pennsylvania and either Illinois or Indiana. If the Democrats could not either resolve or bury the slavery issue, they would go the way of the Whigs and the Know-Nothings, and they knew it.

The house divided

The Dred Scott decision. During the campaign the Democrats had charged that the Republicans were a sectional party devoted to a single issue: the exclusion of slavery from the territories. Once reelected, the Democrats hoped to deprive their opponents of that issue and save their party. In his inaugural address, James Buchanan referred to a momentous case then pending before the Supreme Court that would settle the question of slavery in the territories. He urged the public to accept the verdict, whatever it might be, as final. Actually, Buchanan already knew that Southern Democrats would be pleased with the Supreme Court decision in the case of Dred Scott.

Dred Scott was a black man, once the property of John Emerson, an army doctor who had bought him as a slave in Missouri and had then taken him into Illinois, a free state, and from there into Wisconsin Territory, north of the 36°30′ line of the Missouri Compromise. After Dr. Emerson died, Scott sued in the state courts of Missouri for his freedom, on the grounds that he had lived in free territory. He won his case, but the decision was reversed on appeal. Meantime, Mrs. Emerson remarried, and under Missouri law, the executor of her estate—in this case, her brother John Sanford—could dispose of her property on behalf of the Emersons' daughter. Sanford was a citizen of New York, which gave Scott's lawyers the right to present his case in the federal courts, because Scott, if free, could claim to be a citizen of a different state from Sanford.

The Supreme Court faced two central questions: Did Dred Scott have a right to bring his case into the federal courts? This was another

way of asking whether a Negro, even a free Negro, could be a citizen of the United States. Free blacks had been denied the right to enter claims to Western lands, and they had often been denied passports to travel abroad. Before ratification of the Fourteenth Amendment (1868), there was no constitutional definition of federal citizenship. The second main question for the Supreme Court was whether his sojourn in free territory had made Dred Scott a free man, and that question invited the Court to judge whether the Missouri Compromise of 1820 was constitutional.

Both questions were politically volatile, and the Court might have avoided them by following the formula already used in the Missouri courts: Scott's residence in free territory had not altered his slave status, because he had voluntarily returned to Missouri. The majority of the Supreme Court decided to undertake a broad decision, however, in part because they knew that the public had been expecting such a decision since 1850, and in part because three Justices were determined to get a decision on the Missouri Compromise. The Republican Justices, Benjamin R. Curtis and John McClean, who favored Scott's claim to freedom, would assume that the Missouri Compromise was constitutional, thus vindicating their party's position that Congress, not the people of the territories, had authority over slavery in the territories. Justice James Wayne of Georgia would argue that the compromise was unconstitutional because Congress was not empowered under the Constitution to decide on the question.

Although each Justice followed his own line of argument, the Court ruled six to three against Scott's claim to freedom. Five con-

Dred Scott: he lost his case

curred in the long, involved, but forceful opinion of Chief Justice Roger B. Taney of Maryland, who declared that Scott could not claim the rights of a United States citizen. Negroes, Taney pronounced, had been regarded for more than a century before the Constitution was adopted as "beings of an inferior order" with "no rights which any white man was bound to respect." That statement was not good history, as Justice Curtis pointed out in a brilliant dissent, for in four of the original states free blacks had been entitled to vote. If a majority of the Justices had followed Taney's exact line of reasoning, the Court might have avoided the second question— whether the Missouri Compromise was constitutional. But four Justices, while concurring that Scott's claim to freedom must be denied, did so for reasons different from Taney's and avoided a judgment on whether free blacks could be citizens. Therefore the Court had cast doubt on the first question without actually deciding it and then had proceeded to rule that the Missouri Compromise was unconstitutional. The Fifth Amendment, said Justice Taney, had denied Congress the right to deprive persons of property, and therefore the Missouri Compromise prohibiting slavery north of the 36°30' had violated the Constitution. Slaves were property, and neither Congress nor the territorial governments could deprive citizens of property "without due process of law."

Even mildly antislavery Northerners were outraged by the harshness of Justice Taney's language. Republicans believed that Justice Curtis' powerful dissent had come closer to the truth in pointing out that Congress was given the power to "make all needful rules" for the government of the territories. They observed that most of the Justices were Democrats, many appointed by Andrew Jackson, and that the Northern Democrat, Justice Robert C. Grier of Pennsylvania, who sided with the Southern Justices, was a political associate of President Buchanan. Many Northerners wondered if the Supreme Court and the President were not in conspiracy to extend slavery throughout the nation.

All Democrats had hoped for a decision on the slavery question that would cut the ground from under the Republicans, but Douglas and the Northern Democrats quickly saw that the Dred Scott decision had troublesome implications for their own policy of popular sovereignty. That Congress could not rule on slavery in the territories reinforced the Kansas-Nebraska Act, which they had sponsored; but, Taney had also ruled that the people of the territories could no more exclude slave property than Congress could. This seemed to mean that the people of a territory could take no action against slavery until after the territory was authorized to draw up a constitution in preparation for statehood. Many Northerners feared that slavery might be too deeply entrenched by that time to be abolished.

Lecompton vs. Topeka.

By ruling against the Missouri Compromise the Supreme Court had cast doubt on the constitutionality of popular sovereignty; events in Kansas were making popular sovereignty appear ridiculous in practice. Two governments were operating there: the proslavery government at Lecompton, which enjoyed legitimacy; and the free-state government at Topeka, which commanded the support of the majority of actual settlers. The United States House of Representatives had approved the Topeka constitution, but the Senate would not, claiming that its ratification in Kansas had been irregular.

Soon after his inauguration, President Buchanan sent a fourth governor, Robert Walker, to the territory. Buchanan hoped Walker would be able to get a constitution adopted through a fair vote, so that Kansas could be admitted to statehood. A native Pennsylvanian who had moved to Mississippi and had risen in the Democratic party of his adopted state, Walker seemed qualified to bring harmony to the troubled territory. He undoubtedly counted on strong support from Buchanan in his effort.

Walker knew that, although the free-soil settlers were three times more numerous than the proslavery settlers, the real abolitionists among the free-soilers were few. He hoped therefore to get the free-soilers to cooperate with the proslavery faction long enough to establish a legal government. To that end he called a constitutional convention. Because the proslavery legislature planned the election for delegates, however, the free-soilers refused to participate, claiming that the legislature had divided the voting districts unfairly. Even though they might have won, fraud notwithstanding, the free-soilers would not lend legitimacy to a rigged election. As a result the proslavery delegates dominated the constitutional convention, which met in the village of Lecompton. They drew up a document that attempted to please free-soilers and proslavery voters alike by prohibiting the entry of free blacks into Kansas. Otherwise the Lecompton constitution was thoroughly unsatisfactory to the free-soilers. It included a clause establishing slavery in Kansas, and voters were given the opportunity to vote for the constitution with that clause or without it. There was no way for a voter to indicate that he wanted to eliminate current as well as future slaveholding in the territory. Again the free-state men declined to vote, and the Lecompton constitution was overwhelmingly ratified with the slavery clause.

Though disappointed, Governor Walker continued his efforts to secure free-soil participation. He persuaded the free-soilers to vote in the elections for the territorial legislature, and they handily won a large majority. The new legislature then called a referendum on the Lecompton constitution for January 4, 1858. This time the proslavery men refused to vote, and the constitution was rejected.

One month after the referendum, and much against Governor Walker's wishes, President Buchanan asked Congress to admit Kansas to the Union under the Lecompton constitution. Walker had come east to persuade Buchanan to support him in his efforts to get a constitution acceptable to the majority of Kansas voters. Buchanan refused and Walker resigned. Buchanan had become increasingly submissive to his Cabinet, which was dominated by Southerners. Stephen Douglas was as annoyed with Buchanan as Walker was, for he recognized that the Northern Democrats would not tolerate another capitulation to the Southern wing of the party. Realizing that his own support came from Midwestern Democrats, Douglas defied the President and began building support in the Senate to oppose the Lecompton constitution. For this rebellion, Buchanan forced Douglas out of the chairmanship of the powerful Committee on the Territories.

Although Douglas lost his struggle in the Senate, the Republicans in the House of Representatives blocked the admission of Kansas under the Lecompton constitution. By a compromise, the constitution was then resubmitted to the voters of Kansas. It was again defeated, in August 1858, by a margin of nearly ten to one.

The question of admitting Kansas now receded, and only after much of the South had

Wall Street: the Panic of 1857

seceded did the territory achieve statehood. In the meantime, however, the rupture in the Democratic party had brought the country closer to war.

The Panic of 1857. The slavery question so thoroughly dominated politics that all other questions came to be seen in its light. In 1857 a sharp economic crisis promised briefly to distract the nation's attention from Kansas. Soon, however, sectional partisans, each trying to thrust the blame on the selfishness of the other, were discussing the panic by comparing the relative merits of the Northern and Southern economies.

The failure of the New York branch of the Ohio Life Insurance and Trust Company triggered the panic, and within months foreclosures, bankruptcies, and unemployment spread through the Northeast. The nation slipped into a severe depression from which it did not fully recover for over two years. The fundamental causes of the crisis were complex, deriving from excessive investments in railroads that promised no immediate profits and from a feverish land boom. Speculators invested in lands along the lines of railroads yet to be built, and Americans borrowed as never before to cover investments promising no immediate return. Eventually the flimsy credit institutions of the country collapsed under the strain. International conditions also contributed to the disaster. Basic to the new economic expansion, general throughout the industrialized countries of western Europe as well as the United States, was the discovery of rich new deposits of gold in California and

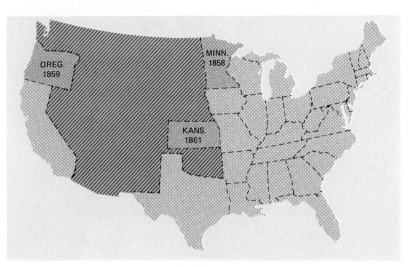

New states, 1858–61

Australia. This new wealth facilitated the flow of goods between nations, and America was becoming increasingly tied to international trade. During the 1850s the American West had benefited from the European demand for its agricultural products. The end of the Crimean War deflated this market, and Western farmers suffered accordingly. Only the market for cotton held firm.

Noticing that the South passed through the crisis relatively unscathed, the Northeast, where suffering was acute, sought explanations. Actually the reliance of the Northeast on an industrialized economy accounted for the greater hardship in that region, but many aggrieved manufacturers blamed the low tariff supported by Southern politicians for their troubles. Had not the "slave power" once more sacrificed the nation's well-being to its own sectional interests? Many believed so. Others, who regarded the revenue-only Tariff of 1857 as the result of a conspiracy, joined the Republican party. Responding to these charges with infuriating smugness, Southern leaders boasted that their economy was superior in that it produced a commodity that Europe had to have and rested on a better organization of labor—namely, slavery.

Although the panic was relatively brief, few have had a greater political impact. The West clamored for homestead legislation to secure financial relief, and the East saw hope in a protective tariff. The Republicans, making these issues their own, attracted many workingmen and farmers who were little moved by the slavery issue. The South was further alarmed for its safety in the Union.

The election of 1858. The Democrats, faced with a congressional election during a depression, tried to dress ranks. It was no use, for President Buchanan and Stephen Douglas had broken irreparably over the Lecompton constitution, and the President had removed Douglas' patronage and purged his followers. Buchanan thought that only stern measures would convince the South of the devotion of the Democratic party. Douglas, though badly handicapped in his fight to retain his Senate seat, knew that his constituents in Illinois would tolerate no further surrenders to Southern pressure on the territorial question. In criticizing the Lecompton constitution as a perversion of popular sovereignty, Douglas believed that he was fighting not only for his own political life but for the survival of the Democratic party, one of the few transsectional institutions left in the country. Only on the basis of popular sovereignty could the party survive.

Douglas' challenger for his Senate seat was Abraham Lincoln, a lawyer from Springfield, Illinois, who two years before had abandoned a long and loyal attachment to the Whig party to join the Republicans. Lincoln was forty-nine years old, largely but splendidly self-educated. A person of many moods but great steadiness of character, Lincoln had an air of melancholy that was broken from time to time by bursts of rough frontier humor. Though Easterners knew little about him, he was no newcomer to Illinois politics. Lincoln had served a term in Congress during the Mexican War, which he strenuously opposed, and in 1852 he had nearly been elected senator. A superb politician, he could surprise and amuse his audiences, establishing his points with homely analogies drawn from the common experiences of the frontier farmers he knew so well. In a time when politicians sometimes doubled as traveling entertainers, even Lincoln's remarkable appearance, though it amused sophisticates, was an asset. People remembered him for his tall frame, his shambling carriage, his plain features. But most of all he impressed his hearers with his sincerity and common sense. Lincoln was not an abolitionist—indeed, he was no extreme advocate of any point of view—but he was deeply convinced that slavery should spread no further. Congress, he believed, had the right and the responsibility to prohibit slavery in the territories. This was the main issue of the senatorial contest in Illinois in 1858, because Senator

I have stated upon former occasions ... what I understand to be the real issue in this controversy between Judge Douglas and myself. On the point of my wanting to make war between the Free and the Slave States, there has been no issue between us. So, too, when he assumes that I am in favor of introducing a perfect social and political equality between the white and black races. These are false issues.... The real issue in this controversy—the one pressing upon every mind—is the sentiment on the part of one class that looks upon the institution of slavery as a wrong, and of another class that does not look upon it as a wrong. The sentiment that contemplates the institution of slavery in this country as a wrong is the sentiment of the Republican party.... They look upon it as being a moral, social, and political wrong; and while they contemplate it as such, they nevertheless have due regard for ... the difficulties of getting rid of it in any satisfactory way and to all the constitutional obligations thrown about it. Yet ... they insist that it should, as far as may be, be treated as a wrong; and one of the methods of treating it as a wrong is to make provision that it shall grow no larger.

From Abraham Lincoln, Speech at Alton, Illinois, October 15, 1858.

We ought to extend to the negro race ... all the rights, all the privileges, and all the immunities which they can exercise consistently with the safety of society. Humanity requires that we should give them all these privileges; Christianity commands that we should extend those privileges to them. The question then arises, What are those privileges, and what is the nature and extent of them? My answer is, that that is a question which each State must answer for itself.... If the people of all the States will act on that great principle, and each State mind its own business, attend to its own affairs, take care of its own negroes, and not meddle with its neighbors, then there will be peace between the North and the South, the East and the West, throughout the whole Union.

Why can we not thus have peace?... The moment the North obtained the majority in the House and Senate by the admission of California, and could elect a President without the aid of Southern votes, that moment ambitious Northern men formed a scheme to excite the North against the South, and make the people be governed in their votes by geographical lines, thinking that the North, being the stronger section, would outvote the South, and consequently they, the leaders, would ride into office on a sectional hobby.

From Stephen A. Douglas, Speech at Alton, Illinois, October 15, 1858.

Douglas still spoke for letting the people decide.

The Freeport Doctrine. In a famous series of debates held at various towns over the state, Lincoln and Douglas discussed the great question of their time. Douglas was badly handicapped by Chief Justice Taney's decision in the case of Dred Scott that slave property could be brought into the territories on the same basis as any other property. When were the people to decide whether they wanted slavery? If a territory could not outlaw slavery until it had become a state, it might then be too late to exclude it. "Letting the people decide" was no longer so appealing a compromise to Northern Democrats as it had once been.

At Freeport, Illinois, Lincoln asked Douglas whether there was any lawful way for the inhabitants of a territory to exclude slavery before achieving statehood. Lincoln was trying to make Douglas state frankly how badly the Dred Scott decision had damaged popular sovereignty. Douglas' answer was not new. People had heard it before, from other Democrats, but for a presidential aspirant it was hazardous. Douglas pointed out that slavery was by its nature an institution that would dissolve unless protected by a slave code and by local police enforcement. Without these defenses slavery could not, Douglas insisted, last a day or even an hour. Therefore the opponents of slavery in a territory simply had to see to it that every effort to enact a slave code was defeated. That answer satisfied pragmatic Northern Democrats, but it antagonized the South. It did no more than state what most thoughtful Southern Democrats knew to be true, especially after the Kansas experience, but it seemed to render meaningless the South's constitutional triumph in the Dred Scott decision. Even the moral victory the decision represented was sullied. Douglas was saying, after all, that slavery couldn't be taken anywhere it wasn't wanted, and his opponents in the South would not forget.

In the campaign Lincoln and Douglas outlined their positions on slavery and race with painful frankness. Resorting to racist demagoguery, Douglas attempted to smear Lincoln as an abolitionist in areas where blacks were disliked and distrusted. Lincoln vigorously denied those charges, saying he did not believe in social or political equality and maintaining the white-supremacy argument. He nevertheless held stubbornly to his belief that slavery was a social wrong that should be contained. Throughout their many debates Douglas evinced an insensitivity to the moral issue that slavery had become for an increasing number of Northern voters.

Lincoln did not win Douglas' seat in the Senate, nor did his party win control of the Senate. Lincoln ran well, however, and the Republicans came out of the election with more seats in the House of Representatives than any other party. If they could win the cooperation of a handful of Know-Nothings, the Republicans would have a majority. Most significantly, the contest had established the reputation of Abraham Lincoln. He had given the principles of the Republican party their most forceful statement, and he had expressed the people's growing concern over the cost of slavery when he likened the nation to "a house divided." "I believe this government cannot endure permanently half *slave*

and half *free*," he told the Republicans at their state convention, adding that he did not expect it to be divided. Douglas and Lincoln assumed positions in 1858 from which neither would retreat in 1860 as they faced each other in the contest for the Presidency of the United States.

By that time several crises had enhanced the validity of Lincoln's position that slavery was a moral wrong that must be contained. Those same crises had made Douglas' position, that slavery concerned only those who had a direct interest in it, seem irrelevant in the South and inadequate to the demands of the times in the North.

Personal liberty laws. As the South lost power in Congress, its leaders, as if insisting on a symbolic recompense, stridently demanded that the Fugitive Slave Law be systematically implemented. Numbers of slaves were returned, but every application of the law in the North aroused more people to the cruelty of slavery. Many citizens helped supposed fugitives to escape. More offensive to the South than those individual actions were the personal liberty laws passed in Northern states to impede the enforcement of the Fugitive Slave Law. By reinforcing the rights of alleged slaves to proper legal defense, and by making illegal the use of state and local police and jails to detain them, angry state legislatures made "slave-catching" a difficult business. The South charged that the personal liberty laws were unconstitutional. In 1859 the Supreme Court endorsed the Southern view.

Early in 1859 tension mounted higher. A Southern commercial convention meeting in Vicksburg in May called for the reopening of the Atlantic slave trade. If Southerners could voice such ideas in the middle of the nineteenth century, then slavery, many Northerners thought, had driven the South into collective madness. While the leading fire-eaters were campaigning ever more openly for secession, voters in Kansas went to the polls and ratified a constitution prohibiting slavery. Congress was not yet ready to act on the admission of Kansas to statehood, but it was evident that Kansas would soon become the nineteenth free state instead of the sixteenth slave state, which meant further decline in Southern representation in the Senate. Even worse fears were soon to surface.

From debate to violence

Harper's Ferry. Ten days after the Kansas voters ratified the free-state constitution, John Brown carried his war on slavery into the South. After the Pottawatomie killings and the guerrilla fighting of the summer of 1856, Brown had escaped authorities and dropped from public view. He had not been idle. With the help of Gerrit Smith, a wealthy abolitionist from upstate New York, Brown secured the backing of a distinguished group of intellectual and financial leaders in the Boston area who called themselves the "Secret Six." With their help, Brown diverted contributions made to the relief of free-soil Kansas settlers to the purchase of guns and ammunition. On the night of October 16, 1859, he led a band of eighteen men from Maryland into Virginia, where he seized hostages among the citizens and occupied the fire-engine house of the federal arsenal at Harper's Ferry. He held the engine house for two days, in a state of siege, before surrendering to a small force of United States marines sent out from Washington under the command of Colonel Robert E. Lee. With many of his men killed and others wounded, John Brown waited quietly in the Charles Town jail, resisting all talk of efforts to rescue him and preparing his own defense.

Although Brown explicitly denied the charge at his trial, evidence indicates that he had intended to raise a slave insurrection. Once in Ralph Waldo Emerson's hearing he had stated that it would be better that every man, woman, and child then living should meet violent death than that "one word" of the Golden Rule or the Declaration of Independence "should be violated in this country." Emerson reflected comfortably that the old man must have been speaking "transcendentally," but he was wrong. Brown believed himself to be God's avenger. Although Brown was sincere in his friendship for the oppressed slave, religious fanaticism best explains his actions from Pottawatomie Creek to Harper's Ferry. Whether that fanaticism extended to insanity, as his friends and relatives hoped to show in presenting his defense, is impossible to judge at this distance. They collected many affidavits attesting to widespread derangement among Brown's close relatives. Their obvious interest in saving Brown from execution cast suspicion on their efforts, however, and the victim himself would have none of that defense.

John Brown knew how to die. From the jail in Charles Town his words stirred many souls who had been impervious to abolitionist arguments. Brown's final appeal to the court expressed a great truth even though it obscured his real intentions: he reminded his hearers that what he had done would have been thought worthy of reward rather than punishment had it been done "in behalf of the rich, the powerful, the so-called great. . . ." In his captivity Brown was magnanimous and cheerful, an altogether credible martyr. The parallels between the crucifixion of Christ and the execution of John Brown were abundant, not least in the conspicuous absence of the Secret Six, who with one exception agreed that Brown could best serve the cause of abolition by dying. In the end John Brown was a better prophet than revolutionary leader. He said on December 2, the day he died, that "the crimes of this guilty land: will never be purged *away:* but with Blood."

Reactions North and South. Although most sober-minded Northerners deplored Brown's actions, Southerners were unaware of that fact. They only heard the tolling bells and memorial services held throughout the North as numbers of citizens (many of them prominent) mourned a man who had tried to free the slaves and who had now become a martyr to the cause of freedom. To most Southerners Brown was no more than a madman who had intended to visit death and destruction upon guilty and innocent alike. The discovery of maps among his belongings showing likely points of assault deep in the southern Appalachians brought Virginia's fears into the Lower South. Edmund Ruffin, a vociferous Virginia fire-eater, distributed among Southern governors nine hundred captured pikes that Brown had had forged from bowie knives and iron staves. It required no paranoid imaginings to see that those crude but quiet weapons were better designed for midnight assassination than for a frontal assault against firearms. In many communities hysteria vented itself in attacks on persons who held unorthodox opinions on slavery. This outburst of hatred showed that the region deeply distrusted outsiders and that there lurked an abiding fear of what the slaves might do if a realistic possibility of freedom presented itself.

John Brown: he thought he was God's avenger

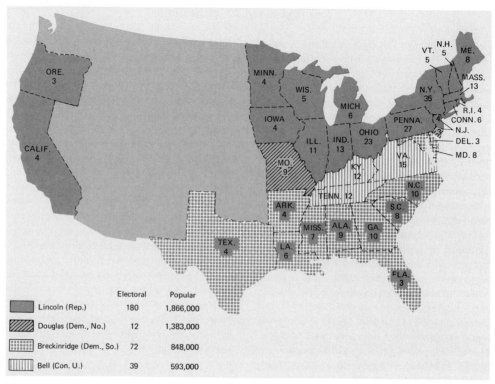

	Electoral	Popular
Lincoln (Rep.)	180	1,866,000
Douglas (Dem., No.)	12	1,383,000
Breckinridge (Dem., So.)	72	848,000
Bell (Con. U.)	39	593,000

The election of 1860

The contest for the Speakership. On the Monday following Brown's execution, Congress convened and set about the routine business of electing a Speaker of the House. This time the task required two months of extravagant recrimination and unprecedented verbal abuse. By combining with Southern Know-Nothings and Whigs, the Democrats prevented the nomination of the Republican choice, John Sherman of Ohio, but they could not command enough votes to elect a Democrat. Sherman would have made an excellent Speaker, but Democrats strenuously opposed him because he had endorsed a controversial book about the South and slavery. Hinton Rowan Helper, the author of *The Impending Crisis of the South,* was a white man from North Carolina who charged that slavery was ruining the nonslaveholders, socially and economically. Helper likened slaveholding to throwing strychnine into a public well, so dangerous was it to the safety of white people. Though he called for immediate emancipation, Helper was not a friend of the blacks. Like many other Republicans, he recommended that emancipated slaves be exported from the country. His book touched a sensitive Southern problem, the economic impotence of non-

slaveholders in a society dominated by the plantation system and by slave masters.

Although Sherman had not seen *The Impending Crisis* after its completion, he had carelessly allowed his name to be used in promoting it after glancing casually at the table of contents. Name-calling was not new in Congress, but there was no humor and no style or eloquence in the verbal duels that followed. Radical Southerners, insinuating that men like John Sherman had provoked Harper's Ferry, angrily renewed their threats to secede from the Union. The Republicans, though more restrained than the Democrats, goaded their opponents from the South by sneering at the threats of secession and by declaring that they would no longer be bluffed by such talk. In this emotionally charged atmosphere, members of Congress began to carry pistols to the stormy sessions. Never able to garner the votes needed to elect Sherman as Speaker, the Republicans at last fell upon a man of inferior talents, John Pennington of New Jersey, who had the necessary Know-Nothing support. In the troubles that lay ahead, the nation might well have used a man of John Sherman's ability as Speaker.

In early February, on the day after Pennington became Speaker of the House, Jefferson Davis introduced in the Senate a series of resolutions that defined the position of extreme Southern Democrats. Davis demanded a national slave code for the protection of slave property in the territories and a congressional declaration that personal liberty laws and attacks on slavery were unconstitutional. After many stormy sessions these resolutions were eventually passed on May 24, nearly four months later. Davis' purpose was to test the Northern Democrats' support of the South and to set forth the program Southern Democrats would insist on in return for party loyalty. Well before Davis' resolutions were adopted, however, the Democrats had tried and failed to nominate a presidential candidate. Their party was destroyed by the principles of Davis' resolutions.

The election of 1860. The Democrats who met in Charleston in April were divided even before they arrived. Senator Douglas was the favorite of most of the Northern Democrats. President Buchanan still opposed him, however, and Administration supporters at the convention found allies among the Southern fire-eaters—men like William Lowndes Yancey—who had come to Charleston to find an excuse for secession. For this reason they demanded the impossible: a party platform calling for federal protection of slavery in the territories. Unfortunately for Douglas the convention took up the platform before nominating a candidate. The majority of the platform committee then brought in a document very like the Davis resolutions that were being debated in the Senate. Since Douglas clearly could not run on such a platform, his supporters had no choice but to fight for the adoption of a minority report. On grounds of principle and politics, they could not recede from the popular-sovereignty position. As H. B. Payne of Ohio warned, if the majority report was adopted, "you cannot expect one Northern electoral vote, or one sympathizing member of Congress from the free states." Without these men the Democrats could not win the Presidency.

After several days of struggle, a compromise was adopted in a vote boycotted by the Southern delegates. After a solemn speech by Yancey in which he detailed Southern grievances, the delegates of the Lower South withdrew. The remaining delegates defeated an

effort to nominate Douglas and at last decided to go home and hold another convention in Baltimore in June.

Seizing on the opportunity presented by the split among Democrats, the Republicans convened in Chicago. On May 18, to a wild ovation, they nominated Abraham Lincoln, the rail-splitter of Sangamon County. Hannibal Hamlin of Maine was nominated as the vice-presidential candidate. Lincoln held firmly to the basic Republican principle that slavery must be contained, but his nomination over William H. Seward represented a victory for the more restrained statement of that principle. Seward's exposure during his career as Senator had given wide circulation to his views on the "irrepressible conflict" between slavery and freedom and to his advocacy of a "higher law" than the Constitution. But Lincoln was nominated largely because he had established himself as a national figure, even winning popularity in Seward's own state of New York. In February Lincoln had come east to speak at Cooper Union in New York City. There he had outlined with powerful simplicity the historical basis for Congress' right to exclude slavery from the territories. "There is a judgment and a feeling against slavery in this nation, which [has] cast at least a million and a half of votes." Destroying Republicans would not destroy that feeling. To striking workers in New England, he had spoken of the rights of free labor, saying he wished all men could quit work when they wished to quit. Lincoln also had a very practical political advantage over Seward. The former governor of New York, who had long fought the Know-Nothings of his state, could not hope to attract members of that party to the Republicans. And yet their votes were essential to victory, especially in Pennsylvania, a key state lost by the Republicans in 1856.

Lincoln campaigned on a platform broader than Frémont's had been. The platform adhered firmly to the basic Republican policy of containing slavery within the states where it existed, but it affirmed also the belief that it should not be disturbed there. It condemned John Brown's raid. The Republicans also gained by the addition of important economic issues. The Democrats, by frustrating Republican efforts to secure homestead legislation, the Pacific Railroad bill, and an elevation of the tariff, had alienated many voters who saw in those measures hope of economic recovery. The Republicans now built those issues into

Republican banner, 1860

The history of the ... Black Republican party of the North is a history of repeated injuries and usurpations, all having in direct object the establishment of absolute tyranny over the slave-holding States. And all without the smallest ... justification.... Every appeal and expostulation has only brought upon us renewed insults and augmented injuries. They have robbed us of our property ... they have set at naught the decrees of the Supreme Court, they have invaded our States and killed our citizens, they have declared their unalterable determination to exclude us altogether from the Territories, they have nullified the laws of Congress, and finally they have capped the mighty pyramid of unfraternal enormities by electing Abraham Lincoln ... on a platform and by a system which indicates nothing but the subjugation of the South and the complete ruin of her social, political and industrial institutions.

From the New Orleans *Daily Crescent,* November 13, 1860.

There never was such a set of arrogant and imperious rulers as the slave-driving captains of this Republic.... Such men cannot be created except by Slavery. It is the institution that makes them.... Of all men, they most need the discipline of reverses and the humiliation of defeat. It is their insolence of temper that forbids them to submit to being fairly beaten in a Presidential election. They will not take the position of a defeated party. They will rule or they will ruin.... They will remain in control of the Government, or they will drag it down about our ears, and bury all in a common destruction.

From J. S. Pike in the New York *Tribune,* January 17, 1861.

their platform. No longer could they be called the party of "one idea."

Halfway between the Democratic fiasco at Charleston and the Republican nomination of Lincoln in Chicago, the Constitutional Union party met in Baltimore. Here was an old party with a new name. Old border-state Whigs, known for their long service to the Union, hoped to head off secession by nominating John Bell of Tennessee, with Edward Everett of Massachusetts as his running mate. The Constitutional Union men declared for "the Constitution of the country, the union of the states, and the enforcement of the laws."

The Democrats, meeting in Baltimore in June, recognized their peril. They even saw the possibility of Southern secession if the Republicans won. Although Douglas would have withdrawn his candidacy in favor of a compromise, he would not retreat from popular sovereignty as the essential plank in the platform. Most Northern Democrats shared his conviction. The convention fell apart almost immediately over the question of accreditation. Bolters from the Charleston convention came to Baltimore and challenged the credentials of the more moderate delegations their states had sent in their stead. Deep South delegates again seceded to a separate convention, and the Democratic rump nominated Douglas to run with Herschel V. Johnson of Georgia. The Southern Democrats nominated John C. Breckinridge of Kentucky, with Joseph Lane of Oregon as their vice-presidential candidate. They called for federal protection of slavery in the territories.

The stage was set for a fateful four-way contest. Whether the nation would move toward war or peace depended on its outcome. The Republicans, capitalizing on their many youthful supporters, organized smart marching bands calling themselves the "Wide Awakes." These bands demonstrated vigorously throughout the North for Lincoln, singing, "Ain't you glad you joined the Republicans?" The campaigners themselves concentrated in each state on the economic issue of greatest concern there. Playing down the sectional question, they claimed that Southern Democrats were once again crying "wolf" with their threats of secession. Douglas knew better; he was the first presidential candidate to undertake a nationwide personal campaign. In the South he urged acceptance of popular sovereignty as the only possible way for the Democrats to save themselves and urged that the South not secede whatever the outcome of the election. He was in Selma, Alabama, when he learned that Lincoln had defeated him.

The Republicans won an overwhelming majority in the Electoral College. Concealed by that majority was a profound division of opinion in the country. Taking only 40 percent of the total ballots cast, the Republicans collected 180 electoral votes, as compared with only 12 for Douglas, 72 for Breckinridge, and 39 for Bell. In the popular vote Douglas won 1,382,713, no disgraceful showing compared with Lincoln's 1,865,593. The South knew that those figures rested on the great increase of population the Middle West had experienced since the last census. Clearly the die had been cast in the North, and the South's electoral votes had been only incidental to the result. With only a third of the total white population in the country, the states of the future Confederacy saw that decisions concerning slavery could now be made without them.

The secession of the Lower South.

Anticipating the outcome of the election, the South Carolina legislature had remained in session until the results were in and then called a state convention. On December 20 that convention, without a dissenting vote, passed an ordinance of secession. By February the entire Lower South had left the Union, and a convention of the seceded states met in Montgomery, Alabama, to form a new government. They called themselves the Confederate States of America.

The urge to secede had been growing steadily for many years, and the extremists who led the movement were seasoned politicians. In the crisis of 1860 such men as Robert Barnwell Rhett of South Carolina, Robert Toombs of Georgia, and even the soft-spoken fire-eater William Lowndes Yancey of Alabama seized the initiative over the Southern Unionists. Secession was very popular throughout the Lower South, and strongest wherever the plantation system and slavery were well developed. Unionism was strongest in the highlands, the upcountry, and the Upper South, where secession was held

to be impractical but not illegal. What the Upper South would do if forced to choose between remaining in the Union and denouncing the constitutional right to secede remained to be seen.

Failure of compromise.

The eight slaveholding states still within the Union were in a precarious situation. The election of a Republican President did not, they believed, require them to abandon the Union, and they distrusted the fire-eating leaders of secession. Yet any effort to coerce the Lower South would involve them; and if the Lower South were not coerced or persuaded to return, they would be left as a small minority in the depleted Union. A compromise that would restore peace and lead to the voluntary return of the seceding states was the best hope of the border-state leaders and of the Upper South generally.

On December 18, two days before South Carolina seceded, John J. Crittenden of Kentucky had introduced resolutions in the Senate that would have prohibited slavery north of the 36°30' line of the old Missouri Compromise and that would have recognized it south of that line, even to protecting it with a federal slave code. The compromise Crittenden proposed called for a series of constitutional amendments to secure those objects and one other: he asked for an "unamendable" amendment that would guarantee slavery forever. The Republicans could not accept those proposals, because they were unwilling to return to the Missouri Compromise. Although few Republicans really feared that slavery would take root in the arid Southwest, they knew that some Southerners wanted to acquire slave territory in the Caribbean. While maintaining a perilous silence himself, Lincoln, the President-elect, warned his followers privately: "Entertain no proposition for a compromise in regard to the *extension* of slavery. The instant you do, they have us under again; all our labor is lost, and sooner or later must be done over. . . . Have none of it. The tug has to come, and better now than later." When it was clear that the Senate would not accept his resolutions, the venerable Crittenden proposed as a last resort that they be offered as a referendum to the people of the country. The Republicans prevented that step. The congressional plans to achieve compromise had failed.

In February the Virginia General Assembly took up the effort for compromise by inviting the delegates of all the states to Washington to seek a solution, but with no better result. Many states boycotted the meeting, including all the Lower South states. In several weeks of discussion the delegates proposed constitutional amendments similar to Crittenden's, but they could not get them adopted by the Senate. Hope for compromise faded.

By this time the Confederate government was established in Montgomery, and the Southern states were seizing federal arsenals and forts. In his annual message, President Buchanan had spoken in conciliatory tones of Southern grievances. He had denied the right of South Carolina to secede but then had disclaimed his own authority to prevent her by force from doing so. Though rightly convinced that the secession threats were in earnest, Buchanan's delay in taking firm measures was a mistake. He acted for peaceful ends but inadvertently encouraged the South to believe that secession could be accomplished without war. Buchanan abruptly changed his course early in the year. When the state-rights Southern members of his Cabinet withdrew, he replaced them with staunch Union men. In his last message to Congress, on January 8, 1861, the President referred to the Union as "a sacred trust" and declared that he would collect federal revenues and protect government property throughout the United States. Even before his annual message he had sent an unarmed merchant ship to Charleston Harbor with supplies for a small force at Fort Sumter under the command of Major Robert Anderson. The South Carolinians fired on the *Star of the West* before she entered the harbor, driving her off. Short on provisions, Fort Sumter became a symbol, along with Fort Pickens in Florida, of all that was left of federal authority in the seceded states. What the new President would do was the question uppermost in the North, where indignation mounted daily.

Two new Presidents. Lincoln's arrival in Washington on February 23 to take the helm of government was in painful contrast with the brilliant reception that had been accorded the President-elect of the Confederacy one week earlier. Informed of an assassination plot, Lincoln came into the city ahead of schedule after a secret ride through the night, avoiding a stop in Baltimore, a city unfriendly to Republicans. President Davis, riding a crest of enthusiasm, brought to his office a long record of public service and an awareness of popular approval. William Lowndes Yancey, introducing him to the crowd in Montgomery, declared, "The hour and the man have met." The leaders of the South were old acquaintances of their President, whereas Lincoln was largely unknown to the men whose support he now urgently required. Unaware of Lincoln's matchless political skill, many Republicans thought he should take advice from men like Seward, his Secretary of State, whose leader-

Jefferson Davis: Confederate man of the hour

Mr. Haley and Tom jogged onward in their wagon, each, for a time, absorbed in his own reflections. Now, the reflections of two men sitting side by side are a curious thing,—seated on the same seat, having the same eyes, ears, hands and organs of all sorts, and having pass before their eyes the same objects,—it is wonderful what a variety we shall find in these same reflections!

As, for example, Mr. Haley: he thought first of Tom's length, and breadth, and height, and what he would sell for, if he was kept fat and in good case till he got him into market. He thought of how he should make out his gang; he thought of the respective market value of certain suppositious men and women and children who were to compose it, and other kindred topics of the business; then he thought of himself, and how humane he was, that whereas other men chained their "niggers" hand and foot both, he only put fetters on the feet, and left Tom the use of his hands, as long as he behaved well; and he sighed to think how ungrateful human nature was, so that there was even room to doubt whether Tom appreciated his mercies. He had been taken in so by "niggers" whom he had favored; but still he was astonished to consider how good natured he yet remained!

As to Tom, he was thinking over some words of an unfashionable old book, which kept running through his head again and again, as follows: "We have here no continuing city, but we seek one to come; wherefore God himself is not ashamed to be called our God; for he hath prepared for us a city." These words of an ancient volume, got up principally by "ignorant and unlearned men," have, through all time, kept up, somehow, a strange sort of power over the minds of poor, simple fellows, like Tom. They stir up the soul from its depths, and rouse, as with trumpet call, courage, energy, and enthusiasm, where before was only the blackness of despair.

From Harriet Beecher Stowe, *Uncle Tom's Cabin: or, Life among the Lowly,* 1852.

---

ship had been proved, or even Salmon P. Chase, Lincoln's new Secretary of the Treasury.

On the day of his inauguration, Lincoln suddenly dispelled the air of ineffectuality that had clung to him from the time of his inglorious arrival in Washington. He pledged that he would maintain the Union, that he would use his office "to hold, occupy, and possess property, and places belonging to the federal government." But he promised not to begin hostilities. The South must decide the "momentous issue of civil war." In a passionate appeal to the patriotism of old, Lincoln voiced his moving hope that "the mystic chords of memory . . . will yet swell the chorus of the Union, when again touched, as surely they will be, by the better angels of our nature." Though his speech was eloquent, and peaceful in intent, it was firm. As one historian has remarked, there was "a clank of metal" in it. The testing time was near.

Fort Sumter. On that same inauguration day, Lincoln learned for the first time that Major Anderson had nearly exhausted his supplies. Forced to choose in haste between surrendering the fort and sending supplies, Lincoln found himself with the initiative, despite his inauguration promise.

Lincoln's new Cabinet gave him advice that reflected the political past of its members. At first only Montgomery Blair, the new Postmaster General, and Salmon P. Chase, Secretary of the Treasury, favored sending supplies. Former Jacksonian Democrats, they undoubtedly remembered the old General's style of dealing with South Carolina in the nullification crisis (see p. 226). The counselors of caution were headed by Seward, who feared that forceful provisioning of Sumter would push the border states to secession. He had on his own authority promised Confederate commissioners in Washington that the government would not reinforce the garrison. Lincoln hesi-

A crest of enthusiasm: the inauguration of Jefferson Davis

Stars and bars above Sumter

without notice, unless of course South Carolina attacked first. He had shifted the decision to Jefferson Davis. Also anxious to avoid bloodshed, Davis instructed General P. G. T. Beauregard, in command in Charleston, to ask Major Anderson to state when he would evacuate the fort and to fire only if Anderson refused to set a time. Major Anderson replied, through three aides-de-camp Beauregard had sent to inquire, that he would leave Sumter by noon on April 15, "should I not receive prior to that time controlling instructions from my government or additional supplies." The aides-de-camp took action without reporting to Beauregard. At 4:30 on the morning of April 12, the Palmetto Guard of South Carolina opened fire on the fort. Forty hours of bombardment damaged Sumter badly; on April 13, with his ammunition gone, Anderson surrendered. His garrison left Charleston aboard the relief ships that had been powerless to assist during the engagement.

The Civil War had begun. It would be exactly four years before Anderson would again raise the United States flag, most ceremoniously, over Fort Sumter. But in April of 1861 no one could know how long the war would last or what toll in blood and treasure the conflict would exact.

tated briefly, but Seward's view was declining in the Cabinet. The President hit upon his own formula.

Lincoln informed Governor F. W. Pickens of South Carolina that he would try to provision Fort Sumter but that he would send no troops

Suggestions for reading

GENERAL

Probably the best introduction to the period covered in this chapter is the early part of J. G. Randall and David Donald, *The Civil War and Reconstruction* (2nd ed., 1961), a learned, judicious, and comprehensive work that is also valuable for its treatment of relevant bibliography. There is a longer account of the years 1854–61, distinguished for its clarity, scope, and the movement of its prose, in the latter part of Allan Nevins, *Ordeal of the Union,* 2 vols. (1947), and its sequel, *The Emergence of Lincoln,* 2 vols. (1950). Of equal importance for the period from 1856, and especially significant for its interpretation of politics and the political process, is R. F. Nichols, *The Disruption of American Democracy** (1948). There are other important points of view in A. O. Craven, *The Coming of the Civil War** (1942); H. H. Simms, *A Decade of Sectional Controversy* (1942); and D. L. Dumond, *Antislavery Origins of the Civil War in the United States* (1939). Bruce Catton, *The Coming Fury** (1961), is a spirited narrative.

THE KANSAS-NEBRASKA ACT AND ITS AFTERMATH

A major concern of the general works cited above, the Kansas-Nebraska Act, receives special analysis in J. C. Malin, *The Nebraska Question, 1852–1854* (1953), and in a splendid essay, R. F. Nichols, "The Kansas-Nebraska Act: A Century of Historiography," *Mississippi Valley Historical Review,* XLIII, 2 (1956). On the aftermath of the act, P. W. Gates, *Fifty Million Acres: Conflicts Over Kansas Land Policy, 1854–1890** (1954), is of major significance, as are two studies of John Brown: J. C. Malin, *John Brown and the Legend of Fifty-Six* (1942), and the essay on that disturbed figure in C. V. Woodward, *The Burden of Southern History** (1960). The best modern biography of John Brown is Stephen Oates, *To Purge This Land with Blood* (1970). Eric Foner, *Free Soil, Free Labor, Free Men** (1970), is the best single analysis of the ideas of

*Available in a paperback edition.

the Republican party. A. W. Crandall describes the birth and growth of the new party in *The Early History of the Republican Party, 1854–1856* (1930), while J. A. Isely, *Horace Greeley and the Republican Party, 1853–1861* (1947), and G. G. Van Deusen, *William Henry Seward* (1967), trace the development of Republicanism in New York State through the lives of individuals. The same is done for Massachusetts in M. B. Duberman, *Charles Francis Adams* (1961), and David Donald, *Charles Sumner and the Coming of the Civil War* (1960). The latter contains a brilliant analysis of Sumner and his controversial caning. On Stephen Douglas see Robert Johannsen, "Stephen A. Douglas and the South," *The Journal of Southern History,* XXXIII,i (1967); for a probing treatment of the Lincoln-Douglas debates see D. E. Fehrenbacher, *Prelude to Greatness: Lincoln in the 1850's** (1962). Allan Nevins' work mentioned above also includes an excellent treatment of Douglas, as do several biographies: Allen Johnson, *Stephen A. Douglas* (1908), G. F. Milton, *The Eve of Conflict: Stephen A. Douglas and the Needless War* (1934), and G. M. Capers, *Stephen A. Douglas, Defender of the Union* (1959).

THE COURT, THE ECONOMY, THE ELECTION

The classic studies of the Dred Scott case appear in two books by C. B. Swisher, *Roger B. Taney* (1935) and *American Constitutional Development* (1943), which can be supplemented with Vincent Hopkins, *Dred Scott's Case* (1951), and, with special profit, relevant sections of the books by Nevins and Nichols cited above. Nevins also handles well the subject of G. W. Van Vleck, *The Panic of 1857: An Analytical Study* (1943). Lincoln's entire life has been studied many times, and all the general studies cited above assign him many pages. The best one to start with is the superb biography by B. P. Thomas, *Abraham Lincoln* (1952). Fehrenbacher's work, mentioned above, is especially helpful for the 1850s. A. J. Beveridge, *Abraham Lincoln, 1809–1858,* 2 vols. (1928), remains useful, and R. H. Luthin, *The First Lincoln Campaign* (1944), has instructive depth. The one-volume edition of Carl Sandburg, *Abraham Lincoln: The Prairie Years* (1929), is a beautiful interpretation of Lincoln the man.

SECESSION AND WAR

Among the many accounts of secession, three of the best are Nevins, cited above; A. O. Craven, *The Growth of Southern Nationalism 1848–1861* (1953); and, R. A. Wooster, *The Secession Conventions of the South* (1962). Two older works are still admirable for their scope and form: D. L. Dumond, *The Secession Movement, 1860–1861* (1931), and U. B. Phillips, *The Course of the South to Secession** (1939). Of special significance is David Potter, *The South and the Sectional Conflict** (1969), the distillation of many years of study by one of the South's great historians. Of equal importance are two volumes of essays by C. V. Woodward, the one cited above and *American Counterpoint* (1971), which include many pieces of special interest to students of the South's movement toward independence. For an interpretation of the Southern position on the eve of the war, see Arthur Bestor, "State Sovereignty and Slavery: A Reinterpretation of Proslavery Constitutional Doctrine," *Journal of Illinois State Historical Society,* LIV (1961). There are two very important and somewhat conflicting analyses of the secession winter of 1860–61 in David Potter, *Lincoln and His Party in the Secession Crisis, 1860–61** (1942), and K. M. Stampp, *And the War Came: The North and the Secession Crisis, 1860–61** (1950). A lively account of Lincoln as President-elect is W. E. Baringer, *A House Dividing* (1945). On the Fort Sumter confrontation see R. N. Current, *Lincoln and the First Shot** (1963). For a spirited scholarly debate on the secession crisis, G. H. Knoles, ed., *The Crisis of the Union, 1860–61* (1965), is very good reading.

*Available in a paperback edition.

Civil war

14

The Civil War tested the strength and exposed the weakness of Americans as nothing before or since has done. It was a savage contest over conflicting ideals waged with weapons far more advanced than were the means of defense against them. The rest of the world, appalled at what Americans were doing to one another, watched with fascination this modern war of ideals and technology.

During the war the federal republic was transformed into a centralized, modern nation. The states were unable to enlist, arm, and pay the great armies engaged on countless battlefields over the four terrible years of combat. And where the states failed, the central government took over.

The war was a catalyst of social revolution as well. Lincoln and the Congress declared that the war would be fought only to preserve the Union, and that the "domestic institutions" of the states would not be disturbed.

Others knew better from the beginning. James L. Pettigru, a staunch Unionist lawyer from Charleston, remarked on learning that South Carolina had fired on the *Star of the West* that slavery would not last five years. Many abolitionists shared that understanding, as did many blacks, both freemen and slaves. Even the followers of William Lloyd Garrison dropped their traditional pacifism and joined in hearty support of a war they believed would inevitably grow into a war on slavery.

In 1860 only a few realized a new nationalism and emancipation were to be the results of the war, for only a few foresaw how long the war would last. Northern leaders underestimated the commitment of the Southerners to their new nation, while Southern leaders underestimated the Northerners' attachment to the old Union and their economic and human resources as well. Only four years of fighting would banish those illusions.

The struggle for the border states

The border states and the call to arms. To most of the nation the strength of those conflicting commitments would be revealed only in battle. But in the vast border region that stretched from Delaware on the Atlantic westward to Missouri, approximately a third of the country then organized into states, it was tested within days after the attack on Fort Sumter. On April 15, 1861, President Lincoln called on the state governors to provide him with seventy-five thousand militiamen for ninety days' service, in order to enforce the law where it was opposed "by combinations too powerful to be suppressed" by ordinary judicial processes. What part would the border states choose to play in the suppression of these "combinations"? Within each of the border states there were historical forces

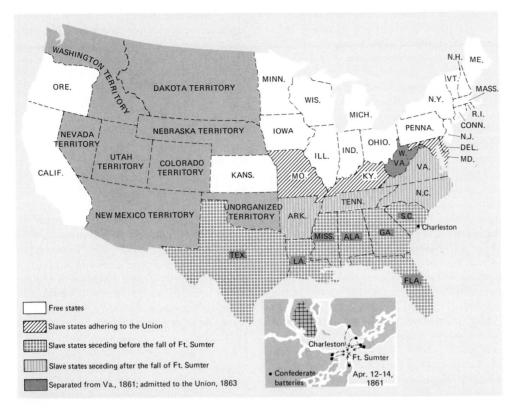

Free states

Slave states adhering to the Union

Slave states seceding before the fall of Ft. Sumter

Slave states seceding after the fall of Ft. Sumter

Separated from Va., 1861; admitted to the Union, 1863

Charleston

Ft. Sumter

Confederate batteries

Apr. 12–14, 1861

The alignment of states in 1861

working for union and those working for secession. The most concrete and formidable on the side of secession was slavery.

The border states had to make their decisions in a cross fire of patriotic enthusiasm that swept the North and the Confederacy. As the South took up arms, the Confederate government sent emissaries to the border states to encourage them to secede. The governors and the people of the North sprang to the defense of the flag that had been fired on at Charleston. Most Northerners of both parties agreed with Lincoln's view that secession was illegal. "The central idea pervading this struggle," Lincoln said, "is the necessity of proving that popular government is not an absurdity. We must settle this question now, whether, in a free government, the minority have the right to break up the government whenever they choose." Lincoln was to state that thought more eloquently two years later when he dedicated the Union cemetery on the battlefield at Gettysburg, Pennsylvania; it was his philosophical justification for the war.

For the moment, however, most people in the border states declined to take part in forcing the seceding states to return to the Union, and a second wave of secession followed. Virginia seceded on April 17, despite nearly unanimous opposition in the state's western counties. This reversal of an antisecessionist vote taken earlier influenced the decision of other border states; Arkansas, Tennessee, and North Carolina soon followed Virginia into the Confederacy. North Carolina based its action on the oldest American justification for war: the right of revolution. Only Delaware, of all the slave states, was safe for the Union.

Maryland, Missouri, and Kentucky. Everything now seemed to hang on the action of Maryland, Missouri, and Kentucky, which faltered between closely matched forces. Lincoln saved those states from secession by a combination of diplomacy and force that was more or less effective depending on how well he understood the Unionist leaders of the wavering states and on the kind of advice they gave him.

On April 19, only a week after Sumter, Maryland pitched directly into crisis. An angry mob in Baltimore, stirred up by pro-Confederate newspapers, attacked the troops of the Sixth Massachusetts Infantry as they changed trains on their way to Washington. Citizens and soldiers were killed in a riot. For more than a week the capital of the United States was set at defiance by a hostile city. On April 27, Lincoln instituted martial law in Baltimore, suspended the writ of habeas corpus, and jailed overt Confederate sympathizers. An ordinance of secession was then defeated in the Maryland legislature, partly because it convened in Frederick, in the northwest part of the state where Unionism was strong, and partly because the delegates from the southern counties en route to the session were impounded at Fort McHenry in Baltimore. Those delegates favored secession. In spite of the harsh measures taken, and in spite of the sympathy for the Confederacy that lived on in Maryland throughout the war, the state was stabilized for the Union within a few months.

Matters were not so well managed in Missouri, where secessionist sentiment was strong and where Unionist leaders precipitated a crisis before they could muster popular support. The secessionist governor, Claiborne Jackson, succeeded in getting a convention, but it refused to adopt an ordinance of secession. The state militia, which was under Governor Jackson's command, was stationed in St. Louis, the site of an important federal arsenal. Francis Blair, then a United States representative from Missouri, surmising that Jackson might attack the arsenal, persuaded Lincoln to let him create a "home guard" to defend the Union position in Missouri. Lincoln agreed, probably because Francis Blair's brother Montgomery, Lincoln's Postmaster General, had persuaded him that the step was essential. The home guard, composed largely of German immigrants, was thrown against Governor Jackson's militia by a hotheaded young captain in the regular army, Nathaniel Lyon. Caught by surprise, the militia surrendered without a fight. But the sight of the Germans marching the militiamen through the streets of St. Louis so enraged the populace that the home guard was mobbed, and many citizens and soldiers were killed in the ensuing melee. Those events alienated even staunch Unionists. Approximately thirty thousand Missourians ultimately fought for the South, and there were Missouri representatives in the Confederate Congress. Until the Battle of Pea Ridge in March 1862, Missouri was not reliable for the Union, and even afterward there

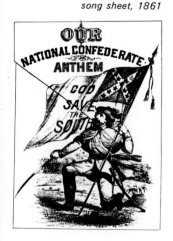

Confederate song sheet, 1861

was intermittent guerrilla warfare in the state. No state emerged from the war with deeper scars or more bitter memories. Greater patience would have permitted latent Union sentiment to develop among Missourians, and a painful heritage might have been avoided that made Reconstruction in Missouri in some respects more difficult than in the former Confederate states themselves.

Lincoln understood better the Unionists of his native Kentucky. Sympathies in the state were hopelessly divided, even within families. Still, the Unionist leaders managed, with Lincoln's help, to scotch secession in spite of a pro-Confederate governor supported by nearly half the citizenry. The Kentucky Unionists simply called for neutrality, knowing that they would be defeated if they asked for firm support of the Union and cooperation with the Union effort to raise an army. A petition demanding neutrality signed by fourteen thousand Kentucky women was presented to the legislature.

Lincoln kept the federal recruiting offices on the Ohio side of the Ohio River and even permitted neutral trade between Kentucky and the South to flourish through the summer. Had Kentucky not been handled so tactfully the Union cause would have suffered; the state was astride a major thoroughfare into the heartland of the Confederacy.

West Virginia. Lincoln capitalized immediately on the divided sympathies of Virginia. In the first months of the war he sent twenty thousand volunteers into western Virginia to secure the lines of the Baltimore & Ohio Railroad. Then, after the Confederates had been driven out of this transmontane region, the federal government began to encourage the separatist feelings of the people, who had long felt themselves neglected by the large landholders and slaveholders of the eastern counties. In November 1861 the western counties formed a government of their own and asked to be admitted to the Union as the state of West Virginia. Congress agreed in 1863. The urgency of securing a route from the East to the Ohio Valley quieted any qualms the members of Congress may have had about the legality of their unprecedented action.

Although Lincoln's border policy was not everywhere successful, he nevertheless retained for the Union by diplomacy or force the key states of Maryland, Missouri, and Kentucky. They were essential to military victory, for they provided easy communications about the periphery of the Confederacy. Moreover, control of those states exposed Tennessee, whose geographic frontier was especially vulnerable, to Union penetration.

A hard economic fact may have counted for even more than Lincoln's tact. By 1860 a dense network of railroads had already developed binding the Middle West, indeed all the states on the Ohio River, with the Northeast. Only a few lines led southward. But secessionist leaders assumed mistakenly that access to the mouth of the Mississippi River was still as important to the trade of the Middle West as ever. Trade still came down the river in seemingly undiminished volume, but the production of raw agricultural products had increased sharply in the 1850s on both sides of the Ohio, and with every year more of those products were rolling eastward on rails, especially over the Chesapeake & Ohio. Even the slave states that remained in the Union benefited from access to the Eastern markets. They soon discovered that being on the periphery of the Union was more profitable than being on the periphery of the Confederacy.

Two nations prepare for war

The two sides compared. When the war began, each section believed that its own peculiar advantages would bring swift victory. Victory had entirely different meanings for North and South, however, and different imperatives.

The North would have to invade, occupy, and hold hostile places and would have to destroy the armies of an enemy state, while the South would have to block such efforts until its enemies gave up trying. Northern confidence at the outset was based on a preponderance of people and on a superior economic potential for making the tools of war. The North also thought that Southern secession did not have wide popular support, that the majority of Southerners had been hustled out of the Union against their will by arrogant leaders. In that view, the Southern people would soon lose the will to fight.

Southerners, convinced that Northerners would not support a long and costly war to impose their will on an unoffending nation, thought that their independence would be recognized if they gave early evidence of stout determination to defend it in battle. In battle the South would have important advantages. Many of the country's high-ranking military officers were Southern-born, and most of them offered their services to their states. Moreover, the young men of the South could be counted on to fight valiantly in defense of their own soil.

The sober-minded leaders of the South were not relying on the imponderables of gifted military leadership or on the fighting qualities of Southern youth. They were relying instead on an economic advantage they believed to be paramount: the cotton export. As early as March 1858 James Henry Hammond of South Carolina had taunted Congress over the world's dependence on Southern cotton. "No power on earth dares make war upon it. Cotton *is* king." When the war came, the dogged confidence that prompted such bombast led Southerners into a diplomacy aimed at winning British recognition of the Confederacy. With recognition would come the financial aid and moral support that the rebellious colonies had received from France during the American Revolution. Surely France and England would see the advantages they would gain by Southern independence. The British, anticipating free trade in Southern ports, could take the middlemen's profits and the carrying trade from Northern businessmen and shippers. Southern enthusiasts could point out that they were fighting for two ideals characteristic of nineteenth-century revolutions: national determination and liberty. In their view of liberty they forgot the slaves, of course; but so did the Northerners, who denied repeatedly that emancipation was a goal of the war. What, asked the South, would deter Europe from recognizing the Confederacy?

Northern advantages. With cotton and the spirit of nationalism on their side, Southern leaders tended to discount the North's formidable economic advantages. Four-fifths of the nation's manufacturing was located in the North, two-thirds of its railroad track, three-quarters of the wealth produced. The share of the wealth produced by the South was largely agricultural, but even that did not mean that the South would be better able to feed her armies. The Middle West had supplied the

Confederate volunteers, 1861

South with much hay and grain before the war, while the South concentrated on producing staple crops for export. Except for rice and corn, the North and West produced far more grain than the South. Although some Southerners had endeavored to diversify their agricultural output, the war caught them frantically importing stocks of bacon and pork from the North. Moreover, the Northern population was more than three times as large as the white population of the South in 1860. Finally, Southerners were primarily an agricultural people, unaccustomed to factory work. On the eve of the war William T. Sherman had warned a Southern friend that ''. . . in all history no nation of mere agriculturalists ever made a successful war against mechanics. . . .'' If the South failed to win victory before the Northern economy could be fully geared to wartime production, its troubles would multiply and all would be lost. But few expected the war would last that long.

The South—a new nation.

To survive as a nation, the Confederacy had to create a viable new government with new institutions, and that government in turn had to persuade the people that it could dispense justice, secure internal peace, and fight a successful war for independence. The Constitution of the Confederate states imitated, in its main structure, the Constitution of 1787. Most Southerners respected the old Constitution and claimed that trouble had arisen not from basic flaws in it but from wrong interpretation of certain clauses. The signal departures of the new document from the old were designed to prevent such misinterpretation in the future. Those changes also showed that the new government was the product of a conservative revolt. Far from being reluctant to mention slavery, as the Founding Fathers had been, the Confederate constitution-makers, who met in February 1861 at Montgomery, gave the peculiar institution every conceivable guarantee short of the restoration of the Atlantic slave trade, which they forbade. The mobility of slave property within the Confederacy was assured through the right of sojourn and transit throughout the Confederacy. The Confederate Congress was obliged to secure the rights of slaveholders in the territories, and the dominant influence of slaveholders in the legislative branch was assured by the retention of the three-fifths ratio for congressional representation (see p. 127). The admission of

new states was made more difficult; protective tariffs and appropriations for internal improvements were made unconstitutional. The President had power to veto individual parts of an appropriations bill, and there was no general-welfare clause. The new Constitution plainly recognized the sovereignty of the states, though it avoided an explicit endorsement of the right of secession.

Jefferson Davis.

The Montgomery convention, composed largely of conservatives, not radical extremists, passed over fiery secessionists for the Presidency and chose Jefferson Davis of Mississippi instead. Although Davis represented the new West, where men could make a fortune and become gentlemen planters in a generation, and though he himself had been born of yeoman stock, he was an instinctive aristocrat. He was also sensitive to criticism, perhaps a lingering mark of his family's rapid rise in the world. Davis, the intellectual in politics, set about forming an ideal Cabinet in which all the states of the Confederacy would be represented. Though his intention was to convince people of his fairness, he managed to create a curious assembly of modest talents who were not always cast in the roles they knew best. His Cabinet members were constantly changing; there were fourteen appointees in six posts over four years, including six Secretaries of War. The ablest and most trusted of all Davis' advisers, Judah P. Benjamin, held three offices in turn—Attorney General, Secretary of War, and Secretary of State.

A responsible public servant, Davis consulted regularly with his Cabinet members and supported them when the press attacked them. Loyalty to subordinates was one of the military virtues Davis had learned at West Point. He had other military habits of mind that did not serve him so well. Regarding himself as a superior strategist, he seemed unable to delegate responsibility to subordinates, either generals or Cabinet officers. Busying himself with trivialities, he was often a tired chief executive. In time of peace he might have served his country better, but in war he demanded more of himself than any man could deliver. Further, he deprived his government of the open counsel of other leaders by interpreting opinions contrary to his own as personal affronts.

Davis' greatest problems arose from his inability to deal effectively with the Confederate Congress. His failure derived not from a lack of respect for Congress' privileges, but from a lack of tact in dealing with legislators and their greed for patronage. He gained little, therefore, by asking Congress to permit him to suspend the writ of habeas corpus, instead of suspending it on his own authority as Lincoln did, and by steadily respecting the constitutional rights of the states. When he asked Congress for measures that touched on state rights, however slightly, his enemies combined to frustrate him. The Confederacy never developed political parties in the usual sense, but there was an anti-Davis party in Congress strong enough to mount vicious attacks in the press and to enact thirty-nine bills he felt obliged to veto. Lincoln vetoed only three.

Davis' opposition centered in the diminutive figure of Alexander H. Stephens, the Vice President, who had abandoned a career as a staunch Unionist to become a reluctant secessionist. Stephens, brilliant and acerb, finding that his talents were not absorbed by his weak office, turned them to obstructionism. It was ironic that the alleged violation of state rights, the ostensible philosophy of the secession, should have become the most potent argument of Stephens and his adherents in Congress in their running attack on the Davis Administration.

Had Davis understood the skillful deployment of patronage as well as Lincoln did, he too might have divided his enemies and developed support in Congress. Lacking it, only popularity with the people could have helped him. This, too, escaped him. To those who knew him well he was not a cold man, but he could not convey his love of country to the people of the Confederacy. "A crippling shyness . . . banked his passion," wrote one historian, "and left him forever a strangely muffled man."

The South prepares for war.
Raising and maintaining the armies required by a modern war imposed grave pressures on the Confederacy's political philosophy of state rights, local liberties, and restraints on central authority. The Conscription Act of 1862, which drafted white men between eighteen and thirty-five for three years' service, passed the Confederate Congress by a substantial majority only because it was regarded as essential to victory. The draft age was subsequently extended to forty-five, and eventually, as the manpower shortage became acute, all males between seventeen and fifty were subject to the draft. Powerful voices spoke out against conscription as a violation of personal freedom, and the inequitable terms of the act fed hostility to the draft as the war went on. Alterations and expansions of the law did not much improve it or placate its critics. The poor found it unjust that a man who could pay the price could send a substitute, and the long list of exemptions made it easy for all but the poorest and least powerful to avoid service altogether. The most demoralizing provision exempted from the draft one white man on a plantation that had twenty or more slaves. Though designed to defend the nation against insurrection and to ensure a steady supply of food, this exemption stirred up latent class antagonisms among whites. Actually very few men were exempted under its terms, but it came to be known among the common people as "the twenty-nigger law." Many a young soldier, deciding against "a rich man's war and a poor man's fight," deserted.

Probably three hundred thousand men, just under a third of all the men who served in the Confederate armies, joined because of the Conscription Act. Some of them were drafted, but many volunteered in order to avoid the onus of being drafted. The draft would have been more effective had it not been for the obstructionism of several governors who made a fetish of state rights. Georgia's Governor Joseph E. Brown, for one, enrolled ten thousand men in the state militia before they could be drafted, exempted from conscription large numbers of civil servants, and insisted that Georgia troops be officered by Georgians.

Despite the resistance of state righters, the armies of the Confederacy increased in size until the summer of 1863, when on the eve of the Gettysburg campaign 261,000 men were reported ready for action. Thereafter the Southern armies dwindled slowly, for there was no way of replacing casualties. To make matters worse, the Northern armies grew steadily until the end of the war, when they had a three-to-one advantage.

An enormous aid to the North was the quickening of immigration during the last two years of the war. New arrivals received strong inducements to enlist. The enrollment of black soldiers from 1863 on also contributed to the manpower of the Northern armies. The South consistently rejected this means of raising troops until the last days of the war, when

Alexander Stephens: brilliant and acerb

provision was made for a draft "irrespective of color." That law stipulated, however, that emancipation would follow military service only with the approval of the slave's master and the state legislature.

Financing the war exposed the weakness of the state-rights philosophy as surely as had the recruitment process. Beginning in 1861 without a treasury, the Confederate government promptly passed a direct tax on property. The tax could be paid by the states themselves, however, and most state governments chose to do so by issuing and selling their own bonds. The tax produced a poor return of $18 million. Further, it did not reach individual property-holders, where it would have damped inflationary spending. Meanwhile the Confederate government was also issuing bonds.

Such practices would not have been crippling in a short war, but continual borrowing in preference to taxing boosted inflation to a perilous level by late 1863. The poor, whose income lagged behind the cost of food and other necessities, steadily lost enthusiasm for the war. The primary cause of inflation was the flood of paper money and treasury notes issued by the Confederate government, by individual states, and even by cities to pay interest on bonds, pay troops, and purchase needed supplies. As prices rose, flour sold at $300 per barrel and men's shoes at $125 a pair. The Confederate government was hardly more timid or cowardly about taxation than other new governments have been, and somehow it managed to feed and transport enormous armies against tremendous odds for four years. Still, the misery inflation engendered eroded the South's will to resist.

One effort to bypass the inflationary spiral and still feed the armies was the "tax in kind," which allowed military authorities to requisition foodstuff directly from the farmers and to pay them a price fixed by the government. Since this price usually was well below the open-market price, and since the practice was widely abused by officers making requisitions, farmers contrived to evade the tax.

Although many Southerners, perhaps half, had been reluctant to secede from the Union, they went to war with high morale. Believing secession constitutional even while questioning its wisdom, most were unified behind a war for independence after the North determined to put down secession as rebellion. Their ultimate disillusionment came, not

through a change of heart, but almost entirely through the failure of their economy to support a long war against a burgeoning industrial power.

The North prepares for war. Abraham Lincoln, confident of his own judgment, appointed what was probably the ablest Cabinet ever assembled by any President. In making his selections he considered talent, but he was especially aware of the need to balance factions and to repay political debts. He knew he would have to make the members of his Cabinet function as a unit in a time of national peril. Few Presidents have understood the use of patronage as well as Lincoln did. Few have needed to, for the Republicans were a new party that had never been obliged to merge discrete factions into a united administration under the public gaze.

As his Secretary of State, Lincoln named William Seward, a prominent former Whig whom the Republicans had regarded as too radical on the slavery issue to qualify as their presidential nominee in 1860; as a Cabinet member, however, Seward advised caution in interfering with slavery. For his Secretary of the Treasury, Lincoln picked Salmon P. Chase, a radical former Democrat whose views on slavery had propelled him into the Republican party. Both Seward and Chase had served as state governors—and both had presidential ambitions. Lincoln recognized their ability, but he knew too that they brought to his Cabinet the potential for discord. Chase, convinced that he would have made a better chief executive than Lincoln, never became an altogether selfless follower of the President. Seward, after vainly trying to maneuver Lincoln into a foreign war that he believed would bring the South back to the old flag, surrendered to Lincoln's leadership and became an excellent subordinate. He was an able if splenetic Secretary of State.

To pay off a campaign debt, Lincoln installed Simon Cameron as Secretary of War. That was an error. Cameron proved inept and was even suspected of venality. Lincoln replaced him in 1862 with the eccentric and brilliant Edwin M. Stanton, who became one of the most dedicated of Lincoln's Cabinet members. Stanton, a hard-working wizard, deserved much of the credit for the eventual victory of Northern arms. Gideon Welles of Connecticut was Secretary of the Navy; Edward Bates, whom some Republicans had

Bounties attracted the poor

pushed as a presidential candidate, was Attorney General; and Montgomery Blair of Maryland was Postmaster General.

Despite their disputes and personal animosities, Lincoln elicited the best from his talented advisers. He averted several crises, usually involving Chase and Seward. But the only major shake-up occurred in 1864, when Lincoln at last accepted Chase's resignation and replaced him with William Pitt Fessenden. Chase became Chief Justice of the Supreme Court of the United States. To soothe Chase's radical supporters, Lincoln also permitted Montgomery Blair, a conservative on slavery and emancipation, to resign. The President's skill in balancing his Cabinet and in seeing that the patronage was distributed to the satisfaction of senators and congressmen was essential to the development of the Republican party and to the teamwork that won the war.

Raising the armies, putting the economy on a war footing, and determining how to pay for the war were the Administration's first tasks. There was some bungling at first because of the illusion that the war would be over soon. Fortunately for the Union, ample resources allowed time for trial and error, and many of the worst difficulties were resolved during the first summer and fall. Though clearly stronger than the South in human and material resources, the North at first squandered that advantage in confusion, dissension, delay, and greed. Inadequate organization complicated the problems of the senior military officers, who were on the whole second-rate men. Before the war ended the Union had found and developed great commanders— Grant, Thomas, Sheridan, and Sherman—but in the beginning the military leaders frittered away the energies of powerful armies in sorry and haphazard campaigns. Even sorrier was the behavior of war-profiteers who overcharged the government for shoddy goods: blankets that disintegrated in the rain, unwholesome meat, inferior rifles, and ships with leaky bottoms.

The first year of the war was marked by conflicts of authority and initiative between the state governors and the Administration in Washington. When Lincoln called for the first seventy-five thousand militiamen to come to the defense of the capital, Northern governors threw themselves with energetic confusion into their traditional role of raising volunteers. The governor of Ohio sent so many troops to

Washington so fast that he lost count. Raising troops in the first flush of patriotic enthusiasm was not dificult, but soon the governors had problems with recruiting. At first the War Department in Washington undertook to reimburse the governors for their expenses in equipping the soldiers, but this scheme, inefficient and subject to graft, had to be abandoned. With the best will in the world, the state governments were unable to cope with the demands of the war, and one by one their traditional responsibilities devolved upon the national Administration. The result was a shift of power away from the states, the very shift that the Confederate states, under the same pressures, resisted so stubbornly.

Realizing sooner than most of his advisers that the Union was in for a long war and that the seventy-five thousand volunteers who reported in April for three months' service would not suffice, Lincoln stretched his constitutional authority as commander in chief. He authorized an increase in the size of the regular army, a power reserved to Congress under the Constitution, and called for forty-two thousand volunteers for three years in the national service. When Congress reconvened in July, the President asked for indemnification for the action he had taken. Congress granted it promptly. By establishing that large volunteer armies would be enlisted for long-term service, Lincoln averted the immediate problem of being left without troops once the three-month militiamen had gone home.

The overwhelming majority of soldiers who served in the Union armies were volunteers encouraged to enlist by generous bounties paid by the federal government, state governments, and local communities. Those bounties were attractive to the poor and the unemployed, especially during the first year of the war. But after the military setbacks of 1862 even generous bounties failed to attract enough volunteers, and in March 1863 the United States passed the first national draft law. Men between twenty and forty-five were subject to conscription for three years' service. There were a few occupational exemptions, and men who were the sole support of dependent families were not obliged to serve. The most detested feature of the law permitted a man to avoid service by hiring a substitute to serve in his stead or by paying a flat fee of $300 to the government. This class legislation was especially resented in areas where the war was unpopular. In September 1863,

He. "Ah! Dearest Addie! I've succeeded. I've got a substitute!"
She. "Have you? What a curious coincidence! And *I* have found one for YOU!"

rioters protesting the draft law disrupted New York City for days.

Although only forty-six thousand men were actually drafted under the Conscription Act, the measure promoted volunteer enlistments, especially in communities anxious to avoid imposing the draft on a resentful populace. Each state was divided into enrollment districts and was assigned a certain draft quota from time to time. If those districts could provide their quota in volunteers, they could avoid the conscription process and the troubles Governor Seymour of New York had encountered. In any case, soldiers preferred the status of volunteer to that of conscript, especially if they could pocket a good bounty. State governors and local authorities, eager to avoid recourse to the draft machinery, borrowed money to raise bounties as high as necessary to fill their quotas. In parts of Illinois the total bounty came to more than $1,000, and in New York a volunteer could get $375 over and above the federal bounty, which was $300 in 1864. Those fat sums led to an abuse known as "bounty-jumping," whereby a man would enlist, desert, reenlist in another district, and collect another bounty.

Yet another abuse followed from the Conscription Act's provision that granted state recruiters the right to go into occupied areas of the South to enlist black soldiers from among former slaves. Recruiting officers exploited that opportunity shamelessly. The poor health of many freedmen, their ignorance in dealing with recruiters, and their gullibility permitted the unscrupulous recruiters to carry people off from their plantations, pocket the "bounty" provided by their state, and give the freedmen over to the army.

Northern finances. Although the North possessed the industrial wealth for fighting a modern war, the government was slow in discovering how to tap that wealth. The Lincoln Administration resorted to the same means of raising money that the Confederacy used: taxation, borrowing, and the issue of paper money. But the North, unlike the South, eventually succeeded with its financial experiments. The assumption that the war would be short at first led the government into the same errors the Confederacy made. The most serious mistake of Treasury Secretary Chase was failing to recommend high taxes to meet a substantial proportion of the government's bills. Such taxes would have lessened reliance

on borrowing and printing money, in itself inflationary, and would have reduced the inflationary buying power of workers, farmers, and managers who were profiting from war-created demands. As it turned out, only a small fraction of the war bill was paid through taxes, and the North, like the South, was subjected to demoralizing inflation.

By far the largest source of money was borrowing. Bankers bought most of the bond issues, the mainstay of the war chest, driving the best bargain they could with Secretary Chase. Chase, however, disliked selling the government's bonds below par, or for long terms, or at high interest. As a result of his struggle with the bankers, bonds were issued from time to time with different dates of maturity and at different rates. In a significant innovation in public finance, Chase enlisted Jay Cooke, a wealthy Philadelphia banker, in a campaign to sell to the general public bonds redeemable in not less than five years or more than twenty—the famous "five-twenties." The Treasury Department had never before used the sale of government bonds to increase popular support of a war.

Early in 1862 the Treasury Department realized that a financial crisis was at hand. The war was costing the government nearly $1.75 million a day, Chase complained, and the Treasury was empty. While expenses were growing, dwindling imports reduced the government's intake from customs, formerly its main source of money. At last Secretary Chase reluctantly asked Congress to make the government's paper money legal tender for all debts, public and private. That request was a bitter step for a former Jacksonian Democrat with hard-money principles. Congress responded with the Legal Tender Act of 1862, which created the "greenbacks." That act was the first phase of a comprehensive plan for financing the war, a plan with far-reaching implications for state rights in the North as well as for the policy of hard-money.

Making paper currency legal tender added to inflation, but it solved the immediate crisis by promptly putting money into the Treasury. Congress went further by passing the Internal Revenue Act, which imposed a tax on incomes over $800—the first income tax in United States history. The act also taxed manufactures and imposed sales taxes and license fees. Although the legislation met little of the cost of the war, it set a comprehensive precedent for a national system of taxation.

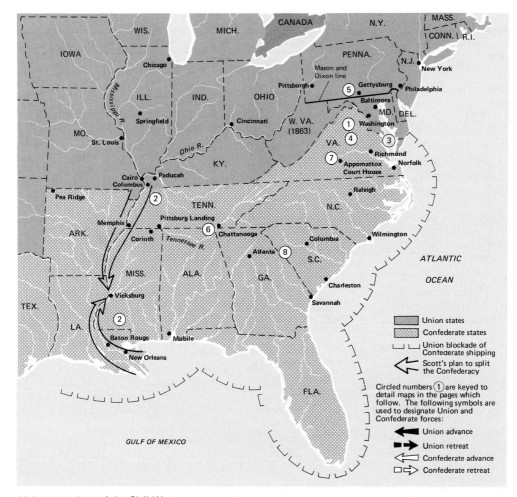

Major campaigns of the Civil War

The National Banking Act of 1863, a further effort to stimulate the sale of war bonds, required all national banks chartered under the act to invest one-third of their capital in federal bonds and to deposit those bonds with the Treasury Department. The banks could then issue bank notes, which would serve as legal tender, up to 90 percent of the market value of the deposited bonds. The banks were also subjected to regular federal inspection to protect depositors. In 1865 Congress brought most of the banks chartered by the states into the national system by imposing a prohibitive 10 percent tax on their bank notes.

The net result of all those financial measures was to enhance the power of the national government at the expense of the state governments. The Legal Tender Act put into circulation $50 million and created the basis for a national currency.

The course of arms

The first offensive: Bull Run. What strategy was Lincoln to follow in destroying the Confederate government and its armies? General Winfield Scott, the aging commanding general of the Union Army, had developed a long-range plan calling for a close blockade of the Confederate coastline and for "containment" of the Confederacy all along its land frontier. An amphibious expedition was to open up the Mississippi Valley, restoring the Middle West's traditional access to the ocean and cutting off Texas, Arkansas, and Louisiana from the rest of the Confederacy. Then separate armies were to strike inland from the

① The first Battle of Bull Run, July 21, 1861

Atlantic and the Gulf of Mexico, progressively fragmenting and ultimately destroying the Southern nation, as a giant serpent, the anaconda, might. General Scott was seventy-four, no longer well, but not unwise. Newspaper strategists eager for military action derided his plan for the slow, remorseless constriction of the enemy. Yet the formula for victory that Union generals eventually stumbled upon after many futile engagements coincided with General Scott's "Anaconda Plan" in all essential features except one: before victory, the Confederate armies had to be destroyed.

One part of General Scott's plan won immediate acceptance: on April 19, 1861, Lincoln declared a blockade of the Southern coastline. By taking that action, Lincoln implicitly recognized that a state of belligerency existed, even though he continued to hold that the war was merely an insurrection on the part of individuals. Clearly, a nation does not blockade its own coastline. And nobody knew how the British would react to a blockade that could not be enforced, whether they might choose to remind the United States of its former condemnation of paper blockades (see p. 168). The question was answered on May 13, when the British recognized the Confederates as belligerents. Lincoln's Administration, deeply disappointed, should not have been surprised. England's ruling classes sympathized with the South, and in any case English interests required a formula that would permit Confederate vessels to be treated as privateers rather than as pirates.

The United States proceeded rapidly with the blockade. Plans were laid for the seizure of forts at Cape Hatteras Inlet, controlling the North Carolina coast, and for the capture of the vulnerable and valuable Port Royal Sound, halfway between Charleston and Savannah. This haven, which had come into Union hands

Victor at Bull Run: P. G. T. Beauregard

by November 1861, provided shelter for the South Atlantic Blockading Squadron in hurricane weather and a station for refueling and repairs. Within a year, owing to the energy of the navy under Gideon Welles' direction, all major Southern ports except Charleston, but including New Orleans, had been taken. The blockade was effective enough to cause the Confederacy considerable annoyance and to deprive it of needed supplies.

Lincoln, rejecting other parts of General Scott's plan, decided to try for a quick victory over the army of P. G. T. Beauregard, who was located in northern Virginia not thirty miles from Washington. He hoped to defeat Beauregard and take Richmond, where the Confederate government had moved after Virginia seceded. On July 21, near a sluggish stream called Bull Run, General Irvin McDowell engaged Beauregard's army in the first major battle of the war. It was a battle of green armies, and McDowell did not even have a good map of the terrain. Although the Northern recruits fought well at first and had the initial advantage of numbers, they failed to carry the day against Confederate reinforcements brought out of the Shenandoah Valley from Joseph Johnston's army in one of the first major uses of railroads for troop transport. When McDowell attempted an orderly retreat, his demoralized men broke ranks and streamed back to Washington. The victors were too stunned by their triumph to give chase. Lincoln and his Cabinet now saw that the road to Richmond would be hard and long.

But Lincoln did not lose confidence in himself as a strategist. Instead he settled into the long process of training the new three-year volunteer army. For this task he picked George B. McClellan. Only thirty-four years old but a superb organizer and administrator, McClellan chose to undertake no new offensive until his troops were fully prepared for combat. Lincoln approved that policy, and throughout the summer and fall an uneasy quiet fell on the land war.

The war opens in the West. Meanwhile, in the West, military threats to Kentucky's proclaimed neutrality led to a campaign that revealed the Confederacy's soft spot (see p. 328). A large Union force was assembling at Cairo, Illinois, under the command of an obscure but tough young officer named Ulysses S. Grant. Major General Leonidas Polk, who watched this development anxiously from the Missouri side of the Mississippi, decided to get his Confederate army into a more strategic position with regard to Grant's force. On September 4, Polk crossed over into Kentucky and occupied high ground overlooking the Ohio River from the Kentucky side. General Grant, grasping the opportunity he had been waiting for, followed hard on Polk's heels with a large force of federal troops, in order, he declared, to defend the state from the Confederates. Thereafter the political standoff in Kentucky cleared with remarkable speed: Union candidates won in the 1861 fall elections, giving Grant and his army the local security they required to drive the Confederates out of Kentucky. Grant quickly gained control of the mouths of the Tennessee and Cumberland rivers as they flowed into the Ohio. Those great waterways, which looped through Kentucky and across the whole of Tennessee, provided a natural highway into the heartland of the Confederacy.

Recognizing the danger, Jefferson Davis appointed the man he regarded as his best officer, General Albert Sidney Johnston, to take command of the Confederate defense. There were now two Confederate armies in Kentucky: Johnston's at Bowling Green, facing a large Union army of eighty thousand under General Don Carlos Buell; and P. G. T. Beauregard's smaller force to the east, at Columbus. But the two armies were not strong enough to hold against the campaign that Grant now launched. Near the end of January 1862 the Union Army began to push the Confederates southward. Early in February, Grant took part of his army along the Tennessee River with a flotilla of gunboats and captured Fort Henry, which guarded the river just below the Kentucky border in Tennessee. This movement, which ruptured the communications of the extended Confederate line, caused General Johnston to withdraw to Nashville, leaving a small force of fifteen thousand to guard Fort Donelson on the Cumberland River. With help from General Henry W. Halleck, who had a small army in Missouri, Grant seized Fort Donelson and captured its garrison. One of the decisive achievements of Union arms, this action cut Johnston's defensive lines and forced a general Confederate retreat back to northern Mississippi. With western Tennessee now secured, the way was open for a Union advance into the Deep South. In February, Lincoln promptly set up

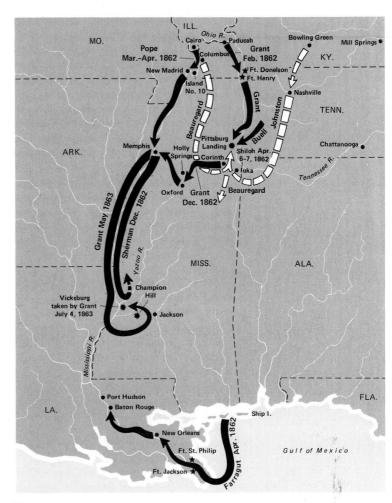

② Grant's campaigns in the Mississippi Valley, 1862–63

a Union government at Nashville and appointed Andrew Johnson, a Tennessee senator who had refused to secede, as governor.

Shiloh. Beauregard and Johnston reunited their armies near the Tennessee-Mississippi line. There they conceived a plan to stop Grant, who had pursued the line of the Tennessee River all the way to Pittsburg Landing in southern Tennessee. Aware that Grant's army was slightly smaller than the total fifty-five thousand men of his own troops combined with Beauregard's, Johnston made a surprise attack on April 6 in a tangle of woodlands and pasture near a country meeting-house called Shiloh. Grant's army, taken by surprise, was nearly driven into the river the first day, but Johnston was killed in the action and reinforcements from Buell's command began arriving in the evening. On the following day the outnumbered Confederates, under Beauregard, had to retreat to Corinth, Mississippi. Shiloh, the greatest battle yet seen on the North American continent, left thirteen thousand Union casualties and more than ten thousand Confederate.

Though the Union victory was not overwhelming, the Confederate gamble to prevent the concentration of the Union armies had been frustrated. It was now a simple matter for General Halleck, who emerged with more credit for the operations than he deserved, to gather his large army of 125,000 men and drive Beauregard out of Corinth, an important railroad center. Now northern Mississippi lay open to Halleck with his great united army, and the Confederate forces in the West were on the brink of disaster.

Support from the Union Navy had been indispensable in that development. Flag Officer David Farragut had pushed his way up the Mississippi to New Orleans and on April 25 had occupied that city. General Benjamin Butler followed to establish a military occupation of New Orleans and its environs and was soon in possession of Baton Rouge as well. Meanwhile, early in June, a fleet of federal gunboats came down the Mississippi and annihilated a Confederate fleet at Memphis, bringing that city into Union possession and opening the upper Mississippi. The Union Navy and Army together now controlled the whole length of the river except for a section between Vicksburg to the north and Port Hudson to the south.

The Monitor and the Merrimac.

The technological advances of the first half of the nineteenth century contributed significantly to naval design. Steamships were already in common use by 1860, and screw propellers, rifled ordnance, and shell guns had been developed. During the war those innovations, widely used, marked the advent of a new era in naval warfare. Early in the war Navy Secretary Welles had contracted to have gunboats on the Mississippi armed with $2\frac{1}{2}$ inches of iron plate, and several of these little ironclad vessels were launched in October and November of 1861. They were available to Grant on the Mississippi and Tennessee rivers in the spring campaign of 1862, and Flag Officer Farragut used ironclads in reducing the defenses of New Orleans.

Suddenly it appeared that armor was of even greater strategic importance for battle-

Union soldiers (sketch by Winslow Homer)

ships than for gunboats. Just after Virginia seceded from the Union, federal authorities had decided, unwisely and precipitately, to abandon the Gosport Navy Yard near Portsmouth, Virginia. In doing so, they scuttled and burned a forty-gun warship named the *Merrimac,* which was then under repair. Confederate Secretary of the Navy Stephen Mallory, alert to the meaning of technology for naval warfare, had the *Merrimac* raised, reconditioned, stripped of its superstructure, and armed in four-inch iron plate made at the Tredegar works in Richmond. Nobody had seen anything like this amazing vessel before. Rechristened the *Virginia,* it appeared in Hampton Roads on March 8, 1862. There it sealed the doom of wooden warships. The ironclad vessel sank the Union frigate *Cumberland,* forced the frigate *Congress* to surrender, drove a big steamer, the *Minnesota,* aground, and threatened to destroy the whole federal fleet around Fort Monroe. Impending disaster was avoided by the timely arrival the next day of the *Monitor,* an ironclad that had just been finished for the Union Navy.

The ability of the Confederates, who had had no navy at all at the outbreak of the war, to come so close to crippling the Union Navy exposed the conservatism of the Naval Board and Congress. Although Union authorities had had ample warning of what was afoot at the Gosport Yard, Secretary Welles had difficulty persuading Congress of the need for haste, and the Naval Board had been slow to see the virtues of ironclad vessels. Had it not been for the passionate advocacy of a Swedish-born engineer named John Ericsson, the *Monitor* might not have appeared in time to challenge the *Merrimac* in her bid for control of the lower Chesapeake. Ericsson laid the keel of the *Monitor* on October 1, 1861, and she was completed according to Ericsson's design just in time.

The *Monitor* and the *Merrimac* fought a wearing battle, demonstrating that warships without armor plate were obsolete. The *Monitor* gained no real advantage, for she was unable to destroy the Confederate ironclad. The *Merrimac* remained in the lower James River, barring the stream to federal shipping and posing a threat to any plan to take Richmond by invasion of the peninsula below the city. Two months later, on May 9, Union forces had occupied the sounds and capes of North Carolina and were threatening Norfolk. The Confederates abandoned the city and

Bridging the Chickahominy

scuttled the *Merrimac* to keep her from Northern hands.

McClellan's peninsular campaign. For so young a general, George B. McClellan was painfully slow and methodical. Or so Lincoln and many of his best advisers thought. Yet McClellan did put his huge army of 150,000 men into good fighting shape during the winter of 1861–62. In the spring he convinced Lincoln that he should take the larger part of his army down the Potomac to the Chesapeake, put his men ashore at Fortress Monroe, and move on Richmond from the southeast. McClellan had "the slows," Lincoln complained. Even though his army outnumbered General Joseph E. Johnston's, which stood between his own and Richmond, McClellan frittered away precious weeks on siege tactics. Johnston quietly withdrew up the peninsula and reestablished himself less then ten miles from Richmond. In late May McClellan, having reached Johnston again, sent part of his army across the Chickahominy, a stream that divided the peninsula; he refused to attack until reinforcements came from Washington. Lincoln had agreed to send troops, provided Washington was not threatened. But by late May Washington appeared to be in danger of Confederate attack. Jefferson Davis and Robert E. Lee, who happened to be in Richmond, had worked out a deception to prevent Lincoln from sending McClellan his reinforcements. They instructed young Thomas J. Jackson, who had earned the nickname "Stonewall" for his stand at the Battle of Bull Run, to engage the enemy vigorously in the Shenandoah Valley and to create the illusion that an attack on Washington was imminent. Jackson carried out his assignment brilliantly. Then, on the last day of May, Johnston attacked McClellan's exposed right flank at Fair Oaks. The battle was indecisive, and Johnston was badly wounded.

Now General Robert E. Lee came out from

③ *The peninsular campaign, 1862*

*Robert E. Lee:
he hated the choice
he had to make*

Richmond to replace Johnston as commander of the Army of Northern Virginia, a post he would retain for the rest of the war. Lee had been a reluctant secessionist, forced, as he wrote a Northern girl who asked for his photograph on the eve of war, ''to side either with or against my section or country. I cannot raise my hand,'' he added, ''against my birthplace, my home, my children.'' He hated the choice he had made because it implied ingratitude to the United States army, which he loved and which had provided the opportunities that launched his career. Like John Brown, ironically, Lee foresaw a terrible war—a war that would be ''a necessary expiation'' for the sins of the country. A daring commander, Lee was at his best in adversity. Resolving to save Richmond, he called on Jackson to bring his troops swiftly east to join him. Jackson's seventeen thousand soldiers came out of the mountains and across the Piedmont at record speed, arriving just in time to help Lee drive the right wing of the Union Army to the southeast in a series of engagements known as the Seven Days' Battle. Though outnumbered at all times, Lee managed, by skillful deployment of his men, to bring to each encounter a superior force. In those battles Lee lost twenty thousand men and McClellan fifteen thousand. Pushed back to Harrison's Landing on the James River, McClellan settled down again to wait for reinforcements. But Lee was determined not to lose the initiative he had gained.

The second Battle of Bull Run. In what must have seemed to McClellan a belated effort, Lincoln called Generals John Pope and Henry Halleck east, placing Halleck in general command of the war and sending Pope southward with his army to help McClellan catch Richmond in a pincer movement. Halleck, failing in his effort to coordinate the two Union armies, at last ordered McClellan to bring his troops north and join Pope. Lee, who had no intention of letting these armies meet, boldly divided his own army to send twenty-five thousand men under Jackson to attack Pope from the rear. On August 28 and 29 he maneuvered Pope into battle on the old field of Bull Run. Wholly undone by Lee's generalship, Pope was driven back to the fortifications around Washington. Lincoln removed Pope from command and asked McClellan to take over, hoping to replace the latter with a more combative general when time allowed.

Time did not allow, or rather Robert E. Lee did not. Lee had already achieved a remarkable reversal of the conflict, shifting the scene of action from the outskirts of Richmond to the banks of the Potomac. Realizing better than most commanders that the Confederacy's survival depended on the destruction of the Union Army, he knew he could not afford to lose time. He struck across the Potomac River. By forcing McClellan to stand between the Confederate Army and Washington, Lee could draw the Union Army out of Virginia, allowing the farmers to harvest their crops in peace. If Lee could win a decisive victory on Northern soil, England and France might be convinced that the South could win independence. This, in turn, might persuade those powers to recognize the Confederacy.

The war at crisis

England and the Confederacy. Neither the Union nor the Confederacy had been entirely satisfied with the official British attitude toward the war. The North was displeased that England had recognized the Confederates as belligerents; the South wanted full recognition of its independence. In the summer of 1862 the French too appeared ready to recognize the Confederacy, waiting only for a signal from England to do so. Lord John Russell, Britain's foreign minister, proposed to the British cabinet that the European powers offer to mediate the American dispute. If mediation were not accepted, Russell indicated, Britain would recognize the Confederacy. Those steps would have provoked war with the United States.

Public attitudes in England were mixed. The upper-class English saw in the Southern cause a defense of conservative values, and many of them would have welcomed the defeat of the world's most important exemplar of popular government. English liberals, especially antislavery reformers, pointed out that the South was defending slavery, which was generally disliked in England. But their conservative opponents replied that the federal government had taken pains to dissociate the war from the issue of slavery. The English working classes tended to side with the Union, even though many of them had been thrown out of work because of shortages of cotton. The need for cotton was not gaining for the Confederacy all that the advocates of "King Cotton diplomacy" had hoped.

There were other reasons for the failure of cotton as a basis for Confederate diplomacy. The rich cotton crop of 1860 had been sold in the Liverpool market before the outbreak of hostilities, and the Union blockade had had slight effect on the•shipment of cotton during the first year of the war. Near the end of the summer of 1862 the stockpile was dwindling. By that time, however, England had developed alternative sources of supply in Egypt and India, thus breaking the Confederate monopoly. England had yet another problem to consider. Poor grain harvests in 1861 and 1862 had made grain purchased from the Northern states very important in feeding her industrial population. So long as the United States refused to make emancipation an aim of the war, only the certainty that the Confederates were actually going to win their independence in battle could budge the British.

England and the Union. The main objective of United States diplomacy was to prevent the British from recognizing the Confederacy. Avoiding hostile encounters that might pitch the British into the Confederate camp was essential.

Actually a dangerous confrontation had already occurred in November 1861, when James Wilkes, captain of the *U.S.S. San Jacinto,* stopped a British mail steamer named the *Trent* and removed two Confederate envoys, James Mason and John Slidell, who were on their way to England. Secretary of State William Seward should have acknowledged that breach of neutral rights promptly, for the United States had historically regarded such seizures as illegal and had in 1812 pointed to similar British actions as one reason for declaring war on England (see p. 170). Lord Palmerston, the prime minister, informed his nervous cabinet that he'd "be damned" if he would let the affront go unnoticed. The popular enthusiasm among Northerners for Wilkes' brash act made it hard for Seward to back down. Congress even voted Wilkes a medal. Demanding a return of the envoys and an apology, even while preparing troops to sail to Canada, the British seemed ready to go to war. The message they sent to Washington might have been even sharper had

Queen Victoria and Prince Albert, who were disposed to be friends with the United States, not suggested a softening of the language. Much of the credit for averting hostilities belonged to two skillful diplomats, America's minister to England, Charles Francis Adams, and the British minister to Washington, Lord Lyons. Since neither nation wanted war, the only question was whether Seward and Lincoln could accept the graceful retreat the English opened up for them. By delaying tactics, the two ministers were able to draw out their negotiations until popular opinion in the United States had cooled. The federal government then released Mason and Slidell and issued an expression of regret to the British.

Tensions between the United States and England nevertheless remained high. With little regard for their duties as neutrals, the British allowed two cruisers built for the Confederacy to escape from Liverpool under British registry. Once on the high seas, the *Alabama* and the *Florida* seriously menaced Northern shipping; before the end of the war they had destroyed $15 million in ships and trade. The Confederacy hoped that these vessels would break the Union blockade, but they never succeeded in doing so.

More ominous plans were developing to break the blockade. Two huge ironclad rams, ships specially designed to attack blockade vessels, were on the ways in a Scottish shipyard, scheduled to be in the water by 1863. Minister Adams now set about preventing their delivery to the Confederacy. How sympathetically the British would listen to him depended in part on whether the United States could reverse the pattern of military defeat. With the British seriously considering mediation and ignoring what was happening in their shipyards, nothing seemed more important to President Lincoln in early September of 1862 than throwing Lee out of Maryland.

The slavery question again. The President needed a victory for another reason. By midsummer of 1862 he had decided to abandon his hands-off policy on slavery and to issue a proclamation freeing the slaves in the seceded states. He was waiting for a victory to make his announcement. Lincoln interpreted his war powers to include the right to emancipate the enemy's property, but he had hesitated long to do so. A merciful man, the President on more than one occasion had said that

"The Engagement between the USS Kearsarge and the CSS Alabama" (oil by Édouard Manet)

he wished that all men could be free, but he had been unwilling to make enemies for the cause of the Union among the many Northern citizens who shared the South's view of racial distinctions even while condemning Southern slavery. The slaveholding border states that had stayed in the Union would, he feared, consider themselves betrayed. Looking for issues in the upcoming congressional elections of 1862, the Democrats would surely charge the government with encouraging a slave insurrection in the South, and few Northerners were willing to visit on the seceded states what they termed "the horrors of servile war."

As the casualty lists lengthened, however, and the war turned against the Union, some Northerners began to ask themselves if they were not enduring an unfair handicap by failing to use that weapon. The Confederate government had employed slaves to build their fortifications, and slave-labor on the plantations released many whites for military service. Scoffing at Lincoln's conservatism and his solicitude for the border-state slaveholders, Wendell Phillips asked, "How many times are we to save Kentucky and lose the war?" Abolitionists like Phillips, once hounded in the North, were enjoying a new popularity among staunch supporters of the war. Only lukewarm patriots showed them the old contempt. Had not abolitionists claimed from the first that slavery was the cause of the war? Northern inability to win victory short of emancipating slaves seemed a signal that they had been right all along.

Fugitive slaves. There were other signs. Especially troublesome for Lincoln was the question of how army officers were to deal with fugitive slaves. In all sectors of the fighting, and from the very beginning of the war, blacks had come over into the Union lines. As long as emancipation was denied as an aim of the war, Southern sympathizers in the North, and all the border-state people, regarded failure to return runaways as hypocrisy. Other Northerners saw no good reason to return slaves who would strengthen the Confederacy.

General Benjamin F. Butler, a soldier-politician from Massachusetts, evolved a formula that served for a time. When Butler led his Massachusetts volunteers through Maryland in the first weeks of the war, he had offered his men to help put down a slave insurrection that was rumored to be imminent;

and he had returned fugitive slaves to their masters. But his action had raised an immediate outcry in Massachusetts, and Butler, never slow to learn a political lesson, found a way to retain the fugitives and use them in the Union cause. He simply suggested that they be regarded as "contraband of war." Some officers followed his lead; some did not. Lincoln tolerated latitude on the part of commanders who faced this dilemma, realizing that their individual responses tended to match their political views.

Lincoln would not allow any officer, however, to make fundamental policy on this sensitive subject. When John C. Frémont, in command of the army in Missouri, proclaimed that the slaves of masters disloyal to the Union were emancipated, Lincoln made him retract the order and shortly removed him from his command. Frémont's order was very popular, nonetheless. Governor Andrew of Massachusetts said Frémont's action gave "the grandest character" to the Union effort, and antislavery people everywhere approved. The border slave states were getting to be, in the words of black abolitionist Frederick Douglass, "a millstone about the neck of the Government." Antislavery Northerners pledged themselves to convert the war into a crusade against slavery.

Time and events were on their side. Union defeats, especially McClellan's failures in the peninsula campaign against Richmond, made Northern citizens, abolitionists or not, less tolerant of the South's advantage in slave-labor. Recognizing in the black man a potential Northern ally, they were beginning to ask why he should not be enlisted in Union armies.

The recruitment of blacks was directly related to the question of emancipation, for no one could expect black men to serve in the army as slaves. With the number of volunteers tapering off in the North, the need for manpower became more pressing. The vigorous new Secretary of War, Edwin M. Stanton, advocated an army of black regiments. Lincoln saw that the time had come for him to test the will of the public on emancipation. Therefore in March 1862, he pointed out to the border states that the war was bringing an end to slavery in areas where it was easy for slaves to run away and urged them to undertake voluntary emancipation with the expectation that Congress would compensate slave owners for their loss. The border states took

Sharpsburg Bridge over the Antietam Creek

no action and neither did Congress. At this point, however, Lincoln's own policy shifted subtly but positively. General David Hunter began to enlist black soldiers in the occupied districts of coastal South Carolina and then, in May 1862, issued a proclamation similar to Frémont's. Instead of removing Hunter from his command, Lincoln simply ordered him to retract his proclamation. It was clear from newspaper comment and from letters to political leaders that public opposition to emancipation and to the enlistment of black soldiers was rapidly diminishing. On July 17, 1862, Congress passed a Confiscation Act that freed the slaves of masters who served in the Confederate Army. It was almost impossible for fugitives to win freedom under this act, however, because they would somehow have to demonstrate that their master was disloyal to the Union. Moreover, the act made no provision for the enforcement of the emancipation clause. The fact that the Confiscation Act of 1862 was passed, however, suggested that Congress was becoming increasingly radical on the slavery question.

Horace Greeley, in a famous letter to the President known as "The Prayer of 20 Millions," urged Lincoln to enforce the Confiscation Act and to convert the war into a war on slavery. The President's answer was firm: he would continue to place the Union ahead of all else. He added that he would consider every possible means to save the Union, including the emancipation of slaves. Actually Lincoln had already decided to issue an emancipation proclamation. He had been working

on the text in the privacy of the telegraph office, where he had hidden himself from office-seekers, and on July 22 he told his Cabinet of his decision. Persuaded by Seward that a proclamation on the heels of McClellan's poor showing in the peninsular campaign would be a demonstration of weakness, Lincoln agreed to await a Union victory.

Now Lincoln learned of Lee's invasion of Maryland. As Lincoln sent McClellan to stop Lee's army, much hung on the outcome. Only emancipation seemed likely to stop the English from thinking about mediation, and emancipation would have to wait upon McClellan's success.

Antietam. The Union and Confederate armies were groping toward one of the crucial encounters of the war. As Lee led his sixty-thousand-man army into Maryland, he deployed part of it under General "Stonewall" Jackson to seize the federal arsenal at Harper's Ferry, Virginia. At this point McClellan had a stroke of incredibly good luck. One of his men happened to pick up three cigars wrapped in what turned out to be a lost dispatch from Lee revealing that his army was momentarily divided. McClellan moved promptly to bring Lee to battle, hoping to defeat him before Jackson could return. On September 17, at Antietam Creek near the small town of Sharpsburg, McClellan made several massive attacks on Lee's lines. In the course of one long ghastly day, three battles were fought on a single field. Very late, but just in time to save the Confederate Army from

*I have ... thought a great deal about the relation of this war to Slavery:
and ... several weeks ago, I read to you an Order I had prepared on
this subject.... I have thought ... that the time for acting on it might
very probably come. I think the time has come now. I wish it were
a better time.... The action of the army against the rebels has not
been quite what I should have best liked. But they have been driven
out of Maryland, and Pennsylvania is no longer in danger of invasion.
When the rebel army was at Frederick, I determined, as soon as it
should be driven out of Maryland, to issue a Proclamation of Emancipation.... I made the promise to myself, and ... to my Maker.... I am
going to fulfill that promise.... I do not wish your advice about the
main matter.... What I have written is that which my reflections have
determined me to say.... I know very well that many others might,
in this matter, as in others, do better than I can; and if I were satisfied
that the public confidence was more fully possessed by any one of
them than by me, and knew of any Constitutional way in which he
could be put in my place, he should have it.... But though I believe
that I have not so much of the confidence of the people as I had
some time since, I do not know that ... any other person has more;
and ... I am here. I must do the best I can, and bear the responsibility
of taking the course which I feel I ought to take.*

From the Diary of Salmon P. Chase, September 22, 1862.

disaster, reinforcements arrived from Harper's
Ferry. With one more attack McClellan might
have defeated the Confederates conclusively,
but he did not attack, and night fell upon a
stalemate.

During that bloodiest day of the entire war,
the Union Army of ninety thousand men had
sustained thirteen thousand casualties, the
Confederate Army nearly eleven thousand. His

army was so weakened that Lee decided to
abandon his drive into Maryland. Most unwisely, McClellan allowed him a whole day
free of harassment, and Lee seized the opportunity to organize an orderly retreat across the
Potomac. For McClellan's blunder Lincoln
eventually removed him from his command,
but for the moment Lincoln deemed the victory sufficient to justify release of the Emancipation Proclamation.

Fortunately the public was prepared for
Lincoln's bombshell; Horace Greeley's letter
and the President's reply to it had helped.
Thousands who had once applauded Lincoln's
caution were by now resigned to the idea of
emancipation as a war measure. Other thousands were comforted to know that the sacrifices of war would advance freedom. Lincoln's
timing was perfect, for a revolution was rising
in public sentiment on emancipation. On September 23 Lincoln released the Emancipation
Proclamation to the newspapers. In plain legal
language, he stated that persons held as
slaves in states that were still in rebellion on
January 1, 1863, would be emancipated. He
specifically exempted most areas occupied by
federal troops, and he declared that the status
of slaves in the Union slave states would be
unaffected. His critics remarked that the proclamation freed slaves only in those areas
where they could not be reached.

④ *Virginia and Maryland, 1862*

Yet the Emancipation Proclamation changed the whole meaning of the war. Territory occupied by federal troops after January 1 would be free territory, and the army was now an army of liberation. The number of runaways increased rapidly wherever federal troops were deployed. The proclamation served notice on the South that the war had become a social revolution; if the cause of secession should fail, the slave-based society of the South would also fail. The Confederacy now renewed its effort to win independence with the energy of desperation.

Emancipation helped the Northern war effort immediately in two important ways. It caused the English to postpone their decision on whether or not to step forward as mediators in the American war. Without the Emancipation Proclamation, the Battle of Antietam might have lent force to the mediationists' argument that the war had become a bloody stalemate. But emancipation ennobled the Northern war effort in the eyes of most Englishmen, and it would now be much harder for the British cabinet to abandon neutrality.

Black men also proved a valuable new source of recruits for the Union Army. By 1863 enlistments were falling off. Congress passed a general Conscription Act in that year, which encouraged localities to redouble their efforts to raise volunteers. But still more men were needed. Governor John Andrew of Massachusetts spearheaded the recruitment of black soldiers by raising the famous Fifty-fourth and Fifty-fifth Regiments of Massachusetts Volunteers. During 1863 a number of significant engagements proved even to the dubious that black troops made good soldiers. At Milliken's Bend, at Port Hudson in the West, and at Battery Wagner in the East, black troops fought valiantly and suffered heavy casualties. The nation learned to be grateful for their sacrifices. By the end of the war nearly 190,000 black soldiers had served in the Union Army.

The election of 1862.

At first it was difficult to judge the impact of emancipation on the Northern people. Repeated defeats and ever lengthening casualty lists had provoked deep distrust of the Administration's handling of the war. In the struggle against disaffection at home and against subversion by the enemy, Lincoln's government, however reluctantly, had made arbitrary arrests and imprisonments, had suspended the writ of habeas corpus, and had censored the press. His severest critics saw Lincoln as a dictator. The "peace" Democrats, who opposed the war, claimed that the President had revealed his true colors by asking citizens to sacrifice their civil liberties in order to emancipate the enemy's slaves. Others too were asking what good was a war that threatened to destroy American freedom. In a mood of fear and despair, the voters handed the Republicans sharp reverses in the congressional elections of 1862.

The election could have gone worse for the Republicans. The government had not actually been defeated, as it might have been had the public had only the debacle of the second Battle of Bull Run, the futility of McClellan's peninsula campaign, and the unfulfilled promise of Antietam to consider. The Emancipation Proclamation, significant in itself, also gave the impression that the President was now totally committed to the war, ready to take every step necessary to win.

Lincoln dramatized that readiness by ridding himself of McClellan and other officers who were not only afflicted with "the slows" but who opposed emancipation. A new vigor seemed to infuse the people. The people of the North were at last accepting emancipation as a goal of the war. Those who approved Lincoln's proclamation outnumbered those who opposed it. For its supporters emancipation gave a noble meaning to the sacrifices demanded at home and the dreadful casualty lists from the field.

The sacrifices were far from over. By the end of the year both the Union and the Confederate armies were settling into a slow war of attrition. Lincoln gave command of the Army of the Potomac to General Ambrose E. Burnside, a dashing officer who had proved his mettle in the North Carolina coastal campaign. Knowing that he had been put in charge in order to give battle, Burnside astonished Generals Lee and Jackson by driving his troops across the Rappahannock River to attack the Confederates entrenched on Marye Heights above the little town of Fredericksburg, about halfway between Washington and Richmond. Burnside had a fault quite different from McClellan's. All day long on December 13 he threw assault after assault against the Confederates, but each time they turned him back with relative ease. At the end of the day a bewildered Burnside counted twelve thousand casualties in his futile exercise. The Confederates had lost half that many.

Battery Wagner: black troops fought valiantly

The two armies dug in for a wet, dreary winter, eyeing each other across the Rappahannock. The Confederates were low on food and clothing; the Union Army was demoralized. The Confederates had plenty of tobacco and no coffee; the Union soldiers had plenty of coffee and no tobacco. In spite of the savage fighting in the days just past, the men of the Army of Northern Virginia and the men of the Army of the Potomac adjusted the imbalance in those homely comforts by shuttling a small carved boat loaded with items in short supply back and forth across the river. Fraternization was a problem for the officers but not for the men; it was one of the most promising signs of what Lincoln sincerely hoped for, that this was "a war with peace in its belly." The two armies sat drinking their coffee and smoking their pipes, waiting for spring and a new campaign. In time, Lincoln appointed a new general, hoping that "Fighting" Joe Hooker would live up to his nickname.

The Kentucky campaign. The fall campaign of 1862 in the West was also indecisive. Confederate General Braxton Bragg conceived of a maneuver to recapture Kentucky. Rather than staying pinned down in northern Mississippi, he would strike north through Tennessee and Kentucky, aiming for Louisville. General Don Carlos Buell would have to follow him to defend the railroad junction at Louisville. En route Bragg could pick his own ground and force the Union Army into battle. It was a brilliant plan that came near succeeding, for Bragg did get his army between Buell and Louisville. All of Tennessee and most of Kentucky now seemed again safe for the Confederacy. But Bragg was afflicted by the same irresolution that blunted George McClellan's genius. Instead of challenging Buell he withdrew, giving Buell time to get into Louisville for reinforcements. Now it was Buell's turn to show reluctance to fight. After an inconclusive engagement at Perryville, Kentucky, in October, Bragg withdrew to Tennessee, followed at some distance by Buell. Buell too had "the slows," Lincoln concluded, and he replaced him with General William Rosecrans, who met Bragg's army in desperate battle at Murfreesboro, Tennessee, on the last day of 1862. After a second engagement, in which the Confederates came off badly, Bragg withdrew to winter quarters. In the West as in the East, the new year began in stalemate.

Behind the lines

Southern problems. The wisest leaders, including both Lincoln and Davis, knew that the South had more to lose in a stalemate than the Union had. Medicine, salt to preserve meat, and leather for soldiers' shoes, wagon harness, and cavalry equipment became scarce early on. The South simply lacked the material resources to sustain a long war. Disaffection mounted with inflation, and unspeakable poverty, even hunger, dogged the families of soldiers conscripted from the poor.

The political system of the Confederacy now began to show strain under the demands of modern war. While the North was being transformed into a modern nation, the Confederacy, organized on the state-rights principle, fell victim to the jealousies of imperious state-rights leaders. Without political parties to moderate their obstructionism, Southern leaders engaged in vicious factional disputes over the policies of Davis' Administration. Vice President Stephens sulked in Georgia, and the governors of several states blocked conscription (see p. 331). When the Confederate Congress convened in January 1863, President Davis spoke some homely truths. The South, he said, must not look abroad for help, and he observed that the Emancipation Proclamation had sparked the North with a new determination. He warned that sterner measures were needed to save the government. The Confederate people would have supported Davis if their leaders had asked them to do so and if they had felt that the burdens of war were fairly distributed. The Congress approved in principle a 10 percent tax in kind on farmers' produce and promised a more generous assessment of goods confiscated from the farmers than in previous impressments. These steps were necessary, but the real wealth of the South was in slaves and cotton and land, and the tax bill that emerged from Congress scarcely touched those bulwarks of privilege. Inflation mounted, morale dipped, and by 1864 the women of Richmond were rioting for bread in the streets.

The Northern war boom. From 1863 on the North gained steadily in material strength. Much of the amateurish experimentation of the first years of the war was distilled into useful knowledge. The North organized. The financial measures taken in 1862 began to show results; the army was paid promptly, and adequate supplies reached the front on time. General Herman Haupt, who was granted full authority to use the railroads to advance the war effort, emerged as a genius of organization. In naval power the Union had enjoyed supremacy even at the start of the war, with 42 effective vessels; by 1863 the figure had grown to a formidable 427.

By 1863 the north had already made its most painful adjustments to the war economy, and the last two years of the war were for the majority of Northerners a time of unprecedented prosperity. The wages of the working poor never quite kept pace with inflation. But for everyone else war contracts meant good jobs, and the enormously expanded production and export of Western grain assured good times for farmers. In almost every area of economic life new energy flowed: mining in copper, silver, and gold; railroad-building; the petroleum trade; and every kind of manufacturing, from iron to flour to woolen cloth. The leather-manufacturing establishments of Newark, New Jersey—once a great center of shoemaking for the slaves of the South—now made shoes for soldiers, and harness and saddles for the army. Immigration, which had slowed down early in the war, now recovered and surpassed prewar levels.

This exuberance was reflected in rampant speculative investment, much of it foolish. Corruption was widespread; employers and profiteers exploited the poor. With capital rapidly accumulating, a speculative psychology overtook the business world. Yet the economic boom, despite its bad features, contributed in manifold ways to Northern victory.

The decisive campaigns of 1863

Chancellorsville. The military might of the Confederacy had reached its peak in 1862, though few recognized the fact at the time. The three great campaigns of 1863 put the South on the defensive and ended Confederate hopes for military victory. In the East, Robert E. Lee once again carried the war into the North; in the West, Ulysses S. Grant pressed to reduce Vicksburg and gain control of the Mississippi; and in Tennessee, the Union at last moved energetically against the Confederate lines at Chattanooga. Those campaigns revealed that the North could achieve victory if it had the patience to push a slow war of attrition to its conclusion.

In Virginia the winter stalemate was broken when General Hooker crossed the Rappahannock River above Fredericksburg; his plan was to outflank Lee's army and force him either to retreat or be caught in a Union net. Once across the river, Hooker failed to move fast enough and fell victim to his own irresolution. Lee then executed one of the most brilliant maneuvers of the war. Splitting his army, he sent "Stonewall" Jackson to attack Hooker's dangerously extended right wing. On May 3, near Chancellorsville, Jackson caught the federal forces by surprise and in smooth cooperation with Lee's diversionary offensive came close to destroying an army of 130,000 men with a force only half as large. The result was not so favorable to the South as it could have been, for the Union Army managed to withdraw north of the Rappahannock. Union losses were heavy, and morale low, but the army was saved. The victory had been costly to Lee as well, for Jackson was mortally wounded the night after the battle by one of his own pickets who failed to recognize him in the darkness.

The extraordinary cooperation between Jackson and Lee, made possible by an absence of vanity surprising in high officers, had been worth regiments to the Confederate cause. With Jackson gone, the Army of Northern Virginia would never be the same again. Even so, Lee began once more to ponder an invasion of the North. President Lincoln, on the other hand, was pondering where he could find a general to match Lee's daring.

Vicksburg and Gettysburg. In the West, Union forces were at last gaining a clear advantage. The greatest fortified point on the Mississippi River still in Confederate control was Vicksburg, which commanded a bluff above a hairpin curve in the river and served as a vital connection between the eastern and western parts of the Confederacy. Late in 1862 Ulysses S. Grant set about reducing Vicksburg

Grant's army at Vicksburg

as well. After fruitless efforts to approach the city over the bayou country to the north, Grant hit on a better plan. He marched his troops down the west side of the Mississippi, ran his naval transports down the river under the Vicksburg batteries to pick the troops up, and brought his army across the river for an approach from the south. Sweeping eastward, Grant prevented reinforcements from reaching Confederate General J. C. Pemberton, who with a force of thirty thousand tried to defend Vicksburg against Grant's approach. Grant caught Pemberton within the defensive lines of Vicksburg and put the city under a six-week siege. Grant gave Pemberton no rest. The defending soldiers were exhausted, and the population of Vicksburg was reduced to near-starvation. Recognizing that no help could reach him, Pemberton surrendered on July 4, 1863. The fall of Vicksburg was followed shortly by the capture of Port Hudson, the last Confederate strong point on the river. Those events marked the turning point of the war in the West. The Confederacy was now split in half.

Grant's strategy and determination brought about the fall of Vicksburg. It was also the result of a strategic decision made by Lee and Davis. To relieve pressure on the Western army under Pemberton they had to choose between two courses of action: either they could send divisions of Lee's army to aid Pemberton, or they could launch a second invasion of the North, which might persuade Lincoln to call part of Grant's army east. Lee and Davis decided that invasion of the North was now the best hope of the Confederacy. England might yet intervene, and the war-weary people of the North might give up their attempt to subjugate the South. In June, the Army of Northern Virginia, ragged but merry, swung into the Shenandoah Valley and again took the road north. This time they were heading for Harrisburg, Pennsylvania.

"Fighting" Joe Hooker followed, keeping his army between Lee and Washington and begging all the way for reinforcements. Actually Hooker seemed reluctant to engage Lee; he complained of petty problems and seized the first opportunity to resign his command. Lincoln, accepting the resignation with alacrity, gave the post to General George G. Meade, who reluctantly accepted. Meade was an able soldier with a good record for skillful deployment of troops. He was hot-tempered enough to earn the nickname "Old Snapping

⑤ *The war in the East, 1863*

Turtle,'' but he had no stomach for a war of attrition.

On July 1 the two armies stumbled toward each other and fell almost by chance into the greatest battle of the war. The fighting began on the northern side of Gettysburg, Pennsylvania, not because either commanding officer had decided upon the spot but because some detached units happened to clash there. With a speed that astonished the Confederates, the new Union commander concentrated his army on a strong position along Cemetery Ridge, south of Gettysburg. Meade's line resembled an inverted fishhook, anchored at its eye by two rocky promontories called Round Top and Little Round Top. To the north the hook nearly encircled Culp's Hill. This was an extraordinarily strong defensive position.

On a line about a mile distant, across an open field, the Confederates held high ground on Seminary Ridge. Lee had to decide whether to risk breaking his lines to encircle the enemy's position or to launch a frontal assault on the Union lines. Confederate cavalry officer J. E. B. Stuart, whose men were the ''eyes'' of Lee's army, had been detached earlier on reconnaissance, and Lee had to

make his decision without knowing what dangers an encircling movement might entail. Against the advice of General James Longstreet, now Lee's second in command, Lee decided on a frontal assault. Hoping Lee would change his mind, Longstreet dragged his feet and unwittingly gave the Union Army time to prepare. On July 3, the Confederates tried to soften the Union lines with the heaviest bombardment they could muster. Those who heard it on that hot, dry afternoon reported that the guns were as loud as any thunderstorm, and that there had never been anything like it in the entire war.

Then Lee made a grievous error of judgment. He launched fifteen thousand men under General George Pickett across the mile-wide field in a futile assault on the Union center. Pickett's Charge was a glorious restaging of the old warfare of legendary valor, flying banners, and disastrous bloodletting. Modern weaponry had made this kind of courage obsolete. In a devastating repulse, federal troops ended Lee's offensive power forever. After a day of mournful waiting for a counteroffensive that never came, the Army of Northern Virginia limped off down the

Chickamauga: a Union view

The march [to Rossville] was a melancholy one. All along the road, for miles, wounded men were lying. They had crawled or hobbled slowly away from the fury of the battle, become exhausted, and lain down by the roadside to die. Some were calling the names and numbers of their regiments, but many had become too weak to do this; by midnight the column had passed by. What must have been their agony, mental and physical, as they lay in the dreary woods, sensible that there was no one to comfort or to care for them and that in a few hours more their career on earth would be ended!...

At this hour of the night (eleven to twelve o'clock) the army is simply a mob. There appears to be neither organization nor discipline. The various commands are mixed up in what seems to be inextricable confusion. Were a division of the enemy to pounce down upon us between this and morning, I fear the Army of the Cumberland would be blotted out.

From John Beatty, *Memoirs of a Volunteer,* 1879.

Shenandoah Valley in a torrential rain. It was July 5, the day after the fall of Vicksburg. Lee had sustained nearly twenty-five thousand casualties in the battle.

The Union losses were as great as those of the Confederacy. Four months later, when President Lincoln dedicated the National Cemetery on the field at Gettysburg, he said of the brave Union dead that they had "nobly advanced" the cause of a new nationalism founded on liberty for all, and that it remained for the living to see that the nation would have "a new birth in freedom." Much hard fighting lay ahead, enough to discourage many patriots, but at Gettysburg the Union war effort had rounded a corner.

The Tennessee campaign. In the West, the evenly matched armies of William Rosecrans and Braxton Bragg faced each other for six months. In spite of frantic urgings from the War Department that he go on the offensive, Rosecrans had delayed interminably. In September 1863 he suddenly sprang into action, and in a series of smart maneuvers he pressed Bragg southward and eastward into northern Georgia. On September 19 and 20, however, the Confederates caught their pursuers off guard and turned on them in one of the most savage engagements of the entire war. Between the two armies nearly thirty-eight thousand casualties were suffered at the Battle of Chickamauga Creek, and the Confederates routed the right flank of Rosecrans' army. Had it not been for the firm stand of General George Thomas, the Virginia-born commander of Rosecrans' left flank, the Union offensive might have been ruined. What the Union owed to Thomas, the victorious Confederates owed to General Longstreet, who had rushed the survivors of the Gettysburg campaign over rickety rails in time to reinforce Bragg's forces.

⑥ *Fighting around Chattanooga, 1863*

Grant and his staff

The Union forces, now under General Thomas, the "Rock of Chickamauga," withdrew to Chattanooga. Bragg followed slowly, supposing that a shortage of supplies would force Thomas to surrender. But late in October Grant arrived with fresh supplies and with Lincoln's commission to take over as supreme commander in the West. Grant infused vigor into the Tennessee campaign. In a tremendous feat of railroad warfare he brought twenty-three thousand troops from the East in two weeks' time. Thus strengthened, on November 24 and 25 Grant drove the Confederates back to the Georgia line and tightened his grip on Tennessee.

The year ended far better for the Union than it had begun. Lee's invasion of Pennsylvania had expended his offensive power; the Union now controlled the entire Mississippi; and Grant's army was poised near the Georgia line ready for further action. The Confederacy was being fragmented and crushed. General Scott's once-rejected "Anaconda Plan" had become the formula for victory.

Lincoln saw that the South was doomed. In the spring he sent for U. S. Grant, the general he had been looking for all along. An aggressive fighter, Grant could be relied on to press the enemy, however heavy the losses, to unconditional surrender. Lincoln named Grant to a newly created post, General of the Armies. The North was building a modern command system, and Grant would direct all theaters of the war. General Henry W. Halleck, called "Old Brains" by friend and foe alike, became the chief of staff, a new position created to clear communications between Grant, Lincoln, and the distant field commanders. Conducting

the war from his field tent, Grant left the tactical details of the Virginia campaign to General Meade, his immediate subordinate, while he himself coordinated the strategy of the Eastern and Western sectors. Grant's plan was to destroy the two great armies of the South.

Both the Union and the Confederacy now shook up their field command. General William Tecumseh Sherman assumed the post Grant had vacated in the West, and Davis at last reinstated Joseph E. Johnston as commander of the Army of Tennessee. In the spring Sherman pressed into northern Georgia. His objective was Atlanta, a center of what was left of the South's dwindling economic power. Grant launched his own offensive against Lee in the East.

Those dogged campaigns brought appalling casualties. The armies of Lee and Grant fought steadily and savagely from the first days of

⑦ Grant's campaign around Richmond, 1864–65

A field nurse reports from Virginia

No one can know the relief one feels in using water after a three days' march, especially when wounded. Some men you could hardly recognize if you knew them intimately.

There has been no day's work that I have done since this campaign that gave such extreme relief as cleansing those poor fellows' faces. All were cases of severe wounds. At dark night while it was raining the long train moved over a newly constructed bridge and loaded the men in transports. In the second Corps hospital the wounded continued rapidly to arrive until they laid out in the open field without any shelter. Here I dressed more wounds than in all my experience before. There were not surgeons near enough who were willing to stay in the sun and attend to the men and it was too awful to leave them uncared for. Just for one moment consider a slivered arm having been left three days, without dressing and the person having ridden in an army wagon for two days with very little food. They mostly arrived at night when all the ladies would fill their stores and feed them as they came in. They would then remain in the ambulance until morning when probably no shelter could be procured for them and here they lay in the scorching sun during $\frac{1}{2}$ the day. It was at this time there was such crying need to dress their wounds, some of which had not been opened for 36 hours. Such tired, agonized expressions no pen can describe. By the time one set of men were got in and got comfortable another set would arrive, and so it continued night and day for about two weeks.

At that time there was a very good opportunity to make a visit to the hospital up at the extreme front. There I stayed for a week, the men were then in the rifle-pits and if they moved out to get a drink of water were shot in the action. I saw them as soon as they were wounded but the custom is here to operate upon the wound and immediately send them to the rear.

From Cornelia Hancock, Letter to Joanna Dickeson, July 18, 1864, in *The South After Gettysburg: Letters of Cornelia Hancock,* edited by Henrietta Stratton Jaquette, 1956.

May into early June—from the Wilderness, to Spotsylvania Court House, to North Anna, and then to Cold Harbor. In just one month Grant sustained nearly sixty thousand casualties and Lee thirty thousand. Grant's efforts to encircle Lee's right flank were continually repulsed, with Lee showing uncanny skill in predicting the direction of Grant's next blow. Like his predecessors, Grant proved unable to destroy the Army of Northern Virginia, but unlike them he kept coming on despite grievous losses. After Cold Harbor, he passed below Richmond and put Petersburg, Virginia, under siege. This vital railroad center anchored Richmond to the Deep South, and Grant understood that without it Richmond would fall. Lee now had to stretch his army to protect the whole line between the two cities. Before it fell, Petersburg sustained a nine-month siege, the longest of the war.

Sherman's task was no easier than Grant's.

Johnston fought a series of superb defensive engagements, and at Kennesaw Mountain, on June 27, he repulsed Sherman in a battle that cost the Union two thousand casualties. But Sherman was gaining ground, and Jefferson Davis once again lost faith in Johnston's generalship. In mid-July he gave the command to John B. Hood, who took the offensive. After two foolish and disastrous pitched battles, on July 20 and 22, Hood withdrew to Atlanta's entrenchments. The Union armies had invested the heart of the Confederacy.

The election of 1864. With the war in Grant's competent hands, Lincoln turned his attention to the fall elections. A Republican triumph seemed essential to military victory, because the Democrats were gaining strength from a peace movement of formidable proportions. Numbers of war-weary Northerners decided that the South would accept a negotiated peace if the slavery issue was abandoned; few realized that the end of the war was near. Northerners who read the ghastly casualty lists from the battles in Virginia called Grant a ''butcher.'' When they reflected on Lincoln's curtailment of civil liberties, they asked if Lincoln himself was not heading a conspiracy to destroy American democracy. The Republicans, by naming a war Democrat, Andrew Johnson of Tennessee, as Lincoln's running mate, hoped to neutralize criticism and win the election. Now they called themselves the Union party.

Lincoln faced disaffection even within his own party. Radical Republicans believed him too soft in his conduct of the war and too gentle in his plans for the readmission of former Confederate states to the Union. Lincoln had already begun his efforts to reconstruct occupied Louisiana, and as Union armies ploughed deeper into the South the question of how the former Confederate states were to be reorganized became a potent political issue. After hostilities ceased, Lincoln's plan would allow returning Southerners to participate in the political rehabilitation of their state if they would merely pledge allegiance to the United States, even though they had supported the Confederacy during the war. Once 10 percent of those in a state who had voted in 1860 had taken such a pledge, the state could, under Lincoln's plan, reorganize. Radical Republicans challenged Lincoln by passing the Wade-Davis bill, which would have limited voting in the Southern states to those who could pledge that they had always been loyal, who could say that they had never given aid or comfort to the Confederate government. Sponsored in the Senate by Benjamin Wade of Ohio and in the House of Representatives by Henry Winter Davis, the bill was a pattern for a harsh and thorough reconstruction of the South. Although Lincoln vetoed that bill, he could not still its sponsors. In a public manifesto denouncing the President's course, the Radical Republicans in Congress accused Lincoln of usurping congressional responsibility by beginning the reorganization of Louisiana on his own initiative. A number of Radicals, challenging Lincoln's nomination, backed the candidacy of John C. Frémont. Lincoln was nervous about the election. ''This morning as for some days past,'' he reflected on August 23, ''it seems probable that this Administration will not be re-elected.''

Fortunately for the Republicans, the Democrats tried to straddle the war issue. They denounced the war as a failure and proposed an armistice and peace negotiations. Yet they nominated the popular George McClellan, who denied that the war had failed. While criticizing the Republicans for making emancipation a goal of the war, McClellan also condemned Democrats who sought peace at the price of disunion.

It was good news from the front that re-elected Lincoln. In late summer 1864, Rear Admiral Farragut captured Mobile Bay. Just before election time, Philip Sheridan routed the troops of General Jubal A. Early from the valley of Virginia. But best of all was the news that Hood had evacuated Atlanta on September 1. Northern spirits soared. Frémont retired from the campaign, and the Radicals closed ranks behind the President.

Lincoln won 55 percent of the popular vote and carried the Electoral College by two hundred twelve to twenty-one. He was supported by a strong coalition of middle-class professional men, farmers, skilled laborers, and conservative Union people who had voted for Bell in 1860. McClellan ran well in areas carried by Breckinridge in 1860, and he attracted most of the immigrant vote.

Lincoln had won a clear mandate for his policies. But the contest had engendered a profound bitterness that lived on into the decade of Reconstruction following the war. The Democrats, in an effort to fix blame for the lengthening casualty lists on Lincoln's emancipation policies, had coupled with their legitimate complaints a sordid appeal to racism. The Administration on its side had made a doubtful play for the soldier vote, allowing voting only in units where Republican sentiment was strong. Voting by voice made it difficult for soldiers in the field to oppose the general will. On the home front, military units were stationed in areas of strong peace sentiment to discourage Democrats from voting. The hatreds and partisanship of the war years had been raised to fever pitch before the polls even opened.

The bitter end. After the election Lincoln's generals moved quickly. Sherman cut loose from his supply base, letting his army feed off the countryside. Leaving Atlanta behind, he headed southeast for Savannah. Lonely chimneys of burned homes and a charred, desolate landscape sixty miles wide marked the route of his famous journey to the sea. Behind his

''Long Abraham: a little longer'': the campaign of 1864

⑧ Sherman's Drive, 1864–65

army followed a throng of black refugees seeking freedom. But in the hearts and minds of the people of the South, this modern soldier left the strongest impression of all. The social system of the South could not withstand the economic might that Sherman's vast well-equipped and well-armed army represented, and after his passing the will to fight died. Hood's futile effort to distract Sherman from his march across Georgia ended in the destruction of that hapless officer's army at the hands of General Thomas in the battle of Nashville. At Christmas Sherman telegraphed Lincoln the news of Savannah's fall.

The Confederacy had no armies left capable of doing harm. As Sherman pushed northward through the Carolinas, Joseph Johnston confessed that he could "do no more than annoy him." In Virginia, Lee failed in a last desperate effort to break the Union lines and had to abandon Petersburg. Federal forces promptly occupied Richmond, and Lee's battered army moved westward. On April 9, at Appomattox Court House, Lee surrendered the Army of Northern Virginia to Grant. Johnston surrendered within a few days, and the remaining Confederate forces followed in short order. After four terrible years, the Civil War was over.

But the Union was not restored. The architects of peace would have to be statesmen, not soldiers. In his moving Second Inaugural Address, Lincoln had pledged to strive for a new Union based on human liberty and justice. The hopes of his countrymen were crushed on the night of April 14, at Ford's Theater in Washington, when a crazed actor, John Wilkes Booth, shot the President. He died the next morning. Gone was the leader who had planned for peace even in the agony of war, and gone with him were the prospects, never bright, that the nation might be reunited "with malice toward none; and charity for all."

Suggestions for reading

GENERAL

Here as in the preceding chapter the best introductory treatment, from the point of view of both its text and its extensive, critical bibliography, is J. G. Randall and David Donald, *The Civil War and Reconstruction* (2nd ed., 1961). A more extended treatment is found in Allan Nevins, *The War for the Union*, 4 vols. (1959–71). For a valuable short synthesis see R. F. Nichols, *The Stakes of Power** (1961), and, especially on military affairs, Bruce Catton, *This Hallowed Ground** (1956).

The literature of the Civil War abounds in good personal accounts. The outstanding Confederate diary is Mary Boykin Chesnut, *A Diary from Dixie** (1961), edited by B. A. Williams. Comparable in depth and grander in scope is R. M. Myers, ed., *The Children of Pride* (1972), the letters of a Georgia family caught in a social revolution. Thomas Wentworth Higginson, *Army Life in a Black Regiment** (1870), is a romanticized but fascinating account of the author's experience as leader of a black regiment; Suzie King Taylor, *Reminiscences of My Life in Camp* (1902), tells the story of a black laundress who taught black troops to read.

THE CONFEDERACY

The outstanding study of the Confederacy is the judicious, trenchant Clement Eaton, *A History of the Southern Confederacy** (1954). E. M. Coulter, *The Confederate States of America, 1861–1865* (1950), is good social history, but less critical. A useful short account is C. P. Roland, *The Confederacy** (1960). The causes of the South's defeat are the subject of a series of incisive essays in David Donald, ed., *Why the North Won the Civil War** (1960). Among many special studies, one of the most engaging is B. J. Hendrick, *Statesmen of the Lost Cause* (1939), which

*Available in a paperback edition.

examines Jefferson Davis and his civilian associates. A more sophisticated treatment of the same subject is in R. W. Patrick, *Jefferson Davis and His Cabinet* (1944). Two works of F. L. Owsley are of the first importance: *King Cotton Diplomacy* (1931) and *State Rights in the Confederacy* (1925). Among the many biographies of significance are Hudson Strode, *Jefferson Davis,* 2 vols. (1955), and R. M. McElroy, *Jefferson Davis: The Unreal and the Real,* 2 vols. (1937), as well as R. R. Von Abele, *Alexander H. Stephens: A Biography* (1946).

LINCOLN AND THE UNION

The general studies cited above and the Lincoln studies listed here afford the appropriate points of departure for understanding the Union during the Civil War. Among additional important works, three bear upon significant diplomatic issues: E. D. Adams, *Great Britain and the American Civil War,* 2 vols. (1925); M. B. Duberman, *Charles Francis Adams* (1961); and the good biography of Seward in S. F. Bemis, ed., *The American Secretaries of State and Their Diplomacy,* 10 vols. (1927–29). See also G. G. Van Deusen's biography of William H. Seward (1967). F. L. Klement, *The Copperheads in the Middle West* (1960), explains the motivation of the group largely in economic terms, whereas disloyalty and danger are stressed by G. F. Milton, *Abraham Lincoln and the Fifth Column** (1942), and Wood Gray, *The Hidden Civil War: The Story of the Copperheads** (1942). The best general account of Lincoln's policies in the border states is E. C. Smith, *The Borderland in the Civil War* (1927). For a superb study of important agricultural developments P. C. Gates, *Agriculture and the Civil War* (1965), is best. For an overview of society in the Union states see E. D. Fite, *Social and Industrial Conditions in the North during the Civil War* (1910). A fine study of an important agricultural state is Frederick Merk, *Economic History of Wisconsin During the Civil War Decade* (1916). Sidney Ratner, *American Taxation* (1942), W. C. Mitchell, *Gold, Prices and Wages under the Greenback Standard* (1908), and R. P. Sharkey, *Money, Class and Party** (1959), treat the financial history of the Union. Indispensable on its subject is J. G. Randall, *Constitutional Problems under Lincoln** (1926). For the impact of the war on the intellectuals, George Fredrickson, *The Inner Civil War** (1965), is peerless. M. E. Massey, *Bonnet Brigades* (1966), recounts the amazing extent of woman's participation in the war, at home and on the front.

There is no end to Lincoln literature. The best short biography is Benjamin Thomas, *Abraham Lincoln* (1952). Among longer biographies, Carl Sandburg, *Abraham Lincoln: The War Years* [abridged version*], 4 vols. (1939), is distinguished for its passion, and J. G. Randall, *Lincoln the President,* 4 vols.* (1945–55), completed by R. N. Current, for its depth and judgment. Among many anthologies, P. M. Angle, ed., *The Lincoln Reader** (1947), stands out for its readability. Two especially incisive collections of essays are David Donald, *Lincoln Reconsidered** (1956), and R. N. Current, *The Lincoln Nobody Knows** (1958). Truly interested students will want to consult R. P. Basler and others, *The Collected Works of Abraham Lincoln,* 9 vols. (1953–55), and the thorough Jay Monaghan, ed., *Lincoln Bibliography, 1839–1939,* 2 vols. (1945). There is a more selective and critical bibliography in P. M. Angle, *A Shelf of Lincoln Books* (1946), and a good selection of Lincoln writings in P. M. Angle and E. S. Miers, eds., *The Living Lincoln* (1955), and R. P. Basler, ed., *Abraham Lincoln: His Speeches and Writings* (1946). Especially significant on Lincoln as a politician are H. J. Carman and R. H. Luthin, *Lincoln and the Patronage* (1943); W. B. Hesseltine, *Lincoln and the War Governors* (1948); and T. H. Williams, *Lincoln and the Radicals** (1941). On Lincoln and military affairs, besides the books listed below, T. H. Williams, *Lincoln and His Generals* (1952), and R. V. Bruce, *Lincoln and the Tools of War* (1956), are particularly rewarding.

BLACKS AND EMANCIPATION

The war almost immediately affected the status of blacks, and J. M. McPherson, *The Negro's Civil War** (1965), tells the story in a fine documentary history. *The Struggle for Equality** (1964) by the same author explains the abolitionists' drive for emancipation during the conflict. For an account of Lincoln's views, see Benjamin Quarles, *Lincoln and the Negro* (1962), and his *The Negro in the Civil War* (1953), a pioneering work in its field. B. I. Wiley, *Southern Negroes, 1861–1865* (1938), is an outstanding early effort to cover a complex subject. For the impact

*Available in a paperback edition.

of the war on one South Carolina community of blacks see W. L. Rose, *The Port Royal Experiment** (1964). The outstanding work on the black man's military contribution is D. T. Cornish, *The Sable Arm** (1956).

MILITARY EVENTS

Just about every significant general, Union or Confederate, and just about every significant engagement at arms, has been the subject of at least one, and ordinarily of several, books or essays. The would-be specialist has no convenient terminus in his reading; the neophyte can begin profitably in any one of many places. For an exciting and informed start, an interested student might turn to the writings of Bruce Catton: *Mr. Lincoln's Army** (1951); *Glory Road** (1952); *A Stillness at Appomattox** (1954); *America Goes to War** (1958); *Banners at Shenandoah** (1965); *Centennial History of the Civil War,* 3 vols. (1961–63); *Grant Moves South* (1960); *This Hallowed Ground** (1956); *U. S. Grant and the American Military Tradition** (1954). See also E. S. Miers, *Web of Victory: Grant at Vicksburg* (1955), and F. D. Downey, *Storming the Gateway, Chattanooga, 1863* (1960). Jay Monaghan, *Civil War on the Western Border, 1854–1865* (1955), provides one of the good accounts available of the trans-Mississippi war, and the Northern navy absorbs several authors, among them R. S. West, Jr., *Mr. Lincoln's Navy* (1957), and C. E. Macartney, *Mr. Lincoln's Admirals* (1956)—both general accounts.

There is also an intriguing but more technical study in J. P. Baxter III, *The Introduction of the Ironclad Warship* (1933). The common soldier has had admirable attention from B. I. Wiley, *The Life of Johnny Reb** (1943) and *The Life of Billy Yank** (1952). Also good on that subject is the anthology, H. S. Commager, ed., *The Blue and the Gray: The Story of the Civil War as Told by Participants,* 2 vols. (1950). *The Personal Memoirs of U. S. Grant,* 2 vols. (1885, 1886) are still an impressive testimony to the author's ability and humility, possibly the best of all Civil War memoirs, but W. T. Sherman, *Memoirs,* 2 vols. (1875), is also first rate; and both men have had talented biographers, in particular Lloyd Lewis in his memorable *Sherman, Fighting Prophet* (1932) and *Captain Sam Grant* (1950). On the Southern side, the literature, like the valor, balances that of the North, and D. S. Freeman stands out as one of the great historians of the conflict in his two classics, *R. E. Lee, A Biography,* 4 vols. (1934–35) and *Lee's Lieutenants,* 3 vols. (1942–44). On Lee's great lieutenant, Frank Vandiver, *Mighty Stonewall* (1957), and Lenoir Chambers, *Stonewall Jackson,* 2 vols. (1959), are readable accounts. The first Western battles of the Confederacy are covered splendidly in T. L. Connelly, *Army of the Heartland: The Army of the Tennessee, 1861–1862* (1967). A short but comprehensive story of the Confederacy with a military emphasis and unforgettable character portrayals is Frank Vandiver, *Their Tattered Flags* (1970).

Finally, not even a list as brief and selective as this should omit mention of the atlases of the Civil War: the most authoritative, H. S. Commager, 1958 ed. of *Atlas to Accompany the Official Records of the Union and Confederate Armies* (1891–95); the more modern, in its design and use of symbols, V. J. Esposito, ed., *The West Point Atlas of American Wars,* 2 vols. (1959); and the motorists' handy J. B. Mitchell, *Decisive Battles of the Civil War** (1955).

*Available in a paperback edition.

15 The aftermath of war

The long war was over. Now the nation, still divided in spirit, plunged into a decade of political and social turmoil. Northern victory had preserved the Union and had ended slavery; the constitutional right of states to secede would never be argued again. But all else was confusion. The Constitution was as silent on how states could be readmitted to the Union as it was on their right to secede. Indeed if Lincoln was correct in holding that states could not secede, then the Southern states had not seceded. They would simply resume their former responsibilities and enjoy their old privileges. The Southern states hoped for just such a simple restoration, even though the bitterness of the war made it unlikely that the North would at once reembrace them.

Uncertainty too marked the future of the blacks emancipated by war. Would the Southern states relegate the freedman to peonage, handicap him legally as they had handicapped free blacks before the war, or grant him full citizenship? That question would have to be resolved by the Southern people, ill equipped to do so, because they had been devastated materially and emotionally by the war. And,

although many Southerners were slow to realize it, their answer would have to satisfy the Northern people.

Northerners faced dramatic changes of their own. Since the 1840s the North had been moving rapidly toward an industrial economy. The war had only diverted the demographic and social changes that accompany industrialism, and with the return of peace those changes sped forward once again. In 1863 immigration resumed its prewar pace, and after the war, for approximately ten years, an average of three hundred thousand new Americans arrived each year at the nation's ports. Every year more workers moved to the city, where they became increasingly dependent on cycles of trade. Unprecedented opportunities for wealth opened for businessmen. The distractions posed by a dynamic economy prevented Northerners from concentrating steadily on the problems of Southern Reconstruction. Then, too, the passions of war were slow to subside, and few politicians of either section could rise above partisanship to disinterested statesmanship. The war lasted four years; winning the peace required twelve.

The problems of recovery

The new nation. The South had seceded from a union of states. It returned to a nation forged by war and vindicated by victory. Although the new spirit of nationalism was evident in many ways, especially in the powers exercised by the President and Congress, it re-

vealed itself most clearly in economic legislation enacted during the war years. The absence of traditional Southern opposition in Congress during the war had made it easy for Republicans to adopt a protective tariff and reduce foreign competition in industry, to create a national banking system, to put through a homestead act, and to start funding a transcontinental railroad. Those measures signaled a new era of expansion in industry, agriculture, and transportation—all under the favoring hand of the national government.

Prosperity fed a mood of confident materialism. Seizing the opportunities of wartime economic expansion and inflation, entrepreneurs concentrated in their own hands new wealth that they now sought to invest. They had not far to look. Technological advances, many inspired by the demands of war, opened thousands of new opportunities to put capital to work. The natural resources of the country, seemingly inexhaustible, were more available than ever; industrialists exploited them fully, often ruthlessly and wastefully. Such vital indexes of industrial growth as the production of pig iron and bituminous coal and the extent of railroad mileage climbed sharply.

The iron horse symbolized the age of energy. The forty thousand miles of railroad track laid in the decade after 1865 stimulated heavy industry and opened the further West to agriculture, supplying the food for an expanding army of industrial workers. Federal loans and land grants had sped the construction of the Central Pacific eastward from California and the Union Pacific westward across the plains. For every mile of track laid the railway company received 6,400 acres of free land. Congress made generous loans on second-mortgage bonds: $16,000 for each mile of level ground covered, $48,000 in the mountains, $32,000 in the high plains, and $22,000 elsewhere. As the two roads raced for their share of the federal subsidies, they sacrificed quality to speed. Still their accomplishment was spectacular. The Union Pacific built 1,089 miles of track; the Central Pacific, 689. They met at Promontory Point, northwest of Ogden, Utah. At ceremonies there on May 10, 1869, the blows of a silver sledge drove in the golden spikes connecting the rails. Now only a week's journey separated the Atlantic from the Pacific.

Demobilization posed problems for the Northern economy. Eight hundred thousand Union veterans were released in six months, and the abrupt cancellation of war contracts threw a million men out of work. Secretary of the Treasury Hugh McCulloch picked this inopportune time to withdraw from circulation nearly $100 million of the greenbacks that had been issued during the war. Constricting the currency when so many were unemployed caused a brief but sharp economic slump in 1867. Within a year, however, railroad construction and expansion of the industries that supplied railroads with essential equipment created new jobs for the unemployed. Until 1873, when a new depression struck, most Americans were optimistic about the future.

The devastated South. In the South there was no such boisterous return to civilian pursuits. Agriculture, the region's economic bulwark, had been ruined wherever armies had clashed and passed. "The country between Washington and Richmond was . . . like a desert," wrote one observer. Another described the path of Sherman's march as "a broad black streak of ruin and desolation." Houses and outbuildings had been burned, crops destroyed, and livestock killed. Seed to plant new crops was often unavailable, and many farmers could not afford to buy it when they found it. Horses and mules to plow the land were even harder to find. Credit was almost unobtainable, and labor was scarce. A quarter of a million soldiers had lost their lives, and many freedmen were reluctant to work for their former masters. They believed, not without reason, that one-time masters would never treat one-time slaves as free men. The freedmen had other problems. Seeking relatives lost in slavery, returning to old homes, and looking for land and jobs, they were much on the road. They long remained a disorganized element in the work force the South required for economic recovery.

The cities fared no better than the countryside. Industry had been crippled or abandoned, financial institutions ruined, and resources for credit wiped out. At one stroke, emancipation had destroyed a credit base made up of billions of dollars invested in slaves. Land values slumped in response to the general devastation and lack of labor. The appearance of cities in the path of the armies was as desolate as the real condition of their industry and commerce. Charleston, South Carolina, was "a city of ruins, of desolation, of vacant houses, of widowed women, of rotting wharves." Columbia lay in ashes, as did most of Richmond.

Most Southerners, accepting defeat with fortitude and resignation, set about rebuilding their land. Many Southern whites expressed relief that slavery had come to an end but were at the same time uneasy about how the races would live together in the future. Long conditioned to rely on slavery as a means of controlling blacks, they were afraid of insurrections in the first year after the war, especially in regions where there were many freedmen. They could not even imagine political equality between the races. The freedmen had to face their own emotional hurdles. Learning to accept the responsibilities of family and self-support was not easy for men who had no land, no money, no education. When freedmen did manage to win some success, few understood the effort success required; when they failed, friend and foe alike were apt to explain it on grounds of inferiority.

The Northerners proved to be generous conquerors, as conquerors go. They executed no one for treason and briefly imprisoned only a few Confederates, one of them Jefferson Davis. They volunteered indispensable relief for the destitute of both races. In the last year of the war they had created the Bureau of Refugees, Freedmen, and Abandoned Lands, commonly known as the Freedmen's Bureau, to aid emancipated slaves. The Bureau frequently aided whites as well. After the war was over the Bureau sent supplies, seed, and rations to planters so farming could begin anew and freedmen could get work. It protected freedmen from exploitative planters and provided them with transportation to reach their families.

But poverty and daily reminders of defeat were hard for white Southerners to bear, and Northern bounty was not always graciously received. Women expressed their bitterness by shunning the army of occupation and by wearing on their gowns the insignia of the Confederacy in the form of buttons taken from the uniforms of husbands and sweethearts. Many young people of the defeated planter class had little hope for the future. "For the first time in my life I feel the pressure of want," wrote one young veteran, struggling vainly to conquer bitterness. "I have no country, no flag, no emblems, no public spirit. . . . I live now simply to live, and for my family." Experienced Southern leaders, however, were eager to reorganize their state governments and regain their lost political rights. They anxiously awaited reassuring signals from the North.

The dilemma of Reconstruction. South-
erners aware of Lincoln's course during the war had reason to be optimistic. Although Lincoln had used military might to reestablish state governments, his plan was generous, its workings swift. As the Northern armies occupied Tennessee, Louisiana, and Arkansas, Lincoln had installed military governors and had sought the support of the loyal minority of citizens in establishing governments loyal to the Union. He had generously pardoned former Confederates who would take an oath of loyalty to the Constitution and the Union. In December 1863, by presidential proclamation, Lincoln outlined a plan for the full restoration of the Southern states to the Union. When in any state one-tenth of the citizens who had voted in the presidential election of 1860 had taken that oath, they could establish a government, without slavery, and the President would recognize it as the "true government." In 1864 Tennessee, Louisiana, and Arkansas had reorganized under Lincoln's "10 percent plan."

The Radical Republicans in Congress had challenged Lincoln's plan by passing the Wade-Davis bill. Moreover, Congress refused to seat congressional delegations from the states Lincoln had reorganized under his plan. In these actions the Radicals had strong support from moderate Republicans who agreed that Lincoln had usurped Congress' authority by taking over Reconstruction and who distrusted the loyalty of the Southern citizenry almost as deeply as the Radicals did (see p. 353). The harsh Wade-Davis bill provided that only after a majority of citizens in a state had taken an oath of loyalty to the United States could their state be reorganized. But only citizens able to take an ironclad oath of past loyalty could vote for representatives to the constitutional conventions. To deny former Confederate officials any role in the new governments, the bill provided that they could not be representatives to the conventions, and that new constitutions must disqualify them from voting and holding office. Lincoln vetoed the Wade-Davis bill, but Congress adamantly refused to seat delegates from the states Lincoln had reorganized. In the Wade-Davis Manifesto the Radicals rebuked Lincoln publicly, instructing him to execute the law and leave the making of it to Congress. The war ended with this conflict unresolved.

The Republicans in Congress faced a serious political problem. By an ironic twist, the late Confederate states stood to gain in defeat more representatives in Congress than they had had before the war. The elimination of slavery meant that blacks, only three-fifths of whom had been counted for purposes of congressional representation while they were slaves, would now be counted to their full number as freedmen. If the freedmen were enfranchised, Republicans might hope they would vote for the party that had emancipated them. To insist that the Southern states enfranchise freedmen before being readmitted to the Union was politically dangerous, however, because even in the North only a few states (those with the fewest blacks) allowed blacks to vote. There was also the danger that Southern planters might use their economic power to influence the votes of their former slaves, thus strengthening the Democrats rather than the Republicans. Beyond these immediate concerns was the Constitution's guarantee that states had the right to regulate their own suffrage requirements, and no one supposed that any Southern state would voluntarily grant the vote to freedmen. Republicans saw no way out of their dilemma. On one point they were firm, however: they had no intention of giving the Democrats the Southern votes they needed to win back their power in Congress. Lincoln himself had hoped to build Republican support among Southern whites, but even he had wavered when he saw Louisiana electing conservatives unwilling to compromise on the race issue.

Republicans seldom spoke openly about the dilemma posed by Southern congressional representation. They stressed instead their distrust of the former rebels and what they pictured as the disloyal behavior of Northern Democrats during the war. Many Republicans, perhaps a majority, believed that the safety of the Union rested on their party's staying in power. They suspected that a combination of former rebels and Northern "Copperheads"— their name for pro-Southern Democrats— might even persuade the federal government to assume the Confederate war debt. For these reasons the Republicans were determined to bar Southern representatives from Congress until the government of the Southern states rested securely in the hands of loyal Unionists, preferably Republicans.

Andrew Johnson: shaped by his harsh past

Johnson takes charge. Lincoln might have untangled the political snarl in which his party was caught. He was a superb politician, deft in maneuver. But before he could devise a workable plan, an assassin's bullet put Andrew Johnson in the White House.

Born to poverty in North Carolina, Johnson moved to Tennessee as a young man and earned his living as a tailor. After he was married, his wife taught him to read and write. By dint of determination and hard work he overcame his background and rose in the politics of his adopted state, serving before the war in both houses of Congress. Johnson never outgrew the attitudes shaped by his harsh past. A belligerent man, he hated aristocrats and special privilege. And yet he had little regard for the freedmen, who in his view were instruments of planter privilege rather than oppressed chattels. Only the destruction of the planter class would, he believed, give power to the poor whites and yeoman farmers, the classes best equipped, in Johnson's mind, to make the South democratic and loyal. Johnson's struggle upward through the rough politics of Tennessee had not taught him the need to compromise. A rigid man, devoted to the Constitution, he was unable to reconcile his literal interpretation of that document with the revolutionary demands of the times. He showed none of Lincoln's flexibility or capacity for growth.

With Congress in recess when the war ended, Johnson seized the initiative. On May 29 he issued two proclamations. The first granted amnesty to former Confederates who would take an oath of loyalty to the Constitution and the federal laws. Their property was to be restored to them, except for slaves and any lands and goods that were already in the process of being confiscated by federal authorities. Fourteen classes of persons were excepted from the general amnesty, however, including the highest-ranking civil and military officers of the Confederacy, all those who had deserted judicial posts or seats in Congress to serve the Confederacy, and persons whose taxable property was worth more than $20,000. Those men were to make individual applications for amnesty, though the President promised to judge each case fairly. In denying automatic pardon to the rich, Johnson seemed as reluctant as the most ardent Radicals to trust Reconstruction to the "bloated aristocrats" he deemed responsible for secession. Still, no one knew what criteria he would use in judging their pleas for amnesty.

The second proclamation, in which Johnson outlined his requirements for the reconstruction of North Carolina, foreshadowed the policy he would follow in future proclamations to other states. He appointed William W. Holden, a well-known Unionist, as provisional governor and directed him to call a convention for the purpose of amending the state constitution "to restore said State to its constitutional relations to the Federal government." Johnson stipulated that only those who had taken the loyalty oath could vote for delegates or serve in that capacity at the convention. Although he did not include the "10 percent" provision, Johnson believed he was following Lincoln's plan of Reconstruction. Indeed, he accepted the governments already established in Arkansas, Louisiana, Tennessee, and Virginia under Lincoln's plan. Only after a public outcry against the leniency of his terms did Johnson require the returning states to disavow their ordinances of secession, repudiate the Southern war debt, and ratify the Thirteenth Amendment. That amendment, which would end slavery forever in the United States, had been approved by Congress in January 1865. Because there were now thirty-six states, approval by some of the former Confederate states was needed to reach the three-fourths that was required for ratification.

The easy terms that Johnson set for the restoration of Southern states to the Union alarmed many Northerners. Southerners heightened that alarm by voting into public office popular former-Confederates, understandably preferring them to wartime Unionists. Johnson might have helped by being more chary of his pardons to Confederate leaders, for without pardons they were not qualified to hold public office. The pardoning process was extremely cumbersome, however, demanding his attention to every case, and the harassed President fell into the habit

of approving all the pardons requested by the provisional governors. Since those governors were Unionists, he followed their advice. Some, like Governor B. F. Perry of South Carolina, forwarded every petition they received. Others requested pardons to reward or to win political friends and withheld them to destroy political foes. Johnson, inundated with petitions, pardoned freely. All too often those he pardoned soon turned up as duly elected congressmen and officers of the restored state governments. Among them was the former Vice President of the Confederacy, Alexander H. Stephens, who was elected senator from Georgia. The stubborn preference of the Southern voters for their former leaders alarmed the North.

There were other signs of Southern obstinacy. Some states refused to repudiate the Confederate war debt. South Carolina merely "repealed" its ordinance of secession, thus refusing to admit that it had been unconstitutional. The Thirteenth Amendment was ratified, but without Mississippi's approval. Southern Unionists and freedmen complained that they were not safe under the Johnson governments.

Clearly Johnson was failing in his plan to transfer leadership to the yeoman farmers. By late summer of 1865 Governor Holden of North Carolina was complaining to the President that there was "much of a rebellion spirit" left in the state. He feared that Johnson's "leniency" had "emboldened" the enemies of the government. Privately Johnson counseled Southern leaders to avoid antagonizing the Radicals in Congress, but he was too stubborn to admit publicly that his plan had misfired. Trapped by his own lavish pardoning policy, he had bestowed political power on the very leaders he had once distrusted most.

Reconstructing the South

Congress acts. When Congress reconvened in December 1865, only the Democrats and a few Republicans were willing to admit the Southern delegates. The majority of Republicans feared that if they seated former champions of the Confederacy they would surrender control over the course of Reconstruction. And yet many of those who voted against admitting the Southern delegates still hoped that Johnson might cooperate with the mod-

erates in Congress by adopting a stronger Southern policy. The moderates were not, in the winter of 1865–66, ready to adopt a radical plan of Southern Reconstruction.

The Radicals, though only a small minority in Congress, had one advantage over the moderates: they held strong opinions on Reconstruction and they knew what they wanted. They believed that, beyond the freedmen, there were few true Unionists in the

Thaddeus Stevens on black suffrage

There is more reason why colored voters should be admitted in the rebel States than in the Territories. In the States they form the great mass of the loyal men. Possibly with their aid loyal governments may be established in most of those States. Without it all are sure to be ruled by traitors; and loyal men, black and white, will be oppressed, exiled, or murdered. There are several good reasons for the passage of this bill. In the first place, it is just. I am now confining my argument to negro suffrage in the rebel States. Have not loyal blacks quite as good a right to choose rulers and make laws as rebel whites? In the second place, it is a necessity in order to protect the loyal white men in the seceded States. The white Union men are in a great minority in each of those States. With them the blacks would act in a body; and it is believed that in each of said States, except one, the two united would form a majority, control the States, and protect themselves. Now they are the victims of daily murder. They must suffer constant persecution or be exiled....

Another good reason is, it would insure the ascendency of the Union party.... I believe ... that on the continued ascendency of that party depends the safety of this great nation. If impartial suffrage is excluded in the rebel States, then every one of them is sure to send a solid rebel representative delegation to Congress, and cast a solid rebel electoral vote. They, with their kindred Copperheads of the North, would always elect the President and control Congress. While slavery sat upon her defiant throne, and insulted and intimidated the trembling North, the South frequently divided on questions of policy between Whigs and Democrats, and gave victory alternately to the sections. Now, you must divide them between loyalists, without regard to color, and disloyalists, or you will be the perpetual vassals of the free-trade, irritated, revengeful South.... I am for negro suffrage in every rebel State. If it be just, it should not be denied; if it be necessary, it should be adopted; if it be a punishment to traitors, they deserve it.

From Thaddeus Stevens, Speech to the United States House of Representatives, January 3, 1867.

South. To ensure the future of the Republican party and the safety of the Union they worked for the rapid advancement of the freedmen and the exclusion of the old Southern leaders from politics. Some Radicals were bent mainly on humiliating the South. But others were truly concerned for the safety of the blacks, most of whom had supported the North during the war, some by serving in the army. All the Radicals, however, wanted to protect Southern Unionists from the ex-Confederate leaders whom Johnson was now restoring to power.

Thaddeus Stevens, a rancorous but able congressman from Pennsylvania, exemplified this mixture of vindictiveness and idealism. He opposed black suffrage (though he was later to endorse it), because he feared that the Southern planters would use their economic power to control the freedmen's votes. Instead

Charles Sumner: he pinned his hopes on suffrage

of the vote, he proposed to give the freedmen land. He would confiscate the holdings of former Confederates and divide it into small freeholds. "Forty acres . . . and a hut," he declared, would "be more valuable . . . than the . . . right to vote." In the coastal areas of South Carolina and Georgia freedmen were already farming land, under "possessory titles," that had been assigned them by the government on estates confiscated during the war. Stevens wanted this policy extended throughout the South.

Charles Sumner, on the other hand, pinned his hopes on suffrage. He called first for votes only for educated blacks and black veterans but soon moved for general black suffrage. He argued that freedmen required the vote for their own protection. Other Radicals, including Salmon P. Chase and Ben Wade, agreed with Sumner. But the moderates, still the ma-

Southern freedmen: objects of the black codes

jority of Republicans, hoped to discover a middle road short of suffrage, between Johnson's simple restoration and the Radicals' more sweeping plans. The moderates dominated the Joint Committee on Reconstruction, which was created in December 1865 to formulate a plan for the South.

As the Joint Committee began its work, signs of Southern intransigence multiplied. Radical congressmen received countless letters from Southern Unionists complaining that they were at the mercy of former rebels. The deepest suspicions were aroused when the Southern states began to pass laws defining the status of blacks. These new "black codes," which looked like the old slave codes, were actually more like the laws governing free blacks in antebellum times. Blacks could now own property, witness, sue and be sued in court, and contract legal marriages. In some states they could even serve on juries. Despite these seemingly liberal provisions, the thrust of the new codes revealed Southern determination to keep blacks in a separate and inferior position. Blacks were segregated; intermarriage was forbidden; in Mississippi blacks could not own land; in several states they had to pay a special license fee in order to engage in certain trades. Everywhere special punishments were prescribed for black vagrants and for those who broke labor contracts. In some states blacks who could show

no means of support could be bound out by the courts as labor apprentices. The most severe codes, drawn up by Mississippi and South Carolina in 1865, reflected the fears of whites during the social chaos of the first six months of peace. Those that followed in the winter of 1865–66 were little better. All were based on the assumption that freedmen would never be anything but dependent farm-workers. Both Radicals and moderates quickly agreed that the black codes must go.

The search for a middle course. In order to counteract the black codes, Congress soon enacted two bills reported by the Joint Committee on Reconstruction. The first, passed in February 1866, extended the life and expanded the powers of the Freedmen's Bureau; the second, passed in April, made a sweeping guarantee of civil rights.

Moderates regarded the Bureau of Refugees, Freedmen and Abandoned Lands as the perfect means of safeguarding Southern Unionists and blacks. Basically a paternalistic agency, the Bureau had been set up in March 1865 primarily to help thousands of displaced persons—refugee white Unionists, and freedmen—get homes, jobs, food, and transportation. The original Freedmen's Bureau Act had empowered the agency to administer lands abandoned by Confederates or confiscated from them and had committed the

*School for freedmen,
Vicksburg, Mississippi*

government to grant freedmen homestead rights to those lands. Under the benevolent administration of Commissioner Oliver Otis Howard, the Bureau provided housing and transportation to Northern schoolteachers who came to the South to teach illiterate freedmen. The Bureau had its faults. The military officers who served as bureau agents sometimes seemed friendlier to the planters than to the freedmen, and a few of them were cruel and even venal. On the whole, however, those who were concerned for the safety of the freedmen knew that the Bureau was indispensable. Only those unsympathetic to the fate of blacks accused the Bureau of "coddling" them. Though Johnson had rendered the land provision in the original act void by returning confiscated property to its owners, the Bureau still had substantial power. The new bill, extending the life of the Bureau, would grant local agents authority to see that free labor contracts were just and that they were enforced, to defend freedmen against unscrupulous employers, and even to conduct courts when they found that freedmen were not receiving justice.

President Johnson held that those provisions would lead to "military jurisdiction," which was unconstitutional in time of peace. Accused persons tried in the Bureau courts would be tried and even convicted, he stated, without benefit of jury, rules of evidence, or right of appeal. And so Johnson vetoed the bill. He used his veto message to rebuke Congress for continuing to exclude the Southern delegates. Although Johnson's observations on the dubious constitutionality of the Freedmen's Bureau bill had some merit, they irritated congressmen who knew that freedmen were not getting justice in Southern courts. Four days after vetoing the bill Johnson harangued a crowd gathered outside the White House to hear him deliver a Washington's Birthday greeting. In a rambling speech he denounced his opponents as traitors, suggested that they wanted to kill him, and compared himself to the crucified Christ. Johnson clearly saw himself as the martyred champion of the Southern states.

Furious, Congress turned to its civil-rights bill. That bill sought to grant freedmen the protection of federal citizenship, thus securing for them the same rights and protection as whites regardless of local statutes. Further, it authorized the use of troops to enforce its privileges and penalties. Again the President resorted to a veto. But this time Congress overrode him and voted the Civil Rights bill of 1866 into law. Heartened by their success, congressional leaders now put through a mildly amended version of the Freedmen's Bureau bill. Once again Johnson vetoed it, and once again Congress overrode his veto. Some Republican senators had sustained Johnson's veto of the first Freedmen's Bureau bill, but only three of them sustained his veto of the amended bill. The broad middle section of the Republican party had joined forces to guarantee civil rights for the freedmen. The President in his obstinacy had consolidated his adopted party in opposition.

The Fourteenth Amendment. In the case of Dred Scott (see p. 311) Chief Justice Robert B. Taney had given his opinion that no black, whether free or slave, could be regarded as a United States citizen or was entitled to the privileges the Constitution granted citizens. Many Republicans, remembering that decision, were afraid to depend on an act of Congress, which would be subject to Supreme Court review, to secure civil rights to the freedmen. They decided that only an amendment to the Constitution would safeguard the freedmen and secure a new electorate in the South loyal to the Union. The Fourteenth Amendment, proposed in April 1866 by the Joint Committee on Reconstruction, was subsequently passed by Congress on June 19. First it defined American citizenship: "All persons born or naturalized in the United States, and subject to the jurisdiction thereof, are citizens of the United States and of the State wherein they reside." The amendment then prohibited states from passing laws "which shall abridge the privileges or immunities of citizens of the United States," from depriving "any person of life, liberty, or property, without due process of law," and from denying "to any person within its jurisdiction the equal protection of the laws." Although the courts in time began to interpret the word "person" to include corporations, the framers of the Fourteenth Amendment had only the freedmen in mind.

The second and third sections of the Fourteenth Amendment attempted to bring about a basic change in the Southern electorate. The second tried to force the states to grant Negro suffrage: either they enfranchised all male citizens or else they would lose seats in the House of Representatives proportionate to the number they excluded. Some Radicals would have preferred a specific guarantee of universal manhood suffrage. Practical politicians realized, however, that such a guarantee might have led to the defeat of the amendment in the North, for only a few New England states had enfranchised blacks. The third section disqualified from officeholding, state and federal, all who before the war had held public office requiring an oath to support the Constitution and who had subsequently supported the Confederacy. Only Congress could remove this disability. Other sections of the amendment disavowed the Confederate war debt, validated the United States war debt, and disallowed all claims for loss of property, including slaves.

The battle joined. The upcoming congressional elections of 1866 caught the voters in a widening rift between President and Congress, with the Fourteenth Amendment as the central issue. The summer and fall witnessed the bitterest congressional election in national history. As with the Thirteenth Amendment, favorable action by some Southern legislatures was needed to secure ratification by the required three-fourths of the states. President Johnson opposed the Fourteenth Amendment and encouraged Southern legislatures to oppose it too. Of all the former Confederate states only Tennessee ratified the amendment. Vainly hoping to prompt other states to follow suit, Congress seated Tennessee's delegates.

Johnson continued to oppose Republican measures, especially the Civil Rights Act and the Freedman's Bureau Act with all the weapons at his command. He used the patronage to reward his friends and hurt his enemies. As commander in chief he replaced military officers serving as agents in the Freedmen's Bureau who showed themselves too enthusiastic in the freedmen's cause. He interpreted acts of Congress passed over his veto in such a way that he almost negated their intent. By cultivating the support of Democrats he angered all Republicans. Though Johnson claimed to be working for peace and reconciliation, he was actually trying to unite moderate and conservative Republicans with willing Democrats in a new National Union party. His purpose was to elect his own supporters to Congress in 1866.

The new party held a convention in Philadelphia in August, but the delegates could do no more than state grand principles. There was no real community of interest in the conglomeration of conservative Republicans, Democrats, and former Confederates who attended. Republicans grew skittish, moreover, at the reappearance of their old enemies, the "rebels" and the "Copperheads." At one point Governor Orr of South Carolina, a huge man, walked down the aisle arm-in-arm with Governor Couch of Massachusetts, a slight man. The scene symbolized the Republican fear that the Southerners were about to overpower the Unionists. The convention was a fiasco.

An even greater fiasco was the President's personal campaign to win support for conservative congressmen. In a "swing-around-the-circle" stump-speaking junket through the Middle West, he met hecklers on their own terms and sacrificed the dignity of his office at every whistlestop. The people grew angry, especially as the President revealed over and over his hostility to blacks. In recent outbreaks of racial violence in Memphis and New Orleans scores of blacks had been killed and hundreds wounded. The President deplored those events, as did most Southerners, but the voters could see nothing in Johnson's restoration policy to prevent them from recurring. In November the Democrats and most of Johnson's supporters were swept out of office. The Republican regulars had won a critical victory.

Congressional Reconstruction. Although the election was more a rejection of Johnson

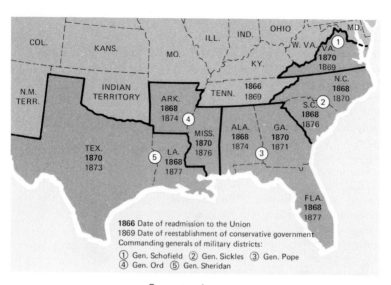

1866 Date of readmission to the Union
1869 Date of reestablishment of conservative government
Commanding generals of military districts:
① Gen. Schofield ② Gen. Sickles ③ Gen. Pope
④ Gen. Ord ⑤ Gen. Sheridan

Reconstruction

than a mandate for extremists, the Radicals eventually gained most of their aims. Even Thaddeus Stevens, though disappointed that Southern estates would not be confiscated and turned over to the freedmen, was pleased with the stringency of the legislation Congress now passed. On March 2, 1867, in its final hours and after long debate, the outgoing Thirty-ninth Congress drove through a bill ''to Provide for the more efficient Government of the Rebel States.'' This Reconstruction Act returned the South, two years after the war, to military rule. The severity of the act was partly owing to the determination of the Radicals, but even more to the unwitting aid of the Democrats who had joined with them to defeat less harsh proposals offered by moderate Republicans. Johnson's veto, not unexpected, condemned the bill as ''utterly destructive'' to the ''principles of liberty,'' but his veto was promptly overridden.

The new law divided the ten Southern states (Tennessee had already been readmitted to Congress) into five military districts, each under the command of an army general backed by troops and armed with full authority over police and over judicial and civil functions. Each commander's immediate task was to secure a new (and verifiably loyal) electorate in his district, to enroll blacks, and to eliminate all persons excluded under the Fourteenth Amendment. Those voters were to elect a constitutional convention, which would draw up a document granting universal manhood suffrage and excluding ''such as may be disfranchised for participation in the rebellion.''

Although the conventions interpreted that requirement variously, most new state constitutions excluded former Confederate leaders from voting and officeholding, and some excluded any who had sympathized with the Confederacy. An estimated 150,000 whites were thus disfranchised. The Reconstruction Act further declared that after a state had presented an acceptable constitution to Congress and had ratified the Fourteenth Amendment, Congress would then admit that state's delegates.

Even after this impressive victory, congressional leaders feared that Johnson might use his authority as commander in chief to subvert their intentions. Some even suspected that he might attempt a military coup. So they passed two more measures to trim his power. The Army Appropriations Act directed the President and the Secretary of State to issue military orders through the General of the Army, U. S. Grant, who was required to maintain his headquarters in Washington. The Tenure of Office Act provided that any officeholder appointed by the President with the Senate's consent was to serve until the Senate had approved a successor. If the President replaced a Cabinet member while the Senate was out of session, the replacement would serve after the Senate reconvened only with its consent; otherwise, the former incumbent would resume his duties. The Tenure of Office Act was designed in general to keep Johnson from using the patronage to destroy those who opposed his views on Reconstruction, in particular to prevent his replacing Edwin Stanton, Secretary of War. Stanton was the only member left in the Cabinet who was friendly to the Radicals, and many Radicals, including Stanton himself, believed that the safety of the nation depended on his remaining in office. The Tenure of Office Act further provided that, unless the Senate approved a change, Cabinet members were to hold office ''during the term of the President by whom they may have been appointed, and for one month thereafter.'' These two acts, the second of dubious constitutionality, were passed on March 2, the day on which the Reconstruction Act was passed.

The Radical program of Reconstruction was now as airtight as its sponsors could make it. In the following months Johnson and the Southern leaders exploited loopholes in the new laws, but Congress promptly closed them by passing three supplementary acts. How-

It is the opinion of your committee—

I. That the States lately in rebellion were, at the close of the war, disorganized communities, without civil government, and without constitutions or other forms, by virtue of which political relations could legally exist between them and the federal government.

II. That Congress cannot be expected to recognize as valid the election of representatives from disorganized communities, which, from the very nature of the case, were unable to present their claim to representation under those established and recognized rules, the observance of which has been hitherto required.

III. That Congress would not be justified in admitting such communities to a participation in the government of the country without first providing such constitutional or other guarantees as will tend to secure the civil rights of all citizens of the republic; a just equality of representation; protection against claims founded in rebellion and crime; a temporary restoration of the right of suffrage to those who had not actively participated in the efforts to destroy the Union and overthrow the government, and the exclusion from positions of public trust of, at least, a portion of those whose crimes have proved them to be enemies to the Union, and unworthy of public confidence.

From the Report of the Joint Committee on Reconstruction, 1866.

The power ... given to the commanding officer over all the people of each district is that of an absolute monarch. His mere will is to take the place of all law. The law of the States is now the only rule applicable to the subjects placed under his control, and that is completely displaced by the clause which declares all interference of State authority to be null and void....

It is plain that the authority here given to the military officer amounts to absolute despotism. But to make it still more unendurable, the bill provides that it may be delegated to as many subordinates as he chooses to appoint, for it declares that he shall "punish or cause to be punished." Such a power has not been wielded by any monarch in England for more than five hundred years. In all that time no people who speak the English language have borne such servitude. It reduces the whole population of the ten States—all persons, of every color, sex, and condition, and every stranger within their limits—to the most abject and degrading slavery.

From Andrew Johnson, Veto of the Reconstruction Act, 1867.

ever unhappily, Johnson at last declared that he would execute the laws.

The Republican South. During the last half of 1867 most of the Southern states wrote acceptable constitutions under military supervision, called their new legislatures into session, and ratified the Fourteenth Amendment. All but three were readmitted to the Union in 1868. There was much foot-dragging over the disfranchisement of former Confederates, who were often the most popular leaders in their states. Endless discussions of this bitter point delayed the writing of constitutions in Virginia and Texas; in Mississippi the constitution was defeated because of it. It was 1870 before those three states won congressional approval of their constitutions and were permitted to reenter Congress. Georgia, admitted in 1868, was cast out again when its new legislature dismissed duly elected black delegates. Georgia, too, had to wait until 1870.

The spectacle of blacks voting
shocked the South

By this time one further requirement had been added for readmission: ratification of the Fifteenth Amendment, proposed by Congress in February 1869. This amendment forbade the states to deny the right to vote "on account of race, color, or previous condition of servitude." Its most immediate effect was to enfranchise Northern blacks; in the South, blacks were already enfranchised under the new state constitutions. Its sponsors hoped, however, that the amendment would prevent unfriendly legislatures from disfranchising freedmen in the future.

The new constitutions of the Southern states were in many respects better than their antebellum constitutions. The states now assumed responsibility for many social services that had formerly been left to local officials and private initiative. States without public-school systems now established them, along with institutions for the care of the indigent, homeless, and the physically handicapped. Tax systems were made more equitable, penal codes more humane, and the rights of women more comprehensive. For the first time in its history, South Carolina now had a divorce law. In states where planters had enjoyed advantages over upcountry farmers, districting for representation in the legislature was made fairer. The new constitutions also empowered state governments to undertake programs of economic recovery, especially for the rebuilding of the ruined railroads. Though not radical, the new constitutions were modern for their time, and they served the Southern states for several decades after the hated Republicans who initiated them had fallen from power.

Southern conservatives denounced the new governments, mainly because they detested the political coalition that had created them and that served in the first legislatures. They dubbed resident Northerners who held office in the new governments "carpetbaggers," suggesting that as transients they had no stake in Southern society. They denounced Southern whites who cooperated with the new regimes as "scalawags," a term suggesting at once disloyalty and a smallness of means and spirit. The spectacle of blacks voting for public officers shocked the white South. Although blacks were not represented in proportion to their numbers, their very presence in government fostered resentment and complaints of "Negro rule."

The assumption behind all this criticism was that none of these groups had any right to participate in the governing of the South. Actually there was little truth in the stereotypes the conservatives fastened on the Republican coalition. Many scalawags were prominent and affluent leaders who found Republican economic policies not unlike the old Whig program. Small farmers sensed that their interests would be better protected than they had been before the war, and they voted accordingly. The carpetbaggers included all sorts of people who had business in the South after the war. Some were military personnel; some were professionals—teachers, ministers, and lawyers; some were planters; and some, of course, were adventuring businessmen and speculators. There were fewer carpetbaggers than there were scalawags and blacks, but their undoubted loyalty to the Union and their connections with the federal government gave them considerable influence. Working through local groups called "Loyal Leagues," they organized the black Republican vote in the South.

The great weakness of this Republican coalition was that it had come to power as a result of revolutionary drives generated outside the South. Members of the once-powerful class of planters, now excluded from public office, would always regard the Republican governments as impostures.

Yet idealism and high purpose marked the early stages of the Republican effort to rebuild the South. Whether the three groups comprising the coalition could stand together against the stresses of biracial politics was uncertain. Uncertain too was the strength of individual Republicans to resist the temptation for easy

The trial of Johnson in the Senate

wealth presented by the rich spending and borrowing programs that were now launched for economic recovery. The Republican leaders, who professed commitment to more genuine democracy than the South had ever known, were under a heavy obligation to conduct themselves as virtuous public servants.

The impeachment of Johnson.

Congress had been right in suspecting that Johnson would use his control of the army to weaken the Reconstruction acts. His behavior was technically correct. But by instructing district commanders not to question the past behavior of those who took an oath of allegiance, he permitted Southerners of doubtful loyalty to regain the vote. He eventually removed three generals who were sympathetic to the Radical program, and he rashly challenged Congress in his December message of 1867 by declaring that he would maintain his rights as President, "regardless of consequences."

Several times the Radicals in Congress had contemplated impeaching Johnson, but they could find no legal ground for action. Their opening came when Johnson resolved to test the constitutionality of the Tenure of Office Act. While Congress was in the 1867 summer recess, he dismissed Edwin Stanton and appointed Grant as temporary Secretary of War. When Congress reconvened, the Senate refused to consent to Stanton's removal. Grant withdrew in confusion, protesting that he had never agreed to join the President in breaking the law. Grant had spoiled Johnson's plan, and his critics suggested that he had done so after a hint from the Radicals that he might

himself become a presidential candidate. Johnson, angry with Grant, now embarked on an *opéra-bouffe* search for a more cooperative general. As stand-in he finally produced General Lorenzo Thomas, but he had no success in installing his protégé in the War Department. Stanton, barricading himself in his office, cooked his own meals and regularly consulted with the Radical leaders.

Confident that most citizens believed Johnson had broken the law, the Republican majority in the House of Representatives voted, on February 24, 1868, to impeach Johnson for "high crimes and misdemeanors in office." The Radicals then drew up a list of specific charges, centering on his alleged violation of the Tenure of Office Act. The most significant was the charge that Johnson had been "unmindful of the high duties of his office . . . and of the harmony and courtesies which ought to exist . . . between the executive and legislative branches." He had attempted to bring Congress into "contempt and reproach." Essentially the House was accusing Johnson of disagreement with congressional policies. A conviction on that charge would have established a precedent for the removal of any President who could not command a majority in the House of Representatives on an important issue. In that event, the American system of balance of powers in government might have given way to the parliamentary system.

To convict the President, two-thirds of the Senate sitting as a court presided over by the Chief Justice would have to agree that Johnson had broken the law (with the implication that he had no right to test the constitutionality of an act of Congress) and that he was not ''fit'' to hold his office. Johnson's able legal defense had no trouble disposing of the first point. Whatever Johnson had done, he had not broken the Tenure of Office Act, because Stanton had been appointed by Lincoln and not by Johnson and had served beyond the term of the President who appointed him. Cautious Senators were troubled by the magnitude of the changes that might follow the removal of a President on the political charge that he had not worked for ''harmony'' with Congress. By a margin of only one vote, the Senate acquitted Johnson. Chief Justice Chase, who presided at the trial, was in sympathy with the President's arguments, and additional Republican senators would have voted for acquittal had their votes been needed. Many of those who voted to acquit the President did so because they distrusted the radicalism of Benjamin Wade, acting President of the Senate, who would have become President if Johnson had been convicted. Wade's views on public finance, labor, and woman suffrage were fully as radical as his views on civil rights for blacks, and they were far more shocking to the moderate Republicans. After Johnson's narrow escape, Stanton resigned and the Senate adjourned.

The Supreme Court and Reconstruction.
During the war much of the power formerly held by the states had gravitated to the national government. It was not clear whether the executive or legislative branch would be the greater beneficiary of this shift. Then, after the war, the struggle over the military phase of Reconstruction severely upset the balance of powers within the federal government itself. Congressional power had reached a high point in the impeachment action against Johnson, but Johnson had won that contest. In another power struggle he failed: he never got a Supreme Court judgment on the Tenure of Office Act, which remained on the books for twenty years. Neither had he managed to get rulings on the two Reconstruction Acts. What was the role of the Supreme Court during this prolonged struggle between the President and the Congress?

The Court had started off boldly late in 1866. In the case of *Ex parte* Milligan it had ruled unanimously that neither Congress nor the President had the power to create military courts to try civilians in areas remote from

war. That noteworthy decision liberated several men who had been condemned by such courts for military subversion in the North during the war. Still, the Milligan decision angered congressional Radicals because it cast doubt on the legality of the courts the Freedmen's Bureau was then sponsoring in Southern states. By passing the Reconstruction Acts in the spring of 1867, Congress delivered an overt challenge to the Court. Unsure of the Court's response, the Radicals began to talk of reducing its size, with some even urging that the Court be abolished. The Supreme Court grew cautious. By a five-to-four decision in the twin cases of *Cummings* v. *Missouri* and *Ex parte* Garland, heard in 1867, it invalidated the use of loyalty oaths, pronouncing them ex post facto and bills of attainder. In the same year, in the cases of *Georgia* v. *Stanton* and *Mississippi* v. *Johnson,* the Court was challenged to rule on the constitutionality of the Reconstruction Acts. In both instances it refused jurisdiction on technical grounds.

The Court's critics charged cowardice. The Justices, they suggested, were afraid that Congress would destroy the Court's power, if it ever elected to use that power, just as it had ridden over the President's prerogatives. But this was not the main reason for the Court's caution. The Court had not been popular in the years following the Dred Scott decision. But when Lincoln replaced the Southern Justices with staunch Unionists, it had grown much stronger in public esteem. By the time Congress and the President clashed, it had no reason to be fearful. Only a few Radicals wanted to destroy the Court. There were more compelling reasons for the Supreme Court's refusal to rule on the Reconstruction Acts: the Justices knew that the country was passing through a revolutionary period marked by questions on which the Constitution was either silent or not clear, and they realized that public opinion in the North demanded a stringent Reconstruction of the South. Moreover, the Justices felt the public good would be best served by judicial restraint. After Radical Reconstruction waned, the Chase Supreme Court reemerged in the early 1870s with strong decisions that had a profound effect on American law for the rest of the century.

Foreign affairs under Johnson.
Although Johnson's Southern policy was a disaster, his conduct of foreign relations under the able direction of Secretary of State William Seward

Seward's ''icebox''

was a credit to his record. During the war the French under Napoleon the Third had affronted the Monroe Doctrine by setting up a puppet government in Mexico under the pliant and ambitious Austrian Archduke Maximilian. Fully occupied with fighting the Confederacy, Lincoln and Seward had denounced the French action but had been unable to challenge Napoleon's bid to restore French imperial power in the Western Hemisphere. Seward lost no time once the war was over. In 1866 President Johnson sent fifty thousand veteran troops to the Mexican border, and Seward demanded the withdrawal of French forces. The French complied, and the Mexicans reestablished their independence.

A vigorous expansionist, Seward believed that trade with other countries would help convince the world of the superiority of American democracy. In 1868 he signed a treaty of friendship and commerce with China. In 1867 he negotiated a treaty to buy the Virgin Islands from Denmark for $7,500,000. The Senate rejected that treaty but at the same time approved one that Seward had arranged with Russia for the purchase of Alaska for $7,200,000. Many Americans joked about Seward's "icebox," for it seemed no more than a frozen wasteland. Time was to demonstrate the strategic value of Alaska and the richness of its resources.

The election of 1868. Johnson's able conduct of foreign affairs was overshadowed by the turbulent issue of Southern Reconstruction, which dominated the presidential contest of 1868. The Republicans, rejecting Johnson's leadership, nominated Ulysses S. Grant as their presidential candidate, with Speaker of the House Schuyler Colfax as his running mate. Grant had no political experience, but he had broken with Johnson over the Tenure of Office Act and had shown himself receptive to the Radicals' advice. Grant's supporters counted on his popularity as a war hero to win over voters who had qualms about the severity of Radical Reconstruction.

The Democrats were thoroughly demoralized. They had yet to rid their party of the taint of disloyalty, and they had no leaders capable of replacing their prewar spokesmen. For President they nominated Horatio Seymour, a wealthy conservative who as war governor of New York had gained an undeserved reputation for disloyalty. His running mate, Francis P. Blair, though recognized as a staunch

Unionist, added little allure to the ticket. The Democratic platform declared the questions of slavery and secession to be settled forever and denounced Republican Reconstruction policies. The party called for amnesty for former Confederates and restoration of the Southern states. Negro suffrage, the Democrats urged, was a matter for the states to settle, not the federal government. This position gained less for the Democrats than it might have, because the Republicans themselves agreed that in the North the suffrage question should be left to the states, while maintaining that black suffrage was essential in the South. The Democratic platform opened the party to the charge that it was soft on the South.

The Democrats' only hope for victory was to focus public attention on the question of money and the repayment of the war debt, which was under hot debate. During the war the government had issued some $450 million in greenbacks. The value of that currency had fluctuated over the years, but it was always below the value of coins and gold-backed currency. Between 1866 and 1868 the Treasury Department had retired some $100 million of greenbacks from circulation. Now the Democrats adopted the "Ohio Idea," sponsored by George H. Pendleton, congressman from that state, who demanded that the notes be reissued to redeem outstanding war bonds not explicitly requiring redemption in gold. This demand for cheap money appealed to debtors, especially farmers with long-term mortgages who stood to benefit from inflation. It appealed also to critics of the "bloated bond-holders," the war-profiteers. The Republicans, on the other hand, pledged themselves to the redemption of the national debt in gold. They knew that conservative financiers would approve this adherence to sound money, and they also understood that Western farmers, however much many of them might prefer cheap money, would, like other Northerners, still remember the passions of war vividly enough to distrust the Democrats' amnesty proposals for the South. The racial demagoguery of the Democratic campaign stirred that memory.

The Republicans worked to keep those passions alive. In the savage campaign of 1868, they concentrated on the alleged treason of the Democrats and waved the "bloody shirt" of war. They knew they could count on the support of the Southern states now dominated by carpetbaggers and on the backing of a multitude of federal officeholders. The Demo-

Campaign cartoon, 1868

crats lost whatever appeal they might have enjoyed from the Ohio Idea when their nominee, Horatio Seymour, repudiated that plank in the platform. Even with all their advantages, however, including the popularity of U. S. Grant, the Republicans just managed to win.

Grant carried the Electoral College by 218 to 80 but received only 52.7 percent of the popular vote. Without the "bloody shirt" and the support of six Southern states, safe in Republican hands, Grant would have lost the election.

The Grant era

Government under Grant. No President had ever come to office so poorly equipped in temperament, intellect, or political experience as Ulysses S. Grant. And it was Grant's fate to come to that office in trying times. The white South, increasingly restive under Republican rule, began to express that restiveness in violence; in the West, farmers were beginning to feel the pinch of a long decline in commodity prices; in the North, a spirit of greedy materialism fostered graft inside the government and out. Grant did not create those problems, but he lacked the statesmanship to meet the first two and the strength of character to resist the third. He had been a great general, with the soldier's virtues of judgment, courage, and loyalty to subordinates. As President he was rudderless and confused by circumstances. His judgment was valueless because it was uninformed. When he found the courage induced by frustration,

he often vented it in the malignant persecution of honest critics. He took everything personally. Loyalty to his subordinates proved his undoing, for he was duped at every turn. His mediocre Cabinet included several rascals who helped themselves to public funds. He was so obtuse in his choice of friends, so easily flattered, that he accepted expensive gifts from favor-seekers and appeared in public as the guest of such notorious stock-market swindlers as Jay Gould and Jim Fisk.

Grant, who had a fatal talent for falling out with the few able men who found themselves in his constantly shifting Cabinet, thereby lost the services of those who might have saved his Administration from shame. The one exception was Hamilton Fish, Secretary of State, an able and conscientious man who conducted foreign affairs with dignity and success.

Through the Treaty of Washington, signed in 1871, Fish opened a new era of friendly relations with Great Britain. Among the many problems that had exacerbated Anglo-American relations in recent years, the most serious had arisen over the extensive damage done to American shipping by the *Alabama* and other raiders that the British had built for the Confederacy. Violent speeches had been made in the Senate by irate patriots like Charles Sumner, who demanded that England be made to pay for indirect damage to American shipping as well as for the actual destruction of property. All those problems were referred, under the Treaty of Washington, to international arbitration. The British expressed "regret" about the *Alabama* and agreed to abide by the decision of the arbitration commission. That decision turned out to be favorable to the United States. Although the commission did not allow the indirect claims, it found that Britain had not exercised "due diligence" over her shipyards and awarded the United States $15,500,000. This successful arbitration of a sore dispute advanced both Anglo-American understanding and international peace.

The President's friends could be proud of little else. In his last annual message, Grant sadly acknowledged the faults of his Administration, blaming many of them on his own inexperience. But he pointed out that his political appointments, disastrous as many turned out to be, had been made "upon recommendations of the representatives chosen directly by the people." The patronage system had failed the President, because those representatives were on the whole true products of their age. The gaudy materialism symbolized by the brightly patterned waistcoats and florid oratory of Senator Roscoe Conkling, the flashy idol of New York, had its counterpart in the cheerful abandon with which Congress disposed of public goods. Politicians ignored the plight of the poor and showered their favors on the wealthy. In 1872, Congress abolished the wartime income tax. The lobbies of industrial interests, however, particularly those of copper and steel, had found Congress receptive to their urgings. In spite of a 10 percent reduction of duties to placate farmers in 1872, many tariff rates that stood at 25 percent in Henry Clay's time had climbed to 500 percent by that year. Still the industrialists were not satisfied.

Neither were the railroad men, nor the congressmen themselves. In the fall of 1872 newspaper-reporters disclosed that prominent congressmen had accepted stock at "token" rates in return for a promise not to investigate the construction company of the Union Pacific Railroad. The Crédit Mobilier's relation to the Union Pacific was wholly fraudulent. Its purpose was to divert the profits from building the Union Pacific to the pockets of the road's promoters. In this way the Union Pacific was relieved of some $23 million in securities appropriated by Congress. Though many were involved in the chicanery—including Vice President Schuyler Colfax and future President James A. Garfield—only one, Oakes Ames, representative from Massachusetts and organizer of the scheme, was censured.

Corruption in Congress was tame compared to the colorful swindles that were taking place elsewhere. Grant's friends, Fisk and Gould, conspired with the President's brother-in-law to corner the available supply of gold in the New York stock market. Assuming they had convinced Grant not to sell government gold, they drove its market price to dizzying heights. Because many transactions had to be made in gold, the nation's business was thrown into panic. At last Secretary of the Treasury George Boutwell destroyed the scheme by selling $4 million of government gold, bringing the market suddenly down to earth. When the crash came on "Black Friday," September 24, 1869, many innocents were ruined but the principal culprits escaped. Gould, probably on the basis of inside information from government bankers, had started selling early; Fisk escaped by the simple expedient of repudiating his debts and then hiring thugs to threaten his creditors.

In New York City, "Boss" William Marcy Tweed of Tammany Hall relieved the city of an estimated $200 million. That figure included the proceeds from fraudulent bond issues and the sale of franchises as well as graft collected from corrupt contractors and merchants dealing directly with the city government. Since the governor of New York was a Tweed henchman, the "Boss," though a Democrat himself, had little trouble silencing the Republican legislature with bribes. Control of the police, the courts, and the district attorney made Tweed almost invulnerable. At last, when the city was nearly bankrupt, Samuel J. Tilden successfully challenged Tweed for control of the Democratic organization in the city, gaining a perhaps inflated reputation for having "smashed" the ring. Tweed's was only the most notorious of the

*Grant:
rudderless and confused*

party machines. Others operated in Philadelphia, Chicago, and Washington. In their heyday they had little trouble winning the cooperation of reputable public figures. Middle-class citizens lamented the decline of civic virtue.

The South experienced the same blight. The corruption of the reconstructed Southern legislatures was particularly disastrous. Governments organized for the first time on the basis of racial equality were hopelessly discredited by association with railroad and printing swindles and eventually fell into bankruptcy. The ideal of political equality suffered in public esteem because it was supported by corruptionists. Bold efforts to rebuild the South's transportation system dissolved in the wholesale theft of railroad stock. In South Carolina even the Land Commission founded to help blacks buy farms ended up as a device for transferring state funds to the private accounts of unscrupulous assessors and their friends in high places. Florida's bill for printing costs in 1869 was more than the entire cost of running the state government in 1860. The list of scandals was long and the crooks were blithe. "Damn it," expostulated Henry Clay Warmoth, carpetbag governor of Louisiana and one of the worst spoilers, "everybody is demoralizing down here. Corruption is the fashion." He had a point. It takes two to make a deal, and many of those who bribed the legislature for favors were native Southerners and Democrats.

Blacks, seldom the beneficiaries of these schemes, were frequently the dupes of those wiser in the ways of the world. Nevertheless the presence of blacks in the legislatures and their loyalty to the carpetbag Republicans enabled disfranchised whites to condemn "Negro rule" and to blame corruption on this experiment in political equality. Even the performance of the honest and efficient Radical government of Mississippi, and of remarkable black leaders like Senator Hiram Revels of that state and South Carolina's Secretary of State Francis Cardozo changed few opinions. Political association with blacks and carpetbaggers became more unpopular as scandals multiplied. Scalawags found themselves ostracized by their neighbors. As one former Whig planter explained when he withdrew from the Republican party, a man with four marriageable daughters could do no less.

White resentment took a vicious turn with the appearance and rapid growth of the Ku Klux Klan. First organized in 1866, the white-hooded nightriders contented themselves for a time with playing pranks on freedmen to frighten them into "good" behavior. But soon the Klan, with its Grand Dragon, "Dens," and "Cyclopses," had spread over the South. Now an instrument of political terror, it attacked the Loyal Leagues, intimidated black voters, and destroyed the effectiveness of local black organizers. Nor did the Klan shun murder. Many able black leaders, including Wyatt Outlaw of North Carolina, lost their lives to the fury of the Klansmen. When the organization was officially disbanded in 1869, it went underground. After an elaborate investigation Congress passed the Ku Klux Klan Act of 1871, empowering the President to suspend the writ of habeas corpus in order to cope with the violence that regularly erupted at elections. The Republican governors were often forced to call on federal troops to keep peace, but critics of the Administration, north and south, abhorred the practice of using soldiers to supervise elections. The North was growing tired of the "autumnal outbreaks," indeed of Southern Reconstruction in general. Before Grant's first term was over, the Republican governments in the South, steeped in corruption and torn by violence, were doomed.

The Liberal Republican movement.

Few doubted that the Republicans would nominate Grant for a second term. In 1872, however, a revolt in the ranks of the party gave the regulars pause. Calling themselves "Liberal Republicans," the dissidents challenged the party regulars on three issues: corruption in government, Grant's financial policies (the high level of tariff protection and the continued use of greenback currency, which delayed resumption of specie payments), and the Radical Southern policy.

To eliminate corruption in government, they demanded a reform of the civil service. As early as 1870 Carl Schurz, a German immigrant and war hero, had led a Liberal Republican revolt in Missouri. There the Radical Republicans had all but proscribed party members who wanted to restore political rights to former Confederates in the state. The victorious Liberals took up the cause of the excluded faction and placed B. Gratz Brown in the governor's chair. Before 1872 the Missouri Liberals had merged with a group of prominent Eastern leaders to form a new party. A number of distinguished journalists

John Sherman on the Ku Klux Klan

---

who had had a hand in exposing scandal lent their talents; E. L. Godkin of the new reform paper, *The Nation,* and two young brothers, Henry and Charles Francis Adams, were among them. Indeed many men of talent and idealism in the East were sympathetic to the movement, and many one-time abolitionists enrolled against Grant. Even Charles Sumner, who had fallen out with Grant over the President's stubborn but futile determination to annex Santo Domingo (see p. 491), joined the Liberals.

The party had its share of office-seekers, however, who at the 1872 convention in Cincinnati were able to kill the nomination of any of several men they feared might fight too well for reform. After a chaotic convention, the Liberals ended up nominating Horace Greeley, the quixotic editor of the New York *Tribune.* Though the Liberals opposed the tariff,

Greeley was a protectionist. During his long, controversial career in journalism, the candidate had himself written the script for those who now attacked him for his contradictory statements on public issues. Greeley understood politics well, but not well enough to know that he was a poor candidate. With his wispy chin-whiskers and cherubic face, he looked anything but a President.

In short, the Liberals had failed to come up with an attractive alternative to Grant. The worst of the Grant Administration scandals were yet to be exposed, and the general's heroic image retained its luster. Few Republicans would abandon him to join hands with the hated Democrats. Moreover, the Democrats gave the kiss of death to the new party of dissident Republicans by weakly endorsing its candidates. The "bloody shirt" was still a potent symbol, and Grant won a great victory.

Greeley died a few weeks later, broken-hearted over his personal defeat and sad that corrupt government had won so thunderous an endorsement.

The collapse. Even though they had lost the election, the Liberals had redefined the goals of the best-informed and most concerned Northern citizens. Northerners were tired of Southern Reconstruction and embarrassed by the Radical governments in the Southern states. To them reform now meant clean government. Civil-service reform took precedence over civil rights for blacks, and the nation became more interested in economic questions than in supporting regimes in the South that regularly sent delegates to Washington to vote with the Radicals.

Republican sensitivity to the Liberals' criticism was demonstrated just before the election of 1872, when Congress passed the Amnesty Act. By its terms political rights were restored to all former Confederates except about five hundred of the most prominent leaders. In the South, Liberal Republican factions charged party regulars with misgovernment and made a bid for white conservative support in a cleanup campaign. They seldom succeeded, because the white conservatives, now rehabilitated politically, preferred new political coalitions to any form of Republicanism. Defecting scalawags promptly joined ranks. Sometimes the new coalition called themselves Democrats, and sometimes simply "conservatives."

Thoroughly factionalized, the Republican state governments in the South fell, one by one, over the next four years. Now Grant sent troops at election time only when he thought there was a strong chance that the Republicans could win. The triumphant conservatives claimed that they had "redeemed" their states from the Radicals. By the time of the 1876 presidential election, only three (South Carolina, Louisiana, and Florida) were still in Republican control.

Less than a year after Grant's second election political scandals and economic distress had destroyed the brittle reputation of his Administration. A congressional committee revealed that the newspaper-reporters had been right about the affairs of Crédit Mobilier. Worse yet, five of Grant's Cabinet officers were exposed as corruptionists. The most notorious was William W. Belknap, Secretary of War, who had accepted bribes from traders

at Indian posts. Benjamin Bristow, Grant's new Secretary of the Treasury, uncovered the Whiskey Ring, a conspiracy of hundreds of distillers who had bribed Treasury officials in order to evade federal taxes. Grant's private secretary, Orville E. Babcock, was implicated in that corrupt adventure. Grant declared, "Let no guilty man escape," but he provided Babcock with a deposition that helped him evade punishment.

Economic disaster followed in the wake of public scandal. In September 1873 a rash of financial failures in New York dragged the country into the deepest depression of its history. The sudden withdrawal of European investments, prompted by the Franco-Prussian War and vast railroad-building abroad, triggered the panic. But Ameriban investment in concerns that produced no immediate or real profits, such as the railroads, rendered bankers unable to cope with the crisis. The failure of Jay Cooke & Co., one of the most respected banking firms in the country, set off a chain reaction. Cooke's firm was deeply involved in financing the Northern Pacific Railroad. Eighty-nine railroads defaulted on their bonds, and eighteen thousand businesses failed in two years. Iron mills and furnaces fell idle, and by 1875 half a million men were out of work. Wages declined, and agricultural prices dropped so low that farmers, unable to pay their mortgages, had to surrender their properties, their homes, their fondest dreams.

Hard times and scandal hurt the Republicans in the congressional elections of 1874. The Democrats elected a majority in the House of Representatives, improved their standing in the Senate, and won control in twenty-three states. Many dissatisfied groups were now blaming Republican financial measures for their problems. As exporters of agricultural products, the South and West disliked the protective tariff. In the West farmers wanted a freer circulation of paper money (the greenbacks issued as legal tender during the war) to ease their burden of debt and to raise farm prices. But businessmen, with some exceptions, favored a retirement of greenbacks and a return to the gold standard, reasoning that these measures would stabilize the value of currency and thus reduce the uncertainty of commerce and exchange.

The legal status of greenbacks was in doubt. In 1870 the Supreme Court, under Chief Justice Chase, who had been, ironically, Secretary of the Treasury when greenbacks were issued, ruled that the Legal Tender Act was unconstitutional. Protesting that decision, Grant's advisers pointed out that it cast doubt on the validity of all contracts calling for payment in money that had been legal tender ever since 1862. They also feared that the abrupt removal of greenbacks would overly contract the supply of money. Grant therefore expanded the Supreme Court by appointing two Justices whose views he knew in advance, and in 1871 the enlarged Court ruled that the government had been within its rights in issuing the paper currency. That opinion settled the legal question but left open the question whether the greenbacks should be kept in circulation.

In 1873, in order to relieve the deflation accompanying the panic, the Treasury Department reissued $26 million of the greenbacks it had retired earlier. But the Administration balked at a further expansion of the currency demanded by Congress the following year. It backed instead a bill designed by John Sherman to give the West and the South a fairer share of the nation's banking facilities. That bill increased the number of national banks and allowed them to augment the amount of bank notes in circulation. It also provided that after January 1, 1879, the Treasury would, on demand, redeem all legal-tender notes in coin. The Specie Resumption Act became law in 1875. In the same year the Republicans, with the help of some Eastern Democrats, restored the protective-tariff duties that had been reduced three years earlier.

The Republicans were now adopting the twin principles of political economy that would become the party's articles of faith in the decades to come—high tariffs and hard money. Those principles endeared the party to business and industry but rendered it increasingly suspect to farmers, debtors, and workers. Advocates of paper money severely criticized the Specie Resumption Act. Overlooking its constructive aspects, they predicted that resumption would precipitate a disastrous contraction. But nothing of the sort happened in 1879, when payments in specie were resumed, because of the coincidental return of prosperity. This accident convinced the Republicans of the merit of their "sound money" policy, but it was too late to mitigate the unpopularity the Grant regime had reaped from the depression and from its steady deference to the propertied interests of the country.

The twilight of Reconstruction.

Scandal and depression during Grant's second term diverted the attention of Congress from the South. Grant, sensing the disenchantment of the public, grew less willing every year to support the toppling carpetbag regimes with troops. Moreover, with most of the older states of the Middle West now safe for the Republicans, a Republican South was no longer essential to their control of the federal government. With federal support withdrawn, the carpetbag governments could no longer withstand the onslaught of the white South. Openly now, without hoods or robes, conservatives organized to intimidate blacks who showed interest in politics, and the few surviving scalawags.

Congress made a last pathetic gesture to the black man whose fate was at stake. Senator Charles Sumner had introduced a civil-rights bill in 1872 that was passed in 1875, after his death, in a much denatured form. Sumner had intended to assure full equality for the freedmen, including political rights, all civil liberties, and the elimination of social segregation. His purpose was frustrated by the ambiguous racial views of Republican moderates and by Northern opinion. The act, as it was finally passed, guaranteed equal accommodations in such public places as inns and theaters and forbade the exclusion of blacks from jury duty, but it provided no practicable means of enforcement. Moreover, school integration, which Sumner had proposed, was quietly dropped from the final bill. What little force the act carried was destroyed in 1883 when the Supreme Court declared invalid those parts of it designed to secure social equality. The Court also ruled that, although the Fourteenth Amendment prohibited the invasion of civil rights by the states, it did not prohibit the invasion of civil rights by individuals unaided by state authority. Blacks might be driven from the polls or otherwise abused by individuals, and the federal government would have no power to intervene.

Although the emasculation of Sumner's program revealed that Republicans were no longer committed to protecting the black man in his citizenship, the Civil Rights Act of 1875 established a significant precedent. In the next century a new generation of crusaders would rediscover the Civil Rights Acts of 1866 and 1875 and in the Fourteenth and Fifteenth Amendments their original purpose. A new Supreme Court would restore their original meaning. But for two generations the black man was to face a lonely struggle. Deprived of legal recourse to defend his freedom and abandoned by Northern public opinion, he was largely ignored by the federal government.

Reconstruction was a story of lost opportunity. Victory in war had opened the grand prospect of a country reunited on the principles of liberty. Sometimes with the best intentions, but often with greed and venom, the nation's leaders allowed the principles of liberty to be smirched by corruption. In restoring the South, they scarred it. In developing the economy, they abandoned power and granted privilege to a grasping few. In dealing with civil rights, they inspired blacks to reach for high goals and then left them to the mercy of demagogues and embittered whites. The fruits of victory were lost in the aftermath of war.

Suggestions for reading

GENERAL

There is a concise analysis of Reconstruction and critical discussion of the bibliography on that subject in J. G. Randall and David Donald, *The Civil War and Reconstruction* (2nd ed., 1961). That volume also covers the Grant years. Three recent and indispensable studies in the rapidly growing scholarship on Reconstruction are W. R. Brock, *An American Crisis** (1963); David Donald, *The Politics of Reconstruction** (1965); and K. M. Stampp, *The Era of Reconstruction* (1965). See also J. H. Franklin, *Reconstruction After the Civil War** (1962); Avery Craven, *Reconstruction: The Ending of the Civil War* (1969); and R. W. Patrick, *The Reconstruction of the Nation* (1967). Another general treatment of the period 1865–78, stressing social and economic conditions, is Allan Nevins, *The Emergence of Modern America, 1865–1878* (1927). The national politics of the period receive detailed but sometimes jaundiced treatment in Matthew Josephson, *The Politicos, 1865–1896** (1938). The national mood concerns P. H. Buck, *The Road to Reunion, 1865–1900* (1937). J. G. Randall, *Constitutional Problems under Lincoln* (rev. ed., 1951), discusses wartime legal decisions that had an impact on postwar reorganization. Clement Eaton, *The Waning of the Old South Civilization* (1968), traces Southern reactions to defeat in war.

Lincoln's views on Reconstruction are discussed in W. B. Hesseltine, *Lincoln's Plan of Reconstruction* (1960), and R. N. Current, *The Lincoln Nobody Knows* (1958). See also Benjamin Quarles, *Lincoln and the Negro* (1962).

JOHNSON, THE RADICALS, AND RECONSTRUCTION

H. K. Beale, *The Critical Year: A Study of Andrew Johnson and Reconstruction* (1930), provides a sympathetic analysis of the President and an interpretation of the Radicals, with emphasis on their economic motives. Johnson is severely criticized in E. L. McKitrick, *Andrew Johnson and Reconstruction* (1960). Of the older studies of Reconstruction, two thorough accounts are marred by their pro-Southern, anti-Negro bias: W. A. Dunning, *Reconstruction Political and Economic, 1865–1877** (1907), and E. M. Coulter, *The South During Reconstruction, 1865–1877* (1947). In *Black Reconstruction,* W. E. B. DuBois imposes a Marxist interpretation, with limited success, on Reconstruction. Two studies of the Freedmen's Bureau are G. F. Bentley, *A History of the Freedmen's Bureau* (1955), and W. F. McFeely, *Yankee Stepfather: General O. O. Howard and the Freedmen* (1968). LaWanda and J. H. Cox, *Politics, Principle, and Prejudice, 1865–1866** (1963), stress civil rights as the basic issue in Reconstruction. Indispensable on its topic is J. M. McPherson, *The Struggle for Equality: Abolitionists and the Negro in the Civil War and Reconstruction** (1964). H. L. Swint, *The Northern Teacher in the South, 1862–1870* (1941), is an account of the activities of antislavery missionaries. W. L. Rose, *Rehearsal for Reconstruction** (1965), records the interaction of Northern missionaries and the freedmen. V. L. Wharton, *The Negro in Mississippi, 1865–1890* (1947), and J. R. Williamson, *After Slavery* (1965), record the experience of blacks in two states. A well-written account of Reconstruction in North Carolina is W. M. Evans, *Ballots and Fence-Rails* (1966).

On the Fourteenth Amendment see J. B. James, *The Framing of the 14th Amendment* (1956),

*Available in a paperback edition.

and Jacobus ten Broek, *The Anti-slavery Origins of the 14th Amendment* (1951). On the Fifteenth Amendment, see W. R. Gillette, *The Right to Vote** (1969). (General and special literature on the South and its postwar problems through 1900 is listed in connection with Chapter 16; on American business, consult the listing following Chapter 18.)

THE GRANT ERA

There is a dearth of truly satisfactory books on this period. A good general study of business is contained in T. C. Cochran and William Miller, *The Age of Enterprise: A Social History of Industrial America** (1942), which also touches intelligently on public policy. Rendigs Fels, *American Business Cycles, 1865–1897* (1959), is authoritative on the Panic of 1873. For the currency question, see Irwin Unger, *The Greenback Era* (1964), and for a balanced and significant analysis of public policy on money and the general economic picture of the period, see R. P. Sharkey, *Money, Class and Party* (1959). Postwar diplomacy has had able attention, especially in Dexter Perkins, *The Monroe Doctrine, 1876–1907** (1937), and Allan Nevins, *Hamilton Fish: The Inner History of the Grant Administration* (1936), which also provides the best account of the topic described by its subtitle. On the scandals of Grant's time and on the responses to them, three worthy studies are D. G. Loth, *Public Plunder: A History of Graft in America* (1938); C. R. Fish, *The Civil Service and the Patronage* (1904); and E. D. Ross, *The Liberal Republican Movement* (1919). There is a first-rate analysis of Grant and the Liberals in the beginning chapters of E. F. Goldman, *Rendezvous with Destiny** (1955). J. G. Sproat, *The Best Men* (1968), describes the liberal reformers of the Gilded Age. See also C. M. Fuess, *Carl Schurz: Reformer* (1932), and G. G. Van Deusen, *Horace Greeley: Nineteenth Century Crusader* (1952).

---

*Available in a paperback edition.

The New South: reunion and readjustment

16

The central theme of American history during the quarter-century following Reconstruction was laissez faire—"let alone." In this period control over public policy was surrendered very largely to private interest. The six chapters that follow will reveal this philosophy at work in all sections of the country, in the city as in the countryside, in economics as in politics. Laissez faire profoundly affected the lot of black freedmen and red Indians, the fate of buffaloes, natural resources, and public lands, the course of railroad operations, industrial management, and labor relations. After 1877 the center of historical forces and the focus of historical interest shift away from Washington. The federal government and the major political parties retreated from responsibility for public policy and fixed their attention narrowly on political maneuvers and trade in public offices.

White Southerners responded with fervor to the doctrine of laissez faire. Their enthusiasm sprang from a revolt against Reconstruction,

an attempt to apply a philosophy that was in certain respects and for a limited period the opposite of laissez faire. Disillusionment with Reconstruction, in fact, was spreading in the North as well as in the South, and Southern conservatives were beginning to hope for support from their former enemies. The great experiment of the Radicals had failed to solve the two problems it was designed to solve: the status of the South in the nation and the status of the Negro in the South. These two problems had torn and agitated the country for more than a generation, and Reconstruction proved no more successful than the Civil War had been in finding a solution. "We have tried for eight years," wrote Joseph Medill, the influential Republican editor of the Chicago *Tribune*, "to uphold Negro rule in the South officered by carpetbaggers, but without exception it has resulted in failure." Patience was running out in 1876, and the demand for some practical solution was growing more and more insistent.

The return to compromise

For sixteen years, ever since Fort Sumter, North and South had settled their differences by armed force—not only during the four years of war but during the twelve years that followed. If the country was ever to give up force and return to peaceful ways of settling sectional disputes, it would have to revive the neglected art of compromise. The opportunity

for a drastic change in relations between North and South and a return to the tradition of compromise on the classic model of 1850 came unexpectedly with the presidential election of 1876.

Tilden versus Hayes. Economic depression, political scandal, and weariness with Grant's

Southern policy clouded Republican prospects in 1876. The election of 1874 had returned the Democrats to control of the House of Representatives for the first time since the Civil War. During the next two years the depression that had started in 1873 deepened, and discontent increased. Throughout 1876 reformers filled the air with exposures of new scandals in the corrupt Grant Administration. Growing disgust with corruption, more than anything else, led to the elimination of the two leading contestants for the Republican nomination. One was President Grant himself, for, incredible as it may seem, the general had permitted the Stalwarts (see p. 464) to persuade him for a time that he would make a logical candidate for a third term. He withdrew, however, before the Republican convention met. The second candidate to be knocked out of the race for the nomination was Congressman James G. Blaine of Maine, formerly Speaker and currently minority leader in the House.

Blaine was known best as the leader of the Half-Breeds, rivals of the Stalwarts, and for his personal enmity with Roscoe Conkling, the Stalwarts' leader. A master of florid oratory and dramatic political maneuver, he commanded a large personal following and an army of political dependents. Blaine's opening maneuver in 1876 was the very opposite of compromise. Taking the floor on January 10, he artfully revived wartime bitterness over the suffering of Northern troops in the South's Andersonville prison camp. Gesturing dramatically, he declared that ''the thumbscrews and engines of torture of the Spanish Inquisition did not begin to compare in atrocity with the hideous crime of Andersonville.'' And he charged that Jefferson Davis was ''the man that organized that murder.'' Here was the classic example of ''waving the bloody shirt''—of stirring up old war hatreds for partisan purposes. Southern congressmen responded heatedly in defense of Davis. Blaine thus succeeded in identifying the Democratic party anew with disloyalty and rebellion and in thereby diverting attention from the scandals of the Republican Administration. His strategy almost won him the Republican nomination and the Presidency.

On the eve of the nominating convention, however, a congressional investigating committee suddenly produced a witness named James Mulligan, who said he had evidence that Blaine, while Speaker of the House, had improperly received $64,000 for granting favors to a railroad company. Boldly seizing the ''Mulligan Letters,'' which contained the alleged evidence, Blaine quoted selectively from them and claimed that he had cleared his name of the charges. In the ensuing convention, however, the Mulligan affair and the disfavor of President Grant and the Stalwarts finally eliminated Blaine from the race.

The Republicans nominated Rutherford B. Hayes, a comparatively obscure figure from the strategically important state of Ohio. Three times governor of his state, Hayes had a creditable war record, an unblemished reputation, and an association with mild civil-service reform. In short, he was the ideal nominee for a party bedeviled by smirched reputations and beset by scandal. Of Whig antecedents and puritanical conscience, Hayes was conservative in his economic and financial views, conciliatory toward Southern whites, and philanthropic toward the freedmen. To balance the ticket, the Republicans chose Congressman William A. Wheeler of New York for Vice President.

Stressing the issue of reform, the Democrats nominated Samuel J. Tilden, governor of New York. Before his election to the governorship in 1874, Tilden had won fame by helping to smash the notorious ring of Boss Tweed, head of Tammany Hall, and by sending Tweed and others to jail; as governor, he had shattered a powerful organization of

Tweed cartoon: ''To the victor belongs the spoils''

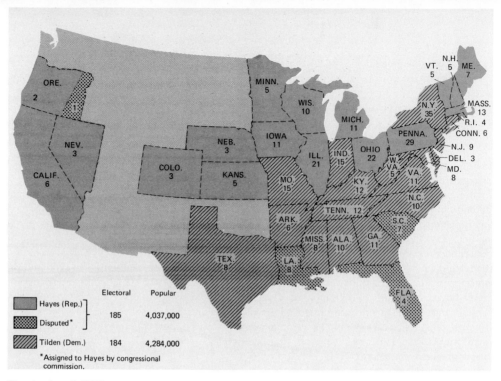

	Electoral	Popular
Hayes (Rep.) ⎤		
Disputed* ⎬	185	4,037,000
Tilden (Dem.) ⎦	184	4,284,000

*Assigned to Hayes by congressional commission.

The election of 1876

grafters known as the Canal Ring. Tilden had made a private fortune as a corporation lawyer serving railroads, and his conservative economic views and hard-money doctrines were more pleasing to the business community of the East than they were to the South and the West. Popular enthusiasm for Tilden's candidacy was further limited by his railroad associations, his secretive habits, and his poor health. In order to make up for these drawbacks, the Democrats named for Vice President Thomas A. Hendricks of Indiana, who had served his state as senator and governor and held soft-money views.

The campaign of 1876 was a struggle of exceptional bitterness and trickery. For the first time in twenty years the Democrats had a reasonable hope of winning a presidential election, and they bore down hard on Republican corruption in high places and misrule in the South. Their opponents countered with bloody-shirt oratory, charging that the Democrats were sympathetic to the rebels and attacking Tilden's personal integrity. When the returns came in, the Democrats seemed to have carried the day, for the majority of popular ballots were cast for Tilden with a quarter of a million to spare. And, while Tilden was conceded 184 electoral votes, only one vote short of the 185 required for election, Hayes was conceded only 165. But nineteen of the

twenty contested electoral votes lay in the three Southern states that were still under Republican government—South Carolina, Louisiana, and Florida. The twentieth vote, from the Republican state of Oregon, was claimed by the Democrats on a technicality. Tilden needed only one of the twenty votes to assure his election, while Hayes had to have them all to win a bare majority of one vote. Republican managers promptly claimed all the votes and announced a Hayes victory. Charging that the Democrats had used intimidation and fraud against black voters, Republican returning boards in the three Southern states threw out enough Democratic popular votes to give those states to Hayes. Both parties had resorted to chicanery in the election, but modern scholars hold that Tilden deserved more than enough of the contested votes to win. On December 6 Republican electors met and cast the votes of the three states for Hayes, but on the same day a rival set of Democratic electors cast the votes of the same states solidly for Tilden.

Congress, with a Democratic House and a Republican Senate, now faced the problem of deciding which returns were authentic and which candidate had won. The Constitution was not explicit on who should count the electoral votes, and the law was silent. As the weeks passed an ominous deadlock ensued, and public anxiety mounted: only sixteen years before, a presidential election had precipitated a civil war, and already there was grave talk of Democratic war veterans organizing for resistance to the seating of Hayes. Probably more people expected a violent outcome in this crisis than in the crisis over Lincoln's election in 1860, but at the same time more people sensed the urgency of finding a peaceful solution.

The compromise of 1877. Shocked by their predicament, the conservatives of North and South, particularly Northern Republicans and Southern Democrats, got together to devise a peaceful way out of the dilemma. They found they had much in common. Just as Old Whigs had risen to the top in the new Republican party of the North, so they had gained prominence and power in the old Democratic party of the South. In both sections they were the people of conservatism, property, and compromise, and they had formerly marched together under the banner of the Whig party. Now they found themselves in opposing camps. Hayes' advisers urged him to attract Southern support by promising a new policy. They would have him abandon the carpetbaggers, scalawags, and Radicals and appeal instead to the ex-Whigs and Conservatives of the South for support in the disputed election as well as for recruits to the Republican party. An ex-Whig himself, Hayes fell in readily with their advice.

Hayes and his friends found other means of attracting Southern Conservatives. War had destroyed Southern capital, depression had dried up sources of Northern investment, and carpetbaggers had exhausted the credit of the states. The only source of capital left was the federal Treasury, and Southern congressmen were knocking at its doors with hundreds of bills for internal improvements—for controlling floods along the Mississippi, for clearing harbors, river channels, and choked canals, for reconstructing depleted railroads, fallen bridges, broken levees, and public buildings. Southerners had already discovered that Republicans were consistently more sympathetic to such requests than were their fellow Democrats of the North, who lectured them sternly about "Grantism," public morals, and reform. Most powerful of the many lobbies promoting Southern measures was the one supporting the effort of Thomas A. Scott, president of the Pennsylvania Railroad, to get a subsidy of more than $200 million for the Texas & Pacific Railroad. General Grenville M. Dodge, the most astute railroad lobbyist of the Grant era, organized the forces behind the Scott bill. Persuaded by intermediaries that Hayes as President would be friendly to the Texas & Pacific, Scott added his powerful influence to that of others seeking to win Southern support for Hayes in the electoral crisis.

In the meantime all the arts of compromise, neglected since 1861, were revived. Congress referred the disputed returns to an electoral commission created for the purpose, consisting of fifteen members drawn in equal numbers from the Senate, the House, and the Supreme Court. Seven were Republicans, seven were Democrats, and one, Justice David Davis, was an independent. At the last moment, however, Justice Davis was elected to the Senate from Illinois and his place on the commission was filled by a loyal Republican. The commission then decided by a strictly partisan vote of eight Republicans to seven Democrats to accept the Republican returns. Enraged at what they denounced as a "conspiracy" to defraud them of victory, many Democrats refused to abide by the vote of the commission and launched a filibuster that threatened to prevent any election whatever and bring on anarchy.

The deadlock was renewed. The Hayes forces intensified their efforts to win over Southern Democrats, thus enabling the latter to demand a higher price for their support. Not only did Hayes promise to withdraw federal troops from the South and leave the state governments in the control of Conservatives, but he agreed to appoint a Southern Democrat to his Cabinet and permit him to hand out patronage to his friends. The Republican candidate and his spokesmen emphasized that the new administration would take a conciliatory attitude toward Southern needs and wishes generally, and particularly toward bills for internal improvements.

These Republican concessions and promises undoubtedly helped persuade Southern Democrats to accept the electoral commission's decision for Hayes, and the South's capitulation influenced many Northern Democrats to abandon the filibuster and accept the loss of a prize they were convinced they had rightfully won. Other influences worked toward the same end, including a patriotic urge to avoid anarchy and a yearning to return to traditional ways of peace and compromise. At

*Rutherford B. Hayes:
President by compromise*

The "strong" government, 1869–77   The "weak" government, 1877–81

President Hayes, sincere in his role as the man of conciliation and faithful to his promises to the South, appointed a Democrat, ex-Confederate General David M. Key of Tennessee, to his Cabinet. After a few weeks of awkward hesitation Hayes withdrew the federal troops from South Carolina and Louisiana, and the last two carpetbagger governments promptly collapsed, never to be restored. All the Southern states and border states as well were now under Conservative control. In his courtship of the South's ex-Whig Democrats, Hayes appointed many of them to federal offices, even though it meant turning down Republican applicants. The Texas & Pacific bill failed in spite of repeated endorsements by the President, but other bills for internal improvements in the South were enacted. Admirers cheered Hayes with the rebel yell during his three visits to the South.

Hayes' policy of conciliation pleased Southern Conservatives and eased somewhat the old tensions between North and South. But certain results of that policy disappointed the President. For one thing the ex-Whig Democrats of the South did not rally in numbers to the Republican standard as he had hoped they would. A ground swell of agrarian discontent and radicalism below the Potomac made it difficult for conservative Democratic leaders there to continue their cooperation with business-minded Republicans. Finally, congressmen of Hayes' own party resisted his policy of appeasing the South and appointing Democrats to office. And so the Republicans returned to the practice of bloody-shirt oratory and to charges of Southern disloyalty. Only a few Republicans seemed disturbed by their party's desertion of the carpetbaggers and the freedmen and its repudiation of the goals of Reconstruction policy.

last Hayes' dubious cause prevailed, and he was declared President only two days before he took office.

The politics of reconciliation. The crisis of 1877 marked the end of one era and the beginning of another. The closing era had dawned with the martial zeal of troops singing ''Let us die to make men free.'' It had reached a crest of revolutionary fervor in 1867. By 1877 that fervor had burned out, the high resolves and ideals had been forgotten, and many of the crusaders had fallen into disgrace. Men of this new era talked of peace at any price, of the need for order, conciliation, and getting on with business. They dismissed high ideals as impractical, used ''politics'' as a term of opprobrium, and insisted that ''business'' was the proper concern of the serious minded.

Subordination of the freedmen

The abandonment of equality. The Radicals, so long as they had the power and so long as the country was in a responsive mood, had made equality for the freedman a war aim as well as freedom for the slave. By constitutional amendment and statutes, the United States was presumably committed to the principle of equal civil and political rights and to the use of federal power to guarantee them. Yet after Reconstruction the country quickly broke this commitment and virtually forgot

about it for two generations. That the North was also remiss was indicated by the conduct of federal troops in the South, the army's treatment of black soldiers, the policies of labor unions, and the discriminatory laws of Northern cities and states. Furthermore, the Radical promise of equality was an embarrassment to Hayes' effort to reconcile the estranged South and to put aside bitter war memories.

In short, the white people of the North and

South were reconciled at the expense of Negroes. When Hayes visited Atlanta in the fall of 1877, he told the freedmen that their "rights and interests would be safer" if Southern whites were "let alone by the general government." This sentiment was greeted with "immense enthusiasm"—by the whites. "Let alone" became the watchword of government policy in race relations as well as in industrial and business affairs. Former champions of the freedmen in the North took up the new slogan and dropped their concern for the rights of the Negro. The *Nation* declared that the federal government should have "nothing more to do with him," and doubted that he could ever "be worked into a system of government for which you and I would have much respect."

The plea for reconciliation, the let-alone philosophy, and the prevailing disillusionment with high ideals and promises also had their effect on the Supreme Court. In a long series of decisions the Court underwrote white supremacy, state rights, and laissez faire and virtually nullified the Fourteenth and Fifteenth Amendments insofar as they applied to the rights of freedmen. In 1876 Chief Justice Morrison R. Waite, in *United States* v. *Cruikshank,* decided that the Fourteenth Amendment "adds nothing to the rights of one citizen as against another" and does not extend federal protection to other rights except when they are infringed by a state. Applying the same interpretation in the *Civil Rights Cases* of 1883, the Court pronounced the Civil Rights Act of 1875 unconstitutional. This act had provided that all persons, regardless of race, were entitled to "the full and equal enjoyment" of all public facilities such as inns and railroads, as well as theaters and other places of amusement. In holding that the Fourteenth Amendment was a prohibition against states only, the Court said in effect that the federal government could not lawfully protect Negroes against discrimination by private individuals. The court joined the President in adhering to laissez faire.

Now, with the official approval of the federal courts, the acquiescence of many Northern liberals and Radicals, and the cooperation of the Republican party, blacks were relegated to an inferior grade of citizenship. Their freedom was not seriously challenged, but their equality most certainly was. There was little they could do about it. Even Frederick Douglass, once the militant leader of the blacks, accepted office under Hayes' Administration, and so did Carl Schurz, one of their most outspoken white liberal friends. The high hopes and fine promises of earlier days were shattered.

The road to segregation. The freedmen were not yet wholly abandoned to their worst enemies nor entirely without friends of a kind. Harder times were to come, but meanwhile they fell under the paternalistic regime of the Southern Conservatives. These men were not wholly insincere in their public pledge to protect the freedman's rights—as they conceived those rights. They thought of the Negro as a subordinate and an inferior but as having limited rights appropriate to his lower status. They did not feel the need for humiliating and persecuting the Negro, as did the men who were to gain control of race relations in the future. The Conservatives professed to feel a paternalistic responsibility for the underprivileged freedmen.

Deserted by their Northern friends and neglected by the federal government, the blacks not unnaturally turned to the Southern Conservatives. They did this, not out of love for their old masters, but out of a real need for protection against worse enemies. They had nowhere else to turn. For their part, the Conservatives partially tamed the antiblack passions they had helped to arouse in overthrowing the carpetbaggers. In politics they sometimes used black votes against agrarian whites who were antagonized by the Whiggish, probusiness policies of the Conservative governments. Such prominent Conservative leaders as Wade Hampton of South Carolina, L. Q. C. Lamar of Mississippi, and Alexander H. Stephens of Georgia invited freedmen's support. Although the Negroes were often coerced, intimidated, or defrauded, they nevertheless continued to vote in large numbers in many parts of the South for two decades after Reconstruction. What is more, they continued to hold minor offices and to keep at least one black congressman in Washington (in all but one term) until after the end of the century. To attract black support to the Democratic party, Governor Hampton of South Carolina appointed eighty-six Negroes to office during his Administration, and Governor Francis R. T. Nicholls of Louisiana also gave minor offices and political favors to blacks. A common device was the "fusion principle," by which the Conservatives helped the black

Frederick Douglass: *militant black*

Carl Schurz: *liberal reformer*

A case for segregation

We consider the underlying fallacy of the plaintiff's argument to consist in the assumption that the enforced separation of the two races stamps the colored race with a badge of inferiority. If this be so, it is not by reason of anything found in the act, but solely because the colored race chooses to put that construction upon it.... The argument also assumes that social prejudices may be overcome by legislation, and that equal rights cannot be secured to the negro except by an enforced commingling of the two races. We cannot accept this proposition.... Legislation is powerless to eradicate racial instincts or to abolish distinctions based upon physical differences, and the attempt to do so can only result in accentuating the difficulties of the present situation. If the civil and political rights of both races be equal one cannot be inferior to the other civilly or politically. If one race be inferior to the other socially, the Constitution of the United States cannot put them upon the same plane.

From Plessy v. Ferguson, 163 U.S. 537, 1896.

A case for equality

The white race deems itself to be the dominant race in this country. And so it is, in prestige, in achievements, in education, in wealth and in power. So, I doubt not, it will continue to be for all time, if it remains true to its great heritage and holds fast to the principles of constitutional liberty. But in view of the Constitution, in the eye of the law, there is in this country no superior, dominant, ruling class of citizens. There is no caste here. Our Constitution is color-blind, and neither knows nor tolerates classes among citizens. In respect of civil rights, all citizens are equal before the law. The humblest is the peer of the most powerful. The law regards man as man, and takes no account of his surroundings or of his color when his civil rights as guaranteed by the supreme law of the land are involved. It is, therefore, to be regretted that this high tribunal, the final expositor of the fundamental law of the land, has reached the conclusion that it is competent for a State to regulate the enjoyment by citizens of their civil rights solely upon the basis of race.

From the Dissent of Mr. Justice John Marshall Harlan, Plessy v. Ferguson, 163 U.S. 537, 1896.

---

against the white wing of the Republican party in return for Negro assistance in the Conservatives' struggle against discontented whites of their own party. By this means the Conservatives strengthened their control over the Democratic party and kept the Republican party divided along racial lines within the South.

For a time this balance of forces restrained extremists who advocated systematic disfranchisement and rigid segregation of the blacks. The idea of racial inferiority had struck roots long before the war, but rigid and universal segregation was incompatible with slavery and rarely required under the system. After the Civil War, blacks withdrew from the white-dominated churches to found their own. Ex-

cept in a few brief experiments, the Radicals did not mix races in the public schools of the South. In transportation and in some other public services, however, the races continued to mingle for two or more decades to an extent that would be unthinkable to a later era of Jim Crow (the popular name for segregation).

The Conservatives themselves were to blame for opening the way to segregation and disfranchisement. In order to defeat the Populists, a radical movement of the early nineties that sought black support (see p. 479), they once again lifted the cry of white supremacy as they had in their struggle to overthrow the carpetbaggers. But this time they could not tame the passions they aroused, and the extremists took over. By 1900 all the Southern

Lynch mob, 1893

states had Jim Crow railroad cars; three required or authorized segregation in railway stations; and one had Jim Crow streetcars. Eventually the harsh rule of segregation spread to all public services and institutions. Little protest came from the North, where the Negro also suffered increasing discrimination. And in 1896, in the case of *Plessy* v. *Ferguson,* the Supreme Court sanctioned segregation by declaring "separate but equal" facilities constitutional.

Two years later, in 1898, the Supreme Court took another step toward laissez faire in the case of *Williams* v. *Mississippi* by approving a Mississippi scheme for depriving the Negro of the ballot. This plan, which had been adopted in 1890, combined the poll tax, the literacy test, and residence requirements to reduce the number of black voters to a handful. South Carolina followed suit in 1895, and the rest of the Southern states during the next twelve years. Each state added minor variations to the Mississippi plan, but everywhere the result was the same. As the Negro disappeared from the polls, he also dropped out of the minor offices and public services on which he had managed to retain some hold. The last black congressman to be elected from the South left Washington in 1901.

By the end of the century, the great laissez-faire reaction had virtually undone the work of Reconstruction. The constitutional amendments guaranteeing equality before the law and at the ballot box had been practically nullified, and life itself was jeopardized by the spread of lynching. This crime reached its peak between 1889 and 1899, when an average of some 187 lynchings a year occurred in the United States as a whole. About four-fifths of the lynchings took place in the South, and the great majority of the victims of the lynch mobs were blacks.

The Atlanta Compromise. Freedom had not emancipated the blacks from labor in the cotton field, for they continued to till the white man's land. At the end of the century a little more than 75 percent of the black farmers in the South were croppers or tenants. Handicapped by prevailing agricultural depression and by their heritage of oppression, they contrived to live little better than they had under slavery. The exodus of the Negro to the North did not begin for more than a half-century after emancipation, but many freedmen did move into the towns of the South. There they went into the trades and crafts and shortly after the war greatly outnumbered white artisans. Employers increasingly discriminated against black workers, often at the insistence of all-white trade unions, which kept up a constant pressure to drive blacks out of the better-paid, more attractive work and confine them to "Negro jobs." Gradually, blacks disappeared from some skilled trades they had traditionally monopolized and were excluded almost entirely from certain of the newer industries, such as textiles. Generally barred from labor unions, black workers were sometimes used as strikebreakers, thereby earning additional ill will from the unions.

By the 1880s the freedmen had become stratified into social and economic classes. The new Negro middle class, consisting largely of professional people and businessmen, was proportionately smaller and commanded far less wealth and power than the corresponding class of white people. Within black society, however, its dominance was quite as strong. The Negro middle class, which reflected many of the attitudes, assumptions, and aspirations of the white middle class, found full expression in Booker T. Washington, the foremost leader of his race in the generation following Reconstruction.

The New South: adjustments

There is a New South, not through protest against the Old, but because of new conditions, new adjustments, and, if you please, new ideas and aspirations.... As ruin was never before so overwhelming, never was restoration swifter. The soldier stepped from the trenches into the furrow; horses that had charged Federal guns marched before the plow....

But what is the sum of our work? We have found out that in the summing up the free negro counts more than he did as a slave. We have planted the schoolhouse on the hilltop and made it free to white and black....

The South found her jewel in the toad's head of defeat.... The Old South rested everything on slavery and agriculture, unconscious that these could neither give nor maintain healthy growth. The New South presents a perfect democracy, the oligarchs leading in the popular movement: a social system compact and closely knitted, less splendid on the surface, but stronger at the core; a hundred farms for every plantation, fifty homes for every palace; and a diversified industry that meets the complex need of this complex age.

From Henry Grady, *The New South*, 1886.

The New South: one Negro's view

Our greatest danger is that, in the great leap from slavery to freedom, we may overlook the fact that the masses of us are to live by the productions of our hands; and fail to keep in mind that we shall prosper in proportion as we learn to dignify and glorify common labor, and put brains and skill into the common occupations of life.... It is at the bottom of life we must begin, and not at the top....

The wisest among my race understand that the agitation of questions of social equality is the extremest folly, and that progress in the enjoyment of all the privileges that will come to us must be the result of severe and constant struggle rather than of artificial forcing. No race that has anything to contribute to the markets of the world is long in any degree ostracized. It is important and right that all privileges of the law be ours, but it is vastly more important that we be prepared for the exercise of these privileges. The opportunity to earn a dollar in a factory just now is worth infinitely more than the opportunity to spend a dollar in an opera house.

From Booker T. Washington, *The Race Problem*, 1895.

Washington became head of an industrial school for blacks at Tuskegee, Alabama, in 1881 but soon attained influence and power that far transcended this modest post and contrasted strikingly with his habitual attitude of humility. The foremost spokesman for his own race, he was also a leader of white opinion on racial policy and a powerful influence in shaping national philanthropic and educational policies. He believed that education for the Negro in that era should stress industrial training rather than intellectual development. In a famous speech delivered in Atlanta in 1895, Washington set forth a philosophy of race relations that came to be known as the Atlanta Compromise.

Washington's compromise in race relations received the support of Southern whites, Northern whites, and many blacks. He conciliated the white South by abandoning the militant Reconstruction demand for equality, emphasizing economic opportunities instead of political rights, and identifying himself and his race with the industrial order established by the Conservatives. To his own race he preached patience, conservatism, and the primacy of material progress. This submissive and compliant doctrine, widely accepted at the time, was rejected as ''Uncle Tomism'' by a later generation.

Anticipating the later militancy of black nationalism, Alexander Crummell, who was educated in England and had spent twenty years in Liberia, preached that American blacks should regard themselves as ''a 'peculiar people' in this land,'' a distinct nation within a nation. And Bishop Henry M. Turner, a leading advocate of African colonization in the late nineteenth and early twentieth centuries, declared that ''a man who loves a country that hates him'' was beneath respect. His agitation produced some black identification with Africa but extremely few emigrants.

Tuskegee Institute: industrial education for the Negro

Politics in the New South

The Redeemers. The new rulers of the South, claiming that they had ''redeemed'' their section from the carpetbaggers, spoke of themselves as the Redeemers. We have already seen that ex-Whigs played a prominent part in this redemption and in the reconstituted Democratic party. It was partly out of regard for their feelings, in fact, that the Democratic party was often called the Conservative party in the South. It deserved that name, for the old Whigs had brought their philosophy with them into their new party.

With some exceptions the Redeemers were businessmen or industrialists rather than planters. Only in Tennessee, Kentucky, and Georgia did the old planter element make a bid for power, but they were unsuccessful in each case. Mississippi, one-time principality of planter-statesmen, was in the hands of five corporation lawyers, two of whom held the governorship for two decades and three of whom shared the state's Senate seats throughout the eighties. Redeemed Georgia was ruled by a triumvirate who speculated in railroads, coal- and iron-mining, and textiles. Virginia, still a countryman's state, was governed by city men for the benefit of bankers, bondholders, and railroad-operators. In Tennessee the leader of the Redeemers was also general counsel of the Tennessee Coal and Iron Company; the first Redeemer governor of the state was president of the company, and his two successors were directors and officials. All were former Whigs and all were industrialists. Similarly, the Redeemers of Alabama were closely associated with the Louisville & Nashville Railroad, which helped put the new

regime in power and won many favors in return. The Louisiana Lottery Company, originally chartered by the carpetbaggers and politically allied with them, turned against its former friends and helped the Redeemers seize power in 1877. The new rulers in return wrote a guarantee of the Lottery monopoly into the state constitution and protected its interests in other ways.

Although the Redeemers were often called Bourbons, they did not really represent the restoration of the old order or cling to its values. They represented instead a new phase of the revolution that had been touched off in the South by the overthrow of the Confederacy, and in that revolution they played a more important and lasting role than the carpetbaggers and the scalawags, who have received far more attention. The Cotton Kingdom of slavery and the Radical regime of equalitarianism proved short and ephemeral compared with the new order of race relations, economic institutions, and politics established by the Redeemers.

The new regime. The new state constitutions framed by the Redeemers embodied a strong reaction against the government interference so characteristic of Reconstruction. They revealed suspicion and distrust of legislatures and placed such hampering restrictions upon government that positive action of any sort became difficult. The constitutions were, above all, laissez-faire documents. The new Southern governments also reacted against Reconstruction through their policy of ''retrenchment,'' which meant cutting taxes and starving or eliminating tax-supported public services. The chief beneficiaries of the tax policy were the railroads, the utilities, and the factories, whose burdens were lightened; and the chief victims were the public schools. The schools, which bore the stigma of carpetbagger support, were gravely crippled by the pinch of Redeemer retrenchment as well as by general poverty and depression. The Redeemers also cut appropriations for other public institutions, but none so drastically as those for prisons. The state governments actually turned prisoners into a source of revenue by leasing them as cheap labor to industrialists with the right political connections. The convict-lease system, often marked by brutal exploitation, became an ugly blot on the reputation of the new regime.

This was an era of corrupt government and lax public morals across the country, and it would be unfair to single out the Redeemers for special censure. They invited such censure, however, by the attack they made on graft and corruption in their campaigns to overthrow the carpetbaggers. Faced with no effective party of opposition, protected by long tenure of office, and consequently immune from criticism and exposure, the Redeemers fell into a laxity that eventually covered some of the state governments with disgrace. In the eighties one scandal after another came to light. Some were exposed only by the absconding of state treasurers, nine of whom were guilty of defalcation or embezzlement, and one of whom defrauded Louisiana of more than a million dollars. Such losses, as an Alabamian said, made a mockery of "niggardly economy in public expenditure."

In national affairs the Redeemers revealed their Whiggish heritage by lining up with conservative Northerners on questions of currency, banks, and internal improvements. In so doing they reversed the sectional diplomacy of Southern Democrats, who traditionally allied themselves with the West, and tied the South instead to the policies of the conservative wing of the party centered in the Northeast. To overcome the unpopularity of this shift in alignment, the Redeemers hushed the discussion of economic issues, stressed issues of race and tradition, and insisted on "white solidarity."

Stirrings of revolt. The "Solid South" won its name prematurely. Hardly had "home rule" been restored when revolt began to stir against the Redeemer regime. Once the pressure of occupation was removed, ancient class, party, and sectional antagonisms within the South began to reassert themselves, and local parties calling themselves Independents, Greenbackers, or Readjusters organized for action. Poorly led, they were often cheated at elections and won only limited success, but they provide a clue to what was seething beneath the surface solidarity of Southern politics.

Many of the issues that prompted revolt against the Redeemer regime were profoundly felt. One source of unrest was resentment over the way the Conservatives used the black vote in the 1870s and 1880s to win political advantage over discontented whites. Upcountry whites in particular resented the huge political power of the white minority in the black belt, the power the carpetbaggers had derived from the same source and had used to the same end. Since the majority of Independents and other third-party men were small farmers, they found the Whiggish policies of the Redeemers little to their liking, particularly the pampering of railroads and corporations. Independents found further cause for resentment in the high-handed rule, the election chicanery, and the treasury scandals that became characteristic of Conservative rule. On national issues they usually sided with Western agrarians in support of soft money, greenbacks, and silver, and therefore rejected the Redeemers' alliance with the Northeast.

But the most disruptive issue of all was the "readjustment," or repudiation, of state debts. So disruptive was it, in fact, that it unseated the Redeemers in some states and threatened the security of the whole regime. By the end of Reconstruction, the Southern states had incurred a total debt of about $275 million, and in nine states there was talk of scaling the debts down or partially repudiating them. In one way or another these nine states contrived to reduce their total liabilities by $150 million. Naturally the states' creditors and bondholders protested bitterly, and in each state a faction of Redeemers fought the debt-readjusters. In Tennessee the fight brought the Republicans back to power, and in Virginia it led to the triumph of a third party calling itself the Readjusters.

The advocates of repudiation argued that much of the debt was a heritage from carpetbagger looting, that the states themselves had derived little benefit from the sale of Reconstruction bonds, and that in any event the section was too impoverished and ravaged to carry the burden of Reconstruction debts. Those who argued that the debt must be repaid—the so-called funders—retorted that the honor of the states was worth any sacrifice. Virginia funders virtually closed the public schools by diverting school funds to bondholders. They starved out other public services and at last provoked their people to rebellion. The Readjusters took charge of the state in 1880, readjusted the debt, and passed a flood of liberal reform measures. The new party, however, quickly fell under the dictatorial control of William Mahone, who was a former Confederate general and subsequently a railroad executive. As soon as the Readjusters elected Mahone to the United States Senate he shifted his allegiance to the Republican party.

Encouraged by the revolt against the Conservative Democrats, the Republicans began to dream of returning to power in the South through an alliance with the local third parties. Even though the Republicans had little in common with these parties save their opposition to Democrats, they put aside President Hayes' commitment to the Southern Conservatives and threw their support to the reformers and debt-repudiators. "Anything to beat the Bourbons" was the Republican policy. The Conservatives responded by reviving the tactics of fraud and intimidation once used against the carpetbaggers, employing them so effectively that by 1883 they had beaten all but the last spark out of the Independent revolt and had shattered Republican hopes of exploiting it. Not for a decade was there to be further talk of insurgency in the South. This was the real period of the Solid South, of exclusively one-party politics, and of the most complete political torpor that ever settled over the region. It was not to be broken until the Populist revolt of 1892.

The doctrine of the New South.

There had long been advocates of industrialism in the South, but before the Civil War they had looked on factories as a means of buttressing the existing social order. Propagandists of the New South, by contrast, sought to replace the old order with an economy like that of the North, a business civilization of cities, factories, and trade, with new values and new aims. This was what the "New South" meant to its champions in the 1880s. "As for Charleston," declared an editor from that city in 1882, "the importation of about five hundred Yankees of the right stripe would put a new face on affairs, and make the whole place throb with life and vivid force."

Propaganda for the New South point of view found full voice during the 1880s and 1890s in such journals as the Baltimore *Manufacturers' Record,* the Louisville *Courier-Journal,* and the Charleston *News and Courier.* But more famous and effective was the Atlanta *Constitution,* edited by orator Henry W. Grady. Full of the bustle and salesmanship of business enterprise, Grady exuded optimism and good will. In an address on "The New South" delivered in 1886 to the New England Society of New York he proclaimed:

> We have sowed towns and cities in the place of theories and put business above politics. We have challenged your spinners in Massachusetts and your ironmakers in Pennsylvania. . . . We have fallen in love with work. . . . We have let economy take root and spread among us as rank as the crab grass which sprung from Sherman's cavalry camps, until we are ready to lay odds on the Georgia Yankee, as he manufactures relics of the battlefield in a one-story shanty and squeezes pure olive oil out of his cotton seed, against any Down-easter that ever swapped wooden nutmegs for flannel sausages in the valleys of Vermont.

As models for young Southerners, Grady held up the businessman, especially the self-made man, the millionaire. What Grady and his friends were preaching was laissez-faire capitalism freed of restraints, a new industrial way of life, and a businessman's scale of values.

One sign of the popularity of the New South doctrine was the Southerner's eagerness for Northern approval. "Beyond all question," declared a Richmond journal, "we have been on the wrong track and should take a new departure." And Henry Watterson, a Louisville editor and orator, thought that "the ambition of the South is to out-Yankee the Yankee." But the appeal of the New South doctrine would have been less compelling had it not been embellished by sentimental tribute to the past: a heritage "never to be equalled in its chivalric strength and grace," as Grady put it. The invention of a legendary Old South and the cult of the "lost cause" revealed the curiously divided mind and the conflicting impulses of the Southern people in the new era. They marched hopefully in one direction and looked back longingly in the other.

The inner tensions of the Southern mind were reflected in the career of the Georgia writer Joel Chandler Harris, author of *Uncle Remus* (1881). A gentle, rather wistful man of humble origins, Harris portrayed the old slave in quaint dialect with humor and affection, casting a spell of charm over memories of the antebellum plantation. But while he was writing his nostalgic stories about the Old South,

Harris was also chief editorial-writer for Grady's Atlanta *Constitution,* doing his daily best to encourage the growth of the New South of business and industry. Both the admirers of the old order and the propagandists of the new advocated sectional "reconciliation," urging that the North abandon its reformist aims and accept the new order in the South. In political terms reconciliation was simply an alliance between conservatives of both regions.

The colonial economy

The agrarian pattern. The dream and design of the new men of the South was to build an urbanized, industrialized society like that of the Yankees. But the habits and economic realities of the Old South were slow to change and hard to shake off. Despite all the factories that were constructed, 96.1 percent of the North Carolinians and 94.1 percent of the Alabamians were still not classified "urban" by the census of 1890. Only 8.5 percent of the population of the South Atlantic states below Maryland was urban in 1890, as compared with 51.7 percent of the population of the North Atlantic states from Pennsylvania up. By 1900 the urban population of those Northern states had further increased by nearly 7 percent, that of the Southern states by only 1 percent. The New South was still the most rural and agrarian section of the country.

On the surface it would seem that deep changes had occurred in the distribution of land ownership in the South. The census of 1880 reported an amazing increase in the number of farms since 1860, and the average farm turned out to be less than half its former size. Optimists concluded that the Civil War had broken up the concentration of land in the hands of planters and had brought about "economic democracy." The truth was, however, that the old plantation lands had been parceled out in small plots among sharecroppers, each plot counting as a new "farm," and that large tracts of new land had been brought under cultivation. The sharecropper had replaced the slave, and his share of the crop depended largely on the tools, work animals, and feed the landlord furnished.

Ownership of the plantations had slipped from the old planters into the hands of merchants or other townsmen. Moreover, whatever efficiency and planning, whatever virtues of proprietorship, had resided in the old plantation system were largely missing from the sharecropper system. The old evils of land monopoly, absentee ownership, soil-mining, and the one-crop system were not only retained but intensified. From a strictly economic point of view, cropping was probably worse for the agriculture of the region than slavery had been.

The most desperate need of the Southern farmer after the war was credit. With no cash in hand, and no banks from which to borrow it, the farmer was at the mercy of merchants who were willing to advance supplies in return for a mortgage or "lien" on his future crop. The farmer pledged an unplanted crop for a loan of unstipulated amount at an undesig-

The increase of farm tenancy in the South

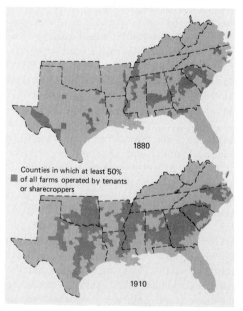

1880

Counties in which at least 50% of all farms operated by tenants or sharecroppers

1910

A map labeled 1860 showing: Little River, Wright's Branch, Gin House, "House", "Quarters", Branch Creek, Syll's Fork

A map labeled 1881 showing: Woods, Gabrina Dalton, Lizzie Dalton, Frank Maxey*, Little River, Joe Bug*, Jim Reid, Nancy Pope*, Cane Pope*, Church, Gub Barrow*, School, Willis Bryant*, Wright's Branch, Lem Bryant*, Gin House, Lewis Watson*, Tom Wright, Reuben Barrow*, Ben Thomas*, "House", Omy Barrow*, Tom Thomas, Handy Barrow*, "Granny", Peter Barrow*, Milly Barrow*, Old Isaac*, Tom Tang*, Calvin Parker*, Woods, Branch Creek, Woods, Beckton Barrow*, Lem Douglas, Syll's Fork, Woods

*Negroes who had lived on plantation as slaves

A Georgia plantation in 1860 and 1881

nated rate of interest. The amount of security fluctuated with the prospects of the harvest, the amount of credit with the hopes of the merchant, the amount of interest with the price of the goods. The lien system was a strange and deplorable makeshift. Once a lien was executed to a merchant, the farmer was bound to him until the debt had been repaid. Since the farmer was forced to part with his crop when prices were lowest, it is no wonder that many farmers failed to "pay out" at the end of the year. Trapped by the system, a man might continue year after oppressive year as a sort of peon, under lien to the same merchant and under the merchant's constant oversight. The lien system, in turn, fostered the stubborn persistence of the one-crop system; for the merchant would advance credit only against such cash crops as cotton or tobacco. The one-crop system was more characteristic of the new agricultural order than it had ever been of the old, and more and more the South had to turn to other sections for supplies that it might have grown itself.

During the last quarter of the nineteenth century farmers were plagued by low prices and chronic depression the country over. The Southern farmer shared these ills with farmers elsewhere, but he also suffered from a combination of burdens peculiar to the South. Among these was the heritage of military defeat, pillage, and occupation that had cost the section every third horse or mule and nearly half its agricultural machinery. On top of these burdens were heaped the ills of sharecropping peonage and the lien system. By the 1890s a spirit of grim desperation had settled on the farmers of the South, a spirit that long manifested itself in a suspicion of city folk and their ways and a resentment of wealth and its display. This spirit was to enter into the soul of the Populist movement in the years ahead (see p. 479).

Industrial stirrings. Toward the end of the 1870s the depression that had settled over the nation in 1873 started to lift. Once again Northern investors began to show interest in opportunities below the Potomac and freed the springs of capital. The propagandists of the New South boasted that the South, like the West, was an empire ripe for exploiting. "The way to clear and large profits is open," announced a Philadelphia editor in 1877. A book appeared in 1888 on *How to Get Rich in the South* and another in 1894 describing

Trapped by the system

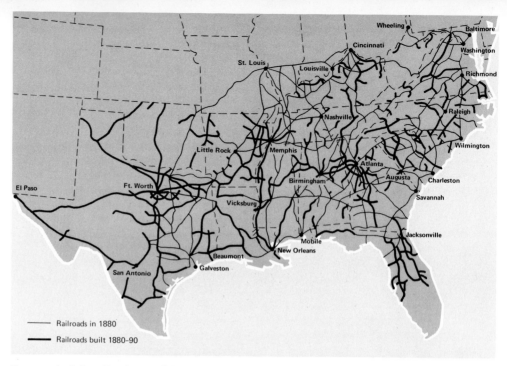

The growth of the railroad network in the South

the South as *The Road to Wealth*. The Redeemers welcomed investors with open arms, tax exemptions, and promises of cheap and docile labor.

With the willing cooperation of Southern legislatures, speculators rounded up huge grants of public lands and mineral resources. Florida granted several million more acres than were in her public domain, and Texas surrendered an area larger than the state of Indiana. In 1877 the law reserving federal lands in five Southern states for homesteaders was scrapped, and the rich Southern empire of timber, coal, and iron was thrown open to unrestricted exploitation. In the next decade nearly 6 million acres of federal lands were sold, most of them to Northern speculators, who indulged in a reckless destruction of forests and a rifling of other resources.

Exploitation of this sort, as well as more laudable schemes of industrial development, would have been impossible without dramatic improvements in transportation. Between 1880 and 1890 railroad mileage in the South as a whole increased from 16,605 miles to 39,108, a growth of 135.5 percent, 50 percent greater than the national rate of growth in mileage in the same period. Railroad development exposed to exploitation the landlocked mineral resources of the South, particularly the iron mines of Tennessee, Virginia, and Alabama. Between 1876 and 1901 pig-iron

production increased seventeen times in the South, as compared with an eightfold increase in the country at large. Alabama, with its unrivaled deposits of iron ore, coal, and limestone in unique proximity, quickly outstripped its Southern competitors, and by 1898 Birmingham was the largest shipping point for pig iron in the country and the third largest in the world.

So long as the Southern economy stuck to its traditional role of supplying raw materials of mine, forest, and farm, it met with encouragement from Northern bankers and investors. Production of lumber and forestry products soared sensationally, as did the output of such fuels as coal and oil, and such ores as iron, sulphur, bauxite, phosphate rock, and manganese. Eastern capital entered each of these enterprises, and Eastern control followed. The modern era of oil production, for example, opened with an unprecedented gusher at Spindletop, near Beaumont, Texas, in January 1901, and soon the newly opened fields of the Southwest became the province of three nominally competing pipeline and refining companies presided over by Standard Oil. The story of the development and control of vast sulphur deposits in Louisiana and bauxite deposits in Arkansas was similar to that of oil in Texas.

The tobacco industry, the oldest in the region, discovered new markets and developed new techniques of manufacture during the new era. Until about 1885 tobacco was processed by the same methods and in the same areas as before the Civil War. But in the next fifteen years the industry was completely revolutionized by changes in consumer tastes, methods of manufacture, and areas of production. Leadership shifted from Virginia to the Carolinas, which grew the bright tobacco that pleased the new cigarette-smokers. By 1900 the invention of new machinery and methods had thoroughly mechanized an industry that had once been largely handicraft. At the same time the size of factories increased dramatically, and control of the industry became highly concentrated. The genius of concentrated control was a tall, rugged, redheaded North Carolinian named James Buchanan Duke, called "Buck," whose rise paralleled that of the industry. He started out in 1865 with two blind mules and a load of tobacco, all the war had left on his father's small farm. "Tobacco is the poor man's luxury," he observed, and on that insight he founded a fortune. By 1889 his firm was producing half the country's cigarettes, and the following year he absorbed his main competitors into the American Tobacco Company.

The true symbol of the New South, however, was the cotton mill, and the zeal of its promoters stirred up a veritable "cotton mill crusade." Actually, the industry was confined largely to the Carolinas, Georgia, and Alabama. Cotton-manufacturing began in the Old South and continued to grow through the Civil War and Reconstruction, but between 1880 and 1900 the amount of capital invested in the Southern mills increased sevenfold. The mill-building fever infected whole communities. Much of the growth came at the expense of New England, which was unable to compete with the vast Southern supply of unorganized workers accustomed to long hours and low pay. The chief textile products of the South were unfinished goods that were sent north for final processing, and in this, as in the use of cheap labor, the cotton mills were typical of the South's new industries.

The colonial status. For all its boasts of industrial progress, the New South lagged far behind the rest of the country. So rapid was the expansion of the North and West that by the end of the century the South had a smaller percentage of the nation's factories and a slightly smaller percentage of the nation's capital than it had in 1860. With few exceptions, the industries that did take root in the South were low-wage industries that gave the first rough processing to the agricultural, forestry, and mining products of the region. Transportation costs made it more economical to do this processing near the source of raw material, and large supplies of cheap, unskilled labor were an even stronger attraction to such industries. Cotton yarn, cottonseed oil, cane sugar, polished rice, fertilizers, liquors, and tobacco, and such forestry products as turpentine, resin, and lumber, constituted the bulk of the South's industrial output. The final processing of these products was usually done in the North, and from the final processing came the greatest profits.

There was no law relegating the South to a raw-material economy, no plot to exclude Southerners from the better-paying jobs and the more profitable industries. What, then, were the reasons for the persistent industrial backwardness of the section? A lost war, a late start, and a lack of capital were some of the reasons. These disadvantages might have been overcome more readily, however, had it not been for certain artificial barriers: a host of practices and rules adopted to suit the convenience of private interests in the North while the South was out of the Union or later when the section was without significant influence in national decisions.

One of these barriers was the system of regional freight-rate differentials adopted in the seventies and eighties by private railway associations and later given legal sanction by the Interstate Commerce Commission. These differentials meant that shippers of manufactured goods in the South and West were charged far higher rates than shippers in the privileged "Official Territory," north of the Ohio and Potomac and east of the Mississippi. The system discouraged the Southern producer from competing in the richest market area, the Northeast, but enabled the Northeastern producer to penetrate the Southern market. At the same time, favorable "commodity rates" were provided for Southern raw materials. Taken together, these rate differentials discouraged the South from developing manufactures of its own and encouraged it to concentrate on raw materials. A price differential imposed on Birmingham steel by the Pittsburgh steel-masters and their allied railroads had a similar effect. "Pittsburgh Plus" meant that buyers of Birmingham steel had to pay the Pittsburgh price *plus* the freight charge from Pittsburgh. Later, the "Birmingham Differential" replaced the freight charge with a straight additional charge of $3 a ton. This scheme protected the Pittsburgh mills and their customers and prevented Southern manufacturers (or potential manufacturers eager to enter the lists against Northern competitors) from taking advantage of the decidedly cheaper steel of Birmingham.

During these years the Northeast assumed something like an imperial power over the other sections, and the national economy fell into a neomercantilism reminiscent of colonial days. The Northeast discouraged the rise of competing manufactures, promoted ample supplies of raw materials for its own factories, monopolized the carrying trade by the combination of regionalized freight rates, steel-price differentials, and patent control, and reduced foreign competition in its domestic markets by the protective tariff. In brief, the Northeast became for a long time the workshop of the nation, reserving for its own coffers the profits of processing, transporting, and distributing goods. The South was left to produce the raw materials for the new economic order, to serve as a tributary of industrial power.

Division of labor was, of course, natural in a national economy, and the South derived real benefits from its role in the form of increased job opportunities, payrolls, and taxable assets. On the other hand, this subordinate economic status imposed grave penalties on the South. As late as 1910 some 62 percent of its workers were engaged in the extractive industries—agriculture, forestry, animal husbandry, fishing, mining. Throughout the country, these industries paid the lowest wages of all, and the wages of Southern workers were even lower than the national average. By 1900 the percentage of Southerners employed in manufactures was still about the same as it had been in all the states east of the Mississippi in 1850.

In wealth, living standards, and general welfare the Union was more a "house divided" now than when Lincoln first used the phrase. In 1880 the estimated per capita wealth in the South was $376 as compared with a national average of $870. No Southern state came within $300 of the national average nor within $550 of the average outside the South. In 1900 the national average in per capita wealth stood at $1,165, and in the South the average was $509. The earliest income estimates, those of 1919, indicate that per capita income in the South was about 40 percent lower than the national average. Little wonder that the region was noted for its "poor whites" and its "poor blacks" as well. Poverty was a characteristic of the regional economy. Closely related to that poverty was a lag in literacy, education, libraries, public health, and living standard.

The South of the New Order was humbled politically as well as economically. Its political abasement, in fact, represents the most striking shift in the geography of power that has ever occurred in American history. In the seventy-two years between Washington and Lincoln, Southerners held the Presidency for fifty years and the title of Chief Justice of the Supreme Court for sixty years. They furnished more than half the Justices and diplomatic representatives to major powers, nearly half the men of Cabinet rank, and more than half the Speakers of the House of Representatives. During the next half-century, by contrast, no Southerner save Andrew Johnson served as President or Vice President, and the South furnished only 14 of the 133 Cabinet members, 7 of the 31 Justices of the Supreme Court, 2 of the 12 Speakers of the House, and fewer than one-tenth of the diplomatic representatives to major powers. From the power and glory of the eighteenth and early nineteenth centuries the South had fallen to a lowly state. In the process of reunion it had lost some of its old distinctiveness, along with much of its disproportionate power, and had become the frontier of a dynamic new order that was expanding southward as well as westward.

Suggestions for reading   The best guide to books on the South is A. S. Link and R. W. Patrick, eds., *Writing Southern History** (2nd ed., 1967). C. V. Woodward, *Origins of the New South, 1877–1913** (1951), concentrates on the post-Reconstruction period. W. J. Cash, *The Mind of the South** (1941), contains provocative interpretations of uneven value. P. M. Gaston, *The New South Creed: A Study in Southern Mythmaking* (1970), is well described by its subtitle. The stresses and strains of sectional adjustment and reconciliation are the subject of P. H. Buck, *The Road to Reunion,*

*Available in a paperback edition.

1865–1900* (1937). C. V. Woodward, *Reunion and Reaction: The Compromise of 1877 and the End of Reconstruction* (1951), investigates the complex national crisis of 1876–77. For the setting of industrial conflict see R. V. Bruce, *1877: Year of Violence* (1959). The development of President Hayes' policy toward the South is traced in Harry Barnard, *Rutherford B. Hayes and His America* (1954); Republican efforts to revive their party in the South are pictured in V. P. De Santis, *Republicans Face the Southern Question: The New Departure Years, 1877–1897* (1959), and S. P. Hirshson, *Farewell to the Bloody Shirt: Northern Republicans and the Southern Negro, 1877–1893* (1962).

The struggles of the blacks after the abandonment of Reconstruction are illuminated in August Meier, *Negro Thought in America, 1880–1915* (1963); J. H. Franklin, *From Slavery to Freedom: A History of Negro Americans* (3rd ed., 1969); and E. F. Frazier, *The Negro in the United States* (rev. ed., 1957). G. M. Fredrickson, *Black Image in the White Mind* (1971), has much to say on this period of racism. Older views of the Negro are revised or discredited in V. L. Wharton, *The Negro in Mississippi, 1865–1890* (1947), G. B. Tindall, *South Carolina Negroes, 1877–1900* (1952), C. E. Wynes, *Race Relations in Virginia, 1870–1902* (1961), and F. A. Logan, *The Negro in North Carolina, 1876–1894* (1964). C. V. Woodward, *The Strange Career of Jim Crow* (2nd rev. ed., 1966), traces the origins and rise of segregation, and R. W. Logan, *The Negro in American Life and Thought: The Nadir, 1877–1901* (1954), depicts the deterioration of Reconstruction ideals of racial equality. Two works written in the period itself are especially recommended: Booker T. Washington's autobiography, *Up from Slavery* (1901), and G. W. Cable, *The Negro Question: A Selection of Writings on Civil Rights in the South,* edited by Arlin Turner (1958).

Insight into the politics of the New South is furnished by biographies of popular leaders, such as F. B. Simkins, *Pitchfork Ben Tillman: South Carolinian* (1944); J. F. Wall, *Henry Watterson: Reconstructed Rebel* (1956); C. V. Woodward, *Tom Watson: Agrarian Rebel* (1938); and N. M. Blake, *William Mahone of Virginia: Soldier and Political Insurgent* (1935). J. P. Maddex, Jr., *The Virginia Conservatives, 1867–1879: A Study in Reconstruction Politics* (1970), and C. C. Pearson, *The Readjuster Movement in Virginia* (1917), are the best studies of the first breach in the Solid South; and A. D. Kirwan, *Revolt of the Rednecks: Mississippi Politics, 1876–1925* (1951), is a colorful account of poor-white revolts. Paul Lewinson, *Race, Class, and Party: A History of Negro Suffrage and White Politics in the South* (1932), shows how the race issue has been exploited. V. O. Key, Jr., *Southern Politics in State and Nation* (1949), treats of twentieth-century politics but sheds a bright light on earlier years.

Industrialization of the South is viewed critically and analytically by H. L. Herring, *Southern Industry and Regional Development* (1941), and from the New South viewpoint by Broadus Mitchell and G. S. Mitchell, *The Industrial Revolution in the South* (1930). N. M. Tilley, *The Bright Tobacco Industry, 1860–1929* (1948), recounts the revolutionary changes that overtook the South's oldest industry in this period. C. C. Rister, *Oil! Titan of the Southwest* (1949), tells of the boom period of a new industry. Broadus Mitchell, *The Rise of Cotton Mills in the South* (1921, 2nd ed., 1968), stresses the "crusading" aspects of the movement for textile-manufacturing. On the freight-rate discriminations W. H. Joubert, *Southern Freight Rates in Transition* (1949), is useful. R. B. Nixon, *Henry W. Grady: Spokesman of the New South* (1943), is an able portrayal of the industrial propagandist. The plight of the Southern farmer is investigated in F. A. Shannon, *The Farmer's Last Frontier: Agriculture 1860–1897* (1945).

Southern men of letters have furnished some of the most profound insights into the life and history of the South. Willard Thorp, who calls the South "the most exotic and exciting region in America," has collected excellent examples in *A Southern Reader* (1955). Of special relevance to this period are some of the works of William Faulkner, foremost of the novelists, particularly *The Hamlet* (1940) and *Go Down, Moses* (1942).

*Available in a paperback edition.

The New West: empire within a nation

17

After the Civil War the American people embarked on the conquest and exploitation of an area greater than all the territory that had been settled since the landing at Jamestown in 1607. Up to this time the settlers of the trans-Mississippi West had occupied only its eastern and western fringes, in one tier of states just beyond the Mississippi and in another tier half a continent beyond along the Pacific coast. Between these two frontiers, separated by fifteen hundred miles, stretched a vast and fabulous expanse of ocean-like plains, spired and towering mountain ranges, grassy plateaus, painted deserts, and breathtaking canyons. Of all the American wests, this was the one that captured the imagination of the world, the one that would be perpetuated in song and story.

Americans had conquered many frontiers in the past, but the New West was different from all the others. The experience of the pioneers there was less like that of their forefathers in taming the forested "wests" of the East and more like the imperialistic adventures of nineteenth-century Europeans in Africa and Asia. America was a nation with a built-in empire, an empire disguised as a nation. What Englishmen and western Europeans had to seek "somewhere east of Suez," their American contemporaries, until the region was tamed and settled, might find somewhere west of the wide Missouri. The impulse behind this late nineteenth-century quest was more than a desire for private gain. It partook of the strange drive that was sending Western man into all the remote corners of the world, mainly in the Southern Hemisphere, to impose his will upon people of color and to master exotic environments. If in Rudyard Kipling's Mandalay there were no Ten Commandments and the best was like the worst, so it was too in Deadwood Gulch and in a hundred mining towns, cow towns, and trading posts of the Wild West.

Subordination of the Indians

The Great Plains environment. The steady westward advance of the American frontier ground to a halt in the 1840s and then (except for Utah, p. 266) skipped all the way to the Pacific coast. What stopped the pioneer in his tracks was the forbidding new environment of the Great Plains. Abnormally dry, almost treeless, and mostly level, the plains had their own peculiar soil, weather, plant life, animal life, and human life. The woodcraft and Indian craft that had enabled the frontiersman to master the humid, forested East were simply inadequate or useless on the treeless, arid plains, and so were his ax, his plow, his canoe, and his long rifle. And so, for that matter, were some of his laws and institutions. As

398

Walter P. Webb writes: "East of the Mississippi civilization stood on three legs—land, water, and timber; west of the Mississippi not one but two of these legs were withdrawn—water and timber—and civilization was left on one leg—land. It is small wonder that it toppled over in temporary failure." Major John Wesley Powell, explorer of the region, wrote in 1879: "The physical conditions which exist in that land and which inexorably control the operations of men, are such that the industries of the West are necessarily unlike those of the East and their institutions must be adapted to their industrial wants."

So harsh and uninhabitable did the plains appear that the Easterner wrote them off as wasteland; in American atlases and geographies from 1820 to 1860 this vast stretch of land was labeled simply "The Great American Desert." The dry winds parched the Easterner's throat, cracked his lips, and made his eyes smart. Everything was different. There were chinooks, or warm mountain winds, northers, blizzards, and hailstorms. All but the chinook could bring distress and disaster. Writing of the Texas plains, Colonel Richard I. Dodge warned: "Every bush had its thorn; every animal, reptile, or insect had its horn, tooth, or sting; every male human his revolver; and each was ready to use his weapon of defense on any unfortunate sojourner, on the smallest, or even without the smallest provocation."

The rivers dried up unexpectedly, and when they flowed, their unpalatable water concealed treacherous sands. The slight rainfall, usually under fifteen inches a year, made traditional methods of farming impracticable and demanded a new extensive agriculture to replace the old intensive type. Not for a generation after they reached the edge of the Great Plains did Americans begin to find satisfactory solutions to the problems posed by the new environment—the problems of water and wood, of fences and transportation, of agriculture and cattle-raising.

The animals native to the plains seemed to need little water—the jack rabbit and the prairie dog apparently none at all. The swift and elusive antelopes, coyotes, and wolves depended on speed for safety and were difficult to bag. The one exception was the most famous, the most numerous, and, for human life, the most important plains animal of all, the buffalo, or American bison. This great, shaggy, lumbering beast, neither swift of gait nor alert to danger, could be overtaken by any good horse and was easy prey to a hunter armed with either bow and arrow or rifle. Though they existed in small numbers far east of the Mississippi in colonial days, the buffaloes found their true home on the Great Plains, from Canada to the Gulf of Mexico. Estimates of the buffalo population around the end of the Civil War range from 12 million to 15 million, and a single herd sighted in 1871 was said to contain at least 4 million.

Once the rebellious South had been put down, Americans turned anew to the conquest of the Great Plains. Here they encountered rebels of a different and even more difficult breed.

The plains Indians. Of some three hundred thousand Indians left in the United States in 1865, more than two-thirds lived on the Great Plains. The frontiersman called them "wild Indians"—and so they were, in comparison with their sedentary cousins of the Eastern forests. The only mounted Indians the white man ever encountered, most of them were nomadic and nonagricultural. Above all, they were fierce, skillful, and implacable warriors—"the most effectual barrier," according to Webb, "ever set up by a native American population against European invaders in a temperate zone." Against all comers—Spanish, French, English, and American—they had held their own as masters of the plains for two and a half centuries.

The Spaniards had introduced horses into Mexico in the sixteenth century and the animals had multiplied and spread northward over the plains in wild herds. Before then, the plains Indian had been a miserable, earthbound creature, hard pressed to earn a living and defend himself. The horse revolutionized the life of the tribesmen and brought on the golden era of the plains Indians—an era that had about reached its peak when the Anglo-Americans first encountered them. The horse made the Indians more mobile and hence more nomadic than ever, less agricultural, more warlike, and above all, far more effective buffalo-hunters. The buffalo was even more indispensable to the plains Indians than the horse, for it provided them with food, clothing, shelter, and even fuel. Necessities, luxuries, ornaments, tools, bedding, their very tepees—all were fashioned from the flesh, bone, and hide of the buffalo. The nomadic tribes moved back and forth across the plains with the great herds and organized their life

Sioux camp, South Dakota

he carried a loosely slung shield made of buffalo hide so tough that it could deflect a bullet. The arrows he used against an enemy, unlike those he used in the hunt, were fitted with heads that came off in the wound when the shaft was withdrawn.

The plains Indians lived on horseback, and in case of emergency even used their mounts as food. They could hang by a heel to one side of the horse and discharge arrows under its neck; they could execute intricate cavalry maneuvers controlled by a secret system of communications and signals that was the envy of white military experts.

Until the white man finally crushed the plains Indians, he was conscious of them mainly as warriors, as ruthless and dreaded enemies who held military supremacy in their own country. The Indian's conception of the conduct of war and the treatment of captives differed from that of the white man. "Cruelty is both an amusement and a study," wrote Colonel Dodge of the plains Indians. "So much pleasure is derived from it, that an Indian is constantly thinking out new devices of torture, and how to prolong to the utmost those already known. His anatomical knowledge of the most sensitive portions of the human frame is wonderfully accurate. . . ." The Indian's reputation for cruelty was probably as much deserved as the white man's reputation for ruthlessness. The military struggle between the two races on the Great Plains was marked by a peculiar ferocity and savagery.

White supremacy in the West. So long as Americans thought of the plains as the "Great American Desert" and as "one big reservation" for the red man, conflict as well as contact between the races was rare. But in the 1850s the situation changed. Mass migrations got under way across the plains to Oregon; miners began to beg for protection; the Kansas and Nebraska territories were organized; and politicians demanded that the Indians be pushed out to north and south to clear the way for transportation and settlement. In 1851 the federal government adopted a new Indian policy of "concentration," under which the chiefs of the plains tribes were persuaded to restrict their people to areas the white man solemnly promised he would never violate. Caught between the mining frontier that, as we shall see, was closing in from the west,

and religion around the hunt. Whatever threatened the buffalo threatened their very existence.

The plains Indians were generally superior in physique to the Indians of other regions. Although their culture varied from that of the peaceful tribes of the pueblos to that of fierce nomadic tribes, all the plains Indians shared the culture of neolithic man, using stone knives, stone scrapers, and bone awls as tools. The warriors carried bows and arrows and fourteen-foot, stone-tipped lances for hunting and warfare. Yet in combat the stone-age man asked no quarter of early industrial man. With his short three-foot bow and a quiver of two-score arrows or more, the Comanche would ride three hundred yards and get off twenty arrows with startling force and accuracy while the Texan was firing one shot and reloading his long and cumbersome rifle. Even the Colt six-shooter, with which the white man began arming himself in the 1840s, did not entirely overcome the Indian's advantage. As armor

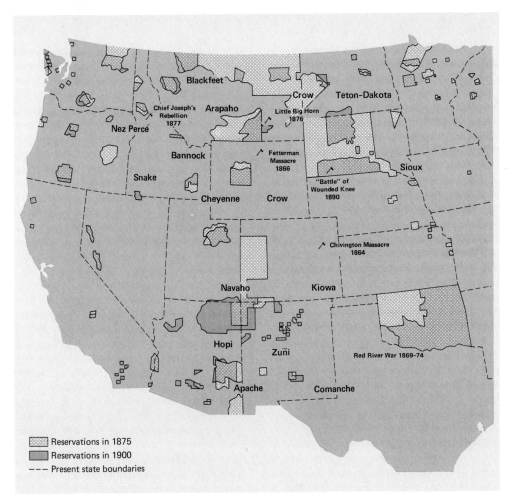

Indian affairs in the West

and an agricultural frontier advancing from the east, the plains Indian was soon to learn what the woods Indian had learned long before: that he could trust none of the white man's promises, however solemn. The red man was further embittered by the behavior of corrupt officials of the Indian Bureau of the Interior Department, who defrauded him of his land, cheated him in trade, and sold him liquor, and by the treachery of a reckless breed of beaver-trappers, gold-prospectors, hunters, and outlaws. Then in 1858 and 1859 the Pike's Peak Gold Rush sent tens of thousands hell-bent for Colorado and trouble, soon to be joined by deserters and draft-dodgers from the Union and Confederate armies.

Indian war broke out in Colorado about the time the Civil War was starting in the East. The immediate provocation was the effort of government officials to force the Arapaho and Cheyenne to abandon all claim to the area that had been granted them forever only ten years before. Many braves rejected the agreement made by their chiefs and took the warpath. After an intermittent warfare of pillaging, home-burning, and murdering that went on for more than three years, they sued for peace. Chief Black Kettle of the Cheyenne, after being assured of protection, was surprised and trapped by a force led by Colonel John M. Chivington on the night of November 28, 1864. Ignoring Black Kettle's attempts to surrender, the militia shot, knifed, scalped, clubbed, and mutilated the Indians indiscriminately until the ground was littered with men, women, and children. Chief Black Kettle and a few warriors escaped, but before a year had passed the Cheyenne and Arapaho, as well as the Kiowa and Comanche, were compelled to surrender their claims and move on to more restricted areas assigned by the white masters.

Hardly had peace been restored to the Southwest in the fall of 1865 when Indian war broke out in the Northwest. The bloody Sioux War of 1865–67 was brought on by many forces, but it was triggered by the demands of miners who had invaded the Sioux country. In response to their request, the federal government announced its intention to build a road through the foothills of the Big Horn Mountains to connect the mining towns of Bozeman and Virginia City with the East. Such a road would spoil one of the Sioux' favorite hunting grounds, and Chief Red Cloud warned that it would be resisted. Sioux warriors ambushed a party of soldiers under Captain W. J. Fetterman near Fort Phil Kearny in December 1866 and slaughtered all eighty-two of its members.

The Chivington and Fetterman massacres, together with scores of minor battles and endless shooting scrapes, prompted the federal government to review its Indian policy in 1867. Easterners clashed with Westerners, humanitarian impulses with fire-and-sword military policies, and at last authority over the Indians was split between the Department of the Interior, which would placate them with gifts, annuities, and reservations, and the War Department, which was accustomed to punish with violence. The Westerner's disgust was reflected in a letter signed "Texas" in the Chicago *Tribune:* "Give us Phil Sheridan, and send Phil-anthropy to the devil." It is hard to say at times whether West or South was in fiercer revolt against the Eastern philanthropists. The East prevailed against the West as it had against the South, however, and sent out a Peace Commission of four civilians and three generals in the autumn of 1867 to end the Sioux War and to inaugurate a new policy of "small reservations" to replace the old one of "concentration." The new policy meant that the Indians were to abandon their way of life, submit to segregation in small out-of-the-way reservations on land spurned by the white man, and accept government tutelage in learning "to walk the white man's road." The Black Hills section of the Dakota Territory was to be set aside for the northern tribes. Poor lands in the western part of what is now Oklahoma, of which the five civilized tribes of the Southeast had just been defrauded on false charges of treason because of their Confederate sympathies, were to be divided among the plains Indians of the Southwest.

The white man's policy toward the red man in these years contrasted strangely with his professed policy toward the black man. The same Congress that devised Radical Reconstruction to bring equality and integration to the Negro of the South approved strict segre-

General George A. Custer

gation and inequality for the Indian of the West. General William T. Sherman, the deliverer of the Southern slaves, instructed General Winfield S. Hancock in 1867 that his principal mission to the Cheyenne and Kiowa was to "impress on them the imprudence of assuming an insolent manner and tone when they visit our posts."

But many Indians refused to renounce their way of life and enter meekly into the reservations. When they took the warpath in the summer of 1868, General Sherman unleashed his troopers and launched a decade of remorseless war against them. "I will urge General Sheridan to push his measures for the utter destruction and subjugation of all who are outside [the reservations] in a hostile attitude," Sherman wrote. "I propose that [he] shall prosecute the war with vindictive earnestness against all hostile Indians, till they are obliterated or beg for mercy. . . ." It took more than two hundred battles from 1869 through 1874 to restore peace, and in the Red River War alone fourteen pitched battles were required to beat the Indians of the Southwest into submission.

In the meantime President Grant was persuaded early in his Administration to place under a dozen religious denominations the control of Indians living on reservations. Supported by government funds, agents chosen by religious bodies sought to educate, "civilize," and assimilate their charges. These actions became known unofficially as "Grant's Peace Policy." Indians refusing to settle on the reservations, however, were mercilessly subjected to the very unpeaceful policy of the United States Army. Coordination of the two policies served to remove most Indians from the path of white settlers and developers.

By the end of 1874 all seemed calm. Then in 1875, when government authorities permitted tens of thousands of gold-prospectors to crowd into the Black Hills, the outraged Sioux and other northern Indians reacted violently. At the Battle of the Little Big Horn on June 25, 1876, the rash young General George A. Custer and 265 men were wiped out in the general's first, and last, stand in the new Sioux War. In spite of this victory, the Indians were compelled to surrender the following fall. Chief Sitting Bull and a few warriors fled to Canada, but, facing starvation, they were forced to sue for peace in 1881. The Nez Percé Indians of Oregon staged a rebellion that was repressed in 1877, and the sur-

Little Big Horn, drawings by Amos Bad Heart Bull

vivors of this once-proud tribe were herded into a barren preserve in Indian Territory to be ravaged by disease and hunger. The last incident of the Indian wars was the sickening "Battle" of Wounded Knee in 1890, in which United States troops mowed down two hundred Dakota men, women, and children.

Long before the fighting ended, the near-extermination of the buffalo herds had hastened the collapse of Indian resistance. At first the indiscriminate shooting of buffalo was motivated by little more than the desire for "sport" or for the diversion of railroad hands and passengers, who might incidentally help to clear the tracks and curb a nuisance. But in 1871, when it was discovered that buffalo pelts and leather could be marketed at a profit, the slaughter was organized on a commercial basis. Now professional hunters and skinners working in teams stepped up the butchery to 3 million buffalo a year. The advance of the railroads hastened the end of the herds. By 1878 the vast southern herd, the larger of the two main herds, had been wiped out. Five years later, when collectors tried to round up a few specimens of what had recently been the most numerous breed of large animals in the world, only remnants of the northern herd could be found in remote parts of Canada.

The slaughter of the buffalo is the classic example of the white man's heedless rapacity in the exploitation of nature; the United States' Indian policy is the classic instance of his racial, cultural, and religious bigotry. Reformers and humanitarians won their fight against the policy of physical extermination of the Indian only to substitute their own policy of relentless attack on Indian society, customs, religion, and tribal unity. This, they were con-

vinced, was necessary if they were to "civilize" the red man, save his soul from "paganism," and integrate him into white civilization. In 1884 the Department of the Interior passed a criminal code forbidding and penalizing Indian religious practices, and in 1887 the Dawes Act struck at tribal authority and organization by breaking up reservation land into small family or individual holdings, with the best of the land usually sold to the whites. All Indians who received grants were to become citizens of the United States.

Thus the oldest residents of the land became the newest citizens. But their government simultaneously deprived them of the basic rights of citizens. Virtually imprisoned and pauperized on the reservations, they were constantly subjected to the withholding of rations—starvation—in an effort to compel them to abandon their tribal customs and loyalties. A government that guaranteed freedom of worship carried its religious persecution of the Indians to the point of espionage and armed violence. The sacred Sun Dance, the supreme expression of tribal unity, was outlawed as "pagan." The notorious corruption of the Indian Bureau and its agents was checked by civil-service reform in the 1880s, but this only meant that the misguided Indian policy was administered more efficiently and destructively than ever before. The real trouble, according to the twentieth-century reformer John Collier, was not corrupt agents but "collective corruption; corruption which did not know it was corrupt, and which reached deep into the intelligence of a nation. It was such a collective corruption that dominated the plains-Indian record and nearly the whole Indian record of the United States."

The era of the bonanzas

Webb in *The Great Frontier* distinguishes between the "primary windfalls" and the "secondary windfalls" that are gleaned from any frontier. The primary windfalls are the first easy pickings—gold, silver, furs—that are gained with little investment of energy or time. The secondary windfalls require more patience and expense. Usually the primary windfalls are grabbed up early in the game. The Spanish mined the precious metals in their quarter of the New World or seized them from the Indians in the sixteenth and seventeenth centuries, and the French gathered their bales of furs in Canada a little later. Entering the continent north of the gold and south of the furs, the Anglo-Americans were obliged to concentrate on secondary windfalls. Then late in the nineteenth century, after the frontier had become a prosaic matter of timber, corn, and cotton, they belatedly entered upon a fabulous phase of frontier history that for the rest of the world had faded into the mists of legend with the conquistadors and the Spanish treasure ships. The beaver pelts had been gathered, and we have seen what happened to the buffalo. But there remained the bonanzas of gold and silver and the lush grass left by the bison.

The miner's bonanza. There had been gold rushes from time to time in the East, but from 1804 to 1866 the five-state Appalachian gold field had yielded only $19,375,890. An entirely new scale was set by the California yield of $555 million in a single decade, 1848–58. In the 1860s and 1870s the turbulent gold rush of the forty-niners (see p. 276) was to be repeated with variations time and again in the mountain areas of Nevada, Colorado, Arizona, Idaho, Montana, and Wyoming. Since the experienced Californians usually led the invasion of these areas, the mining frontier advanced eastward instead of westward. The Californians also developed the primitive technology of "placer" mining, by which "pay dirt" was washed in pans, "cradles," or sluice boxes. Armed with nothing more than a pick and shovel and a crude pan, the lucky prospector could gather up loose gold that had washed down through debris to bedrock. The richer deposits of gold, usually in deep-lying veins of quartz, could only be mined with machinery that was beyond the means of the prospector and had to await the corporation.

It has been estimated that by 1868 placer miners, with their wasteful methods, had lost beyond recovery nearly $300 million in precious metals. During the sixties placer mining was more and more superseded by quartz mining.

The lure of the bonanza—even the hope of modest pay dirt—was enough to keep thousands of prospectors feverishly exploring gulches and canyons for three decades. Working in groups—the lone prospector is largely mythical—they crisscrossed the vast mountain area in their obsessive quest. Few of them were qualified to interpret the evidence they uncovered, and some of the richest lodes were discovered by chance. Prospectors were entitled by law to one claim by preemption and one by discovery; latecomers were entitled to only one claim. The typical claim ran from side to side of a gulch and was one hundred feet wide. Only the exceptional claim really paid off, but the promise of fabulous riches and the wild thrill of discovery seemed reward enough. After the discovery came the inevitable leak of the secret and the headlong scramble by other prospectors to stake a claim. One such rush in 1861 was described by a witness:

> On Friday morning last, when the news of the new diggings had been promulgated, the store of Miner and Arnold was literally besieged. As the news radiated—and it was not long in spreading—picks and shovels were thrown down, claims deserted and turn your eye where you would, you could see droves of people coming in "hot haste" to town, some packing one thing on their backs and some another, all intent on scaling the mountains through frost and snow, and taking up a claim in the new El Dorado. In town there was a perfect jam—a mass of human infatuation, jostling, shoving and elbowing each other.

The prospectors' invasion of the interior was touched off by discoveries in Colorado and Nevada. A party of Southerners bound for California in 1849 had found signs of gold in Colorado, and two of them, John Beck and W. Green Russell, returned with a party of a hundred in 1858 to prospect more thoroughly. During the summer they made a number of small strikes in the vicinity of what was later to become Denver. Rumors of these finds, wildly and perhaps deliberately exag-

"The Gold Bug," by Frederick Remington

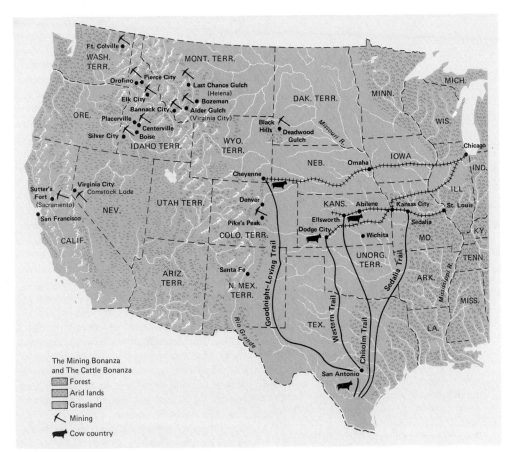

The Great Plains environment

gerated, spread rapidly through the frontier region and started a rush for the Pike's Peak country that fall. During the winter news of the strike spread more widely, and by midsummer the Pike's-Peak-or-Bust rush had started some one hundred thousand people toward the new diggings. A new discovery in May 1859, followed by several smaller ones, had offered some justification for the excitement, but the great majority of fortune-hunters were doomed to disappointment. The dejected horde returning from Pike's Peak symbolized the disillusioned gold-rusher of the period. Thousands of the unsuccessful miners, however, stayed on to become settlers and future citizens of Colorado.

In the meantime prospectors had struck it rich on the eastern slope of the Sierras in Nevada opposite the California fields on the western slope. Two Irishmen named Patrick McLaughlin and Peter O'Riley accidentally turned up a vein of bluish rock while digging a water reservoir for their modest placer operation. They were promptly bluffed out of a large share of their find by a loud-mouthed scamp named Henry Comstock, who sold out before he had more than an inkling of the treasure he had acquired: the incredibly rich Comstock Lode, the biggest bonanza of them all! At the first rumor, a thundering stampede of fifteen thousand claim-stakers blanketed the Washoe district. But most of the gold and silver was locked in veins of quartz, and little mining could be done until quartz mills and mining machinery were brought in. Not until 1873, after heroic tunneling operations and giant engineering feats under the direction of John W. Mackay and his partners, was the greatest lode of silver and gold struck. From 1859 to 1879 the total output of the Comstock mines was $350 million, of which 45 percent was in gold and 55 percent in silver. No deposits of equal richness have ever been recorded in ancient or modern mining history.

Perched on the roof of this subterranean treasure house on the steep side of Mount Davidson, seventy-two hundred feet above sea level, was Virginia City, the most celebrated

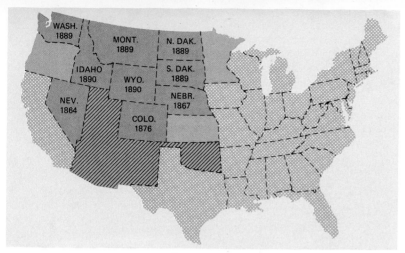

New states, 1864–90

of the Western mining towns. Mark Twain, who arrived at the diggings in the early days, described the town in *Roughing It:*

> Virginia [City] had grown to be the "livest" town, for its age and population, that America had ever produced. The sidewalks swarmed with people—to such an extent, indeed, that it was generally no easy matter to stem the human tide. The streets themselves were just as crowded with quartz wagons, freight teams and other vehicles. The procession was endless. So great was the pack, that buggies frequently had to wait half an hour for an opportunity to cross the principal street. Joy sat on every countenance, and there was a glad, almost fierce, intensity in every eye, that told of the money-getting schemes that were seething in every brain and the high hope that held sway in every heart. . . . a dozen breweries and half a dozen jails and station-houses in full operation, and some talk of building a church. The "flush times" were in magnificent flower!

After Comstock one strike followed another in western Nevada. None was so rich as Comstock, but all served to attract an unstable population to the territory and to increase the demand for statehood. Eight days before the election of 1864 Nevada became a state and promptly furnished three electoral votes for Lincoln.

In the meantime the future states of Washington, Idaho, and Montana were the scene of gold rushes and flush times. During the tragic years from Bull Run to Appomattox "yonder-siders" from California joined "pilgrims" from the East and seasoned prospectors from Nevada in stampedes to Orofino, Pierce City, Elk City, Boise, Placerville, Cen-

terville, and Silver City. Some remained in Idaho as permanent settlers, but only fifteen thousand were living there in 1870. Many joined the great Montana gold rush around Bannack City, then jumped on to the spectacular diggings in Alder Gulch that produced $30 million of gold in three years, and ended up at Last Chance Gulch, where Helena was first laid out as a mining camp. A few more strikes after the war turned up the last surface gold in Idaho and Montana; then the placer miners passed on, leaving scarred hills and ghost towns behind them. As in Nevada, the richest deposits lay in deep veins of quartz that could be reached only by expensive shafts and crushed only by heavy mills. Eastern capital moved in and opened up new mines in the seventies and eighties, one of which, the Bunker Hill and Sullivan Mine, discovered in 1885, yielded a quarter of a billion dollars in silver and lead.

During the early days of the gold rushes a motley and cosmopolitan assortment of humanity accumulated on the mining frontier. The population of one camp was somewhat unscientifically classified as "Saxon, Celt, Teuton, Gaul, Greaser, Celestial, and Indian." The 206 souls of another camp were more carefully tabulated as 73 American white citizens, 37 Chinese, 35 British subjects, 29 Mexicans and Spaniards, 8 Negroes, and the rest assorted Europeans. Every camp of any size attracted its share of lawless outcasts—jailbirds, gamblers, prostitutes, deserters, desperadoes, stagecoach-robbers. And every town had to decide whether or not to let the outcasts take over. As one observer described life in Last Chance Gulch in 1864: "Not a day or night passed which did not yield its full fruition of fights, quarrels, wounds, or murders. The crack of the revolver was often heard above the merry notes of the violin. . . . Pistols flashed, bowie knives flourished, and braggart oaths filled the air. . . ." The United States government was far off and preoccupied with other matters, and its arm was not always long enough to reach into Nevada and Idaho. As a result the miners developed their own informal codes of law and their own informal means of enforcement. Throughout the region there was a generous and sometimes loose resort to vigilantism, a more or less formalized lynch law intended to terrify the desperadoes.

The old mining frontier had its last mad fling in the Black Hills of what later became South

Dakota. The army had finally given up as hopeless its effort to keep the insistent horde of prospectors out of the Sioux reservation, and in October 1875 it threw open the district to all who were willing to enter at their own risk. Thousands of prospectors, still hopeful after two decades of disappointments, rushed in for one last chance. In a grand finale at Deadwood Gulch the miners' frontier outdid itself in a lurid caricature of its reputation. The curtain was rung down on the rowdiest brawls, the wildest desperadoes, and the most vigilant vigilantes of them all. After the Black Hills rush the prospectors and their supporting casts trooped off the scene, leaving mining to heavy investors and engineers. The frontier's "primary windfall" of precious metals had been stripped off, though the serious business of mining had only begun.

The cattleman's bonanza. The windfall of the early cattlemen was almost as rich and free as that of the early miners. The cows harvested the free crop of grass, turned it into beef and hides, transported these commodities to market on the hoof, and dropped calves along the way as replacements.

For a brief interlude between the passing of the Indian and the buffalo and the entry of the farmer and the barbed-wire fence, the Great Plains witnessed the most picturesque industrial drama ever staged—the drama of the open range and the cattle ranch. If the Southern planter could once claim that cotton was king, the Western cattleman could proclaim with equal fervor that grass was king. For the time being, at least, the plains were one limitless, fenceless, gateless pasture of rich, succulent, and ownerless grass that was his for the taking. Within an incredibly short period the red man's herds of bison had been replaced and outnumbered by the white man's herds of cattle.

The miner's invasion of the mountain and plains country came mainly from the Far West: the cattleman, his animals, and his ranch culture invaded from the South. Herdsmen had acquired some of the cowboy's arts and lingo on their long trek across the Gulf states and the antebellum Southwest, but it was not until they had reached Texas and had begun to handle Spanish cattle from horseback that the craft took on its Mexican flavor and exotic style. A diamond-shaped area at the tip of Texas, with San Antonio at its apex, was the cradle of the future cowboy and his

Deadwood, South Dakota, 1876

long-horned charges. The bulk of the cattle, a Spanish stock, grew up wild and were said to be "fifty times more dangerous to footmen than the fiercest buffalo." A tough, stringy, durable breed, wonderfully adapted to the plains, they multiplied so rapidly that they became a pest. Within just one decade the cattle population of Texas increased over 1,000 percent, and by 1860 cattle were estimated at nearly 5 million in that state alone.

Even before the Civil War Texas cattlemen had made a few inconsequential drives to Northern markets, and after the war inducements multiplied. During the 1860s the population of the United States increased 22 percent, while the number of cattle in the country decreased about 7 percent. But industrialization was piling up big meat markets in the cities and pushing the railroad out to the plains. At the end of the war cattle that brought $3 to $5 a head in Texas could be sold for $30 to $50 a head in Northern markets. Fantastic profits had recently induced speculators to bring Confederate cotton through armed ranks of blue and gray to Yankee mills, and Texans were not to be daunted by the mere twelve or fifteen hundred miles that separated them from the fabulous meat markets in the North. In 1866 they set forth on the long drive north with more than a quarter of a million head. Taking the most direct route to the nearest railhead, Sedalia, Missouri, the cattlemen fell into the hands of thieves along the wooded parts of their route. Thereafter they kept to the open plains. The first town founded for the specific purpose of receiving cows for shipment was Abilene, Kansas, established by J. G. McCoy on the Hannibal and St. Joe Railroad in 1867. Of Abilene and its reputation, Webb has written:

The West: cowboys

Those first trail outfits in the seventies were sure tough.... They had very little grub and they usually run out of that and lived on straight beef; they had only three or four horses to the man, mostly with sore backs, because old time saddles eat both ways, the horse's back and the cowboy's pistol pocket; they had no tents, no tarps, and damn few slickers. They never kicked, because those boys was raised under just the same conditions as there was on the trail—corn meal and bacon for grub, dirt floors in the houses, and no luxuries. In the early days in Texas, in the sixties, when they gathered their cattle, they used to pack what they needed on a horse and go out for weeks, on a cow-hunt, they called it then. That was before the name roundup was invented, and before they had anything so civilized as mess wagons....

In person the cowboys were mostly medium-sized men, as a heavy man was hard on horses, quick and wiry, and as a rule very good-natured; in fact it did not pay to be anything else. In character their like never was or will be again.

From E. C. Abbott and H. H. Smith, *We Pointed Them North*, 1955.

Abilene was more than a point. It is a symbol. It stands for all that happened when two civilizations met for conflict, for disorder, for the clashing of great currents which carry on their crest the turbulent and disorderly elements of both civilizations—in this case the rough characters of the plain and of the forest. On the surface Abilene was corruption personified. Life was hectic, raw, lurid, awful. But . . . if Abilene excelled all later cow towns in wickedness, it also excelled them in service—the service of bartering the beef of the South for the money of the North.

Other cow towns followed—Wichita, Ellsworth, Dodge City—pushing farther and farther westward with the railroad, an indispensable adjunct to the cattle kingdom. The Texas trails themselves pushed in the same direction toward the Texas Panhandle and eastern New Mexico and Colorado. The trails shifted during the years of the long drive, to take advantage of the best grazing and water supplies. Some of them—the Goodnight-Loving Trail, the Western Trail, and the Chisholm Trail—left broad, brown, beaten tracks across hundreds of miles of grasslands. Riders of the long drive, beset by heartbreaking misfortunes, watched helplessly as the weight of their droves dwindled on the way to market. Nevertheless, the cowboys drove more than 6 million head of cattle northward over these trails between 1866 and 1888.

Not all the Texas cattle were sold directly for beef. Of the record drive of six hundred thousand in 1871 only half could find buyers and the rest spent the winter as "feeders" in the neighboring areas. It was mainly from this surplus of the Texas drives, many of them crossed with Hereford bulls to produce the white-faced hybrid, that the Great Plains area was stocked. Many herds were driven directly to the ranges of New Mexico, Arizona, Colorado, Wyoming, Montana, and the Dakotas to feed mining camps and railroad-builders and to supply the ranchers' demand for fresh stock. Some Eastern cattle, called "pilgrims" (as were the miners from the East), contributed slightly to the stocking of the plains. In the amazingly brief period of fifteen years, by 1880, the cattlemen and their ranches had spread over the whole vast grassland from the Rio Grande into Canada as well as up into the recesses of the Rockies.

With the boom of the 1880s, the monarchs of the cattle kingdom became intoxicated with the magnificence of their domain and its immediate prospects. The depression of the seventies had been rolled aside, the Indians had been driven into reservations, the railroads were coming on, and neither the homesteader nor barbed wire had yet arrived in menacing quantity. Beef prices were soaring and the grass was growing higher by the hour. No wonder the cow king got a wonderful feeling that everything was going his way. His optimism spread abroad, and investors from the four corners of the earth rushed to the plains to seek their fortunes, money hot in their pockets. Cheyenne, where a new cowman's club served caviar and rare wines, was described in 1882 by a local journalist:

Sixteenth Street is a young Wall Street. Millions are talked of as lightly as nickels and all kinds of people are dabbling in steers. The chief justice of the Supreme Court has recently succumbed to the contagion and gone out to purchase a $40,000 herd. . . . A Cheyenne man who don't pretend to know a maverick from a mandamus has made a neat little margin of $15,000 this summer in small transactions and hasn't seen a cow yet that he has bought and sold.

As a symbol of this spectacular adventure, the public took to its heart not the cow king but his hired hand, and there the cowboy has remained enshrined, his cult faithfully tended by votaries of screen and television. Known sometimes as "cowpoke" or "cowpuncher," names derived from an early method of prodding lagging critters with long poles, the cowboy is more popularly identified with the lariat and the branding iron. His picturesque accouterments—sombrero, spurs, long-heeled boots, chaps, gloves, and saddle, which he called his "workbench"—were strictly functional, not ornamental, and strictly adapted to life on horseback. There, indeed, much of his life was spent—eighteen hours or more a day during phases of the long drive or the roundup. Each cowboy had a "mount" of from eight to fourteen horses, depending on the work he was doing and the class of horses. Normally a hardworking man of Spartan and sober habits, the cowboy has come to share with the sailor a public image derived from his rare escapades of frantic recreation after long ordeals. The cowboy's two or three months in the saddle on the long drive built up as big a head of steam as a long voyage built up for the sailor. As for the cowboy's addiction to lethal six-guns, it was exaggerated.

Violence of the shooting-iron sort, however, was unavoidable in the open-range cattle kingdom. With millions of dollars' worth of property wandering at large on public lands, unfenced and poorly marked, rustlers found the temptation overwhelming. Since government was remote and undependable, cattlemen resorted to private associations for protection and self-government in matters of roundup, branding, and breeding. These associations sometimes furnished all the government there was. The sort of justice they dispensed and the methods they used are suggested by a laconic item in the obituary of John S. Chisum of New Mexico, who died in 1884. Annoyed by Indians who had stolen some of his sixty thousand cattle in 1877, he armed a hundred men, moved against the presumed offenders, and "killed 175."

Even with free pasturage and virgin grassland, cattle-raising on the open range was extravagant and uneconomical. It exposed the herds to weather hazards, made adequate care of animals impossible and improvement of breeds difficult, encouraged rough and wasteful handling of cattle, and provoked costly and sometimes bloody range disputes. The approaching doom of the free range was further hastened by the expanding railroads and their loads of settlers, who staked claims and ran fences, and by the sheep-herders, who fouled the water holes and stripped the grazing land. But the cattlemen contributed to their own downfall. They resorted to land fraud, monopoly, and ruthless violence to protect their interests. They even adopted for their own use that concrete denial of the open range, the barbed-wire fence: Charles Goodnight ran one all the way across the Texas Panhandle into New Mexico. Worse still, they overstocked and overgrazed the range.

The day of reckoning dawned in 1885, when beef prices started to tumble. On top of that, during the severe winter of 1885–86 up to 85 percent of the herds on the southern ranges either starved or froze to death. A bad drought the following summer scorched the grass and left the animals in poor condition. Then the legendary winter of 1886–87 fastened its cruel grip on the plains and brought panic to men as well as animals. When the thaw finally came, the emaciated corpses of enormous herds were left stacked up against fences or piled deep in coulees. A few grisly survivors staggered about on frozen legs.

The disaster spelled the end of the great beef bonanza. It ruined the larger corporations and many individual ranchers and took the heart out of the enterprise. There was little left of the reckless confidence with which cattlemen had greeted the great risks of the open range in its heyday. When nature smiled again and the public domain beckoned, some of the more hardy ranchers carried on in the old manner through the depressed nineties. But there was a steady and unmistakable retreat of investment to the security of privately owned pasturage and a deliberate avoidance of the wild gambles and risks of the old days. Cattle had become a sober business instead of a high, wide, and handsome adventure.

The farmer moves West

Ever since 1607 American farmers had been moving west to break new ground. But in the last three decades of the nineteenth century they occupied and brought under cultivation more land than in all the years before 1870. It might seem natural to attribute this rapid expansion to the free-homestead policy adopted in 1862 (see p. 358). Before we jump to such a conclusion, however, it would be well to review that policy.

American land policy. The number of farms in the United States increased from some 2,000,000 in 1860 to 5,737,000 in 1900. And yet fewer than 600,000 homesteads were patented in those years, and they accounted for only 80,000,000 acres out of the more than 430,000,000 acres that were added to the total land in farms. Thus even if all the farmers who filed claims had been bona fide homesteaders, they would have accounted for fewer than one-sixth of the new farms and a little more than one-sixth of the added acreage. Actually, a great number of the so-called homesteads fell into the hands of large landholders and did not become farms until they were sold to settlers by speculators.

Nothing could have been further from the intention of the framers of the Homestead Act than the promotion of land monopoly. On the contrary, by distributing the bounty of free land among needy people they had hoped to defeat land monopoly. In practice, however, the great American promise of free land—a promise that was published around the world—turned out to be pretty much a delusion. One trouble was that few prospective homesteaders could afford to take advantage of the opportunity, because they lacked the capital to transport their families and possessions to the public domain, stock up with expensive machinery, and stick it out for years until the farm became self-supporting. Fewer still understood the new type of agriculture required on the arid plains. Two-thirds of all homestead claimants before 1890 failed at the venture. Speculators hired men to stake out homesteads, falsely claim they had fulfilled the required conditions, and then turn over the land to their employer.

But the fundamental weakness of the Homestead Act was that it simply was not appropriate to the region where it applied. The law covered all public lands, of course, but by the time the act was passed the great bulk of public lands available for homesteading lay on the Great Plains and beyond. The Eastern congressmen who framed the law for the plains knew little about the needs of the people who were eventually going to live there. To the farmer back in the humid East a 160-acre tract seemed ideal for a family-sized farm—a good deal larger than the average, in fact. In the arid or semiarid West, however, land was useful only for intensive irrigated farming, extensive dry farming, or grazing. A 160-acre tract was too small for grazing or dry farming and too large for irrigated farming. Of the last there was little anyway, so the great Western complaint was against the smallness of holdings. If the East persisted in writing laws for the West that did not work, said the Westerners, then the West was justified in ignoring or violating them. Reflecting the ranchman's point of view, Webb writes: "He violated every land law made, in order that he might survive."

In land policy, as in Indian policy, it proved difficult to reconcile the views of East and West—particularly since the Eastern outcry was against land monopoly and the Western demand was for larger and larger units of land. One attempt to adjust land policy to Western needs was the Timber Culture Act of 1873, which permitted the homesteader to add another 160 acres of relatively treeless land to his holdings provided he would plant trees on one-quarter of it within four years. The law failed to increase rainfall, however, and nine out of ten claimants are said to have made no serious effort to forest their holdings.

A more absurd law was the Desert Land Act of 1877, which offered 640 acres to anyone who would pay 25 cents an acre down and promise to irrigate the land within three years. Upon presenting proof of irrigation and paying an additional dollar per acre the claimant could close the deal. The trouble here was that the law required irrigation where no water was to be had. Cattlemen seized on the Desert Land Act to enlarge their holdings, but at least 95 percent of the "proofs" of irrigation were estimated to be fradulent.

The Timber and Stone Act of 1878 permitted any citizen, or any alien with first papers, to buy at $2.50 an acre 160 acres of land "unfit for cultivation" and valuable chiefly for

Railroad broadside

The beauty and wealth of the American continent greeted the first Europeans to settle in the area that is now the United States, the first to see the Hudson Valley or the Florida jungle. Unspoiled wealth greeted successive generations as they spread westward from the east coast. The very abundance of the land—as the late, great historian David Potter observed—invited the habit of waste, for most Americans could not believe they would ever exhaust the plenty that lay before them.

Thomas Chambers, *The Hudson Valley, Sunset:* National Gallery of Art; gift of Edgar William and Bernice Chrysler Garbisch

The land and the people: the national environment

Winslow Homer, *Jungle in Florida*, 1904: courtesy of the Fogg Art Museum, Harvard University; gift of Mrs. Charles S. Homer in memory of the late Charles S. Homer, brother of Winslow Homer

Indeed as they first used their resources—on farms, in forests, on the ocean—beauty and productivity went hand in hand.

Winslow Homer, *The Hudson River Logging:* watercolor in the collection of the Corcoran Gallery of Art

Charles C. Hofmann, *View of Benjamin Reber's Farm:* National Gallery of Art; gift of Edgar William and Bernice Chrysler Garbisch

Winslow Homer, *The Herring Net:* courtesy of the Art Institute of Chicago

During the nineteenth century and later, the growth of commercial farming (facilitated by federal land policy), the concurrent neglect of the soil, and the application of machinery to increase production marred the countryside. Only after 1900, and especially during the 1930s, did government begin energetically to promote scientific farming techniques—contour plowing, crop rotation, and irrigation among them.

Generation after generation, Americans also recklessly spent their subsoil wealth. Gold-miners in California despoiled river valleys there more than a century before oil spills damaged wildlife and oil rigs punctuated the coast of Alaska with hideous exclamation points. Copper-mining had bored deep into the once virgin land of Utah. Kentucky and other states were scarred by strip miners who extracted coal without regard for the ugliness they created or the wastage they left behind.

As they used their water, Americans spoiled it too. While population remained small relative to the vastness of the country, there was ample water to provide power for machinery in a mill, or to carry steamers along their routes, or just for pleasure. By the middle of the twentieth century, however, population growth, manufacturing, and new technologies

Winslow Homer, *Long Branch, New Jersey*; courtesy of the Museum of Fine Arts, Boston; Charles Henry Hayden Fund

George Catlin, *St. Louis from the River*; National Collection of Fine Arts, Smithsonian Institution

had taxed the nation's water resources, often beyond repair.
Industrial waste polluted rivers and streams, even as large
a body of water as Lake Erie. Nuclear power plants made
thermopollution a hazard for all life. The sheer number
of people seeking recreation on hot summer days littered
public beaches with human bodies.

The development of communities in America proceeded in patterns that often reflected haphazard growth rather than private or public planning. The Indian village gave men a way of living and working together. So did the New England town and the Southern plantation, both of which profited from their founders' sense of the relationship of form to function. But the towns that simply grew up behind the edge of the frontier were characteristically bleak—cluttered predecessors of latter-day highway strips. The early cities, usually ports like Baltimore and Detroit, had a simplicity and attractiveness that vanished when growth occurred, as in St. Louis, without rational direction from those who had to live with urban crowding and disorder.

Adrian Persac, *Olivier Plantation:* courtesy of the Louisiana State Museum

That absence of direction, a function of public indifference and
a failure of public policy, opened the way to the wasteland of
steel cities like Pittsburgh and Gary, and of textile towns like Berlin,
New Hampshire. Urban blight gradually produced a reaction, a series
of efforts, beginning in the mid-nineteenth century, to make
cities into places where people could once again live with comfort

and beauty. To that end, Frederick Olmsted planned Central Park as an oasis for New York's millions. In the twentieth century Pittsburgh with its Golden Triangle, Philadelphia with its Independence Mall, Chicago along its lakefront turned to public action to attempt to reconcile the needs of industry and commerce with the desirability of grace and open space.

Space—the long reach of the continent, the broad spans between cities and their hinterlands—made quick and reliable transportation a special necessity for Americans. Better than any previous means of transport, railroads answered that national need. In its early years, the locomotive, symbol of power to the poet Walt Whitman, was a welcome convenience to travelers, an effective instrument in the penetration of the West, a favorite toy of American children. From the first, the train also symbolized the demise of a quiet, slow, pastoral America and its presumed virtues. Those who cherished that culture resented the engine and all it portended. Had they lived long enough, they would have found their fears fulfilled in the squalor of a locomotive cemetery, in railway yards with their sprawl and noise, in suburban tracks cutting unlovely corridors through the Eastern megalopolis.

PIERCE-ARROW

Dual-Valve Six

As with the train, so later with the automobile, the promise of convenience was accompanied by the prospect of destruction. The coach moving across primitive roads through heavy forests was uncomfortable, uncertain, and slow. The splendid cars of the 1920s, the first decade of the automobile age, excited Americans as had no other product of modern industry. They were thrilled, too, by the vision of broad intercity highways. But too many cars, the property of millions of men and women, crowded those highways until the traffic often stopped, jamming the cities that they also filled with cacophony and foul exhausts. Reckless or careless drivers carried themselves and their passengers to sudden death or left worn-out vehicles in heaps of scrap that dotted the national landscape.

The Cleveland waterfront, the Chicago railroad yards, a Los Angeles factory typified the modern urban environment. No less offensive to the eye and ear were the commercial artifacts of the automobile culture that stretched from the outer perimeter of the cities into the burgeoning suburbs.

Even when the nation was young, the wilderness men, determined to be alone, escaped from civilization. During the Gilded Age, the very rich, like the Vanderbilts, effected a partial and elegant escape in their palaces on the still rural Hudson. In contemporary America, it remained possible to feel almost alone in places like Block Island. But that possibility rapidly diminished. Levittown, Pennsylvania, one of many suburbs built after the Second World War, afforded little privacy in its ticky-tacky houses and along its crowded roads. Postwar hotels and condominiums engulfed Miami Beach, as they did so much of Florida and California, and even on ski slopes there was no relief from too much company.

Under those circumstances, more and more Americans saw the need to restore and to beautify the environment so long wasted and defaced. The progressives of the early twentieth century had given high priority in public policy to the preservation of natural beauty, as in Yellowstone Park, and the conservation of national resources. So had the New Dealers. While governor of New York, Franklin Roosevelt moved the state to build the Taconic Parkway according to a plan that exposed, instead of violating, the gentle landscape. Now again preservation and conservation had their champions. Responsible lumbermen, prompted both by self-interest and the national mood, stepped up their programs for planting trees and protecting timberlands. In Columbus, Indiana, enlightened corporate management assisted the city in hiring adventurous architects whose buildings, among them Venturi's Firehouse 4, made the community a showplace of perceptive modernity. The federal government cultivated life in its fish hatcheries and protected natural space from the ravages of development in preserves like that on Cape Cod.

The most spectacular achievements of the New Deal remained
monuments to the effectuality of multipurpose public
planning. Boulder Dam provided facilities for recreation,
water for drinking and for irrigation, electric power
for domestic and industrial use. The Tennessee Valley
Authority duplicated those achievements in its series of dams
and also instructed the residents in the area it served
in reforestation and scientific agriculture.

Yet the American people,
by and large, persisted in
what they appeared to consider
their freedom to litter.
Indiscriminate dirtiness made
rubbish the trademark
of the American scene,
urban and rural.

War, the most wasteful and destructive American
experience, necessarily left rubble in its wake. In the 1940s
it despoiled tiny atolls in the Pacific and littered
the beaches of Normandy, as in 1918 it had littered French
roads. The ruins of Richmond in 1865 offered a preview of the
ghastly devastation of Hiroshima eighty years later.

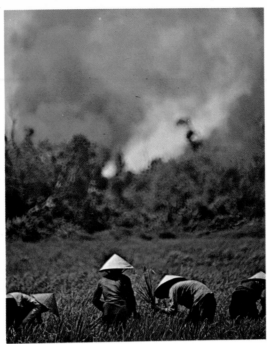

Yet never before the involvement in Vietnam
had the American government embarked so self-righteously
as it then did on a policy of wanton,
irreparable destruction of people and of nature.

Though they were no longer a people of plenty,
Americans in the 1970s had yet clearly to decide
how to treat the environments they entered.
In their immediate past they had ruined a small
foreign nation; they had left litter on the
moon. They had also begun to clean up their
neighborhoods, to husband their resources, to
worry about the growth of population, to fight
pollution, and to place pockets of green acres
in the concrete fabric of their cities.

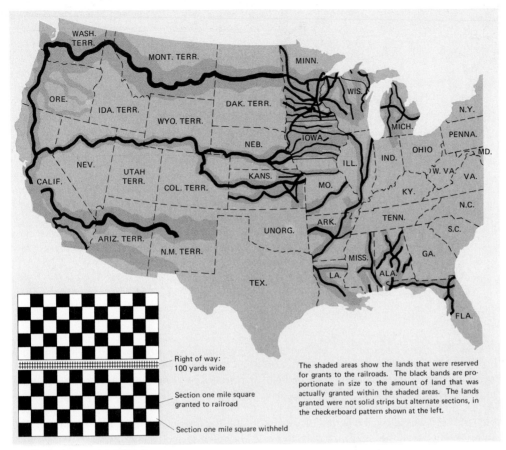

Federal grants to the railroads

Right of way: 100 yards wide

Section one mile square granted to railroad

Section one mile square withheld

The shaded areas show the lands that were reserved for grants to the railroads. The black bands are proportionate in size to the amount of land that was actually granted within the shaded areas. The lands granted were not solid strips but alternate sections, in the checkerboard pattern shown at the left.

timber and stone. This act was as enticing an invitation to the timber barons as the Desert Land Act had been to the cattlemen. Using dummy entrymen to claim quarter-sections and deed them promptly to the corporation that paid them, lumber monopolists gobbled up vast empires of forest lands.

The laissez-faire philosophy of the period speeded the land-speculator to the more desirable lands and locations well ahead of the homesteader. Taking advantage of cash sale and public auction of government lands, the speculator moved in early and cornered the choice lands, the probable town sites, and lands along streams and roads to hold for high prices. When the bona fide homesteader finally arrived on the scene to stake out his claim, he usually had to choose from the least desirable and worst located tracts or else pay the speculator's price. In addition to about 100 million acres bought from the federal land office, the land-jobbers bought up another 100 million acres from shrinking Indian reservations that became available under the govern-

ment's policy of concentration and 140 million acres from state land holdings. This accounted for some 340 million acres that were beyond the reach of homestead privileges.

Between 1850 and 1871 the federal government and the states had given railroad corporations 181 million acres of land to encourage construction (see p. 358), making the railroads the largest land-jobbers of the West. But the form of the federal grants meant that many millions of acres in addition to the actual land granted were withheld from settlement. The railroad lands lay on both sides of the track, up to forty square miles for every mile of track laid in the territories and up to twenty for every mile laid in the states. This land was not arranged in solid strips, however, but in alternate sections, checkerboard fashion. But the whole solid strip was commonly withheld from settlement until the railroad chose its right-of-way and decided which alternate sections to keep. Great belts of land on either side of the tracks were placed beyond the homesteader's reach. At one time or another some

Here had sprung up in two weeks, as if by the touch of Aladdin's Lamp, a city of three thousand people; there were regular squares arranged into five wards, a city government of mayor and aldermen, a daily paper, and a volume of ordinances for the public health. It was the end of the freight and passenger, and beginning of the construction, division; twice every day immense trains arrived and departed, and stages left for Utah, Montana, and Idaho; all the goods formerly hauled across the plains came here by rail and were reshipped, and for ten hours daily the streets were thronged with motley crowds of railroad men, Mexicans and Indians, gamblers, "cappers," and saloon-keepers, merchants, miners, and mule-whackers. The streets were eight inches deep in white dust as I entered the city of canvas tents and pole-houses; the suburbs appeared as banks of dirty white lime, and a new arrival with black clothes looked like nothing so much as a cockroach struggling through a flour barrel.

It was sundown, and the lively notes of the violin and guitar were calling the citizens to evening diversions. Twenty three saloons ... and five dance-houses amused our elegant leisure.

From J. H. Beadle, *The Undeveloped West*, 1873.

three-tenths of the area of the country, and a much greater proportion of the West, was forbidden to use. Homesteaders were obliged either to accept areas remote from the rails or to pay the price the railroads asked. In 1887 this evil was alleviated by the Cleveland Administration (see p. 472), which threw open to settlement most of the land thus withheld.

The advance of settlement.

The railroads became the principal colonizers as well as the biggest landowners of the New West. Rapid settlement along their lines meant larger revenues from passenger fares and freight charges and bigger profits from land sales. Railroads and states sold settlers nearly six times as much land as the farmers were able to obtain by homesteading. Each Western road had its land department and its bureau of immigration, and each Western state its agency to advertise and exaggerate opportunities for settlers. Steamship companies with an eye to emigrant passengers joined in the campaign abroad; working with railroad agents, they plastered Europe with posters and literature calculated to attract settlers to the "Garden of the West." The railroads provided what the Homestead Act had neglected: credit terms, special passenger rates, and agricultural guidance and assistance for prospective purchasers and settlers. The success of the railroad

colonizers was striking, and their campaigns in Europe infected whole countries with the "American fever." From Norway, Sweden, and Denmark, which were especially susceptible, peasants by the millions emigrated to the Northwest. By 1890 Minnesota had four hundred towns bearing Swedish names. Irish and German colonies were sprinkled across Minnesota, Nebraska, and Dakota Territory.

As in the past, however, the states immediately to the east of the advancing frontier furnished a large proportion of the new settlers. In the 1870s some 190 million acres, an area equal to that of Great Britain and France combined, were added to the cultivated area of the country, mostly just to the west of the Minnesota-Louisiana tier of states. The line of settlement surged westward irregularly, first along the river valleys, rapidly along the growing railroad lines, and out over the rolling plains. A frontier in Kansas that had not budged perceptibly in two decades forged rapidly ahead in the seventies, and both Kansas and Nebraska had filled out to the edge of the semiarid plains by 1880. To the north the frontier advanced in a succession of three "Dakota Booms" roughly coinciding with three contemporaneous gold rushes. A demonstration of how to make a 100 percent profit in wheat-growing, put on by the Northern Pacific Railway after the Panic of 1873, started a rush that covered three hundred miles of the Red River Valley with "bonanza

To the frontier the American intellect owes its striking characteristics. That coarseness and strength combined with acuteness and inquisitiveness; that practical, inventive turn of mind, quick to find expedients; that masterful grasp of material things, lacking in the artistic but powerful to effect great ends; that restless, nervous energy; that dominant individualism, working for good and for evil, and withal that buoyancy and exuberance which comes with freedom—these are traits of the frontier, or traits called out elsewhere because of the existence of the frontier. Since the days when the fleet of Columbus sailed into the waters of the New World, America has been another name for opportunity, and the people of the United States have taken their tone from the incessant expansion which has not only been open but has even been forced upon them. He would be a rash prophet who should assert that the expansive character of American life has now entirely ceased. Movement has been its dominant fact, and, unless this training has no effect upon a people, the American energy will continually demand a wider field for its exercise. But never again will such gifts of free land offer themselves.

Turner on the frontier

From Frederick Jackson Turner, "The Significance of the Frontier in American History," 1893.

---

farms" ranging up to one hundred thousand acres in size, a remarkable commentary on the supposedly democratic land system. Further north in Dakota Territory was the special province of James J. Hill, inspired colonizer of the Northwest and head of the Great Northern Railway. Hill planned and directed the settlement of thousands of pioneers along the tracks of his road to the Pacific. By 1885 all of Dakota east of the Missouri River was settled, and the population had increased 400 percent in five years. The mountainous territories to the west, except for the Mormon settlements of Utah, were slower in attracting settlers, but by the mid-eighties homesteaders in western Nebraska and Wyoming were challenging the cattlemen there.

In the meantime settlers of the Southwestern frontier were pushing ahead. The number of farms in Texas more than doubled during the seventies. As both the Texas and the Kansas frontiers approached the semiarid country to the west, avid land-seekers began to eye the tempting lands of the Indian Territory between the two states. Egged on by railroad companies with actual or projected lines in the territory, agitators defied the troops guarding the boundaries, repeatedly invaded the territory, and besieged Congress with demands to throw the cowed and defeated Indian tribes out of their last refuge. Congress yielded to their demands and on April 22, 1889, threw open some 2 million

acres of the Oklahoma District in the heart of the territory. At the signal, a hundred thousand "Boomers" and "Sooners," riding on every conceivable vehicle, including fifteen trains with passengers jamming the roofs, swarmed into the district, staked it off in claims, and founded two cities—all within a few hours. Congress yielded to pressure again and created the Oklahoma Territory on May 2, 1890. In succeeding years one strip after another was opened—the largest, the 6 million acres of the Cherokee Outlet, in 1893— until the entire area of Oklahoma had been settled.

The superintendent of the census of 1890 discovered after the returns were in that something was missing: the long-familiar frontier. "Up to and including 1880," he reported, "the country had a frontier of settlement, but at present the unsettled area has been so broken into by isolated bodies of settlement that there can hardly be said to be a frontier line." Three years later Frederick Jackson Turner, a young historian from Wisconsin, undertook to interpret the meaning of this development in a paper entitled "The Significance of the Frontier in American History." A devoted son of the West, Turner maintained that contact with the frontier created the continuous rebirth and rejuvenation of democracy—a conclusion not easy to reconcile with the way land was distributed and the frontier advanced.

"Boomers" in business: Oklahoma, 1889

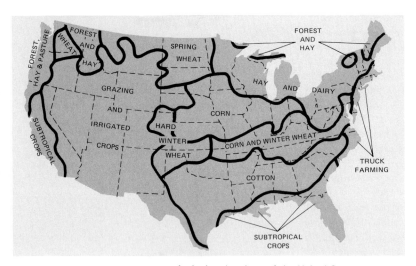

Agricultural regions of the United States

New farms and new methods. The tribulations of the new pioneers of prairie and plain rivaled those of the Jamestown settlers in the early seventeenth century. Like the plagues that the God of Moses sent against the Egyptians, new calamities visited Western farmers with each season. Hardly had the winter blizzards ceased when melting snow brought flash floods to menace man and beast. Summer temperatures soared to 118°; drought and hot winds seared corn to crisp blades and whitened men's faces with the salt of sweat. Worst of all were the grasshoppers, especially during the terrible plagues of the midseventies. The insects came in clouds that darkened the sun, cracked the limbs of trees with their weight, and covered the ground inches deep. After they had chewed the crops down to the roots, they stripped the few trees of leaves and tender bark and even consumed the curtains at the farmers' windows. Prairie fires, dust storms, marauding Indians, claim-jumpers, and rattlesnakes further chastened the spirit of the pioneers and discouraged all but the sturdiest.

Mrs. Abigail Scott Duniway, woman suffrage leader in the Northwest, never forgot the death of her mother, who was a victim of frontier hardship in Dakota. She described her own lot later in a pioneer community of Oregon: "To bear two children in two and a half years from my marriage . . . to sew and cook, and wash and iron; to bake and clean and stew and fry; to be, in short, a general pioneer drudge, with never a penny of my own, was not pleasant business for an erst-while school teacher."

Gradually inventiveness and industry solved many of the problems of soil and climate and overcame the lack of wood and water. In his first few years the homesteader lived in a miserable sod house, half buried in the prairie and roofed with slabs of cut turf. But later, when the railroads brought down the cost of lumber, he built a frame house. The problem of how to fence his land in a woodless, railless, stoneless region was solved by the invention of barbed wire. Of the several types devised, the most successful was patented by Joseph F. Glidden, an Illinois farmer, in November 1874. Joining forces with a wire-manufacturer, Glidden began mass production two years later, and by 1883 the Glidden factory was turning out six hundred miles of barbed wire a day. Farmers and cattlemen strung it up as fast as it was produced.

The problem of water supply was harder to solve. The only reliable sources of supply lay far below the surface, too deep to reach by open, hand-dug wells. And even when a well was drilled, pumping the water up two hundred to eight hundred feet by hand was impractical. The obvious solution was to harness the free power of the winds that steadily swept the plains, and by 1880 scores of small firms were producing windmills adapted to this purpose. The cost of digging a well ran up to $2 per foot, and this expense, plus the cost of the windmill, tower, tank, and reservoir, kept that solution beyond the means of the homesteader and the small farmer until near the end of the century. The big rancher, however, might have several windmills drawing water for his cattle.

To meet the problem of cultivating soil in semiarid country without irrigation, Westerners developed the technique of "dry farming." They plowed deep into the earth to bring subsurface moisture up to the plant roots and then harrowed the surface into fine particles to slow down evaporation. To break the tough soil of the plains and cultivate larger farms where labor was scarcer than ever, the farmer needed a new type of machinery. A revolution in farm machinery had started before 1860, and most of the basic patents had been granted by that year. But the mass production of machines came only after the Civil War.

The plow that most successfully broke the plains was devised by James Oliver of Indiana. After working on it for twenty-five years, by 1877 he had perfected the modern chilled-iron plow and smooth-surfaced moldboard.

On bonanza farms in California before 1900 huge steam tractors were pulling sixteen plows, four harrows, and a seed drill, simultaneously breaking and planting as much as fifty acres a day.

Machine harvesting of wheat was improved in 1880 by a mechanical twine-binder that tied up the cut bundles. An even speedier device, used in drier parts of the West, was the header, which cut off the heads of the grain and left the stalk for pasturage or plowing under. The threshing machine was improved over the years by refinements that increased its capacity and efficiency, and in 1884 a blowing device was developed for stacking straw.

The soft winter wheat of the East could not withstand the rigors of the new climate and was replaced by a new variety imported from northern Europe and by Turkey Red from the Crimea. To mill the hard grain of the new varieties, the basic idea of the roller mill was borrowed from Hungary, and chilled-iron rollers were added by 1879. By the early seventies the storage, loading, handling, and transporting of wheat had all been reduced to mechanical processes.

The most striking results of mechanized farming were achieved in wheat production. An acre that had required 61 hours to farm by hand took only 3 hours to farm by machine, and where one man could farm only $7\frac{1}{2}$ acres by old methods he could take on 135 acres in the nineties. Mechanization released men from drudgery and stupefying toil. On the other hand, in the very states where mechanization was most prevalent there was a remarkable growth of tenancy in the last two decades of the century and a corresponding decline in the percentage of farmers working their own farms. The farmers, like the placer miners and the range cattlemen, were destined in the late eighties for trouble and disenchantment with the Golden West. They fell victims to their own illusions—the illusion of inexhaustible resources and the illusion of unlimited markets.

The illusions of the farmer were part of a great national illusion dating from the early years of the republic. This was what Henry Nash Smith in *Virgin Land* has called "The Myth of the Garden"—the myth that the West was a realizable utopia, an agrarian Eden where free land and honest toil would produce a virtuous yeomanry and the good life. According to the myth, the West was the true

Black homesteaders, Nebraska, 1887

source of national regeneration, the means of realizing the ideals of democracy and equality, and it was celebrated by poets, novelists, and historians alike. "All of the associations called up by the spoken word, the West," wrote the Western novelist Hamlin Garland in 1891, "were fabulous, mythic, hopeful." To the frontier West Frederick Jackson Turner attributed "that buoyancy and exuberance which comes with freedom."

But the stark contrast between the hopes fostered by the myth and the harsh realities of experience could not escape even the dullest farmer. Far from utopian were the sod house, the dust storm, the grasshopper plague. "So this is the reality of the dream!" exclaims a character in a Garland novel. "A shanty on a barren plain, hot and lone as a desert. My God!" Far from equalitarian or democratic was a land system that fostered monopoly in the guise of distributing free land. It was a curious "safety valve" for the urban discontent of the East that sent homesteaders flocking to the city to escape the rural discontent of the West. The disillusionment with the Myth of the Garden that dates from these years helps explain the bitterness of the agrarian revolt that burst forth toward the end of the century.

Whether as myth or as reality, whether as the last stand of the first American or as the last frontier of miner, cattleman, and farmer, whether as man's last hope of equality or as a disillusioning experience with monopoly and inequality—this last of the nation's many wests left a profound imprint upon the American mind and the American legend.

Suggestions for reading   Two readable and comprehensive surveys of Western history are R. A. Billington, *Westward Expansion: A History of the American Frontier* (1967), which stresses the Turner thesis, and T. D. Clark, *Frontier America: The Story of the Westward Movement* (2nd ed., 1969), which disclaims the thesis. The thesis itself appears in an essay by F. J. Turner, "The Significance of the Frontier in American History," in his *The Frontier in American History** (1920). R. A. Billington, *America's Frontier Heritage** (1967), is a synthesis of recent thought on the subject. W. P. Webb, *The Great Plains** (1931), is the most provocative study of regional culture and environmental influences in our literature; his *The Great Frontier* (1932, rev. ed., 1964), examines the world significance of the New World frontiers since the Age of Discovery. H. R. Lamar, *The Far Southwest, 1846–1912** (1966), is an excellent history of territories. J. C. Malin, *The Grassland of North America* (1947), brings agricultural and geographical science to the aid of historical understanding. Wayne Gard, *The Great Buffalo Hunt** (1959), is the best book on this dramatic subject. Allan Nevins, *The Emergence of Modern America, 1865–1878* (1927), has excellent chapters on the West. The West as symbol and myth in American thought is brilliantly analyzed in H. N. Smith, *Virgin Land** (1950).

Two general histories of the Indians are recommended: W. T. Hagan, *American Indians** (1961), and J. R. Swanton, *The Indian Tribes of North America* (1953). On the plains Indians in particular Dee Brown, *Bury My Heart at Wounded Knee: An Indian History of the American West* (1970), is readable. F. G. Roe, *The Indian and the Horse* (1955), and Robert Utley, *Last Days of the Sioux Nation* (1963), are first rate. Two champions of the red man's rights have left moving accounts: H. H. Jackson, *A Century of Dishonor** (1881), a stirring indictment, and J. J. Collier, *The Indians of the Americas** (1947), by a leader of policy reform. L. B. Priest, *Uncle Sam's Stepchildren: The Reformation of United States Indian Policy, 1865–1887* (1942), defends the reformers against their critics. H. L. Fritz, *The Movement for Indian Assimilation, 1860–1890* (1963), treats the philanthropists. Revealing books on military activities are R. G. Athearn, *William Tecumseh Sherman and the Settlement of the West* (1956); E. I. Stewart, *Custer's Luck* (1955); and C. C. Rister, *Border Command: General Phil Sheridan in the West* (1944).

On mining, the best reading on this period is R. W. Paul, *Mining Frontiers of the Far West, 1848–1880** (1963), and W. S. Greever, *The Bonanza West: The Story of the Western Mining Rushes, 1848–1900* (1963). G. C. Quiett, *Pay Dirt: A Panorama of American Gold-Rushes* (1936), stresses the more colorful and violent parts of the story. C. H. Shinn, *The Story of the Mine* (1896) and *Mining Camps: A Study in American Frontier Government** (1885), are based on firsthand experience. For colorful reminiscences, see Mark Twain, *Roughing It** (1872), and Dan De Quille, *History of the Big Bonanza** (1876, reprinted 1947).

The cattleman's bonanza is briefly surveyed in E. S. Osgood, *The Day of the Cattleman** (1929, reprinted 1957), and more fully in E. E. Dale, *The Range Cattle Industry* (1930, reprinted 1969). Maurice Frank, W. T. Jackson, and A. W. Spring, *When Grass Was King* (1957), is a roundup of scholarship. Lewis Atherton, *The Cattle Kings* (1961), is thoughtful and sympathetic. Also helpful are G. M. Gressley, *Bankers and Cattlemen* (1966), and R. R. Dykstra, *The Cattle Towns** (1970). Of the vast cowboy literature, Andy Adams, *The Log of a Cowboy** (1927), and J. F. Dobie, ed., *A Texas Cowboy* (1950), contain firsthand experiences; J. B. Frantz and J. E. Choate, *The American Cowboy: The Myth and the Reality* (1955), is a realistic analysis.

The best histories of agriculture in this period, especially in the West, are F. A. Shannon, *The Farmer's Last Frontier: Agriculture, 1860–1897** (1945), and Gilbert C. Fite, *The Farmer's Frontier, 1865–1900** (1966). On the history of American land policy and its administration, two works of value are P. W. Gates, *History of Public Land Development* (1968), and R. M. Robbins, *Out Landed Heritage: The Public Domain, 1776–1936** (1942). The history of the new farm machinery is found in Waldemar Kaempffert, *A Popular History of American Invention* (1924), and R. M. Wik, *Steam Power on the American Farm* (1953). The pioneer farm on the Western frontier is pictured in Everett Dick, *The Sod-House Frontier, 1854–1890* (1937). Vivid fictional accounts are Willa Cather, *O Pioneers!** (1913) and *My Antonia** (1918), O. E. Rølvaag, *Giants in the Earth** (1927), and Mari Sandoz, *Old Jules** (1935).

*Available in a paperback edition.

18 The ordeal of industrialization

"The truth is," Senator John Sherman wrote his brother General William T. Sherman in November 1865, "the close of the war with our resources unimpaired gives an elevation, a scope to the ideas of leading capitalists, far higher than anything ever undertaken in this country before. They talk of millions as confidently as formerly of thousands." The high hopes and towering schemes of the industrial capitalists continued to mount over the decades, and before the end of the century they were talking of billions where they had once spoken of millions. There was reason for their optimism. Of all the nations that have industrialized their economies through capitalistic rather than socialistic methods, the United States offered its businessmen the greatest encouragement and the fewest obstacles.

While industrial growth slowed down in some respects during the Civil War years, the expansion immediately following was tremendous. The war proved a great smasher of barriers and opener of opportunities. "Such opportunities for making money," wrote Judge Thomas Mellon of Pittsburgh in 1863, "had never existed before in all my former experience." But the great war did more than give rein to fortune-builders. It created new attitudes and expectations on the part of the public, the government, and industry. It accustomed bankers, bookkeepers, and manufacturers to nationwide operations and large-scale organization. It pointed the way to mass markets and mass production, and it taught the government habits of openhanded and reckless generosity toward private enterprise that sought control of public funds and public resources.

Throughout the last third of the nineteenth century the federal government was controlled by men who were not only responsive to the wishes of the business community but eager to further its interests. They used the prevailing philosophy of laissez faire to justify the lack of a positive public policy and the virtual absence of restraints and regulation of business to protect public welfare and safeguard public health. M. I. Ostrogorski, a distinguished foreign scholar, concluded that the Americans were in this period essentially an ungoverned people:

> From one end of the scale to the other, the constituted authorities are unequal to their duty; they prove incapable of ensuring the protection of the general interest, or even place the power which has been entrusted to them by the community at the disposal of private interests. The spring of government is weakened or warped everywhere.

When the government intervened at all, it was to extend loans, grant subsidies and franchises, hand over public resources, or protect home industries from foreign competitors. The Civil War eliminated the Southern planter as a rival of the industrialist for control in Washington, and no other class offered serious competition. Unlike European businessmen, the Americans had no heritage of canon law and feudal custom with which to contend. No royal prerogatives or aristocratic privileges barred them from certain fields of enterprise, and no pampered courtiers controlled vital trade routes. For the time being, the industrial entrepreneur was the lord of all he surveyed.

What he surveyed was a built-in empire, rich in coal, iron, oil, waterpower, lumber— most of the resources essential for great industrial power. Of bituminous coal, the unrivaled fuel of nineteenth-century industry, the United States had the greatest known deposits in the world. Petroleum fields in Pennsylvania had been tapped already, and the vast oil fields of the Southwest were yet to be discovered. Employers had already learned to draw on European resources for their labor supply, and after the Civil War immigrants came swarming to the New World in unprec-

edented numbers. Within the boundaries of the United States was the greatest free-trade market in the world, and around it Congress had erected a high protective-tariff barrier.

It is no wonder that an economy that had already been expanding rapidly before the Civil War grew with explosive force in the decades that followed. In 1860 the United States was a second-rate industrial country, lagging behind the United Kingdom, and perhaps France and Germany. But by 1890 the United States had stepped into first place, and the value of its manufactured goods almost equaled the combined production of all the three former leaders. Between the eve of the Civil War and the eve of the First World War, American manufacturing production multiplied twelve times over.

The railroad empire

"The generation between 1865 and 1895 was already mortgaged to the railways," reflected Henry Adams, "and no one knew it better than the generation itself." This was the generation that planned, built, financed, and made the first attempts to control the most extensive railroad network in the world. The headlong haste and heedless ethics of its experience are caught in the national expression "railroaded through." No one, not even the enemies of the railroad, could be found in that age to deny its importance. Everyone believed it was the key to mass production and mass consumption, to the utilization of natural resources and the creation of a national market, and to the binding together and settlement of a two-ocean land mass. The railroad dominated the imagination, the politics, the economy, and the hopes of a generation, and the outsized cowcatcher and smokestack of the old-fashioned steam locomotive might well be taken as the symbol of the age. The poet William Ellery Leonard, who was born in 1876, entitled an autobiographical work *The Locomotive-God,* and the popular ballad-makers lavished a devotion on the iron horse they had formerly reserved for the flesh-and-blood steed and the sailing ship.

Building the network. The laying of rails, which until the eighties were mainly iron rather than steel, went forward in fits and starts, impeded by panics and depression and spurred on by speculative booms and pros-

perity. Starting with only about 35,000 miles of railway at the end of the Civil War, during which less than 5,000 miles were laid, the country had doubled its mileage before the Panic of 1873. The next six years of depression added only some 16,000 miles. The 1880s, the great decade of railway expansion, opened with some 93,000 miles and ended with 166,000, an increase of more than 73,000 miles in ten years. By the end of the century the United States had a total of nearly 200,000 miles, or more than all Europe including Russia. In the meantime the ungainly little "bullgine" with the disproportionate funnel had evolved into a giant that could master mountain and plain, a giant that dwarfed any foreign make of locomotive. Greatly improved by the Westinghouse air brake and other inventions, the trains carried more passengers in 1900 than they did in any year of the decade beginning in 1932.

To build this vast railway network was an undertaking comparable in magnitude to the construction of a navy, and for the United States it was even more costly and probably more essential to the national interest. European governments assumed responsibility for building and running their railroad establishments as readily as for their military establishments. In America, apart from a few state-owned roads of antebellum origin, initiative and management were left primarily in the hands of private enterprise. Even by 1880, before half the network was completed, an

The Union Pacific meets the Central Pacific, 1869

investment of more than $4,600 million had gone into the nation's railroads. By 1897 their stocks and bonds totaled $10,635 million as compared with a total national debt of less than $1,227 million. Edward Kirkland, the economic historian, concludes that the handling of railroad finances had "a greater effect upon the economy than the management of the national finances." Since such huge sums were far more than private American investors could supply, promoters turned to foreign investors and to local, state, and federal governments. Foreign investment reached its peak earlier, but in 1898 Europeans, mainly British, owned $3,100 million worth of American railroad securities, about one-third of the whole.

While public enthusiasm for railroad-building was at its height, government at all levels fairly thrust credit and resources upon the railroad-promoters. Villages, towns, cities, and counties came forward with $300 million, and states with some $228 million more in the form of bonds and other commitments. The federal government lent approximately $65 million to six Western railroads and extended even more important aid through grants of public land. In all, Congress committed 155,500,000 acres of the public domain, of which the railroads actually received more than 131,000,000 acres. In addition they received 49,000,000 acres from the states. There is no way of estimating realistically the dollar value of these lands and the resources upon them. Their main value to the railroads was not the cash they brought from sales but the credit and security they supplied for bond issues. Although government subsidies were often obtained through bribery and were responsible for much corruption, the policy of subsidizing the railroads with grants of public land was probably justified in the long run. By attaching conditions to the land grants that obliged the railroads to furnish cheap transportation for mail and military shipments, the government has enjoyed substantial savings over the years. Actually, less than 10 percent of the railroad mileage of the country was built with federal land grants. And most of that mileage was on the roads built across the Great Plains, where investment was slow in yielding returns and where some form of public credit was essential.

The transcontinental lines called for the most heroic efforts and attracted some of the ablest—and some of the most unscrupu-

Depot on the Erie line, 1876

lous—enterprisers. The completion of the Union Pacific-Central Pacific in 1869 (see p. 358) realized the antebellum dream of spanning the continent with rails, and within the next quarter of a century four more lines flanked the original one, two on either side: the Southern Pacific and the Santa Fe to the south and the Northern Pacific and the Great Northern to the north. Each line excited intense rivalries and ambitions in the cities they connected and the sections they served, as well as among the railroad-builders and promoters.

Collis P. Huntington, one of the Californians behind the Central Pacific, took the leading role in pushing through the Southern Pacific, the second and southernmost of the transcontinentals. Like many railroad barons of his generation, Huntington was tough and cynical about business and politics and ruthless in his methods. He talked about bribing and buying congressmen as he would about the purchase of so many cattle. The son of a large and unprosperous Connecticut family, he grew up with little schooling, became a peddler, and went west with the California gold rush of 1849. He did not strike gold, but he made money as a merchant and a fortune as a builder of the Central Pacific. His next ambition was to build the Southern Pacific southward from San Francisco through California and eastward across Arizona, New Mexico, and Texas. This enterprise brought a head-on

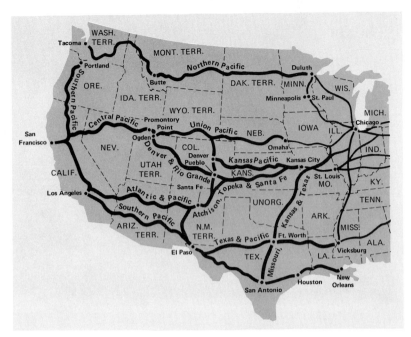

Early Pacific railroad lines, about 1884

Jay Gould: land pirate

influence in the Southern Pacific. The Gould and Huntington lines joined near El Paso in 1882, and two years later the Southern Pacific reached New Orleans.

About the same time another major system, the Atchison, Topeka, & Santa Fe, usually known simply as the Santa Fe, entered the Southwest and threatened the Huntington-Gould monopoly. Financed by Boston capital, this road cut across Kansas and a corner of Colorado to reach Santa Fe, New Mexico. Huntington and Gould cleverly thwarted the Santa Fe's efforts to gain direct access to the coast by buying up its charter. In 1883 the Southern Pacific, on its own terms, permitted the Santa Fe to enter California on Southern Pacific lines. The competing Santa Fe was then subordinated to the monopoly, and by 1890 Gould was the virtual dictator of transportation in the Southwest.

The Northwest was somewhat more fortunate in its railroad pioneers and masters. The Northern Pacific had been chartered to build a line from Lake Superior to Puget Sound, but construction was halted in 1873 when Jay Cooke and Company as well as the railroad it was financing went bankrupt. Reorganized in 1875, the Northern Pacific was acquired in 1881 by Henry Villard, a German-born capitalist with large holdings in Oregon. Villard completed the line to Tacoma, Washington, in 1883, but he was never able to enjoy a monopoly of transportation in the Northwest. In 1878 a competing line under the management of James J. Hill had begun to push westward from St. Paul, parallel to the Northern Pacific. A Canadian by birth, Hill had a long-cherished dream of colonizing the Northwest. First he had acquired the two-hundred-mile track of the bankrupt little St. Paul & Pacific, and then had started building westward through Minnesota, North Dakota, Idaho, and across Washington for 2,775 miles to the Pacific. The Great Northern, as he renamed this line, had no land grant such as the Northern Pacific enjoyed. Consequently, in order to build up traffic and revenue, Hill had to rely on Canadian and American capital and his own efforts to settle the country. "We consider ourselves and the people along our line as co-partners in the prosperity of the country we both occupy," said Hill. He completed his line to Puget Sound in 1893. Built more carefully and solidly than its competitor, financed more soundly, and integrated more thoroughly into the economy of the region it served, Hill's

clash with Thomas A. Scott, who was equally determined to build the Texas & Pacific over roughly the same route. Scott was president of the Pennsylvania Railroad and as powerful and ruthless a man as Huntington. The effect the Scott lobby had on the presidential election of 1876 has already been noted (see p. 383). But in spite of President Hayes' support of Scott's bill for a $200 million government subsidy for the Texas & Pacific, Congress failed to pass it. There were several reasons for the failure, but one important reason was Huntington, who once remarked, "It costs money to fix things so that I would know his bill would not pass." Huntington would stop at nothing, and nothing could stop him. In defiance of a War Department order he laid rails across an Indian reservation and then boasted to the President of his defiance. Scott continued to resist, but Huntington kept laying rails until at last he forced the Southern Pacific into El Paso, Texas, in 1881, and Scott decided to give up the struggle.

In the course of the contest with Scott, however, Huntington met his match in Jay Gould, the most notorious land pirate of all the railroad barons. Gould won control of the Texas & Pacific, forced his way into the Southern Pacific, and threatened to block Huntington's way through the state of Texas. He relented only after exacting a traffic-sharing agreement from Huntington and a large

Great Northern was the only transcontinental road to pull through the Panic of 1893 and the depression that followed.

East of the Mississippi, railroads, with exceptions such as the New York Central, were built mainly to serve local needs and to promote the interests of particular cities. Hundreds of small lines using a variety of gauges were built after the Civil War, many without connections. The South alone had four hundred companies averaging not more than forty miles apiece. One task of the postwar generation was to fill in the gaps between lines and to weld them into an integrated national network. Through consolidation by lease, purchase, or merger, nearly two-thirds of the country's railroad companies were absorbed by the other one-third. In 1880 alone, 115 companies lost their identity, and between 1880 and 1888 some 425 companies were brought under the control of other roads. The Pennsylvania Railroad by 1890 was an amalgamation of 73 smaller companies and some five thousand miles of rail.

One result of combination was the emergence of a few dominant systems in each section. In the Northeast, in addition to the Pennsylvania, were the New York Central, the Erie, and the Baltimore & Ohio. All competed to some degree, and all shared the same general aim of connecting the Eastern ports with the Western rivers and the Great Lakes. In the South the largest system was the Richmond & West Point Terminal (later the Southern Railway), which by 1890 had pieced together by financial jobbery some eighty-five hundred miles of lines. Competing with it for north-south traffic were the Atlantic Coast Line and the Seaboard Air Line, smaller companies that were themselves the result of combinations of more than a hundred small lines. West of the Appalachians the powerful Louisville & Nashville served the mining and industrial areas of Kentucky, Tennessee, and Alabama; and the Illinois Central paralleled the Mississippi River down to New Orleans and connected with the Atlantic coast at Savannah.

Consolidation sometimes, but not always, brought improvements: steel rails to replace iron rails, safety precautions such as double-tracking and the block signal, and cheaper, more reliable, and more punctual service. In the last half of the century, real passenger charges fell nearly 50 percent and freight rates much more. In 1883 the American Railway Association divided the country into four time zones with an hour's difference between each and, in spite of outraged advocates of "God's time," regularized their timetables. The standard gauge of 4 feet 8½ inches for rails became virtually nationwide in May 1886, when the Southern roads moved one rail three inches closer to the other.

Competition and disorder.

In spite of all these improvements, the American railroads were in serious difficulties. They were under heavy criticism and attack from the public, and they were suffering from grave and uncontrolled disorders within the industry itself. The troubles of the railroads were inherent in the very nature of American industry in the age of unrestricted competition. The mania for construction in the seventies and eighties provided all the major transportation areas with an overdeveloped network of railroads, much greater than was needed at the time. In the same period the looting by buccaneer operators saddled the railroads with heavy fixed costs due to wasteful construction and overcapitalization. In 1885 *Poor's Manual*, an authority on railroads, estimated that nearly one-third of the capitalization in that year represented "watered stock," that is, stock issued in excess of the value of assets. Railroad-managers, faced with the need to make regular payments on swollen bonded indebtedness, with the demand to make profits on overcapitalized stock, and with the pressing need for traffic when there was not enough to go around, resorted to ruinous competitive wars of line against line. Between St. Louis and Atlanta, for example, shippers could choose between twenty competitive routes. Competitors and interlopers paralleled each other's lines for purposes of blackmailing or ruining rivals. Railroads offered fantastic "rebates," secret rates below the published tariffs, to secure the traffic of big shippers and overcharged outrageously to compensate where they had no competition. They often charged less per mile for a long haul than for a short haul, resorted to all kinds of rate jugglery and deception, and trusted neither client nor competitor. "No wonder that railroad managers accused each other of fraud and deception," testified one manager before a Senate committee in 1885. "Men who in all other relations of life were blameless winked at falsehoods, and dallied with deception, not because they were morally debased, but ac-

James J. Hill: empire builder of the Northwest

"The Scourge of the West"

tually because they knew not the way out of the toils."

Competition under such circumstances, instead of being "the life of trade" and benefiting enterprise as well as the public, proved a curse to both. The railroads themselves suffered heavily from the rate wars, for they were often driven to cut rates below the cost of handling the business and thereby imperiled the dividends, if not the solvency, of the firm. Obviously the railroads had to find some way to stop the piratical practices of rebate, rate-cutting, and blackmail. They sought solutions in treaties and solemn agreements—most of which proved unenforceable. A more formal device of railroad cooperation was the pool, an agreement to divide traffic on some proportional basis and charge uniform rates. But the pool agreements were also difficult to enforce and were always breaking down. The temptation to gain advantage over competitors by violating agreements often proved irresistible. As Charles Francis Adams, Jr., a keen student as well as an executive of railroads, described the demoralization:

> Honesty and good faith are scarcely regarded. Certainly they are not tolerated at all if they interfere with a man's getting his "share of the business." Gradually, this demoralizing spirit of low cunning has pervaded the entire system. Its moral tone is deplorably low. . . . That healthy, mutual confidence which is the first essential to prosperity in all transactions

between man and man, does not exist in the American railroad service taken as a whole.

If the railroad industry could not set its own house in order, then order would have to be imposed from outside. The problem was nationwide, but the federal government continued through the years of the worst railroad anarchy to practice laissez faire. The state governments took the initiative and made the first experiments in regulation and control. Their laws and commissions are often attributed to the "Granger movement," the work of a farmers' organization (see p. 477), and associated with the Middle West. But the movement to regulate railroads was limited to no one class or section. Massachusetts and New York made important contributions, and states in the Southeast, the Southwest, and the Far West also participated. Merchants, wholesale dealers, and manufacturers were more prominent and effective than farmers in pressing for regulation in several areas. If pools were an unsatisfactory solution from the point of view of the railroads, they were even more offensive from the point of view of consumers, who had to pay the exorbitant rates charged and submit to the abuses practiced. Shippers of all kinds suffered from the abuses and disorders of the railroads. In particular they resented rate and service discrimination between persons and places, favoritism that gave unfair advantages to powerful shippers and to cities where railroads had competition. Small men resented bigness and the power it gave the railroads over legislatures, governors, and judges and correctly charged some roads with using bribes and free passes to corrupt or influence public officials. The low reputation railroads acquired by the underhanded means they had used to secure land grants, subsidies, and charters from federal and state governments continued to cling to them.

Popular resentment of abuses found expression in numerous state laws. In 1869 Massachusetts established a commission to supervise railroad activities and investigate grievances and made Adams a member. Within the next ten years a dozen more states established commissions modeled on that of Massachusetts. Several state legislatures in the Middle West adopted more thoroughgoing measures of regulation. Illinois, for example, laid down explicit and detailed provisions against discrimination and went further to give its commission power to bring suit "against any railroad corporation which may violate the provisions of this act." The Supreme Court upheld the constitutionality of the legislation in the case of *Munn* v. *Illinois* (1877) and declared that when private property is "affected with a public interest" it "must submit to be controlled by the public for the common good" and that in the absence of federal policy states could act. Railroads nevertheless waged relentless war against such legislation, which in some states was carelessly drawn, and limited its effectiveness from the start. Then in the Wabash case of 1886 (*Wabash, St. Louis, & Pacific Railway Co.* v. *Illinois*) a more laissez-faire Supreme Court reversed earlier decisions and held an Illinois statute invalid on the ground that it was the exclusive power of Congress to regulate interstate commerce. With the states thus excluded, any effective regulatory action would have to be taken by the federal government.

A second spur to federal action in 1886 was the report of a Senate committee headed by Senator Shelby M. Cullom of Illinois, which denounced railroads sharply for the "reckless strife" of their competition and for "unjust discrimination between persons, places, commodities, or particular descriptions of traffic." Railroad-leaders themselves urged federal regulation, for they acknowledged the necessity for measures to end the anarchy in which they struggled. The Republican platform of 1884 had declared that "the principle of the public regulation of railroad corporations is a wise and salutary one." The Interstate Commerce Act, which eventually grew out of demands for regulation, was a milestone in American history, but it was not a triumph of radicals over conservatives or of the people over the corporation.

The Interstate Commerce Act, passed by large majorities in both houses of Congress and signed by President Grover Cleveland on February 4, 1887, forbade railroads to engage in discriminatory practices, required them to publish their rate schedules, prohibited them from entering pooling agreements for the purpose of maintaining high rates, and declared that rates should be "reasonable and just." The act placed enforcement in the hands of an Interstate Commerce Commission of five members, who were to hear complaints and issue orders to the railroads to "cease and desist." For enforcement of its orders, however, the commission had to appeal to the courts, and there the advantage was consistently with the railroads. During the first eighteen years after the act was passed the Supreme Court heard sixteen cases brought before it by the Interstate Commerce Commission and decided fifteen for the railroads and against the commission. As an assertion of the federal government's right to regulate private enterprise and as a precedent for more effective measures in the future, the Interstate Commerce Act was important. But it did not provide any immediate solution to the problem of cutthroat competition. It was a conservative measure, based on the old belief that competition was beneficial rather than harmful and adopted mainly to alleviate public anxieties.

Morgan and banker control. Within a year of the passage of the Interstate Commerce Act, the railroads began to return to the discriminatory practices that were now illegal. They were somewhat more secretive about rebates and blackmail competition, but it quickly became evident that the law had no teeth and that there was nothing to fear from the courts. With no effective government control, the industry appeared as anarchic as ever and management as quick to resort to speculative looting and stock-watering. Railroads generally continued to make profits and pay dividends through the 1880s and the early 1890s, but, after decades of waste, mismanagement, and folly, many of them were in a shaky financial plight and in no condition to weather hard times. Railroad speculation and overexpansion had prepared the way for the panics of 1857 and 1873, and the first signal of the Panic of 1893 was the bankruptcy of the Philadelphia & Reading Railroad, on February 20. This panic was less closely connected with railroad overexpansion than the earlier panics. Railroad failures were not the only index of calamity, but by the middle of 1894 there were 192 railroads in the hands of the receivers. "Never in the history of transportation in the United States," reported the Interstate Commerce Commission at that time, "has such a large percentage of railway mileage been under the control of receiverships." There were 40,818 miles of railway insolvent then, and 67,000 miles, or about one-third of the total mileage of the country, were foreclosed by the middle of 1898. Among the failures were some of the greatest systems in the country, including the Erie, the

B&O, the Union Pacific, and the Northern Pacific. To obtain the funds needed for reorganization, the distressed railroads turned to the bankers. They received not only reorganization but a measure of control that neither they themselves nor the state and federal governments had so far been able to contrive.

Numerous bankers took part in the railway reorganizations of the nineties, but none took so prominent and conspicuous a part as J. Pierpont Morgan, the dominant investment banker of his time. For the quarter of a century ending with his death in 1913, this tall, massive figure with piercing eyes and fiery nose was the very symbol of American financial power. Morgan began life near the top of the economic and social ladder, the son of a rich merchant from Hartford, Connecticut, who established a bank in London during the Civil War. He grew up with all the advantages of wealth, including a good education, travel and residence abroad, and study at the University of Göttingen in Germany. He established his firm and his family in New York during the seventies in princely fashion and began to collect treasures of art and rare books. His elegant steam yacht, *Corsair* (165 feet long at the water line), or its successors, *Corsair II* (204 feet) and *Corsair III* (302 feet), always awaited his pleasure in the harbor. Aboard his yacht or in the library of his home at 219 Madison Avenue the titans of industry and finance met at his call and submitted to agreements that made history in the world of business and sometimes in the world of politics as well. At such meetings he brought to bear his passion for order and his interest as a seller of securities. Morgan enhanced his reputation as a masterful peacemaker among railroads when in 1885 he intervened in a reckless war of blackmail competition between the New York Central and the Pennsylvania and persuaded them to abandon the destructive operation of parallel lines. It was natural that the managers of the sick railroads of the nineties should come to him, as to a famous surgeon, for the strong medicine and heroic surgery the bankrupt roads needed for recovery.

Other investment banking firms, such as Kuhn, Loeb & Company, employed the same methods as Morgan and charged huge fees for their services. First they ruthlessly pared down the fixed debt of the railroad, then assessed holders of the old stock for working funds, and next issued lavish amounts of new stock, heavily watered. To assure control along lines that suited them and to veto unwise expansion plans, the bankers usually installed a president of their own selection and placed members of their own houses on the boards of railroad directors. Between 1894 and 1898 the House of Morgan reorganized the lion's share of big railroads, including the sprawling, demoralized Richmond Terminal, which became the Southern Railway, as well as the Erie, the Reading, the Norfolk & Western, the B&O, the Cincinnati & Ohio, and, in alliance with James J. Hill, the Northern Pacific. Banker control was not the ideal solution or the final answer to the problems of competition and control, but it did curb prevailing anarchy, whether or not it improved the management and efficiency of railroad service.

Industrial empire

Carnegie and steel. The new industrial order of America was based on steel, and by 1870 the techniques of production, the supply of raw materials, and the home market were sufficiently developed to make the United States the world's greatest steel-producer. A cheap and practical process of making steel by forcing a blast of cold air through molten iron to clean it of impurities had been invented by Henry Bessemer, an Englishman, in 1857. A rival patent for the same process was held by one William Kelly, a Kentucky ironmaster who claimed to have made the discovery before Bessemer. The two patents were merged in 1866, and the following year the first steel rails in the country were rolled for commercial use. In 1867 the United States made 1,643 tons of steel ingots; in 1897 it made 7,156,957. In the meantime new discoveries of ore deposits in the fabulous Lake Superior district opened exciting prospects for the ironmasters. Government surveyors in 1844 had discovered the Marquette Range in Michigan, including "a mountain of solid iron ore, 150 feet high." In 1868 the rich Vermilion Range in Minnesota was discovered, and in 1875 it was tapped by a railroad. Within the next decade the Menominee, the Gogebic, and the Mesabi mines—all within close proximity to Lake Superior and cheap water transportation—were opened up. Together they constituted the greatest iron-ore district in the world.

These opportunities brought a multitude of entrepreneurs into the field of iron and steel in quest of profits. By 1880 there were 1,005 iron companies in the nation, all of them subject to the competitive struggle under which the railroads labored, with all its uncertainties, anxieties, and ruthlessness. In fact, the spread of the railroads intensified the competitive struggle in iron and steel by breaking down the protection against competition provided by distance, creating a national market. Like railroad operators, the iron and steelmasters resorted to cutthroat tactics, price-slashing, and blackmail. Faced with large fixed costs, they sometimes ran their plants at a loss rather than let them remain idle. They sought rebates and unfair advantages and rushed into pools, combinations, and mergers to hedge against competition. Out of the melee emerged one dominant figure, Andrew Carnegie, the most articulate industrialist America ever had.

Quite untypical of industrial leaders of his day in several respects, Carnegie was of immigrant and working-class origin, a voluble speaker, a facile writer, and a religious skeptic. He came to the United States from Scotland with his family when he was thirteen years old and went to work immediately to earn a living. At eighteen he became a telegraph clerk in the office of Thomas A. Scott, then a rising official of the Pennsylvania Railroad, and won his employer's favor and confidence. His service with Scott, which lasted through the Civil War, not only brought valuable acquaintance with the foremost railroad and industrial leaders of the country, but guided him in making shrewd and extremely profitable investments. With a salary of only $2,400 a year, he was receiving a millionaire's income from investments when he was twenty-eight years old. He was drawn into the iron business and then in 1872 into a venture for building a huge steel plant on the Monongahela River, twelve miles from Pittsburgh, a site with excellent river transportation and service from both the Pennsylvania and the B&O railroads. The new plant rolled its first rail in 1875.

Without pretense of engineering or technological skill, Carnegie was first of all a superb salesman with a genius for picking the right subordinates to supervise production. He was personally acquainted with all the railroad barons of the day and, as he said, simply "went out and persuaded them to give us orders." He did not have to remind them that steel rails lasted twenty times as long as iron. The supreme example of the industrial capitalist, Carnegie refused to permit his company to become a corporation, maintained it as a limited partnership, and retained a majority of the shares himself. Giving no hostages to the bankers, he used the firm's enormous profits to construct new plants, acquire raw materials, buy out competitors, and win fights with organized labor. His independent resources enabled him to go on building and spending even during depressions and thus to approach his goal of establishing an "integrated industry." He bought ore deposits in the Mesabi Range and ore ships on the Great Lakes, and he acquired docks, warehouses, and railroad lines to supply his great furnaces and mills with raw materials.

Carnegie had a remarkable gift for finding able lieutenants—men like Henry Clay Frick, Charles M. Schwab, Laurence C. Phipps, and Alexander R. Peacock. He pitted these men against one another in jealous competition, rewarding the successful with shares and partnerships. Like other capitalists of his day, he benefited from pools, rebates, and protective tariffs, but in time his power and resources became great enough to make him virtually independent of such devices. At the crest of his power he held the whole steel industry in his grasp. His trail to the top was strewn with ruined competitors, crushed partners, and broken labor movements. His bloody victory over labor at Homestead (see p. 438) had reestablished the twelve-hour day. Carnegie increased his annual production from 322,000 tons in 1890 to 3,000,000 tons in 1900. Over the same decade he and his lieutenants increased the annual profits of the Carnegie Steel Company from $5,400,000 in 1890 to $40,000,000 in 1900. Carnegie's own share of the 1900 profits was approximately $25,000,000.

In the meantime Pierpont Morgan turned his attention from railroads to steel, and the bankers challenged the industrialists for the control of heavy industry. The American Steel and Wire Company, the first big combination in steel, was constructed without his help. Then in the summer of 1898 Morgan swung his support to Judge Elbert H. Gary of Chicago and other Midwesterners who merged several big concerns to form the Federal Steel

Andrew Carnegie: steelmaster

Company, second in size only to Carnegie Steel. Quickly other mergers between hitherto competing steel firms sprang into being, "as if a giant magnet had moved over the surface of the industry," observed one historian. The next obvious move in the drive for mergers was to combine the combinations, that is, consolidate the whole industry into one vast supercorporation, the greatest in the world. Blocking that dream was the mighty Carnegie Steel Company and the known prejudice of its head against banker control. Even Morgan threw up his hands when it was proposed that he buy up Carnegie Steel outright; "I don't believe I could raise the money," he said. The new combinations for making finished steel products then decided in the summer of 1900 to produce their own raw steel, free themselves from dependence on Carnegie, and cancel their contracts with him. Carnegie's response was a cable from Skibo Castle, his summer home in Scotland, declaring open war: "Have no fear as to result. Victory certain." He proposed to go into the production of finished steel products himself and to drive all his competitors to the wall.

Alarmed at the prospect of a war that would place the new steel combinations in deadly peril and demoralize the whole industry, Morgan determined to buy out Carnegie and consolidate the supercorporation. After a night-long conference in the famous Morgan library, Charles M. Schwab agreed to take the matter up with Carnegie. The Scotsman scribbled a few figures on a scrap of paper, and Schwab took it to Morgan. The banker glanced at it and said, "I accept." There was no bargaining. The figure was nearly a half-billion dollars. In a few weeks Morgan pushed and pulled the big steel companies into combination and, on March 3, 1901, announced the organization of the United States Steel Corporation. The new concern brought under a single management three-fifths of the steel business of the country and was capitalized at nearly a billion and a half dollars.

Although U. S. Steel was never without competition within the industry, the uneasy popular sentiment about the gigantic deal was reflected in the words the humorist Finley Peter Dunne put in the mouth of his Irish saloonkeeper, "Mr. Dooley":

Pierpont Morgan calls in wan iv his office boys, th' presidint iv a national bank, an' says he, "James," he says, "take some change out iv th' damper an' r-run out an' buy Europe f'r me," he says. "I intind to re-organize it an' put it on a paying basis," he says. "Call up the Czar an' th' Pope an' th' Sultan an' th' Impror Willum, an' tell thim we won't need their savices afther nex' week," he says. "Give thim a year's salary in advance."

Rockefeller and the trusts. An industrial giant of power and influence comparable to that wielded by Carnegie was John D. Rockefeller, who did for oil what the Scotsman did for steel. The two contemporaries were strikingly different in temperament and taste: Carnegie was exuberant and communicative, Rockefeller silent and taciturn; Carnegie was a skeptic and an agnostic, Rockefeller a Bible-class teacher and a devout Baptist. In their business methods and their achievements, however, there were many similarities. Both men showed the same astuteness in selecting lieutenants and putting them in the right jobs, the same abhorrence of waste and gambling, the same ability to transform depressions into opportunities for building, buying, and expanding. The Standard Oil Company, founded in 1872 with Rockefeller its head, made ruthless use of railroad-rate discrimination, espionage, bogus companies, price-slashing, and other reprehensible practices. On the other hand, it had positive achievements to its credit, including improved and standardized products, the elimination of waste, and efficiency in distribution.

Rockefeller was the outstanding American exponent of consolidation in industry. Of the trend toward consolidation he wrote:

This movement was the origin of the whole system of modern economic administration. It has revolutionized the way of doing business all over the world. The time was ripe for it. It had to come, though all we saw at the moment was the need to save ourselves from wasteful conditions. . . . The day of combination is here to stay. Individualism has gone, never to return.

By "wasteful conditions" he meant the glutted markets in crude and refined oil and the disorder, uncertainty, and wild fluctuation of prices and profits that attended free competition among thousands of small producers and hundreds of small refiners. Rockefeller hated free competition and believed that monopoly was the way of the future. His early method of dealing with competitors was to gain unfair

John D. Rockefeller: consolidator

Standard Oil: "Wealth vs. Commonwealth"

advantage over them through special rates and secret rebates exacted from railroads.

The most notorious device of the sort was the short-lived South Improvement Company, by means of which Standard joined a few other oil companies in 1872 to demand special rates and secret advantages from the leading railroads in the Pennsylvania oil fields. They received not only large rebates on their own shipments but cash rebates on all shipments made by rivals outside the combination, as well as full and valuable reports on their competitors' business. The South Improvement scheme was soon exposed and had to be abandoned, but Standard continued to receive special advantages from the railroads and to use them to threaten or eliminate competitors. By such methods Standard Oil acquired some seventy-four refining companies and by 1878 was manufacturing a very large percentage of the national product of oil. When pipelines threatened the advantage gained through railroad favors, Standard quickly consolidated most of the pipelines in the Appalachian field into the United Pipe Lines Company, in which Standard had controlling interest. Independent producers and refiners sought to escape the monopoly by building a pipeline across the Appalachian Mountains to the seaboard. Standard waged unrelenting war on the independent Tidewater Pipe Company, which succeeded in completing its line, but in 1883 it signed an agreement that gave Standard 88½ percent of the business.

Rockefeller and his associates dealt competitors crushing blows with their nationwide marketing organization, which could put irresistible pressure on competitors and force surrender. They strengthened their position further by manufacturing all commodities necessary to the trade, from barrels to bungs. Referring to his competitors, Rockefeller said: "They had not the means to build pipe lines, bulk ships, tank wagons; they couldn't have their agents all over the country; couldn't manufacture their own acid, bungs, wicks, lamps, do their own cooperage—so many things; it ramified indefinitely." He was convinced that small-unit enterprise and free competition were things of the past.

Standard Oil speeded up the progress of consolidation and the suppression of competition by forming a trust, first set up in 1879 and then revised in 1882. The trust was an old legal device, but Standard Oil lawyers put it to new use. They created a board of nine trustees and persuaded all stockholders of twenty-seven competing oil companies to turn over their capital stock to the board and receive trust certificates in return. The trustees were now in a position to harmonize and direct the affairs of a huge aggregation of capital, for according to the Standard Oil Trust agreement they were authorized "to hold, control, and manage the said stock and interests for the exclusive use and benefit" of the parties to the agreement. With competition thus brought under control, profits soared.

The Standard Oil Trust became the model for many imitators. Other American industries were plagued by much the same anarchy that had prompted the leaders in railroads, steel, and oil to force consolidation upon warring competitors. They had tried associations, agreements, and pools, but the trust had obvious advantages over the older devices. With the Standard Oil Trust as a pattern, some fifteen new trusts appeared during the 1880s, including the American Cottonseed Oil Trust, the National Linseed Oil Trust, the National Lead Trust, the Whiskey Trust, and the American Sugar Refining Company.

The trust movement encountered active popular suspicion and hostility from the start. The American creed, bred of an agrarian heritage, held that business should be organized in small units, that competition should be unfettered, and that opportunity should be open to all. The trusts were an affront to this traditional faith: they were gigantic, powerful, even awe-inspiring. To the public, the trusts were the product of an evil plot born of greed, and that was the way the cartoonists pictured them in the newspapers and journals and the way popular political leaders described them in their speeches in the eighties. The popular attitude was not without foundation, for the trusts often did use their enormous power to the detriment of both consumers and small businessmen. A demand for government action against the trusts grew as rapidly as the trusts themselves. Even the big-business community, increasingly aware that mergers and trusts were not likely to stabilize and control industry, looked to the federal government for the answer.

As in railroad regulation, the state legislatures took the lead against the trusts. The laws they passed were never very effective, however, and the Wabash decision of 1886 limited the states here as it did in the regulation of railroads and left the problem up to the federal government. The growth of the trusts had stirred uneasiness in the East and the South as well as the West, and by the campaign of 1888 all political parties of significance had inserted antitrust planks into their platforms. In that year John Sherman of Ohio submitted an antitrust bill in the Senate, one of many similar bills introduced that year. Debate in Congress revealed concern for the interests of both the consumer and the small business-proprietor. It illustrated both the "folklore" of the old capitalism and apprehension about the new. The so-called Sherman Antitrust Act became law on July 2, 1890.

On the face of it the new act would seem to have spelled the end of every trust or trust-like combination. In effect it wrote common-law doctrine against monopoly into a federal statute. The opening sentence of the first section declares, "Every contract, combination in the form of trust or otherwise, or conspiracy, in restraint of trade or commerce among the several States, or with foreign nations, is hereby declared to be illegal." And the second section pronounces guilty of a misdemeanor "every person who shall monopolize, or attempt to monopolize, or combine or conspire with any other person or persons, to monopolize any part of the trade or commerce among the several States, or with foreign nations." The word "person" was specifically defined to include corporations, and the act fixed penalties, as the Interstate Commerce Act had not, for violations.

Efforts to enforce the act during the 1890s were not very vigorous, and clever lawyers found loopholes and various ways of evading its provisions. Some trusts merely reorganized as huge corporations, while others pointed the way to the future by finding refuge in holding companies—that is, giant financial structures that held enough stock in member companies to control their policies. In the first five years after the act was passed, twenty-five new combinations came into being. Then in 1895 the first case under the Sherman Act was decided by the Supreme Court. A suit against the E. C. Knight Company of Philadelphia charged that in selling out to the American Sugar Refining Company it was guilty of furthering monopoly. Although the purchase rounded out one of the most complete monopolies in the country, the court decided that it did not violate the antitrust act. The court's reasoning was that manufacturing was not "commerce" within the meaning of the law, and that monopoly of manufacturing without "direct" effect on commerce was not subject to regulation by the federal government. *United States* v. *Knight* was an extreme instance of laissez-faire interpretation of the Constitution. After this signal that the law offered virtually no obstacle, consolidation went forward with a rush, and literally hundreds of new combinations sprang up in the next five years.

The course of Standard Oil from trust to holding company illustrates the trend. The company formally abandoned the trust agreement of 1882 under an Ohio court order in 1892, but in practice the same nine men who had served as trustees continued to conduct the business of the member companies for five years after the trust was formally dissolved. Charged with evading the court order, the trust reorganized in 1899 as a holding company under the laws of New Jersey, which permitted corporations of that state to own and control corporations of other states. The Standard Oil Company of New Jersey simply increased its stock some tenfold and exchanged it for stock of the member companies. These in turn elected directors of the New Jersey company, who carried on in the place of the old trustees. With concentration of control unimpaired and power enhanced instead of diminished, Standard made money as never before. In the eight years following its reorganization as a holding company, annual dividends on its stock varied between 30 and 48 percent.

The merger movement was restricted mainly to a minority of the dominant American industries and lasted only a few years. It reached its peak in 1899, when 1,208 firms disappeared and merger capitalizations rose to $2,263 million. It declined sharply after that, in spite of the formation of U. S. Steel in 1901. Contrary to expectation, most of the mergers brought neither greater profit nor less competition.

The technology of centralization.
Concentration of ownership did not always mean centralization of control. But the management of a vast railroad network, a continent-wide industry, or an international market required a new technology of business administration and communication. American inventors outdid themselves to meet these demands. The number of patents issued to inventors jumped from fewer than two thousand a year in the 1850s to more than thirteen thousand a year in the 1870s and better than twenty-one thousand a year in the 1880s and 1890s. In those days the typical inventor was not a trained engineer in an industrial or university laboratory but an individual tinkerer who frequently operated on a shoestring.

Such a man was Christopher L. Sholes, printer and journalist from Pennsylvania and Wisconsin, who invented a typewriter in 1867. He sold his rights to the Remington Arms Company, which put the typewriter on the market in 1875. The year Sholes invented the typewriter, E. A. Callahan of Boston developed a superior stock ticker. In the summer

Alexander Graham Bell: he made iron talk

of 1866 Cyrus W. Field employed new techniques to repair and improve his transatlantic cable, broken since 1858, and stock quotations spanned the ocean. Numerous other inventions, including the adding maching (1888), quickened the pace of business transactions.

None of these inventions, however, could rival the importance of the telephone. This was the work of Alexander Graham Bell, a Scotsman who was educated in Edinburgh and London, emigrated to Canada in 1870, when he was twenty-three, and then to Boston two years later. As a teacher of speech to the deaf, he formed the ambition to "make iron talk"—to transmit speech electrically. His experiments over three years resulted in the magnetoelectric telephone. He transmitted the first intelligible sentence on March 10, 1876, and a year later conducted a conversation between Boston and New York. The inventor and his supporters organized the Bell Telephone Company in 1877 and promptly plunged into law suits to defend their patent. The most formidable challenger was the Western Union Telegraph Company, which had originally spurned an opportunity to buy the patent for the "scientific toy" for a mere

Thomas Alva Edison: he built his own invention factory

$100,000. Western Union settled out of court and left the field to Bell and his company, which continued to win hundreds of suits, improve the telephone, buy out competitors, and expand facilities. In 1885 the directors of Bell, led by Theodore N. Vail, organized the American Telephone and Telegraph Company. By 1900 it had become the holding company for the whole system, with some thirty-five subsidiaries and a capitalization of a quarter of a billion dollars.

The use of electricity for light is justly linked with the name of Thomas Alva Edison, who outdid his contemporary Bell as an inventor. The son of a Canadian who settled and prospered in Ohio, Edison grew up without formal schooling. He became a telegraph-operator and while still quite young made some very profitable inventions to improve transmission. He then established himself as a businessman-inventor and built his own "invention factory," forerunner of the modern industrial-research laboratory, at Menlo Park, New Jersey, in 1876. There in 1877 he invented the phonograph, and in later years his laboratories turned out hundreds of inventions or improvements, including the storage battery, the motion-picture projector, an electric dynamo, and an electric locomotive. The electric light required a vacuum bulb with a durable filament. Edison made one that burned for forty hours in 1879 and improved it until it was commercially practicable. With the backing of J. Pierpont Morgan he organized the Edison Illuminating Company and moved to New York City to install an electric-light plant.

On September 4, 1882, in the presence of Morgan, Edison threw a switch and the House of Morgan, the New York Stock Exchange, the New York *Times,* the New York *Herald,* and many smaller buildings in lower Manhattan began to glow with incandescent light.

Edison's plant used direct current, but in order to transmit electricity any distance its voltage had to be stepped up and then stepped down again. For this purpose alternating current and transformers were necessary. George Westinghouse of Pittsburgh, who had invented the railroad air brake in 1869, developed a power plant and a transformer in 1886 that could transmit high-voltage alternating current efficiently, safely, and cheaply over long distances.

For this type of current to be converted into mechanical power, an alternating-current motor had to be developed. In 1888 Nikola Tesla, a Hungarian engineer who immigrated to the United States in 1884, invented such a motor. Westinghouse and his associates bought the patent, improved it with the aid of Tesla, and dramatically demonstrated the practicability of alternating current by illuminating the Columbian Exposition at Chicago in 1893 and by harnessing the might of Niagara Falls and transmitting the power over the countryside. While American industry continued to depend mainly upon steam and water for power until the end of the century, factories no longer had to hover around waterfalls and coal supplies. They were now ready for the electrical revolution that came in the twentieth century.

Laissez-faire conservatism

The Gospel of Wealth. A survey of private fortunes conducted in 1892 revealed that there were 4,047 millionaries in the United States. These were new fortunes; very few of them dated from before the Civil War, when a millionaire was a rarity. Only eighty-four of the millionaires of 1892 were in agriculture, and most of those were cattle barons. The fortunes of the new plutocracy were based on industry, trade, railroads. The new plutocrats were the masters and directors of the economic revolution that was changing the face of American society.

To say that these men were conservative is to put a strain on customary usage of the word, for conservatives are usually opposed

to change and devoted to tradition. Yet these men flouted tradition and preached progress. To confuse customary usage further, they adopted the slogan "laissez faire," which was traditionally the doctrine of Jeffersonian and Jacksonian liberals and radicals. In one of the strangest reversals in the history of political thought, the new conservatives took over virtually the whole liberal vocabulary of concepts and slogans, including "democracy," "liberty," "equality," "opportunity," and "individualism," and turned it against the liberals. In short, they gave an economic and material turn to ethical and idealistic concepts. Man became economic man, democracy was identified with capitalism, liberty with property and

The question of motive enters into any consideration either of economic vision or of business ethics; and it is important because some writers of the muckraking school have grievously misconstrued the motives ... of a whole generation of business leaders. They sum up these motives in the word ''greed,'' as if it were greed which led Carnegie to build steel mills, Rockefeller to organize the oil industry, Westinghouse to develop the electrical industry, and Ford to manufacture motor cars. If we wish to misuse the word greed we can apply it in many contexts. We can say that Shakespeare was greedy for fame, Lincoln greedy for political power, and Duse greedy for applause. But such a word means nothing in the analysis of motive. What these figures were really interested in was competitive achievement, self-expression, and the imposition of their wills on a given environment. And these were precisely the motives which actuated Carnegie, Westinghouse, and Rockefeller.... The men who built the really towering economic structures were not thinking primarily of dollars, or they would have halted at the first story.

From Allan Nevins, *John D. Rockefeller,* 1940.

If our civilization is destroyed ... it will not be by ... barbarians from below. Our barbarians come from above. Our great money-makers have sprung in one generation into seats of power kings do not know. The forces and the wealth are new, and have been the opportunity of new men. Without restraints of culture, experience, the pride, or even the inherited caution of class or rank, these men, intoxicated, think they are the wave instead of the float, and that they have created the business which has created them. To them science is but a never-ending repertoire of investments stored up by nature for the syndicates, government but a fountain of franchises, the nations but customers in squads, and a million the unit of a new arithmetic of wealth written for them. They claim a power without control, exercised through forms which make it secret, anonymous, and perpetual. The possibilities of its gratification have been widening before them without interruption since they began, and even at a thousand millions they will feel no satiation and will see no place to stop. They are gluttons of luxury and power, rough, unsocialized, believing that mankind must be kept terrorized.

From Henry Demarest Lloyd, *Wealth Against Commonwealth,* 1894.

the use of it, equality with opportunity for gain, and progress with economic change and the accumulation of capital. God and nature were thus in league with the Gospel of Wealth.

The new doctrine was conservative, however, in the sense that it was bent on defending the status quo, conserving the privileges by which vast accumulations of wealth were gained, and preventing government interference with those privileges. The laissez-faire conservatives naturally found comfort in classical economics, and those who had heard of them found special fascination in the biological theories of Charles Darwin and the socio-logical theory of Herbert Spencer. The ideas of the great English biologist, which were taken up by American scientists after the Civil War, found early acceptance in the older colleges and were spread abroad by popular writers and lecturers. Herbert Spencer, an English philosopher, found zealous American apostles in John Fiske, a prolific writer and lecturer, and Edward L. Youmans, self-appointed salesman of Spencer's ideas. Spencer applied biological concepts, especially the concept of natural selection, to social principles and justified the unimpeded struggle for existence on the ground that ''survival of the fittest'' made for human progress. State interference in behalf of the weak would only impede progress. The tooth-and-claw competition of the postwar American economy prepared the perfect market for ideas that glorified laissez faire as the secret of progress. The people could readily see the industrial struggles around them in terms of the Darwinian jungle. It is not surprising that Darwin and Spencer were more readily acclaimed and more widely admired in America than they were in their native England. ''The peculiar condition of American society,'' wrote the preacher Henry Ward Beecher to Spencer, ''has made your writings far more fruitful and quickening here than in Europe.'' By 1903 more than 368,000 volumes of Spencer's works had been sold in the United States, and many Americans who had never opened one of them or even heard of the author spoke glibly of ''the struggle for survival,'' ''natural selection,'' and ''the survival of the fittest.'' So thoroughly did these concepts become associated with laissez-faire conservatism that the new doctrine has appropriately been called ''social Darwinism.''

Professors, clergymen, and intellectuals, as well as businessmen, were captivated by the new philosophy. Professor William Graham Sumner of Yale, the most articulate and influential exponent, in an essay called ''The Concentration of Wealth: Its Economic Justification,'' wrote,

> What matters it then that some millionaires are idle, or silly, or vulgar. . . . The millionaires are a product of natural selection, acting on the whole body of men to pick out those who can meet the requirement of certain work to be done. . . . They get high wages and live in luxury, but the bargain is a good one for society.

William Lawrence, the Episcopal Bishop of Massachusetts, announced, ''Now we are in a position to affirm that neither history, experience, nor the Bible necessarily sustains the common distrust of the effect of material wealth on morality. . . . Godliness is in league with riches. . . . The race is to the strong.'' Rockefeller said, ''The growth of a large business is merely a survival of the fittest . . . the working out of a law of nature and a law of God.'' Carnegie admitted that while this ''may sometimes be hard for the individual, it is best for the race, because it insures the survival of the fittest in every department.''

By the time it had become fully elaborated, the Gospel of Wealth and its corollaries of social Darwinism included many propositions widely accepted. Among them were the following: (1) that the American economy was controlled for the benefit of all by a natural aristocracy and that these leaders were brought to the top by a competitive struggle that weeded out the weak, the incompetent, and the unfit and selected the strong, the able, and the wise; (2) that politicians were not subject to rigorous natural selection and therefore could not be trusted to the same degree as businessmen; (3) that the state should confine itself to police activities of protecting property and maintaining order and that if it interfered with economic affairs it would upset the beneficent effect of natural selection; (4) that slums and poverty were the unfortunate but inevitable negative results of the competitive struggle and that state intervention to eliminate them was misguided; (5) that the stewardship of wealth obliged the rich to try to ameliorate social injustice.

Though these ideas may be regarded as a rationalization of the rule of a privileged group, they were by no means confined to members of that group. They also became the common assumption of millions, a sort of folk faith. The popular demand for success stories like those in the novels of Horatio Alger, whose 119 books were filled with rags-to-riches heroes for boy readers, suggests that the mass of Americans were as firm in their faith in the Gospel of Work as they were in their faith in the Gospel of Wealth. The business creed absorbed and fostered both faiths for its own purposes.

In the Supreme Court the Gospel of Wealth found institutional support of great prestige and incomparable value. Under the persistent tutelage of Justice Stephen J. Field, the court had been converted by the late eighties to the view that Herbert Spencer's *Social Statics* coincided remarkably well with the will of the Founding Fathers and the soundest moral precepts of the ages. Interpreting the ''due process'' clause of the Fourteenth Amendment as a protection intended to cover the substantive interests of corporate enterprise, the Court proceeded to declare state regulatory measures unconstitutional on the ground that they deprived corporations of property without due process of law. By the end of the century, the Court's laissez-faire interpretation of the Constitution had debarred the states in

This, then, is held to be the duty of the man of wealth: To set an example of modest, unostentatious living, shunning display or extravagance; to provide moderately for the legitimate wants of those dependent upon him; and, after doing so, to consider all surplus revenues which come to him simply as trust funds, which he is called upon to administer, and strictly bound as a matter of duty to administer in the manner which, in his judgment, is best calculated to produce the most beneficial results for the community—the man of wealth thus becoming the mere trustee and agent for his poorer brethren, bringing to their service his superior wisdom, experience, and ability to administer, doing for them better than they would or could do for themselves.

From Andrew Carnegie, *The Gospel of Wealth and Other Essays,* 1901.

Andrew Carnegie: the duties of wealth

What constitutes the rightful basis of property? What is it that enables a man justly to say of a thing, ''It is mine''? From what springs the sentiment which acknowledges his exclusive right as against all the world? Is it not, primarily, the right of a man to himself, to the use of his own powers, to the enjoyment of the fruits of his own exertions? Is it not this individual right, which springs from and is testified to by the natural facts of individual organization—the fact that each particular pair of hands obey a particular brain and are related to a particular stomach; the fact that each man is a definite, coherent, independent whole—which alone justifies individual ownership? As a man belongs to himself, so his labor when put in concrete form belongs to him....

If production give to the producer the right to exclusive possession and enjoyment, there can rightfully be no exclusive possession and enjoyment of anything not the production of labor, and the recognition of private property in land is a wrong.

From Henry George, *Progress and Poverty,* 1879.

Henry George: the nature of property

many fields from the exercise of ancient police powers for the protection of the public interest and the welfare of workers.

Social critics and dissenters. The Gospel of Wealth and the Darwinian apology for unrestrained capitalism did not meet with universal acceptance, however, for those doctrines were challenged by social critics, economists, and clergymen. The dissenters themselves were influenced by Darwin, but they interpreted the social implications of his theories in a different way. They rejected the survival-of-the-fittest concept of social progress and found a place for ethical values in economic theory, as well as a need for governmental intervention to restrain the strong and protect the weak. A strong religious impulse often motivated the nonclerical as well as the clerical critics of social Darwinism.

Lester Frank Ward, one of the founders of sociology in America, was an outspoken critic of Spencer's theories. Ward took a job in a Washington bureau in 1865, after service in the Union army, and remained in government work for some forty years. Largely self-educated, he compensated for his impoverished background by astonishing feats of learning. He mastered ten languages and several fields of science in addition to sociology, and, when he finally found acceptance in academic life, he entitled a course he gave at Brown University ''A Survey of All Knowledge.'' His first book, *Dynamic Sociology* (1883), was a prodigious work of fourteen hundred pages that was not easily or widely read. He never achieved the acclaim or the influence his conservative rival, Professor Sumner, did. Ward pointed out that there was a difference between animal and human economics. Bears have claws, but men have intelligence. Darwinian laws governed the former, but the human mind transformed the environment of human economics and substituted rational choice for natural selection. This was as it should be, for nature was terribly wasteful in her crude methods of evolution. Unrestrained competition actually prevented the fittest from surviving, and the doctrine of laissez faire killed off whatever benefits competition conferred by encouraging monopoly and by leaving no competitors to compete. For competition to survive, government regulation was necessary. Ward believed in social planning and had great faith in education. "Thus far," he wrote, "social progress has in a certain awkward manner taken care of itself, but in the near future it will have to be cared for." The caring, he said, should be done by social engineers, scientific planners, and managers of society.

A second self-taught social philosopher of the age, and one of the most original economists of the time, was Henry George, author of the famous book *Progress and Poverty* (1879). Born in Philadelphia, George traveled in the Orient and in 1868 settled in California, where he had ample opportunity to observe the land speculation, land monopoly, and social distress that played so important a part in his economics. Addressing himself to the problem of unequal distribution of wealth, he inveighed against the "shocking contrast between monstrous wealth and debasing want." Wealth is produced, he concluded, by applying labor to land, and capital is the surplus above the cost of labor. Labor therefore creates all capital. But capital, by withholding advantageous land sites until their value has been enhanced by labor in adjacent areas, reaps a profit out of all proportion to its contribution. This profit George called the "unearned increment." Since land should no more be monopolized than air and sunshine, George's solution was to tax land in such a fashion as to appropriate the unearned increment. This was to be done by a "single tax," which would make other taxes unnecessary. After 1885 he put aside the hope that this would result in common ownership of the land

by the people. George's book and his lectures won him a political following at home and abroad and enabled him to make a strong showing as candidate for mayor of New York in 1886.

Another political aspiration born of a book was the Nationalist movement; this time the book was Edward Bellamy's *Looking Backward* (1888). The most successful of several utopian novels published during the eighties, Bellamy's book "looked backward" to the benighted 1880s from the collectivized society of the year 2000 A.D. By that time selfishness has been eliminated by the abolition of corporate property and the nationalization of industry. Competition is seen to have killed nineteenth-century society and its individualism. "Competition," says the protagonist, "which is the instinct of selfishness, is another word for dissipation of energy, while combination is the secret of efficient production." Bellamy's attack on the ethic of "survival of the fittest" appealed to a wide variety of people, who for a time sought to maintain a political organization. Nationalist clubs and periodicals fostered municipal ownership of utilities and public ownership of railroads. As agrarian reform mounted in the nineties, however, the Nationalists tended to join the farmers' parties and abandon their own organization.

From the viewpoint of a later day, the debate over laissez-faire doctrine and social Darwinism appears confused and paradoxical. If free competition was the goal of laissez faire, the industrialists who hated competition and sought to restrain it would seem to have embraced the wrong doctrine. If social Darwinism taught hands off by the government, the businessmen who sought subsidies, protection, and favors from the government again seemed inconsistent. But insofar as these doctrines were useful for the defense of the status quo and the discouragement of efforts to reform or change society by conscious purpose the conservatives were right in embracing them and the radicals in rejecting them.

The house of labor

Man and the machine. In the long run industrialization raises the living standard and increases the opportunities of labor, but around the world labor has discovered that the revolution that establishes industrialization

comes at heavy cost and that the worker's adjustment to the machine and the factory way of life is often painful and difficult. In America the labor shortage that had persisted since colonial times had kept the level of wages higher than the level that prevailed abroad; and yet the American worker had his full share of troubles in the grim iron age of industry.

Many of the adjustments the worker had to make were hard to understand and painful to accept, for they meant loss of status and surrender of independence. The skilled craftsman who owned the tools he used was likely to be an individualist who took pride in the quality of his product and enjoyed a strong bargaining position. The new factory discipline offered a humbler role and a lower status. In the factory the worker surrendered his tools, nearly all the creative pride he took in his product, most of his independence, and much of his bargaining power. He became the tender of a machine that set the work pace and the employee of owners whom he probably never met and never saw. The craftsmanship that had been the skilled worker's source of pride and security was no longer of any significance, for his place at the machine could be taken by an unskilled worker. The growing impersonality of his relations to his work and his employer and the ever increasing size of the industrial organization meant a sacrifice in security, identity, and the satisfactions that bestow meaning and value on work.

Adjustment would have been easier had the change been less swift and the worker better prepared. But the mechanization and expansion of the factory system hit a breathtaking pace during the 1880s. Between 1880 and 1890 the total capital invested in the production of machinery increased two and a half times, and the average investment in machinery increased 200 percent for each establishment and 50 percent for each employee. The manufacturer, with all his capital tied up in new machinery, was driven to seek a rapid return on his investment, generally at low prices in a highly competitive market. Real wages actually rose, but the hard-pressed employer often made economies at the expense of the unskilled factory workers, who suffered from working conditions that impaired their safety, their comfort, and their health. The great body of legislation that now protects factory workers had not yet been written in the eighties and nineties. Employers thought nothing of using detectives and armed force to thwart the organization of labor unions, and in "company towns," where all houses, stores, and services were company-owned, employers subjected workers to end-

less harassments and petty tyranny. There was nothing but the urging of conscience and the weak protest of labor to keep employers from cutting costs at the expense of their workers.

The average weekly wages of common laborers remained less than $9 throughout the nineties, and farm laborers got less than half that amount. After the depression of the seventies, however, there was a fairly steady increase in real wages—for those who had jobs. The rise in real wages helps explain labor's attachment to the system and its relative indifference to socialism. The millions who suffered unemployment during the depressions of the last three decades of the century were not even enumerated, much less assisted, by the government. The most insistent demand of organized labor was for the eight-hour day, but the main result was the adoption of a federal law passed in 1869, and amended in 1892, limiting the work day of federal employees to eight hours. In private industry, however, most workers continued to work a ten-hour day and a six-day week, and in steel and other industries they worked even longer. The accident toll taken by heedless negligence, and the damage done to workers' health by poor ventilation and lighting, dust and fumes—in so far as the facts were known at all—were charged off as the cost of progress.

A special handicap of American labor was its lack of homogeneity. Workers were fragmented by race and color, as well as by geography, philosophy, concepts of organization, style of protest, and national origin. Some formed exclusive groups to protect their own privilege and to keep underprivileged groups at bay. Between 1882 and 1900 there were fifty strikes waged against the employment of black labor. Blacks sometimes served as strikebreakers, thereby increasing the resentment of white workers.

Immigrants formed the largest segment of the American labor force, except in the South, where few of them settled. There had been immigrant workers from the start in the United States, and while the percentage in the labor force remained about the same as it had been since the Civil War, immigrants were coming in greater numbers and from different parts of Europe, mainly the southern and eastern countries. Nineteenth-century immigration reached high tide in the 1880s, when nearly $5\frac{1}{4}$ million immigrants arrived, $2\frac{1}{2}$ million more than had come in the seventies and $1\frac{1}{2}$

million more than were to come in the nineties. Set apart by language and culture, accustomed to lower wages and living standards, the newcomers often concentrated as ethnic groups in certain industries—Slavs in anthracite, Jews in the garment industry. Native workers often looked down on them with contempt and spoke of work for which they were suited as "foreign jobs." The new immigrants crowded into the coal-mining and steel industries, with each wave pushing the earlier comers a step up the ladder. The bitterest and most implacable labor opposition to immigrants was directed at the Asiatics, particularly the Chinese of California. Supported by labor organizations in the East, the Californians persuaded Congress in 1882 to suspend admission of Chinese immigrants for ten years.

Unions and strikes. For a long time the attitude of American labor toward unions and collective bargaining was typically that of the skilled craftsman or the small shopkeeper. Native workers, and many immigrants as well, were reluctant to abandon the American dream of rising higher and higher in the social scale. Instead of accepting the new industrial order and its conditions, they looked back nostalgically to the past and longed for the good old days. Longings of this sort found expression in such slogans as "every man his own master" or "every man his own employer." Labor unions remained very weak throughout the nineteenth century, embracing not more than 1 or 2 percent of the total labor force and less than 10 percent of the industrial workers.

During and after the Civil War the typical national trade union was designed primarily to protect the status of skilled craftsmen. In 1866 William H. Sylvis, an iron-molder of Pennsylvania, attempted to unite the trade unions into a single organization called the National Labor Union. This organization, of which Sylvis became president in 1868, bore no resemblance to modern labor unions. It was led by visionaries and idealists who did not believe in strikes and who were unconcerned with the immediate needs of working people, apart from the eight-hour day. Sylvis stressed long-range reforms and humanitarian demands, and admitted farmers' societies and advocates of women's rights as members. The organization changed its name to the National Labor party in 1871, and after a feeble show-

ing in the election of 1872 the new party went to pieces.

With many of the same generous impulses and naive assumptions, the Noble and Holy Order of the Knights of Labor was founded in 1869. A secret fraternal order with high-flown titles and elaborate rituals, the Knights sought to unite all labor and welcomed all "toilers" of whatever color, race, nationality, or craft, whether skilled or unskilled. They excluded only gamblers, bankers, liquor-dealers, and a few others—apparently on moralistic grounds. Utopian and nostalgic in many of their views, the Knights frowned on the use of the strike and promoted dreams of restoring the past. Their labor program, however, included demands for a federal bureau of statistics, equal pay for both sexes, the eight-hour day, and the abolition of child and prison labor. The two hundred or more consumer and producer cooperatives the Knights founded elicited great enthusiasm but little profit. Many of their political demands resembled those of contemporary farmers' organizations, for they included paper money, an income tax, abolition of the national bank, and Prohibition.

The Knights, like Sylvis, however, grasped one important fact of the new economy: that the consolidation of industry made necessary the consolidation of labor. They founded their General Assembly in 1878 with a view to centralizing control over labor in order to combat the monopolistic power of corporations. In 1879 they elected Terence V. Powderly as their Grand Master Workman. The dominant figure in the Order during the years of its power and influence, Powderly was described at a labor convention in 1886 as elegantly dressed in "double-breasted, black, broadcloth coat, stand-up collar, plain tie, dark trousers and narrow small shoes," surrounded by "horny-fisted sons of toil" and acting "like Queen Victoria at a national Democratic convention." Powderly constantly preached against strikes, and yet it was as a result of strikes in 1885–86 that the Order made its most sensational gains. These were spontaneous revolts rather than organized strikes, but under their stimulus membership soared from about one hundred thousand to over seven hundred thousand. The strength of the Order quickly ebbed after the upheavals of 1886, and two years later its membership had fallen to two hundred thousand. By 1893 it was virtually defunct.

William H. Sylvis:
unionizer

Terence V. Powderly:
Knight of Labor

In the meantime the American Federation of Labor, founded in 1881, was hammering out a labor philosophy somewhat more closely related to the realities of the industrial economy and more in harmony with the future. Rejecting the utopian radicalism of the Knights of Labor, the AFL foreswore political goals for economic objectives. Instead of embracing the brotherhood of all workers, it devoted its attention to gaining concrete benefits for skilled workers organized along craft lines. It was a loose alliance of national trade unions, each of which retained a large amount of autonomy, with jurisdiction over its own affairs and with the power to call its own strikes. Unlike the Knights, the AFL did not hesitate to acknowledge the strike and the boycott as legitimate means of collective bargaining. These principles were fully formulated by 1881 and reaffirmed when the AFL was reorganized in 1886.

As its first president the AFL elected Samuel Gompers, who retained the office for nearly forty years. An immigrant boy, born in London in 1850, Gompers grew up in the trade-union movement. Under the impact of his experience in America he gradually put aside his earlier leanings to socialism and slowly shaped a more conservative approach to the problems of labor. He felt that labor should accept the economic system and should try to win for itself a respectable place as a ''legitimate'' group within that system, as legitimate as business or the church. And to do so, he argued, labor would have to struggle day by day for higher wages and lower hours. Gompers strove to impose order by resolving jurisdictional disputes between unions and by consolidating local unions in state and national federations. The AFL grew as the Knights declined; in fifteen years its membership topped the million mark.

Labor's struggle to win acceptance and to improve its lot was marked by an extraordinary number of strikes and lockouts, conflicts that sometimes flared into bloodshed, particularly in time of depression. In July 1877 a series of wage cuts and abortive strikes provoked an upheaval of insurrectionary violence along the trunk lines of three big railroads. In the first show of violence, along the B&O, federal troops were called in after a mob intimidated state militia. In Pittsburgh the community joined the strikers against the Pennsylvania Railroad and destroyed $5 million worth of property before

Chicago anarchists, 1886

being dispersed with heavy loss of life. Other disturbances broke out in Philadelphia, Harrisburg, Reading, Scranton, Buffalo, and Toledo, and farther west in St. Louis, Chicago, and San Francisco. Scores of people lost their lives, and property valued at millions of dollars went up in flames. The courts clamped down, the police became more ruthless, and the public began to withdraw its sympathy from the labor movement. Another upsurge of labor militancy occurred during the mid-eighties. With the Knights of Labor at the peak of their strength the loose rhetoric of labor solidarity ceased to be merely verbal and materialized in general strikes, sympathetic work stoppage, and nationwide boycotts and political demonstrations. During 1886, a climactic year in labor history, 610,000 men were out of work because of strikes, lockouts, or shutdowns due to strikes, more than three times the average of the five preceding years. Then on May 4, during an anarchist demonstration against police brutalities at Haymarket Square in Chicago, a bomb was thrown that killed a policeman and fatally wounded six other persons. A jury found eight anarchists guilty, and four were hanged, though the identity of the bomb-thrower was never established. The incident smeared the whole labor movement,

Troops at the Pullman strike, 1894

especially the Knights, with the charge of anarchism and subjected labor to public suspicion and hostility.

Resort to violence was common in the turbulent nineties, but often labor was merely replying to force with force. In the remote Coeur d'Alene district of Idaho, company guards and miners fought it out in 1892 with rifles and dynamite until at last federal troops came in, crushed the strike, and turned the miners' jobs over to strikebreakers. At Carnegie's Homestead steel plant in Pennsylvania the same year thirty-eight hundred members of the Amalgamated Association of Iron and Steel Workers struck over wage cuts and working conditions. As a preparation for breaking the strike, Henry C. Frick, the manager, imported three hundred Pinkerton detectives. When they arrived at the plant on barges, the strikers resisted and a gun fight ensued that resulted in the death of three detectives and ten strikers, the wounding of a much larger number, and the surrender of the detectives. The sufferings of the workers stirred great public sympathy, a sympathy that was not entirely alienated by the attempt of an anarchist, who had no connection with the strike, to assassinate Frick. In the end, however, the strike failed miserably, and its failure destroyed unionism in the steel industry for many years to come.

The great depression that started in 1893 (see p. 482) brought on a new wave of wage cuts, layoffs, and strikes. More men were thrown out of work by strikes in 1894, a year of exceptional unemployment and labor violence, than in any previous year. The most important strike of that year, and of many years to come, was the big railroad strike centering in Chicago. It originated not among railway workers but among factory workers in George M. Pullman's "model" company town just south of Chicago. The men were driven to desperation by five wage cuts in one year and no reduction in the high rents charged for company houses. The Pullman workers had recently joined the New American Railway Union, headed by Eugene V. Debs and frowned on by the older Railway Brotherhoods of the AFL. Although Debs urged caution, his union voted to refuse to handle Pullman cars if the management would not accept arbitration of the strike. Pullman rejected all arbitration, and the General Managers Association came to his aid by dismissing switchmen who boycotted his cars. The union then struck against the railroads and by the end of June 1894 nearly all railroad men on roads west of Chicago were on strike.

Acting for the railroads, the General Managers Association then appealed directly to the federal government to intervene with armed force and end the strike. There had been no violence so far, and federal intervention with troops was a move that Governor John P. Altgeld strongly opposed. Railroad lawyers had no trouble persuading President Cleveland and Attorney General Richard Olney that intervention could nevertheless be justified on the ground that the strike had obstructed the delivery of United States mail. Actually, the railroads themselves refused, against the union's wishes, to attach mail cars to trains boycotting Pullman cars. Nevertheless, Olney secured an injunction against the union, and on July 4 Cleveland sent some two thousand troops to Chicago to enforce the injunction and protect the mails. After the troops arrived, the union completely lost control of the situation, and mobs of looters destroyed cars and burned and stole property. Twelve people were killed and many arrested at the scene, but none was a striker. The effect of the troop action was to break the strike, a result that Olney, by his own confession, intended to accomplish.

The failure of the Pullman strike had important consequences for the future of American labor. Debs and other union officials were tried and sentenced to jail for contempt of court in disobeying the injunction against the union. The Supreme Court in upholding the sentence gave the use of the injunction in labor disputes a prestige it had never before enjoyed. And the government in suggesting that a strike might be construed as a conspiracy in restraint of trade under the Sherman Antitrust Act placed a powerful weapon in the hands of management for use against unions. Another unforeseen consequence of the Pullman strike and the court's decision was to bring into national prominence for the first time the name of Eugene V. Debs. Within a few years he became the foremost leader of the socialist movement in the country, a position he held during the years when that movement enjoyed its greatest strength.

Any realistic account of the ordeal of industrialization in America will tell of heedless waste and ruthless exploitation, of cutthroat competition and consolidation. Whatever economic progress came out of the grim struggle—and undoubtedly much was gained—was purchased at a high cost in brutalized labor, wasted resources, and deterioration in business and public ethics. Historians who emphasize the necessity for industrialization and the advantages ultimately derived from it remind us that the costs of industrialization have never been low and that when reckoned in human suffering and social turmoil the price has been even more appalling in other countries than in the United States. And in all fairness, the American ordeal should be judged in comparison with that of England, which preceded it, and that of Russia, which came after it. In neither case does the American record, as bad as it was, suffer by comparison.

Suggestions for reading

E. C. Kirkland, *Industry Comes of Age: Business, Labor, and Public Policy, 1860–1897** (1961), is a survey of superior quality. A much briefer sketch of value is S. P. Hays, *The Response to Industrialism: 1885–1914** (1957). J. A. Garraty, *The New Commonwealth, 1877–1890** (1968), R. H. Wiebe, *The Search for Order: 1877–1920** (1968), I. M. Tarbell, *The Nationalizing of Business, 1878–1898* (1936), and T. C. Cochran and William Miller, *The Age of Enterprise** (1942), contain excellent chapters. Two older books still worthwhile are L. C. A. Knowles, *Economic Development in the Nineteenth Century* (1932), and D. A. Wells, *Recent Economic Change* (1890). William Miller, ed., *Men in Business** (1952), has illuminating essays.

The railroad establishment of the period is described in G. R. Taylor and I. D. Neu, *The American Railroad Network, 1861–1890* (1956). The importance of railroads to the economy is questioned by R. W. Fogel, *Railroads and American Economic Growth: Essays in Econometric History** (1964). Railroading in the West is treated in R. E. Riegel, *The Story of the Western Railroads** (1926), and R. C. Overton, *Burlington West* (1941), and *Gulf to Rockies* (1953); in New England by E. C. Kirkland, *Men, Cities and Transportation*, 2 vols. (1948); and in the South by J. F. Stover, *The Railroads of the South, 1865–1900* (1955). On consolidation and management see E. G. Campbell, *The Reorganization of the American Railroad System, 1893–1900* (1938). Matthew Josephson, *The Robber Barons** (1934), stresses the misdeeds of the capitalists, and T. C. Cochran, *Railroad Leaders, 1845–1890* (1953), emphasizes their attitudes and problems. New light on government regulation comes from Lee Benson, *Merchants, Farmers, and Railroads* (1955), and Gabriel Kolko, *Railroads and Regulation, 1877–1916** (1965).

On technological developments, Lewis Mumford, *Technics and Civilization** (1934), is suggestive. H. J. Habakkuk, *American and British Technology in the Nineteenth Century** (1962), is a comparative study. An authoritative work of reference is Charles Singer, *et al.*, eds., *A History of Technology, Vol. V: The Late Nineteenth Century, c. 1850 to c. 1900* (1958). Roger Burlingame, *Engines of Democracy* (1940), is a narrative of inventions, and Waldemar Kaempffert, *A Popular History of American Invention*, 2 vols. (1924), is full of interesting detail. A good biography of a major inventor is Matthew Josephson, *Edison** (1959). Heavy industry and manufacturing generally are treated in V. S. Clark, *History of Manufactures in the United States from 1607–1928*, 3 vols., Vol. II (1929); a briefer account is Malcolm Keir, *Manufacturing Industries in America* (1920). H. C. Passer, *The Electrical Manufacturers, 1875–1900* (1953), reveals much about technical change and economic growth.

*Available in a paperback edition.

On the steel industry, Andrew Carnegie, *Autobiography* (1920), and J. F. Wall, *Andrew Carnegie* (1970), are highly informative. Oil and Rockefeller are the subject of more exhaustive studies, including Allan Nevins, *John D. Rockefeller,* 2 vols. (1940); R. W. Hidy and M. E. Hidy, *Pioneering in Big Business, 1882–1911: History of the Standard Oil Company, New Jersey* (1955); and P. H. Giddens, *Early Days of Oil* (1948). For contrasting points of view on Rockefeller, see Earl Latham, *John D. Rockefeller: Robber Baron or Industrial Statesman?** (1949). Jonathan Hughes, *The Vital Few* (1966), is another study of big-business leaders. The trust and early regulatory legislation are most fully treated in H. B. Thorelli, *The Federal Antitrust Policy* (1955); but see also W. Z. Ripley, *Trusts, Pools and Corporations* (1905), John Moody, *The Truth about the Trusts* (1904), and H. D. Lloyd, *Wealth Against Commonwealth** (1894).

The business philosophy of laissez faire is perceptively treated in E. C. Kirkland, *Business in the Gilded Age* (1952) and *Dream and Thought in the Business Community, 1860–1900** (1956), and by R. G. McCloskey, *American Conservatism in the Age of Enterprise, 1865–1910** (1951). Chapters in R. H. Gabriel, *The Course of American Democratic Thought* (1940), are illuminating. Richard Hofstadter, *Social Darwinism in American Thought** (1944, rev. ed., 1959), throws much light on both laissez faire and its critics; and so does Sidney Fine, *Laissez Faire and the General-Welfare State: A Study of Conflict in American Thought, 1865–1901** (1956). On utopian thought, see G. N. Grob, *Workers and Utopia* (1961). The authority on Henry George is C. A. Barker, *Henry George* (1955). See Samuel Chugerman, *Lester F. Ward: The American Aristotle* (1939), and A. E. Morgan, *Edward Bellamy* (1944), for the best treatment of these men.

For detailed history, J. R. Commons, *et al., History of Labour in the United States,* 4 vols. (1918–35), is indispensable; Vol. III is on this period. For source material see J. A. Garraty, ed., *Labor and Capital in the Gilded Age** (1968). A useful brief survey is Henry Pelling, *American Labor** (1960). On the Knights of Labor, see N. J. Ware, *The Labor Movement in the United States, 1860–1895** (1929), and on its great rival see Philip Taft, *The A. F. of L. in the Time of Gompers* (1957). An important study is Lloyd Ulman, *The Rise of the National Trade Union* (1955). Autobiographies of the two foremost leaders of labor are T. V. Powderly, *Thirty Years of Life and Labor, 1859–1889* (1890), and Samuel Gompers, *Seventy Years of Life and Labour,* 2 vols. (1925).

Industrial life and business struggles have been the subjects of such novels as Henry James, *The American** (1877); John Hay, *The Breadwinners* (1883), an antilabor work; W. D. Howells, *The Rise of Silas Lapham** (1885), the study of a businessman; and Theodore Dreiser, *The Financier** (1912) and *The Titan** (1914), portraits of industrial tycoons. Edward Bellamy, *Looking Backward, 2000–1887** (1888), is a utopian novel that started a reform movement.

*Available in a paperback edition.

19 The urban society

"The United States was born in the country and has moved to the city." A great deal of American history is summed up in this observation by Richard Hofstadter. Old America was rural by birth, by breeding, and in outlook. The Founding Fathers, their children, and their grandchildren were typically country men, and it was inevitable that their problems, their values, and their myths should have been shaped by the setting in which they lived. It was just as inevitable that the problems, values, and myths of modern America should be shaped by the urban environment that eventually replaced the old agrarian setting. The new environment created new problems and strained old institutions. It compelled new adjustments in politics, religion, education, and economic life, and it left a profound imprint upon the whole style of American life, including arts and literature.

America moves to town

The pull of the city. In 1790, the year of the first census, only 3.35 percent of the population lived in towns of eight thousand or more. By the end of the nineteenth century ten times that percentage, a third of the population, was classified "urban" by this definition. The cities grew with the nation, of course, but after about 1820 they grew much faster than the nation. Between 1800 and 1890 the population of the entire country increased twelvefold, but over the same period the urban population multiplied eighty-seven fold. In 1800 there were only 6 cities with more than eight thousand people; by 1890 there were 448, and 26 of them had a population greater than one hundred thousand. More striking still was the rise of the American metropolis, the big city of more than half a million. The ancient world produced only two of that size, Rome and Alexandria, and western Europe had only two by the end of the seventeenth century, London and Paris. By 1900 there were six cities that large in the United States and three of them had a population of over a million. Rapid urbanization was not limited to this country, but the pace was faster in the United States than in Europe. The New World metropolis grew at a pace unprecedented in history. Chicago more than tripled its size between 1880 and 1900, when it had more than $1\frac{1}{2}$ million, and New York grew from not quite 2 million to nearly $3\frac{1}{2}$ million in those two decades. Buffalo, Detroit, and Milwaukee more than doubled, and St. Paul, Minneapolis, and Denver more than quadrupled their size.

Urban growth was very unequally distributed, and some parts of the country did not really participate in the movement significantly until the twentieth century. In fact, half

Cities of more than 8,000 inhabitants

1870

America moves to town, 1870

the entire urban population in 1890 was in the North Atlantic states and only 7.7 percent was in the South Atlantic states. More than half the nation's city-dwellers lived in the five states of New York, Pennsylvania, Massachusetts, Illinois, and Ohio. Four-fifths of them lived north of the Ohio and Missouri rivers. While by 1900 six out of ten people in the North Atlantic states and three out of ten in the Middle West lived in cities, scarcely one out of ten was an urbanite in the South. Urbanization affected all parts of the country, even the most remote, but in large areas toward the end of the century it was less an immediate experience than a distant and powerful lure.

The depopulation of the countryside was especially noticeable in the Middle West and the North Atlantic states. Some of it was due, as in the past, to the lure of the West. But the pull of the city was growing stronger and stronger. Between 1880 and 1890 more than half the townships of Iowa and Illinois declined in population, and yet both states gained substantially in total number of inhabitants. Rural decline was even greater in the North Atlantic states, where the flight to the city had long been in progress. In New England 932 out of the total of 1,502 townships, including two-thirds of those in Maine and New Hampshire and three-fourths of those in Vermont, declined in population during the

eighties. Thousands of farms were abandoned, houses were left to decay, and scores of villages were completely deserted. Yet in that decade New England, largely through the growth of her cities, actually gained 20 percent in total population. As early as 1890 the number of industrial wage-earners in the whole country almost equaled the number of farm-owners, tenants, and farm laborers combined.

Rural defenses against the ancient lure of the city reached a new low in the eighties and nineties. Those were the worst decades of agricultural depression (see Chapter 20), when everything seemed to go wrong with the farming economy. Crop prices were lower, debts greater, and mortgages heavier than ever before. At the same time the glamour and attraction of the city were enhanced by the glitter of the new electric lights, as well as by the telephones, the trolley cars, and a thousand other wonders. The city was the only place one could enjoy such amenities, for they did not begin to penetrate the countryside and soften the contrast with urban comforts to any extent until well into the twentieth century. The contrast between rural ills and urban felicity made the farmer regard his harsh lot and isolation as even more intolerable than ever before, as indeed they were. Many farmers resorted to political rebellion for relief. A great many others simply moved to town.

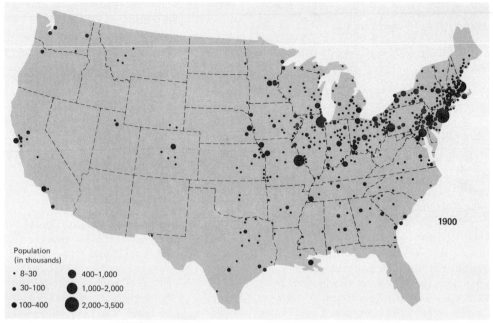

America moves to town, 1900

Population
(in thousands)

- 8–30   ● 400–1,000
- 30–100 ● 1,000–2,000
- 100–400 ● 2,000–3,500

1900

City lights and cesspools. The new technology and the factories probably produced more discomforts and inconveniences than comforts and amenities for the city-dweller of the late nineteenth century. But to the outsider the advantages and attractions were more readily apparent. First among these were the bright lights that were replacing the dim gas lamps in the streets and the kerosene lamps and gas jets indoors. Cleveland and San Francisco led the way in 1879 by installing brilliant electric arc lamps in their streets, and their example was quickly followed in cities across the country. The noisy, sputtering arc lamp was impractical for indoor use, but for that purpose the incandescent light bulb patented by Edison in 1880 (see p. 430) became available in a few years and spread as swiftly as the growth of power plants permitted. In 1882 there were only thirty-eight central power stations in the whole country, but before the end of the century there were three thousand. Improved lighting not only made cities safer at night but enabled factories to run night shifts, proved a boon to theaters and other amusement houses, and extended the hours of libraries, shops, and schools.

Electrical power provided the answer to a city problem that was even more pressing than that of lighting—the problem of moving vast numbers of people rapidly through the streets at rush hours. The old horse cars or mule-drawn coaches, the prevalent means of public transportation into the eighties, were much too slow as well as too small, smelly, and crowded. New York City, later imitated by Brooklyn, Chicago, and Boston, built an overhead railroad with four cars pulled by a tiny steam locomotive. But the heavy elevated roadway was expensive to build and shut out light from the streets, and the locomotives sprinkled pedestrians with soot and hot coals. To master her steep, hill-climbing streets, San Francisco developed cable roads, with the cars pulled by an endless cable sunk under the track level. Midwestern and Eastern cities also used them successfully in their level streets.

In the meantime, inventors had tinkered for years with the idea of an electric street railway, but Lieutenant Frank J. Sprague was the first to install and profitably operate one, a short line built at Richmond, Virginia, in 1887. The success of the experiment started a revolution in urban transportation, for the electric trolley cars were faster, cheaper, and more comfortable than any of the older types. By 1895 some eight hundred fifty lines, using ten thousand miles of tracks, were in operation. Boston in 1897 was the first city to put electric cars underground, and New York opened her subway to the public in 1904.

Cities took to the telephone eagerly and naturally, for without it the congestion and concentration of people that was to follow

Elevated railroad

would have been insupportable. Within two years after Bell invented the instrument in 1876 (see p. 429), New Haven had set up the first commercial switchboard, and in two more years eighty-five cities had telephone exchanges. The first telephone connection between cities was effected in 1877 between Boston and New York. Before the end of the century the whole country was laced with interconnecting lines, and eight hundred thousand phones were in use—double the number in all of Europe.

Technology and invention were slower to yield solutions to city problems that were traditionally assigned to the public domain, such as street-paving, water supply, and sewage disposal, and in these matters progress was halting. In the seventies the streets even of the larger cities were poorly paved—usually with cobblestones or granite blocks along the eastern seaboard, with wooden blocks in the Middle West, and with gravel or macadam in the South. Brick became popular as pavement in the mid-eighties, especially in cities where it was manufactured. The national capital in 1878 set the pace in adapting asphalt to street-paving, the method that eventually proved the favorite, and by 1900 Washington was pronounced the best-paved city in the world.

Water supply and sewage disposal lagged far behind the demands and needs of mushrooming city populations. The typical urbanite of the seventies relied on the rural solution of individual well and privy or cesspool: Washington had fifty-six thousand cesspools in the mid-seventies, and Philadelphia even more. Improvement was slow, and large cities of the

East and South depended mainly on drainage through open gutters to the end of the century. Pollution of water supplies by sewage as well as by the dumping of industrial waste accounted in large measure for the wretched public-health records and staggering mortality rates of the period. The number of public waterworks multiplied more than fivefold in the eighties, but filtering and purification were slow to be adopted. Throughout the nineties the American city remained poorly prepared to accommodate the hordes that continued to pour in upon it.

The immigrant and the city. The cities grew at the expense of the European as well as the American countryside and village. For the pull of America was felt in Europe more powerfully than ever before, and the great majority of the immigrants crowded into the nation's cities. Like the new native city-dwellers, the immigrants were also country men. In spite of the distance they had come, they were usually no more familiar with city ways and city life than Americans fresh from the farm, and for the immigrants the uprooting was even more of a shock and a bewilderment. Neither they nor native Americans were prepared to understand or cope with the urban crisis intensified by their sudden convergence upon the city from the ends of the earth.

Many observers have singled out the immigrants as the primary cause of the urban crisis. Actually, the percentage of foreign born in the total population remained about the same; the immigrants came from much the same social class as they always had; and they came for the same old reason—to better their lot. As always, a large percentage returned permanently to Europe. But there were significant changes. For one thing they began to come in far greater numbers than ever before. From 1850 to 1880 about $2\frac{1}{2}$ million had arrived per decade, with the rate falling off a bit in the sixties but picking up again in the seventies. Big passenger ships, built for the purpose, altered immigration in many ways. In the eighties the number more than doubled, with nearly $5\frac{1}{4}$ million arriving during that decade, and with nearly $3\frac{3}{4}$ million more landing in the next. For another thing immigrants showed a greater tendency than ever to congregate in the large Eastern cities and less disposition to disperse over the countryside. This concentration naturally made them more conspicuous. And finally there came a shift to what was called "new" immigration—from southern and eastern Europe—as contrasted with the "old" immigrants from northern and western Europe. The old immigrants had come typically from Britain, Ireland, Germany, or one of the Scandinavian countries, and they were usually Protestant. The new immigrants were Italians, Austrians, Hungarians, Poles, Serbs, and Russians; they were Catholic or Jewish in religion and had habits and ways that appeared outlandish to older Americans. Immigrants of the new type had made up only 1.4 percent of the total immigration of the sixties and less than 20 percent in the eighties; but in the nineties their proportion suddenly climbed to more than 50 percent and in the next decade to more than 70 percent. This increasing proportion of new immigrants coincided with, and provided stimulation for, two tendencies: (1) an increasing concern over the ills of urban life and (2) an increasing tendency to stress racial differences. Because of this coincidence, the new immigrants were blamed for many serious city problems that had little to do with racial or national origin.

There could be no doubt, however, that the foreigner and the immigrant had become conspicuous in American life. By 1890 one-fourth of the Philadelphians and one-third of the Bostonians and Chicagoans were of foreign birth, and in Greater New York four out of five residents were of foreign birth or foreign parentage. Of the male population of the eighteen largest cities in the country there were two and a half times as many of foreign birth or foreign parentage as there were of the

The lure of America

older American stock. New York City had half as many Italians as Naples and two and a half times as many Irish as Dublin. Understandably, the newcomers tended to huddle together clannishly by nationality. Jacob Riis, a New York journalist and reformer who had emigrated from Denmark in 1870, pictured a map of Manhattan in 1890 colored according to races and nationalities:

> Between the dull gray of the Jew, his favorite color, and the Italian red, would be squeezed in on the map a sharp streak of yellow, marking the narrow boundaries of Chinatown. Dovetailed in with the German population, the poor but thrifty Bohemian might be picked out by the sombre hue of his life. . . . Dots and dashes of color here and there would show where the Finnish sailors worship their *djumala* (God), the Greek pedlars the

Sources of immigration, 1871–1910

ancient name of their race, and the Swiss the goddess of thrift.

Less colorfully, Jane Addams described the map of Chicago:

> Between Halsted Street and the river live about ten thousand Italians—Neapolitans, Sicilians, and Calabrians, with an occasional Lombard or Venetian. To the south on Twelfth Street are many Germans, and side streets are given over almost entirely to Polish and Russian Jews. Still farther south, these Jewish colonies merge into a huge Bohemian colony, so vast that Chicago ranks as the third Bohemian city in the world.

Slums and palaces. The city was the way of the future. But there was much about the city of the late nineteenth century to justify the old antiurban prejudice of agrarian America, the prejudice Jefferson voiced when he called the city "a sore on the body politic." To many the city did indeed seem a product of disease rather than a source of social health. The city of that period was the very embodiment of laissez-faire doctrine, for it grew without plan, with a minimum of control, guided mainly by the dictates of industrial enterprise and private greed. Even with an alert and informed citizenry and an honest and efficient municipal government a city would have faced staggering difficulties, and few cities could boast either asset.

The foulest product of the haphazard laissez-faire growth was the city slum, an old evil that took on new life and descended to new depths in 1879 with the invention, in New York City, of the "dumbbell" tenement house, so named for the shape of its floor plan. Designed to get the maximum return for the landlord, the new tenement was no better than a barracks honeycombed with rooms, many of them with no direct access to light or air. Lacking sanitary facilities, privacy, or health precautions, these tenements rapidly degenerated into human pigsties, vile smelling and vermin infested. According to Jacob Riis, in 1890 there were thirty-seven thousand tenement houses of this type in New York, and more than 1.2 million people lived in them— half the city's population.

William Dean Howells, a realistic novelist, admitted in 1896 that from a distance the tenement might sometimes appear picturesque:

But to be in it, and not have the distance, is to inhale the stenches of the neglected street, and to catch the yet fouler and dreadfuller poverty-smell which breathes from the open doorways. . . . It is to see the work-worn look of mothers, the squalor of the babes, the haggish ugliness of the old women, the slovenly frowziness of the young girls.

The worst of the tenement slums in New York, which had their counterpart in every urban community in the United States, were known by such names as Bandit's Roost, Misery Row, and Murderer's Alley. Crime and prostitution flourished in these noisome horrors, and organized gangs operated securely within their protection. In years when the homicide rate in England and Germany was less than half that in the United States and when the rate in Europe was declining, the ratio in the United States was increasing, and lawlessness was growing at an alarming pace. Extremes of human misery and degradation had become common sights.

In the eighties and nineties the gulfs between social classes were dramatically emphasized rather than concealed. It was no accident that the economist Thorstein Veblen, in his *Theory of the Leisure Class* (1899), hit on the expression "conspicuous consumption." Displaying habits of consumption that were competitive as well as conspicuous, Chicagoans sported liveried servants and dwelt in lavish palaces built in plain view. The contrast with conspicuous poverty was glaring and unconcealed; squalor and splendor paraded the same streets. The palaces of the wealthy that lined New York's Fifth Avenue were paralleled a few blocks away by the desolation of Shantytown, inhabited by Irish paupers and goats and stretching along the East Side for sixty blocks or more. In the same year in which Jacob Riis published his shocking study of the slums, *How the Other Half Lives* (1890), Ward McAllister published his *Society As I Have Found It* (1890), lovingly recounting the extravagances of New York's Four Hundred, the self-elected social élite. One exploit of this set, a favorite example among protest groups, was the Bradley Martin costume ball, staged in the Waldorf Hotel at a cost of $368,200. It took place on February 10, 1897, near the depths of the depression, when thousands of unemployed roamed the street, and was attended by guests decked in costumes costing as much as $10,000. Scenes of this sort help

Jacob Riis: journalist and reformer

to explain the violence in the rhetoric of Populism and other protest movements of the nineties.

Howells, in a poem called "Society" (1895), compared the violent social contrasts of his day with "a splendid pageantry of beautiful women and lordly men" playing and dancing upon a magnificent floor that barely covered the crushed and bleeding bodies of the oppressed:

And now and then from out the dreadful
  floor
An arm or brow was lifted from the rest,
As if to strike in madness, or implore
For mercy; and anon some suffering breast
Heaved from the mass and sank; and as
  before
The revellers above them thronged and
  prest.

The foulest product of urban growth

The awakening of the social conscience

The city was a shock to the American conscience, not merely because of violent contrasts, abuses, and evils, but because the national conscience had taken shape in an agrarian culture and a rural past. So had national values, ideals, morals, folkways, and political institutions. American country men or European peasants who emigrated were repelled as well as fascinated by the city; they accepted it and rejected it at the same time. Their feelings were torn and their consciences were bruised by the experience.

The challenge of the bosses. Probably the most flagrant offense against public morals in the last quarter of the nineteenth century was the corruption of city government. At least it seemed more conspicuous. The politician bent on corruption could hardly have dreamed of a more promising combination of circumstances. The rapid growth of cities had made necessary the large-scale expansion of public utilities of all sorts—water, gas, transportation, electricity—as well as the construction of public buildings, sewage systems, docks, street and sidewalk pavement. For this work a multitude of valuable contracts, franchises, monopolies, subsidies, and privileges had to be granted. Such prizes were worth the ransom of kings, and there were plenty of predatory operators ready with the price. The corrupt politician was aided in his operations

by an antiquated and complex form of municipal government modeled on that of the state. Clumsy city charters saddled the government with inappropriate legislative machinery, weak executive authority, and disorganized courts, making responsibility so difficult to fix that crime went unpunished. State legislatures, by interfering excessively with city affairs, added to the confusion and increased the opportunities for corruption.

Not surprisingly, the cities were excessively burdened with debt. By 1880 city and town indebtedness ran to more than three-quarters of a billion dollars, more than three times the amount of state indebtedness. Yet for all their heavy expenditures the cities often received wretched service from the utilities they subsidized and were cynically and repeatedly defrauded by the public servants they elected. "With very few exceptions," wrote Andrew D. White, president of Cornell, "the city governments of the United States are the worst in Christendom—the most expensive, the most inefficient, and the most corrupt." And James Bryce, a generous but well-informed English critic, pronounced city government "the one conspicuous failure of the United States," far more serious, in his opinion, than the shortcomings of state and federal government.

The city machine dominated politics, and the boss dominated the machine. Never has a more colorful set of politicians wielded such power as the great bosses of this period. With

The immigrant and the boss

What tells in holdin' your grip on your district is to go right down among the poor families and help them in the different ways they need help. I've got a regular system for this. If there's a fire ... any hour of the day or night, I'm usually there with some of my election district captains as soon as the fire-engines. If a family is burned out I don't ask whether they are Republicans or Democrats, and I don't refer them to the Charity Organization Society, which would investigate their case in a month or two and decide they were worthy of help about the time they are dead from starvation. I just get quarters for them ... and fix them up till they get things runnin' again....

Another thing, I can always get a job for a deservin' man. I make it a point to keep on the track of jobs, and it seldom happens that I don't have a few up my sleeve ready for use....

And the children—the little roses of the district! Do I forget them? Oh, no! They know me, every one of them, and they know that a sight of Uncle George and candy means the same thing. Some of them are the best kind of vote-getters.

From William L. Riordon, *Plunkitt of Tammany Hall*, 1905.

a disposition toward large girth, shiny hats, and heavy jewelry, the boss played the role of a freehanded spender, the Robin Hood of the masses. High in the annals of bossdom are the names of "Honest" John Kelley and Richard Croker of New York, Christopher L. Magee and William Finn of Pittsburgh, Ed Butler of St. Louis, "King" James McManes of Philadelphia, and "Czar" Martin Lomasney of Boston. Revenue flowed into their coffers from office-seekers, contractors, public utilities, railroads, prostitutes, gamblers—anybody who happened to need protection or favors. Even pushcart-peddlers and garbage-collectors paid tribute to New York's Tammany. Boss McManes, as head of Philadelphia's gas trust, had 5,630 public jobs at his disposal; he died leaving an estate of more than $2 million.

The city boss and his lieutenants in the wards and precincts found their most reliable supporters among the immigrants. These new voters certainly had no monopoly on ignorance and apathy, and many of them were intelligent and useful citizens. But they were usually unaccustomed to the ballot, unpracticed in the ways of democracy, and bewildered by city life in a strange land. Moreover, the great majority of them were unskilled laborers who lived close to the margin of existence and were often in need of a job and a friend. The boss dealt primarily in jobs and votes. He had sprung from the immigrant community himself, shared its sense of solidarity, knew its members by name, and re-

mained one of them. He was in fact the natural leader of the immigrants, and they responded to him with group loyalty and devotion. They knew him as a man who "got things done," a man to whom they could always take their troubles. The boss made it his business to know their needs and to give them tangible evidence of his interest in them. His favors took the form of getting them jobs, intervening with the law in their behalf, bailing them out of jail, paying burial money, distributing free coal, and handing out Christmas baskets. In short, he performed services for which there was as yet no public agency and which no one else was ready to perform.

Irish politicians were especially adept at these arts, and it was a prevailing conviction that, as one writer put it, "The function of the Irishman is to administer the affairs of the American city." A glance at the names heading the roster of bosses supports this conviction. One of them put his political theory in these words: "I think that there's got to be in every ward a guy that any bloke can go to when he's in trouble and get help—not justice and the law, but help, no matter what he's done." Theodore Roosevelt, who studied the matter, concluded that urban reformers would have to create social agencies to fulfill the role the boss played before they could replace him.

As the reformers found out for themselves, after a little experience, many "good" people supported the bosses and machines—educated, respectable, middle-class people

The immigrant in the city

who had been natives for at least three generations. Some of these ''good'' people were businessmen who were quite willing to cooperate with the machine to secure the favors, privileges, and exemptions they desired. Other respectable citizens voted regularly, if regretfully, for the machine because of their sincere devotion to the national party with which the machine was identified and their desire for a party victory. In short, city machine and city boss were buttressed by some of the strongest as well as by some of the weakest elements of the population. Anyone who undertook to change the system would need to be very powerful indeed.

Humanitarians and reformers. The conscience of the middle class was eventually stirred to indignation and action by the misery and degradation of the city. But first the middle class had to discover what poverty was. Early humanitarians and reformers did not understand the poor—the ''depraved classes,'' as they called them. Attributing their plight to moral shortcomings, they sent agents of the Charity Organizations Society to discover which of the poor were ''deserving.'' But it was the young social workers, nearly all of them women, patiently investigating and visiting the sweatshops and tenement firetraps, who began to establish contact between the middle class and the working class.

Inspired by English social-reform literature and a visit to Toynbee Hall in the slums of London, Jane Addams, the most famous American woman of her time, took up the settlement-house idea and established Hull House on Halsted Street in Chicago in 1889. She wished, she said, ''to share the lives of the poor'' and to make social service ''express the spirit of Christ.'' One such house had already been established in New York in 1886, and in the next ten years some fifty or more were founded in Northern and Eastern cities. They offered a variety of services, maintained playgrounds, nurseries, club rooms, libraries, and kindergartens, and conducted classes in various subjects. But perhaps of more significance was the education they provided for the young middle-class social workers who came to live in the slums to gain firsthand knowledge of the workers' problems. Within a few years the settlement houses had become the spawning ground of women reformers. Among them were Lillian Wald, founder of the Henry Street Settlement in New York, Florence Kelley, leading spirit in the National Consumers League, and Frances Perkins, with a great future as a Progressive leader.

On the political front the battle for municipal reform began under leaders recruited from the solid and substantial middle class. These included Seth Low and George William Curtis in New York, Edwin U. Curtis and Thomas W. Higginson in Boston, Lyman J. Gage in Chicago, and Joseph W. Folk in St. Louis. Good-government clubs, committees, commissions, and reform organizations for municipal improvement proliferated rapidly in the eighties.

Every city of any size had one such organization, and the larger cities had several. One of the most prominent was the National Civil Service Reform League, founded in 1881, which published the magazine *Good Government* to promote its prime object, the merit system for city employees. In the early stages these organizations wasted a good deal of time in mass meetings that drafted wordy resolutions and accomplished nothing except to make the reformers look ineffectual if not ridiculous. Cynics called the good-government people the "goo-goos." Their efforts to expose corruption met with more success than their attempts to break the power of machine politics, but they kept up a running fight to lower the cost of city administration, to encourage law enforcement, and to improve public sanitation and education. They stirred up a good bit of excitement on occasion, but for a long time they seemed to be getting nowhere.

Not until after 1890 did the municipal reformers become an effective force for change and improvement. The cumulative experience of scattered reformers began to point the way to a concerted program, and the National Municipal League was launched on a wave of public interest in 1894. Within two years more than two hundred branch leagues were founded. The league put forward as its program a model city charter that embodied such advanced reforms as the short ballot, greater freedom from state interference, limited franchise for utilities, separate city and state elections, the merit system, government by experts, and, above all, more authority for the mayor. In 1880 only one of the nation's twenty-three principal cities was dominated by the mayor, but by 1900 there were twelve. By that year the battle for municipal reform was in full swing. The reformers still had much to learn, but they had aroused the electorate, and they had gained experience and confidence through substantial victories. In 1894 the embattled hosts of reform in New York overthrew Boss Richard Croker and elected William L. Strong mayor, though Tammany returned to power after a brief period. Reformers in Chicago, Boston, and St. Louis also scored significant victories over their machines in the next few years.

Vassar commencement, 1875

The rights of women. Women reformers responded to the social problems of the city, as we have seen, but another of their preoccupations was the plight of their own sex in a male-dominated society. Their bill of grievances, well documented and long-standing, included political disfranchisement, legal discrimination, economic exploitation, cultural and educational deprivation, and domestic drudgery. If blacks had their "place," women had their "sphere," and to many women its limitations seemed increasingly oppressive. Woman's sphere was The Home, and beyond its walls she ventured, save on religious missions, only at the risk of breaching "the cult of true womanhood"—piety, purity, submissiveness, and domesticity. For a growing number of middle-class women technology—gas lighting, domestic plumbing, manufactured ice, and improved furnaces, stoves, washtubs, and sewing machines—provided some escape from the domestic treadmill. For others cheap domestic servants from the immigrant ships furnished release. New women's colleges and older men's colleges turned coeducational were graduating larger numbers of women—2,500 a year by 1890. But they were educated to fill places that, save for underpaid teaching, did not yet exist. Like their sisters who were venturing out of the "sphere," they found themselves in a society that had no use for them.

Turning to organization to battle their frustrations, women established hundreds of clubs, most of them devoted to "self-culture." Founded in 1882, the Association of Collegial Alumnae remained small and exclusive for a long time, limited in 1889 to the graduates of the fourteen colleges that met their rigorous standards. At the opposite extreme of inclusiveness was the sprawling General Federation of Women's Clubs. Organized in 1890, it federated hundreds of clubs, had 150,000 members by 1900, and was soon to top a million. Mainly limited to "self-culture" and entertainment, most members were middle-aged, middle-class, conservative women. The General Federation took pains to avoid antagonizing the cautious rank and file, many of them antisuffragists, and did not endorse woman suffrage until the eve of victory. The leaders of the Federation were usually suffragists, however, and their movement furnished the hard core of feminism. Split into two organizations since the struggle over black suffrage in the 1860s, the rival groups resolved their differences and merged as the National American Woman Suffrage Association in 1890.

A new generation of women leaders had arrived by this time, though veterans like Susan B. Anthony, Elizabeth Cady Stanton, and Lucy Stone were still on the scene. Like them, Anna Howard Shaw met working women as equals, but she was an exception. "The younger women," As Eleanor Flexner writes, "were not, for the most part, distinguished by the breadth of their social views." This was true of Carrie Chapman Catt, May Wright Sewall, Rachel Foster Avery, and Harriet Taylor Upton. They reflected the drift of their times toward conservative views on labor and race relations and were more concerned with decorum in pressing their cause. Rejecting their radical origins, the new feminists also turned away from the disturbing and fundamental questions that their contemporary, Charlotte Perkins Gilman, asked in her book *Woman and Economics* (1898). Instead they narrowed their objectives to suffrage, submerged all women's rights in the political struggle, and as a consequence came to exaggerate the value of the ballot as the sovereign remedy for women's ills.

By 1890 seventeen states and territories had given women limited suffrage in school elections, but not until that year did Wyoming enter the Union as the first state with full suffrage for women. Three more underpopulated Western states followed suit, Colorado in 1893 and Utah and Idaho in 1896, but not for fourteen years did another state adopt woman suffrage. Congress gave formal hearings to pleas for a federal woman suffrage amendment, but neither house reported the bill favorably after 1893, and the question disappeared from Congress as an issue for twenty years. Women kept up their campaigns for state action, waging hundreds of them, many heroically under adverse conditions. Among their arguments were some that appealed to nativism and racism. The 1893 convention of the Woman Suffrage Association urged suffrage with literacy instead of sex qualifications, since there were "more white women who can read and write than all negro voters; more American women who can read and write than all foreign voters." For all that they continued to be rewarded with defeat after defeat until the First World War.

The conscience of the church. The church community was eventually to respond both in faith and in works to the human needs and social problems of city and industry. But in 1876, as Henry May has observed, "Protestantism presented a massive, almost unbroken front in its defense of the status quo." Slums, depressions, and unemployment were but necessary steps to progress, and suffering was the lot of man in good, orthodox theology. Religion was a spiritual and individual, not a social, concern, and salvation came through the striving of the individual with sin and conscience, not through social welfare and betterment. The church, middle class in outlook, was dedicated to the early social creed of individualism and laissez faire, and the mightiest preachers of that era expressed these attitudes forcefully and repeatedly. There was no better exponent of laissez faire and social Darwinism than Henry Ward Beecher in his Brooklyn pulpit.

Revivalism and professional revivalists were usually powerful propagators of the old-time religion—orthodox fundamentalism—and had very little or no social awareness. Throughout the eighties and nineties the annual revival was a regular feature of the program of Methodist, Baptist, Presbyterian, Congregational, and smaller churches. The most famous of the professional revivalists was Dwight L. Moody, an impressive figure of two hundred eighty pounds who got his start with a successful campaign in Britain during the seventies. Returning to America in 1875, he set out with Ira D. Sankey, his equally weighty singer, to "evangelize the world in this generation." Moody brought into play all his great executive and publicity talents to attract huge crowds and with forceful and colloquial sermons converted sinners by the thousands in all parts of the United States. His popularity continued unflagging until his death in 1899. Moody and another famous revivalist, T. DeWitt Talmage, along with numerous imitators, set a new record for professional revivalism in America. Whether as a result of their work or for some other reason, Protestant churches grew rapidly in the last two decades of the century, increasing their membership from somewhat over 10 million to almost 18 million.

In spite of this growth, clergymen complained constantly that the working people were drifting away from the church. Moved either by the pulpit's lack of sympathy for their plight or by the elegance of the clothing they saw in the pews, workingmen found the churches of the older Protestant denomi-

Wyoming voters, 1888

nations less suited to their tastes than they once had been. Investigators reported that large working-class districts in the cities were without church facilities of any kind. Some of the poor and the lowly, as they had in the past, sought solace in new sects founded to restore the lost purity or the original doctrine of the old sects. Many of these "holiness" people were recruited from the Methodists, Baptists, and other Protestant churches. Usually originating in the country and then moving to the city, a dozen or more pentecostal and millennial sects sprang up in the eighties and nineties.

A new sect of a different sort was the Church of Christ, Scientist, usually called Christian Scientist, which was chartered by a small group of the followers of Mary Baker Eddy in 1879. The prophet of the new faith was born in 1821 to a New England family of the pious, humble sort to which Joseph Smith, the Mormon prophet (see p. 266) had been born fifteen years earlier. Inspired by the help she received from a faith healer in her own rather complex health problems, she developed the belief that "disease is caused by mind alone." At the end of her long life in 1910, adherents of her church numbered a hundred thousand, her book *Science and Health* (1875) had sold four hundred thousand copies, and her estate was appraised at more than $2½ million.

Addressing its appeal to the downtrodden, the Salvation Army invaded America in 1879 under the command of George Railton and seven women officers. Founded the year before in London by William Booth, it was born of his desire to reach the city poor. Using revivalist methods and brass bands to attract crowds, the uniformed army and its lassies preached repentance to "rumdom, slumdom and bumdom." Within a decade after the invasion they began to supplement repentance sermons with a social-service program and sent "slum brigades" into the tenement districts to bring relief as well as the gospel to the poor.

It would have been impossible for the Catholic Church to ignore the working class and the social problems of the city. Since the "new" immigration was overwhelmingly Catholic, working class, and urban, the American Catholic Church of the late nineteenth century became more than ever the church of the city, the worker, and the immigrant. The number of Catholics in the country increased from over 6 million to more than 10 million in the last two decades of the century. Responsibility for training and adjusting the new Americans to their country compelled the Church to adjust its social policy to urban needs and persuaded James Gibbons, then in Rome to be installed as cardinal, to defend the cause of American labor before the Holy See in 1887. American Catholics found support for their social policy in the loyalty of their communicants, which contrasted strongly with the defection and alienation of the masses of which European Catholics complained. The papal encyclical *Rerum novarum,* of May 1891, enunciated social ideals and responsibilities for Catholics that gave additional sanction to the social views of the Americans.

In the meantime a small group of Protestant clergymen, at first responding as individuals to the social crises and labor struggles of the seventies, eighties, and nineties, had begun to shape a reinterpretation of their religion that in later years came to be known as the Social Gospel. Turning away from the traditional emphasis on spiritual and moral concerns, the new gospel stressed the social and pragmatic implications of Christian ethics and called for good works in social reform and betterment. The Reverend Josiah Strong's book *Our Country* (1885), which sold half a million copies in twenty years, has been called the *Uncle Tom's Cabin* of the movement. But Washington Gladden, a Congregational minister who wrote *Applied Christianity* (1886), was probably the most influential leader. Next in importance was R. Heber Newton, a liberal New York Episcopalian and an advocate of more sweeping reform. The Episcopal Church, the most aristocratic denomination and yet the one most influenced by the mildly socialistic doctrines then gaining attention in the parent Church of England, took most readily to the new gospel, while the Methodist Church, traditionally the church of the common man, tended to cling to rural individualism and resisted the Social Gospel at first. With a similar following and the additional restraint of such wealthy benefactors as John D. Rockefeller, the Baptists nevertheless moved earlier toward the Social Gospel under the inspiration of Walter Rauschenbusch. By 1895 the influence of the Social Gospel was being felt throughout American Protestantism and in secular thought as well. Its main impact, however, was not to come until the following century.

Salvation Army, 1880

The spread of learning

Public schools and mass media. The national determination to educate everybody was best reflected in the growth of public schools, which increased at an unprecedented speed after 1870. Free education for all became a foremost article in the American faith, and the schools were unfairly expected to solve all of democracy's problems, from poorly cooked meals to poorly adjusted races. Growing cities expected the schools to take over many functions that parents, police, and priests had once performed and along the way to Americanize the children of the new immigrants. One measure of the hopes and aspirations thus aroused was the rapid expansion of the school system, especially in the cities. In 1870 only $69 million, or an average of about $15 per pupil, was spent on public education, while in the first school year of the new century $250 million, or nearly $23 per pupil, went into the school budget. By 1900 all but two of the states outside the South had compulsory school-attendance laws of some sort, and both the average school attendance and the length of the average school year had increased markedly. There were only one hundred sixty public high schools in the whole country in 1870, but by the end of the century there were more than six thousand. The cities, with a more concentrated school population and better transportation than rural communities, reaped the greatest benefits from the public-school expansion. More and more of them extended public schools to include kindergartens, normal schools, night classes, and adult and vocational education.

Under the sway of the new theories of education the public schools gradually put aside the old authoritarian ways of the drillmaster and disciplinarian in the one-room country school. Just as the preceding generation imported the progressive doctrines of Pestalozzi, the new generation brought from Germany the theories of Johann Friedrich Herbart, who believed that education could be made into a science. The Herbartians encouraged the abandonment of corporal punishment and the teaching of ''practical'' subjects such as manual training.

Private schools still held on, particularly in the Eastern states, and certain ethnic and religious groups resisted being integrated into a uniform public-school system. Unable to win public support for their own educational efforts, the Catholics in 1884 determined upon an elaborate expansion of their parochial schools and increased their number to nearly four thousand by 1900. The program was mainly designed to educate the immigrants of that faith in the cities, and most of the schools were located in New England and the Middle Atlantic states.

The federal government had made a gesture of assistance to public schools in 1867, when Congress laid the foundation of a bureau of education, but the Blair Bill for federal aid distributed according to the proportion of illiterates in a state was defeated in the 1880s. Since support of the schools was left to local communities, improvement and growth varied widely with the distribution of wealth. In general, the rural districts lagged behind the urban areas and the West and South behind the East. But the South had a staggering burden of special disadvantages. In the first place it had about twice as many children per adult as the North, and it had considerably less than half the per capita taxable wealth with which to educate them. To complicate the matter, Southerners were not concentrated in cities and towns but scattered thinly over the countryside. And on top of that, at the insistence of the whites, two separate school systems were maintained for the segregation of the races. At the century's end the schools of the South were still miserably supported, poorly taught, and wholly inadequate. Efforts to improve them accomplished little until the next decade.

In spite of the physical growth of the educational plant and the millions of dollars poured into public education, the average American adult by the turn of the century had only about five years of schooling. Illiteracy had been reduced, however, from around 17 percent in 1880 to about 11 percent twenty years later. For all the faddism and quackery, in spite of the low-paid teachers and the attempt to saddle them with all the problems of democracy, the public schools continued to increase in number and grow in popular esteem.

The popular faith in education and the craving for its benefits were reflected in other ways as well. One of these was the highly popular Chautauqua movement, which was started in 1874 at Lake Chautauqua, New York, by Methodist laymen as a camp meeting for training Sunday-school teachers. The idea

Education: article of American faith

spread over the country as a sort of informal adult-education movement. It retained its pious, middle-class emphasis on temperance and morality and often made use of Methodist camp-meeting grounds. Small-town audiences sweated earnestly through long lectures on science and religion, thrilled to the illustrated travel lectures of John L. Stoddard, or relaxed with James Whitcomb Riley and Swiss bell-ringers. To supplement the summer meetings a home-study circle was formed in 1878, and ten years later a Chautauqua College began to offer correspondence courses and hand out degrees via the postman.

These years also brought a dramatic expansion of public libraries. Librarians laid claim to professional standing in 1876, when they organized the American Library Association. State and local tax money was tapped, and private donors began to put large amounts into library-building: Andrew Carnegie, the most munificent of them, launched his library benefactions at Pittsburgh in 1881. In the 1890s six library buildings costing more than a million dollars had been either started or completed. The most splendid were the Boston Public Library and the New York Public Library, both opened in 1895, and the Library of Congress, the largest and most costly in the world, opened in 1897. By 1900 there were more than nine thousand public libraries in the country, with a total of more than 45 million volumes.

The repetitive theme of ''more and more and more'' that drums through all phases of American life in the eighties and nineties (along with *more* unemployment and *more* depression) was nowhere so striking as in journalism, especially in periodicals. In the last fifteen years of the century the number of periodicals published increased by twenty-two hundred, most of them devoted to trades and special interests. More striking was the increase in the number and circulation of periodicals for the general reader. There were only four such monthly magazines in the country in 1885 with circulations of a hundred thousand or more, and they were usually priced at 35 cents a copy. Twenty years later there were twenty such magazines with an aggregate circulation of more than 5½ million, and all but four of them sold at 10 to 15 cents a copy. The 10-cent monthlies created a vast new reading public. More than price was involved in the expansion, however. The older journals, such as the *Century,* the *Atlantic,*

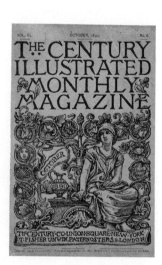

and the *North American Review,* were sedate, leisurely, rather aloof, and upper class in appeal and sympathy. The new 10-cent competitors, such as *Munsey's, McClure's,* and the *Cosmopolitan,* were lighter in tone, with shorter articles and many illustrations. News-mindedness was an innovation of *Public Opinion* (1886), *Current Literature* (1888), and the *Literary Digest* (1890), and reform-mindedness was the theme of the *Forum* (1886) and *Arena* (1889), as well as the older *Nation* (1865) and *Independent* (1848).

Growing cities, increasing literacy, and expanding population combined to create greater and greater markets for newspapers and to heighten the temptation to vulgarize the product in order to exploit the potential market. The number of daily papers, largely confined to the cities, more than doubled, and the number of weekly and semiweekly papers increased more than 50 percent between 1880 and 1900, while subscribers increased even more rapidly. The growth of daily newspapers came as follows:

Year	Number of Dailies	Total Daily Circulation
1860	387	1,478,000
1870	574	2,602,000
1880	971	3,566,000
1890	1,610	8,387,000
1900	2,226	15,102,000

By the end of the century the United States had more than half the newspapers in the world. Two potent influences were at work to change the character of American newspapers: one was advertising, which surpassed sales as a source of revenue in the nineties, and the other was the mass audience. To reach the masses the news columns became more sensational and vulgar. The father of the new school of journalists was Joseph Pulitzer, who bought the New York *World* in 1883 and ran its circulation up from fifteen thousand in 1883 to over a million by 1898. The assault on privacy and taste was continued and intensified by his imitator, William Randolph Hearst of the New York *Journal.*

The higher learning. For all the crassness and materialism that earned for it the name of ''Gilded Age,'' the period could boast of substantial advances in higher education and scholarship. There was obviously much room for improvement. American colleges of 1870, even the better ones, were likely to be strongly sectarian, provincial, and undistinguished. The typical college professor of that year was harshly, but not very unfairly, described as "a nondescript, a jack of all trades, equally ready to teach surveying and Latin eloquence." The traditional curriculum, designed for the training of ministers, did not permit specialization or allow time for research. Library and laboratory facilities were inadequate, and the natural sciences were neglected. There were no graduate schools and no professional schools to speak of beyond theological seminaries. Collegiate pedagogy, like the Victorian family, was heavily authoritarian, with emphasis upon rules, discipline, rote learning, and recitations.

With Harvard in the vanguard and with Charles W. Eliot at its head, a small group of academicians undertook to reform the old collegiate order. The reforms they made were not universally acknowledged to be improvements in their day, nor are they yet, but they were widely if slowly imitated. One of them was the elective system, which resulted in a proliferation of courses and subjects from which the student chose according to his fancy. Additional reforms, such as an increase in the number of science courses and in the use of the laboratory method of instruction, were taken up rapidly, as were discussion periods as substitutes for rote recitation. Colleges were slower to follow Harvard's example of abolishing compulsory chapel attendance (1886) and relaxing student discipline. But there were numerous signs that the old collegiate system that had prevailed for centuries was passing. Among these signs were the decline of authoritarian norms and traditional curricula and a decrease in the proportion of clergymen on boards of trustees and in presidents' offices.

Accompanying these changes and reflecting the shift to a secular and scientific emphasis was an increase in German influence in academic circles. During the nineteenth century more than nine thousand Americans studied at German universities, all but about two hundred of them after 1850. In the 1880s some two thousand Americans were studying in Germany. The Johns Hopkins University, opened in Baltimore in 1876 with an inaugural address by Thomas Huxley, the Darwinian, was an expression of both English and German influence. Nearly all the faculty of the new university had studied in Germany, and

the policies pursued by President Daniel Coit Gilman expressed many of the academic ideals of that country's universities. Among these were a stress on research and graduate study and a shift from the attitude that professors and students were mere conservers of learning to the attitude that they were searchers and advancers of knowledge. The new emphasis implied an increase in the scholar's stature, freedom, and prestige. Inspired more or less by the example of Johns Hopkins, fifteen major graduate schools or departments had been established by the end of the century.

Nearly three thousand students registered in American graduate schools in 1890, as compared with a mere handful two decades before. As quick as their fellow countrymen to organize themselves in national associations, the professional scholars founded scores of learned societies in the seventies and eighties: the Archaeological Institute of America (1879), the Modern Language Association (1883), and in the next ten years the American Historical Association, the American Economic Association, the American Mathematical Society, the American Physical Society, and the American Psychological Association, to mention only a few. Learned journals and books equal to Europe's best began to appear in America, and American-trained scholars began to acquire international reputations.

Medical and legal education was still primitive in the seventies and eighties. None of the schools of medicine or law required a college degree for admission, and the typical medical school turned its graduates loose on a helpless public after only a few months of haphazard lectures. Both medical and legal degrees could easily be bought. Between 1876 and 1900 eighty-six new medical schools were founded, but the Johns Hopkins Medical School, opened in 1894, was the first to require a college degree for admission and the first to have a full-time teaching staff. By the end of the century many states had established boards of medical examiners that tightened license requirements, and the schools themselves began to raise their standards in response. Comparable improvement in law schools was to come only later.

This was an era prolific in the birth of new institutions of higher learning, both public and private. In the last two decades of the nineteenth century the total number of colleges and universities in the country increased by nearly one hundred fifty, though many of them had no valid claim to academic status and were often short lived. Ten new state universities, all of them coeducational from the start, were founded between 1882 and 1895. In the East, where coeducation was slower to win acceptance, Vassar was opened in 1861, Smith in 1871, and Bryn Mawr in 1885, while several of the older men's colleges opened affiliated women's colleges nearby. Numerous land-grant colleges, taking advantage of the Morrill Act of 1862, sprang up to teach both agricultural and mechanical arts. A fraction of the new industrial and commercial fortunes of the age went into the founding of universities bearing the names of Cornell (1868), Vanderbilt (1873), Hopkins (1876), Tulane (1884), Stanford (1885), and Clark (1887). The University of Chicago (1891) was one of the few that did not take the name of its benefactor, in this case John D. Rockefeller.

The history of higher learning of this period was not, however, purely a story of expansion and improvement. A mistaken conception of democracy led to the assumption of equality among all academic pursuits and justified the teaching of courses in almost any subject, however trivial. Charlatans were often commissioned to teach such courses, and almost anyone could take them. Institutions became overexpanded, overcrowded, and absurdly bureaucratized by a new species of academician known as the administrator. A misguided deference to the opinions of alumni, sports enthusiasts, and the unlettered public generally led to an anarchical confusion of values and grotesque distortions of academic purpose. For the first time in recorded history institutions of higher learning assumed the function of providing mass entertainment in spectator sports, and the comparative distinction of a university came to depend on its success in pursuing these commercial enterprises.

The businessmen who replaced the clergymen on the college boards of trustees were slow to acknowledge the status claimed by the new scholar and were sometimes quite unable to distinguish between their relation to faculty members and their relation to "other employees." The trustees of seven well known universities approved a statement published in the Chicago *Tribune* in 1899 to the effect that college professors "should promptly and gracefully submit to the determination of the trustees" in deciding what should be taught, and that "if the trustees err it is for the patrons and proprietors, not for the employees, to change either the policy or the personnel of the board." During the 1890s nine prominent faculty members were dismissed for presuming to express their opinions on such subjects as labor, railroads, and currency. Though there was no legitimate excuse for the gaucheries that for a time made American colleges a laughingstock of informed world opinion, we must remember that America was trying to spread the benefits of learning far more widely (and as a result more thinly) than had ever been attempted before.

Arts, letters, and critics

Artists and their work. In matters of taste the Gilded Age has acquired and in part deserved a deplorable reputation. Whether it was because the molders of fashion were insecure in their social position or new to their wealth or for some other reason, their taste ran to excesses in all things—in their clothing, their jewelry, and their houses, in interior décor and exterior ornament. They overloaded their rooms with bric-a-brac, their dresses with bustles, and their houses with gingerbread. They had no trouble finding architects, painters, and sculptors of the sort that would cater to their preferences, but the work these people left behind need not detain us.

Beneath the crass surface and behind the clutter of imitative art, however, there were genuinely original and creative spirits at work in the land. Artists, engineers, architects, sculptors, and painters honestly faced the realities of the new urban, industrial society and contrived original and powerful answers to its problems. It was the new city that gave them both their challenge and their opportunity. The bold spirit with which they met the challenge and seized the opportunity is caught in a statement by a Georgia-bred architect, John Wellborn Root, who did his work in Chicago:

> In America we are free of artistic traditions. Our freedom begets license, it is true. We do shocking things; we produce works of architecture irremediably bad;

Amid the immense number and variety of living forms, he [Louis Sullivan] noted that invariably the form expressed the function, as, for instance, the oak tree expressed the function oak, the pine tree the function pine, and so on through the amazing series. And, inquiring more deeply, he discovered that in truth it was not simply a matter of form expressing function, but the vital idea was this: That the function created or organized its form. Discernment of this idea threw a vast light upon all things within the universe, and condensed with astounding impressiveness upon mankind, upon all civilizations, all institutions, every form and aspect of society, every mass-thought and mass-result, every individual thought and individual result.... The application of the idea to the Architectural art was manifest enough, namely, that the function of a building must predetermine and organize its form.

From Louis H. Sullivan, *The Autobiography of an Idea*, 1924.

Modern architecture: the principle

It became evident that the very tall masonry office building was in its nature economically unfit as ground values steadily rose. Not only did its thick walls entail loss of space and therefore revenue, but its unavoidably small window openings could not furnish the proper and desirable ratio of glass area to rentable floor area.

Thus arose a crisis, a seeming impasse. *What was to do?... The need was there, the capacity to satisfy was there, but contact was not there. Then came the flash of imagination which saw the single thing. The trick was turned; and there swiftly came into being something new under the sun. For the true steel-frame structure stands unique in the flowing of man and his works; a brilliant material example of man's capacity to satisfy his needs through the exercise of his natural powers....*

The social significance of the tall building is in finality its most important phase. In and by itself, considered solus *so to speak, the lofty steel frame makes a powerful appeal to the architectural imagination where there is any. Where imagination is absent and its place usurped by timid pedantry the case is hopeless. The appeal and the inspiration lie, of course, in the element of loftiness, in the suggestion of slenderness and aspiration, the soaring quality as of a thing rising from the earth as a unitary utterance.*

From Louis H. Sullivan, *The Autobiography of an Idea*, 1924.

Modern architecture: the application

we try crude experiments that result in disaster. Yet somewhere in this mass of ungoverned energies lies the principle of life. A new spirit of beauty is being developed and perfected, and even now its first achievements are beginning to delight us. This is not the old thing made over; it is new. It springs out of the past, but it is not tied to it; it studies the traditions, but is not enslaved by them.

One achievement of the age that was daring and magnificent enough to meet Root's description was the Brooklyn Bridge, a suspension such as had never before been built, with granite towers 276 feet high and with a central span of 1,600 feet. Sketched by John A. Roebling, who died before construction began, the great bridge was completed by his son Washington A. Roebling in 1883. A product of the new industrialism down to the last of the nineteen strands of steel cable and the last riveted girder, the bridge soared out of the soot and slums of Manhattan, monumental proof that the new society could produce a thing of beauty out of its materials. In the same city a landscape architect named Frederick L. Olmsted demonstrated that it was not necessary for a city to be the seat of an

Brooklyn Bridge: symbol of the new industrialism

absolute monarch in order to create in its very center spacious, lovely, and exquisitely designed parks, such as Central Park, Olmsted's masterpiece. It was not his only great park, however, for he designed many more and left scarcely a major city in the country untouched by his influence.

The architect whom Root singled out to illustrate the new spirit in American art was Henry Hobson Richardson. Born in New Orleans but educated at Harvard and abroad, Richardson was a man of gargantuan ambitions and appetites, full of zest for any problem and equally ready to design churches, railroad stations, department stores, libraries, office buildings, anything. "The things I want most to design," he said, "are a grain elevator and the interior of a great river steamboat." Although he died in 1886 at the age of forty-eight, he left his buildings scattered across the country from Trinity Church in Boston to a monument on the Wyoming plains.

The problem of the skyscraper, called into being by the fantastic extravagance of unplanned city growth and overcrowding, could not be solved by masonry. What was required was a steel skeleton for support and walls reduced to mere fireproof curtains instead of supporting buttresses. With contributions from engineers and steelmasters as well as architects, Chicagoans achieved a solution in the Tacoma Building in 1888. With the arrival of the electric elevator and vertical transportation, the age of the skyscraper begins, and with that age the name of Louis Sullivan is intimately associated. Ranking with Richardson as one of the giants of the period,

Sullivan was a capricious genius who commanded the respect of the ablest critics: Frank Lloyd Wright referred to him as *Der Meister.* Sullivan had been called the "father of the skyscraper," and yet he revealed the inner conflicts of his generation's adjustment to the city when he characterized the structure as "profoundly antisocial."

It is curious that Chicago, which contributed so many new and original architectural techniques, should also have been the host and creator of the White City at the Columbian Exposition of 1893, which represented a return to Renaissance classicism and eclecticism in the extreme. Although Daniel H. Burnham of Chicago supervised the building, the White City was mainly the work of Easterners, particularly the firm of Charles F. McKim, William R. Mead, and Stanford White. The architects were assisted by the most famous American sculptor of the period, Augustus Saint-Gaudens, and by Olmsted, whose landscaping included the lovely lagoon surrounded by gleaming white-plaster buildings. The ephemeral dream city was undoubtedly an impressive spectacle, but Sullivan, who designed the only nonclassical structure in the Exposition, regarded it as "an appalling calamity" whose influence would "last for half a century." What he feared was a reversion to the academic, classical models of architecture; in the "Federal" style sponsored by McKim, Mead, and White in the national capital and elsewhere in the ensuing era, Sullivan's fears were justified. On the other hand the example of a city intelligently planned for comfort and beauty stimulated the "city beautiful" move-

New spirits: Richardson and Sullivan built for Chicago

ment, and under Burnham's guidance Washington, Cleveland, San Francisco, and Manila made impressive achievements in the art of city-planning.

Some of the fine arts in what Lewis Mumford has called the "Brown Decades" were creditably served by American artists. John La Farge, a gifted interior-decorator and art critic, executed thousands of stained-glass windows and won the admiration of Richardson, for whom he did the windows of Trinity Church in Boston. Winslow Homer, a serious illustrator, occasionally struck the note of greatness in his paintings of the weather-beaten ruggedness of common life. But to find American painters who deserve to rank with the best of their European contemporaries one must turn to Thomas Eakins and Albert Pinkham Ryder. Eakins worked in relative obscurity outside fashionable currents and left a house full of unsold paintings at his death. A friend of Walt Whitman, whose portrait he painted, he had a salty contempt for pretense and loved to paint boxers, oarsmen, and surgeons at their work. Ryder was a painter of the sea and the night and has been compared with Melville in the symbolic and lyrical qualities of his art. Among his great symbolic paintings are *Death on a Pale Horse, The Flying Dutchman, Jonah,* and *Macbeth and the Witches*—all eerie, mystic, and tragic.

Beginnings of realism.

In letters as in arts the post-Civil War decades have had a poor reputation. Their writers have been tagged with the "genteel" label and condemned for complacency and blindness to the glaring faults of their society. Their reputation for shallowness, complacency, and prudery is not wholly unjustified, but the age was often as blind to its literary merits as to its social faults. It sometimes overlooked and sometimes misunderstood its best talent. Contemporaries of Emily Dickinson, the greatest American poet of the age, and one of the subtlest, never even heard of her, for she lived the life of a recluse and published only two poems before her death in 1886. They mistook Mark Twain, their greatest satirist, for a funny man and a writer for boys. They were misled by the surface mildness of William Dean Howells, their major critic and their leading realist, and they misunderstood (when they did not neglect) Henry James, their greatest artist. But any age that could produce Dickinson, Twain, Howells, and James should command respect and serious attention.

More completely and richly than any other writer, Mark Twain, who was christened Samuel Langhorne Clemens, embodied in his life and writings the sprawling diversity, the epic adventures, the inner tensions, and the cross-purposes of post-Civil War America. A Southerner by birth and heritage, he became a Westerner while the West was wildest and settled in New England to live out his life. He was a child of the frontier and, like his America, a country man who moved to the city, a provincial who was thrust into a strange new world. His literary record of the experience documents a whole epoch. "I am persuaded," the playwright George Bernard Shaw wrote Mark Twain, "that the future historian of America will find your works as

Mark Twain, 1835–1910

Henry James, 1843–1916

indispensable to him as a French historian finds the political tracts of Voltaire.''

Mark Twain's American odyssey started in Missouri on the banks of the Mississippi, where the East bordered on the West and the South overlapped the North. He joined the Confederate army when the war broke out, but, after a trivial accident that involved no fighting, he gave up the war and joined his brother in the Far West. He recorded his adventures in the Nevada mining camps in *Roughing It* (1872) and gave the period a name that has stuck in *The Gilded Age* (1873), a broad political and social satire. His boyhood and his later experience as a pilot on the great river found expression in two of his works, *The Adventures of Tom Sawyer* (1876) and *Life on the Mississippi* (1883). But he surpassed all his other work in *The Adventures of Huckleberry Finn* (1884), the finest expression of the age in fiction and a masterpiece of American literature. A composite of satire and nostalgia, it dips deeper into irony than was characteristic of the age, for it aligns the sympathies of every decent reader with Huck, the river rat, against civilization itself and fixes the primitive, superstitious Nigger Jim as one of the noblest figures in American fiction. Mark Twain wrote a great deal more, but like the miners of his Nevada adventure and America itself, he was a spendthrift with his resources and could not always tell the stuff that glittered from real gold.

Howells, the friend of Twain and the generous friend of every creative spirit in letters of his time, was even more prolific. He wrote thirty full-length novels and five volumes of short stories, not to mention an endless stream of literary criticism. In his time he was rightfully called the dean of American letters and the foremost exponent of American realism. Rejected by a later generation that unfairly associated him with complacency and materialism, Howells deserves better from the present perspective. In mid-life he reached a turning point marked by his reaction to the Haymarket executions in 1886, against which he conducted virtually a one-man protest among the intellectuals. The experience coincided with his reading of Tolstoy and Henry George, and he began calling himself a socialist and demanding a sterner realism that would confront the injustice and suffering of industrial society under plutocratic control. His fiction began at once to reflect his views. *Annie Kilburn* (1889) is an indictment of social injustice and the inadequacies of charity in a New England community, and *A Hazard of New Fortunes* (1890) the best expression of Howells' new phase and the climactic work of American realism, centers around a violent strike. *A Traveler from Altruria* (1894) is a utopian novel that exposes and attacks social injustice.

Henry James continued to develop as a writer after Howells and Twain began to decline. His wonderfully productive life carried over into the twentieth century, though the bulk of his work appeared before 1900. Unlike Howells and Twain, he was not interested in the common man. His typical subjects are Americans and Europeans of cultivated minds, usually in a cosmopolitan setting. *The American* (1877), *The Europeans* (1878), and *Daisy Miller* (1879) are treatments of national attitudes in transatlantic society. This was only the beginning of four decades of writing that included such masterpieces as *The Portrait of a Lady* (1881), *The Ambassadors* (1903), and *The Golden Bowl* (1904). Henry James was the most completely dedicated and probably the most wholly fulfilled American writer and artist of his time.

The age affords posterity one unflattering but fascinating portrait of itself drawn by a philosopher-historian who stands in a class by himself: Henry Adams, descendant of the two Presidents whose name he bore. Every serious student of the period must make his own acquaintance and his own peace with this querulous and opinionated critic. His main writing dealt with the history of another period, that of Jefferson and Madison. But his novels *Democracy* (1880) and *Esther* (1883) and more particularly his autobiographical *Education of Henry Adams* (1918) and *The Degradation of the Democratic Dogma* (1919) are the keys to his incisive critique. It was characteristic of him that he had the first two books published anonymously and the last two posthumously. Having mastered those, one is then better prepared to find Adams, in *Mont-Saint-Michel and Chartres* (1913), searching the monuments of the Middle Ages for their meaning to modern America, and projecting lines of change from the year 1200 to the year 1900.

After the end of the century and near the end of his life, Henry Adams looked back philosophically over the American experience since the Civil War. He was astonished at how much history had been telescoped into that brief span of years and how frightfully the pace of change had accelerated. At the outset of the period, in his youth, his fellow citizens were still grappling with stone-age men on the Great Plains and debating the issue of African slavery in their midst. America had been a land of villages and farms, a provincial outpost of Western civilization. But now, as he steamed into New York Harbor in 1902, remembering his return from Europe in 1868, he searched in vain for landmarks of the earlier era. "The outline of the city became frantic in its effort to explain something that defied meaning," he observed. Titanic, uncontrollable forces "had exploded, and thrown great masses of stone and steam against the sky. . . . A Traveller in the highways of history looked out of the club window on the turmoil of Fifth Avenue, and felt himself in Rome, under Diocletian. . . . The two-thousand-years failure of Christianity roared upward from Broadway, and no Constantine the Great was in sight." Henry Adams' fellow Americans, less troubled by historical perspective and premonitions of things to come, called the spectacle "progress" and greeted the dawn of the twentieth century with a confidence that was apparently unbounded.

Suggestions for reading

C. M. Green, *The Rise of Urban America** (1965), is a short history, and Blake McKelvey, *The Urbanization of America, 1860–1915* (1963), and C. N. Glaab and A. T. Brown, *A History of Urban America** (1967), are general studies. A. M. Schlesinger, *The Rise of the City, 1878–1898** (1933), furnishes an introduction to the social history of urban America in this period. A. F. Weber, *The Growth of Cities in the Nineteenth Century** (1899), compares statistics of city growth in Europe and America. Lewis Mumford, *The Culture of Cities** (1938), *The City in History** (1961), and several other studies, transcends national history to study the phenomenon theoretically. Max Weber, *The City** (1958), is another theoretical study. Several cities are examined as types by C. M. Green, *American Cities in the Building of the Nation** (1956).

Contemporary sources on urban slums and poverty include Jacob Riis, *How the Other Half Lives** (1890), *The Children of the Poor* (1892), and *The Battle with the Slum* (1902); see also Josiah Strong, *The Twentieth Century City* (1898), as well as Jane Addams, *Twenty Years at Hull House** (1910). A good history of American attitudes toward poverty is R. H. Bremner, *From the Depths: The Discovery of Poverty in the United States** (1956). A sensitive analysis of immigration is Oscar Handlin, *The Uprooted** (1951). On the new immigrants see particularly I. A. Hourwich, *Immigration and Labor* (1922); on their reception in the United States consult Barbara Solomon, *Ancestors and Immigrants** (1956), and John Higham, *Strangers in the Land** (1955). M. A. Jones, *American Immigration** (1960), is an expert synthesis.

On the boss, the machine, and the reformer a contemporary account, James Bryce, *The American Commonwealth,* 2 vols* (1888), is a classic. For reformers of the period, see J. G. Sproat, *The Best Men: Liberal Reformers in the Gilded Age* (1968). A muckraker who deals with this period informatively is Lincoln Steffens, *The Shame of the Cities** (1904). Later studies of value are F. J. Goodnow, *Municipal Problems* (1907), Clifford W. Patton, *The Battle for Municipal Reform: Mobilization and Attack, 1875–1900* (1940), and A. B. Callow, Jr., *The Tweed Ring** (1966).

On women's rights and the suffrage movement see William L. O'Neill, *Everyone Was Brave: The Rise and Fall of Feminism in America* (1969), Eleanor Flexner, *Century of Struggle: The Woman's Rights Movement in the United States** (1959), and A. S. Kraditor, *The Ideas of the Woman Suffrage Movement, 1890–1920* (1965).

The reaction of the Protestant churches to social problems is discussed in several books, notably H. F. May, *Protestant Churches and Industrial America** (1949); A. I. Abell, *The Urban Impact on American Protestantism, 1865–1900* (1942); and C. H. Hopkins, *The Rise of the Social Gospel in American Protestantism, 1865–1915** (1940). On evangelists, see B. A. Weisberger, *They Gathered at the River: The Story of the Great Revivalists and Their Impact upon Religion in America** (1958), and J. F. Findlay, Jr., *Dwight L. Moody: American Evangelist, 1837–1899* (1969). On the Catholics there is a fine brief account in J. T. Ellis, *American Catholicism** (1956),

*Available in a paperback edition.

and a longer study in Theodore Maynard, *The Story of American Catholicism** (1941). Allan Johnson's long sketch of Mary Baker Eddy in the *Dictionary of American Biography* is helpful on the origins of Christian Science. W. W. Sweet, *Revivalism in America: Its Origins, Growth and Decline** (1944), is a useful survey, and his *The Story of Religion in America* (1939, rev. ed., 1950) is also helpful.

The history of higher learning has been surveyed by Frederick Rudolph, *The American College and University, A History** (1962), elaborated upon by L. R. Veysey, *The Emergence of the American University* (1965), and much illuminated by Richard Hofstadter and Walter Metzger, *The Development of Academic Freedom in the United States* (1955). For a stiff and amusing indictment see Thorstein Veblen, *Higher Learning in America** (1918). Merle Curti, *Social Ideas of American Educators** (1935), is instructive, as is H. K. Beale, *Are American Teachers Free?* (1936). R. H. Shryock, "The Academic Profession in the United States," *Bulletin of the American Association of University Professors* (Spring 1952), is most important.

The history of public education receives vigorous and needed reinterpretation in L. A. Cremin, *The Transformation of the School: Progressivism in American Education, 1876–1957** (1961). A. E. Meyer, *An Educational History of the American People* (1957), is a useful reference work. On the South see C. W. Dabney, *Universal Education in the South,* 2 vols. (1936). R. O. and Victoria Case, *We Called It Culture: The Story of Chautauqua* (1958), is the best account of that movement. F. L. Mott, *A History of American Magazines, 1885–1905* (1957), is an exhaustive and excellent history. The newspapers are treated in W. G. Bleyer, *Main Currents in the History of American Journalism* (1927).

On the graphic arts there are several studies of value, notably Lewis Mumford, *The Brown Decades: A Study of the Arts in America, 1865–1895** (1931); John Kouwenhoven, *Made in America: The Arts in Modern Civilization** (1948); and O. W. Larkin, *Art and Life in America* (1949, rev. ed., 1960). On architecture, see Wayne Andrews, *Architecture, Ambition and Americans** (1955), and on the growth of cities, Christopher Tunnard and H. H. Reed, *American Skyline** (1955).

Literary history in this era is treated by Larzer Ziff, *The American 1890s: Life and Times of a Lost Generation** (1966), Everett Carter, *Howells and the Age of Realism* (1954), who discusses Howells' contemporaries as well, and Kermit Vanderbilt, *The Achievement of William Dean Howells: A Reinterpretation* (1968). E. H. Cady, *The Realist at War* (1958); G. N. Bennett, *William Dean Howells* (1959); and V. W. Brooks, *New England: Indian Summer, 1865–1915** (1940) and *The Confident Years, 1885–1915* (1952), are full of biographical incident. Alfred Kazin, *On Native Grounds** (1942), starts his account at 1890 but has two illuminating chapters on that decade. Some good biographies are Justin Kaplan, *Mr. Clemens and Mark Twain** (1966); Ernest Samuels, *Henry Adams: The Middle Years* (1958) and *Henry Adams: The Major Phase* (1964). H. M. Jones, *The Age of Energy: Varieties of American Experience, 1865–1915* (1971), contains essays on the cultural scene.

*Available in a paperback edition.

20

Political stalemate and agrarian revolt
1877–1896

National politics had normally been the vital center of American civilization, the arena in which the future was determined and important issues of the present were resolved. Under Presidents Hayes, Garfield, Arthur, Cleveland, and Harrison, Americans still worked up a great deal of excitement over national politics, and voters turned out in great numbers, but it was the excitement more of spectators than of participants. The outcome of the contests meant more to the contestants than to the spectators, for the elections determined which party would enjoy the spoils of victory—and often little else. Great issues were sometimes debated, but most of them were settled around the council tables of industrialists and financiers rather than in the halls of legislatures and in the meetings of cabinets. The doctrine of laissez faire, so popular among businessmen, was just as popular among politicians, for it spared them a great deal of trouble. Literally applied, it meant permitting men of power to have things their own way so long as they appeared to stay within the law, with little regard for the social consequences. The political game played under these rules attracted men of great skill, but none of true greatness.

The business of politics

The party equilibrium. Politics in the post-Reconstruction period was more a business than a game, a highly competitive business with the two major parties as the evenly matched competitors. The Democrats managed to elect only one of their candidates President (for two terms) in the fifty-two years between 1860 and 1912. And yet this gives a misleading impression of the relative strength of the Democratic and Republican parties. Actually, there was an extraordinarily narrow margin of difference in the popular vote the two parties polled in the two decades following 1876. In none of the presidential elections from 1876 to 1892 did the Republicans carry a majority of the popular votes, and

in only one, that of 1880, did they receive a plurality—but even that plurality was less than one-tenth of 1 percent. In three of the five elections, in fact, the difference between the popular votes for the two major-party candidates was less than 1 percent, and in that of 1876, even though the Democrats received a majority of nearly 3 percent, they lost the election. In the Electoral College votes, on the other hand, majorities ranged from 1 in 1876 to 132 in 1892. The narrow margin between victory and defeat encouraged the laissez-faire tendency of politicians, the tendency to avoid vital issues and take few chances.

The Republican party was a loose alliance of regional and interest groups with different

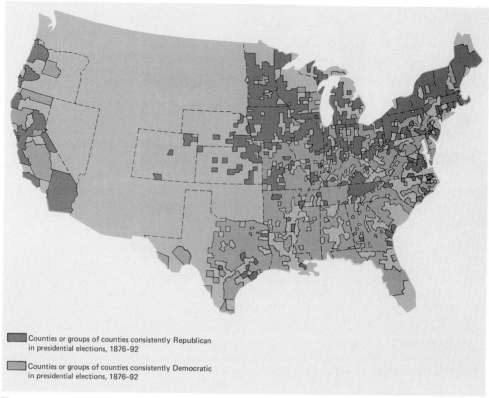

Counties or groups of counties consistently Republican
in presidential elections, 1876–92

Counties or groups of counties consistently Democratic
in presidential elections, 1876–92

The consistency of the vote, 1876–92

and sometimes conflicting interests. The basic regional alliance was between the Northeast and the Middle West—an alliance that had been consolidated in 1860 and had fought and won the Civil War. It hung together afterward partly because of wartime loyalties and memories of the heroic days of Lincoln, when the party had emancipated the slaves and saved the Union. Two other large groups traced their attachment to the party back to the Civil War: the freedmen and the Union army veterans. The blacks remained loyal to the party of emancipation and continued to send one or two congressmen to Washington from the South, but after the Republicans abandoned them in 1877 the political power of the freedmen diminished rapidly. On the other hand the political significance of the war veterans increased as the Grand Army of the Republic grew as a pressure group and as Congress responded with larger and larger pensions for veterans. Economic conflict and political rivalry opened breaches in party unity. Republican policies such as high tariffs, sound money, and favors for railroads pleased Eastern industrialists, but Western grain-growers often resented these policies and

threatened revolt. The noisiest quarrel within Republican ranks was the running war between the Half-Breeds, led by James G. Blaine of Maine, and the Stalwarts, led by Roscoe Conkling of New York. The long-winded battles between these factions fascinated the multitude, but there was no significant difference between them over any policy or issue that troubled the country—only over which of them should get the spoils of office. Each demanded all the offices.

The post-Reconstruction Democratic party was even more regional than the Republican. Its most reliable sources of support were the South and the machine-dominated cities of the Northeast. And the disparity of outlook and interest between the provincial, Protestant cotton-farmers of the South and the underprivileged, Catholic, immigrant, industrial workers of the big cities was almost as great as that between the impoverished Negro and the affluent capitalist supporters of the Republican party. The Democrats also received support from Northeastern merchants and bankers who opposed the protective tariff and favored contraction of the currency—''sound-money'' men, they called themselves.

The leaders of the party in the South, many of them of Whig background, preferred to be called Conservatives, and were often called Bourbons by their opponents. They had much in common with the dominant Democratic leaders in the Middle West, who were also business-minded conservatives and were also known as Bourbons. Rank-and-file Democrats, farmers, industrial workers, and small businessmen in the West, the South, and the East, were often restive and sometimes rebellious under such leaders, but conservatives generally had things their way in the party until the mid-nineties.

On major issues no important differences existed between the two old parties, which were under equally conservative leaders. Politics became the art of blurring or avoiding issues. Not that there was any lack of important issues. To appreciate the emptiness and bankruptcy of national politics in this period, one has only to recall the recurrent industrial crises and depressions of the period and the desperate plight of the victims. Their problems cried out for vigorous government action. But if they got a hearing in the political arena, it was through small third parties. The major parties preferred to avoid live issues and revive dead ones. In the North the Republicans "waved the bloody shirt," accusing the Democrats of rebellion and treason, and in the South the Democrats invoked the menace of "Negro rule" and called for white supremacy. It is true that a vast amount of lung power was devoted to the "platform" and its "planks" during campaigns, but the wind seems to have whistled over the heads of the voters. Yet the rate of voter turnout was unusually high in these years.

"The American, like the Englishman," observed James Bryce in 1888, "usually votes with his party, right or wrong, and the fact that there is little distinction of view between the parties makes it easier to stick to your old friends." Party allegiance during these years was in fact remarkably rigid. In Indiana, for example, thirty-two counties remained unswervingly Republican from 1876 to 1892, and thirty-nine counties stuck as unswervingly with the Democrats, with neither group varying more than 3 percent. In spite of much population mobility, only twenty-one counties shifted parties at all, and with third parties in the picture neither of the major parties could muster a reliable majority in those counties until 1896. The same pattern had prevailed

for years: two-thirds of the Democratic counties had been voting Democratic since 1844, and over four-fifths of the Republican counties had gone down the line for the old party since its founding in 1856. These rigid loyalties carried Hoosier voters right through war and peace, through a wide variety of candidates and policies, and through all the economic and social upheavals of the passing years.

Party loyalties seemed less affected by national issues and policies, such as the tariff, than by matters closer to the daily life and experience of voters. And party identifications were more strongly influenced by cultural than by economic interests. Substantive issues such as prohibition versus the "saloon power," Sabbath observance versus "desecration," and public versus parochial schools reflected and symbolized religious and ethnic values. These values and symbols divided "pietists" from "ritualists" and Protestants from Catholics. The Republicans of the period are described as the "Party of Piety," and Democrats as the "Party of Personal Liberty." Men took their party identifications seriously because they did not take their religious values lightly.

Neither party was strong enough, however, to rely for victory on the allegiance of certain states or parts of states that could be counted "in the bag." There were always the "doubtful states"—that is, states with enough shifting voters to turn the tide either way. These states were thought to be Connecticut, New York, New Jersey, Ohio, Indiana, and Illinois, but the key states were New York and Indiana. In the 1880s the Republicans had to carry New York and all three of the doubtful Midwestern states to elect their candidate President. Since the whole contest hinged on a few states, it is no wonder that they commanded great bargaining power, absorbed most of the "slush funds" from the campaign treasuries, and gained desirable offices for their politicians. The strategic importance of the few doubtful Midwestern states also helps to explain why five of the six Republican candidates for President from Grant to McKinley came from those states, including three from Ohio and one from Indiana. And as a running mate for their Midwestern candidate, the Republicans almost invariably chose a man from New York. The Democrats, on the other hand, usually reversed the regional order, though they picked their nominees from the same doubtful states. Their presidential nominees, with one exception, all came from New York—three of them had been governors of the state—and their vice-presidential nominees from Ohio, Illinois, or Indiana. In 1876, 1880, and 1884 the second place on the Democratic ticket went to the "strategic" state of Indiana.

The spoilsmen and the reformers.

From Grant to McKinley the power and influence of the presidential office were at low ebb. One reason was that no President between 1865 and 1897 enjoyed the advantage of having his own party in control of both houses of Congress throughout his tenure of office, so rapidly did control seesaw back and forth between the evenly matched parties. But more than that, the Presidency was slow in recovering from the blows struck by Congress in its bitter fight with President Johnson and from President Grant's continual acquiescence in the domination of Congress. For a generation congressional supremacy and presidential subordination remained the rule. Senator John Sherman of Ohio, himself a perpetual aspirant to the office, wrote that the President "should be subordinate to the legislative department" and should merely "obey and enforce the laws." Ordinarily the President did not even have a voice in preparing the annual budget, and he was certainly not given the staff or the money to play the role of a real chief executive. To a large degree, Congress itself took care of administration. As Leonard D. White, a leading administrative historian, puts it, "The established course of the public business went on its appointed way, for the most part without requiring or inviting the collaboration of the man who sat in the White House."

Politics was really controlled by oligarchies of party bosses, many of them United States senators, who headed state machines and commanded armies of henchmen whom they paid off with public offices. In addition to Senators Blaine and Conkling were such potentates as Senator Zachariah Chandler, the fat, coarse, and cynical boss of Michigan, and Senator John A. "Black Jack" Logan of Illinois, a power in the Grand Army of the Republic. The patronage system placed at the disposal of the bosses the whole public service, an enormous booty in federal, state, and local offices, the "spoils" of political victory. The spoilsmen sometimes sold offices to the highest bidder, but more regularly they distributed them among faithful workers for service rendered and systematically taxed the holders for "contributions." After the Civil Service Reform Act of 1883 (see p. 470) began to curb patronage as a source of revenue, politicians increasingly turned to big business for money and support. A new type of boss then began to replace the old flamboyant "stump politician," a quieter, more efficient "desk politician," who employed the methods of the corporation executive and worked hand in glove with the lobbyists and leaders of public utilities, railroads, heavy industries, and manufactures. Matthew Quay, who kept a card index of the foibles of Pennsylvania politicians; "Easy Boss" Tom Platt, who succeeded Conkling in New York; Arthur P. Gorman, the friend of business in Maryland; Henry G. Davis and his son-in-law Stephen B. Elkins, who ran respectively the Democratic and Republican parties of West Virginia; and Marcus Alonzo Hanna, Ohio industrialist turned politician, were bosses of the new type.

Not all the public men of the age were cynics and spoilsmen. A group of liberal reformers called Mugwumps by their deriders kept up a running crusade against patronage and corruption in office for two decades. Earnest and élitist, the Mugwumps were men of high social position and conservative economic views, usually of Republican background. Foremost among them was George William Curtis, scholarly editor of *Harper's Weekly,* whose cartoonist Thomas Nast made a career of ridiculing and caricaturing the corrupt. Carl Schurz, who called Curtis "the intellectual head, the guiding force" of the movement, was himself a hero of the Mugwumps. Another of the luminaries was E. L. Godkin, editor of the *Nation.* Devoted to laissez-faire principles and unconcerned over the deeper ills of the economy, the reformers of this school confined their economic program to tariff reform and sound money and fixed their hopes on achieving honest and efficient government through civil-service reform. Spoilsmen sneered at "snivel service," and Senator Conkling described the reformers as "the man milliners, the dilettanti and *carpet knights* of politics" and accused them of "canting self-righteousness."

The influence of the Mugwumps was largely confined to the literate upper class, for they were isolated from the mass of voters by their attitudes and their social position. The various

The Boss

reform movements of the period were not on speaking terms with one another, or they spoke different languages. Grangers, Greenbackers, and Alliancemen of the West and the South (see pp. 477–78) demanded reforms in the currency, banking, and credit systems that chilled the blood of Eastern reformers. Agrarian reformers were at the same time divided among themselves: Northerner against Southerner, Republican against Democrat. Both the urban Mugwumps and the rural agrarians had trouble understanding the impulses and strivings of labor reformers. The cause of reform, its forces divided and mutually suspicious, languished and faltered through the eighties.

The conservative ascendancy

Hayes in the White House. We have already seen how the means used to elect Rutherford B. Hayes cast widespread doubt on his title to the Presidency (pp. 383–84). He did not strengthen his position when he announced that he would not run for reelection. Hayes was never an astute politician, but he did not lack courage and determination. From the start of his Administration he set out resolutely to redress the balance between the executive and legislative branches and regain for the Presidency some of the powers that Congress had preempted, particularly the powers of appointment and removal of officeholders.

The nominations for the Cabinet that he sent to the Senate were his first challenge to congressional dominance, for they included names unwelcome to the bosses—notably the name of Carl Schurz for Secretary of the Interior. "Hayes has passed the Republican party to its worst enemies," said Senator Zach Chandler. The Senate balked and refused confirmation on the whole list at first but later yielded to the President. An old device that the House used to coerce the President was the "rider," a piece of legislation the President had to approve in order to secure the needed appropriation to which it was tied. The Democratic majority of the House used the rider repeatedly in an attempt to force Hayes to accept the repeal of Reconstruction laws providing federal protection of elections. Determined to resist the pressure and make the executive "an equal and independent branch of the Government," Hayes vetoed seven such bills, compelled acceptance of his independence, and gained a clear-cut victory over congressional encroachment.

Hayes struck at the spoils system in its most powerful entrenchment, the New York Custom House Ring, the center of Senator Conkling's machine. A commission appointed by the President in 1877 and headed by John Jay of New York investigated the Custom House patronage system and reported that it was "unsound in principle, dangerous in practice, demoralizing in its influence on all connected with the customs service," and ridden with "ignorance, inefficiency, and corruption." Conkling's lieutenants, Collector of the Port Chester A. Arthur and naval officer Alonzo B. Cornell, refused to clean up the corruption and declined to resign. At Conkling's demand the Senate refused to confirm appointment of the successors whom Hayes nominated, but the President stubbornly persisted, dismissed Arthur and Cornell while the Senate was in recess, and eventually filled their places with men of his own choice. Hayes had won a battle with the spoilsmen, but not a war. His orders that officeholders not be assessed for political contributions or required to do political campaigning were ignored. His promise of "thorough, radical and complete" civil-service reform remained unfulfilled, and the spoilsmen continued to rule the roost.

Economic crises and social protest in the worst years of the depression caught the Hayes Administration without a policy and without real comprehension of what was happening. The first great industrial conflict in our history started with a strike on the B&O Railroad in July 1877 (see p. 437). The strike spread spontaneously and rapidly throughout all sections save New England and the South, affecting two-thirds of the railroad mileage in the country. At the request of four state governors, Hayes set the fateful precedent of using federal troops to intervene in a strike and restore order. The President incurred additional ill will from labor, especially on the West Coast, by vetoing a bill passed in 1879 to restrict Chinese "coolie" immigration. He vetoed the bill because it violated the Burlingame Treaty of 1868, but after the veto he began negotiations for a new treaty with China. The Treaty of 1880 acknowledged the right of restriction, and in 1882 Congress passed a bill putting an end to Chinese immigration for the following decade.

Monetary policy in politics. The President also took the unpopular side in a series of debates over national currency policies that divided both parties during his Administration. Hayes held the conservative, laissez-faire doctrine that the sole duty of the government was to maintain the value of currency and that the only way to do this was by the demonstrated ability of the Treasury to redeem currency at face value in gold. His opponents held, on the other hand, that it was the duty of the government to manage the currency so as to prevent or correct injustice and to relieve distress and suffering. While this was not the only explanation for the growing agricultural distress of the time, the farmer was perfectly right that crop prices were falling and that monetary policy was related to this decline.

The first clash between Hayes and the discontented agrarians occurred over a movement to repeal the Specie Resumption Act of 1875, which obliged the Treasury to resume the redemption of legal-tender notes in specie at full face value by January 1, 1879, and to reduce the number of greenbacks in circulation. The measure thus contracted the currency and at the same time appreciated its value, the two things most complained of by farmers and debtors. Advocates of repeal, called Greenbackers, argued that fulfillment of the act would further depress prices and increase the burden of private and public debt. They denounced as outrageous the proposal to redeem war bonds that had been bought with greenbacks worth less than 40 cents to the dollar with currency worth 100 cents to the dollar. A National Greenback party had polled an insignificant vote in the election of 1876, but in the following year the movement gained recruits from labor and additional support from farmers and in February 1878 reorganized as the Greenback Labor party. In the fall elections the new party polled a remarkable total of 1,060,000 votes and elected fourteen representatives to Congress. Resisting all pressure, much of it from his own party, Hayes clung to the policy of resumption and supported Secretary of the Treasury John Sherman in building up a gold reserve to redeem the currency. Two weeks before the deadline of January 1, 1879, however, greenbacks became worth their face value in gold and no run on the gold reserve developed.

Resumption was an accomplished fact. The Greenbackers nominated James B. Weaver of Iowa for President in 1880, but their issue was dead, and they attracted little attention.

Inflationist sentiment, by no means dead, found a new outlet in the movement for the free coinage of silver just as the greenback cause was becoming hopeless. Once again Hayes took the unpopular side. The silver question was to become one of the most hotly debated issues in the history of American politics during the next two decades, but before 1875 it attracted no popular interest. The official government ratio of sixteen to one—sixteen times as much silver in a silver dollar as there was gold in a gold dollar—had undervalued silver ever since the gold rush of 1849 had lowered the price of gold. As a consequence, silver-miners sold their product commercially rather than offer it to the Treasury at a loss, and silver dollars virtually disappeared from circulation. Foreseeing a drop in silver prices, a few monetary experts persuaded an ill-informed Congress to abolish the coinage of silver dollars and put the country on the gold standard in 1873. New silver mines in Nevada, Arizona, and Colorado soon flooded the market, and the price of silver began to drop. Miners then discovered that the Treasury rejected their product and that their European market had been reduced by widespread adoption of the gold standard abroad. Denouncing demonetization of silver as the "Crime of 1873," urban publishers of the Midwestern and Middle Atlantic states, not Western miners, started the demand that free coinage at the old ratio be restored. Inflationists eventually took up their cry because they saw in silver a means of halting currency contraction, getting cheaper money, raising crop prices, and securing debtor relief.

So rapidly did the silver movement spread that by the fall of 1877 an overwhelming majority of the lower house of Congress voted for a bill for the "free and unlimited coinage of silver" introduced by Representative Richard "Silver Dick" Bland of Missouri. The Bland bill would have stopped the sale of government bonds for gold and driven that metal out of circulation, since it would have produced silver dollars worth less than 90 cents (and still falling in value) and made them legal tender. Yet the bill commanded so much support in both houses that Hayes knew it would be passed over his veto. Before the Senate acted, however, Senator William B.

Allison of Iowa amended and weakened the bill, and in that form it was passed over Hayes' veto in February 1878. The Bland-Allison Act deprived the inflationists of their objective of ''unlimited coinage,'' and substituted the requirement that the Treasury buy not less than $2 million and not more than $4 million worth of silver per month and coin it into dollars. The act did not have the effects that the conservatives feared and the inflationists desired. For one thing the government consistently purchased the minimum amount of silver required by the act and stood ready to redeem the silver coin and notes in gold. And for another, the depression lifted in 1879, gold flowed in from abroad, and crop prices improved temporarily for reasons other than monetary policy. Silverites were to return to the battle in stronger force, but for more than a decade they made no change in the law.

In spite of the unpopularity of his stand on silver and quarrels with Congress, Hayes ended his Administration on an upswing of confidence and respect. Ordinarily such an upturn would have overcome his announced intention to retire, but no such movement developed. His party virtually ignored him, and he became scarcely more than a spectator during the struggle to nominate his successor.

The Garfield tragedy. The Republicans brought their bitter feuds to the Chicago nominating convention under the banners of rival candidates. The Stalwarts were united under Conkling's leadership to name Grant for a third term. The Half-Breeds were determined to have the prize for their own leader, Blaine; and Secretary of the Treasury John Sherman maneuvered to make himself available as a compromise candidate. When it became clear that none of the three could marshal a majority, the Blaine and Sherman forces joined on the thirty-sixth ballot and nominated Congressman James A. Garfield of Ohio as a dark horse. Garfield had managed Sherman's campaign and led the anti-Grant forces at the convention. To conciliate the defeated faction, the convention then nominated Conkling's lieutenant, Chester A. Arthur, the deposed spoilsman of the New York Custom House, for Vice President.

Prospects for revenging Governor Tilden by nominating him in 1880 looked promising to the Democrats, but Tilden, like Hayes, declined to run for the Presidency again. The party nominated instead General Winfield

James A. Garfield: victim of spoilsman politics

Scott Hancock, a Pennsylvanian and a Union hero in the Battle of Gettysburg. Hancock had no political experience, but his nomination was an effective answer to the charge of disloyalty that was so often thrown at his party. His running mate was William H. English, from the ''doubtful'' state of Indiana. The platforms of the two parties were nearly indistinguishable, their nominees almost equally undistinguished, and the campaigns they waged demagogic and sometimes unprincipled. The Republican managers did the most decisive work of the campaign in the doubtful states of Ohio, New York, and Indiana, using large amounts of money to carry Indiana by a bare seven thousand votes and New York by twenty thousand. Garfield won by a scant margin of less than forty thousand popular votes in the country at large, though his electoral vote was 214 to 155 for Hancock.

President Garfield's brief tenure in the White House began with embarrassments, continued with unhappiness, and ended in tragedy. A handsome, massive figure of a man, with a reputation for courage under fire in the war and for resourcefulness as party-leader in the House, Garfield was not without a degree of integrity. Under the extraordinary pressures of his new office, however, he wavered in purpose. His first impulse was to conciliate all the warring Republican factions and please as many people as possible. He knew that his major obligation for his office was to Blaine, however, and he acknowledged it by making the senator Secretary of State. Blaine promptly used his influence over the President to undermine and destroy the power of his sworn enemy Conkling. Garfield's most aggressive move against the Stalwarts was to replace the man whom Hayes had made collector of the port of New York (in the name of civil-service reform) with the leading opponent of the Conkling faction in New York. This precipitated a violent war between the factions of the spoilsmen and a torrent of abuse and charges of bad faith against the President.

At the very height of the furor over spoils and corruption, on July 2, 1881, Charles J. Guiteau, a crazed and disappointed office-seeker, shot the President in the back. Garfield died of the wound on September 19, and the next day Stalwart Chester A. Arthur became President.

The Arthur interlude. The new President was a wealthy, easygoing man with expensive tastes, elegant clothes and carriages, and twenty years of experience as a spoilsman in the Conkling camp of New York politics. His first year as President did little to dispel the fear that Garfield's martyrdom had been in vain and that the spoils system was there to stay. He did not turn over patronage to Conkling, as many expected, but after Blaine resigned the President filled the Cabinet with friends of Grant and Conkling. Arthur did prosecute with vigor the criminals charged with post-office frauds, one of whom claimed to have provided the money for carrying Indiana for Garfield and Arthur. But the guilty men escaped punishment, and the President's efforts not only failed to win over the reformers but alienated his former followers. The fall elections of 1882 drove his party from control of the House of Representatives and gave the Democrats a majority of nearly a hundred seats.

One cause of the Democratic landslide was the nation's shock over Garfield's assassination and revulsion against the system of patronage and spoils associated with the tragedy. Popular indignation put new power behind the demands of the small band of reformers who, having fought the spoilsmen since the 1860s, had in 1881 organized the National Civil Service Reform League, with George William Curtis as president. It was ironic that "Chet" Arthur, long the very symbol of spoils politics, should be cast in the role of civil-service reformer, but he firmly told Congress that "action should no longer be postponed" and promised his full cooperation. In January 1883 large bipartisan majorities in both houses of Congress passed a Democratic bill sponsored by Senator George H. Pendleton of Ohio. The Civil Service Act (often called the Pendleton Act) established a bipartisan Civil Service Commission of three members, appointed by the President with Senate confirmation, who were to administer competitive examinations and select appointees on the basis of merit and an apportionment among the states according to population. Arthur demonstrated his good faith by naming as head of the commission Dorman B. Eaton, an outstanding reformer who drafted the act, and appointing two prominent friends of reform as the other commissioners. At first the act affected only some fourteen thousand officials, about one-tenth of the total number of federal employees, but it empowered the President to expand the proportion of "classified" posts—jobs subject to the merit system. By the end of the century 40 percent were classified, and the federal civil service was securely established.

While the Civil Service Commission was the most important achievement of the Arthur Administration, it was not the President's only assertion of independence and conscience, nor his only praiseworthy effort. Two such efforts, both of them futile as it turned out, were in response to the problem of a surplus of over $100 million accumulated in the United States Treasury by excessive tax revenues. The solution favored by Congress was to spend the surplus in lavish appropriations for river and harbor improvements and pork-barrel handouts. Arthur vetoed one such bill, only to have Congress pass it over his veto. The President's solution to the Treasury surplus included the reduction of taxes, particularly the high protective tariff duties. To this end he appointed a Tariff Commission that made an elaborate study and recommended a moderate reduction of about 20 percent in the revenues, but a lobby of industrialists frustrated the President's plans for reform. As an incidental means of reducing the Treasury surplus, Arthur's naval-construction program was more successful. The navy had deteriorated since the Civil War to a collection of wooden antiques with cast-iron guns and rotten hulls. It did not boast a steel vessel or a rifled gun afloat. The Arthur Administration awakened Congress out of its indifference and started the construction of new fighting ships. The three cruisers begun in his Administration had numerous defects, but he is properly credited with sweeping away barriers of ignorance and clearing the way for a modern navy. In this as in other ways Arthur proved worthier of the office he held than anyone had reason to believe when he took it.

Changing the conservative guard.

The chances of Arthur's succeeding himself as President in 1884, never very strong in any case, were greatly weakened by the Democratic tidal wave of 1882, in which he lost control of his own state. He later won approval from the reform, especially the Mugwump, element, but not their support, and he proved unable to unite his own faction of the party behind his candidacy. Blaine remained the dominant figure in the Republican party, and his nomination seemed more and more likely as the convention approached. Curtis, Schurz, and other Mugwumps spurned Blaine and supported their own candidate, Senator George Edmunds of Vermont, to the end. Ignoring the reformers and overriding the Arthur supporters, the Blaine men nominated their candidate without difficulty and named John A. Logan, favorite son of Illinois, for Vice President. The Yankee Mugwumps promptly decided to bolt the party provided the Democrats nominated the rising hope of the reformers, Grover Cleveland, governor of New York.

Cleveland's rise in New York politics had been recent but rapid. Elected mayor of Buffalo in 1881, he accepted the Democratic nomination for governor in 1882 and won an easy victory because of the split in the Republican party of the state. A burly figure of two hundred forty pounds, determined jaw, and hard eyes, he was known for his rugged honesty and his habits of hard work and thrift—the common man turned reformer. But Cleveland was a thoroughgoing conservative as well, a believer in sound money and a defender of the right of property. As governor he enhanced his reputation for scorn of popularity by vetoing a popular bill reducing the fare on Jay Gould's elevated railroads in New York City to 5 cents. Similarly, he risked the wrath of labor by vetoing a bill limiting the working day of New York streetcar-conductors to twelve hours, and with even greater recklessness he defied "Honest" John Kelley, boss of Tammany Hall. Businessmen, middle-class taxpayers, and reformers of the Mugwump school admired the independence and integrity of Cleveland. The nomination of Blaine and the promise of Mugwump support made Governor Cleveland the logical standard-bearer for the Democrats in 1884. He was nominated with the aid of state bosses and financed in his campaign by corporate wealth. His running mate was Thomas A. Hendricks, yet another available candidate from the shifting counties of Indiana.

The presidential campaign of 1884 was one of the most sensational and frenzied in our history, and yet it managed to avoid all vital issues. "The public is angry and abusive," wrote Henry Adams. "Every one takes part. We are all doing our best, and swearing like demons. But the amusing thing is that no one talks about real interests." Cleveland said little at all, and Blaine talked a great deal without saying very much. There was no significant difference between the party platforms. In the absence of public issues, popular attention focused on the private life and personal morals of the candidates. Democrats and Mugwumps took the initiative by reviving the Mulligan Letter charges (see p. 381) that had deprived Blaine of the nomination in 1876 and by publishing additional Mulligan letters to prove that Blaine had been guilty of underhanded deals with railroad-promoters. George William Curtis declared that the issue was "moral rather than political." Thereupon the Republicans retaliated with charges that Cleveland was the father of an illegitimate son. The campaign deteriorated into scandalmongering that became more and more irresponsible.

Cleveland had to carry New York to win the election, and the extreme closeness of the contest in that state concentrated attention on a number of intangible factors, any one of which might conceivably be decisive. Whatever the explanation, the tide turned narrowly in Cleveland's favor. In addition to all the Southern states, he carried the doubtful states of Indiana, New Jersey, Connecticut, and New York—the last by a plurality of a mere 1,149 votes. His share of the votes in the country as a whole was only slightly greater than Blaine's. Mugwumps and reformers rejoiced at the victory, but it is a mistake to conclude that a moral crusade had defeated Blaine. Actually, he polled about the same percentage of the total vote as Garfield had in 1880 and a larger percentage than the Republican candidates were to poll in 1888 and 1892. At any rate, the long Republican rule was at an end, and the Democrats were back in power for the first time in twenty-four years.

A sensational campaign

Cleveland in command. No one could be sure of the new President's views on any of several leading issues, but everyone could be sure he was a conservative. His inaugural address promising adherence to ''business principles'' bore this out, and so did his Cabinet appointments, which included representatives of the most conservative and business-minded wing of the party in the East and South. The new Administration signified the return of the party of the ''outs'' and the political rehabilitation of the South but no break with the past on fundamental issues.

If there was any policy to which Cleveland had a clear commitment, it was civil-service reform, and it was over this issue that he came near to wrecking his Administration. He came to office with two masters to please: the Mugwump reformer and the hungry spoilsman of his own party with an appetite for office whetted by twenty-four years of anticipation. The President's first moves delighted the reformers. Defying the Democratic bosses and spoilsmen, he retained in office some able Republicans and personally examined applications for office far into the night. Party-leaders besieged the President with patronage demands and insisted that he accept their definition of civil-service reform, which, according to one senator, ''meant turning out of office of Republicans and putting honest Democrats in their places''—*all* their places. The party press thundered against his ''ingratitude.'' Within a few months he yielded to pressure, and Republican heads began to roll. Carl Schurz wrote, ''Your attempt to please both reformers and spoilsmen has failed,'' and Cleveland broke with the Mugwumps. By the end of four years he had removed about two-thirds of the 120,000 federal officers. He did increase the list of classified jobs to 27,380, nearly double the number when he took office, but he filled the Civil Service Commission with weak and incompetent men.

In the role of Treasury watchdog and thrifty steward of public funds, Cleveland showed more independence and consistency than he did as civil-service reformer. For one thing, he sternly rebuked a scandalous pensions racket run by a powerful lobby for Union veterans of the Civil War. Agents of this lobby used private bills to push through Congress thousands of dubious claims, hundreds of them obviously fraudulent. Previous Presidents, who feared the Grand Army of the Republic, had always signed these bills, but Cleveland called a halt and took to investigating individual claims himself, vetoing many of them, often with sarcastic comment. In January 1887, Congress passed a Dependent Pension Bill that provided a pension for all honorably discharged disabled veterans who had seen as much as ninety days of service if they were unable to work, regardless of the cause of their disability. The President defied the wrath of the GAR and its half-million members and vetoed the bill.

Cleveland believed that, except in rare circumstances, the President should confine himself to the execution of the laws and was not obliged to furnish leadership to Congress. In spite of the storms of social protest in the mid-eighties, Congress enacted little legislation of lasting significance, and the President's influence upon that was largely negative. His Secretary of the Interior, L. Q. C. Lamar, showed initiative in compelling railroads and cattle barons of the West to give up 81 million acres of public lands that they illegally withheld from settlement. But Cleveland himself deserves no credit for what was probably the most important act passed during his Administration, the Interstate Commerce Act of 1887 (see p. 423). He regarded the whole idea with suspicion and signed the bill reluctantly and ''with reservations.''

In his fight for tariff reform, however, Cleveland rose to the full heights of leadership that earned him the distinction of being the outstanding President between Lincoln and Theodore Roosevelt. The forthright stand he eventually took on this issue may have contributed to his defeat for reelection, but it fulfilled his promise of rugged integrity and dedication to duty. Typical of the man was his reply to an adviser who counseled compromise and caution: ''What is the use of being elected or re-elected, unless you stand for something?'' To appreciate the risks he ran and the foes he encountered, one needs to glance back over the history of the tariff issue.

The tariff in politics. The issue was as old as the republic, but since the Civil War it had taken on a new importance and complexity and was treated with caution and evasiveness by politicians of both parties. The tariff acts of the Civil War had been justified on the grounds that high internal war taxes on American industries put them at a competitive disadvantage that had to be offset with protective tariff duties to enable Americans to compete

Grover Cleveland: defender of the right of property

with foreign manufacturers on equal terms. Beginning with modest rates of 18.8 percent on dutiable goods in 1861, a succession of acts raised the average to 40.3 percent in 1866. No politician at the end of the war would admit publicly that these rates were anything but a temporary expedient. But, while the American producers were soon relieved of the burden of internal war taxes, the protective tariff remained unrepealed. American industry quickly adjusted to the prices, dividends, and profits made possible by freedom from competition from abroad. Producers who enjoyed or desired these advantages organized to press their needs on Congress. Politicians learned the great power of the tariff lobby, and both major parties, the Republicans explicitly and the Democrats tacitly, accepted the principle of protection—though with dissent in each party.

From time to time a President would make a gesture of reform, but Congress would regularly respond with jugglery that left the situation unchanged or made a mockery of reform. The Tariff Act of 1870 reduced the duties on coffee, tea, spices, and other articles not produced in this country but left the protective duties virtually unaltered. Regulars joined reformers in 1872 and actually effected a reduction of 10 percent in the protective duties, but the cut was quietly restored three years later on the ground that the Panic of 1873 had reduced federal revenues. Two Democratic bills for reform in 1876 and 1878 never got out of committee. We have already seen (p. 470) how President Arthur's efforts on tariff reform came to naught in 1883.

Cleveland hesitated for three years to take an aggressive stand. He knew that a minority of some forty Democratic congressmen had combined with Republicans to defeat tariff-reform bills in 1884 and 1886, and Democratic leaders assured him that an all-out fight on the issue would split the party and lose the next election. Finally deciding, however, that a bold stand was his duty, the President went the whole way and devoted his entire annual message of December 1887 to the tariff question. He made a slashing attack on the injustice, inequity, and absurdity of existing rates, ridiculed the need to protect century-old ''infant industries,'' and denounced high rates as ''the vicious, inequitable and illogical source of unnecessary taxation.'' The House of Representatives, with a Democratic majority, responded to the President's demand by adopting a bill sponsored by Roger Q. Mills of Texas. Far from radical, it did place such raw materials as lumber, wool, and flax on the free list and made moderate reductions of about 7 percent in rates for finished goods. The Republican-controlled Senate then rejected the Mills bill, as expected, and adopted a highly protective bill that was buried in the House committee by the Democrats. The deadlock of tariff reform produced the first clear-cut economic issue between parties since Reconstruction and provided the leading issue of the 1888 election.

For their presidential candidate the Republicans chose Benjamin Harrison of Indiana, whose chief attractions were that he came from a doubtful state and that he was the grandson of former President William Henry Harrison, ''Old Tippecanoe,'' of log-cabin and hard-cider fame. His running mate was Levi P. Morton, a wealthy New York banker. The Democrats naturally renominated President Cleveland, and for their vice-presidential candidate they chose the elderly and ailing ex-senator Allen G. Thurman of Ohio.

Although the Democratic platform endorsed Cleveland's demand for tariff reform, the party made a protectionist the chairman of its national committee. The campaign for Cleveland's reelection was handicapped, therefore, by halfhearted and ineffective leadership. By contrast, the Republican campaign had a vigorous leader in Senator Matt Quay, boss of a ruthless machine in Pennsylvania. With the support of such industrialists as those aroused by Cleveland's challenge to the tariff, Quay collected and spent a huge campaign fund. Republican strategists made telling use of this fund to purchase votes and rig elections in Indiana and New York.

In spite of much talk about tariff reform, the election did not turn on that issue. Cleveland actually carried the manufacturing states of New Jersey and Connecticut, and the Democrats gained ground in Michigan, Ohio, and California, normally protariff states. Cleveland polled a plurality of almost one hundred thousand popular votes, but Harrison won the electoral vote 233 to 168. It was an extremely narrow victory for the Republicans. As usual, the outcome had hung on a few evenly divided states—Indiana, New York, Rhode Island, and Ohio—and Harrison had carried them all, each by a few thousand votes. Prominent factors in what was probably the most corrupt presidential election of national

Cutting the tariff

history appear to have been trickery in Indiana and New York and division within the Democratic party.

Harrison and reaction. President Harrison complained that he could not name his own Cabinet because party-managers "had sold out every place to pay the election expenses." Heavy obligations to Blaine dictated his appointment as Secretary of State, and other appointments paid off regional bosses, high-tariff groups, and donors to the campaign fund. John Wanamaker, a wealthy Philadelphia merchant, became Postmaster General and promptly turned over the Post Office patronage to hungry spoilsmen. In spite of his commitment to civil-service reform, Harrison watched the process in silence.

For the first time since 1875 the Republicans in 1889–91 held the Presidency and a majority in both houses of Congress. Each majority was extremely slight, however, and under existing House rules the Democratic minority could frustrate the majority by simply not answering roll call and thereby depriving the House of a quorum. Speaker Thomas B. Reed of Maine earned the title of "Czar" by sweeping aside the rules over the indignant protest of the minority, strengthening party responsibility, and running House proceedings with an iron will. Under Reed in the House and the protectionist Senator Nelson W. Aldrich of Rhode Island in the Senate, the Republican majority won the name of the "Billion Dollar Congress." Their solution for the growing Treasury surplus was not to lower the tariff revenues that produced it but to give away the surplus to their friends. With this policy they greeted the protectionist lobby, the veterans'-pension lobby, and the pork-barrel lobby with open arms.

The American Iron and Steel Association, the Industrial League, and other protectionists were the first to benefit. Reed appointed William McKinley, a high-tariff representative from Ohio whom he had just defeated in a contest for the speakership, as chairman of the House Ways and Means Committee, and the new chairman assumed the task of fulfilling Republican pledges of higher tariff rates. The McKinley tariff bill, which became law on June 10, 1890, raised an already scandalously high tariff scale even higher, an *ad valorem* increase of about 4 percent. Its purpose was not merely to be protective but to be prohibitive; not merely to discourage foreign compe-

tition but to eliminate it; not merely to protect infant industries but to call new industries into being. To aid the Sugar Trust, the bill put raw sugar on the free list but granted American sugar-growers a compensatory subsidy of 2 cents a pound. As a rather hypocritical gesture of help to farmers, duties were raised on farm products that generally needed no protection anyway. Finally, there was a "reciprocity" clause intended not as a means of lowering tariffs but as a threat to raise them in this country if other countries did not lower theirs.

Faced with an indignant reaction in the agricultural sections against the favoritism of the McKinley Tariff, Republican congressmen now hastened to take steps of appeasement. Representatives from the silver-mining states and the Western states in favor of currency expansion had been promised that the party would "do something for silver" in return for their reluctant support of the tariff bill. The measure finally contrived to fulfill this commitment was the Sherman Silver Purchase Act, named for the senator from Ohio. It was designed to replace the Bland-Allison Act of 1878 (see p. 469), which had fixed a minimum amount of silver that the federal Treasury was required to purchase each month in dollars. Under this law the Treasury had put about $378 million in silver into circulation without relieving the scarcity of currency. The Sherman Act fixed the amount of silver to be purchased in ounces rather than dollars: $4\frac{1}{2}$ million ounces per month, approximately the amount of current production of the metal. The silver was to be paid for in Treasury notes of full legal-tender value, which could be redeemed in either gold or silver at the discretion of the government. The bill was passed by a straight party vote, with Democrats opposing on the grounds that it provided no adequate relief. As it turned out, the government subsequently chose to redeem the notes only in gold, and as the price of silver dropped the Treasury was required to spend fewer and fewer dollars to purchase the stated number of ounces. The act produced no more currency expansion than its predecessor had. The product of weak and shifty statesmanship, it pleased neither side and contributed nothing of importance toward solving the currency problems of the nation.

Another reform act passed about the same time, the Sherman Antitrust Act, bearing the name of the same Ohio senator, became law in July 1890 (see p. 428). Although many congressmen were absent when the vote was taken, the Sherman Antitrust Act was adopted with only one vote against it in the Senate and none in the House. It had little effect during the following decade, for no administration during those years showed much interest in enforcing it.

In order to please Union veterans of the GAR, Harrison appointed Corporal James Tanner, a cynical pensions lobbyist, as commissioner of pensions. The new commissioner publicly declared that he favored ''an appropriation for every old comrade who needs it,'' and as quickly as he could in a brief term of office he added millions to the pension budget. Congress assisted him with the Dependent Pension Act of 1890, similar to the one Cleveland had vetoed in 1887, which declared all Union veterans with at least ninety days' service in the Civil War eligible for a pension if they were unable to provide for themselves for any reason at all. Their widows and children were also made eligible for pensions. The number of pensioners increased by one-third in three years and reached nearly a million, more than the number of Union veterans surviving at the time.

The legislative program of the Billion Dollar Congress did wonders in taking care of the Treasury surplus. The prohibitive tariff rates set by the McKinley Act reduced income, and the combination of excessive pensions and silver purchases increased expenditures. Still in a mood of generosity and still finding some of the surplus left, Congress hastily devised more handouts in the form of subsidies to steamship lines, lavish pork-barrel bills for river and harbor improvements, enormous premiums for government bondholders, and the return of federal taxes paid during the Civil War by Northern states. These handouts and the onset of depression wiped out the surplus in the Treasury by 1894, and the Treasury-surplus problem has never troubled the United States since.

The first Congress of the Harrison Administration promoted the interests of politicians and businessmen—that is, if they belonged to the right party or were engaged in the right business. To other interests, particularly farmers and small businessmen, Congress appeared a wasteful dispenser of favors to the privileged. The congressional elections of 1890 came as a severe rebuke. The Republicans were overwhelmed by a revolt that penetrated traditional strongholds in Ohio, Michigan, Illinois, Wisconsin, and Kansas, even Massachusetts. The shift began in 1889 in Ohio and Massachusetts. Local and cultural issues determined the outcome in several states. Republicans were reduced to 88 seats in the House of Representatives, the smallest number in thirty years, while the Democrats took 235 seats. Republicans hung on to a small majority in the Senate. But the election of 1890 ran up danger signals for conservative leaders of both the old parties, a depression was on the way, a third-party revolt was shaping up, and a new era of reform was in the making.

The agrarian revolt

The decline of agriculture. The spirit of revolt flamed up most fiercely in the agricultural sections of the South and the West, and it was fed by acute economic distress and a deep sense of grievance. American farmers reached the lowest point in their history in the 1890s. The past was not the golden age they sometimes dreamed of, but they had certainly been better off before and were to be much better off in the future. But ever since the 1860s agriculture had been slipping backward, while the cities and factories had been surging forward. Farmers knew they were being left behind, and they suspected the government of indifference, if not hostility, to their interests. They searched everywhere for the causes of their plight and the cure for their troubles. Some of their guesses were shrewd and accurate, but they never grasped the larger causes of their troubles.

What the American farmers did not see was that they were caught up in an international crisis that afflicted agriculture in many parts of the world and provoked rebellion abroad as well as at home. The crisis for producers of export staple crops resulted from a revolution in communication and transportation that created a worldwide market for agricultural products. Ships first steamed through the Suez Canal in 1869, the year locomotives first steamed across the North American continent. The network of railroad and steamship lines was swiftly paralleled by a network of telegraph and telephone lines and transoceanic cables that linked continents and tied the world together. In the meantime vast new tracts of land were brought under cultivation in South America, Australia, and Canada, as well as in the trans-Mississippi West, and simultaneously a new technology of mechanized cultivation increased productivity enormously.

Forced to compete in a world market without protection against their competitors or control over output, American farmers watched the prices of their product decline as productivity mounted. It did not seem fair: the more they grew, the less they earned. And as their income diminished, their expenses increased. They had to buy expensive farm machinery in a protected market and sell their crops in an unprotected market. As the gap between income and expenses widened, farmers were increasingly forced to mortgage their land or borrow money to cover the gap. They were therefore chronically in debt, and debtors always suffered most keenly from deflationary monetary policies, such as those the government had pursued ever since the resumption of specie payments in 1879 (see p. 468). Contracting the amount of currency in circulation resulted in lowering the price that crops brought and increasing the difficulty of paying off debts. Farmers in debt had reason for opposing contraction and demanding expansion of currency.

It was no wonder that agrarian discontent was most bitter in the South and the West, for the growers of the staple crops of those sections were most dependent on exports. Eastern and Midwestern farmers had different problems and were sometimes at odds with farmers of other sections. The price of cotton and wheat had been falling steadily for two decades. From 1870 to 1873 cotton had averaged about 15.1 cents a pound; from 1894 to 1898 it dropped to an average of 5.8 cents. Over the same period wheat prices dropped from 106.7 to 63.3 cents a bushel, and corn from 43.0 to 29.7. These were market prices, after transportation and warehouse charges had been paid, not the lower prices the farmer received. In 1889 corn was actually selling for 10 cents in Kansas, and farmers were burning it for fuel. Georgia farmers were getting 5 cents a pound for their cotton at a time when economists were estimating that it cost about 7 cents a pound to produce. During several of these years the nation's farmers were running a losing business. Western farmers were

kept going sometimes by the appreciation of land values and Southern farmers mainly by sheer habit and the momentum of generations, for in the South land values were declining as well as crop prices.

The ills of agriculture were reflected in the growing number of mortgages (not always an evil) and tenant farmers. Nearly a third of the country's farms were mortgaged by the end of the nineties—45 percent of those in Wisconsin, 48 percent in Michigan, and 53 percent in Iowa. In Kansas, Nebraska, North Dakota, South Dakota, and Minnesota there were by 1890 more mortgages than families. In the Southern states mortgages were far fewer, but only because land was such a drug on the market that it could not be mortgaged. The South's substitute was the lien system, the worst credit system of all (see p. 392). Fewer and fewer farmers owned the land they worked, and more and more labored for a landlord, often an absentee landlord. The number of tenant farms increased from 25.8 percent of all the farms in 1880 to 35.3 percent at the end of the century.

Understandably, the farmer blamed others for his woes. He singled out the railroads as the archenemy, and the offenses he attributed to them were by no means wholly imaginary, though sometimes exaggerated. The complaint that it took one bushel of wheat or corn to pay the freight on another bushel was no exaggeration. The chief complaints of rate discrimination came from the South and the West, where rates were frequently two or three times what they were between Chicago and New York. On the other hand, Eastern farm groups also complained of rate discrimination and charged favoritism for Western competitors. Railroads favored large over small shippers and one locality over another and flagrantly dominated politics and bought up legislatures. The national banks were also a natural target for agrarian abuse, for they were located and run for the convenience of city people, not for countryfolk. They were concentrated in nonagricultural areas, and their rules forbade them to lend money on real estate and farm property. Farmers believed that they manipulated banknote currency against agricultural interests and were indifferent to seasonal needs for money for the movement of crops.

Few could deny the validity of the complaint that the farmer bore the brunt of the tax burden. Stocks and bonds could easily be concealed from the view of the tax-collector, but not livestock and land. Railroads and corporations could pass the taxes on to the consumer, but the farmer could not pass on his taxes. The tax laws, like the bank laws, worked to the farmer's disadvantage. And so did the tariff. Southerners, with their long antitariff tradition, felt this more keenly than did the Westerners, and they lost no opportunity to press their views that farmers were doubly victimized by the tariff—as sellers in a free-trade market and as buyers in a protected market. Sharing none of the benefits of protection, they were compelled as consumers to foot the bill and pay the additional cost of protected goods. The injustice was all the harder to bear for those who believed that the tariff was "the mother of trusts." By fixing prices and defeating competition at home, trusts levied tribute on the consumers of all types of goods. Antitrust and antimonopoly feeling ran high in all farmer organizations. While agrarian theorists were wrong in attributing their plight to a conspiracy, they were right in their contention that they had a number of legitimate grievances against a system that worked so consistently to their disadvantage.

In their more desperate moods the farmers sometimes felt that nature herself was conspiring with their oppressors. In the late eighties and early nineties natural calamities came one on top of another with stunning impact—droughts on the plains that not merely damaged the crops but destroyed them; floods in the lower Mississippi Valley that not merely destroyed the crops but left the land unusable; grim, blizzard-bound winters on the high plains that destroyed not merely domestic animals but wild ones as well and threatened the survival of man himself. Less spectacular, but contrasting sharply with the new urban way of life, was the loneliness, the drudgery, and the isolation of rural life in America in those years. This was the ancient lot of farmers, but the growing glitter of the city made it less tolerable than ever, especially when coupled with the grinding, ceaseless pressure of economic ills and grievances. To Thomas E. Watson of Georgia, who was to whip agrarian wrath into a frenzied crusade, the farmers of his region seemed to move about "like victims of some horrid nightmare . . . powerless—oppressed—shackled." It is not surprising that their protests sometimes sounded a bit irrational.

Grange cartoon: the railroad menace

Agrarian protest. There was nothing irrational, however, about the farmers' impulse to organize and protest against their lot. The Patrons of Husbandry, organized in local "granges" and better known as the Grangers, served as a model for later and more powerful movements. Founded in 1867 by Oliver Hudson Kelley, a government employee in Washington who was moved by the plight of Southern farmers, the Grange grew slowly until the pinch of depression quickened interest in the early seventies. By 1874 the estimated membership was about $1\frac{1}{2}$ million, and growth continued into the next year. In 1875 the Grange was strongest in the Middle West, the South, the Southwest, and the border states of Missouri and Kentucky. It was officially described as a secret social order for "working together, buying together, selling together, and generally acting together for . . . mutual protection and advancement."

Seeking to eliminate the profits of the middleman, Grangers founded cooperatives for buying and selling, for milling and storing grain, even for banking and manufacturing. These enterprises often suffered from inexperience and lack of capital, but some of them flourished and saved their members money. Membership fell off rapidly after 1875, but the Grangers left their imprint upon law and politics. While their order officially declared itself "nonpolitical," individual members joined agrarian third parties and swelled the farmer's influence in state legislatures. They actually received more credit than they were due for the so-called Granger laws that were adopted in the early seventies by Midwestern states to regulate grain elevators and railroads. Eight "Granger cases" came before the Supreme Court in 1877, and in *Munn* v. *Illinois,* the most significant of them, the Court upheld the "police power" of state regulation (see p. 428). Curtailed and hampered by subsequent decisions, the right of the public to control great corporations nevertheless held securely in the future.

The Grange dropped out of political prominence in the late seventies after inspiring a number of similar and smaller agricultural societies. Easily the most important was the Farmers' Alliance, really two organizations of independent origins, a huge one in the South and a much smaller one in the Middle West. Each of them underwent changes of names with reorganizations but were commonly known as the Southern Farmers' Alliance and the Northwestern Farmers' Alliance. The Southern Alliance had originated in 1875 in a frontier county of Texas, but it amounted to little until it launched a program of rapid expansion in 1886 under the energetic leadership of Dr. C. W. Macune. The Alliance took in several rival agricultural societies, including the Agricultural Wheel, with its home base in Arkansas, and the Farmers' Union of Louisiana. Agents spread out through all the cotton-growing states and found farmers everywhere eager to join. And they joined by the hundreds of thousands—at one time the national organization claimed as many as 3 million members, though it never made a really accurate count. Affiliated with them was a separate Colored Farmers' National Alliance and Cooperative Union that claimed $1\frac{1}{4}$ million black members.

The Southern Alliance took in tenants and landowners, as well as rural mechanics and other classes of country people. With a highly centralized national organization, it established its own press, which was supported by hundreds of local weekly papers, and a lecture bureau that kept reform ideas circulating among its members. The Alliance went in for cooperatives even more extensively than the old Grange. Hundreds of Alliance stores and warehouses, marketing agencies, gins, tanneries, and mills sprinkled the South, though most of them were short-lived.

The Northwestern Alliance, organized by Milton George of Chicago in 1880, did not agree with the Southern Alliance in its policies of secrecy, centralized control, and separate organization for blacks and resisted pressure to join it for fear of being overwhelmed by the larger society. But in 1889 the Southern Alliance changed its name to the National Farmers' Alliance and Industrial Union and persuaded the three strongest state alliances of the Northwestern Alliance, those of Kansas and North and South Dakota, to join it. In the same year the Alliance gained the endorsement of the Knights of Labor and formed a political combination with that organization.

The character of the Alliance is reflected in the "demands" drawn up at its annual conventions. The Ocala Demands, for example, voted at the convention in Ocala, Florida, in 1890, called for the government to establish a "Subtreasury System." This would permit farmers to store nonperishable crops in government warehouses or elevators and receive Treasury notes lending them up to 80 percent of the local market value of the grain or cotton deposited. The government loan was secured by the crops and repaid when they were sold, thus enabling the farmer to hold his produce for the best price.* Other demands were for the abolition of national banks, a substantial increase in the amount of money in circulation, the free coinage of silver, a federal income tax, the reduction of tariff rates, the direct election of senators, "rigid" control of railroad and telegraph companies—and, if that did not work, "government ownership" of both.

Though the Alliance, like the Grange, professed to be strictly "nonpolitical," it was clear that its demands could be realized only by political means. Using their demands (similar to the ones adopted later that year at Ocala) as a yardstick, Southern Alliancemen required all Democratic candidates in the 1890 elections to "stand up and be measured." As a result, the Alliance seemed at the time to have come near taking over the Democratic party in the South, for it elected four governors, secured control of eight legislatures, and elected forty-four congressmen and three senators who were pledged to support Alliance demands. Instead of working within one of the old parties, Alliancemen in the West hastily set up independent third parties, the names of which differed from state to state, and nominated their own candidates. Their most striking successes were in Kansas, where they elected five congressmen and a senator;

*The idea was embodied in the New Deal measure of 1936 creating the Commodity Credit Corporation.

in Nebraska, where they took control of both houses of the legislature and elected two congressmen; and in South Dakota, where they elected a senator. In other Western states their vote came largely at the expense of the Republicans and accounted in part for the large number of Democratic congressmen elected in 1890. The election served notice on both old parties that the farmers were on the march.

The Populist crusade. Their successes in 1890 inspired Westerners with the ambition to form a national third party to promote Alliance ideas. Southerners hung back, however, in order to try out their plan of working within the Democratic party. They were quickly disillusioned, for all the Southern Democratic congressmen elected on an Alliance platform, with the exception of Tom Watson, entered the Democratic caucus and voted for a conservative anti-Alliance Georgian for Speaker. Thereupon Watson, redheaded and a rebel by temperament, left his party and became the "People's party" candidate for Speaker with the support of eight congressmen from the West. Thus the new party, often called the Populist party, had a congressional delegation before it had a national organization. The National Alliance, however, under the leadership of President Leonidas L. Polk of North Carolina, was moving rapidly in the Populist direction. On February 22, 1892, a huge Confederation of Industrial Organizations met at St. Louis, attended by delegates from the Knights of Labor, the Nationalists, the Single-Taxers, Greenbackers, Prohibitionists, and other curiously assorted reform groups, but dominated by delegates from the National Alliance. The delegates officially founded the People's party and called for a convention to nominate a ticket for the presidential election of 1892.

Shortly before the convention met in Omaha on July 4, the Populists were deprived of their strongest candidate by the death of Polk. The party nominated the old Greenback campaigner of 1880, General James B. Weaver of Iowa, for President, and, to balance the Union general with a Confederate one, chose General James G. Field of Virginia as his running mate. The platform emphatically reiterated Alliance principles on money, credit, transportation, and land and evoked the wildest enthusiasm for its planks on government ownership of railroads and monetary

Anti-Populist cartoon, 1892

reform. Populist principles, embodying the agrarian reform ideas of two decades, had become a sacred creed. The fervor and violence of Populist rhetoric is illustrated by the following excerpt from the preamble to the platform, written and delivered by Ignatius Donnelly of Minnesota, foremost Populist writer and orator:

> . . . we meet in the midst of a nation brought to the verge of moral, political, and material ruin. Corruption dominates the ballot-box, the legislatures, the Congress, and touches even the ermine of the bench. The people are demoralized. . . . The newspapers are largely subsidized or muzzled, public opinion silenced, business prostrated, homes covered with mortgages, labor impoverished, and the land concentrated in the hands of capitalists. . . . The fruits of the toil of millions are boldly stolen to build up colossal fortunes for a few. . . .

Eastern conservatives were frightened by the Populist tone and built up a distorted image of the movement as an insurrection of hayseed anarchists or hick communists. The very nicknames of Populist leaders lent themselves to such propaganda—names such as Lemuel H. "Calamity" Weller of Iowa, Congressman "Sockless" Jerry Simpson of Kansas, Governor Davis H. "Bloody Bridles" Waite of Colorado, and orator James H. "Cyclone" Davis of Texas—not to mention the endlessly quoted advice of Mary E. Lease of Kansas to "raise less corn and more hell." It is quite true that some of the Populist leaders were fanatical and narrow-minded, and that the majority of Populist voters were provincial and ill-informed folk with a poor under-

A vast conspiracy against mankind has been organized on two continents, and it is rapidly taking possession of the world. If not met and overthrown at once, it forebodes terrible social convulsions, the destruction of civilization, or the establishment of an absolute despotism.

We have witnessed for more than a quarter of a century the struggles of the two great political parties for power and plunder, while grievous wrongs have been inflicted upon the suffering people. We charge that the controlling influences dominating both these parties have permitted the existing dreadful conditions to develop without serious effort to prevent or restrain them. Neither do they now promise us any substantial reform. They have agreed together to ignore in the coming campaign every issue but one. They propose to drown the outcries of a plundered people with the uproar of a sham battle over the tariff, so that capitalists, corporations, national banks, rings, trusts, watered stock, the demonetization of silver, and the oppressions of the usurers may all be lost sight of. They propose to sacrifice our homes, lives and children on the altar of mammon; to destroy the multitude in order to secure corruption funds from the millionaries.

From The Omaha Platform of the People's Party, 1892.

What's the matter with Kansas?

We all know; yet here we are at it again. We have an old mossback Jacksonian who snorts and howls because there is a bathtub in the State House; we are running that old jay for Governor. We have another shabby, wild-eyed, rattle-brained fanatic who has said openly in a dozen speeches that "the rights of the user are paramount to the rights of the owner"; we are running him for Chief Justice, so that capital will come tumbling over itself to get into the state....

Oh, this is a state to be proud of! We are a people who can hold up our heads! What we need is not more money, but less capital, fewer white shirts and brains, fewer men with business judgment, and more of those fellows who boast that they are "just ordinary clod-hoppers, but they know more in a minute about finance than John Sherman"; we need more men who are "posted," who can bellow about the crime of '73, who hate prosperity, and who think, because a man believes in national honor, he is a tool of Wall Street. We have had a few of them—some hundred fifty thousand—but we need more.

From William Allen White, "What's the Matter with Kansas?" 1896.

standing of the troubles that beset them. Populists tended to oversimplify issues, to embrace panaceas, to talk loosely of "conspiracy" against them, and to use violent and desperate language.

It is only fair to the Populists, however, to recall that the plight of the people for whom they spoke was desperate. We must recall also that their conservative opponents, much better educated as a rule, entertained absurd monetary and economic theories of their own and talked wildly of conspiracies and subversives themselves (see p. 488). To their credit it should be remembered that the Populists

were the first important movement in this country to insist that laissez-faire economics was not the final solution to industrial problems and that the federal government had some responsibility for social well-being. Most of the Populist demands that seemed so wild at the time were accepted as respectable within a surprisingly short time and were eventually written into law. The Populists' main service was to usher in a long-needed and long-delayed era of reform and to reveal the empty pretense of the political game as played by the old parties.

The first task of the Populists was to bridge

Kansas House of Representatives, 1895

the cleavages between parties, sections, races, and classes that kept apart the forces of reform that they wished to unite. First they sought to revive the old agrarian alliance between South and West that had been effectively broken by the Civil War. Second, they felt that both the Republicans and the Democrats were bent on keeping natural allies divided and sought to replace the old parties with a third party. Third, they tried to unite farmers of the South who were divided by racial barriers, and both whites and blacks worked hard at the effort. Finally, the Populists sought to create an alliance between farmers and labor. The Populists enjoyed some success with all four of these alliances, but sectional animosities were kept alive by the bloody-shirt issue, old party loyalties were hard to break, racial antagonism was inflamed by white-supremacy propaganda, and labor did not always see eye to eye with the farmer. In view of all these handicaps the Populists made a surprisingly good showing in their first appearance at the polls. They cast a little more than a million votes for their presidential candidate and broke into the Electoral College with twenty-two votes. They also elected ten representatives, five senators, three governors, and some fifteen hundred members of state legislatures.

The depression and the silver issue

Cleveland and the silverites. Somewhat sobered by the Populist threat, the Democrats and the Republicans conducted their 1892 campaigns with more dignity than usual. Cleveland, the choice of conservative Democrats, was nominated by the first ballot of his party's convention, and Harrison was the equally predictable nominee of the Republicans. Adlai E. Stevenson* of Illinois became Cleveland's running mate, and Whitelaw Reid, editor of the New York *Tribune,* was the Republican nominee for Vice President. Both

*Grandfather of the Democratic candidate for President in 1952 and 1956.

platforms were evasive on the monetary issues that stirred the greatest interest among voters. Cleveland improved his poll of 1888, and 1884 as well, winning 5,555,426 votes to 5,182,690 for Harrison, and 277 electoral votes to Harrison's 145. The Democrats carried not only the doubtful states of New York, New Jersey, Connecticut, and Indiana but the normally Republican states of Illinois, Wisconsin, and California. It was not quite a landslide, but it was the most decisive victory either party had won in twenty years.

President Cleveland moved back into the White House and surrounded himself with a thoroughly conservative Cabinet of Easterners and Southerners who were as completely out of touch with the radical discontent of the country as he was himself. Almost immediately the financial panic of 1893 shattered his peace and ushered in the worst depression the nation had experienced up to that time. The panic had actually started ten days before Harrison left office, when the Philadelphia & Reading Railroad went bankrupt and the New York Stock Exchange was shaken by the greatest selling spree in its history. Two months after Cleveland's inauguration the market collapsed. Banks called in their loans, and credit dried up. Unstable financial conditions abroad, especially the failure of Baring Brothers of London in 1890, had started a drain on the gold reserve that became increasingly severe after 1893. One great railroad after another—the Erie, the Northern Pacific, the Union Pacific, the Santa Fe—went down in failure. "Mills, factories, furnaces, mines nearly everywhere," reported the New York *Commercial and Financial Chronicle* in August, "shut down in large numbers, and commerce and enterprise were arrested in an extraordinary degree." By the end of the year five hundred banks and more than fifteen thousand business firms had fallen into bankruptcy. Populist Donnelly's apocalyptic picture in 1892 of "a nation brought to the verge of ruin" seemed about to be translated into reality.

Learned economists still argue about the causes and remedies of depressions, and there can be no doubt that the causes of the depression that settled over the country in 1893 were highly complex. But President Cleveland had a simple explanation and a simple remedy, and never did a dogmatist cling more tenaciously to his theory. His explanation was that the Sherman Silver Purchase Act (see p. 474) had caused the depression, and his remedy was to repeal the act and maintain the gold standard at all costs—that is, continue to redeem all United States Treasury notes in gold. The economic consequences of Cleveland's remedy do not appear to have been decisive one way or the other, but the political consequences were disastrous. No issue since slavery had divided the people more deeply than silver. It split both old parties, disrupted Populism, and caused a revolution in the Democratic party that overthrew conservative control.

The trouble was that Cleveland's theory clashed head on with a more popular theory held with equal dogmatism by the silverites. According to them, the cause of the economic disaster lay in the "Crime of '73" that demonetized silver, and the remedy lay in the free and unlimited coinage of silver at a ratio of sixteen to one of gold. The arguments and the sources of support for the silver movement had not changed since the Bland-Allison Act of 1878 (see p. 474), but the movement had acquired new strength and additional recruits. The admission of six new Western states— Montana, North Dakota, South Dakota, and Washington in 1889 and Idaho and Wyoming in 1890—brought reinforcements to the silverites in Congress, especially in the Senate. In the meantime American silver-producers suffered additional reductions in their market from the demonetization of silver in Europe and India and became more desperate for relief through free coinage in the United States. At the same time debtor agrarians saw free coinage of silver as one hope of relief from deflation and currency contraction and increased their cry for "free silver." In place of the inadequate relief provided by the Sherman Silver Purchase Act, they demanded unlimited and free coinage.

Cleveland stubbornly insisted, on the other hand, that the Sherman Act was the whole cause of the trouble and demanded its repeal. The only way to restore confidence and prosperity, he held, was to maintain the gold standard, and that required the maintenance of a gold reserve of $100 million in the Treasury. There was a case to be made in favor of the gold standard in the 1890s, but there were many causes for the drain on the gold reserve, and there were many causes of the depression other than the threat to the gold standard. But under relentless pressure by the President, Congress finally repealed the Sherman Act. Cleveland got his way by relying on Republican support and splitting his own party.

Repeal of the Sherman Act seemed to have no effect, for the drain on the gold reserve continued unabated, and so did the depression. Business confidence was not restored, and the hoarding of gold increased. The Treasury surplus that the Billion Dollar Congress had been so eager to spend was no more, and the McKinley Tariff had sharply reduced tariff revenues. Holders of gold and silver certificates, doubting the ability of the government to maintain the gold standard, started a run on the Treasury; and panic in

Europe caused continual withdrawals. The President resorted to a series of highly unpopular bond sales to recoup the gold reserves. The third bond sale, in February 1895, caused the greatest indignation of all. This time the President yielded to the demand of J. Pierpont Morgan that the sale be kept private, and the syndicate of bankers that handled the loan drove a hard bargain for their services and were accused of making large profits, though Morgan refused to reveal how much. The bond issue yielded over $65 million to the government, half of it from Europe, and the bankers scotched some of the drain on the gold reserve. Nevertheless, another issue was necessary in January 1896. The four bond sales did save the gold standard, but they did not stop the decline of the gold reserve or restore prosperity. Each one further intensified the silverites' hatred of the President. These bond sales enhanced Cleveland's reputation for courage but not for wisdom: they failed to cure the depression, and they led to political disaster.

The politics of depression. The blight that had been familiar to farmers for years now began to fall on the factory and the city. Railroad construction fell off drastically, dividends halted, and investment in all businesses declined sharply. Bankers, businessmen, and employers seemed stricken with a failure of nerve. They laid off men, cut wages, closed factory doors, and swelled the army of jobless men. A hundred thousand of them shuffled through the streets of Chicago, and visitors to the "dream city" at the Exposition in 1893 wondered at the miles of sleeping men who lined the tracks of the elevated railway. "What a spectacle!" exclaimed Ray Stannard Baker, a cub reporter, "What a human downfall after the magnificence and prodigality of the World's Fair."

The year 1894 was the most brutal of the depression. Between 2½ and 3 million, perhaps as many as one out of five workers, were thought to be unemployed, but no one really knew, and the unemployed felt that no one in the government really cared. Some cities provided a little work relief, but this was wholly inadequate, and when hungry men turned to the federal government they were met with cold indifference or angry rejection. Jacob S. Coxey of Massillon, Ohio, a well-to-do businessman who was a Populist and was quite untypical of his class in other ways,

"Coxey's Army" on the march

proposed a plan of federal work relief on public roads to be financed by an issue of $500 million in legal-tender Treasury notes. The "good roads" bill was designed to end the depression by providing monetary inflation and internal improvements as well as work relief for the unemployed. When Congress refused to pass it, Coxey declared, "We will send a petition to Washington with boots on." "Coxey's Army" marched peacefully from Massillon to the Capitol, picking up sympathizers on the way, including a hundred students from Lehigh University and a few visionaries and eccentrics, and paraded into Washington on May Day, about five hundred strong. They were cheered by crowds, but Coxey and his lieutenants were arrested by the police, and some fifty people were beaten or trampled. No fewer than seventeen "industrial armies" started for Washington in 1894, and some twelve hundred men arrived. They were peaceful and sober as a rule, but it was the obvious sympathy they stirred over the country that frightened the government, even

Richard Olney:

The constitutional objection [is] nothing but a call upon the judicial department of the government to supplant the political in the exercise of the taxing power; to substitute its discretion for that of Congress.... It is inevitably predestined to failure unless this court shall, for the first time in its history, overlook and overstep the bounds which separate the judicial from the legislative power—bounds, the scrupulous observance of which it has so often declared to be absolutely essential to the integrity of our constitutional system of government.

James C. Carter:

Nothing could be more unwise and dangerous—nothing more foreign to the spirit of the Constitution—than an attempt to baffle and defeat a popular determination by a judgment in a lawsuit. When the opposing forces of sixty millions of people have become arrayed in hostile political ranks upon a question which all men feel is not a question of law, but of legislation, the only path of safety is to accept the voice of the majority as final.

From Pollock v. Farmers' Loan and Trust Co., 157 U.S. 429, 1895.

President Cleveland, into the mistaken idea that a spirit of rebellion threatened to bring on mob rule.

Not only the government but private employers resorted to violence in countering labor protest. An extraordinary number of strikes, some fourteen hundred in all, occurred during 1894, many of them provoked by wage cuts. More than 660,000 men were thrown out of work by strikes or lockouts. Management countered by using violence, employing secret police, or securing injunctions from friendly courts. In the Pullman strike of July, as we have seen (p. 438), the federal government used troops of the regular army to crush the workers. Cleveland earned as much hostility from labor by his use of troops as he had from agrarians by his sale of bonds.

In the meantime, the only serious piece of reform the second Cleveland Administration undertook, the reform of the tariff, met with complete failure. To fulfill their campaign pledges, the Democrats did put through the House a bill, framed by William L. Wilson of West Virginia, containing modest reductions in the tariff. But in the Senate the protectionists of both parties fell upon it with six hundred amendments that restored the old rates and actually raised some of them. The Wilson-Gorman Act, which Cleveland denounced as "party perfidy and party dishonor" and allowed to become law without his signature, made a mockery of the Administration's pre-tenses of tariff reform. The only sop to reformers was an amendment, slipped in by the agrarians and deplored by the President, that provided for a small income tax of 2 percent on incomes over $4,000. The Supreme Court, which shared Cleveland's unpopularity as an agency of reaction, promptly declared the income tax unconstitutional by a vote of five to four. For relief of suffering among the unemployed, on the farms, and in the cities, for restoring credit, and for assisting industry afflicted by depression, Cleveland's Administration refused to take any responsibility beyond maintaining the gold standard.

The spirit of despair and resentment abroad in the land was perfectly suited to the appeal of the Populists. In the fall elections of 1894 the third party increased the vote it polled in 1892 by 42 percent. In the West the Populists lost Nevada, which went over to the Silverites, a new party, and Colorado and Idaho went Republican, so that the overall strength of the party declined. But in the South Populists exploited hatred of Cleveland, and with evangelistic campaigns and camp-meeting techniques they piled up gains that frightened the Democrats. In spite of violence and fraud and racist propaganda more blatant than the Democrats had used since the overthrow of Reconstruction, the Populists captured North Carolina, with Republican aid, and mustered more strength in the supposedly conservative states of Georgia and Alabama than they commanded in any Western state save Nebraska.

Joseph H. Choate:

You cannot hereafter exercise any check if you now say that Congress is untrammelled and uncontrollable. My friend says you cannot enforce any limit. He says no matter what Congress does ... this Court will have nothing to say about it. I agree that it will have nothing to say about it if it now lets go its hold upon this law....

I have thought that one of the fundamental objects of all civilized government was the preservation of the rights of private property. I have thought that it was the very keystone of the arch upon which all civilized government rests, and that this once abandoned, everything was in danger.... According to the doctrines that have been propounded here this morning, even that great fundamental principle has been scattered to the winds....

If it be true, as my friend said in closing, that the passions of the people are aroused on this subject, if it be true that a mighty army of sixty million citizens is likely to be incensed by this decision, it is the more vital to the future welfare of this country that this court again resolutely and courageously declare, as Marshall did, that it has the power to set aside an act of Congress violative of the Constitution ... no matter what the threatened consequences of popular or populistic wrath may be.

From Pollock v. Farmers' Loan and Trust Co., 157 U.S. 429, 1895.

After the defeats of 1894 the Democrats retained only technical control of the Senate and suffered heavy losses in the House. Many prominent Democratic congressmen went down to defeat as the Republicans recouped their losses in the previous election and took control of the House with a majority of one hundred forty seats. No Democrats at all won national office in twenty-four states, and only one each in six others. New York, Illinois, and Wisconsin returned to the Republican fold, and only one Democratic congressman was elected in New England. The elections of 1894 brought about the largest congressional gains and one of the most widespread political realignments in the nation's history. It was this election and not that of 1896 that marked the fall of the Democrats and the beginning of the long Republican ascendancy.

The Democratic party was, in fact, in the midst of revolution almost as profound as that of 1860. Again it was a sectional split, but this time it was the Northeast that was isolated instead of the South. West and South joined hands in the name of the free coinage of silver, but silver merely served as a symbol for dozens of other sectional issues. And Grover Cleveland became the personification of the Northeastern conservatism against which the two agrarian regions were in revolt. Never since Andrew Johnson had a President

been so detested and abused by members of this own party as was Cleveland. Southern and Western Democrats deserted him in droves and outdid the Republicans and Populists in denouncing him. "He is an old bag of beef," Democratic Congressman "Pitchfork" Ben Tillman told his South Carolina constituents, "and I am going to Washington with a pitchfork and prod him in his old fat ribs."

Early in 1895 prominent Democrats in the South and West set to work systematically to use the silver issue as a means of taking over control of their party and unseating Cleveland and the conservatives. With financial support from the silver-miners, they held silver conventions all over the South and West to which they invited Populists and urged them to give up their more radical demands and "come down to silver." They distributed great quantities of silver propaganda, such as Ignatius Donnelly's *The American People's Money* (1895) and the famous booklet by William H. "Coin" Harvey, *Coin's Financial School* (1894). In the latter, "Professor Coin" laid bare the "conspiracy of Goldbugs," proponents of the gold standard, and "proved" that the free and unlimited coinage of silver was the panacea for all economic ills. The work of the silver Democrats against Cleveland was so effective that after the state conventions in

Sound money cartoon

the summer of 1896 no state Democratic organization south of the Potomac and only three west of the Alleghenies remained in the hands of the President's friends. There was no longer any doubt that the silverites would be able to wrest control of the national Democratic convention from Cleveland.

McKinley and gold versus Bryan and silver.

Nor was there any doubt that the Republican convention would nominate William McKinley of Ohio when it met at St. Louis in June. McKinley's nomination had been assured by the systematic and patient work of his devoted friend Marcus Alonzo Hanna, who not only rounded up the necessary votes before the convention but financed and managed his friend's preconvention campaign. A blunt and forthright businessman from Cleveland, Hanna had made a fortune in coal, iron, banking, shipping, and street railways before he retired from business in 1895 to devote full time to fulfilling his ambition of putting McKinley in the White House. McKinley's nomination rolled forward as planned on the first ballot, and Garret A. Hobart, a relatively unknown corporation lawyer from New Jersey, was the vice-presidential nominee. A protectionist platform was obviously called for, since McKinley's name had become synonymous with high tariff. The only doubt was how explicit the plank on the gold standard should be. Hanna had already decided upon a forth-

right endorsement, but he cleverly hung back at the convention and permitted himself to be "persuaded" by Eastern delegates to accept the statement that "the existing gold standard should be preserved." Upon the adoption of the gold plank, Senator Henry M. Teller of Colorado led a small group of Western silver Republicans from the hall, and they withdrew from the party.

Eastern Republicans had reason to doubt McKinley's firmness on gold. In the political lingo of the battle of standards, politicians were classified as "Goldbugs," "Silverbugs," or "Straddlebugs," and the Ohioan was often classed with the third group. He had voted for both the Bland-Allison Act and the Sherman Silver Purchase Act and continued to speak kindly of silver as an American product that deserved "protection" and to favor compromise when compromise had become untenable. In 1896, however, he accepted his party's decision for gold. He was an experienced and skillful politician who had served in Congress from 1876 to 1892, with the exception of one term, and had been governor of Ohio for two terms, completing the second in 1895. A kindly, impressive-looking, rather solemn man, McKinley sincerely shared Hanna's devotion to the interests of American business. The campaign caricature of McKinley as the spineless puppet of the millionaire boss had no foundation in fact, for the evidence is that Hanna constantly deferred to his friend and respected his wishes.

The Democratic convention at Chicago exhibited all the disorder and spontaneity that the Republicans had been spared under Hanna's direction. Cleveland-supporters, still full of fight, arrived from the East to clash with red-hot silver orators from the South and the West amid a din of hisses and catcalls and rebel yells in which only the leather-lunged could make themselves heard. But the Easterners had neither the strength to control the convention nor a suitable candidate to put before it, and the agrarian rebels rode over them roughshod. They adopted a platform strongly influenced by Governor John P. Altgeld of Illinois, the friend of the Pullman strikers and the pardoner of the Haymarket-riot anarchists. The platform, which denounced virtually everything Cleveland stood for, also struck out fiercely at the protective tariff, the national banks, trusts, and the Supreme Court; it demanded an income tax and, most important of all, free coinage of silver at the ratio of sixteen ounces of silver to one of gold.

Altgeld was disqualified as a candidate by foreign birth, and the convention passed over Congressman Richard P. "Silver Dick" Bland, the most prominent contender. At the strategic moment a handsome young ex-congressman, William Jennings Bryan of Nebraska, captured the attention and the imagination of the silver forces with a speech that mounted to a thrilling peroration: "You shall not press down upon the brow of labor this crown of thorns, you shall not crucify mankind upon a cross of gold." Bryan was nominated on the fifth ballot, and, to balance the ticket, Arthur Sewall of Maine, a banker and businessman who opposed the gold standard, was nominated for Vice President.

While he was only thirty-six and little known in the East, Bryan was already widely known as a peerless orator in the West and the South, where he had been campaigning for three years to prepare the revolt of the silver forces. Bryan had some naive ideas about money and harbored suspicions of the East, "the enemy's country," as he once called it. He was no radical, and his ties were with the simple agrarian past rather than with the complex future. But conservatives were wrong to dismiss him as a one-idea fanatic. He had an intuitive grasp of the deep mood of protest that stirred the mass of voters, and he expressed that mood in a moral appeal to the conscience of the country. His real service was to awaken an old faith in social justice and to protest against a generation of plutocratic rule.

In their next maneuver, the silver-leaders of the "revolutionized" Democrats persuaded the Populist party, which held its convention in St. Louis after the Democratic convention had met, to make Bryan its candidate as well. The proposal deeply divided the Populists, who neither wanted to split the reform forces with a separate ticket nor give up their own party identity. Western Populists were eager to nominate Bryan, but Southern members, always more radical and less devoted to silver, wanted a separate Populist ticket and no compromise. Bryan's nomination was at last secured when Senator William V. Allen of Nebraska, chairman of the convention, told the Southerners that the Democrats had agreed to withdraw Sewall and accept Thomas E. Watson as their vice-presidential nominee if the Populists would nominate Bryan. South-

ern radicals bitterly resisted fusion with the Democrats, whom they had been fighting for four years. But when their hero Watson agreed to compromise, they reluctantly consented and nominated Bryan and Watson. Only later did they learn that the Democrats refused to withdraw the banker Sewall.

Two more parties were created out of bolters from the old parties. The National Silver Republicans endorsed the Democratic candidates. Later on, the gold Democrats, with encouragement and financial support from Hanna, organized the National Democratic party and nominated a separate ticket that was intended to contribute to Bryan's defeat.

The contest between McKinley and Bryan in 1896 has taken on the legendary character of the combat between Goliath and David—except that it turned out quite differently. Bryan played the David role admirably—the lone youth armed with nothing but shafts of oratory pitted against the armored Gold Giant and all his hosts. Actually, reformers of many schools rallied to Bryan's cause, including Henry George of the Single-Taxers, Edward Bellamy of the Nationalists, W. D. P. Bliss of the Christian Socialists, Eugene V. Debs of the Railway Union, and Samuel Gompers of the American Federation of Labor, all of whom campaigned for him. Bryan's chief reliance, however, was upon his own voice. In a campaign without precedent at that time, he traveled eighteen thousand miles by train, made more than six hundred speeches, and talked to some 5 million people. He spoke not only of silver but of the price of crops, the cost of mortgages, the need for credit, and the regulation of railroads. The powerful popular response to his campaign aroused great hopes for victory.

It also aroused a hysterical wave of fear among conservatives and facilitated Hanna's collection of campaign funds. He exacted tribute from every great trust, railroad, bank, and tycoon with any stake in the outcome and built up a treasure chest undreamed of before that time. The fund has been estimated everywhere between $3.5 million and $15 million (the latter an exaggeration)—as against a mere $300,000 at Bryan's disposal. Hanna spent the money lavishly but shrewdly, sending out propaganda by the ton and the carload and speakers by the battalion. He also transported trainloads of people from representative groups, all expenses paid, to hear McKinley read well-prepared speeches from

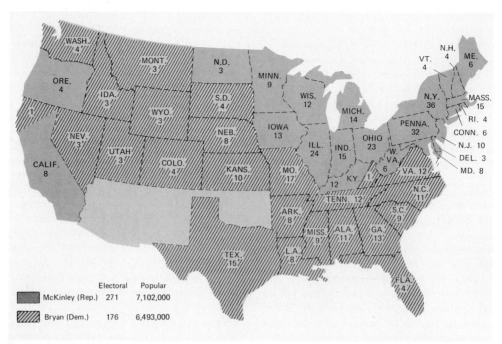

	Electoral	Popular
McKinley (Rep.)	271	7,102,000
Bryan (Dem.)	176	6,493,000

The election of 1896

his front porch in Canton, Ohio, from which the candidate never stirred. The press assisted Hanna with blasts of ridicule and charges of socialism and anarchism against Bryan. The Philadelphia *Press* described the "Jacobins" of the Chicago convention as "hideous and repulsive vipers." President Cleveland called them "madmen" and "criminals," and the New York *Tribune* referred to Bryan as a "wretched, rattle-pated boy." Employers of labor joined in with threats to close up shop or cut wages if Bryan was elected.

The combination of powers was too much for the resources of Bryan. He polled 6,492,559 votes, more votes than any victorious candidate had ever polled before, nearly a million more than Cleveland polled in 1892, but it was still not enough. McKinley won with 7,102,246 votes, a plurality of 609,687, and an electoral vote of 271 to 176. Bryan did not carry a single state north of the Potomac or east of the Mississippi above its juncture with the Ohio. He did not even carry the farming states of Iowa, Minnesota, and North Dakota. What is more significant, he carried no industrialized, no urbanized state. This may well be the main reason for Bryan's defeat. In spite of widespread unrest among labor, Bryan did not win labor's support, which might have given him victory. He really had little to offer either labor or the cities. Like many other

American reformers of his day, he had something of significance for the present, but his true ties were with the past. McKinley and Hanna may not have been looking very far into the future, but they clearly had a firmer grip on the present. They were also able to influence labor (by threats as well as promises), and they evidently won the confidence of the urban middle class. Their victory at the polls meant a return to conservatism and yet another businessman's regime.

The aftermath of '96. The election was followed by a brief revival of the economy and three years later by the end of the long depression. The upturn had little if anything to do with the saving of the gold standard or the victory of McKinley. The price of wheat had started to climb before the election, though hardly enough to have influenced the outcome. But in 1897 the European wheat crop fell off 30 percent, and American farmers doubled their exports of the previous year. Prices continued to rise, and the whole economy began to revive. Discoveries of gold in Australia and Alaska revived the flow of gold into the country, and gold production was further increased by discoveries of pay dirt in South Africa and the development of the cyanide process for extracting the metal from ore. The inflation that the agrarians and silverites had demanded came, ironically enough, not through silver but through gold. The influx of gold and capital stimulated industrial expansion, and that in turn touched off a boom in iron and steel.

With a Republican majority in both houses, McKinley called a special session of Congress in the summer of 1897 to further additional protective tariffs. The Wilson-Gorman Tariff of 1894 was already high enough for most protectionists, but Congress passed a bill framed by Nelson Dingley of Maine, which raised duties to an average of 52 percent. McKinley avoided action on the gold standard until gold was flowing in and silver sentiment was waning. But in his annual message of 1899 he called for legislation, and Congress adopted by a party vote the Gold Standard Act, which he signed on March 14, 1900. The act declared that the gold dollar was henceforth the sole standard of currency, thus writing an end to a generation of controversy, but without producing any significant economic effect, either good or bad.

One significant but often overlooked result of the election of 1896 and the return to prosperity was the demoralization of the Populist movement. Fusion with the enemy party and abandonment of principle for the sake of silver had demoralized the Populists and all but destroyed their party. "The sentiment is still there, the votes are still there, but confidence is gone," thought Tom Watson. The following decade was to see a new upsurge of reform and the realization of many of the old Populist demands, but they were achieved under urban, not rural, leadership. Nineteenth-century agrarian radicalism made its last significant bid for leadership of a national reform movement in 1896.

Suggestions for reading

The political history of this period is treated by H. W. Morgan, *From Hayes to McKinley: National Party Politics, 1877–1896* (1969), and by Matthew Josephson, *The Politicos, 1865–1896** (1938); less readably in E. P. Oberholtzer, *A History of the United States Since the Civil War,* 5 vols. (1917–37). A revisionary estimate of politicians is D. J. Rothman, *Politics and Power: The United States Senate, 1869–1901** (1966). On the nineties, a helpful synthesis is H. U. Faulkner, *Politics, Reform and Expansion, 1890–1900** (1959). W. E. Binkley, *American Political Parties: Their Natural History* (1943, 4th rev. ed., 1963), is interpretative; E. H. Roseboom, *A History of Presidential Elections* (1957, rev. ed., 1970), is factual; and C. A. M. Ewing, *Presidential Elections from Abraham Lincoln to Franklin D. Roosevelt* (1940), is analytical. Richard Hofstadter, *The Age of Reform: From Bryan to F. D. R.** (1955), is revisionary and challenging. Two sectional studies are Paul Kleppner, *The Cross of Culture: A Social Analysis of Midwestern Politics, 1850–1900* (1970), and R. J. Jensen, *The Winning of the Midwest: Social and Political Conflict, 1888–1896* (1971).

Key biographies are Harry Barnard, *Rutherford B. Hayes and His America* (1954); R. G. Caldwell, *James A. Garfield: Party Chieftain* (1931); G. F. Howe, *Chester A. Arthur* (1934); D. S. Muzzey, *James G. Blaine: A Political Idol of Other Days* (1934); Allan Nevins, *Grover Cleveland: A Study in Courage* (1933); and H. J. Sievers, *Benjamin Harrison: Hoosier Statesman* (1959). (On Bryan and McKinley, see below.) See also J. G. Sproat, *The Best Men: Liberal Reformers in the Gilded Age* (1968), and C. E. Rosenberg, *The Trial of the Assassin Guiteau: Psychiatry and Law in the Guilded Age* (1968).

On the politics and issues of reform the literature is rich. On reformist mentality, see Eric Goldman, *Rendezvous with Destiny: A History of Modern American Reform** (1952, abr. & rev. ed., 1956), and the book by Hofstadter cited above. Ray Ginger, *Age of Excess** (1965), is an interpretative study. Civil-service reform is the subject of three excellent works: L. D. White, *The Republican Era: 1896–1901** (1958); P. P. Van Riper, *History of the United States Civil Service* (1958); and Ari Hogenboom, *Fighting the Spoilsmen* (1961). Still valuable on tariff reform are F. W. Taussig, *The Tariff History of the United States** (1894, 8th ed., 1967), and I. M. Tarbell, *The Tariff in Our Times* (1911). Pensions for veterans are treated by J. W. Oliver, *History of the Civil War Military Pensions* (1917), and W. H. Glasson, *History of Military Pension Legislation in the United States* (1900). Monetary controversies of the period are examined in Milton Friedman

*Available in a paperback edition.

and A. J. Schwartz, *A Monetary History of the United States, 1867–1960* (1963); Irwin Unger, *The Greenback Era: A Social and Political History of American Finance, 1865–1879** (1964); W. T. K. Nugent, *Money and American Society, 1865–1880* (1968); and Allen Weinstein, *Prelude to Populism: Origins of the Silver Issue, 1867–1878* (1970).

Agricultural conditions and movements are authoritatively examined in F. A. Shannon, *The Farmer's Last Frontier: Agriculture, 1860–1897** (1945). For light on farmers' organizations, see chapters in Allan Nevins, *The Emergence of Modern America, 1865–1878* (1927); and for greater detail, S. J. Buck, *The Granger Movement** (1913); J. D. Hicks, *The Populist Revolt** (1931); Norman Pollack, *The Populist Response to Industrial America** (1962); W. T. K. Nugent, *The Tolerant Populists: Kansas Populism and Nativism* (1963); R. B. Nye, *Midwestern Progressive Politics: A Historical Study of Its Origins and Development, 1870–1958** (1951, rev. ed., 1959); and Theodore Saloutos, *Farmer Movements in the South, 1865–1933** (1960). A suggestive survey is C. C. Taylor, *The Farmers' Movement, 1620–1920* (1953); and a special study is F. E. Haynes, *Third Party Movements Since the Civil War, with Special Reference to Iowa* (1916).

The depression of the nineties and its political repercussions are intelligently discussed in G. H. Knowles, *The Presidential Campaign and Election of 1892* (1942); and economic causes of the trouble in F. B. Webeg, *The Background of the Panic of 1893* (1929). The serious student will be fascinated by source materials in Hamlin Garland, *Main-travelled Roads** (1891), for agrarian ills; W. H. Harvey, *Coin's Financial School** (1894), and Ignatius Donnelly, *The American People's Money* (1895), for silver propaganda; and H. D. Lloyd, *Wealth Against Commonwealth** (1894), for an exposure of monopoly. Scholarly studies of labor protest are D. L. McMurry, *Coxey's Army** (1929), and Almont Lindsey, *The Pullman Strike** (1943). On the latter event, see also Harry Barnard, *"Eagle Forgotten": The Life of John Peter Altgeld** (1938), and Ray Ginger, *Altgeld's America—The Lincoln Ideal Versus Changing Realities** (1958).

On Populism, Bryanism, McKinleyism, and the crisis of 1896, many books already mentioned are relevant. In addition, see Stanley Jones, *The Presidential Election of 1896* (1964); J. R. Hollingsworth, *The Whirligig of Politics: The Democracy of Cleveland and Bryan* (1963); and P. W. Glad, *McKinley, Bryan, and the People** (1964). The best biographies are Margaret Leech, *In the Days of McKinley* (1959); H. Wayne Morgan, *William McKinley and His America* (1963); and Paolo E. Coletta, *William Jennings Bryan, Political Evangelist, 1860–1908* (1964). Bryan's own account, *The First Battle* (1897), is worth consulting. Still the best book on McKinley's great friend is Herbert Croly, *Marcus Alonzo Hanna* (1912). Agrarian leaders prominent in 1896 are pictured in C. V. Woodward, *Tom Watson: Agrarian Rebel** (1938), and F. B. Simkins, *Pitchfork Ben Tillman: South Carolinian** (1944).

*Available in a paperback edition.

21 *Empire beyond the seas*

The United States was not born in isolation, nor with any bias against expansionism. On the contrary, the long colonial experience was lived out in the midst of international rivalries. Independence itself was painfully won and precariously defended by taking shrewd advantage of those rivalries. Expansionism was a fundamental policy in the new nation's negotiations with foreign powers. Louisiana, Florida, Texas, New Mexico, California, Oregon, the Gadsden Purchase, and the Alaska Purchase—in fact the acquisition of all the continental area of the country beyond the original colonies—are dramatic evidence of expansionism, vigorously and steadily pursued.

After about a century, ending in 1867 with the purchase of Alaska, the nation lapsed into what might almost be called isolationism, though a better term would probably be withdrawal, or preoccupation. At any rate, the United States called a halt to territorial expansion for a quarter of a century or more. In the 1880s, however, expansionism reawakened in a new form—overseas expansion—and concern over foreign affairs revived. A war with Spain, though not itself prompted by expansionism, actually brought overseas possessions, colonies, millions of colonial subjects, protectorates—a whole empire. A republic became an empire, a country long preoccupied with internal affairs turned into a world power. One phase of isolationism ended, and with it one phase of American innocence.

Withdrawal and return

The period of withdrawal. The United States' withdrawal from world affairs was not due to any lack of advocates of aggressiveness. William H. Seward, Secretary of State under Lincoln and Johnson, proposed, among other things, intervention in Korea, acquisition of the Hawaiian Islands, and adventures in the Caribbean. He could muster no support for these undertakings, however, and only with difficulty persuaded Congress to accept the Alaska bargain offered by Russia. Moved by scheming friends, President Grant devised a treaty for the annexation of Santo Domingo, though the Senate rejected

it in 1870. Other expansionists agitated in vain for the annexation of Canada, for intervention in the Cuban rebellion in 1868–78, for securing a naval station in Samoa in the seventies, and for grabbing naval harbors in Haiti during the eighties. The standard arguments against such schemes were that it was against American principles to govern without the consent of the governed, that we should abstain from foreign entanglements, avoid large naval commitments and expenditures, and refrain from absorbing peoples of alien race and tradition. One name for this policy was ''continentalism''—the idea that the nation should acquire no territory outside its continental limits.

Preoccupation with domestic concerns did not blind Americans entirely to opportunities and temptations abroad. The Administrations of Garfield and Arthur sought to advance limited and overlapping goals of prestige, markets, and security, especially in the Caribbean and Central America. Reciprocity trade agreements with countries of these areas were made with a view to exerting economic control over approaches to the proposed isthmian canal region. Arthur's Secretary of State Frederick T. Frelinghuysen pointed out that this would confer "upon us and upon them [Puerto Rico and Cuba] all the benefits which would result from annexation were that possible." Less typical of that period, but suggesting expansionist impulses to come, were the negotiation of a treaty with Korea in 1882 opening up that country to the non-Asian world, and the United States participation in the Berlin Conference of European powers on trade rights in the Congo in 1884–85.

The fact remains, however, that Americans in the seventies and eighties were mainly preoccupied with their built-in empire of the West and their economic colonialism in the South, absorbed in political and economic problems of a domestic character, largely content to stay at home. When Cleveland became President in 1885 the State Department had only sixty employees, including clerks. Secretaries of State were usually political appointees with little knowledge of foreign affairs. Until the 1880s the United States navy was an obsolete and antiquated collection of wooden ships that provoked foreign ridicule. The American merchant marine had virtually disappeared from the seas, and the army was reduced to a handful of Indian-fighters. America still enjoyed—complacently took for granted—nature's marvelous boon of security, which was not only effective but relatively free. Wide oceans, weak neighbors, and rivalries that kept her potential enemies divided accounted for this blessing of free security. No other great nation enjoyed it, and only the habit of relying upon it can account for the tendency of the United States to engage in heated disputes with foreign powers in which her threats and boasts were out of all proportion to her military strength.

Some of these disputes were with Great Britain, then the mightiest power in the world, and any such dispute was likely to become a game between the major political parties. The game was to see who could "twist the lion's tail" the hardest and who could curry the most favor with the Irish and other anti-British elements. One of the disputes during Cleveland's first Administration was merely a renewal of the perennial bickering over fishing rights along the coasts of British North America. Off the western shores of the continent the United States and Canada were simultaneously embroiled in another dispute—this one over the fur-seal industry in and out of the Bering Sea. The United States advanced an arrogant claim to exclusive jurisdiction over the Bering Sea with the contention that the seals were domestic animals that had wandered out of bounds. The American position was in obvious conflict with the traditional policy of "freedom of the seas." A court of arbitration rejected the American claims and prescribed regulations for the industry that were put into effect by both governments.

The only other embroilment to ruffle the relatively calm waters of foreign affairs during Cleveland's first Administration occurred in the Samoan Islands of the remote South Pacific. The splendid harbor of Pago Pago on Tutuila Island had stirred the interest of naval officers of the United States and other countries. In 1878, after rejecting the proposal of annexation or guardianship made by a Samoan chieftain, the Hayes Administration negotiated a treaty granting the United States the right to establish a naval station at Pago Pago. Germany and Great Britain secured similar treaties the following year, granting them naval-station rights in the same harbor and elsewhere. Competition among the traders of these three nations, and the intrigues of their consuls with rival native chieftains, precipitated a tropical squall of international temper in the mid-eighties. Alarmed by the threat of bloodshed, Cleveland called a conference among the three powers that met in Washington in the summer of 1887 but accomplished nothing. Conditions grew worse when Germany set up a new regime in the islands, and seven warships anchored at Samoa prepared for hostilities. A sudden storm of hurricane force in Apia Harbor brought peace unexpectedly by sinking all but one of the warships on March 15, 1889, less than two weeks after Cleveland's term ended. Harrison's Administration worked out a tripartite protectorate of the islands with Germany and Great Britain.

In spite of all these flurries and alarms, little had happened down to 1889 to divert Cleveland from his determination, announced in his first annual message to Congress in 1885, to adhere to "the tenets of a line of precedents from Washington's day, which proscribe entangling alliances," and to oppose "acquisition of new and distant territory or the incorporation of remote interests with our own." Yet the old tradition of isolation, abstention, and withdrawal was near its end, for America was now about to plunge into imperialism and world affairs.

Manifest Destiny revived. The old doctrine of Manifest Destiny (see p. 260) that sped the conquest of California and Oregon in the 1840s had been based on a rather simple faith in the superior vitality of the American people and the beneficence of their political institutions. The new-model manifest destiny that flourished in the late nineteenth century was ornamented by fashionable ideas and scientific notions. Imperialists of the bookish sort found in Darwinism a source of support and rationalization. Practicing imperialists such as Blaine and McKinley found no need for Darwin to justify imperialism. But if industrialists could justify the rise of monopoly in terms of "natural selection," the imperialists could use the same defense for their conquest of "natives" and "backward peoples" in tropical climes. The domination of the "fittest" was thus given the sanction of reputable science. Impulses of aggression and mastery were part of nature's plan for the evolution of man, and to resist them was to go against the law of the universe. Ordinary rules of right and wrong did not apply in this sphere, for responsibility was shifted from conscience to nature. Moreover, the ethics of war and international relations were even more primitive than those of business, for there one was dealing with "the lesser breeds without the law" rather than with civilized adversaries.

Nor did the question of who was the "fittest" present the imperialists with any problem: those who were the fittest to rule were those who had the power and craft to do so. The concept of a superior breed of rulers was perfectly attuned to prevailing ideas about race and racial superiority, particularly to the cult of Anglo-Saxon superiority that prevailed among the upper classes of the East and, with a different emphasis, among the whites of the South. Some preferred the term "Teutonic" and others "Aryan" to describe the superior race, but the terms were often used interchangeably and were sufficiently vague to cover almost all white people with whom one shared friendly feelings.

Religiously inclined exponents of racial superiority believed it had divine sanction. Josiah Strong, an evangelical leader and social reformer, felt this to be a moral obligation. He wrote in his popular book *Our Country* (1885) that the Anglo-Saxon was "divinely commissioned to be, in a peculiar sense, his brother's keeper" and pictured the American branch of the family moving "down upon Mexico, down upon Central and South America, out upon the islands of the sea, over upon Africa and beyond." Professor John W. Burgess of Columbia University assigned the Teutonic nations "the mission of conducting the political civilization of the modern world." A Darwinian lecturer and writer, John Fiske, shared with many historians and philosophers of his time the conviction that it was the "manifest destiny" of the English-speaking people to establish sovereignty of the seas and to bestow the blessings of benevolent rule and superior institutions on less fortunate people around the globe.

But such a grand mission could hardly be accomplished with an antiquated navy. No one was more aware of this fact than Captain Alfred T. Mahan, the foremost exponent of navalism in his time. Mahan was the author of such books as *The Influence of Sea Power upon History* (published in 1890 but delivered as a series of lectures at the new Naval War College in 1886) and *The Interest of America in Sea Power* (1897). "Whether they will or no," wrote Mahan in 1890, "Americans must now begin to look outward." He advanced a program of mercantile imperialism that included the building up of foreign markets, the expansion of the merchant marine, the construction of a navy to protect it, and the acquisition of overseas bases that would enable the fleet to operate in distant seas. Only by these means, he argued, could America keep pace with rival nations. Mahan was the prophet of world power for the United States, and he spoke a language of hard realism that was new to his fellow countrymen. "When he speaks," wrote an admirer, "the millennium fades, and this stern, severe, actual world appears." His books were translated into many languages, he was honored in England, and he was studied assiduously in Germany

The Anglo-Saxon
mission

It is not necessary to argue ... that the two great needs of mankind, that all men may be lifted into the light of the highest Christian civilization, are, first, a pure, spiritual Christianity, and, second, civil liberty. Without controversy, these are the forces, which in the past, have contributed most to the elevation of the human race, and they must continue to be, in the future, the most efficient ministers to its progress. It follows, then, that the Anglo-Saxon, as the great representative of these two ideas, the depositary of these two great blessings, sustains peculiar relations to the world's future, is divinely commissioned to be, in a peculiar sense, his brother's keeper. Add to this the fact of his rapidly increasing strength in modern times, and we have well nigh a demonstration of his destiny.... It seems to me that God, with infinite wisdom and skill, is training the Anglo-Saxon race for an hour sure to come in the world's future.

From Josiah Strong, Our Country, 1885.

American interests

Indications are not wanting of an approaching change in the thoughts and policy of Americans as to their relations with the world outside their own borders.... The interesting and significant feature of this changing attitude is the turning of the eyes outward, instead of inward only, to seek the welfare of the country. To affirm the importance of distant markets, and the relation to them of our own immense powers of production, implies logically the recognition of the link that joins the products and the markets—that is, the carrying trade; the three together constituting that chain of maritime power to which Great Britain owes her wealth and greatness. Further, is it too much to say that, as two of these links, the shipping and the markets, are exterior to our own borders, the acknowledgment of them carries with it a view of the relations of the United States to the world radically distinct from the simple idea of self-sufficingness? We shall not follow far this line of thought before there will dawn the realization of America's unique position, facing the older worlds of the East and West, her shores washed by the oceans which touch the one or the other, but which are common to her alone.

From Alfred T. Mahan, The Interest of America in Sea Power, 1897.

and Japan. He was a prophet with honor at home as well as abroad, for his influence was strong in shaping naval policy in Washington and in molding opinion and inspiring ambitions among such rising statesmen as Henry Cabot Lodge and Theodore Roosevelt.

Big-navy agitators worked hard and effectively through the eighties. In 1881 Congress established a Naval Advisory Board, which began at once to press for larger naval appropriations, and in 1883 Congress authorized the Secretary of the Navy to construct three cruisers and in 1886 two battleships, the *Maine* and the *Texas*. This construction was still guided by the concept of the navy as a defensive force, but the Naval Act of 1890, which authorized the building of three more battleships, the *Indiana*, the *Massachusetts*,

and the *Oregon*, all heavier and more powerful ships, announced the intention of the government to have a navy that could meet a potential enemy anywhere on the high seas. Before the end of the century the United States had moved up from twelfth to third place among naval powers. Thereafter the big-navy advocates began to reap the cumulative benefits of an expanding fleet: new bases and coaling stations, a stronger argument for a canal to connect the Atlantic and the Pacific, an even larger navy to protect the additional bases, and even more bases to accommodate the larger navy.

Another stimulus that quickened America's response to imperialist propaganda was the example set by the European nations that were carving up Africa and Asia, snatching island kingdoms in the Pacific, and casting eyes on South America. Driven by lust for power and greed for trade, they made protectorates of Morocco, Algeria, Tunis, and Libya in North Africa. The British worked southward from the Sudan and northward from the Cape to realize Cecil Rhodes' dream of an African empire. French, Germans, Belgians, and Italians took all the rest, save Ethiopia. The predatory powers moved in on the crumbling dynasty of China from bases already established in Asia: the French from Indochina, the British along the Yangtze Valley, and the Russians from Siberian possessions. Japan felt cheated when, after her victory over China in 1894, she received only Formosa as booty. Americans began to wonder if they were not falling behind the times, whether they would ever be able to protect their interests if they did not enter even belatedly into the imperialist adventure and "take up the white man's bur-den" along with the rewards and plunder that went with it.

Domestic affairs furnished further arguments for foreign adventure. The Indians had been subdued and the built-in empire of the West had been "settled" by 1890—at least according to formal census reports. The South had resumed control of the domestic "white man's burden." Some theorists, including young Theodore Roosevelt, believed that foreign adventures might divert farmers and laborers and the nation from preoccupation with economic ills.

All these impulses—the doctrine of racial superiority, the sense of national mission, and the excitement of the Darwinian struggle, along with an expanding navy, an interest in foreign markets, and the example set by old and admired European nations—combined to prepare America for a new era of involvement in foreign affairs.

The new diplomacy

Imperialistic stirrings. The break with the old tradition was finally made by James G. Blaine, Secretary of State under Harrison. Blaine had served briefly in the same office eight years earlier under Garfield and revived the tradition of earlier Republican expansionism under Seward and Grant. Like them he also sought naval bases in Santo Domingo and Haiti, though with no more success. His followers expected him to pursue a "spirited policy" in keeping with his nickname of "Jingo* Jim." Actually Blaine exerted a moderating influence in the settlement of the Samoan incident with Germany and Great Britain held over from the previous Administration. The three-power protectorate over the islands to which he agreed was, however, without precedent and constituted one of the first steps toward overseas imperialism.

Closer to Blaine's interests was Latin America, especially the promotion of United States trade with her sister republics, the obtaining of naval bases in the Caribbean, and the construction of an isthmian canal. Eight years earlier he had urged calling an international conference of the American republics, and the idea materialized when he became Secretary of State for the second time. Delegates arrived in the fall of 1889 and were treated to a six-thousand-mile barnstorming tour of the country, but when they settled down to consider Blaine's proposals on trade and arbitration treaties they could not agree. All they would accept was the setting up of an information center, which later became the Pan-American Union. More than a half-century was to pass before Pan-American conferences would finally accept the sort of agreements Blaine tried to effect in 1889.

In the early nineties a new martial spirit in America found expression in a succession of chauvinistic outbursts, "jingoism" it was called. One such outburst almost brought the United States to the point of war with Chile, a republic with not one-twentieth its population. In October 1891, when a party from the cruiser *Baltimore* went on shore leave in Valparaiso, a mob of Chileans killed two of the American sailors and injured seventeen others. President Harrison inserted a sword-rattling passage in his annual message to Congress and followed this with another message to Congress virtually inviting it to declare war at a time when the apologies he had demanded from Chile were hourly expected. Chile fortunately capitulated with apologies

*The word was originated in England and popularized in America by a jingle printed in the Detroit *News* during the fisheries dispute with Great Britain and Canada:

> We do not want to fight
> But, by jingo, if we do
> We'll scoop in all the fishing grounds
> And the whole Dominion, too.

The Venezuelan crisis: "Keep off!"

and indemnities, and the war scare passed over.

The bellicose mood of the jingo editors and politicians did not pass over, however. Rather, it continued to mount during the nineties. "The number of men and officials in this country who are now mad to fight somebody is appalling," said the anti-imperialist editor of the *Nation*, E. L. Godkin, in 1894. "Navy officers dream of war and talk and lecture about it incessantly. The Senate debates are filled with predictions of impending war and with talk of preparing for it at once." The irresponsible warmongering of the period was indeed appalling, though it should be remembered that nineteenth-century Americans knew nothing of the total wars to come. They regarded the Civil War as an exception and still thought of war as a heroic affair filled with splendor and glory. It was an illusion slow to die.

Even the antiexpansionist Cleveland was not immune to the new spirit, as he showed in his handling of relations with Britain in the dispute over the boundary between British Guiana and Venezuela. It was an old dispute that went back into the colonial history of Venezuela, but the discovery of gold in the disputed territory, combined with a bit of Venezuelan propaganda suggesting that British aggression was a challenge to the Monroe Doctrine, stirred up the Anglophobia and pugnacity of the jingo editors of the United States. In 1895 Cleveland's Secretary of State, Richard Olney, demanded that Great Britain conform to the Monroe Doctrine, as he very broadly interpreted it, by submitting the boundary dispute to arbitration. He accom-

panied this demand with the truculent assertion that the United States today "is practically sovereign on this continent, and its fiat is law upon the subjects to which it confines its interposition." The tone of the note, coupled with his request for a quick reply, gave it the flavor of an ultimatum.

The British foreign minister, Lord Salisbury, took his time in replying, and when he did reply four months later he repudiated Secretary Olney's interpretation of the Monroe Doctrine and flatly refused to submit the dispute to arbitration. After receiving this rebuff, Cleveland sent a special message to Congress deploring "a supine submission to wrong and injustice and the consequent loss of national self-respect." He asked that he be authorized to appoint a commission to determine the boundary and that the commission's decision be enforced at whatever cost. Congress promptly complied, and war sentiment mounted. "Let the fight come if it must," wrote Theodore Roosevelt, who hoped to participate personally. "I rather hope that the fight will come soon. The clamor of the peace faction has convinced me that this country needs a war." The risk was altogether disproportionate to the American interest at stake, but it was not at all disproportionate to the chauvinistic mood of the day. Fortunately Britain saw fit to back down. Suddenly finding herself in trouble in South Africa with no ally in Europe on which she could count for support, Great Britain decided to court a friend instead of make an enemy in the New World. She switched to a conciliatory tone and signed a treaty with Venezuela providing for arbitration, which turned out to be mainly in her favor. The upshot of the incident was to enhance American nationalist feeling, but paradoxically it also ushered in an era of Anglo-American understanding.

The Hawaiian question. When it came to expansion overseas, however, Cleveland clung consistently to traditional views and stood firm against the annexation of Hawaii. American interest in these islands dated back to the China trade in the late eighteenth century. Traders were followed by American missionaries, who converted the native Polynesians to Christianity in the second quarter of the nineteenth century, and the missionaries were followed by American sugar-growers. Efforts to annex the islands under President Pierce and again under Secretary Seward failed, but in 1875 a reciprocity treaty was signed opening a free market in the United States to Hawaiian sugar-planters. Sugar production in the islands multiplied tenfold in the next twenty years in response to the free American market. So dependent did the industry become on this market, however, that when the McKinley Tariff of 1890 admitted other foreign sugar on the same terms and subsidized domestic producers, the blow precipitated an economic crisis in the island kingdom and contributed to a political crisis.

King Kalakaua, the next to last of the reigning family, had been forced by the white business community in 1887 to accept a new constitution that curbed his power, made his ministers responsible to the legislature, and brought the legislature under control of the propertied classes. The dissolute old king was succeeded in 1891 by his sister Liliuokalani, who made it apparent that she was determined to overthrow the constitution her brother had accepted, shake off white control, and restore royal prerogatives. In January 1893 a committee of businessmen-revolutionaries demanded that she abdicate. Thereupon United States Minister John L. Stevens, an annexationist whom Blaine had picked for the office, ordered marines ashore from the cruiser *Boston* and raised the American flag. The queen then capitulated, as she said, "to the superior force of the United States of America." A month later, on February 15, Harrison sent to the Senate a treaty annexing the islands. It might have gone through then and there had it not been for the declared preference of Cleveland, who was to begin his second Administration in a few days, that the matter be held over until his inauguration. As soon as he became President again he dispatched a special commissioner to investigate the situation in the islands. The commissioner's report convinced Cleveland that the great majority of the natives supported the queen. Cleveland therefore not only withheld the annexation treaty but insisted that it was his duty to restore "Queen Lil." The revolutionary provisional government refused to step down, however, and continued to rule, biding its time until a more imperialist-minded Administration came to power.

Cleveland's firm resistance to annexation, as compared with Harrison's receptive attitude, helped to make the question something of a party issue. The Republican platform of 1896 contained a plank favoring Hawaiian annexation, and though McKinley had previously shown no interest in the matter he was quickly won over after he became President in March 1897. Comparing him with Cleveland, commissioners from Hawaii reported that there was "the difference between daylight and darkness." On June 16, 1897, Secretary of State John Sherman signed a treaty of annexation and McKinley sent it to the Senate. Congress was strongly interested in Hawaii and alarmed by the interest Japan was manifesting in the islands, but the sentiment against overseas expansion was still too strong to be overcome, and the treaty languished for more than a year without action. Only in July 1898, after the war with Spain had opened the floodgates of expansionism, was Hawaii annexed.

Queen Lil

War with Spain

The Cuban crisis. The expansionists and imperialists did not cause the war with Spain. They merely exploited it for their own purposes. The war itself grew out of deplorable conditions in Cuba that seemed intolerable to an aroused popular sentiment in the United States. Spanish misgovernment of the island had given rise to numerous revolts and a Ten Years' War, 1868–78, that brought little relief for Cuban ills. A new civil war broke out in February 1895. As in the case of the Hawaiian revolution, American tariff policy contributed to the uprising, for the tariff law of 1894, by imposing a duty on raw sugar, had added economic suffering to political discontent.

Both the Cubans and the Spaniards used savage methods. The Cubans systematically destroyed sugar mills, cane fields, and other property. Early in 1896 the Spanish commander, General Valeriano Weyler, resorted to the brutal policy of "reconcentration." This meant driving the entire population of large areas of Cuba—including women, children, and old people—into cities and towns fortified with barbed wire and under armed guard. Left without food or sanitation, the prisoners fell victim to famine and disease. Within two years two hundred thousand, or approximately one-eighth of the total population, were estimated to have been wiped out.

The American press exaggerated the Spanish atrocities, but the sufferings of the rebels were horrible enough in any case to arouse deep sympathies among Americans. The sufferings, moreover, were those of a neighbor, and they were incurred in a fight for independence from a manifestly unjust imperial ruler. Little more was required to whip up popular sympathy for the Cuban patriots and animus against Spain, especially in years when the public mind was as susceptible to jingoism as it had recently proved to be in far less serious disputes with Chile and Great Britain. Indications were abundant that influential Americans were "spoiling for a fight," and the Cuban junta that established itself in New York to dispense propaganda, solicit aid, and arouse sympathy was not without support. Those with long memories recalled that the United States had expressed great interest in Cuba since the early years of the century and since 1823 had implicitly regarded European control of the island as unnatural.

One strong ally of the interventionists was the "yellow press" of New York City. Led by William Randolph Hearst's New York *Journal* and Joseph Pulitzer's New York *World,* which were currently engaged in a war for circulation, the press sent a corps of reporters and artists to cover the Cuban conflict and supply the papers with vivid human-interest stories and pictures. The barbarities of the Spaniards were played up and the atrocities of the Cubans glossed over, with the result that the newspaper coverage constituted powerful propaganda for the rebel cause. Waves of sympathy for the insurgents swept the country, and when the struggle continued to drag on with no prospect of Spain's relenting, much of the sympathy began to turn into a demand for American intervention and war with Spain.

American businessmen did not originally share the interventionist sentiment, though important segments of the business community became converts before the intervention. Protestant religious journals and both Republican and Democratic newspapers clamored loudly for intervention and war, though they insisted that they did so on purely humanitarian grounds and disclaimed any desire to annex Cuba or gain territory. Theirs was a moralistic aggression, with imperialism disavowed. Outright imperialists, including Roosevelt, Lodge, and Mahan, were also for war, but for the express purpose of conquest,

expansion, and military glory. Two contrasting sets of aggressive impulses, both frustrated in the nineties, sought outlet in an idealistic crusade for Cuban freedom. One set embraced the impulses of protest and humanitarian reform; the other embraced the impulses of national self-expression, aggressiveness, and expansion. The first was embodied in Populism, utopianism, the Social Gospel, and radical labor movements—all of which had suffered frustrations in the nineties, most recently in the downfall of Populism and Bryan and the triumph of conservatism and McKinley. The second group included the big-navy advocates, the patriotic societies, and the statesmen and propagandists of imperialism, whose programs had been blocked by cautious business interests and the antiexpansionist foreign policy that had prevailed since Grant's Administration. The convergence of these two groups in support of intervention in Cuba goes far toward explaining why Americans worked themselves up into a mood for war with Spain.

American intervention. When Grover Cleveland was President, he had opposed intervention in Cuba on every front. He had resisted pressure from Congress to accord the insurgents belligerent rights, had sought to suppress gun-running into Cuba from the States, and had tendered his good offices to Spain to settle the colonial war. In the summer of 1896, however, Cleveland underwent a change, and in his last annual message to Congress he came near to laying down a rationalization for America's intervention. McKinley tried hard to curb the jingoes and halt the drift to war. Six months after he took office a satisfactory settlement seemed to be in the making. A change of government in Spain brought in a prime minister who recalled General Weyler and offered Cuba a considerable measure of self-government in local affairs. The offer proved unacceptable, however, since the Spaniards in Cuba opposed rule by native Cubans and the insurgents refused to settle for anything short of complete independence. Further hopes for a peaceful solution were disrupted by a series of fateful incidents, or accidents, that brought relations between the United States and Spain to the breaking point.

The first incident was the publication on February 9, 1898, of a stolen private letter from the Spanish minister in Washington,

William Randolph Hearst: spoiling for a fight

EDITION FOR GREATER NEW YORK

NEW YORK JOURNAL
AND ADVERTISER.

NO. 5,571. — Copyright, 1898, by W. R. Hearst — NEW YORK, WEDNESDAY, FEBRUARY 16, 1898.—16 PAGES. — PRICE ONE CENT In Greater New York, Elsewhere and Jersey City. | TWO CENTS.

MAINE BLOWN TO ATOMS IN HAVANA HARBOR;
OVER ONE HUNDRED OF HER CREW KILLED.

Three Million Dollar Battleship Destroyed by a Terrific and Mysterious Explosion While Her Men Are Sleeping.

Dupuy de Lôme, who indiscreetly described President McKinley as "weak and a bidder for the admiration of the crowd" and said that the Cuban rebels should be suppressed by force. Dupuy de Lôme resigned before his government had time to respond to Washington's inevitable request for his recall. Then, six days later, the battleship *Maine* blew up in Havana Harbor with a loss of two hundred sixty officers and enlisted men. The Spanish government hastened to offer condolence and propose a joint investigation. An investigation by American naval officers reported that the *Maine's* bottom plates had been thrust inward, indicating an external explosion, but the cause of the tragedy was never discovered. It is highly improbable that the Spanish government would have plotted such an act, but the jingo press held Spain guilty and raised the cry "Remember the Maine!" Before the report of the *Maine* explosion was completed, Congress unanimously voted a defense appropriation of $50 million, and on March 19 Senator Redfield Proctor of Vermont delivered a speech painting the shocking conditions he had found in Cuba during a recent unofficial visit. His calm tone, his reputation for moderation, and his matter-of-fact manner convinced many who had heretofore been skeptical of the lurid stories in the yellow press that action was indeed necessary.

On March 27 McKinley proposed to Spain a peaceful settlement in which she would abandon her reconcentration policy at once, grant an armistice until October 1, and enter into peace negotiations with the insurgents through his offices. This was not an ultimatum, though he followed it the next day with a telegram saying that independence would be the only satisfactory outcome of the peace negotiations. Spain was confronted with a cruel dilemma: if she rejected McKinley's demands she faced a disastrous war, and if she complied with them she faced a revolt that might overturn the government and possibly the throne. Her appeals for support from European powers won sympathy, but the only tangible response was a visit to President McKinley by the ambassadors of six powers who begged him not to intervene with armed force. Despairing of European aid, Spain replied on March 31 to McKinley's proposals by agreeing to abandon reconcentration and to grant an armistice upon the application of the insurgents. She hedged on the point of independence but volunteered to submit to arbitration the question of who was responsible for sinking the *Maine*. She followed up on April 9 by declaring an armistice on her own without waiting for the insurgents to take the initiative. The following day the American minister in Madrid cabled that he believed Cuban independence and a solution satisfactory to all could be worked out during the armistice.

Spain had gone far toward meeting the President's demands, far enough according to his minister in Madrid to assure a peaceful solution. But ignoring these assurances, caught up in the popular cry for war, McKinley on the day after receiving his minister's cable, April 11, sent a warlike message to Congress. He alluded to Spain's concessions to American demands in passing, but did not stress them. There was, it is true, ground for doubt that the Spanish government could make good its promises. Congress paused only to debate whether it should recognize the insurgent government as well as the independence of Cuba, decided on the latter only, and adopted the resolution on April 19 by a vote of 42 to 35 in the Senate and 311 to 6 in the House. An amendment to the resolution, which was prepared by Senator Henry

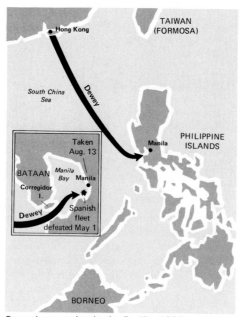

Dewey's campaign in the Pacific, 1898

M. Teller of Colorado and adopted at the same time without dissent, renounced any intention of annexing or governing Cuba and promised to "leave the government and control of the Island to its people." The Teller Amendment proclaimed American righteousness and abstention with respect to Cuba but, as the author of the resolution carefully pointed out, left the country a free hand "as to some other islands" that also belonged to Spain. Spain responded by declaring war on April 24, and Congress followed suit the next day. The American declaration of war was made retroactive to April 21, since the President had established a blockade of the Cuban coast on April 22.

The little war. Within ten weeks of the declaration of war the fighting was over and the victory assured. For the country at large—and the readers of headlines in particular—it could not have been a more "splendid little war," as John Hay described it, or one conforming more completely with the romantic imagination of the budding imperialists. The whole war seemed to have been fought to the stirring music of "The Stars and Stripes Forever," the battle song of the war, played by a marine band in dress uniform. Even the participants chose to remember it in the manly prose of Richard Harding Davis or in the heroic sketches of Frederic Remington, two of the numerous writers and artists who "cov-

ered" the story of one of the best-publicized wars in history. The Spanish-American War was, in short, the most popular of all American wars. Disillusionment takes a bit of time, especially among noncombatants, and this war was over even before weariness could set in—save among combat troops.

The most hardened skeptics were thrown off balance less than a week after the war started by Commodore George Dewey's dazzling naval victory in Manila Bay on the opposite side of the globe. Assistant Secretary of the Navy Theodore Roosevelt, who had secured the commodore's assignment to the command, had taken advantage of his superior's temporary absence to direct Dewey two months earlier to be thoroughly prepared for action. McKinley approved this order the next day. On receiving news of the war and his final instructions, Dewey had immediately steamed out of Hong Kong, slipped through the straits of Boca Grande during the night of April 30, and at dawn opened fire on the weak and inferior Spanish squadron at Manila. Before breakfast, and without losing a man, he had sunk the whole fleet to the last of its ten ships. Dewey had crushed Spanish power in the Pacific.

Unfortunately the army was not as well prepared as the navy, but the public did not learn about that until later. the account of the expeditionary force to Cuba that the public read and gloried in was the sort supplied by the debonair reporter Richard Harding Davis:

> It was a most happy-go-lucky expedition, run with real American optimism and readiness to take big chances, and with the spirit of a people who recklessly trust that it will come out all right in the end, and that the barely possible may not happen. . . . As one of the generals on board said, "This is God Almighty's war, and we are only His agents."

That was one way of putting it. At least Davis was accurate about the expedition's optimism and recklessness. The army, with only some twenty-six thousand men at the start of the war, had no adequate plans, equipment, or supplies. The War Department was crippled by antiquated methods, utterly incompetent administration, and inefficient and negligent officers. General William R. Shafter, a three-hundred-pound Civil War hero, presided over the chaos at Tampa preceding the embarkation of the expeditionary force. Transportation broke down and confu-

The Rough Riders and their colonel

sion reigned. The thousands of volunteers who rushed to the colors eager for glory could not be supplied with guns, tents, or blankets. With hopeless inefficiency they were clad in heavy woolen winter uniforms for a summer campaign in the sweltering tropics. Food was inadequate, repulsive, and sometimes poisonous, sanitation was conspicuously wanting, and medical supplies were almost nonexistent. Over the expeditionary force there spread the stench of dysentery and illness and eventually the horror of plague, the yellow jack. The fact was that blundering inefficiency brought the army to the brink of disaster.

The Spaniards blundered badly, too, but with an unstable government, a tradition-bound leadership, and a backward economy, they had more excuse for inefficiency than the Americans, who had none of these handicaps. Yet for all their pride in industrial progress and their reputation for bustling efficiency and technological know-how, the Americans made a mess of their war effort. The government seemed unable to adopt the vigorous administrative methods that would have made effective use of the country's vaunted industrial superiority. The scandal reflected a quarter-century of federal lassitude and bureaucratic stagnation. As it turned out, the real explanation of the quick American military success lay in the even more incredible inefficiency and blundering of the Spaniards.

The enemy obliged by immobilizing his

Cuban naval power, a small force of four cruisers and three destroyers under the command of Admiral Pascual Cervera, in Santiago Harbor, where it was immediately blockaded by a vastly superior fleet commanded by Admiral William T. Sampson. The blockade ended the threat to the landing of an expeditionary force, and after much backing and filling and countermanding of orders a force of some eighteen thousand regulars and volunteers got under way from Tampa, partly equipped, partially trained, and poorly led. The most publicized unit of volunteers was the Rough Riders, commanded by Colonel Leonard Wood, who was loudly supported by

The Cuban campaign, 1898

WAR WITH SPAIN   **501**

"Charge of San Juan Hill," by Frederick Remington

Lieutenant Colonel Theodore Roosevelt, second in command. The landing force blundered slowly ashore on June 20 and somehow established a beachhead at Daiquiri, a few miles east of Santiago.

With some two hundred thousand troops in Cuba, the Spaniards could have destroyed the Americans utterly. But they had only about thirteen thousand men at Santiago and were so handicapped in transportation that they could not bring their superior forces to bear and so unfortunate in military leadership that they could not employ what power they had at hand to their best advantage. Even so they came near inflicting a disaster upon the invaders. The American objective was to capture the ridges, known as San Juan Hill, that surrounded Santiago and then to take the town in whose harbor Admiral Cervera was blockaded. So poorly was the command organized, however, that the American units were largely without coordinated control in their attack. It was in the capture of Kettle Hill, a flanking outpost of San Juan Hill, that Theodore Roosevelt established his reputation for martial zeal and heroism. Later he was to describe the attack volubly and frequently as a "bully fight" that was "great fun," something of a rollicking skylark. Actually the fight, in which his was by no means the only part, was a pretty desperate and bloody affair marked by a reckless display of courage and a great many needless casualties. The capture of the heights proved decisive in the land fighting, for Santiago was now closely invested. But, under counterattack and without supplies, the American troops were soon in a dangerous plight. On July 3 Roosevelt wrote Lodge, "We are within measurable distance of a terrible military disaster," in desperate need of reinforcements, food, and ammunition.

On that very morning, however, Admiral Cervera hoisted anchor and steamed out of Santiago Harbor to face his doom for the honor of Castile. He knew perfectly well that he was far outclassed and outgunned by the four United States battleships awaiting him just outside the harbor, but he gave battle rather than surrender without a fight. The American battle line opened up with its thirteen-inch guns, and one after another the Spanish ships went down gallantly, guns ablaze. It was all over in a few hours, with four hundred enemy killed or wounded and with only one American killed. The next day was the Fourth of July, and orators had not had such an opportunity since the day after Gettysburg and Vicksburg.

The enemy ashore was now powerless, and the Spanish forces surrendered Cuba on July 16. Puerto Rico was taken within the next two weeks virtually without resistance, and on August 12 a peace protocol was signed. The next day Manila fell to the troops that were sent over after Dewey's victory in May, and the war was over. In actual battle casualties the price of victory was comparatively small. But only after the close of the war did the major losses begin to mount: losses due to disease, mainly typhoid, malaria, and yellow fever. By the end of the year the total deaths in the American army in all theaters of war had risen to 5,462, only 379 of which were the direct result of combat or wounds.

The white man's burden

Mr. McKinley and his duty. The armistice deliberately left open the question of the disposition of the Philippine Islands. They had scarcely figured at all in the war motives of most Americans, who, in Reinhold Niebuhr's phrase, were bent on fighting a ''pure-minded war.'' To seize those possessions and to rule them by force without consent of their inhabitants would be to violate both the humanitarian motives that prompted the war and the oldest and profoundest American political traditions. Knowing these things in their hearts, whether they admitted them or not, the imperialist-minded minority scarcely dared hope at the onset of the war that their dreams would materialize. As it turned out they were on the eve of sensational success.

Hawaii was the first sign. In the spring before the war the cause of annexation had looked fairly hopeless. But in the excitement of the Dewey and Sampson victories the traditional arguments were swept aside and the ''large policy'' of Hay, Lodge, Mahan, and Roosevelt prevailed. The New York *Tribune* maintained that Hawaii was ''imperative'' as a halfway station to the Philippines, and another expansionist argued later that the Philippines were imperative as an outpost for Hawaii. On June 15 the House of Representatives, and on July 6 the Senate, adopted a joint resolution annexing Hawaii. The large policy was now on the way to further enlargement.

The enlargement was facilitated by the flexible conscience of President McKinley, who once regarded forcible annexation as ''criminal aggression'' but now saw in it ''the hand of Almighty God.'' He advanced his insights in the form of such epigrams as, ''Duty determines destiny,'' but he did not answer the New York *Evening Post*'s query, ''Who determines duty?'' At any rate the destiny of the Philippines was becoming pretty manifest as McKinley's epigrams and actions multiplied. Even before Dewey's victory was confirmed he sent a force to capture and hold Manila, and before the end of May Lodge was writing Roosevelt, ''The Administration is now fully committed to the large policy that we both desire.''

The President was swimming with the tide, as he usually did. And the commercial and industrial interests now helped swing the tide toward expansionism. Though they had opposed the war at first for fear of its effect on recovery and the gold standard, once the war started and news of the victories poured in and the potentialities of expansion for the advancement of trade became manifest, the business community swung about in support of the policies it had once opposed. Big business saw the Philippines as a key to the China trade and listened appreciatively to Senator Albert Beveridge's declaration that ''the trade of the world must and shall be ours.''

At the same time the religious press, with the support of the missionary movement, stepped up support for the ''imperialism of righteousness.'' Annexation would further the cause of world evangelization, extend the blessings of civilization and sanitation, and ''civilize'' more of the heathens. It was this sentiment that McKinley reflected later in recounting how he had reached his decision through prayer ''to educate the Filipinos, and uplift and civilize and Christianize them, and, by God's grace, do the very best we could by them, as our fellow men for whom Christ also died.''

A more cynical approach to imperialism was that of editor Henry Watterson, who proposed to ''escape the menace and peril of socialism and agrarianism'' by means of ''a policy of colonization and conquest.'' One popular way of thinking, however, was to attribute imperialism to a determinism of some sort: the hand of God, the instinct of race, the laws of Darwin, the forces of economics and trade—anything but rational and responsible decision. Though many Americans seemed willing to surrender to imperialist policies, few would admit they did so because they wanted to.

McKinley revealed his intentions pretty clearly by the choice of commissioners he sent to negotiate with Spain at the peace conference held in Paris. Three of the five peace commissioners were open and avowed expansionists. Another indication was his seizure of Spain's island of Guam—whose inhabitants mistook the American bombardment for a salute and apologized for having no ammunition with which to return it. In his instructions to the peace commissioners the President took the moral position that ''without any desire or design on our part'' the United States had assumed duties and responsibilities that it must discharge as became a nation of noble destiny. Impressed by the popular response

William McKinley:
''Duty determines destiny''

to speeches he made along this line of "responsibility," he instructed the commissioners in October with regard to the Philippines that "duty requires we should take the archipelago."

John Hay, who had recently become Secretary of State, cabled the delegation in Paris to hold out for the whole of the Philippine Islands. The Spanish commissioners resisted the demand to the point of risking a renewal of hostilities. McKinley stuck to his position that we should "not shirk the moral obligation of our victory" but made one concession, an offer to pay $20 million for the Philippines. The Spaniards capitulated, and the treaty was signed December 10, 1898. By its terms Spain was to give up control over Cuba and surrender Guam, Puerto Rico, and the Philippine Islands to the United States.

In thus abandoning American tradition and his own earlier convictions, President McKinley showed little evidence of grasping the implications of his decision for American foreign policy and future involvement in power rivalries and wars in the Far East. There is little reason, however, to doubt the sincerity of the reasons he offered a year later, though some critics question that they came to him in a flood of prayerful illumination. The reasons he offered were that it would be cowardly and dishonorable to give the Philippines back to Spain, "bad business and discreditable" to let France or Germany seize them, impossible to leave them to their own devices since they were unfit for self-rule, and absolutely necessary to follow the humanitarian impulses to "civilize and Christianize" the Filipinos by taking possession of their land. He did not see fit to propose the establishment of a protectorate over the islands with the promise of self-government and later independence.

What McKinley had in mind in his reference to the designs of European powers on the Philippines was a bit of recent history. In November 1897, Germany landed troops at Kiaochow, and a Russian fleet anchored at Port Arthur. The following March the two European powers forced China to sign agreements giving Germany exclusive rights in Shantung province and Russia exclusive rights in Manchuria. Japan had occupied Korea, and France was established in Kwangchau Bay.

The debate on the Philippines. The treaty with Spain committed the country to open imperialism in the Far East and the Caribbean. But first it had to be ratified by the Senate, and the question of ratification precipitated a debate that spread far beyond the Senate chamber and cast more light on the issues of annexation than had the President's speeches and the expansionists' slogans. After the drums of war were silenced and the people began to think more soberly, it became apparent that there was formidable opposition to the President's policy, perhaps enough to defeat it. Far more opposition came from Democrats than from Republicans, and the sentiment was strong enough to unite even such Democratic extremes as Bryan and Cleveland. But prominent members of McKinley's own party, including Speaker Reed of the House and Senator George F. Hoar of Massachusetts, broke with the Administration over the question, as did Senator Eugene Hale of Maine. To the very last it was doubtful whether the President could muster the two-thirds of the Senate required to ratify his treaty.

Even before the treaty was signed an Anti-Imperialist League was organized that attracted the support of many distinguished men. As president, the league elected George S. Boutwell, formerly Grant's Secretary of the Treasury and later Republican senator from Massachusetts. Among the vice-presidents were such contrasting figures as Grover Cleveland and Samuel Gompers, Andrew Carnegie and Carl Schurz, John Sherman and Charles Francis Adams. Intellectuals, novelists, and poets rallied to anti-imperialism in great numbers, among them President Eliot of Harvard and President David Starr Jordan of Stanford, along with William James, William Dean Howells, William Graham Sumner, Hamlin Garland, William Vaughn Moody, and Mark Twain. In a bitter satire Mark Twain assured his countrymen that the "Blessings-of-Civilization Trust" had the purest of motives. "This world-girdling accumulation of trained morals, high principles, and justice cannot do an unright thing, an unfair thing, an ungenerous thing, an unclean thing," he wrote. "It knows what it is about. Give yourself no uneasiness; it is all right."

Some of the anti-imperialist arguments showed remarkable prescience. George Boutwell foresaw a war with Japan as a consequence of American expansion in the western Pacific, and following that the rise of a warlike China in potential alliance with Russia that

We are making no new departure. We are not taking a single step which in any way affects our institutions or our traditional policies. From the beginning we have given widely varying degrees of self-government to our different Territories, according to their needs.

The simple truth is that there is nothing even remotely resembling 'imperialism' or 'militarism' involved in the present development of that policy of expansion which has been part of the history of America from the day when she became a nation. The word means absolutely nothing as applied to our present policy in the Philippines; for this policy is only imperialistic in the sense that Jefferson's policy in Louisiana was imperialistic; only military in the sense that Jackson's policy toward the Seminoles or Custer's toward the Sioux embodied militarism; and there is no more danger of its producing evil results at home now than there was of its interfering with freedom under Jefferson or Jackson, or in the days of the Indian wars on the plains.

From Theodore Roosevelt, Letter Accepting the Nomination as Vice President, September 15, 1900.

Acquisition of the Philippines: Theodore Roosevelt

Our opponents, conscious of the weakness of their cause, seek to confuse imperialism with expansion, and have even dared to claim Jefferson as a supporter of their policy.... The acquisition of the Louisiana Territory, Florida, Texas and other tracts which have been secured from time to time, enlarged the Republic, and the Constitution followed the flag into the new territory. It is now proposed to seize upon distant territory already more densely populated than our own country, and to force upon the people a government for which there is no warrant in our Constitution or our laws....

A colonial policy means that we shall send to the Philippines a few traders, a few task masters and a few office holders, and an army large enough to support the authority of a small fraction of the people while they rule the natives.

If we have an imperial policy we must have a large standing army as the natural and necessary complement. The spirit which will justify the forceable annexation of the Philippines will justify the seizure of other islands and the domination of other people, and with wars of conquest we can expect a certain if not rapid, growth of our military establishment.

From William Jennings Bryan, Speech Accepting the Presidential Nomination, August 8, 1900.

Acquisition of the Philippines: William Jennings Bryan

would turn against American holdings. A favorite argument was based on the doctrine of the Declaration of Independence: no government without the consent of the governed. We had fought the Revolution for that principle and had intervened in Cuba on the same ground; how could we now shamelessly adopt the doctrines we fought to overthrow? Or, as Senator Hoar put it, how could we "strut about in the cast-off clothing of pinchbeck emperors and pewter kings?" Other objections were that the Asiatic people could not be assimilated into our tradition, that imperialism would lead to militarism and racist

dogma at home, that overseas expansion was unconstitutional and inconsistent with the Monroe Doctrine. Populistic opponents of empire in the South and West never fully understood those of the Northeast. Southerners viewed the new imperialism as a revival of carpetbaggery and warned of the difficulties of reconciling races of contrasting color and heritage. Racist arguments were used both for and against imperialism.

The imperialist-minded defenders of the treaty revived with new assurance their old arguments of naval strategy, world power, and commercial interests and incorporated the moralistic line of McKinley on duty, destiny, humanitarianism, and religious mission. In the latter vein Senator Beveridge declared, ''It is God's great purpose made manifest in the instincts of our race, whose present phase is our personal profit, but whose far-off end is the redemption of the world and the Christianization of mankind.'' Senator Lodge dismissed the consent-of-the-governed argument as of no account because that principle had been ignored or violated before, notably in the Louisiana Purchase, in order to advance the national interest. He emphasized and exaggerated the supposed economic advantages of the Philippines: their resources, their trade, and their relationship to the international struggle for China and its trade. He stressed the political expediency of keeping the islands: they were not ready for self-government, would lapse into anarchy, or would be seized by more ruthless powers.

In the meantime the Senate continued its deliberations, the outcome still in doubt. Before the end of the debate the anti-imperialists were confused by a strange maneuver and strategic blunder of William Jennings Bryan. Although he was a strong opponent of the acquisition of the Philippines, he decided that the Senate should approve the treaty to assure peace and should leave the future disposition of the islands to be decided at the polls. He undoubtedly believed that this move would provide him with a winning issue in the presidential election of 1900, but he miscalculated. Approval of the treaty confronted the voters with a *fait accompli.* Bryan's advice won some Senate votes over to the side of the Administration, though not enough to assure victory. On February 5, 1899, the very day before the final ballot was set, the drama of the decision was complicated and intensified by the arrival of news that the Filipinos had taken up arms in open revolt against the United States. There could be no more doubt of their desire for freedom or that the United States was now in the same position formerly occupied by discredited Spain. The effect of this news is impossible to estimate. The issue remained in doubt until the roll call the next day recorded fifty-seven in favor of the treaty and twenty-seven against. Two more than the necessary two-thirds majority.

In the meantime the American army remained in control of Cuba, and the government refused to withdraw until the Cubans incorporated into their constitution a permanent treaty with the United States, the so-called Platt Amendment, proposed by the United States Senate in 1901. This limited the power of Cuba to make treaties, borrow money, or change certain policies established by the occupation forces and required the sale or lease of lands for a naval base. More important, the United States was granted the right to intervene at will ''for the preservation of Cuban independence'' and ''the protection of life, property, and individual liberty.'' Having no choice, Cuba submitted.

The motives that prompted America to ''take up the white man's burden,'' as Rudyard Kipling urged her to do, were even more complex than the motives of the war that prepared the way for the decision. Part of the motivation was fear, the fear of appearing silly and playing the fool in the eyes of the world. Part of it was an uglier impulse of aggression. ''The taste of empire is in the mouth of the people even as the taste of blood in the jungle,'' said the Washington *Post*.

John Hay: promulgator of the Open Door

Beyond the Philippines. What the other great imperial powers of the world were currently doing to China was a cause more of alarm than of emulation in America. Even before the Cuban war, John Hay had pressed upon President McKinley the common interest of the United States and Great Britain in forestalling exclusion from the China trade. Now the trade opportunities promised in the Far East by the acquisition of Hawaii and the Philippines were threatened by the impending dissolution of China and its partition among imperial powers. A small pressure group of American exporters interested in the China trade added their influence to that of Britain to move the State Department into action.

To meet the problem, Secretary Hay sent his ''Open Door'' notes to Great Britain, Germany, and Russia in September 1899 and later to Japan, Italy, and France, inviting them to agree to three principles: (1) that no power would interfere with the trading rights of other nations within its sphere of influence, (2) that Chinese tariff duties (which gave America most-favored-nation rights) should be collected on all merchandise by Chinese officials, and (3) that no power should levy discriminatory harbor dues or railroad charges against other powers within its sphere. Great Britain agreed conditionally, Russia equivocated, and Germany, France, Italy, and Japan agreed on

American troops in Peking, 1900

condition of full acceptance by the other powers. It was a chilling response, but Hay saved face by blandly announcing that since all powers agreed on the American proposals, their assent was considered "final and definitive." Since Russia had not agreed, and Britain only with conditions, and since the others made acceptance conditional on full acceptance by all powers, Hay's claims were not very impressive. His proposals at this point did not undertake to preserve the territorial integrity or independence of China.

In May 1900, two months after Hay announced his interpretation of the response to the Open Door notes, the Boxers, an organization of fanatical Chinese patriots, incited an uprising that took the lives of 231 foreigners and many Christian Chinese. In June the Boxers began the siege of the legations in Peking and cut the city off from the outside world for a month. The Western powers and Japan then sent in a military force, to which the United States contributed five thousand troops. This expeditionary force relieved the besieged legations on August 4.

During the Boxer Rebellion crisis, Secretary Hay labored successfully to prevent the spread of war, limit the extent of intervention, assure the rapid withdrawal of troops, head off the extension of foreign spheres of influence, and keep down punitive demands on China. On July 3, 1900, Hay issued a circular stating it to be the policy of the United States "to seek a solution which may bring about permanent safety and peace to China, preserve Chinese territorial and administrative entity," and protect all trade rights mentioned in the Open Door notes in all parts of the empire. This was an important extension of American policy in the Far East. Although only Great Britain, France, and Germany responded favorably to Hay's circular, its effect was to help soften the punitive terms imposed on China. Unwilling to risk the general war that might be precipitated by a struggle to divide China, the intervening powers were persuaded to accept indemnity in money rather than territory. The United States' share of the reparations was $25 million, more than enough to settle the claims of her nationals. In fact, the United States returned a balance of more than $10 million, and the Chinese government, as a gesture of gratitude, placed the money in trust for the education of Chinese youth in their own country and in the United States.

McKinley's vindication of 1900. It was Bryan's mistake, in planning to make the election of 1900 a popular referendum on imperi-

An English view of American expansion

alism, to believe that the anti-imperialist sentiment of the great debate of 1898–99 could be sustained or even revived, much less strengthened. Nearly two years were to pass between the ratification of the treaty and the presidential election, and by that time much water had passed under the bridge. Empire was no longer a dangerous menace to tradition and a decision that had to be worried out; it was an accomplished fact to which the people were growing accustomed. They did not like the war that was being waged to suppress Emilio Aguinaldo and his Filipino patriots, even though censorship kept some of its worst aspects from them. That war was to drag on for three years, during which the United States was to use more men to suppress freedom in the Philippines than it had used to bring freedom to Cuba. And the new American rulers were to repeat in grotesque imitation the tortures and brutalities of their Spanish predecessors. But all that was taking place on the other side of the widest of oceans. When pressed, people admitted, "Peace has to be restored."

At home there were plenty of distractions to divert a burdensome conscience. The most important one was the gradual return to prosperity. The war itself served as an additional stimulus. Business regained its nerve, trade quickened, and the economy bustled into activity.

As the farmers and laborers sloughed off the burden of depression, their radicalism declined. "The Spanish War finished us," wrote Tom Watson of the Populist party. "The blare of the bugle drowned the voice of the reformer." The war, coupled with returning prosperity, mounting racism, and the legacy of the Populists' demoralizing fusion with Bryanism in 1896 (see p. 487), did just about finish the party. In the 1900 campaign it split into two feuding factions, neither of which could make a substantial showing. Many of the Populists of the Southwest and Middle West were attracted to the new Social Democratic party, which was founded in 1900 and nominated Eugene V. Debs of Pullman-strike fame as its presidential candidate.

Although McKinley's policies had little to do with the revival of the economy, he was billed as "the advance agent of prosperity," and he prospered politically with the return of good times. With a Cabinet that was if possible even more conservative than he was himself, McKinley's first Administration had proved as willing and cooperative as Hanna and the business community could have hoped. The Dingly Tariff of 1897 raised the rates to a new high, and the gold standard was now safe.

The presidential nominees of the two major parties in 1900 were pretty much a foregone conclusion. The Republicans had no hesitation about McKinley, but only with some difficulty did they settle upon the military hero and New York governor, Theodore Roosevelt, whom neither McKinley nor Hanna wanted, for Vice President. The Democrats returned to Bryan and picked the Silverite Adlai E. Stevenson, who had been Cleveland's running mate in 1892, for second place. The Democratic platform stressed imperialism as the "paramount issue" and on Bryan's insistence revived the demand for free silver. His strategy of uniting silverites of West and South with gold men of the Northeast in a coalition against imperialism came to grief. Bryan soon discovered that he had two fairly moribund issues on his hands and therefore shifted his emphasis to monopoly and special privilege.

Bryan, in a poorer showing than he had made in 1896, lost his own state of Nebraska, as well as Kansas, South Dakota, Utah, and Wyoming—all silver states he had carried before. The election neither revived the silver issue nor provided a mandate on imperialism. Even if the voters opposed imperialism, they could express their disapproval only by voting against prosperity. To the majority of voters in 1900 McKinley meant prosperity rather than imperialism or gold, and with him conservatism was triumphant once more.

The general histories of American diplomatic relations by Bemis, Pratt, and Bailey see this period Suggestions *for* *reading* from somewhat different points of view. F. R. Dulles, *The Imperial Years** (1956), is an informed and perceptive general study beginning with Cleveland's first Administration. E. R. May, *Imperial Democracy* (1961), reveals how America emerged as a great power. J. A. S. Grenville and G. B. Young, *Politics, Strategy, and American Diplomacy: Studies in Foreign Policy, 1873–1917* (1966), and Walter LaFeber, *New Empire: An Interpretation of American Expansion, 1860–1898** (1963), contribute insights on this period. A neglected period is covered in D. M. Pletcher, *The Awkward Years: American Foreign Relations under Garfield and Arthur* (1962). The world context of imperialism is seen in P. T. Moon, *Imperialism and World Politics* (1926); and the American variant and its rationalization are described and richly illustrated and exposed in A. K. Weinberg, *Manifest Destiny** (1935). On Latin American affairs the most informative studies are S. F. Bemis, *The Latin American Policy of the United States: An Historical Interpretation** (1943), and Dexter Perkins, *The Monroe Doctrine, 1867–1907* (1937); and on the Far East a helpful work is A. W. Griswold, *The Far Eastern Policy of the United States** (1938). W. A. Williams, *The Tragedy of American Diplomacy* (1959), stresses economic expansion.

The revival of the expansionist impulse is traced in Harold and Margaret Sprout, *The Rise of American Naval Power, 1776–1918** (1939), and reflected in many works of the period, particularly Josiah Strong, *Our Country* (1885), and A. T. Mahan, *The Influence of Sea Power upon History, 1660–1783** (1890). Leading expansionists of the 1880s and 1890s are portrayed in W. D. Puleston, *Mahan* (1939); H. K. Beale, *Theodore Roosevelt and the Rise of America to World Power** (1956); and H. F. Pringle, *Theodore Roosevelt: A Biography** (rev. ed., 1956). C. A. Beard and G. H. Smith, *The Idea of National Interest** (1934), takes a skeptical view of expansionism. See also S. K. Stevens, *American Expansion in Hawaii, 1842–1898* (1945). The crisis in Cuba and the war with Spain are treated by Julius W. Pratt, *The Expansionists of 1898** (1936), with emphasis on motives; by Walter Millis, *The Martial Spirit** (1931), with coverage of diplomatic and military aspects; and by Frank Freidel, *The Splendid Little War* (1958), with many wonderful photographs and contemporary sketches. R. S. West, Jr., *Admirals of the American Empire* (1948), is useful on naval aspects of the war. The influence of newspapers is examined in M. M. Wilkerson, *Public Opinion and the Spanish-American War* (1932), and J. E. Wisan, *The Cuban Crisis As Reflected in the New York Press, 1895–1898* (1934). Orestes Ferara, *The Last Spanish War* (1937), uses Spanish sources. Penetrating analysis of the theories and motives of American imperialists are found in Richard Hofstadter, *Social Darwinism in American Thought** (rev. ed., 1959), and by the same author, "Manifest Destiny and the Philippines," in Daniel Aaron, *America in Crisis* (1952). G. F. Kennan, *American Diplomacy: 1900–1950** (1951), has sober reflections on this crusade. Valuable discussions of the peace negotiations and the aftermath of the war are Tyler Dennett, *John Hay* (1933); F. E. Chadwick, *The Relations of the United States and Spain,* 2 vols. (1909–11); and J. W. Pratt, *America's Colonial Experiment* (1950). England's example and approval are pictured in C. S. Campbell, *Anglo-American Understanding, 1898–1903* (1957). Matthew Josephson, *The President Makers, 1896–1919* (1940), throws light on the election of 1900; and Margaret Leech, *In the Days of McKinley* (1959), illuminates not only the same subject but also many aspects of the war with Spain. On opponents of American imperialism, see R. L. Beisner, *Twelve Against Empire: The Anti-Imperialists, 1898–1900* (1968); and on China policy, see M. B. Young, *The Rhetoric of Empire: America's China Policy, 1895–1901* (1968), and Thomas McCormick, *The China Market** (1967).

*Available in a paperback edition.

Theodore Roosevelt and the progressive movement

22

"That which strikes the visitor to America today," a friendly English observer wrote soon after the turn of the century, "is its prodigious material development." Industry was growing more swiftly than ever before. Cities spread, wealth increased, and so did "the stress and rush of life." Yet the United States, as another Englishman had noted, was still a "land of stark, staring, and stimulating inconsistency." While technology advanced, rural ways of life and habits of mind persisted. Americans had yet to accommodate to the social and cultural changes stimulated by industrial and urban growth. They had yet to adjust their laws and their techniques of government to an age of large and complex private organizations. Americans had yet to recognize the international implications of their national wealth.

They had yet to fulfill their national promise of individual dignity, liberty, and decency for all men.

The unprecedented productivity of the economy made comfort potentially available to all Americans. That possibility in turn highlighted the striking contrasts between the few and the many, the white-skinned and the dark, the urban and the rural—the striking contrast between national aspiration and national achievement. Out of an awareness of that contrast, out of the tensions of material development, out of a consciousness of national mission, there emerged the efforts at adjustment and reform that constituted the progressive movement, a striving by men of good will to understand and improve the society in which they lived.

A land of growth and contrasts

National wealth and the business elite.
During the first decade of the twentieth century the number of people in the United States, their average age, and their average per capita wealth and income all increased. This growth gave confidence to most members of a generation that tended to measure progress in terms of plenty.

There were almost 76 million Americans in 1900, almost 92 million in 1910. Advances in medicine and public health, resulting in a declining death rate, accounted for most of the increase, which was accompanied by a continuing movement of people within the United States. In the West the rate of growth was highest—along the Pacific slope, more

510

than 73 percent. But growth occurred everywhere, especially in the cities, where it proceeded three times as fast as in rural areas. The cities, in the pattern of the past (see p. 444), absorbed almost all of the 8 million immigrants who came largely from central and southern Europe. Usually swarthy and unlettered, ordinarily Catholics or Jews, these newcomers differentiated the cities further and further from the patterns of life that rural America remembered and revered.

Spurred by the pace of private investment, the nation was recovering from the depression of the nineties. During the first decade of the century, capital investment more than doubled and the total value of the products of industry rose over 76 percent. By a larger margin than ever before the average per capita income of Americans led that of all other nations. But not all groups shared equally in national wealth. Though unemployment became negligible, the average real income of wage-earners was falling, partly because prices rose faster than wages, partly because an increasing percentage of business profits was going to investors.

Those who were already rich were at once the agents and the beneficiaries of the process of industrial expansion and consolidation, which followed the patterns of the 1880s and 1890s. Corporate mergers and reorganizations gave a dominant influence to a few huge combinations in each of many industries—among others, railroading, iron and steel and copper, meatpacking, milling, tobacco, electricals, and petroleum. By 1909, 1 percent of all the business firms in the nation produced 44 percent of all its manufactured goods. The consolidators had become the richest and in some ways the most powerful men in the United States. They guided the process of investment. They controlled the boards of directors of the great American banks and industries. Further, they interpreted the startling growth and burgeoning product of industry as a demonstration of their own wisdom and their optimism about the economic future of the United States.

The "leaden-eyed." The magnificence of American wealth contrasted sharply with the sorry lot of the American poor, whom society, as the poet Vachel Lindsay put it, had made "oxlike, limp, and leaden-eyed." In 1910 the nonagricultural laboring force consisted of more than 30 million men and 8 million women, most of whom worked too long,

Population 1900

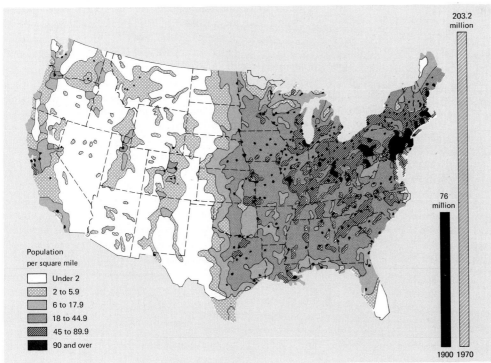

Population per square mile

- Under 2
- 2 to 5.9
- 6 to 17.9
- 18 to 44.9
- 45 to 89.9
- 90 and over

203.2 million

76 million

1900 1970

511

The widest and most varied opportunities for play have surrounded the child for centuries in the country life.... The growth of large cities has deprived the child of these opportunities.... The street is all that is left to the playing child, and the street gang is his organization for purposes of play.... They have no purpose except to play, and this means ... to "steal, to destroy, even to stab or shoot".... The collapse of home life ... and the necessity which compels both mother and father ... to work early and late, bereave the child of every good influence.... Our gardens are given a place apart; flowers and plants are tended ... by wise hands ... but the childhood of our city is without its place, without its tending, and without its guidance.

From Robert Hunter, *Poverty,* 1904.

Garment worker: few finished high school

earned too little, and lived meanly. While the richest 1 percent owned 47 percent of the national property and received 15 percent of the annual national product, a large part of the industrial population, between one-third and one-half, lived in poverty. Their children ordinarily left school to find work—only one-third of the American children enrolled in primary schools completed their courses; less than one-tenth finished high school.

Work for men, women, and children was arduous. Four million laborers were on the job between fifty-four and sixty hours each week; at least half a million, between sixty and seventy-two hours. Industrial accidents were common and conditions of work unhealthy and sometimes despicable. Usually the worker had to suffer his disasters alone. Employer-liability laws, where they existed, were inadequate; there was no social insurance against accident, illness, old age, or unemployment. And the slums, where most workers lived, were as bad as they had been in the 1890s.

Skilled laborers fared better. The craft-union movement, well launched in the nineties, made significant gains during the early years of the twentieth century. Membership in the affiliates of the American Federation of Labor rose from 548,000 in 1900 to 1,676,000 in 1904 and, in the face of strong resistance from employers, to about 2,000,000 by 1914, though even then some 90 percent of industrial workers remained unorganized. The unions and the railroad brotherhoods continued to strive for the objectives Samuel Gompers and their other leaders had defined earlier. Especially in the building and metals trades, they were able to win from management agreements providing for collective bargaining, higher wages, shorter hours, and safer conditions of work.

The craft unions were effective but in some respects selfish agencies of change. Though they excited opposition from business-managers not yet prepared to grant labor any voice in industrial decisions, they had little quarrel with the concentration of industrial power. Indeed their leaders recognized that labor had benefited from the stability produced by the restriction of competition. The American Federation of Labor did, however, demand the right to organize workers into national trade unions, consolidations that would parallel the consolidations of capital. In order to organize, labor needed to be unshackled from state and federal prohibitions on the strike and the boycott—and needed, too, state and federal protection from anti-union devices. The unions welcomed legislation setting standards of safety and employer liability, but otherwise they preferred to rely on their own power, rather than on the authority of the state, to reach their goals. They continued to distrust the federal government, for it had so often in the past assisted in breaking strikes, and they were eager to enlarge their own power even at the expense of those they had no intention of organizing. So it was that Gompers and his associates persisted in opposing legislation on wages and hours, matter that they intended to settle through collective bargaining.

Bargaining, even when possible, assisted only union members, and the craft unions were generally unconcerned with the unskilled bulk of the labor force. Indeed Gompers, along with other labor-leaders, looked down on the unskilled, particularly the immigrants (though he himself was one of them). Craft-leaders feared that management would hire unskilled and unorganized immigrants and blacks to replace skilled workers (though in fact skilled workers were competing less with the unskilled than with an advancing technology and mechanization). This fear intensified prejudices against Asians, blacks, and southern and eastern Europeans—prejudices that fed growing sentiments for the restriction of immigration and for racial segregation. Organized labor condoned Jim Crow and sparked the agitation that led in 1902 to the permanent exclusion from the United States of Chinese immigrants and in 1907 to the effective exclusion of Japanese.

In short, the unions did no more than management or landlords to help the majority of workers. Within that majority were numbered the American blacks, of whom almost 90 percent still lived in the South, but more and more in the cities there. In 1910 almost a third of all blacks were still illiterate; all were victimized by the inferior facilities for schooling, housing, traveling, and working that segregation had imposed upon them. Worse still, the incidence of lynchings and race riots remained high—a shameful condition dramatized by mass killings in Atlanta in 1906 and by riots in Abraham Lincoln's own Springfield, Illinois, in 1908. As racist concepts spread in the North as well as the South, the American Negro experienced his darkest hours since the Civil War. A few black intellectuals, led by W. E. B. DuBois, a Harvard Ph.D., in 1905 organized the Niagara movement. Abandoning the program of Booker T. Washington, DuBois and his associates demanded immediate action to achieve political and economic equality for blacks. With some support from informed whites, the Niagara movement was transformed in 1909 into the National Association for the Advancement of Colored People. But the NAACP, though a hopeful portent for legal redress of black grievances, was some years from becoming an influential instrument of reform.

With varying success women, too, intensified their struggle for political, economic, and social status equal to that of men. Sarah Platt Decker, president of the General Federation of Women's Clubs, converted the energies of that middle-class organization to agitation for improving the conditions of industrial work for women and children (see p. 450). That objective received a stronger thrust from Florence Kelley's National Consumers' League, which sponsored state legislation for minimum wages and maximum hours. In New York City, the International Ladies' Garment Workers Union, financed in part by wealthy matrons, conducted a prolonged strike in 1909 that won limited gains in spite of opposition from employers and police. Tiny when the strike began, the union had become the third largest in the AFL by 1914. With the woman suffrage movement gaining strength, Carrie Chapman Catt astutely focused its efforts on demands for federal action, and by 1910 she was close to achieving the goal of a constitutional amendment guaranteeing women the right to vote. Meanwhile some women radicals, among them Margaret Sanger and Emma Goldman, had begun to advocate free and open instruction in birth control. Birth control, they argued, by gradually reducing the size of the working force, would soon enhance labor's ability to bargain with capitalists. Interest in birth control, however, spread largely among middle-class women who recognized the physical, social, and psychological advantages of family planning and who were eager to be freed from the constraints of the ordinary American home. Under their auspices, the National Birth Control League in 1915 began its attempt through education and lobbying to effect the repeal of state and federal laws that forbade as obscene the dissemination of information about birth control. But like the NAACP, the NBCL was still many years from becoming an effective political force.

Throughout the country, conscientious middle-class men and women, long engaged in sporadic battles for political reform, tended to blame the immigrants and blacks for the shameful conditions that still characterized urban government (see p. 448). Yet the candidate for a reform administration needed the votes of the poor. The continuing struggle for political reform and for restrictions on wealth forced the polite to learn more about the unfortunate. With that learning, whetted by compassion, came a larger understanding of the need to improve the lives of those whom machine politics, in its own way, exploited.

Politics had not created the glaring inequities in American life, but politics did reflect and sustain them. Politics might also erase them, and during the first decade of the twentieth century there occurred a flowering of remedial political ideas and of remedial social ideas that politics could implement. The thoughtless and extravagant behavior of the very people who profited most from American wealth and productivity was generating a corrective discontent.

Protest and reform

Agrarian demands. The new century brought unparalleled prosperity to American farmers. As domestic and world markets revived, the prices of farm products and the value of farm land just about doubled within a decade. The farmer was still suspicious of bankers, of industry and middlemen, of cities and foreigners. But prosperity tempered farmers' hostilities, softened their rhetoric, turned them from outright attack to flanking maneuvers by which they sought to procure for themselves a larger share both of urban culture and comforts and of the business profits of agriculture.

Farm organizations continued to press for political reforms designed to give voters a stronger and more direct voice in government. The reforms, they hoped, would help them obtain public policies that would aid agriculture—better roads and marketing facilities, cheaper credit, technical advice on planting and cultivation, more and cheaper electric power, assistance to cooperatives, lower taxes on land, and tariff adjustments that would facilitate sales abroad. Those practical goals, some of which entailed special privileges for farmers, challenged the special privileges and the superior power big business had long enjoyed.

In Washington farm spokesmen continued to urge the creation of agencies to monitor the growth and the practices of the great consolidations. Reflecting the agrarian bias against monopoly, they also argued that industrial power should be splintered by enforcing the languishing antitrust laws. Many farm leaders believed that controls should extend to the treatment accorded to labor. Thus the objectives of farm politics sometimes merged with the objectives of urban reformers.

Art and literature of protest. Those objectives took shape as artists, journalists, and social workers exposed the conditions of filth and misery that violated the ideals of middle-class Americans. Realistic literature and art, candid and conscientious journalism, reached the hearts of ladies and gentlemen of good will and helped enlist them in the causes of reform.

Theodore Dreiser, an immigrant's son schooled in poverty, used his powerful novels to describe the barren life of the poor "as simply and effectively as the English language will permit." His *Sister Carrie* (1901), *Jennie Gerhardt* (1911), *The Financier* (1912), and *The Titan* (1914) revealed the human tragedy of inadequate wages, of insecure, hopeless, mechanical existence. Most of Dreiser's characters, driven by greed or sex to bestial violence, tried to fight their way into more splendid circumstances, but he made it poignantly clear how great were the odds against them, how cruel the cost of success, how sorry the lot of those success left behind. Frank Norris, a lesser talent than Dreiser, made his novel *The Octopus* (1901) a vehicle for condemning the inhumane policies of the Southern Pacific Railroad. In spite of the evils he recounted, he professed a faith that "all things . . . work together for good," but he continued his indictment of wealth in *The Pit* (1903). Jack London, a socialist, was optimistic only about the ultimate triumph of those who had lived, as he had, in "the unending limbo of toil." His fellow socialist and novelist Upton Sinclair, writing *The Jungle* (1906) in a similar vein, showed how those who labored in the poisonous world of the Chicago packing-houses "hated their work . . . the bosses . . . the owners . . . the whole place, the whole neighborhood." The poet Carl Sandburg railed at the stockyards and at "Pittsburgh, Youngstown, Gary—they made their steel with men."

Realistic painters, representatives of the "ash-can school," produced canvases that one of their number, John Sloan, called "unconsciously social conscious." Sloan, Robert Henri, William Glackens, George Luks, and others, experimenting with new brush techniques and new relationships of form, found compelling subject matter in dirty alleys, dank saloons, and squalid tenements—"chapters out of life," which they interpreted with beauty that expressed the sorrow and injustice of an experience previously unrecorded in fashionable galleries.

The art of men like Sloan, Sandburg, and Dreiser, for whom social criticism was often a secondary purpose, supplemented and sharpened the message of outraged authors of a deliberate literature of exposure. Social workers, sociologists, and economists recited the facts of poverty in the magazine *Charities and the Commons;* in reports like *The Tenement House Problem* (1903); in books like Robert Hunter's *Poverty* (1904), Father John

Tenement: a chapter out of life

A. Ryan's *A Living Wage* (1906), John Spargo's *The Bitter Cry of the Children* (1906), Walter Rauschenbusch's *Christianity and the Social Crisis* (1907), and Frances Kellor's *Out of Work* (1915). Those documents demonstrated that between half and two-thirds of all working-class families had incomes too small to buy food, shelter, and clothing—incomes that left nothing for recreation or education, little even for union dues or church contributions. No thoughtful student of the facts could any longer believe that poverty was a function of sloth or moral turpitude; clearly there was something wrong with a society that permitted so much misery while it pretended to a Christian ethic and a generous standard of living.

Tragedy confirmed that lesson. In 1911 fire at the Triangle Waist Company in New York resulted in the death of 146 employees, mostly girls, who could not escape from the building where management had been as stingy about safety as about wages (four or five dollars for a seventy-hour week). This shocking episode provoked official investigations that led ultimately to new factory laws and immediately to broader support of organizations already advocating remedial legislation.

But humanitarian striving, effective though it was, influenced fewer Americans than did the hortatory, often sensational, journalism of exposure. *McClure's* set the pace for inexpensive, middle-class magazines. It published Ida M. Tarbell's devastating account of the business methods of the Standard Oil Company, Lincoln Steffens' exposés of the role of respectable citizens as well as ward politicians in the corrupt government of a dozen cities and states, Burton J. Hendrick's disclosures of the fraudulent practices of various insurance companies, and Ray Stannard Baker's indictments of railroad mismanagement, labor-baiting in Colorado, and race discrimination in the South. Though other "muckrakers" (the phrase was Theodore Roosevelt's) sometimes enlivened their work with willful exaggerations, they had no need to distort. The bare facts stirred the awakening conscience of middle-class Americans. Disenchantment with the mighty, like compassion for the poor, swelled the ranks of reform.

Protests of the intellectuals. Meanwhile, American intellectuals were formulating the

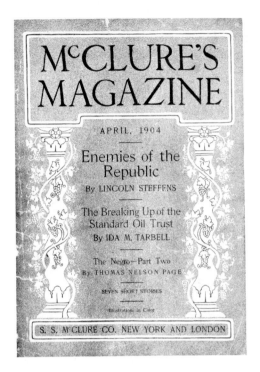

attitudes and techniques on which reform was to rely. These new attitudes, taken together, suggested the need for skepticism about rigid, formal systems of thought. They suggested also the importance of rigorous, dispassionate inquiry as a foundation for knowledge and of constant testing of hypotheses and modification of them on the basis of experience. These principles, derived from the methods of science, were expected to yield ideas for social action. Indeed for the innovative proponents of the developing philosophy of pragmatism, the value of any idea depended on its utility for the thinker and his society.

Among the influential intellectuals of the early century, none better stated the case for enlightened skepticism than did Justice Oliver Wendell Holmes, Jr., who recognized that the prejudices of judges often determined their interpretations of the law. Explaining the divergences between law and ethics, Holmes questioned the propensity of courts to upset the decisions of popularly elected legislatures. Though he understood the fallibility of the majority, he preached judicial restraint, for he understood also the judiciary's fallibility and its tendency to artificiality and arrogance.

The artificiality and formalism of prevalent theories of social Darwinism invited the attack of William James and John Dewey, the fathers of American pragmatism. A psychologist as well as a philosopher, James emphasized the vagaries and the resilience of the mind, and warned against imprisoning intellectual creativity within arbitrary or mechanistic systems. For him the truth of an idea or an action lay in its consequences, as it did also for Dewey, who conceived of philosophy as an instrument for guiding action, an instrument he himself used in advocating experimentation in education and government. Tolerance and freedom of belief and of expression, Dewey noted, were essential if ideas were to enjoy a competitive chance to prove their merit.

Thorstein Veblen continued to strip away the façade of contemporary institutions as he had in the nineties. His *The Theory of Business Enterprise* (1904) explained the cultural and economic importance of the machine process, and his *The Instinct of Workmanship* (1914) showed that wasteful and destructive monopolistic practices frustrated man's basic drive to create. Veblen's uncompromising analyses contained insights from which reformers, economists, and sociologists were then and later to borrow freely and with reward.

Other less angry and less probing students of contemporary economic institutions directed attention to reform. The writings of John R. Commons on labor, Jeremiah W. Jenks on industry, and William Z. Ripley on railroads were characteristic of moderate, but perceptively critical, scholarship. These experts, often counselors to state and federal regulatory or investigatory commissions, understood that business-managers were not ordinarily bad men but that they were too often timid or limited men, lacking in power and imagination. With Ripley, the economists Henry C. Adams, Richard T. Ely, and Simon Patten viewed man not as the creature of deterministic forces but as the maker of beneficent change. They urged that the principles of management be applied to government and that the state be empowered to solve the public problems business could not.

All in all, American intellectuals were growing more and more skeptical about their culture and society and more and more confident in the ability of free, informed, alert minds to conceive and to achieve a better world. Their impatience for change accorded with the restlessness of a self-critical era and animated the diverse social thrusts that constituted progressivism.

Progressivism in the cities and the states.

Democratic government had failed most blatantly in American cities. Now municipal-reform organizations, many of them founded in the nineties, succeeded gradually in winning home-rule charters and permission to regulate franchises or to provide for public ownership of vital services. The experiments of Galveston, Texas, with a commission form of government, and of Staunton, Virginia, with a city-manager, demonstrated how efficient these substitutes for an aldermanic system could be. Over a hundred cities had copied them by 1910. The form of government, however, was less important than its spirit, which in city after city drew inspiration from the examples set by mayors like Hazen Pingree of Detroit and Samuel "Golden Rule" Jones of Toledo.

Those developments impinged continually on state government, partly because urban reform could not proceed without improvements in state laws. A wave of reform in the agricultural Middle West began in Wisconsin with the election of Robert M. La Follett as governor in 1900. "Battle Bob," who set precedents for the entire region, had tried for years to overcome the regular Republican machine. A loyal party man, he built his own faction of those who shared his rural democracy. Before he became United States senator in 1906, La Follette made his administration a model of honesty and efficiency, established a fruitful liaison between the government and the state university, whose distinguished faculty included many valuable advisers on public policy, and overcame the opposition of the Old Guard in the legislature. At the governor's urging, Wisconsin passed laws providing for a direct primary, civil service, restrictions on lobbying, conservation, apparent control of railroads and banks, higher taxes on all corporations (previously undertaxed), and the first state income tax. Wisconsin had become, as Theodore Roosevelt later said, "the laboratory of democracy."

As in Wisconsin, progressive government also drew heavily on rural support in Iowa, Minnesota, the Dakotas, Oregon, Arkansas, Mississippi, Georgia, and South Carolina. Progressive administrations limited the privileges of corporations, especially railroads, and put into effect sundry devices of popular democracy—the direct primary, the popular election of United States senators, the initiative and referendum, penalties for corrupt

"The System":
Wisconsin

But there was the good State of Wisconsin ruled by a handful of men who had destroyed every vestige of democracy in the commonwealth. They settled in private conference practically all nominations for important offices, controlled conventions, dictated legislation, and had even sought to lay corrupt hands on the courts of justice....

The pass abuse had grown to extraordinary proportions in Wisconsin, and the power to give passes, franks on telegraph and telephone lines, free passage on Pullman cars, and free transportation by express companies had become a great asset of the machine politicians....

Clubs were formed in Madison where members of the legislature could be drawn together in a social way and cleverly led into intimate associations with the corporation men who swarmed the capital. In one of the principal hotels a regular poker game was maintained where members who could not be reached in any other way, could win, very easily, quite large sums of money. In that way bribes were disguised.... It was notorious that lewd women were an accessory to the lobby organization. Members who could not be reached in any other way were advised that they could receive good positions with railroad corporations after the legislative session was over.

From Robert M. La Follette, *La Follette's Autobiography,* 1913.

"The System":
Pittsburgh

Boss Magee's idea was not to corrupt the city government, but to be it; not to hire votes in councils, but to own councilmen; and so, having seized control of his organization, he nominated cheap or dependent men for the select and common councils. Relatives and friends were his first recourse, then came bartenders, saloon-keepers, liquor dealers, and others ... who were ... dependent ... upon the maladministration of law....

Business men came almost as cheap as politicians, and they came also at the city's expense.... The manufacturers and the merchants were kept well in hand by many little municipal grants and privileges, such as switches, wharf rights, and street and alley vacations.... A foundry occupies a block, spreads to the next block, and wants the street between....

As for the railroads, they did not have to be bought or driven in; they came, and promptly, too. The Pennsylvania appeared early, just behind Magee, who handled their passes and looked out for their interest in councils and afterwards at the State Legislature.

From Lincoln Steffens, *The Shame of the Cities,* 1904.

political practices, and frequently woman suffrage.

Progressivism won similar victories in industrial states, though here much of the impetus for reform came from the middle class of cities and suburbs. In New Jersey the "New Idea" arose among prosperous suburbanites who were fighting to prevent valuable rapid-transit and other franchises from falling into exploitative hands, to empower a state commission to regulate commutation fares, to extract taxes from corporations (instead of from real estate alone) to defray the costs of public schooling. Objectives like these, along with the characteristic middle-class hostility toward machine politics, brought the New Idea into alliance with the reform mayor of Jersey City, who had built his strength among the workingmen he befriended. In 1904 the resulting coalition of independent Republicans began to convert New Jersey into the progressive community that in 1910 elected the Democrat Woodrow Wilson as governor and that during his administration completed, under bipartisan auspices, the program of the New Idea.

New York, New Hampshire, Michigan, California, and to a lesser degree Ohio, all states with important industrial centers, had political experiences not unlike New Jersey's, though none elected a governor who was so quickly and dramatically successful as Wilson. Reform in these and other industrial and semi-industrial states led to major improvements for the working force, which cast some of the crucial votes for progress. Before 1915, twenty-five states passed employer-liability laws; five limited the use of injunctions preventing strikes or boycotts; nine passed minimum-wage laws for women; twenty granted pensions to indigent widows with children; others restricted hours and conditions of work.

The progressive attitudes and motives.

The strivings of the progressives revealed a great deal about the progressives themselves—their faith in democratic processes, their hostility to large aggregations of private power, their confidence in public regulatory agencies, their humanitarian temper. And yet they were a diverse group, and their movement was a concatenation of similar but independent movements. In rural areas, it borrowed much from Populism, and it retained an agrarian flavor modified by time, experience, and prosperity. In the cities, where the poor were increasingly conscious of the need to remedy their lot by political action, progressivism was more visible as a political expression of the attitudes of liberal intellectuals and social critics of the nineties and the early twentieth century. The middle-class men who absorbed those attitudes and swelled the ranks of reform were both goodhearted and worried. They partook of the long national heritage of humanitarian democracy, but where they had long been inactive in public matters, they now mobilized, partly because they had gained a better understanding of the urgency of social reform, partly because they saw that change was needed if they were to preserve the things they valued. The unrest of the nineties had been a searing experience. Violence, trembling below the surface of society, had threatened the comfortable middle-class world. And with prosperity returned and violence abating, the middle class had a chance to remove the inequities that had bred disquiet. Further, the state (as middle-class men often viewed it) and especially expert agencies created by the state would mediate the tensions between rich and poor that had troubled the nineties.

Professional men, white-collar men, and small businessmen, moreover, felt their status and their well-being threatened by the advancing power of big business, big city machines, and—more rarely—big labor. They had to organize to protect themselves and their standing and to monitor their giant rivals. Mostly native Americans, they resented the immigrant or second-generation political boss. Mostly men of modest means and often men of old family, they resented the purchased prestige and paraded vulgarity of the newly rich. Though some of them were bureaucrats, successful servants of big business and finance, more of them were the victims of bigness and consequently anxious to regulate it. Where labor unions were strong economically and politically, as in California, they too became targets for the attack on power. But more often the attack was pointed toward corporations that dealt directly with many customers—monopolies or near-monopolies selling transportation, utilities, and food—or that were saddled (sometimes unjustly) with especially bad reputations.

Some managers of large corporations realized that reform sentiment might work to their own advantage. Such men, eager to protect the industrial stability they had achieved, worried about the possibility of renewed competition. They recognized that limited and benign federal regulation—for example, of railroading, of lumbering, of banking, or of the manufacture of pharmaceuticals—could restrict the sharp practices of their smaller but aggressive business rivals. Public policy, in that view, instead of being merely permissive or primarily antimonopoly, had the potentiality of providing positive guidance for industrial behavior, guidance compatible with the interests of big business. Spokesmen of big business who were also reformers—distinctly a minority of their kind—acted in some cases in pursuit of selfish advantage, in some cases out of a sense of social obligation, in some cases out of both motives.

Whatever their motives, they often reasoned from the unstated, paradoxical premises that were characteristic of progressive thought. They had a sense of their own elite status—whether of wealth or social standing or talent—which they felt they deserved. They also believed in representative government, in the agencies it created, and in the electorate to which it was responsible. They reconciled those beliefs with the comforting, private assumption that they and men sympathetic to them would win and hold the confidence of the people. In that assumption, for those leaders of big business who championed reform, there was little to fear from federal regulation of industry, for the regulators would appreciate the problems of the regulatees.

The urban progressives, men of many stripes, included many middle-class men, but not all—or even most—middle-class men were progressives. Those who were, were the most socially conscious, perhaps the most anxious, but also, by and large, the younger men, educated, ambitious, and adventurous. They drew much of their inspiration from the most dynamic national exponent of their spirit and purpose, President Theodore Roosevelt. Without Roosevelt, progressivism would doubtless have happened, but it would not have been nearly so much fun.

The Republican Roosevelt

In September 1901 McKinley died, the third President to be assassinated in less than forty years. His successor, Theodore Roosevelt, whom Mark Hanna had called "that damned cowboy," had set his political course for the White House long before McKinley's death. "It is," wrote Roosevelt, "a dreadful thing to come into the Presidency this way; but it would be a far worse thing to be morbid about it." The gift of the gods to Roosevelt—at forty-two the youngest chief executive in American history—was joy in life, and for eight exciting years he brought that joy to his office.

The son of patrician parents, a graduate of Harvard, an accomplished ornithologist and an enthusiastic historian, Roosevelt chose early in life to make politics his career, for he wanted to rule—and he chose to work not as an independent but as a loyal Republican, for he wanted to win. He served successfully, with occasional time out as a rancher in the Dakotas, as an assemblyman in New York, a United States Civil Service commissioner, a New York City police commissioner, Assistant Secretary of the Navy, colonel of the celebrated Rough Riders, and governor of New York. Senator Thomas C. Platt, the long-time boss of the state Republicans, developed serious apprehensions about Roosevelt's successful ventures in reform and managed in 1900 to get him out of New York by arranging his nomination for Vice President, a position Roosevelt accepted with somewhat resigned grace but with characteristic vigor.

Roosevelt and the Presidency. As a campaigner Roosevelt displayed the qualities that were to give him during his Presidency an enormous influence with the people. As had no President since Jackson, he captured their imagination. To the Americans who acclaimed him he was many wonderful things—policeman, cowboy, hero in arms, battler for the everlasting right. He was that toothy grin, that animal energy, that squeaky voice exhorting the worthy to reform. Roosevelt was also a learned man, receptive to the advice of the men of ideas whom he brought to Washington. As one Englishman put it, he was more remarkable than anything in the United States, except perhaps Niagara Falls.

Roosevelt was also a skilled politician who made the Presidency a great office and used it boldly. He conceived of the President as "a steward of the people bound actively and affirmatively to do all he could for the people"; he set out therefore as President to define the great national problems of his time, to propose for each a practicable solution, to win people and Congress to his proposals, and to infuse the executive department with his own dedication to efficient enforcement of the laws.

Roosevelt summoned to federal service a remarkable group of advisers and subordinates. The President's example and support inspired them; his reorganizations of federal agencies gave scope to their talents. They included, among others, Elihu Root, McKinley's Secretary of War whom Roosevelt continued in that office and later made Secretary of State; William Howard Taft, Root's successor in the War Department; Chief Forester Gifford Pinchot and Secretary of the Interior James R. Garfield, eminent conservationists; and United States District Attorney Henry L. Stimson, who was to serve in various capacities under five other Presidents.

In filling dozens of lesser federal offices, Roosevelt assured his own control of his party. He manipulated patronage so deftly that Mark Hanna had lost control of Republican affairs months before he died in February 1904. By that time Roosevelt could count on the support of every important state delegation to the forthcoming national convention. He could rely, too, on the influential party-leaders, for he had satisfied the most urgent demands of the liberal wing without offending or frightening the stand-patters.

Roosevelt and the trusts. Roosevelt, always a gradualist, fashioned a circumspect domestic program, which he dressed in a pungent rhetoric. At the outset of his Administration he indicated that he would accept the advice of the Old Guard in the Senate on tariff and monetary policies, matters about which they were most sensitive. He was himself much more worried about the problems of industrial consolidation. The "absolutely vital question," Roosevelt believed, "was whether the government had power to control" the trusts. The Supreme Court's decision in the E. C. Knight case (1895) suggested that it did not (see p. 428). Seeking a modification of that interpretation, Roosevelt in 1902 ordered his Attorney General, Philander C. Knox, to bring suit for violation of the Sherman Act against the Northern Securities Company.

The President had chosen his target carefully. The Northern Securities Company was a mammoth holding company for the Northern Pacific, the Great Northern, and the Chicago, Burlington, & Quincy railroads. A battle for the stock of the Northern Pacific, key to control of transportation in the Northwest, had led in 1901 to panic on Wall Street. The antagonists made peace by creating the Northern Securities Company for the immediate purpose of quieting the market and for the ultimate purpose of monopolizing the railroads of a rapidly growing region. Those who had fought and then made their profitable peace were titans of finance: J. P. Morgan and Company, the Rockefeller interests, James J. Hill, and E. H. Harriman. The panic they had brought on, a calamity for many brokers, drew attention to their ruthless speculation; the holding company they formed, in which 30 percent of the stock represented only intangible assets, cast a long shadow of fear over the Northwest, where farmers, suspicious as ever of monopolies, expected freight rates to soar.

While several states initiated legal action against the holding company, Roosevelt began his preparations in secret. Announcement of the federal government's suit stunned Wall Street. Morgan, with the arrogance of an independent sovereign, tried in vain to have his lawyer settle things with the Attorney General. His failure, like Roosevelt's attack, symbolized a transfer of power from lower New York to Washington, where it belonged. In 1903 a federal court ordered the dissolution of the Northern Securities Company, a decision the Supreme Court sustained the next year. Heartened by the outcome, most Americans agreed with Roosevelt that it was "impossible to overestimate the importance" of the case.

The government proceeded against forty-four more corporations during Roosevelt's term in office. In 1902 action began against the "beef trust," so unpopular with sellers of livestock and buyers of meat; equally unpopular were four defendants in cases started in 1906 and 1907, the American Tobacco Company, the Du Pont Corporation, the New Haven Railroad, and the Standard Oil Company.

Roosevelt's revival of the Sherman Act won him a reputation as a "trust-buster," but he never believed that the fragmentation of industry could solve the nation's problems. He had, he felt, to establish the authority of the federal executive to use the antitrust law in cases of monopoly or flagrant misbehavior. Trust-busting, however, was in his view an ultimate weapon, inappropriate in the case of most enterprises that had reduced the cost of production and had won for the nation the industrial leadership of the world. The growth of industry was, he argued, natural, unavoidable, and beneficial. Breaking up corporations whose only offense was size would be impossible unless the government also abolished steam, electricity, large cities, indeed all modern conditions. The need was for continuous, informed, and expert regulation, which only the federal government could properly undertake.

The Square Deal. In December 1901 Roosevelt made his first modest recommendations to Congress for creating the efficient system of control on which, he believed, the orderly development of industrial life depended. He asked for an act to expedite antitrust prosecutions, which Congress passed in 1903. Without opposition it then also enacted his proposal for forbidding the granting or receiving of rebates, a practice that powerful shippers had forced upon unwilling railroads. There

J. Pierpont Morgan: field marshal of industry

was, however, serious resistance to Roosevelt's major objective, the creation of a new Department of Commerce and Labor with a Bureau of Corporations empowered to gather and release information about industry. Such a bureau was essential if the government was to learn what businesses to regulate and how. On that account, conservative Republican senators blocked Roosevelt's bill. The President saved it by announcing that John D. Rockefeller was secretly organizing the opposition to it. The culprit was actually one of Rockefeller's subordinates, but the purport of Roosevelt's charge was accurate, and the consequent public clamor accelerated the passage of the controversial law.

The act gave Cabinet status to the Bureau of Labor, primarily a fact-finding agency that had demonstrated its usefulness to Roosevelt and to workingmen by its fair reporting during the strike of anthracite-coal miners that began in May 1902 and lasted until October. The managers of the Eastern coal-carrying railroads that owned most of the mines would not negotiate with the union, the United Mine Workers, which was demanding recognition, an eight-hour day, and a 10 to 20 percent increase in pay. Labor's orderly conduct and willingness to arbitrate won growing public approval, particularly after the intransigent owners, speaking through George F. Baer, the president of the Reading Railroad, insisted that "God in his Infinite Wisdom has given control of the property interests" to the directors of large corporations. This attitude invited public antagonism at a time when fuel was short and the days were growing chilly.

Roosevelt, sympathetic to the workers and worried about the coal shortage, had hesitated to enter the dispute only because his advisers felt that he lacked the legal authority. Early in October he summoned the mine-operators and John Mitchell, the union chief, to the White House. Mitchell again offered to submit to arbitration, but the owners remained obdurate. Indeed, they demanded that the President issue an injunction and, if necessary, use the army to end the strike. Their "arrogant stupidity" provoked Roosevelt instead to let them know indirectly that he was prepared to use troops to dispossess them and produce coal. With this kind of intervention in the offing, Mark Hanna, Elihu Root, and other conservative men who were already working for peace quickened their efforts, enlisted the help of J. P. Morgan himself, and on October

13 persuaded the mine-owners to accept a compromise settlement. By its terms the miners resumed work, and a commission appointed by the President arbitrated the questions at issue. In March the commission awarded labor a 10 percent raise, a reduction in working hours to nine and in some cases eight per day, but not recognition of the union. The owners in return received a welcome invitation to raise coal prices 10 percent. Roosevelt was the first President to bring both labor and capital to the White House to settle a dispute, the first to get them both to accept the judgment of a commission appointed by the executive, the first to coerce the owners of a crucial industry by threatening to take it over. All this contrasted vividly with the course of the federal government during the Pullman strike (see p. 438).

Roosevelt, however, in other labor episodes insisted on the open shop for government-workers and resisted not only all radical unionism but also the principle of the union shop in industry. He believed, as he put it, in "the right of laboring men to join a union . . . without illegal interference." This was less than Gompers advocated, but it was more than most businessmen or conservative politicians were yet willing to concede. It was a position characteristic of Roosevelt—advanced but not radical, cautious but not timorous.

His purpose during the coal strike, Roosevelt explained during the campaign of 1904, had been to give both sides a "square deal." The phrase became a familiar label for his first Administration, and for his intention to abolish privilege and enlarge individual opportunity. His "natural allies," he said, were "the farmers, small businessmen and upper-class mechanics," middle-class Americans "fundamentally sound, morally, mentally and physically." Like him, they abhorred extremes; like him, they judged in moral terms. They were not radicals, but they were fed up with the behavior of the Rockefellers and the Baers. They warmed, therefore, to Roosevelt's fusillades against those he later called the "malefactors of great wealth." They accepted and cheered his image of himself as a champion of fairness.

Queue for coal, Autumn 1902

The election of 1904. That was the basis of his campaign for reelection. It was the basis, too, for his appointment to office of qualified men from minority groups, blacks,

Catholics, Jews, Americans of Hungarian and German and Irish extraction. His appreciation of the inherent dignity in every man encouraged him to invite to the White House Booker T. Washington, the Negro educator who doubled as an adviser on patronage. There was, to be sure, a happy compatibility between Roosevelt's conscience and the needs of politics, but that did not detract from his conscience, though it manifestly strengthened his campaign. He took no chances. A new pension order, making age alone a sufficient qualification for eligibility, held the GAR to the GOP. The official platform contained standard Republican platitudes about the tariff and prosperity, sops to the Old Guard, as was the lackluster nominee for Vice President, Senator Charles W. Fairbanks of Indiana. But the real platform was Roosevelt's record, and the real issue was the man.

That made things difficult for the Democrats. As Bryan complained, Roosevelt had captured his banner. The Republicans now marched as the party of reform. Conservative Democrats returned to the formulas of Grover Cleveland's days, to a platform emphasizing strict construction of the Constitution and a candidate—Judge Alton B. Parker—chosen for his safe views and close ties to New York wealth.

Parker conducted a dull campaign until the vision of impending defeat persuaded him to charge that Roosevelt's campaign-manager, George B. Cortelyou, was blackmailing corporations for contributions. Cortelyou, who had been Secretary of Commerce, had indeed had access to the findings of the Bureau of Corporations, but he neither resorted to blackmail nor needed to. Wealthy Republicans, loyal party men in spite of their reservations about Roosevelt, had responded without stint to the usual appeals for funds. Parker's charges reminded the electorate that Roosevelt's campaign was well endowed but served otherwise only to provoke from the President an indignant denial. Indeed Roosevelt directed his party treasurer to return any contributions that had come from predatory wealth. The treasurer ignored the order, just as the voters by and large ignored Parker's accusations. Roosevelt could have won without much financial support. In a landslide victory, he received 57.4 percent of the popular votes (7,628,461) to Parker's 37.6 percent (5,084,223), and 336 electoral votes to the Democrat's 140.

Roosevelt and reform

The regulation of business. When Congress convened in December 1904, the progress of reform in Washington and in the states was gathering momentum. President now in his own right, Roosevelt took advantage of the mandate he had helped to create. His prime objective was railroad regulation. Decisions of the Supreme Court had stripped the Interstate Commerce Commission of authority over railway rates or rebates, which the roads continued to grant in spite of the government's efforts to enforce the antirebate act of 1903. The only feasible remedy was to give the commission power to set reasonable and nondiscriminatory rates and to prevent inequitable practices. Farmers and small businessmen and their representatives were increasingly demanding that remedy. But most railroads, their privileged customers, and the devotees of conservative economic theory opposed federal rate-making, which would for the first time in American history give the national government authority to determine prices, the sacrosanct prerogative of private enterprise.

For Roosevelt, laissez-faire theory was not sacred, but moral corporate behavior was. In 1904 and 1905 he urged Congress to endow the ICC with the power to adjust rates against which shippers had complained. During the long debate that ensued, Roosevelt advanced his purpose skillfully. Concentrating on the railroad issue, he gave up a tentative plan to press for a downward revision of the tariff, which agrarian Republicans as well as Democrats favored. The President had never considered the tariff a vital matter, for in his opinion it was not a moral question. It was, however, an issue that divided his party. So, rather than risk division, he conceded to the Old Guard on tariff reform. At least partly on that account, the House of Representatives passed the President's railroad bill by an overwhelming margin.

Handling the Senate was more difficult, for the Old Guard delayed a vote while the railroads underwrote a national publicity campaign, which Roosevelt answered in a series of vigorous speeches. In 1906 he outmaneu-

On the prairies nearby ... were hundreds of farms which supplied the city with milk; and all the cows that developed lumpy jaw, or fell sick, or dried up of old age—they ... shipped them to this place to be canned. Here came also cattle which had been fed on ''whiskey-malt,'' the refuse of the breweries, and had become ... covered with boils.... It was a nasty job killing these, for when you plunged your knife into them they would burst and splash foul-smelling stuff into your face; and when a man's sleeves were smeared with blood, and his hands steeped in it, how was he ever to wipe his face?... It was enough to make anybody sick, to think that people had to eat such meat as this; but ... the canners were going on preparing it, year after year.

From Upton Sinclair, *The Jungle*, 1906.

Chicago packinghouses: the indictment

There were many other things that we did.... One of the most important was the passage of the meat-inspection law because of scandalous abuses shown to exist in the great packing-houses.... There was a curious result of this law, similar to what occurred in connection with the law providing for effective railway regulation. The big beef men opposed the law.... Yet three or four years after these laws had been put in the statute-books every honest man ... in the beef business ... came to the conclusion that they worked good and not harm to decent business concerns. They hurt only those who were not acting as they should have acted.

From Theodore Roosevelt, *Autobiography*, 1913.

The packinghouses: a progressive view

The basic purpose of Sinclair's exposé, to improve the conditions of the working class in the packing houses, could have been achieved either through better wages or socialism. Although they now had cleaner uniforms at work, their homes and living conditions were no better than before....

If the packers ... actually opposed the bill, it is difficult to explain the magnitude of the vote for it. The reality of the matter ... is that the big packers were warm friends of regulation, especially when it primarily affected their ... small competitors.... Swift & Co. ... told the public in large ads ''It is a wise law. Its enforcement must be universal and uniform.''

From Gabriel Kolko, *The Triumph of Conservatism*, 1963.

The packinghouses: a revisionist view

Cleaving pork at Swift & Co.

vered his opponents and, after few modifications, the Hepburn Act carried. It gave the ICC the authority upon complaint from a shipper to set aside existing rates and to prescribe substitutes, subject to court review. This was less than the most vocal critics of the roads had wanted, for they suspected the courts of pro-business bias and advocated the physical valuation of railway properties as the proper basis for rate-making. But the act was just what Roosevelt was after. It was a keystone in his intended system of continuous, expert federal regulation of American industry.

Congress in 1906 passed several notable laws. One was an employer-liability act for the District of Columbia and all common carriers. Another was a pure-food-and-drug bill of which the chief exponent was Dr. Harvey W. Wiley of the Department of Agriculture. For several years this measure, twice approved by the House, had faltered. Now a series of articles by Samuel Hopkins Adams exposed the dangers of patent medicine, aroused public opinion, and speeded the enactment of the legislation. In a similar way, the publication of Upton Sinclair's *The Jungle,* with its description of the scandalous conditions in meatpacking houses, led Roosevelt to order a special investigation. This confirmed Sinclair's findings and precipitated the passage of a federal meat-inspection law, which, like the pure-food-and-drug legislation, took a first step toward federal controls that would later have to be enlarged.

In 1906 Roosevelt also sent Congress a series of recommendations on which it did not act, including proposals for federal control of railway securities and for the abolition of child labor. Labor problems were much on his mind. The National Association of Manufacturers had won a number of victories in its drive to cripple unions by obtaining injunctions against strikes and boycotts, the unions' most effective weapons. The NAM was also exhorting legislators to oppose all labor legislation. Fighting back, Gompers and his associates submitted to Roosevelt and the Congress a Bill of Grievances voicing their traditional demands, especially for relief from injunctions granted under the Sherman Act. The American Federation of Labor struck politically as well, campaigning in 1906 against congressmen unfriendly to labor, most of whom were Republicans. Caught between his growing sympathy for labor's goals and his partisan loyalties, Roosevelt endorsed all Republican candidates but exhorted them to mend their ways.

New ideas and the Old Guard. The gulf between the President and the Old Guard widened in 1907 and 1908. They especially differed about conservation. In 1902 Roosevelt, an ardent conservationist, had spurred the passage of the Newlands Act, which set aside a portion of receipts from the sale of public lands for expenditures on dams and reclamation. Pushing on, largely on the advice of Gifford Pinchot, he had withdrawn from private entry valuable coal and mineral lands, oil reserves, and waterpower sites. He had proceeded vigorously against cattlemen and lumbermen who were poaching on public preserves. These policies offended the Western barons who had become rich by exploiting the nation's natural resources (see p. 411). In 1907 their representatives attached a rider to an appropriation bill for the Department of Agriculture that prevented the creation of new forest reserves in six Western states without the consent of Congress. Roosevelt had to sign the bill, for the department had to have funds, but before signing he added 17 million acres to the national reserves. He later vetoed bills that granted waterpower sites to private interests but that did not provide for federal supervision of waterpower development.

In 1908 Roosevelt called a National Conservation Congress, which forty-four governors and hundreds of experts attended. It led to annual meetings of governors and to the creation of state conservation commissions. Congress, more and more hostile, ignored recommendations for river and flood control made by the Inland Waterways Commission, which Roosevelt appointed, and refused to provide funds to publish the report of another of his boards, the Country Life Commission, which advocated federal assistance for rural schools and roads and for farmers' cooperatives. Yet Roosevelt had succeeded in making the conservation of human and natural resources an issue of the first importance to thousands of Americans. The spirit of reform stressed the ability of the mind and will of man to alter and improve his environment. Conservation provided an obvious laboratory for testing that belief.

Roosevelt's policies jarred many businessmen who blamed him for the financial panic that occurred in the autumn of 1907 and for the brief depression that preceded and fol-

*The gravely significant attitude toward the law and its administration
recently adopted by certain heads of great corporations renders it
desirable that there should be additional legislation as regards certain
of the relations between labor and capital....*

*It is to be observed that an employers' liability law does not really
mean mulcting employers in damages. It merely throws upon the
employer the burden of accident insurance against injuries which are
sure to occur. It requires him either to bear or to distribute through
insurance the loss which can readily be borne when distributed, but
which, if undistributed, bears with frightful hardship upon the unfortunate victim of accident....*

*It is all wrong to use the injunction to prevent the entirely proper
and legitimate actions of labor organizations in their struggle for industrial betterment.... It is futile to concede, as we all do, the right and
the necessity of organized effort on the part of wage-earners and yet
by injunctive process to forbid peaceable action to accomplish the
lawful objects for which they are organized.*

From Theodore Roosevelt, Special Message to Congress, 1908.

---

lowed it. The basic causes of the slump were
beyond his control. Productive facilities had
expanded beyond the country's immediate
capacity to consume, but the differential
would probably have led to no serious trouble
if the nation's banking and monetary systems
had been stronger and if financiers had not
been guilty of speculative excesses. Panic
began only after depositors learned that several New York trust companies had failed in
an expensive attempt to corner the copper
market. As runs began on these and other
(sound) banks, some had to close and all had
to call in loans from creditors in New York and
throughout the country. J. P. Morgan, at his
most magnificent in this crisis, supervised a
pooling of the funds of the leading Manhattan
banks to support the threatened institutions.
Undoubtedly this action prevented general
disaster.

Morgan and his fellows could not have succeeded without assistance from Washington.
Their complex maneuvers depended in part on
the purchase by the United States Steel Corporation of controlling shares of stock in the
Tennessee Coal and Iron Company. That
transaction, however, was unthinkable if there
was any danger that it might lead immediately
to an antitrust suit. So informed, Roosevelt,
without making "any binding promise,"
urged Morgan's associates to proceed. The
government had earlier given the banks more
important but less dramatic help through the
United States Treasury.

Though the panic quickly subsided, it had
demonstrated the urgency of financial reform.
It was ridiculous for a great nation in a time
of crisis to have to fall back on Morgan or any
other private banker. And it was vital to relax
the general monetary stringency that intensified the crisis. Both the President and his
detractors endorsed the action of Congress
authorizing a commission, with Senator Nelson Aldrich as chairman, to study and report
on monetary and banking policy.

Roosevelt meanwhile had condemned the
"speculation, corruption and fraud" that contributed to the panic. His messages to Congress of December 1907 and January 1908
disclosed his zeal for further reform. After
repeating many of his earlier recommendations, the President called for federal
incorporation and regulation of all interstate
business, federal regulation of the stock market, limitation of injunctions against labor,
compulsory investigation of labor disputes,
extension of the eight-hour law for federal
employees, and personal income and inheritance taxes. He went on to castigate the courts
for declaring unconstitutional a workmen's-
compensation law and to condemn "predatory wealth" for its follies and its unscrupulous opposition to "every measure for honesty
in business." An avid foe of socialism, which
was then gaining adherents, Roosevelt in private warned that a revolution would break out
if rich men and blind judges made the lot of
the worker intolerable. Without reform, capitalism could not survive.

The goals Roosevelt defined and the principles he enunciated were the chart and compass of progressives in 1908 and for many years thereafter. He did not invent them, but he gave them effective expression, put the dignity of his high office at their service, and converted to them the thousands who felt the integrity and the vitality of his person. All this he did with a faith in the progress that conserves; a belief that power properly inheres in the federal government rather than in any private group; a conviction that the holder of power has an obligation to promote justice and enforce orderly and moral behavior; and a confidence in his own ability to handle power to those ends. Those beliefs and that confidence also guided his foreign policy.

Roosevelt and world power

National power and responsibility. During the first decade of the twentieth century, more and more Americans, including those who considered themselves progressives, subscribed to a new doctrine of manifest destiny (see p. 493). Along with these concepts there grew up other ideas about the international role of the United States. The writings of Alfred T. Mahan, the experience of the Spanish War, and awareness of the swelling ambitions and power of Germany and Japan persuaded an influential minority of Americans of the importance of naval preparedness and national defense. Some, like Roosevelt, Root, and Senator Henry Cabot Lodge, also believed that every powerful nation had a stake in world order and an obligation to preserve it; that a great country like the United States could not escape involvement in international affairs.

Roosevelt as President continually reminded his countrymen of the oneness of the world. Nineteenth-century progress in transportation, communication, and production, he warned, had created situations of potential chaos in which only the availability of power and, when necessary, the application of force could establish a tolerable equilibrium. He therefore preached preparedness to his frequently reluctant countrymen. For Roosevelt, preparedness was not simply militarism. It entailed, too, the preservation and development of natural and human resources. Sharing the Anglo-Saxon bias of his time, Roosevelt urged Americans of old stock to increase their birth rate. But all Americans, regardless of national origin, could contribute, he maintained, to national well-being if they saw to their physical fitness and cultivated clear minds, clean souls, and brave hearts.

High character and the strenuous life were not in themselves enough, for preparedness ultimately involved the size, equipment, and leadership of the military services. The President heartily supported the reform of the outmoded army organization that Secretary of War Root had begun to plan under McKinley. Root set up an Army War College, demanded rigorous tests for the promotion of officers, and in 1902 asked Congress to authorize the creation of a general staff and the incorporation of the state militia into the regular army. Congress hesitated, partly because the national guard and its aggressive lobby, as well as some senior regular officers, opposed incorporation of the guard, partly because of the belief, especially among rural Americans, that the militia was a democratic institution and a general staff a "Prussian" agency. Roosevelt and Root had to give up their plan for the militia, but Congress approved a modification of the general-staff plan that permitted the proposed modernization of the army to get under way.

Roosevelt also demanded the construction of a modern navy strong enough to protect American interests and to further his "large view" of national obligations. The United States, he realized, could no longer depend on the British fleet for protection. It had to keep pace with the building programs of Japan and Germany and with rapid changes in naval technology. Before he left office, Congress acceded to his constant prodding. The navy and army profited, too, from the enthusiastic recognition the President gave to military service and to dedicated and imaginative commanders like General Leonard Wood and Commander William S. Sims.

His zeal for discipline and morale, however, led him to discharge without honor the black troops who refused to reveal the names of the few soldiers who had allegedly shot up the anti-Negro town of Brownsville, Texas, in 1906. That hasty, unjust decision, which American blacks properly resented, was reversed by Secretary of the Army Robert F. Froehlke in 1972.

Elihu Root: champion of a modern army

It is idle to assume, and from the standpoint of national interest and honor it is mischievous folly for any statesman to assume, that this world has yet reached the stage, or has come within measurable distance of the stage, when a proud nation, jealous of its honor and conscious of its great mission in the world, can be content to rely for peace upon the forbearance of other powers.... Events still fresh in the mind of every thinking man show that neither arbitration nor any other device can as yet be invoked to prevent the gravest and most terrible wrongdoing to peoples who are either few in numbers, or who, if numerous, have lost the first and most important of national virtues—the capacity for self-defense....

I can not recommend to your notice measures for the fulfillment of our duties to the rest of the world without pressing upon you the necessity of placing ourselves in a condition of complete defense.... There is a rank due to the United States among nations which will be withheld, if not absolutely lost, by the reputation of weakness. If we desire to avoid insult, we must be able to repel it; if we desire to secure peace, one of the most powerful instruments of our rising prosperity, it must be known that we are at all times ready for war.

From Theodore Roosevelt, Special Message to Congress, 1908.

T. R. on preparedness

A strong nation, in the view of Roosevelt and others who subscribed to the new manifest destiny, had the duty of imposing civilization and justice in the backward territories it ruled. In the Insular cases of 1900 and 1901, the Supreme Court held that inhabitants of the recently acquired American empire were not American citizens and did not have a right to the liberties guaranteed by the Constitution unless Congress expressly conferred them. Except for Hawaii and Alaska, which were destined for statehood, the Court's rulings left the determination of colonial policy to the Roosevelt Administration. It adopted a variety of expedients. The navy administered Guam and Tutuila, where it had coaling stations. Puerto Rico elected its own house of delegates, though its decisions had to be confirmed by a council and executed by a governor appointed in Washington. The American protectorate in Cuba ended in May 1902 with the inauguration of the first government under Cuba's new constitution. The next year, however, a formal treaty between Cuba and the United States provided for American intervention in the event of a foreign threat or domestic disturbance. Insurrection in Cuba in 1906 persuaded Roosevelt reluctantly to exercise the right of intervention. After three years of gentle rule, the Americans withdrew. Earlier, the President had insisted that in return for the rights accorded by the Cuban treaty, the United States had a moral duty to aid the Cuban economy by granting special tariff rates to Cuban sugar, a concession he wrung from protectionist congressmen after a stiff legislative struggle in 1903.

He was unable, in spite of repeated attempts, to obtain tariff concessions for the Philippines. Those islands presented a number of difficult problems. Occasional episodes of cruelty by the American army during the suppression of the independence movement (see p. 506) had whetted native resentment. It began to abate (though for a brief time the revolt continued) when Congress in 1902 passed an organic act for the Philippines, Roosevelt abolished the office of military governor, and William Howard Taft, the first civilian governor, proclaimed a general amnesty. A patient proconsul, Taft got along well with the elected assembly and furthered municipal home rule, improvements in public health, civil affairs, education, and transportation. He was successful, too, in delicate negotiations with the Vatican and Catholic friars in the islands for the purchase of lands that the Church claimed but the Filipinos held and deserved to keep. Like Roosevelt and Root, Taft did not believe the Philippines would be ready for independence for many years. Though native patriots and American anti-imperialists remained impatiently committed to that goal, Taft's benign administration gradually won the confidence of the islanders, assisted the development of their economy,

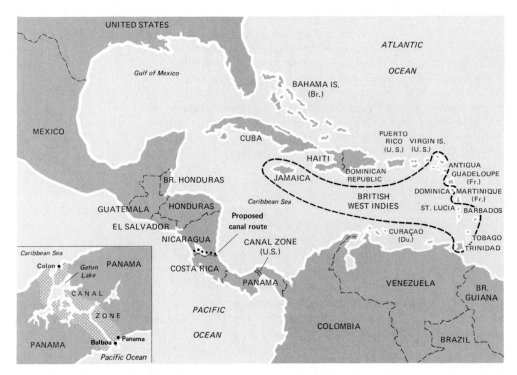

International interests in the Caribbean

and helped them prepare for ultimate self-government. Still, the inability of Roosevelt and his associates to understand the urgency of sentiment for self-government among subject peoples made American policy, as it developed, essentially indistinguishable from the imperialism of European powers.

Policing the hemisphere. Roosevelt's foreign policies, like his colonial policies, were derived from his assumption that it was ''incumbent on all civilized and orderly powers to insist on the proper policing of the world.'' This was, of course, a highhanded assumption, which Roosevelt defended when he had to by arguing that only with stability could there be justice. An imperious manner characterized his methods as well as his objectives. As President, he believed, he had to conduct foreign policy himself, for in that field the Congress and ''the average American'' did not ''take the trouble to think carefully or deeply.''

Stretching his constitutional authority to its limits, Roosevelt intervened to preserve stability and American hegemony in the Caribbean, where, with Mahan, he felt the United States could not afford a rival. Like the other small states in that area, Venezuela had borrowed money in Europe, which Cipriano Castro, her prodigal dictator—Roosevelt considered him

a ''villainous little monkey''—lacked either the means or the will to repay. In December 1902 England, Germany, and Italy, demanding payment for their citizens, blockaded Venezuela and fired on one of her ports. Venezuela asked the United States to arrange arbitration, to which England and Germany agreed. But a German ship again bombarded a port, infuriating the President and many other Americans, and later Germany briefly opposed referring the dispute to arbitration. During the controversy Roosevelt implied to the German ambassador that the United States would insist on that solution. He recalled years later that he threatened, if necessary, to dispatch a naval squadron under Admiral George Dewey. His memory probably exaggerated his role but whatever he actually did he certainly was indignant over Germany's conduct.

The best way to keep Europe at home, the President believed, was to keep order in the Caribbean. Yet a selfish conception of order gave Roosevelt a flimsy basis for incontinent behavior in Panama. In December 1901 the Senate ratified the second Hay-Pauncefote Treaty by which England acknowledged the right of the United States alone to build and fortify an isthmian canal, so long an American dream. Such a canal would facilitate inter-

Building the Panama Canal

coastal shipping and would make it easier for the navy to move from ocean to ocean. The preferred route had at one time been through Nicaragua, where a sea-level canal could be built, but the commission of experts that Congress had authorized had come to prefer a lock canal through Panama, which would provide the cheapest and shortest route between the coasts of the United States. Accordingly, in June 1902 Congress directed the President to negotiate with Colombia for the acquisition of a strip of land in Panama, provided that the old French canal company, which had begun work decades earlier, agreed within a reasonable time and on reasonable terms to sell the United States its titles and equities in the area. Members of the American commission had valued the French holdings at not more than $40 million. This was only half of the company's own official estimate, but the company gratefully accepted the revised figure.

With that matter settled, Roosevelt pressed Colombia to surrender control of the land in return for $10 million and an annual rental of $250,000. A treaty to that effect was rejected by the Colombian government, which wanted more money and greater rights of sovereignty in the zone. Roosevelt, outraged at what he considered "blackmail," though the Colombian request was scarcely that, let it be known privately that he would smile upon insurrection in Panama. Predictably, in November 1903 insurrection occurred (if it had not, the President was prepared to ask Congress for authority to take the zone from Colombia). The United States aided the revolutionists, used a warship to prevent Colombian forces from landing, and immediately recognized the new, independent Republic of Panama, which promptly accepted Roosevelt's terms for a canal zone.

Roosevelt boasted that he "took Panama," and most Americans at the time condoned his behavior. But the episode was a national disgrace. There was even suspicion of scandal. Agents of the French company, eager to unload their otherwise worthless assets, had influenced the State Department and members of Congress to favor the Panama route and had helped to foment the insurrection. Roosevelt had no personal stake in their game, but his ruthless pursuit of his own interpretation of national advantage was no more ethical than was their pursuit of profit. Yet he persuaded himself that his conduct was impeccable, for, he argued, he had stamped out lawlessness in Colombia and disorder in Panama. Thus he perverted his insistence on stability in the Caribbean into a rationalization for imperialism.

That perversion took much of the gloss off his message to Congress of December 1904, in which he announced that the United States would not interfere with Latin American nations that conducted their affairs with decency, but that "brutal wrongdoing" might require intervention by some civilized power, and that the United States could not "ignore this duty." The Monroe Doctrine told Europe to stay out of the Americas; the Roosevelt Corollary asserted that the United States had a right to move in. In 1905 Roosevelt interceded in Santo Domingo to end the cycle there of debt, revolution, and default. He imposed American supervision of customs collections and finance and established a trust fund to repay the European-held debt. The convention containing those terms was blocked in the United States Senate, which was growing restive under the President's single-handed conduct of foreign affairs, but Roosevelt substituted an executive agreement that protected his policy until the Senate accepted a modified treaty in 1907.

The balance of power. The international police power that Roosevelt arrogated to the United States he expected other civilized nations to exercise elsewhere—Japan in Korea, England in Egypt and India. Stable and prosperous nations, however, had in his view no right to proceed against one another. World order depended on their restraint and on the shifting balances of their power. British restraint preserved the growing Anglo-American entente during a dispute about the Alaskan boundary. Canada in 1902 claimed Alaskan lands that cut off newly discovered Canadian gold fields from the sea. Roosevelt rightly judged the claim weak, but he wounded Canadian sensibilities by his blustering refusal to arbitrate (for, he said, arbitration usually resulted "in splitting the difference"). To help Canadian officials save face, in 1903 he submitted the issue to negotiation but instructed the commissioners he appointed to concede nothing. He also took pains to inform London of his order. The single English commissioner voted with the three Americans against the two Canadians, thereby straining temporarily the bonds of empire but serving both the merits of the issue and the cause of transatlantic friendship.

As he contemplated the balance of power in Europe, Roosevelt was grateful for England's friendship, dubious about Russia's immediate strength (though he recognized her great potentials), and more and more anxious about Germany. Had the Kaiser had the "instinct for the jugular," Roosevelt thought, he would have kept a sharp eye on Russia. As it was, Germany was more jealous of France and England, and the Kaiser entertained "red dreams of glory" that might disrupt Europe and thus the whole world.

Aware of the network of European alliances that would engage every major continental power in a contest between any two, the President worried about the tensions that flared in 1905 over French and German rivalry in Morocco. The Kaiser secretly asked Roosevelt to persuade England not to support France. Roosevelt at first hesitated to intervene, for, as he put it, the United States had "no real interest in Morocco." It did have a major stake in preserving peace, however, and Roosevelt overcame his disinclination to appear "a Meddlesome Mattie" and carried on the difficult negotiations that brought all parties, including the United States, to a conference at Algeciras, Spain, in January 1906.

Roosevelt's instructions to the American delegates revealed his anti-German bias, his conviction that the entente cordiale between France and England preserved the essential balance of power in Europe. Though American participation had little effect on the outcome of the conference, at which France won a diplomatic victory, Roosevelt's role was nevertheless significant. He had served peace. Furthermore, he had demonstrated to Europe and to the American people, many of whom criticized his departure from the course of isolation, that the President of the United States recognized the nation's unavoidable concern in any European crisis.

In Asia, Roosevelt judged, slumbering China was of no account, but to prevent dislocations of power he accepted the prevailing fiction of her territorial integrity, and he gave lip service to the principle of the Open Door. He was little interested in Chinese markets, but to stabilize the Orient politically he counted on a balance between Russia and Japan. He welcomed an Anglo-Japanese defensive alliance of 1902, which committed both signatories to preserve the status quo in Asia, but in 1904, when the Russo-Japanese War began, he brooded about its "immense possibilities . . . for the future." A Russian triumph, he concluded, would be "a blow to civilization"; on the other hand, the elimina-

The Big Stick

tion of Russia's "moderative influence" on Japan would be equally unfortunate. That possibility seemed imminent after Japan's initial naval and land victories and the outbreak of revolution in Russia. Though Roosevelt was partial to the Japanese, he intensified his effort through mediation to arrange a peace that would preserve an equilibrium. Proceeding without the knowledge of Congress, he worked secretly and deftly through personal friends in the diplomatic corps of Japan, Germany, and Great Britain. By the summer of 1905 Russian distress and Japanese financial infirmity brought both belligerents to accept a peace conference at Portsmouth, New Hampshire.

The President's brilliant diplomacy continued at the conference, which produced a settlement that suited his purpose and earned him a Nobel Prize for Peace. Japan took over the southern half of the island of Sakhalin, Port Arthur, and the South Manchuria Railroad, but Manchuria remained legally a part of China where the Open Door still presumably permitted all nations to trade and invest. Russia retained effective control over northern Manchuria and all of Siberia, the source of her basic weight in Asian politics. The Japanese failed to get the huge indemnity they had wanted, which made the treaty and Roosevelt the object of considerable public criticism in Japan. But her government was satisfied, particularly because the United States, like Russia, had recognized Japan's primacy in Korea.

Also in 1905 Taft and Japanese Foreign Minister Taro Katsura reached an agreement by which the United States permitted Japan to occupy Korea. This, too, was a victory for the President's realistic and essentially cautious diplomacy. Though he sometimes sounded fierce, he never undertook ventures beyond his means to execute them. The United States, he knew, lacked the means to interfere in Korea, and Japan had to be kept friendly or she could easily conquer the Philippines, which Congress would not arm.

Japanese-American relations might have remained excellent had it not been for the problem of immigration. In 1900 Tokyo agreed to deny passports to emigrant laborers bound for the United States. But Japanese workers continued to make their way to the West Coast through Hawaii, Mexico, and Canada. Especially in California, where deep-rooted prejudice against all Asians had resulted in the national exclusion of Chinese immigrants, anti-Japanese feeling rose, revealing itself in the press, in the debates of the legislature, and in race riots. In 1906 San Francisco segregated Asian school children. The proud Japanese protested officially to Washington. Roosevelt assured them that he had no sympathy with the "outrageous agitation" of the Californians. He could not, however, silence the yellow press or control the "idiots" in the California legislature, nor could he prevent racial discrimination by barring the immigration of all laborers, for Congress opposed so stringent a law. Yet he was wholly unwilling to ask the Japanese to concede any racial inferiority. The State Department resolved the crisis by negotiating the "Gentlemen's Agreement" of 1907, an official but informal understanding that bound both countries to stop unwanted immigration between them.

This crisis focused attention on the whole immigration question. Roosevelt understood why organized labor objected to unrestricted immigration, Asian or European, and to a degree he shared the middle-class prejudice against the unrestricted entry of southern and eastern Europeans. Still, he feared that a general debate about immigration in 1906 would complicate relations with Japan and possibly divide the Republicans, some of whom were urging enactment of a literacy test for immigrants. He recommended the appointment of a fact-finding commission, a solution that would delay debate, appease the restrictionists, and, he believed, throw light on a complex subject. Modifying his proposal, Congress in 1907 authorized a commission of nine members, of whom three were to be selected by the President, three by the Speaker of the House, and three by the President of the Senate. Those who were appointed to the commission, of which Senator Dillingham became chairman, approached the task with a formidable bias for the restriction of immigration.

Besides provoking a debate on immigration policy, the Japanese-American crisis stirred up loose talk of war. There was probably less in Japan than in the United States, where racists spoke of irreconcilable conflict and where the President was apparently worried in 1907 that Japan intended to provoke war. His anxiety may have been contrived to stir Congress into pushing ahead with the naval building program. In any case, there was no need for alarm, although years later Roosevelt said that he had detected "a very, very slight undertone of veiled truculence" in Japan's communications. "It was essential," he then decided, "that we should have it clearly understood by our own people especially, but also by other peoples, that the Pacific was as much our home waters as the Atlantic." He sailed the battle fleet around the world to make his point clear.

Had Japan been belligerent, she could have demolished the American ships that entered Tokyo Bay. Instead she welcomed them heartily. Yet Roosevelt believed their presence curbed any Japanese urge toward aggression and was therefore "the most important service" he ever rendered to peace. It was certainly a fine example of one of his favorite adages: "Speak softly but carry a big stick." Good will rather than fear led the Japanese ambassador to propose a declaration of friendship. In the Root-Takahira Agreement of 1908, both nations promised to uphold the status quo in the Pacific and to respect the Open Door and China's territorial integrity.

"A council of war never fights," Roosevelt wrote in his *Autobiography*, "and in a crisis the duty of a leader is to lead." As President he personally conducted the nation's foreign policies, acting sometimes with skill, sometimes with daring, sometimes with scant regard for the opinion of public or Congress or for the rights or sensitivities of other nations. His magisterial manner and imperialistic ventures set potentially dangerous precedents that his critics deplored. Still, as he knew, and as he instructed, the United States had become part of an interdependent world; the use of force could keep isolated trouble spots from erupting into general war; power was a pervasive element in world affairs; and the United States, a powerful nation, had an obligation to keep its power in a state of readiness and, when necessary, to use it intelligently but with restraint.

The election of 1908. No harm came from the concentration of power in one man's hands, Roosevelt observed, "provided the holder does not keep it for more than a certain, definite time, and then returns it to the people from whom he sprang." An American President, he believed, should serve only two terms. So he had announced in 1904 that he would not run again, and, though he gloried in his office, he resisted the strong sentiment for his renomination in 1908 and used his power in the party to ensure the nomination of William Howard Taft, whom he had selected as the man most able to perpetuate his policies.

Some progressive Republicans would have preferred New York's governor, Charles Evans Hughes, but the President's endorsement and Taft's own excellent reputation kept the party united. With the tide of progressivism rising, the Democrats turned again to Bryan, who ran with more prudence but less vigor than before. He had the support of the leaders of organized labor, who applauded the Democratic plank urging the restriction of injunctions, and he made what he could of an attack on the Republican tariff. But Taft polled 52.0 percent of the popular vote and carried the Electoral College 321 to 162. Taft's identification with Roosevelt elected him. In 1901 Roosevelt had inherited a conservative administration. Increasingly he had enlisted with reform. When he bowed out in 1909, off to hunt in the African jungles, a majority of Americans had come to adulate him and his policies. It remained to be seen what Taft would do with his inheritance.

Suggestions for reading

GENERAL

G. E. Mowry, *The Era of Theodore Roosevelt** (1958), provides the best comprehensive account of the developments during the first twelve years of this century. There is a stimulating interpretation of progressivism and its adherents in Richard Hofstadter, *The Age of Reform** (1955). Another spirited account appears in the relevant chapters of Eric Goldman, *Rendezvous with Destiny** (1952), which should be compared to C. Lasch, *New Radicalism in America, 1889–1963** (1965). S. P. Hays, *The Response to Industrialism** (1957), and R. H. Wiebe, *The Search for Order: 1877–1920** (1966), offer interpretations suggested by their titles. G. Kolko, *The Triumph of Conservatism** (1963) and *Railroads and Regulation, 1877–1916** (1965), attributes the reforms of the progressive era largely to conspiratorial and selfish influences of big-business leaders while R. H. Wiebe, *Businessmen and Reform** (1962), emphasizes divisions of opinion about reform issues within the business community.

*Available in a paperback edition.

PROGRESSIVISM

The various aspects of progressivism have received wide contemporary and historical treatment. One of the best places to begin reading is in a lucid study of the underprivileged and their champions, R. H. Bremner, *From the Depths** (1956). Two of those champions revealed their concerns in J. A. Riis, *How the Other Half Lives** (1890), and Jane Addams, *Forty Years at Hull House** (1935). The contributions of the churches receive a thorough analysis in H. F. May, *Protestant Churches and Industrial America** (1949). Philip Taft, *The A. F. of L. in the Time of Gompers* (1957), provides a systematic, friendly account of the trade unions. Two contrasting accounts of the struggle for women's rights are W. L. O'Neill, *Everyone Was Brave: The Rise and Fall of Feminism in America* (1969), and D. M. Kennedy, *Birth Control in America: The Career of Margaret Sanger** (1970). Among the important interpretations of progressive intellectuals, besides the volumes listed in the preceding paragraph, are Daniel Aaron, *Men of Good Hope** (1951); Morton White, *Social Thought in America: The Revolt Against Formalism** (1949); D. W. Noble, *The Paradox of Progressive Thought* (1958); Sidney Fine, *Laissez Faire and the General-Welfare State** (1956); and H. F. May, *The End of American Innocence** (1959). These should be read in conjunction with the contemporary works mentioned in the text, with A. and L. Weinberg, eds., *The Muckrakers** (1964), and with such revealing autobiographies as those of Lincoln Steffens and William Allen White. Progressive ferment and achievement in various regions, states, and cities have had excellent treatment in C. V. Woodward, *Origins of the New South, 1877–1913** (1951); R. B. Nye, *Midwestern Progressive Politics, 1870–1958** (1951, rev. ed., 1959); G. E. Mowry, *The California Progressives** (1951); R. E. Noble, *New Jersey Progressivism Before Wilson* (1947); R. M. Abrams, *Conservatism in a Progressive Era: Massachusetts Politics, 1900–1912* (1964); H. L. Warner, *Progressivism in Ohio, 1897–1917* (1964); and Arthur Mann, *Yankee Reformers in the Urban Age: Social Reform in Boston, 1880–1900** (1954).

ROOSEVELT AND HIS ADMINISTRATION

The best introduction to Theodore Roosevelt remains his autobiography, which can be profitably supplemented by reading in his voluminous collected works (the National Edition [1926] is handiest) and published letters, E. E. Morison, ed., *Letters of Theodore Roosevelt*, 8 vols. (1951–54). Carleton Putnam provides a glowing account of Roosevelt in *Theodore Roosevelt: The Formative Years* (1958). Henry Pringle, *Theodore Roosevelt** (1931), for all its discernment, tends to see its subject from the point of view of the depression years in which it was written. A more learned biography is W. H. Harbough, *Power and Responsibility** (1961). J. M. Blum, *The Republican Roosevelt** (1954), focuses on Roosevelt as politician and President, and H. K. Beale, *Theodore Roosevelt and the Rise of America to World Power** (1956), offers an informed analysis of Roosevelt's foreign policy. Among other special studies of important public policies in Roosevelt's time, some of the most rewarding are E. L. Peffer, *The Closing of the Public Domain* (1951), which should be supplemented by Gifford Pinchot's autobiography; O. E. Anderson, Jr., *The Health of a Nation* (1958); B. H. Meyer, *History of the Northern Securities Case* (1906); and relevant chapters from W. Z. Ripley, *Railroads: Rates and Regulations* (1915). There is a wealth of good autobiography by and biography of the men around Roosevelt. Besides those autobiographies noted earlier, Robert La Follette's is important, and among the most readable and instructive biographies those that most successfully introduce the period are: C. G. Bowers, *Beveridge and the Progressive Era* (1932); the contrasting John Braeman, *Albert J. Beveridge* (1971); N. W. Stephenson, *Nelson W. Aldrich* (1920), a sympathetic treatment of a great conservative; P. C. Jessup, *Elihu Root*, 2 vols. (1938), a distinguished and detailed work; Henry Pringle, *The Life and Times of William Howard Taft*, 2 vols. (1939), which is both learned and laudatory; and E. E. Morison, *Admiral Sims and the Modern American Navy* (1942).

*Available in a paperback edition.

Progressivism in crisis and triumph

23

Republicans celebrating the inauguration of William Howard Taft in March 1909 had no cause for complacency. Their party had won four successive presidential elections, and its national leaders had preserved the alliances on which its majority rested. But the partners in those alliances—the Old Guard, urban progressives, and Western agrarians—were growing uneasy with one another. The Demo-crats, secure in the South and in many North-ern cities, were gaining strength among labor unions and farmers. In 1906 and 1908 the Republicans had lost seats in the House of Representatives, and in 1908 they had also lost several governorships. If they hoped to remain in power, they would have to satisfy their restive factions and close ranks against their opposition.

Insurgency

William Howard Taft: kindly conservative

President Taft. Taft, the new President and head of the party, had excellent intentions. A kindly, learned man, he saw the need for social-welfare legislation, understood the pur-poses of the Roosevelt reforms, for which he had worked with skill, and meant to keep his promise to preserve and further his prede-cessor's program. He was also a loyal Repub-lican who hoped to strengthen his party, which in his opinion was the only fit instru-ment of government. In a placid time he might have done well.

He was, however, seriously handicapped for the job he had to do. Taft was almost a car-icature of the fat man—genial, usually easy-going, often lazy. He was also untrained in politics, for his career had been on the bench and in appointive administrative offices. He had no instinct for manipulation, no nerve for controversy. His reluctance to use the full powers of the Presidency grew out of his interpretation of the Constitution, which led him to believe that he should not interfere in the course of legislation, something that in any case he found uncomfortable. He was uncomfortable, too, in the company of men who did not share his background of old fam-ily, personal means, and Eastern education. He preferred talking with Nelson Aldrich to conversing with La Follette, whom he consid-ered one of the party's troublemakers.

The President was by nature and conviction a conservative whose highest confidence was in the law as he and other judges had shaped it. The bench, he believed, was the appro-priate arbiter of social issues. He was suspi-cious of direct democracy, because he did not trust the majority to make laws. He was also cautious about enlarging the power of the executive for fear that it might encroach upon the traditional authorities of the other branches of government.

Taft was not unresilient. He accepted the need for change. But he did not particularly

534

So much in the President's character can be explained by his complacency. He believes that many things left to themselves will bring about the same result as if he took a hand himself in their settlement. He acts with promptness and vigor when he has got to act, but he would rather delay trouble than seek it.... While it is useless to guess what will ... take place in the next four years, it is of interest ... that the President, while endorsing the Roosevelt policies ... did consort with the men most obnoxious to Mr. Roosevelt.... The President is not over-indulgent toward reformers, especially that class ... who are suspicious of everyone who does not agree with their pet schemes.

From *Taft and Roosevelt, The Intimate Letters of Archie Butt, Military Aide,* 1930.

President Taft: 1909

like it, and he did not at all like to be rushed. Yet he came to his office when the progressives were in a hurry. And they expected him, on the basis of his commitment to Roosevelt's programs, to keep pace with them. He held his own view of that program, expecting an easy pace, an advance in which each forward step was measured carefully against the footprints trailing through the past.

The tariff. Taft began boldly by calling a special session of Congress to revise the tariff. He and Roosevelt had insisted upon a plank in the Republican platform promising modification of the tariff, and his speeches had suggested that he preferred a moderate downward revision. Republican representatives of manufacturing interests were still wedded to high protectionism, but the Midwestern farmers and their party spokesmen were convinced that the Dingley duties (see p. 489), by protecting the trusts from foreign competition, were sustaining artificial prices for manufactured goods. Furthermore, as proponents of the "Iowa Idea" argued, Europeans had to sell in the American market in order to earn dollars to buy American agricultural surpluses.

The Western progressives counted on the President's support in getting the tariff lowered, but even before the special session got under way they experienced their first disappointment. Taft appointed a Cabinet of conservatives, five of them corporation lawyers. He also turned down young George Norris of Nebraska and other insurgents in the House of Representatives who appealed for his support in their effort to restrict the power of the Speaker, "Uncle Joe" Cannon of Illinois, an arch-Tory and protectionist. And when debate on the tariff began, Taft made no gesture in behalf to the revision he had advocated.

The House of Representatives passed a tariff bill that made modest concessions to reform. It reduced some duties and imposed an inheritance tax graduated from 1 to 5 percent.

In the Senate, however, the Old Guard carried the day. The Finance Committee struck out the inheritance tax, made over eight hundred amendments to the House bill, and even slightly increased the average rates of the Dingley Tariff. On the floor of the Senate, progressives attacked the swollen tariff schedules one by one and joined the Democrats in urging an income tax. Taft's intercession fostered a compromise that set a 2 percent tax on corporate income and assured passage of a constitutional amendment authorizing a personal income tax. But the compromise little affected the tariff itself. A conference committee of the two houses made modest changes in a number of schedules, but most of those revisions benefited manufacturers rather than farmers or consumers.

The bill as it finally passed was a triumph for the protectionists. During the struggle Taft had alienated the insurgent Midwesterners and their constituents. Stubbornly, the President in September widened the breach. In a series of implausible speeches he scolded the progressives who had voted against the tariff, which he declared the best the party had ever enacted.

A divided party. When Congress met again in 1910, the insurgents no longer expected help from the White House. Attacking at once, Norris and his associates made common cause with the Democrats and passed a resolution transferring much of Speaker Cannon's authority to the House Rules Committee. The insurgents then joined the Democrats to amend Taft's railway bill, though the President

"Uncle Joe" Cannon: Republican protectionist

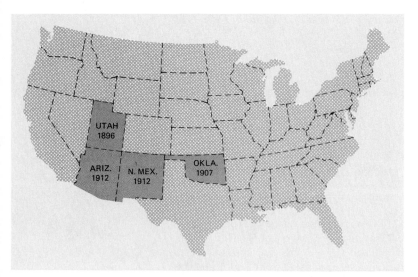

New states, 1896–1912

made support of that bill a test of party loyalty. The measure empowered the Interstate Commerce Commission to fix rates on its own initiative. But it established a Court of Commerce with broad powers of review over the commission's decisions, thereby giving the traditionally conservative judiciary a determining veto. The bill also permitted railroads to acquire competing lines. The Democratic-progressive coalition supported the first of those three provisions, attacked the others, and succeeded in eliminating the third. It further amended the bill to bring telephone and telegraph companies under the commission's jurisdiction and to provide for the physical valuation of railway properties as a basis for determining fair rates.

In the Senate Aldrich eliminated the provision calling for physical valuation and preserved the Commerce Court by making a trade with the Democrats. In return for their help on the railway bill, he agreed to the admission of Arizona and New Mexico, which were sure to elect four Democratic senators in 1912. This was a Pyrrhic victory: it saved the Administration's face, but it did not long prevent a physical-valuation law (which Congress passed early in 1913), and it precipitated open warfare within the Republican party. The insurgents had defied the President, who had unwisely raised the question of party regularity. Now he retaliated by denying them patronage and starting a campaign to defeat them in the fall elections.

Meanwhile Taft had got caught up in a damaging controversy. With his approval, his Secretary of the Interior, Richard A. Ballinger had reopened to private sale millions of acres of public land and many valuable waterpower sites that Gifford Pinchot, Roosevelt's trusted friend, had previously arranged to have closed. Pinchot, still chief forester of the United States, became suspicious of Ballinger's motives when he learned from Louis R. Glavis, an investigator in the General Land Office, that Ballinger had been instrumental in selling certain government coal lands in Alaska to a wealthy syndicate controlled by J. P. Morgan and David Guggenheim. Pinchot took the case to Taft, who ruled for Ballinger on every count and discharged Glavis. Though he considered Pinchot a "crank," Taft politely urged him to drop the issue and stay in office.

The indignant Pinchot had other plans. He supplied material for two magazine articles attacking Ballinger. He also wrote a letter praising Glavis that was read to the Senate. Taft had no choice but to dismiss Pinchot, though he knew that in so doing he would seem to oppose Roosevelt's conservation policies and possibly antagonize the Colonel. His worst fears materialized. A joint congressional committee in 1910 exonerated Ballinger, but Louis D. Brandeis, counsel for the opposition, made a brilliant case against both the secretary and the President. Though Taft was an effective conservationist, Brandeis' arguement cost him his laurels and again identified him with reaction. The political damage was compounded when Pinchot greeted Roosevelt after the Colonel emerged from the African jungles. In the future Roosevelt always saw the matter Pinchot's way.

The election of 1910. Taft felt that Roosevelt's friends had plotted to cause a rupture between him and their hero. After Roosevelt's triumphant return to New York, the insurgents set out for his home at Oyster Bay to enlist his help. Roosevelt, who was temperamentally incapable of remaining out of politics and who was sensitive to a coolness on Taft's part, now decided that his principles needed defending. He embarked on a speaking tour during which he endorsed the Administration but gave stronger praise to Beveridge and other insurgents. He also reemphasized the points he had made in his last messages to Congress. At Osawatomie, Kansas, invoking the spirit of John Brown, Roosevelt announced his New Nationalism, a program of social welfare, federal regulation of business and industry, and direct democracy. In that address he frightened conservatives by attacking the courts for having invalidated progressive labor legislation.

The friction within the Republican party contributed to its losses in the elections of 1910. The Democrats in many states managed to identify themselves with progressivism and to identify the Republican tariff with the rising cost of living, a particularly sensitive issue among city-dwellers. The Democrats won several governorships, including those of New York and New Jersey, which had been safely Republican for many years. For the first time since 1892, the Democrats elected a majority to the House of Representatives. The Republicans' loss of New York and the defeat of Senator Beveridge in Indiana saddened Roosevelt. The Democratic victories over Old Guard candidates in the East and the victories of progressive Republicans in the West repudiated Taft. Overall, the returns suggested that only an insurgent could save the Republicans in the presidential election of 1912, but the Old Guard, tense and defensive, prepared to resist the temper of the time.

Taft's closest political associates began in 1911, by the adroit use of patronage, to strengthen their factions in the North and to wrap up the Republican organizations in the South. At the same time, La Follette began to recruit support for his own candidacy, which was endorsed by many progressives. Some of them, however, privately hoped to draft Roosevelt, whose personal appeal remained strong even after his announcement that he had retired from politics.

A divisive foreign policy. During the year Taft succeeded in intensifying party discord and stirring the Colonel to action. In January 1911 the President submitted to Congress a reciprocity agreement with Canada. It put on the free list many agricultural products, including important raw materials for industrial use, and some manufactured goods. Western progressives, fearing the competition of Canadian farmers, opposed the measure. So did most high-tariff advocates, who objected to any breach in the wall of protection. Together they rejected the agreement. But Taft called a special session in April during which the Democrats, delighting in the discomfort of the Republicans, helped Administration forces to

put the measure through. The Canadians, however, disturbed by the prospect of economic competition and Americanization, in September repudiated the agreement. Another tariff debate had produced only more wounds. The Democrats kept them open, with help from Republican insurgents, by passing a series of bills reducing specific schedules—"pop-gun" tariffs that the President systematically vetoed.

Taft's foreign policy also aroused opposition. His Secretary of State, Philander C. Knox, negotiated treaties with Nicaragua and Honduras providing for the assumption of their European-held debt by American investors and for the appointment of Americans to direct their finances and thus assure the collection of those debts. Though the Senate rejected the treaties, Knox pursued his policy throughout the Caribbean with considerable success.

Taft and Knox also emphasized the possibilities for American investments in China. At the instigation of the State Department, American bankers agreed to join in various commercial projects there, including an international railway consortium. Roosevelt disapproved of that "dollar diplomacy." He had urged Taft to abandon commercial competition with the Japanese in China. It was more important, the Colonel argued, to cultivate Japanese friendship and to arrange a clearer understanding about Japanese immigration.

Roosevelt also opposed arbitration treaties that Taft negotiated with France and England. Taft was confident that international problems could be solved by courts of law. In the summer of 1911 he submitted to the Senate treaties with France and Great Britain that bound the signatories to arbitrate all differences "susceptible of decision by the application of the principles of law or equity." Those treaties excited the hopes of the thousands of Americans who considered them an important step toward avoiding wars. But Roosevelt wrote angry articles denouncing the arbitration of questions involving "territory" or "national honor," and he cooperated with like-minded senators who succeeded in amending the treaties so drastically that the President scrapped them. Taft was dismayed by the outcome and offended by Roosevelt's scathing language.

Roosevelt revolts. Roosevelt in turn was offended by Taft's antitrust policies. The Su-

La Follette in Wisconsin, his laboratory of democracy

If the anti-trust people really grasped the full meaning of what they said, and if they really had the power or the courage to do what they propose, they would be engaged in one of the most destructive agitations that America has known. They would be breaking up the beginning of a collective organization, thwarting the possibility of cooperation, and insisting upon submitting industry to the wasteful, the planless scramble of little profiteers. They would make impossible any deliberate and constructive use of our natural resources, they would thwart any effort to form the great industries into coordinated services, they would preserve commercialism as the undisputed master of our lives....

It is said that the economy of trusts is unreal. Yet no one has ever tried the economies of the trust in any open, deliberate fashion. The amount of energy that has had to go into repelling stupid attack, the adjustments that had to be made underground—it is a wonder the trusts achieved what they did to bring order out of chaos, and forge an instrument for a nation's business.

From Walter Lippmann, *Drift and Mastery,* 1914.

preme Court in 1911 in the Standard Oil and American Tobacco cases, both of which had been initiated during Roosevelt's Administration, found that the corporations were monopolies guilty of violating the Sherman Act. Yet the decisions also pronounced the "rule of reason," which held that only unreasonable restraints of trade were unlawful. That was a necessary corollary to antitrust law, for an undiscriminating application of the Sherman Act would destroy the structure and impede the functioning of American business. But whereas Taft was content to have the Court take upon itself the authority to define reasonableness, Roosevelt believed that an administrative agency should make that judgment and should base it on considerations of economic efficiency and business behavior.

This difference of opinion was exemplified in the case of the United States Steel Corporation, then the largest of all holding companies, which Taft chose to prosecute. Roosevelt, who considered the company guiltless, concluded that Taft had acted largely to embarrass him, for the prosecution, which resulted ultimately in an acquittal, and the congressional hearings that it provoked, publicized Roosevelt's negotiations of 1907 with J. P. Morgan (see p. 525).

Taft's antitrust and foreign policies gave Roosevelt a chance to rationalize what he would undoubtedly have done anyway. In February 1912 he announced that his hat was in the ring. A furious battle for the Republican presidential nomination was under way.

The struggle was really between Roosevelt and Taft, who denounced each other with unrestrained personal vehemence. Though La Follette remained in the race, most of his supporters of 1911 deserted him for Roosevelt. Now just as progressive and vastly more sophisticated and popular than La Follette, Roosevelt had in his New Nationalism formulated a program that promised to distribute the abundance of industrialism, while controlling and preserving the institutions which had made that abundance possible. Roosevelt stood an excellent chance of winning the election. Taft had no such chance, but his dander was up, and the Old Guard cared more about nominating him, defeating Roosevelt, and dominating the party than about beating the Democrats.

The Taft forces, moreover, had in their hands the party apparatus through which they could control the convention. In some states Roosevelt's supporters managed to pass legislation establishing preferential primaries for the nomination, but in the end only thirteen states held such elections. They gave 36 delegates to La Follette, 48 to Taft, and 278 to Roosevelt—an overwhelming mandate for the Colonel. Taft, however, controlled the South, New York, and the crucial national committee, which with its affiliates disposed of 254 contested seats at the convention. With a cynical disregard for the merits of the contestants, it allotted 235 of the contested seats to Taft delegates. The rigged convention then renominated the President on the first ballot.

I think we are in a position, after the experience of the last 20 years, to state two things: in the first place, that a corporation may well be too large to be the most efficient instrument of production and of distribution, and, in the second place, whether it has exceeded the point of greatest economic efficiency or not, it may be too large to be tolerated among the people who desire to be free. I think, therefore, that the recognition of those propositions should underlie any administration of the law....

It seems to me that there is a distinct peril in the community in having one organization control a very large percentage of the market.... Where there is found to be a combination in restraint of trade, if the combination controls 40 per cent or more of the market, that creates a presumption of unreasonableness. I am inclined to think that an inquiry into our experience of the last 20 years would justify making of that presumption irrefutable, and that no corporation ought to control so large a percentage if we desire to maintain competition at all.

A case against bigness

From Louis D. Brandeis, Testimony Before the Committee on Interstate Commerce, 1911.

The Bull Moose. Before the balloting took place, most of the Roosevelt men bolted, crying fraud. In August they reconvened as delegates of the new Progressive party. To that convention there came social workers, feminists, intellectuals, and industrialists attracted by Roosevelt's personality and program, and Republican politicians disenchanted with their factional rivals—all imbued with a revivalist spirit that led them to choose "Onward, Christian Soldiers" as their marching song. Roosevelt, "strong as a Bull Moose," told them they were standing at Armageddon battling for the Lord and accepted the nomination they tendered with thundering unanimity.

The Progressive party was a politician's Gothic horror, hastily and inadequately organized but with a powerful leader. Roosevelt probably knew in his heart that by splitting the Republican party he was assuring the election of a Democrat. He and Taft, however, had by June gone too far to turn back toward compromise, which the events of four years had in any case made difficult. The split was much more than just a personal falling out. Taft's adherents by and large stood for the status quo. Some, to be sure, were of a progressive mind but were unwilling to break with their party. Many were genuinely frightened by Roosevelt's advocacy of the recall of state judicial decisions by referendum, a proposal that in their view would substitute the fickle and untutored will of the majority for the presumed majesty of the courts. For the most part they stayed with Taft because they

considered him and his sponsors safe, whereas they considered Roosevelt, along with his friends and his platform, downright alarming.

The Bull Moose platform was incontestably adventurous, a charter of progressive reform for its own time and for years to come. It advocated the familiar devices of popular democracy—presidential primaries, woman suffrage, the initiative and referendum, and popular election of United States senators. It advocated, too, a comprehensive social-welfare program—conservation of natural and human resources, minimum wages for women, the restriction of child labor, workmen's compensation, social insurance, a federal income tax,* and the limitation of injunctions in labor disputes. Finally, in keeping with Roosevelt's ideas about the proper role of government, it called for expert federal commissions to adjust the tariff and to regulate interstate business and industry. Party and candidate alike stood for social justice and popular rule, and stood, too, for the application of efficiency to the management of public problems, an objective attractive at once to many progressives and to many men of affairs. As it developed, however, they faced formidable competition as champions of reform from a united and inspired Democratic party.

*The Sixteenth Amendment, which provided for an income tax, was already before the states, as was the Seventeenth, providing for popular election of senators. Both were ratified in 1913.

Progressivism at zenith

Woodrow Wilson. The Democratic candidate in 1912 had found his way into politics by an unusual route. Woodrow Wilson, the son of a Southern Presbyterian minister, had abandoned a brief and unrewarding career in law for one in education. After earning his doctorate at The Johns Hopkins University, Wilson taught history and political science at Bryn Mawr, Wesleyan of Connecticut, and Princeton, his own alma mater, of which he became president in 1902. He first won national attention for his writings, especially his earliest book, *Congressional Government* (1885), which criticized the weakness of the executive and the inefficiencies of Congress and praised the British parliamentary system. As president of Princeton Wilson initiated a number of celebrated educational reforms, but he lost his battle with faculty members and wealthy alumni over plans for a graduate school. That struggle brought on his resignation but also gave him a reputation as a champion of democracy in education.

Wilson resigned in 1910 to accept the Democratic nomination for governor of New Jersey. He had always had political ambitions; now he owed his nomination to Democratic machine leaders who were impressed, as were his wealthy New York friends, by his stature and his presumably conservative economic views. But during the campaign Wilson adopted the program of New Jersey progressives. As governor he made a brilliant record that put New Jersey in the van of progressive states (see p. 517) and put Wilson in the lead for the Democratic presidential nomination.

But in 1912 the Democrats, like the Republicans, were caught in a momentous struggle over selecting a candidate. Wilson had offended his conservative sponsors, who now helped organize a movement to defeat him. In spite of his appeal to many Southern progressives, his opponents were particularly successful in the South, where they captured most of the state delegations. In the East, the city machines, alarmed by Wilson's treatment of their counterparts in New Jersey, embarrassed him by publicizing sections of his *History of the American People* (1902), which disparaged the new immigrants. In the farming West, moreover, the favorite candidate was Champ Clark, the folksy "Ol' Hound Dawg" of Missouri. Bryan Democrats there rightly judged that Wilson was not one of them.

During the national convention at Baltimore Bryan, probably more to further his own ambitions than Wilson's, took the floor to castigate any candidate supported by Tammany. Tammany had just moved New York into the Clark column, thus contributing to his majority. But it took a two-thirds vote to nominate, and Wilson's floor-leaders gradually made the deals that turned the convention their way. One of those deals assured the vice-presidential nomination to Thomas R. Marshall of Indiana, a politician best remembered for his fetching assertion that what the country needed was "a good five-cent cigar." On the forty-third ballot Wilson won a majority of the votes; on the forty-sixth, the nomination.

The election of 1912. The basic contest in 1912 was between the Democrats and the Progressives. Certain of the South, assisted elsewhere by the Republican schism, the Democratic leadership took pains to preserve party unity by placating the factions that had opposed Wilson and by appealing to the urban ethnic groups that had long sustained the party's political machines. But Wilson, though the odds were with him, could not take Roosevelt for granted. He had to meet the challenge for progressive votes.

In many respects the Bull Moose and Democratic platforms were similar, but there were several significant differences between them. Where the Progressives endorsed a protective tariff, the Democrats called for sharp downward revision. Where the Progressives demanded powerful federal regulatory agencies, the Democrats emphasized state rights. The Democrats did not spell out a broad social-welfare program, but they did advocate limiting the use of injunctions against labor unions. The party's continuing insistence on that issue held the allegiance of Gompers and most of his associates in the American Federation of Labor. Moreover, farmers responded enthusiastically to Democratic promises to make loans for agriculture cheaper and more readily available.

More than the platforms, the attitudes of the candidates marked the differences between the parties. Roosevelt's New Nationalism assumed that the consolidation of the economy was inevitable and healthful. He welcomed big business but demanded big government to

Woodrow Wilson:
"Free men need no guardians"

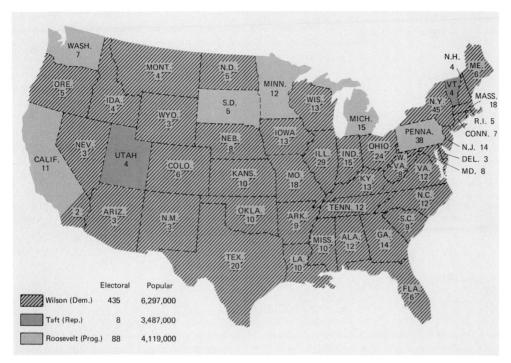

		Electoral	Popular
	Wilson (Dem.)	435	6,297,000
	Taft (Rep.)	8	3,487,000
	Roosevelt (Prog.)	88	4,119,000

The election of 1912

supervise it and to promote the welfare of nonbusiness groups. The political theorist Herbert Croly expressed these ideas forcefully in *The Promise of American Life* (1909), an influential book that helped Roosevelt and like-minded men articulate their principles. It demanded positive, comprehensive federal planning for the national interest and for social reform.

Wilson had reached dissimilar conclusions. There lingered in his mind a complex of ideas he had cherished since youth. He was a devout Presbyterian who held men individually responsible to God for their actions. Guilt in business affairs, he believed, was also personal guilt. Where a corporation misbehaved, his instinct was to punish its officers as the Lord punished sinners. He was more the stern prophet than the stern promoter. He was also convinced that laissez-faire principles of economics would work if only the state would protect and encourage competition. It should, he felt, act as a handicapper resolved to make the race equitable at the start and as a policeman determined to keep the runners in their lanes. An enemy of political and business corruption, a believer in popular democracy, a proponent of regulation to prevent industrial abuses, Wilson was a progressive, but of a type uncomfortable with Croly's formulations.

Another able intellectual, Louis D. Brandeis of Massachusetts, one of the splendid legal thinkers of his time, helped Wilson organize his developing ideas. The great corporations, Brandeis argued, controlled credit, raw materials, and markets. They prevented competition and guarded their own inefficient methods, excessive profits, and overcapitalized values. They had corrupted government, Brandeis went on, and had to be prosecuted and broken up. He also urged that the rules of competition be defined by law and that federal programs be launched to provide credit for small and new businesses. His ideas and the data with which he supported them confirmed Wilson's own theories, which the candidate set forth in the program he called the New Freedom.

Roosevelt's plans, Wilson said, would result in "partnership between the government and the trusts." The Democratic alternative would ensure a free economy and preserve free government. "Free men," he asserted, "need no guardians." Indeed they could not submit to guardians and remain free, for submission would produce "a corruption of the will."

Wilson called for "regulated competition" in preference to "regulated monopoly." He feared that individuals were being "swallowed up" by great organizations, and he con-

We have itemized with some degree of particularity the things that ought to be altered and here are some of the chief items: A tariff which cuts us off from our proper part in the commerce of the world, violates the just principles of taxation, and makes the Government a facile instrument in the hands of private interests; a banking and currency system based upon the necessity of the government to sell its bonds fifty years ago and perfectly adapted to concentrating cash and restricting credits; an industrial system which, take it on all its sides, financial as well as administrative, holds capital in leading strings, restricts the liberties and limits the opportunities of labor, and exploits without renewing or conserving the natural resources of the country; a body of agricultural activities never yet given the efficiency of great business undertakings or served as it should be through the instrumentality of science taken directly to the farm, or afforded the facilities of credit best suited to its practical needs; water courses undeveloped, waste places unreclaimed, forests untended, fast disappearing without plan or prospect of renewal, unregarded waste heaps at every mine.

From Woodrow Wilson, First Inaugural Address, 1913.

demned what he considered "an extraordinary and very sinister concentration in . . . business." He demanded "a body of laws which will look after the men . . . who are sweating blood to get their foothold in the world of endeavor." Roosevelt called Wilson's program "rural Toryism." In a sense it was. But Wilson affirmed the hopes of the farm, of the small town, of middle-class America.

Wilson won a telling victory, though he got only 41.9 percent of the popular vote and a smaller total vote than Bryan had in 1908. Roosevelt received only 27.4 percent and Taft only 23.2. In the electoral count Wilson led his rivals 435 to 88 and 8, and the Democrats carried both houses of Congress. The Democrats, who ran best in the areas of their traditional strength, had needed the Republican division to win. The returns were just as clearly a triumph for reform. Taft's miserable showing revealed the voters' disdain for standpat government, while the dissatisfaction with existing conditions was evidenced by the nearly 1 million votes for Socialist candidate Eugene V. Debs and by the remarkable support won by the Bull Moose party in its initial test.

Edward M. House: urbane Texan

Wilson and the tariff. Wilson realized that he could work most efficiently through his own party. Indeed he considered himself a party-leader in the English style, with the right to hold party members in Congress to his programs and, if necessary, to appeal over their heads to the electorate. From the first he set out to unite the Democratic factions— the Southerners, the Northern city machines, the progressives; to use his united party to legislate; and to endow it with a record and reputation that would make a majority of Americans prefer it to any rival.

Wilson, however, had neither the temperament nor the experience to get along with professional politicians. A tense and angular man, he was incapable of displaying good fellowship he did not feel. But he knew his limitations and compensated for them by selecting a group of skilled advisers. Among others they included Bryan, the new Secretary of State, influential as always with the agrarian liberals; Albert S. Burleson, Postmaster General, a veteran Southern congressman popular among the party regulars on the Hill; Secretary of the Treasury William G. McAdoo, a progressive businessman who had the confidence of those who had made Wilson's nomination possible; Joseph P. Tumulty, the President's private secretary, a young Irishman wise in the ways of machine politicians and professional journalists; and Colonel Edward M. House, an urbane Texan who attached himself to Wilson and became his "second personality." Though House had neither title nor office, he quickly acquired important responsibilities as a liaison man between the President and leaders of the party and the Congress as well as between the President and foreign heads of state.

Informed and assisted by his subordinates,

Wilson made his own major decisions and gave a personal stamp to his executive leadership. Right after his inauguration he called a special session of Congress to fulfill the Democratic pledge of tariff revision. He dramatized the session and his intended role by appearing personally, as had no President since Jefferson's time, to address the Congress. He had already begun a fruitful cooperation with the committees responsible for tariff recommendations. In May 1913, only a month after the President's address, the House passed a bill reducing average *ad valorem* rates about 11 percent; adding a number of consumer goods to the free list; and eliminating the protection of iron, steel, and various other products of the trusts. To make up for the attending loss in revenue, the bill levied a modest graduated income tax, which ratification of the Sixteenth Amendment had legalized two months earlier.

The test of Wilson's leadership came in the Senate, where the Democrats had a majority of only three votes. Democratic senators from sugar- and wool-producing states were reluctant to leave those products on the free list where the House had placed them. Wilson urged them to vote with their party, but they wavered, and lobbyists for protection tried to exploit the chance for logrolling. The President then called on public opinion to "check and destroy" the "intolerable burden" of "insidious" lobbyists. His statement helped to initiate an investigation of the private interests of all senators, some of whom, it developed, stood to profit personally from the protection of wool and sugar. With a refreshed sensitivity to public opinion, all but two Democrats voted for the party's bill. It kept sugar and wool on the free list and reduced the general level of rates another 4 percent. It also, thanks to the efforts of progressives in all the parties, doubled the maximum surtax on personal incomes.

The tariff of 1913, the Underwood-Simmons Tariff, removed an accumulation of privileges and, without abandoning protection, reduced previously swollen schedules to dimensions that permitted a healthy international trade. It also made a significant modification in the federal tax structure by shifting some of the burden to those best able to bear it. It was a convincing demonstration that the Democrats could achieve the goals of the New Freedom, and it was an acknowledged triumph for Wilson's leadership.

Banking reform. Pressing his gains, the President had urged the special session of Congress to correct the nation's anachronistic money and banking system. The Panic of 1907 (see p. 524) had underscored the inflexibility of currency and the inelasticity of credit. The events of the panic also suggested that financial power was concentrated in the hands of a small group of Eastern private bankers. That situation had been the subject of investigation by a House committee chaired by Congressman Arsène P. Pujo. Its findings, later popularized in Louis Brandeis' *Other People's Money* (1914), persuaded many progressives that there existed a "money trust."

Southern and Western farmers had long assumed that there was a bankers' conspiracy against their interests and had long agitated for monetary reform. By 1913 the bankers themselves were in favor of reform, but of their own kind. The experience of the panic and the report of Aldrich's Monetary Commission (see p. 525) led most of them to advocate central control of the banking system and the creation of a currency responsive to, and partly based on, the expansion and contraction of commercial paper—that is, loans that banks made to business.

The bankers, taking as their models the Bank of England and the controversial Second United States Bank, wanted a central bank to be authorized by the government but privately controlled. They also wanted it to issue currency on its own liability. The conservative Democrats modified those proposals by replacing a single central bank with a number of regional banks supervised by a federal board. This modification, the plan Wilson at first favored, failed to satisfy the party's progressive and agrarian factions. To meet their minimum demands, the President agreed that the government should appoint the supervising board and that the bank notes issued by the new system should be obligations of the United States.

Those concessions fell short of the program advanced by Southern farmers. They called for a prohibition of interlocking directorates, for public control of the regional banks, for permitting reserve banks to discount agricultural paper, and for preventing the use of commercial paper as a basis for currency. Bryan mediated their differences with Wilson, who saw that he had to meet them part way. Accordingly he conceded the discounting of agricultural notes and promised later to take care of interlocking directorates. In return, the militants supported the rest of the bill, which the House passed in September 1913.

There was resistance again from conservatives in the Senate. Wilson overcame some of it by another appeal for party responsibility and by a timely use of patronage. Again he took his case to the people, asserting that bankers were trying to defeat the measure by creating artificial fears of impending panic. Although Senate conservatives managed to increase the percentage of gold reserves required for the issue of bank notes and to reduce the authority of the Federal Reserve Board, the Democrats were sufficiently united to pass the bill without further changes in December 1913.

The Federal Reserve Act was the most significant statute of Wilson's Administration. The Federal Reserve Board and the regional Reserve Banks gave the United States its first efficient banking system since the time of Andrew Jackson. Their power over currency and credit put into responsible hands the means to provide the flexibility of short-term credit that was so badly needed. Though private banking interests dominated the regional banks with their large powers, the regulatory authority of the board assured a greater degree of public control over banking than ever before. Indeed the act remedied almost all the deficiencies in American banking and currency that informed men then recognized. Without the new system the country could not have adjusted to the financial strains of the First World War. There was still need to ease long-term agricultural credit and (though it was not yet understood) to endow public authorities with effective instruments to modulate the business cycle. But the new law was nonetheless impressive. Americans of all points of view and parties applauded it and the President's "great exhibition of leadership" in guiding it through Congress.

The New Freedom completed. When Congress met in regular session in 1914, Wilson presented his program for regulating industry. The tariff had furthered the New Freedom by reducing protection for the products of the trusts. The Federal Reserve Act had made credit more readily available to small and new enterprises. The obvious drift of public opinion and public policy had helped to persuade the Morgan partners to resign from many of their directorates. Now the President asked Congress to make it impossible for interrelated groups to control holding companies, to create a commission to help dissolve corporations found in restraint of trade, and to define unfair business practices.

Those recommendations, too strong for conservatives, did not satisfy either labor-leaders, who urged that unions be exempted from the Sherman Antitrust Act, or Bull Moosers, who advocated a strong regulatory agency. Louis Brandeis had moved closer to the Bull Moose point of view, and he now drafted a bill that Wilson supported. It created a Federal Trade Commission to prevent the unlawful suppression of competition. The measure passed, but only after Southern conservatives had helped the Republicans amend it to provide for broad court review of the commission's orders.

A companion measure, the Clayton Bill, was also amended before enactment. As the House passed it, it followed the prescriptions of Wilson's message, defined unfair practices, and forbade interlocking directorates. Senate conservatives modified that prohibition by exempting instances that did not tend to decrease competition. That standard gave the courts great latitude in deciding antitrust cases. It was also in the Senate, however, that friends of labor added to the bill a statement declaring that labor was not to be considered a commodity, a mere article of commerce. The House had earlier included a clause exempting labor unions and farm organizations from antitrust prosecutions, but only when those groups were lawfully pursuing legitimate aims. As the courts were to interpret the Clayton Act, the reservation about legitimate aims just about canceled the exemption.

The antitrust laws of 1914 failed to prescribe business conduct to the extent Wilson had sought, and they failed to give unions the freedom of activity Gompers had urged. The Federal Trade Commission, moreover, had less power than many progressives had recommended. But the weaknesses of the legislation were not immediately apparent, and in any event the laws constituted another, though limited, victory for the Administration. In less than two years Wilson had reached the major statutory goals of his new freedom.

The voters responded favorably in the elections of 1914. Superficially the Democrats suffered that year, for the Republicans made sizable gains. But the Democrats retained control of both houses of Congress. The collapse of the Progressive party helped the Republicans in the Northeast, where they made their best showing. Elsewhere the Democrats picked up progressive support, and in the new Congress that sat in 1915 and 1916 Southern and Western farmers had a larger voice than they had had before. The returns convinced perceptive Democratic strategists that they could carry the nation in 1916 only by winning the progressives of the West. Once more, reform had won a mandate.

In behalf of social justice. This mandate made an impression on Wilson, who had given signs of turning toward the right. Before the election he had blocked bills that outlawed child labor and that established federal banks to make long-term loans to farmers. His appointments to the Federal Reserve Board and the Federal Trade Commission had on the whole been conservative. After the election he adjusted to the demands of congressional and national politics. He encouraged the progressive Democrats, who in 1916 succeeded in passing the Federal Farm Loan Act and the Child Labor Act. Though he also endorsed legislation permitting firms engaged in export trade to combine to meet foreign competition, he did so primarily in order to strengthen American competition against foreign cartels.

On matters of international trade the President had come to respect the arguments of the Progressive party, and he supported an act in 1916 creating a nonpartisan, expert tariff commission designed, among other things, to prevent the dumping of unprotected goods on the American market.

In 1916 Wilson also practically ordered Congress to establish the eight-hour day at ten-hour pay for railway labor. Congress responded with the Adamson Act. In this case the President acted largely to prevent a threatening strike that would have tied up shipments of war materials for France and England, but his intercession won plaudits from organized labor. Labor-leaders and reformers had earlier found convincing evidence of Wilson's progressive intentions in his nomination of Louis D. Brandeis as Associate Justice of the Supreme Court.

Wilson's effective use of influence to overcome the opposition to the Brandeis appointment symbolized the President's commitment to progressivism. He had moved a long way from his position of 1912 toward that of Roosevelt and the Bull Moose. Indeed he had a right to boast that the Democrats had opened their hearts to "the demands of social justice" and had "come very near to carrying out the platform of the Progressive Party" as well as their own.

Wilson and moral diplomacy

The force of moral principle. In making foreign policy Wilson and Secretary of State Bryan were guided by attitudes they shared with most progressive Americans, particularly rural reformers, social workers, and Protestant Social Gospelers. "The force of America," the President said during one crisis, "is the force of moral principle." Moral principle, as he interpreted it, involved a duty to work for peace both by example and through diplomacy. It also involved obedience to the law. Wilson and Bryan felt that they had a mission to teach semideveloped countries to live according to the kind of legal and constitutional system that existed in the United States. They believed that that system was not only especially efficient but also especially ethical. They believed, too, that there was a definable body of international law that moral nations should obey in their relations with one another. And

they placed their hope for peace, as well as for American commercial interests, in that law rather than in systems of alliances or in defensive or deterrent military buildups.

Those attitudes led Wilson and Bryan to distrust the career men in the navy, the army, and the State Department, whom they considered conventional and even cynical. The President and the Secretary of State were willing to risk offending the experts in order to strike out along new diplomatic paths. Bryan launched his program in 1913 and 1914 by negotiating treaties with Great Britain, France, Italy, and twenty-seven lesser powers. Those treaties provided for submitting all disputes among the signatories to permanent commissions of investigation. For one year, while investigation proceeded, the parties to the treaties promised that they would neither go to war nor increase their armaments. At the end of that year they could either accept or reject the findings of the investigation, but Bryan expected the "cooling-off" period to remove the chance of war. Though Roosevelt ridiculed the plan, humanitarians throughout the Western world applauded the treaties and the spirit that produced them.

That spirit impelled Wilson in 1913 to withdraw American support from the Chinese railway consortium that Taft had helped to arrange (see p. 537). The United States, Wilson said, could not be a partner to foreign interference in Chinese affairs. He also recognized the new Republic of China, the first major recognition that government received.

The most imminent threat to China's national integrity was Japan, whose relations with the United States had deteriorated because of the troublesome race issue. Wilson had characteristic Southern prejudices about race. During his Administration there was increasing segregation of Negroes within the federal service. Never an enemy of Jim Crow, Wilson made no effort to dissuade California politicians who were in any case determined in 1913 to prohibit Japanese from owning land in their state. On the President's advice, they passed a statute which achieved that end indirectly, and without violating American treaty obligations. But the Japanese were nonetheless humiliated. Their ambassador protested to the State Department; there were anti-American disturbances in Japan; and the Joint Board of the Army and Navy, deeming war probable, advised Wilson to move warships into Chinese and Philippine waters. The President resorted instead to conciliatory diplomacy. The ensuing exchange of notes

eased the crisis and ended talk of war, but the issue remained unresolved, and the Japanese remained understandably resentful.

That resentment contributed to a new controversy in 1915. The preoccupation of European powers with the war then raging on their own continent gave Japan a chance to make twenty-one extraordinary demands of China. Had China agreed to the treaty containing the demands, she would have become a political and economic dependency. American protests, supplemented by pressure from England, persuaded the Japanese temporarily to moderate their terms. The episode revealed how tenuous the balance of power in Asia had become. It also disclosed Bryan's commitment to long-standing national policies. The United States, he warned Japan in a portentous note, could not recognize any agreement impairing the Open Door policy, the treaty rights of Americans, or the political or territorial integrity of China.

Confusion in Latin America. As in Asia, so in Latin America, Wilson intended to abandon "dollar diplomacy" with its attendant intrusions on the sovereignty of weak nations. He hoped also, while preserving the strategic lifeline to the Panama Canal, to cultivate the friendship of Latin American peoples and to help them achieve a higher standard of living and a more democratic government. He began convincingly by negotiating a treaty with Colombia providing both apology and indemnity for Roosevelt's Panamanian adventure. But Roosevelt's friends in the Senate prevented approval of that treaty, and the Administration's benign purposes soon produced policies that seemed imperialistic to those they were designed to assist.

A combination of circumstances made moral diplomacy difficult. The small nations in and around the Caribbean were, as they had long been, impoverished and turbulent. Unwilling to have the United States government assume and service their debts, Wilson relied on private bankers, whose motives he suspected. He could not permit turmoil in the area to breed revolutions or European intercessions that might endanger the approaches to the isthmus. Consequently he turned to American troops and American dollars to keep order. Since the local forces of order were often also the forces of reaction, Wilson at times resisted reform. Further, he let Bryan send to the Caribbean area "deserving Democrats" lacking any qualifications except faithful party service.

Yet the President tended to attribute qualities of justice and legality to the reactionary government Bryan supported in Nicaragua and to the protectorates the Administration established in Santo Domingo and Haiti. Wilson never fully appreciated the intensity of the anti-American feeling his policies provoked. That feeling impeded his efforts to establish a Pan-American pact, to which Chile and Argentina were in any event unready to subscribe.

The President also plunged into Mexican affairs. During the late nineteenth century, large landholders, the army, the hierarchy of the Church, and foreign investors had sustained a dictatorial government in Mexico that had suppressed the landless, uneducated, impoverished peasants and workers. In 1911 a revolution overthrew the government, but in 1913 General Victoriano Huerta engineered a *coup d'état* that restored a reactionary regime under his domination. The revolutionists, who called themselves Constitutionalists, continued to resist under Venustiano Carranza, their able and implacable leader. Though his forces controlled much of the country, the major European powers recognized the Huerta government. President Taft had delayed recognizing the Huerta regime only because he hoped first to settle various outstanding American claims.

Americans with financial interests in Mexico urged Wilson to recognize Huerta, but the President would have no formal dealings with a government of assassins. He therefore refused to appoint an ambassador to Mexico.

He did, however, send a series of special agents, whose reports intensified his dislike for the regime but also led him erroneously to believe that the United States could decree a solution to her neighbor's problems.

Wilson followed a policy of "watchful waiting" until October 1913, when Huerta, supported by British oil interests, proclaimed himself military dictator. The President then demanded that Huerta retire. The United States, he assured the Mexicans, sought no territory but only the advancement of "constitutional liberty."

To cut off the dictator's support, Wilson promised to protect British property if a Constitutionalist victory endangered it. He also, in 1914, drove through Congress a law repealing the exemption from tolls for American coastal shipping using the Panama Canal. That exemption, as the British had argued, violated an Anglo-American treaty that pledged the United States not to discriminate against British shipping using the canal. In full agreement, Wilson timed his action to serve his Mexican policy as well as international good faith. The danger of war in Europe made the British particularly solicitous of American friendship, and in March 1914 they withdrew their recognition of Huerta.

Meanwhile Wilson had told Carranza that the United States would join him in war against Huerta if he would keep the revolution orderly. Opposed to any American interference, Carranza rejected the indiscreet offer. But, since he needed the arms that an American embargo denied all Mexicans, his representatives assured Wilson that he would respect property rights. Somewhat skeptically, the President lifted the embargo in February 1914.

Armed conflict in Mexico. Soon thereafter Wilson seized an excuse for intervention. On April 10, 1914, an Huertista colonel arrested some American sailors who had gone ashore at Tampico. Though the Mexicans immediately apologized, they refused to make a formal salute to the American flag. Wilson therefore prepared to occupy Vera Cruz, Mexico's most important port. On April 20 he asked Congress for authority to use military force "to obtain from General Huerta . . . the fullest recognition of the rights and dignity of the United States."

The next day, before Congress could act,

"CONSIDER MY SIDE, SENOR SAM"

Pancho Villa: brazen bandit and friends

Wilson ordered the navy to seize Vera Cruz in order to prevent a German merchant ship from landing arms for Huerta. Several Americans were killed in the action that followed. While American newspapers predicted war and Wilson ordered war plans drawn up, the Constitutionalists as well as the Huertistas denounced the violation of their national sovereignty.

Fortunately both countries accepted an offer of mediation from Argentina, Brazil, and Chile. The resulting proposals were never signed by the Constitutionalists, who had become the dominant faction in Mexico. Huerta abdicated in July, and Carranza marched into Mexico City in August 1914, angry with the United States and disdainful of Wilson.

During 1915 the revolution in Mexico reached high pitch. Violence sometimes accompanied reform. The destruction of private property and attacks on priests and nuns excited American demands for intervention, especially among Catholics, Republicans eager to embarras Wilson, and jingoes spoiling for a war. The President had no affection for Carranza, but he resisted the pressure of the jingoes, partly because he respected Car-

ranza's objectives, partly because he dared not let embroilments in Mexico tie his hands in the crisis then developing with Germany. In October 1915 he recognized the Constitutionalists as the *de facto* government.

Within a few months the bandit leader Pancho Villa created a new crisis. An opponent of Carranza, Villa had earlier won some support from Wilson. In January 1916, however, Villa murdered a group of Americans whom he had removed from a train in Mexico. In March he killed nineteen more during a raid on Columbus, New Mexico. Again there were demands in the United States for war, but Wilson tried to contain the situation. He ordered an expedition to cross the border and punish Villa but to avoid engaging the Constitutionalists.

The futile pursuit of Villa aroused Mexican tempers. In April Carranza insisted the Americans leave his country. Wilson refused. When Villa brazenly raided Texas, the President called up the national guard for service on the border and commissioned plans for a full-scale invasion. Twice there were serious skirmishes between American and Constitutionalist soldiers. Carranza, however, needed to devote

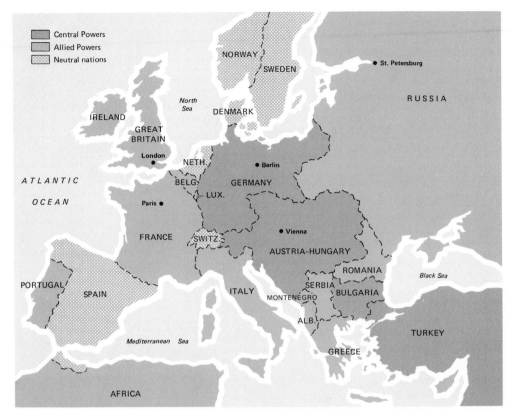

The European powers at war

his full energies to his domestic affairs, and Wilson had growing problems in Europe. Both men, moreover, genuinely desired peace. In July 1916 they agreed to appoint a joint commission to resolve their differences. Although Carranza later rejected its decision, the danger of war had passed. In January 1917 Wilson called the troops home, and two months later he granted the Constitutionalists *de jure* recognition.

In the balance Wilson's restraint outweighed his impulsiveness. In attempting to impose American standards upon the Mexicans, the President offended those he wanted to help. But he also succeeded in withstanding the demands for war that he had inadvertently fanned. He succeeded most of all in grasping the need for reform in Mexico. The American people in varying degree shared his confusions and his distaste for the excesses of revolution. Most of them, however, also shared his sympathy for Mexico's troubles and his reluctance to permit disagreement and discord to grow into war.

Problems of neutrality

War in Europe. In August 1914 a crisis within the empire of Austria-Hungary brought on the war in Europe that had been brewing for more than a decade. Ambitious Germany dominated the alliance of the Central Powers, including Austria-Hungary and Turkey. On the other side were the western powers, France and England, their ally, Russia, and soon also Italy, a partner bought by promises of more lands.

Though most Americans had known that war was threatening, they were shocked by the outbreak of hostilities and unprepared to face the problems war imposed on them. Relieved that war seemed so far away, they had yet to learn that distance alone could not insulate the United States. Most progressives tended to believe that selfish commercial rivalries had moved the European nations toward disaster. They believed, too, that the United States could serve the world best by concentrating on further reform at home, by

The war at sea

setting a noble example of peace and democracy. Even those who were not progressives were slow to recognize the intensity of nationalistic emotions that war bred, slower still in seeing how those emotions blocked a return to peace. Americans, like other Western men, had no experience with the shocks of total war, calculated brutality, and mass hatred.

The Administration's initial statements of policy gave official sanction to attitudes that prevailed throughout the nation. Wilson expressed his faith that the United States could play "a part of impartial mediation," and he urged his countrymen to be "neutral in fact as well as in name." But impartiality of sentiment was impossible. Many Americans of various national origins identified themselves with the loyalties of their forebears. The German- and Irish-Americans particularly supported the Central Powers. British-Americans favored the western Allies. The similarities between British and American speech and institutions, furthermore, fostered widespread sympathy for England. Wilson himself had long been an admirer of England's culture.

Belligerents in both camps tried to enlist American emotions. The Germans circulated stories alleging that the British blockade was causing mass starvation; the British published accounts of atrocities allegedly committed by German soldiers. Both sides exaggerated, but propaganda won few converts. The course of the war itself, however, made a deeper impression. Germany's invasion of Belgium in August 1914, which violated a treaty pledging Germany to respect Belgian neutrality, offended many Americans. Propaganda could not erase that evidence of German ruthlessness, and evidence was to come of German

intrigue within the United States. The Allied cause gradually gained adherents, though very few even among them favored American participation in a war across the Atlantic.

Neutral rights. While Wilson remained firm in his purpose to be neutral in fact, he upheld neutral rights to trade and to the use of the ocean. Those traditional objectives of American diplomacy had, the President believed, a clear basis in law and morality. His standards for defining neutral rights were "the existing rules of international law and the treaties of the United States." But those rules were uncertain, especially under the unprecedented conditions created by the tactics of the submarine, the novel weapon on which Germany counted heavily. Particularly with Germany, but also with England, troubles arose over Wilson's interpretations of American neutral rights.

The British, who controlled the seas, were determined that the Allies alone should receive munitions and other essential war materials from the United States. They therefore established a tight blockade of Germany and narrowly limited the kinds of goods that American ships could carry to neutral ports from which they could be sent on to Germany. The British also diverted suspect shipping to their own ports, confiscated many cargoes, interfered with American mail in order to intercept military and economic information, and ultimately forbade British subjects to do any business with American firms "blacklisted" for violating British rules.

Wilson protested often and vigorously against these and other British practices that infringed upon traditional neutral rights. The British, engaged in total war, considered him peevishly legalistic. But, since they had to have American supplies, they made the basic objective of their diplomacy "the maximum blockade that could be enforced without a rupture with the United States."

The success of that policy owed much to the increasing good will Americans felt for England. It owed something, too, to the growing importance of war production for the American economy. Allied demands for war materials stimulated American heavy industry and provided a market for American agriculture. Indeed, with a wise solicitude the British even provided funds to help stabilize the price of cotton at a level satisfactory to the Democratic South.

There were no international rules against selling war materials to the Allies. And if Wilson had refused to permit such sales, he would have indirectly aided the Central Powers. Nor were there any rules to prevent American bankers from making loans to finance Allied purchases. Bryan at first maintained that such loans violated "the true spirit of neutrality," but early in 1915, when the Allies were desperate for funds, he partially reversed himself. Before the end of that year the State Department had approved enormous loans, arranged by American financiers, without which England and France could not have continued to buy the materials they had to have. Thereafter almost every segment of the national economy would have suffered from a diplomatic rupture with the Allies or from a German triumph.

The Germans, who were unable to transport supplies through the British blockade, protested against American sales of war materials to the Allies and against British interpretations of maritime law. They also sent out submarines to destroy Allied shipping. These U-boats created the issue on which German-American relations ultimately foundered.

The submarine problem. Submarines could not operate according to the traditional rules governing the conduct of ships bent on destroying commerce. Their effectiveness depended upon surprise. They could not warn their prospective targets before attacking them or remove crews or passengers from stricken ships. They were too small to rescue survivors of their sinkings. Yet Wilson insisted, as most Americans thought he should, that the Germans observe traditional international law.

The submarine issue arose in February 1915, when Germany proclaimed a war zone around the British Isles. Enemy ships, she warned, would be sunk on sight, and neutral ships would be in danger of misidentification. In a sharp reply Wilson called the sinking of merchant ships without visit and search "a wanton act." The destruction of an American ship, he declared, or the loss of American lives on belligerent ships, would be regarded as "a flagrant violation of neutral rights." It would be an offensive act for which he would hold Germany to "strict accountability." His note expressed the horror most Americans felt toward the barbarity of modern weapons. It left the Germans with a choice between abandon-ing their strategic plan or risking American antagonism.

They chose to take the risk. In April 1915 an American went down aboard a British ship. On May 1 an American ship was torpedoed. Six days later the Germans sank the British passenger liner *Lusitania* and with her died hundreds of men, women, and children, many of them Americans whom the Germans had warned not to embark. That sinking shocked the nation. A minority wanted to break off relations with Germany, which in their view was guilty of "murder" and "piracy," as Theodore Roosevelt put it. Most men of that mind hoped soon to see the United States at war. At the other extreme, those who sympathized with Germany and those who considered war the worst possible calamity were eager to arbitrate the issue, if necessary to prohibit travel on the ships of belligerents. The majority of Americans were angry, determined to win some redress, but anxious to avoid hostility. Like Wilson, they hoped the problem could be negotiated away.

"There is such a thing," the President told one audience, "as a man being too proud to fight. There is such a thing as a nation being so right that it does not need to convince others by force." In that spirit he began his negotiations. It did not matter, he told Berlin, that the *Lusitania* carried munitions as well as passengers. That was a secondary consideration. The United States was concerned with the "sacred . . . rights of humanity," particularly "the right to life itself." The sinking was an "illegal and inhuman" act, and Wilson demanded an apology and reparations. Since submarines could not be used without violating "principles of justice and humanity," he also by implication demanded that they should not be used at all.

The extremists were dissatisfied. Roosevelt called the President "yellow." Bryan, who had urged Wilson to adopt the principles of the "cooling-off" treaties, considered the notes to Germany too harsh. Sadly he resigned from the Cabinet, to be replaced by Robert Lansing, a New York lawyer with a talent for diplomatic phraseology. As he and the President continued to negotiate, the Germans met them part way. They would not admit the illegality of the sinking, but in February 1916 they offered an apology and an indemnity. By and large the American people were relieved. As Lansing put it, they desired only honorable friendship.

Captured U-boat: effectiveness depended on surprise

Peace with honor. So long as the war continued, however, the submarine issue might involve the United States. The national interest as well as the interests of the besieged people of Europe impelled Wilson to attempt to arrange a peace. He had sent Colonel House to Europe in January 1915 to investigate the possibility of mediation, but House had found the Germans adamant in their decision to hold Belgium and to destroy England's naval power. In October, however, the Colonel concocted a plan for peace, which Wilson approved. They intended to force Germany to negotiate by warning that otherwise the United States might enter the war on the Allied side. If the Germans were agreeable to negotiations, House hoped to bring them to reasonable terms at the conference table. Again, failure, according to the plan, would invite American participation in the war. In London in January and February 1916 House made progress toward his goal. Indeed it looked as if the British would accept an offer from Wilson for a peace conference in the autumn. But the enterprise collapsed when Lansing tried to revise American policy toward the submarines.

Wilson and Lansing had decided to ease the submarine issue by attempting to persuade the Allies not to arm their merchantmen. In that event the U-boats could issue warnings before attacking. The Germans naturally welcomed the idea, for their purpose was not to kill sailors but to destroy cargoes and bottoms. To their delight, just as House was completing his negotiations in England, Lansing suggested that Allied merchantmen be disarmed. The British of course refused. Lansing had earlier suggested to the Germans that if the Allies declined, Germany might declare unrestricted submarine warfare against all armed ships. In February 1916 the Germans made precisely that declaration. But Lansing then doubled back, reasserted Wilson's original submarine policy, and announced that the United States would not warn Americans against travel on armed ships. "Strict accountability" still applied.

The conflicting strands of American diplomacy had increased the chances of national involvement in the war. The Roosevelt Republicans prepared to make a major campaign issue during 1916 of the embarrassment the President had caused the Allies. At the opposite pole of opinion, Bryan, La Follette, and other agrarian progressives saw a "sort of

moral treason" in letting American citizens create crises by sailing on endangered ships. Resolutions forbidding such travel failed in Congress only because Wilson exerted all his influence to defeat them.

One month later, in March 1916, a German submarine without warning torpedoed an unarmed French steamer, the *Sussex*. The President's policy seemed to have failed completely. But he did not retreat from his principles. After much reflection, in April he sent Germany an ultimatum. Unless it immediately abandoned "its present method of submarine warfare," the United States would "sever diplomatic relations." The Kaiser's advisers decided that since they lacked the submarines to conduct a useful blockade of England, it was more important to keep the United States neutral. In May Germany acceded to Wilson's demand. Submarines would observe the rules of visit and search, the Germans said, but they might remove that limitation unless the United States compelled England to obey international law.

In spite of the threat that Germany might revert to its earlier tactics, most Americans were again relieved. Unaware of the reasons for the German decision, they felt that the President had avoided war, maintained justice, and conquered the submarines with his pen. The *Sussex* pledge seemed to promise peace with honor—a happy formula, especially in a campaign year.

Americanism and preparedness. As the war went on, it revealed to Americans as well as to Europeans the terrors of organized brutality and the dangers of organized passions. Intelligence and decency and orderliness gave way before the strains of continual fear. Though the United States was far from the fields of battle, even here timid men sought some symbol that would protect them from the disturbances around them. Other men seized the chance to create symbols they could use for their own selfish ends. So it was that the most avid foes of labor unions underwrote a campaign to equate the open shop with "Americanism." So it was that those who distrusted blacks or Catholics or Jews now did so in the name of Americanism. It was a word that the opponents of woman suffrage used, a word used also by the advocates of a literacy test for immigrants. The Senate blocked an amendment to enfranchise women, and Congress in 1915 passed a bill establishing a literacy test. Wilson vetoed it, pointing out that it abridged the traditional right of asylum and tested education rather than talent.

The President resisted the spirit of frightened conformity that Roosevelt exalted in the name of Americanism. The name, however, had a political magic no politician could safely ignore, and Wilson himself used it to describe his foreign policy. In 1915, condemning the sabotage of munitions production for the Allies, he attributed it to extremists among the German- and Irish-Americans. Calling on all others to dedicate themselves to the national honor, the President planned to make his version of Amercanism the keynote of his campaign for reelection.

The position Wilson and his party took on preparedness also accorded with the middle-of-the-road attitudes of most Americans. Even after the war began, they tended, like the President, to consider arms and munitions the unnecessary tools of evil men. Again like the President, they had an instinctive dislike for widespread military training and a large standing army, neither of which had any place in the American tradition. That tradition persisted, in spite of the nature of modern war, in defining the militia and a citizen-soldiery as proper safeguards for national security. Four months after the sinking of the *Lusitania*, Wilson expressed a popular sentiment when he said he saw no need ''to stir the nation up in favor of national defense.''

Moved by the possibility of war in Europe and Mexico, a vocal minority began to preach about the need to prepare, pointing out that it took time to produce weapons and to train armies and navies for twentieth-century warfare. Theodore Roosevelt led these advocates of preparedness. He was sometimes too strident to be convincing, but more moderate men gradually put their ideas across. During 1915 Secretary of War Lindley M. Garrison and his three Republican predecessors all urged preparedness. It had become a political issue, and Wilson's Democratic advisers warned him that he had better do something about it.

In July 1915 the President instructed the armed services to make plans for expansion. In November, asking for much less than they had recommended, he proposed a volunteer army of four hundred thousand men who were to serve only a few months in each of several successive years. Even this modest proposal met opposition from rural liberals in Congress, most of them Democrats, some of them with great influence. Preparedness also incurred the hostility of a passionate peace party, its membership recruited not least from among women who saw all war as a needless exercise of raw masculinity. To win more moderate support for his program, Wilson went on a speaking trip that took him halfway across the continent. During that tour he came out for a ''navy second to none.''

Yet in 1916 the President had to make concessions to his opponents. Still close to the middle of the road, he first rejected the War Department's plan for creating a large reserve force under the regular army, and he appointed a new Secretary of War,* Newton D. Baker, a progressive with a reputation for antimilitarism. Wilson and Baker then worked out a compromise that satisfied the Congress. The resulting law of May 1916 doubled the regular army but left the national guard still largely independent of the authority of the War Department. The President's influence helped, too, to carry a measure accelerating the building of a strong navy.

The agrarians scored one success: in the face of Administration opposition, they fashioned the revenue legislation to pay for the defense program. It increased surtaxes on personal income and put new taxes on inheritances. Those best able to pay would have to foot the bill for preparedness.

Taken together, the army, navy, and tax laws of 1916 satisfied the majority of Americans. The Democrats had given the preparedness issue a progressive stamp and had identified their party with national defense. The measures fell short of the demands of the armed services, but they met the most urgent requirements of a nation that still hoped and expected to remain at peace.

The election of 1916. For the Republicans one major problem in 1916 was how to reassimilate the Progressive party. Roosevelt had kept it alive largely to further his own ambitions, but the Old Guard would not countenance his nomination on the Republican ticket, and the Colonel cared more about defeating Wilson than about nursing old grudges. In order to regain Bull Moose votes, the Republicans selected a candidate with a

---

*Garrison had resigned partly because of his view on national defense, partly because he opposed Wilson's policy for increasing home rule in the Philippines.

Charles Evans Hughes: candidate with a progressive record

progressive record, Charles Evans Hughes. He had been a successful reform governor of New York and in 1912, as an Associate Justice of the Supreme Court, had stayed neutral in the party split. He was an able man and a strong candidate whose cause may have been hurt rather than helped by Roosevelt's obsessive attacks on Democratic foreign policy.

Although Wilson had planned to run on the issues of Americanism and progressivism, foreign policy became a central factor in the campaign. At the Democratic convention, as the keynote speaker described the recurrent crises in foreign policy, he explained how Wilson had resolved each one and concluded each time with the phrase: "We did not go to war." Each time the delegates responded jubilantly. The party-managers sensed that their most effective slogan would be: "He kept us out of war." Its effectiveness probably grew as Roosevelt sounded more and more bellicose and as Hughes explained that he would have been tougher on Mexico and Germany than Wilson had been. The President himself told the voters that he was "not expecting this country to get into war," and

Democratic propagandists advertised: "Wilson and Peace with Honor? or Hughes with Roosevelt and War?"

There were, of course, other issues. The Irish-American and German-American extremists embarrassed Hughes by supporting him openly; but he failed to repudiate them publicly, while Wilson deliberately attacked them. The Democrats had made a progressive record that was especially persuasive with those from the defunct Bull Moose who could not yet tolerate the idea of voting Republican again.

By and large, rural America voted for Wilson, as did labor, the liberals, and most intellectuals. The contest was so close that it hinged on the ballots in California and Minnesota, which were counted only after early Eastern returns had put Hughes ahead. Hughes went to bed election night thinking that he had won. But the South and the West reversed the verdict. Wilson received 49.4 percent of the popular vote to Hughes' 46.2 percent and carried the Electoral College 277 to 254. The mandate was narrow, but the appeal of peace and progressivism had prevailed.

The road to war

Wilson knew very well how tenuous was the nation's hold on peace. Before election day the British had tightened their regulations on neutral trade, and the Germans had intensified their submarine campaign against the Allies. The war could not be contained much longer. Either Wilson had to find ways to end it or else he would have to sacrifice peace or honor—or both.

The President planned to send a dramatic note to the belligerents. He was ready, his draft said, to pledge the "whole force" of the United States to end the "war of exhaustion and attrition" and to keep the future peace. The draft asked each side for "a concrete definition" of the objectives for which it was fighting. It also demanded that a peace conference be called immediately. Furthermore, Wilson intended to employ every pressure short of war to assist the more reasonable side. While he was still reworking his draft, in December 1916, the German chancellor announced his government's readiness to negotiate. For a brief time Wilson was encouraged.

The offer, however, hid a calculating spirit. The Germans made the gesture out of confidence of impending victory. Masters of the eastern front, where the Russians were collapsing, the Germans expected to smash France and England if their terms were rejected. They had also secretly decided that, if negotiations failed, they would resume unrestricted submarine warfare. And their secret terms were harsh—they would insist on territory along the Baltic, in the Congo, and in Belgium, France, and Luxembourg.

Slowly Wilson discovered the truth. He dispatched the note he had been drafting, but the Germans replied that they wanted no neutral at the peace table. The Allies publicly rejected the President's proposal but privately let him know they would negotiate if the German conditions were reasonable. Then in January 1917 the Germans at last revealed their greedy terms and announced that their submarines would sink at sight all ships, belligerent or neutral.

For several weeks Wilson would not admit that he had either to surrender his principles

The world must be made safe for democracy. Its peace must be planted upon the tested foundations of political liberty. We have no selfish ends to serve. We desire no conquest, no dominion. We seek no indemnities for ourselves, no material compensation for the sacrifices we shall freely make. We are but one of the champions of the rights of mankind. We shall be satisfied when those rights have been made as secure as the faith and the freedom of nations can make them....

It is a fearful thing to lead this great peaceful people into war, into the most terrible and disastrous of all wars, civilization itself seeming to be in the balance. But the right is more precious than peace, and we shall fight for the things which we have always carried nearest our hearts,—for democracy, for the right of those who submit to authority to have a voice in their own governments, for the rights and liberties of small nations, for a universal dominion of right by such a concert of free peoples as shall bring peace and safety to all nations and make the world itself at last free.

From Woodrow Wilson, War Message to Congress, 1917.

Program for a just war

or go to war. He broke off relations with Germany, but he told Congress he wanted no conflict. He remained outwardly temperate even after learning on February 25 that Germany was plotting against the United States. That day the British communicated to Washington secret orders of the German foreign minister, Arthur Zimmermann, which they had intercepted. Those orders told the German minister to Mexico that, in the event of war with the United States, he should invite Mexico and Japan to join the Central Powers.

Wilson, while still hoping to avoid war, had meanwhile pressed his interpretation of neutral rights. He had asked Congress for authority to arm American merchant vessels and to employ any other means that might be necessary to protect American ships and citizens at sea. To win votes for his proposal, he made the Zimmermann note public on March 1, 1917. A wave of anti-German sentiment swept the country, but the Democratic House of Representatives withheld the broad authority the President wanted, and in the Senate a dozen antiwar progressives talked a stronger bill to death.

That "little group of willful men," as Wilson called them, struggled in vain. The Zimmermann note had dissolved the myth that the war was strictly European. The President on his own ordered the merchantmen armed, and on March 18, two weeks after his second inauguration, U-boats sank three American ships. Moreover, the first Russian revolution established a limited monarchy and a respon-

sible parliament, temporarily destroying the despotism that had made Americans reluctant to associate with the Allied cause. And the Allies could no longer fight without American men, money, and material. The combination of events convinced even the most ardent peace advocates in the Cabinet of the necessity for war.

Wilson was agonized by a conclusion he could not escape. War, he allegedly told one confidant, "would overturn the world we had known," lead to "a dictated peace," require "illiberalism at home." Sadly he predicted that "the spirit of ruthless brutality" would enter the very "fibre of our national life." His pain was shared by every progressive, for progressivism had based its faith on the peaceful, reasonable improvement of the lot of man in a world of quiet and intelligence. It was also, however, a moral faith, and in the view of Wilson and other progressive intellectuals, Germany had violated moral principles. She had forced war on France and Belgium. She was bent on conquest. Whatever the definitions of neutral rights, no one was immune from German aggression, and there could be no real peace while it went unpunished.

With those thoughts in mind, Wilson on April 2 addressed the special session of Congress he had summoned. On April 4 the Senate by a vote of 82 to 6, and on April 6 the House of Representatives by a vote of 373 to 50, passed a resolution recognizing the existence of a state of war with Germany.

Suggestions for reading

GENERAL

The best general account of the Taft years and of the breakup of the Republican party is in G. E. Mowry, *The Era of Theodore Roosevelt** (1958). A. S. Link, *Woodrow Wilson and the Progressive Era** (1954), covers the succeeding years to the American entry into the war. Both books are challenged by Gabriel Kolko, *The Triumph of Conservatism** (1963). Also useful are relevant parts of Eric Goldman, *Rendezvous with Destiny** (1952), and Richard Hofstadter, *The Age of Reform: From Bryan To F. D. R.** (1955). An older book of G. E. Mowry, *Theodore Roosevelt and the Progressive Movement** (1946), contains a more detailed account—and less friendly to T. R.—than that in the same author's later work.

PROGRESSIVES AND REGULARS

The case for Taft is set forth in Henry Pringle, *Life and Times of William Howard Taft,* 2 vols. (1938), but that study should be compared with the Roosevelt biographies listed in connection with the preceding chapter and with A. T. Mason, *Bureaucracy Convicts Itself* (1941), which takes Pinchot's part in his controversy with Ballinger. For an understanding of progressive social ideas, it is essential to read Herbert Croly, *The Promise of American Life** (1909); Walter Weyl, *The New Democracy** (1912); and Walter Lippmann, *Drift and Mastery** (1914); as well as the autobiographies of La Follette* and William Allen White. See also O. Graham, Jr., *Encore for Reform: The Old Progressives and the New Deal** (1967). Two significant studies of progressive thought, besides those referred to in the previous chapter, are Walter Johnson, *William Allen White's America* (1947), and C. B. Forcey, *The Crossroads of Liberalism** (1961). There are no comparable studies of conservative thought, but that subject gets useful treatment in Richard Leopold, *Elihu Root and the Conservative Tradition** (1954), and in the introduction by E. E. Morison to Vol. V of *The Letters of Theodore Roosevelt* (1952).

WILSON

The outstanding work on Wilson is A. S. Link's multivolume biography. Two brief studies of Wilson are J. M. Blum, *Woodrow Wilson and the Politics of Morality** (1956), and J. A. Garraty, *Woodrow Wilson** (1956). These are less sympathetic than two older works: H. C. F. Bell, *Woodrow Wilson and the People* (1945); and R. S. Baker, *Woodrow Wilson: Life and Letters,* 6 vols. (1927–37). Of the special studies of Wilson's diplomacy, the best are A. S. Link, *Wilson the Diplomatist** (1957), and N. G. Levin, Jr., *Woodrow Wilson and World Politics** (1968). There are keen analyses of the issues of American foreign policy in R. E. Osgood, *Ideals and Self-Interest in America's Foreign Relations** (1953), and E. R. May, *The World War and American Isolation 1914–1917** (1959). The European scene gets thorough treatment in S. B. Fay, *Origins of the World War,* 2 vols.* (1930), and B. E. Schmitt, *The Coming of War, 1914,* 2 vols. (1930). The case for isolation imbues both C. C. Tansill, *America Goes to War* (1928), and Walter Millis, *The Road to War: America* (1935). Of the various studies of the Wilsonians, one is indispensable: Charles Seymour, ed., *The Intimate Papers of Colonel House,* 4 vols. (1921–28). Also useful, particularly on domestic issues, is A. T. Mason, *Brandeis: A Free Man's Life* (1946). J. A. Garraty, *Henry Cabot Lodge* (1953), presents an understanding account of one of Wilson's foremost antagonists. The literature on Wilson and his time has been richly expanded with the continuing publication of his letters and papers under the editorship of A. S. Link.

*Available in a paperback edition.

24 _War and its sequel_

The American nation was unprepared for the First World War. To begin with, the nation had no clear sense of purpose. Many German- and Irish-Americans were unreconciled to fighting on the side of the Allies. Smaller groups of pacifists saw no excuse for any fighting, and some progressives believed that the United States had no business involving itself in what they considered to be a struggle between European imperialists. The majority of Americans were in full accord with the decision to go to war, but they were confused about its origins and objectives. Like the President, they had hoped to remain neutral. Like the President, they regarded the submarine issue as a matter of morality. They had little if any understanding of world politics.

Indeed the moral temper of the times led men to seek utopian rather than realistic reasons for the actions to which they were committed. To accommodate that temper, and to convert the dissenters, Wilson defined Ameri-

can war aims in idealistic terms. The spirit of his war message and later addresses was noble as well as persuasive. It helped transmute the fervor of progressivism into the selfless bravery of the "great crusade." But it also turned some fervor into frenzy, and it led men to expect a paradise that no war could give them. The failure to achieve that expectation tinged the persisting frenzy of the immediate postwar years with bitterness and vindictiveness.

The United States was also unprepared for the total mobilization demanded by modern war and for the special strengths required to fight a war overseas. The nation lacked the necessary army, the plans and facilities to raise it, the guns and tanks and airplanes to equip it, the ships to transport it, and even the tools and the organization to produce the materials of war. In every respect—emotional, economic, military—mobilization was urgent but erratic.

The armed forces on land and sea

Selective service. The President and his military advisers agreed that conscription was the only efficient and democratic way to recruit a large army. Yet the Speaker of the House and the Chairman of the Military Affairs Committee, both Democrats, led the opposition to the Administration's selective-service bill. Many of the bill's opponents considered conscription a threat to democracy. Others had a romantic attachment to the tradition of voluntary military service. But if war had ever

been romantic it was no longer so, and selective service, as Wilson argued, spread the obligation to serve among all qualified men without regard to their social position. The House passed the bill in May, but only after mollifying American mothers by raising the minimum draft age from nineteen, which the army recommended, to twenty-one.*

*It was necessary in 1918 to lower the minimum age to eighteen.

Gas? What do you know of it, you people who have never heard earth and heaven rock with the frantic turmoil of the ceaseless bombardment? A crawling yellow cloud that pours in upon you, that gets you by the throat and shakes you as a huge mastiff might shake a kitten, leaves you burning in every nerve and vein of your body with pain unthinkable; your eyes starting from their sockets; your face turned yellow-green.

Rats? What did you ever read of the rats in the trenches? Next to gas, they still slide on their fat bellies through my dreams.... Tens of thousands of rats, crunching between battle lines while the rapid-firing guns mow the trench edge—crunching their hellish feasts....

Stench? Did you ever breathe air foul with the gases arising from a thousand rotting corpses? Dirt? Have you ever fought half madly thru days and nights and weeks unwashed, with feverish rests between long hours of agony, while the guns boom their awful symphony of death, and the bullets zip-zip-zip ceaselessly along the trench edge that is your sky-line—and your death line, too, if you stretch and stand up?

Quoted in the *Independent,* June 19, 1916.

In the Senate the Republicans wasted three weeks in a futile effort to force the Administration to accept the volunteer division Theodore Roosevelt was organizing. Roosevelt and his admirers believed that even though his troops were half-trained they would make up the deficiency in dash. Wilson prudently preferred professional to political generals. The Selective Service Act finally passed by the

Selective Service:
over 24 million men registered

Senate left Wilson free to dispose of volunteer units as he saw fit, and he saw fit to reject Roosevelt's.

Early in June 1917 over 9 million men registered quietly with the local officials whom the War Department authorized to supervise the draft. Before the war ended, over 24 million had registered and almost 3 million had been inducted into the army. There was no significant opposition to conscription, and the drafted troops fought as heroically as the 2 million volunteers who enlisted in the various armed services.

The army's top command was strictly professional. Bypassing General Leonard Wood, an intimate of Roosevelt, Wilson made General John J. Pershing head of the American Expeditionary Force and gave his decisions consistent support. "Black Jack" Pershing, a laconic, stern West Pointer, pursued two controversial policies. He refused to send troops into battle until they had completed their training, and he insisted on preserving a separate identity for the American Expeditionary Force, though the French and British were impatient for reinforcements and eager to merge American units with their own.

The war in the west. In the fall of 1917 German offensives routed the Italians and destroyed the Russian army. The Bolshevik Revolution of November removed Russia from the war and left the western front, manned by war-weary French and British troops, ex-

The Meuse-Argonne: extraordinary expenditures of nerve and flesh

posed to the full attack Germany was certain to mount the following spring. The alarmed Allies created the Supreme War Council to direct their resistance and urged Pershing to supply men, trained or untrained. But Pershing still declined. In the spring, however, as the Allied lines crumbled before a furious German offensive, Wilson agreed to the appointment of French Marshal Ferdinand Foch as supreme commander, and Pershing put his four available divisions at Foch's disposal.

During May 1918 the Germans pushed the French back to the Marne River, only fifty miles from Paris. Foch then called up one American division and a few regiments of marines who met the Germans at Chateau Thierry, carried the intensive battle there, and in June drove the enemy out of Belleau Wood.

Gambling for a quick victory before more American forces could reach France, the Germans in July struck at the sector of the Marne between Rheims and Soissons. Here some eighty-five thousand Americans helped to turn the attack, and eight divisions of Yanks participated in the French counteroffensive that cleaned out the sector early in August. The American First Army under Pershing then took over the southern front near St. Mihiel and routed the Germans there in an independent offensive in September. Late that month Pershing attacked the German lines between Verdun and Sedan. This Meuse-Argonne engagement produced a costly but crucial American victory. Along with the success of French and British forces on the northern and central

fronts, it crushed the German army and set the stage for an armistice (see p. 565).

The triumph exacted extraordinary expenditures of nerve and flesh, for in some respects the First World War was the most ghastly in history. Casualties ran high, particularly during offensives, and American troops, along with their allies and foes, suffered a high incidence of shell shock, a form of battle fatigue, and of tuberculosis, a companion of the poi-

*American operations
on the western front, 1918*

New knights of the air

son gas and the mud, cold, wet, and filth of the trenches. For most soldiers the war was an awful combination of fear, drudgery, and exhaustion.

The signal exceptions were the aviators. Their craft were simple and slow, their tactics rudimentary. Yet the new knights of the air wrote a chapter of military history in their man-to-man combat in the skies, and American aces dramatized for their countrymen the potentialities of aerial warfare.

The Yanks had reached France just in time. The Allies needed the new manpower to stop the Germans' gamble for victory—a gamble that would probably have succeeded had reinforcements failed to appear. Yet the Americans, indispensable during the last months of war, and gallant and effective then, arrived only after the Allies had held the Germans for almost four terrible years. Over 50,000 Americans died in France, but the war took the lives of 3 million English, French, and Russian soldiers. The role of the American army was both relatively small and absolutely vital.

The war at sea. So too was the role of the American navy. In all but one respect the war at sea had been won by the success of the British navy in bottling up the German fleet. As the British Admiralty admitted, however, the German submarines also had to be brought under control. During 1917 U-boats sank more than twice the tonnage of shipping that the Allies and Americans built that year.

Hard pressed to supply themselves, the British could not guard the American lines of supply to Europe, and the Americans could not afford to risk transporting an army aboard ships unprotected from enemy submarines.

The United States navy had the ships and the men to take over the patrol of the Western Hemisphere and to assist the English in patrolling the waters around the British Isles. But the Allies lacked the antisubmarine vessels to root the U-boats out of the ocean. An American plan proved to be at least as important as the ships themselves. Admiral William S. Sims, the ranking American naval officer in Europe, was the primary exponent of the idea of using destroyers and other men-of-war to escort convoys of merchantmen across the Atlantic. Though British skippers preferred to sail alone rather than to proceed in formation under naval command, Sims in the summer of 1917 overcame their objections and the resistance of the British Admiralty. By the end of 1917 the use of convoys had cut shipping losses in half.

The escorted convoys and the patrolling American destroyers were so effective that not one American soldier was lost in transit to Europe. The bridge of ships to France carried the troops and supplies that the Germans had expected to destroy, and the miracle of transportation turned the tide of war. That great American achievement was possible only because the British also provided bottoms for men and equipment, and only because the Yanks at the front could use Allied cannon, tanks, and airplanes.

The home front

Problems of production. By themselves the eventual prodigies of American war production would have been too little and too late for victory. Since there were no precedents for economic mobilization, the Administration had to feel its way along in creating agencies to supervise production and distribution and to allocate vital goods and services. When war came, the army did not even have information about the uniforms and shoes it would need. There was no inventory of national resources, no adequate plan for priorities or for stockpiling critical materials. Most of the first nine months of the war were spent in learning about mobilization, and in tooling up for production.

The lost time was especially serious for the aviation program. American planners were so slow in designing and manufacturing aircraft that American aviators had to fly in British and French machines all through the war. The situation was almost as desperate in the production of artillery and tanks. The building program for transports and cargo vessels collapsed completely, and the government had to rely on ships seized from neutrals or purchased from private industry.

These and other difficulties spurred the Senate Military Affairs Committee to investigate the conduct of the war. As 1918 began, the Democratic chairman of that committee asserted publicly that the military effort had been impeded by waste and inefficiency. Republican senators, joined by several Democrats, urged that a war cabinet of three distinguished citizens be set up to exercise the powers that Congress had conferred upon the President. If that measure had passed, Wilson would have become a figurehead. Even as it was, the Senate committee was close to assuming the role of its predecessor that had harassed Lincoln during the Civil War.

The President, however, had already begun to solve the problems of mobilization. Neither during 1917 nor later, moreover, did any scandal taint the administration of the war. Aware of the threat from the Senate, Wilson prepared a bill giving him sweeping authority to reorganize and manage all executive agencies. This measure, which Senator Lee S. Overman sponsored, passed Congress in April 1918 and enabled the President to complete his own plans.

Economic mobilization. As those plans matured, the Administration put the nation's economy on a satisfactory war footing. In the spring of 1917 England, France, and Italy urgently needed food. Stretching the mandate of the Council of National Defense, which Congress had authorized the year before, the President established a food-control program in May under Herbert C. Hoover, who had acquired an international reputation as director of the Belgian Relief Commission. Wilson also asked Congress for emergency authority over agricultural production and distribution. The Lever Act of August 1917 granted him that authority, together with limited power to control the prices of certain scarce commodities. Wilson at once created the Food Administration. With Hoover at its head, that agency controlled prices to stimulate the production of wheat and pork, managed the distribution of those and other foodstuffs, and persuaded the public to observe meatless and breadless days. To that last objective, as to the selling of war bonds, American women contributed impressive energy. The success of Hoover's policies made possible the victualing of the nations fighting Germany.

To put American industry on a wartime footing proved more difficult. The General Munitions Board, another offshoot of the Council of National Defense, showed itself incapable of coordinating the conflicting demands of the American armed services and the Allied purchasing commissions. Conse-

quently, in July 1917 Wilson appointed a War Industries Board with authority to pass on all American and Allied purchasing, to allocate raw materials, to control production, and to supervise labor relations. The WIB, however, failed to elicit the cooperation of the armed services. In March 1918 the President rewrote its charter and named a new chairman, the wealthy and influential Democrat, Bernard M. Baruch, who enlisted the help of some hundred outstanding business-leaders. Now concerned largely with establishing industrial priorities, the WIB eliminated bottlenecks and speeded the conversion of plants to war production. The agency was helped in its task by a reorganization of the general staff of the army into functional divisions with each under an experienced officer selected without regard to seniority. With the army and the WIB cooperating, the abundance of the country could now be funneled into the war effort.

As in agriculture and industry, so in fuel, transportation, and labor, peacetime practices faltered under the stress of war. To relieve the critical coal shortage, the Lever Act empowered the President to fix the price of coal high enough to encourage operators to work marginal mines. In August 1917 he established the Fuel Administration under Harry A. Garfield, president of Williams College. The agency set an attractive price for coal, and the resulting production was ample for the nation's needs. Snarls in railway transportation, however, impeded coal deliveries, and for four days in January 1918 Garfield closed all East Coast plants that used coal for any but vital purposes.

That emergency order underlined the crisis in railroading. The roads had tried to handle the extraordinary wartime traffic on the basis of voluntary cooperation, but in the absence of unified authority delays became worse and worse, and the snow and freezing weather of December 1917 precipitated a total collapse of internal transportation. With congressional approval, Wilson therefore established the United States Railway Administration under William G. McAdoo. Exercising an even greater authority than Baruch had over industry, McAdoo improved the railways' equipment, strengthened their finances, and successfully adjusted their operations to the demands of war.

Labor in wartime. In April 1918 the President created the National War Labor Board,

William G. McAdoo: railway administrator

which unified the various agencies that had been established to prevent labor disturbances and the attending losses in production. Under the joint chairmanship of former President Taft and Frank P. Walsh, a labor lawyer, the WLB heard more than twelve hundred cases and forestalled many strikes, but it lacked the information it needed to set labor policies for the entire country. To remedy that deficiency, Wilson in May 1918 appointed the War Labor Policies Board under Felix Frankfurter, a young law professor who had been the War Department's labor adviser. The WLPB surveyed national labor needs and practices and standardized wages and hours. At its recommendation, the President created the United States Employment Service, an agency that placed almost 4 million workers in essential war jobs.

While keeping the country free from serious strikes, the government's labor agencies and policies also advanced the peacetime objectives of social reformers and union-leaders. Industry hired more women, though by no means enough to satisfy the reasonable expectations of American feminists. Membership in the American Federation of Labor grew more than 50 percent, reaching over 3,200,000 by 1920. The government demanded an eight-hour day for war industry wherever it could and insisted on decent working conditions and living wages. Even though the cost of living rose 50 percent, booming wages and full employment permitted a gratifying increase of 20 percent in average *real* income. Though management groups hostile to labor were impatient with wartime controls, their profits were high. The overall experience demonstrated dramatically that enlightened federal labor policies could bring to the laboring force unprecedented comfort and personal dignity without damping business enterprise.

Indeed the wartime experience confirmed the insights of men like Herbert Croly (see p. 541). Working together in the emergency agencies, businessmen and public servants refined the techniques of organization and administration and applied them vigorously in the national interest. The organization of agriculture and labor proved to be as rewarding as the organization of industry, which had proceeded so much further during the days of peace. The wartime experience provided an efficient pattern for organizing a government beset by emergency.

War worker

Propaganda, public opinion, and civil liberties. This very increase in efficiency, however, gave some of the wartime agencies a dangerous authority over the minds of men. A week after war was declared, Wilson created the Committee on Public Information to mobilize public opinion. George Creel, chairman of the CPI, worked out with newspapermen a voluntary censorship that kept the public reasonably well informed while safeguarding sensitive information. He also hired hundreds of artists and writers to mount a propaganda campaign without precedent in American history.

The CPI stressed two major points. One argued, as Wilson did, that the United States was fighting only for freedom and democracy. The other maintained that the Germans were all Huns, diabolic creatures perpetrating atrocities in an effort to conquer the world for their lust and greed. The releases of the Creel committee intensified the unreasoning attitudes of a nation at war. They hinted that German spies had an ear to every wall. Often they carried antiunion overtones, labeling as treason all work stoppages, whatever their real cause. More often they implied that all dissent was unpatriotic and that pacifists and socialists had hidden sympathies for the enemy.

This propaganda helped to sell war bonds, combat absenteeism in the factories, and reconcile some doubters to the war. But the price was high. The attitudes the CPI encouraged were the same as those fostered by private vigilante groups like the National Protective Association, which cultivated a kind of war-madness. There were continual spy scares, witch hunts, even kangaroo courts that imposed harsh sentences of tar and feathers. The innocent victims were usually German-Americans or antiwar radicals. The orgy of hatred had its ridiculous as well as its outrageous side. Americans stopped playing German music and stopped teaching or speaking the German language; they called sauerkraut "liberty cabbage"; and in Cincinnati they even removed pretzels from the free-lunch counters of saloons.

It was essential, of course, to protect the country from espionage and sabotage, but wartime legislation and its administration exceeded reasonable bounds. The Espionage Act of 1917, which Wilson requested, provided penalties of up to twenty years in prison and a $10,000 fine for those who helped the enemy, obstructed recruiting, or incited rebellion within the armed services. One section gave the Postmaster General authority to deny the use of the mails to any publication that in his opinion advocated treason or forcible resistance to the laws. The Trading-with-the-Enemy Act, which Congress passed in October 1917, added sweeping authority to censor the foreign-language press.

In 1918 Congress went still further. The rising hysteria was stimulated by the demands of the Attorney General and by the violence of the syndicalists in the Industrial Workers of the World, who had tried to tie up copper production. Copying state statutes, Congress passed the Sabotage Act and the Sedition Act, which empowered the federal government to punish any expression of opinion that, regardless of whether or not it led to action, was "disloyal, profane, scurrilous or abusive" of the American form of government, flag, or uniform. Subsequent systematic persecution effectively destroyed the Wobblies.

The recklessness of Congress in stocking such an arsenal had its source in the frenzy of the people. Timid in the face of public opinion, state and federal officials and judges made a mockery of the right of freedom of speech and belief. Just as those administering the draft subjected conscientious objectors to needless humiliations, often imprisonment, so those administering the espionage, sedition, and other wartime laws made conformity a measure of loyalty. The mails were closed to publications whose only offense was a statement of socialism, a plea for feminism, or anti-British bias. Men were haled into court who had done no more than criticize the Red Cross or the financing of the war or who had merely declared that war was contrary to the teachings of Jesus Christ. Of over fifteen hundred arrests for sedition, only ten were alleged to be for actual sabotage. The government's own immoderation and its failure to control private vigilantes shocked men of good will and good sense, blemished the Administration's war record, and exaggerated passions that long outlived the crisis itself.

Politics in wartime. Those exaggerated passions sometimes found expression in partisan, sectional, and factional politics. Though Wilson expressed the wish that politics might be adjourned for the duration, wartime problems raised conflicts of interest and irresistible opportunities to pursue partisan advantages. The Republicans, determined to prevent the Dem-

ocrats from getting all the credit for American successes, criticized the conduct of the war. But that criticism, much of it valid, hurt the Democrats less than did the behavior of a few Southerners in key congressional posts who consistently voted against war legislation.

Southern agrarians and Western progressives demanded heavy income, inheritance, and excess-profits taxes to prevent war profiteering. Conservatives, in contrast, preferred federal borrowing and excise or sales taxes of various kinds. They argued that future generations should share the cost of a war fought in the national interest and that taxes on consumption would help check wartime inflation. The Administration took a sensible middle position. In all, the war cost about $33.5 billion, of which $10.5 billion was raised by taxes, the balance by Treasury borrowing. Secretary of the Treasury McAdoo had intended taxes to carry a larger share, but the soaring cost of the war upset his calculations. As it was, wartime taxes were heavier than they had ever been in the United States. The Revenue Act of October 1917 imposed new and larger excise and luxury taxes, a graduated excess-profits tax on business, and increased estate and personal income taxes. It raised the maximum surtax on income to 63 percent, and the Revenue Act of 1918 lifted it and the excess-profits tax still higher.

The revenue measures passed during the war established a truly progressive tax structure, which placed a heavy but equitable burden on those best able to carry it. They paid, but they also complained. And, especially in the Northeast, Republican politicians won middle-class support by contending that the agrarian Democrats were deliberately punishing the nation's industrial regions. By 1918 the tax issue was being hotly debated by moneyed men who had once supported less expensive progressive policies.

The Republicans also made gains among Midwestern farmers who had defected to the Democrats in 1916. The Lever Act empowered the Administration to control the price of wheat but not the price of cotton, and the Western farmers resented the larger profits of their Southern brethren and the Democratic votes in Congress that made those profits possible.

The Democratic coalition of 1916 was hurt by other issues as well. Southern votes were crucial in overriding Wilson's veto of an act of 1917 establishing a literacy test for immi-

Women, war, and the vote	*Suffragists are asking now for the passage of the Federal amendment as a war measure in order that this country may escape the charge that it has bargained with its women.... Suffrage for women is a part of the complete democracy so aptly named by Mr. Wilson as the object of this war. It is belittling to the government, not to the women of the country, to withhold grudgingly what it must ultimately give. The government ... must start about setting the world right for democracy by giving American women the franchise for democracy's sake.*

From *Women Citizen,* 1919.

grants. The urban laboring force found the Southerners' support of Prohibition even more exasperating. Advocates of the prohibition of the manufacture and consumption of alcoholic beverages had been gaining strength since 1900, and during the war they achieved their goal. First, a section of the Lever Act limited the production of whiskey and a section of the Selective Service Act limited its sale near army camps. Later, in December 1917, Congress adopted the Eighteenth Amendment—the Prohibition Amendment—and submitted it to the states for ratification (completed in January 1919).

Northern liberals, disturbed by the Administration's threats to civil liberties, were also irritated by Southern resistance to the woman-suffrage amendment, which senators from Dixie blocked to Wilson's disappointment. As he had learned from the suffragists, democratic principles included the right of women to vote. But only in January 1919 did Congress remove the injustice of limiting suffrage on the basis of sex. (Ratification followed in August 1920).

As the coalition of interests that had elected Wilson in 1916 fell apart, the Republicans effected a powerful reorganization of their party under the direction of their aggressive national chairman, Will Hays. They approached the elections of 1918 (see p. 565) with more confidence than they had had in a decade, and their campaign threatened not only Democratic control of Congress but the program for a liberal peace on which Wilson pinned his most fervent hopes.

Constructing the peace

A liberal program. During the war, sentiment for a liberal peace developed on both sides of the Atlantic, especially in England and the United States. The plans of various humanitarian groups differed in detail, but they usually advocated four common principles: the substitution of an international comity for the alliance system; the substitution of arbitration for armaments; the institution of self-government among all peoples; and the avoidance of seizures of territories and of demands for reparations.

Wilson embraced these objectives. In 1916 he publicly advocated the idea of a league of nations. In 1917 he began to meditate seriously on the components of a generous peace—a peace without victory. Soon after the United States declared war, he assigned the task of preparing detailed peace plans to Colonel House and a staff of experts. While they were at work, the President in a series of addresses spelled out his own goals, which reflected the principles that had previously characterized his New Freedom and his neutrality policies.

It was necessary, Wilson believed, to remove the military party, including the Kaiser, from authority in Germany, to divest Germany of power over other peoples, to establish democratic self-government in Germany and among each of the national groups rescued from her domination or the domination of her allies. It was necessary then to bring all nations into a world parliament whose collective democratic judgment would guard the peace. "Peace," he said, "should rest upon the rights of peoples, not the rights of governments—the rights of peoples great or small . . . to freedom and security and self-government and to . . . economic opportunities."

This grand vision underestimated the role of power in world affairs and the selfishness of nations torn by war. Even so, Wilson might have won commitments from the Allies to a liberal peace if he had tried. He did not. By his own choice the United States had fought not as one of the Allies but as an "associated" belligerent, with the others but not of them. This was the Administration's way of paying tribute to the questionable tradition of avoiding "entangling alliances." Wilson chose, too, to avoid facing squarely the punitive intentions of the Allies, intentions that they had recorded in secret treaties. He simply ignored the existence of those treaties, with their clauses providing for the division of German, Austrian, and Turkish territories and for the exaction of huge indemnities. Apparently he felt no need to insist that America would help the Allies only if they agreed to give up those plans.

The course of revolution in Russia focused the attention of the world on the problems of peace. After taking over the government in November 1917, the Bolsheviks began to arrange a separate and humiliating surrender to Germany. They also set out, in the midst of ruthless civil war, to solidify their hold at home and to advance the communist revolution elsewhere. In order to embarrass the Allies, they disclosed the terms of the secret treaties they found in the czar's archives. Both David Lloyd George, the British prime minister, and Wilson countered by reasserting their dedication to a just peace.

In January 1918, while the war was still raging, Wilson announced his celebrated Fourteen Points. Five were broad: open diplomacy, by which he meant an end to secret agreements; free use of the seas in peace and war; the reduction of armaments; the removal of barriers to free trade; and an impartial adjustment of colonial claims. Eight points pertained to the principle of national self-determination: German evacuation of Russian territory; the restoration of Belgian independence; the return to France of Alsace-Lorraine (which Germany had conquered in 1870); the establishment of an independent Poland; and the autonomous development of each of the peoples of Austria-Hungary and European Turkey. The fourteenth and crowning point called for forming "a general assembly of nations" to afford "mutual guarantees of political independence and territorial integrity."

Those objectives conflicted not only with the ambitions of the Allies but with the attitudes of many Americans. Though there was much enthusiasm for the President's ideals, there was also opposition from those who wanted protective tariffs, from those who resisted internationalism of any kind, and particularly from those whose war-born hatreds demanded revenge, a march on Berlin, and gallows for the Kaiser.

The armistice and the election of 1918.

The President was by no means soft. In October 1918, as the Allies drove through the German lines, the German high command urged the chancellor to propose an armistice to Wilson on the basis of the Fourteen Points. During the ensuing exchange of notes, Wilson took a position charitable enough to lead the Germans on, but firm enough to make them admit defeat. This satisfied all the Allied chiefs of state and military commanders except Pershing, who urged unconditional surrender. The British and French, exhausted by four years of war and frightened by the westward surge of Bolshevism, were eager for an armistice so long as it gave them security.

Aware of those views, Wilson demanded withdrawal of German forces from all invaded territory and immediate cessation of aerial and submarine warfare. When the Germans acceded to these conditions, which were designed to make renewed hostilities impossible, Wilson on October 23 opened negotiations with the Allies and suggested to the Germans that reasonable terms would depend on their establishing a democratic government. This suggestion precipitated the overthrow of the Kaiser, who abdicated on November 9.

The Allied leaders chafed at the Fourteen Points; the British explicitly rejected the point on the freedom of the seas, and the French demanded reparations for civilian damages. They would have insisted on further changes had Colonel House not threatened to make a separate peace if they did not assent to the rest of the Fourteen Points, which were to be the basis for an armistice. The Americans for their part ultimately agreed to add terms forcing the Germans to withdraw well beyond the east bank of the Rhine and to surrender vast quantities of war materials, including their submarines.

Those were tough conditions. But even so the Republicans attacked the President's foreign policy, insisting, as Roosevelt put it, on dictating peace to the hammer of guns instead of to the clicking of typewriters. This demagoguery frightened many Democratic leaders who, with a congressional election coming on, were tempted to seek votes by flag-waving. But Wilson refused to let politics interfere with his carefully devised program. He yielded, however, to his advisers' demand for a blanket endorsement of all Democratic candidates. Angry himself at the onslaughts of men like Roosevelt, Wilson on October 25 urged the people to vote Democratic if they approved of his policies at home and abroad. The return of a Republican majority, he said, would be a repudiation of his leadership.

This appeal made Wilson's foreign policy more than ever a partisan issue. It infuriated the Republicans, and though it helped some Democratic candidates it did not prevent the Republicans from gaining control of both houses of Congress. The Republicans profited from many issues, but their leaders later claimed that it was foreign policy that had determined the outcome. On November 11, 1918, only a few days after the election, men of all parties rejoiced at the news that an armistice had been arranged. Now, as Wilson turned to negotiating the terms for peace, he had to reckon with a Republican majority in the Senate, where partisanship could delay or even prevent approval of any treaty he submitted.

Negotiating peace

The background of the Paris conference. Wilson failed to appoint any influential Republican to the American delegation preparing to leave for the peace conference at Paris. To advance his liberal program he chose to head the delegation himself, thus becoming the first President to go overseas on a diplomatic mission. Though his critics complained that he would slight his duties at home, his able performance at Paris justified his decision. Wilson named to the delegation Secretary of State Lansing and Colonel House, in his view obvious choices, and two others: General Tasker H. Bliss, a military expert, and Henry White, a career diplomat, ostensibly a Republican but in no sense a politician or a representative of the Senate. The delegation was to be Wilson's instrument, under his domination, but any advantage this control gave him during negotiations was overshadowed by the disadvantages inherent in slighting the Republicans.

Wilson also slighted public opinion. He had little talent for dealing with journalists, many of whom distrusted his official press representative, George Creel. Moreover, at the peace conference he had to yield to the other negotiators' insistence on secret sessions. The American press interpreted this decision as a violation of the principle of open diplomacy, even though there was no secret about the decisions reached at the conference. If Wilson's press relations had been better, American newspapers could have helped explain the President's difficulties to a public that did not fully understand the necessity for give-and-take.

Wilson had to bargain endlessly with the Allies, for their objectives often conflicted with his. He felt strongly that the Fourteen Points should be accepted as guides for the peace settlement. He did not expect a perfect peace, but he thought that a league of nations could continually improve the terms of a peace treaty, and he counted on enlisting the moral force of the world behind the league. His optimism grew during his tour of Europe before the conference opened. Crowds greeted him as a savior, and he mistook their gratitude for victory as an endorsement of his goals.

Actually, the peoples of Europe and Asia, with unimportant exceptions, supported the demands of their own spokesmen. Four of these men were, with Wilson, the major architects of the peace. There was the inscrutable and resourceful Count Nobuaki Makino of Japan, ambitious for territory, as was the cultured and adroit Vittorio Orlando of Italy; there was the perspicacious but shifty British prime minister, David Lloyd George, who has promised his electorate vast reparations; there was the French premier, Georges Clemenceau, cynical, tenacious, weary, aloof, determined to crush Germany forever. These men were bound by treaties to support one another's claims. Their armies, moreover, actually held most of the lands they planned to annex or assign.

Over large parts of the world neither they nor Wilson could exercise much influence. The Bolshevik Revolution had made Russia unwelcome at the conference, and she stood apart brooding, dissatisfied, a mighty and ominous force. There was, furthermore, continuing war within her borders while the peace conference sat. British troops in the northern

Dover, England: crowds greeted Wilson as a savior

part of European Russia were trying to assist anti-Bolsheviks there, and in Siberia a Japanese army was pushing west with an eye to conquest. In order to keep watch on them the United States also sent troops to Siberia. The Bolsheviks, resenting the presence of foreigners, believed the Japanese and the Americans were agents of counterrevolution, as some authorities in Washington, London, and Tokyo intended them to be.

Revolution and counterrevolution infected all of Russia's European neighbors. The empire of Austria-Hungary had simply ceased to exist. In the territories it once had ruled, the quarrels of self-conscious ethnic groups, complicated by the conniving of communists, were forging the new states that were to speckle the map of central and eastern Europe whether the men at Paris willed it or not. Within Germany the new republican government faced revolution at the borders, Red plots within, and a populace exasperated by a food shortage imposed by the continuing Allied blockade. With the world in turmoil and Europe exhausted by war, the Paris conference had an unpropitious setting. With the Allies opposed to a liberal peace, moreover, the odds against Wilson's program were enormous.

The League of Nations. Wilson's plans for a charter for a league of nations included the disposition of former German colonies. In order to bring about an impartial and equitable settlement of colonial claims, as the Fourteen Points promised, Wilson hoped to put the German colonies under the guardianship of small neutrals like Switzerland and Sweden. These neutrals were to be trustees for the league and were to help the backward colonial peoples to move toward independence.

The British and Japanese, however, would not surrender the territory in Africa and the Pacific that they had seized during hostilities. According to a secret treaty between them, German islands in the Pacific north of the equator were to go to Japan and islands south of the equator were to go to Australia and New Zealand. Wilson prevented the outright transfer of colonies by persuading the Allies to accept instead a system of "mandates," which obliged their holders to render annual accountings and theoretically to help subject peoples to stand alone. The compromise gave the Allies a pocketful of territory, but it also subjected them to some surveillance in their administration of that territory. Though the mandate system was imperfect, Wilson felt that the league would gradually better it.

Yet the concepts of a league met opposition from the French, who wanted a military alliance of the victors against Germany. Japan further complicated Wilson's negotiations by demanding a statement of racial equality pledging member nations of a league not to discriminate against the nationals of other members. But the President had help from the Italians, who were pleased by his endorsement of the northern boundary they wanted, and from the British, who shared his hopes for the league. The racial pride of the Japa-

Fear of the League *This treaty ... imperils what I conceive to be the underlying, the very first principles of this Republic. It is in conflict with the right of our people to govern themselves free from all restraint, legal or moral, of foreign powers.... Next to the tie which binds a man to his God is the tie which binds a man to his country, and all schemes, all plans, however ambitious and fascinating they seem in their proposal, but which would embarrass or entangle and impede or shackle her sovereign will, which would compromise her freedom of action I unhesitatingly put behind me.*

Since the debate opened months ago those of us who have stood against this proposition have been taunted many times with being little Americans. Leave us the word American, keep that in your presumptuous impeachment, and no taunt can disturb us, no gibe discompose our purposes.

From William E. Borah, Speech in the United States Senate, November 1919.

nese was assuaged by their new mandates, and the French accepted the idea of a league after they realized that they could obtain their objectives elsewhere in the treaty. Wilson in return let the French and British dodge the question of self-disarmament. In the end his draft served as the basis for the Covenant of the League of Nations, which the responsible committee approved and reported to the peace conference in February 1919.

It was a simple document. Each signer of the treaty was to have one vote in a Body of Delegates of the League. Larger authority rested with the Executive Council, which was to consist of representatives from the United States, the British Empire, France, Italy, Japan, and four states selected by the Body of Delegates. Decisions of the council required a unanimous vote except when a council member was itself a party to a dispute. The covenant also established a permanent secretariat, an international Bureau of Labor, and the mandate system. It provided for the admission of new members by a two-thirds vote of the delegates and for amendment by a three-fourths vote.

The main purpose of the League was to keep the peace. To that end the covenant obliged signatories, before they resorted to war, to submit disputes either to inquiry by the council or to arbitration by the Permanent Court of International Justice which the council was to create. Member nations were to punish any breach of this article by severing economic relations with the offending state. The council, moreover, might recommend that members of the League contribute mili-

tary and naval units to protect its principles. And the council was to advise on means of ensuring that member nations lived up to Article 10, which Wilson considered the heart of the covenant. This article bound signatories "to respect and preserve against external aggression the territorial integrity and . . . political independence of all members of the League."

The League was not a superstate. It could only recommend, but not compel, the recruitment and use of military force. Its deliberations would not bind Germany or Russia until the victorious powers invited them to join. Those powers had sufficient authority, moreover, to use the League to try to perpetuate the status quo. But the covenant did create the first promising international organization in modern history. It also fulfilled Wilson's purpose of recognizing war and the threat of war as everybody's business and of providing a forum for the nations of the world to discuss problems that might lead to conflict. In his view, the covenant organized the moral force of the world.

Consequently the President was distressed by the opposition to the League that he confronted during a brief trip home. The essence of that opposition was Republican partisanship, but it fed on other attitudes as well. Many German-Americans still resented the war and its outcome. Many Irish-Americans believed Wilson should have insisted on Irish independence. The President pointed out that that was a question for England to resolve, but he was pointedly cool toward his Irish critics. He was even less patient with those Americans

America is going to grow more and more powerful; and the more powerful she is the more inevitable it is that she should be trustee for the peace of the world.... All Europe knew that we were doing an American thing when we put the Covenant of the League of Nations at the beginning of the treaty.... The most cynical men I had to deal with ... before our conferences were over ... all admitted that the League of Nations, which they had deemed an ideal dream, was a demonstrable, practical necessity. This treaty cannot be carried out without the League of Nations....

The rest of the world is necessary to us, if you want to put it on that basis. I do not like to put it on that basis. That is not the American basis. America does not want to feed upon the rest of the world. She wants to feed it and serve it. America ... is the only national idealistic force in the world, and idealism is going to save the world.... That is the program of civilization.

From Woodrow Wilson, Speech at Helena, Montana, November 1919.

Need for the League

---

who hesitated to depart from what to them was a national tradition of isolation from Europe. They thought of the past as having been sterilized from the Old World, and they viewed the covenant as an "entangling alliance." These and other sentiments bred susceptibility to the propaganda of Wilson's opponents.

On March 4, 1919, the day before the President returned to Paris, Senator Henry Cabot Lodge produced a round robin signed by thirty-seven Republican senators, four more than were needed to defeat the treaty. It stated that the covenant was unacceptable and insisted that consideration of the League be deferred until after a treaty had been completed. In a speech that night, Wilson condemned the "careful selfishness" of his critics and their "ignorance of the state of the world." The covenant would be intimately tied to the treaty itself, he said. That interrelationship was essential for working out the problems of the conference, and the President was understandably annoyed. But his strong language intensified the partisanship that provoked it.

The Treaty of Versailles. Though Wilson would not separate the League from the treaty, he realized that the covenant would have to be modified to meet the suggestions of American moderates. The revisions the President sponsored on his return to Paris would certainly have been demanded by the Senate in any event. They defined procedures for withdrawal from the League, stated that

the acceptance of mandates was optional, and excluded from the purview of the League domestic issues such as immigration and regional agreements such as the Monroe Doctrine. By reopening the question of the covenant, however, Wilson exposed himself to the bargaining of his associates, who once more pressed their demands for Europe and Asia. The President secured his revisions, but only at an inflated price.

Clemenceau, still determined to assure French security, insisted that Germany be dismembered. He urged that two new states, Poland and Czechoslovakia, be set up on Germany's eastern border. Both states would absorb some German land and population. He also asked for the creation of a Rhenish buffer state, to be splintered off from Germany's west, and for the cession to France of the Saar Basin, a bountiful source of coal and iron, as well as of Alsace-Lorraine. Wilson balked at these extreme demands and argued that the League itself would protect France from German aggression. Clemenceau scoffed and called the President pro-German. For ten days the conference stalled. Early in April Wilson cabled for the *George Washington* to stand by to take him home. This threat to depart, though perhaps petulant, was effective, for Clemenceau bowed to the proponents of compromise.

The treaty drew generous boundaries for Poland and Czechoslovakia, but it also arranged for the League to conduct a plebiscite to determine the disposition of a part of Silesia coveted by both Germans and Poles. To give Poland access to the sea, the treaty drew a

Europe in 1920

narrow corridor through Germany that put some Germans under Polish rule, but Danzig, the port within the corridor, was made a free city under League supervision. France received Alsace-Lorraine and temporary economic concessions in the Saar, but the League was to administer the Saar and after fifteen years was to conduct a plebiscite there. France could also occupy the Rhineland for fifteen years; after that time the area was to be demilitarized but left a part of Germany. The German army was limited to a token force of one hundred thousand.

Furthermore, Wilson and Lloyd George agreed to a special security treaty pledging their nations to assist France if she were attacked. Clemenceau realized, even if Wilson did not, that the United States Senate would reject the special treaty, but in that case the Rhineland could be occupied indefinitely. All in all, Clemenceau obtained as much safety for France as any treaty could reasonably provide.

The French and the English also pushed Wilson into accepting their demands for reparations far in excess of what Germany could pay and in violation of the prearmistice agreement to limit payments to the cost of civilian damages. The President let the Allies include the cost of pensions, which later permitted the reparations commission to calculate that the Germans owed some $120 billion, the fantastic figure that had been the British objective. The reparations clause of the treaty, moreover, specifically attributed the cause of war to "the aggression of Germany," a phrase that rankled in German minds for years to come, however accurate it may have been. Along with the economic dislocations that were bound to grow out of the exorbitant reparations imposed on Germany, the war-guilt clause proved to be an emotional threat to future peace.

At the time, however, the President's troubles with Italy seemed more ominous. Before the conference Wilson had agreed to a northern frontier for Italy at the line of the Brenner Pass, which put two hundred thousand Austrians under Italian rule. This left him with nothing left to trade when the Italians also insisted on taking Fiume, an Adriatic port surrounded by Yugoslav land. When the Italians discovered that all the powers were antagonistic to their claim to Fiume, they boldly marched into the city. Wilson appealed to the Italian people in the name of justice, but they, with their leaders, resented the President's miscalculated intrusion. The Italians left Paris in a rage, and, though they returned to sign a treaty that did not give them Fiume, the incident confirmed the Italians in their pursuit of deceitful diplomacy, alienated Italian-Americans from Wilson's treaty, and almost disrupted the conference.

The Japanese seized on the confusion to advance their own claims. They were seeking endorsement for their economic ambitions in China and for their assumption of the German leasehold at Kiaochow and of German economic privilege in the Shantung Peninsula. The Chinese, of course, opposed the whole program, which Japan's secret treaties with France and England condoned. Furthermore, late in 1917 Secretary of State Lansing had reached an understanding with Viscount Kikujiro Ishii by which Japan affirmed her support of the Open Door and of China's territorial integrity; but in return the United States recognized Japan's special interest in Chinese provinces adjoining Japanese possessions. Since Shantung was just such a province, Wilson found it hard to oppose the Japanese demands, especially after the whole confer-

ence seemed about to disintegrate. He accepted a compromise that by and large restricted the Japanese to former German holdings, less Kiaochow, which Japan promised to surrender. Though many Americans, including two of the delegates, thought the President conceded too much, he felt he had obtained a solution ''as satisfactory as could be got out of the tangle.''

The same could be said of the whole treaty that the victors and the vanquished signed at Versailles in 1919. It was punitive, but Germany had lost the war she had expected to win, and the Allies were much less severe than she would have been. The treaty followed the Fourteen Points as closely as world conditions permitted. Wilson had conceded little, if anything, more than he had to. Europe had a new map that approximated ethnic groupings as closely as possible. This, to be sure, involved some compromises of the principle of self-determination and created some boundaries that conflicted with the military defense and the economic needs of the new states. But these difficulties and others could be negotiated later in the forum of the League. As Wilson had predicted, the League was inextricably part of the treaty, a ''convenient, indeed indispensable'' instrument. He had yet, however, to bring two-thirds of the Senate over to his way of thinking.

The struggle over ratification

The Senate and the treaty. Wilson brought the treaty home to a people initially predisposed in its favor. Though few Americans were familiar with the whole long document, most had learned something about the League, and millions were enthusiastic about it. But the people could not vote on the treaty. The question of its approval, and therefore the portentous question of what direction American foreign policy would take, were for the Senate to debate and decide.

Of the ninety-six senators forty-nine were Republican, but only fourteen were irreconcilably against the League and the treaty. The other thirty-five were resolved to Republicanize Wilson's work. They intended not to reject the treaty but to make its adoption contingent on a number of reservations, of which the most significant had to do with Wilson's League of Nations. Twenty-three Republicans favored a list of strong reservations drafted

and sponsored by Senator Lodge; twelve were willing to settle for milder reservations. Since only four of the forty-seven Democrats opposed the treaty, a coalition of Democrats and moderate Republicans would have commanded a majority vote. And a majority was all that was needed to settle the kind of reservations that would be demanded. Such a coalition, moreover, could probably have attracted the necessary two-thirds vote for approval. But the crucial coalition was never formed.

The Democratic leaders knew they had to make concessions to their opponents, but they felt that they also had to wait for instructions from the President. They never received those instructions, for Wilson refused to compromise an issue he considered both personal and moral.

It was Lodge who had made the issue personal. Lodge had endorsed the round robin and the strategy of insisting on reservations; Lodge had packed the important Foreign Relations Committee with irreconcilables and strong reservationists. Lodge, the majority leader of the Senate, was determined to hold his party together and to win in 1920. Further, he honestly believed that the League as Wilson had planned it was a threat to national sovereignty. He put his faith in armies and navies and the balance of power, the "large view" of his old friend Theodore Roosevelt, who had just died. A ruthless, often exasperating man, Lodge was also moved by mean considerations, including the prejudices of his many Italian- and Irish-American constituents. He was a formidable antagonist who hated Wilson as Wilson hated him.

Lodge's reservations struck the President as unnecessary and immoral. Wilson objected to the very idea of making the approval of the treaty subject to reservations. He also held that reservations would mean that the treaty would have to be renegotiated, though the British, the French, and the State Department did not think so. Two of the reservations would have made Congress the sole judge of whether the United States should accept a mandate and whether it should withdraw from the League. Two others reserved to the United States exclusive authority over tariff policy, immigration, and the Monroe Doctrine. Wilson argued that the revised covenant already covered those issues. Another reservation exempted the United States from any decision of the League on which any member and its self-governing dominions had cast in the aggregate more than one vote. The American veto in the council, Wilson noted, made superfluous such an ungracious protest against the seats of the British dominions in the Body of Delegates. The President especially opposed the reservation on Article 10, which stated that the United States would assume no obligation to preserve the territorial integrity or political independence of any other country without the approval of Congress. To Wilson this would be a violation of the essential spirit of the League—the moral obligation to protect the peace of the world.

In the abstract Wilson may have been right, but the politics of the Senate made compromise necessary. Even if Lodge's reservations did make the United States seem timid and selfish, they would have damaged the League far less than would outright rejection of treaty and League alike. Senator Gilbert Hitchcock,

the Democratic minority leader, advised Wilson to work out some sort of compromise with Lodge, as did Colonel House, Robert Lansing, Bernard Baruch, and many other friends of the President.

But Wilson would not listen, and his personal efforts to persuade individual Republicans to adopt his point of view were futile. Moreover, as the days passed, the public tended to become bored with the whole question and amenable to Lodge's purpose. Wilson had advocated a degree of national involvement in foreign affairs greater, in all probability, than most Americans, after reflection, were willing to accept. And their willingness gradually shrank. The idealism of wartime was fading into the problems of the postwar period. Inflation, unemployment, and fears of Bolshevism deprived Wilson of the public enthusiasm for a generous peace and for a genuine internationalism on which he had relied.

The President's collapse. In order to arouse new enthusiasm for the League, Wilson set out in September 1919 on a speaking tour across the country. He hoped to stir up a passion for his program that the Republican senators would not be able to withstand. His train moved through the strongholds of isolationism, over eight thousand miles, stopping thirty-seven times for him to address the voters. As he proceeded through the Middle West to the Pacific Coast, then south, and then east, he was greeted by larger and larger crowds. But their applause did not change one vote in the Senate. Indeed Wilson's attacks on his opponents stiffened their resolution to resist, and his absence from Washington impeded Democratic efforts to find a basis for compromise. The President was superbly eloquent but his strenuous efforts taxed his limited strength without achieving his political purpose.

On September 25 Wilson spoke at Pueblo, Colorado. That night his head hurt mercilessly. Frightened by the President's exhaustion, his physician canceled the remainder of the trip. Back in Washington Wilson was too tired to work, too tense to rest. On October 2 he fell to the floor unconscious, the victim of a cerebral thrombosis, a blood clot in his brain.

The stroke did not kill the President, but it paralyzed his left side, thickened his speech, totally disabled him for almost two months, and prevented him thereafter from working more than an hour or two at a time. For six months he did not meet with the Cabinet. For six weeks he could not execute the minimum duties of his office. Though his mind was not injured, he became petulant, suspicious, and easily moved to tears. He was unable to assess men or situations with accuracy. His collapse was a tragedy not only for himself but for a nation facing a momentous crisis in foreign policy.

On November 6, while Wilson was still bedridden, Lodge presented his reservations to the Senate. It was obvious that the Republicans had the votes to adopt them but not the two-thirds needed to approve the treaty after the reservations had been attached. The Democratic leaders hesitated to move without the President's consent, and he gave stringent orders on November 18 that they were to reject the treaty so long as it was shackled by the Lodge reservations. They were then to move that the treaty be accepted either as it stood or with mild interpretive reservations of which Wilson approved. This order conceded nothing to the Republican moderates, who stood behind Lodge. Though nonpartisan friends of the League preferred accepting Lodge's reservations to rejecting the whole treaty, the Democrats on November 19 voted to reject the treaty with those reservations. Consequently the resolution to adopt the treaty as Lodge had modified it failed by 39 to 55. Lodge blocked debate of the interpretive reservations that the Democrats then proposed, and minutes later a resolution to approve the unamended treaty also failed, 38 to 53.

The final rejection. But the treaty was still not dead. The moderate Republicans and the Democrats were stunned by what they had done and felt they had to try again. Furthermore, organizations representing some 20 million Americans petitioned for compromise and ratification. The same hope was voiced by the British and French press and by the British government. Influential Democrats without exception tried to persuade the President to relieve his party of the hopeless battle to defeat the Lodge reservations.

But Wilson, the victim of fantasies produced by ill health, would still not hear of concessions. Instead, on January 8, 1920, he wrote a blistering letter to his fellow Democrats. The majority of the people wanted ratification, he said. Let the Senate accept the treaty without

tampering with it or else reject it. If there was any doubt about public opinion, Wilson warned, the issue could be resolved at the next election, which would be "a great and solemn referendum."

This was the counsel of a deluded man, for presidential elections turn on many issues, not just one. The Democratic party had been losing strength for three years, and the treaty, if the Senate rejected it again, would be impossible to resuscitate. Recognizing the folly of Wilson's position, Senator Hitchcock and other Democrats tried to work out a satisfactory compromise on the reservations. They failed, partly because the Republican irreconcilables warned Lodge against compromise, partly because Lodge himself probably did not want to rescue the treaty. The President, increasingly peevish, on March 8 again instructed the Democrats to hold the line.

His adherents prevailed. The Lodge reservations, only slightly modified, were adopted, this time with some Democratic help. On March 19, the day of the final test, half the Democrats voted to approve the treaty with the reservations. But twenty-three Democrats, twenty of them Southerners, did the President's bidding. Together with twelve irreconcilables, they voted against approval and thus prevented by a margin of seven the two-thirds majority needed for adoption.

There was to be no "solemn referendum." The Democratic presidential nominee in 1920, James M. Cox, supported the League, but sometimes with hesitation. The Republican plank on the treaty was deliberately vague, as was the Republican candidate, Warren G. Harding. Though Harding enjoyed the full support of both Republican isolationists and Republican internationalists, he chose to consider his smashing victory a repudiation of the treaty.

The Senate had made the telling decision. In rejecting both treaty and League, the Senate had for the while turned America's back to Europe. The rejection destroyed the best available chance for developing world peace. Perhaps the irreconcilables, the forceful spokesmen of isolation, could have defeated the treaty in any event, but it was not they who did so, though they helped. Wilson's stubbornness and Lodge's partisanship helped even more. Indeed partisanship was the real culprit, and the outcome of the fight revealed how severely domestic politics could damage foreign policy.

The fight over the League: internationalism or imperialism?

The damage, in the end, affected the whole world, for without the United States the League became an instrument for preserving the status quo. It never had a chance to fulfill Wilson's vision. That vision, which rested on the moral intent of the President's peace program, was the most compelling image democracy could offer to the world. With the defeat of the treaty, a great democracy seemed to have renounced its persuasive claims to the imagination of men everywhere.

And its renunciation came just at the time when Bolshevism was advancing its revolutionary claims more effectively than ever before. The American retreat opened the way for both the advocates of reaction and the advocates of communism. It cost the United States the true fruits of a gallant victory. It left her allies unchecked to use the League as they would, for their own ends. It made a travesty of the noble effort to create a world safe for the democracy Americans cherished.

Transition from war

Demobilization. When the war ended, the government had no plans for demobilization. It simply lifted the controls it had imposed on the economy during the war. In accord with public sentiment, it hastened the discharge of the soldiers, many of whom were unable to find jobs when they returned to civilian life. Though unemployment declined after February 1919, it persisted in troubled areas for another half-year, and it soured thousands of veterans who had expected a hero's welcome to include a job.

Immediately after the armistice the War Industries Board began to close up shop, confident that private industry would be able to switch back to a peacetime economy with no help or direction from the federal government. That was a miscalculation. While industry bid for new plants and machinery, consumers dug out their wartime savings to make the purchases they had long postponed. Inflation struck the country. During 1919 the cost of living climbed 77 percent above prewar levels; during 1920, another 28 percent.

The government developed only piecemeal and inadequate remedies for unemployment and inflation. There was as yet no body of economic ideas to explain the need for overall federal policies that would ease the process of reconversion. Wilson, moreover, was preoccupied with peacemaking and hampered by an opposition Congress. Yet the Revenue Act of 1919 carried on the policy of progressive taxation, ensured the government the income it needed, and helped check inflation.

Both Congress and the public were anxious to settle the question of what should be done with the railroads, which the government was still running. Private management wanted them back, but labor had found that public administration was more generous and more efficient. An attorney for the railway brotherhoods, Glenn E. Plumb, proposed a plan for nationalizing the roads. The AFL supported the Plumb plan, but elsewhere it evoked little enthusiasm. Congress, in the Transportation Act of 1920, extended the tradition of mixed capitalism by turning the railroads back to their private owners while subjecting them to increased but deliberately benign supervision. In a similar spirit, the Water Power Act of 1920 set up a Federal Power Commission, consisting of the Secretaries of War, Agriculture, and the Interior, to license the building and operation of dams and hydroelectric plants. This clumsy arrangement by its very failure drew attention to the need for genuine public control.

Labor strife. In the years right after the war, the once-progressive fervor of Americans seemed to have spent itself. The nation's policy-makers, like the American people, turned more and more to the past. The Administration, which had sympathized with organized labor for so long, now began to favor management. This policy reversal was prompted by several forces: Wilson's advisers were growing impatient with the strikes that continued to cripple the nation's industries; management had launched a successful campaign to associate all unions with radicalism; and the country at large was infected by an almost hysterical fear of radicalism in any form.

The enforced wartime truce between labor and management ended in 1919. The unions then set out to consolidate their gains and to bring wages into line with the rising cost of living. And the National Association of Manufacturers and other management groups set out to reestablish the open shop, which they

Rounding up strikers in Boston: Coolidge called out the national guard

liked to call "the American way." Management propaganda extolled the beneficence of business and warned that unions and union demands were inspired by foreign and radical influences. Nevertheless, many of the first strikes after the war were successful, notably those of clothing, textile, telegraph, and telephone workers.

The AFL faced its crucial test in the steel industry. Unfortunately it selected as secretary of its organizing committee William Z. Foster, whose record seemed to confirm management's charges of labor radicalism. Still, the steelworkers had grave grievances. Most of them put in a twelve-hour workday in return for subsistence wages. After attracting a substantial minority of workers, the union called a strike in September 1919, for management had rejected its demands for recognition, an eight-hour day, and decent pay. Episodes of violence punctuated the strike. Public opinion, misled by the steel companies' propaganda, condoned the widespread use of state and federal troops to prevent picketing. United States Steel alone used thousands of strikebreakers. In January 1920 the union gave up, thoroughly beaten.

Meanwhile, in November 1919 the bituminous-coal miners had walked out under the leadership of their new and colorful president, John L. Lewis, who was radical only in his pugnacious manner. A wartime agreement had governed wages in the mines, but the union claimed that the armistice had made that agreement inapplicable. As Lewis observed, there was no ceiling on the rising price

of coal. The miners demanded a 60 percent wage increase, a six-hour day, and a five-day week. When the operators refused to negotiate, the miners prepared to strike. With Wilson's approval, Attorney General A. Mitchell Palmer ruled that the wage agreement was still in effect and obtained an injunction against the union. Lewis then called off the strike because, as he put it, "we cannot fight the government." Still the miners refused to go back to work until the government ordered an immediate 14 percent increase in pay and set up an arbitral commission, which ultimately awarded another 27 percent. The miners' other demands were denied.

The most celebrated postwar strike had run its course two months earlier. The Boston police found that they could not stretch their prewar wages to cover postwar living costs. Denied a raise and restive because of other grievances, they secured a charter from the AFL and threatened a strike in August 1919. The mayor appointed a citizens' committee, which suggested that most of the policemen's demands, except recognition of their union, be granted. The police commissioner, however, a declared enemy of organized labor, rejected the suggestion and fired nineteen of the union's leaders. On September 9 the policemen went out on strike. Volunteer vigilantes were unable to control the gangs of looters who brought Boston to the point of anarchy. The American middle class was shocked and scared. But just then the governor of Massachusetts, Calvin Coolidge, called out the national guard to restore order.

The strike failed, and many of the police were dismissed.

The whole episode was as unnecessary as it was lamentable. Coolidge could have supported the mayor and overruled the police commissioner before the strike began. The police for their part permitted their frustrations to overcome their professional obligation to protect the city. Certainly there was nothing in the episode for anyone to be proud of. Coolidge, however, won a national reputation by putting down the strike. The American people knew little about the facts of the case, but they long remembered the governor's somewhat irrelevant response to Gompers' request that the policemen be reinstated: "There is no right to strike against the public safety by anybody, anywhere, any time."

Race hatred. Old prejudices, whetted by new fears, provoked a wave of persecution and violence that engulfed American blacks. In response to wartime labor shortages, several hundred thousand blacks had moved from the South to Northern industrial centers. Segregated there in urban slums, they were the continuing objects of the race hatred of their white neighbors, especially of unskilled immigrants who viewed blacks as competitors for their jobs. More and more blacks, for their part, educated by the experience of military service, by the war's avowedly democratic aims, and by the inequities they met in the North, began to demand rights long denied them, particularly higher wages, equal protection under the law, and the chance to vote and hold political office. Those were key goals of the increasingly militant National Association for the Advancement of Colored People and of its foremost leader, W. E. B. DuBois. Yet white supremacists were determined "to keep the Negro in his place," by force if necessary, and many of them applauded irresponsible statements of men like Congressman James F. Byrnes of South Carolina, who warned that the Reds were inciting a black uprising in the South.

Turning to terrorism, lynch mobs in the South made victims of more than seventy blacks in 1919, ten of them veterans in uniform. The new Ku Klux Klan (see p. 594), committed to the intimidation of blacks, gained some one hundred thousand members. In 1919 South and North alike saw the worst spate of race riots in American history to that time. Two of the most tragic occurred in Washington, D.C., where a majority of the offenders were white veterans, and in Chicago, where for thirteen days a mob of whites rampaged through the black slums. Before the year ended, twenty-five race riots had resulted in hundreds of deaths and injuries and millions of dollars of property damage.

Many blacks resisted their attackers, as the NAACP advised them to, and liberal whites organized to fight intolerance and to lobby for antilynching laws, but most blacks were neither hopeful of remedy nor yet ready to campaign in their own behalf. Instead, by 1923 about half a million blacks had joined the Universal Negro Improvement Association of Marcus Garvey, a Jamaican black nationalist who proposed to create a new empire in Africa with himself on the throne. That wild scheme collapsed, but its transient appeal to American blacks rested on the need they felt for self-identity, racial pride, and an escape from a society that denied them dignity, opportunity, and even personal safety.

The Red scare. American radicals also felt the sting of old prejudices and new fears. There was, to be sure, genuine cause for concern over the spread of Bolshevism in Europe. In March 1919 Soviet leaders organized the Third International as an agency for world revolution, and during the rest of that year the communists made striking gains in Germany, Hungary, and along Russia's frontiers. The International fed on the postwar disintegration of eastern Europe—a disintegration the United States did little to check.

Within the United States, however, communism was feeble. In 1919 the Socialist party, its ranks depleted and its morale low, broke into three factions. Some forty thousand moderates retained the old name. One left-wing faction of about twenty thousand, almost all of them immigrants, formed the Communist Labor party. Another militant group of between thirty thousand and sixty thousand, also largely immigrant, joined the Communist party of America under native-born leaders. Some of these leaders—John Reed, a successful journalist and former Harvard cheerleader, for one—made a good deal of noise, but the three groups together constituted less than half of 1 percent of the population.

During the war public and private propaganda had generated hatred and fear of the Germans, and Americans had already begun to fight the shadows of their anxieties. In the postwar months they transferred much of this hate to the nation's immigrants, whom the suspicious middle class had long stereotyped as radical. Hysteria reached pathological proportions under the influence of business propaganda that branded all labor as radical, under the spur of politicians who exploited the mood of the nation for their own advantage, and under the stimulus of sporadic episodes of violence.

There were early outbreaks of hysteria in February 1919, when the Seattle Central Labor Council called a general strike to support shipyard-workers who had walked out in quest of higher pay and shorter hours. Some of the Seattle labor-leaders were unquestionably radical, and a general strike was itself a radical technique. But Mayor Ole Hanson grossly exaggerated the Red menace and used troops to stamp out the strike.

Scare headlines and legislative investigations of alleged Red activity kept the public edgy. In April the handiwork of a few lunatic radicals created near-panic when bombs were mailed to Mayor Hanson, Senator Thomas W. Hardwick of Georgia, and thirty-six other eminent citizens, including John D. Rockefeller, Justice Holmes, the Postmaster General, and the Attorney General. The Post Office intercepted all the bombs except one, which wounded Hardwick's maid. In June there were several direct bombings. One weapon exploded in front of the Washington home of Attorney General A. Mitchell Palmer, damaging the building and dismembering his would-be assassin, an Italian anarchist.

The bombings of April and June had been plotted by dangerous criminals. They were not, however, a part of communist strategy, for the leaders of international communism recognized that simple terror would be an ineffective weapon for overturning a strong capitalist state. But most Americans did not differentiate among radicalisms. They grew more frightened every day, and they saw Red on everything they feared or disliked.

The mood of the nation endorsed the witch hunts conducted by Attorney General Palmer. A Quaker, a progressive Democrat who had worked effectively for woman suffrage and labor reforms, an enthusiast for the League of Nations, Palmer had enjoyed a deserved reputation as a liberal until he took office in March 1919. Then he threw his department, especially the Federal Bureau of Investigation, into a strenuous campaign against aliens and radi-

cals. He may have been hoping to advance his candidacy for the Democratic presidential nomination in 1920. If so, he overreached himself. But he did succeed in violating the Anglo-American heritage of civil liberties.

Congress refused to pass a sedition bill that Palmer had drafted, but the Attorney General on his own authority ordered a series of raids beginning in November 1919. During the first raid his agents arrested 250 members of the Union of Russian Workers and beat many of them up, but the Justice Department could find cause to recommend that only 39 of them be deported. In December Palmer cooperated with the Labor Department in deporting 249 aliens to Russia, most of whom had committed no offense and were not communists. A nationwide raid on January 1, 1920, led to the arrest of some 6,000 people, many of whom were American citizens and noncommunists. They were herded into prisons and bull pens; some were seized on suspicion only, taken without warrants from their homes, and held incommunicado. The raids revealed no evidence of a grand plot. Nevertheless, few Americans spoke out against the highhanded tactics of the Attorney General, the chief legal officer of the United States.

His ambitions soaring, Palmer continued to warn the nation about Red plots. But the outbreak he predicted for May 1, 1920, failed to materialize, and gradually the public began to tire of his unfounded alarms. The tide of Bolshevism had started to recede in Europe, and Palmer and his imitators had made themselves ridiculous. They could, of course, also be ruthless, as was the New York legislature, which expelled five innocuous Socialists, all properly elected members of the Assembly. This travesty on the American elective system evoked sharp denunciations, the most influential from Charles Evans Hughes. By the summer of 1920 the Red scare was lagely over, the hysteria spent. In September Americans were horrified by a bomb explosion at the corner of Broad and Wall Streets in New York; but they accepted the episode for what it was, the work of a crazed individual, not the product of a Bolshevik conspiracy as Palmer maintained.

The Red scare left ugly scars. The constitutional rights of thousands of Americans had been violated. Hundreds of innocent people had been deported. Many states had enacted sedition laws even more extreme than those passed during the war. And there lingered a less strident but still pervasive nativism that in the years ahead was to condone the new Ku Klux Klan, an organization dedicated to the hatred of blacks, Catholics, Jews, and foreigners. Nativism set the stage for a major reversal of immigration policy, which had for so many decades kept the gates of America open to newcomers. In February 1921, over Wilson's veto, Congress passed a law limiting the number of immigrants in any year to 3 percent of the foreign-born of each national group who had been living in the United States in 1910. Even this restrictive quota, which just about choked off immigration from Asia and central and southern Europe, was later to be reduced (see p. 594).

Hatred of aliens and radicals made a mock-ery of justice in the celebrated case of two Italians, confessed anarchists, Nicola Sacco and Bartolomeo Vanzetti. They were arrested, tried, and convicted for murdering two employees of a shoe company in South Braintree, Massachusetts, during a payroll robbery in 1920. Yet there was no conclusive evidence against them, and they were condemned essentially for their language and their beliefs. The judge who conducted the trial referred to them privately as "those anarchist bastards." Many Boston patricians felt the same way, and most of them, including the presidents of Harvard and M.I.T., approved the decision to deny a retrial. Felix Frankfurter, the novelist John Dos Passos, the poet Edna St. Vincent Millay, and other defenders of justice tried for six years to save Sacco and Vanzetti, but they failed. The cause attracted attention throughout the world and engaged the hearts of men who were to provide liberal leadership in the years to come. But in 1927, when Sacco and Vanzetti were electrocuted, the wounds of the Red scare festered again. The forces of respectability and conformity and regression seemed to be united against justice and decency and democracy.

The election of 1920. The Red scare drained away the last vestiges of progressive zeal. Americans, weary of public matters great and small, withdrew to a private world of pleasure, entertainment, and sensationalism. The political parties reflected the nation's fatigue and selfishness. The confident Republicans met in Chicago to select their presidential nominee from a large group of aspirants, among whom probably the best known was General Leonard Wood, who claimed the mantle of Roosevelt and stood for nationalism, militarism, and hell fire for radicals. Senators Hiram Johnson of California and Robert La Follette of Wisconsin appealed to the outnumbered progressives, as did Herbert Hoover, who had announced that he would accept nomination.

The professionals who controlled the party machinery had plans of their own. They intended to name a candidate they could manage. After six ballots, the bosses met in the Blackstone Hotel suite of George Harvey, a New York editor, once a friend but now a bitter foe of Wilson. In this, the most celebrated of smoke-filled rooms, they arranged for the nomination to go to Senator Warren G. Harding of Ohio. The convention selected Harding on the tenth ballot, and then the delegates, ignoring the orders of the bosses, named Calvin Coolidge for Vice President.

Harding was a handsome, semieducated political hack with a modest talent for golf; a larger taste for women, liquor, and poker; a complaisant disposition; an utterly empty mind; and an enduring loyalty to the Republican creed of 1890. He was probably the least-qualified candidate ever nominated by a major party. His platform fitted his creed exactly. It promised lower taxes, a higher tariff, restriction of immigration, and—with opportunistic generosity—aid to farmers. It damned the League of Nations but called vaguely for an "agreement among nations to preserve the peace"—a phrase that made the isolationists

happy and that Harding's wordy speeches did nothing to clarify.

The Democrats were at odds with themselves. The failure of President Wilson, in spite of his illness, to disclaim ambition for the nomination impeded the candidacy of his son-in-law, William G. McAdoo, probably the ablest of the hopefuls. Attorney General Palmer had begun to run out of gas before the convention met. And in any event the Democratic bosses, almost as powerful as their Republican counterparts, wanted no candidate who was identified with the Wilson Administration. They preferred Governor James M. Cox of Ohio, a good vote-getter and an opponent of Prohibition.

After thirty-seven ballots Palmer released his delegates, but McAdoo still could not muster the necessary two-thirds vote; on the forty-fourth ballot the convention selected Cox. As his running mate, the delegates chose a young Wilsonian with a magic political name, Assistant Secretary of the Navy Franklin D. Roosevelt. The platform was pro-League (though it allowed for amendments to the covenant), in favor of tax reduction and Philippine independence, noncommittal about Prohibition, and otherwise undistinguished. So, except in contrast to Harding, was the Democratic candidate. Cox had about him a pleasant way, a certain prim yet persuasive manner, and a satisfactory record; but he also had a quality of littleness, at least in comparison with the national candidates of the preceding decade.

The movement toward the Republicans, still the normal majority party, had begun in 1918 (see p. 563), and it accelerated in 1920. Midwestern farmers, alienated by wartime controls, were now troubled by falling prices. Much of the once-progressive middle class had come to resent high taxes and labor strife. Urban Democrats of the North were suspicious of Southern "drys," and Irish-Americans were hostile toward Wilson's foreign policy. Many independents could not forgive Palmer his behavior or Wilson his sometimes open endorsement of it.

All these factors combined to produce a Republican "earthquake," as one Democrat put it. Harding received 61 percent of the popular vote, which now included women, carried every state outside the South and also Tennessee, and led Cox by 404 to 127 in the Electoral College. The Republicans also swept the congressional elections, obtaining a ma-

Sacco and Vanzetti: "You will kill the brave men"

jority of 22 in the Senate and 167 in the House of Representatives. Not only had the voters repudiated Wilson and internationalism; they had repudiated progressivism. They restored to power the Republicans who had stuck with the party when Roosevelt bolted in 1912. Harding, for all his limitations, had caught the purpose of his constituency when he called for a return to "not nostrums, but normalcy."

Normalcy

All the advantages. Harding, his Secretary of State, Charles Evans Hughes, and the Republican majority in the Senate quickly buried the issue of the Treaty of Versailles. In his first message to Congress the President stated that the United States would have nothing to do with the League of Nations, not even with its health program. Since the rejection of the treaty left the United States still technically at war with the Central Powers, the Senate passed again a resolution establishing a separate peace with Germany—a resolution that Wilson had vetoed. Harding signed it in July 1921, and Hughes then negotiated peace treaties with Germany, Austria, and Hungary. Like the resolution, these treaties claimed for the United States all the rights and advantages, but none of the responsibilities, of the Paris settlement.

The pursuit of advantages without responsibility—in Wilson's words "an ineffaceable stain upon . . . the honor of the United States"—also engaged the Harding Administration as a diplomatic partner to American oil companies. Their pressure persuaded the President to champion a treaty with Colombia, ostensibly designed only to indemnify that republic with $25 million for her loss of land and honor when Roosevelt assisted the Panamanian revolt. The treaty had been under consideration for several years, but Roosevelt's friends had blocked it while he still lived. In 1921, two years after his death, Colombia was preparing to withdraw all private rights to subsurface oil deposits. That possibility helped to move even Lodge to seek the good will that would permit Standard Oil to obtain concessions from the Colombian government. In April 1921 the Senate approved the treaty; Colombia ratified it in 1922; and American investments there, largely in oil, grew from about $2 million to $124 million by 1929. The State Department opened even richer prospects for profit by persuading the British to share with American companies the enormous oil fields of the Middle East.

The outstanding diplomatic venture of Harding's term was a 1921 conference on naval disarmament, which the President was rather reluctant to summon. At the time of his inauguration, the Navy Department was urging the completion of the vast building program that had been launched five years earlier (see p. 553). But businessmen were impatient to cut federal expenses so that taxes could be reduced, and they grumbled about the cost of the program. Continued naval expansion, moreover, was provoking an armament race with two recent associates, Great Britain and Japan, sea powers who were unwilling to stand idly by while the American navy grew. Senator William E. Borah of Idaho suggested a three-power meeting on naval limitation. In his view, for which there was growing popular support, the Republicans could make disarmament the fulcrum for world peace. Though Harding disagreed, large majorities in both houses of Congress endorsed Borah's scheme in a resolution attached to the naval-appropriations bill of 1921.

This move was welcomed by the British government, which foresaw trouble in the naval rivalry between Japan and the United States. Britain was also eager to terminate the defensive alliance she had made with Japan in 1902, an alliance that the dominions, especially Canada, disliked. The agreement bound both powers to respect each other's interests in the Orient and to assist each other should the interests of either be attacked by two other countries. The British felt that the arms race was intimately associated with stability in the Far East, particularly because the United States and Japan had been at odds over such questions as China's future, the Siberian intervention, and the disposition of former German islands in the western Pacific. Harding proposed a conference on naval limitations on the same day the British called for a conference on the Far East. They agreed to discuss both matters at a single meeting in Washington.

The double agenda made it necessary to invite all the major naval powers—the United

Harding in Florida: a complaisant disposition

Washington Conference, 1921: a considerable achievement

States, Great Britain, Japan, France, and Italy—as well as smaller powers with interests in the Far East—China, Portugal, Belgium, and the Netherlands. Everyone agreed that Bolshevik Russia, though a Pacific power, should be excluded, and her protests were ignored. Of the powers that were invited, only Japan was hesitant, but she accepted on the condition that the conference would not consider matters that constituted accomplished facts.

The delegates assembled on November 11, 1921, to commemorate the third anniversary of the armistice. The next day Harding greeted them with an emotional speech. Then they heard an address by Secretary of State Charles Evans Hughes, who had been named presiding officer. Instead of dealing in the usual platitudes of such occasions, Hughes presented the conference with a detailed plan for naval disarmament. The United States was to scrap thirty capital ships, half old and half being built; the British were to give up twenty-three; Japan, seventeen. This destruction of more than 1,878,000 aggregate tons afloat, on the ways, or planned, would establish a capital-ship tonnage ratio among the three nations of 5:5:3. The ratio was to persist for ten years, during which the powers would observe a moratorium on the construction of capital ships. France and Italy were each to have one-third the tonnage allotted the United States and Great Britain.

Hughes' speech, one of the most dramatic in diplomatic annals, stirred the amazed delegates to cheers. The Japanese, however, dis-liked being on the short end of the ratio, which wounded their pride and might threaten their national security. Starting with a demand for a 10:10:7 ratio, they bargained successfully to keep their newest battleship, which Hughes had destined for the junk heap. They accepted the Five Power Naval Treaty only after the United States and England had agreed not to fortify their possessions in the western Pacific.

Another agreement, the Four Power Treaty, bound the United States, Great Britain, Japan, and France to respect each other's rights affecting insular possessions in the Pacific, to refer disputes in that area to a joint conference, and to consult each other in the event of a threat from another power. Moreover, the treaty specifically supplanted the Anglo-Japanese alliance.

Now Hughes pressed on to conclude a Nine Power Treaty that committed all the nations at the conference to observe traditional American policies in the Far East. They agreed to respect the territorial and administrative integrity and the independence of China and to uphold the Open Door.

The Washington treaties were a considerable achievement. As the British had intended, and as the United States later maintained, they were integrally related to each other, and together they reduced tension in the Far East. Indeed, in the wake of the treaties, Japan restored Shantung to China's sovereignty, withdrew from Siberia, and granted the United States cable rights on the former German island of Yap. The naval treaty, moreover, marked the first time in history that major powers had consented to disarm. Hughes had made a virtue of necessity, for he had really given up nothing he had any reasonable chance of getting. The economy-minded Congress, as Lodge reported, would not have continued to expand the navy and would have looked askance at the cost of fortifying Guam or the Philippines.

Yet the Washington settlement also had shortcomings. It left the powers free to construct auxiliary naval vessels, such as destroyers, cruisers, and submarines, which were to prove vital weapons in the future. It provided no mechanism for policing the islands of the western Pacific or for protecting China. Thus it largely perpetuated the postwar status quo, for the western Pacific was still a Japanese lake. Japan when she chose could build up her fleet, fortify her mandate islands, and encroach upon China, unless the United States and the other powers were prepared to defend their stated policies. The test of the settlement lay not in its terms but in whether or not the powers chose to honor them. As Wilson had asserted, peace was a matter of continuous negotiation and accommodation. And, as Roosevelt had preached, power was ever a factor in the affairs of nations.

Hughes had done remarkably well, but the spirit with which Americans greeted his accomplishment was ominous. In ratifying the Four Power Treaty, the Senate added a reservation asserting that the United States recognized ''no commitment to armed force, no alliance, no obligation to join in any defense.'' Congress in 1922 and for years thereafter was unwilling to maintain the navy even to treaty strength. In short, the American people accepted words as realities, and the Washington settlement proved to be another case of seeking all the advantages and none of the responsibilities.

The best minds. Advantages rather than responsibilities were also the goal of the representatives of business and finance who shaped the domestic policies of the Harding Administration. The President had promised to recruit for government the ''best minds'' of the country. Hughes met that standard, as did Secretary of Agriculture Henry C. Wallace, who had long devoted himself to the cause of agricultural reform. But Wallace's influence was outweighed by that of Herbert Hoover, the new Secretary of Commerce, who used his depart-

ment to promote the interests and enlarge the markets of American business. Hoover, in Harding's view, had proved his worth by acquiring a magnificent fortune. That was the President's surest criterion for finding the ''best minds.''

Foremost among Harding's advisers was Secretary of the Treasury Andrew Mellon, a reticent multimillionaire from Pittsburgh whose intricate banking and investment holdings gave him, his family, and his associates control, among many other things, of the aluminum monopoly. A man of slight build, with a cold and weary face, Mellon exuded sober luxury and contemptuous worldliness. ''The Government is just a business,'' he believed, ''and can and should be run on business principles.''

Great businesses, as Mellon knew, thrive on innovation and expansion. Yet the only business principle he considered relevant to government was economy. With small regard for the services that only government could furnish the nation, Mellon worked unceasingly to cut federal expenditures. Expenses had to be cut if he was to achieve his corollary purpose: the reduction of taxes, especially taxes on men of means. It was better, he argued, to place the burden of taxes on lower-income groups, for taxing the rich inhibited their investments and thus retarded economic growth. A share of the tax-free profits of the rich, Mellon reassured the country, would ultimately trickle down to the middle- and lower-income groups in the form of salaries and wages. Robert La Follette paraphrased this regressive theory succinctly: ''Wealth will not and cannot be made to bear its full share of taxation.''

The quest for economy in government had some beneficial results. In 1921 Harding signed the Budget and Accounting Act, which improved the budgeting procedures of the federal government. It also served Mellon's purpose, for Harding's first Director of the Budget, Charles G. Dawes, a Chicago banker, made economy the touchstone of the budget that was presented to Congress in 1922.

Primarily to hold expenditures down, Harding opposed a veterans'-bonus bill that Congress debated in 1921, and he vetoed it when it passed the next year. The American Legion, an organization of World War veterans, led the lobby that demanded ''adjusted compensation'' for all servicemen. The Legion argued that soldiers had fought for a pittance

To the average man, it seems not unfair that the taxpayer with an income of over $200,000 a year should pay over half of it to the Government.... Taxation, however, is not a means of confiscating wealth but of raising necessary revenues for the Government.

One of the foundations of our American civilization is equality of opportunity, which presupposes the right of each man to enjoy the fruits of his labor after contributing his fair share to the support of the Government, which protects him and his property. But that is a very different matter from confiscating a part of his wealth, not because the country requires it for the prosecution of a war or some other purpose, but because he seems to have more money than he needs. Our civilization, after all, is based on accumulated capital, and that capital is no less vital to our prosperity than is the extraordinary energy which has built up in this country the greatest material civilization the world has ever seen. Any policy that deliberately destroys that accumulated capital under the spur of no necessity is striking directly at the soundness of our financial structure and is full of menace for the future.

From Andrew W. Mellon, *Taxation: The People's Business,* 1924.

while civilians were drawing high wartime wages. The bonus was to set matters right. Perhaps veterans did indeed deserve something more than gratitude from their country, but this bonus was little more than a raid on public funds supported by the American Legion, an energetic and increasingly influential pressure group. The newly created Veterans Administration was already taking care of the disabled. Veterans were not necessarily the neediest candidates for public assistance. Yet the veterans were simply acting in the spirit of the time when they continued to seek special advantages. Congress overrode a second veto in 1924 and granted a bonus in the form of paid-up twenty-year insurance policies, against which the veterans could immediately borrow limited funds.

Meanwhile, Mellon had advanced the tax program of the business community. In 1921 he urged Congress to repeal the excess-profits tax and to reduce the surtax on personal income from a maximum of 65 percent to 32 percent for 1921 and 25 percent thereafter. These proposals would have prevailed had it not been for the opposition of a group of Western Republican senators who joined with the Democrats to preserve the progressive principles of wartime revenue legislation. Though the Revenue Act of 1921 did eliminate the excess-profits tax, it fell short of Mellon's other goals. It held the maximum surtax on personal income at 50 percent, and it granted some tax relief to lower- and middle-income groups by raising exemptions for heads of families and their dependents.

The Administration had better luck with its tariff policy. Following the tradition of their party, Republican leaders set out at once to restore the protective rates that had prevailed before 1913. Though they experienced some delay, two developments eased their way. The spread of industry in the South had dispelled much of the traditional Democratic resistance to tariff protection. More important, farm representatives had concluded that they would profit from protective rates on farm products. This was a delusion, for the farmer really needed larger markets abroad and help at home in marketing his produce and obtaining credit. But during the discussion of the tariff the leaders of the farm bloc, except for Senators William E. Borah, George Norris, and Robert La Follette, rivaled the spokesmen of industry in their zeal for protection. Consequently there was no spirited debate on the tariff, as there had been in 1909.

With no significant dissent, Congress in 1922 passed the Fordney-McCumber Act, which reestablished prohibitive tariff rates. The act did instruct the Tariff Commission to help the President determine differences in production costs between the United States and other nations. And it did empower the President to raise or lower any rate by 50 percent, on the commissions' recommendation. In practice, however, the commission was strongly protectionist, and of the

A virtuous poor?   The standard furnished by the statute ... is so vague as to be impossible of practical application with any reasonable degree of accuracy. What is sufficient to supply the necessary cost of living for a woman worker and maintain her in good health and protect her morals is obviously not a precise or unvarying sum—not even approximately so.... Morality rests upon other considerations than wages; and there is, certainly, no such prevalent connection between the two as to justify a broad attempt to adjust the latter with reference to the former.... Nor is there ground for distinction between women and men, for, certainly, if women require a minimum wage to preserve their morals, men require it to preserve their honesty. For these reasons, and others which might be stated, the inquiry in respect of the necessary cost of living and of the income necessary to preserve health and morals, presents an individual and not a composite question, and must be answered for each individual considered by herself and not by a general formula prescribed by a statutory bureau.

From Adkins v. Children's Hospital, 261 U.S. 525, 1923.

thirty-seven rates that were altered during the life of the act, thirty-two were actually increased.

The Tariff of 1922 enriched American industrialists, but it damaged foreign trade. By preventing Europeans from selling their goods in the United States, it made it impossible for them to buy American products, including agricultural surpluses, except by borrowing dollars and thus increasing the large debts they had incurred during the war. This was an unhealthy situation both for the United States and for Europe.

Nullification by administration. The restoration of tariff protection was only one part of a concerted effort by the Administration to restore the conditions of the nineteenth century. Wherever they could, Harding and his associates rolled back the accomplishments of the progressive movement.

The President could not tear down the apparatus that had been constructed for regulating business and industry, but he succeeded in rendering that apparatus useless by turning it over to the very interests it had been designed to regulate. His appointments to federal commissions, as Senator Norris said, "set the country back more than twenty-five years." They achieved "the nullification of federal law by a process of boring from within."

The Administration also stood aside while management continued its attack on labor unions and labor legislation. In 1922 Harding interceded to stop the violence that attended

a nationwide coal strike. The report of the commission of inquiry he appointed revealed the pitiful, even desperate, state of life in the coal towns. The commission supported neither compulsory arbitration, which the operators wanted, nor complete unionization, which the miners had advocated. Instead, it recommended various federal controls over the mining industry, but Congress and the Administration ignored the report. In the same year, the national Railway Labor Board approved a 12 percent reduction in the wages of railway shopmen, a decision that precipitated a strike that lasted two months. It ended only when the Attorney General got an injunction that forbade the union to picket or in any way to encourage workers to leave their jobs.

In this and other rulings the federal courts, acting in the spirit of the executive establishment, took advantage of the permissiveness of the Clayton Act (see p. 544). Contrary to Gompers' hopes, the injunction was still a handy instrument for breaking strikes. In the same spirit, the courts sustained "yellow-dog" contracts that bound employees not to join unions. The courts' hostility toward labor not only helped management's campaign for the open shop but destroyed social legislation designed to protect the poorest and weakest workers. The Supreme Court in 1922, in the case of *Bailey* v. *Drexel Furniture Company*, declared unconstitutional a federal statute levying a prohibitive tax on products manufactured by children. The Court had ruled earlier, in *Hammer* v. *Dagenhart* (1918), that federal laws to control child labor were an unconstitutional invasion of the police powers of the states. In the Bailey case, it said that Congress could not use its tax power to accomplish this unconstitutional purpose. The decision perpetuated child labor, especially in the Southern textile mills.

The Supreme Court was just as opposed to regulation of wages, hours, and working conditions. In 1923, in *Adkins* v. *Children's Hospital,* it held unconstitutional a District of Columbia statute establishing minimum wages for women. Ignoring the social and economic arguments for the act, the majority of the Court found it a violation of the freedom of women to contract to sell their labor as they pleased. The Adkins decision contravened the spirit of the Clayton Act, which asserted that labor was not a mere commodity. The decision also left labor defenseless, for neither federal nor state governments could insist on minimum standards of health and decency, and the attitudes of the courts denied the unions much of their opportunity to recruit membership or to strike for fair treatment.

The farmers fared better politically, but not economically, under the Harding Administration. In 1922 agricultural prices began to recover from their postwar slump, but the farmers were harassed by high interest charges on mortgages and by heavy taxes on land. Advancing technology raised production and expanded surpluses even though the number of farms and of agricultural workers was steadily declining. And advancing industrialism continuously reduced the farmers' share of the national income. Agriculture during the early 1920s was not generally impoverished, though segments of it were. But even the more privileged farmers were anxious about their future and resentful of their diminishing influence on American life. They were jealous, too, of the conveniences, especially electricity, automobiles, and entertainment, that were becoming more and more common in the cities.

In 1921 and 1922 the discontent of farmers generated considerable political force in the South and the Middle West, and the farm bloc in Congress won a series of victories. With few exceptions, however, the leaders of the farm bloc failed to understand the basic difficulties. They made their mark instead where the objectives of the fading progressive movement helped them to define their goals. Legislation in 1921 authorized the Secretary of Agriculture to compel commission merchants, grain

merchants, and stockyard owners to charge reasonable rates. An act of 1922 exempted farm cooperatives from the antitrust laws, and Congress added a representative of agriculture to the Federal Reserve Board. In 1923 the Agricultural Credits Act established twelve Intermediate Credit Banks to make loans to cooperatives and other farm groups for six months to three years. The loans were to help cooperatives to withhold crops from the market when prices were temporarily low. These statutes strengthened the farmer's ability to conduct his business, and they created instruments for controlling the middlemen to whom he sold his produce. But they did not provide him with new markets or ease his mortgage burden, and they helped the small farmer, sharecropper, and farm laborer not at all.

In the off-year elections of 1922, agrarian dissent carried anti-Administration candidates to victory in Republican primaries in most of the West. In November the resurgent Democrats reduced Republican majorities to eight in the Senate and eighteen in the House. And, of the Republicans who were elected, so many were disenchanted that the Administration no longer controlled Congress. The elections assured key committee assignments to strong men in both parties who were dubious about the Administration's program and methods. Those men, using Congress' power of investigation, soon exposed the Harding regime to publicity it could not afford.

The Harding scandals. The President of the United States sets the tone of his Administration. The first two decades of the twentieth century had been marked by McKinley's kindness, Theodore Roosevelt's strenuosity, Taft's decent ineffectuality, and Wilson's soaring idealism. Warren Harding brought to government the qualities of his own weak person. He was an ignorant, naive, confused man whose loose standards made him particularly vulnerable to his intellectual deficiencies and to the corrupt character of the hail-fellows with whom he instinctively surrounded himself.

Harding was ruefully aware of some of his limitations. As he once admitted, he did not know whom to trust. Though a few members of his Cabinet—Hughes, Hoover, and Mellon in particular—were men of large talent, more of his advisers were distinguished by their lack of qualifications. Uncomfortable with the ''best minds,'' Harding preferred the kind of tawdry companionship he had known in his

John, I can't make a damn thing out of this tax problem. I listen to one side and they seem right, and then—God!—I talk to the other side and they seem just as right.... I know somewhere there is a book that will give me the truth, but, hell, I couldn't read the book. I know somewhere there is an economist who knows the truth, but I don't know where to find him and haven't the sense to know him and trust him when I find him. God! what a job.

From William Allen White, *Masks in a Pageant*, 1928.

native Marion, Ohio. As head of the Veterans Bureau he selected Charles R. Forbes, whom he had met by chance during a jovial holiday in Hawaii. For the office of Secretary of the Interior the President chose Senator Albert B. Fall of New Mexico, a bitter partisan with a reputation for shiftiness. The new Attorney General was Harry M. Daugherty of Ohio, who had advanced his own career largely by promoting Harding's. Daugherty's intimate, Jesse Smith of Ohio, came along as an unofficial influence. These, and a few others, constituted the "Ohio gang" who met continually with Harding at a house on K Street. There councils of state had an incidental but insinuating part in the rounds of poker, whiskey, and women that made the President feel at home.

For two years the Ohio gang flourished. Early in 1923, however, Daugherty decided he had to tell Harding of the rumors he had heard about Charles Forbes. The cheerful head of the Veterans Bureau had pocketed an impressive fraction of the $250 million his agency spent lavishly for hospitals and hospital supplies. Harding permitted Forbes to go abroad and resign, but in March a Senate committee began to investigate the Veterans Bureau, whose legal adviser, lacking the courage of his rascality, committed suicide. Yet ultimately Forbes was exposed, tried, convicted, and sentenced to prison.

There was a second suicide in May. Jesse Smith had been selling his influence at the Justice Department to lawbreakers who paid handsomely for forgiveness or immunity. When stories of his dealings finally reached the obtuse President, he told Daugherty that Smith had to leave. Briefly Smith returned to Ohio, but on May 23, back in Daugherty's familiar apartment, he killed himself.

It was later revealed that one of Smith's ventures involved Thomas W. Miller, Harding's alien-property custodian, who had agreed to a dubious disposition of the control of the American Metal Company. The attorney in that transaction was John T. King, the Republican national committeeman from Connecticut. King funneled part of his large fee to the Attorney General. Eventually Miller went to jail for accepting a bribe, but two divided juries in 1926 saved Daugherty, who refused to testify on his own behalf for fear of self-incrimination.

Albert Fall was less fortunate. In 1921 he persuaded Harding to transfer to the Interior Department control over naval oil reserves at Elk Hill, California, and Teapot Dome, Wyoming. The next year Fall secretly leased Elk Hill to the oil company of Edward L. Doheny and Teapot Dome to the company of Harry F. Sinclair. But the leases could not be kept secret very long. In October 1923 a Senate committee under the chairmanship of Thomas J. Walsh, a Montana Democrat, began an investigation, which a special commission completed in 1924. The inquiries disclosed that Doheny had "lent" Fall $100,000 and that Sinclair had given the Secretary of the Interior a herd of cattle for his ranch, $85,000 in cash, and $223,000 in bonds. In 1927 the government won a suit for cancellation of the leases. Though another remarkable verdict acquitted Doheny, Sinclair, and Fall of conspiracy to defraud the government, Sinclair was convicted of tampering with a jury, and in 1929 Fall was convicted of bribery, fined $100,000, and sentenced to a year in jail. He was the first Cabinet officer ever to go to prison.

Harding knew of the exploits of only Forbes and Smith. In June 1923, before setting out on a speaking tour through the West, the President unburdened himself to William Allen White: "My God, this is a hell of a job. I have no trouble with my enemies. . . . But my damned friends, my God-damned friends . . . they're the ones that keep me walking the floor nights!'' Depressed and tired, Harding grew ''nervous and distraught'' as he traveled. Late in July, while in Seattle on the way home from Alaska, the President suffered acute pain. Dr. Sawyer diagnosed it as indigestion, but other physicians in the party believed that Harding had had a heart attack, a diagnosis that was confirmed by a San Francisco specialist. On August 2, in a room at the Palace Hotel, Harding died, the victim of a coronary or cerebral thrombosis.

Sawyer's incompetent and unconvincing diagnosis bred doubts on which melodrama thrived. One Nan Britton, who claimed to have been Harding's mistress and to have borne him an illegitimate daughter, suggested that he had been poisoned by his jealous wife. The cheapness of Harding's life made the story plausible, but the truth was less exciting. A middle-aged man, overweight, with a tendency toward high blood pressure and an immoderate taste for booze, tired, disappointed by his friends, despondent, had died of a bad heart and poor circulation. Only death saved him from sharing the disgrace of his companions.

Vulgarity and scandal were the sordid fruits of normalcy, of a government that sought all the advantages of power but none of the responsibilities, of organized self-interest that sought special favors in bonuses, bounties, lower taxes, and higher tariffs. The scandals passed, but the spirit that nurtured them lived on. It was a spirit that satisfied the ''best minds'' during the decade that followed the great war; a spirit that contradicted the best hopes cultivated during that war and in the years of progressivism preceding it.

Suggestions for reading

THE WAR

Historians have given the experience of the United States during the First World War less attention than it merits. The biographies of Wilson and the Wilsonians, noted in connection with the preceding chapter, provide some useful data and insights. More complete is F. L. Paxson, *American Democracy and the World War,* 3 vols. (1936–48). There are adequate discussions of economic mobilization in B. M. Baruch, *American Industry in War* (1941) and *The Public Years** (1960). The relevant chapter of Sidney Ratner, *American Taxation* (1942), is important on its subject. On congressional developments, see S. W. Livermore, *Politics Is Adjourned** (1966). On the administration of the War Department, Frederick Palmer, *Newton D. Baker,* 2 vols. (1931), offers considerable information; the Navy Department receives perceptive treatment in Frank Freidel, *Franklin D. Roosevelt: The Apprenticeship* (1952). The most rewarding of the war memoirs is J. J. Pershing, *My Experiences in the World War,* 2 vols. (1931), but there are more useful accounts of military developments in J. G. Harbord, *The American Army in France* (1936), and E. E. Morison, *Admiral Sims and the Modern American Navy* (1942). There are a number of admirable studies of propaganda, censorship, and civil liberties in wartime, including J. R. Mock and Cedric Larson, *Words That Won the War: The Story of the Committee on Public Information, 1917–1919* (1939); H. C. Peterson, *Propaganda for War* (1939); H. C. Peterson and G. C. Fite, *Opponents of War, 1917–1918** (1957); and the classic Zechariah Chafee, *Free Speech in the United States** (rev. ed., 1941).

THE PEACE

The student of peacemaking and of the American rejection of the peace treaty has at his disposal a voluminous literature that is continually growing. One excellent place to begin reading is in the penetrating analysis of H. R. Rudin, *Armistice, 1918* (1944). On the significance of the Bolsheviks in the fashioning of peace terms, see A. J. Mayer, *Political Origins of the New Diplomacy, 1917–1918** (1959) and *Politics and Diplomacy of Peacemaking** (1968). Two detailed accounts of the negotiations at Paris, which applaud Wilson's efforts, are D. F. Fleming, *The United States and the League of Nations, 1918–1920* (1932), and Paul Birdsall, *Versailles Twenty Years After* (1941). On the United States and the Soviet Union, there are two superb volumes by G. F. Kennan, *Russia Leaves the War: The Americans in Petrograd and the Bolshevik Revolution** (1956) and *The Decision to Intervene: The Prelude to Allied Intervention in the Bolshevik Revolution** (1958). Also laudatory, and essential on its topic, is R. J. Bartlett, *League to Enforce Peace* (1944). There is a critical but persuasive analysis in T. A. Bailey, *Woodrow Wilson and*

*Available in a paperback edition.

the Lost Peace* (1944). The same author, in *Woodrow Wilson and the Great Betrayal** (1945), provides a trenchant study of the rejection of the treaty. Also significant on that subject are: N. G. Levin, Jr., *Woodrow Wilson and World Politics** (1968); J. A. Garraty, *Henry Cabot Lodge* (1953); R. W. Leopold, *Elihu Root and the Conservative Tradition** (1954); and M. C. McKenna, *Borah* (1961). There are conflicting views about the conduct of government during Wilson's illness in E. B. Wilson, *My Memoirs* (1938), and J. M. Blum, *Joe Tumulty and the Wilson Era* (1951). Among the accounts of contemporaries friendly to Wilson, two of the most valuable are D. F. Houston, *Eight Years with Wilson's Cabinet, 1913–1920,* 2 vols. (1926), and Herbert Hoover, *The Ordeal of Woodrow Wilson** (1958). Two important unfriendly statements appear in H. C. Lodge, *The Senate and the League of Nations* (1928), and J. M. Keynes, *Economic Consequences of the Peace* (1919). Several of the books here listed cover the question of the League in the election of 1920, a subject further explored in J. M. Cox, *Journey Through My Years* (1946), and Frank Freidel, *Franklin D. Roosevelt: The Ordeal* (1954).

THE RED SCARE

R. K. Murray, *The Red Scare** (1955), contains the most comprehensive narrative about the subject. It has to be supplemented, however, by the perceptive biography by S. Coben, *A. Mitchell Palmer: Politician* (1963); the lucid treatment of civil liberties in Zechariah Chafee, cited above; the masterful analysis of G. L. Joughin and E. M. Morgan, *The Legacy of Sacco and Vanzetti** (1948); the excellent studies of labor in Irving Bernstein, *The Lean Years** (1960), and D. Brody, *Labor in Crisis: The Steel Strike of 1919** (1965); the analysis of the Negro in A. I. Waskow, *From Race Riot to Sit-In, 1919 and the 1960s** (1966), E. D. Cronin, *Black Moses** (1955), and N. I. Huggins, *et al., Key Issues in Afro-American Experience,* 2 vols. (1971); and the penetrating treatments of nativism in John Higham, *Strangers in the Land** (1955), and Oscar Handlin, *Race and Nationality in American Life** (1957) and *The American People in the Twentieth Century** (1954, 2nd rev. ed., 1966). For an opposite point of view, interesting but unpersuasive, on the temper of the times, see D. Felix, *Protest: Sacco-Vanzetti and the Intellectuals* (1965).

HARDING AND NORMALCY

W. E. Leuchtenburg, *The Perils of Prosperity, 1914–32** (1958), provides a crisp and thoughtful account of the Harding period. Also lively, but less judicious, is F. L. Allen, *Only Yesterday** (1931). There is a short but incisive evaluation of the Harding years in A. M. Schlesinger, Jr., *The Crisis of the Old Order** (1957), and a fuller narrative in J. D. Hicks, *Republican Ascendancy, 1921–1933** (1960). The economy and its problems receive able handling in George Soule, *Prosperity Decade: From War to Depression, 1917–1929** (1947); but for a richer discussion of taxation and agriculture, respectively, the relevant chapters of R. E. Paul, *Taxation in the United States* (1954), and Theodore Saloutos and J. D. Hicks, *Twentieth Century Populism: Agricultural Discontent in the Middle West, 1900–1939** (1951), are particularly valuable. The Harding scandals get the treatment they merit in S. H. Adams, *Incredible Era** (1939), and Karl Schriftgiesser, *This Was Normalcy* (1948). A. Sinclair, *The Available Man** (1965), tries to redeem Harding's reputation, as does R. K. Murray, *The Harding Era* (1969). Two stimulating accounts of the Washington Conference are H. H. and M. T. Sprout, *Toward a New Order of Sea Power* (1946), and J. C. Vinson, *The Parchment Peace: The United States Senate and the Washington Conference, 1921–1922* (1950). Also important are the pertinent parts of A. W. Griswold, *The Far Eastern Policy of the United States** (1938), and F. R. Dulles, *Forty Years of American-Japanese Relations* (1937). Two biographers have given first-rate attention to the diplomacy of Harding's Secretary of State: M. J. Pusey, *Charles Evans Hughes,* 2 vols. (1951), and Dexter Perkins, *Charles Evans Hughes and American Democratic Statesmanship* (1953).

*Available in a paperback edition.

25

A new age of business

Calvin Coolidge believed in the kind of luck that Horatio Alger had immortalized. If a man worked hard, saved his pennies, respected the authorities, and kept his mouth shut, an invisible hand would contrive an occasion to make his reputation. Coolidge took no chances while he waited for his breaks. The son of a Vermont storekeeper, he worked his way through Amherst College, studied law in Northampton, Massachusetts, and entered politics there, winning successively those minor state offices on which undistinguished politicians build their ordinary careers. His patient course endeared him to the Massachusetts Republicans, who valued his unquestioning acceptance of things as they were, his unwavering preference for inaction, and his obvious personal honesty.

In 1919, twenty years after he first won public office, Coolidge achieved national prominence for his role in stopping the Boston police strike. His delay in dealing with that episode invited anarchy, but his friends used his new reputation to generate the boom that made him the Republican choice for Vice President. In that post Coolidge dispatched his ceremonial duties with quiet pleasure, warned Americans against the ''Reds in Our Women's Colleges,'' and awaited his next break. When Harding died, Coolidge's luck had him at home, where his father, a notary public, administered the oath of office. The event was a blessing for the most privileged Republicans, for the accession of Calvin Coolidge gave them a new President who cloaked normalcy with respectability.

A new cult of enterprise

Coolidge and the business creed. Personally neat, even prim, deliberately laconic and undemonstrative in public (though given in private to temper and garrulity), Coolidge scrubbed the White House clean of the filth that Harding had left. Grace Coolidge, the new first lady, erased scandal with her natural dignity, charm, and warmth. The President chose two lawyers of impeccable integrity to prosecute the rascals in government. When the mounting evidence against the Attorney General forced his retirement in March 1924, Coolidge named to his place an eminent for-

mer dean of the Columbia Law School, Harlan Fiske Stone, whose appointment completed the shift from obscenity to virtue.

In other respects Coolidge left the national government unaltered. As much as Harding, Coolidge subscribed to the creed of American business. ''The business of America is business,'' Coolidge believed. ''The man who builds a factory,'' he once said, ''builds a temple. . . . The man who works there worships there.'' The President himself worshiped wealth and those who had it. Worldly possessions were for him evidence of divine election.

An adman? Let us begin by asking why he was so successful in mastering public attention and why, in contrast, his churches are less so?... In the first place he recognized the basic principle that all good advertising is news. He was never trite or commonplace; he had no routine. If there had been newspapers in those days, no city editor could have said, "No need to visit him to-day; he will be doing just what he did last Sunday." Reporters would have followed him every single hour, for it was impossible to predict what he would say or do; every action and word were news....

Can you imagine the next day's issue of the Capernaum News, *if there had been one?...*

PROMINENT TAX COLLECTOR JOINS
NAZARETH FORCES

MATTHEW ABANDONS BUSINESS TO
PROMOTE NEW CULT

GIVES LARGE LUNCHEON

Every advertising man ought to study the parables of Jesus ... schooling himself in their language.... They are marvelously condensed, as all good advertising should be.... Jesus had no introductions. A single sentence grips your attention; three or four more tell the story; one or two more and the application is driven home.

From Bruce Barton, *The Man Nobody Knows*, 1925.

Coolidge cloaked normalcy with respectability

He stood in awe of Andrew Mellon. He took a smug delight in his own eminence, but he was absolutely euphoric when his office commanded for him the deference of the rich. Coolidge, as William Allen White put it, was "sincerely, genuinely, terribly crazy" about wealth.

This passion coincided exactly with the theories of business spokesmen. There were, they preached, a superior few and an inferior many. And they were easy to distinguish, for "a man is worth the wages he can earn." Material success marked the elite, and to them the others should leave the important decisions about society. The 1920s witnessed a renaissance of the conservative dogmas of the 1880s, now clothed in new metaphors. Bruce Barton, a magnificently successful advertising man, gave the gospel its most popular phrasing in his best-seller of 1925, *The Man Nobody Knows*. To his infinite satisfaction, Barton, the son of a minister, discovered that Christ was a businessman. "Jesus," he wrote, ". . . picked up twelve men from the bottom ranks of business and forged them into an organization that conquered the world." The parables made incomparable advertisements; the gospel, an incomparable business school.

Coolidge was devoted to the dominant values of his time, to business, materialism, elitism, and their corollaries. If only the rich were worthy, it followed that government should beware the counsels of the majority. Since poverty was the wage of sin, government should not tax the virtuous rich in order to assist the unworthy poor. And since the rich best understood their own interests, government should not interfere with the businesses they ran, though it should help promote them.

No devotee of laissez faire ever abhorred government more than Coolidge did. "If the Federal Government should go out of existence," he said, "the common run of people would not detect the difference . . . for a considerable length of time." Government's grandest service was to minimize itself, its activities, and its expenditures. So persuaded, Coolidge slept more than any other President in this century. He also said and did less when he was awake. "Four-fifths of all our troubles in this life," he told one agitated senator, "would disappear if we would only sit down and keep still." Silence, inactivity, gentility, complacency—those were the sum and the substance of the Coolidge calculus. He was shrewd and self-righteous and marvelously representative of the mood of an acquisitive society.

Productivity and plenty. The extraordinary prosperity of the 1920s cast a mantle of credibility over the doctrines of business and its representative President. It was easy for him and others of like mind to interpret prosperity as majestic proof of their beliefs. As the country came out of the short slump of 1921, unemployment became negligible except in sick industries like textiles and coal. By 1923 the average money wages of industrial workers were twice what they had been in 1914, and they continued to advance through 1928. Real wages rose, too, steadily though less dramatically. By 1928 they were about one-third higher than they had been fourteen years earlier. Several factors accounted for those increases. Many employers had begun to realize that higher wages removed one of the incentives that prompted workers to join unions and also provided purchasing power that swelled the market for industrial products. Wages stretched further as prices fell, especially the price of food and of goods manufactured in industries where mechanization pushed productivity to new peaks.

The profits that came with mechanization invited investment in new plants and new tools. Investment was encouraged also by the growing national market, by the permissive climate of inactive government, and by Mellon's gradual success in persuading Congress to reduce taxes on large incomes. While investment provided the means for building more and more productivity into American industry, management was mastering new ways to use machinery and to organize production more effectively.

The American system of manufacturing that flowered during the 1920s had deep roots. It depended on the concept of continuous fabrication, by which raw materials entered a plant to emerge after multiple operations as finished products. That concept was at least as old as the first Lowell textile mills. It depended also on machine tools capable of producing standard, complex artifacts with interchangeable parts—the kinds of tool and the kind of standardization that Eli Whitney had developed for guns a century before Coolidge's inauguration. More immediately, the American system of manufacturing depended on two recent and interrelated developments. One was the emerging profession of industrial engineering, with its concern for continuous process, improved machinery, specialization of jobs, and time-motion studies of performance. The other was an emerging cult of productivity, a rationalization of the glories of making and distributing and consuming ever more bountifully. Americans had long honored that objective, but never more avidly than in the 1920s.

The founding father of "scientific management" was Frederick W. Taylor. Born into a comfortable family in Germantown, Pennsylvania, in 1856, Taylor had to interrupt his gentleman's education at Harvard because of poor eyesight. Moving into an entirely different environment, he learned the trades of patternmaker and machinist and in 1878 went as a common laborer to the Midvale Steel Company. By 1885 he had earned his Master of Engineering degree at Stevens Institute; a year later he became chief engineer at Midvale. His driving concern was with making machines and the men who attended them produce more and faster. Those interests led him to establish his own consulting practice on production, on "systematizing shop management."

Taylor's system started with a close study of every step in manufacturing. By applying the resulting data, by breaking the process of manufacturing into separate parts, and by specializing the function of the man and machine involved in each part, he could substantially increase the rate of production. His classifications of jobs and of capacity, he believed, would lead also to higher wages as workers first met and then exceeded their calculated goals. The aim of every establishment, Taylor wrote in *Shop Management* (1911), should be to give each workman the highest grade of work of which he was capable, to call on each to turn out his maximum, and to pay each in accordance with his product. "This means," he argued, "*high wages* and *low labor cost.*" It also meant time-motion studies, discipline, pressure, and incentives for speedup. For Taylor efficiency was a fetish, but he got results. Before he died in 1915 (with a watch in his hand, John Dos Passos surmised), he had caught the attention of management and had aroused the fears of labor-leaders, who suspected that piecework and the speedup would grind profits out of workers' fatigue. In spite of those fears, Taylorism spread. It was praised by Louis Brandeis and other progressives, and institutionalized by a Taylor Society.

Taylor was the philosopher of the machine process; Henry Ford was its commanding general. In 1911 Ford opened his plant at

Assembly line: Ford Motor Company

Highland Park, Michigan. There he and his fellow executives arrived at Taylor's principles along their own routes and began to turn out automobiles at prodigious rates. The Ford Motor Company outsped all industry in specializing the tasks of men and machines. After 1913 it also applied the idea of continuous motion, using conveyor belts, gravity slides, and overhead monorails to feed the machinery by which workers stood. The modern assembly line turned out the Model T's that put America on wheels. As his production and market grew, Ford cut prices and increased wages. To be sure, the wages he claimed to pay did not reach all his workers, the speedup at the Ford company was notorious, and the company tolerated no unions. But the $5 day that Ford announced in 1914 seemed to mark the dawn of a new era, and so did Ford's staggering profits. In the mid-1920s Ford had become, in the phrase of Upton Sinclair, the Flivver King.

By that time Ford's production techniques had become standard in the automobile and other industries. The Model T was a very stark car, but America's machines were also producing more comfortable, more sumptuous, and more complex mechanisms. During Coolidge's tenure in office, for the first time in the history of any nation, a mass market developed for cars, for radios, for refrigerators and vacuum cleaners. There was, in a sense, no longer any problem of production. The available stocks of American raw materials, workers, machines, and techniques could saturate the nation, and much of the world, with the necessities and conveniences of modern civilization.

A market developed for radios

Businessmen, however, were interested in more than just the science of production. Their restrictive labor policies during the 1920s kept the rise in real wages well below the rise in profits. And they guarded their market jealously, trying to produce only as much as the market could absorb without a break in prices. Large firms in heavy industries had long since learned the importance of administered, noncompetitive pricing and had long since contrived the consolidations that made for industrial stability. During the 1920s the tendency toward consolidation proceeded at an accelerating tempo, in old industries as well as new. And, as consolidation advanced, managers became more and more skillful in governing costs, price, and output.

These developments disturbed Americans for whom the production and distribution of wealth were more precious objectives than amassing profits. The Nobel Prize-winning novelist Sinclair Lewis, in *Dodsworth* (1929), told of an automobile-manufacturer who was forced to sell out to a giant holding company, a fictional General Motors. Dodsworth, deprived of the satisfaction of producing cars himself, and unwilling to serve as a subordinate in a great corporation, sought vainly to find new satisfactions in the culture of Europe. But in the end he came back to the United States to embark on the manufacture of mobile homes. He was the kind of business engineer who adhered to a commitment to production that Lewis felt ordinary business-managers were destroying.

Thorstein Veblen made the most devastating comparisons between those who made goods and those who made money. In *The*

Engineers and the Price System (1921) and *Business Enterprise* (1923) he condemned businessmen for artificially curtailing output for the sake of profit—a practice he labeled "sabotage." He called for a revolution of technicians, of men committed to production, who would free industry of pecuniary restraints and use the machine process to provide plenty for all mankind. There was a legacy of Populism in Veblen's ideas, a naiveté in his attitude toward competition, and a strong dose of Marxism. But his simplifications had both merit and influence. Whereas business-managers often planned only for profit, Veblen urged public planning for the general welfare. His message helped to bridge the space between the progressive era and the next era of reform.

Republican symbols: 1924. In the Coolidge era, however, the impulse for reform flagged. The spirit of that time saw no conflict between profits and productivity. It found a symbol in the person of Herbert Hoover, who seemed to have walked right out of American mythology. Son of an Iowa farmer, descended of pioneer stock, orphaned at ten, Hoover went west, worked his way through Stanford University, married a banker's daughter, and as an engineer in Asia earned his first million before he was forty. He was the hero of Belgian relief, the successful Food Administrator of Wilson's war Cabinet, and, in the opinion of one London newspaper, "the biggest man . . . on the Allied side" at Paris. By 1920 Hoover's name stood for personal success, for food for the hungry, and for rigor in administration. His reputation reached its height while he was serving under Harding and Coolidge as Secretary of Commerce.

To that office Hoover applied, as it were, the principles of scientific shop management. His department studied business trends, fought economic waste through its Office of Simplified Practice, and promoted American commerce and investment abroad. Concurrently it encouraged trade associations to sustain prices and profits by adjusting production to demand. Hoover personally organized the relief of victims of the Mississippi flood of 1927, avoided associating with politicians, and harbored an ambition as broad and inconspicuous as his conservative blue suits. He stood at once for laissez-faire doctrines, humanitarian endeavor, and quiet and humorless

efficiency. Coolidge, increasingly jealous of Hoover's reputation, could barely tolerate "the wonder boy."

The President did not suffer any rival kindly. A shrewd political manipulator, he rapidly brought the machinery of the Republican party under his control. As the nominating convention of 1924 approached, he had only one serious, though unlikely, opponent—not Hoover, who was biding his time, but Henry Ford. The Flivver King had run as a Democrat, and lost, in the race for senator from Michigan in 1918. His publicity men, who wrote much of what he signed, had begun in 1922 to suggest that he might be available as a Republican candidate for the White House. The prospect was both preposterous and alarming. Away from his machines, Ford was a ludicrous, semiliterate figure, the captive of folk prejudices. He was opposed to tobacco, liquor, and ballroom dancing. He had published and circulated anti-Semitic propaganda. He detested labor unions and Wall Street, both of which he felt were the tools of an international Jewish conspiracy. But this nonsense had an unfortunate appeal to the uneducated, and a third of those who were polled by *Collier's* in a straw ballot of 1923 named Ford as their first choice for President.

Ford's candidacy may not have been serious, though many people thought it was. He was, however, deadly serious in his proposal to take over the government dam, nitrate plant, and other facilities constructed during the war at Muscle Shoals on the Tennessee River. He proposed to purchase the nitrate works for less than 5 percent of what they had cost the government, to lease the waterpower facilities for a hundred years for less than 10 percent of what it would cost the government to complete them, and to have the government pay him simply by issuing new paper money. In return, he hinted that he would be able to produce fertilizer for American farms at half its current price. As Senator Norris said, this was the "most wonderful real estate speculation since Adam and Eve lost title to the Garden of Eden."

Norris exposed and defeated the scheme, which would have destroyed his cherished plans for the public development of the Tennessee. Yet before the chimera vanished, Coolidge, after talking with Ford, recommended that Congress sell Muscle Shoals to private interests. Ford himself soon put an end to his presidential boomlet by announcing that the nation was "perfectly safe with Coolidge." There may have been no bargain, but the coincidence of events suggested that both men were trading in character.

It was a striking commentary on the times that Ford's nitrate project was even proposed. It was no less striking that Ford's candidacy seemed to be the only barrier to Coolidge's renomination. Robert La Follette and Hiram Johnson, dedicated, doughty old progressives, could muster between them only forty-four votes at the Republican convention that gave Coolidge over a thousand votes on its first and decisive ballot. Only a dozen years earlier almost half the Republicans had cast their lot with Theodore Roosevelt.

One nation divisible

For white Protestants only. The temper of the twenties was marked by narrowness and provincialism as well as by prosperity and complacency. The attitudes on which the Red scare had fed survived the passing of the scare itself. Among many Americans there lingered an intolerance of all "isms," a distrust of foreign nations, and a dislike, often bordering on hatred, of people of foreign origins. Much of the farm community had long been susceptible to those feelings, and organized labor had endorsed the racial as well as the economic arguments of those who advocated that immigration be restricted.

In 1924 Congress adopted the recommendations of the Dillingham commission (p. 531) and passed the National Origins Act. This based annual immigration quotas temporarily on the proportion of descendants of each nationality resident in the United States in 1890 and limited immigration after 1927 to 150,000 a year, selected on the proportion established by the census of 1920. Those quotas ended all but a trickle of immigration from southern and eastern Europe. The act, furthermore, included a provision that West Coast racists had been urging for years. It forbade the immigration of Asians, thus terminating the Gentlemen's Agreement (see p. 531) and insulting the race-sensitive Japanese. "It has undone the work of the Washington Conference," Charles Evans Hughes wrote, "and implanted seeds of . . . antagonism."

Asians, blacks, Catholics, and Jews were all victims of the prejudice based on the ethnic self-consciousness of white, Protestant Americans of older stock. Even many educated and comfortable people, who should have known better, attributed to race, religion, or national origin varying qualities of character and intelligence, always with the assumption that Americans of old stock were a superior breed. That kind of bigotry thrived among Southern whites, but it also appealed to the poorer and semieducated who lived or had grown up in rural or small-town America. They tended, as they had for at least half a century, to blame their personal disappointments on the growth of cities and industry and to express their anxieties in hostility toward those who peopled the cities.

Those prejudices were the stock in trade of the Ku Klux Klan, an organization founded in Georgia in 1915 on the model of its Reconstruction predecessor. It recruited only "native born, white, gentile Americans," and it gave them a sense of importance by admitting them to membership in a group dedicated to persecuting an alleged enemy within the country. It also gave them a uniform, a hierarchy, and a ritual.

In 1920 two professional fund-raisers organized a membership drive and arranged to share with local officers the profits from increased initiation fees and from the sale of uniforms and insignia. By 1925 membership approached 5 million. The Klan used floggings, kidnapings, cross-burnings, arson, even murder to terrorize whole communities. It was especially vicious in its treatment of Catholics. An Alabama jury acquitted a Klansman who had murdered a priest; a Klan mob burned a Roman Catholic church in Illinois; the Klan and its sympathizers attempted to crush parochial schools in Oregon; and in Oklahoma they inspired the impeachment of a governor who had declared martial law in a brave effort to rout the organization. Increasingly powerful in politics, the Klan held the balance of power in several states.

At its zenith in 1923 and 1924, the Klan by its very excesses attracted increasing opposition. In 1924 William Allen White, its implacable enemy, lost the Kansas governorship to one of the Klan's friends, but White's campaign set a sensible example. In some states the Klan began to fade, especially after

The remoter and more forlorn yokels have risen against their betters—and ... their uprising is as hopeless as it is idiotic. ... The truth is that the strength of the Klan, like the strength of the Anti-Saloon League ... has always been greatly overestimated. Even in the most barbarous reaches of the South ... it met with vigorous challenge from the start, and there are not three Confederate States to-day in which, on a fair plebiscite, it could hope to prevail. The fact that huge hordes of Southern politicians jumped into night-shirts when it began is not proof that it was actually mighty; it is only proof that politicians are cowards and idiots. Of late all of them have been seeking to rid themselves of the tell-tale tar and feathers; they try to ride the very genuine wave of aversion and disgust as they tried to ride the illusory wave of popularity. As the Klan falls everywhere, the Anti-Saloon League tends to fall with it.

From H. L. Mencken, *Prejudices: Sixth Series*, 1927.

"Dragon" David Stephenson of Indiana kidnaped and assaulted his secretary and connived to keep her from medical attention after she took poison. Convicted in 1925 of second-degree murder and sentenced to life imprisonment, Stephenson demanded a pardon from his fellow Klansman, Governor Ed Jackson. When Jackson refused, the vindictive "Dragon" opened a "little black box" whose contents provided evidence that sent one congressman, the mayor of Indianapolis, and various lesser officers to jail. Most important, the Klan, which had pretended to guard civic purity and feminine virtue, now stood exposed for what it was—corrupt, sordid, and licentious.

Prohibition. The Prohibitionists, who were always strongest in rural areas and particularly among fundamentalist sects, considered liquor an instrument of the devil. Unaware of the complex personal and social problems that provoke excessive drinking, they insisted that alcoholism was created by alcohol itself and by the saloonkeepers who sold it. Whiskey and beer seemed to them, moreover, the potions of immigrants and political bosses, the poison of the corrupt city.

The Prohibition Amendment of 1919 also drew strength from the delusion of many Americans that legislation could somehow control personal behavior of all kinds. Yet before long only the most rabid or stubborn "drys" failed to recognize the difficulties of enforcement. The Prohibition commissioner, in his quest to prevent the manufacture, transportation, and sale of alcoholic beverages (defined by the Volstead Act of 1919 as one-half of 1 percent by volume), had to depend on a small force of agents who were often third-rate political appointees with neither the background nor the intelligence to resist bribes or needless violence. They simply could not police the millions of Americans who wanted to drink and who either made their brews at home or, more often, bought their beer or whiskey from the hundreds of "bootleggers" who earned an illegal, sometimes dangerous, but remunerative living supplying it.

Smugglers brought whiskey in across the Canadian border, or on fast boats from the Caribbean. To supplement the supplies of these "rum-runners," there were countless domestic distillers of illicit whiskey, much of it bad and some of it poisonous. It was easy to buy whiskey by the case, the bottle, or the drink. Indeed "speakeasies," illegal saloons, did business in every major city, and obliging policemen and cab-drivers were glad to tell strangers where they were.

The traffic in bootlegging provided a new and rich source of income and influence for organized crime. In 1920 the most notorious gangland chief, "Scarface" Al Capone, moved to Chicago, where within seven years he had established a $60-million enterprise in whiskey, drugs, gambling, and prostitution. His private army of about a thousand gangsters, who were charged with protecting his domain, accounted for most of the one hundred and thirty murders in the Chicago area in 1926–27. Such was Capone's influence that not a single murderer was convicted. In New York, Philadelphia, Kansas City, and elsewhere, gangsters put high public officers

*"Now then, all together,
'My country 'tis of thee'"*

Darrow and Bryan at Dayton:
creation took centuries

on their payroll and transformed machine politics into agencies for crime.

Prohibition, manifestly unenforceable, had not created organized crime, but it had given gangland a vast privilege to exploit—a privilege that repeal of Prohibition would at least remove. Urban "wets," who had opposed Prohibition from the first, led the movement for repeal, supported by more and more former "drys." The most adamant foes of repeal were the moralists of the countryside who had failed to distinguish between liquor and crime and who identified both with immigration and the city.

Last-ditch fundamentalism.

Rural hostility to urban culture also showed itself in matters of the mind. The unsophisticated have always fallen prey to antiscientism, partly because they do not understand the methods of science, partly because they resent many of the changes that science and technology bring about. Though most Americans admired the technological advances of the 1920s and recognized them as the products of earlier scientific strivings, some were distressed by the complexities and uncertainties of a machine civilization, by its speed, its capacity for destructive as well as constructive power, its overwhelming challenge to the ways of the "good old days." To those Americans science seemed threatening and mysterious. In the

rural areas that modern culture had just begun to reach, Protestant fundamentalism seized on science as an archenemy.

The fundamentalists insisted that the Bible must be accepted as literal truth. More than sixty years after the publication of Darwin's *Origin of Species,* they still rejected the concept of biological evolution and attacked those who taught it. In the postwar years William Jennings Bryan, a "dry," a fundamentalist, a folk hero of a kind, and now an old and frustrated man, enlisted in the antievolutionist crusade. Strengthened by his leadership, the antievolutionists scored partial victories in several Southern states. Bryan himself in 1925 assisted the lobby that pressured the Tennessee legislature into passing a statute making it illegal to teach any theory that denied the account of creation recorded in Genesis.

The American Civil Liberties Union, responding to this challenge to the freedom of inquiry, offered counsel to any Tennessee teacher who would test the law. More in amusement than in anger, John T. Scopes of the mountain town of Dayton lectured from a Darwinian text and was arrested. Among the lawyers who defended him were Clarence Darrow, the most famous pleader of the time, and Arthur Garfield Hays, a celebrated advocate of civil liberties. Assisting the prosecution was Bryan, who had been retained by the World's Christian Fundamental Association. The all-star cast in the Dayton "monkey trial" engaged the interest of the entire nation.

The prosecution contended that the only issue was Scopes' violation of the law, but the defense raised the question of the validity of the law itself. The case reached its climax when Bryan took the stand as an expert on the Bible. Joshua had made the sun stand still, the Commoner said; the whale had swallowed Jonah; if it was in the Bible, it was so. As Darrow pressed the cross-examination, Bryan revealed an invincible ignorance of modern learning. Exhausted by the strain of testifying and by the laughter of the spectators, he died, heartbroken, soon after the trial.

Scopes was convicted for violating the law, but the state supreme court reversed the decision on a technicality, and the constitutionality of the statute could not be tested. There was no longer any reason to test it. Bryan had admitted in his testimony that creation took centuries; a "day" in Genesis might be an eon. That admission cost the fundamentalists their argument, and the ridicule of Bryan's performance had lost them their cause.

But by 1925 the blind innocence of fundamentalism, together with the pernicious zeal of the Klan, had estranged the ordinary citizen from the intellectual and had divided the underprivileged of the farms from the underprivileged of the cities. Protestant laborers had been set against Jewish and Catholic laborers, whites against blacks. Americans whom prosperity either did not reach or did not beguile had been sealed off into separate and often hostile groups.

The election of 1924. This estrangement made it difficult for the Democratic party to select a national candidate in 1924. One of the two leading contenders was William G. McAdoo, who had won the acclaim of liberals for his administration of the railroads during the war (p. 561), but who had lost their favor by taking a job as counsel to Edward L. Doheny, one of the scoundrels of Teapot Dome. Yet McAdoo, ardently "dry" and equivocal about the Klan, held the support of the South and the West. His major rival, Alfred E. Smith, the governor of New York, was a "wet," a Catholic, and a Tammany man. The darling of the Eastern cities, Smith was anathema to the rural delegates in spite of his progressive record.

The convention met in New York's Madison Square Garden during a July heat wave. To the party's shame a motion not to include a plank in the platform condemning the Klan by name passed by $543\frac{3}{20}$ to $542\frac{3}{20}$. There followed a nine-day deadlock over the nomination. Through ninety-five ballots the hoarse voice of the aged Bryan vied with the raucous noise of the Tammany gallery, and the contest was relayed by radio to millions of American homes. The split in the party had become irremediable; the sweltering delegates had become exhausted. At last Smith and McAdoo withdrew by mutual agreement. On the 103rd ballot the convention nominated John W. Davis for President and Charles Bryan as his running mate. They were an unlikely brace. Davis, who had served as Solicitor General and briefly as ambassador to Great Britain during the Wilson Administration, was a cultivated gentleman and an eminent corporation lawyer identified with the House of Morgan. The liberals who disdained him could find small solace in Bryan's younger brother Charley, at best a cockboat in the wake of the

Commoner's leaky man-of-war. Wall Street and Nebraska could not be squeezed onto a single ticket, but the prolonged bitterness of the convention had made a saner choice impossible.

A third nomination stirred wider interest. The resurgence of reform candidates in the congressional election of 1922 had owed much to the Conference for Progressive Political Action, an organization of farm leaders, social workers, former Bull Moosers, and Socialists. Now the leaders of the Conference began to talk about running a separate ticket in 1924. The communists forced their hand by taking over the Farmer-Labor party and offering its nomination to "Battle Bob" La Follette. Then almost seventy, iron-gray, still the indomitable Daniel in the lion's den of "the interests," La Follette scorned the offer. That response prompted his supporters to form a new Progressive party, which named La Follette and the liberal Montana Democrat Burton K. Wheeler as its national candidates.

La Follette's candidacy attracted a host of tireless battlers for reform, among them Felix Frankfurter, John R. Commons, and Jane Addams. It was endorsed by the American Federation of Labor and, curiously, by the Socialists. La Follette stood for conservation, public ownership of waterpower, increased taxes on wealth, curbing the authority of the Supreme Court, limiting the use of injunctions in labor disputes, the popular election of judges, the direct election of Presidents, the end of child labor, and a national referendum on declarations of war. But he emphasized the evil of monopoly, ringing again the changes of his early campaigns in Wisconsin. The *Wall Street Journal* called his platform "Wisconsin Bolshevism"; the head of the Communist party in the United States called it "the most reactionary document of the year." Both statements were nonsense. The platform and the campaign were simply refurbished Grangerism, rather seedy and out of place in 1924, yet still appealing to many farmers, and the only haven for those who could stomach neither Coolidge nor Davis.

The Republicans ignored Davis and harped on La Follette's radicalism. They need not have worked so hard as they did nor have spent the millions they poured into the campaign, for the nation voted overwhelmingly to "keep cool with Coolidge." The President carried thirty-five states to Davis' twelve and La Follette's one, Wisconsin. Coolidge won

382 electoral votes to his opponents' 149. And his popular vote, over 15,000,000, exceeded the combined total of Davis, who polled less than 8,500,000, and La Follette, who had slightly more than 4,800,000. Prosperity and "Silent Cal" had enjoyed a major triumph.

Yet the new Progressive party had made a point, though it died in 1925 with La Follette. The point was simply that there was room in politics for dissent from the business creed. The lesson was not lost on the Democrats, who realized that they had to close ranks and reconstruct a coalition that welcomed men of all colors, all parentages, all sections. If the Democrats were to win in the future they would have to be "unequivocally the party of progress and liberal thought." That phrase was Franklin Roosevelt's, who saw small chance for a victory before 1932.

Grandiose illusions

Incomparable clown: Charlie Chaplin

The "It" girl: Clara Bow

The good life. Americans were optimistic during Coolidge's second term. The middle class in particular, more comfortable than ever before, experienced a sense of well-being. They admitted no limit to a personal success symbolized by material possessions. They neither liked nor trusted the "knockers," but preferred the "boosters," the men with their eyes and hearts set on the rosy future.

Some of the boosters channeled their optimism into the expanding advertising profession. National advertising flourished in the twenties. It offered an attractive substitute for more painful forms of competition, like price-cutting, which, in any event, were being curtailed by trade agreements and informal arrangements among manufacturers. Advertising also helped identify brands for consumers, who were buying more and more of their goods in stores and producing fewer and fewer at home. Advertising men believed they were "inspiring citizens to live a more abundant life." They were creating new wants and encouraging discontent with possessions outmoded but not necessarily outworn. Advertisers sold the ingredients of the good life—health in orange juice, cleanliness in soap, popularity in deodorants, romantic love in voguish clothes.

As one General Motors executive put it, advertising had to make people "healthily dissatisfied with what they have. . . . The old factors of wear and tear . . . are too slow." Built-in obsolescence paved the road to business success. Manufacturing prettier, more comfortable cars than Ford did, changing models annually (while also meeting competitive standards in engineering), General Motors won primacy in the automobile industry largely by catering to luxury and fashion.

Advertising also created and sold reputations, both corporate and personal. Public-relations experts, taking over the new game of ballyhoo as their own, fabricated heroes on demand. Some of the celebrated athletes of the 1920s, for example, owed part of their fame to sheer ballyhoo. To be sure, Bobby Jones in golf, Bill Tilden in tennis, Jack Dempsey in boxing, and Babe Ruth in baseball were athletes of genuinely heroic proportions. But their proportions were overdrawn, and cynical public-relations men learned to conceal the boorish behavior of Ruth, among others, by planting stories of fictitious noble deeds.

The prospering tabloid newspapers catered to a mass audience that delighted in sensationalism and hero worship. The art of sham was especially effective when it could concentrate on sex. It publicized the new heroes and heroines of the booming motion-picture industry—Rudolph Valentino, the Casanova of the silent films, whose untimely death broke thousands of adolescent hearts; Clara Bow, the "It" girl, whose curves and curls entranced a male multitude; Mary Pickford, the sweet charmer whom a plucky lad could more properly admire; and Charlie Chaplin, the incomparable clown.

Outside of Hollywood, standard success stories followed classic forms—farm boys conquered the city while remaining pure, poor boys struggled and saved their way to wealth, nice boys met and married beautiful rich girls. The protagonist's gleaming teeth, curly hair, lithe muscles, humility, and hard work assured a happy ending. And ordinary Americans could do just as well through diligent use of the right toothpaste, hair lotion, and correspondence course. But the plot was used too often to boost sales and circulation, and it was beginning to wear thin. Just then a real hero revived the faith.

In the spring of 1927 there was startling

The spirit of Lindbergh

news of a young man flying solo, eastward across the Atlantic, in a small monoplane. No one before had made that flight alone. The prayers of the nation followed Charles A. Lindbergh, Jr., to France. His safe landing set off a jubilee; Coolidge sent a cruiser to bring him home; New York extended ecstatic greetings. Briefly, sham and commercialism hid from authentic daring and clean-cut youth. Lindbergh took it calmly. After writing another stanza to his saga by marrying Anne Morrow, the daughter of a Morgan partner, he tried to escape the tabloids and the confetti. Myths need a foundation in truth, and the Lindbergh story had been as genuine as it was refreshing. When it faded from the headlines, myth fed once again on the exploits of hired muscle men who drew crowds to mammoth stadiums and testified about the proteins packaged in breakfast cereals.

Advertising and public relations and ballyhoo, like the newspapers and magazines and radio that carried them, exported urban ways to rural people. They disseminated a common set of symbols to diverse groups. They told farmers and laborers and suburbanites to admire the same success stories and buy the same cars and cosmetics. They told them all to spend their money to increase their comfort, to prove their mettle, to live "the good life." They encouraged installment buying to ensure the sale of an expanding national product. They helped Americans with rising wages to forget about the frustrations of their dull and routine jobs. The spurious self-esteem that sprang from possession and fashion

would endure only so long as Americans could count on steady income and easy credit; but so long as prosperity lasted, advertisers gilded the promises of a commercial culture, the only brand of Americanism they really understood. This crass and transient boom was rooted in illusion, in calling things by the wrong names and then accepting the names as true. The illusions of public life were similarly deceiving.

The image of America abroad. The Coolidge Administration was continually involved in Latin American affairs. But often it succeeded only in obscuring national purpose and generating ill will among Latin Americans. Secretary of State Hughes, moved by a concern for peace and order, had helped bring about the peaceful settlement of several Latin American boundary disputes. During his tenure, the United States also sponsored a conference of Central American powers, which agreed to withhold recognition from any government established by a *coup d'état.* But this genuflection to stability ignored the realities of Central American politics, for where the government in power had complete control over elections, a *coup d'état* or revolution was the only means of ousting it.

In Nicaragua Coolidge acted unilaterally. First, in 1925, he withdrew a token force of marines from that nation, which then seemed capable of servicing its foreign debt and preserving its internal stability. But the appearance was deceptive. Almost at once revolution broke out, and Coolidge again landed the marines, in time some five thousand. Regrettably, in its quest for order the United States chose to support the reactionary faction, whose identification with large landowners and foreign investors had helped provoke the revolution in the first place.

The marines contained the fighting, but they could not bring it to an end. American bankers were lending money to the conservative faction for the purchase of munitions in the United States, and the rebels were receiving some arms from sympathetic Mexico. Increasingly uncomfortable, Coolidge in 1927 named Henry L. Stimson as his personal emissary to negotiate a peace. Stimson succeeded in arranging an effective truce and an honest election, in which the rebel general triumphed. The marines, however, remained until 1933. They also remained in Haiti but in 1924 left the Dominican Republic, where President Wilson had sent them.

Though the United States had no territorial ambitions, Yankee investors were seeking bonanzas in Latin America, and Latin Americans resented the Yankee habit of intervening in their local affairs. At the Pan-American Conference of 1928 the Argentine delegation sponsored a proposal that "no American country have the right to intervene in any other American country." The United States succeeded in defeating the proposal but in doing so heightened the resentment. Late in 1928 the State Department concluded that intervention was not justified by the Monroe Doctrine or by the interests of American investors. But it was still not ready to announce that conclusion or to surrender its claim to unilateral intervention. This offense to the sensitivities of Latin Americans continued to cloud hemispheric friendship.

*Dwight W. Morrow:
patient negotiator*

Latin American liberals, moreover, identified the United States with the forces of reaction. Even more than the Nicaraguan episode, developments in Mexico contributed to that view. In 1925 Plutarco Elias Calles, the new president of Mexico, revived the spirit of the revolution of 1910, which had for several years been in eclipse. He sponsored laws that permitted foreigners to acquire land only if they renounced the protection of their own government, and laws that defined all subsoil deposits as the inalienable property of the Mexican nation. Oil companies, American and other, were required to apply for a renewal of their concessions before 1927. Four large American companies refused. Their spokesmen in the United States, asserting that

Mexico was on the road to Bolshevism, demanded military intervention. They were supported by some American Catholics incensed by Calles' anticlericalism. The clumsy diplomacy of Coolidge's ambassador to Mexico complicated the situation, but in January 1927 the United States Senate by unanimous vote passed a resolution demanding the peaceful settlement of all contested issues— by arbitration, if necessary.

Several months later Coolidge appointed a new ambassador, Dwight W. Morrow, with the overriding commission "to keep us out of war with Mexico." Morrow's patient negotiations led to a temporary relaxation of the Mexican land laws and to an uneasy accord between the Mexican government and the Catholic Church. Those holding operations restored friendly relations. Yet Morrow's admirable performance could not erase the hostility created by earlier American diplomacy. To reformers south of the border American amity was colored by oil.

Europeans resented a different kind of diplomacy of the dollar. During the First World War the United States had lent the Allies $7 billion and after the war another $3.3 billion. The recipients had spent their loans almost entirely on American military products and relief supplies. With the return of peace, they regarded the loans merely as one part of the total Allied resistance to Germany, an American contribution toward a victory to which Europeans had given a larger share of flesh and blood. So they were reluctant to repay either the loans or the interest on them. And even those who wanted to square accounts found it difficult to pay. The European nations had depleted their own reserves before borrowing from the United States, and now they found it impossible to replenish those reserves in an American market sealed off by the tariff.

The only way they could meet their obligations to the United States was to draw on the huge reparations that had been imposed on Germany at Versailles. But Germany lacked both the means to pay and the will to scrimp in order to exonerate a war guilt she did not really accept. In 1923 she defaulted, and French and Belgian troops occupied the Ruhr Valley. The Germans there cut down coal production, while the German government inflated its currency recklessly, and the resulting economic distress in both France and Germany seemed to forebode economic collapse and possibly even armed conflict.

The crisis commanded American as well as European attention. Earlier, Charles Evans Hughes had suggested that an international commission of experts, including Americans, be appointed to examine the whole reparations problem. The deadlock in the Ruhr now persuaded the French to agree. The committees that then met recommended what was called the Dawes Plan, in recognition of the participation of Charles Gates Dawes, who was soon to become Coolidge's running mate. That plan, which went into effect in 1924, arranged for an international loan to stabilize German currency and for a flexible, graduated scale of reparations payments. Five years later another American, Owen D. Young, headed a second committee, which substantially reduced the payments. The Allies, satisfied by these terms and concurrent European political agreements, withdrew their forces from the Ruhr and the Rhineland.

American money, however, played a more significant role in the European crisis than did either Dawes or Young. Between 1924 and 1931 Germany managed to meet her payments only because her government, her municipalities, and her businessmen were able to borrow $2.6 billion in the United States. In turn, only the reparations collected by the Allies enabled them to keep up their payments on their American war debts. The interdependence of debts and reparations payments was obvious, but the United States refused to acknowledge it. Most Americans, moreover, most of their congressmen, and certainly their President rejected the notion that the debts had in any sense been offset by the Allied losses in battle. For Coolidge, as for most of his constituents, the debts were business obligations pure and simple. When the French proposed that the burden of debt be eased, the President unhesitatingly turned them down. "They hired the money," he said. The spirit behind that phrase overshadowed all the efforts of Dawes and Young. So long as it prevailed, Europe regarded Uncle Sam as Uncle Shylock.

Deluded diplomacy.

The Administration resisted the facts of international politics as strongly as it resisted the facts of international economics. Like most Americans, Coolidge believed in disarmament, not only because he knew that it would reduce federal expense, but also because he presumed that it would assure peace. But he did not understand, or at least would not admit, the continuing importance of power in international affairs.

Further, the conventional men in control of the army and the navy husbanded their meager appropriations and resisted spending anything on airplanes and submarines, even though those weapons had clearly made traditional military tactics and strategy obsolete. The failure to develop aircraft infuriated General William ("Billy") Mitchell of the Army Air Service, whose bombers had sunk a battleship in 1921. In an oracular report two years later, he warned the authorities of the vulnerability of battleships. In 1925, after the navy's sheer incompetence had resulted in the destruction of a dirigible, Mitchell attacked his superiors in public and urged the creation of a separate air command. A court-martial suspended him from duty for five years. The flurry over the episode persuaded Coolidge to appoint a civilian board of inquiry under Dwight Morrow, but it shrugged off Mitchell's arguments. The Administration denied public funds to promote commercial aviation as well. By 1929 the productive capacity of the American aircraft industry had fallen to seventy-five hundred planes a year, little more than a third of the capacity available at the war's end. In the absence of responsible public policy, the United States alone of the major powers slept smugly through the morning of the air age.

Coolidge was less complacent about international naval competition. The Five Power Treaty had applied only to battleships and aircraft-carriers, and the signatories had continued to build auxiliaries. Late in 1924 Congress authorized the construction of eight cruisers. Hoping to avoid the expense of further construction and to end the naval rivalry, the President invited the powers to a conference in 1927. Italy, already infected by Mussolini's fantasies of military glory, refused to attend. So did France, unhappy with the small ratio she had already received at Washington and reluctant, in the face of Italian resurgence, to commit herself to further self-restraint. Coolidge, dedicated to a policy of isolation from European affairs, had failed to assess these obstacles to disarmament. He failed also to negotiate a preliminary understanding essential to any agreement with the British. As a consequence, the English-speaking delegates at the 1927 conference wrangled to no purpose, while the Japanese stood contentedly aside.

Coolidge had already retreated from an

Vice President Charles G. Dawes

earlier, cautious gesture toward internationalism. The Permanent Court of International Justice called for by the League of Nations Covenant had been established in 1921. The purpose of this World Court was to adjudicate certain types of case, to render advice whenever the League requested it, and to arbitrate cases brought before it. Americans had long hoped for the development of a body of law that could be applied to international affairs, and in 1923 Harding, influenced by Hughes, recommended conditional American adherence to the court. Coolidge made the same recommendation in his first annual message. But, even though Hughes had drafted four reservations to the court's protocol to protect the United States from contact with the League itself, the isolationists in the Senate balked. After a long delay the Senate adopted a fifth reservation that would limit the court's right even to render advisory opinions to the League. Further, the court could give no opinion, without American consent, on any question in which the United States claimed an interest. In 1926 the Senate finally voted adherence to the court on those conditions. When the members of the court then tried to clarify the meaning of the reservations, Coolidge declared that clarification constituted rejection and that there was no prospect of American adherence to the court.* That denouement, followed by the failure of the naval-armaments conference, left the Administration's diplomatic record singularly barren.

During his last months in office, however, Coolidge's diplomacy won wide acclaim. Salmon O. Levinson, a Chicago lawyer, had been recommending that the great powers sign an agreement condemning war. Professor James T. Shotwell, who had been advancing the same suggestion independently, also proposed sanctions to enforce such an agreement. The idea of outlawing war caught the attention of many Americans, including William E. Borah, chairman of the Senate Committee on Foreign Relations, Shotwell urged it upon Aristide Briand, the French foreign minister, who promptly used it for his own purposes. In April 1927, in a gesture of good will to compensate for Franco-American friction over disarmament and war debts, Briand wrote an address to the American people in which he proposed a pact outlawing

*Both Hoover and Franklin Roosevelt later recommended adherence to the court on terms like those contemplated by Hughes. But the Senate declined.

war. Coolidge was irritated by Briand's resorting to irregular channels to announce his scheme, but the popular enthusiasm for the proposal forced the President's hand. The State Department asked Briand to submit his plan formally.

Secretary of State Frank B. Kellogg now outflanked Briand. Intent on avoiding a bilateral agreement that would imply some sort of alliance between the United States and France, Kellogg recommended instead "an effort to obtain the adherence of all the principal powers of the world to a declaration renouncing war as an instrument of national policy." While Briand stalled, the Secretary of State circulated the draft of a declaration he had drawn up on his own. He also let it be known that the United States would consent to sign the pact in Paris. Briand then accepted the American scheme, and in August 1928 fifteen nations meeting in Paris endorsed a treaty by which they renounced war and promised to settle all disputes, whatever their nature, by "pacific means."

Americans were jubilant over the banishment of war—so jubilant that they tended to ignore qualifications made in diplomatic notes exchanged by the signatories. These set down reservations safeguarding France's interpretations of her own self-defense and Great Britain's obligations to her empire. In recommending ratification of the pact, the Senate Foreign Relations Committee reported that ratification would not, in its view, curtail the right of the United States to self-defense and to its own interpretations of the Monroe Doctrine, nor would ratification oblige the United States to take any action against a violator of the Kellogg-Briand pact. So interpreted, the pact won approval by a vote of 85 to 1. But so interpreted, it was, in the words of Senator Carter Glass of Virginia, "worthless, but perfectly harmless."

For most Americans the Paris pact constituted a triumph. To declare perpetual peace without assuming the responsibility for preserving it suited the nation's mood. Now the nation could cut its expenditures, disarm, collect its debts, and trust to reassuring words for sunny safety. Yet the hocus-pocus that sold peace in multilingual print was not unlike the hocus-pocus that sold beauty in a bottle.

Get rich quick. Of all the grandiose illusions of the 1920s none was more beguiling than the prospect of easy riches. It rested on the

Miami: population doubled in five years

simple faith that the value of property would constantly increase, and that the man who bought today could sell tomorrow at a handsome profit. Those who had property to sell nourished this faith, and they were helped by the ready credit that enabled speculators to borrow what they needed. The hucksters and the boomers, moreover, made the allure of speculation a favorite fantasy of the time.

For a while in the mid-twenties the quest for a bonanza drew thousands of Americans to ventures in Florida real estate. The population of Miami more than doubled between 1920 and 1925, and other Florida cities and resorts along the Atlantic and Gulf coasts also mushroomed. Florida's boomers pointed to the warm winter climate, the ready accessibility of their region to vacationers from the North, the prospect of an American Riviera. Imagination covered swamps and barren sands with towns and building lots. As the greedy rushed to buy the dream, a few who invested early and sold at the peak of the boom made fortunes. Their success lured others. Most of the transactions took the form of binders—agreements to buy property, which could be had for a fraction of the value of the property itself. The binders could be sold and sold again, each time for more money.

For every sale, of course, there had to be a buyer. The trade in binders was profitable only so long as someone came along to bid them up, and once people began to compare the dream with the reality the buyers were bound to disappear. The balloon began to deflate in the spring and summer of 1926. That fall it burst when a hurricane swept through the Miami area, destroying develop-ments that had emerged from the dream stage, and wrecking the railroad to Key West. The grand plans of the boomers were laid away; the millions of dollars in speculative profits were wiped out; and the Florida craze was over.

But a much larger boom was already under way. During the prosperous twenties most of the gains from increased productivity and from the growing market for manufactured goods were funneled into corporate profits. And as profits rose, enhanced by Mellon's tax favors to business, so did the value of corporate shares. Initially that rise reflected a genuine increase in the worth of corporate properties and in the earning potential of the corporations themselves. In the mid-twenties, however, the price of stocks began to soar at a dizzying pace. Investors who were looking for securities that would give them a reasonably safe return now had to compete with speculators who were after overnight fortunes. To meet the demand for stocks, promoters organized investment trust and multitiered holding companies whose only assets were hope and good will. They offered their new issues to eager buyers deluded by greed and by a naive confidence in the surging market. In 1923 new capital issues totaled $3.2 billion; in 1927, $10 billion, much of it purely speculative. The volume of sales on the New York Stock Exchange leaped from 236 million shares in 1923 to 577 million in 1927 and to 1,125 million a year later.

Corporations themselves speculated. As the market rose, corporations found that they earned less by investing their reserves in new facilities than by putting them into brokers' loans—that is, loans that brokers made to

Coolidge on the stock market: January 6, 1928

I am not familiar enough with the exact workings ... of the Federal Reserve System so that comments that I might make relative to the amount of brokers' loans and so on would not be of very much value. I do know in a general way that the amount of securities in this country has increased very largely in recent years.... The deposits in banks also are larger. And those two things together would necessarily be a reason for doing more business of that kind that is transacted by brokers and would naturally result in a larger sum of money being used for that purpose. Now, whether the amount at the present time is disproportionate to the resources of the country I am not in a position to judge accurately, but so far as indicated by an inquiry that I have made of the Treasury Department and so on I haven't had any indications that the amount was large enough to cause particularly unfavorable comment.

From H. H. Quint and R. H. Ferrell, Eds., *The Talkative President: The Off-the-Record Press Conferences of Calvin Coolidge*, 1964.

their customers to enable them to gamble far beyond their cash resources. In "buying on margin," as this practice was called, customers relied on brokers' loans to cover most of the cost of their stock purchases. Brokers and customers alike expected that the growing value of the stocks would make it easy enough to repay the loans. Meeting the pressing demand for brokers' loans, or "call money," corporations emptied their surpluses into the money market, where they received staggering returns.

Instead of tempering the boom, public officials encouraged it. The Federal Reserve System had two means of tightening credit—that is, of making loans more expensive. It could contract the supply of money by selling government securities or by raising the rate of interest at which banks borrowed from the Federal Reserve. But the Federal Reserve chose to use its power to keep interest rates low. It did so for good reason—in order to discourage the import of gold from Europe and to facilitate American loans to Europe, then still in need of investment funds for economic rehabilitation and development. (If interest rates had gone way up, Europeans and Americans would both have tended to invest more of their money within the United States.) Even if the Federal Reserve had tightened credit, however, it could not have controlled the call-money market that the corporations were feeding, for speculators were willing to borrow at usurious rates to finance their march to riches.

In the absence of federal authority over either credit or the chicanery of promoters, the best weapon available to the government was simple candor. There was, however, none of that. Secretary of the Treasury Mellon knew exactly what was going on; indeed he was himself deep in speculation. Yet whenever sober businessmen questioned the state of the market, he or his colleagues in the Administration invariably responded with soothing reassurances. And Coolidge went along. Early in 1927 William Z. Ripley, a Harvard economist, lectured the President on the prevalent "double-shuffling, honey-fuggling, hornswoggling and skulduggery." Coolidge, feet on desk and cigar in teeth, asked gloomily: "Is there anything we can do down here?" Ripley answered that the regulation of securities was the responsibility of the states, not of the federal government. Relieved, the President relaxed and put the incident out of his mind.

By the end of the year brokers' loans had reached nearly $4 billion. In January 1928 Coolidge reassured the dubious few by announcing that this volume of loans was perfectly natural. Shortly thereafter Roy Young of the Federal Reserve Board, a close friend of Herbert Hoover, told a congressional committee that the loans were "safely and conservatively made." Those sanctions hastened the tempo of the boom and gave a Midas touch to 1928, an election year.

To Coolidge the ascending figures on the ticker tape were evidence of the nation's prosperity and of his own sagacity. He was as much honey-fuggled as hornswoggling. Like the brokers and speculators, he was at once the prisoner and the propagator of the grandiose myths that bemused the nation.

Nonconformity and dissent

The Jazz Age. Some Americans, however, were repelled by materialism and its delusions. Disappointed by a progressive faith that seemed to have failed, they were alienated by the emptiness of business civilization. They were equally cynical about serving mankind and about striving for worldly success. Finding only futility in the past and the future, they chose to seek out the pleasures of the present, to live for their private selves and for immediate self-expression.

Those men and women, many of them young, were no more immoral or promiscuous than men and women had been before. But they dropped pretense. They revealed their impatience with traditional standards of conduct openly and often. One symbol of their protest was jazz, with its sensuality, its spontaneity, its atavistic rhythms, and with the sinuous and intimate dancing it inspired. Jazz was ungenteel, even un-Caucasian, above all uninhibited. It expressed not only protest and art of a kind but also a controversial change in sexual mores.

That change sprang largely from the ways in which city living altered family life. The nuclear family of the city and suburb (man, wife, children) existed in a private world quite different from that of the kinship family of the country, where grandparents, aunts, uncles, and cousins provided support and where community was more common than aloneness. The very impersonality of the city obliged its inhabitants to meet and resolve the problems of their lives with neither help nor impediment. Not every marriage was equal to the challenge.

Having won the vote, women now demanded equal rights to jobs, to income, to their own apartments, to cigarettes, to whiskey, and to sexual satisfaction in matrimony or sometimes outside it. Much of the energy of feminism concentrated on the birth control movement. That movement, so Margaret Sanger claimed, freed the mind from "sexual prejudice and taboo." Not the least of its functions was to increase the quantity and quality of sexual relationships. Sexual mores were also affected by changing attitudes toward divorce. Unhappy men and women, at one time without escape from oppressive marriages, each year sought more and more divorces under laws that grew increasingly lenient. Probably the incidence of premarital

and extramarital sexual experience also rose. To some extent, especially for young people, adventures in sex released part of a rebellion against the reigning culture and its neopuritanical code.

During the twenties, moreover, even the unrebellious were learning to understand the significance of sex in human nature. The most important contributions to that understanding were made by Sigmund Freud, whose doctrines had first reached America in the years before the war. After the war Freudian psychology rapidly became a national fad, ordinarily in vastly simplified and distorted forms. Freud himself, while demonstrating that neurotic symptoms and behavior could usually be attributed to sexual origins, did not advocate promiscuity. His first concern was with creating a system of analysis that would enable a doctor to help a patient find the emotional sources of his disorders, behavioral or somatic. On the basis of that discovery sick people could then reconstruct their lives.

His popularizers, however, often concentrated on the libido, the antisocial, the powerful and personal and sexual instinct in man, rather than on the social experiences that contained it or permitted it constructive release. Further, Freud spoke much more to the anxieties and the behavior of men than of women, and his popularizers persisted in his unconscious masculinity. The average American met Freudian ideas only in the tabloids, which made headline news of almost any escape from sexual starvation.

In their undistorted form, Freudian doctrines did not excuse adultery or condone lechery, but they did explain the importance of sex, which prudery was reluctant to admit. They also called attention to the need for latitude and compassion in judging behavior, sexual or otherwise. And, incidentally, they demonstrated the harrowing inadequacy of the values of a pecuniary culture.

A literature of alienation. "Society was something alien," Malcolm Cowley wrote about himself and his literary contemporaries of the 1920s. "It was a sort of parlor car in which we rode, over smooth tracks, toward a destination we should never have chosen for ourselves." Gertrude Stein called the young writers of the time "a lost generation." It was lost, Cowley later concluded,

Margaret Sanger: free from sexual taboo

Langston Hughes

Jazz and the black artist

Jazz to me is one of the inherent expressions of Negro life in America: the eternal tom-tom beating in the Negro soul—the tom-tom of revolt against weariness in a white world, a world of subway trains, and work, work, work; the tom-tom of joy and laughter, and pain swallowed in a smile. Yet the Philadelphia clubwoman ... turns up her nose at jazz and all its manifestations—likewise almost anything else distinctly racial.... She wants the artist to flatter her, to make the white world believe that all Negroes are as smug and as near white in soul as she wants to be. But, to my mind, it is the duty of the younger Negro artist ... to change through the force of his art that old whispering "I want to be white," hidden in the aspirations of his people, to "Why should I want to be white? I am a Negro—and beautiful."

From Langston Hughes, "The Negro Artist and the Racial Mountain," *The Nation*, 1926.

F. Scott Fitzgerald

Ernest Hemingway

Gertrude Stein

because its training had prepared it for another world than existed after the war . . . because it accepted no older guides to conduct and because it had formed a false picture of society. . . . The generation belonged to a period of transition from values already fixed to values that had to be erected. . . . They were seceding from the old and yet could adhere to nothing new.

This generation of artists turned its back on progress, on economics, on Main Street, and on Wall Street. "It was characteristic of the Jazz Age," said novelist F. Scott Fitzgerald, one of its high priests, "that it had no interest in politics at all." And the editor of *The Smart Set,* H. L. Mencken, wrote: "If I am convinced of anything, it is that Doing Good is in bad taste."

These men and their fellows detested the business culture. Many of them fled, some to Paris, others to Greenwich Village, still others to an impenetrable privacy of creativity. And they attacked the civilization they hated. Sinclair Lewis peopled the Middle West with confused men and women, trapped by their own futile materialism and unthinking gentility, narrow, unhappy, stifled. Lewis' *Main Street* (1920) and *Babbitt* (1922) created satirical symbols of American life that persisted for a quarter of a century, not in the United States alone, but in Europe as well.

Sherwood Anderson exercised a large influence on his literary compatriots. A compassionate critic of small-town America, Anderson abandoned a business career, after a nervous breakdown in 1912, to devote himself to writing. His *Winesburg, Ohio* (1919) was a moving, autobiographical novel of alienation. Perhaps more important, he exemplified the religion of art, for he had escaped Babylon and had succeeded in his career of the spirit.

Seeking in art a distillation of experience, the young masters experimenting with literary form gave a new beauty and vitality to American letters. Encouraged particularly by Ezra Pound and Gertrude Stein and inspired by their prewar poetry, the novelists Ernest Hemingway and William Faulkner and the poet T. S. Eliot raised the national literary reputation to its all-time zenith. Hemingway's *The Sun Also Rises* (1926) and *A Farewell to Arms* (1929) expressed a deep revulsion against nineteenth-century standards of conduct and idealizations of war. In *The Sound and the Fury* (1929) Faulkner used Freudian insights and adventurous prose to expose the awful tensions between self and society and the exacerbation of those tensions in the culture of the Deep South. Eliot's "The Love Song of J. Alfred Prufrock" (written in 1911, published six years later) made impotence the weary symbol of modern man. His *The Waste Land* (1922), probably the most emulated poem of the decade, provided a text in fragmentation and despair.

All these works were vastly more significant for their form than for their content. They revealed alienation and spoke of protest, but their authors were first, and most self-consciously, artists. So, too, were the other Americans who shared in the extraordinary literary renaissance of the period. They included an impressive number of talented black artists and authors, among them James Weldon Johnson, Countee Cullen, and Langston Hughes. Though some of the prose and poetry of the "Harlem Renaissance" repudiated black themes, much of it borrowed self-consciously from black culture, and the best of it, like the poetry of Hughes, ranked with the best work of white Americans.

The great outburst of artistic creativity had begun before 1920; it continued beyond 1929; but it came to a crescendo during the Coolidge era. The experimental forms of literature and of the fine arts were themselves a break with tradition. They were based on the deliberate artistic manipulation of concepts of time, of man, of sound, of meaning. Art, if it was not a distillation of all experience as its devotees believed, was at least a distillation of aesthetic expression without equal in the American past. And the artist's alienation from society freed his creative mind, which enriched the perceptions and satisfactions of generations yet unborn.

But the religion of art could also be as futile as materialism itself. Alienation ordinarily denied social responsibility. The artists who rejected their national culture also accepted most of its claims. They turned away from the Coolidge era not because of its inequities but because of its superficial accomplishments. In contrast to the progressive intellectuals who had preceded them, they sought private escapes and private satisfactions, and they surrendered society to its shortsighted masters. This escapism deprived the nation of the assistance of many of its most imaginative minds.

Worse still, some Americans cast off democracy along with materialism. They took at their word the Mellons and the Fords and the Coolidges who believed that the business cult was the democratic ideal. They concluded that democracy necessarily generated a vulgar, selfish, pecuniary civilization. The critic Van Wyck Brooks, in his *The Ordeal of Mark Twain* (1920), wrote about the Gilded Age, with the twenties much in mind, as "a horde-life, a herd-life, an epoch without sun and stars," which condemned the artist, and the soul, to frustration. Eliot also scorned democracy and remained rootless until he found salvation in the church, as Brooks did in sentimentality. H. L. Mencken was more acid. He ridiculed not only Prohibition, the Ku Klux Klan, and censorship, but the whole American people, whom he considered a sodden, brutish, ignorant mob. Democracy, for him, was government by orgy. As for democracy as a theory, "all the known facts lie flatly against it." Irving Babbitt, who formulated an aristocratic doctrine of the "inner check," had no patience with the "sickly sentimentalizing of the

lot of the underdog," no confidence in social reform, no hope except in pseudo-Platonic comforts, and thus no real hope. The price of complacent materialism was alienation; and the bill of despair that went with alienation was ominously high.

Progressive still. Yet disenchantment did not lead all critics to alienation. Some drew on the legacy of progressivism and on their own undaunted spirit to point out anew the paths toward a good society. John Dewey (see p. 516) continued to examine the practical consequences of social policies in *Human Nature and Conduct* (1922) and *Individualism Old and New* (1929). These books urged experimentation in education for selfless citizenship, and public rather than private planning for social rather than pecuniary goals. Charles Beard in his *The Rise of American Civilization* (1927) stressed optimistically the historical significance of economic change. A year later he called for social engineering, national planning, to organize advancing science and technology for the general good. John R. Commons (see p. 516) worked out theories and techniques for social insurance, and among his fellow economists Irving Fisher showed that the government had to manage the nation's money supply if it was to achieve desirable social and economic ends. William T. Foster and Waddill Catchings advanced even more novel ideas. They attacked the beliefs that savings flowed automatically into investment and that business cycles righted themselves. If the nation was to avoid depressions, they insisted, government would have to resort to public spending when private investment faltered.

In public life, too, the progressive faith persevered—not least within the nonpartisan League of Women Voters—though it suffered major setbacks. In 1926, when Mellon again advocated tax relief for the rich, his dwindling opponents could find no telling argument against cutting taxes. Federal revenues were then more than ample for the costs of government, and no one had yet developed a cogent program for spending to improve the nation's housing, roads, and natural resources. Without difficulty, the Administration put through Congress a revenue act that cut in half the estate tax and the maximum surtax on individual incomes. Two years later Congress eased the tax on corporations. Mellon had carried the field.

Private utility companies were almost as successful. Sales of electric power doubled during the twenties, and ingenious promoters with very little cash managed to monopolize the industry by setting up complex holding companies. By the end of the decade ten utility systems controlled approximately three-fourths of the nation's light and power business. The promoters kept the cost of electricity unreasonably high and through financial sleight of hand manipulated securities at the expense of bewildered stockholders. They also carried on a massive propaganda campaign and financed a powerful lobby to beat back demands for public supervision and for public distribution of electrical power.

The reformers were led by George Norris. They included Governor Smith of New York and his successor, Franklin Roosevelt, who advocated state ownership and operation of public power. Gifford Pinchot, governor of Pennsylvania, organized a survey in 1923 that paved the way to public rural electrification. Many municipalities built or acquired their own power plants, and Nebraska, Norris' home state, established a public power system.

Prosperity won in '28

Farm politics particularly exercised Washington during Coolidge's second term, when farmers stepped up their demands for a government marketing plan. Such a plan had first been suggested in the lean years right after the war. Now it became the basis for legislation sponsored by Senator Charles L. McNary of Oregon and Representative Gilbert N. Haugen of Iowa. At the heart of the proposal was a two-price scheme—a high domestic price and a low foreign price for staple crops. By purchasing farm surpluses, the government was to sustain a balance of supply and demand that would keep commodity prices at "parity" (see p. 632). In that manner the government would be underwriting the prosperity of the American farmers. The government would sell farm surpluses abroad for whatever price it could get, and any loss would be offset by an equalization tax levied on farmers or on those who processed and transported farm products.

Congress rejected the McNary-Haugen bill in 1924. But it passed a revised measure in 1927 and another one in 1928. Coolidge vetoed both versions. The bill, he said, would create a vast and clumsy bureaucracy, would improperly delegate taxing power from Congress to the administrators of the program,

and would involve the government in trying to fix prices. Such prices, he argued, would be artificial and would encourage farmers to overproduce. Moreover, if the American government began to dump farm surpluses abroad, foreign governments would be bound to retaliate. The last two objections were undoubtedly sound, but Coolidge's concern for minimized government and a laissez-faire economy was unconvincing. After all, the government used the tariff, which was simply one kind of taxation, to aid industry. And the tariff, combined with the marketing practices of big business, led to artificial prices for manufactured goods. Those very prices kept farmers' costs high while their incomes lagged. Coolidge's vetoes, as the economist Rexford G. Tugwell put it, revealed "a stubborn determination to do nothing."

The debate over farm policy, like the debate over public power and taxation, highlighted the policy issue that dominated the late twenties: Was the federal government to be the handmaiden of business, the servant of the wealthy? Or was the government to treat all men equitably, and to build a society in which all could obtain a fair share of the nation's wealth? Intellectuals like Dewey and Commons and politicians like Norris and Smith insisted on the second alternative. They were insisting that Americans, both in their private lives and in their conduct of public affairs, accept a responsibility that the spirit of the times rejected.

The election of 1928. Calvin Coolidge announced that he "did not choose to run" in 1928. He might have been persuaded to accept a draft, but the Republican convention nominated Herbert Hoover on its first ballot. Professional politicians had little liking for Hoover, who was never one of them, and Midwestern farmers had little enthusiasm for a man who had opposed the McNary-Haugen bill precisely as Coolidge had. But businessmen trusted Hoover; his reputation for efficiency and humaneness was at its peak; and his personal success more than compensated for his lack of public glamour.

Hoover stood stolidly on a platform that attributed good times to Republican rule, praised the protective tariff, endorsed Prohibition, offered only platitudes to labor, and warned farmers of the evil of "putting the government into business." In his campaign

I am unable to understand how anything I was taught to believe as a Catholic could possibly be in conflict with what is good citizenship. The essence of my faith is built upon the Commandments of God. The law of the land is built upon the Commandments of God. There can be no conflict between them....

What is this conflict about which you talk? It may exist in some lands which do not guarantee religious freedom. But in the wildest dreams of your imagination you cannot conjure up a possible conflict between religious principle and political duty in the United States except on the unthinkable hypothesis that some law were to be passed which violated the common morality of all God-fearing men. And if you can conjure up such a conflict, how would a Protestant resolve it? Obviously by the dictates of his conscience. That is exactly what a Catholic would do. There is no ecclesiastical tribunal which would have the slightest claim upon the obedience of Catholic communicants in the resolution of such a conflict.

From Alfred E. Smith, Article in the *Atlantic Monthly,* May 1927.

A Catholic for President

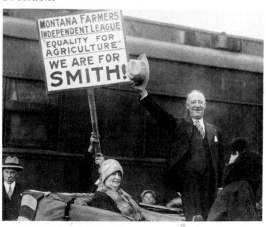

speeches Hoover emphasized the virtues of individualism and ''the American system'' of free enterprise. There lay the source of prosperity. ''We in America,'' Hoover said, ''are nearer to the final triumph over poverty than ever before in the history of any land. . . . Given a chance to go forward with the policies of the last eight years, we shall soon with the help of God be in the sight of the day when poverty will be banished from this nation.''

The Democrats nominated Al Smith. Those who had kept the nomination from him in 1924 could no longer deny his claims. As governor of New York he had made a record for efficiency as compelling as Hoover's. He had reordered the state's finances and reorganized its administration. He had promoted public health and public recreation, workmen's compensation, and civil liberties. As a national candidate, Smith stood for public ownership of the principal power sites and generating plants, and he endorsed the McNary-Haugen Plan.

''Socialism,'' Hoover retorted. But Smith was no radical. Indeed, he blurred his own liberalism by deferring to the temper of the time. He accepted the need for protective tariffs. He chose as his campaign-manager John J. Raskob, a Republican industrialist, identified with Du Pont and General Motors. The Democratic campaign may have reassured the conservatives, but it converted almost none of them, and it disappointed the liberals.

Raskob's appointment, furthermore, reopened the party wounds of 1924, for, like Smith, Raskob was a Catholic and a ''wet.'' Rural America dug out its old suspicions of the city, booze, Tammany, and the pope. Particularly in the South, fundamentalist preachers associated Smith with all the old fears and hates. Smith explained that his religion had not and would not affect his policies, and his record confirmed his words. But the suspicious took their cue instead from his East Side accent, his brown derby, his open advocacy of repeal, his unabashed cityness. Hoover, for his part, made no convincing effort to dispel the religious issue. And with the ethnic issue he had no real quarrel: Smith accepted men for what they were; Hoover was a dedicated ''lily white.''

More than bigotry, prosperity defeated Smith, for probably no Democrat could have outraced Santa Claus. Smith received only 87 electoral votes to Hoover's 444; some 41 percent of the popular vote to Hoover's 58. Five Southern states and all the border states went Republican. The Grand Old Party had won another landslide.

The returns, however, were not that unambiguous. Smith polled twice as many votes as Davis had in 1924. He carried the dozen largest cities, which the Republicans had won handily four years before. The Democrats also cut into the traditionally Republican agricultural vote in the West. The farmers had doubts about Santa Claus, and in the cities the ethnic issue cut both ways, helping the Democrats in the urban North as much as it hurt them in the rural South. In 1928, as in 1924, the vote dramatized the need for Democratic unity and for a positive commitment to social reconstruction. But the prospects seemed poor, for the Coolidge era ended much as it had begun. Prejudice had divided the underprivileged, and prosperity had obscured public irresponsibility. Most Americans, as they had shown at the polls, were remarkably content. And confident, too. The stock market boomed as it awaited Hoover's inauguration and the nation's final triumph over poverty.

Suggestions for reading

GENERAL

The outstanding general accounts of the Coolidge years and their implications are in A. M. Schlesinger, Jr., *The Crisis of the Old Order** (1957), which focuses on the culture and the politics of the time, and W. E. Leuchtenburg, *The Perils of Prosperity, 1914–32** (1958), which is shorter but more inclusive. F. L. Allen, *Only Yesterday** (1931), while often rather casual, has charm and flair; and J. D. Hicks, *Republican Ascendancy: 1921–1933** (1960), is sober and usually solid. The most entertaining and perceptive biography of Coolidge is W. A. White, *A Puritan in Babylon** (1938); the President emerges as a hero in C. M. Fuess, *Calvin Coolidge* (1940); he speaks often but rarely well in H. H. Quint and R. H. Ferrell, eds., *The Talkative President: The Off-the-Record Press Conferences of Calvin Coolidge* (1964).

BUSINESS ENTERPRISE

The economics of prosperity are described in George Soule, *Prosperity Decade: From War to Depression, 1917–1929** (1947); the institutions of business, in T. C. Cochran, *The American Business System: A Historical Perspective, 1900–1955** (2nd ed., 1957); the business creed, in J. W. Prothro, *The Dollar Decade: Business Ideas in the 1920's* (1954); and the techniques of advertising, in Otis Pease, *The Responsibilities of American Advertising* (1958). On the Ford Motor Company, its master, and the automobile industry in general, the preeminent works are Allan Nevins and F. E. Hill, *Ford: The Times, the Man and the Company* (1954) and *Ford: Expansion and Challenge* (1957). There is also an acid and scintillating analysis in Keith Sward, *The Legend of Henry Ford** (1948). The best introduction to F. W. Taylor is his own *The Principles of Scientific Management** (1907). Siegfried Giedion, *Mechanization Takes Command: A Contribution to Anonymous History* (1948), offers brilliant observations about technology, which is handled on a more elementary level in Stuart Chase, *Men and Machines* (1929). By far the fullest and best account of labor during the 1920s is in Irving Bernstein, *The Lean Years** (1960). Two studies of the first rank on corporate concentration and on the business cycle, respectively, are A. A. Berle, Jr., and S. F. Means, *The Modern Corporation and Private Property** (1932, rev. ed., 1969), and Thomas Wilson, *Fluctuations in Income and Employment* (1948). E. A. Goldenweiser, *American Monetary Policy* (1951), deals expertly with its subject.

IDEALS AND IDEOLOGIES

The works mentioned in the text, and other works of the authors noted there, provide a good point of departure for studying the artists and intellectuals of the 1920s. For that purpose, Malcolm Cowley, *Exile's Return** (1934), is rewarding; and so are Alfred Kazin, *On Native Grounds** (1942), and Edmund Wilson, *The Shores of Light** (1952) and *The American Earthquake** (1958). The outstanding anthology of the social and cultural expressions of the time is Loren Baritz, *The Culture of the Twenties** (1969). Among the helpful literary studies are Mark Schorer, *Sinclair Lewis** (1961); G. Smith, Jr., *T. S. Eliot's Poetry and Plays: A Study in Sources and Meaning** (1956); C. Brooks, *William Faulkner: The Yoknapatawpha Country** (1963); F. J. Hoffman and O. W. Vickery, eds., *William Faulkner: Three Decades of Criticism** (1960); and H. D. Piper, *F. Scott Fitzgerald: A Critical Portrait* (1965). See also C. A. Fenton, *The Apprenticeship of Ernest Hemingway** (1954), and C. H. Baker, *Hemingway: The Writer As Artist* (1956). American anti-intellectuals and bigots receive their just rewards in N. F. Furniss, *The Fundamentalist Controversy, 1918–1931* (1954); Ray Ginger, *Six Days or Forever?** (1958), on the Scopes trial; and J. M. Mecklin, *The Ku Klux Klan* (1924). More sympathetic is W. B. Gatewood, Jr., ed., *Controversy in the Twenties* (1969). Among the engaging works on the ideology and politics of Prohibition, and on the crime it helped to spawn, are Andrew Sinclair, *Prohibition:*

*Available in a paperback edition.

The Era of Excess* (1962); Herbert Asbury, The Great Illusion (1950); Charles Merz, Dry Decade* (1932); Virginius Dabney, Dry Messiah: The Life of Bishop Cannon (1949); F. D. Pasley, Al Capone (1930); and Raymond Moley, Tribunes of People (1932).

PUBLIC ISSUES AND PUBLIC MEN

Two important accounts of major federal public policies in the period 1923–29 are in the pertinent parts of R. E. Paul, Taxation in the United States (1954), and Theodore Saloutos and J. D. Hicks, Twentieth Century Populism: Agricultural Discontent in the Middle West, 1900–1939* (1951). Agricultural matters also receive useful treatment in J. D. Black, Agricultural Reform in the United States (1930), and M. R. Benedict, Farm Policies of the United States, 1790–1950 (1953). On the campaign of 1924, there is a brief review in R. B. Nye, Midwestern Progressive Politics, 1850–1958* (1951, rev. ed., 1959), and a longer analysis in K. C. MacKay, The Progressive Movement of 1924 (1947). The fullest study of the election of 1928 is E. A. Moore, A Catholic Runs for President (1956). Oscar Handlin, Al Smith and His America* (1958), is short and thoughtful, while M. and H. Josephson, Al Smith: Hero of the Cities (1969), is laudatory. Among the autobiographies and biographies of other public men of the time, some of the more rewarding are B. C. and Fola La Follette, Robert M. La Follette, 2 vols. (1953); Frank Freidel, Franklin D. Roosevelt: The Ordeal (1954); A. Mann, La Guardia: A Fighter Against His Times, 1882–1933* (1959); G. W. Norris, Fighting Liberal* (1945); Herbert Hoover, Memoirs, 3 vols. (1951–52); E. E. Morison, Turmoil and Tradition: A Study of the Life and Times of Henry L. Stimson* (1960); and H. L. Stimson and McGeorge Bundy, On Active Service in Peace and War (1948). The last two shed significant light on the foreign policy of the Coolidge years, on which R. H. Ferrell, Peace in Their Time (1952), and Hicks, cited above, are also useful; for an influential, opposing point of view, see W. A. Williams, The Tragedy of American Diplomacy* (1959).

*Available in a paperback edition.

The end of an era

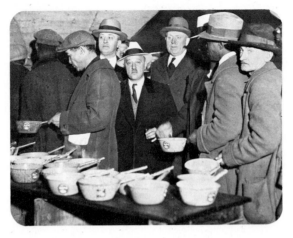

26

The United States met the new year of 1929 with a smile and a swagger. The national habit of confidence had grown during three decades in which both the reformers of the early century and the merchants of the new age of business believed they were fashioning a national Eden. A college graduate of the class of 1901, fifty years old in 1929, could believe with them that they had succeeded. As evidence of success, he might point to the statutes left over from progressivism, the great war won, the apparent unlikelihood of future war, the excitement of new inventions, and the largess of good times. Not since the mid-nineties, not for a generation, had the nation suffered a serious depression.

President Hoover

Business plans. "I have no fears for the future of our country," the new President announced at his inauguration. "It is bright with hope." There was no nonsense about Hoover, none of T. R.'s boyishness or Wilson's dreaminess, none of Harding's incontinence or Coolidge's folksiness. The President was a serious man who kept in shape by playing medicine ball in the early morning. He would, most people thought, keep the nation in shape and lead it to ever higher plateaus of prosperity.

Hoover approached his office like a businessman with a business plan. He reorganized the inefficient presidential staff by creating a secretariat in which each member was assigned a specific place and duty. Government was to be neat. It was also to be respectable. Hoover appointed a Cabinet of men who stood for what the business community admired. With one exception, they were distinguished only for that stance. The exception was Secretary of State Henry L. Stimson, a conservative, to be sure, but also a man whose superior perceptions soon made him as uncomfortable as he was valuable. Andrew Mellon continued as Secretary of the Treasury. Among the others were Secretary of Agriculture Arthur M. Hyde, whom few farmers considered a friend, and Secretary of War James W. Good, a former utilities lawyer who preserved his private loyalties while serving, by virtue of his office, as head of the Federal Power Commission.

The utilities had other reasons for rejoicing. Hoover himself, according to the solicitor of the Federal Power Commission, interceded to prevent private companies from being regulated rigorously. The President also proposed that the federal government withdraw its control from all public lands and from all new reclamation and irrigation projects. The states, he said, were "more competent to manage . . . these affairs." This was a debatable assertion, but it suited Hoover's purpose. In conservation, as in most other matters, he was determined to keep federal government small in both size and power.

Hoover's farm program reflected that determination. Still, he recognized the need for some aid to agriculture, and he summoned a special session of Congress to provide it. The President suggested that the best way to help the American farmer would be to raise the tariff and to give him federal assistance in marketing his produce—policies that would not, he said, undermine the farmer's initiative. In the Agricultural Marketing Act of 1929, Congress acted on Hoover's suggestions. It created a Federal Farm Board of nine members, who were to be advised by committees representing the cooperative associations that marketed each of the major commodities. It also provided a revolving fund of $500 million from which the board could make loans to cooperatives to help them market their crops more effectively. Another provision, inserted by the farm bloc, permitted loans to be made to stabilization corporations "for the purpose of controlling any surplus." In other words, these corporations could influence prices so long as the Farm Board lent them enough money. But the Farm Board had no control over production. Consequently, not even generous loans for stabilization could long sustain prices if they should begin a major decline in the face either of gross overproduction or of adverse general economic circumstances. From the first, farmers were dissatisfied with the legislation of 1929.

They gained nothing at all from Hoover's proposal to give them more tariff protection. The President lacked the political skill to guide a tariff bill through Congress. In 1929 Congress put the matter aside. In 1930 industrial lobbyists and their friends in the Republican majority carried protection to its all-time high. The Hawley-Smoot Tariff of that year raised average *ad valorem* rates from about 32 percent to about 40 percent. It increased rates on some seventy farm products and over nine hundred manufactured goods. More than a thousand economists urged Hoover to veto the bill. It would, they pointed out, raise the cost of living, encourage inefficient production, hamper American export trade, including trade in agricultural surpluses, and provoke foreign bitterness and retaliation. Though those arguments were entirely correct, Hoover signed the measure. It reflected the continuing influence of business interests in Washington and their continuing shortsightedness.

The crash. Dramatic evidence of that shortsightedness had already appeared in the stock market, the barometer of prosperity. It soared during the early months of 1929, but unbridled speculation began to worry conservative financiers and the President too. He privately urged the New York Stock Exchange to curb the manipulation of securities, but with no success. Hoover would not ask Congress to interfere, for he "had no desire to stretch the powers of the Federal Government" that far. Instead he supported the Federal Reserve Board when it warned banks against making loans for speculative purposes, and he approved the board's 1 percent increase in the interest rate first in June and again in August 1929. But the higher cost of funds for speculation did not check the speculative fever.

Gamblers in stocks paid no heed to other warnings. The first signs of danger began to appear during the summer of 1929. Residential construction, important for the many industries that supplied its needs throughout the nation, fell off more than a billion dollars; business inventories trebled; the rate of advance in consumer spending dropped some 400 percent. From June onward, industrial production, employment, and commodity prices declined steadily. Indeed the August increase in the interest rate came at a time when legitimate enterprise could ill afford it.

Yet the stock market boomed on. Ignoring the evidence of industrial decline, undeterred by the advancing costs of brokers' loans, speculators bid shares to new peaks. The morning after Labor Day the New York *Times* average of selected industrial stocks stood at 452, up more than 200 points since early 1928. American Telephone and Telegraph had reached 304; General Electric, 396; Radio Corporation of America, 505. The market seemed strong, but it was sustained only by deluded confidence. In one week brokers' loans had risen $137 million and New York banks had borrowed $64 million to carry the weight of speculation.

During September and most of October the market wavered, moving gently downward. Some days were worrisome, but none of the captains of finance in New York or their lieutenants in Washington voiced alarm. Then on October 23 security prices crumbled in a wave of frenzied selling. Panic was temporarily averted when a group of New York bankers met next morning at J. P. Morgan and Company and agreed to pool their resources to hold the market up. The senior Morgan partner assured reporters that the heavy selling

Herbert Hoover: "I have no fears for the future of our country"

Had there been a better distribution of the current income from the national product—in other words, had there been less savings by business and the higher-income groups and more income in the lower groups—we should have had far greater stability in our economy. Had the six billion dollars, for instance, that were loaned by corporations and wealthy individuals for stock-market speculation been distributed to the public as lower prices or higher wages and with less profits to the corporations and the well-to-do, it would have prevented or greatly moderated the economic collapse that began at the end of 1929.

From M. S. Eccles, *Beckoning Frontiers: Public and Personal Recollections*, 1951.

had been "due to a technical condition," not to any basic cause. The following day President Hoover announced that "the fundamental business of the country . . . is on a sound and prosperous basis."

They were wrong. During the next fortnight the market shuddered to collapse. As values fell, all the bets made on a rising market paid off in panic. An uncontrollable decline swept past the support the bankers had organized. By mid-November the New York *Times* average had fallen to a shattering 224. In less than a month the securities listed on the New York Stock Exchange lost $26 billion—more than 40 percent—of their face value. Nor was the descent over. In July 1932 the *Times* average hit bottom at a mere 58.

Contrary to Hoover's assertion, the fundamental business of the country was unsound. Excessive industrial profits, along with skimpy industrial wages, were distributing one-third of all personal income to 5 percent of the population. Some two years before the crash, the annual rate of increase of national investment (as contrasted to speculation) had started downward, not the least because corporations and their executives had diminished expectations for profits from an economy in which purchasing power could no longer keep pace with productivity. That rate of increase of investment, as economists came to understand a decade later, had to continue to rise if economic growth was to be sustained. The shortage of purchasing power among consumers had a particularly bad effect on the vital construction and automobile industries. But in the 1920s the level of economic intelligence, like the level of both private and public economic policy, was still relatively low. The surfeit of disposable income among the rich, together with the swollen profits of corporations, had encouraged speculation. When trouble came, the jerry-built corporate structures of many businesses, especially the utilities, toppled. Nor could the American banking system meet the strain, for bankers, though they had been aware of the loose practices of their profession, had long refused to discipline themselves.

Business had failed to keep its house in order. Even worse, it had persuaded the government to follow the unwise economic policies of the decade preceding the crash. The crash itself brought the sagging economy down. It wiped out savings and confidence alike. The mood of despair that settled over the nation stifled any renewal of private investment that might have encouraged recovery. It also dispelled the confidence of Americans in the business elite. The dominance of businessmen and industrialists, in government and out, had brought, not a new Eden, but a panic that marked the onset of the most baleful depression in all history.

The onset of depression

The Hoover policies: first phase. Few of the leaders of American business and politics, either Republican or Democrat, had expected the crash. And when it came, very few of them understood what had caused it or foresaw the severity of the depression it was to bring.

Most of them agreed with the head of Bethlehem Steel, who announced in December 1929 that "never before has American business been as firmly entrenched for prosperity as it is today." Most of them agreed also with Andrew Mellon, who recommended letting the economy run down to the depths, from which it would presumably recover automatically, as it had in the 1870s and 1890s. That policy would entail great suffering, but those who believed that the economy operated according to mechanical laws believed too in the inexorability of business cycles and in the wisdom of leaving them alone, suffering or no. "Liquidate labor," Mellon advised, "liquidate stock, liquidate the farmers."

Hoover knew better. Though he remained convinced that the economy was basically sound and that government should not interfere with business, he took steps to prevent the spread of depression. In a series of conferences he tried to persuade business-leaders to keep wages and prices up voluntarily. He called on the Federal Reserve to make it easy for business to borrow. He encouraged the Farm Board to provide funds to help the stabilization corporations in their efforts to sustain commodity prices. Above all, he hoped, by offering private advice and by making public pronouncements, to restore the nation's confidence in business.

Hoover welcomed the Tariff Act of 1930 (see p. 613), for he was convinced that business would be encouraged by a continuation of protection. To hearten businessmen further, he recommended, and Congress in 1930 provided, cuts in personal and corporate income taxes. The reductions gave the wealthy more disposable income to use for investment, but they gave lower-income groups little additional money to spend on consumption. In the absence of confidence in business, the investments were not forthcoming. Following Hoover's advice, Congress did make modest appropriations for public works. These gave some boost to the sick construction industry and to the heavy industries that supplied it, and indirectly to the men who were employed in those industries.

But those efforts were too meager to check the contraction in private spending, investment, and employment that followed the crash. Both Hoover and the Federal Reserve Board opposed a rapid, deliberately inflationary expansion of currency and bank deposits, which the board might have attempted with some possible healthy effect. The President would not countenance any more spending, because he was determined to keep the federal budget balanced, or as close to balanced as possible. This, he believed, as did most Americans, was sound finance, and it was also

an unshakable article of business faith. Large federal deficits, like inflation, would have frightened the business community, which the President wanted to soothe. To that purpose, during 1930 the President continually applied the balm of official optimism. True, official gloom would have caused further alarm; but Hoover, while privately dubious, acted as if his conferences with business-leaders had succeeded, whereas wages and prices actually continued to decline.

The blight of depression.

"We have now passed the worst," Hoover announced wishfully in May 1930, "and . . . shall rapidly recover." The statistics told a different story. In 1929 new capital issues in the United States, a rough yardstick of investment, had totaled $10 billion; in 1930 they dropped to $7 billion. As the depression deepened, the figure reached $3 billion in 1931 and $1 billion in 1932. Investment was discouraged by the decline in corporate profits, which fell off steadily from $8.4 billion in 1929 to $3.4 billion in 1932. At the same time, the rate of business failures rose—over 100,000 businesses went under in the period 1929–32. And banks were failing too. In 1929, 659 banks with total deposits of about $200 million closed their doors; in 1930, 1,352 banks with deposits of $853 million; in 1931, 2,294 banks with deposits of almost $1,700 million, at the rate of almost 200 a month. Each collapse buried the cash and savings of depositors, most of whom had no other resources.

By the last quarter of 1930, industrial production had fallen 26 percent below the 1929 level. By mid-1932 it was off 51 percent from that level. Unemployment mounted: 4 million in October 1930; nearly 7 million a year later; almost 11 million by the fall of 1932. Even those who kept their jobs were earning less and less. Between 1929 and 1933 the total annual income of labor dropped from $53 to $31.5 billion. Average manufacturing wages came down 60 percent, average salaries 40 percent. Farmers fared even worse: their income declined from $11.9 to $5.3 billion. In 1929 national income touched $81 billion; by 1932 it had shrunk to $49 billion.

Liquidation carried a frightful burden of human suffering. Thousands of middle-class families, their incomes dwindling, sometimes entirely gone, lost next their savings, then their insurance, then, unable to pay their mortgages, their very homes. The optimism

Andrew Mellon:
"Liquidate labor,
liquidate stock,
liquidate the farmers"

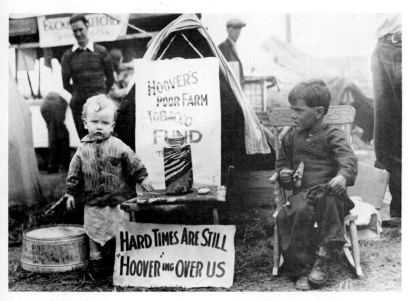

No rent, no joy, no hope

of the twenties gave way to gloom and fear. The times were even harder on laboring men and their families. The lost job, the fruitless search for work, the shoes worn through and the clothes worn thin, the furniture and trinkets pawned, the menu stripped of meat and then of adequate nutrition, no rent, no joy, no hope; and finally the despair of bread lines—these visited every city, leaving in their path sullen men, weeping women, and hungry children. So, too, on the farm—vanished incomes, foreclosures, tenancy, migrancy, and with them, as in the cities, the death of self-respect.

Hoover had predicted the abolition of poverty in America. Instead, within two years there mushroomed around America's cities settlements of shacks built of empty packing boxes, where homeless men squatted, reduced to desultory begging. A new Eden? "Brother, can you spare a dime?"

The Hoover policies: second phase. In the congressional elections of 1930 the Democrats conducted a rousing campaign against Hoover, though they offered no clear alternatives to his policies. The intensification of depression hurt the Republicans, as depression had always hurt the party in power. Though Hoover had been by no means unenlightened, he was, by virtue of his office, the most exposed target for abuse. The Democrats made his name a synonym for hardship. A "Hoover blanket" was yesterday's newspaper; a

"Hoover flag" was an empty pocket turned inside out. Rough tactics and national discontent produced a slim Democratic victory, the first since 1916. The Republican majority in the Senate was reduced to a single vote, leaving that body dominated by a coalition of Democrats and Western agrarians. The Democrats won a bare majority in the House.

The new Congress was not to meet for a year (see Twentieth Amendment, Section 5), but in December 1930 the Democratic minority of the old Congress (which had been elected in 1928) used the rump session to develop a program for unemployment relief. Hoover, irritated by the Democratic campaign and appalled by its success, reasserted his own policies.

The President felt that relief was strictly a local problem. The cities, he insisted, with help from private charity, should and could take care of the needy. This was a fallacious assumption, for nowhere in the nation was there an adequate system of relief. Local public funds in 1929 paid three-fourths of the cost of relief (by 1932, four-fifths), but the localities had neither the means to raise revenue nor the capacity to borrow to defray their mounting obligations. Their relief agencies and programs, moreover, had concentrated on helping unemployables, people unable to work. Local administrators had neither the experience nor the facilities to cope with mass unemployment, and private charity was incapable of meeting the nation's massive need for immediate relief.

As the winter of 1930–31 came on, cold and hunger moved into the homes of the unemployed. Relief payments were only $2.39 a week for a family in New York and even less in most other cities. Two Texas cities barred relief for blacks. Detroit, unable to tax or borrow, dropped a third of the needy families from its relief rolls; St. Louis cut off half, and children there combed the dumps for rotting food.

In October 1930 the President appointed an Emergency Committee for Employment under Colonel Arthur Woods. Though Hoover told the committee that relief was a local responsibility, Woods recommended a federal public-works program. The President rejected it, and in April 1931 Woods resigned.

Meanwhile Senator Robert Wagner, a New York Democrat, had introduced bills providing for federal public works and a federal employment service. Along with Wagner, Senator

For years it has been an article of faith with the normal American ... that America, somehow, was different from the rest of the world.... The smash of 1929 did not, of itself, shake this serene conviction.... It looked, at the time, just because it was so spectacular and catastrophic, like a shooting star ... disconnected with the fundamental facts.... So the plain citizen, no matter how hard hit, believed. His dreams were shattered; but after all they had been only dreams; he could settle back to hard work and win out....

Then he found his daily facts reeling and swimming about him, in a nightmare of continuous disappointment. The bottom had fallen out of the market, for good. And that market ... had a horrid connection with his bread and butter, his automobile, and his installment purchases.... Worst of all, unemployment became a hideous fact, and one that lacerated and tore at self-respect....

That is the trouble that lies ... at the back of the American mind.... If America really is not ''different,'' then its troubles, the same ... as those of Old Europe, will not be cured automatically. Something will have to be done—but what?

From M. A. Hamilton, *In America Today,* 1932.

Robert M. La Follette, Jr., ''Battle Bob's'' son and successor, and Republican Senator Bronson Cutting of New Mexico urged federal spending for public works and relief. All this Hoover opposed on the ground that federal action was unnecessary.

Instead, in February 1931 Hoover expressed his continuing dedication to individualism, local responsibility, and mutual self-help. But in the face of depression, the virtues of economic individualism and private charity were drowned out by the demands of the helpless. Hoover's dedication to keeping the federal government small in size and small in power was breaking the lives of 4 million unemployed and their families. The President was an honest man whose convictions had glued him to inaction.

Hoover's interpretation of the economic ups and downs of 1931 strengthened his convictions. Between February and June of that year the economic indexes rallied slightly, partly because of a normal seasonal upturn. The gains, though tiny, persuaded the President, and others bent on optimism, that recovery was under way. Then in the spring and summer of 1931 financial panic swept over Europe. The American crash had precipitated the collapse abroad by drying up the loan funds on which the European economy and the interrelated reparations and war-debt payments had come to depend. And the European collapse in turn drove foreigners to dump American securities in their scramble for dollars,

thereby driving American stock prices down even further. Moreover, shortages in exchange forced one European nation after another to devalue its currency. This action disrupted international trade, and the prices of American agricultural commodities plummeted. Before the end of the summer, the indexes had resumed their decline. Again the depression deepened.

The fault, Hoover concluded, lay in Europe. All the calamities since 1929, he came to believe, had originated in the Old World. The war had taxed the world economy beyond repair; the United States had regrettably become involved not only in war but in a morass of bad loans as well. European bankers had collaborated with their New York associates to create the easy-money conditions on which speculation had fed (see p. 604), and from that collusion was born the Panic of 1929. Then, just as recovery beckoned, European disaster in 1931 had reversed the gains so arduously won. This view of the causes of the depression reasserted the persistent myth of American innocence—even wounded innocence—for as Hoover saw the situation American business shared little of the blame; he himself shared none. Hoover's theory, moreover, excused him from embracing the domestic policies he had rejected, for if the basic cause of depression lay outside the United States the most appropriate action would be to ease the strains abroad and to protect the American economy from them.

Diplomacy in depression

A set of good intentions. The foreign policies on which the Hoover Administration embarked in 1929 were marked by good will and peaceful purpose. The President and his able Secretary of State, Stimson, believed, as had their immediate predecessors, that the world had fought its last major war a decade earlier. Europe, they expected, could take care of itself, as could Asia and Latin America, with occasional advice from the United States. The aroused morality embodied in the Kellogg-Briand pact would prevent aggression and discourage militarism. Indeed Hoover expected the powers to put an end to their arms race in the very near future.

Initially Hoover and Stimson made some progress toward their benign goals. While still President-elect, Hoover had carried friendship to Latin America during a ten-week tour that publicized the "good neighbor" policy.* In Argentina he promised to abstain from intervention in the internal affairs of the nations south of the border. He kept his word. In 1930 Stimson announced that the United States henceforth would grant diplomatic recognition to *de facto* governments. Moreover, Hoover set about withdrawing the marines from Nicaragua, a task that was completed in 1933, and he arranged to remove them from Haiti.

In 1930 the President formally repudiated the Roosevelt Corollary to the Monroe Doctrine (see p. 530). A memorandum written by former Assistant Secretary of State J. Reuben Clark, which Hoover ordered published, denied that the doctrine justified American intervention in Latin America. Nor did Hoover regard the doctrine as a mandate for collecting the private debts of Americans. Some fifty revolutions or attempts at revolution shook the "good neighbors" of the hemisphere during his Administration. But he kept hands off, even though those disturbances often resulted in the repudiation of debts owed to American citizens and in the nationalization of their properties. Although the State Department fell into argumentative negotiations that ran on for many years, the United States did not resort to force. By abandoning dollar diplomacy and protective imperialism, Hoover initiated a new era of hemispheric friendship and solidarity.

This success contrasted with the Adminis-

*A phrase later used by and ordinarily associated with Franklin Roosevelt.

tration's diplomatic disappointments in Europe and its agonies in Asia. Intent on naval disarmament, Hoover welcomed the cooperation of Ramsay MacDonald, the head of the new Labor Cabinet in England. Their preliminary negotiations prepared the way for the multipower conference that met in London in 1930. There the Americans, the British, and the Japanese extended the "holiday" on the construction of capital ships, and American and British representatives evolved a formula for limiting the construction of cruisers, destroyers, and submarines. Naval experts of the English-speaking nations, however, deplored a compromise that increased Japan's ratio for cruisers and destroyers and gave her equality in submarines. In effect, this arrangement recognized her primacy in the western Pacific. She would have accepted nothing less, and neither the Hoover nor the MacDonald government wanted to engage in an expensive naval race. Neither, moreover, considered Japan unfriendly. They confirmed, therefore, only what they had already conceded.

Even so, they failed to close the door on a naval race. The French, frightened by the militarism of fascist Italy, refused to limit their naval program unless the United States promised to help France in the event of aggression. Such a pledge was unthinkable to Hoover, the Senate, or the American people. When France and Italy would not subscribe to significant parts of the London treaty, England insisted on adding a clause permitting her, the United States, or Japan to expand their fleets if their national security was threatened by the building program of some other power. This "escalator" clause meant that naval limitation was conditional upon the self-restraint of a resurgent Italy and an alarmed France. Yet the Hoover Administration and the American people accepted disarmament as a fact.

Monetary diplomacy. When the panic struck European banks and security markets in 1931 (see p. 617), the focus of Hoover's diplomacy shifted to money. American investors, hard hit by the depression, cut off the loans to Germany that had so far enabled her to pay reparations for her part in the First World War. Without this source of income, the former Allies were unable to keep up payments on their debts to the United States. Even before the distressed German president appealed for help in the spring of 1930, Hoover had begun to think about a one-year moratorium on all intergovernmental debts and reparations payments. The idea was admirable, but Hoover said nothing about it until he had made sure of congressional support, and he failed to consult the French. When he announced his proposal late in June, England and Germany endorsed it, but France held back, still hopefull of collecting reparations. The French also suspected that the American proposal was partly designed to enable Germany to pay back private debts she owed in the United States. During the two weeks before France endorsed the moratorium, the accelerated flight of funds from Germany forced widespread bank failures.

To his shock, the President discovered that Europe's distress directly embarrassed American banks. They had lent some $1.7 billion, on a short-term basis, without collateral, to central European banks, especially in Germany. Bank runs in Europe meant that those loans could not be collected, and the solvency of the American banks that had made them was threatened. The loans were part of a complex network of obligations among banks in many countries. In order to stop demands for payments back and forth among them, Secretary Stimson and other American representatives in July 1930 negotiated an emergency "standstill" agreement. It was later extended to September 1931, and again to March 1933. The standstill agreements froze private debts just as the moratorium had frozen public debts. This gave financiers time to try to protect the banks of the Western world from bankruptcy, and time to delay putting pressure on borrowers for loans due.

But the freezing came too late to stop panic. Depositors, their confidence in banks shaken, demanded their money, which they intended to hoard. A run on the Bank of England, for decades the world's foremost symbol of financial stability, drained its gold and forced Great Britain off the gold standard in September 1931. That nation made gold the property of the government, refused to convert paper currency into gold except under conditions the government set, and devalued the pound— that is, increased the cost of gold in terms of British currency. England also established a special government fund to manage the value of the pound in terms of other currencies. By the end of 1931 every major power except Italy, France, and the United States was also forced off the gold standard, and each depreciated its currency and attempted to control its value in international exchange. These efforts at control were often designed to produce selfish advantages in trade, as were the prohibitive tariffs that invariably accompanied devaluation. Exchange controls and high tariffs actually impeded world trade and, worse still, gave rise to international suspicion and distrust.

Hoover had shown commendable initiative in arranging the moratorium and the standstills, but he never saw to the bottom of the problem. He failed to recognize that America's high protective tariffs were among the first and worst impediments to world commerce. And he would not support the cancellation of war debts. At the Lausanne Conference of 1932, England and France finally admitted Germany's bankruptcy and agreed to scale reparations down to an insignificant sum provided that the United States would scale war debts down equivalently. Most American bankers favored that plan, as did Stimson, who urged cancellation of "these damn debts." But Congress, reflecting public opinion, would not even consider a new debt commission, and Hoover, equivocal himself, demanded that the European nations resume payments on their debts after the moratorium expired. The debtor nations—except for Finland, whose obligation was tiny—had no choice but to default.

The defaults, like the demand that forced them and the long stalemate over debts and reparations that preceded them, engendered ill feeling on both sides of the Atlantic. The resulting distrust weakened the will of the democracies to resist the black forces gathering around them.

Fire bells in the Orient. Japan broke the peace of the world. Since her victory over Russia in 1905, she had dominated the economy of southern Manchuria, the northeastern section of China. Tokyo was willing to acknowledge China's political claim to the area so long as it did not collide with Japanese military interests and economic privileges. During the late twenties such a collision grew increasingly likely. In China Chiang Kai-shek took over the central government and broke with the communists who had been his allies. Chinese nationalists hoped soon to have the whole country under their control. But the Russians still managed the Chinese Eastern

Fire bells in the Orient: Japanese troops near Shanghai

Railway and were developing its Pacific terminus, the Siberian city of Vladivostok. Alarmed by the construction there, Japan resolved to reinforce southern Manchuria. Here she confronted Chiang Kai-shek, who was determined to yield nothing further to any foreign power.

In the fall of 1931 the Japanese army in effect took over the Tokyo government. In September Japanese troops occupied Mukden and other Manchurian cities and moved rapidly to establish political control over the province. This violation of the Nine Power Treaty and the Kellogg-Briand pact was perfectly timed. China turned to the League of Nations for help, but the West was paralyzed by depression.

Even in good times Japan would probably have had little to fear. The British were opposed to any strong action in Manchuria. American public opinion, though it condemned Japan's behavior, was vehemently against any measures that might precipitate war. Hoover, anxious to avoid war at any cost, rejected Stimson's suggestion that the United States might have to cooperate with the League in imposing economic sanctions on Japan.

At Hoover's insistence, Stimson proceeded cautiously. He hoped at first to strengthen the civilian moderates in the Japanese cabinet and to persuade them to end the occupation of Manchuria. But in January 1932 the Japanese army drove on. Now Stimson resorted to moral condemnation, the only weapon Hoover would countenance. In identical warnings to China and Japan, he revived the doctrine Bryan had enunciated in 1915. The United States, Stimson warned, would not recognize any change brought about by force that im-

paired American treaty rights or Chinese territorial integrity. Japan scoffed politely.

Before the end of January the Japanese invaded Shanghai, bombarded the city, and killed thousands of civilians—all on the pretext that they were retaliating against a Chinese boycott. America's warning had proved no deterrent. Yet once again Hoover refused to consider economic sanctions. Stimson could turn only to sterner words.

In February he published a long letter to Senator Borah, in which he reiterated his nonrecognition doctrine and lamented the failure of other nations to endorse it. He also recalled the interdependence of the various Washington treaties of 1922. Stimson wrote:

> No one of these treaties can be disregarded without disturbing the general understanding and equilibrium. . . . The willingness of the American government to surrender its commanding lead in battleship construction and to leave its positions at Guam and in the Philippines without further fortification, was predicated upon, among other things, the self-denying covenants contained in the Nine Power Treaty.

Stimson had hoped that his letter would encourage China, inform the American public, exhort the League and Great Britain, and warn Japan. But sentiment did China no good. Americans, like the League and its members, shared Hoover's determination to confine deterrence to words, and Japan was confident that neither the President nor his constituents were prepared to heed Stimson's counsel.

In 1932 the Assembly of the League, with Japan abstaining, unanimously adopted a resolution incorporating the nonrecognition doctrine. A year later a League commission of inquiry named Japan the aggressor in Manchuria and called on her to return the province to China. Japan simply withdrew from the League, though she left Shanghai temporarily.

Stimson, a disciple of Theodore Roosevelt, believed that power and the will to use it were essential to world peace. The vast majority of his countrymen, including Congress, disagreed. In the early weeks of 1933 Congress passed a bill granting independence to the Philippine Islands, largely in response to pressure from American interests eager to raise the tariff barrier between themselves and their Filipino competitors. The measure, enacted over Hoover's veto, demonstrated that Congress was willing to throw the islands to the mercy of Japan, and it canceled the veiled warning in Stimson's letter to Borah.

The story was very much the same in Europe, where the German Nazis were marching to power. At a World Disarmament Conference in Geneva in 1932, the French proposed that an international army be established and that all powers submit to the compulsory arbitration of disputes. Hoover countered with a plan for the immediate abolition of all offensive weapons and the reduction by one-third of existing armies and navies. But with the United States still unwilling to guarantee their security, the French were unimpressed by the arithmetic of arms reduction, and the conference adjourned in July with nothing accomplished. In 1933 Germany was Hitler's.

Good will and high moral purpose had no meaning in the Germany of the Nazis or the Japan of the Imperial Army. For men who hoped for disarmament and peace and the rule of law, the hour of peril was close. Neither the American people nor their leaders had brought mankind to the edge of disaster, nor could they alone have prevented the collapse of world order. But the foreign policies of the United States lacked the force to check depression or aggression.

The depths of depression

The Hoover policies: third phase. Hoover, William Allen White once said, was "constitutionally gloomy, a congenital pessimist who always saw the doleful side of any situation." The President took no joy in his office or in its potentialities for leadership. As he put it himself, "I can't be a Theodore Roosevelt." Grim and aloof, Hoover was nonetheless resolute. Just as he tried to halt the panic in Europe in 1931, so did he try to buttress the United States against the effects of that panic. By the fall of that year he had reached certain conclusions that were to shape his policies during the coming months. He intended to do everything he could to keep the nation on the gold standard, in his view an indispensable condition of economic health. The business and financial community shared that belief passionately, as it had for almost a century. The President also intended, again with ardor and with the blessing of men of means, to strive for economy and a balanced budget. He was prepared, however, to use federal funds and federal authority on an unprecedented scale to rescue the banks and industry from their troubles. The effects of their recovery, he thought, would reach down to the farmers and laborers, who were to receive little direct aid from the federal government.

The new Congress convened in December 1931. At Hoover's suggestion it appropriated $125 million to expand the lending powers of the Federal Land Banks. Also at his urging, but not until July 1932, it established a system of home-loan banks with a capital of $125 million for discounting home mortgages. The purpose of this scheme was to enable savings banks, insurance companies, and building-and-loan associations to obtain cash for the mortgages they held instead of having to foreclose them. The act not only helped to keep the assets of the lending institutions liquid but also, as Hoover said, spared hundreds of Americans the "heartbreaking . . . loss of their homes." And it set a significant precedent for more extensive legislation later on.

In February 1932 Congress amended the Federal Reserve Act of 1914 as requested by the President and Secretary of the Treasury Ogden Mills. (Hoover had rid himself of the increasingly unpopular Mellon by appointing him ambassador to Great Britain.) The act of 1914 had required that Federal Reserve currency be backed by gold or certain safe kinds of commercial paper—bank loans to business. By 1932 there was so little commercial activity that gold had come to form almost 70 percent of the reserve stock. Yet foreigners were withdrawing gold at an increasing rate, and domestic hoarding had reached alarming proportions. Hoover and Mills therefore recommended making government bonds and larger classes of safe commercial paper acceptable as collateral for Federal Reserve notes.

The new law, the Glass-Steagall Act, freed about a billion dollars' worth of gold to meet the demands of Europeans who were converting their dollars to gold. This enabled the United States for the time being to retain enough gold to remain on the gold standard without putting controls on gold movements or on transactions in foreign exchange. Yet the continuing outflow of gold even further reduced bank reserves and thus the availability of bank loans to business. That situation further depressed prices and added to the burden of debts contracted when prices were high. To hold to the gold standard was in keeping with the theories of classical economics, with their emphasis on the automatic workings of domestic and international trade and of the business cycle. Yet now that mechanism spun the business cycle downward and helped depression feed upon itself.

In spite of the Glass-Steagall Act, moreover, many banks remained weak. To supplement their resources, Hoover in the fall of 1931 persuaded New York bankers to create a National Credit Association with a $500-million pool. But the halfhearted use of this fund doomed the effort to failure. The President then gave in to the urgings of Eugene Meyer, governor of the Federal Reserve Board and formerly head of the War Finance Corporation established in 1918. Meyer proposed reviving that agency in order to rescue American finance. Hoover, hoping that the psychological lift provided by this scheme would justify the cost of financing it, made it the keystone of his recovery policy in 1932.

In January Congress created the Reconstruction Finance Corporation with a capital stock of $500 million and the power to borrow three times that sum in guaranteed, tax-free bonds. It was authorized, as Meyer and Hoover had recommended, to lend money to banks and insurance companies and, with the approval of the Interstate Commerce Commission, to railroads. Most of the $1.5 billion the RFC disbursed before March 1933 went to banks and trust companies. The RFC, however, could lend funds only against adequate collateral, and it could not buy bank stock. Its

loans increased bank indebtedness, but it could not satisfy the banks' basic need for new capital.

The RFC kept its transactions secret for five months, largely because Hoover feared that publicity would incite runs on the weak banks that were receiving the loans. More than half of the $126 million that the RFC dispersed during those months went to three large banks. One of them was the bank of Charles G. Dawes, who resigned as president of the RFC only a month before the loan went through. In July 1932 the Democrats in Congress, to Hoover's dismay, put through an amendment compelling the RFC to report its transactions. Thereafter the number of loans made to large institutions fell off.

The muddle of relief. Late in 1931 Hoover appointed a new committee on unemployment with Walter S. Gifford as its head. Gifford, the president of the American Telephone and Telegraph Company, agreed with Hoover that relief was the responsibility of local government and private charity. Yet Gifford could not convincingly defend this view. In January 1932 he confessed to a Senate committee that he did not know how many people were out of work; he did not know how many needed help, how much help they needed, or how much money localities were raising or could raise. But of one thing he seemed certain: the "grave danger" of taking "the determination of these things into the Federal Government."

The gravest danger, in the view of the President and most congressmen of both parties, was that the budget might be thrown further out of balance. Yet throughout 1932 the need for federal spending increased. In the words of Senator Edward P. Costigan, Colorado's progressive Republican, "nothing short of federal assistance . . . can possibly satisfy the conscience and heart and safeguard the good name of America." With La Follette, Costigan introduced a bill granting a modest $375 million for relief, but the Administration blocked it. Sensing the political importance of the issue, the Democratic leadership now began to press for direct federal aid to the unemployed and for deficit spending for public works.

Hoover, however, insisted on limiting any relief program to RFC loans to localities and on limiting public works to self-liquidating projects, like bridges and housing, which could return enough income from tolls or

I want to tell you about an experience we had in Philadelphia when our private funds were exhausted and before public funds became available....

One woman said she borrowed 50 cents from a friend and bought stale bread for 3½ cents per loaf, and that is all they had for eleven days except for one or two meals.

With the last food order another woman received she bought dried vegetables and canned goods. With this she made a soup and whenever the members of the family felt hungry they just ate some of the soup....

One woman went along the docks and picked up vegetables that fell from the wagons. Sometimes the fish vendors gave her fish at the end of the day. On two different occasions this family was without food for a day and a half....

Another family did not have food for two days. Then the husband went out and gathered dandelions and the family lived on them.

From Hearings Before a Subcommittee of the Senate Committee on Manufactures, 1932.

Urban distress

There was an air of immense earnestness about the farmers. They had been swung completely out of their usual orbit, but they are absolutely sure of the righteousness of their cause. An old man with white mustache said:

"They say blockading the highway's illegal. I says, 'Seems to me there was a Tea-party in Boston that was illegal too. What about destroying property in Boston Harbor when our country was started?'" He sets the note of the evening.

"If we farmers go down bankrupt," says one of the younger men, "everything in this country goes down. If we get enough to live on, everybody's going to go to work again." ... There is a cry:

"Truck!"

They hurry out in the roadway. All of them carry heavy stakes, some made from axe handles.... Beside the road, handy to use, are heavy spiked logs and planks bristling with spikes to throw in front of trucks. This truck is empty. There is a short conference. The truck passes on its way.

"Good-night, boys," calls the driver. "Good luck!" He is one of them, part of the movement that is just beginning to realize its power.

From Mary Heaton Vorse, "Rebellion in the Cornbelt: American Farmers Beat Their Plowshares into Swords," *Harper's Magazine,* December 1932.

Rural violence

rentals to pay back the initial cost of construction. But many states had nearly exhausted their legal authority to borrow from any source, and few projects had emerged from the drawing board. Consequently the President's restrictions put a low ceiling on spending.

Even so, Hoover endorsed a federal program without precedent in American history. After a partisan wrangle, on July 21, 1932 he signed a bill that authorized the RFC to lend $1.5 billion for local self-liquidating public works and $300 million at 3 percent interest to supplement local relief funds.

The relief loans, the President said, were to be based on "absolute need and evidence of financial exhaustion." That limitation kept them small. The governor of Pennsylvania asked for a loan of $45 million (three-fourths of the sum, he noted, that would allow the jobless in the state a mere 13 cents apiece a day for food for a year). The RFC let him have only $11 million (enough for little more than 3 cents a person a day). By the end of 1932 the RFC had allotted only $30 million for relief loans and even less for public works.

The outlook of the nation's farmers seemed as hopeless as that of the unemployed workers

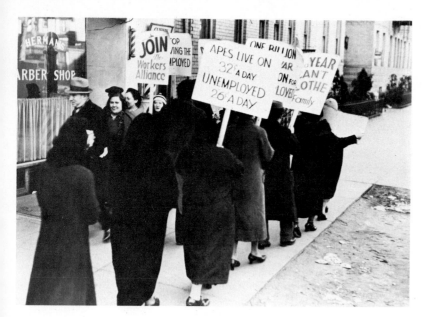

"Absolute need":
relief parade, the Bronx, 1932

in the cities. Even before the depression destroyed the European market for farm commodities, the Federal Farm Board had recognized that it could never stabilize farm prices
without some control over farm production.
When in 1932 American prices followed world
prices down to bewildering lows, the stabilization corporations made a brief but futile effort
to brake the decline. They lost $354 million
in market operations, accumulated huge
stocks of unsalable commodities, and finally
in the summer simply gave up. Wheat, which
had brought $2.16 a bushel in 1919 and
$1.03 in 1929, sank to 38 cents. Cotton,
corn, and other prices suffered comparably.
Farmers found themselves without enough
income to meet their mortgage payments or
even to buy food for their families. And certainly they lacked the money to buy manufactured goods, which still sold at prices sustained by industry.

In December the members of the Federal
Farm Board urged Congress to do something
about regulating acreage and production as a
first step in setting up some sort of program
for boosting farm prices. The only alternative
was agricultural bankruptcy. Yet Hoover and
Secretary of Agriculture Hyde rejected the
idea of imposing federal controls on agriculture. Before the year ended, farmers were
burning corn in Nebraska to keep warm, forming angry posses in Minnesota to prevent
foreclosures, and joining Milo Reno's militant

Farmers' Holiday Association in Iowa to block
the shipment of produce until prices rose.

Moods of despair. Father John Ryan, the
Catholic social reformer, despaired for the
state of the nation. "I wish," he said, "we
might double the number of Communists in
this country, to put the fear, if not of God,
then . . . of something else, into the hearts
of our leaders." Communism had a particular
appeal for the intellectuals who had been
alienated by the culture of the Coolidge era,
men like Malcolm Cowley and Sherwood
Anderson. But the theories of Karl Marx had
little appeal for the general public. The communists organized "hunger marches" in
Washington and Detroit and preached revolution elsewhere, but Communist party membership was little more than one hundred
thousand.

Though desperate Americans spurned communism, they gave way to hatred and violence. Farmers, brandishing shotguns to prevent foreclosures, defied the law to defend
their homes. The president of the Farmers'
Union damned the rich as "cannibals . . . who
live on the labor of the workers." Some of
the prosperous took out "riot and civil commotion insurance" and began to suggest that
the United States needed a fascist dictator like
Mussolini.

In the spring of 1932 some fifteen thousand
unemployed veterans converged on Washington from every region of the country. They
announced that they planned to stay in the
capital until Congress voted full and immediate payment of the bonus. The year before,
over Hoover's veto, Congress had authorized
loans up to 50 percent of the value of each
adjusted service certificate (see p. 582). But
those funds had been spent, and the unemployed veterans, like all other unemployed
Americans, were in dire need of help. When
the Senate voted down the bonus bill, half the
veterans went home. But the rest had no place
to go and no way of getting there, so they
camped in a muddy shantytown on Anacostia
Flats and in vacant government buildings.

Their plight evoked the sympathy of the
chief of the District of Columbia police, who
treated them generously and intelligently. But
their presence worried the Administration.
Hoover, anxious to get rid of them, had Congress pass a bill that permitted them to borrow
against their bonus certificates in order to get
funds for transportation home. Still most vet-

erans waited around after Congress adjourned, hoping at least for a conference with the President.

Late in July the Administration ordered the eviction of all squatters from government buildings. In the ensuing melee, brought about largely by the small corps of communists among the veterans, two men were killed and several policemen wounded. Secretary of War Patrick Hurley had been looking for just such an incident. At his request, the White House now called in the army—four troops of cavalry and four infantry companies, with six tanks, tear gas, and machine guns. Under the personal command of General Douglas MacArthur (whose junior officers included Dwight D. Eisenhower and George Patton), the troops rode into Anacostia Flats, drove out the veterans and their families, and burned their shacks. Crowing over his triumph, MacArthur called the veterans "a mob . . . animated by the essence of revolution." The Administration published reports claiming that most of them had been communists and criminals.

Neither a grand jury nor the Veterans Administration could find evidence to support those charges. The bonus marchers were destitute men. Whether or not they merited special treatment, they deserved, as did unemployed Americans everywhere, compassion and assistance. They received first indifference and veiled hostility, then vicious armed attack. That treatment appalled the nation.

With government callous and blundering, with the business elite defensive about the disrepute it had brought on itself, with depression still spreading, Americans began to fear that the whole political and economic system might collapse. Yet they waited patiently, as they had so often before in times of trouble, to see whether the presidential campaign would give them a vote for a brighter future.

The changing of the guard. In the summer of 1932 the Republicans renominated Hoover and his Vice President, Charles Curtis. A minority of the delegates to the convention were dissatisfied with the Administration's policies but were unwilling to repudiate the President. The convention was listless, for the delegates realized that the electorate, rightly or wrongly, blamed the party for the depression and regarded Hoover as the symbol of the party.

Bonus army:
the burning of Anacostia Flats

The Democrats, in contrast, sniffed victory ahead. A majority of the delegates came to Chicago pledged to Franklin D. Roosevelt, who had been the front runner for the nomination since his spanking reelection as governor of New York in 1930. He had the nerve for politics, the sense of fun, and the zest with people that had once made his distant cousin, Theodore Roosevelt, the most popular man in America. Franklin Roosevelt, moreover, had worked effectively with Tammany Hall, had made friends with the masters of other Northern machines, and yet had always preserved close relations with the Southern wing of the party. Though conservative in his economic thinking, Roosevelt believed in positive, active, humane government.

Roosevelt stood to the left of his serious opponents. Their one hope was to organize a coalition to keep him from getting the two-thirds vote necessary for nomination. Al Smith, still a favorite of the machines, hoped to be nominated once again. Ambition had soured Smith's best instincts. When Roosevelt before the convention called for help for "the forgotten man at the bottom of the economic pyramid," Smith remarked testily, "This is no time for demagogues." But Smith lacked allies. The McAdoo faction still opposed him and now backed Speaker of the House John N. Garner. After Roosevelt had failed to win the necessary vote in three ballots, McAdoo, evening up the old scores of 1924 (see p.

The proposals of our opponents will endanger or destroy our system.... I especially emphasize that promise to promote "employment for all surplus labor at all times." At first I could not believe that anyone would be so cruel as to hold out a hope so absolutely impossible of realization to these 10,000,000 who are unemployed. And I protest against such frivolous promises being held out to a suffering people. It is easily demonstrable that no such employment can be found. But the point I wish to make here and now is the mental attitude and spirit of the Democratic Party to attempt it. It is another mark of the character of the new deal and the destructive changes which mean the total abandonment of every principle upon which this government and the American system is founded. If it were possible to give this employment to 10,000,000 people by the Government, it would cost upwards of $9,000,000,000 a year.... It would pull down the employment of those who are still at work by the high taxes and the demoralization of credit upon which their employment is dependent.... It would mean the growth of a fearful bureaucracy which, once established, could never be dislodged.

From Herbert Hoover, Campaign Address in New York, October 1932.

597), switched California's critical delegation to the New York governor. This put Roosevelt across and in return his lieutenants arranged second place on the ticket for Garner.

In a characteristically dramatic gesture, Roosevelt broke precedent by flying to Chicago to accept the nomination before the convention adjourned. "Let it . . . be symbolic that . . . I broke traditions," he told the cheering delegates. "Republican leaders not only have failed in material things, they have failed in national vision, because in disaster they have held out no hope. . . . I pledge you, I pledge myself to a new deal for the American people."

Roosevelt began to define that New Deal during his campaign. He was often deliberately vague and took pains to avoid offending any large bloc of voters. He hedged on the tariff. He made much of his party's demand for the repeal of the Eighteenth Amendment: Prohibition was still an important political issue in 1932, but it had no immediate bearing on the depression, which was the overriding concern of Americans. But he also set forth strong lines of attack on the nation's economic ills. At the Commonwealth Club in San Francisco, Roosevelt said that "government . . . owes to everyone an avenue to possess himself of a portion of that plenty sufficient for his needs, through his own work." In its dealings with business, government was to "assist the development of . . . an economic constitutional order." And such

Roosevelt's arrival in Chicago, 1932: "Let it . . . be symbolic that . . . I broke traditions"

an order, he pointed out, demanded national planning.

Roosevelt's plans drew on the ideas reformers had nurtured throughout the twenties and promised assistance to the victims of depression. He called for strict public regulation of the utilities and federal development of public power. He advocated federal controls on agricultural production as a part of a program to support commodity prices and federal loans to refinance farm mortgages. He expressed interest in the schemes for currency inflation that agriculture-leaders were urging as a means to raise prices and reduce the weight of debt. He appealed to the business community by demanding cuts in government spending in order to balance the budget, but in the same speech he also promised to incur a deficit whenever human suffering made it necessary.

Roosevelt's oratorical flair and personal ebullience contrasted with Hoover's heavy speech and grim manner. The President emphasized his dedication to budget-balancing and the gold standard, defended his record, and charged his opponent with recklessness. The policies Roosevelt advocated, Hoover said, "would destroy the very foundations of our American system." If they were adopted, "grass will grow in the streets of a hundred cities, a thousand towns."

That rhetoric reflected Hoover's gloom. It obscured his own expansion of federal control, and it exaggerated Roosevelt's intentions.

We have two problems: first, to meet the immediate distress; second, to build up on a basis of permanent employment.

As to ''immediate relief,'' the first principle is that this nation, this national Government, if you like, owes a positive duty that no citizen shall be permitted to starve....

In addition to providing emergency relief, the Federal Government should and must provide temporary work wherever that is possible. You and I know that in the national forests, on flood prevention, and on the development of waterway projects that have already been authorized and planned but not yet executed, tens of thousands, and even hundreds of thousands of our unemployed citizens can be given at least temporary employment....

Third, the Federal Government should expedite the actual construction of public works already authorized....

Finally, in that larger field that looks ahead, we call for a coordinated system of employment exchanges, the advance planning of public works, and unemployment reserves.

From Franklin D. Roosevelt, Campaign Address in Boston, October 1932.

Actually the Democrat's campaign disappointed many intellectuals who felt, as Walter Lippmann earlier had, that Franklin Roosevelt was ''a highly impressionable person . . . without strong convictions. . . . a pleasant man, who, without any important qualifications for the office, would very much like to be President.''

But there were significant differences between the two candidates and their ideas, between Hoover's pessimism and Roosevelt's effervescence, between Hoover's belief that the origins of the depression lay outside the United States and Roosevelt's belief that they were internal, between Hoover's impulse toward caution and Roosevelt's impulse toward experiment, between Hoover's identification with industry and finance and Roosevelt's identification with the forgotten men and with the intellectuals and social workers who championed them. Hoover in his last campaign speech was right in associating Roosevelt with Norris and La Follette, right in asserting that the contest was between two philosophies of government. Both philosophies were fundamentally American, but Hoover's looked backward, while Roosevelt's looked eagerly ahead.

The people had a real choice when they went to the polls in November. Dismissing radicalism (the Socialists—rent by factionalism—polled 881,951 votes, the Communists, only 102,785), they swept the Democrats into office. Roosevelt won over 57 percent of the popular vote and carried the Electoral College 472 to 59. The Democrats also gained a large majority in both houses of Congress. The vote, a protest against the Administration, gave Roosevelt a clear mandate for change. He lost only six states—Maine, New Hampshire, Vermont, Connecticut, Delaware, and Pennsylvania. He carried the agricultural West as well as the South; he carried the great cities by majorities larger than Smith's in 1928.

Depression had stripped the American people of most of their illusions. After twelve years the farmers and the workers once again had the determining voice in Washington. They had repudiated business and its policies and servants, had thrown out the Old Guard, and had taken the direction of government back into their own hands.

HOOVER AND HIS POLICIES
Arthur M. Schlesinger, Jr., *The Crisis of the Old Order** (1957), provides a critical and detailed analysis of the Hoover Administration and its problems. Also critical, though the authors intend to be sympathetic, are H. G. Warren, *Herbert Hoover and the Great Depression** (1959), and J. A. Schwarz, *The Interregnum of Despair* (1970); the relevant chapters in J. D. Hicks, *Republican*

*Available in a paperback edition.

Ascendancy: 1921–1933[*] (1960), are unsympathetic and those in W. E. Leuchtenburg, *The Perils of Prosperity: 1914–32*[*] (1958), lucid but brief. The most ardent defense of the Administration appears in Herbert Hoover, *Memoirs: The Great Depression, 1929–1941* (1952), which may be supplemented by another book of similar spirit, R. L. Wilbur and A. M. Hyde, *The Hoover Policies* (1937). On Hoover's foreign policies, there is significant material in both W. A. Williams and the biographies of Stimson mentioned in connection with the preceding chapter, and in R. H. Ferrell, *American Diplomacy in the Great Depression: Hoover-Stimson Foreign Policy, 1929–1933*[*] (1957).

DEPRESSION

All the volumes noted above of course deal with the depression. Its impact is also poignantly revealed in the pertinent parts of I. Bernstein, *The Lean Years*[*] (1960); C. Bird, *The Invisible Scar*[*] (1965); B. Sternsher, ed., *Hitting Home*[*] (1970); and D. A. Shannon, ed., *The Great Depression*[*] (1960). There are excellent descriptions of the stock-market crash in F. L. Allen, *Only Yesterday*[*] (1931), and J. K. Galbraith, *The Great Crash, 1929*[*] (1955). The skillful analysis of the latter should be compared with the also able view in Thomas Wilson, *Fluctuations in Income and Employment* (1948), and with the special view of central banking policy in M. Friedman and A. J. Schwartz, *The Great Contraction, 1929–1933*[*] (1965). Within his excellent general study of American radical intellectuals, *Writers on the Left*[*] (1961), Daniel Aaron discusses the influence of the depression on the spread of radicalism.

F. D. R. AND 1932

Franklin D. Roosevelt's governorship and first presidential campaign receive important treatment in A. M. Schlesinger's work, mentioned above, which is brilliant and panoramic on those subjects, and in Frank Freidel, *Franklin D. Roosevelt: The Triumph* (1956), a work of outstanding scholarship. Less comprehensive but still useful are parts of J. M. Burns, *Roosevelt: The Lion and the Fox*[*] (1956), and R. G. Tugwell, *The Democratic Roosevelt*[*] (1957).

[*]Available in a paperback edition.

27

The New Deal

During the winter of 1932–33, the despair born of depression gripped the United States ever more tightly. The four-month interval between the November election and the inauguration of March 1933 found Hoover without influence and Roosevelt without power. Hoover frustrated any chance of collaboration with his successor by insisting on policies Roosevelt had condemned. In February, when the President called on Roosevelt to make a series of conservative declarations, he privately wrote a Republican senator, "I realize that if these declarations be made by the President-Elect, he will have ratified the whole major program of the Republican Administration." The incoming President, recognizing Hoover's invitation as a request for capitulation rather than cooperation, naturally rejected it, as he was, in any event, inclined to.

Without making public commitments to any program, Roosevelt awaited his day to take charge. Americans, worried and gloomy, also awaited the change of command, their anxieties deepened by an attempt upon Roosevelt's life by a madman in Miami, Florida, in February. The electorate had no sure sense of what a new deal might bring them, but they had clinching evidence that the old deal was ending in disaster.

The spreading panic was beginning to concentrate on one of the weakest links in the economy—the banking system. As the economy continued downward, more and more people played it safe by converting their savings to cash. The mounting pressure on financial institutions, the lines of depositors waiting to draw out their savings, the threat of further runs on the banks, led the governor of Michigan in mid-February to proclaim a bank holiday—that is, to order the temporary closing of the banks in his state. That act set off a chain reaction in other states. On the last day of Hoover's Administration, with banks shutting their doors across the land, the retiring President said, "We are at the end of our rope. There is nothing more we can do."

Franklin D. Roosevelt

His background. The new President was fifty-one years old. Like his distant cousin Theodore, he had come from a patrician background that gave him both a high sense of civic responsibility and a certain disdain for those whose chief achievement was making money. Like Theodore, Franklin Roosevelt was a man of charm, vivacity, and energy. He had been much influenced by Theodore, and their careers offered curious parallels. Both had made their political debuts in the New York legislature; both had served as Assistant Secretary of the Navy in Washington; both had been governor of New York; both had been candidates for the Vice Presidency.

Unlike Theodore, Franklin was a member of

629

the Democratic branch of the Roosevelt family. He was less of an intellectual than Theodore, but he was also less moralistic and evangelical. His urbane and conciliatory manner, indeed, led some observers to suppose him too compliant for hard responsibilities and decisions. His record suggested otherwise. As second in command in the Navy Department during the First World War, he had been a resourceful executive. As candidate for Vice President in 1920, he had been a vigorous campaigner. In 1921 he had been stricken by an acute attack of poliomyelitis. That illness deprived him of the use of his legs; many thought it would end his public career. The iron determination of his comeback revealed an inner spirit that was not only gallant but tough. He had been an imaginative governor of New York; no state had taken so many positive measures to meliorate the effects of depression. His capture of the Democratic nomination in 1932 was the work of a seasoned politician.

The superficial affability of Roosevelt's manner actually concealed a complex personality—at once light-hearted and somber, candid and disingenuous, open and impenetrable, bold and cautious, decisive and evasive. Throughout his life he pursued certain public ends—especially the improvement of welfare and opportunity for the great masses of people—with steadiness of purpose; but the means he employed to achieve those ends were often inconsistent and occasionally unworthy. Yet his capacity to project the grand moral issues of his day—and his readiness to use the resources of presidential leadership to prepare the country for necessary action— enabled him to command the confidence of a great majority of Americans during his terms in office, despite the persistent opposition of a powerful minority.

His ideas. Roosevelt was a child of the progressive era. Theodore Roosevelt and Woodrow Wilson had been his early inspirations. Government seemed to him a necessary instrument of the general welfare, and he had no inhibitions about calling on the state to redress matters when "rugged individualism" left parts of the population or sections of the country without adequate protection. But the problems of 1933 were novel. Progressivism had been a gospel of social welfare rather than a program for economic growth, and progres-

sives were no less baffled than conservatives by economic collapse. But, where faith in the sovereign virtue of laissez faire constrained conservatives from taking positive government action, progressives like Roosevelt, with activist temperaments and an adventurous attitude toward social policy, were ready to invoke affirmative government to bring about economic recovery.

In economics, Roosevelt had leanings rather than theories. In his campaign for the Presidency, he had identified himself with two main ideas—action and planning. As to what should be tried, his views were sometimes incompatible.

Certain of his advisers had more clear-cut ideas. A group of college professors, mostly recruited from Columbia University, had served as his campaign brain trust. A book of 1932, *The Modern Corporation and Private Property,* by Adolf A. Berle, Jr., and Gardiner C. Means, provided the foundation for their analysis. The trend toward economic concentration, they contended, was irreversible. Already it had transformed great parts of the old free market of classical economics into "administered" markets, in which basic economic decisions were made, not by equations of supply and demand, but by the policies of those who ran the great corporations. In Berle's and Means' opinion this change in the structure of the market rendered classical laissez-faire theory obsolete.

So persuaded, another Columbia economist, Rexford G. Tugwell, urged the President-elect to bold conclusions. If concentration was inevitable, Tugwell argued, then control over the nation's economic life could not be safely left in private hands. Such private control had brought about the depression; in the twenties the gains of economic productivity had gone into profits, savings, and speculation when they should have gone into a buildup of purchasing power through the payment of higher wages to workers and higher prices to farmers. The only way to operate the modern integrated economy at capacity, in Tugwell's view, was organized public planning.

Men like Berle, Tugwell, Means, and Raymond Moley, who acted as nominal head of the brain trust, were in a sense heirs of Theodore Roosevelt's New Nationalism. Their predisposition toward new institutions for central planning was reinforced by the views of those who, recalling America's last national emergency, the First World War, reverted to wartime economic agencies in the battle against depression. The Reconstruction Finance Corporation of the Hoover Administration was itself a revival of Wilson's War Finance Corporation (see p. 622). Now men who had once been associated with the War Industries Board, men like Bernard Baruch, Hugh S. Johnson, and George N. Peek, began to sponsor schemes of industrial and agricultural planning, though with little of Tugwell's zeal for accompanying social reform.

Not all those around Roosevelt accepted the virtues of national planning. Others close to him—especially Associate Justice Louis D. Brandeis of the Supreme Court and Professor Felix Frankfurter of Harvard—were heirs of Wilson's New Freedom. They rejected the thesis of inevitable economic concentration, distrusted the idea of central planning, and advocated policies designed to encourage more competition. Still others, though these were more powerful in the Democratic party in Congress than in the President's immediate circle, were inflationists in the tradition of William Jennings Bryan. And others, like Lewis W. Douglas, whom Roosevelt was about to appoint Director of the Budget, were sound-money, laissez-faire Democrats deeply committed, like the Republicans, to the gold standard and the annually balanced budget. As now one, now another, of these groups exerted a telling influence, the resulting policies on occasion clashed.

Roosevelt, concerned more with action than consistency, presided benignly over the clash of debate and policy alike. Disagreement stimulated him, enabled him to compare the merits of competing arguments and personalities, and reassured him that crucial questions would come to him for decision. His choice of Cabinet members reflected his desire for a variety of views and his confidence that he could control men of divergent opinion. To the State Department he named Cordell Hull, a Tennessee Democrat who had sponsored the Income-tax Amendment during the Wilson Administration but who was now cautious in his views except as a passionate foe of international trade barriers. Two vigorous progressive Republicans—Henry A. Wallace of Iowa and Harold L. Ickes of Illinois—were appointed to Agriculture and Interior; the first woman in history to go into the Cabinet, Frances Perkins of New York, a veteran social worker, became Secretary of Labor; and the other posts were filled by Democratic politicians or, in the case of the Treasury, by William Woodin of New York, a flexible-minded businessman.

The Hundred Days

The inauguration. On March 4, 1933, millions of Americans clustered around their radios to hear the new President deliver his inaugural address. "Let me assert my firm belief," Roosevelt began, "that the only thing we have to fear is fear itself." Then he assailed the business-leaders whose incompetence and misconduct, he said, had been largely responsible for the economic disaster. "This Nation asks for action, and action now," he concluded, adding that he would seek from Congress "broad Executive powers to wage a war against the emergency, as great as the power that would be given to me if we were in fact invaded by a foreign foe."

Action itself was quick to follow. Immediately after the inauguration, Roosevelt declared a national bank holiday and called Congress into special session. When Congress convened on March 8, it received at once a special message on the banking crisis and a draft of emergency banking legislation, on which Roosevelt's advisers had collaborated with some of Hoover's outgoing Treasury staff. In less than eight hours the House and Senate shouted through the bill and returned it to the President for signature. The unprecedented combination of decision and speed in the passage of the act electrified the country.

Quick to seize advantage of the national mood, the President put forward a bill calling for the reduction of government expenses, including veterans' pensions. He followed his economy message with a call for the amendment of the Volstead Act to legalize light wines and beers. The prompt enactment of both the economy and beer bills meant, among other things, the defeat of the two most powerful lobbies in the nation's capital—the veterans and the Prohibitionists. All this activity increased the national sense of exhilaration. "In one week," wrote Walter Lippmann, "the

Inauguration Day, 1933: action was quick to follow

nation, which had lost confidence in everything and everybody, has regained confidence in the government and in itself."

Planning for agriculture. So far the Roosevelt program had been dashing in style but orthodox in content. Now, focusing on the problem of recovery, the President followed the path of the planners who advocated using the power of the federal government to "rationalize" and to help to manage agriculture and industry. On March 16, Roosevelt sent to Capitol Hill a message calling for a bold national policy in agriculture. "I tell you frankly that it's a new and untrod path," he warned Congress, "but I tell you with equal frankness that an unprecedented condition calls for the trial of new means."

The condition was indeed unprecedented. The per capita cash net income of the American farmer had declined from $162 to $48 between 1929 and 1932; farm prices had fallen 55 percent; and, since industrial prices had not fallen correspondingly, the farmer's purchasing power was only about 60 percent of what it had been in 1929. The farmer's fixed charges—especially the burden of mortgage debt assumed at higher price levels—weighed more heavily than ever on him. In some areas, the farmer was not even able to clear the cost of production. Since the individual farmer saw no way to fight falling prices except to increase his production, he put more produce on the market and drove prices down faster and further.

The central idea in the Administration proposal was "agricultural adjustment." This plan aimed to increase farm income by controlling production; and it aimed to control production by offering benefit payments to farmers who agreed to regulate their plantings according to a national plan. The adjustment programs were to be financed by processing taxes collected at the flour mill or textile mill or packinghouse. No program would go into effect until a majority of farmers indicated they wanted it by voting in a referendum; and the local administration of the plan was to be as much as possible in the hands of the farmers themselves. The ultimate object was to restore to the farmer substantially the terms of trade he had had in 1909–14—that is, to give his produce the same exchange value it commanded in the years directly before the First World War. This concept was known as "parity."

The agricultural-adjustment bill that emerged from conferences between the Department of Agriculture and leading farm organizations incorporated, in addition to benefit payments, a number of other approaches to the farm problem. It gave the government authority, for example, to maintain prices through loans on or purchase of nonperishable crops, which would then go into government storage; it also conferred authority to withdraw land from cultivation through leasing and to regulate the release of commodities for sale through marketing agreements and quotas. Through the use of those powers the government could not only prevent gluts on the market but could build up reserves against lean years, and, in the phrase of Henry Wallace, maintain an "ever normal granary." The inflationists in Congress added an important amendment giving the President power to issue greenbacks, to remonetize silver, and to alter the gold content of the dollar. In the meantime, the Farm Credit Administration provided quick and effective mortgage relief.

While Washington laid its plans, trouble was mounting on the countryside. In late April a mob marched on a judge in Le Mars, Iowa, who had refused to suspend foreclosure proceedings and nearly lynched him. The Farmer's Holiday Association, the most radical of the farmers' groups, renewed its threat of a farm strike. Alarmed by the rising agrarian wrath, the governor of Iowa called out the national guard and placed half a dozen counties under martial law.

Those developments speeded passage of the Agricultural Adjustment Act on May 12. It established the Agricultural Adjustment Administration and opened the New Deal's campaign to raise farm income. The first task was to cut down production in areas already overwhelmed by surpluses. Thus a carry-over from previous years of 8 million bales of cotton had driven cotton prices down to 5 cents a pound. Yet, by the time the act had passed, some 40 million acres had already been planted in new cotton. The only way to save the cotton-grower was to persuade him to plow under the planted crop in return for benefit payments. This the AAA proceeded to do in a whirlwind plow-up campaign of some 10 million acres in the spring and summer. Acting on the recommendation of the Farm Bureau and the Grange, the AAA dealt with the market glut in corn and hogs by buying and slaughtering some 5 million little pigs.

No one perceived more sharply the irony of destroying plenty in the midst of want than the men who ordered the job to be done. "To destroy a standing crop goes against the soundest instincts of human nature," said Henry Wallace. Yet industry, the Secretary of Agriculture pointed out, had in effect plowed under much of its potential output after 1929 by cutting down on production; how, in all logic, could agriculture be denied the same right of self-protection?

The terrible logic of scarcity worked. As production declined—aided, in the cases of wheat and corn, by the searing droughts of 1933–34—prices rose. Between 1932 and 1936 gross farm income increased by 50 percent, and cash receipts from marketing (including government benefit payments) nearly doubled. The parity ratio rose from 55 in 1932 to 90 in 1936. The chief beneficiaries were commercial farmers, owners of large holdings and recipients of a disproportionate share of benefit payments. To reduce acreage, they often forced their tenants or sharecroppers off the land and into migrancy, usually as itinerant farm-laborers or unemployed newcomers to the cities. But many owners of family-sized farms also benefited, and though the AAA was occasionally disturbed by top-level policy conflicts, it conducted its complex administrative operations with smoothness and effect.

Planning for industry. Agricultural planning covered only the lesser part of the American economy. By 1933 American industry was employing some 5 million fewer workers than in 1929 and producing less than half the value of goods. Businessmen, striving to maintain a margin of profits, saw no choice but to cut costs—that is, to lower wages and lay off employees. But the more wages and employment were reduced, the more mass purchasing power declined.

There was increasing agreement that the only way to stop the industrial decline was through joint planning by government and business. This view was backed not just by Tugwell, with his belief in public management of the economy, and by Johnson, with his memory of the War Industries Board. Powerful voices in business, especially the United States Chamber of Commerce, now urged that private trade associations be given authority to fix prices, divide markets, and "stabilize" industrial production. Recovery, they argued,

depended on limiting the play of what Johnson called "the murderous doctrine of savage and wolfish individualism."

In the spring the Administration worked out a so-called national-industrial-recovery bill, divided into two parts. The first part was designed "to promote the organization of industry for the purpose of cooperative action among trade groups" through codes of fair competition carrying with them exemption from the antitrust laws; an important provision—the celebrated Section 7a—sought to win labor support by offering federal guarantees of the right of trade unions to organize and bargain collectively. The second part of the bill provided for the establishment of a Public Works Administration with an appropriation of $3.3 billion. Roosevelt signed the bill on June 16, calling it "a challenge to industry, which has long insisted that, given the right to act in unison, it could do much for the general good which has hitherto been unlawful. From today it has that right."

Two agencies were set up under the National Industrial Recovery Act—the National Recovery Administration, with General Johnson as head, and the Public Works Administration under Harold L. Ickes. Johnson combined considerable knowledge of the workings of the economy with showmanship and evangelism. He saw the NRA as a national crusade designed to restore employment and regenerate industry in an excitement of torchlight processions and giant rallies. Finding the negotiation of codes with specific industries disappointingly slow, Johnson came up in July with the idea of a "blanket code" in which cooperating employers would pledge themselves to observe NRA standards on minimum wages and maximum hours; the Blue Eagle, modeled on the Indian thunderbird, became the symbol of compliance. Briefly, in the revivalist atmosphere conjured up by Johnson, the Blue Eagle soared. Two million employers accepted the blanket code, and the great industries of the country, one by one, began to accept special codes.

Protected from competition by those codes, managers were able to stop cutting prices and with them wages. But the codes also protected marginal firms that might best have been allowed to fail, as well as strong firms that could have produced at a profit at prices lower than those that tended to obtain. Further, by limiting production the codes decreased the probability of investment in new, improved facilities. Yet new capital investment would have helped to stimulate the overall economy.

Those liabilities were balanced in part by the attempts of the NRA to pursue some of the long-term objectives of American reformers. In the economic field, it hoped to bring about permanent reemployment by raising wages and shortening working hours. In the social field, it sought the abolition of child labor, an improvement of working conditions, an encouragement of labor organization, an extension of fair-trade practices.

Soon the NRA began to overextend its efforts. Instead of concentrating on codification in the major industries, it allowed itself to be tempted into setting up codes for local and service trades. There was good humanitarian reason for this effort, for these were precisely the trades where the sweatshop was most deeply entrenched. But it involved the NRA in a host of petty enforcement problems, which at once distracted its energies and dissipated its credit. Johnson was reluctant to use the NRA's coercive powers, since he wanted to avoid a court test of the NRA's constitutionality. Consequently his chief reliance against those whom he denounced as "chiselers" was the compulsion of public opinion. So long as the nation felt itself in acute crisis, this compulsion worked. But as soon as economic conditions began to grow better, more and more employers tried to beat the codes.

Within the NRA, moreover, there was constant pressure from trade associations to use the code mechanism as a means of raising prices. Many businessmen felt that price-fixing would be an appropriate *quid pro quo* for their concessions on wages, hours, and collective bargaining. On the other hand, many inside the NRA and out argued that excessive price increases would defeat the whole policy of expanding purchasing power; they feared, moreover, that price-fixing would turn the codes into a vehicle for precisely the sort of monopoly Congress had tried to outlaw in the Sherman Act. An investigation by a special committee in 1934 under the chairmanship of Clarence Darrow, the criminal lawyer, seemed to substantiate the charge that the NRA had become the instrument of monopoly.

In the meantime the labor provisions in Section 7a had given a great stimulus to trade-union organization, and this embittered many employers. Hugh Johnson's unstable personality and his increasingly erratic course further complicated the NRA's existence. Roosevelt forced him out in the fall of 1934 and replaced him by a five-man board. By now the NRA had lost its allure. In 1933 nearly everyone had been for giving it a chance. By 1935 most people—except for the trade associations and the trade unions—were against it. When the Supreme Court finally declared the National Industrial Recovery Act unconstitutional in 1935, the Administration accepted the verdict with relief. From the outset it had been seeking other roads to recovery and reform.

The end of the Hundred Days. The AAA and the NRA set the pattern of national planning and were, in this sense, crucial measures of the early New Deal. But they by no means exhausted the achievement of the special session of 1933. During the Hundred Days after March 4, 1933, Roosevelt sent fifteen messages to Congress and saw fifteen major bills through to enactment.

Advocates of inflation, strongest in Congress but vocal also within the executive branch, were eager to relieve the burden of debt contracted when the price level was much higher. Since the closing of the banks and the Economy Act had a deflationary impact, the Administration looked, too, for means to induce a general price increase. Conservative officials, especially Budget Director Douglas, profoundly opposed anything that savored of inflation. On the other hand, many Southern and Western congressmen demanded either a massive printing of greenbacks or an extensive monetization of silver. Those prospects had broad support among farmers and even some members of the business community. Roosevelt himself had no desire for currency inflation, but he was determined to bring about a rise of prices—not so fast as to absorb the increases in wages and farm income but fast enough to reduce the drag of debt on the economy. It seemed increasingly evident to him that the United States had to choose between the old gold standard and the price-raising policy, and he had no hesitation about the choice. On April 18, 1933, the President determined to abandon the gold standard officially by executive orders authorizing the control of the flow of gold from the United States. In a few weeks Congress confirmed the departure from gold by passing a resolution providing for the abrogation of the gold clause in public and private contracts.

In the meantime, the inflationist amendment to the Agricultural Adjustment Act (see p. 632) had bestowed a variety of monetary powers on the President. He protected the independence of American monetary policy by refusing at the London Economic Conference in July to peg the dollar at a fixed value in international exchange, and, when farm prices sagged in November, Roosevelt, always eager for action, embarked on a gold-purchase program designed to raise the level of prices, especially commodity prices, by Treasury purchases of gold. The economics of this program was of doubtful validity. But the exercise did little harm, and it permitted Roosevelt to retain control of monetary policy at a time when both inflationists and bankers were demanding that he take action that he deemed positively harmful. By January 1934 the experiment had obviously failed to raise prices, but the pressure for inflation had abated. The Administration then stabilized the dollar at $35 for an ounce of gold, 59.06 percent of the pre-1933 gold value. Roosevelt also guided through Congress the Gold Act of 1934, which gave the Treasury large new authority in managing the value of the dollar abroad and the conditions of credit at home.

The gold policy, along with the banking and securities legislation of 1933–34, shifted the financial capital of the nation from Wall Street to Washington, a significant reform. Further, the adventure in inflation and the Treasury's use of its new powers established a continuing policy of ''cheap money''—that is, low interest rates. Those low rates made private borrowing more attractive and the financing of government borrowing less expensive. But the inducement to private or public investment proved inadequate, for the private sector still envisaged small opportunities for profit and the Administration still hesitated deliberately to incur heavy deficits. Like planning for industry, inflation and cheap money did not produce recovery. They did establish public authority over an area of economic activity which private power had previously dominated.

Other actions of the Hundred Days were designed to strengthen the banks and to reduce the human cost of depression. The Home Owners' Loan Act, one of the most popular of New Deal measures, saved countless homes by providing means for the refinancing

of mortgages. That refinancing, along with the similar operations of the Farm Credit Administration for agricultural mortgages, not only protected homes and farms from foreclosure but helped banks and insurance companies as well. In return for mortgages that were not being paid, those lending institutions received government bonds which they could always convert to cash and on which regular interest payments were assured. Still another New Deal measure, the Federal Deposit Insurance Corporation, set up a system for the insurance of savings and demand deposits and thereby helped restore confidence in the banks.

Even more precedent-breaking was the Federal Emergency Relief Act, which established for the first time a system of federal relief. Under the resourceful direction of Harry L. Hopkins, a New York social worker, a succession of agencies (the best known, launched in 1935, was the Works Progress Administration) tackled the problem of aid for the unemployed. In Hopkins' view the solution lay in ''work relief'' rather than in ''doles''—that is, in jobs rather than in cash handouts. Though the work-relief program led to a certain amount of made work, known invidiously

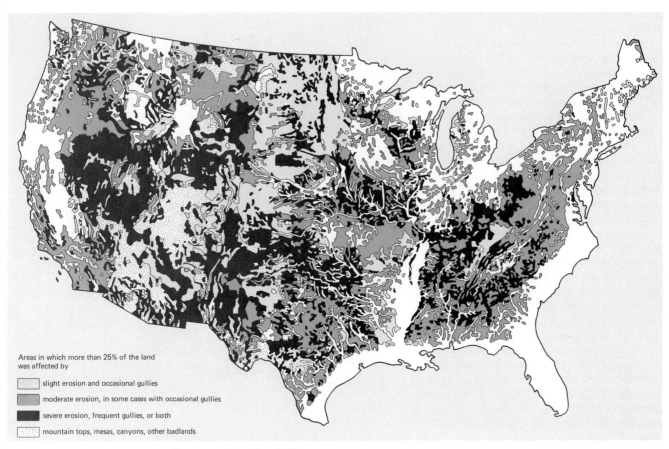

Areas in which more than 25% of the land was affected by

- slight erosion and occasional gullies
- moderate erosion, in some cases with occasional gullies
- severe erosion, frequent gullies, or both
- mountain tops, mesas, canyons, other badlands

The extent of erosion, 1935

as "boondoggling," it also built roads, airports, and schools, improved parks and waterways, produced plays and concerts, maps and guidebooks, and sustained the morale and preserved the skills of millions of Americans unable through no fault of their own to find private employment. Where Hopkins' WPA specialized in light public works, Ickes' Public Works Administration concentrated on heavy and durable projects, ranging from dams and bridges to irrigation projects and aircraft-carriers. The activities of PWA not only gave some stimulation, albeit inadequate, to the national economy but permanently improved the national estate in many ways.

Another measure of the Hundred Days linked work relief to the conservation of natural resources. This was the Civilian Conservation Corps, an organization that recruited young men between the ages of eighteen and twenty-five to work in the countryside. CCC camps were set up in all parts of the country, and CCC boys played a useful role in protect-

ing and developing reservoirs, watersheds, forests, and parks. The dust storms of the early thirties, whirling up from the parched and eroded land of the Great Plains, emphasized the need for a revitalized national conservation policy. A "shelterbelt" of trees was planted along the one-hundredth meridian from Canada to Texas; other measures were undertaken to promote reforestation, to control overgrazing, and to encourage farmers to plant soil-improving crops and adopt other soil-conservation practices.

In some respects the most striking innovation of the Hundred Days was an effort to rescue an entire region. The Tennessee Valley was a conspicuous example of what later generations would know as an "underdeveloped" territory. Recurrent floods washed away the topsoil; the forests were thin and overcut; income was less than half the national average; and in the highland counties, over half the families were on relief. Only two out of every hundred farms had electricity. Yet the Valley also contained one of the most valuable

TVA: new life and new hope

power sites in the country, at Muscle Shoals, Alabama; and some people, especially Senator George W. Norris of Nebraska, saw in cheap electric power the means of transforming life in the valley. But Norris' bills providing for government operation of hydroelectric plants had fallen under the vetoes of Republican Presidents.

Many factors converged in the Valley: not only electric power and conservation but fertilizer production, flood control, inland waterways, and, above all, the hopeless cycle of human poverty. In a bold change of perspective, Roosevelt now saw all these elements as parts of a single problem. The answer, he believed, was not a collection of separate and unrelated reforms but multipurpose development under the direction of a single authority. In April 1933 he called on Congress to establish "a corporation clothed with the power of Government but possessed of the flexibility and initiative of a private enterprise" charged with "national planning for a complete river watershed."

Despite the opposition of the power companies of the area, whose executives claimed that the Valley already had all the power capacity it could absorb for years to come, Congress passed the bill establishing the Tennessee Valley Authority in May 1933. The TVA proved to be one of the most dramatically successful of all New Deal undertakings. Seeking at every opportunity to win local collaboration under TVA director David E. Lilienthal's slogan of "grassroots democracy," the TVA built dams and powerhouses, cleared the rivers, replenished the soil, rebuilt the forests, and brought the magic of electricity into the farthest corners of the Valley. Grassroots democracy in the Valley proved to be for whites only. Without protest from Washington local agencies working with TVA systematically excluded blacks from participation and benefits. Yet for whites at least the region vibrated with a new life. Soon visitors came from all over the world to inspect the result. No other New Deal agency had such an international impact.

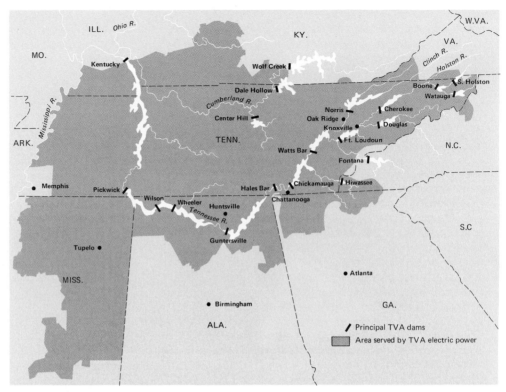

The Tennessee Valley Authority

The struggle for recovery

The conquest of fear. The Hundred Days induced a tremendous revival of confidence. In this revival the personality of the President himself played a basic role. As late as the 1932 campaign, Franklin Roosevelt had still been a hazy figure. Now his speeches, his radio "fireside chats," his twice-a-week press conferences made him seen almost a constant presence in the homes of Americans who had suffered too long under presidential indifference. He radiated energy, decision, and good cheer; and his superb personal faith, along with the explosion of administrative inventiveness and political audacity in Washington, convinced the people that they had a chance to recover control of their economic destiny.

During 1933 Roosevelt enjoyed almost universal support. As the crisis receded, however, opposition began to emerge—first from the business community on Roosevelt's right, then in a clamor of discordant voices on his left. At the start his critics made little dent in his popularity. The congressional election of 1934 provided an almost unprecedented na-

tional endorsement of the President's program. The Administration actually increased its strength in both the House and the Senate, and the Republicans were left with the governorship of only seven states. Many of the new Democrats came to Congress from urban districts and were especially responsive to labor and welfare concerns.

Critics, right and left. Roosevelt confronted the congressional session of 1935 with top-heavy majorities in both houses, but the policy momentum of 1933 had begun to slacken. Full economic recovery still seemed distant, and the voices of criticism were now speaking out with new confidence. The American Liberty League, an organization formed in 1934 by a group of conservative businessmen and politicians, offered the most active opposition on the right. On the left the most powerful of the new leaders was Huey Long of Louisiana.

As governor of Louisiana, Long had brought new roads and schools and textbooks to the state; but the price of his impressive program of social improvement was spreading corruption and repression. By 1935 he ruled his native state almost as a dictator. In national politics, Long's role was more purely that of a demagogue. His "Share Our Wealth" movement, which stressed heavy taxation of the rich and large handouts to the poor, rested upon no serious economic theory. It was rather a means of stirring existing resentments over the maldistribution of wealth in the hope that the Kingfish, as Long fondly called himself, could be propelled into the Presidency.

Another rising leader was a California physician, Dr. Francis E. Townsend, who proposed a two-hundred-dollar monthly pension for all over sixty-five. No group in the population save the blacks had suffered more from the depression than the aged, and the Townsend Plan seemed for a while in 1935 to be developing genuine mass support. Both Long and Townsend were openly hostile to the New Deal. A third leader, Father Charles E. Coughlin, the famous "radio priest" of Royal Oak, Michigan, had originally endorsed Roosevelt and the New Deal but by 1935 was drifting into opposition. He established in that year the National Union for Social Justice, an organization that appealed especially to the Populist and inflationist traditions of the Middle West and to the Irish-Catholic masses of the great cities. Coughlin's particular nostrum was the nationalization of the banks.

Long, Townsend, and Coughlin were hawking competing patent medicines for the nation's economic ills. But they drew their following from much the same audience—baffled and disoriented members of the old-American lower-middle class who were seeking attention and protection. The emergence of these new movements signified a discontent that the President could hardly ignore.

Stalemate in 1935. Though the policies of the Hundred Days had ended despair, they had not produced recovery. The gross national product, though nearly $20 billion larger than in 1933, was still $30 billion less than in 1929. Four million more workers were employed in 1935 than in 1933, but 9 million were still unemployed. Roosevelt was still in economic trouble and, as the clamor of the demagogues and the fractiousness of the new Congress in the first months of 1935 made clear, might well be in increasing political trouble. He needed a new forward thrust of policy if he was to maintain his control.

The Supreme Court further increased the pressure against the policies of 1933. For two years the Administration had delayed tests of the constitutionality of New Deal legislation, but at last the dam was breaking. Early in 1935 the Court invalidated a provision of the National Industrial Recovery Act prohibiting interstate shipment of "hot" oil—that is, oil produced in violation of production quotas

1935: a million were still unemployed

The Act establishes a compulsory retirement and pension system for all carriers subject to the Interstate Commerce Act.... The Act is invalid because several of its inseparable provisions contravene the due process of law clause of the Fifth Amendment.... The Act is not in purpose or effect a regulation of interstate commerce within the meaning of the Constitution....

The petitioners' sole reliance is the thesis that efficiency depends upon morale, and morale in turn upon assurance of security for the worker's old age.... The question at once presents itself whether the fostering of a contented mind on the part of an employee by legislation of this type, is in any just sense a regulation of interstate transportation. If that question be answered in the affirmative, obviously there is no limit to the field of so-called regulation....

We feel bound to hold that a pension plan thus imposed is in no proper sense a regulation of the activity of interstate transportation. It is an attempt for social ends to impose by sheer fiat ... a means of assuring a particular class of employees against old age dependency.

From the Majority Opinion of the United States Supreme Court by Mr. Justice Owen J. Roberts, Railroad Retirement Board v. Alton Railroad Co., 295 U.S. 300, 1935.

---

fixed by state laws. A few weeks later, the gold resolution of 1933, one of the foundations of the nation's monetary policy, barely escaped judicial veto in a bitter and somewhat ambiguous 5 to 4 decision. Then the Court, in another 5 to 4 decision, declared against the whole idea of a federal pension act for railroad employees. And on May 27, 1935, the celebrated "Black Monday" of New Deal annals, the Court in three sweeping decisions killed a farm-mortgage-relief act, rebuked the President for what it declared to be an illegal exercise of his removal power, and condemned the entire National Industrial Recovery Act as unconstitutional.

The NRA case, irreverently known as the "sick chicken" case, involved some Brooklyn poultry-dealers, the Schechter brothers, who had been charged with violations of the Live Poultry Code. The Court pronounced unanimously against the Recovery Act on two grounds: that it delegated excessive powers to the executive and that it ascribed to Congress powers of economic regulation that could not be justified under the commerce clause. This second objection was particularly devastating. The language used in the decision seemed to say that the Court regarded mining, manufacturing, agriculture, and construction as "essentially local" activities. In a press conference a few days later Roosevelt concluded, "We have been relegated to the horse-and-buggy definition of interstate commerce."

New directions in policy. In invalidating the NRA, the Supreme Court knocked out the keystone of the early New Deal experiment in national planning. Moreover, the Court's action came at a time when Roosevelt himself was perhaps losing faith in the efficacy of national planning and when the New Dealers most identified with the planning idea were beginning to lose their political usefulness. Roosevelt had little choice now but to seek new ideas and new men. Always the activist, he turned to those best prepared to offer him a convincing program of action. He found this program in the Brandeis-Frankfurter group (see p. 631).

During the Hundred Days, that group had played a subordinate though hardly negligible role. They contributed to the enactment of two important laws: the Securities Act of 1933, requiring full disclosure of relevant information in the issuance of new securities; and the Glass-Steagall Banking Act, providing for the separation of commercial and investment banking. But they disapproved of the NRA, rejecting both the philosophy of irreversible economic concentration on which it was based and the program of national planning to which it led. During 1934 Brandeis, Frankfurter, and their like-minded friends moved a little more to the forefront. Two members of the group in particular, Thomas G. Corcoran and Benjamin V. Cohen, revealed exceptional skill as legislative draftsmen and congressional persuaders. They wrote, with some unavoid-

I am unable to concur in the decision of this case. The gravest aspect of the decision is that it does not rest simply upon a condemnation of particular features of the Railroad Retirement Act, but denies to Congress the power to pass any compulsory pension act for railroad employees....

The fundamental consideration which supports this type of legislation is that industry should take care of its human wastage, whether that is due to accident or age. That view cannot be dismissed as arbitrary or capricious. It is a reasoned conviction based upon abundant experience. The expression of that conviction in law is regulation. When expressed in the government of interstate carriers, with respect to their employees likewise engaged in interstate commerce, it is a regulation of that commerce....

The power committed to Congress to govern interstate commerce does not require that its government should be wise, much less that is should be perfect. The power implies a broad discretion and thus permits a wide range even of mistakes.

From the Minority Opinion of the United States Supreme Court by Chief Justice Charles E. Hughes, Railroad Retirement Board v. Alton Railroad Co., 295 U.S. 300, 1935.

The scope of congressional power: a permissive view

able concessions to congressional and Wall Street influences, the Securities Exchange Act of 1934, which carried the fight against deceit and scandal in the securities market a further step by establishing new standards of behavior and a new agency—the Securities and Exchange Commission—to enforce them. In 1935 Roosevelt began to adopt more and more of the recommendations of the Brandeis-Frankfurter group.

The President's support in February of a bill to deconcentrate public-utility holding companies demonstrated a growing interest in the idea of breaking up big business instead of accepting it as an economic necessity. Roosevelt was still unwilling for some months to move unequivocally along the new lines, but the mounting hostility of business and the Court's condemnation of the NRA cut his remaining ties with the Hundred Days. Moving on, in a message to Congress on June 19, 1935, calling for a new tax law, the President committed himself to the view that "without . . . small enterprises our competitive economic society would cease. Size begets monopoly." The New Deal had abandoned the faith in "concentration and control" and was moving into a new phase.

With the revival of Roosevelt's leadership, the 1935 session broke the log jam that had blocked action for months. The result was a stunning program of legislative achievement. A new $4.8 billion relief bill, establishing the Works Progress Administration, had already

passed in April. But the elimination of the NRA had created an urgent need for new laws continuing elements of the NRA program. Thus the Wagner Labor Relations Act, to which the President now gave his support, replaced Section 7a of the National Industrial Recovery Act; by giving new authority to the National Labor Relations board, the Wagner Act provided more reliable guarantees for collective bargaining. The Public Contracts Act applied NRA wage and hour standards to firms doing business with the federal government. The Guffey Coal Act tried to put the NRA Coal Code into constitutional form. No one could be sure whether these laws would survive the Supreme Court, though they had been drawn up to avoid the more obvious defects of the National Industrial Recovery Act.

Most important, the Congress passed in August the Social Security Act, setting up the Social Security Board to operate both a national plan of contributory old-age and survivors insurance and a federal-state plan of unemployment compensation. Both programs were of inestimable importance in providing men and women a measure of protection against hazards and vicissitudes beyond their control. They laid the basis for what later was to be termed the "welfare state." In addition, the Social Security Act, along with other measures of the session, helped further to consolidate a political alliance between the New Deal and organized labor.

Other acts of the 1935 session were designed to restore competition to the economy. The Public Utilities Holding Company Act, passed in late August after weeks of violent altercation and high-pressure lobbying, struck at financial concentration in public utilities, especially at the exaggerated development of holding companies, which had so often arisen in response, not to the needs of efficient operation, but to the desire for financial gain. The much disputed "death sentence" provision limited each holding company after 1938 to a single integrated public-utility system unless it could make a convincing economic case for holding more than one system. The tax law of 1935, with its increased surtaxes and estate taxes and its substitution of a graduated for a uniform corporation income tax, sought to discriminate in favor of small business and the small taxpayer. The tax act of 1936, deeply resented by business, made an attempt that congressional conservatives tempered to force management to distribute most corporate profits to shareholders. Once distributed, those profits would be subject to the high personal surtax rates. Most important, the forced distribution of profits would reduce the power of management and enhance the options of shareholders who might spend their larger incomes or seek alternative, more attractive investments. Still another tax act in 1937 aimed to close the loopholes through which Andrew Mellon, Alfred Sloan, the du Ponts, and other rich men had been escaping taxes. And the Banking Act of 1935, by giving the Federal Reserve Board control over "open-market operations"—that is, the purchase or sale of government securities in order to enlarge or contract the base of the money supply—reduced the power of private bankers over the money market.

The philosophy of the later New Deal.

The early and later New Deals were two phases in a continuing drive for economic recovery and social reform. They diverged somewhat in their ideas and methods, partly as a consequence of the change in national mood between 1933 and 1935. The desperation of 1933 seemed to demand sweeping economic measures; at the same time, it produced a large measure of political unity. The partial recovery of 1935 increased political disunity and decreased the desire for radical economic change.

Consequently the second phase of the New Deal was economically more conservative but politically more radical than the first. It was economically more conservative in its abandonment of inflationary adventures. More important, while the first New Deal had accepted the logic of the administered market and tried to invent new institutions to do what competition had once done to keep the economy in balance, the second New Deal revived the classical model of a freely competitive market as the objective of policy. It was politically more radical in the sense that, while the first New Deal had sought government-business cooperation to achieve national objectives, the second New Deal, persuaded that free competition could be restored only through rigorous government enforcement of the rules of the competitive game, was zestfully antibusiness in rhetoric. If "a concentration of private power without equal in history" was the great menace to the American economy, as Roosevelt told Congress in 1938, then the way out was a program "to stop the progress of collectivism in business and turn business back to the democratic competitive order." His basic thesis, Roosevelt said, was "not that the system of free enterprise for profit has failed in this generation, but that it has not yet been tried." In 1938 the antimonopoly drive picked up new speed with the appointment of Thurman Arnold as head of the Antitrust Division of the Department of Justice and with the establishment of the Temporary National Economic Committee to survey the concentration of economic power.

The fight against economic concentration, however, constituted only part of the second phase of the New Deal. A new philosophy of recovery through the use of the federal budget was beginning to emerge within the Administration. The chief spokesman for this new view was Marriner Eccles of the Federal Reserve Board, who contended that, when the decline of private spending brought about a depression, it was the obligation of government to offset the decline by increasing public spending. Eccles felt that the deliberate creation of compensatory government deficits would stimulate capital formation and purchasing power until the consequent rise in national income produced enough revenue to bring the budget once again into balance. In 1935 these ideas were still tentative and unorthodox, even among New Dealers. The New Deal was spending large sums and was running budgetary deficits (the largest in the prewar years was $4.5 billion, in 1936); but it was doing these things in response to conditions, not to theories. Further, the deficits were too small effectively to spur recovery. In 1936 the English economist John Maynard (later Lord) Keynes gave Eccles' approach its first ex-tended theoretical justification in his influential book *General Theory of Employment.* Younger New Dealers found Keynesian ideas increasingly congenial, and their alliance with the compensatory spenders was decisive in the final evolution of New Deal policies.

The 1936 election

The estrangement of business. The emergence of big government and big labor in the early thirties meant that the business community no longer enjoyed unchallenged primacy in American society. Resentment over loss of status, resentment over government regulation and taxation, resentment over uncertainty and strain—all these emotions, joined in many cases to a sincere conviction that the New Deal was a first step toward a totalitarian state, gradually produced among businessmen a state of bitter opposition to Roosevelt's Administration. In alienating businessmen, the New Deal also discouraged them from new investment, but they had not invested while Hoover cultivated their interests and solicited their confidence. Further, had the New Deal ignored social problems, and had it used taxation not to redistribute income and reform business but instead to provide favors for business, the Administration would have surrendered the social interests of the whole people to the possibility, by no means certain, of a recovery beneficial primarily to the wealthy. Even if recovery had occurred under those conditions, it would have left unaltered the many injustices of American society in the twenties. New Deal social reforms may have involved some short-run economic and political liabilities, but, for the long run, Roosevelt's emphasis was indispensable for preserving democratic possibilities in the United States.

Still the attitude of the Supreme Court seemed to validate the notion of businessmen that the New Deal was using unconstitutional means to achieve unconstitutional objectives. When the Court returned in 1936 to its assault on the New Deal—vetoing the Agricultural Adjustment Act in January, the Guffey Coal Act and the Municipal Bankruptcy Act in May, and a New York minimum-wage law in June—its actions deepened convictions on both sides that an impassable gulf existed between the America of individualism and the America of reform. Hoover denounced the New Deal as an attack on ''the whole philoso-phy of individual liberty.'' The family of J. P. Morgan told visitors not to mention Roosevelt's name in his presence lest it excite his blood pressure. Some conservatives began to trace the New Deal to subversive foreign ideas—to fascism or, more generally and fashionably, to communism. At the height of the holding-company fight, and on occasion thereafter, rumors were even put into circulation that Roosevelt was a madman given to wild bursts of maniacal laughter.

The 1936 campaign. The ''hate-Roosevelt'' feeling, the conviction that the New Deal represented the end of the American way of life, permeated the conservative wing of the Republican party. Other Republicans, however, recognizing the hard fact of Roosevelt's popularity and, in many cases, agreeing with his policies, opposed Hoover's notion of making the 1936 campaign an all-out fight against the New Deal. This view prevailed in the Republican convention of 1936. The Republicans nominated Governor Alfred M. Landon of Kansas, a former Bull Moose Progressive, who, while conservative on matters of public finance, had shown himself tolerant of many aspects of the New Deal. Frank Knox, a newspaper-publisher from Chicago, was chosen as Landon's running mate. The Democrats meanwhile renominated Roosevelt and Garner. The forces of Coughlin, Townsend, and Long (Long himself had been assassinated in September 1935) coalesced in the Union party and nominated Congressman William Lemke of North Dakota for the Presidency.

At the start Landon took a moderate line, accepting New Deal objectives but arguing that only the Republican party could achieve them thriftily and constitutionally. In the later stages of the campaign, however, he found himself making more and more extreme accusations, until in the end his line was almost indistinguishable from Hoover's. In a moment of last-minute desperation the Republican

Sunrise Extra

Nation's Verdict

The Washington Post

The Weather

'NO. 22,056

WASHINGTON: WEDNESDAY, NOVEMBER 4, 1936 **** XX

THREE CENTS

President Roosevelt Is Reelected in Landslide; Victory May Assure Him All But Two States; Democrats Increase Big Majority in Congress

Easy Control Of the House For Roosevelt Program Due

New Deal Will Hold Present Membership, May Increase It.

Captures 3 Seats In Pennsylvania

Other Gains Reported From N. Y., Maine, R. I., Connecticut.

The Post's Institute Poll Forecast Of Election, Most Nearly Correct

Mother of President Is Happy; Mrs. Landon Smiles Amid Tears

G. O. P. Faces Loss of Many Senate Seats

Hastings Runs Behind in Delaware; Barbour Trails in Jersey.

Green Leading Metcalf in R. I.; Norris and Borah Ahead.

Reelected by Landslide

Reprisals 'Out,' Landon Admits Farley Asserts, Defeat, Sends Hailing Victory President Wire

New Hampshire Conceded to F.R. By Knox Paper

Landon's Defeat Is Worst Suffered by Candidate Since Taft's in 1912; Roosevelt's Popular Ballot Rises.

high command even decided to make an issue of the social-security program, which was due to go into effect on January 1, 1937. The Social Security Act, declared Frank Knox, "puts half the working people of America under federal control." The Republican national chairman said that every worker would have to wear metal dog-tags carrying his social-security number.

Such efforts were unavailing. Roosevelt conducted his campaign in a mood of buoyant confidence. He was aware, however, of the bitterness of feeling against him; and, in indignation over the social-security panic, he gave vent to bitterness of his own before the campaign was over. "Never before in all our history have these forces [of selfishness and greed] been so united against one candidate as they stand today," he said. "They are unanimous in their hate for me—and I welcome their hatred." The election revealed that the attacks on Roosevelt had made little impression on the voters. In a victory without precedent in American politics, Roosevelt carried every state except Maine and Vermont. The Republicans were routed, and the Union party sank without a trace. In 1936, the celebrated Roosevelt coalition—farmers west and south, workingmen of all ethnic origins, reform-minded intellectuals, and a newly confident middle class—had emerged in its full strength.

The Supreme Court fight

The Court versus the New Deal. Roosevelt opened his second Administration by issuing a vigorous call for an extension of the New Deal. "I see one-third of a nation ill-housed, ill-clad, ill-nourished," he said in his inaugural address. But he faced a formidable roadblock in his determination to push ahead his reform program. That roadblock was the Supreme Court. By the end of its 1936 term the Court had heard nine cases involving New Deal legislation. In seven of these cases a majority of the Court had found the legislation unconstitutional, though three verdicts of unconstitutionality were by the narrow margin of 5 to 4 and two more by 6 to 3. In addition, the Court, having in 1923 (*Adkins* v. *Children's Hospital*) denied the federal government power to set minimum wages, had now denied that power to the state of New York, thereby apparently saying that no power existed in the United States to outlaw the sweatshop.

So sustained and devastating a use of the judicial veto to kill social and economic legislation had never before occurred. Moreover, the minority, which in several cases had affirmed its belief in the constitutionality of the disputed laws, comprised by far the more distinguished members of the Court—Louis D. Brandeis, Benjamin N. Cardozo, Harlan F. Stone, and, on occasion, Chief Justice Charles Evans Hughes. "Courts are not the only agency of government that must be assumed to have a capacity to govern," Stone had warned his conservative brethren.

The whole future of the New Deal appeared uncertain. Such laws as the Social Security Act, the Wagner Act, and the Holding Company Act seemed the next candidates for execution by the Court. And, so long as the majority's narrow reading of the Constitution prevailed, there was little chance that the New Deal could take further steps to meet the problems of the forgotten third of a nation. During 1936 Roosevelt and his Attorney General, Homer Cummings of Connecticut, came to feel that, before anything else could be done, something had to be done about the

Court. They considered and then dismissed the idea of a constitutional amendment, partly because of the difficulties of the ratification process, partly because the amendment itself would be at the mercy of judicial interpretation. In any case, the trouble seemed to lie, not with the Constitution, which they regarded as a spacious charter of government, but with the Court majority. They concluded that the best solution would be to do something directly about the personnel of the Court.

"Packing" the Supreme Court. In February 1937 Roosevelt sent a message to Congress calling for the reorganization of the federal judiciary. He contended that the Supreme Court could not keep up with its work burden, and that the interests of efficient administration required the appointment of an additional justice for each justice aged seventy or over. The argument about overcrowded dockets was disingenuous and gave the Court plan an air of overslickness from which it never recovered. Chief Justice Hughes was soon able to demonstrate that the Court had, in fact, been keeping abreast of its responsibilities. In two speeches in March, Roosevelt tried to wrench the debate back to the real issue. The Court, he said, had "cast doubts on the ability of the elected Congress to protect us against catastrophe by meeting squarely our modern social and economic conditions." His object was "to save the Con-

stitution from the Court and the Court from itself." But it was too late. The protest against the measure was now too great to be diverted.

Those who had disliked the New Deal from the start found in the Court plan verification of their claim that Roosevelt was trying to destroy the American system. And many who had supported the New Deal were genuinely shocked both by the idea of "packing" the Court and by Roosevelt's circuitous approach to his objective. The proposal set in motion a bitter national debate. In Congress the Republicans held back and allowed dissident Democrats to lead the fight against the President. The measure might have carried in some form, however, had not the Court itself suddenly changed its attitude toward New Deal legislation. On March 29, 1937, the Court in effect reversed its decision of 1936 and affirmed the constitutionality of a Washington minimum-wage law. Two weeks later it sustained the Wagner Act. Plainly the Court majority had abandoned the narrow ground of 1935–36; in Robert H. Jackson's phrase, it had retreated to the Constitution. The way had apparently been cleared for the New Deal without the appointment of a single new justice. And the resignation of one of the conservative justices in June, giving the President his first Supreme Court appointment, made his plan of enlarging the Court seem less necessary than ever. The bill was defeated, though Roosevelt could later claim with some justice that if he had lost the battle he had won the war.

ALL I SAID WAS GIMME SIX MORE JUSTICES!

Social and economic crises

The rise of the CIO. The Court battle had struck a blow at Roosevelt's prestige and at the unity of the Democratic party. And the surging militance of organized labor was creating new problems. The NRA had given the trade-union movement its first impetus to mass organization since the First World War. Under the leadership of John L. Lewis and the United Mine Workers, a great campaign had begun in 1933 to organize the unorganized in the mass-production industries. This campaign soon led to a major conflict within the labor movement itself. The American Federation of Labor was dominated by craft unions; under the craft theory, the automobile industry, for example, was to be organized, not by a single union, but by as many different

unions as there were different crafts involved in making a car. But Lewis, as head of one of the few industrial unions in the AFL, thought instinctively in terms of organization, not by craft, but by industry. Moreover, craft unionism had signally failed to organize the basic industries, to which industrial unionism seemed peculiarly adapted. The consequence was a fight within the AFL between craft unionism and industrial unionism, culminating in the expulsion of Lewis and his associates in 1936 and their formation of a rival labor federation, the Congress of Industrial Organizations.

The CIO came into existence at a time when workers throughout the country, especially in the mass-production industries, were hunger-

John L. Lewis:
United Mine Worker

*Steel strike: there were
shocking moments of violence*

ing for organization in unions of their own choosing. The spontaneous character of the labor uprising was shown in 1936 and 1937 by the development of a new strike technique, frowned upon by national labor leadership—the "sit-down strike," in which workers sat down by their machines in factories and refused to work until employers would concede them the right of collective bargaining. To many employers, the sit-down strike threatened property rights and smacked of revolution; its vogue led them to fight all the more savagely against any recognition of industrial unions as bargaining agents.

But the CIO pushed its organizing campaigns ahead vigorously, especially in automobiles and steel. There were shocking moments of violence. In May police shot and killed ten pickets outside the Republic Steel plant in Chicago. In Detroit Walter Reuther and other leaders of the United Automobile Workers were brutally beaten by company guards at Henry Ford's River Rouge plant. But the decision of General Motors to negotiate with the UAW in February 1937 and of United States Steel to negotiate with the Steel Workers Organizing Committee in March dated the beginning of the end. The battle for collective bargaining was substantially won. Union membership, which had been less

than 3 million in 1933 and barely over 4 million at the start of 1937, grew to 7.2 million by the end of the year and to 9 million by 1939.

The recession of 1937–38. The years 1935 and 1936 had been years of slow but steady economic improvement. So marked was the trend that leading bankers began to worry about inflation, though resources and labor were still widely underemployed. Under pressure from the bankers, the Federal Reserve Board tried to put on the brakes by raising reserve requirements and thus interest rates in 1936 and 1937. This action had some effect. But it was less significant in arresting the upward swing than the decline between 1936 and 1937 in the federal government's net contribution to the economy. In 1936 the payment of the veterans' bonus of $1.7 billion on top of relief and public-works expenditures and the normal costs of government resulted in a net government contribution of $4.1 billion. In 1937 several factors—the collection of taxes under the Social Security Act as well as the attempt to reduce public spending and to move toward a balanced budget—resulted in a decrease of the net government contribution to $800 million, a drop of $3.3 billion in a single year. Private business spending, contained by the apprehensions of investors, did not fill the gap created by the contraction of public spending.

The collapse in the months after September 1937 was actually more severe than it had been in the first nine months of the depression. National income fell 13 percent, payrolls 35 percent, durable-goods production 50 percent, profits 78 percent. The increase in unemployment reproduced scenes of the early depression and imposed new burdens on the relief agencies.

The recession brought to a head a policy debate within the Administration. One group, led by Henry Morgenthau, Jr., the Secretary of the Treasury, had supported the policy of government retrenchment and favored balancing the budget as soon as practicable. Those steps, they believed, though historical evidence contradicted them, would restore business confidence and lift private investment. Another group, led by Hopkins of the WPA and Eccles of the Federal Reserve Board, urged the immediate resumption of public spending. Roosevelt himself favored for a while the first group; but, as the downward slide speeded up, he reluctantly accepted the necessity for spending. In March 1938 a new spending program was announced. Again too small to achieve its intended results, this program, which included as much as Congress would tolerate, did begin to reverse the decline. It sopped up some unemployment and by 1939 effected a gross national product larger than in 1937. The recession, however, killed Roosevelt's hope of attaining full economic recovery before the end of his second term.

1938 and the purge. The Court fight, the new aggressiveness of organized labor, and the resumption of the spending policy all tended to widen the gap between the liberal and the conservative wings of the Democratic party. The liberals were mostly Northerners, the conservatives mostly Southerners, and other events of 1938 hastened the alienation of the Bourbon Democrats from the New Deal. Southern employers were bitterly opposed to the Administration's Fair Labor Standards (or Wages and Hours) Act, which was finally passed in June 1938; they objected that its policy of setting minimum wages and maximum hours and outlawing child labor would increase labor costs. Southern planters were equally bitter against the Farm Security Administration and its activities on behalf of tenant farmers and sharecroppers. The release in August 1938 of a government report on economic conditions in the South and Roosevelt's description of the South as "the nation's No. 1 economic problem" seemed to express a determination to extend the New Deal into the South. Conservative Democrats in Congress prepared to resist; and the alliance between Southern Democrats and Northern Republicans tentatively initiated in 1937 during the Supreme Court fight, began to harden in 1938 into a major obstacle to further New Deal legislation. The House Committee on Un-American Activities, dedicated under the chairmanship of Martin Dies of Texas to the harrying of radicals in and out of government, became an instrument of conservative retaliation against the New Deal.

The defection of the Southern conservatives raised difficult problems for the Administration. Roosevelt felt that many conservative Democrats had taken a free ride on the popularity of the New Deal; their refusal to support liberal policies, in his judgment, served to blur

"The nation's No. 1 economic problem"

essential distinctions in American politics. "An election cannot give a country a firm sense of direction," he said in June 1938, "if it has two or more national parties which merely have different names but are as alike in their principles and aims as peas in the same pod." Accordingly he decided to make the New Deal itself an issue in the Democratic primary elections. In August he began to intervene personally in state primaries in the hope of replacing anti-New Deal Democratic senators and congressmen with liberals. Such intervention was a striking departure from precedent, and his opponents were quick to denounce it as a "purge." The almost complete failure of Roosevelt's efforts was a prelude to Administration setbacks in the general election: the Republicans gained seven seats in the Senate and eighty in the House.

The year 1938 marked the end of the forward thrust of the New Deal. The public demand for reform seemed to be slackening, Congress was now controlled by a conservative coalition, and the drift toward war in Europe was leading both the President and the people to shift their attention to foreign policy. In his state-of-the-union message in January 1939 Roosevelt spoke significantly of the need "to invigorate the processes of recovery in order to *preserve* our reforms."

The American people in the depression

The trauma of depression. The depression had been a severe shock to the American people—to their expectations, their values, and their confidence in themselves and their future. Mute evidence of a declining faith in their prospects was the sudden slowdown of the marriage and birth rates. Population grew at a rate of less than a million a year; the total population increase (to 131.7 million in 1940) was hardly more than half that of the preceding decade. In 1938 there were 1.6 million fewer children under ten than there had been five years before. With the increase in life expectancy (from fifty-six in 1920 to sixty-four in 1940), the proportion of people over sixty-five increased from 5.4 percent in 1930 to 6.9 percent in 1940. In the perspective of depression America began to look like an aging country, its future limited. The demographic trend led economic theorists to argue that the nation had reached "economic maturity" and could not hope to resume growth without aggressive government intervention.

Americans brought up in the tradition of the bright future and the happy ending found it hard to adjust to bread lines, government relief, and mass unemployment. Some fell into listlessness and apathy. Others, unwilling to concede that the old story had come to an end, flocked behind one or another of the social demagogues with their promises of miraculous deliverance. A few believed that depression was an inherent and ineradicable evil of the capitalist system and concluded that the only way out was to abolish capitalism.

Some of these, excited by the success of fascism in Italy and Germany, formed fascist groups, bearing such names as the Silver Shirts. In a vivid novel, *It Can't Happen Here* (1935), Sinclair Lewis showed how a 100 percent American fascist movement might take over the United States. But, though the American fascists diligently imitated many of the Nazi techniques and appeals (including anti-Semitism), they had little impact on American life.

More of those who despaired of capitalism turned toward Marxism. In 1932 just under a million Americans voted against the capitalist system. Most of the votes went to the Socialist party, a reformist group under the appealing leadership of Norman Thomas; but over one hundred thousand voted for the Communist party ticket. The communist movement, the more serious of the two, was controlled by a hard core of disciplined devotees, faithfully conforming to the turns and twists of the party line laid down in Moscow. Not all those who joined the party, however, were aware of its whole nature. At one time or another during the decade, a large number of people passed rather quickly through the movement, attracted primarily by the apparent idealism of communist promises but soon bored by the sectarian inflexibility of communist analysis or repelled by the ruthless dishonesty of communist performance, especially in Europe. Secret communists had some success in penetrating certain labor unions and even a few government offices, though without significantly influencing American policy.

The shake-up of the people. If depression induced despair, it also compelled change. In particular, it discredited and disrupted the structure of status and prestige that had ruled the United States in the twenties. The businessman had been the culture hero of the prosperity decade. In 1929 his New Era had exploded in his face. In the thirties his pretensions to wisdom were derided, his leadership rejected, and he himself often dismissed as a fool if not a crook. A midget perched impudently on the knee of the mighty J. P. Morgan at a congressional investigation became the symbol of the new skepticism about men of wealth.

People from outside the business community—especially politicians and intellectuals—were now in power. Still smarting from their own sense of inferior status in the twenties, they often took undue pleasure in rubbing the nose of the once-arrogant businessman in the mess he had helped create. And in their wake came a rush for status of the "forgotten men" of America—men who had been denied opportunities in the past because of their class or ethnic origin. The New Deal, by revising the structure of status, brought about both a social and an ethnic revolution.

The social revolution. Organized labor's rise to respectability typified the tendencies of the decade. In 1933 the presidents of the six great steel companies blanched and fled when Secretary of Labor Frances Perkins proposed to introduce them to William Green of the American Federation of Labor for a discussion of the NRA steel code. Four years later, when United States Steel signed up with the CIO, labor had achieved substantial recognition. The business community had reluctantly accepted the right of other groups to participate in national economic decisions. Even though the depression continued to restrict economic opportunity, members of once-marginal groups—not only wage-earners but tenant farmers, sharecroppers, old folks, and even intellectuals and women—now had larger chances for fulfilled lives.

The social revolution also enhanced the quality of life, particularly in the countryside. Though the Supreme Court knocked out the original AAA in 1936, the principle of national responsibility for the agricultural economy was established and reaffirmed in legislation of 1938. No other federal agency had such an impact on the quality of country life as did the Rural Electrification Administration. When it was founded in 1935, only about one farm in ten had power-line electric service, and these were mostly in the neighborhood of towns or cities. Through low-interest loans to cooperatives, the REA enabled farmers to build their own power lines and generate their own electricity. The spread of electricity transformed the countryside. Had distribution been kept in the hands of privately owned utilities, this expansion would not have taken place so quickly.

While the price-support and rural-electrification programs made life far more tolerable for commercial farmers, they left untouched wide areas of rural poverty, especially among subsistence farmers. Toward the end of the decade, poor farmers and agricultural workers displaced by changes in agricultural technology began to head west in a pathetic search for new employment. John Steinbeck's *The Grapes of Wrath* (1939) offered a memorable picture of the exodus of the "Okies" (from Oklahoma) and the "Arkies" (from Arkansas). This migration was part of a general westward shift of people that resulted, for example, in nearly doubling the population of California between 1920 and 1940. In time and with economic recovery, many of the migrants were absorbed in the new communities.

The ethnic revolution. Immigration substantially stopped in the thirties (except for refugees from fascism toward the end of the decade). The last wave of immigrants, mostly

Migratory workers: the grapes of wrath

from southern and eastern Europe, in the earlier part of the century had not yet achieved full acceptance in American society; the upheaval of depression gave many Italians, Poles, South Slavs, and Jews their first opportunities. Where craft unions, for example, had often discriminated against the "wops" and the "hunkies," as against the blacks, the industrial unions of the CIO opened their doors to them. Similarly the New Deal gave them their first chance in politics and public service.

Roosevelt himself had no patience with the old American attitude of superiority toward more recent immigrants. "Remember, remember always," he once told the Daughters of the American Revolution, "that all of us, and you and I especially, are descended from immigrants and revolutionists." Of the 214 federal judges appointed by Harding, Coolidge, and Hoover, only 8 were Catholics; of the 196 appointed by Roosevelt, 51 were Catholics. Political figures in the great cities, like Mayor Fiorello La Guardia of New York, acted as brokers in gaining recognition for ethnic minorities previously shut out from political preferment. Concurrently there was a notable decline in the foreign-language press

The New Deal neglected many Americans—sharecroppers, tenant farmers, migratory workers and farm laborers, slum dwellers, unskilled workers, and the unemployed Negroes. They were left outside the new order....

*Perhaps this is one of the crueller ironies of liberal politics, that the marginal men trapped in hopelessness were seduced by rhetoric, by the style and movement, by the symbolism of efforts seldom reaching beyond words. In acting to protect the institution of private property and in advancing the interests of corporate capitalism, the New Deal assisted the middle and upper sectors of society. It protected them, sometimes, even at the cost of injuring the lower sectors. Seldom did it bestow much of substance upon the lower classes. Never did the New Deal seek to organize these groups into independent political forces.... Liberalism, by accepting private property and federal assistance to corporate capitalism, was not prepared **effectively** to reduce inequities, to redistribute political power, **or to** extend equality from promise to reality.*

From Barton J. Bernstein, *Towards a New Past*, 1967.

We saw government conducted by ''emergencies,'' purges, propaganda, bureaucracy, hate, the turmoil of class conflict.... We saw an era of the deepest intellectual dishonesty in public life. We saw the growth of executive power by the reduction of the legislative arm.... We saw the Congressional power over the purse practically abandoned. We saw the subjection of the Supreme Court to the collectivist ideas of the executive. We saw the independence and responsibility of the states undermined by huge Federal subsidies directly to the citizens.

Thus the four great pillars of free men were weakened. As a result of eight years of the New Deal, there was not more but less liberty in America. And ... we had not ended the Great Depression....

From Herbert C. Hoover, *Memoirs: The Great Depression*, 1952.

---

and a more effective assimilation of ethnic minorities into American life.

Most striking of all, perhaps, was the rise in expectations of American blacks, for many years the victims of economic and political neglect. During the depression, the Negro was, in the phrase of the day, ''the first man fired and the last man hired.'' And, though he had voted Republican since the Civil War, the Republican administrations had shown little concern for his welfare; black leaders had denounced Hoover as ''the man in the lily-White House.'' Roosevelt brought to Washington an unprecedented sympathy for black problems. New Deal agencies generally conformed to local folkways that perpetuated segregation and discrimination within the CCC and in the distribution of work relief in the South, for two of many examples. But the New Dealers appointed many able blacks to senior administrative positions from which

they were able not only to symbolize new opportunities for their race but to mount programs to assist their fellows. Roosevelt himself repeatedly denounced lynching, though he would not provide direct support to the Northern Democrats in the Senate who took the initiative in sponsoring bills to make lynching a federal crime. The New Deal did far less for American blacks than their circumstances warranted, but it did far more than had any administration since Reconstruction. By 1936 black voters had begun to shift to the Democratic party.

The recovery of American faith. The release of energy brought about by the New Deal, the invigorating sense that the ''forgotten man'' could still make a place for himself in American life—all this gradually began to heal the trauma of depression. The sense of America as an exhausted nation gave way to the image of a purposeful society capable of meeting its problems with energy and conviction.

In the twenties, the intellectuals who scorned the American present had turned to "debunking" the American past. In the thirties, when the American present was acquiring purpose and dignity, they began to read this purpose and dignity back into American history. The title of John Dos Passos' book *The Ground We Stand On* (1941) summed up the new attitude. "In times of change and danger," Dos Passos wrote, "when there is a quicksand of fear under men's reasoning, a sense of continuity with generations gone before can stretch like a lifeline across the scary present." Other skeptics of the twenties joined Dos Passos in taking a more affirmative view of American traditions. Van Wyck Brooks, who had once seen American culture as pinched and sterile, now portrayed it, in *The Flowering of New England* (1936) and succeeding volumes, as rich and abundant. Even H. L. Mencken, though he took small comfort in the America of the thirties, dedicated his main energies to bring up to date his loving study of *The American Language* and to writing his own nostalgic recollections of an earlier America. The publication of a number of important biographies helped meet the new national desire to repossess the past in all its solidity. This impulse came into happy conjunction with the New Deal in the valuable series of state guidebooks produced by the WPA.

The new pattern of American society. The recovery of American faith in the thirties both derived from and contributed to the capacity of the American people to reassert a measure of control over their social and economic destiny. In so doing, American society was countering the prevailing ideologies of the day. Both laissez faire and Marxism were philosophies of economic determinism with narrow views of social possibility. The New Deal, with all its improvisations, contradictions, sentimentalisms, and errors, did have the signal advantage of rejecting economic fatalism. By affirming a faith in intelligent experiment, it expanded the range of social possibility and helped lead America toward a new society beyond classical capitalism and beyond classical socialism.

By Roosevelt's second term the essential pattern of the new society was complete for his generation. The American nation had renounced laissez faire without embracing socialism. Government had acquired the obligation to underwrite the economic and social health of the nation. The budget provided the means by which the government through the use of fiscal policy could compensate for a decline in private economic activity. The state had abandoned efforts aimed at the direct control of industrial production, but industry had to accept ground rules covering minimum standards of life and labor; and the state continued to intervene to maintain, in modified form, the free play of competition. Special areas of economic activity required more comprehensive government control—banking, transportation, public utilities, agriculture, oil. Human welfare was to be protected through various forms of public insurance. A collection of "built-in stabilizers"—minimum wages, unemployment compensation, farm-price supports, social-security payments—were to help secure the economy against future crashes like that of 1929.

Was a middle way possible? These measures involved more government intervention in the economy than some had thought the economy could stand and still remain free. This was the critical question raised by the New Deal—whether a policy of limited and piecemeal government intervention in economic life was feasible; whether a mixed system was possible that gave the state power enough to assure economic and social security but still not so much as to create an all-powerful dictatorship or so little independence as to remain uncorrupted by the large influence of powerful industrial, labor, and agricultural groups.

The New Deal especially assisted the American middle class. It protected their savings, homes, and farms. It opened the way to middle-class comforts and status for previously stigmatized ethnic groups and many clerical and blue-collar workers. But the New Deal also knew many failures. It did not achieve recovery. It did not sufficiently redistribute income and wealth, though it proposed more effectual policies than Congress would accept. It did not bring American blacks an equitable share in the country's social and economic life. It could not overcome the conservative social and regressive economic policies of most American states. It could not permanently insulate its new regulatory agencies from the tendency of regulators to develop excessive sympathy for those they were supposed to control.

Those failures, clearer in retrospect than at the time, suggested that the particular middle way of the Roosevelt years would later need modifications. But to the question of the viability of any middle way, doctrinaires returned a categorical *no* through the decade. Ogden Mills stated the issue with precision for the conservatives: "We can have a free country or a socialistic one. We cannot have both. Our economic system cannot be half free and half socialistic. . . . There is no middle ground . . . between tyranny and freedom."

In such sentiments, at least, the critics of capitalism agreed enthusiastically with the conservatives. "Either the nation must put up with the confusions and miseries of an essentially unregulated capitalism," said a radical weekly in 1935, "or it must prepare to supersede capitalism with socialism. There is no longer a feasible middle course." The proponents of individualism and the proponents of collectivism agreed on this if on nothing else:

no regulated capitalism was possible, no mixed economy, no middle way between laissez faire and socialism.

But the New Dealers cheerfully rejected the conclusion. They believed that there was more on heaven and earth than could be found in any ideology. Roosevelt himself was blithe and humane in his undeviating rejection of any all-encompassing doctrine. He might have undertaken social experiments either more or less bold than those he chose. But his aim was consistent—to steer between the extremes of individualism and statism by moving always, in a favorite phrase, "slightly to the left of center," avoiding alike "the revolution of radicalism and the revolution of conservatism." The New Deal faith in intelligence, compassion, and experiment demonstrated in the end that a managed capitalist order could combine personal freedom and economic growth. For the generation that lived through it, the decade of the New Deal, with all its confusion and recrimination, rekindled confidence in free society, not in America alone, but throughout the Western world.

Suggestions for reading

GENERAL

The most comprehensive account of domestic developments, 1933–36, is in A. M. Schlesinger, Jr., *The Coming of the New Deal** (1959) and *The Politics of Upheaval** (1960). W. E. Leuchtenburg, *Franklin D. Roosevelt and the New Deal, 1932–40** (1963), provides the best short account. There are valuable insights in J. M. Burns, *Roosevelt: The Lion and the Fox** (1956). Paul Conkin, *The New Deal** (1967), criticizes Roosevelt and his policies from the point of view of the disenchanted revisionists of the 1960s and 1970s. For a trenchant analysis of that point of view and of various others, see O. L. Graham, Jr., ed., *The New Deal: The Critical Issues** (1971).

MEMOIRS AND BIOGRAPHIES

Memoirs of the New Dealers and biographies based on their papers throw important light on Roosevelt and his problems. R. E. Sherwood, *Roosevelt and Hopkins: An Intimate History** (1948, rev. ed., 1950), provides a view of an important friendship and a favorable account of relief policies. Frances Perkins, *The Roosevelt I Knew** (1946), is significant for its compassion; R. G. Tugwell, *The Democratic Roosevelt** (1957), for its retrospective reflections; *The Secret Diary of Harold L. Ickes,* 3 vols. (1953–54), for its gossip and atmosphere. On politics, two illuminating memoirs are J. A. Farley, *Behind the Ballots* (1938), and Edward Flynn, *You're the Boss** (1947). J. M. Blum, *Roosevelt and Morgenthau** (1970), recounts in detail the activities of the Secretary of the Treasury, one of the President's influential advisers. H. S. Johnson, *The Blue Eagle* (1935), presents a contemporary view of the National Recovery Administration. There is a valuable contemporary critique of the early New Deal in Raymond Moley, *After Seven Years** (1939); this may be supplemented by his retrospective *The First New Deal* (1966). In *Beckoning Frontiers* (1935), M. S. Eccles provides an important account of the evolution of economic policy. Samuel Rosenman writes as a close counselor to the President in his *Working with Roosevelt* (1952). R. G. Tugwell's work, cited above, is an important memoir-history, as is his *The Brain Trust** (1968). There is indispensable personal material in Eleanor Roosevelt, *This I Remember** (1949), and in J. P. Lash, *Eleanor and Franklin* (1971). Though there is no useful edition of Roosevelt's

*Available in a paperback edition.

private papers, one vital source for study of the man and his times is Samuel Rosenman, ed., *The Public Papers and Addresses of Franklin D. Roosevelt,* 13 vols. (1938–50).

NEW DEAL POLITICAL THOUGHT

Students wishing to study New Deal political thought in the important works of the time should consult, as the text suggests, at least the following influential sources: A. A. Berle, Jr. and G. C. Means, *The Modern Corporation and Private Property** (1932, rev. ed., 1969), significant on economic concentration; M. S. Eccles, *Economic Balance and a Balanced Budget* (1940), significant on countercyclical spending; R. G. Tugwell, *The Battle for Democracy* (1935), and H. L. Ickes, *The New Democracy* (1934), both important on social goals and public planning, as is H. A. Wallace, *New Frontiers* (1934); and D. E. Lilienthal, *TVA** (rev. ed., 1953), on regional development. Two incisive books by Thurman Arnold—*The Symbols of Government** (1935) and *The Folklore of Capitalism** (1937)—well express the iconoclastic and deflationary side of the New Deal. For a revisionistic view, see H. Zinn, *New Deal Thought** (1966).

SPECIAL STUDIES

Outstanding studies of economic problems in the 1930s include the analytical T. Wilson, *Fluctuations in Income and Employment* (1948); K. D. Roose, *Economics of Recession and Revival: An Interpretation of 1937–38* (1954); and R. E. Paul, *Taxation in the United States* (1954). Some of the most useful of more recent works are I. Bernstein, *Turbulent Years** (1970), which describes the labor movement; R. Lekachman, *The Age of Keynes** (1966), which discusses the rate and range of acceptance of the ideas of the new economics; and E. W. Hawley, *The New Deal and the Problem of Monopoly** (1966), which analyzes pressure-group influences on federal policies. O. L. Graham's work, cited above, includes an excellent bibliography of still other good studies.

There are stimulating essays about social and intellectual currents in Isabel Leighton, ed., *The Aspirin Age: 1919–1941** (1949). For a thoughtful account of the appeal of communism, especially to artists and writers, see D. Aaron, *Writers on the Left** (1961), and the forthcoming volume on the Communist party during the 1930s by T. Draper. R. G. Swing, *Forerunners of American Fascism* (1935), offers a contemporary account of the lunatic right, which is modified in A. P. Sindler, *Huey Long's Louisiana** (1956), and challenged by T. H. Williams, *Huey Long** (1969). On the problems of blacks during the 1930s, see B. Sternsher, ed., *The Negro in Depression and War: Prelude to Revolution** (1969).

Samuel Lubell, *The Future of American Politics** (1952), identifies important political changes in the period. A. M. Bingham, *Insurgent America* (1935), describes the radical politics of the mid-thirties; and George Wolfskill, *The Revolt of the Conservatives* (1962), displays the reaction on the right, as does his volume with J. Hudson, *All But the People* (1969). On the Supreme Court fight, four especially rewarding studies are R. H. Jackson, *The Struggle for Judiciary Supremacy** (1941); A. T. Mason, *Harlan Fiske Stone* (1956); Joseph Alsop and Turner Catledge, *168 Days* (1938); and M. J. Pusey, *Charles Evans Hughes,* 2 vols. (1951). The same subject is treated by one of the masters of constitutional history, E. S. Corwin, in his *Twilight of the Supreme Court* (1934), *Court over Constitution* (1938), and *Constitutional Revolution, Ltd.* (rev. ed., 1946). New and important studies on the Court are soon to be published by W. E. Leuchtenburg and P. A. Freund.

*Available in a paperback edition.

The decay of the peace

28

When Franklin D. Roosevelt became President, the American democracy was absorbed in gloomy domestic problems. The crusading internationalism of 1917 was a distant, and for most a distasteful, memory. The rejection of the League of Nations had been followed by growing disenchantment about the motives and results of the First World War; and the renewed American determination to go it alone in world affairs was only slightly tempered during the twenties by such symbolic gestures as the Kellogg-Briand pact and the Stimson Doctrine. If the Republican Administrations sought to enlarge world markets for American products, they simultaneously undercut the policy of commercial expansion by raising tariffs and thereby denying foreign nations the opportunity to earn dollars for the purchase of American goods. After 1929 depression intensified tariff warfare and eco-

nomic nationalism in both America and Europe. By 1933 isolationism, both political and economic, was the dominant American mood.

There were multiplying intimations, however, that the uneasy peace established after the First World War was in jeopardy. Japanese expansionism in East Asia was soon accompanied by German militancy in Europe. On January 30, 1933, Adolf Hitler became the new chancellor of Germany. In March, nineteen days after Roosevelt's inauguration, the Reichstag gave the Nazi leader dictatorial powers to carry forward his program of rearmament, anti-Semitism, and messianic nationalism. The German *Führer's* fanatical resolve to overthrow the system established at Versailles in 1919 offered an ominous challenge to the whole postwar structure of international order.

Roosevelt and world affairs

Preparation for statesmanship. Few American politicians could rival Roosevelt in the breadth of his world experience. Between 1885 and 1931 he had made thirteen trips to Europe, and, though he had never visited the Far East, family tradition—his maternal grandfather had been active in the China trade—gave him a lively interest in Asia and especially in China. He had come of age, moreover, when the United States, under

Theodore Roosevelt, was first beginning to recognize the opportunities of world power. As a young man, he was also greatly influenced by the strategic philosophy of Admiral Alfred T. Mahan.

His service under Woodrow Wilson as Assistant Secretary of the Navy provided him varied experience in international affairs. Almost alone among the members of the Administration, he instantly perceived the catastrophic implications of the events of the summer of 1914. While Wilson strove to maintain American neutrality, young Roosevelt made no secret of his desire to build up American naval power or of his passionate belief in the Allied cause. When America entered the war, he dealt effectively both with problems of economic mobilization at home and with problems of coalition strategy and diplomacy abroad.

But the war did more than give him a chance to apply the principles of strategy he had learned from Mahan. It placed those principles in a new setting. To Mahan's realism, Roosevelt now added Wilson's idealism: the combination defined his own future approach to foreign affairs. He became an ardent supporter of Wilson in his fight for the League, and he made the League a key issue in his campaign for the Vice Presidency in 1920. He retained his sharp concern with the actualities of national power but now saw power in the context, not of nationalist self-assertion, but of international order.

During the twenties Roosevelt opposed the drift toward isolationism and moralism in foreign affairs. He condemned the Republican tariff policy, derided the pretensions of the Kellogg pact, and constantly pleaded the case for international collaboration. "If the World War showed anything more than another," he said, "it showed the American people the futility of imagining that they could live in smug content their own lives in their own way while the rest of the world burned in the conflagration of war." But, as depression accentuated the isolationist mood after 1929, Roosevelt moved somewhat with the prevailing winds. In 1932 he announced that in existing circumstances he no longer favored American participation in the League.

The Roosevelt style in foreign policy. At bottom, however, Roosevelt retained faith in internationalism. He signalized this by naming as Secretary of State Cordell Hull, an unregenerate Wilsonian and low-tariff man. "In pure theory," he once wrote Hull, "you and I think alike but every once in a while we have to modify principle to meet a hard and disagreeable fact!" Roosevelt was far more ready than Hull to modify principle, but he respected his Secretary of State's capacity to recall him to the true faith.

Toward the State Department itself, Roosevelt's attitude was one of disdain. He instinctively understood the problems of military as of political leaders, but he was often impatient with the professional diplomat. Foreign-service officers, he tended to believe, represented a narrow social group and knew little of American life.

This attitude molded his own style in foreign affairs. His conduct of foreign policy was marked by imagination, insight, and also a certain dilettantism and insouciance. He remained the brilliant amateur, better in the main than the professionals, bolder, more creative, more compelling, but often deficient in steadiness and follow-through. Given this attitude, he tended toward personal diplomacy. He used his own agents and emissaries to bypass the professionals, and his basic preference, not always realizable in practice in these early years, was for direct negotiation among heads of state.

Uniting the Western Hemisphere

The good neighbor. "In the field of world policy," Roosevelt said in one of the scant references to foreign affairs in his inaugural address, "I would dedicate this Nation to the policy of the good neighbor—the neighbor who resolutely respects himself and, because he does so, respects the rights of others—the neighbor who respects his obligations and respects the sanctity of his agreements in and with a world of neighbors." Though this thought was evidently intended to be general in its import, its immediate sphere of application was Latin America. Soon the Good Neighbor policy came to refer specifically to United States policy in the Western Hemisphere.

Latin Americans had not recently considered the United States a good neighbor. After Theodore Roosevelt laid down his Corollary to the Monroe Doctrine (1904), Washington insisted on a "right" in circumstances of local disorder to intervene in Latin American republics. This intervention took a variety of forms from economic pressure to military occupation. Roosevelt himself had participated in such intervention when United States marines occupied Haiti during the Wilson Administration. In the twenties, however, Roosevelt

The Montevideo Conference: a new epoch in hemispheric relations

and other North Americans—among them his old friend Sumner Welles, a former diplomat—had become critical of the policy of intervention. In the meantime, accumulating resentment throughout the hemisphere resulted in a sharp rebuff to the United States at the Havana Conference of 1928. The Hoover Administration, recognizing the gravity of the situation, began to recede from the Theodore Roosevelt Corollary and to withdraw American troops from Nicaragua and Haiti.

Roosevelt's Latin American policy got off to an ambiguous start. Welles, recalled to public service, went to Cuba as ambassador to get rid of the brutal Machado dictatorship. The dislodgment of Machado, however, eventually brought into power a revolutionary government that the United States declined to recognize. In response to the American attitude, a conservative regime received recognition. Though Roosevelt at the same time speeded up plans for withdrawing the marines from Haiti, Latin Americans in the fall of 1933 were convinced that policy in Washington was as bad as ever.

From Montevideo to Buenos Aires. The Seventh International Conference of American States met at Montevideo in December 1933 in an atmosphere of extreme hostility toward the United States. The American delegation, however, led by Cordell Hull with Welles' able assistance, soon induced a change in Latin American attitudes. The United States, reversing its policy of five years before in Havana, now accepted (with minor qualifications) a proposal declaring that "no state has the right to intervene in the internal or external affairs of another." The Montevideo Conference, by establishing inter-American relations on the principle of nonintervention, brought into

being a new epoch in hemispheric relations.

The United States proceeded to show that it meant to live up to its Montevideo pledge. In May 1934 it abrogated the unpopular Platt Amendment, thereby abandoning its treaty right to intervene in the affairs of Cuba. In 1934 in El Salvador, it abandoned the policy of nonrecognition of revolutionary governments in Central America. The establishment of the Export-Import Bank the same year provided a means of extending credit to Latin American states. The Panama Treaties of 1936 renounced the right to intervene in Panama and recognized Panama's responsibility in the operation and protection of the canal. A treaty of 1940 terminated United States financial controls in the Dominican Republic.

Relations with Mexico provided a test of the new policy. The hostility of the radical Mexican government toward the Roman Catholic Church in the early thirties had produced demands in the United States that Washington intervene in Mexico. The expropriation of foreign-owned petroleum companies renewed this pressure in 1938. Washington declined to intervene, however, confining its activities to urging the Mexican government to provide American owners their due compensation. A State Department memorandum of 1939 summed up the new attitude: "Our national interests as a whole far outweigh those of the petroleum companies."

This attitude, verified by Roosevelt's progressive actions in his own country, helped inspire confidence throughout the hemisphere in the reality of the Good Neighbor policy. By December 1936, when Roosevelt himself attended the Inter-American Conference at Buenos Aires, the warmth of his reception attested to a transformation in Latin American attitudes toward the colossus of the north.

Early relations with Europe

The London Economic Conference. American relations with European nations had been bedeviled since 1919 by the question of war debts. Pressure for the cancellation of these debts mounted as the depression deepened. A good deal of this sentiment emanated from the international banking community, and Roosevelt suspected that the bankers wanted to wipe out intergovernmental debts to make it easier to collect private debts owed to themselves. In any case, the European nations, feeling that America had contributed dollars to a cause to which they had contributed blood, increasingly resented "Uncle Shylock's" insistence on getting his money back. Beginning in 1933, most European nations, except for Finland, began to suspend payment. War debts thereafter became a dead issue—except to the United States Congress, which retaliated in 1934 by passing the Johnson Act prohibiting loans to defaulting governments.

From the European viewpoint, war debts were only a part of the larger problem of world economic relations. In the panic of depression, governments everywhere were building walls of protection in the hope of defending their national economies against the worldwide decline. Economic nationalism took more than one form, however. The Hoover version was nationalist in trade, internationalist in finance: Hoover thus advocated raising the protective tariff to new levels and at the same time argued that recovery depended on the restoration of a world gold standard. In this belief, he agreed to United States participation in an international economic conference favored by the gold-bloc nations and scheduled for London in the spring of 1933.

Roosevelt and the early New Dealers, on the other hand, believed that recovery was to be achieved primarily through domestic planning. "I shall spare no effort to restore world trade by international economic readjustments," the new President said in his inaugural address, "but the emergency at home cannot wait on that accomplishment." The New Dealers consequently mistrusted the international gold standard as a threat to national programs for recovery. Yet, unlike Hoover, they rejected the steeply protective tariff, favoring instead the system of reciprocal trade agreements, which Hoover assailed in 1932 as "a violation of American principles."

The Roosevelt version of economic nationalism was thus internationalist in trade, nationalist in finance.

When the London Economic Conference opened in June 1933, it became evident that the gold bloc, led by France and Italy, was determined to force through an agreement stabilizing foreign exchanges. By now the American government was fully committed to its program of raising commodity prices through reducing the value of the dollar—a policy obviously incompatible with immediate stabilization of the dollar in terms of an international standard. Roosevelt therefore declined to subordinate his domestic policy to international stabilization. This view emerged only gradually in the course of the conference; meanwhile the antics of an odd American delegation had dissipated American influence in London. As the gold bloc continued to press for stabilization, Roosevelt, in what he conceived as an effort to recall the conference to more fruitful topics, sent a testy message scolding the conference for succumbing to the "old fetishes of the so-called international bankers." This "bombshell" message threw the conference into consternation. Though some Englishmen, among them J. M. Keynes and Winston Churchill, defended Roosevelt, the predominant reaction was to criticize him for "wrecking" the conference.

Liberalizing American trade. Roosevelt soon made it clear that his opposition to the international gold standard did not mean that he believed in economic self-containment. In March 1934 he asked Congress for authority to enter into commercial agreements with foreign nations and to revise tariff rates in accordance with such agreements up to 50 percent either way. This proposal for the executive negotiation of reciprocal trade agreements raised a storm of opposition, partly because some congressmen—and the protectionist lobbies—objected to the weakening of the congressional role in tariff-making, partly because businessmen feared the new system would result in lower rates. Senator Arthur H. Vandenberg of Michigan condemned the proposal as "Fascist in its philosophy, Fascist in its objective." Only two Republicans supported the bill in the House, only three in the Senate. But, with Hull's devoted backing, the bill became law in June 1934.

Reichstag, 1933: Hitler meant war

By the end of 1935, reciprocal trade agreements were in effect with fourteen countries; by 1945, with twenty-nine countries. While the program did little in the thirties to relieve the balance-of-payments problem between the United States and foreign countries (indeed, debts owed to the United States grew steadily during the thirties), it did display America's hope of bringing about a larger measure of economic internationalism.

Disarmament. In an effort to compose matters after the breakup of the London Economic Conference, Roosevelt wrote to Ramsay MacDonald, the British prime minister, "I am concerned by events in Germany, for I feel that an insane rush to further armaments in Continental Europe is infinitely more dangerous than any number of squabbles over gold or stabilization or tariffs." From an early point—earlier, indeed, than any European statesman of comparable rank—Roosevelt was convinced that Hitler meant war. Yet, while he saw the approaching horror with clarity, he also saw it with aloofness. This was partly the result of geography, which conferred on the United States the luxury of de-

tachment; partly the result of politics, for Roosevelt had little choice but to defer to the isolationist preferences of the vast majority of the people; partly the result of the depression, which gave the American domestic scene first claim on his attention.

The combination of concern and aloofness produced a basic contradiction in the heart of his foreign policy. Roosevelt addressed himself to two problems: first, how to stop the world drift toward war; and, second, if that drift proved irresistible, how to make sure that the United States would not be involved. Plainly the goals of international peace and national isolation—of world disarmament and American neutrality—were in latent conflict. World disarmament implied American cooperation in a world system. Rigid neutrality implied a systematic reduction of America's international commitments. In 1933 and 1934 the tension between these two ideas complicated the conduct of America's foreign policy.

Disarmament had been a major theme of foreign affairs in the twenties, when a succession of conferences established a system of tonnage quotas governing the naval strength of the great powers. Efforts to work out formulas for land armaments had proved less successful. A new disarmament conference, beginning in Geneva in 1932, had bogged down because of Germany's demand for equality in armed strength—a demand the Germans based on Article 8 of the League covenant with its call for general arms reduction. It had proved impossible to reconcile the German position with the insistence of other nations, especially France, on having reliable protection against a possible recurrence of German aggression.

The replacement of the Weimar Republic by the Nazi regime now gave the German demand for equality an ominous cast. In May 1933 Roosevelt authorized the American representative at Geneva to say that, if a substantial reduction of armaments was effected by international agreement, the United States was prepared to consult with the other states in case of a threat to peace. If the other states identified an aggressor and took measures against aggression, the United States, if it concurred in their judgment, would "refrain from any action tending to defeat such collective effort which these states may thus make to restore peace." In other words, the United States would forgo its traditional insistence on neutral rights, including the freedom of the seas, in the interest of supporting measures of collective security. But, when the Administration asked Congress to pass a resolution authorizing the executive at his discretion to embargo arms shipments to aggressor nations, the Senate Foreign Relations Committee amended the resolution to compel the President to embargo arms shipments to *all* nations involved in a war. This amendment destroyed the original purpose of the resolution, which was to discriminate against aggressors. Its effect would now be to strengthen those who had arms already and to abandon those who had none.

The Administration tried in vain to defeat the amendment. Failing, it dropped the resolution itself, thereby canceling the effect of the American initiative at Geneva. What the President had proposed the Congress had now disowned. This frustration of the Roosevelt Administration's first effort to throw American power in the balance against world aggression confirmed the deep-seated skepticism in European chancelleries over the seriousness of American diplomacy.

It seems unlikely, however, that even congressional approval of the arms embargo could have saved the Geneva conference. Hitler, now hell-bent on rearmament and committed to a revolt against the entire Versailles system, would probably not have accepted international disarmament on any terms. When Germany walked out of the League in October 1933, land disarmament was dead. And the withdrawal of Japan from the League in 1933 and the Japanese decision in 1934 to terminate the Washington Naval Treaty signaled the end of naval disarmament. By 1934 the hope of averting war through disarmament had gone.

The American government had been prepared to cooperate in the supervision of a disarmed world. It was not prepared to cooperate in keeping the peace at the risk of war in a world intent on rearmament. If disarmament had failed, the alternative, in the American view, was neutrality.

Relations with Great Britain and the Soviet Union.
The collapse of disarmament was accompanied by a deterioration in American relations with the leading anti-Hitler powers. Roosevelt's bombshell message had exasperated London, and the policies of the British government now exasperated Washington. An important faction in the British Cabinet, led by Neville Chamberlain, the chancellor of the exchequer, so deeply distrusted the United States that in 1934 it seriously considered whether Britain should base its strategy on cooperation with Japan instead of with the United States. At this point Roosevelt instructed his roving emissary, Norman Davis, to impress British Foreign Secretary Simon "and a few other Tories" with the fact that

> if Great Britain is even suspected of preferring to play with Japan to playing with us, I shall be compelled, in the interest of American security, to approach public sentiment in Canada, Australia, New Zealand and South Africa in a definite effort to make these Dominions clearly understand that their future security is linked with us in the United States.

Happily, the Japanese themselves soon took care of the problem by presenting the British with rearmament demands so extreme that even the pro-Tokyo Cabinet members had to abandon their policy.

Roosevelt's efforts to establish friendly relations with the Soviet Union were hardly more successful. Support for the recognition of the communist regime had been growing for some time before 1933. Businessmen saw in Russia a market for American surplus production. The renewal of Japanese aggression argued for a normalization of Soviet-American relations as a means of restraining the Japanese. "The world," Cordell Hull told Roosevelt, "is moving into a dangerous period both in Europe and in Asia. Russia could be a great help in stabilizing this situation."

In October 1933 Maxim Litvinov, the Soviet commissar for foreign affairs, came to Washington. After a series of talks Roosevelt and Litvinov worked out a set of agreements. In one document Litvinov gave a remarkably detailed pledge to refrain from any intervention in American internal affairs—a pledge that covered not only the Soviet government itself but any organizations "under its direct or indirect control." Another memorandum provided what seemed to be a formula for the settlement of Russian debts to the United States. The discussions concluded in the establishment of formal relations between the two governments.

Despite this beginning, relations soon returned to the prerecognition state of mistrust. The attempt to make the Soviet government live up to its promises on propaganda and debts led to interminable negotiation, recrimination, and frustration. American representatives in Moscow encountered harassment and hostility. Finally, when American communists came to Moscow in July 1935 for the seventh congress of the Comintern, their presence seemed, in the view of the American ambassador, to constitute "a flagrant violation of Litvinov's pledge" and a justification for the severance of diplomatic ties. Though the government did not go this far, relations with Soviet Russia thus reached a low ebb less than two years after recognition.

Isolationism at flood tide

The rout of the internationalists. The breakdown of attempts to strengthen relations with Britain and the Soviet Union coincided with a crystallization of isolationist sentiment in the United States. By the early 1930s, few Americans were prepared to make an all-out defense of Wilson's decision of 1917. "Revisionist" historians had launched a reconsideration of such problems as German "war guilt" and American entry into the war. Their scholarship seemed to reveal the war, not as a struggle of democracy against autocracy, but as a sordid scramble among imperialist powers. If this was so, then the United States had been drawn into the war under false pretenses.

The next question was: Who had drawn the United States in and why? The new disillusion was clinched in 1934 and 1935 by the work of a Senate committee set up under the chairmanship of Gerald P. Nye of North Dakota to investigate the munitions industry. The Nye Committee unearthed a wealth of documentation purporting to show that the United States had been shoved into war when international bankers, especially the House of Morgan, saw no other way to guarantee repayment of the vast credits they had granted to the western Allies. To demonstrate that no President could be trusted with discretionary power in matters of war and peace, Nye charged Wilson with duplicity in pretending to be ignorant of the secret treaties.

The Nye Committee completed the work of consolidating the isolationist philosophy. The isolationists could conceive of no world war that would present a moral issue between the antagonists or a strategic threat to American security; in fact, they were convinced that American freedom could not survive participation in another holocaust. America's best contribution to peace and democracy, in their judgment, lay in absolute rejection of the power struggles of Europe and Asia.

Roosevelt was quickly to learn the new power of organized isolationism. In January 1935, a short time after the stunning Democratic victory in the 1934 elections, he sent the Senate a recommendation that the United States join the World Court. "At this period in international relationships," he said, "when every act is of moment to the future of world peace, the United States has an opportunity once more to throw its weight into the scale in favor of peace." Joining the World Court could hardly have been a more innocuous act, and the Administration confidently supposed that it could command the necessary two-thirds vote. But the isolationist bloc staged an extraordinary appeal to public opinion, and an outpouring of protest defeated the resolution. Roosevelt wrote to Elihu Root, who had proposed a world court at The Hague a generation before, "Today, quite frankly, the wind everywhere blows against us."

The design of neutrality. The next problem, as Nye, Arthur Vandenberg, and their Nye Committee colleagues saw it, was to make sure the forces that had brought about American participation in the First World War would never have their way again.

If America had been drawn into that war to ensure the repayment of debts owed to American bankers and munitions-makers, then to keep out of war it would be necessary to forbid loans and the export of arms to belligerents. If America had been drawn into that war because American ships carried supplies to belligerent nations or because American citizens insisted on traveling on belligerent ships, then to keep out of war such actions should be prohibited. If America had been drawn into war by the unneutral decisions of a President with too much discretion in the conduct of foreign policy, then the President should be denied the opportunity to tamper with neutrality. The Nye group demanded a new American neutrality policy—one that might even involve the surrender of certain classical neutral rights, such as the freedom of the seas.

The Administration, yielding to isolationist pressure, agreed that the President should have authority to prohibit American ships from carrying arms and munitions, to withdraw the protection of the government from Americans traveling on belligerent vessels, and to impose an embargo on arms and loans. But the Administration wanted the President to be able to use these powers at his discretion; the senators, with the image of the perfidious Wilson in their mind, wanted to make it mandatory that he use them against *all* belligerents—which would, of course, nullify American influence in the case of conflict. In the end the Senate passed a mandatory bill, the House a discretionary bill. The resulting compromise of August 31, 1935, contained a mandatory arms embargo but made it good only until March 1, 1936; in other respects— such as American travel on belligerent ves-

Senator Nye and witness: the committee was inflexible

sels—it gave the President discretion. The Administration decided to accept the measure rather than risk further exacerbation of isolationist sentiment through a veto. On signing the bill, Roosevelt warned that "the inflexible provisions . . . might have exactly the opposite effect from that which was intended."

Neutrality on test

Italy invades Ethiopia. Early in October 1935 Italian troops crossed the frontier into Ethiopia. In his message to Congress in January 1936, Roosevelt outspokenly indicted nations that had the "fantastic conception that they, and they alone, are chosen to fulfill a mission and that all the others among the billion and a half of human beings in the world must and shall learn from them and be subject to them." At the same time, he issued a proclamation of neutrality and invoked the mandatory arms embargo.

The supposition in Washington was that the embargo would hurt Italy more than Ethiopa, since Ethiopa lacked dollars to buy arms in the United States and ships to carry them away. Actually the arms embargo did Italy little initial harm, since it had its own munitions industry. Where the restriction of American exports really could hurt the Italian warmaking capacity was in raw materials, especially in oil. But the Neutrality Act covered only implements of war. Roosevelt accordingly followed up the arms embargo with a call for a voluntary restriction of other exports. This action initiated the experiment in what became known as the "moral embargo."

The moral embargo aroused the protests of the Italian government as well as of American oil companies, and moral suasion did not turn

out to be effective. Oil shipments to Italy were 600 percent larger in August and September 1935 than they had been for the same two months in 1934. Nevertheless, the American policy preceded by many weeks any comparable action by the League, and it strengthened the hands of those in Geneva contending for economic sanctions against Italy. The League decision was finally taken in a limited way (not including oil, for example) on November 18, 1935.

When Congress convened in 1936, one of its first tasks was to replace the neutrality resolution of 1935. The Administration tried to increase the presidential role in the management of neutrality; but the legislative situation grew hopelessly confused, and in the end it seemed simpler to extend the existing act until May 1, 1937, with an amendment banning credits to belligerents. One apparently minor change did, however, increase executive discretion; it was now up to the President to decide that a state of war existed before the act could be invoked.

"One cannot help feeling," Roosevelt wrote his ambassador to France in the midst of the neutrality debate of 1936, "that the whole European panorama is fundamentally blacker than at any time in your lifetime or mine." The outbreak of civil war in Spain on July 17,

1936, deepened Roosevelt's sense of a general European disintegration. In a speech at Chautauqua, New York, four weeks later, he set forth with earnestness his hatred of war, his commitment to neutrality, and his determination to resist the forces that might draw the United States into another world conflict. His private correspondence reflected a belief that somehow a conference among heads of state might avert the drift to Armageddon; but he found no formula that offered any promise of success and thus took no action.

The attempt of Spanish fascists under General Francisco Franco to overthrow the democratic government of Spain created new problems. The mandatory embargo applied to wars between nations, not to civil wars; so, early in January 1937, Congress, with Roosevelt's full support and with but one negative vote in both houses, enacted a resolution aligning the United States with Britain and France in a program of nonintervention and in banning shipments of implements of war to either side in Spain.

Then Congress faced once again the question of renewing or rewriting the existing neutrality legislation. The main innovation in the 1937 debate was the so-called cash-and-carry proposal, which provided that, once the President had proclaimed the existence of a state of war, no nonmilitary goods could be shipped to a belligerent until the purchaser acquired full title and took them away himself. The Administration supported this idea in order to head off a drive for an automatic embargo on all goods. Ironically, the amendment would clearly have the unneutral effect of favoring the maritime powers, notably Britain and Japan, and of closing American markets to inland nations, notably Germany and China. Nevertheless, Congress adopted the provision by sweeping majorities.

Aggression in the Far East

The problem of China. For many Americans the problems of Europe had come to seem more remote, or at least less America's business, than the problems of the Far East. As far back as the announcement of the Open Door doctrine, the acquisition of the Philippines, and Theodore Roosevelt's mediation of the Russo-Japanese War, America had conceived of itself as playing a direct role in the affairs of East Asia. By the First World War Washington had concluded that the great threat to the Open Door would come from Japan. Both the Washington Naval Conference and the Stimson Doctrine were designed to restrain Tokyo's imperial aspirations.

In addition, years of missionary endeavor had given many Americans warm sympathy with China in its struggle for nationhood. Roosevelt, who shared this sympathy, himself endorsed the Stimson Doctrine. Then the Tangku truce of May 1933 suspended hostilities between China and Japan. But in April 1934, Eiji Amau, spokesman for the Japanese foreign office, demanded a free hand in China for Japan and warned the West against coming to China's assistance. Soon Japan denounced the Five-Power Treaty.

An aggressive Japan confronted America with perplexing problems. Some historians have argued that the American motive was to secure markets and investment outlets in China for American capitalism. But American trade with China was negligible, and American investment there far below British. Japan, indeed, was a far more profitable American market. Nor was the tendency of the Roosevelt Administration to carry out the desires of the business community ever marked. What concerned Roosevelt was the Japanese challenge to international order—the fear that, if aggression ran on with impunity, the peace system would collapse and war might engulf the United States. The preservation of that system therefore seemed a vital American interest. In addition, an expanding Japan could deny the United States strategic materials, like natural rubber, that were essential to national security.

But what could America do? To the State Department, the cornerstone in a containment policy had to be the buildup of the United States navy. So long as America remained weak in Asian waters, Cordell Hull reasoned, any attempt to oppose the Japanese or to help the Chinese would be pinpricks that would serve only to provoke Tokyo unnecessarily. Naval superiority became, in short, not only the indispensable condition for a future American policy in East Asia but a powerful argument against present action. Thus the State Department generally opposed proposals to condemn Japan or aid China.

Interventionism: an economic interpretation

The renewal of Japanese aggression. In the meantime, the Chinese, under the leadership of Chiang Kai-shek, were making impressive progress toward the unification of their nation. Perhaps wishing to halt the process before it went too far, the Japanese used troop clashes at the Marco Polo Bridge in July 1937 as an excuse for a new invasion of China. By the end of the month, Japanese soldiers had seized Peking and Tientsin. The subsequent bombing of Shanghai by Japanese planes and the appalling sack of Nanking in December horrified Americans. The Chinese retreated to the interior, established their capital at Chungking, and prepared to keep up their resistance.

Popular sympathy in the United States was wholly with the Chinese, but official reaction was cautious. Britain and America warded off Chinese pressure for invocation of the Nine-Power Treaty (see p. 581) and instead allowed the matter to go to the League for perfunctory condemnation. The President, however, displayed his solicitude for the Chinese cause by refusing to proclaim the existence of a state of war between China and Japan. Without such a proclamation, the arms embargo and the cash-and-carry provision for nonmilitary commodities would not go into effect. Most observers felt that these provisions would hurt China, which had to import implements of war, more than they would Japan, which had ample stockpiles and a productive capacity of its own. Thus between July and November 1937 the value of licensed munitions shipments to China was $86 million; to Japan, $1.5 million. Moreover, an arms embargo would not cut off what Japan needed most— oil and scrap metal. And cash-and-carry would favor Japan as a naval power.

Shanghai, 1937

Awakening the nation

The quarantine speech. The disintegration of the peace system promised to loose war upon the world—a war contemporaries believed would be vastly more destructive than the war of 1914–18. Moreover, as the peace system collapsed, Nazi Germany might well seize control of the power and resources of Europe; and this Roosevelt regarded as a mortal threat to the security of the United States. In 1814 Jefferson had said he preferred war to ''seeing the whole force of Europe wielded by a single hand.'' When that hand would be

F. D. R.:
the contagion
of war

It seems to be unfortunately true that the epidemic of world lawlessness is spreading.

When an epidemic of physical disease starts to spread, the community approves and joins in a quarantine of the patients in order to protect the health of the community against the spread of the disease....

War is a contagion, whether it be declared or undeclared. It can engulf states and peoples remote from the original scene of hostilities. We are determined to keep out of war, yet we cannot insure ourselves against the disastrous effects of war and the dangers of involvement. We are adopting such measures as will minimize our risk of involvement, but we cannot have complete protection in a world of disorder in which confidence and security have broken down....

Most important of all, the will for peace on the part of peace-loving nations must express itself to the end that nations that may be tempted to violate their agreements and the rights of others will desist from such a course. There must be positive endeavors to preserve peace.

From Franklin D. Roosevelt, Speech at Chicago, October 1937.

Gerald P. Nye:
the contagion
of isolationism

There can be no objection to any hand our Government may take which strives to bring peace to the world so long as that hand does not tie 130,000,000 people into another world death march.

I very much fear that we are once again being caused to feel that the call is upon America to police a world that chooses to follow insane leaders. Once again we are baited to thrill to a call to save the world.

We reach now a condition on all fours with that prevailing just before our plunge into the European war in 1917. Will we blindly repeat that futile venture? Can we easily forget that we won nothing we fought for then—that we lost every cause declared to be responsible for our entry then?

From Senator Gerald P. Nye, Statement in the New York *Times,* October 1937.

Adolf Hitler's, the danger seemed greater than that posed by any previous external threat in American history. Fearing the strategic consequences of Nazi expansion, detesting the cruel and tyrannical Nazi ideology, American leaders watched Hitler with increasing anxiety. Roosevelt even proposed a personal meeting with Neville Chamberlain, the British prime minister. But Chamberlain had no confidence in the United States—"it is always best and safest," he said in 1937, "to count on nothing from the Americans but words"—and he dedicated himself instead to the hope of making Hitler reasonable through a program of appeasement.

The renewal of warfare in China now heightened the sense of international urgency. It apparently also turned Roosevelt's attention to an idea that had been in the back of his mind for many years—the deterrence of aggression by holding over potential aggressors the threat (as he had put it in a "Plan to Preserve World Peace," written for a prize competition in 1923) of "the severance of all trade or financial relations, and the prohibition of all intercourse." Carrying his campaign to alert the nation to the heart of American isolationism, Roosevelt, in a speech at Chicago in October 1937, declared that "the present reign of terror and international lawlessness" had reached a stage "where the very foundations of civilization are seriously threatened." If aggression continued, he said, "let no one imagine America will escape." In a cryptic passage, he compared "the epidemic of world lawlessness" to an epidemic of physical disease and advocated a "quarantine" to protect the community against the contagion.

Aftermath of the quarantine speech. Roosevelt's main purpose was undoubtedly educational: he wanted to awaken the nation to the dangers of world war. A secondary purpose was very likely to explore the readiness of the American people to support some form of boycott of aggressors—moral, diplomatic, perhaps economic.

In the international sphere, the quarantine speech encouraged the British to call the signatories of the Nine-Power Treaty to a conference at Brussels to deal with the new Sino-Japanese conflict. But first the British sent word to Washington that they could do nothing about imposing sanctions against Japan unless they received "assurance of military support" in the event of Japanese retaliation. Roosevelt declined to give such guarantees; the British declined to act without them; and the Brussels Conference came to nothing.

In the meantime, Under Secretary of State Sumner Welles suggested that Roosevelt follow up his quarantine speech by convening a conference of neutral nations to set forth a peace program based on certain standards of international behavior. But Neville Chamberlain, wholly absorbed in the appeasement policy, rejected the American initiative on the ground that it ran the danger of "cutting across our efforts here." Winston Churchill later wrote that Chamberlain's decision was "the loss of the last frail chance to save the world from tyranny otherwise than by war."

Within the United States the first reaction to the quarantine speech was not unfavorable. But most Americans, while sharing their President's detestation of dictators, detested war even more. When Japanese planes sank the American gunboat *Panay* in the Yangtze River in December 1937, the nation accepted Japanese apologies and indemnification with relief. Interest was rising in a constitutional amendment offered by Congressman Louis Ludlow of Indiana proposing that declarations of war be subject to popular plebiscite except in case of invasion. The country, moreover, was sinking into an economic recession, and the Administration needed congressional support for its new recovery program.

The quarantine idea, vague enough at best, now perished between American reluctance and British indifference. It left a mark, however, on the popular consciousness as the nation struggled to define the issues of totalitarianism and aggression.

The road to war

The end of appeasement. In 1936 Germany moved into the Rhineland. In March 1938 it invaded and annexed Austria. In the following months Hitler began to use the plight of the German minority in the Sudetenland as a pretext for demands on the government of Czechoslovakia.

As the Czech crisis deepened in September, Chamberlain requested a personal conference with Hitler. There followed a series of meetings attended by Hitler, Chamberlain, Prime Minister Daladier of France, and eventually Mussolini. No representatives of Czechoslovakia were present. In the interval between the talks at Godesberg (September 23) and those at Munich (September 29), when it seemed as if Chamberlain was standing firm against Hitler, Roosevelt sent him an encouraging cable ("GOOD MAN") and brought pressure on Hitler to resume negotiations. But the Munich meeting produced an abject capitulation of the democratic powers. Czechoslovakia had no choice other than to acquiesce bitterly in the result.

The first reaction in the United States was one of heartfelt relief: the appeasement policy seemed to have averted war. But in a short while people began to compute the price of appeasement: not just the establishment of German hegemony in Central Europe, but the incentive offered everywhere to intimidation and aggression. "There can be no peace," Roosevelt said in a speech on October 26, 1938, "if national policy adopts as a deliberate instrument the threat of war."

Rearmament. During the 1920s the regular army had fallen well below the size authorized by the National Defense Act of 1920 and the navy below the levels permitted by the various international agreements. When Roosevelt came into office in 1933, the army ranked seventeenth in the world in active strength. From the start of his Administration, he had tried to rebuild American military and naval power. Thus the Public Works Administration constructed cruisers and aircraft-carriers; and in 1935 Congress authorized the army to increase its enlisted strength to 165,000. In a message to Congress in January 1938 Roosevelt called for larger defense appropriations. In May Congress passed the Naval Expansion

Munich:
an abject capitulation

Aggressions leading to the Second World War in Europe

Act. In the months after Munich, he requested vast increases in the defense budget and encouraged British and French purchasing missions to place defense orders in the United States.

In other respects Roosevelt began to tighten his ship in preparation for storms ahead. Following the failure of his "purge" in 1938 (see p. 647), he moved toward a tacit political truce, moderating his liberal objectives in the hope of gaining support for his foreign and defense policies. He also gathered support in the American hemisphere. In December 1938 in the Declaration of Lima the American republics announced their collective determination to resist fascist threats to peace.

The Neutrality Act remained the greatest obstacle to a positive policy; and in 1939, as the Munich settlement seemed to be growing increasingly unstable, Roosevelt considered how he might modify the neutrality system in order to make American aid available to dem-

ocratic nations. Hitler's invasion of Czechoslovakia on March 15, 1939, persuaded even Neville Chamberlain of the bankruptcy of appeasement. The State Department denounced Germany's "wanton lawlessness," and the Administration stepped up its campaign for the modification of the arms embargo. As Cordell Hull put it, the law "plays into the hands of those nations which have taken the lead in building up their fighting power. It works directly against the interests of the peace-loving nations." But isolationist senators, confident there would be no war in 1939, insisted that the matter be laid over to the next session of Congress.

In Europe events rushed toward climax. The invasion of Czechoslovakia was followed by the German occupation of Memel (March 23), the collapse of the Spanish Republic (March 28), and the Italian invasion of Albania (April 7). Through the summer Hitler carried on a war of nerves against Poland, using a German

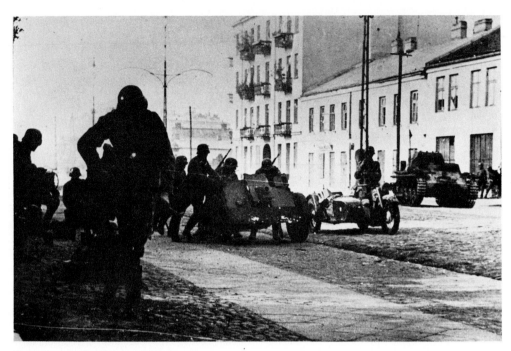
German troops in Warsaw, 1939

minority in Danzig as his tool. In the meantime his emissaries were secretly negotiating a nonaggression pact with the Soviet Union. On August 23 the German-Russian pact was signed in Moscow. The next day Britain and Poland signed a pact of mutual assistance. On September 1 Germany attacked Poland. Two days later Britain and France declared war on Germany. The Second World War was under way.

America and the war

First reactions. "When peace has been broken anywhere," Roosevelt said in a fireside chat on the evening of September 3, 1939, "the peace of all countries everywhere is in danger." He reaffirmed his determination "to use every effort" to keep war out of America. But, in marked contrast to Wilson's appeal in 1914 that his countrymen be "neutral in fact as well as in name," he added that he could not ask that "every American remain neutral in thought. . . . Even a neutral cannot be asked to close his mind or his conscience." When he issued the proclamation of neutrality, he also indicated that he would call Congress into special session in order to repeal the arms embargo.

The isolationist leaders in the Senate, backed by former President Hoover and by such national figures as Colonel Charles A. Lindbergh, as well as by the American Communist party (following the Soviet-Nazi pact), declared that Roosevelt's course was leading straight to war. The opposition was strong enough to compel the Administration to accept restrictive compromises in exchange for the elimination of the embargo. Thus hedged around, the neutrality-revision bill passed Congress, and the President signed it on November 4, 1939. The new law placed the arms trade on a cash-and-carry basis. Where the previous legislation had favored Germany, with its well-established war industries, the new law enabled Britain and France to buy war materials in the United States so long as they were willing to pay cash and to carry their purchases away in their own ships.

Meanwhile the Nazi air force and Panzer divisions had subdued Poland in a three-week campaign. The French and British had been able to do little to create a diversion on the western front, and the war now settled into an aspect of apparent quiescence that won it the derisive name of "the phony war." While public-opinion polls showed an overwhelming

*What was pushing behind Communism? What behind Fascism in
Italy? What behind Naziism? Is it nothing but a "return to barbarism,"
to be crushed at all costs by a "crusade"? Or is some new, and
perhaps even ultimately good, conception of humanity trying to come
to birth, often through evil and horrible forms and abortive attempts?...
I cannot see this war, then, simply and purely as a struggle between
the "Forces of Good" and the "Forces of Evil." If I could simplify
it into a phrase at all, it would seem truer to say that the "Forces
of the Past" are fighting against the "Forces of the Future"....*

*Somehow the leaders in Germany, Italy and Russia have discovered
how to use new social and economic forces.... They have felt the wave
of the future and they have leapt upon it. The evils we deplore in
these systems are not in themselves the future; they are scum on the
wave of the future.... There is no fighting the wave of the future, any
more than as a child you could fight against the gigantic roller that
loomed up ahead of you.*

From Anne Morrow Lindbergh, *The Wave of the Future*, 1940.

public preference in America for the western
Allies against Germany (in October 1939, 62
percent of the population favored all possible
aid to the Allies short of war), less than 30
percent favored American entry into the war
even if Britain and France were in danger of
defeat.

American emotions were perhaps more
deeply engaged when the Soviet Union, having advanced into eastern Poland in September, moved into the small Baltic republics of
Latvia, Estonia, and Lithuania in October and
invaded Finland in late November. The American people, remembering Finnish punctilious-
ness in the payment of war debts, grew particularly indignant over the onslaught on the
"gallant little Finns." Roosevelt sharply condemned "this dreadful rape." Isolationists,
however, were alert not to let emotion over
Finland drag the nation closer toward war. The
Administration's cautious program of aid to
Finland encountered strong opposition in
Congress and had hardly gone into effect
when the Winter War came to an end in
March 1940.

German paratrooper

Blitzkrieg. Hitler was already preparing the
blow that he hoped would break the will of
his western antagonists. On April 9, 1940,
Germany attacked Denmark and Norway. An
Anglo-French attempt to land forces in Norway miscarried, and by the end of the month
Norwegian resistance was broken. Popular
discontent in Britain over the Chamberlain
government now reached new heights. Cham-

berlain was forced to resign, and Winston
Churchill, who had long criticized the appeasement policy and, after the outbreak of
war, had served as first lord of the admiralty,
became prime minister.

Chamberlain was in the course of resigning
on May 10 when Nazi mechanized divisions
invaded the Netherlands, Belgium, and Luxembourg. In a week they were thrusting deep
into northern France. The British and French
were unable to cope with the speed of the
German attack. The main part of the British
forces retreated to Dunkirk, where they were
evacuated across the British Channel by a
heroic flotilla of small boats conjured up from
British ports. In a few days Italy joined the
war, invading France from the south. "The
hand that held the dagger," Roosevelt said
grimly, "has struck it into the back of its
neighbor." Soon Paris fell, Marshal Pétain
became head of the French government, and
on June 22 France and Germany signed an
armistice at Compiègne. The next day, from
London, General Charles de Gaulle pledged
continued French resistance.

The success of the Nazi blitzkrieg had a
stunning effect on American opinion. Citing
"the almost incredible events of the past two
weeks," Roosevelt asked Congress for more
than a billion dollars in additional defense
appropriations, calling in particular for the
annual production of fifty thousand war-
planes. He also set up a National Defense
Advisory Commission to plan defense production. And he began to consider how he could
aid Britain, now standing alone against the

Evacuation at Dunkirk, 1940

Berlin-Rome Axis. Churchill's rise to power meant the end of the glumness that had marked Anglo-American relations during the Chamberlain period. Roosevelt, who had for some months exchanged letters with the new prime minister, recognized him as a man of congenial temperament and stature. When Churchill offered his own people nothing but "blood, toil, tears and sweat," when he promised to "wage war by sea, land and air, with all our might and with all the strength that God can give us," he made a profound appeal to the American imagination.

But Britain needed more than sympathy. On May 15 Churchill sent Roosevelt a long list of specific requirements, including old destroyers, new aircraft, and materials of war. For the moment Washington could do little, partly because of America's own defense needs, partly (as in the case of the destroyers) because it was feared that congressional assent would not be forthcoming. After Dunkirk the American government did scrape together small arms and ammunition for the British to use in the desperate eventuality of a German invasion. But the problems of American policy were now further complicated by the approach of the 1940 presidential campaign.

The election of 1940

The third term. The struggle between isolationists and interventionists cut across party lines. Thus Roosevelt found some of the most effective supporters of his foreign policy in the ranks of internationalist Republicans—a fact he acknowledged in June 1940, when he appointed Henry L. Stimson of New York as Secretary of War and Frank Knox of Illinois as Secretary of the Navy. However, the basic sentiment of the Republican party was isolationist. When the Republicans gathered in Philadelphia to select a presidential candidate, they read Stimson and Knox out of the party and prepared to choose between two candidates, Senator Robert A. Taft of Ohio and Thomas E. Dewey of New York, both identified with isolationism.

They did not allow, however, for the enthusiasm with which a group of internationalist Republicans rallied support for a dark-horse candidate, Wendell L. Willkie of Indiana. Willkie, an affable and articulate businessman, had magnetic qualities of personality that justified the title of "the rich man's Roosevelt." As president of Commonwealth & Southern, a leading public-utilities holding company, Willkie had won attention as an antagonist of the New Deal during the fight over the Tennessee Valley Authority. Actually he had been a Democrat himself most of his life; his personal views and values were on the liberal side; and, most critically of all in 1940, he sympathized with the Roosevelt policy of aid to Great Britain. To general astonishment, the

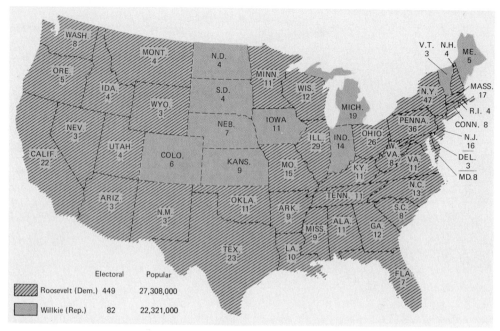

The election of 1940

Electoral | Popular
Roosevelt (Dem.) 449 | 27,308,000
Willkie (Rep.) 82 | 22,321,000

Willkie forces staged a blitzkrieg of their own at Philadelphia, and the former Democrat emerged as the Republican candidate.

As for the Democrats, Roosevelt had failed, whether through design or negligence, to develop an heir apparent. For many months ardent New Dealers had demanded that he stand himself for a third term. Conservative Democrats, led by Vice President Garner and Postmaster General Farley, sought to organize opposition on the ground that a third term

The U.S.-British destroyer-bases agreement, 1940

would violate a sacred American tradition. But the international urgencies made Roosevelt seem to most Democrats the indispensable candidate. The Democratic convention accordingly renominated him at Chicago in July, though it swallowed rather hard at his insistence on Henry A. Wallace, the Secretary of Agriculture, for Vice President.

Foreign policy and the campaign. While Americans concerned themselves with presidential politics, the German Luftwaffe launched a savage air war against England. The Royal Air Force put up a magnificent defense in what became known as the Battle of Britain. But if Britain hoped to repulse an anticipated German invasion—as well as maintain its own lines of supply—it needed immediate reinforcement of its battered destroyer fleet. Churchill, renewing his request for American destroyers, cabled Roosevelt on July 31, "I must tell you that in the long history of the world this is a thing to do *now.*"

Though the United States had overage destroyers to spare, the Naval Appropriations Act required prior approval of the Chief of Naval Operations before they could be released. Moreover, Roosevelt feared the political repercussions in a campaign in which he was already under attack for unneutral acts. But he was persuaded that he could legally release the destroyers without amending the

Wendell Willkie: "the rich man's Roosevelt"

law, and he received assurances that Willkie, the Republican candidate, would not oppose the transaction. Accordingly, on September 2 the United States by executive agreement transferred fifty destroyers to Britain in exchange for ninety-nine-year leases of bases in Newfoundland and the Caribbean.

Willkie's support of conscription also enabled the Administration to obtain a Selective Service Act in August. Still, though Willkie's internationalism minimized the role of foreign policy in the campaign, it did not altogether eliminate peace and war as an issue. Indeed, as the campaign wore on, the Republican candidate, rattled both by his own inexperience and by discordant counsel among his advisers, assailed Roosevelt's foreign policy more and more extravagantly in terms which he would later dismiss as "campaign ora-

tory." Soon he predicted that Roosevelt, if elected, would have the nation in war by April 1941. By the end of the campaign Roosevelt was himself assuring American parents: "I have said this before, but I shall say it again and again and again: Your boys are not going to be sent into any foreign wars."

The election showed that Roosevelt still retained the national confidence. He received 27 million popular votes against 22 million for Willkie; the Electoral College margin was 449 to 82. But he received only 54.8 percent of the vote as against 60.8 percent in 1936. Because of the equivocal way in which both candidates had presented the foreign issues—had, indeed, somewhat misrepresented their own convictions—the election did not serve either to clarify public thinking or to produce a setting for future action.

Aid short of war

The Lend-Lease Act. Through 1940 Britain had been able to get the goods it needed under the system of cash-and-carry. But, as Churchill urged on Roosevelt in December, both features of the system were in peril—"cash" because Britain's supply of American dollars was nearing exhaustion, "carry" because of the effectiveness of the German submarine campaign against British shipping.

"The thing to do," Roosevelt now told Secretary of the Treasury Morgenthau, "is to get

away from a dollar sign. I don't want to put the thing in terms of dollars or loans." As he explained to his press conference, if a neighbor's house was on fire, you would not waste time arguing about the cost of the hose; you would put the fire out and get the hose back afterward. Why not say to England, "We will give you the guns and the ships you need, provided that when the war is over you will return to us in kind the guns and ships we have loaned to you"?

Lend-Lease: the opposition

We confront a terrible emergency; yes. But the worst of the emergency, in my view, is the insinuating proposal that to keep others free, we must become less free ourselves.... This so-called lending-leasing bill not only invites us closer to the grim event of war itself.... but it lends essential congressional prerogatives to the President and leases a new portion of the Constitution to the White House—and all unnecessary in order to aid England short of war....

This bill hands the President ... all these vital American resources ... plus the authority to purchase or manufacture or "otherwise procure" war supplies, as he sees fit, either at home or abroad.... He can lease these resources or lend them or give them away on whatever terms may suit his fancy. He is almoner and armorer to the world....

This is a license to arm half or more of the earth out of our arsenals at a moment of grave danger, when we have not yet been able adequately even to arm ourselves.... I reject and deny the novel doctrine ... that our American defense is thus at the mercy of any such far-flung manipulation of power politics in the Old World.

From Senator Arthur H. Vandenberg, Speech in the United States Senate, February 1941.

Lend-Lease: the defense

These are the provisions which it is said set up a dictatorship in the United States. But, may I ask, what other officer of the Government of the United States than the President could or should be empowered to do these things? Congress cannot execute its own laws. That must be done by the Executive established by the Constitution.... The President ... is also the Commander-in-Chief of the Army and Navy of the United States. Congress cannot divest him of this official character by statute. There is no other appropriate person or officer than the President who can carry out the will of Congress....

It has been suggested that the bill itself ought to name the countries which are to receive the aid which it provides. If the situation now existing were permanent, and not subject to daily or weekly changes, such a provision might be safe. But the situation is not permanent. We have seen one after another of the small nations of Europe overrun. At present England ... Greece ... and China ... are the defenders of their right to exist. Tomorrow it may be some other nation.

From Senator Alben W. Barkley, Speech in the United States Senate, February 1941.

In January 1941 the Administration introduced the so-called lend-lease bill to carry out Roosevelt's intention. The measure authorized the President to sell, transfer, exchange, lend, lease, or otherwise dispose of war equipment and other commodities to the "government of any country whose defense the President deems vital to the defense of the United States." So sweeping a proposal aroused bitter isolationist opposition. "The lend-lease-give program," said Senator Burton K. Wheeler, "is the New Deal's triple A foreign policy; it will plow under every fourth American boy." (Roosevelt called this "the rottenest thing that has been said in public life in my generation.") Among those who testified against the bill were Charles A. Lindbergh, Charles A. Beard, the historian, and Joseph P. Kennedy, the former ambassador to England; Wendell Willkie led a parade of witnesses in its favor. But public sentiment strongly supported the proposal, and it became law on March 11, 1941. "Through this legislation," Roosevelt said, "our country has determined to do its full part in creating an adequate arsenal of democracy."

The Battle of the Atlantic. The Lend-Lease Act decisively committed the economic power of the United States to the support of Britain. More than this, it implied at least a partial commitment of American naval power; for, if

America deemed aid to Britain vital to American security, then clearly America had better make sure that goods intended for Britain actually arrived there. Shortly after the passage of lend-lease, the Germans joined the challenge by extending the North Atlantic war zone westward to the coast of Greenland. Through the spring of 1941 the Germans were destroying half a million tons of merchant shipping a month; ships were sinking twice as fast as they could be replaced. It is, Churchill told Roosevelt, "in shipping and in the power to transport across the oceans, particularly the Atlantic Ocean, that in 1941 the crunch of the whole war will be found." In response, Roosevelt proposed an eastward extension of the area in which American naval and air patrol was clearly legitimate. While this move lessened, it by no means resolved, Britain's problem of the Atlantic lifeline.

Lend-lease for the Soviet Union

Unlimited national emergency. Roosevelt's policy of aid to Great Britain was not limited only by the fear of an adverse public reaction. It seems likely that the President himself cherished the hope, which many around him had abandoned by the spring of 1941, that Hitler might be defeated without direct American military involvement.

Yet he confronted the hard fact that Britain's situation seemed to be growing steadily worse. And in the United States itself the attitude of business as usual impeded full mobilization of the economy for defense production. The Office of Production Management had succeeded the National Defense Advisory Commission in January 1941, but the new agency lacked adequate authority over allocations and priorities. Many businessmen were disinclined to convert their facilities to defense needs. Strikes in defense industries, some of them instigated by communists, further kept the country from living up to its full responsibility as the "arsenal of democracy." Some positive step seemed necessary to galvanize America and to reassure Britain. On May 27, 1941, the President addressed a forceful speech to the nation, concluding with a proclamation "that an unlimited national emergency exists and requires the strengthening of our defense to the extreme limit of our national power."

Isolationism's last stand

The great debate. The slow unfolding of American policy had been accompanied by an intensification of public debate. In 1940 the Committee to Defend America by Aiding the Allies was established under the chairmanship of the Kansas editor William Allen White to argue the moderate interventionist position; in 1941 the Fight for Freedom Committee contended for American entry into the war. On the other side, the America First Committee argued that Hitler's victory would not menace American security. Each side took its case to the public through newspaper advertisements, radio broadcasts, and mass meetings.

The resulting debate became more bitter even than the arguments of the thirties over the New Deal. It was, in addition, unpredictable, cutting across political, economic, and geographical lines. Isolationists were to be found in all parts of the country, in all social classes, and in all political parties. Still, to a considerable degree, isolationism as a political force represented the conservative Republican wing of the business community, with special strength in the Middle West. Progressives like Burton K. Wheeler, Socialists like Norman Thomas, and the communists also criticized Roosevelt's policies. The German-American Bund and the fringe of pro-Nazi groups in America endorsed the isolationist position.

Nazi tanks move east, June 20, 1941

The isolationist dilemma. Most Americans remained uncertainly in the middle of the violent debate. "I am 100 percent plus against our participation in this criminal war," wrote Josephus Daniels, the old Wilsonian, once Roosevelt's chief as Secretary of the Navy in the First World War, now ambassador to Mexico, "but, of course, I trust that Europe will be delivered from totalitarian governments and the scourge of force." This was the isolationist dilemma: at some point, the two sentiments were bound to collide. George W. Norris, the patriarch of American liberalism, told an interviewer that he was the only one left of the six senators who had voted against war in 1917:

The first summit: Argentia, 1941

> viewing the aftermath of the war, I feel justified in what I did. Yet now . . . I do not like to think how a future generation called upon to combat this terror will feel about us who did not nip it in the bud. . . . If the policies of Hitler or Mussolini or Japan are carried out to their logical conclusion, the civilized world will ultimately have to contend against the barbarous conduct they have inaugurated.

An analysis of votes in Congress during these years shows, not a rigid isolationist-interventionist division, but a large middle bloc trying to steer a course between the two extremes. Most members of Congress, like most Americans, wished that all-out support of Britain short of war would somehow bring British victory without American participation.

In providing Britain such support, they edged steadily toward involvement. Yet involvement was not their purpose; it was rather the last resort they earnestly hoped to avoid. Men like Henry L. Stimson, Harold L. Ickes, and the members of the Fight for Freedom Committee felt that Roosevelt himself, by refusing to call for an American declaration of war, was engaged in self-delusion. Still, the President's policy of hoping for the best while preparing for the worst expressed the predominant sense of the American people in 1941.

Hitler widens the war. After the Soviet Union attacked Finland, Roosevelt had condemned Stalin's regime as "a dictatorship as absolute as any other dictatorship in the world." Nonetheless, American diplomats, noting growing evidence of tension between Germany and Russia, told a skeptical Kremlin in the winter of 1940–41 that a German attack might be in the making. Stalin remained impervious to warnings, however; and, when Hitler, despairing of an early defeat of Britain, decided to eliminate the potential threat of Russia by a sudden blow, the Soviet regime was taken by surprise. The Nazi invasion of the U.S.S.R. on June 22, 1941, brought the European war into a new phase.

Winston Churchill had long since decided that, in such an eventuality, he would offer Russia full British support. "I have only one purpose," he said, "the destruction of Hitler. . . . If Hitler invaded Hell, I would make at least a favorable reference to the Devil in the House of Commons." Roosevelt was ready to accept this policy. Despite warnings that Russia could not be expected to hold out against the Nazi onslaughts, he sent Harry Hopkins to Moscow in July. Hopkins' relatively optimistic report confirmed Churchill and Roosevelt in their decision to do what they could to stiffen Soviet resistance.

Most Americans supported this decision. The American communists, of course, rapidly called off their antiwar agitation and became passionate proponents of national defense. From an isolationist viewpoint, however, Hitler's new embroilment strengthened the case against American participation.

The Atlantic Charter. In August, Roosevelt and Churchill met on a warship off Argentia on the coast of Newfoundland. While Roosevelt avoided military commitments, he did agree with Churchill on "certain common principles in the national policies of their respective countries on which they base their hopes for a better future for the world." In the Atlantic Charter, Britain and the United States now disclaimed territorial aggrandizement, affirmed the right of all peoples to choose their own form of government and to express freely their wishes concerning territorial changes, assured all states equal access to trade and raw materials ("with due respect to their existing obligations"), proposed collaboration among all nations in the economic field, and promised "after the final destruction of the Nazi tyranny" the disarmament of all aggressor nations "pending the establishment of a wider and permanent system of general security."

In the meantime, American troops had moved to Greenland in April and Iceland in July. Although this was done in agreement with the governments of both Denmark and Iceland, isolationists denounced Roosevelt for acting without congressional authority. American destroyers now could escort convoys as far as Iceland, leaving the British navy to conduct them the rest of the way. The question of what American ships should do if they encountered a German raider was left un-

answered until a U-boat fired on the destroyer *Greer* early in September. Saying the time had come for "active defense," Roosevelt instructed the navy to "shoot on sight" any Axis ships in the American neutrality zone. In October the Germans badly damaged one American destroyer and sank another, the *Reuben James,* with considerable loss of life. In November Congress revised the Neutrality Act to allow merchantmen to carry arms and to proceed to British ports.

Both the Argentia meeting and the new Atlantic policy goaded the isolationists into ever more impassioned attacks on the Administration. In an angry speech at Des Moines, Iowa, in September, Charles A. Lindbergh declared that "the three most important groups who have been pressing this country toward war are the British, the Jewish and the Roosevelt administration." He went on to say of the Jews, "Their greatest danger to this country lies in their large ownership and influence in our motion pictures, our press, our radio, and our government." Though most isolationists disowned the Lindbergh line, a disturbing strain of anti-Semitism began to appear in isolationist discourse. Some observers felt that the dynamics of isolationism was propelling many of its supporters in a pro-Nazi direction.

Thunder in the East

The Japanese dilemma. Despite the Japanese occupation of coastal China in 1937 and the failure of the Brussels Conference (see p. 665), the Chiang Kai-shek government and the Chinese communists under Mao Tse-tung had kept up stalwart resistance. The Chinese plight increasingly enlisted the sympathy of the United States and Britain. Though both governments were reluctant to provoke Japanese retaliation, they began in 1938 to seek ways to get financial assistance to China.

The Japanese response was less explosive than the State Department had predicted. One reason for this restraint was the extent to which the Japanese war effort had itself become dependent on the United States. In 1938, for example, the United States supplied Japan with 90 percent of its metal scrap, 91 percent of its copper, and 66 percent of its oil. This trade confronted Washington with embarrassing problems. It was sanctioned by the Japanese-American commercial treaty of

1911, and the commodities involved were beyond the reach of existing neutrality legislation. To call for a "moral" embargo of the sort used in the Italo-Ethiopian conflict would penalize China as well as Japan. Its hands thus tied, the United States was left in the position of fueling a war machine of which it profoundly disapproved. In an effort to regain freedom of action, Washington informed Tokyo in July 1939 of its intention to terminate the commercial treaty, though, it added in January 1940, it would not for the time being disturb the existing trade.

Then the Nazi successes in Europe transformed the situation. The expansionists in Tokyo felt their long-awaited opportunity had come to seize the colonial empires of France and the Netherlands, even perhaps of Britain. The relatively moderate government was overthrown. In its place came a tough government, dominated by the military and dedicated to the achievement of a "new order in

Cordell Hull and Japanese representatives, November 17, 1941

reappraisal in Tokyo. Prime Minister Konoye, a moderate, favored one more attempt to reach an agreement with the United States. But there was no assurance that the civilians in Tokyo could deliver the military; and the military, haunted by the decline in Japan's oil reserves, believed time to be against them. At an Imperial Conference in early September, the Japanese leaders reached their decision: "If by the early part of October, there is no reasonable hope of having our demands agreed to in the diplomatic negotiations . . . we will immediately make up our minds to get ready for war." Their minimum demands included the abandonment of China by the United States and the restoration of normal commercial relations, with renewed delivery of oil and scrap metal. Roosevelt, vigorously backed by Churchill, concluded that acceptance of these demands would betray and doom China, embolden the Japanese to exact further concessions, and enfeeble the western capacity to act in the Far East; moreover, by cutting off rubber from Indonesia, Japan could in the future gravely weaken the defense position of the United States.

Greater East Asia." In September Japan joined Germany and Italy in the Tripartite Pact. The Axis now extended to Asia.

The American response. The American response was an embargo on essential materials, especially aviation gasoline and scrap metal. Since this action could be justified in terms of America's own defense needs, it did not have the flavor of an open affront to Japan. Behind the scenes, American representatives took part in staff discussions with British and Dutch officials to consider plans for the defense of the western Pacific in case a Japanese attack forced the United States into war.

Roosevelt, however, was primarily concerned with the crisis in Europe. He therefore wished to stave off a showdown with Japan. Accordingly 1941 was marked by long, intricate, and repetitious discussions between the two countries. Then in mid-July 1941 Japanese troops invaded southern Indochina and occupied Saigon. Roosevelt told the Japanese ambassador that if Japan withdrew from Indochina he would secure its neutralization and assure Japan access to its raw materials. If Japan persisted in its course, and especially if it moved into the Dutch East Indies, the United States would help the Dutch and probably cut off oil exports to Japan. When Japan did not reply, Roosevelt on July 26 froze Japanese assets in the United States and a few days later embargoed oil shipments.

These actions brought about a moment of

The Rising Sun over the Pacific. In mid-October Konoye resigned, to be replaced by General Tojo, the minister of war. On November 5 the new government set as its final deadline November 25 (later November 29). It also prepared a final offer to Washington along the line of the minimum demands of September. Tojo told Admiral Nomura, the Japanese ambassador, that other matters would be negotiable but that Japan could never yield on the question of China.

By decoding secret Japanese messages, the Americans had been able to follow some of the Japanese moves. Officials in Washington realized that the end was drawing near. Late in November American forces in the Pacific, including those in Hawaii, were sent the first of a number of alerts ordering them onto a war footing. Everyone expected attack, but the conviction was absolute that the Japanese would move toward the south. In Washington, Cordell Hull continued to meet with Japanese representatives. On December 6 Roosevelt sent a final appeal to the emperor.

In the meantime, a striking force of Japanese aircraft carriers had left the Kuriles on November 26 and was making its way toward Pearl Harbor. On December 7, 1941, while discussions continued in Washington, the

Japanese launched a devastating attack on the fleet and air force in Hawaii. An epoch in American history had come to an end.

"In the past few years—and, most violently, in the past few days—we have learned a terrible lesson," said Franklin Roosevelt two days later. "We must begin the great task that is before us by abandoning once and for all the illusion that we can ever again isolate ourselves from the rest of humanity." He added, "We are going to win the war, and we are going to win the peace that follows."

Suggestions for reading

THE MAKING OF AMERICAN FOREIGN POLICY

Selig Adler, *The Uncertain Giant: American Foreign Policy Between the Wars** (1966), and R. A. Divine, *The Reluctant Belligerent: American Entry into World War II** (1965), cover the main events of the period. For a cogent transatlantic view, see Jean-Baptiste Duroselle, *From Wilson to Roosevelt: Foreign Policy of the United States, 1913–1945* (1963). J. E. Wiltz, *From Isolation to War, 1931–1941** (1968), provides an incisive discussion of leading issues. R. E. Osgood, *Ideals and Self-Interest in America's Foreign Relations** (1953), offers a stimulating analytical framework from which to view American foreign policy. See also G. F. Kennan, *American Diplomacy, 1900–1950** (1951), and Walter Lippmann, *U.S. Foreign Policy: Shield of the Republic* (1943).

For Roosevelt's first term, the raw material of foreign affairs can be conveniently found in E. B. Nixon, ed., *Franklin D. Roosevelt and Foreign Affairs*, 3 vols. (1969). Merze Tate, *The United States and Armaments* (1948), describes the frustrations of disarmament in the years between the wars. The story from 1937 to Pearl Harbor is splendidly recorded in two magistral volumes by W. L. Langer and S. E. Gleason, *The Challenge to Isolation** (1952) and *The Undeclared War** (1953). 1941 is well covered in J. M. Burns, *Roosevelt: The Soldier of Freedom* (1970). For military aspects, see M. S. Watson, *Chief of Staff: Prewar Plans and Preparations* (1950).

Cordell Hull, *Memoirs,* 2 vols. (1948) supplies the view from the office of the Secretary of State. It may be supplemented by J. W. Pratt, *Cordell Hull,* 2 vols. (1964). Sumner Welles, *A Time for Decision* (1964), and Herbert Feis, *Seen From E. A.: Three International Episodes** (1947), amplify the State Department view. For H. L. Stimson, there are three works: his own book with McGeorge Bundy, *On Active Service in Peace and War* (1948); a perceptive biography by E. E. Morison, *Turmoil and Tradition** (1960); and a prosecutor's brief by R. N. Current, *Secretary Stimson* (1954). R. E. Sherwood, *Roosevelt and Hopkins** (1948, rev. ed., 1950), is vivid and penetrating; and the second volume of J. M. Blum, *From the Morgenthau Diaries: Years of Urgency* (1965), is invaluable for the years before Pearl Harbor.

Two waves of revisionism have washed over these years. The old isolationist school can be consulted in two books by C. A. Beard—*American Foreign Policy in the Making, 1932–1940* (1946) and *President Roosevelt and the Coming of War, 1941* (1948). C. C. Tansill sums up the isolationist case in *Back Door to War* (1952). In *Roosevelt: From Munich to Pearl Harbor* (1950), Basil Rauch provides a careful rebuttal. The contemporary school of revisionism, committed to the thesis that American foreign policy has always been the expression of the imperialist necessities of American capitalism, is represented in L. C. Gardner, *Economic Aspects of New Deal Diplomacy** (1964), and in the relevant chapters of W. A. Williams, *The Tragedy of American Diplomacy** (1959; rev. ed., 1962).

THE POLITICS OF FOREIGN POLICY

Selig Adler, *The Isolationist Impulse** (1957), Manfred Jonas, *Isolationism in America, 1935–1941** (1966), and Samuel Lubell, *The Future of American Politics** (1952), consider the sources of isolationism. Frank Waldrop, *McCormick of Chicago* (1966), is an illuminating essay on the isolationist mood. J. K. Nelson, *The Peace Prophets: American Pacifist Thought, 1919–1941** (1967), discusses the peace movement. Congressional reactions to foreign affairs can be traced in F. L. Israel, *Nevada's Key Pittman* (1963), M. C. McKenna, *Borah* (1961), B. K. Wheeler, *Yankee from the West* (1962), and W. S. Cole, *Senator Gerald P. Nye and American Foreign*

*Available in a paperback edition.

Relations (1962). See also J. E. Wiltz, *In Search of Peace: the Senate Munitions Inquiry, 1934–1936* (1963); for the neutrality debate, R. A. Divine, *The Illusion of Neutrality** (1962); and for Willkie, D. B. Johnson, *The Republican Party and Wendell Willkie** (1960).

The angry controversy of 1939–41 is well covered in Walter Johnson, *The Battle Against Isolationism* (1944), M. L. Chadwin, *The Hawks of World War II* (1968; in paperback as *The Warhawks: American Interventionists before Pearl Harbor*); and W. S. Cole, *America First: The Battle Against Intervention* (1953). The musings of a leading isolationist can be followed in C. A. Lindbergh, *Wartime Journals* (1970).

EUROPE

J. W. Gantenbein, *Documentary Background of World War II* (1948), lives up to its title. For interpretations, Keith Eubank, *The Origins of World War II** (1969), sums up the accepted view; and A. J. P. Taylor, *The Origins of the Second World War** (1962), is a stimulating essay in heterodoxy. W. S. Churchill's classic volumes, *The Gathering Storm** (1948) and *Their Finest Hour** (1949), are majestic and indispensable.

Alan Bullock, *Hitler: A Study in Tyranny** (1952), is the best biography. Five useful works discuss Nazi Germany and America: H. L. Trefousse, *Germany and American Neutrality* (1951); J. V. Compton, *The Swastika and the Eagle* (1967); Alton Frye, *Nazi Germany and the Western Hemisphere, 1933–1941* (1967); A. A. Offner, *American Appeasement: United States Foreign Policy and Germany, 1933–1938* (1969); and Robert Dallek, *Democrat and Diplomat: The Life of William E. Dodd* (1968). For American relations with the Soviet Union, see R. P. Browder, *The Origins of Soviet-American Diplomacy** (1953); Beatrice Farnsworth, *William C. Bullitt and the Soviet Union* (1967); and E. M. Bennett, *Recognition of Russia: An American Foreign Policy Dilemma* (1970). Brice Harris, *The United States and the Italo-Ethiopian Crisis* (1964), displays the American response to the events of 1935; and F. J. Taylor, *The United States and the Spanish Civil War* (1956), and Allen Guttmann, *The Wound in the Heart: America and the Spanish Civil War* (1962), consider the problems of 1937–38. Four books throw light on Anglo-American relations at various points: Herbert Feis, *1933: Characters in Crisis* (1966); W. F. Kimball, *'The Most Unsordid Act': Lend-Lease, 1939–1941* (1969); T. A. Wilson, *The First Summit: Roosevelt and Churchill at Placentia Bay, 1941* (1969); and H. D. Hall, *North American Supply* (1955).

FAR EAST

Dorothy Borg, *The United States and the Far Eastern Crisis of 1933–1938* (1964), is a basic work. The Japanese problem is assessed from various angles in Herbert Feis, *The Road to Pearl Harbor** (1950); D. J. Lu, *From the Marco Polo Bridge to Pearl Harbor: Japan's Entry into World War II* (1961); P. W. Schroeder, *The Axis Alliance and Japanese-American Relations* (1958); and Robert Butow, *Tojo and the Coming of the War** (1961). For American diplomatic reactions, see Walter Johnson's rendering of the papers of J. C. Grew, *Turbulent Era: A Diplomatic Record of Forty Years*, 2 vols. (1952), and W. H. Heinrichs, *American Ambassador: Joseph C. Grew and the Development of the United States Diplomatic Tradition* (1967).

LATIN AMERICA

Bryce Wood, *The Making of the Good Neighbor Policy** (1961), is the best historical account; Laurence Duggan, *The Americas: Search for Hemispheric Security* (1949), is the testimony of a participant. David Green, *The Containment of Latin America* (1971), is a revisionist critique of the Good Neighbor policy.

*Available in a paperback edition.

29

The world in flames

The bitter wreckage of ships and planes at Pearl Harbor ended the illusion that the United States could be a world power and remain safe from world conflict. In the shocking strike from the placid Hawaiian skies, the Japanese crippled the Pacific fleet, destroyed nearly 200 planes, and killed nearly 2,500 men. The navy lost three times as many men in this single attack as it had lost in the Spanish-American and First World Wars combined. Four days after Pearl Harbor, on December 11, 1941, Germany and Italy declared war on the United States. America was now committed to global war.

America organizes for war

Arms for global war. War ushered in a series of massive changes in American society. The first problem was to produce the machines and weapons for global warfare. In 1941 military spending had reached a monthly rate of about $2 billion; but only 15 percent of industrial output had gone for military purposes, and businessmen had resisted pressure to shift to war production. Roosevelt now laid down unprecedented objectives for 1942—60,000 planes, 45,000 tanks, 20,000 antiaircraft guns, 8 million tons of shipping—and set up the War Production Board under Donald Nelson to convert the economy to a war basis.

In the first six months of 1942, the government placed over $100 billion in war contracts—more goods on order than the economy had ever produced in a single year. The structure of central control buckled under the strain. An effective priority system was essential, but sometimes more priorities were issued than there were goods to satisfy them. In the confusion the military, who had already gained authority over procurement, demanded control over production. Nelson, backed by the President and Congress, fended off this proposal. In 1943 the WPB's Controlled Materials Plan finally introduced order into the allocation of critical materials.

Though the WPB thus preserved civilian control over production, Roosevelt, in his characteristic style, assigned important areas of authority to other civilian agencies. In December 1942 the War Food Administration assumed direction of the nation's food program. Shortages in oil and rubber brought about the appointment, also outside the WPB, of "czars" with exceptional powers to expedite production. The War Manpower Commission supervised the mobilization of men and women for both civilian and military purposes.

Assembly line at the Vultee plant

And the Office of Scientific Research and Development, under the direction of Dr. Vannevar Bush, conducted scientific and technical mobilization; its scientists and engineers were responsible for short-range rockets (especially the "bazooka"), the proximity fuse, and other remarkable gains in military technology.

In 1942 the proportion of the economy committed to war production grew from 15 to 33 percent. By the end of 1943 federal expenditures for goods and services constituted a sum larger than the total output of the economy when Roosevelt took office a decade earlier. The gross national product grew from $99.7 billion in 1940 to $211.9 billion in 1945 (in 1971 dollars, from about $275 billion to about $425 billion). The WPB continued to be shaken by feuds, both internal and external; Nelson himself was forced out in 1944. Still, in one way or another, the WPB succeeded in releasing and guiding the productive energies of the economy to enable America in a surprisingly short time to outproduce all other nations in the world.

The fight for stabilization. This extraordinary feat was a result of the stimulus provided by government spending to the productive talents of American managers and workers. Federal purchases of goods and services rose from $6 billion in 1940 to $89 billion in 1944. Total federal spending during the war years came to over $320 billion—an amount twice as great as the total of all previous federal spending in the history of the republic.

How was this prodigious expenditure to be paid for? The first resort was to a broadening and deepening of the tax structure. In October 1942, for example, Roosevelt by executive order limited salaries to $25,000 net after taxes. By the end of the war surtaxes were taking away 94 percent of net income in the highest brackets; and people at every level were paying taxes that would have seemed inconceivable a short time before. Total tax revenues in the war years came to about $130 billion. This was far less than Roosevelt had requested, however, and, as a result, the government was able to meet only about 41 percent of the cost of the war on a pay-as-you-go basis—not enough, though a much larger proportion than during the First World War.

The rest of the defense bill was made up by borrowing. In 1944 alone the excess of expenditures over receipts amounted to more than $50 billion—a figure over twice the total size of the accumulated debt in 1941. By the end of the war the national debt had grown to about $280 billion, nearly six times as large as it had been when bombs fell on Pearl Harbor. The budgetary deficits so loudly bewailed in New Deal days now seemed negligible compared to the deficit spending of war. An incidental effect was to prove the Keynesian argument that public spending would end the depression: unemployment rapidly vanished in 1941 and 1942, and old New Deal agencies like the Works Progress Administration gave up the ghost. The problem became, not to find jobs for people, but to find people for jobs.

The tremendous increase in public spending released strong inflationary pressures. The shift from civilian to war production meant that the quantity of goods available for purchase was shrinking just as the quantity of money jingling in people's pockets was increasing. By 1944, for example, the production of civilian automobiles, of washing machines and other consumer durables, of nondefense housing and the like had virtually come to an end. Unless prices were to soar out of sight, means had to be found to hold the volume of spendable money down to the volume of available goods.

One recourse was to fiscal and monetary policies. Taxation was an obvious means of reducing the supply of spendable money in people's hands. The war-bond drive was another way by which the government sought to persuade people to put their money away instead of using it to bid up prices; nearly $100 billion worth of the various series of war bonds were sold in these years. But it was evident from an early point that indirect measures would not be enough to eliminate the "inflationary gap"—the gap, that is, between too few goods and too much money. As early as August 1941 Roosevelt had accordingly established the Office of Price Administration under the direction of Leon Henderson, a hard-driving New Deal economist.

Price control presented one of the toughest problems of war administration. Every economic interest wanted rigid policing of the other fellow's prices but tended to regard attempts to police its own prices as subversive of the free-enterprise system. In April 1942 the OPA imposed a general price freeze, joining to this a system by which necessities of life in short supply—meat, gasoline, tires—were rationed to the consumers through an allotment of coupons. The farm bloc, however, succeeded in gaining exceptions for agricultural prices; and the increase in the cost of food brought about demands for wage increases. The War Labor Board, set up in January 1942, sought to meet this problem by the Little Steel formula of July, permitting wage increases to keep pace with the 15 percent rise in the cost of living since January 1941. In September Roosevelt requested new authority to stabilize the cost of living, including farm prices and wages. The Stabilization Act of 1942 established the Office of Economic Stabilization under the direction of former Supreme Court Justice James F. Byrnes.

Special interests nevertheless continued unabashed guerrilla warfare against price control in their own sectors. The farm bloc was unrelenting in its demand that exceptions be made for itself. John L. Lewis led the United Mine Workers in a fight against the Little Steel formula; for a time in 1943 the government was forced to seize and operate the coal mines. Henderson, who had affronted Congress by the unquenchable zeal of his war against inflation, had been forced to resign in December 1942. But a "hold-the-line" order

in April 1943, followed by a campaign in May to "roll back" food prices, helped bring the price level to a plateau by mid-1943. For the rest of the war the OPA, under the able direction of Chester Bowles, was able to maintain substantial price stability. From October 1942 to the end of the Pacific war, consumers' prices rose only 8.7 percent. For all its unpopularity, especially among businessmen, politicians, and farm leaders, the OPA was one of the war's brilliant successes.

The problem remained of concerting the efforts of various agencies dealing with production and stabilization. In May 1943 Roosevelt set up the Office of War Mobilization and put Byrnes in charge. Employing his judicial and political skill to intervene when operating agencies disagreed, Byrnes did an effective job in pulling together the infinitely ramified strands of America's domestic war effort.

The people behind the lines. The attack on Pearl Harbor ended the isolationist-interventionist debate and caused a surge of national unity. Throughout the war popular confidence in the government remained high. Nevertheless, like any period of war, this was a time of upheaval and anxiety.

To combat the threat of enemy activity within the United States, Roosevelt gave new authority to the Federal Bureau of Investigation, including the power to tap wires in national security cases. Under the astute direction and relentless self-advertisement of J. Edgar Hoover, the FBI had already established itself in congressional and public opinion; its new mandate encouraged it to widen its investigations into the beliefs as well as the deeds of Americans. But the years 1941–45 were not marred by the widespread assaults on civil freedom that had characterized the years 1917–20 (see pp. 576–79). Perhaps because the issues now seemed ideological rather than national, German-Americans and Italian-Americans were not subjected to jingoistic harassment. The tragic exception to this general tolerance was the fate of the over one hundred thousand Japanese-Americans— the Nisei—who were brutally removed from their homes along the Pacific Coast and relocated in internment camps in the interior—an act of national hysteria wholly unjustified and subsequently profoundly regretted.

Of native Americans suspected of sympathy for fascism, some had their publications—for example, Father Coughlin's *Social Justice*—

Nisei evacuees: victims of American brutality

Black power: 1942   *We know that our fate is tied up with the fate of the democratic way of life. And so, out of the depths of our hearts, a cry goes up for the triumph of the United Nations. But we would not be honest with ourselves were we to stop with a call for a victory of arms alone.... Unless this war sounds the death knell to the old Anglo-American empire systems, the hapless story of which is one of exploitation for the profit and power of a monopoly capitalist economy, it will have been fought in vain. Our aim then must not only be to defeat nazism, fascism, and militarism on the battlefield but to win the peace, for democracy, for freedom and the Brotherhood of Man without regard to his pigmentation, land of his birth or the God of his fathers....*

While the March on Washington Movement may find it advisable to form a citizens committee of friendly white citizens to give moral support ... it does not imply that these white citizens ... should be taken into the March on Washington Movement as members. The essential value of an all-Negro movement such as the March on Washington is that it helps to create faith by Negroes in Negroes. It develops a sense of self-reliance with Negroes depending on Negroes in vital matters. It helps to break down the slave psychology and inferiority-complex in Negroes which comes and is nourished with Negroes relying on white people for direction and support. This inevitably happens in mixed organizations that are supposed to be in the interest of the Negro.

From A. Philip Randolph, Keynote Address to the Policy Conference of the March on Washington Movement, September 1942.

---

denied the mails. Toward the end of the war, an effort to convict a number of American fascists in a mass sedition trial miscarried. In the meantime, the Department of Justice had taken effective steps against Nazi agents and organizations. So far as is known, no acts of enemy sabotage were committed in the United States during the war. In the main, Attorney General Francis Biddle strove with success to maintain an atmosphere of moderation.

If war meant anxiety, it also meant opportunity. It uprooted people from familiar settings, exposed them to new experience, changed the direction of their lives. The rise in output and employment was accompanied by a tremendous increase in real income. Wartime tax policies strengthened the tendency toward income redistribution that had begun under the New Deal. The most wealthy 5 percent of Americans had received 30 percent in 1929 and 24 percent in 1941; by 1944 their share was down to 20.7 percent.

Black America benefited particularly from reemployment. The income gap between whites and nonwhites, though still considerable, contracted somewhat during the war years. More important, war became a lever in

the black struggle for equal rights. A government rallying its citizens to fight a master race in Europe could hardly admit the idea of a master race in America. War idealism was thus the Negro's ally when, entering the armed forces or defense industries, he found himself shunted off to menial tasks, often under rigidly segregated conditions. As black bitterness grew, A. Philip Randolph, president of the Brotherhood of Sleeping Car Porters, organized the March on Washington Movement to demand integration in the armed services, equality in employment, and industrial democracy. To persuade Randolph to call off the march, Roosevelt in June 1941 issued his historic executive order 8802 forbidding discrimination in hiring by defense industries and establishing a Fair Employment Practices Commission. The FEPC, its task facilitated by labor shortages, worked effectively during the war to enlarge job opportunities for blacks. Randolph's March on Washington Movement prefigured the later strategy of black protest in several ways—in its mass character, in its reliance on direct, nonviolent action, in its exclusion of whites, and in its advocacy of radical economic policies.

Progress was also made in reducing segregation in the armed services. Very little was achieved, however, in the desegregation of civilian facilities. Wartime conditions increased racial tensions; a shameful series of riots in Detroit in June 1943 resulted in the death of over thirty persons, white and black. But the war years saw striking black advances in a self-reliant assertion of rights. It marked, as James Baldwin later wrote, "a turning point in the Negro's relation to America."

Early politics of the war. Political developments after Pearl Harbor quickly refuted the isolationist prediction that war must doom democracy and free discussion. In Congress the dominating conservative coalition of Republicans and Southern Democrats seized the opportunity to liquidate New Deal agencies that appeared to have lost their function. On the other hand, Congress also provided responsible counsel on many aspects of the war effort—most notably in the Senate War Investigating Committee, which, under the able chairmanship of Harry S. Truman of Missouri, exposed waste and confusion in the defense effort and made many valuable recommendations to the executive.

Relations with Congress presented Roosevelt with difficult problems. The 1942 congressional election took place in an atmosphere suffused with wartime irritations, especially over the OPA's efforts to hold prices and rents down. It resulted in striking Republican gains—ten seats in the Senate, forty-seven in the House. This outcome confirmed the conservative complexion of the Congress and filled the Republicans with high hopes for the presidential election of 1944.

The war in Europe

Beat Hitler first. The manifold activities at home, however, only provided the backdrop for the essential problem of war—victory over the enemy. For the United States there were two enemies—the Japanese, advancing rapidly into Southeast Asia in the weeks after Pearl Harbor; and the European Axis, now engaged in savage warfare on the Russian front and presumably preparing an eventual invasion of England. The immediate problem for the United States was whether to throw its military might against Germany or against Japan.

American military planners had already concluded by March 1941 that, if the United States entered the war, American strategy must be to beat Hitler first. There were several reasons for this decision. For one thing, Germany, with its command of most of the western coast of Europe and its access to the Atlantic, presented a direct threat to the Western Hemisphere; there was particular concern over Axis penetration of Latin America. For another, Germany seemed far more likely than Japan to achieve some revolutionary breakthrough in military technology. In addition, Great Britain was fully engaged in fighting the Axis, while in the Far East, China was both less active in its resistance to Japan and less accessible to outside support.

The Nazi attack on the Soviet Union in June 1941, far from reversing the Europe-first argument, was considered to reinforce it; for the Russo-German war increased both the chance of defeating Germany and the urgency of doing so before Germany conquered Russia. Nor did the Japanese attack on Pearl Harbor shake the American decision. When Winston Churchill came to Washington in December 1941, he found complete agreement on his proposition that "the defeat of Germany, entailing a collapse, will leave Japan exposed to overwhelming force, whereas the defeat of Japan would not by any means bring the World War to an end."

Diverging strategies in Europe. The agreement between the United States and Britain on beating Germany first was not matched, however, by agreement on the best way of doing it. The British strategy was to postpone direct assault on Germany until a combination of naval blockade, aerial bombing, psychological warfare, and military attack on the Axis periphery had sufficiently weakened Germany's capacity to resist. In Churchill this strategy had an exceptionally eloquent and resourceful champion. The British prime minister had long been identified with the circuitous approach to the German foe. "No plan could be more unpromising than the plan of frontal attack," he had written in his history of the First World War. "It is a tale of the torture, mutilation, or extinction of millions of men, and of the sacrifice of all that was best and noblest in an entire generation."

My advice is: As soon as your Chiefs of Staff have completed the plans for the northern offensive to your satisfaction, you should send them by a most trusted messenger and advocate to Churchill and his War Council as the American plan which you propose and intend to go ahead with if accepted by Britain....

And then having done that, you should lean with all your strength on the ruthless rearrangement of shipping allotments and the preparation of landing gear for the ultimate invasion.... It should be pushed with the fever of war action, aimed at a definite date of completion not later than September. The rate of construction of a number of landing barges should not be allowed to lose the crisis of the World War. And yet that is the only objection to the offensive that, after talks with British critics here, I have heard made.

If such decisive action is once taken by you, further successful dispersion of our strength will automatically be terminated. We shall have an affirmative answer against which to measure all such demands; while, on the other hand, so long as we remain without our own plan of offensive, our forces will inevitably be dispersed and wasted.

From Henry L. Stimson, Letter to President Roosevelt, March 1942.

Where the British strategy was to attack the enemy where he was weakest, the American was to attack the enemy where he was strongest. From the American viewpoint, the Churchill plan of "pecking at the periphery" would waste resources without winning victory. As Roosevelt used to observe when Churchill advocated a landing at one or another European point remote from Germany, "All right, but where do we go from there?" The American Joint Chiefs of Staff, ably led by General George C. Marshall, felt that only a massive thrust across the English Channel and France into the heart of Germany would achieve victory. In their view—a view generally shared by Roosevelt—all Anglo-American efforts should be concentrated on establishing a second front in France.

Detour to North Africa. The Soviet Union, in desperate need of relief from the hammer blows of the German army and air force, brought strong pressure for a second front in 1942. But, though the British accepted a cross-Channel invasion in principle, they continued to object in practice. They felt that the Americans underestimated the difficulties of amphibious landings on fortified coasts; they regarded American troops as untried; and they doubted whether the American economy could quickly achieve the production levels necessary to sustain a great invasion. There were particularly ominous shortages in land-

Troops disembarking in North Africa

ing craft and in modern tanks. Accordingly, when the American Joint Chiefs submitted in the spring of 1942 a plan for the invasion of France later that year, the British turned it down.

Still, something had to be done in 1942, if only to reassure the hard-pressed and bitterly disappointed Russians. Churchill consequently proposed an invasion of North Africa. The American Joint Chiefs felt that a North African diversion, by committing Anglo-American forces to a Mediterranean campaign as well as by preempting necessary men and materiel, would delay the invasion of France, perhaps until 1944. But Roosevelt accepted Churchill's argument that an invasion of North Africa in 1942 could be a preliminary to a cross-Channel attack in 1943. In July the decision was made to invade North Africa in the autumn. The operation was placed under the command of General Dwight D. Eisenhower.

On November 8, 1942, Anglo-American forces disembarked at Casablanca in Morocco and at Oran and Algiers in Algeria. The landings achieved tactical surprise. Within short order, local resistance came to an end. But military success raised political problems. The collaborationist regime of Marshal Pétain, established at Vichy and in control of unoccupied southern France, exercised nominal authority in North Africa. The United States, which had maintained diplomatic relations with the Vichy government, had some hope

Across the Channel in '42: the opposition

of winning the support of pro-Vichy officials and military leaders in Algeria and Morocco. Roosevelt and Churchill supposed that General Charles de Gaulle, commander of the Free French in London, would be unacceptable to the North African French, who had sworn oaths of loyalty to Pétain. But the Americans believed that General Henri Giraud, who had recently escaped from a German prison camp, would be exempt from de Gaulle's unpopularity. The situation was further complicated when, by pure accident, the invasion happened to catch in Algiers Admiral Jean François Darlan, a prominent French collaborationist and Pétain's successor-designate.

Giraud's prestige in North Africa turned out to be much overrated. Darlan, on the other hand, proved as ready to collaborate with the Americans in 1942 as he had been with the Germans in 1940; and on November 11 he signed an armistice agreement. As part of the arrangement, Eisenhower recognized Darlan as *de facto* political chief in North Africa—an action that provoked a storm of criticism in England and the United States from those who feared that it inaugurated a policy of making deals with fascists. Roosevelt defended Eisenhower's action as "a temporary expedient, justified solely by the stress of battle." The Darlan deal undoubtedly accelerated the Anglo-American military success in Algeria and Morocco, and Darlan's assassination on December 24 spared Roosevelt and Churchill

what would have been a vexing political embarrassment.

In the meantime, Hitler, after ordering the occupation of Vichy France, rushed German troops by sea and air to Tunisia. Eisenhower promptly advanced into Tunisia from the west, while the British Eighth Army, under the command of General Bernard Montgomery, entered from Tripoli to the east. The Anglo-American forces encountered the brilliant generalship of Field Marshal Rommel, who came to be known as the Desert Fox. Nonetheless, the Anglo-American vise closed inexorably. On May 12, 1943, the Axis troops surrendered. The British and Americans had not only captured or destroyed fifteen Axis divisions; they had regained the Mediterranean for their shipping and had thereby laid open to attack what Churchill called the "soft underbelly" of the Axis.

The Mediterranean or France? "All right, but where do we go from there?" Roosevelt had asked. As the Joint Chiefs of Staff had feared, the British advocated moving on into Sicily and Italy in order to maintain the initiative in the Mediterranean. The Americans reluctantly accepted this logic. The result was the invasion of Sicily in July and of Italy in September. At first, when Mussolini toppled from his dictatorial seat and the new Italian government, under Field Marshal Pietro

The Second World War

Badoglio, made haste to surrender, it seemed as if this campaign would produce quick results. But, despite the Italian collapse, the German forces in Italy put up dogged resistance; and the Italian front soon was marked by the most bitter and bloody fighting of the European war. When Allied progress up the spine of Italy was stopped at Monte Cassino early in 1944, an attempt was made to circumvent the enemy by amphibious landings at Anzio near Rome late in January. But for many weeks Allied troops could not break out of the Anzio beachhead, and Rome itself did not fall for another four months. In the end, the Italian campaign—especially beyond Rome—cost more and achieved less than its proponents had expected.

In the meantime, argument continued over the invasion of France. The British service chiefs still wanted to delay Overlord (the code

Quebec Conferences
Aug. 1943
Sept. 1944

Signing of the
Atlantic Charter
Aug. 1941

Casablanca Conference
Jan. 1943

Yalta Conference
Feb. 1945

Teheran Conference
Nov. 1943

Cairo Conferences
Nov., Dec. 1943

GREENLAND

ICELAND

NORWAY
SWEDEN
FINLAND
Murmansk
Leningrad
Moscow
SOVIET UNION
Stalingrad

GREAT
BRITAIN
London
GERMANY
FRANCE
ITALY
SPAIN
Yalta
TURKEY
SYRIA
IRAQ
Teheran
IRAN
CHINA

Quebec
Argentia

New York
Washington

Casablanca
MOROCCO
TUNISIA
ALGERIA
LIBYA
Cairo
Suez
Canal
EGYPT
SAUDI
ARABIA
INDIA

ATLANTIC

FRENCH
WEST AFRICA
NIGERIA
SUDAN
ETHIOPIA

VENEZUELA
COLOMBIA
ECUADOR
OCEAN
FR. EQ.
AFRICA
BELGIAN
CONGO
KENYA
TANG.

PERU
BOLIVIA
PARAGUAY
BRAZIL
ANGOLA
NO. RHO.
INDIAN
OCEAN
MADAGASCAR
MOZAMBIQUE

CHILE
URUGUAY
ARGENTINA
S.W.
AFR.
BECH.
SO.
RHO.
UNION
OF SOUTH
AFRICA

	Allied nations		Axis powers
	Neutral nations		Area of maximum Axis control
——	Allied supply lines		Area of German submarine operations
– – –	U.S. air supply lines		

name for the cross-Channel operation) for the sake of new adventures in the Mediterranean. But the American Joint Chiefs, with Soviet backing, insisted on a firm commitment to a second front in France. At the end of November 1943, Churchill finally consented to May 1944 as a target date.

The actual invasion, scheduled, as Churchill said, "mainly by the moon and the weather," did not take place until June 6. The Germans,

deceived by elaborate stratagems, did not expect an attack in Normandy. The Allied forces were thus able to consolidate their position and fan out for movement along a larger front. On July 25 General George Patton's Third Army broke through into Brittany. The war in France now developed extraordinary mobility. American and British divisions raced toward Paris, which was liberated on August 25; and by September 13 Allied forces had

Normandy beachhead, June 6, 1944

penetrated deep into Belgium and crossed the German frontier at Aachen.

These developments, on top of the long-sustained Anglo-American air offensive against Germany, made Hitler's situation more desperate every day. From 1942, when the British and American air forces took substantial command of the air, Germany had been subjected to a series of devastating air raids. By the autumn of 1944, Allied air attacks—which by the end of the war amounted to 1.5 million bomber sorties and 2.7 million tons of bombs dropped—were exerting a heavy toll on German production (most essentially, of fighter aircraft), rail and road transportation, and civilian morale. In addition, a Soviet offensive, timed to coincide with the Anglo-American landings in France, was driving the Germans back in the east; indeed, on D-day, there were 165 German divisions on the eastern front as against 131 in the west and south. An attempt on Hitler's life on July 20, 1944, provided heartening evidence of resistance within Germany.

General Montgomery, the top British commander in the west, now urged Eisenhower to concentrate all Allied resources on ending the war by a single decisive thrust into Germany. Eisenhower, looking at Allied port and trucking facilities, concluded that logistic support was lacking for the Montgomery plan. Accordingly, in a controversial decision, he settled instead for a "broad-front" strategy of building up strength along the entire western front in preparation for a general advance into Germany.

Southern France or the Ljublana Gap? A final argument over strategy remained. The Americans had long wished to follow up the invasion of Normandy with troop landings in southern France; Eisenhower regarded this as essential to the invasion of Germany. The

Winning the war in Europe

British wanted to switch the whole operation to the east and mount instead an invasion through Trieste and the Ljublana Gap of Yugoslavia toward Vienna.

It was this debate that gave rise to the subsequent myth that Churchill, wishing to forestall the Soviet advance into Eastern Europe, favored a Balkan invasion rather than a second front in France. Actually Churchill's Mediterranean strategy of 1942–43 was based on military considerations; Churchill himself never claimed—nor has historical research revealed—that this strategy was designed to thwart Soviet expansion. Moreover, Churchill never advocated an invasion of the Balkans, as an alternative to the second front or otherwise. As he wrote Roosevelt in October 1943, "I have never wished to send an army into the Balkans, but only by agents, supplies, and Commandos to stimulate the intense guerrilla prevailing there"—and the guerrillas he wished to stimulate were the Yugoslav partisans under the leadership of the communist Tito. Indeed, the only recorded champion of a second front in the Balkans was Stalin himself, who urged this course on Churchill in 1940. The proposed attack through the Ljublana Gap in 1944—the "stab in the Adriatic armpit," as Churchill called it—would have left most of the Balkans untouched.

By 1944, it is true, Churchill was becoming increasingly concerned over the spread of Soviet power, and a definite object of the Ljublana plan was to beat the Russians to Vienna. The Americans rejected the proposal, partly because of the logistic difficulties presented by an Istrian campaign, partly because of their indifference to postwar political considerations. And so the invasion of southern France took place according to schedule on August 15, 1944. With the fresh Allied advance up the Rhone Valley, the iron ring around Germany was drawing tight.

The war in the Pacific

Holding the line. Though the European theater of war had acknowledged priority, the United States and Great Britain did not neglect the Far East. Pearl Harbor had marked only the beginning of a period of exultant Japanese aggression. ''For three months after the Pearl Harbor attack,'' Admiral Samuel Eliot Morison has written, ''the Pacific was practically a Japanese lake.'' One after another the bastions of western empire fell to the Japanese: Guam, Wake Island, and Hong Kong in December 1941; Singapore in February 1942; Java in March; the Philippines in May. Japanese forces were moving into Burma and threatening advances as far to the west as India and to the south as Australia. Japanese politicians were looking forward to the formation of the Greater East Asia Co-Prosperity Sphere, where Japan would mobilize the power of East Asia behind a wall of air and naval defense.

The Allied forces in the Pacific felt themselves the stepchildren of the war. Still, even when they believed themselves starved for supplies, their situation was by no means hopeless. The Japanese had failed to destroy a single aircraft-carrier at Pearl Harbor; and the American carrier striking force was not only able to secure the South Pacific supply line between Hawaii and Australia but could conduct sporadic harassments of the enemy (including an air raid on Tokyo in April 1942).

Moreover, the Japanese themselves, instead of pausing for consolidation, struck out

The Second World War in the Pacific

on ambitious new programs of conquest in the spring of 1942. Japanese political leaders hoped to extend the sway of the emperor by isolating and perhaps invading Australia; and Admiral Yamamoto, the chief Japanese sea lord, wished to force the American Pacific Fleet into a final engagement before it had a chance to recoup the losses of Pearl Harbor. In May 1942, therefore, the Japanese occupied Tulagi in the Solomon Islands and launched a naval expedition across the Coral Sea toward Port Moresby in Papua, New Guinea. But an American carrier task force intercepted the Japanese ships, and, in an extraordinary battle of carrier-based aircraft, the Americans turned back the enemy. This was the first sea battle in history in which the ships involved exchanged no shots—indeed, did not even come within sight of one another.

The Battle of the Coral Sea marked the high point of Japanese initiative in the south. Yamamoto now shifted his operations to the north-central Pacific. A month later, the bulk of the Japanese navy—some two hundred ships—headed toward Midway Island and the western Aleutians. But the Americans, having broken the Japanese code, were able to anticipate enemy intentions. There followed the decisive naval battle of the war, in which the American fleets, brilliantly led by Admirals Spruance and Fletcher, destroyed four Japanese aircraft-carriers and many other ships and forced the enemy into disorderly retreat. The Japanese never again had sufficient naval air strength to take the long-range offensive.

The road to Tokyo. The threat to communications from Hawaii to Australia remained, however, so long as the Japanese held bases in the Solomons and the Bismarcks. Moreover, the Bismarck Barrier, a chain of small islands, gave the Japanese a powerful defense block athwart the road to Tokyo. Intelligence reports that the Japanese were building an airstrip on the island of Guadalcanal in the Solomons precipitated American action in August 1942. There followed six months of grueling combat in the steaming, fetid jungles of Guadalcanal and in the serene waters around the island. By February 1943 the Japanese abandoned Guadalcanal.

In January 1943 the Joint Chiefs, noting that only 15 percent of Allied resources was applied to the Pacific, argued for enough additional strength to permit the launching of an offensive. The British acquiesced, stipulating

only that Pacific operations should be kept within such limits as would not handicap the war against Germany. The American planners—for the Pacific war was accepted as essentially an American responsibility—now considered the question of the best route to Tokyo.

If European strategy was a compromise between diverging American and British views, Pacific strategy was a compromise between the diverging views of the American army and navy. General Douglas MacArthur, who had been American commander in the Philippines and had been evacuated to Australia early in 1942 to take command of the army in the South Pacific, argued forcefully for an advance on Japan along what he called the "New Guinea-Mindanao Axis"—that is, from the South Pacific through New Guinea to the Philippines and thence to Japan. Admiral Chester Nimitz, on behalf of the navy, contended for an advance through the central Pacific—the Gilbert, Marshall, Caroline, and Mariana Islands—to Formosa and the Chinese coast, and thence to Japan. MacArthur protested that this would be a gravely mistaken diversion of limited resources. But the navy responded persuasively that a single axis of advance would allow the Japanese to concentrate their defensive action. In the end the Joint Chiefs in Washington decided on parallel offensives along both routes.

The invention of new tactical techniques facilitated the American offensive. In March 1943, in the Battle of the Bismarck Sea, General George Kenney's bombers destroyed a Japanese troop convoy headed for New Guinea—an action that dissuaded the Japanese thereafter from attempting to move large bodies of troops within range of Allied air power. As a consequence, American forces could simply bypass the stronger Japanese bases, knowing that the Japanese would not risk large-scale reinforcement, and leave them to wither on the vine. This "leapfrogging" technique became the basic pattern of the American counteroffensive.

By March 1944 Nimitz' forces had leapfrogged at Tarawa and Kwajalein, and MacArthur's forces had broken the Bismarck Barrier. Nimitz was now moving into the Marianas; in June the Pacific Fleet under Admiral Spruance smashed the Japanese navy again in the Battle of the Philippine Sea; MacArthur continued to press along the northwest coast of New Guinea toward the

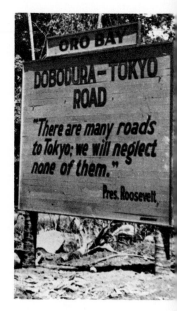

ORO BAY

DOBODURA-TOKYO ROAD

"There are many roads to Tokyo; we will neglect none of them."

Pres. Roosevelt

General Douglas MacArthur: "I have returned"

Philippines. The time was approaching for a final decision about the road to Tokyo.

Luzon or Formosa? MacArthur insisted on the recapture of the Philippines, and especially of Luzon, as the indispensable preliminary. He invoked not only strategic arguments—that Luzon would be a safer staging area for invasion than Formosa (Taiwan)—but political and emotional arguments; as he put the question to Roosevelt, was the President willing "to accept responsibility for breaking a solemn promise to eighteen million Christian Filipinos that the Americans would return?" Admirals King and Nimitz, on the other hand, advocated leapfrogging part or all of the Philippines in the interest of an immediate attack on Formosa. In a conference at Pearl Harbor in July 1944, Roosevelt leaned toward the MacArthur view but did not settle the question in MacArthur's favor until early October.

Once given the signal, MacArthur lost no time. On October 20 he disembarked on the beach at Leyte, saying, "People of the Philippines: I have returned." A few days later, in the Battle of Leyte Gulf, the American navy in the Philippines completed the destruction of Japanese naval striking power; in number of ships engaged, this was the greatest naval battle of all history. MacArthur's troops mean-

while pressed on toward Manila, while Nimitz' forces were making their way toward Japan from the central Pacific. Japan itself was now under a stern naval blockade and ever more devastating air attacks.

The riddle of China. Washington had hoped that China could play a leading role in the war against Japan. Indeed, through the war, Roosevelt, despite Churchill's skepticism, persisted in treating China as if it were a major power. However, the Nationalist regime of Chiang Kai-shek—driven into the interior, cut off from sources of supply, exhausted by four years of war, and demoralized by inflation, intrigue, and graft—was increasingly incapable of serious action.

Keeping China in the war nevertheless remained a major American objective. In 1941 and 1942 the Chinese government, now established in Chungking, received a trickle of supplies flown over the "hump" of the Himalayas from India. Then in 1943 an assortment of Chinese, Indian, and American troops, under the command of General Joseph W. Stilwell, began to construct a road and pipeline across northern Burma to Kunming. Soon Stilwell was sent to Chungking as commander of the American forces in China, with orders to maximize the Chinese contribution to the war against Japan. But, where Stilwell saw only one enemy, he discovered that Chiang Kai-shek saw a second—the increasingly powerful Chinese communists, spreading out from their base in Yenan.

Seeking particularly to mobilize the poverty-stricken and land-hungry peasants, the communists won respect, even among Westerners, as an embodiment of reform, austerity, and discipline. War sharpened the contrast between the self-indulgence of Chungking and the dedication of Yenan. Chiang himself seemed to be paying less and less attention to Japan in his preoccupation with the threat of Mao Tse-tung and his Eighth Route Army. By 1944 four hundred thousand Nationalist troops had been diverted to check the spread of communist influence. Stilwell, eager to get as many Chinese divisions as possible—whatever their politics—into action against the Japanese, soon came to consider Chiang a main obstacle to the fulfillment of his mission.

In June 1944 The Fourteenth Air Force began to attack Japan from Chinese airstrips. This action provoked the Japanese into counterattacking the bomber bases and renewing their offensive against Chungking. Now the difficulties between Stilwell and Chiang came to a head. A brave, narrow, intense man, Stilwell was devoid of diplomatic skill and baffled by the unfathomable depths of Chinese politics. When the Joint Chiefs recommended that the Chinese army be placed under Stilwell's command, Chiang instead demanded his dismissal. Roosevelt complied. The military potential of China was disappearing in the swirl of Chinese civil discord.

The fourth term

Politics as usual. The congressional elections of 1942 brought into office the most conservative Congress Washington had known for a decade. Congressional refusal in the spring of 1943 to continue the National Resources Planning Board was a symbolic rejection of the whole idea of New Deal planning. Passage in June of the Smith-Connally Act over Roosevelt's veto bestowed on a reluctant government new powers to crack down on trade unions in labor disputes. Congress repealed the $25,000 net-salary limitation, liquidated the National Youth Administration, harassed the Farm Security Administration, and sought in a variety of ways to curtail social functions and expenditures.

Roosevelt himself gave ground before the conservative attack. In a press conference in December 1943 he explained that the New Deal had come into existence because the United States was suffering from a grave internal disorder. But in December 1941 the patient had been in a bad external smashup. ''Old Dr. New Deal didn't know 'nothing' about legs and arms. He knew a great deal about internal medicine, but nothing about surgery. So he got his partner, who was an orthopedic surgeon, Dr. Win-the-War to take care of this fellow who had been in this bad accident.'' Roosevelt went on to praise the ministrations of Dr. New Deal but added, ''At the present time, obviously, the principal emphasis, the overwhelming first emphasis should be on winning the war.''

The occupation of the White House by Dr. Win-the-War meant a certain disenchantment in the American liberal community. Though Roosevelt retained the essential confidence of liberals, he was no longer articulating their day-to-day hopes. In their frustration, they listened to other voices. They found consolation in particular in Vice President Henry Wallace, with his celebration of ''the century of the common man,'' and, more surprisingly, in Wendell Willkie, the Republican presidential candidate of 1940 (see p. 669). In the years after his defeat, Willkie had shown himself a political leader generous in disposition and courageous in utterance. His book *One World,* published in 1943 after his trip as a presidential emissary to Britain, the Soviet Union, the Middle East, and China seemed to sum up the best aspirations of America in its sturdy assertion of liberal internationalism.

The campaign of 1944. As the titular leader of the Republican party, Willkie retained hopes of a second presidential nomination in 1944. But his liberal tendencies, on top of a chronic political maladroitness, had estranged most of the leaders of his party. After suffering a bad defeat in the Wisconsin presidential primary in April, he withdrew from the race. Thomas E. Dewey, who had been elected governor of New York in 1942, was now emerging as the favored Republican contender. A young man—he had just passed his forty-second birthday—he had already gained a reputation for executive efficiency and vigor. The Republican convention, meeting in Chicago at the end of June, promptly nominated Dewey on the first ballot. To balance Dewey's growing inclinations toward liberalism and internationalism, Governor John W. Bricker of Ohio, a conservative isolationist, was named for second place.

The Democrats renominated Roosevelt without suffering the trauma of 1940. ''For myself, I do not want to run,'' he wrote the chairman of the Democratic National Committee in July. ''All that is within me cries to go back to my home on the Hudson. . . . But as a good soldier . . . I will accept and serve.'' The struggle was over the vice-presidential nomination. Wallace, with the ardent support of the labor-liberal wing of the party, sought renomination. But the Democratic bosses opposed him, and, though Roosevelt said he ''personally'' would vote for Wallace if a delegate, it was evident that he was not insisting on Wallace's renomination. Roosevelt's personal preference seems to have been James

Dewey in California, 1944

F. Byrnes. When Ed Flynn of New York and Sidney Hillman of the Amalgamated Clothing Workers vetoed Byrnes, Roosevelt said he would be "very glad to run" with either Senator Harry S Truman of Missouri or Justice William O. Douglas of the Supreme Court. The contest narrowed down to Truman and Wallace, and Truman won on the third ballot.

The campaign was overshadowed by the war. The initial restraint of Dewey's speeches failed to stir the electorate. He stepped up the harshness of his attack, but his main achievement was to force Roosevelt himself into the arena. An uproariously successful speech before the Teamsters Union in Washington on September 23 showed that the old campaigner had lost none of his magic. In October he sought to meet doubts about his health by riding around New York City all day in an open car through pouring rain. In the meantime, he spoke with eloquence about the need for liberalism and internationalism in the postwar world. On November 7 Roosevelt received 25.6 million popular and 432 electoral votes as against 22 million and 99 for Dewey. The Democrats lost one seat in the Senate, gained twenty in the House, and captured five governorships. The election was a categorical confirmation of Roosevelt as America's chosen leader for the peace.

The diplomacy of coalition

The question of war aims. Even before Pearl Harbor Roosevelt had outlined his broad ideas on the postwar settlement. In his message to Congress on January 6, 1941, he said that the United States looked forward to a world founded upon "four essential human freedoms—freedom of speech and expression, freedom of worship, freedom from want, freedom from fear." In August of the same year, the Atlantic Charter (see p. 675) further particularized the American conception of the postwar world, laying stress on national self-determination, equal access to trade and raw materials, and a lasting peace to be achieved through a permanent system of general security. On January 1, 1942, twenty-six nations (led by the United States, Britain, the Soviet Union, and China) signed a joint declaration subscribing to the Atlantic Charter, pledging their full resources to victory, promising not to make a separate peace, and dedicating themselves to "defend life, liberty, independence, and religious freedom, and to preserve human rights and justice in their own lands as well as in other lands." Roosevelt called this a "declaration by United Nations," and his phrase was employed thereafter to describe the grand alliance.

In practice, three of the United Nations— the United States, Britain, and the Soviet Union—were more important than the rest. The United States and Britain, with common traditions and interests, had little difficulty in establishing partnership. Roosevelt and Churchill regarded each other with mutual respect and delight and were almost immediately on intimate terms. The formation of the Anglo-American Combined Chiefs of Staff in December 1941 guaranteed close military coordination; combined boards were subsequently set up in other fields. Friction, of course, was not entirely eliminated. There were persistent differences over European strategy, and Churchill quickly made it clear that he had no intention of applying the Atlantic Charter to British possessions. "We mean to hold our own," he said. "I have not become the King's First Minister in order to preside over the liquidation of the British Empire." Nonetheless, disagreements were held within a framework of reciprocal confidence.

With regard to the postwar world, Churchill, though by instinct a balance-of-power man, was prepared to go a considerable distance with Roosevelt's determination to make the United Nations the keystone of a peace system. Renewing the Wilsonian dream, Roosevelt declared that peace must "spell the end of the system of unilateral action, the exclusive alliances, the spheres of influence, the balances of power, and all the other expedients that have been tried for centuries—and have always failed." A reversion to these bad old principles, the Americans believed, would create the conditions for future wars; it would also mean the repudiation of the Atlantic Charter, the Four Freedoms, and the universalist values for which the war had presumably been fought. So, by this universalist view, all nations had an equal interest in all the affairs of the globe (except Latin America, where the United States deemed itself more equal than the rest). International prosperity was to be assured by the reduction of barriers to an expanding world trade, and the security of each nation was to be provided for by the universal peace organization, the United Nations, under the leadership of the Big Four—America, Britain, Russia, and China.

The Russians, on the other hand, saw the world only in terms of spheres of influence and balances of power. They placed little confidence in the United Nations. Their physical safety, as they read their bitter historical experience, demanded the absolute guarantee that all states along the Russian border in Eastern Europe should have "friendly governments," by which they meant governments reliably subservient to Moscow. They had no intention of allowing other states a role in Eastern Europe. In 1939 the Soviet-Nazi pact had enabled Russia to begin to fulfill part of what it considered its security requirements through the acquisition of the Baltic states, Karelian Finland, and eastern Poland. In November 1940 Moscow had pressed further demands on Hitler—a free hand in Finland, predominance in Romania and Bulgaria, bases in the Dardanelles. After the German attack, Stalin hoped to gain from the West what Hitler had not dared yield him.

These were traditional Russian objectives not dependent on ideology. But ideology intensified the possibilities of discord. The Soviet view, grounded in the Marxist-Leninist analysis of history, excluded the idea of long-term peace between communist and capitalist states. The very existence of the United States as the citadel of capitalism was, by definition, a deadly threat to the security of the Soviet Union; even the existence of independent communist states, like Yugoslavia, turned out to be intolerable to Stalin. While short-term accommodations with capitalism might be undertaken for tactical reasons, such arrangements would at best be an armed truce. But Stalin was not necessarily the helpless prisoner of this ideology. He saw himself less as the disciple of Marx and Lenin than as their fellow prophet. Sensing that Stalin was the only force capable of overcoming Stalinism, Roosevelt placed great emphasis on his personal relations with the Soviet leader.

So long, however, as Russian survival depended on the establishment of a second front, Moscow's purposes, whether strategic or ideological, were muted. Thus the Soviet government adhered to the Atlantic Charter (though with a reservation about adapting its principles to "the circumstances, needs, and historic peculiarities of particular countries") and acquiesced in the British refusal, under American pressure, to recognize the Soviet conquest of the Baltic republics. But Stalin's basic hope, as expressed in a proposal to Britain at the end of 1941, was for a straight sphere-of-influence deal. The British foreign secretary, Anthony Eden, noting Cordell Hull's Wilsonian opposition to this approach, expressed the British attitude: "Soviet policy is amoral; United States policy is exaggeratedly moral, at least where non-American interests are concerned."

The early wartime conferences. It soon became evident that the diplomacy of coalition required not only constant communication among the nations but periodic face-to-face meetings among their leaders. Thus Churchill followed his Washington visit in December 1941–January 1942 with a visit to Moscow in August, where he explained to an angry Stalin the reasons for the postponement of the second front ("Now they know the worst," he wrote Roosevelt, "and having made their protest are entirely friendly; this in spite of the fact that this is their most anxious and agonizing time").

The successes in North Africa at the end of 1942 opened a new phase of the war and emphasized the need for a conference among all three leaders. Stalin, however, felt that he could not leave the Soviet Union; so Roosevelt and Churchill met with their staffs at Casablanca on the Atlantic coast of Morocco in January 1943. The Casablanca Conference laid plans for future military action in the Mediterranean. Roosevelt and Churchill also sought, with little success, to unite the anti-Vichy French by bringing about a reconciliation between General de Gaulle and General Giraud. The main contribution of Casablanca, however, was the doctrine of "unconditional surrender."

By unconditional surrender Roosevelt meant no more than the surrender by Axis governments without conditions—that is, without assurance of the survival of the political leadership that had brought on the war. "It does not mean," he explained at Casablanca, "the destruction of the population of Germany, Italy, or Japan, but it does mean the destruction of the philosophies in those countries which are based on conquest and the subjugation of other people." Uncondi-

The return from Casablanca, 1943: the decision was for unconditional surrender

tional surrender was not a last-minute improvisation. It had been discussed in the State Department since the preceding spring and had been raised with Churchill (who, in turn, raised it with the British War Cabinet) before the press conference at which it was announced. The doctrine was designed partly to overcome misgivings generated by the Anglo-American willingness to deal with Darlan but even more to prevent Hitler from breaking up the Allied coalition by playing off one side against the other. The fear that the Soviet Union might seek a separate peace with Germany haunted British and American policy-makers in 1942–43, and unconditional surrender seemed the best insurance against such an eventuality.

Critics have subsequently claimed that unconditional surrender stiffened Axis resistance and prolonged the war. While this argument has an initial plausibility, it is not easy to substantiate with regard to the European war. Thus unconditional surrender had no effect at all in delaying the Italian surrender. In the case of Germany, no one seems to have been deterred from surrendering who would have surrendered otherwise, and up to the last moment such Nazi leaders as Goering and Himmler were sure they could work out their own deals with the Allies. An associated argument that unconditional surrender played into the hands of the communists seems odd in view of the fact that Stalin tried hard in 1944 to persuade Roosevelt and Churchill to modify the doctrine.

From Big Two to Big Three. Roosevelt and Churchill met again in Washington May 1943, and in Quebec in August. Both meetings dealt mainly with Anglo-American military questions. The Soviet Union still remained outside the conference circuit until October, when Cordell Hull and Anthony Eden journeyed to Moscow to pave the way for a meeting of the Big Three.

Relations between the Soviet Union and its western allies were now somewhat ambivalent. On the one hand, a temporary recession of ideology was evident when Stalin, in order to rally his people against the invader, replaced the appeal of Marxism with that of nationalism. "We are under no illusions that they are fighting for us," he once observed to Averell Harriman, the American ambassador. "They are fighting for Mother Russia." In May 1943 the Comintern, the instru-

mentality of communist revolution, was dissolved.

On the other hand, shadows of future problems were casting themselves ahead, especially in the liberated nations. The Soviet Union protested its exclusion from the Allied Control Commission for Italy. It had made clear its disinclination to relinquish the part of Poland it had seized in 1939, and in April 1943 it broke off relations with the Polish government-in-exile in London because the Poles asked the International Red Cross to investigate German charges that the Russians had massacred several thousand Polish officers at Katyn. In Yugoslavia, the communist partisans, led by Marshal Tito, were already in conflict with a monarchist resistance movement of Chetniks led by General Mihailovich. A similar feud between communist and noncommunist guerrillas divided the resistance movement in Greece.

But such events remained in the background when the foreign secretaries met in October. Molotov, the Soviet foreign secretary, went agreeably along with a statement of pieties advocated by Hull and soon issued as the Declaration of Moscow; this included affirmation of "the necessity of establishing at the earliest practicable date a general international organization . . . for the maintenance of international peace." The Moscow Conference also established the European Advisory Commission to plan for German collapse.

The next step was the long-delayed meeting of the three leaders, arranged for Teheran in late November. This was preceded by a separate conference in Cairo where Roosevelt and Churchill met with Chiang Kai-shek; Stalin did not take part because Russia was not in the Far Eastern war. The Cairo Declaration promised to strip Japan of its conquests, to free Korea, and to return Manchuria and Taiwan to China. The Teheran meeting concentrated on military problems, but it also considered the future of Germany, problems in Eastern Europe and the Far East, and the shape of the postwar peace system. "We came here with hope and determination," the three leaders wrote in the Declaration of Teheran. "We leave here, friends in fact, in spirit and in purpose."

Postwar planning. More progress was made in defining the structure of the future international organization when the Allies met at

Dumbarton Oaks in Washington in August–September 1944. But the creation of broad frameworks for postwar collaboration did not solve the concrete problems of the postwar settlement. The fate of Germany posed especially perplexing questions. All members of the Big Three had played at one time or another with notions of German dismemberment; this approach seemed to prevail as late as Teheran. But when the European Advisory Commission took over, dismemberment receded into the background. The EAC concentrated instead on determining the zones of Allied occupation. In the end, Britain took the northwestern zone, America the southwestern, and Russia the eastern. Berlin, though situated in the Soviet zone, was to be jointly held; the question of access to Berlin was left, on military advice, to the commanders in the field.

As for the German economy, the most drastic proposals came from the United States Treasury Department in August 1944. Secretary Morgenthau urged both territorial transfers and partition; in addition, he recommended the dismantling of German heavy industry and the transformation of Germany into an agricultural state. For a moment Roosevelt fell in with the Morgenthau plan. Even Churchill accepted it briefly during the second Quebec Conference in September. But in a few weeks this scheme dropped by the wayside.

Growing doubts about Soviet policy compounded the uncertainty over the future. The Polish question was more acute than ever. Churchill, in an effort to restore the position of the Polish government-in-exile in London, had been urging that government to accept Soviet territorial demands, including the Curzon line to the east and (in compensation) the Oder-Neisse line to the west; in November 1944 the British government pledged support for the Oder-Neisse line even if the United States refused to go along. But Stalin, who saw Poland as "the corridor for attack on Russia," considered the Polish question as "one of life and death" and refused to accept the London regime. In August the Polish Home Army, whose affiliations were with London, set off a revolt against the Germans in Warsaw. The Red Army, a few miles outside the city, declined to aid the uprising; the Soviet Union would not even permit planes carrying supplies to Warsaw from the west to land on Russian soil. This seemed a calculated attempt to destroy noncommunist Poles. In addition, the Soviet Union was setting up a group of procommunists in Lublin as the nucleus of a postwar Polish government. And, citing the Anglo-American example in Italy, the Russians, after the surrender of Bulgaria, denied the western Allies any role in the Bulgarian Control Commission.

In October Churchill paid another visit to Moscow. His effort to bring about a reconciliation between the London and Lublin Poles failed; but he and Stalin agreed on a scheme for southeastern Europe, according to which in the period after liberation Britain would recognize Russia's predominant interest in Romania, Bulgaria, and Hungary, and Russia would recognize Britain's predominant interest in Greece, with Yugoslavia split fifty-fifty. Roosevelt went along with this only as a temporary wartime arrangement, but Stalin and perhaps Churchill too probably expected it to register postwar realities.

Triumph and tragedy

The Big Three at Yalta. Roosevelt's reelection in November 1944 found the Allied forces pressing hard down the last mile to victory. But bloodshed was far from over. With Eisenhower's forces deployed along the length of the Siegfried line, the Germans saw an opportunity in December 1944 to launch an attack in the Ardennes Forest. The desperate German offensive resulted in some early breakthroughs, but the Americans held at Bastogne, and, after weeks of severe fighting, the Battle of the Bulge came to an end in January. On the other side of the world, the Japanese continued their resistance. Manila was not liberated until February 1945; and the forces of Admiral Nimitz coming in from the central Pacific had to fight every step of the way before they could gain such islands to the south of Japan as Iwo Jima (in February) and Okinawa (in April).

The approach of victory did not simplify the political problems of the triumphant coalition. In December communist resistance groups revolted against the British-backed provisional government of newly liberated Greece. Though Stalin, respecting the October agree-

Yalta, 1945: hopeful assumptions were soon to be falsified

the population and pledged to the earliest possible establishment through free elections of governments responsive to the will of the people.'' With regard to Germany, the conference postponed decisions on dismemberment and on future frontiers, endorsed the EAC provisions for zonal occupation (adding a zone for France) and for an Allied Control Council, and evaded a Soviet demand of $20 billion for German reparations while conceding the figure as a ''basis for discussion.''

The Yalta discussions also dealt with the Far East, where the American Joint Chiefs were anxious to secure from Stalin a precise commitment about entering the war. While Stalin had said vaguely in 1943 that the Soviet Union would declare war on Japan after the defeat of Germany, some feared that Russia would let the United States undertake a costly invasion of Japan and then move into Manchuria and China at the last minute to reap the benefits of victory. Moreover, the military estimated that the invasion of Japan, scheduled for the spring of 1946, might cost over a million casualties to American forces alone —another reason for desiring early Soviet participation. In discussions with Roosevelt, Stalin agreed to declare war on Japan within two or three months after the surrender of Germany on condition that the Kurile Islands and southern Sakhalin be restored to Russia and that the commercial interest of the Soviet Union in Dairen and its rail communications be recognized. When Roosevelt obtained the assent of Chiang Kai-shek to these measures, the Soviet Union would agree ''that China shall retain full sovereignty in Manchuria'' and would conclude a treaty of friendship and alliance with the Chiang Kai-shek government.

A third topic at Yalta was the organization of the United Nations. Here the Soviet Union accepted American proposals on voting procedure that it had opposed at Dumbarton Oaks and agreed that a United Nations conference should be called at San Francisco in April to prepare the charter for a permanent organization. With British support, the Russians also secured votes in the General Assembly for Byelorussia and the Ukraine. Roosevelt attached great importance to the apparent Soviet willingness to collaborate in a structure of international order and doubtless supposed that the United Nations would provide the means of remedying the omissions or errors of the various summit conferences.

Roosevelt and Churchill returned from Yalta

ment, made no objection to Churchill's military intervention in Greece, the fact that local communists had taken such initiative seemed a poor omen. The Polish tangle showed no signs of unraveling. The fate of Germany remained undecided. The future of Eastern Europe and the Far East was still swathed in obscurity. The persistence of these problems argued for another meeting of the Big Three. They met in a conference at Yalta in the Crimea in February 1945.

Some of the decisions taken at Yalta pertained to Europe. The most critical of these had to do with the liberated nations of Eastern Europe. Roosevelt and Churchill rejected Stalin's proposal that they accept the Lublin government in Poland. Instead, the three leaders agreed on a reorganization of the Polish government to include leaders from abroad—this provisional government to be ''pledged to the holding of free and unfettered elections as soon as possible.'' For liberated Europe in general, the conference promised ''interim governmental authorities broadly representative of all democratic elements in

The Premier of the Union of Soviet Socialist Republics, the Prime Minister of the United Kingdom and the President of the United States of America ... jointly declare their mutual agreement to concert during the temporary period of instability in liberated Europe the policies of their three governments....

The establishment of order in Europe and the re-building of national economic life must be achieved by processes which will enable the liberated peoples to destroy the last vestiges of Nazism and Fascism and to create democratic institutions of their own choice. This is a principle of the Atlantic Charter—the right of all peoples to choose the form of government under which they will live—the restoration of sovereign rights and self-government to those people who have been forcibly deprived of them by the aggressor nations.

To foster the conditions in which liberated peoples may exercise these rights, the three governments will jointly assist the people in any European liberated state... (a) to establish conditions of internal peace; (b) to carry out emergency measures for the relief of distressed peoples; (c) to form interim governmental authorities broadly representative of all democratic elements in the population and pledged to the earliest possible establishment through free elections of governments responsive to the will of the people; and (d) to facilitate where necessary the holding of such elections....

When, in the opinion of the three governments, conditions ... make such action necessary, they will immediately consult together on the measures necessary to discharge the joint responsibilities set forth in this declaration.

From Declaration on Liberated Europe, Yalta Conference, February 1945.

The Big Three on Eastern Europe

well satisfied. Churchill told the House of Commons:

> The impression I brought back . . . is that Marshal Stalin and the Soviet leaders wish to live in honourable friendship and equality with the Western democracies. I feel also that their word is their bond. I know of no Government which stands to its obligations, even in its own despite, more solidly than the Russian Soviet Government.

It is true that during the war the Soviet government had discharged its military commitments with commendable promptitude. The Yalta agreements, however, represented the first experiment in postwar political collaboration. Here, as Churchill himself later wrote, "Our hopeful assumptions were soon to be falsified. Still, they were the only ones possible at the time." If the United States and Britain had proceeded at Yalta on the opposite assumption—that is, of Soviet postwar hostility—before sufficient evidence was in to convince the world of the correctness of that assumption, then the onus for starting the Cold War would have rested on the West.

After the war right-wing critics wrote that Roosevelt and Churchill had perpetrated a "betrayal" at Yalta, selling Eastern Europe and China "down the river" in a vain effort to "appease" Stalin. The Yalta text makes it hard to sustain such charges. Had the agreements been kept, Eastern Europe would have had freely elected democratic governments and Chiang Kai-shek would have been confirmed in control of China and Manchuria. Far from facilitating Soviet expansion, Stalin had to abandon his pledges in order to achieve his purposes. Communism, moreover, gained no territory as a result of Yalta (except the Kurile Islands) that was not already, or about to be, in communist hands as a result of military operations—and such operations could have been checked only by countervailing force from the West.

In more recent years left-wing critics have made opposite charges: that Stalin conceded more at Yalta than did Roosevelt and Churchill, that it was America which failed to fulfill its agreements after Yalta, and that behind American policy was an aggressive determination to dominate the world, promote

Allied victory in Europe

Area controlled by Axis May 8, 1945

counterrevolution and, in particular, make Eastern Europe and the Far East safe for American capitalism. Again the Yalta documents fail to sustain such charges. Roosevelt remarked at Yalta that "two years would be the limit" for keeping American troops in Europe; and the evidence suggests that the western Allies would have been wholly satisfied with an Eastern Europe composed of nations friendly to Russia and (in the words of a State Department analysis) "in favor of far-reaching economic and social reforms, but not, however, in favor of a left-wing totalitarian regime to achieve these reforms."

Victory in Europe. For the Soviet Union, cooperation with noncommunists had been a response to the rise of Nazism. The Yalta Conference, taking place in the shadow of the Ardennes counteroffensive, reflected the still dangerous Nazi military threat. But the pic-

ture began to alter rapidly. A fortnight after Yalta, the United States Ninth Army had reached the Rhine at Düsseldorf. With the end of the war in sight, the Soviet need for wartime cooperation was disappearing: it was now time to begin the postwar struggle for Europe. Within a few weeks the Soviet Union took swift action in Romania and Poland to frustrate the Yalta pledges of political freedom. Stalin himself opened up a political offensive against the West, charging that the United States and Britain were engaged in separate peace negotiations with Germany. Roosevelt replied with indignation that he deeply resented these "vile misrepresentations."

At the end of March 1945 Roosevelt cabled Churchill that he was "watching with anxiety and concern the development of the Soviet attitude"; this attitude portended danger not only for immediate issues, but for "future world cooperation." The President sent stern warnings to the Soviet leader and on April 6 told Churchill, "We must not permit anybody to entertain a false impression that we are afraid. Our Armies will in a very few days be in a position that will permit us to become 'tougher' than has heretofore appeared advantageous to the war effort." But Roosevelt, worn out by long years of terrible responsibility, was reaching the end. On April 12 he died of a massive cerebral hemorrhage, as truly a casualty of war as any man who died in battle. The world greatly mourned his loss.

These ominous political developments put military problems in a new context. As the Anglo-American armies plunged ahead into Germany, Churchill argued in March and April that they should race the Russians to Berlin. "From a political standpoint," he said, "we should march as far east into Germany as possible." But General Eisenhower replied, "I regard it as militarily unsound . . . to make Berlin a major objective." The imperative consideration, in the view of the American Joint Chiefs, was the destruction of the German armed forces; and this, Eisenhower believed (incorrectly, as it turned out), required the pursuit of the remaining German troops to a supposed last stand in the south.

A month later, Churchill renewed his pleading, this time in connection with Prague. The Allied liberation of Prague, he said, might "make the whole difference to the postwar situation in Czechoslovakia." He went on to propose that Allied forces remain as far east as they could until Soviet Russia clarified its intentions with regard to Poland and Germany. Harry S Truman, who had succeeded to the American Presidency, hesitated at suggestions for deeper American involvement in Central Europe, partly because of a fear of prejudicing future Soviet cooperation with the United Nations, partly because of the need for redeploying American troops to the Pacific. He accordingly treated the problem as a tactical one to be decided by the commander in the field. Eisenhower, for his part, declined to abandon strictly military criteria in the absence of orders from above. Though he could have put American troops into Prague far in advance of the Red Army, he refused to do so. It is by no means clear that Churchill's plan would have basically changed the postwar balance in Europe. But it seems evident that the American generals, as General Omar Bradley later wrote, "looked naïvely on this British inclination to complicate the war with political foresight and non-military objectives."

By now events in Europe were rushing to climax. Hitler's thousand-year *Reich,* racked by months of Allied bombing and now overrun by Allied armies from both west and east, was falling to pieces. The German dictator himself took refuge in his bunker in Berlin and on April 30 committed suicide. On May 3 the process of piecemeal German surrender began, culminating in a final ceremony of unconditional surrender at Eisenhower's headquarters in Rheims on May 7. As Churchill later wrote, the end of hostilities was "the signal for the greatest outburst of joy in the history of mankind." He added somberly that he himself moved amid cheering crowds "with an aching heart and a mind oppressed by forebodings."

Victory in the Far East. While the European war was coming to its troubled end, American forces continued to make steady progress in the Pacific. But Japanese resistance grew every day more fanatical. The use of kamikaze suicide planes and the last-ditch fighting in Iwo Jima and Okinawa seemed to confirm the horrendous American estimates of casualties to be expected in an invasion of the homeland. Within civilian Japan, though, sensible people recognized that the war was irretrievably lost.

In the meantime, an extraordinary new factor entered into American calculations. In 1939 the scientist Albert Einstein had called Roosevelt's attention to the possibility of using

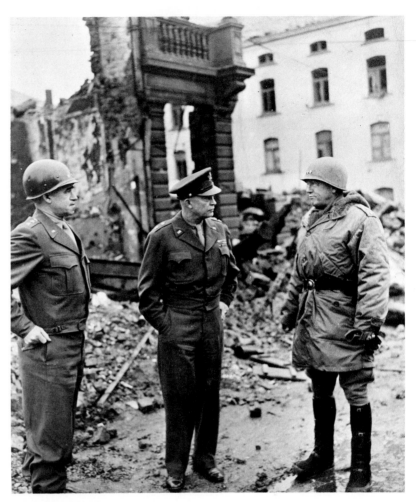

Bastogne, 1945: Generals Bradley, Eisenhower, and Patton

atomic energy for military purposes. In the next years the government sponsored a secret $2 billion operation known as the Manhattan Project to attempt the building of an atomic bomb. A brilliant group of physicists, working under the direction of J. Robert Oppenheimer in Los Alamos, New Mexico, steadily broke down the incredibly complex scientific and technological problems involved in the production of the weapon. On April 25, 1945, Secretary of War Stimson could tell President Truman, "Within four months we shall in all probability have completed the most terrible weapon ever known in human history, one bomb of which could destroy a whole city."

The next question was how and when this frightful weapon should be employed. On June 1 a special committee recommended to the President that the bomb be used against Japan as soon as possible. Many Manhattan

The atomic bomb: a plea for restraint

The development of nuclear power not only constitutes an important addition to the technological and military power of the United States, but creates grave political and economic problems for the future of this country.

Nuclear bombs cannot possibly remain a "secret weapon" at the exclusive disposal of this country for more than a few years. The scientific facts on which their construction is based are well known to scientists of other countries. Unless an effective international control of nuclear explosives is instituted, a race for nuclear armaments is certain to ensue following the first revelation of our possession of nuclear weapons to the world. Within ten years other countries may have nuclear bombs.... In the war to which such an armaments race is likely to lead, the United States, with its agglomeration of population and industry in comparatively few metropolitan districts, will be at a disadvantage compared to nations whose population and industry are scattered over large areas.

We believe that these considerations make the use of nuclear bombs for an early unannounced attack against Japan inadvisable. If the United States were to be the first to release this new means of indiscriminate destruction upon mankind, we would sacrifice public support throughout the world, precipitate the race for armaments, and prejudice the possibility of reaching international agreement on the future control of such weapons.

From the Committee on Social and Political Implications, Report to the Secretary of War, June 1945.

The atomic bomb: the President's view

I realize the tragic significance of the atomic bomb.

Its production and its use were not lightly undertaken by this Government. But we knew that our enemies were on the search for it. We know now how close they were to finding it. And we know the disaster which would come to this nation, and to all peaceful nations, to all civilizations, if they had found it first.

That is why we felt compelled to undertake the long and uncertain and costly labor of discovery and production.

We won the race of discovery against the Germans.

Having found the bomb we have used it. We have used it against those who attacked us without warning at Pearl Harbor, against those who have starved and beaten and executed American prisoners of war, against those who have abandoned the pretense of obeying international laws of warfare. We have used it in order to shorten the agony of war, in order to save the lives of thousands and thousands of young Americans.

We shall continue to use it until we completely destroy Japan's power to make war. Only a Japanese surrender will stop us.

From Harry S Truman, Radio Address, August 1945.

Project scientists, intimately aware of the ghastly character of the weapon, opposed this recommendation, favoring a preliminary demonstration to the world in a desert or on a barren island. But this course was rejected, partly because of the fear that the bomb might not go off, partly because only two bombs would be available by August and it seemed essential to reserve them for direct military use.

Within Japan, a new government was looking for a way out. In July it requested Soviet mediation to bring the war to an end, though it added, "So long as the enemy demands unconditional surrender, we will fight as one man." Moscow was cold to this request while

Hiroshima: the decision was tragic

Stalin departed for a new Big Three meeting at Potsdam, near Berlin. At the same time, the American government, following the Japanese peace explorations through decoded cable intercepts, came to the conclusion that the best way to hasten the end of the war would be to issue a solemn plea to the Japanese to surrender before it was too late. This warning was embodied somewhat cryptically in a declaration issued at Potsdam by Truman and Clement Attlee, who had succeeded Churchill as British prime minister, urging the Japanese to give up or face "the utter devastation of the Japanese homeland." The Japanese government was inclined to accept this ultimatum, but the military leaders angrily disagreed. On July 28 the Japanese prime minister, in a statement designed for domestic consumption, pronounced the Potsdam Declaration "unworthy of public notice."

Truman had already been informed while at Potsdam that the first bomb test in New Mexico on July 17 had been a triumphant success. The rejection of the Potsdam Declaration now convinced him that the militarists were in control of Tokyo and that there was no point in delaying the use of the bomb against Japan. On August 6, in a blinding flash of heat and horror, the first atomic bomb fell on Hiroshima, killing nearly one hundred thousand people, fatally injuring another hundred thousand through blast or radiation, and reducing the city to rubble.

Even after this appalling blow the Japanese military vetoed the civilian desire to accept the Potsdam Declaration. Two days after Hiroshima, the Red Army invaded Manchuria and, on the third day, with no word from Tokyo, the Americans dropped a second bomb on Nagasaki. In Tokyo the military still objected to unconditional surrender. It finally required the personal intervention of the emperor to overcome their opposition. With Japanese acceptance of Potsdam conditioned on the preservation of the imperial prerogatives, the act of surrender took place on September 2, 1945.

The decision to drop the atomic bomb was the most tragic in the long course of American history. It is true that only so drastic a step would have achieved unconditional surrender so rapidly. On the other hand, thoughtful observers have wondered whether the American government, with Japan essentially beaten and on the verge of capitulation, had exhausted all the possible alternatives before at last having recourse to the bomb—whether there were not resources of negotiation or demonstration that, even at the cost of prolonging the war, should have been first attempted, with the bomb held in reserve as a weapon of last resort. Here perhaps the doctrine of unconditional surrender had terrible consequences. Certainly, though the bomb terminated the war, it also placed America for many years in an ambiguous position before the world as the only nation to have employed so horrible a weapon.

Victory thus came—but in a way that converted triumph into tragedy. The Second World War ended. More than 25 million persons, soldiers and civilians, had died during the five years. Sixteen million Americans— more than 10 percent of the population—had been under arms; total casualties amounted to over a million, with nearly three hundred thousand deaths in battle. Now, in the autumn of 1945, the world stood on the threshold of a new epoch in human history—an epoch incalculably rich in hazards and potentialities. With apprehensive steps, mankind was entering the atomic age.

Suggestions for reading

THE SECOND WORLD WAR: THE HOME FRONT

R. E. Sherwood, *Roosevelt and Hopkins* (1948, rev. ed., 1950), remains the most vivid account of Roosevelt as a war-leader; it should be supplemented by J. M. Burns' valuable study, *Roosevelt: The Soldier of Freedom* (1970). For war mobilization, see the Bureau of the Budget, *The United States at War* (1946); Eliot Janeway, *The Struggle for Survival** (1951); and H. M. Somers, *Presidential Agency: OWMR* (1950); on price control, L. V. Chandler, *Inflation in the United States, 1940–1948* (1951); Chester Bowles, *Promises to Keep* (1971); and, for the penetrating reflections of a leading controller, J. K. Galbraith, *Theory of Price Control** (1952). The mobilization of science and technology is incisively depicted in J. P. Baxter, III, *Scientists Against Time** (1946); R. G. Hewlett and O. E. Anderson, Jr., *The New World* (1962), is authoritative on the development of the atomic bomb. Volume III of J. M. Blum, *From the Morgenthau Diaries: Years of War, 1941–1945* (1967), throws light on a variety of issues.

For American society in wartime, see F. E. Merrill, *Social Problems on the Home Front* (1948); Jack Goodman, ed., *While You Were Gone: A Report on Wartime Life in the United States* (1946); Richard Polenberg, *War and Society: The United States, 1941–1945* (1972); and Richard Polenberg, ed., *America at War: The Home Front, 1941–1945** (1968). Francis Biddle provides thoughtful discussion of the civil-liberties problems he faced as Attorney General in *Democratic Thinking and the War* (1944) and in his distinguished memoir *In Brief Authority* (1962). For black Americans, see Herbert Garfinkel, *When Negroes March* (1959); Louis Ruchames, *Race, Jobs and Politics: The Story of FEPC* (1953); R. M. Dalfiume, *Desegregation of the United States Armed Forces* (1969); and, of course, the magistral study by Gunnar Myrdal, *An American Dilemma** (1944, rev. ed., 1962).

THE SECOND WORLD WAR: MILITARY OPERATIONS

A. Russell Buchanan, *The United States and World War II,* 2 vols.* (1964), is a survey. For able analyses of American strategy, see S. E. Morison, *Strategy and Compromise** (1958); Louis Morton, *Strategy and Command* (1962); K. R. Greenfield, ed., *Command Decisions* (1959); and K. R. Greenfield, *American Strategy in World War II: A Reconsideration** (1963). The role of the American services is intensively portrayed in three multivolume series: Office of the Chief of Military History, *The United States Army in World War II;* S. E. Morison, *History of United States Naval Operations in World War II* (summarized in *The Two-Ocean War,* 1963); and W. F. Craven and J. L. Cate, *The Army Air Forces in World War II,* 7 vols. (1949–58). There is indispensable background in the six volumes of W. S. Churchill, *The Second World War** (1948–53); in two volumes on the Secretary of War: H. L. Stimson and McGeorge Bundy, *On Active Service in Peace and War* (1948), and E. E. Morison, *Turmoil and Tradition** (1960); and in the biography of the Chief of Staff, F. C. Pogue, *George C. Marshall,* 2 vols. (1963–66). Among the formidable number of American war memoirs, the most useful on the European theater are those of Dwight D. Eisenhower, Omar Bradley, H. H. Arnold, W. Bedell Smith, and Mark Clark; on the Pacific theater, those of Douglas MacArthur, Joseph Stilwell, Claire Chennault, Albert Wedemeyer, Courtney Whitney, Robert Eichelberger, W. F. Halsey, George C. Kenney, Walter Kreuger, and, as recounted by Walter Whitehill, Ernest J. King.

For the American military role in Europe, C. B. MacDonald, *The Mighty Endeavor: American Armed Forces in the European Theater in World War II* (1969), offers a comprehensive account. For strategic debates in Europe, see Chester Wilmot, *The Struggle for Europe* (1952); S. E. Ambrose, *The Supreme Commander: The War Years of General Dwight D. Eisenhower* (1970); Michael Howard, *The Mediterranean Strategy in the Second World War* (1968); and two volumes by Trumbull Higgins: *Winston Churchill and the Second Front, 1940–1943* (1957) and *Soft Underbelly: The Anglo-American Controversy Over the Italian Campaign, 1939–1945* (1968). John Toland, *The Last Hundred Days** (1966), and Cornelius Ryan, *The Last Battle** (1966), cover the fall of Germany. For the Pacific war, see John Toland, *The Rising Sun: The Decline and Fall of the Japanese Empire** (1970); Barbara Tuchman, *Stilwell and the American Experience in China, 1911–1945* (1971); T. H. White and Annalee Jacoby, *Thunder Out of China* (1946); John Hersey,

*Available in a paperback edition.

*Hiroshima** (1946); W. S. Schoenberger, *Decision of Destiny* (1970); and various volumes in the Army history, especially those by Louis Morton, C. F. Romanus, and Riley Sunderland.

The GI's view of the war is candidly portrayed in the gritty newspaper reporting of Ernie Pyle, *Here is Your War* (1943) and *Brave Men* (1944), and the sardonic cartoons of Bill Mauldin, *Up Front* (1945). See also the *New Yorker Book of War Pieces* (1947), and such novels as J. G. Cozzens, *Guard of Honor** (1949); Norman Mailer, *The Naked and the Dead** (1948); James Jones, *From Here to Eternity** (1951); William Styron, *The Long March** (1952); and Joseph Heller, *Catch-22** (1961). S. A. Stouffer, *et al., The American Soldier,* 2 vols.* (1949), contains important sociological data.

THE SECOND WORLD WAR: DIPLOMACY

J. L. Snell, *Illusion and Necessity: The Diplomacy of Global War** (1963), and Gaddis Smith, *American Diplomacy During the Second World War** (1965), are useful surveys. The volumes of Herbert Feis—*The China Tangle** (1953), *Churchill, Roosevelt, Stalin** (1957, 2nd ed., 1967), *The Atomic Bomb and the End of World War II** (rev. ed., 1966)—provide brilliant coverage of diplomatic questions. Two books by R. A. Divine, *Roosevelt and World War II** (1969) and *Second Chance: The Triumph of Internationalism in America** (1967), deal with war and postwar issues. For a left-revisionist view of American policy, see Gabriel Kolko, *The Politics of War: The World and United States Foreign Policy, 1943–1945** (1969). On Yalta, E. R. Stettinius, *Roosevelt and the Russians—The Yalta Conference* (1949), defends Administration policy, W. H. Chamberlin, *America's Second Crusade** (1950), attacks it from the right, and D. S. Clemens, *Yalta* (1970), questions it from the left. On relations with Russia, see W. H. McNeill, *America, Britain and Russia** (1953); J. L. Gaddis, *The United States and the Origins of the Cold War* (1972); Adam Ulam, *Expansion and Coexistence** (1968); J. R. Deane, *The Strange Alliance* (1953); P. E. Mosely, *The Kremlin and World Politics** (1960); Martin Herz, *Beginnings of the Cold War* (1966); and W. A. Harriman, *America and Russia in a Changing World* (1971). On relations with France, see W. L. Langer, *Our Vichy Gamble** (1947), and Milton Viorst, *Hostile Allies* (1965). On China, see Tang Tsou, *America's Failure in China, 1941–1950** (1963).

Particularly useful memoirs are Cordell Hull, *Memoirs,* 2 vols. (1948); W. D. Leahy, *I Was There* (1950); J. F. Byrnes, *Speaking Frankly* (1950) and *All in One Lifetime* (1958); Sumner Welles, *The Time for Decision* (1944) and *Seven Decisions That Shaped History* (1951); Robert D. Murphy, *Diplomat Among Warriors* (1964); J. C. Grew, *Turbulent Era: A Diplomatic Record of Forty Years,* 2 vols. (1952); G. F. Kennan, *Memoirs, 1925–1950* (1967). Indispensable glimpses of American policy from foreign perspectives can be found in the memoirs or diaries of Winston Churchill, Charles de Gaulle, Joseph Goebbels, Albert Speer, Galeazzo Ciano, Milovan Djilas, Ivan Maisky, Lord Avon (Anthony Eden), Lord Halifax, Lord Montgomery, Harold Macmillan, Lord Alexander, Lord Tedder, Sir Frederick Morgan, Sir John Slessor, Sir Alexander Cadogan, Harold Nicolson, Lord Casey, and Sir Robert Menzies.

*Available in a paperback edition.

The Cold War

30

The United States emerged from the Second World War a relatively unified, powerful, and confident nation, restored from the demoralization of the Great Depression, ready to take an active part in the affairs of the greater world. Victory gave Americans an uncritical pride in the productivity of their economy, in the prowess of their armed forces, in the rectitude of their motives, and in the strength of their liberal ideals.

At the same time, victory brought relief rather than euphoria. The Americans of 1945 did not, like their parents of 1918, suppose that, once war was won, they could retire from international responsibility. Their nation was now inextricably mixed up in world affairs and could no longer escape world burdens and opportunities. It had to make peace with the defeated states. It had to help war-ravaged nations in the tasks of reconstruction. It had to tame the unleashed power of the atom. It had to explore the foundations for an enduring structure of world order. It had to meet new threats to the peace, real and imagined. And at home it had to prevent a repetition of the economic depression, the political hysteria, and the intellectual complacency that had followed the First World War.

Truman takes over

The new President. Moreover, the nation faced these problems under a new and inexperienced leader. ''I feel as though the moon and all the stars and all the planets have fallen on me,'' Harry S Truman told newspapermen on the April day in 1945 when he heard the report of Roosevelt's death. ''Please, boys, give me your prayers. I need them very much.'' An inconspicuous back-bencher from Missouri who had barely retained his own seat in the Senate four and a half years before, he had to fill the mighty place of the man who had dominated the affairs of the United States and the world for a dozen years. And he had to do all this as a comparative unknown, without a Cabinet of his own choosing, without a personal following in Congress or in the country, without even adequate instruction on his government's policies and objectives.

His past did not throw great light on his potentialities. On the record he seemed a Missouri courthouse politician of a familiar sort, a beneficiary of the notorious Pendergast machine in Kansas City, a Democratic wheel horse in the Senate, an old-time political pro whose chief attribute was loyalty to his organization and his President. On the other hand, those who knew him valued the spontaneous sense of decency that had led him to fight the Ku Klux Klan at the height of its power in Missouri, the courage in adversity that had enabled him to hold his Senate seat in 1940, and the dedication to popular welfare he had displayed throughout his public career. Even back in Kansas City, for all his machine associations, his personal record was spotless. As chairman of the Senate Committee to Investigate the National Defense Program, he had discharged a delicate job with intelligence and responsibility. He kept on his desk a motto from Mark Twain: "Always do right. This will gratify some people, & astonish the rest." No one could tell what the chemistry of the Presidency would do with this strange mixture of human elements.

The first Truman months. Initial impressions were not encouraging. In his fourth week as President, Truman casually signed an order that abruptly stopped the delivery of goods under the lend-lease program. During the war, the United States had sent abroad over $50 billion worth of goods under that program, of which 60 percent had gone to Great Britain and 22 percent to the Soviet Union. The sudden termination of these deliveries caused resentment abroad and some real hardship. "This experience brought home to

me," Truman subsequently wrote, "not only that I had to know exactly where I was going but also that I had to know that my basic policies were being carried out. If I had read that order, as I should have, the incident would not have occurred. But the best time to learn that lesson was right at the beginning of my duties as President."

The candor, the humility, and the cockiness were all characteristic. Though he never totally divested himself of a tendency to shoot from the hip, Truman gradually developed authority in his new role. His wide knowledge of history gave him a vigorous sense of the dignity and power of the Presidency. He worked hard. He accepted responsibility: he used to say of the presidential desk, "The buck stops here." He sifted his advisers until he found those he could trust. Rapidly he transformed a Roosevelt Administration into a Truman Administration. By July 1945 at Potsdam, Winston Churchill, calling on Truman the morning after his arrival, was impressed with "his gay, precise, sparkling manner and obvious power of decision."

Experiment in world order

The postwar atmosphere. This power of decision was almost immediately put to the test. For war had left the international order in a condition of acute derangement. With the Axis states vanquished, the European Allies battered and exhausted, the colonial empires in dissolution, and the underdeveloped world in tumult, great gaping holes appeared in the structure of world power. And war had also left only two states—the United States and the Soviet Union—with the political dynamism, ideological confidence, and military force to flow into these vacuums of power. The war had accustomed both states, moreover, to thinking and acting on a world scale.

The war's end thus saw a geopolitical rivalry between America and Russia as well as a clear-cut difference over the principles on which the peace should be organized— whether in terms of great-power spheres-of-influence or United Nations universalism (see pp. 694–95). And the factor that transformed this structural conflict into something akin to a religious war and began to give it apocalyptic overtones was the apparently irreconcilable ideological disagreement between the two superpowers. With the prewar world in pieces,

America and Russia appeared in 1945 as the first truly global powers in the history of man, exerting their influence everywhere around the planet, encountering no serious opposition anywhere, except from each other—each, as Tocqueville had prophesied in *Democracy in America* a century earlier, seemingly "marked out by the will of Heaven to sway the destinies of half the globe."

Launching the United Nations. Nevertheless war had bound the victors together in coalition; and the Dumbarton Oaks conference of 1944 had laid down the main lines for a postwar structure. On April 29, 1945, representatives of fifty nations met at San Francisco to adopt a United Nations Charter and create a permanent UN organization.

The charter, essentially an American product, was in the direct line of descent from the Covenant of the League of Nations. It was dominated by the belief that the best way to keep peace was through conciliation, backed up when necessary by collective military strength. The principal UN organs were the General Assembly, the Security Council, the

707

Economic and Social Council, the Trusteeship Council, and the Secretariat. Of these, the Assembly and the Security Council had the widest authority. The Assembly was the general legislative body of the organization, though its powers were limited to discussion and recommendation. The Security Council was the agency of action; it was to this body that the architects of the UN assigned, in the language of the charter, "the primary responsibility for the maintenance of international peace and security." The Security Council consisted of five permanent members—the United States, Britain, Russia, France, and China—with six further members to be elected each year by the General Assembly. The charter gave the Council authority to settle international disputes by peaceful means— through investigation or mediation or whatever method seemed suitable. If such methods failed, Chapter 7 of the charter authorized the Council to determine whether there existed a threat to the peace and to take appropriate measures against any state that broke the peace. If necessary, it might use armed force supplied by the member states.

However, the charter also limited the Council's authority to invoke these powers. The most notable limitation was the provision giving each permanent member a veto. While neither the United States nor the Soviet Union would have joined the UN without this means of protecting its interests, the effect of the provision was to render the Council impotent to deal with infractions by the great powers. By 1972 the Soviet Union had used its veto one hundred eight times, the United States once. Hobbled by the veto, the Security Council declined for a time in importance. By the end of the 1950s, as total membership in the UN more than doubled, the General Assembly began to be the focus of decision and attention.

Collective economic effort. Surrounding the UN was a constellation of subsidiary agencies, among which the United Nations Relief and Rehabilitation Administration had particularly urgent responsibilities. Established in 1943 to bring food, clothing, medicine, and other supplies to liberated countries, UNRRA disbursed $2.7 billion over the next five years combating hunger and other ravages of war. Its director and many of its agents were American, and the United States contributed nearly three-quarters of its financial support.

While UNRRA tackled the immediate crisis, the western Allies, meeting in July 1944 at Bretton Woods, New Hampshire, planned for the long-term international economic framework. Bretton Woods led to the establishment of two institutions: the International Monetary Fund, designed to create a world monetary system based on fixed exchange rates; and the International Bank for Reconstruction and Development (better known as the World Bank), designed to supply capital for investment and trade in underdeveloped areas. The Soviet Union, regarding these institutions as the instruments of international capitalism, declined to participate.

It did, however, join other specialized UN agencies—the Food and Agricultural Organization, the International Trade Organization, the World Health Organization, and the International Labor Organization (taken over from the League). In addition, the newly organized United Nations Educational, Scientific, and Cultural Organization (UNESCO) fostered international efforts to raise cultural standards and promote intellectual exchange.

Except for UNRRA, however, these international agencies could do little to meet immediate economic problems. Countries whose economies had been disrupted by war desperately needed imports from the United States but lacked the dollars to pay for them. The cessation of lend-lease forced them to buy goods on international account, and the result was an extraordinary imbalance in international payments. In 1946 the rest of the world owed the United States $7.7 billion; in 1947, $11.5 billion. To meet this yawning "dollar gap," the United States resorted to a number of expedients—a $3.75 billion loan to Great Britain in 1946, loans by the Export-Import Bank, sales of surplus property on credit, and so on.

The challenge of the atom. The most fateful responsibility confronting the United Nations was to bring the incalculable new force of atomic energy under control. The United States still enjoyed a monopoly of nuclear power, and in the winter of 1945–46 a sharp debate had gone on in Washington over whether the atomic program should be military or civilian. Truman believed that the government had to have an absolute monopoly of the ownership and production of all fissionable materials and that the program should be run by civilians. This view was embodied in

Test at Bikini: the new world

the McMahon Act, which, among other things, set up a civilian Atomic Energy Commission. Truman designated as its first chairman David E. Lilienthal of the Tennessee Valley Authority.

In the meantime, the government was developing a plan for the international control of atomic energy through the United Nations. This proposal, presented in June 1946 to the United Nations Atomic Energy Commission by Bernard Baruch, the American delegate, called for an International Atomic Development Authority empowered to own and operate the materials and facilities involved in the production of atomic energy. The proposed agency was to have power to punish violations of its rules, and it was to be exempt from the great-power veto.

The imaginative sweep of the plan, especially its elimination of the veto, forecast a tremendous stride forward toward international cooperation. But the Russians always resisted international inspection. Their counterproposal called for the cessation of production and the destruction of stockpiles *before* the imposition of controls. It also retained the veto. These provisions were unacceptable to the United States. Though the United Nations Commission adopted the American plan, the threat of Soviet veto prevented further action. Atomic negotiations entered an impasse from which they were not to emerge for years.

The Cold War begins

The coalition in trouble. The United Nations could only register the realities of international life. It could not by fiat abolish profound disagreements in interest and ideology. These disagreements, held in check during the war by common opposition to Hitler, now found new nourishment in postwar difficulties.

For Stalin the overriding concern remained the security of the Soviet Union. He was determined to safeguard the Soviet frontiers by keeping Eastern Europe under Soviet control. He was also determined to stay in power inside Russia. As later described by his closest collaborators, he was a man with marked psychopathic traits, especially vengefulness, morbid suspicion, and an obsession with conspiracies. His country had been unsettled by a war that the Russian people had fought for national rather than for ideological reasons and that had exposed them to a seductive variety of foreign influences. Both his political problems and his personality may have disposed him to seize on the idea of an external capitalist threat as the best means of reestablishing internal ideological and personal control.

As for Eastern Europe, Stalin doubtless construed the Yalta agreement in terms of the sphere-of-influence deal he had made with Churchill at Moscow four months before. In addition, he probably believed at first that the free elections promised at Yalta would produce reliably pro-Soviet regimes. But events soon made it clear that he had overestimated

Stalin, Truman, and Churchill at Potsdam: "New perils loomed and glared"

Soviet popularity in Eastern Europe and underestimated western concern over the extension of Soviet power into Central Europe. When after Yalta Stalin moved to fasten a procommunist regime on Poland, the new American President, only a few weeks in office, conveyed his disapproval in salty language to V. M. Molotov, the Soviet foreign minister. In May 1945 Truman sent Harry

The partition of Germany and Austria

DENMARK — SWEDEN — U.S.S.R.
U.S. and Br.
EAST PRUSSIA
NETH.
POLAND
Berlin
Oder R.
(Joint occupation by four powers)
Neisse R.
GERMANY
CZECHOSLOVAKIA
FRANCE
Vienna
AUSTRIA — HUNGARY
SWITZ.
ITALY — YUGOSLAVIA

Occupied by U.S.   Occupied by U.S.S.R.
Occupied by France   Transferred to Poland
Occupied by Gr. Britain

Hopkins to Moscow to emphasize that Poland had become the "symbol" of the ability of Russia and the West to work out their problems and to warn that "if present trends continued unchecked the entire structure of world cooperation . . . would be destroyed." As Churchill later described the mood in the summer of 1945, "The agreements and understandings at Yalta, such as they were, had already been broken or brushed aside by the triumphant Kremlin. New perils, perhaps as terrible as those we had surmounted, loomed and glared upon the torn and harassed world."

It was in this atmosphere that Truman, Stalin, and Churchill met at Potsdam outside Berlin at the end of July to consider the peace settlement with Germany and its satellites as well as the war with Japan. The western powers acquiesced in a temporary Polish occupation of Germany up to the Oder-Neisse line, with the final territorial decision to be reserved for the peace conference. The task of drawing up peace treaties with the minor Axis powers was assigned to a Council of Foreign Ministers. The talks on Japan led to the Anglo-American Potsdam Declaration.

Occupation of Germany. Of all the power vacuums created by the war, the most vital was in the heart of Europe. Not trusting the Germans to fill this vacuum themselves, the three powers proposed a joint occupation by the United States, Britain, Russia, and France. Each nation was to supervise its own zone of occupation, but each was also to participate in an Allied Control Council responsible for matters affecting Germany as a whole. The objectives of the occupation included disarmament, demilitarization, de-Nazification, the trial of war criminals, the breaking up of cartels, the democratization of politics, and the encouragement of libertarian ideals.

Though the Potsdam Conference marked a retreat from the punitive proposals considered a year earlier at Quebec, the American occupation authorities at first imposed severe political and economic measures on Germany. American troops were forbidden to "fraternize" with Germans. An International Military Tribunal established at American instigation tried twenty-two top Nazis in Nürnberg from November 1945 to October 1946; nineteen were convicted, of whom twelve were sentenced to death. Restrictions on the economy kept German living standards low.

The curtain falls. Potsdam was the last meeting between Stalin and the western leaders. When the Communist party received only 17 percent of the vote in the free Hungarian elections of November 1945, Stalin decided to consolidate the communist position in Eastern Europe without further regard for local or western sensibilities. There followed in the next years the atrocious extermination of political dissenters and dissent through staged trials, forced confessions, and executions. At first the Soviet purge concentrated on non-communist leaders—Bela Kovacs in Hungary, Nikola Petkov in Bulgaria, Julius Maniu in Romania—but by 1949 it began to sweep through the Communist parties themselves, liquidating leaders suspected of inadequate loyalty to Stalinism, such as Laszlo Rajk in Hungary, Traicho Kostov in Bulgaria, and Rudolf Slansky in Czechoslovakia.

As the Russians hardened their grip on Eastern Europe, the expectation arose that they would use their zone, not just to secure their own frontiers, but as a springboard from which to dominate Central and Western Europe, now lying economically prostrate and politically vulnerable before them. The Soviet threat to democratic Europe was not seen at this point in military terms. Stalin's instrumentality, it was supposed, would be the obedient Communist parties of France, Italy, and Germany through which he might, without Russian military action, promote the Stalinization of the continent and thereby succeed where Hitler failed in wielding the whole force of Europe by a single hand.

In Asia, moreover, the Soviet Union declined at the end of 1945 to carry out its promise (as Great Britain and America already had done) to withdraw its troops from Iran six months after the end of the war. In December pro-Soviet Iranians established a revolutionary regime in the northern province of Azerbaijan. In January 1946 Iran charged before the UN Security Council that Russia was interfering in her internal affairs. The Soviet Union rejected these charges and a new deadline for troop withdrawal as well. A protest from Truman finally brought a change in Soviet policy, and the troops left in May.

To American eyes, the Russian movement into Europe and Asia, along with the brutal extinction of civil freedoms in areas already under Russian control, seemed to portend a new phase in the world struggle between democracy and totalitarianism, with communism

Nürnberg trials: nineteen top Nazis were convicted

inheriting the mantle just relinquished by fascism. Communism in the forties did not particularly imply—as it might in later years—popular movements determined to reclaim political and economic independence for their nations. For most Americans, communism meant Stalinism, the system that ruled Soviet Russia, a system correctly seen as not only extraordinarily cruel and repressive at home but also in secure command of most Communist parties through the world. Though past dislike of Russian communism had been submerged during the war by honest admiration for the Red Army and by sentimental effusions about the great Soviet ally, a rational anti-Stalinism now arose, gradually to be enveloped by an obsessive anticommunism, often finding crude and doctrinaire expression.

In an important speech on February 9, 1946, Stalin was understood to be saying that the capitalist system rendered war inevitable. On March 5, Churchill, speaking at Fulton, Missouri, with Truman beside him on the platform, responded by warning against the "expansive tendencies" of the Soviet Union. "From Stettin in the Baltic to Trieste in the Adriatic," he said, "an iron curtain has descended across the Continent." What should the West do to meet the Russian challenge? "I am convinced that there is nothing they admire so much as strength, and there is nothing for which they have less respect than weakness, especially military weakness."

The Cold War hardens

The western reaction. There thus developed what came to be known by 1947 as the Cold War, an intricate, interlocking, reciprocal process, involving authentic differences in principle, real and supposed clashes of interest, and a wide range of misunderstanding and misperception. Each superpower believed with passion that its own safety as well as world peace depended on the success of its peculiar conception of world order. Each superpower, in pursuing its own clearly expressed and ardently cherished principles, only confirmed the fear of the other that it was bent on aggression. Soviet behavior in Eastern Europe, Iran, and Berlin and the activity of Communist parties elsewhere seemed to confirm the western notion of an expansive Soviet Union. American postwar policy, especially in its expressions of concern about Eastern Europe, assumed a threatening aspect for the Russians. Each superpower persevered in corroborating the fears of the other. Together they proceeded to deepen the Cold War.

In retrospect, it seems probable that the Soviet Union was not bent on military aggression or "world conquest." Stalin, indeed, carefully refrained from committing the Red Army outside his own sphere of vital interest. In exchange for a free hand within that sphere, Stalin, while not forgoing the pleasures and benefits of communist intrigue and subversion in other parts of the world, was prepared to concede America and Britain free hands in their spheres of vital interest, including the freedom to suppress communist revolutionary activities. He was even perhaps prepared to place Greece and China within western zones of vital interest.

Nor, on its part, was the United States bent on a policy of military or ideological domination. Hostility to the Soviet Union was not a premeditated American purpose. No nation in history had ever conducted so swift a demobilization of its conventional military forces. By the summer of 1946, the army and navy were down to 1.5 million and 700,000 men respectively. Nor was Congress willing to compensate by accepting Truman's recommendation for universal military training, though it agreed to continue selective service. Even as relations grew worse, the United States continued to cut back its armed forces until they were reduced to almost an eighth of their wartime size. Nor did Washington heed those who like the British philosopher Bertrand Russell urged the use of the atomic bomb to compel the Russians to good behavior.

The American leaders in the forties were not obsessive anticommunists. In China, for example, Truman worked for a coalition between Chiang Kai-shek and Mao Tse-tung. Nor were they dominated by economic motives—by the quest for markets, investment outlets, and raw materials. While they desired a freely trading world, it was not this desire that prompted American concern about Soviet policy in Eastern Europe, where the American stake in markets, investment outlets, and raw materials was slight indeed. Nor were they opposed to socialism. Washington worked closely in these years with the democratic socialist governments of Great Britain, France, and Scandinavia; much of this time the British foreign minister, Ernest Bevin, who had deeper roots in the working-class movement than any leader on either side, considered American reaction to Soviet pressure unduly and naively slow.

Nor did Washington reject the Soviet insistence on pro-Soviet regimes along the Russian frontier. The western powers would have been satisfied if the Russians had been willing to settle for the Finnish pattern throughout Eastern Europe—that is, to permit each nation internal freedoms so long as its foreign policy was linked to Moscow. Nor was Washington in these years opposed to anticolonialism in much of the Third World. Washington supported the independence of India and Indonesia and nationalist revolutions in Egypt and elsewhere. Acquiescence in the French return to Indochina was a lamentable and fateful exception. The fundamental issue, as the American government saw it, lay not between capitalism and revolution but between democracy and Stalinism.

The Axis states. So the interacting process of suspicion and countersuspicion, action and counteraction, gathered speed. The first casualty was any hope of close collaboration in the postwar settlement. Germany remained a crucial issue. Each side came to feel that, if it did not fill the power vacuum, the other would and that this would constitute an unacceptable threat; so each began to sponsor German revival in its own zone. By 1949 the German Federal Republic was established in the west; the German Democratic Republic in the east.

Potsdam had assigned to the Council of Foreign Ministers the task of drawing up peace treaties with Axis satellites. In December 1946 James F. Byrnes, now Truman's Secretary of State, finally came to an agreement with Moscow on treaties with Italy, Bulgaria, Hungary, Finland, and Romania. Though the Eastern European treaties all contained solemn pledges to preserve political and intellectual freedom, in effect they turned the countries (except for Finland) over to Soviet-dominated governments. No agreement was reached on Austria until 1955, when the superpowers agreed on Austrian neutralization.

By these treaties the western powers acquiesced in Soviet control of Eastern Europe. In tacit exchange, the Soviet Union now acquiesced in American control of occupied Japan. There, as in Germany, the American occupation began in severity and, as circumstances changed, became progressively more benign.

At first General Douglas MacArthur, as supreme Allied commander, instituted a series of political and economic purges, culminating in the establishment of an International War Crimes Tribunal and the trial and punishment under standards more stringent than at Nürnberg of leading officials in previous Japanese governments. At the same time he imposed on Japan a number of reforms designed to transform the defeated country into a model western democracy. A new constitution, adopted under American direction in 1946, renounced war as a sovereign right, adding that "land, sea and air forces, as well as other war potential, will never be maintained." The *zaibatsu*, the great family trusts, were threatened with dissolution; trade unions were encouraged, women were given the vote, land was redistributed among the peasants, the educational system was reorganized, and Shinto was abolished as the state religion.

After 1947 American policy began to change. As in the case of Germany, the United States began to look with favor on the idea of permitting an increase in Japanese production in order to reduce the burden on American taxpayers. At the same time, the growing aggressiveness of the Soviet Union raised the question of whether a disarmed Japan would not leave a dangerous power vacuum in the Far East. A peace treaty with Japan, finally negotiated in 1951, registered the altered American attitude. The treaty terminated the occupation, conceded to Japan as a sovereign nation "the inherent right of individual or collective self-defense," and opened the way for American troops to remain in Japan through bilateral agreement.

The experience of military occupation in general, and especially the supposed success of MacArthur's reconstruction of Japan, increased the confidence of Americans in their capacity to build and rebuild nations around the world.

Confusion on the home front

The process of reconversion. At home, Truman decided, as soon as the war ended, to dissipate all doubts about where he stood on domestic issues. His message to Congress on September 6, 1945, was his answer to the question (as he later wrote) of whether "the progress of the New Deal [was] to be halted in the aftermath of war as decisively as the progress of Woodrow Wilson's New Freedom had been halted after the first World War." In this document and in six additional messages in the next three months, Truman laid out the main elements of what was called after 1948 the Fair Deal—full-employment legislation, public housing, farm-price supports, the nationalization of atomic energy, health insurance, a permanent Fair Employment Practices Commission, and an updating of New Deal legislation on conservation, social security, and minimum wages. Truman evidently saw himself as both the continuator and the consolidator of Roosevelt's brilliant improvisations. A man of orderly administrative habits, he tried to systematize the Presidency and to rationalize the recently expanded government.

At the same time, he was faced with the problem of reconverting the nation's economy from war to peace without creating depression. Predictions of 8 or 10 million unemployed had been common in 1945. But the American economy showed far more resilience than anyone expected. Between 1945 and 1946 government purchases of goods and services declined from $83 billion to $31 billion, a sum equal to almost one-quarter of the gross national product. This decline, according to theorists, should have brought in its wake a disastrous fall in the national output and a rise in unemployment. But the gross national product declined by only $4 billion in the same period, and employment actually increased by 3 million.

This extraordinary achievement was due in great part to the pent-up demand for consumer goods after the deprivations of the war years. It was also due to sensible government policy. The Servicemen's Readjustment Act of 1944, known popularly as the G.I. Bill of Rights, assisted veterans in a variety of ways to find employment, education, and medical care; between 1945 and 1952 the government provided veterans with $13.5 billion for education and training alone. In addition, Congress considered in the winter of 1945–46 a so-called full-employment bill, committing the government to use federal investment and expenditure to assure "a full employment volume of production." Though conservative opposition succeeded in diluting the Murray-Wagner bill, the Employment Act of 1946, enacted in February, established the Council of Economic Advisers and charged the federal government with responsibility for maintaining a high level of economic activity.

Inflation rather than depression was the greater threat. With the war over, the nation was chafing more than ever under price and wage controls. Businessmen evaded the system through black markets; labor, seeking wage increases after years of wartime denial, went out on strike. When a railroad strike paralyzed the economy in the spring of 1946, Truman asked Congress for power to draft strikers into the army—a request that even conservatives deemed intemperate and that the Senate rejected. Congress subsequently extended the OPA but so weakened its authority that Truman vetoed the bill. There followed an interval in July 1946 with no controls at all, during which time prices shot up almost 25 percent. When Congress passed another bill a few weeks later, it was too late to put back the lid. The assault on OPA was, in the end, responsible for the largest price rise in a single year in American history. Wholesale prices increased more from 1946 to 1947 than they had during the entire Second World War.

The election of 1946. As the midterm congressional election approached, Truman seemed to have lost control of the economic and political situation. Labor resented his violent reaction to the railroad strike, farmers his attempt to roll back meat prices. Conservatives disliked his professions of liberalism; liberals distrusted his faltering performance and were dismayed by the elimination of New Deal personalities, like Harold Ickes and Henry Wallace, from the Administration. Republicans asked with penetrating effect, "Had enough?" "To err is Truman" became a popular joke.

To no one's surprise, the Republicans carried both houses of Congress for the first time since 1928 and won governorships in twenty-five states. In the eyes of the nation, Truman had been repudiated. Some observers—even a thoughtful Democratic senator, J. William Fulbright of Arkansas—proposed that the President resign.

Truman assumes the initiative

The Truman Doctrine. But Truman had no intention of resigning. And, with Soviet pressures against the West assuming more definite shape, the need for executive energy was growing urgent. Truman had already shown his determination to maintain personal control over foreign policy when he reprimanded his Secretary of State, James F. Byrnes, for not keeping him adequately informed during the Council of Foreign Ministers meeting in Moscow in December 1945. At the end of 1946, Byrnes resigned because of ill health, and Truman appointed General George C. Marshall to take his place. Marshall's unique national eminence helped remove the discussion of foreign policy from a partisan context. So too did the collaboration of Arthur H. Vandenberg, a Republican senator from Michigan, whose prewar record as an isolationist gave his views special weight among conservatives.

In the meantime communist pressure was mounting against Greece and Turkey; and early in 1947, Great Britain, in acute economic straits itself, notified Washington that in five weeks it must end financial support to

The Soviet challenge

a Greek government besieged by communist guerrillas receiving support from Yugoslavia and other Soviet satellites. Though Stalin had not in fact instigated the Greek uprising, this was not known in the West, which supposed that the collapse of Greece would embolden Moscow to press an offensive against Italy and France. Truman accordingly decided that America must take up the burden. Recalling the hard fight for a loan to Britain itself a year before, Truman feared that a conventional request for aid to Greece and Turkey would not pass the Congress. Accepting Vandenberg's judgment that he had to scare the hell out of the country, he went to Capitol Hill in person to urge what soon became known as the Truman Doctrine. "I believe," Truman said, "that it must be the policy of the United States to support free peoples who are resisting attempted subjugation by armed minorities or outside pressures." Some, within the Administration and without, flinched at the sweeping language. But Congress responded to presidential evangelism and in May 1947 passed a bill granting $400 million in aid to Greece and Turkey over the next fifteen months. Though the subsequent collapse of the Greek insurgency was due as much to Tito's break with Stalin as to American assistance, the apparent efficacy of the Truman Doctrine in its initial application strengthened America's belief in both its ability and its responsibility to serve as guardian of freedom in the world.

The containment policy. The American return to Europe under the Truman Doctrine was the first application of a philosophy that had been evolving for some time in the minds of American policy-makers. The most extended statement was made by George F. Kennan, a member of the foreign service with long experience of the Soviet Union. Writing anonymously in *Foreign Affairs* in July 1947, Kennan argued that Soviet communism was like "a fluid stream which moves constantly, wherever it is permitted to move, toward a given goal." American policy, Kennan proposed, must be that of "the firm and vigilant containment of Russian expansive tendencies." The purpose of containment was not to enter the Russian sphere or overthrow the Soviet regime but rather to block the Soviet effort to flow into "every nook and cranny available to it in the basin of the world." In time this would force a measure of circumspection on the Kremlin and "promote tendencies which must eventually find their outlet in either the break-up or the gradual mellowing of Soviet power."

The containment idea provoked heated debate in the United States. On the right, traditional isolationists, led by Senator Robert A. Taft of Ohio, doubted America's financial or moral capacity to sustain an activist international policy. In the center, commentators like Walter Lippmann feared that the containment psychology might lead people to see the Soviet Union as primarily a military threat to be

Soviet-American relations: a dissenting view

We are reckoning with a force which cannot be handled successfully by a 'Get tough with Russia' policy. 'Getting tough' never bought anything real and lasting—whether for schoolyard bullies or business-men or world powers. The tougher we get, the tougher the Russians will get.... I believe that we can get cooperation once Russia under-stands that our primary objective is neither saving the British Empire nor purchasing oil in the Near East with the lives of American sol-diers....

On our part, we should recognize that we have no more business in the political affairs of Eastern Europe than Russia has in the political affairs of Latin America, Western Europe and the United States. We may not like what Russia does in Eastern Europe. Her type of land reform, industrial expropriation, and suppression of basic liberties offends the great majority of the people of the United States. But whether we like it or not the Russians will try to socialize their sphere of influence just as we try to democratize our sphere of influence.... We cannot permit the door to be closed against our trade in Eastern Europe any more than we can in China. But at the same time we have to recognize that the Balkans are closer to Russia than to us—and that Russia cannot permit either England or the United States to dominate the politics of that area.... Under friendly peaceful competition the Russian world and the American world will gradually become more alike. The Russians will be forced to grant more and more of the personal freedoms; and we shall become more and more absorbed with the problems of social-economic justice.

From Henry A. Wallace, Speech at Madison Square Garden, September 12, 1946.

met by military means and might involve the United States beyond its sphere of direct and vital interest. On the left, Americans unwilling to surrender the idea of the innocence or vir-tue of Stalin denounced the policy as aggres-sive and provocative. This group, which had some strength within the labor movement and the liberal community, found a spokesman in Henry Wallace, who had resigned from Truman's Cabinet in protest against the hard-ening of policy toward the Soviet Union.

The Marshall Plan. The Truman Doctrine was an emergency effort to shore up crum-bling positions in Greece and Turkey. It had been made necessary by a larger economic problem—the hard-pressed condition of Brit-ain, confronted by a staggering deficit in its international balance of payments, as well as by acute shortages in food and power. And Britain's plight was symptomatic of the plight of all Western Europe. With UNRRA coming to an end, with crops damaged or destroyed over millions of acres by severe winter weather, with little evidence of industrial re-covery, with Communist parties and the So-viet Union threatening political and economic

action, Western Europe faced a frightening crisis. European city dwellers were living on less than 2,000 calories a day. The cradle of Western civilization seemed to Winston Churchill in 1947 "a rubble heap, a charnel house, a breeding ground for pestilence and hate." "The patient is sinking," said Secretary Marshall, "while the doctors deliberate."

But Congress was likely to balk at more foreign credits along the line of the British loan of 1946. In an address at the Harvard commencement on June 5, 1947, Marshall accordingly set forth a revolutionary new pro-posal. After describing the European crisis, he called on the European countries themselves to draw up a plan for European recovery. "This is the business of the Europeans. . . . The role of this country should consist of friendly aid in the drafting of a European pro-gram and of later support. . . . The program should be a joint one, agreed to by a number, if not all, of European nations." Marshall added, significantly, "Our policy is directed not against any country or doctrine but against hunger, poverty, desperation, and chaos."

This was the proposal that, as British For-eign Secretary Ernest Bevin later told Parlia-

The truth of the matter is that Europe's requirements for the next 3 or 4 years of foreign food and other essential products—principally from America—are so much greater than her present ability to pay that she must have substantial additional help, or face economic, social, and political deterioration of a very grave character.

The remedy lies in breaking the vicious circle and restoring the confidence of the European people in the economic future of their own countries and of Europe as a whole. The manufacturer and the farmer throughout wide areas must be able and willing to exchange their products for currencies the continuing value of which is not open to question.

Aside from the demoralizing effect on the world at large and the possibilities of disturbances arising as a result of the desperation of the people concerned, the consequences to the economy of the United States should be apparent to all. It is logical that the United States should do whatever it is able to do to assist in the return of normal economic health in the world, without which there can be no political stability and no assured peace.

From George C. Marshall, Commencement Speech at Harvard University, 1947.

The Marshall Plan

ment, he "grabbed . . . with both hands." Within three weeks, representatives of European states, West and East, met in Paris to discuss the Marshall offer. The prospect of Soviet and East European participation, however, was quickly disappointed when the Russians pulled out of the Paris meeting, taking their satellites with them. Four months later Moscow set up the Communist Information Bureau (Cominform), a new version of the Comintern with the special mission of coordinating the European Communist parties, including those of France and Italy. A pro-Soviet coup in Czechoslovakia in February 1948— itself conceivably an overreaction to the Marshall Plan—completed the division of Europe. It also smoothed the way for the passage of the plan by the American Congress in March.

The sixteen remaining states (including Turkey) now formed the Organization for European Economic Cooperation to begin integrated economic planning. With generous contributions by the United States—$12.5 billion in four years—the West European economy was restored in a strikingly short time. By 1951 the Marshall Plan countries had raised their industrial output 40 percent over 1938. The stimulus provided by the Marshall Plan and the OEEC led both to continued economic expansion and to further experiments in European integration—especially the European Coal and Steel Community (1952) and the European Economic Community, better known as the Common Market, established

by the Rome Treaties in 1957. The dramatic economic recovery both reduced the power of communism in Western Europe and gave that region a more independent voice in world affairs.

The first Berlin crisis. The Marshall Plan checked the Soviet hope that economic disintegration might strengthen communism in Western Europe. In response Moscow in 1949 organized the Council for Mutual Economic Assistance (COMECON) in Eastern Europe. And in the spring of 1948 the Soviet Union presented the West with a new challenge when it cut off West Berlin by blockading all highway, river, and rail traffic into the former German capital. The evident purpose was to force the western powers out of Berlin.

The West now had several choices, all unattractive. If it retreated, it would encourage the Soviet Union to believe that it could win its objectives through a show of force. If it tried to break the blockade by sending armed convoys to Berlin, it ran the risk of a third world war. General Lucius Clay, the American commander in Germany, proposed a third course—that the West circumvent the blockade by supplying West Berlin through an airlift. Truman adopted Clay's suggestion. On June 26, 1948, the airlift went into operation. By October American and British planes were flying in nearly five thousand tons a day. When it became apparent that even winter weather could not halt the airlift, Moscow developed second thoughts. After negotiations in the early months of 1949, the Russians finally, on May 12—321 days after the start of the airlift—ended the blockade.

The Berlin crisis, following so closely on the communist coup in Czechoslovakia, convinced many western Europeans of the need for some sort of regional defense agreement against possible Soviet aggression. Led by Bevin of Britain and Spaak of Belgium, Britain, France, Belgium, the Netherlands, and Luxembourg joined in March 1948 to sign the Brussels Pact providing for military and economic collaboration. The Senate expressed American approval of such arrangements by passing the Vandenberg Resolution in June. Bevin argued, however, for more explicit American commitments; and Truman agreed that only "an inclusive security system" could dispel the fear that communism might overrun Western Europe before effective help could arrive. Accordingly, negotiations on such a

system began in Washington in July. By October the countries involved had agreed in principle on a North Atlantic alliance in which (in the language of Article 5 of the final pact) "an armed attack against one or more of them in Europe or North America shall be considered an attack against them all." The treaty was signed in Washington on April 4, 1949, by the United States, Britain, France, Italy, Belgium, the Netherlands, Denmark, Norway, Portugal, Luxembourg, Iceland, and Canada. The creation of the North Atlantic Treaty Organization (NATO) completed the work of the Marshall Plan in immunizing Western Europe against Soviet aggression.

The spring of 1948 also saw the prompt American recognition of the new Republic of Israel, proclaimed on May 14 when the British mandate in Palestine came to an end. Truman's action, though unpopular in the national security bureaucracy, won general acclaim.

The Eightieth Congress at home

The resurgence of conservatism. Despite his setback in the 1946 election, Truman had compiled an impressive record of achievement in foreign affairs. In domestic policy, however, the Eightieth Congress proved a bulwark of conservatism. Its dominant figure was Robert A. Taft of Ohio, son of the former President and a senator of inexhaustible energy, knowledge, and self-confidence. His admirers regarded him as the epitome of old-fashioned American wisdom; his critics said he had the best mind in Washington until he made it up.

Taft had long been concerned with ending what he regarded as the privileged position created for organized labor by the Wagner Act of 1935. He now sponsored legislation outlawing the closed shop and reviving the government injunction as a means of dealing with labor disputes. Though the bill as amended permitted a measure of union security through the "union shop" (that is, a contract requiring workers to join the union after being hired—as distinct from the closed shop, which demands that they join before being hired), its Section 14B legalized so-called right-to-work laws by which states could forbid the requirement of union membership as a condition of employment. Labor leaders denounced the law rather extravagantly as a "slave-labor" measure, and Truman vetoed it. But in early

1947 Congress promptly passed the Taft-Hartley Act over his veto.

The conservatives also passed in 1947 a proposed amendment forbidding presidential third terms—a belated act of vengeance against Franklin D. Roosevelt. The Twenty-second Amendment was ratified by the required thirty-six states in February 1951. In other areas the Eightieth Congress ignored Truman's legislative recommendations and passed more bills, including a major tax reduction in 1948, over his veto.

Truman fights back. As the 1948 presidential election approached, Truman's advisers, especially his White House counsel, Clark Clifford, concluded that his only hope for reelection lay in the militant advocacy of a liberal program. The President agreed and in early 1948 bombarded Congress with a series of reform proposals. Much of this was a reaffirmation of New Deal objectives; but in the field of racial justice he broke new ground.

Though he had grown up according to the Southern customs of a border state, Truman was a man of humane instinct. He was also aware of the considerable change in the position of black America wrought by the New Deal and the war. Recognizing the validity of black aspirations, he had appointed in 1946

To strengthen the right to equality of opportunity, the President's Committee recommends:

1. In general:

The elimination of segregation, based on race, color, creed, or national origin, from American life.

The separate but equal doctrine has failed in three important respects. First, it is inconsistent with the fundamental equalitarianism of the American way of life in that it marks groups with the brand of inferior status. Secondly, where it has been followed, the results have been separate and unequal facilities for minority peoples. Finally, it has kept people apart despite incontrovertible evidence that an environment favorable to civil rights is fostered whenever groups are permitted to live and work together. There is no adequate defense of segregation.... We believe that federal funds, supplied by taxpayers all over the nation, must not be used to support or perpetuate the pattern of segregation in education, public housing, public health services, or other public services and facilities.... A federal Fair Employment Practice Act prohibiting discrimination in private employment should provide both educational machinery and legal sanctions for enforcement purposes.

From the President's Committee on Civil Rights, *To Secure These Rights,* 1947.

---

a President's Committee on Civil Rights. A year later the committee recommended a permanent commission on civil rights, a mandatory FEPC, antilynching and anti-poll-tax laws, and a strengthening of civil-rights statutes and enforcement machinery. In an eloquent message on February 2, 1948, Truman made these proposals part of his executive program. This attempt to realize the promises of the Declaration of Independence for all Americans, regardless of race or color, represented Truman's boldest initiative in the domestic field.

The civil-rights proposals alienated the conservative Democrats of the South. In the meantime, the Truman Doctrine and the Marshall Plan outraged communist sympathizers in the North, as well as liberals like Henry A. Wallace, whose concern for world peace led them to overlook the implications of Stalinism. A new anticommunist liberal group, Americans for Democratic Action, while deeply opposed to Wallace, was skeptical of Truman. Old-line Democratic bosses shared this skepticism. As the Democratic convention drew near, a "dump-Truman" movement gained momentum

The anti-Truman forces were unable to agree on an alternative, however, and in the end Truman won renomination with little difficulty. The choice of Senator Alben Barkley of Kentucky for the Vice Presidency was excep-

tionally popular. The adoption of a strong civil-rights plank after a floor fight brought the Truman-Barkley ticket the enthusiastic support of Northern liberals. Then Truman himself concluded a fighting acceptance speech with a promise to call a special session of Congress to test the readiness of the Republicans to live up to their platform pledges.

The 1948 campaign. The Republicans had once again nominated Governor Thomas E. Dewey of New York. Governor Earl Warren of California received the vice-presidential nomination. Dewey campaigned with the quiet confidence of a man who could not lose. Republican optimism swelled even further when a communist-dominated Progressive party nominated Wallace for the Presidency and when the die-hard Southern Democrats formed the States Rights Democratic party (better known as the Dixiecrats) and nominated Strom Thurmond of South Carolina.

Only Truman thought he could win. The special session of Congress adjourned without doing anything, thus providing him with the issue he needed. He began a lively "give 'em hell" campaign across the country, telling audiences at every whistlestop that the record of the "do-nothing, good-for-nothing" Republican Eightieth Congress proved the worthlessness of Republican campaign prom-

The conclusion was premature

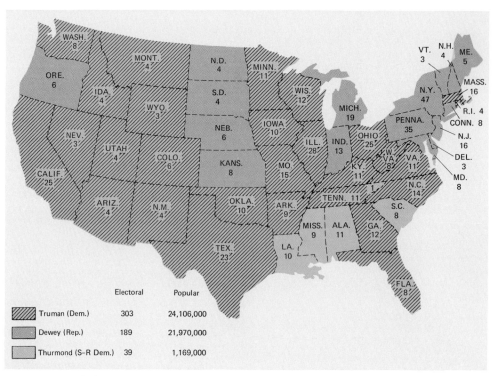

The election of 1948

	Electoral	Popular
Truman (Dem.)	303	24,106,000
Dewey (Rep.)	189	21,970,000
Thurmond (S-R Dem.)	39	1,169,000

ises. A fall in the price of corn and hogs alarmed the farmers; this, reinforced by the fear that the Eightieth Congress, in cutting funds for the Commodity Credit Corporation, had left inadequate storage space for grain, turned the Corn Belt toward the Democrats. The Dixiecrat revolt confirmed the blacks in their Democratic allegiance, while the Wallace movement eliminated communism as an issue between the major parties and kept Catholics in the Democratic camp. Neither Dewey's personality nor his campaign roused much enthusiasm, even among his supporters. Truman, on the other hand, emerged as a pungent orator, an indomitable fighter, and —in contrast to his opponent—an intensely *human* being. By late October, shouting crowds greeted Truman's appearances with the joyful cry, "Pour it on, Harry." By election

day he had traveled 31,700 miles and had delivered 356 speeches.

Public-opinion polls forecast a sure Republican victory. The Chicago *Tribune* put out an election extra announcing Dewey as the next President. But Truman received 24.1 million popular votes against 22 million for Dewey, and 303 electoral votes against 189. Thurmond carried four states (South Carolina, Mississippi, Alabama, and Louisiana) and polled 1.2 million votes. Wallace also polled 1.2 million votes but carried no states. In addition, the Democrats captured both houses of Congress. Truman had at last established himself as President in his own right. As for the pollsters, one wit observed, "Public opinion polls reach everyone in America, from the farmer in his field right up to the President of the United States, Thomas E. Dewey."

The Fair Deal

Return to frustration. An English magazine entitled its postelection editorial, "Roosevelt's Fifth Term." Truman himself regarded his victory as a mandate for liberalism. "We have rejected the discredited theory that the fortunes of the nation should be in the hands of a privileged few," he said in January 1949.

"Instead, we believe that our economic system should rest on a democratic foundation and that wealth should be created for the benefit of all. The recent election shows that the American people are in favor of this kind of society and want to go on improving it." His state-of-the-union message was a ringing summons to a new era of social reform. "Every segment of our population and every individual," he concluded, "has a right to expect from his government a fair deal."

But his Fair Deal roused fierce opposition. Secretary of Agriculture Charles F. Brannan's plan for the support of farm income through production payments and Federal Security Administrator Oscar Ewing's proposal for national health insurance were condemned as "socialistic." Congress refused to repeal the Taft-Hartley Act and rejected Truman's requests for federal aid to education and for middle-income housing. A Senate filibuster killed the FEPC. On the other hand, though thwarted in his legislative program for civil rights, Truman was able through executive action to combat segregation within the government and the armed services. And, though Congress turned down the more spectacular Fair Deal proposals, it did enlarge the federal effort in low-income public housing, slum clearance, soil conservation, public power, flood control, and rural electrification.

The year 1949 was marked by the first serious economic troubles since the war. The gross national product fell about $9 billion; unemployment reached 4.6 million, or 7 percent of the labor force. By the middle of the year, however, the tide had begun to turn. Though the Eightieth Congress had not reduced taxes in 1948 for Keynesian reasons, the effect was to release funds for consumer spending. With this fiscal stimulus, reinforced by increased government expenditures, the economy began to right itself before the downturn could develop momentum.

The Fair Deal abroad. Though Truman's primary concern in 1949 was with domestic affairs, he did not see the Fair Deal as merely a domestic policy. In a listing of points in his inaugural address, he placed particular emphasis on Point Four—"a bold new program for making the benefits of our scientific advances and industrial progress available for the improvement and growth of underdeveloped areas." With Western Europe presumably secure against communism, the next priority was to prevent the uncommitted third of the world from falling into communist hands. "There will be no quick solution for any of the difficulties of the new nations of Asia and Africa," he said, "—but there may be no solution at all if we do not press forward with full energy to help these countries grow and flourish in freedom." The war against poverty "is the only war we seek."

The Point Four program of technical assistance to underdeveloped countries was a first response to what was evolving as a major challenge to the West—the "revolution of rising expectations" sweeping through Asia, Africa, and Latin America and producing an intense desire for political independence, economic growth, and social modernization. By 1952 America's "technical missionaries" were at work in thirty-three countries, improving agricultural productivity, fighting typhus and malaria, launching irrigation and hydroelectric projects, and teaching people to read and write.

Revolution in China. The most conspicuous communist gain in the Third World was not the result of premeditated Soviet design. Stalin seems to have believed nearly as firmly as the United States in the capacity of the Nationalist regime of Chiang Kai-shek to organize China. If he had not, he would hardly have stripped Manchuria of nearly a billion dollars' worth of industrial equipment in 1945. But both superpowers underestimated the revolutionary possibilities in China—the ancient resentments against foreign domination, the pent-up demand for agrarian reform, the growing revulsion against the corruption and autocracy of the Kuomintang, and the skill and tenacity with which the Chinese communists under Mao Tse-tung were to exploit these discontents.

When the Japanese surrendered, China was battered and exhausted. In the north the communist armies, fanning out from Yenan, were in control; in the center were the Japanese armies; in the southwest corner were the armies of Chiang Kai-shek. American policy still looked to Kuomintang-communist cooperation under Chiang's leadership; but, to bring this about, it was considered first necessary to establish the primacy of the Nationalist regime. Accordingly, an American airlift operation dropped Nationalist armies from the skies to occupy such key cities as Peking and Shanghai. Then at Yalta Stalin recognized Chiang as the ruler of China—a recognition confirmed by the Sino-Soviet pact of August 1945 (in which the Nationalist government made concessions to the Soviet Union opposed by the State Department and beyond anything required by Yalta).

The next step in Washington's view was

coalition with the Chinese communists. As so resolute an anticommunist as General Claire Chennault put it, "There is only one way out. . . . That is for us to sponsor thorough political reconstruction at Chungking, followed by true unification between Chungking and Yenan." Generals Wedemeyer and MacArthur joined in a similar recommendation in December 1945. The new American ambassador to China, General Patrick J. Hurley, took enthusiastic personal charge of this effort. When a disenchanted Hurley resigned in November 1945, Truman appointed General George C. Marshall to continue his work.

For a time Marshall appeared to be making progress. But the Nationalists believed that they could win a civil war; the communists were committed by ideology to domination. In January 1947 Marshall abandoned his mission, blaming its failure on both the reactionaries in the Kuomintang and the communists.

Though the Nationalists scored early military successes, they disregarded the counsel of their American military advisers and soon began to overextend themselves. The communists, welded by quasi-religious conviction and helped by the increasing popular hatred of the Nationalist government, now started to win victories. With each victory they captured more arms and attracted more deserters. In 1947 Truman sent Wedemeyer to China on a fact-finding tour. "The only basis on which national Chinese resistance to Soviet aims can be revitalized," Wedemeyer reported, "is through the presently corrupt, reactionary and inefficient Chinese National government." Therefore the United States should aid that

government. But "until drastic political and economic reforms are undertaken United States aid cannot accomplish its purpose."

The United States continued economic and military assistance, but Chiang made no serious attempt at reform. In 1947 and 1948 the Nationalist armies began a retreat from Manchuria. By January 1949 they had abandoned Peking and Tientsin. Shanghai fell in May, Canton in October. By the end of the year, the Nationalist regime, driven from the mainland, had withdrawn to the island of Formosa (Taiwan).

The collapse of the Nationalist regime later provoked a bitter political debate in the United States. Some contended that anti-Nationalist prejudice—if not outright treason—in the State Department caused the "loss of China" and that more American money and arms would have saved Chiang. But, as Wedemeyer explained the Nationalist defeat, it was "lack of spirit, primarily lack of spirit. It was not lack of equipment. In my judgment they could have defended the Yangtze with broomsticks if they had the will to do it." It was Chiang's failure to retain the support of his own people that brought about his defeat—this plus the efficiency, incorruptibility, and fanaticism of Mao Tse-tung and the Chinese communists. The American government accepted the result without undue surprise, put out a white paper placing the blame on Chiang, pronounced Taiwan in January 1950 a part of mainland China, declared American neutrality even if the communists sought to take the island by force, and adopted a general policy of "letting the dust settle."

Limited war

The dilemma of deterrence. If the rhetoric of the Truman Doctrine seemed to call for a worldwide program of containing the communists, Truman himself did not construe the doctrine in any such crusading way, applying it neither to China nor to Eastern Europe as it was applied to Greece and Turkey. Even with regard to Russia, he could make amiable public reference to Stalin in 1948 as "Uncle Joe." In 1949 he seemed to view the contest with the Soviet Union without alarm. The forward drive of communism in Europe had been stopped, in Berlin as well as in Western Europe. The dust was settling in China. All this

encouraged the President to continue to clamp down on the defense budget.

The National Security Act of 1947 established a unified defense establishment, creating a Secretary of Defense, a permanent Joint Chiefs of Staff, a National Security Council, and a Central Intelligence Agency. But Truman kept national-security expenditures under tight control; in 1947–50, they averaged only $13 billion a year. By 1949 the army was down to ten active divisions. The capacity to fight small wars had dwindled. Deterrence rested on the idea of a retaliatory air-atomic strike against the Soviet Union.

This was not the military posture of a state bent on establishing a world empire. The Truman defense policy placed the United States in an all-or-nothing military position. If war broke out, it seemed that Washington faced the choice either of doing nothing or of blowing up the world. Observers feared that this situation might invite communist aggression in some marginal area where the United States would not wish to respond by atomic war and lacked the means to respond otherwise.

The end of the atomic monopoly.

Then in September 1949 evidence reached Washington that an atomic explosion had occurred in the Soviet Union. With one stroke the Russians had not only broken the atomic monopoly but had proved to the world their own technological capacity. The era of American invincibility had come to an end.

In response, Truman concluded a bitter argument among his scientific advisers by directing the Atomic Energy Commission to proceed with the construction of a hydrogen bomb, a weapon even more fearful than the atomic bomb. At the same time, he instructed the National Security Council to undertake a basic reappraisal of America's strategic position. The result was a document known as NSC 68, which called for an increase in military expenditures from 5 to, if necessary, 20 percent of the gross national product and more ample capacity to deal with conventional and local wars. But, before NSC 68 could be translated into concrete policy, a new development reinforced the thesis that air-atomic power by itself would not assure American security.

War in Korea.

When American and Soviet troops entered Korea after the collapse of Japan in 1945, they had accepted the thirty-eighth parallel as a military dividing line. Time and the Cold War converted the military demarcation into a political frontier. In 1948 the Russians set up a People's Democratic Republic in North Korea, while the Americans recognized the Republic of South Korea. In June 1949 the bulk of the American army of occupation withdrew from South Korea. The position of the new republic in the American security system was not altogether clear. Both General Douglas MacArthur and Dean Acheson, who had now succeeded Marshall as Secretary of State, declared that South Korea

The shifting front in Korea

lay outside the American defense perimeter in the Pacific; should an attack occur, Acheson said, "The initial reliance must be on the people attacked to resist it and then upon the commitments of the entire civilized world under the Charter of the United Nations."

At just this time Kim Il-sung, the communist dictator of North Korea, came to Moscow to seek Stalin's support for a North Korean invasion of South Korea. Misled perhaps by the MacArthur and Acheson statements, persuaded that the war would be over before America had time to intervene, Stalin gave Kim a green light. On June 25, 1950, North Korean troops crossed the thirty-eighth parallel in a surprise invasion.

Truman was confronted with what he later recalled as the toughest decision he ever had to make. He was convinced that the invasion could not have taken place without Soviet approval and might well have taken place at Soviet instigation. If the United States did not react in Korea, he believed, the Russians would sponsor similar thrusts elsewhere; and the result might be a third world war. Without hesitation, he committed American forces under General MacArthur to the defense of South Korea. At the same time he brought the matter before the United Nations Security

Truman and Acheson

Council. The fortunate absence of the Soviet delegate, who was boycotting the Security Council in pique over its refusal to seat a delegate from Communist China, made it possible for the UN to condemn the North Korean aggression without running the risk of a Soviet veto.

The original UN intention in South Korea was simply to repel the North Korean invasion. At first the communists drove the UN troops—made up of ROK (Republic of Korea) forces and American troops, soon to be reinforced by a smattering of units from other nations, especially Great Britain and Turkey—back to the southeastern corner of the peninsula. But on September 15, in a daring move, MacArthur landed an amphibious force at Inchon behind the enemy lines. By September 27 the UN forces were in Seoul, and by October 1 they had recovered almost all of Korea below the thirty-eighth parallel.

Crossing the thirty-eighth parallel.
Mac-Arthur's brilliant generalship now raised the question whether the UN forces, having repelled the invader, should pause at the frontier, or whether they should pursue the enemy into North Korea. Despite warnings from Peking that crossing the thirty-eighth parallel might provoke Chinese intervention, the UN General Assembly, "recalling that the essential objective was the establishment of a unified, independent, and democratic Korea," authorized UN forces on October 7 to move into North Korea.

On October 15 Truman and MacArthur met at Wake Island. When the President asked the General about the chances of Chinese or Soviet intervention in Korea, MacArthur replied, "Very little. . . . If the Chinese tried to get down to Pyongyang there would be the greatest slaughter." He added that he believed all enemy resistance would end by Thanksgiving. Superbly confident, MacArthur ignored cautions from Washington and deployed his forces in a thin line across North Korea. On November 24 he declared that his final drive to end the war was "now approaching its decisive effort." Two days later, a Chinese communist army drove a wedge through the central sector. The UN forces retreated in disarray two-thirds of the way down the peninsula. MacArthur gloomily announced, "We face an entirely new war."

Relations between MacArthur and Washington, not easy in victory, now became prickly in defeat. Years of proconsulship had charged a naturally proud and flamboyant personality with a conviction of independent authority. In particular, MacArthur showed a disposition to issue public statements at variance with official policy and often in criticism of it. A barrage of messages after his November defeat suggested that the blame lay, not in his own faulty intelligence or tactics, but in the Washington decision to limit the war to Korea and to forbid attack on Chinese bases in Manchuria. This "privileged sanctuary," said MacArthur in one public *démarche,* was "an enormous handicap, without precedent in military history." On December 6 Truman ordered MacArthur to clear all subsequent statements with Washington.

No substitute for victory?
The tension between MacArthur and Truman reflected a fundamental disagreement over the purpose of the war. MacArthur believed that the United States must pursue the Korean conflict to a victorious conclusion. If this required an escalation of the war—the bombing of Manchurian bases, the blockade and bombing of China, the entry of the Nationalist Chinese—then so be it. "In war there is no substitute for victory. . . . War's very object is victory, not prolonged indecision."

The Administration, on the other hand, saw the conflict as a limited war for limited objectives. If Manchuria was a privileged sanctuary, so were Okinawa and Japan. To commit American military strength to the mainland of Asia might abandon Europe to Soviet aggression. To transform a limited war into a general war against Communist China would be, in General Omar Bradley's phrase, to fight "the wrong war, at the wrong place, at the wrong time, and with the wrong enemy."

The Administration was content to achieve the original objective of its intervention—the integrity of South Korea. And a reversal of military fortunes now gave hope that this limited goal could be won. General Matthew B. Ridgway, who had taken command of the 8th Army in December, rallied the UN forces and began to recover the initiative. By March most of South Korea was once again free of communists, and Ridgway's troops were pressing on the thirty-eighth parallel. The time seemed right for negotiation.

On March 20 Washington informed MacArthur that the United States and the United Nations felt that "further diplomatic efforts

G. I. in Korea

Retreat in Korea, January 1951: an entirely new war

toward settlement should be made before any advance with major forces north of the thirty-eighth parallel." MacArthur's reply, a defiant public statement calling for enemy surrender, killed the President's move toward negotiation. "By this act," Truman later said, "Mac-Arthur left me no choice—I could no longer tolerate his insubordination." When on April 5, Congressman Joseph Martin of Massachusetts, the Republican leader in the House, produced a new and provocative MacArthur letter, Truman relieved MacArthur of his command.

Truman's decision caused an outburst of public indignation. Senator Joseph McCarthy of Wisconsin ascribed MacArthur's recall to the machinations of a White House clique besotted by "bourbon and benzedrine." Senator William Jenner of Indiana declared, "This country today is in the hands of a secret inner coterie which is directed by agents of the Soviet Union." The fever reached its pitch on April 19 when MacArthur, returning to the United States for the first time in fourteen years, addressed a joint session of Congress. He concluded with a reference to a barracks-room ballad popular in his youth "which proclaimed most proudly that 'old soldiers never die; they just fade away.' And like the old soldier of that ballad," he went on, "I now close my military career and just fade away, an old soldier who tried to do his duty as God gave him the light to see that duty."

There followed an extraordinary inquiry into the circumstances of MacArthur's dismissal by the Senate Foreign Relations and Armed Services committees. Beginning on May 3, MacArthur, Acheson, Marshall, Bradley, and other military and civilian leaders underwent a congressional interrogation that, in time, canvassed the most basic problems of global strategy. When the hearings ended on June 25, over 2 million words had been transcribed. This ventilation of the issues dispelled much of the turbulence. MacArthur permitted the Administration to persuade the country that the President and the Joint Chiefs, having the global interests of the country in view, might have been justified in overruling Mac-Arthur's local recommendations. In a short time, Truman rode out the storm; and Mac-Arthur in due course began to fade away.

The Korean War: repercussions

Could the Cold War have been avoided?
By now the Cold War was in full swing. In retrospect it seems probable that each of the superpowers in these years was acting more on defensive grounds and on local considerations than the other realized. Neither nation had a master plan for world dominion. Yet the American government could hardly have been certain that Soviet aims would have remained local and limited had counterpolicies not developed. Acheson wrote twenty years after, "A school of academic criticism has concluded that we overreacted to Stalin, which in turn caused him to overreact to policies of the United States. This may be true. Fortu-nately, perhaps, these authors were not called upon to analyze a situation in which the United States had not taken the action which it did take."

In retrospect the hard questions remain: could the democracies really have relied on the self-restraint of an increasingly unstable Stalin if there had been no western resistance—no Truman Doctrine, no Marshall Plan, no NATO, no rearmament, no response to the Berlin blockade or to the invasion of South Korea? Had the democracies not rallied, would not Moscow have had an irresistible temptation to keep moving, always on the pretext of rendering its own borders even more secure?

There thus seems even in retrospect an awful inevitability about the start of the Cold War. "In what is truly tragic," wrote Hegel, "there must be valid moral powers on both the sides which come into collision. . . . Both suffer loss and yet both are mutually justified."

The globalization of containment. Though the limitations imposed on the Korean War showed that the defense of Western Europe remained the top American priority, the fact that the war was fought at all expressed the growing American belief that Soviet expansion, if blocked in the main theater, would break out in secondary theaters. Korea thereby resulted in the transformation of containment from a selective European policy into a general global policy. Interpreting the North Korean invasion as part of a worldwide communist offensive, Truman proceeded to batten down hatches all around the world.

The image of an aggressive Russia commanding a highly centralized world communist movement—an image not altogether false in the age of Stalin—now fastened itself dogmatically on the American mind. The new China, for example, began to be perceived simply as an extension of Soviet power. Three days after the North Korean attack, Truman canceled the policy of neutrality in the Chinese civil war, declared that the seizure of Taiwan by "communist forces" would threaten American security in the Pacific, and ordered the Seventh Fleet to prevent a mainland attack on the island (and also to prevent a Nationalist attack on the mainland). By 1951 Assistant Secretary of State Dean Rusk could speak of the Mao regime as a "colonial Russian government—a Slavic Manchukuo."

The nationalist uprising against French control in Indochina was incorporated into the larger pattern. During the Second World War Roosevelt had opposed the restoration of Indochina to French rule, favoring instead an international trusteeship to prepare Indochina for independence. This wise suggestion was forgotten after his death, and the return of the French colonial government produced dogged resistance on the part of Ho Chi Minh and the so-called Viet Minh. Though Ho had served the Comintern for twenty years, he was a nationalist as well as a communist; and the Viet Minh were seen by most Indochinese as leaders of a movement for national independence. Washington had paid little attention to the fighting in Indochina until the fall of mainland China roused anxieties about wholesale communist expansion in Asia. When the French government made token concessions to a client regime in Saigon, the Truman Administration began to give the French military and economic assistance. After Korea the State Department, condemning Ho as "an agent of world communism," pronounced the French role in Indochina "an integral part of the world-wide resistance by the Free Nations to Communist attempts at conquest."

In the United States, the Korean War brought about a quick reversal of the policy of military retrenchment. Major national-security expenditures increased to $22.5 billion in 1950–51 and to $44 billion in 1951–52; only 33 percent of the budget in 1950, they reached 67 percent in 1952. Two years after the attack on South Korea, the nation had 3.6 million men under arms—an increase of nearly 2.2 million. The army doubled its number of divisions, the air force grew from forty-eight to ninety-five wings, and the navy doubled its number of big carriers. With American financial backing, Britain and France launched rearmament programs, and in September 1950 Acheson persuaded his European allies to go along with a measure of rearmament in Germany. In 1951 NATO forces were integrated under the command of General Eisenhower, and the United States agreed to station four additional American divisions in Europe.

Domestic repercussions. The Korean War had its impact both on the American economy and on the national psychology. Stimulated by increased military spending, the gross national product rose from $264 billion in 1950 to $339 billion in 1952. At the same time, between the invasion of South Korea and the beginning of general price and wage controls in January 1951, the cost of living rose, on the average, nearly 1 percent per month and wholesale prices more than 2 percent per month. Prices then steadied, partly because of price-wage controls and partly because tax increases offset inflationary tendencies.

It was easier to contain the economic than the psychological consequences of Korea. With the intensification of the Cold War, many Americans demanded to know why the nation they deemed so powerful and so safe in 1945 should now, five years later, appear in deadly peril. Some, resenting the complexity of history, found a satisfactory answer by tracing all troubles to the workings of the communist conspiracy—unsleeping, omnipresent, and diabolically cunning. Unquestionably there had been communist penetration of the American government, the labor movement, and the intellectual community, and there were now multiplying disclosures of communist espionage in Canada and other countries. Recognizing the reality of the problem and at the same time hoping to keep public reaction under control, Truman in 1947 had set up a federal loyalty program. "Disloyal and subversive elements must be removed from the employ of government." Truman said. "We must not, however, permit employees of the Federal government to be labelled as disloyal . . . when no valid basis exists for arriving at such a conclusion."

Despite these injunctions, the loyalty program—as a consequence of overzealous investigators, ignorant or malicious informers, and apprehensive loyalty boards—began to assume a drastic and promiscuous character. By December 1952, 6.6 million people had been checked for security. Of the 25,750 who received full FBI field investigations, 5,900 withdrew before or during adjudication and 490 were dismissed as ineligible on loyalty grounds. No cases of espionage were uncovered by the investigations. The outcome was an impressive testimonial to the public service, but it was purchased in many cases at a pitiful human cost. "It was not realized at first," Acheson later wrote, "how dangerous was the practice of secret evidence and secret informers, how alien to all our conceptions of justice and the rights of the citizen. . . . Experience proved again how soon good men become callous in the use of bad practices."

The government also initiated prosecutions against the eleven top communist leaders under the Smith Act of 1940, which prohibited groups from conspiring to advocate the violent overthrow of the government. Throughout the country, citizens anxious to protect their communities against the dread infection sometimes, in ardor or panic, failed to distinguish between communism and traditional American radicalism or mere dissent.

The denunciation in 1948 of Alger Hiss, a former State Department official, as a communist spy and his conviction for perjury in January 1950 increased popular apprehension. If Hiss, a man of apparently unimpeachable respectability, was a communist agent, who might not be? The Administration compounded its troubles when Truman called the Hiss affair a "red herring" and Acheson, after Hiss' conviction, said, "I do not intend to turn my back on Alger Hiss." Then in February a little-known senator from Wisconsin, Joseph R. McCarthy, gave a speech in Wheeling, West Virginia. "I have here in my hand a list," he said—a list of communists in the State Department; whether he said there were 205 or 81 or 57 or "a lot" of communists (and this was a question around which much controversy would revolve) was in the end less important than his insistence that these communists were "known to the Secretary of State" and were "still working and making policy." With this speech, a remarkable figure began a brief but lurid career on the national stage.

The rise of McCarthyism. McCarthy's charges prompted an astonished Senate to appoint a subcommittee under Senator Millard Tydings of Maryland to look into his allegations. After weeks of hearings, the Tydings Committee declared that McCarthy had worked a "fraud and a hoax." Yet, for all the apparent failure of his charges, the hearings also revealed the facility, agility, and lack of scruple with which McCarthy operated. His most characteristic weapon was what Richard Rovere called the "multiple untruth"—a statement so complicated, flexible, and grandiose in its mendacity as almost to defy rational refutation. To this McCarthy added unlimited impudence, an instinct for demagoguery, and an unmatched skill in alley-fighting. If the Tydings Committee thought it had disciplined McCarthy, it was wrong. In the election of 1950, McCarthy's intervention in Maryland, marked by a broad hint that Tydings, a conservative Democrat whom Roosevelt had tried in vain to purge in 1938, was procommunist, brought about Tydings' defeat. From that moment, the Wisconsin senator became a formidable figure in the Senate.

The Korean War meanwhile wrought a significant change in the public atmosphere. It created a climate that transformed McCarthy's crusade from an eccentric sideshow, like that of Martin Dies, into a popular movement. If communists were killing American boys in Korea, why should communists be given the

Alger Hiss: January 1950

benefit of the doubt in the United States? In some quarters a storm of near-hysteria blew up, and for a moment membership in any liberal or internationalist organization seemed to provide grounds for indicting a man's loyalty to his country. Politicians who knew better quailed, especially when they noted the fate of Tydings in 1950 and of William Benton of Connecticut, McCarthy's next major senatorial opponent, in 1952.

Though Truman's loyalty program had in some respects overridden traditional safeguards of civil freedom, it did not go nearly far enough for McCarthy and his followers. In September 1950, Congress passed the McCarran Internal Security Act, establishing a Subversive Activities Control Board to follow communist activities in the United States and setting up bars against the admission to the country of anyone who had once been a member of a totalitarian organization.* Truman vetoed the bill: "We need not fear the expression of ideas—we do need to fear their suppression. . . . Let us not, in cowering and foolish fear, throw away the ideals which are the fundamental basis of our free society." But Congress passed the bill over his veto.

The spectacle of McCarthyism infuriated the President. "All this howl about organizations a fellow belongs to gives me a pain in the neck," he wrote when someone attacked Secretary of the Air Force Thomas K. Finletter for the crime of belonging to the United World Federalists. He told the American Legion:

> Slander, lies, character assassination—these things are a threat to every single citizen everywhere in this country. When even one American—who has done nothing wrong—is forced by fear to shut his mind and close his mouth, then all Americans are in peril. It is the job of all of us—of every American who loves his country and his freedom—to rise up and put a stop to this terrible business.

The 1952 election

Truman in retreat. But, in the backwash of the Korean War, the movement of opinion favored McCarthy. The Administration and its leading officials—especially Secretary of State Acheson—fell under unsparing attack as communist sympathizers. Conservatives asked "Who lost China?", as if China had been America's to lose, and replied that it was a group of traitors in the State Department. The Republicans scored impressive gains in the congressional elections of 1950 and looked forward with increasing confidence to 1952.

Their confidence grew with revelations of corruption within the Administration. A congressional investigation of the Reconstruction Finance Corporation in 1951 exposed collusion and payoffs—mink coats and deep freezes—in RFC loans. Soon the phrase "five percenter" became the colloquialism for the fixer who would arrange profitable transactions with the government for a 5 percent fee.

In a few months, further exposures revealed extensive corruption in the Bureau of Internal Revenue and in the tax division of the Department of Justice. In addition, the Senate Crime Investigation Committee, under the chairmanship of Estes Kefauver of Tennessee, set forth before rapt television audiences the connections between politics and organized crime in big cities.

"There are two Trumans," Elmer Davis once said, "—the White House Truman and the courthouse Truman. He does the big things right, and the little things wrong." The disclosures of 1951–52 called attention to the decline that had taken place in the governmental service from the relatively incorruptible thirties—a decline brought about in part because Truman's ill-concealed scorn for the "professional liberal" had driven many of the old New Dealers from government to be replaced by party hacks. When the facts got out, moreover, Truman, constrained by loyalty to old political associates, seemed grudging in his response; and, though the necessary house-cleaning finally took place, it took place too late for him to recapture public confidence. All this strengthened the idea of a "mess in Washington" and helped substantiate a growing national conviction that the Democratic party had been in power too long.

---

*A second McCarran Act, also passed over Truman's veto, was the Immigration and Nationality Act of 1952. While this bill finally abolished the Asian-exclusion provisions of 1924, it retained the national-origins quota system, which discriminated in favor of immigrants from northern and western Europe and which critics condemned as a form of racism built into federal law. It also required that foreigners visiting the United States go through so complicated a system of loyalty checks that many came to feel that the United States regarded them as potential criminals.

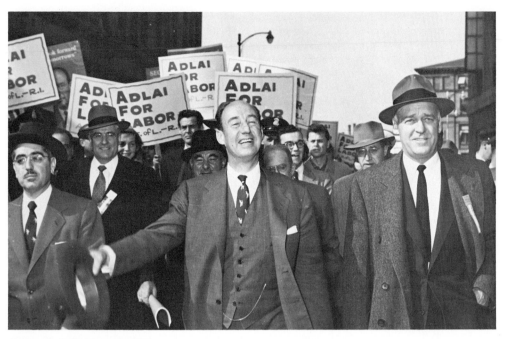

Stevenson in Providence, 1952

The campaign of 1952.

Robert A. Taft's triumphant reelection to the Senate in 1950 over determined liberal and labor opposition made him the leading contender for the Republican nomination in 1952. But the powerful Eastern wing of the party, fearing that the Ohio senator was too strong, too isolationist, and too conservative, turned to General Dwight D. Eisenhower. The contest between the Taft and Eisenhower forces reached its angry climax at the Chicago convention in July. There the Eisenhower supporters outmaneuvered their opposition in a battle over contested delegates. Eisenhower was nominated on the first ballot. Senator Richard M. Nixon of California, who had played an important part in the exposure of Alger Hiss, became his running mate.

Truman had meanwhile withdrawn from the Democratic contest. Though his choice for the Democratic nomination—Governor Adlai E. Stevenson of Illinois—at first demurred, the Democratic convention in Chicago drafted Stevenson for the top place on the ticket. Little known to voters outside Illinois, Stevenson in the next three months established himself as a brilliant, literate, and eloquent candidate. His campaign pledge was to ''talk sense to the American people.'' He explained in a series of remarkable speeches that the problems of the age had no easy solution and called for restraint and sacrifice. Labor backed him, and he won particular support among intellectuals.

The Republican campaign was based on the themes of ''Korea, communism, and corruption.'' Nixon, a more experienced campaigner than Eisenhower, developed these themes with particular relish, referring to the Democratic candidate, for example, as ''Adlai the appeaser . . . who got a Ph.D. from Dean Acheson's College of Cowardly Communist

The election of 1952

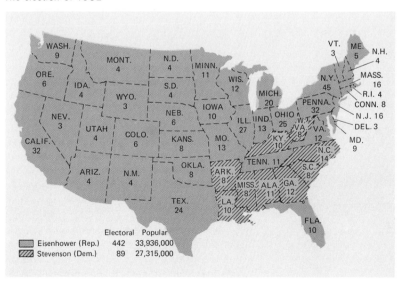

	Electoral	Popular
Eisenhower (Rep.)	442	33,936,000
Stevenson (Dem.)	89	27,315,000

Eisenhower: the crusade

From the beginning we will bring into government men and women to whom low public morals are unthinkable. Thus, we will not only drive wrong-doers and their cronies out of government. We will make sure that they do not get into government in the first place....

Then we will begin to move forward. With that accomplished, we will make these our objectives, our immediate aims for the government of the United States:

First, to save: That means an administration which knows how to practice the wiser spending of less of the people's money;

Second, to streamline: That means an administration which knows how to make government the more efficient servant of the people;

Third, to decentralize: That means an administration which is determined effectively to bring government close to the people. It means, also, faith in the people to act more wisely in their own behalf than can a bureaucrat removed a thousand miles from the scene of action.

Fourth, to unify: That means an administration able to make the whole government a joint, cooperative enterprise for the whole people's benefit.

From Dwight D. Eisenhower, Campaign Address at St. Louis, September 1952.

Stevenson: a new day

Government has three duties.

First, government is an umpire, denying special privilege, ensuring equal rights, restraining monopoly and greed and bigotry....

Second, government has the duty of creating an economic climate in which creative men can take risks and reap rewards, so that our economic life will have a continuous flow of fresh ideas and fresh leadership; and, of course, it means the building of solid defenses against the greatest threat to that flow—depression....

Third, government has the duty of helping the people develop their country.

The Federal Government made the Louisiana Purchase, and on that land a nation grew to greatness. No private corporation would have built Grand Coulee Dam, yet in the Grand Coulee country people are building their homes and establishing their private business, and farmers are converting desert into garden....

We take our stand upon the fundamental principle that the role of government is, to sum up, just this: To remove the roadblocks put in the way of the people by nature and by greedy men; to release the energies of the people, so that free men may work the miracles of the future as they have worked the miracles of the past.

From Adlai E. Stevenson, Campaign Address at St. Louis, October 1952.

Containment." "I further charge," Nixon added, "that Mr. Truman, Dean Acheson and other administration officials for political reasons covered up this Communist conspiracy and attempted to halt its exposure." Intellectual supporters of Stevenson were dismissed as "eggheads."

The campaign was interrupted by a revelation that Nixon had been a beneficiary of a fund collected on his behalf by California businessmen. For a moment, Eisenhower considered asking Nixon to resign from the ticket. But a histrionic television speech in an autobiographical vein enabled the vice-presidential candidate to regain his partner's confidence. When Eisenhower, late in the campaign, declared his intention to go to Korea if elected, he clinched his victory. The popular vote showed 33.9 million for Eisenhower, 27.3 million for Stevenson; the margin in the Electoral College was 442 to 89. Twenty years of Democratic rule had come to an end.

GENERAL

Truman's *Memoirs,* 2 vols.* (1955–56), are pungent, revealing, and sometimes controversial; his *Mr. President* (1952), William Hillman, ed., offers more informal glimpses of his Presidency. Jonathan Daniels, *The Man from Independence* (1950), is perceptive on Truman's formative years. B. J. Bernstein and A. J. Matusow, *The Truman Administration: A Documentary History* (1966), is a useful compilation. Cabell Phillips, *The Truman Presidency: The History of a Triumphant Succession** (1966), gives a generally favorable appraisal; for dissent from the left, see B. J. Bernstein, ed., *Politics and Policies of the Truman Administration** (1970). R. E. Neustadt, *Presidential Power** (1960), has penetrating insights.

FOREIGN POLICY

Seyom Brown, *The Faces of Power** (1968), provides a cogent general analysis with special attention to military and economic factors. For the development of the Cold War, W. H. McNeill, *America, Britain and Russia* (1953), and Herbert Feis, *Churchill, Roosevelt and Stalin** (1957), remain fundamental works; Feis, *From Trust to Terror* (1970), L. J. Halle, *The Cold War as History** (1967), and André Fontaine, *History of the Cold War,* 2 vols.* (1968–69), carry the story forward. A brilliant contemporaneous critique is Walter Lippmann, *The Cold War* (1947). The revisionist view is stated with moderation in Walter La Feber, *America, Russia, and the Cold War, 1945–1966** (1967); with impassioned detail in Joyce and Gabriel Kolko, *The Limits of Power* (1971); less carefully in D. F. Fleming, *The Cold War and Its Origins, 1917–1960,* 2 vols. (1961), and in Gar Alperovitz, *Atomic Diplomacy: Hiroshima and Potsdam** (1965); see also T. G. Paterson, ed., *Cold War Critics** (1971). Two useful compilations—L. C. Gardner, Arthur Schlesinger, Jr., and Hans Morgenthau, *The Origins of the Cold War** (1970), and J. V. Compton, ed., *America and the Origins of the Cold War* (1972)—give some flavor of the historiographical controversy.

On Soviet policy, R. A. Medvedev, *Let History Judge: The Origins and Consequences of Stalinism* (1972), is a rich account by an anti-Stalinist Soviet scholar. Strobe Talbott, ed., *Khrushchev Remembers* (1970), is fascinating but to be used with caution. For stimulating interpretations by American scholars, see Adam Ulam, *Expansion and Coexistence** (1968) and *The Rivals: America and Russia Since World War II* (1971); M. D. Shulman, *Stalin's Foreign Policy Reappraised* (1963); and Zbigniew Brzezinski, *Ideology and Power in Society Politics** (1961).

Dean Acheson, *Present at the Creation** (1969), is an able and massive memoir. Other significant books by policy-makers include J. F. Byrnes, *Speaking Frankly* (1947) and *All in One Lifetime* (1958); Walter Millis and E. S. Duffield, eds., *The Forrestal Diaries* (1951); A. H. Vandenberg, Jr., and J. A. Morris, eds., *The Private Papers of Senator Vandenberg* (1952); G. F. Kennan, *Memoirs, 1925–1950* (1967); C. E. Bohlen, *The Transformation of American Foreign Policy** (1969); W. A. Harriman, *America and Russia in a Changing World* (1971). L. C. Gardner, *Architects of Illusion* (1970), assesses the policy-makers from a revisionist viewpoint. For contemporaneous Republican views, consult J. F. Dulles, *War or Peace* (1950), and R. A. Taft, *A Foreign Policy for Americans* (1951).

On economic relations with Britain, R. N. Gardner, *Sterling-Dollar Diplomacy* (1956), is the standard work. J. M. Jones, *The Fifteen Weeks** (1955), describes the origins of the Truman Doctrine and the Marshall Plan; H. B. Price, *The Marshall Plan* (1955), reviews the plan in operation. Germany is discussed from various viewpoints in L. D. Clay, *Decision in Germany* (1950); John Gimbel, *The American Occupation of Germany* (1968); W. P. Davison, *The Berlin Blockade* (1958); Edgar McInnis, *et al., The Shaping of Postwar Germany* (1960); J. E. Smith, *The Defense of Berlin* (1963); and Robert McGeehan, *The German Rearmament Question* (1971).

For the Japanese settlement and occupation, see Herbert Feis, *Contest Over Japan** (1967), and E. O. Reischauer, *The United States and Japan* (3rd ed., 1965). Tang Tsou, *America's Failure in China, 1941–1950** (1963), and J. K. Fairbank, *The United States and China** (rev. 3rd ed., 1971), are two excellent works. G. D. Paige, *The Korean Decision: June 24–30, 1950** (1968), is meticulous and authoritative. David Rees, *Korea: The Limited War** (1964), is a good summary;

*Available in a paperback edition.

see, in addition, useful works by two generals, M. B. Ridgway, *The Korean War* (1967), and J. L. Collins, *War in Peacetime* (1969); and also Allen Whiting, *China Crosses the Yalu** (1960). J. W. Spanier is detached in *The Truman-MacArthur Controversy and the Korean War** (1959), and Trumbull Higgins takes a skeptical view in *Korea and the Fall of MacArthur* (1960). General MacArthur is discussed adoringly in Courtney Whitney, *MacArthur* (1956), and in Douglas MacArthur, *Reminiscences* (1964), and more coolly in R. H. Rovere and Arthur Schlesinger, Jr., *The General and the President* (1951; reissued as *The MacArthur Controversy,** 1965).

For the beginnings of the Indochina imbroglio, see J. T. McAlister, *Vietnam: The Origins of Revolution** (1969); G. M. Kahin and J. W. Lewis, *The United States in Vietnam** (1967); Marvin Kalb and Elie Abel, *Roots of Involvement* (1971); and Ellen Hammer, *The Struggle for Indochina* (1954). Edward Friedman and Mark Selden, eds., *America's Asia: Dissenting Essays on Asian-American Relations** (1971), offers a revisionist critique of American Far Eastern policies.

For atomic energy, the authorized but judicious studies by R. G. Hewlett and O. E. Anderson, Jr., *The New World* (1962) and *Atomic Shield* (1969), are indispensable. For more personal views, consult B. M. Baruch, *Baruch, The Public Years* (1960), and the second volume of D. E. Lilienthal, *Journals: The Atomic Energy Years* (1964). On the United Nations, see Trygve Lie, *In the Cause of Peace* (1954), and J. G. Stoessinger, *The United Nations and the Superpowers** (1965).

DOMESTIC AFFAIRS

Samuel Lubell, *The Future of American Politics** (1952), is a penetrating analysis of the political currents of the Truman years; and John Gunther, *Inside U.S.A.* (1951), gives a vivid rendition of political and regional dramatics. S. K. Bailey, *Congress Makes a Law** (1950), deals with the origins of the Employment Act of 1946, while E. S. Flash, Jr., *Economic Advice and Presidential Leadership* (1965), reports on the Council of Economic Advisers in action. Specific aspects of Truman's domestic policy are considered in R. A. Lee, *Truman and Taft-Hartley* (1967); A. F. McClure, *The Truman Administration and the Problems of Postwar Labor* (1969); A. J. Matusow, *Farm Policies and Politics of the Truman Administration** (1967); R. O. Davies, *Housing Reform During the Truman Administration* (1966); P. H. Douglas, *Ethics in Government* (1952); and Estes Kefauver, *Crime in America* (1951). For the 1948 election, see Irwin Ross, *The Loneliest Campaign** (1968); and for the 1952 election, A. E. Stevenson, *Speeches* (1952), and J. B. Martin's authoritative biography of Adlai Stevenson (1973).

M. R. Konvitz, *Expanding Liberties** (1966), assesses progress in civil rights; Walter White, *A Man Called White* (1948), and A. M. Rose, *The Negro in Postwar America** (1950), provide contemporaneous analyses of the situation of black Americans.

For the communist problem, Earl Latham, *The Communist Conspiracy in Washington** (1966), is the most sober guide. R. H. Rovere, *Senator Joe McCarthy** (1959), is brilliantly critical; W. F. Buckley, Jr., *McCarthy and His Enemies* (1954), is affectionately admiring; M. P. Rogin, *The Intellectuals and McCarthy** (1967), gives the most solid explanation of McCarthy's grassroots strength; Robert Griffith, *The Politics of Fear* (1970), discusses McCarthy and the Senate; and Daniel Bell, ed., *The Radical Right** (1963), strives, not altogether persuasively, for sociological illumination. Thoughtful contemporaneous discussions are to be found in Francis Biddle, *The Fear of Freedom* (1951), and Alan Barth, *The Loyalty of Free Men* (1951). Whittaker Chambers, *Witness** (1952), and Alger Hiss, *In the Court of Public Opinion* (1957), present contrasting views. For anti-Stalinist liberalism, see Reinhold Niebuhr, *The Children of Light and the Children of Darkness** (1944) and *The Irony of American History** (1952), and Arthur Schlesinger, Jr., *The Vital Center** (1949); a critique of this position is to be found in Christopher Lasch, *The New Radicalism in America** (1965).

*Available in a paperback edition.

31

Years of repose

By 1952 the American people had endured nearly a generation of unrelenting crisis. In the years since 1929 they had experienced the worst depression in their history, the worst hot war, the worst Cold War, the worst limited war. During these years, moreover, they had followed Presidents who believed strongly in affirmative government and vigorous action. But a nation's capacity for innovation and crusading is limited. Just as the first two decades of the twentieth century—the activist decades dominated by Theodore Roosevelt and Woodrow Wilson—left the people with a yearning for normalcy, so the high-tension thirties and forties produced a fresh desire for respite. The new pursuit of normalcy, though, took place in stormier times and within the frameworks established by depression and war. Communist challenge and revolutionary ferment abroad, minority aspirations and population growth at home, confronted the nation with problems it could not easily ignore.

The Eisenhower mood

The new President. President Dwight D. Eisenhower embodied the popular mood. Sixty-two years old on his inauguration, he was already a national hero, long beloved by his countrymen. After quiet years in the peacetime army, Eisenhower had been one of that group of remarkable military men who emerged during the Second World War. His service as supreme commander of the Allied Forces in Europe was followed by a postwar tour of duty as Chief of Staff. President of Columbia University in 1948, he yielded to Truman's request in 1950 that he return to Europe as supreme commander of NATO. He resigned this post to seek the Republican nomination in 1952.

The appearance of being "above" politics was an important source of Eisenhower's popular strength. People weary of the "mess in Washington" and wanting an end to the con-

troversies of the New Deal era saw him as the man to heal the nation's wounds. His appointed role, wrote Walter Lippmann, was "that of the restorer of order and peace after an age of violence and faction." His affable personality and accommodating temperament qualified him as national conciliator. Actually his surface geniality and imprecision concealed much political cunning, an instinct for self-protection, and considerable ability, not always employed, to enforce his will.

Eisenhower and the Presidency. He had been the candidate of what would later be termed the Eastern establishment against the Midwestern, small-town, isolationist Republicans who had favored Robert A. Taft; and he was expected to lead his long-embattled party to accept both the international policies and the social reforms of the Roosevelt-Truman

Under the Constitution the President of the United States is alone responsible for the "faithful execution of the laws." Our government is fixed on the basis that the President is the only person in the executive branch who has the final authority. Everyone else in the executive branch is an agent of the President. There are some people, and sometimes members of Congress and the press, who get mixed up in their thinking about the powers of the President. The important fact to remember is that the President is the only person in the executive branch who has final authority, and if he does not exercise it, we may be in trouble. If he exercises his authority wisely, that is good for the country. If he does not exercise it wisely, that is too bad, but it is better than not exercising it at all.

Yet our government is so vast that branches of the administrative machinery do not always tie in smoothly with the White House. The Cabinet represents the principal medium through which the President controls his administration. I made it a point always to listen to Cabinet officers at length and with care, especially when their points of view differed from mine.

I never allowed myself to forget that the final authority was mine. I would ask the Cabinet to share their counsel with me, even encouraging disagreement and argument to sharpen up the different points of view. On major issues I would frequently ask them to vote, and I expected the Cabinet officers to be frank and candid in expressing their opinions to me. At the same time, I insisted that they keep me informed of the major activities of their departments in order to make certain that they supported the policy once I had made a decision.

From Harry S Truman, *Memoirs*, Vol. I, *Year of Decisions*, 1955.

epoch. In foreign policy this anticipation was sound. But the new President had little interest in domestic matters, assigned them low priority, and, though he had no hope of dismantling the New Deal, was in some respects more conservative than Taft.

An exponent of the Whig theory of the Presidency, Eisenhower rejected the idea of strong presidential leadership. Roosevelt and Truman, he felt, had aggrandized the executive branch at the expense of the other branches of government. It was his duty now to "restore" the constitutional balance. In dealing with Congress, he believed that his responsibility was simply to propose policies; thereafter members of Congress could "vote their own consciences." Even within his official family, he did not, save in rare cases, insist on his own views. He once said of his Cabinet, "I have given way on a number of personal opinions to this gang." He was not, he liked to remark, the desk-pounding sort of President. Though disposed to complain about the Republican party in private, he realized that he was far more popular than the party and therefore did not propose to risk his public

Inauguration, 1953: more problems than respite

standing by acting as a party-leader. "In the general derogatory sense," he observed in 1955, "you can say that, of course, that I do not like politics."

In running the Presidency, Eisenhower rejected the informal methods of his civilian predecessors in favor of the military staff system. Former Governor Sherman Adams of New Hampshire, as chief of the executive staff, controlled the flow of domestic information and recommendations to the President; in foreign affairs, Secretary of State John Foster Dulles had a similar monopoly. "I don't want people springing things on me!" the President often said. Commitment to the staff system tended to confine Eisenhower's knowledge of public matters. He seldom read the daily newspapers, and he drew on fewer sources of information and ideas than some of his predecessors.

Some observers welcomed what they regarded as a necessary institutionalization of the Presidency. Others were more skeptical. Sam Rayburn, House Democratic leader, once said of Eisenhower as President: "No, won't do. Good man, but wrong business."

I think any President who tries to follow what he believes to be public opinion will in the long run come a cropper.... The President, I think, always has a job, day in and day out—not merely in times of crisis—but trying to get an informed public opinion.... I went to the people in every way I could....

I have not much patience with the desk-pounding type of leadership.... Leadership is a matter of influencing people. And you sometimes have to influence people who are hostile as well as friends.

From Dwight D. Eisenhower, Interview on CBS-TV, February 1962.

The Presidency: D. D. E.

The job of the next President will be the hardest since Roosevelt, and I think Roosevelt had the hardest of all except Lincoln and perhaps Washington. The job will be tremendous, and a great responsibility will center on the President. The real dilemma we face is whether a free society in which each of us follows our own self-interest can compete over a long period of time with a totalitarian society....

There are many short-term advantages which a totalitarian possesses in that kind of competition.... The responsibility of the President, therefore, is especially great. He must serve as a catalyst, an energizer, the defender of the public good and the public interest against all the narrow private interests which operate in our society. Only the President can do this, and only a President who recognizes the true nature of this hard challenge can fulfill this historic function....

Congress is quite obviously not equipped to make basic policy, to conduct foreign relations, to speak for the national interest in the way that a President can and must.... I ... believe that in the next two or three decades there will be greater demands upon the President than ever before—and the powers are there, if the man will use them.

Quoted in James M. Burns, *John Kennedy: A Political Profile,* 1959.

The Presidency: J. F. K.

Republican foreign policy

Ending the Korean War. Fulfilling his campaign pledge, Eisenhower visited Korea in the interval between his election and the inauguration. Though this trip produced no miracles, it expressed the theme of conciliation that would be the President's personal contribution to the conduct of foreign affairs. Cease-fire negotiations, initiated in July 1951, continued to drag on, however, as did hostilities; indeed, some of the heaviest fighting of the war took place around Porkchop Hill in the Chorwon area in July 1953.

The sticking-point was whether, and how, prisoners of war should be repatriated. Many of the 173,000 North Koreans in United Nations hands had made clear that they did not want to return to North Korea. United Nations negotiators accordingly rejected communist insistence on compulsory repatriation. In the spring of 1953, exasperated by the deadlock,

Eisenhower decided to let the communists understand. "that, in the absence of satisfactory progress, we intended to move decisively without inhibition in our use of weapons, and would no longer be responsible for confining hostilities to the Korean Peninsula." Whether because of this threat of nuclear war, or for other reasons, the North Koreans now accepted voluntary repatriation. President Syngman Rhee of South Korea, seeing the collapse of his hopes for a united Korea, opposed the end of hostilities and even ordered the unilateral release of twenty-five thousand North Korean prisoners. But an armistice was finally concluded at Panmunjom on July 27, 1953.

The armistice provided for a demilitarized zone between the opposing armies, established a Neutral Nations Supervisory Commission to carry out the armistice terms, and called for a political conference to settle remaining questions, including the future of Korea and the fate of prisoners of war who refused to return to their homelands. But the conference was never held, and during the next few years each side repeatedly charged the other with violations of the armistice agreement. The United States signed a mutual-defense treaty with South Korea in 1954 and kept an uncertain hand in South Korean affairs. The increasingly capricious actions of the aging Syngman Rhee caused widespread protest both in South Korea and in Washington, culminating in the overthrow of the Rhee regime in April 1960 and the establishment of a new government with American support.

The Korean War had lasted three years and one month. During that time 33,629 Americans had lost their lives in battle, along with about 3,000 from other UN countries and about 50,000 South Koreans. Total communist battle casualties were estimated at 1.5 million. For all the bitterness and frustration the war produced at home, it had stopped aggression in Korea, strengthened the authority of the United Nations, and shown the communist world that the democratic nations were prepared to meet military challenge.

Eisenhower and Dulles. Ending the Korean War marked a first success for Eisenhower as a man of peace. His pacific instincts and pragmatic temper, however, were somewhat at odds with the ideological militancy of his party and especially of his Secretary of State. The differences should not be exaggerated. Eisenhower fully accepted the premises of the Cold War (as, indeed, did Adlai Stevenson), reposed complete confidence in John Foster Dulles, and granted him exceptional authority over the day-to-day conduct of foreign policy, reserving only the right to intervene in extreme cases. Nevertheless, as Sherman Adams later wrote, "The hard and uncompromising line that the United States government took toward Soviet Russia and Red China between 1953 and the early months of 1959 was more a Dulles line than an Eisenhower one."

As for Dulles, few Americans had ever seemed so well prepared by inheritance and experience for such responsibility. The grandson of one Secretary of State (John Foster) and nephew of another (Robert Lansing), he had begun his diplomatic career as his grandfather's secretary at the Hague Conference of

John Foster Dulles: a penchant for moralism

1907. He had been at Versailles in 1919; and, though an isolationist in the thirties, he had emerged by 1944 as the leading Republican spokesman on foreign affairs. By profession a lawyer and by avocation an eminent Presbyterian layman, Dulles united a talent for close legal argument with a penchant for righteous moralism. Critics found him legalistic and sanctimonious. One British foreign secretary, Herbert Morrison, spoke of his "duplicity," and another, Harold Macmillan, questioned his "intellectual integrity."

Though identified with many aspects of the Truman-Acheson foreign policy, Dulles had grown violently critical of that policy as the 1952 election drew near. Now he felt that containment would commit the United States to a policy of indefinite coexistence with communism, whereas the proper goal, in his view, was not to coexist with the communist threat but to end it. Containment was, as he put it in the Republican foreign-policy plank, "negative, futile and immoral." "We will abandon the policy of containment," Dulles said, "and will actively develop hope and resistance spirit within the captive peoples." The mere statement by the United States "that it wants and expects liberation to occur would change, in an electrifying way, the mood of the captive peoples." By such means the Cold War could be brought to an end; moreover, the cost would be far less than the cost of containment. In short, the infusion of "dynamism" into American foreign policy would both push back communism and balance the budget.

Thus Eisenhower in his first state-of-the-union message canceled Truman's 1950 order to neutralize the Straits of Formosa, thereby "unleashing" Chiang Kai-shek and his Nationalist forces for presumed reconquest of the mainland. He also reaffirmed the Republican platform pledge to repudiate "all commitments contained in secret understandings such as those of Yalta which aid Communist enslavement." However, Chiang's forces were, in effect, "re-leashed" by the mutual-security pact of 1955 with Nationalist China; the publication of the Yalta documents revealed no secret agreements; and American inaction in face of anti-Soviet upheavals in East Germany in 1953 and Hungary in 1956 ended talk of "liberation."

The alliance system. In abandoning liberation, Dulles had no choice but to fall back on containment. But, where Truman had at first

SEATO Conference, 1954

applied his doctrine sparingly, Dulles now boldly generalized it. Seeing the atheistic communist conspiracy as both evil in itself and the source of all the world's troubles, he absolutized the philosophy of the Cold War. Assuming that the Soviet Union would exploit situations of local military weakness everywhere, he concluded that aggression could be restrained only if such situations were shored up at every point by visible military force.

Dulles' central idea was to arrest the advance of communism by setting up NATO-like alliances in other parts of the world. In 1954 he brought together three Asian states (Thailand, Pakistan, and the Philippines) with the United States, Britain, France, Australia, and New Zealand in a new Southeast Asia Treaty Organization (SEATO). SEATO's provisions were, however, far less explicit and binding than those of NATO. Instead of stipulating that an attack on one signatory would be regarded as an attack on all, it called only for consultation among the signatories in case of communist subversion and for action by each state "in accordance with its constitutional processes" in case of armed attack.

In the Middle East, Dulles pursued a similar strategy, inducing the British to create a regional defense organization under the Baghdad Pact of 1955 (later known as CENTO—the Central Treaty Organization). Though the United States continued its aid

program to underdeveloped countries, that program became subordinate to the mutual-security system. The aid itself was predominantly military—the Point Four idea receded, the very name being dropped—and it went in the main to such embattled states as South Korea, Formosa, and South Vietnam. Denouncing neutralism as "immoral," Dulles hoped to force all nations to choose sides in the Cold War. Some observers felt that he had undue faith in the capacity of military pacts to stabilize underdeveloped areas. Critics referred acidly to his "pactomania."

Behind the alliance system stood the military power of the United States. Eisenhower, however, rejected the recommendation of the Truman Administration that the United States diversify its military establishment. Fearing that an attempt to provide limited-war forces would unbalance the budget and weaken the American economy, Eisenhower restored the atomic bomb as the center of American strategy. "My feeling was then," he wrote in 1963, "and still remains, that it would be impossible for the United States to maintain the military commitments which it now sustains around the world (without turning into a garrison state) did we not possess atomic weapons and the will to use them when necessary."

As Dulles defined the "new look" in 1954, it "was to depend primarily upon a great capacity to retaliate, instantly, by means and at places of our choosing." He explained that this meant rejecting the policy of "meeting aggression by direct and local opposition" in favor of "more reliance on deterrent power and less dependence on local defensive power." In other words, local aggression was presumably to be countered in the future, not by limited war, but by a threat to retaliate directly against the Soviet Union or Communist China. The threat by itself, Dulles apparently thought, would be sufficient to stop aggression. As he put it on another occasion, the "necessary art" was "the ability to get to the verge without getting into the war. . . . If you are scared to go to the brink, you are lost." The doctrine of "massive retaliation" would lower the cost of national defense, bringing "more bang for the buck."

The institutionalization of the Cold War.

The absolutist philosophy soon took root in a group of government agencies—the State Department (purged by Dulles of active dissenters), the Defense Department, the National Security Council, the Central Intelligence Agency—all of which developed vested institutional interests in the idea of a militarily expansionist Soviet Union. The Cold War conferred power, appropriations, and public influence on these agencies; and, by the natural law of bureaucracies, their stake in the conflict steadily increased.

Restrained from local military action by the massive-retaliation strategy, restrained as well by Eisenhower's own circumspection, the government now employed the CIA as the routine instrument of American intervention. The fact that Allen W. Dulles, head of the CIA, was the Secretary of State's brother ensured close coordination with American diplomatic objectives. In these years the CIA mounted a series of ambitious clandestine operations—helping to overthrow governments regarded as communist or procommunist in Iran (1953) and Guatemala (1954), failing to do so in Indonesia (1958), helping to install supposedly prowestern governments in Egypt (1954) and Laos (1959), organizing an expedition of Cuban refugees against the Castro regime (1960). Such activity doubtless fed the American government's conviction both of its ability and its right to decide the destiny of other nations.

The same institutionalization had long since taken place in the Soviet Union, where the Russians were already equipped with a dogma of inevitable conflict and with the means of local intervention. This meant on both sides by the 1950s a propensity to perceive local conflicts in global terms, political conflicts in moral terms, and relative differences in absolute terms. Each side saw mankind as divided

Europe, North Africa, and the Middle East

Funeral of Stalin: feuds were to follow

between forces of light and forces of darkness. Each assumed that the opposing bloc was under the organized and unified control of the other. Washington supposed that what was then called the free world should reshape itself on the American model; Moscow that the communist world should reshape itself on the Russian model.

Crisis in East Asia. The American concern with the underdeveloped world, expressed in the Dulles pacts and the CIA interventions, corresponded to modifications in Soviet foreign policy, forecast by Stalin in a statement to the Nineteenth Party Congress in October 1952. Stalin's death on March 5, 1953, was followed by harsh and obscure feuds among Soviet leaders, resulting in the victory of N. S. Krushchev by 1957–58. During these years, however, the communists steadily carried forward Stalin's 1953 injunction to pick up "the banner of nationalism where it had been dropped by the bourgeoisie." They launched major campaigns to win over the new nations first of Asia and the Middle East, then of Africa, and, by the end of the decade, of Latin America. The Soviet claim that communism offered the best road to modernization acquired some plausibility in the fifties because of both the Russian rate of industrial growth, averaging about three times that of the United States, and unexpected Soviet technical breakthroughs—the hydrogen bomb (1953), the first intercontinental ballistic missile and Sputnik, the first earth satellite (1957), the first moon satellite (1959), and the first man in space (1961).

Especially striking was the emergence of China, the most populous nation in the world, as a communist state. Washington assumed Communist China to be a Soviet subsidiary and therefore a new instrument in the monolithic communist plan of world conquest. Concern over China now heightened American interest in Indochina. Here, Eisenhower later wrote, the conflict "began gradually, with Chinese intervention, to assume its true complexion of a struggle between Communism and non-Communist forces rather than one between a colonial power and colonists who were intent on attaining independence." By 1954 the United States was paying nearly 80 percent of the French cost of the continuing war against Ho Chi Minh and the Viet Minh. The French position, however, had grown desperate. The war was bitterly unpopular in the homeland, while in Indochina the guerrillas under the astute leadership of General Giap were spreading across the country. In March 1954, with substantial French forces under siege in the valley of Dienbienphu in western Tonkin, Paris asked Washington for armed intervention.

In the preceding August the National Security Council had said, "The loss of Indochina would be critical to the security of the United States." Eisenhower himself now remarked in a press conference that Indochina was of "transcendent" concern; "you have a row of dominoes set up, you knock over the first one. . . . You could have the beginning of a disintegration that would have the most profound influences." Admiral Arthur Radford, chairman of the Joint Chiefs of Staff, proposed the use of the atomic bomb to raise the siege of Dienbienphu. When General Ridgway, now Army Chief of Staff, strongly opposed this plan, Radford recommended a massive air strike from American carriers. Though Ridgway opposed this too, Dulles favored it, and Eisenhower agreed on condition that Congress and the British went along. Vice President Nixon suggested to a conven-

French reinforcements parachuting into Dienbienphu

tion of newspaper editors the possibility of "putting American boys in," and Dulles tried to sell the Radford plan on Capitol Hill and in London. But leading senators, among them Lyndon B. Johnson and John F. Kennedy, were highly skeptical. Nevertheless the Administration made preparations for a strike on April 28. Then Winston Churchill, once again British prime minister, rejected and killed the plan. "What we are being asked to do," he told his cabinet, "is assist in misleading the Congress into approving a military operation which would be in itself ineffective, and might well bring the world to the verge of major war."

Dienbienphu fell, after fifty-six days, on May 7. Four days later Eisenhower informed Paris that he would seek authority from Congress to send troops to Indochina if the French would make political concessions to anticommunist nationalists. Serious preparations were made for American intervention even without British participation. Soon, however, Pierre Mendès-France came to power in Paris with a pledge to end the war in a month. In the next weeks negotiations at Geneva, from which the United States stood aside, produced a provisional settlement. Under pressure from their respective large-power patrons, both Vietnamese factions reluctantly accepted the temporary partition of their nation at the seventeenth parallel—this to be a "military demarcation line" and "not in any way [to] be interpreted as constituting a political or territorial boundary"—with reunification to come through general elections scheduled for July 1956.

Washington had watched the negotiations with grim disapproval, and the National Security Council now pronounced the result a "disaster . . . a major forward stride of Communism which may lead to the loss of Southeast Asia." The organization of SEATO was part of the strategy designed to avert this latter possibility; a special protocol extended the organization's protection to South Vietnam, Laos, and Cambodia. The Administration decided to give assistance to the Saigon government of South Vietnam and its new premier Ngo Dinh Diem, a devout Catholic and stubborn nationalist whose strength of purpose had impressed many Americans, liberal and conservative, during his American stay in 1950-53. In 1955 Diem rejected the elections provided for in the Geneva accords. Soon he deposed Emperor Bao Dai and, as president of the new Republic of Vietnam, moved to extinguish political opposition, abolish village self-government, and confirm his personal control. American aid continued, and a fatal involvement deepened.

In the meantime, the mutual-security pact with Nationalist China enlarged Dulles' ring of alliances. Once unleashed, Chiang Kai-shek had put troops on islands in the Straits of Formosa, notably Quemoy, Matsu, and the Tachens. When the Chinese communists started bombing Quemoy in September 1954, Eisenhower supplemented the mutual-security pact by persuading Congress in January 1955 to pass the Formosa Resolution authorizing American action to defend the offshore islands if the United States considered an attack on these islands to be part of an attack on Taiwan.

The Administration continued to insist it was reversing the Truman-Acheson policies. "Isn't it wonderful," said Vice President Nixon in 1954, "finally to have a Secretary of State who isn't taken in by the Communists, who stands up to them?" But observers were more impressed by continuities than by reversals. Though the Dulles tone was more moralistic and ideological than that of his predecessors and his proposals more bellicose, his militancy was offset by the President's caution and optimism; and the actual results were essentially an extension and elaboration of the Truman-Acheson idea of containment.

Modern Republicanism at home

Eisenhower's domestic purposes. The preference for inaction that served Eisenhower so well in foreign affairs proved less fortunate at home. He came to the Presidency at a time of unexpected population growth. The fall in the birth rate during the Depression had led demographers to predict that the nation's population would soon level off. Instead, the return to prosperity in the war years produced a swing to earlier marriages and larger families. At the same time, medical advances—the introduction of penicillin and other antibiotics, of antipolio vaccines, and of new surgical techniques—brought about a steady drop in the death rate. Between 1935 and 1957 the birth rate rose from 16.9 to 25 per thousand, the death rate fell from 10.9 to 9.6, and life expectancy rose toward 70. Furthermore, about 2.25 million immigrants entered the country in the fifties—more than in any decade since the twenties. The nation's population had grown only about 9 million in the thirties; it grew 19 million in the forties and 28 million in the fifties. The increase in the fifties alone was almost equal to the total population of the country a century earlier.

To cope with the consequent strain on the institutions and facilities of American society, Eisenhower offered only what he called "modern Republicanism" or "dynamic conservatism." This meant in practice an acceptance of the social and economic framework of the New Deal tempered by a determination to preserve the value of the dollar and to cut back the activity of the federal government. Inexperienced in domestic problems, Eisenhower tended to defer to those whose superior wisdom, in his view, was certified by their financial success. His Cabinet was dominated by Secretary of the Treasury George M. Humphrey, an Ohio businessman who reinforced deeply conservative views with a strong and genial personality. When the new Secretary of Defense, Charles E. Wilson of General Motors, was asked whether he foresaw a conflict between his business and official commitments, he replied, "I cannot conceive of one because for years I thought what was good for our country was good for General Motors, and *vice versa.*" The Secretary of the Interior, Douglas McKay of Oregon, summed up the general attitude when he said, "We're here in the saddle as an Administration representing business and industry." The conspicuous exception was the Secretary of Labor, Martin Durkin of the Plumbers Union, whose appointment prompted the remark that the Cabinet consisted of "eight millionaires and a plumber." His presence displeased prominent Republicans like Taft (who termed the appointment "incredible"); and after eight months of vain effort to persuade the Administration to go along on Taft-Hartley revision, Durkin resigned.

McCarthy: zenith and decline. Some voters had supported Eisenhower in the belief that a Republican President would be better able to control McCarthy than a Democrat. Eisenhower's campaign, however, had not been reassuring on this point. In 1951 McCarthy had denounced General Marshall as part of "a conspiracy so immense and an infamy so black as to dwarf any previous venture in the history of man." Later Eisenhower, to avoid offending McCarthy, deleted a paragraph of praise for Marshall from a campaign speech in Wisconsin. This action foreshadowed the President's reluctance to engage himself personally in the McCarthy issue. As he later put it, "I will not get in the gutter with *that* guy."

For over a year, President Eisenhower tried to get along with McCarthy. The Wisconsin senator, agile and unscrupulous as ever, took full advantage of the Administration's indulgence. Before 1953 only the bully of the Senate, he now began, as chairman of the Senate Committee on Government Operations, to swagger without challenge through the executive branch in pursuit of communists and fellow travelers.

A main target was the State Department. He began with an investigation of the Voice of America, the government agency for foreign broadcasts. On the basis of rumors provided by disgruntled employees, McCarthy and his chief counsel, Roy Cohn, proceeded to disrupt the Voice's operations and demoralize its personnel. Next McCarthy moved in on the International Information Administration and for a few months exerted direct control over its appointments and policies. Cohn, accompanied by his committee colleague, G. David Schine, made a whirlwind tour of United States information offices in Europe, plucking offending books from the shelves and terrorizing employees.

Determined to propitiate the right wing, John Foster Dulles was ready to collaborate with McCarthy and even to anticipate his demands. Veteran foreign-service officers whose political reporting had aroused McCarthy's ire were drummed from the service. A McCarthy disciple, W. Scott McLeod, was appointed chief of State Department personnel. The Secretary ordered State Department libraries to remove books by "authors who obviously follow the Communist line or participate in Communist front organizations." Such books as the thrillers of Dashiell Hammett, *The Selected Works of Tom Paine,* and even Whittaker Chambers' *Witness* were banned; a number of the proscribed books were actually burned. By June 1953 the panic had spread so widely that the President himself intervened to arrest it. "Don't join the book burn-

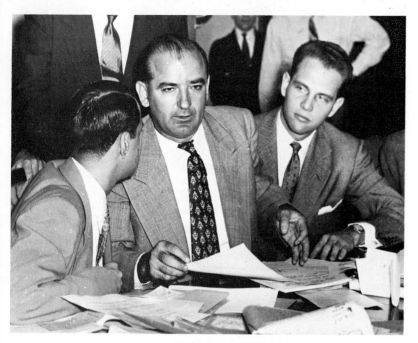

*McCarthy with Cohn and Schine:
the army fought back*

ers,'' he said. ''Don't think you are going to conceal faults by concealing evidence that they ever existed.''

Meanwhile posses of road-company McCarthys sprang up across the land. What was conceived as an effort to guard the national security became a heresy hunt employing the techniques traditionally used to ferret out nonconformists—guilt by association, loyalty oaths, testimony of secret informers, blacklists, suppressions of speech and assembly, interrogation and intimidation by legislative committees. In the 1954 campaign Vice President Nixon boasted of the number of ''security risks'' who had been driven from government. One notable victim was the great physicist Dr. J. Robert Oppenheimer, the father of the atomic bomb, whose security clearance was withdrawn in 1953 on the basis of information well known to security officers a decade before when Oppenheimer was heading the Manhattan Project. A review board declared that the Oppenheimer case ''demonstrated that the Government can search . . . the soul of an individual whose relationship to his Government is in question.'' It added that national security ''in times of peril must be absolute.''

Thoughtful people began to wonder whether such ideas as these might not be the most subversive of all. George Kennan said

that ''absolute security'' was an unattainable and self-devouring end—that its frenzied pursuit would lead only to absolute tyranny. Judge Learned Hand summed up the feelings of many Americans:

> I believe that that community is already in process of dissolution where each man begins to eye his neighbor as a possible enemy, where nonconformity with the accepted creed, political as well as religious, is a mark of disaffection; where denunciation, without specification or backing, takes the place of evidence.

If the Korean War had given McCarthy his opportunity for influence, the end of that war in July 1953 brought about his decline. As war frustrations receded, McCarthyism began to lose its emotional base. By now, in his increasingly erratic course, McCarthy had become embroiled with the army, launching a sensational, if unproductive, search for communists and spies in the army signal-corps installation at Fort Monmouth, New Jersey. The matter was further complicated by the efforts of Roy Cohn to obtain favored treatment for his sidekick Schine, who had recently been drafted. For a time Vice President Nixon tried to reconcile McCarthy and Secretary of the Army Robert Stevens. But, goaded beyond endurance, the army finally fought back. The denouement took place in a series of televised hearings from April 22 to June 17, 1954.

The Army-McCarthy hearings were a compelling spectacle, marked by vivid and sharply etched personalities and passages of passion and conflict. They commanded a fascinated audience, amounting at times to 20 million people. Viewers trained through long exposure to TV westerns to distinguish between good and bad guys had little trouble deciding to which category McCarthy belonged. After thirty-five days of the grating voice, the sarcastic condescension, the irrelevant interruption (''point of order, Mr. Chairman, point of order''), and the unsupported accusation, McCarthy effectively achieved his own destruction. The spell was at last broken. On December 2, 1954, the Senate censured McCarthy by a 67 to 22 vote. The Wisconsin senator was finished. His death in 1957 merely ratified his political demise.

Eisenhower economics: inflation. Now liberated from serious harassment on the far right and strengthened by the collaboration of the moderate conservative leader Robert A. Taft (until his death in July 1953), the Eisenhower Administration prepared to reorder American society according to the values of ''modern Republicanism.''

The commitment to price stability dominated economic policy. One consequence was a feeling within the Administration that if recession set in the government should let events take their course, even at the cost of unemployment, rather than risk inflation through reduction of the interest rate or increase in public spending. Indeed, the influential Secretary of the Treasury actually believed that cutting government spending was the best way to offset decline.

This fear of stimulative measures was no doubt a factor in the decline in the rate of economic growth from 4.3 percent in the years 1947–52 to 2.5 percent in the years 1953–60. A good deal of this slowdown resulted from recessions in 1953–54, 1957–58, and 1960–61. The 1953–54 recession was occasioned by an $11-billion drop in government spending at the end of the Korean War. The 1957–58 recession was both sharper and shorter. Unemployment rose to 7 percent of the labor force. The federal deficit for the fiscal year 1958–59, which pumped $12.4 billion into the economy, was probably responsible for bringing this setback to a quick end.

Yet, despite the Administration's conservative policies, prices mounted through the decade. Though the inflation caused by the Korean War was followed by comparative price stability in 1952–55, prices rose in 1955–58 by 8 percent. The climb persisted—contrary to the expectations of orthodox economic theory—even through the recession of 1957–58. Moreover, the true extent of inflation was disguised by a drop in farm prices. If farm prices had risen along with other prices, the price index would have been about eight points higher by 1960.

Economists concluded that changes in the structure of the market had removed key industrial prices from the play of market forces. ''Administered'' prices—that is, prices and wages set in concentrated industries by decisions independent of the market—could not be effectively controlled by policies designed to repress aggregate demand, like raising the interest rate, controlling the money supply, or cutting public spending. Given its faith in ''free enterprise,'' the Eisenhower Administration was unwilling to interfere with business decisions through guidelines or other forms of federal intervention.

Eisenhower economics: big government.

Eisenhower had a fear of ''statism'' and cited such projects as the Tennessee Valley Authority as examples of ''creeping socialism.'' He promised what he called a ''revolution'' in the federal government, ''trying to make it smaller rather than bigger and finding things it can stop doing instead of seeking new things to do.'' The intention was to cut federal activity in every direction—spending, taxation, regulation—and stimulate local and private activity.

At first this shifting of the burden met with some success. While the per capita national debt declined from $1,697 in 1950 to $1,595 in 1958, the per capita state and local government debt rose from $159 to $336. In power development, the Administration favored corporate over public activity. The great power site at Hell's Canyon on the Snake River went to the Idaho Power Company, a Maine corporation, for the construction of three low dams in place of the high multipurpose federal dam urged by public-power advocates. In an evident effort to check the expansion of TVA, the Administration arranged with the newly formed Dixon-Yates syndicate to erect a steam-power plant in Arkansas to provide electricity for TVA customers. The circumstances in which the Dixon-Yates contract was negotiated were so disreputable, however, that the Administration was finally forced to repudiate it and eventually sued for its cancellation as ''contrary to public policy.'' Offshore oil lands were turned over to the adjacent states. In 1955 the Department of Health, Education and Welfare even refused during the polio season to distribute free shots of scarce Salk vaccine to school children. In keeping with the same principle, regulatory commissions were now staffed more largely by men sympathetic to the industries they were supposed to regulate.

Particularly close to the President's heart was the vision of transferring countless functions from the federal government to the states. When his Commission on Intergovernmental Relations failed to come up with a comprehensive program for such transfers, Eisenhower in 1957 appealed personally to the Governors' Conference for action. After working for a year, the resulting committee of governors and federal officials could find only two minor programs, costing $80 million, to recommend for transfer from federal to state hands.

The notion of a sweeping shift of federal functions either to state and local governments or to private business seemed doomed to frustration. In 1960 the size and structure of the federal government were much what they had been in 1952. Indeed, for all the concern with budget-balancing, the Eisenhower Administration achieved a budgetary surplus less than half the time and piled up an overall deficit of $18.2 billion as well as the largest peacetime deficit (in 1959) thus far in American history. This record disturbed the more conservative members of the Administration. When Eisenhower sent Congress a $72-billion budget in 1957, Secretary of the Treasury Humphrey said that, if the "terrific" tax burden were not reduced, "I will predict that you will have a depression that will curl your hair."

The battle of desegregation. The gravest domestic issue, however, lay in social rather than economic policy. The struggle to assure blacks their full rights as American citizens had resumed, after a long quiescence, during the New Deal and had gathered momentum during and after the Second World War. Though most of President Truman's civil-rights program was rejected by Congress, his fight for that program established civil rights as a national issue.

Thwarted in Congress, the champions of civil rights now turned to the courts. The Supreme Court, once chary of taking on cases involving Negro rights, started doing so after the war. One important decision (*Shelly* v. *Kraemer*, 1948) removed government sanction from restrictive covenants—that is, private efforts to exclude ethnic minorities from buying houses in specified neighborhoods. Others required state educational institutions to admit blacks when the training available to them in black institutions was not demonstrably equal (*Sipuel* v. *University of Oklahoma*, 1948; *Sweatt* v. *Painter*, 1950). These decisions reflected the Fabian tactics of the Court under Chief Justice Fred M. Vinson of Kentucky (1946–53). The Vinson Court sought to work toward equal rights within the inherited legal framework—that is, by accepting the *Plessy* v. *Ferguson* doctrine (see p. 386) of "separate but equal," construing it

literally, and rejecting separate facilities when they were not in full and exact fact equal.

After 1953 the Eisenhower Administration completed the process of ending segregation in the government and the armed services. But Eisenhower was skeptical about what the government could do to promote equal rights: "It is difficult through law and through force to change a man's heart." Since the Administration did not advance civil-rights legislation with vigor, black organizations turned even more to the courts for remedy. Beginning in 1952 attorneys for the National Association for the Advancement of Colored People (NAACP) argued before the Supreme Court against state laws requiring the segregation of children in public education. On May 17, 1954, in the case of *Brown* v. *Board of Education of Topeka*, the Court, speaking through Earl Warren, the new Chief Justice, responded with a unanimous decision reversing *Plessy* v. *Ferguson* and interpreting the Fourteenth Amendment as outlawing racial discrimination in public schools. "We conclude," the Court said, "that in the field of public education, the doctrine of 'separate but equal' has no place. Separate educational facilities are inherently unequal." A year later, the Court called on school authorities to submit plans for desegregation and gave local federal courts the responsibility of deciding whether the plans constituted "good faith compliance." The Court concluded by ordering action "with all deliberate speed."

The border states moved toward compliance. But in South Carolina, Georgia, Alabama, and Mississippi, resistance began to harden, especially after the spread in 1955–56 of the militantly segregationist White Citizens' Councils and a manifesto by Southern congressmen, on March 11, 1956, condemning the decision. Some Southern states passed laws to frustrate the Supreme Court ruling. A favorite device was to divert state funds to what might be passed off technically as a private school system. Extreme segregationists revived the pre-Civil War doctrine of nullification under the more mellifluous name of "interposition." Fanatics incited violence, as in Clinton, Tennessee, in 1956.

The crisis of Little Rock. The strategy of resistance came to a climax in 1957 in Little Rock, Arkansas. Governor Orval Faubus, contending that integration would threaten public order, mobilized the Arkansas national guard

Little Rock, 1957: separate but equal had no place

in an effort to deny nine black students enrollment in the Central High School. Up to this time, Eisenhower had been reluctant to take action in support of the desegregation decision. The year before, he had said, "We must all . . . bring about a change in spirit so that extremists on both sides"—meaning apparently both those who wanted extremely to carry out the law and those who wanted extremely to block it—"do not defeat what we know is a reasonable, logical conclusion." But Faubus' open challenge compelled the President to defend the Constitution. After a face-to-face discussion with Eisenhower, Faubus withdrew the national guard. When the black boys and girls then entered Central High School, they were mobbed by crowds of angry whites. On September 24, 1957, Eisenhower sent federal troops into Little Rock. Order was restored, and black children entered the school.

In the meantime, Congress was finally taking action on behalf of racial justice. The Civil Rights Act of 1957, the first of its kind since Reconstruction, authorized the Department of Justice to seek injunctions on behalf of black voting rights. A second act, in 1960, provided for the appointment of federal referees to safeguard voting rights. For its part, the Warren Court extended the principle of the *Brown* case to new fields, striking down segregation over the next years in interstate commerce, in public buildings, in airports and interstate bus terminals, in parks and other public recreational facilities. Both Congress and the Court,

by concentrating on segregation as embodied in law, left untouched the wide and bitter realm of *de facto* discrimination; but at the same time, by accepting and, in the Court's case, declaring the moral necessity of equality, they were changing the values of American society.

Blacks themselves were increasingly taking the lead in the struggle. Lawyers like Thurgood Marshall of the NAACP argued the constitutional cases. In the South new leaders emerged to urge the assertion of black rights through nonviolent resistance. Beginning in December 1955, the blacks of Montgomery, Alabama, under the inspiration of a young minister, Dr. Martin Luther King, Jr., boycotted the city's segregated bus system. King, who was strongly influenced by Thoreau and Gandhi, counseled his followers to avoid provocation and to confront "physical force with an even stronger force, namely, soul force." The boycott, reinforced by suits in the federal courts, achieved the desegregation of the bus system in a year. Passive resistance was widely used in the winter of 1959–60 to challenge the refusal to serve blacks at Southern lunch counters. The rapid spread of "sit-in" demonstrations through the South and the support they evoked in the North and among moderate Southern whites testified to the rising moral force of the protest against segregation.

By 1960 blacks were still far from the goal of integration. But, if only limited progress had been made in school desegregation and

The assertion of black rights: Martin Luther King, Jr., and friends, Montgomery, 1956

Kefauver, Truman, Stevenson, 1956

in assuring the right to vote, vast progress had been made in gaining acceptance for the moral case against discrimination. The rather pallid Southern filibuster against a civil-rights bill in 1960 was marked by the fact that, with one or two exceptions, no one tried any longer to argue the philosophy of white supremacy.

The Warren Court. When Eisenhower appointed Earl Warren, he did not realize what sort of Chief Justice he was getting. The former Republican governor of California turned out to have a spacious view of the Constitution; and his humane approach received support and elaboration from three other Eisenhower appointees—John M. Harlan, Potter Stewart, and, most consistently, William J. Brennan—as well as from distinguished holdovers from the Roosevelt Court, Hugo Black, Felix Frankfurter, and William O. Douglas.

In addition to its initiatives in the field of racial justice, the Warren Court, especially in the 1956–57 term, sought to mend the holes McCarthyism had made in the fabric of civil freedom. The *Watkins* and *Sweezy* cases, with their condemnation of exposure "for the sake of exposure," restricted legislative investigations to questions deemed pertinent to a legislative objective. The *Yates* case, reversing

one count in the conviction of a group of California communists, construed the Smith Act of 1940 as distinguishing between "the statement of an idea which may prompt its hearers to take unlawful action, and advocacy that such action be taken." The *Jencks* case required that Federal Bureau of Investigation reports, if used by the prosecution in a criminal trial, be made available to the defense.

These decisions stirred up passing furor and led to congressional rage at the Court. In the longer run their impact was less drastic than civil libertarians hoped or that the heirs of McCarthy feared. Indeed, the Court itself sharply qualified the *Watkins* and *Sweezy* rulings by the *Barenblatt* and *Uphaus* decisions in 1959 and 1960, affirming a wide scope for federal and state legislative investigations in the area of communism.

Thoughtful critics felt at times that the activism of the Warren Court was carrying the judiciary into decisions that properly belonged to legislative or executive processes. Defenders replied that legislative and executive inertia had created a vacuum of power, which, if not filled by the Supreme Court, would have severely strained the bonds of social order.

The second term. As a national hero, above politics, Eisenhower enjoyed a popularity far exceeding that of his party. In 1954, the Democrats took control of both the House and the Senate. In spite of a coronary thrombosis in 1955 and ileitis in 1956, Eisenhower decided to run for reelection. "Some of my medical advisers," he said, "believe that adverse effects on my health will be less in the Presidency than in any other position I might hold." Most voters accepted with sympathy his need for a more carefully regulated life, made affectionate jokes about his long hours on the golf course, and accorded him undiminished confidence. Though Eisenhower several times suggested to Nixon that he might prefer a Cabinet post, his Vice President declined the hint and secured renomination.

The Democrats, over the brief opposition of Harry Truman, renominated Adlai Stevenson, whose penetrating comment on national issues had kept him in the forefront among the party leaders. Estes Kefauver, who had been Stevenson's chief rival till shortly before the convention, received the vice-presidential nomination. Eisenhower won decisively, carrying the popular vote by 35.6 to 26 million and the Electoral College by 457 to 73.

If Eisenhower's first term had seen the end of both the Korean War and McCarthyism—if, indeed, only a Republican could perhaps have presided so tranquilly over the liquidation of these angry issues—his second term proved less successful. The Administration's reluctance to move swiftly against the recession of 1957–58 damaged confidence, and its claim to moral rectitude was tarnished in a series of scandals. These scandals forced the resignation of the Secretary of the Air Force, the chairman of the Republican National Committee, the chairman of the Interstate Commerce Commission, the General Services Administrator, the Public Buildings Administrator, a number of lesser officials, and, finally, in September 1958, Sherman Adams, the Assistant to the President.

The 1958 elections brought a Democratic landslide. The Democratic majority in the House—282 to 153—was the largest since 1936. In addition, the Democrats gained a 62 to 34 majority in the Senate. But the Democratic sweep had little effect on the President's conservative policies. The departure of the moderate Adams, ironically, gave Eisenhower's more conservative inclinations free play. In his last two years in office he succeeded, through the use or threat of the veto, in blocking most of the Democratic welfare and public-investment proposals. His posture in domestic affairs remained to the end one of dogged defense of the budget. In what a later decade would regard as wasted years, little was done to tackle the problem of the cities, of the environment, of racial relations, and of social order at a time when these problems were still relatively manageable.

The American people in the fifties

A homogenized society? The quiescence of government expressed the national mood. People did not want to be bothered by public issues. They sought security rather than adventure, comfort rather than challenge. Society seemed to reward those who lacked rough edges, eschewed eccentricity, excited no suspicion, and played the company game. In a training film circulated by a leading chemical firm, the sound track said, as the camera panned over men in white coats at a Monsanto laboratory, "No geniuses here; just a bunch of average Americans working together." More and more people were spending their whole lives in organizations—their days in great corporations, their nights in great suburban enclaves. Both corporation and suburb appeared to foster a pervasive, benign, and invincible conformity. It had become, it was said, a case of the bland leading the bland.

The new and compelling medium of television advanced the process of homogenization. Originally developed in the 1930s, television went on the popular market in the late forties. By 1960 nearly 90 percent of American households had television sets—more than had running water or indoor toilets. It was estimated that these families spent five hours a day watching the tiny screen. From the age of three, according to one survey, the average child dedicated between one-sixth and one-seventh of his waking hours to television.

"The strongest sustained attention of Americans," said Dr. Frank Stanton, president of the Columbia Broadcasting System, "is now, daily and nightly, bestowed on television as it is bestowed on nothing else." Programing was dominated by three large networks and a collection of advertising agencies. The result dismayed thoughtful viewers. Edward R. Murrow, who himself did much to elevate the medium, wrote, "Television in the main is being used to distract, delude, amuse and insulate."

Most striking of all was the hold the mood of quiescence seemed to have on the young. Older generations, recalling their springtimes of revolt—cultural in the twenties, political in the thirties—looked with incredulity on this "uncommitted generation" composed of prudent young men and women who shunned risk and subordinated everything to a steady job, a house in the suburbs, and a company retirement plan—a generation apparently fearful of politics, mistrustful of ideas, incurious about society, desperate about personal security.

The boom in religion. Even the church threatened to become an instrument of the new acquiescence. Though religious statistics are notoriously unreliable, it appears that in the second quarter of the century church membership grew twice as fast as population. In 1940 total church membership was estimated at 64.5 million; in 1950 at 86.8 million; and in 1958 at 109.6 million. Never before in American history had so many persons claimed religious affiliation. When public-opinion polls inquired into religious affiliation, 95 percent of the respondents declared themselves Protestants, Catholics, or Jews, and 97 percent asserted a belief in God. The militant, free-thinking tradition, from Ethan Allen through Robert G. Ingersoll to Clarence Darrow, seemed to have disappeared.

The religious boom had diverse manifestations. During the fifties, for example, the President opened his Cabinet meetings with prayer. Special rooms were set aside for religious meditation in the Capitol and the United Nations, in airports, and in factories. Revivalists, headed by the popular Dr. Billy Graham, staged extraordinary mass meetings. The words "under God" were added to the pledge of allegiance to the flag. Religious songs even appeared on the Hit Parade.

This religiosity was conspicuously indifferent, however, to historical religion. According to one public opinion poll, 80 percent of those responding claimed they regarded the Bible as the revealed word of God but only 35 percent could name the four Gospels and over half could not name one. Belief was deemed good in general. As President Eisenhower said, "Our government makes no sense unless it is founded in a deeply felt religious faith— and I don't care what it is." Religion became a part of "belonging," a convenient way to establish social identity.

In place of the austere intellectual structure of the traditional faiths, the best-selling religious books of the period purveyed a "cult of reassurance"—Rabbi Joshua Loth Liebman's *Peace of Mind* (1946), Bishop Fulton J. Sheen's *Peace of Soul* (1949), the Reverend Norman Vincent Peale's *The Power of Positive Thinking* (1952). These and other books portrayed God as the man upstairs, someone up there watching over me, the everlasting source of protection and comfort. The new, nondoctrinal faith seemed designed to dispel anxiety, to induce self-confidence, to guarantee success for the individual in his professional career and victory for the nation in its struggle against atheistic communism.

Stirrings under the surface. Yet the break between decades is never sharp, and under the complacent surface of the fifties other tendencies were at work. Novelists and social critics portrayed American conformism in such books as *The Man in the Gray Flannel Suit, The Status Seekers,* and *The Lonely Crowd.* In *The Organization Man* (1956), W. H. Whyte, Jr., argued that, under the pressure of the large organization, the old Protestant-individualist code of nineteenth-century America was giving way to a new collective ethic, based on the notion that the group was the source of creativity and that "belongingness" rather than personal fulfillment should be the individual's aspiration. In *The Affluent Society* (1958), J. K. Galbraith questioned the "conventional wisdom" that put forward the maximization of economic growth as the answer to all problems, pointing out that in America this had produced a combination of private opulence and public squalor and had notably failed to eradicate poverty.

In such terms the intellectual community weighed the decade and found it smug and torpid. And, as the rise of the "lost generation" had expressed a rejection of Babbittry by the youth of the 1920s, so the rise of the "beat generation" expressed a dissent by the youth of the fifties from the ethos of affluence. The rebels of the fifties were more chaotic and pitiful than their lighthearted and talented predecessors. The "beat generation" included both "hipsters"—proletarian in origin, sometimes criminal in inclination, apostles of inarticulate and violent revolt—and the middle-class "beatniks"—descendants of the bohemians of an earlier day, vindicating their withdrawal by experiments in verse, sometimes intoned to the accompaniment of a jazz band, and by an addiction to Zen Buddhism. Hipsters and beatniks congregated in San Francisco and New Orleans, shared a special vocabulary, admired "cool cats" like James Dean and Marlon Brando, and lost no opportunity to exhibit their biting contempt for the "squares" of the world. Sympathetic observers saw in these "antiheroes" a brave attempt to heighten the integrity of individual experience and to reject the suffocating embrace of a conformist society. Others saw in them a tiresome conformity of their own and dismissed them as "rebels without a cause," dedicated to an aimless and pathetic flight from responsibility. As the beat novelist Jack Kerouac put it in an exchange between two characters in *On The Road* (1957), "We gotta go and never stop going till we get there." "Where we going, man?" "I don't know, but we gotta go."

Nationalism and the superpowers

Nationalism in the Middle East. In the world outside, America and Russia continued for a decade after 1945 to reign as superpowers. The only states able to fill the vacuums of power created by the Second World War, they now sought to consolidate their positions around the planet—America through its pacts, Russia through its parties. But competing forces began to arise—above all, the force of nationalism, acquiring special vitality in the Third World where peoples long subject to colonial or neocolonial control were demanding political and economic independence.

The rise of nationalism presented a complex challenge to the superpowers. As they tried to enlist the new nationalist states on one side or the other in their Cold War, the new states tended to respond by using the Cold War as a means of getting aid for themselves or by playing off one superpower against the other. Despite pretenses and alliances, the new states—even, it developed, those that pronounced themselves communist—responded in the end to their own national interests and purposes.

In the Middle East, Arab nationalism, now surging in unprecedented force, posed problems in a part of the world where Britain and France had traditional interests and which Russia had long coveted. The United States watched this area with growing concern. This was partly because of extensive American oil investments and even more because of the republic of Israel, which had shown its tough capacity for survival when it defeated the assault of neighboring Arab states in 1948–49 and which, with the fervent support not only of the American Jewish community but of many other Americans, had come to seem a particular American charge.

The center of Arab nationalism was the new regime in Egypt, installed by revolution in 1952 and, after 1954, under the purposeful leadership of Colonel Gamal Abdel Nasser. When the Baghdad Pact exalted Egypt's chief Arab rival, Iraq, and portended Egypt's diplomatic isolation, Moscow established relations with Nasser, sent Egypt arms, and proposed to subsidize the construction of a great dam at Aswan on the Nile. Washington responded by offering to arrange western financing for the dam. Nasser already dominated Syria; he was stepping up Egyptian raids across the Israeli border; in March 1956 he incited a revolution in Jordan. On the understanding that the Soviet Union could not after all finance the dam, Dulles withdrew the American offer in July 1956 just as Egypt was about to accept it. He did so in a manner calculated to humiliate Egypt. Nasser retaliated by nationalizing the Suez Canal.

Britain and France regarded Nasser's seizure of the canal as a threat to western Europe's vital supplies of oil. Moreover, Sir Anthony Eden, now British prime minister, saw Nasser in the image of Hitler and believed that appeasement would only inflame his ambitions and invite the spread of Soviet influence. France felt that Nasser's support was helping to prolong a nationalist revolt in Algeria. Together, Britain and France determined to overthrow Nasser.

Eden understood Dulles to agree with him that Nasser must be made to "disgorge what he has swallowed." But despite shows of private indignation, Dulles really felt that the use of western force against Nasser would only alienate the new nations of Asia and Africa. By October, communication between London and Washington had pretty well broken down.

In the meantime, another element in a complicated drama was approaching its climax—Israeli resentment over the Egyptian border raids and Israeli fear that Egyptian rearmament would permanently alter the balance of power in the Middle East. In October, British and French officials met secretly with Israeli leaders in France. On October 29, Israel attacked Egypt. Two days later Britain and France entered the war against Egypt on the patently spurious excuse of trying to localize the conflict. Ironically, one of the effects of the Anglo-French intervention was to save the Egyptian forces from probable defeat by the Israelis.

The situation was further complicated by a nationalist uprising against Soviet domination in Hungary beginning on October 24. Though deeply involved in the brutal suppression of this revolution, the Soviet Union threatened to use force—including the hint of long-range missiles against Western Europe—to "crush the aggressors" in Egypt. This threat, along with the fear of estranging the ex-colonial world, led Eisenhower to bring intense personal pressure on Eden to call off the Suez expedition. At the same time, a run on Britain's gold reserves threatened the pound, and Secretary of the Treasury Humphrey informed London that Britain could expect no financial aid from the United States until a statement on withdrawal had been made. On November 6 Eden ordered a cease-fire.

The American government now initiated immediate action in the United Nations—backed by the Soviet Union and opposed by Britain and France—to condemn Israel as the aggressor. While the rigid American line in the UN resulted in the rescue and reinstatement of Nasser without rebuke for past Egyptian harassment of Israel, the Anglo-French adventure was nonetheless ill-conceived and ill-prepared, and Dulles was right in supposing that gunboat imperialism was obsolescent.

Still, despite the power of Arab nationalism, Dulles persisted in regarding Soviet penetration as the essential Middle Eastern problem. "The existing vacuum in the Middle East," Eisenhower told Congress in January 1957, "must be filled by the United States before it is filled by Russia. . . . Considering her announced purpose of dominating the world, it is easy to understand her hope of dominating the Middle East." Eisenhower asked Congress to declare a vital American interest in preventing such domination and to authorize the commitment of American forces to aid Middle Eastern nations "requesting such aid, against overt armed aggression from any nation controlled by International Communism." Congress by joint resolution passed the so-called Eisenhower Doctrine in March 1957. In April Eisenhower sent the Sixth Fleet to Jordan when King Hussein was threatened by a pro-Nasser movement and in July 1958 landed 14,000 troops to protect a prowestern government in Lebanon. In neither case did the American military presence lead to hostilities.

Nationalism in Latin America. In Latin America nationalist aspirations struck at the political and economic domination of the United States. In the years since the Second World War, the Good Neighbor policy of the thirties had suffered neglect. In the 1940s, Latin America was swept by nationalist ferment. Everywhere historic oligarchies were challenged by rising popular groups. The wave of unrest affected most of the Central American states and all the South American republics except Paraguay. The resulting revolutions sometimes (as in Argentina) took authoritarian, sometimes (as in Venezuela)

A triumphal tour: Castro in Washington

democratic, forms. Then toward the end of the forties a counterrevolutionary reaction set in, beginning in Ecuador in 1947. By 1954 thirteen Latin American presidents were military men. Now a new surge of protest arose against dictatorships, bringing the overthrow of, among others, Perón of Argentina in 1955, Pérez Jiménez of Venezuela in 1958, Batista of Cuba in 1959, and Trujillo of the Dominican Republic in 1961.

All through this ebb and flow, Washington, insofar as it thought about the hemisphere at all, tried to fit it into the framework of the Cold War. The Truman Administration concentrated on a program of inter-American military cooperation—a program that was expanded under the Eisenhower Administration. The Eisenhower Administration also placed great reliance on foreign private investment, a policy that led it to favor authoritarian regimes in Latin America. The Administration thus granted a loan to the Perón regime in Argentina. Vice President Nixon, visiting Cuba in 1955, praised the "competence and stability" of the Batista dictatorship. In November 1954 Eisenhower himself presented the Legion of Merit to two Latin American dictators—Pérez Jiménez of Venezuela (for his "sound foreign-investment policies") and Manuel Odría of Peru. When Nixon visited these two countries in May 1958, after the dictators had been thrown out, the people's resentment against United States identification with the hated regimes led to mob violence. The fact that the Vice President of the United States should be stoned and spat upon in Latin America revealed how far relations had deteriorated since the high noon of the Good Neighbor policy.

The course of the Cuban revolution of 1958–59 was even more ominous. The hemisphere hailed the overthrow of the Batista regime and welcomed the advent of a revolutionary government led by Fidel Castro. In 1959 Castro's visit to the United States was something of a triumphal tour. In Cuba he initiated a long-needed program of social and agrarian reform. But he combined this program with a terrorism which, if less than that of his predecessor, still showed a brutal disregard for the processes of justice. A romantic Marxist nationalist rather than a disciplined communist, Castro needed the United States as his enemy and therefore rebuffed conciliatory American gestures. For its part, Washington grew obsessed with the expropriation of American property in Cuba.

In time, surrounded increasingly by communists and lashed by the intensities of his own turbulent personality, Castro led Cuba into the Soviet camp. Fearful of a Soviet satellite in the Western Hemisphere, Eisenhower in March 1960 agreed to a CIA proposal to arm and train a force of Cuban exiles for possible use against Castro. When Castro ordered the United States to cut its embassy to eleven persons, the Eisenhower Administration broke relations in January 1961.

For all his excesses, Castro became for a moment a hero through much of Latin America. The rapid spread of the *fidelista* enthusiasm, especially among poverty-stricken workers and underemployed intellectuals, suggested the magnitude of the problem the United States faced in coming to terms with the Latin American demand for economic development, social reform, and national self-assertion. When President Kubitschek of Brazil proposed "Operation Pan America" and an Inter-American Development Bank in 1957, Washington had shown no interest; but by 1960 Under Secretary of State Douglas Dillon and Milton Eisenhower, the President's brother, persuaded the Administration to offer "a broad new social development program for Latin America" based on the Inter-American Development Bank. The Organization of American States endorsed the Dillon program in the Act of Bogotá in September 1960.

Nationalism in Southeast Asia. Nationalism continued to thrive in Southeast Asia. In Vietnam, though President Diem in Saigon had been a consistent opponent of French rule, he could not compete with Ho Chi Minh in Hanoi as a nationalist leader. Moreover, the discontent aroused by Diem's increasingly arbitrary and authoritarian regime now gave the Vietnamese communists a new chance to seize power. In 1958 a communist-nationalist movement soon called the National Liberation Front or, more popularly, the Viet Cong, began guerrilla warfare against Diem. This development alarmed Washington. "The loss of South Vietnam," said Eisenhower on April 4, 1959, "would set in motion a crumbling process that could, as it progressed, have grave consequences for us. . . . We reach the inescapable conclusion that our own national interests demand some help from us in sustaining in Vietnam the morale, the economic progress, and the military strength necessary

to its continued existence in freedom." From 1955 to 1961 military aid to South Vietnam averaged $200 million annually.

It was in Laos, however, that the military crisis was more acute and American intervention more active. Regarding the upper Mekong Valley as the gateway to Southeast Asia, the United States put nearly $300 million into Laos between the period of the Geneva Accords and the end of 1960—more aid per capita than it sent to any other country. Nearly all went for military purposes. The Pathet Lao, a communist-led guerrilla movement, was roaming the countryside; and the United States in 1958 vetoed the effort of Prince Souvanna Phouma to establish a neutral Laos under a coalition government with Pathet Lao participation.

In 1959 the CIA installed General Phoumi Nosavan as head of a prowestern government in Vientiane. When Phoumi was overthrown by a nationalist revolt in 1960, Souvanna regained power and, rebuffed by the Americans, established relations with Russia. At the end of the year, Phoumi, with American support, put an army into the field. American policy now forced Souvanna, the neutralist, into reluctant collaboration with the Pathet Lao. When Eisenhower, before leaving office, briefed his successor, he did not mention Vietnam but spoke earnestly about the danger to Laos, which, he said, was the key to all Southeast Asia.

In the meantime, the Chinese communists, who had not abandoned their hope of annexing Formosa to mainland China, began heavy bombardment of the islands of Quemoy and Matsu, now occupied by a hundred thousand Nationalist soldiers, in August 1958. Though Eisenhower was irritated by Chiang Kai-shek's increased troop commitment to the offshore islands, he saw no alternative but to convince Peking that the United States would intervene, "perhaps using nuclear weapons," if the communists attempted an invasion. After three months the shelling tapered off, and the crisis passed. Under American pressure Chiang eventually reduced the size of his forces on the islands, "but not," Eisenhower subsequently wrote "to the extent I thought desirable."

Vicissitudes of the Cold War. Eisenhower had a genuine desire for conciliation and peace. Though he never questioned the premises of the Cold War, he strove in his circuitous

Ho Chi Minh

and intermittent way to mitigate its intensity and to improve relations with the Soviet Union. The death of Stalin in 1953 had given new opportunity to western diplomacy as well as new outlet both to energies of normalization stirring within Russia and to energies of nationalism spreading elsewhere in the communist empire. Hoping for a less rigid Soviet leadership, Churchill wanted a summit meeting at once. But Dulles, forever fearful that a reduction in tension would relax the western guard, successfully opposed the idea. In 1953–54 the West may well have lost a chance to test significant new Soviet proposals, especially regarding the neutralization of Germany.

By early 1955 Churchill finally persuaded Dulles to drop his opposition to a summit conference. When the Soviet Union, after a decade's stalemate, agreed to sign an Austrian peace treaty in May, omens for the Big Four meeting seemed auspicious. The meeting itself, taking place at Geneva in July, produced no substantive results. But, as the first of its sort since Potsdam, it did restore personal contact among the heads of the powers, and the "spirit of Geneva" diminished for a moment the ideological ferocity of the Cold War. Though Suez and Hungary dealt blows to the precarious equilibrium of peace in October–November 1956, the two episodes offset each other: with both sides preoccupied with internal troubles, each refrained from exploiting the other's difficulties.

Other currents seemed to be carrying the Cold War into a season of thaw. At the Twentieth Party Congress in 1956, Khrushchev gave his famous "secret speech" denouncing the crimes of Stalin. He also amended the Leninist doctrine of the inevitability of war; in the nuclear age, he said, the conflict between capitalism and communism would be decided by peaceful competition between social systems. Soviet as well as western leaders were increasingly impressed by the incalculable perils presented by nuclear weapons—by the fact, for example, that a single plane could deliver more destructive power than all the planes in all the air forces delivered during the Second World War. Also the problem of radioactive fallout had come sharply to the world's attention in 1954, when both the United States and the Soviet Union tested large-yield nuclear weapons in the atmosphere. As scientists analyzed the long-term effects of radioactive contamination on the bones, blood, and germ plasm of man, concern mounted over the continuation of nuclear testing. In March 1958 the Soviet Union suspended testing, and the United States and Britain followed suit in October (while Russia briefly resumed). A permanent test ban, as well as the prevention of surprise attack, were for some years under inconclusive negotiation between Russia, Britain, and the United States at Geneva.

Khrushchev's dilemma. If Khrushchev was determined to limit the risk of nuclear war between the superpowers, he also seems to have felt he could not admit this determination without revealing a sense of Soviet weakness that might increase western intransigence. He therefore evidently hoped to obtain the risk-limiting measures, such as the denial of nuclear weapons to West Germany, by threats rather than by persuasion. Moreover, he was under increasing secret pressure from Communist China, which regarded his policy of "peaceful coexistence" as a betrayal of Marxism-Leninism and which might soon challenge Russia for the leadership of the international communist movement. And Khrushchev himself was temperamentally something of a plunger, fond of the spectacular and the audacious, unable to resist targets of opportunity created by western confusion or disarray.

All these factors led him to transform the defensive Cold War of Stalin into what the West perceived as a more far-flung and aggressive contest. "While Stalin conducted a Cold War of position," Hans Morgenthau later wrote, "Khrushchev conducted a Cold War of movement." His speeches were boastful and truculent, and the launching of Sputnik seemed to verify his horrendous claims about Soviet superiority in intercontinental ballistic missiles. He liked to tell small countries how many bombs would be required to destroy them, and he did not hesitate (as in 1956 against England and France over Suez and later against the United States in Cuba) to threaten war against great powers. He greatly increased Soviet activity in the Middle East, Southeast Asia, Latin America, and Africa and appeared eager to exploit every western vulnerability. Confronted by inflammatory rhetoric and worldwide intrusion, the West did not appreciate his more pacific purposes. Moreover, if Khrushchev could secure "peaceful coexistence" (from which he always rigorously excluded ideological coexistence), he confidently predicted the withering away of capitalism and the triumph of communism by peaceful means. This is what he meant when he told the western democracies, ''We will bury you''—not that the communists would kill their adversaries but that they would outlive them.

His policy thus bounded back and forth between belligerence and conciliation. Hoping perhaps to end up with a denuclearized Germany, Khrushchev reopened the Berlin question in October–November 1958, demanding that West Berlin be made a demilitarized free city under international control with access to the West guaranteed by East Germany, and that West Berlin agree not to tolerate ''subversive activity'' against East Germany. If the West failed to negotiate a new status for West Berlin within six months, Khrushchev threatened, Russia would sign a separate treaty with East Germany. The western powers replied by stating their firm determination ''to maintain their position and rights in Berlin, including the right of free access.''

Khrushchev grew conciliatory again early in 1959; and, on the strong recommendation of Prime Minister Macmillan after a visit to Moscow in February, the West in March accepted a summit meeting in principle. Even Secretary of State Dulles, now ravaged by cancer, acquiesced in the drift toward negotiation. In April Dulles resigned, to be replaced by Christian A. Herter; five weeks later Dulles was dead. Though a foreign ministers' meeting in Geneva in May resulted in a deadlock over Berlin, the movement toward the summit continued. In the summer of 1959 Nixon paid a visit to Russia and Poland, and Anastas Mikoyan, a veteran Soviet leader, toured the United States. This exchange paved the way for an extraordinary visit to the United States by Khrushchev. The Khrushchev tour, marked by a series of picturesque incidents, reached its climax in private talks between Khrushchev and Eisenhower at Camp David, in Maryland. Following these talks, the United States agreed to a summit meeting, and Khrushchev agreed to drop his deadline on Berlin. For a moment the ''spirit of Camp David'' seemed to renew the ''spirit of Geneva.''

Though little noticed at the time, the Antarctic Treaty of 1959, which in effect internationalized the only uninhabited continent, was a useful step in cooperation. A dozen interested nations, including America and Russia, suspended their territorial claims and set up

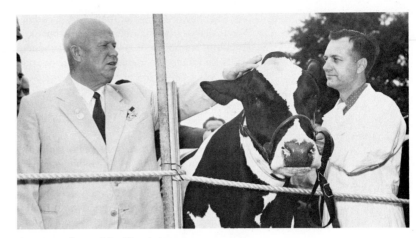
An extraordinary visit: Khrushchev on tour

a mutual inspection system to prevent military activities in the area, including nuclear testing.

The dark year. After protracted preliminaries, the summit meeting was scheduled for Paris on May 16, 1960. Then on May 5 Khrushchev announced the shooting down of an American plane over the Soviet Union. He gave no details, and Washington promptly said that the plane had somehow strayed from course on a meteorological flight. On May 7 Khrushchev gleefully sprang his trap. The pilot was alive, he said, and had confessed that he was engaged in espionage. Khrushchev added, ''I am quite willing to grant that the President knew nothing about the plane.''

The story was indeed true. At irregular intervals for about four years, the CIA had been sending the U-2, an aircraft capable of flying at exceptional heights, on missions over the Soviet Union. At this point the Administration decided to take an unusual step, unprecedented in modern history: it owned up to the act of espionage. Secretary Herter went on to argue that the United States was morally entitled to conduct such flights in order to protect the ''free world'' from surprise attack. Herter and, soon, Nixon implied that the flights would continue. Eisenhower, rejecting Khrushchev's proffered escape clause, accepted full responsibility. Khrushchev now came to Paris demanding that Eisenhower apologize for the flights and punish those responsible. Eisenhower rejected these demands, and the summit collapsed.

It is not clear whether sharpening Chinese criticism had already persuaded Khrushchev before the U-2 incident that he had better refurbish his revolutionary image, or whether

Nixon with Khrushchev, Moscow, 1959

the Eisenhower Administration, with its addiction to clandestine methods, had unexpectedly undercut his policy. In any case Khrushchev, while continuing to defend peaceful coexistence within the communist world (as at a meeting of eighty-one Communist parties in Moscow in October–November 1960), made it clear that he would have no serious dealings with Washington until there was a new American President.

End of the Eisenhower era

The election of 1960. The electorate faced the election of 1960 in a troubled state of mind. After the U-2 fiasco, the request of the Japanese government that, in view of anti-American riots in Tokyo, Eisenhower cancel a scheduled presidential visit provided further evidence of a decline in American influence. The fact that since 1958 the United States balance of payments had been in deficit and that gold was flowing out of the country deepened anxiety. Within the United States, the persistence of economic stagnation and the rise of unemployment toward 6 percent of the labor force caused further problems for the Republicans.

Nevertheless a confident Republican convention gave the presidential nomination to Vice President Nixon with Henry Cabot Lodge of Massachusetts as his running mate. The Democrats turned to Senator John F. Kennedy of Massachusetts, who had established himself as the most popular candidate in the primaries. The Democratic Senate leader, Lyndon B. Johnson, who had run second to Kennedy in the convention balloting, accepted the vice-presidential nomination. A movement to draft Adlai Stevenson evoked fervent support but failed to attract enough delegates.

The 1960 campaign was marked by an innovation in American politics—a series of television debates in which the two candidates responded to questions put to them by news-

The election of 1960

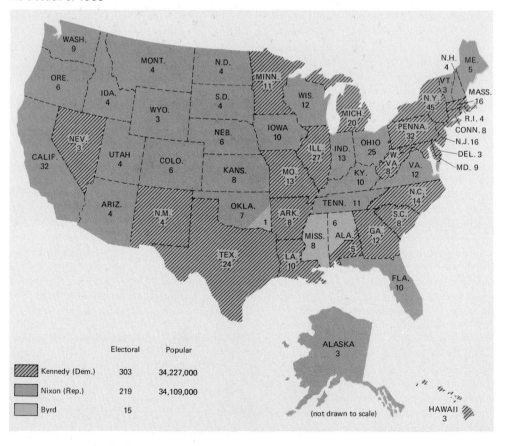

	Electoral	Popular
Kennedy (Dem.)	303	34,227,000
Nixon (Rep.)	219	34,109,000
Byrd	15	

(not drawn to scale)

papermen. Observers believed that Kennedy's poise and command in these confrontations destroyed the Republican argument that he was too young and inexperienced for the Presidency. The campaign itself revolved around the question of America's condition as a nation. "Militarily, economically and diplomatically," Nixon declared, "we maintain and have a position of strength unparalleled in the history of this country." In foreign affairs, "Communist prestige in the world is at an all-time low and American prestige is at an all-time high." Kennedy, in contrast, found the national situation disturbing, even perilous. The United States, he contended, was falling behind both in the world competition with communism and in meeting its own goals of economic growth and social progress. The process of decline could be reversed only by a "supreme national effort" under strong presidential leadership to "get the country moving again"—a "New Frontier."

The popular vote was the closest since 1888. With the admission of Alaska (January 3, 1959) and Hawaii (August 21, 1959), there were now fifty states in the Union. Kennedy's popular margin was only 119,057 out of 68.3 million votes; taking into account the votes for splinter-party candidates, he was a minority victor. The margin in the Electoral College was more decisive—303 for Kennedy to 219 for Nixon (with 15 Southern votes for Senator Harry F. Byrd of Virginia).

The Eisenhower record. Like Washington and Jackson, Eisenhower left behind a testa-

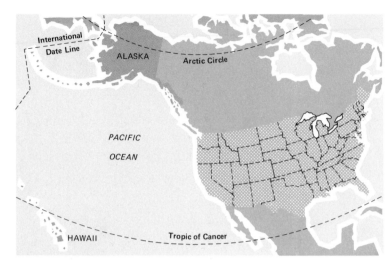

New states, 1959

ment for the American people in the form of a farewell address. Speaking with unaccustomed directness, he said that public policy could become "the captive of a scientific-technological élite" and warned against "the acquisition of unwarranted influence, whether sought or unsought, by the military-industrial complex." Though these had not been themes of his own Administration, they identified salient problems of the future.

As he left the White House, Eisenhower told his young successor that, if the United States could not persuade others to join in saving Laos from communism, then it should be willing "as a last desperate hope, to intervene unilaterally." Mentioning the Cuban refugees under training by the CIA in Guatemala, he

Kennedy and Nixon debate: an innovation in politics

recommended that "this effort be continued and accelerated," saying it was "the policy of this government" to aid anti-Castro forces "to the utmost." Yet, for all the bellicosity of this valedictory counsel, his own Administration had been a rare interlude of peace in an age of continous war. Whether through good luck or good management or a combination of both, the American government concluded one war and began no others during the Eisenhower Presidency. The people would remember the man of war as a man of peace. Whether passivity served the nation as well at home as it may have abroad was a question that the next decade would have to decide.

Suggestions for reading

GENERAL

Dwight D. Eisenhower's two volumes of memoirs—*Mandate for Change** (1963) and *Waging Peace* (1965)—are valuable if predictable. Herbert Parmet, *Eisenhower: The Necessary President* (1972), is the best historical survey. R. L. Branyan and L. H. Larsen, eds., *The Eisenhower Administration, 1953–1961: A Documentary History*, 2 vols. (1972), is a useful compilation. Revealing accounts by participants in the Eisenhower Administration include Sherman Adams, *Firsthand Report** (1961); E. J. Hughes, *The Ordeal of Power** (1963); and Arthur Larson, *Eisenhower: The President Nobody Knew* (1968). See also R. M. Nixon, *Six Crises* (1962); L. L. Strauss, *Men and Decisions** (1962); E. T. Benson, *Cross Fire* (1962). K. S. Davis, *Soldier of Democracy* (1952), is a good biography of Eisenhower up to his election. R. J. Donovan, *Eisenhower: The Inside Story* (1956), and R. H. Rovere, *Affairs of State: The Eisenhower Years* (1956), offer illuminating sidelights on the first term. For not unfavorable comments from the left, see I. F. Stone, *The Haunted Fifties** (1964).

FOREIGN AND MILITARY POLICY

Seyom Brown, *The Faces of Power** (1968), provides a trenchant discussion of the main issues. For contemporaneous views by participants, see M. B. Ridgway and H. H. Martin, *Soldier: Memoirs of Matthew B. Ridgway* (1956); J. M. Gavin, *War and Peace in the Space Age* (1958); and Maxwell Taylor, *Uncertain Trumpet* (1959); and for commentaries by "defense intellectuals," H. A. Kissinger, *Nuclear Weapons and Foreign Policy** (1956) and *The Necessity for Choice** (1961); S. P. Huntington, *The Common Defense** (1961), and, ed., *Changing Patterns of Military Politics* (1962); and R. E. Osgood, *Limited War* (1957). On Dulles, see Richard Goold-Adams, *The Time of Power* (1962), and, for a sympathetic account by his sister, Eleanor Dulles, *John Foster Dulles: The Last Year* (1965). For the role of the CIA, L. B. Kirkpatrick, Jr., *The Real CIA* (1968), is the generally favorable view of a former official; David Wise and T. B. Ross, *The Invisible Government* (1964), is a less admiring report by two well-informed journalists; and H. H. Ransom, *Can American Democracy Survive Cold War?** (1963), discusses issues raised by secret intelligence operations. On particular CIA capers, see Miles Copeland, *The Game of Nations* (1970), and David Wise and T. B. Ross, *The U-2 Affair* (1962).

Hugh Thomas' two works—*Suez** (1967) and *Cuba* (1971)—provide invaluable background. R. E. Neustadt, *Alliance Politics* (1967), has an incisive analysis of the Suez affair in the context of Anglo-American relations; see also J. C. Campbell, *Defense of the Middle East* (2nd ed., 1960). P. W. Bonsal, American ambassador to Cuba in 1959–60, gives an objective and authoritative account of the evolution of Castro's relations with the United States in *Cuba, Castro, and the United States* (1971); his predecessor E. E. T. Smith is less objective in *The Fourth Floor* (1962). See also Theodore Draper, *Castroism: Theory and Practice** (1965). Milton Eisenhower, *The Wine Is Bitter* (1963), describes the awakening of the Eisenhower Administration to the problem of Latin America.

The best analysis of the American experience in Vietnam is Frances FitzGerald, *Fire in the Lake* (1972). See also, in addition to books cited in Chapter 30: Victor Bator, *Vietnam: A Diplomatic Tragedy* (1965); Melvin Gurtov, *The First Vietnam Crisis** (1967); Robert Shaplen, *The Lost Revolution** (1965); Jean Lacouture, *Vietnam: Between Two Truces** (1966). On Laos, see Arthur Dommen, *Conflict in Laos* (1964, rev. ed., 1971), C. A. Stevenson, *The End of Nowhere* (1972),

*Available in a paperback edition.

and, for documents, Nina Adams and Alfred McCoy, eds., *Laos: War and Revolution* (1970); on Cambodia, Jonathan Grant, ed., *Cambodia: The Widening War in Indochina** (1971). Other useful documentary collections are M. G. Raskin and B. B. Fall, eds., *The Viet-Nam Reader** (1965); Marvin Gettleman, ed., *Vietnam: History, Documents and Opinions** (2nd ed., 1970); Marvin and Susan Gettleman, Lawrence and Carol Kaplan, *Conflict in Indochina** (1970). A selection from the Pentagon history of the American involvement in Vietnam is to be found in Neil Sheehan, *et al., The Pentagon Papers** (1971).

DOMESTIC ISSUES

On McCarthyism at high noon and at twilight, see, in addition to the books mentioned in Chapter 30, Michael Straight, *Trial by Television* (1954); J. A. Wechsler, *The Age of Suspicion* (1953); P. M. Stern, *The Oppenheimer Case* (1969); and Samuel Stouffer, *Communism, Conformity and Civil Liberties* (1955).

On economic issues, J. K. Galbraith, *The Affluent Society** (1958), is a penetrating critique of prevailing conceptions. Three useful works on the Eisenhower economic policy are E. L. Dale, *Conservatives in Power: A Study of Frustration* (1960); A. H. Hansen, *Economic Issues of the 1960's** (1960); and S. E. Harris, *The Economics of the Political Parties* (1962). F. M. Bator, *The Question of Government Spending* (1957), is an incisive analysis. P. M. Stern, *The Great Treasury Raid** (1964), offers a disenchanted look at tax policy.

P. L. Murphy, *The Constitution in Crisis Times: 1918–1969* (1972), provides a general conspectus. R. H. Saylor, B. B. Boyer, and R. E. Gooding, Jr., eds., *The Warren Court: A Critical Analysis* (1969), give an informed and sympathetic account; A. M. Bickel, *The Supreme Court and the Idea of Progress* (1970), and P. B. Kurland, *Politics, the Constitution and the Warren Court* (1970), enter thoughtful dissents. Anthony Lewis, *Portrait of a Decade** (1964), describes the aftermath of the school desegregation decision of 1954; J. B. Martin, *The Deep South Says Never* (1957), the immediate impact of that decision; and E. F. Morrow, *Black Man in the White House** (1963), the reaction of the Eisenhower Administration. M. L. King, Jr., *Stride Toward Freedom** (1958), contributes a central document in the black revolution; August Meier, Elliott Rudwick, and F. L. Broderick, eds., *Black Protest Thought in the 20th Century** (2nd ed., 1971), a valuable anthology; Harold Cruse, *The Crisis of the Negro Intellectual** (1967), a perceptive if uneven historical essay; L. E. Lomax, *The Negro Revolt** (1963), an astute journalistic account; and Talcott Parsons and K. B. Clark, eds., *The Negro American* (1966), a useful collection of analytical essays.

On politics, Samuel Lubell, *The Revolt of the Moderates* (1956), is a searching contemporaneous statement. For Adlai Stevenson, see, in addition to the J. B. Martin biography cited in Chapter 30, his own book, *The New America* (1957); and, for a revisionist view, Bert Cochran, *Adlai Stevenson: Patrician Among Politicians* (1969). T. H. White gives a lively picture of the 1960 election in *The Making of the President, 1960** (1961).

For appraisals of American society in general, Eric Larrabee, *The Self-Conscious Society* (1960), is a useful review. The more enduring works include J. K. Galbraith, *American Capitalism: The Concept of Countervailing Power** (1952) and *The Affluent Society** (1958) (both reissued in revised editions); David Riesman, *et al., The Lonely Crowd** (1952); F. L. Allen, *The Big Change: America Transforms Itself** (1952); W. H. Whyte, Jr., *The Organization Man** (1956); David Potter, *People of Plenty** (1954); and, for an eclectic and thoughtful synoptic view, Max Lerner, *America As a Civilization** (1957). The values of the business community are discussed in F. X. Sutton, *et al., The American Business Creed** (1956), and the impact of advertising in Martin Mayer, *Madison Avenue, USA** (1958); Vance Packard, *The Hidden Persuaders** (1957); and, in a larger context, D. J. Boorstin, *The Image** (1962). On the religious boom, see Will Herberg, *Protestant-Catholic-Jew* (2nd ed., 1960), and W. L. Miller, *Piety Along the Potomac: Notes on Politics and Morals in the Fifties* (1964). Bruce Cook, *The Beat Generation* (1971), is an effective account.

*Available in a paperback edition.

Years of revolt

32

John F. Kennedy, forty-three years old in 1960, was the youngest man as well as the first Roman Catholic elected to the American Presidency. A son of the millionaire Joseph P. Kennedy, who had been the first chairman of Franklin Roosevelt's Securities and Exchange Commission and later ambassador to London, young Kennedy graduated from Harvard with honors, served heroically in the war, and won election from Massachusetts to the House of Representatives in 1946 and to the Senate in 1952. His book *Profiles in Courage* received the Pulitzer Prize for biography in 1957, though critics questioned whether Kennedy himself had shown much courage when he evaded the McCarthy issue in the Senate. Handsome in appearance and graceful in manner, cool, lucid, and ironic in play of mind—he once described himself as an ''idealist without illusions''—activist in temperament and purpose, he had an affirmative view of the Presidency and a high sense of America's national and world responsibilities. He was proficient in the game of politics, but he also hoped, in the manner of Wilson and Roosevelt, to tap resources of idealism he felt had been too long repressed in American society. He attracted and sought out men and women of ideas; intellectuals and academics now entered government in unprecedented numbers.

In particular, his election represented both in America and in the world the rise of a new generation to power. As he put it in his eloquent inaugural address, ''Let the word go forth from this time and place, to friend and foe alike, that the torch has been passed to a new generation of Americans—born in this century, tempered in war, disciplined by a hard and bitter peace.''

The Thousand Days

Kennedy and the Cold War. The new President lacked the ideological passions of the preceding Administration and, though a child of the Cold War, saw it not as a religious but as a power conflict. In power terms, though, the Cold War still seemed active enough, especially after the more than usually truculent speech Khrushchev delivered on January 6, 1961, two weeks before Kennedy's inauguration. The Soviet leader portrayed communism as riding the crest of history to inevitable triumph, promised that Russia would outstrip America in volume of production by 1965 and in per capita production by 1970, and, in the passages that made the greatest impression in Washington, pledged unreserved Soviet support for ''national liberation wars.'' Citing Vietnam, Algeria, and Cuba as examples, Khrushchev called Asia, Africa, and Latin America ''the most important centers of revolutionary struggles against imperialism.'' He added, ''Communists are revolutionaries, and it would be a bad thing if they did not take advantage of new opportunities."

In retrospect it is possible to surmise that Khrushchev's bellicosity was intended less as a challenge to the United States than as part of a complex maneuver involving China. For he also took occasion to reaffirm his rejection of nuclear war and his belief in "peaceful coexistence"—views the Chinese continued to reject. By placing these reaffirmations in a context of militancy, he may have been trying to show the communist movement that coexistence was not incompatible with the support of revolution in the Third World. In this way, he could head off the Chinese, while at the same time his talk of coexistence would signal the Americans—as he also may have tried to do by releasing two American fliers who had been shot down over the Arctic—that his intentions were not immediately hostile. But few in the West realized the extent of Russian-Chinese differences; nor did many, as they recalled Khrushchev banging his shoe on his desk at the UN General Assembly the previous autumn, suppose him a subtle man. So Washington missed his subtleties, if indeed they were there, and heard only boasts and threats.

Reading the speech as a declaration of hostility, Kennedy's inaugural address was, in effect, a reply. Dealing exclusively with foreign affairs, he saw an "hour of maximum danger" and said somewhat grandiloquently, "Let every nation know, whether it wishes us well or ill, that we shall pay any price, bear any burden, meet any hardship, support any friend, oppose any foe, in order to assure the survival and the success of liberty." He concluded: "And so, my fellow Americans, ask not what your country can do for you: Ask what you can do for your country."

The irony of this exchange was that both leaders, probably because they understood better than most the horror that waited at the end of the line, wanted to escape from the upward spiral of the arms race. If Khrushchev was twisting and turning in his hope of diminishing the risk of nuclear catastrophe without losing ground to Communist China, Kennedy felt equally that nuclear war would mean the end of civilization. His inaugural address condemned the arms race, asked to "bring the absolute power to destroy other nations under the absolute control of all nations," emphasized that "civility is not a sign of weakness," and declared: "Let us never

negotiate out of fear. But let us never fear to negotiate."

Moreover, Kennedy had a vivid sense of the limitations of American power to shape the world as it wished. Nine months after the inaugural address he asked the American people to "face the fact that the United States is neither omnipotent nor omniscient—that we are only 6 percent of the world's population—that we cannot impose our will upon the other 94 percent of mankind—that we cannot right every wrong or reverse each adversity—and that therefore there cannot be an American solution to every world problem."

From "massive retaliation" to "flexible response." In the grim mood induced by the Khrushchev speech, Kennedy proceeded to reorganize American security policy to prepare for crises ahead. His Secretary of State, Dean Rusk, was experienced in foreign affairs and held hard and tenacious Cold War views. Adlai Stevenson, who was moving beyond his Cold War positions of the fifties, was made ambassador to the United Nations. The new Secretary of Defense, Robert S. McNamara, was a professor turned industrial manager who concentrated his energy and intelligence on the control of the defense establishment and the reformulation of American strategy. Often frustrated in his dealings with the State Department, Kennedy turned increasingly to his White House staff and especially to McGeorge Bundy, a Harvard intellectual who became his Special Assistant for National Security.

The new President's first decision, in face of Khrushchev's Cold War of movement, was to minimize the chance of nuclear war by abandoning the defense strategy that relied on nuclear weapons as a deterrent to local as well as general aggression. Under McNamara's direction, the guiding strategic doctrine shifted from "massive retaliation" to "flexible response"—that is, to the diversification of forces so that the level of deterrence could be precisely graduated to meet the level of threat. This shift was designed to enable the West to respond to Soviet aggression in Europe by means other than nuclear war; and it required above all the expansion of conventional warfare capabilities. However, imprisoned by a fallacious "missile gap" notion he himself had encouraged during his campaign and reluctant to take on the Joint Chiefs of Staff at a time when McNamara was trying to establish

Inauguration, 1961: "idealist without illusions"

759

control over the military establishment, Kennedy yielded to military pressure and also requested more long-range missiles.

The missile buildup of 1961, as some in the Administration felt at the time and most felt later, was an overreaction to the Khrushchev speech. It was more than American security demanded; it ended any hope of freezing the rival military forces at relatively low levels; and it sent the wrong message to Moscow, probably causing Khrushchev to feel that, for his own security and prestige, he had to increase Soviet missile strength. Though Kennedy also made a serious effort to negotiate a test-ban agreement, the Russians hardened their position; indeed, the Soviet Union—the first state to do so since 1958—began in September 1961 an extensive series of tests in the atmosphere, exploding in October a device nearly three thousand times more powerful than the bomb dropped on Hiroshima.

For the longer run, Kennedy, with McNamara's strong backing, wanted to stop the arms race. Speaking before the United Nations in September, he presented a plan for general and complete disarmament. This goal, he said, was "no longer a dream—it is a practical matter of life or death. The risks inherent in disarmament pale in comparison to the risks inherent in an unlimited arms race. . . . Mankind must put an end to war— or war will put an end to mankind." But the appeal fell on deaf ears; and, with reluctance, Kennedy himself resumed atmospheric testing in April 1962. So the two superpowers, still in the lockstep of the Cold War, proceeded to intensify the arms race.

Struggle for the Third World.

Both Kennedy and Khrushchev agreed that, with the stalemate in Europe, the Third World had become the decisive battleground between democracy and communism. The new Administration rejected the condemnation of neutralism as "immoral" and took a number of steps in the United Nations and elsewhere to indicate American sympathy with the new states struggling to achieve political and economic identity. The foreign-assistance program underwent a significant revision in concept so that an increasing share of aid would go to modernize economies rather than to build armies. The Peace Corps—an undertaking especially close to Kennedy's heart— channeled the idealism of individual Americans into face-to-face cooperation with

Peace Corps worker in Pakistan: face-to-face cooperation

underdeveloped countries. An expanded Food for Peace program under George McGovern used American agricultural abundance to foster development in emergent nations.

Kennedy's basic purpose was to persuade the Third World that democratic methods offered the best means of development and independence. But there remained the problem of protecting the democratization process, so often disruptive in its initiation and gradual in its impact, against communist interruption and subversion—a problem spotlighted by Khrushchev's fervent espousal of national-liberation wars. The American view was that, the nuclear standoff having rendered nuclear war unlikely, national-liberation wars now created the main problem. If only Moscow could be restrained from supporting or instigating such wars, then the world could look forward to an era of peace.

Hence a strategy for national-liberation wars became a Washington obsession. Though "flexible response" had been adopted for European reasons, an important side effect was to create capabilities that could be employed in local wars elsewhere around the world. To strengthen the American ability to deal with national-liberation wars, Kennedy ordered the development of "counterinsurgency" forces. Counterinsurgency doctrine was propounded, schools were set up, and the President himself took a personal interest in the organization of élite counterguerrilla units, notably the Green Berets. The theory was that counterinsurgency would operate within a context of social reform, defending governments seeking to carry out structural changes essential to modernization. But the political component did not take root, and the counterinsurgency mystique primarily nourished the American belief in the capacity and right to intervene in foreign lands.

Latin America: crisis and hope.

Kennedy's main reliance, however, was on the use of American economic assistance to advance democratic reform in underdeveloped countries—a program he quickly applied to Latin America when he set forth the Alliance for Progress in March 1961. Building upon Latin American proposals, like Kubitschek's Operation Pan America, and greatly extending last-minute efforts within the Eisenhower Administration, he called for a concerted, hemisphere-wide effort to accelerate economic growth and raise living standards. Most novel was the insistence—against the wishes both of North American business and Latin American oligarchies—on the necessity for social reform within a democratic framework. "Those who make peaceful revolution impossible," as he told the Latin American diplomatic corps, "will make violent revolution inevitable." At an inter-American conference at Punta del Este, Uruguay, in August 1961 the Latin American states (except for Cuba) subscribed to the goals of the Alliance.

The Alliance was accompanied by a determined effort to support progressive democratic forces in Latin America and to oppose military dictatorship. This, reinforced by the fact that no President since Roosevelt had shown such interest in the hemisphere, resulted in a notable change in Latin attitudes toward the United States. In November 1961, when American naval units appeared off the Dominican Republic to strengthen a transition regime against an attempt by brothers of the late dictator Trujillo to seize power, the American flag was cheered by prodemocratic crowds. When a military coup nullified the results of a presidential election in Peru in 1962, Kennedy suspended diplomatic and economic relations until the military junta restored political freedom and pledged new elections. Kennedy's dramatically successful visits to Venezuela, Colombia, Mexico, and Central America enabled the United States for a moment to recover its popularity of Good Neighbor days in the southern half of the hemisphere.

These gains took place, however, against the vociferous opposition of the Castro regime in Cuba and despite a disastrous episode taking place a few weeks after the announcement of the Alliance for Progress. Among other inheritances from the preceding Administration was the force of anti-Castro Cubans that had been trained and equipped by the CIA in Guatemala. Confronted with the choice of disbanding this group or permitting it to try an invasion of their homeland, Kennedy accepted the recommendation of the Joint Chiefs of Staff, the Secretaries of State and Defense, and the CIA that he should let the exiles go ahead. A Cuban Revolutionary Council, organized in March 1961, served as the ostensible sponsor of the action. Its membership consisted of the liberal (as against the communist) wing of the original revolutionary movement; its chairman, Miro Cardona, had been Castro's first prime minister.

On April 17, 1961, about twelve hundred Cubans landed at the Bahia de Cochinas (Bay of Pigs), on the southern coast of Cuba. After three days of fighting, the invasion collapsed. To the world, and to many Americans, the Bay of Pigs was an indefensible exercise in intervention, and for a moment the bright promise of the new Administration seemed blighted. Refusing escalation, Kennedy resisted proposals that he send in the marines and took full responsibility for the fiasco, remarking wryly that victory had a hundred fathers but defeat was an orphan. In the longer run, he pursued a policy directed toward the economic and diplomatic isolation of Cuba. Pinprick raids sponsored by the CIA had little effect, except to irritate Castro who avowed his commitment to Marxism-Leninism and continued to stimulate guerrilla action against democratic regimes in Latin America, especially Venezuela.

Trouble in Southeast Asia. Another troubling inheritance was the crisis in Laos. Kennedy, who felt in general that the United States was "overcommitted" in Southeast Asia, felt in particular that neither superpower had enough at stake in Laos to justify armed confrontation. He consequently decided to reject Eisenhower's counsel of unilateral American military intervention—a decision facilitated by his disenchantment with the military advice of the Joint Chiefs of Staff after the Bay of Pigs—and to reverse the Eisenhower effort to build a bastion of the West in the Asian jungle. Instead he sought the neutralization of Laos under the leadership of Prince Souvanna Phouma.

Protracted negotiations conducted by the veteran diplomat Averell Harriman in Geneva in 1961–62 finally resulted in Soviet-American agreement on a tripartite Laotian regime headed by Souvanna Phouma and including the prowestern faction of General Phoumi and the communist Pathet Lao as well as Souvanna's neutralists. The neutralization proclaimed at Geneva was not, however, achieved. North Vietnam continued to send men and supplies to the Viet Cong in South Vietnam via the Ho Chi Minh trails in southeastern Laos and maintained a military presence in Laos to protect the infiltration effort. In response, a CIA mission aided the coalition government in Vientiane. When Pathet Lao ministers withdrew from the government in 1963, the Pathet Lao insurgency resumed in the northeast. The result was *de facto* partition of the country.

Perhaps fearful that his refusal to send American troops into Cuba and his retreat from Laos might be construed in Moscow as weakness, Kennedy decided to increase support to the government in South Vietnam, where the situation appeared militarily more manageable. In the spring Vice President Johnson, on a visit to Vietnam, pronounced Diem the Churchill of South Asia; and on his return, while recommending against American combat involvement, he said, "We must decide whether to help these countries to the best of our ability or throw in the towel in the area and pull back our defenses to San Francisco." In the meantime, Kennedy sent a small force of Green Berets to instruct the South Vietnamese army in the black arts of counterinsurgency and authorized minor clandestine operations against North Vietnam. But despite the great numerical superiority of the South Vietnamese forces—250,000 in November 1961 against 15,000 Viet Cong—the situation of the Saigon government was growing worse. That same month a presidential mission, headed by General Maxwell Taylor, recommended the dispatch of an American task force—perhaps 10,000 men—and urged the consideration of air strikes against the "ultimate source of aggression" in North Vietnam.

Kennedy rejected these recommendations. Sending in troops, he remarked, was "like taking a drink. The effect wears off, and you have to take another." Nevertheless, while declining to commit American combat units, he accepted the theory that the assignment of American military "advisers" to South Vietnamese units would improve their tactics and stiffen their resistance. In early 1962 the advisers began to arrive, and soon American helicopters and personnel were taking a part in the fighting. At the same time, aware that lack of popular support was a central cause of Diem's difficulties, Kennedy urged the regime to enlarge its base by political and economic reform. Diem, profoundly authoritarian by temperament, disdained such advice.

Two clashing views arose within the government over Vietnam policy. One group, led by Harriman, now Assistant Secretary of State for Far Eastern Affairs, saw the issue as primarily political and local; the crisis had resulted, this group believed, from Diem's reactionary policies in face of a communist-managed peasant insurrection. The other group, centered in the Pentagon, conceived the situation as one not of civil war but of external aggression, attributing the crisis to the instigation and support of the Viet Cong by Hanoi and, beyond this, by China and Russia. This group, supported by the American ambassador and the general in charge of the military advisory group in Saigon, agreed with General Earle Wheeler, the Army Chief of Staff, who said in November 1962, "The essence of the problem in Vietnam is military."

In 1962 the military adviser policy seemed to be working. Even the communists called it "Diem's year." "Every quantitative measurement we have," McNamara said on his first visit to Vietnam in 1962, "shows we're winning the war." In his January 1963 state-of-the-union message, Kennedy summed up the prevailing optimism: "The spearpoint of aggression has been blunted in South Vietnam."

Kennedy and Khrushchev. The central problem remained the Soviet Union. Meeting Khrushchev in Vienna in June 1961, Kennedy tried to persuade the Soviet leader that their two nations must avoid head-on collision in an era of change and uncertainty. Therefore each superpower should refrain from actions that, by upsetting the existing balance, would invite miscalculation and compel reaction by the other. This concept of a status quo, Kennedy emphasized, did not exclude revolutionary change within nations in each bloc, but such change should take place without transferring power from one bloc to the other. Probably misled by the Bay of Pigs into seeing Kennedy as irresolute, Khrushchev brusquely rejected the idea of a global standstill (except in Laos, where he agreed to neutralization) and adopted an intransigent, even bullying, attitude. He too believed in the status quo, but this, he explained, was the revolutionary process itself; to block revolution, he told Kennedy, was really to interfere with the status quo.

For Khrushchev, Germany was the critical issue. He was determined to relieve the pressure on East Germany (where the flow of refugees west was reaching thirty thousand a month), to expel the West from Berlin, and to prevent West Germany from acquiring nuclear weapons; at the same time, he wanted to strengthen his position against China within the communist world by producing a success of his own. He therefore reopened the question of Berlin, telling Kennedy that by the end of the year he would conclude with East Germany a peace treaty that would extinguish western occupation-and-access rights in West Berlin and establish West Berlin as a free city. Kennedy replied that the abandonment of West Berlin would mean the abandonment of Western Europe and that so drastic an alteration in the world balance of power was unacceptable; Khrushchev himself would not accept a comparable shift in favor of the West. Khrushchev said, if America wanted war over Berlin, there was nothing the Soviet Union could do about it; he was going to sign the treaty by December 31. When the two men parted, Kennedy commented, "It will be a cold winter."

Returning to the United States, Kennedy in July 1961 requested a further increase in the defense budget, called out 150,000 reservists, and announced a program, which set off an ugly outburst of near-panic and which he soon regretted, of fallout shelters for protection against nuclear attack. Though these measures, especially the last, soon came to seem an overreaction, all of them, including the last, may have persuaded Khrushchev that he could not solve the Berlin question by intimidation. In addition, Kennedy, acknowledging Russia's security interests in Central and Eastern Europe, declared his readiness to work out arrangements "to meet these concerns." On August 13 the East Germans erected the Berlin Wall, thereby stopping the refugee flow. Though Khrushchev continued to deliver bellicose speeches and resumed nuclear testing, he postponed his treaty deadline in October; and the Berlin crisis, for a moment so frightening to the world, subsided.

In Western Europe, Kennedy hoped for steady movement toward unification, particularly through the admission of Great Britain to the European Economic Community (see p. 717). To this end, he secured the passage in September 1962 of the Trade Expansion Act, creating authority to negotiate tariff reductions up to 50 percent for the purpose of bargaining with an enlarged Common Market. But Kennedy's so-called grand design for Europe was frustrated by President de Gaulle's veto in January 1963 of British membership—an action precipitated by the French president's resentment of what he considered the British effort at the Nassau Conference of December 1962 to maintain its "special relationship"

with the United States and caused more generally by de Gaulle's unrelenting opposition to what he saw as an American attempt to dominate the military and economic arrangements of the new Europe.

The missile crisis. Khrushchev had by no means abandoned his goal of driving the West out of Berlin. In the summer of 1962, carrying his Cold War of movement to its ultimate audacity, he decided to establish in Cuba bases for nuclear missiles targeted against the United States—an unprecedented step for the Russians, who had never before placed their missiles in any other country. If successful, the operation would not only protect Cuba from American invasion—the objective later alleged by Khrushchev (though this could have been more simply achieved by stationing Soviet troops on the island)—but would give Russia a potent bargaining counter when it chose to reopen the Berlin question. Moreover, by making shorter-range missiles effective against American targets, it would double Soviet nuclear first-strike capacity and do so without additional strain on the Soviet budget; it would deal America a shattering political blow by showing the Soviet capacity to penetrate the American sphere of influence; and it would strengthen the Russian hand against the militant Chinese by proving Moscow capable of bold action in support of a communist revolution.

Secrecy and speed were of the essence. Washington had not objected to Russian supply of defensive weapons to Cuba; but Kennedy warned in September 1962 that, if there were evidence of "significant offensive capability either in Cuban hands or under Soviet direction . . . the gravest issues would arise." Khrushchev repeatedly denied both publicly and privately that he had any such intention; nor did Washington suppose him capable of so imprudent an action. Then, on October 14, a U-2 overflight found conclusive evidence that Khrushchev had lied and that a Soviet nuclear buildup was well under way.

Kennedy's first decision was that, one way or another, the missiles would have to be removed. Later critics have suggested that he should have accepted the Soviet missiles without protest. After all, the Americans had their Jupiter missiles in Turkey (though this was because the State Department had delayed in executing Kennedy's order that they be withdrawn). Moreover, the United States

Berlin, 1961:
East German soldier
leaps to the West

"USS Barry" on inspection: the missiles went back

would still retain decisive nuclear superiority even after the Cuban buildup. But Kennedy felt that to acquiesce in so gross an intrusion into what the Russians, with their sensitivity to spheres of influence, well knew to be the American sphere, would, by displaying American impotence in its own zone of vital interest, convince both Khrushchev and the western allies that the Russians could get away with almost anything and would tempt Moscow into more recklessness to which in the end America would be compelled to respond by force. The attempted nuclearization of Cuba, as Kennedy saw it, was "a deliberately provocative and unjustified change in the *status quo* which cannot be accepted by this country if our courage and our commitments are ever to be trusted again by either friend or foe."

For six days Kennedy and a small group of advisers debated behind locked doors how best to get the missiles out. One faction, led by Dean Acheson and the Joint Chiefs of Staff, advocated the destruction of the bases by surprise air attack. The other, led by Attorney General Robert F. Kennedy, the President's brother, and Secretary of Defense McNamara, sharply opposed this course on moral grounds—as a Pearl Harbor in reverse against a small country—and on practical grounds—because it might kill Russians at the missile sites and force the Soviet Union into drastic retaliation. Naval blockade, this group argued, would both show the American determination to get the missiles out and allow Moscow time

and room to pull back without undue humiliation. President Kennedy announced his course in the first public disclosure of the crisis on October 22—to establish a naval quarantine against further shipments; to demand the dismantling of the bases and the removal of the missiles; and to warn that any nuclear attack launched from Cuba would be regarded "as an attack by the Soviet Union on the United States, requiring a full retaliatory response upon the Soviet Union."

The days that followed were more tense than any since the Second World War. Moscow continued to deny the presence of nuclear weapons until, in a dramatic moment before the United Nations, Ambassador Adlai Stevenson confronted the Soviet delegate with blown-up aerial photographs of the nuclear installations. Meanwhile work was continuing day and night to make the bases operational. An American invasion force was massing in Florida. Soviet ships, presumably carrying more missiles, were drawing near the island; Kennedy kept the interception line close to Cuba to give Khrushchev maximum time for reflection. Finally, after indescribable suspense, Soviet ships began to turn back. "We're eyeball to eyeball," said Dean Rusk, "and I think the other fellow just blinked."

It remained for negotiation to complete the resolution of the crisis. On October 26 Kennedy received a long, passionate letter from Khrushchev dilating on the horror of nuclear war and offering to remove the missiles and send no more if the United States would end the quarantine and agree not to invade Cuba. But on the following morning there arrived a second letter from Khrushchev, harder in tone and proposing an entirely different trade: the Soviet missiles in Cuba for the American missiles in Turkey; a Soviet guarantee of Turkish integrity for an American guarantee of Cuban integrity. Robert Kennedy now recommended that his brother ignore the second letter and respond to the first. The President followed this advice. Robert Kennedy took the American restatement of the first Khrushchev proposal to the Soviet ambassador, who then asked him about the Turkish missiles. The Attorney General replied that, while this could be no *quid pro quo*, his brother had ordered their removal some time back, "and it was our judgment that, within a short time after this crisis was over, those missiles would be gone." The next day, October 28, a favorable reply came from Khrushchev.

Khrushchev's bluff had failed. In short order the bases were dismantled and the missiles on their way home. Castro's resistance, however, made it impossible to establish the UN inspection to which Khrushchev had agreed, and the United States never formally completed the reciprocal pledge not to invade Cuba. But in substance the deal went into effect anyway. U-2 overflights, which the Russian antiaircraft batteries made no attempt to stop, took the place of UN inspection; the Jupiter missiles left Turkey; and the United States, which had no intention of invading Cuba in any case, now ended hit-and-run raids by Cuban refugees from American territory. In the autumn of 1963 Kennedy began secret explorations through the United Nations looking toward a normalization of relations with Cuba.

The world of diversity. The American success—Kennedy forbade gloating and refused to claim a triumph—was the result of Kennedy's combination of toughness and restraint and of his precise understanding of the uses of power. He now hoped he had made to Khrushchev the point he had tried to make in Vienna—that neither side dare tamper carelessly with the complex and explosive international equilibrium.

In this hope he renewed his quest for a test-ban treaty. "I am haunted," he said in March 1963, "by the feeling that by 1970, unless we are successful, there may be ten nuclear powers instead of four, and by 1975 fifteen or twenty." Negotiations bogged down during the spring. In an effort to break the deadlock, Kennedy, in a notable speech at American University in June 1963, called on Americans as well as Russians to rethink the Cold War: "We must reexamine our own attitude—as individuals and as a Nation—for our attitude is as essential as theirs." He rejected the "holy war" idea: "No government or social system is so evil that its people must be considered as lacking in virtue." Both sides, he said, were "caught up in a vicious and dangerous cycle in which suspicion on one side breeds suspicion on the other, and new weapons beget counterweapons." He specified a nuclear test ban as a first means of breaking this cycle.

Khrushchev, who later described the American University address as "the greatest speech by any American President since Roosevelt," came back with the proposal of a limited ban designed to outlaw tests in the atmosphere, in outer space, and under water—in environments, in other words, where violations could be detected without physical inspection. Kennedy sent Harriman to Moscow; and, after arduous negotiations, Washington, London, and Moscow agreed in July on the text of the treaty. In September it was ratified by the Senate. Though France and China declined to sign it, the test-ban treaty represented the most significant formal step toward peace since the onset of the Cold War. And the warm reception given in his own country to the American University speech, with its quiet rejection of clichés of the Cold War, signified the change Kennedy's reliance on reason had wrought in national attitudes toward foreign policy.

Not all Americans agreed. Some clung to the old simplifications, denouncing acceptance of communism as a "no-win" policy and demanding a program of "total victory." Under the urging of Robert Welch, a candy-manufacturer who professed his "firm belief that Dwight Eisenhower is a dedicated, conscious agent of the Communist conspiracy," such people joined Welch's John Birch Society. The John Birch Society, however, was a zany minority; and the leadership was far less formidable than Huey Long in the thirties or Joe McCarthy in the early fifties.

As against the belief of the Dulles decade in an eternal contest between the "Free World" and the communist conspiracy, Kennedy felt that the policy of the two blocs was finished, the world of the superpowers in dissolution. "The revolution of national independence," he said in 1962, was bringing a "world of diversity" into existence, "a world where, within the framework of international cooperation, every country can solve its own problems according to its own traditions and ideals." Communism might well be one element in this pluralist world, but diversity, he added, was "incompatible" with the communist belief that all the roads of history had "a single destination." No one could "doubt that the great currents of history are carrying the world away from the monolithic toward the pluralist idea—away from communism and toward national independence and freedom." Indeed, nationalism was already breaking up the centralized communist empire. And the world of diversity, "far from being opposed to the American conception of world order," expressed "the very essence of our view of the future." As he summed up his policy at American University, in a conscious revision of Wilson's famous line, "If we cannot end now all our differences, at least we can help make the world safe for diversity."

Deeper into the quagmire. There remained the problem of national liberation wars, and Kennedy continued to see them as threats to the world of diversity. There remained, above all, Vietnam. The optimism of 1962 came to seem hollow early in 1963. The South Vietnamese army showed little interest in fighting, Diem even less interest in rallying popular support. The Viet Cong insurgency gained both internal strength and external assistance. In the spring Buddhist protests against the Saigon government and Diem's angry retaliation demonstrated the regime's instability. Diem's brother Ngo Dinh Nhu, a political mystic, urged Diem on to further repression.

Belatedly perceiving that Vietnam was as much a political as a military problem, Kennedy brought new pressure on Diem to reform his regime. Henry Cabot Lodge, sent to Saigon in August as American ambassador to carry out this policy, was confronted by new outrages against the Buddhists. Dissident Vietnamese generals soon asked him whether, if there was a coup, a new regime would receive American support. Lodge believed that, unless Diem got rid of Nhu, which was unlikely, the Saigon government would only plunge on to disaster. The Harriman group in Washington agreed, and Kennedy, with some dubiety, backed Lodge in selective measures designed to force Diem to drop Nhu and undertake reforms. In October, with Lodge's knowledge, the generals prepared for a coup. On November 1 they overthrew and murdered Diem and Nhu, and South Vietnam moved into a new phase of turmoil.

Buddhist monk protests: Saigon, 1963

Kennedy never fully clarified his views on Vietnam. On the one hand, he accepted the domino theory; "for us to withdraw," he said in July 1963 ". . . would mean a collapse not only of South Vietnam but of Southeast Asia." On the other hand, he laid down in July 1962 a plan for the phased withdrawal of American forces by the end of 1965—a plan that remained in effect until March 1964. Though he gradually increased the number of American "advisers"—there were 16,300 American troops in Vietnam at the end of 1963—only 73 Americans were killed in combat during his Presidency.

While regarding the United States as overcommitted in Southeast Asia, Kennedy felt that, the commitment having been made, America could not let South Vietnam fall cheaply to the communists. How far he would have gone to prevent this outcome no one can know. His memory of the French predicament a decade before had persuaded him that too large an infusion of white soldiers would only unite Vietnamese nationalism against the alien presence; and he had shown at the Bay of Pigs his capacity to refuse escalation and cut losses. "In the final analysis," he said in September of the people of South Vietnam, "it is their war. They are the ones who have to win it or lose it. We can help them, we can give them equipment, we can send our men out there as advisers, but they have to win it, the people of Vietnam."

Space. The competition between the superpowers produced at least one benign by-product. In April 1961 the Russians put the first man, Yuri Gagarin, into space orbit. Ten months before the Gagarin flight, a government scientific committee had proposed that the United States send a manned expedition to the moon before 1970; but Eisenhower had little sympathy with space exploration. Observing the prestige conferred on the Soviet Union by its space successes, Kennedy, on May 25, 1961, took up the proposal and declared that the United States "should commit itself to achieving the goal, before this decade is out, of landing a man on the moon and returning him safely to earth." The idea was greeted with disapproval by those who thought the money should be spent in meeting human needs on earth and with skepticism by those who doubted whether the project could be carried out.

Nonetheless, Kennedy pushed ahead. In February 1962 John Glenn became the first American to enter space orbit; and National Aeronautic and Space Administration (NASA) scientists in the Apollo program were already hard at work breaking down the technical problems of a moonshot. Seven years later, on July 16, 1969, the moonship Apollo 11 was launched from Cape Kennedy, Florida. On July 20 Captain Neil A. Armstrong became the first man to walk on the moon. "That's one small step for a man," Armstrong said "one giant step for mankind."

Beating Russia to the moon was not Kennedy's main interest. Indeed, he suggested at

Vienna in 1961 and again at the UN in 1963 that the Americans and the Russians go to the moon together. He was responding rather to the newest of new frontiers, to the ultimate challenge and mystery of space itself. "Why, some say, the moon? . . . The great British explorer George Mallory, who was to die on Mount Everest, was asked why did he want to climb it, and he said, 'Because it is there.' Well, space is there, and . . . the moon and planets are there, and new hopes for knowledge and peace are there." Kennedy's sense of history was surely right. When all else about the twentieth century is forgotten, it may still be remembered as the century when man first burst his terrestrial bonds and began the endless voyage, beyond planet and galaxy, into the illimitable dark.

The New Frontier. In domestic policy, Kennedy, elected by an exceptionally narrow popular margin and confronted by the powerful coalition of Republicans and Southern Democrats that had dominated domestic policy since 1938, had to proceed with circumspection. The 1962 congressional election—the most successful for any incumbent Administration since 1934—strengthened his popular mandate but did not significantly improve his parliamentary situation.

Nonetheless, Kennedy strove perseveringly to achieve his aim of getting the country moving again. In economic policy he relied heavily on Walter Heller, an economist who served as chairman of the Council of Economic Advisers, as well as on Douglas Dillon, the liberal Republican whom he appointed Secretary of the Treasury. In February 1961 the gross national product was down to $500 billion—nearly $9 billion less at uniform prices than a year earlier. 8.1 percent of the labor force, $5\frac{1}{2}$ million people, were unemployed. Though conditions improved by the end of 1961, largely because of the increase in government cash contributions to the economy, the first months of 1962 saw business investment again fall off. Worried by this relapse, by the inflationary bias produced by concentrated corporate and labor power, and by the continuing problem of the nation's balance of payments, the Council of Economic Advisers urged business and labor to keep wage increases within the limit of advances in productivity.

This standard, later the basis of the "wage-price guideposts," was urged with particular

force in the case of the steel industry, which exerted a bellwether effect on industrial costs. The steelworkers accepted a noninflationary contract on the tacit assumption that the steel companies would forgo a price increase. When the companies, led by United States Steel, announced a major price rise in the spring of 1962 without warning or consultation, Kennedy reacted with anger and, through a variety of pressures, forced the companies to retract their action. The episode—especially Kennedy's off-the-record remark, "My father always told me that all businessmen were sons-of-bitches, but I never believed it till now"—provoked a wave of business criticism of Washington reminiscent of the Roosevelt years.

A stock-market slump in May 1962 aggravated the economic situation. But, despite business clamor, Kennedy, the first Keynesian President, steadily pursued expansionist policies: in 1962, liberalized depreciation allowances and the investment credit; in 1963, the proposal of general tax reduction, enacted in 1964. These Keynesian measures fostered the longest peacetime expansion of the American economy in history, with an average annual increase in the gross national product of 5.6 percent in the Kennedy years.

While fiscal stimulation increased output and employment, it did not solve the question of localized and structural poverty. The contemporary poor, unlike the ambitious immigrants of the nineties or the angry unemployed of the thirties, were largely a demoralized and inarticulate minority who in many cases had inherited their poverty and accepted it as a permanent condition. In 1962 Michael Harrington's *The Other America* provided a powerful account of the distress of the invisible poor. Kennedy had already begun to attack the problem through the Area Development Act of 1961 and through programs directed at Appalachia, an eleven-state region stretching from Pennsylvania to Alabama and centering in eastern Kentucky and West Virginia; and in 1963 he reached the conclusion that, if the forgotten Americans were to be helped, tax reduction required a counterpart in the form of a comprehensive war against poverty.

Kennedy also pressed bills for federal aid to education and for medical care for the old through the social-security system (popularly known as Medicare). Though these were defeated in Congress, the work of public educa-

A giant step for mankind

Harassment in Birmingham, 1963

tion began in these fields, and he was able to make legislative gains in improving social security and the minimum wage and in housing.

The black revolution. In the urgent area of civil rights, Kennedy concentrated at first on executive rather than legislative action. His brother, Attorney General Robert F. Kennedy, took new steps to end segregation in interstate transportation and to secure the right of blacks to vote. In October 1962 the President sent federal troops into Oxford, Mississippi, in order to protect James Meredith, a black student, in the right, assured him by the courts, to attend the University of Mississippi. In addition, an unprecedented number of blacks received federal appointments.

But these actions fell behind the pace of the black revolution. "This Administration," said Martin Luther King, Jr., "has outstripped all previous ones in the breadth of its civil rights activity. Yet the movement, instead of breaking out into the open plains of progress, remains constricted and confined. A sweeping revolutionary force is pressed into a narrow tunnel." As black discontent grew, there was a comparable increase in Southern resistance.

The Civil Rights Commission reported early in 1963, "Citizens of the United States have been shot, set upon by vicious dogs, beaten and otherwise terrorized because they sought to vote." In April 1963, when King began a campaign to end discrimination in shops, restaurants, and employment in Birmingham, Alabama, Police Commissioner Eugene "Bull" Connor harassed King's marchers with firehoses, electric cattle prods, and growling police dogs.

The Birmingham episode caused a surge of indignation throughout the nation. Then, in June, Governor George Wallace of Alabama personally tried to block the admission of two black students to the state university, but he folded under federal pressure. That night Kennedy went on television to pronounce the civil-rights question "a moral issue . . . as old as the scriptures and . . . as clear as the American Constitution," and to commit the nation to the proposition "that race has no place in American life or law." With this speech he launched a fight for new and more sweeping civil-rights legislation.

Later that same night, Medgar Evers, the head of the Mississippi NAACP, was shot

Martin Luther King, Jr., and Roy Wilkins: mourning for Medgar Evers

down by a white killer. A few months later four little girls were murdered in the bombing of a black church in Alabama. But, despite such incidents, the civil-rights movement clung to the faith that the righteousness of their cause made success inevitable. In August Dr. King led a quarter of a million people, black and white, on a great march in front of the Lincoln Memorial in Washington, where they listened to King's moving eloquence ("I have a dream") and sang the old Baptist hymn the civil-rights movement had made its own, "We Shall Overcome." "In the process of gaining our rightful place," King said, "we must not be guilty of wrongful deeds. Let us not seek to satisfy our thirst for freedom by drinking from the cup of bitterness and hatred. . . . The marvelous new militancy which has engulfed the Negro community must not lead us to a distrust of all white people, for . . . their freedom is inextricably bound to our freedom. We cannot walk alone." But in the same year the black novelist James Baldwin, in his bitter warning to white America, *The Fire Next Time*, wrote that the Negro "no longer believes in the good faith of white Americans." Time was running out.

Kennedy and America. In the White House Kennedy's directness and openness of mind, his faith in reason, and his compassionate vision of American life helped break the intellectual as well as the political crust that had settled over American society in the fifties. He communicated not only an insistence on personal excellence but a sharply critical attitude toward ideas and institutions that most Americans in the preceding decade had regarded with vast self-satisfaction. Kennedy's message was that abroad the old Cold War was played out, that at home the American way of life was in bad shape, that the nation was neglectful of its young and its old, callous toward its poor and its minorities, that its cities and schools and landscapes were a mess, and that national motives were tending toward meanness and materialism.

Kennedy's words and actions encouraged a great new release of critical energy throughout American society. A new literature of protest examined hitherto sacrosanct or shadowed corners of American life, casting a harsh light on suppressed issues like poverty and racial injustice and freely assailing such national ikons as television, the cigarette, the pesticide, billboards, the funeral parlor, the

Washington, 1963: "We shall overcome"

automobile, and the brand-name drug. The outpouring of social criticism was comparable to that of the Progressive period and the New Deal. Like the Roosevelts, Kennedy, by the strength of his personal attitude, helped the nation see itself with new eyes. "There wasn't a point," one writer said, "where he didn't upset some preconception of every group in the country."

He gave people the belief that things could be done and that public policy must be determined by open and reasoned discussion. For a moment he made politics seem in truth (in a phrase he cherished from John Buchan's *Pilgrim's Way*) "the greatest and most honorable adventure." He was greatly admired and trusted in the black community, and he was the first President since Roosevelt who had anything to say to the young. With his more radical younger brother, Robert Kennedy, the intimate partner in the great decisions of his Administration, he produced an image of concern and courage. Not only his purpose but, in the much abused word of the time, his "style" seemed to open up new vistas for his nation.

On November 21, 1963, he left for a trip

to Texas. The next day, while traveling with his wife in an open car through Dallas, he was shot and killed. Kennedy's murder sent a wave of incredulity, shame, and grief across the United States and around the planet. In his brief thousand days in the Presidency, he had done much to wipe away the world's impression of his country as an old nation of old men, weary, played out, fearful of ideas, everywhere committed to the status quo, and had revived the idea of America as a young, questing, creative land, facing the future with confidence and hope.

He had faced the future with confidence

The Johnson years

The Great Society. The Presidency now descended to a political leader of an older generation, Lyndon Baines Johnson. A Texan, fifty-five years old, Johnson had come to the Vice Presidency from twenty-three years in the Congress as representative and then senator, ending as Democratic leader of the Senate. No President since Polk had had such impressive legislative experience. He was also the first Southern President since Andrew Johnson a century before. A fervent New Dealer who had become more conservative in his middle years, he still retained an entirely authentic concern for the poor and, though a Southerner, for black America. His admirers rejoiced in the power of his formidable personality, the sincerity of his social concern, and the resourcefulness with which he pursued his purposes; others found him egotistical, histrionic, secretive, devious, and vindictive.

In the national shock after Dallas the new President took over his responsibilities with firmness and strength. He soon appointed a commission under Chief Justice Warren to investigate his predecessor's assassination. The commission reported in 1964 that the murderer was a rootless and embittered former communist named Lee Harvey Oswald, though later critics challenged both the commission's procedures and its conclusions.

In other respects, Johnson made clear his determination to carry forward his predecessor's policies and (unlike Truman in 1945) to continue his predecessor's Cabinet. His experience and inclination led him toward the field of domestic affairs. Both the tax-reduction and civil-rights bills were on their way to

Lyndon B. Johnson, November 23, 1963: grief and determination

enactment at the time of Kennedy's death, and the rush of national remorse assured them speedy passage. The Civil Rights Act of 1964 prohibited discrimination in the use of federal funds and in places of public resort and established an Equal Employment Opportunity Commission to prevent discrimination in employment. A subsequent act in 1965 strengthened the right to vote by authorizing the federal government to register those whom the states refused to put on the voting lists.

Seeking a distinctive name for his domestic program, Johnson in May 1964 called for a Great Society—"a place where the city of man serves not only the needs of the body and the demands of commerce but the desire for beauty and the hunger for community." The Great Society, he said in his annual message of 1965, "asks not only how much, but how good; not only how to create wealth, but how to use it; not only how fast we are going, but where we are headed. It proposes as the first test for a nation: the quality of its people." The Great Society incorporated and soon extended Kennedy's New Frontier, especially with the passage of the Economic Opportunity Act of 1964, which carried into legislation Kennedy's vision of a war on poverty.

The Great Society provided the central issue of the 1964 presidential campaign. The Republicans nominated Senator Barry Goldwater of Arizona, a likable businessman with rigidly conservative views. Convinced that the danger to freedom came from the activity of government, Goldwater had proposed in his book *The Conscience of a Conservative* (1960) that the graduated income tax be abolished and that the federal government withdraw from the bulk of its public programs at a rate of 10 percent a year. He had also urged the sale of the TVA and had questioned the social-security system. Though Goldwater's personal dash and his campaign slogan—''In your heart you know he's right''—evoked ardent enthusiasm among his followers, the bulk of the voters were disturbed by the spirit that led him, in accepting the Republican nomination, to proclaim: ''Extremism in the defense of liberty is no vice.''

For his part, Johnson, carefully snuffing out a movement in favor of Robert F. Kennedy, selected as his running mate the veteran liberal senator, Hubert Humphrey of Minnesota. The Johnson-Humphrey ticket won 61.1 percent of the popular vote and carried all but six states—the most decisive presidential triumph since 1936.

Johnson brought in with him nearly forty northern Democratic congressmen—enough to assure, for the first time since 1938, a working progressive majority in the House of Representatives. This enabled him in 1965–66 to compile the most impressive record of

domestic legislation in a single session for thirty years. Long-sought bills for federal aid to education and for Medicare were at last enacted. In addition, Congress authorized the establishment of a new federal department, the Department of Housing and Urban Development (to which Johnson appointed Robert C. Weaver, the first black to serve in the Cabinet); it passed a new Housing and Urban Development Act; it sought to restrict billboard advertising through the Highway Beautification Act and to prevent water pollution through the Water Quality Act; it liberalized the immigration laws; it passed a new civil-rights act; and it institutionalized Kennedy's experiments in federal support for the arts in the National Foundation on the Arts and Humanities Act. In 1966, though it rejected a civil-rights bill banning discrimination in the sale or rental of housing, Congress passed Johnson's rent-subsidy and model-cities programs and gave the government authority to set safety standards for automobiles and highways.

Among Great Society programs the most original and distinctive was the war on poverty, conducted by the Office of Economic

Victory, 1964:
L.B.J. and H.H.H.

The election of 1964

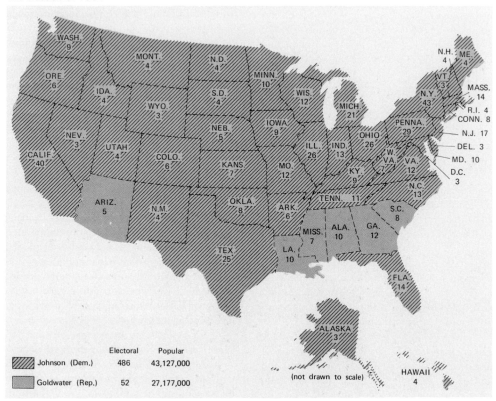

		Electoral	Popular
Johnson (Dem.)		486	43,127,000
Goldwater (Rep.)		52	27,177,000

Opportunity. Headed by Sargent Shriver, Kennedy's brother-in-law and former head of the Peace Corps, OEO included a Job Corps for dropouts from the educational system; a Neighborhood Youth Corps for unemployed teen-agers; the Volunteers in Service to America (VISTA), in effect a domestic Peace Corps; a Head Start program for young children; an Upward Bound program to send bright children to college; and, in its most controversial feature, a Community Action program designed to secure the "maximum feasible participation" of the poor in planning and running the antipoverty effort. A venture so unprecedented could not avoid experiment and confusion. Local politicians particularly saw Community Action as a threat to their own prerogatives, and other critics felt that OEO gave professionals in the social-welfare field undue opportunity to impose their own ideas on the helpless poor.

Between 1965 and 1970 nearly $10 billion was committed to OEO programs. In 1959 39.5 million Americans—22.4 percent of the population—had been below the poverty line (a shifting line, defined in 1967 as an annual income of $3,130 for an urban family of four, $2,190 for a farm family); ten years later, the figure had fallen to 24.3 million or 12.2 percent. Most of this improvement probably resulted from the general rise in the level of economic activity. Of those left below the line in 1969, 16.7 million were white—9.5 percent of the total white population; the 7.6 million nonwhites below the line represented 31.1 percent of the nonwhite total in the country.

The Great Society programs brought about an increase in federal spending for health, education, and social purposes from $54 billion in 1964 to $98 billion in 1968—an increase paid for out of new revenues generated by economic growth (itself stimulated by the $11.5 billion tax cut of 1964). The Great Society also meant, for a time, an increase in presidential rhetoric—to an extent that roused expectations that the programs themselves, oversold and underfunded, could not meet. As time went on, moreover, Johnson's increasing absorption in foreign affairs diverted his attention from domestic problems.

Foreign policy: Latin America. In one of his first appointments, Johnson placed the conservative Thomas Mann in charge of Latin American policy. A long-simmering dispute

with Panama over the 1903 treaty providing for the Canal Zone resulted, after a few months of acrimony, in an agreement to negotiate a new treaty. But the Alliance for Progress now began to change its character, losing its reform content; and American policy in general involved greater accommodation both to North American business and to right-wing governments in Latin America. Thus Washington welcomed the military coup that established authoritarian government in Brazil in 1964.

The reversion to older ways in dealing with Latin America received its most spectacular expression in Johnson's response to civil war in the Dominican Republic in 1965. Followers of the progressive democratic leader Juan Bosch rebelled against a conservative regime; and, in the confusion, Johnson became convinced on the basis of much disputed evidence that, as he told the nation, "What began as a popular democratic revolution, committed to democracy and social justice. . . . was taken over and really seized and placed into the hands of a band of communist conspirators." Without consulting with the Organization of American States or seeking Latin American support, Johnson ordered United States Marines to land in the Dominican Republic.

In a short time 22,289 American troops were deployed on the embattled island. After failing to establish a new conservative regime, the American government tacitly backed away from the theory of a communist takeover of the rebellion and worked out a compromise based on both rebel and loyalist factions. Though this eventual outcome was generally applauded, the size, the unilateral character, and the impetuosity of American intervention caused deep concern throughout Latin America, reviving the mistrust that Roosevelt's Good Neighbor policy and Kennedy's Alliance for Progress had striven to dispel. The intervention also began to break up the consensus Johnson had laboriously forged in the United States. Liberals, including some associated with the Kennedy Administration, saw the action as the expression of a tendency to use American power not with precision but with extravagance—a foreign policy, it was believed, of overkill.

Vietnam: the war Americanized. These same apprehensions became crucial in the controversies over the most intractable item in Johnson's inheritance—the war in Indo-

MEXICO

Mexico City •

UNITED STATES

Miami •

Havana •

BAHAMAS
(Br.)

Batista overthrown 1959
Attempted anti-Castro invasion 1961
Soviet military aid, U. S. quarantine 1962

Magloire overthrown 1956
Duvalier dictatorship 1957

CUBA

JAMAICA   HAITI   REP.

DOMINICAN

U. S. broke diplomatic ties 1960
Trujillo assassinated 1961
Diplomatic ties restored 1962
U.S. military intervention 1965

BR. HONDURAS

GUATEMALA   HONDURAS

EL
SALVADOR   NICARAGUA

COSTA
RICA

PANAMA

Caribbean Sea

PUERTO
RICO

Rojas Pinilla forced out 1957

TRINIDAD

Arbenz overthrown 1954
Castillo Armas assassinated
1957

CANAL
ZONE

Caracas •

VENEZUELA   GUYANA

Pérez Jiménez overthrown 1958
Anti-Nixon riots 1958

Diaz
overthrown 1956

Bogotá •

FR.
GUIANA

Anti-U. S. riots 1959
U.S.-Panama Canal Zone
Negotiations 1964
Revolution 1968
Torrijos takes over 1969

COLOMBIA

SURINAM

• Quito

ECUADOR

PERU

BRAZIL

Odria overthrown 1956
Anti-Nixon riots 1958
Military coup 1962
Military-nationalist revolution
1968

• Lima

Quadros resigned 1961
Military coup 1964

• La Paz

• Brasília

BOLIVIA

Revolution 1952
Che Guevara's guerrilla effort 1967

PARAGUAY

• Asunción

• Rio de Janeiro

CHILE

Chavez
overthrown;
Stroessner
dictatorship
1954

Vargas overthrown
1954

PACIFIC
OCEAN

Santiago •

URUGUAY

Left-wing Allende regime
1970

ARGENTINA

Buenos Aires •

• Montevideo

Punta del Este Conferences
1961, 1962

Perón overthrown 1955
Frondizi overthrown 1962
Military rule 1966

ATLANTIC
OCEAN

Central and South America, 1952–70

china. For the public, Vietnam still seemed a marginal issue. Johnson barely mentioned it in his January 1964 state-of-the-union address and gave it little more than a hundred words a year later. This lack of public emphasis, however, was perhaps due less to presidential indifference than to a desire to minimize de-

bate and manage the situation without congressional interference.

For the overthrow of Diem had failed to bring stability. Neither General Minh, who led the coup and was himself ousted in January 1964, nor his successor General Khanh proved capable of rallying the South Vietnamese people behind the war. Concerned over the growing strength of the Viet Cong, now presumed to number nearly one hundred thousand, Johnson laid on in February the "A-34" program of clandestine hit-and-run military operations against North Vietnam, organized but not conducted by American personnel. The Joint Chiefs of Staff had meanwhile been urging American bombing strikes against North Vietnam, and in May Johnson's advisers drafted but did not submit a congressional resolution authorizing American military action.

When South Vietnamese commandoes under A-34 raided two islands in the Gulf of Tonkin at the end of July, North Vietnamese PT boats, pursuing the raiders, encountered the destroyer *Maddox* on electronic intelligence patrol and fired on it on August 2. Two days later another American destroyer was reported under attack in the Gulf. Though subsequent investigations raised the greatest doubt about the second report, the Administration without full attempts at verification seized on the pretext, claimed two unprovoked attacks, ordered retaliatory air strikes against North Vietnamese targets, and sent Congress the Southeast Asia resolution authorizing the President to "take all necessary steps, including the use of armed force" to assist South Vietnam and prevent aggression. To popular applause the Senate passed the Tonkin Gulf resolution, as it was promptly known, by a vote of 88 to 2, the House by 416 to 0.

Two days after signing the resolution, Johnson, now turning his attention to Senator Goldwater, who had been urging escalation in Vietnam, said, "Others are eager to enlarge the conflict. They call upon us to supply American boys to do the job that Asian boys should do. They ask us to take reckless action which might risk the lives of millions and engulf much of Asia." Through the campaign he continued to condemn those who "say that we ought to go north and drop bombs." Johnson was doubtless honest in his hope of avoiding direct American intervention. But early in 1965 Washington was persuaded that the army of South Vietnam, though it still outnumbered the Viet Cong by at least six to one, was on the verge of collapse. Something, it was felt, had to be done to save the situation; and a Viet Cong mortar attack killing American advisers at Pleiku on February 7 provided a new pretext. Johnson instantly ordered reprisal bombing against northern

targets, and this in March swelled into the Rolling Thunder campaign of systematic and gradually escalating air war against North Vietnam. In April he decided to increase American forces in South Vietnam and, for the first time, use American combat units in offensive action.

Up to this point, Hanoi's role in the war had been to infiltrate men into South Vietnam—4,400 to 7,400 in 1964, according to American estimates, and mostly native southerners. Now, evidently in response to American escalation, units of the North Vietnamese regular army began for the first time to appear in South Vietnam. In June General William C. Westmoreland, the American commander in Saigon, requested the dispatch of 200,000 American troops and their commitment to ground war in South Vietnam. Despite some dissent in the Administration, notably from Under Secretary of State George W. Ball, Johnson in July announced his response to Westmoreland: "We will meet his needs." With the sending of American bombers into North Vietnam and American combat units into South Vietnam, the Indochina War entered a new and fatal phase. By the end of 1965 there were 184,300 American troops in Vietnam.

The Johnson rationale. The immediate reason for the Americanization of the war was to revive morale in Saigon by offering assurance of the American determination to stay the course. In February 1965 General Khanh gave way to General Nguyen Van Thieu; after June 1965, Thieu as chief of state shared power with his prime minister, the flamboyant Air Marshal Nguyen Cao Ky. Following an election in September 1967 (which Ky later denounced as "a farce"), Thieu and Ky served in uneasy tandem as president and vice-president.

A second reason was the hope that bombing would break the will of the North Vietnamese and induce them to order the National Liberation Front (who were thought to be under their control) to call off the war. Though the experience of the Second World War and of Korea had demonstrated the limitations of strategic bombing, and though these limitations would presumably be even greater in the case of guerrilla warfare, Johnson simply could not conceive that, if pounded long enough, North Vietnam would not have a breaking-point; that, if American power were applied, the problem could not be solved. As W. W. Rostow, who soon succeeded Bundy as the Special Assistant for National Security, put it, American influence on the outcome "flows from the simple fact that we are the greatest power in the world—if we behave like it."

At the same time it was believed that bombing, if it could not altogether stop the infiltration of men and supplies into South Vietnam, would at least make the cost of infiltration prohibitive. Since most infiltration took place along the Ho Chi Minh trail network, American planes began in 1964 to carry out bombing missions against North Vietnamese units in Laos, while the CIA had already organized an army of Meo tribesmen to prevent the Pathet Lao and the North Vietnamese from overrunning the Plaine des Jarres. A secret war in Laos thus developed alongside the open war in Vietnam.

The Americanization of the war, it was supposed, would quickly force Hanoi into a negotiated settlement. For the next years negotiating efforts punctuated the process of escalation, most notably during the thirty-seven-day bombing pause of December 1964–January 1965. Unfortunately, acts of escalation repeatedly undercut and raised doubt about the attempts at negotiation. In any case, American proposals always included the preservation of the Saigon regime and the withdrawal of North Vietnamese forces prior to American withdrawal; and acceptance of such terms would, from the viewpoint of Hanoi and the National Liberation Front, amount to unconditional surrender.

The larger reason for the Americanization of the war lay in the assumption, inherited from previous Administrations and not re-examined now, that the defense of South Vietnam from communist takeover was vital to the security of the United States. Johnson accepted the universalized Dulles version of the Truman Doctrine and felt that concessions to communism in Indochina would encourage communist aggression first in South Asia and eventually all along the frontiers of freedom. "Ike has made a promise," he would say. "I have to keep it." Keeping American commitments in Vietnam thus became a test of American will and credibility everywhere. "We learned from Hitler at Munich," said Johnson, "that success only feeds the appetite of aggression. . . . To withdraw from one battlefield means only to prepare for the next."

Since it was hard to see in Ho Chi Minh and North Vietnam a threat comparable to that presented by Hitler at Munich, the Administration contended that the "free world" was confronted by a premeditated plan of Chinese expansion, of which the NLF and North Vietnam were only the spearhead. "Over this war, and all Asia," said Johnson, "is another reality: the deepening shadow of Communist China. . . . The contest in Vietnam is part of a wider pattern of aggressive purpose." This view found sustenance in the misreading of a 1965 article by Lin Piao, the Chinese Minister of National Defense, outlining Mao Tse-tung's "village-encircle-city" strategy of world revolution. (Lin Piao also noted, however, in passages ignored in Washington, that a "people's war" could succeed only on the basis of a "policy of self-reliance.") In 1967 Secretary of State Rusk invoked the specter of "a billion Chinese on the mainland, armed with nuclear weapons," and Vice President Humphrey said, "The threat to world peace is militant, aggressive Asian communism, with its headquarters in Peking, China."

Beyond all this, the American effort had a positive goal. The experience of military occupation after the Second World War had given Americans undue faith in their talent for "nation-building." Johnson, the old New Dealer, talked about TVAs on the Mekong and compared Marshal Ky to Rexford G. Tugwell; similarly, Humphrey saw "a tremendous opening here for realizing the dream of the Great Society in the great area of Asia, not just here at home." Social evangelism thus provided a further reason to justify the American adventure.

Nor did Johnson see the war as reason for hostility toward the Soviet Union; rather, he believed that, if the problem of national-liberation wars could be solved in Vietnam, relations with the Soviet Union would be stabilized. In October 1964 Khrushchev had been replaced by the collective leadership of L. I. Brezhnev (who in time became the dominant partner) and A. N. Kosygin. Johnson, seeking to thaw the Cold War, announced a policy of "bridge-building" to Eastern Europe. In 1966 he joined with the Soviet Union in supporting a UN outer-space treaty, modeled on the Antarctic Treaty and providing for the internationalization and demilitarization of space. In 1967 he secured the ratification of a consular convention with Russia and met with Kosygin in Glassboro, New Jersey. In

Chemical defoliation: a land of ruin and wreck

lion tons of explosives on this hapless land (as against a total of 2 million tons on all fronts in the Second World War and 635,000 tons in the Korean War). The result was a country gutted and devastated by bombs, burned by napalm, turned into a wasteland by chemical defoliation, a land of ruin and wreck. "It became necessary to destroy the town to save it," said an American major standing in the rubble of Ben Tre; and for more and more Americans this summed up the ghastly logic of the American intervention. The technological war was too gross to cope with guerrilla warfare: it was like trying to weed a garden with a bulldozer. Bombing failed to stop the movement of troops and supplies; instead of breaking the spirit of the enemy, it succeeded, if anything, in hardening Hanoi's will. In August 1967, McNamara, who had developed grave doubts about the war and had become the main proponent of negotiation within the Administration, told the Senate Armed Services Committee that air power had failed.

Johnson nevertheless escalated the bombing, though not enough to suit the Joint Chiefs of Staff, always the tireless advocates of further escalation. Insisting that military means had not yet received a fair try, the Chiefs wanted to bomb the centers of Hanoi and Haiphong, to mine Haiphong harbor, to invade Cambodia, Laos, and even North Vietnam. But Johnson, fearing that too rapid or too drastic escalation would bring China into the war, maintained political restrictions over ultimate military action. Within the United States escalation received enthusiastic support from "hawks" in Congress and the country. But, as the national debate intensified, the "doves," who called for American disengagement and a negotiated solution, spoke out with increasing passion.

Though sizable majorities backed escalation in public-opinion polls until 1968, the protest movement against the war, arising in universities with the "teach-ins" of the spring of 1965, grew steadily in strength. In the Senate, where Ernest Gruening of Alaska and Wayne Morse of Oregon had been alone in their opposition to the Tonkin Gulf resolution, doubts about the war now began to find effective lodgment, especially in the Foreign Relations Committee, whose chairman, J. William Fulbright, became a caustic and increasingly influential critic. Soon Robert F. Kennedy, now senator from New York, added a powerful voice. In February 1966 Kennedy proposed

1968 he concluded with Russia and fifty other nations a treaty on the nonproliferation of nuclear weapons. His hope of visiting Russia himself in October 1968 perished when the Red Army invaded Czechoslovakia in August in order to throw out a liberal communist regime.

"Hawks" and "doves." Vietnam remained Johnson's most urgent problem. Despite an endless series of optimistic assurances from General Westmoreland, the Americanization of the war did not produce the expected results. The number of American troops steadily grew—385,300 by the end of 1966; 485,600 by the end of 1967; 536,100 by the end of 1968—but Westmoreland's "meatgrinder" strategy of victory through "attrition" made no progress against the capacity of the NLF and the North Vietnamese, benefiting from the 10 to 1 ratio of guerrilla war, to replenish their losses and match every escalation. In the meantime, American casualties also grew: deaths in combat rose from 1,130 in 1965 to 4,179 in 1966, 7,482 in 1967, and 12,588 in 1968.

The bombing increased too. By the end of 1968 American planes had dropped 3.2 mil-

Vietnam, 1966: almost 400,000 American troops

*It has been U.S. policy to sustain the independence of Southeast Asia
from potentially hostile control. But sacrifice for a policy that cannot
succeed is meaningless or worse. What have the sacrifices since 1965
achieved?... The domino theory was not just a theory in the first seven
months of 1965; every observer of the scene knew the dominoes were
about to fall unless American power was rushed into the balance.
Then, at the end of July, 1965, President Johnson moved to commit
American forces. Now, six years later, there is a different Asia.*

*South Vietnam has harvested the greatest rice crop in its history
and is about to conduct its second presidential election under a democratic constitution. Well over 90 per cent of its population live under
reasonably reliable government administration. Indonesia is independent and advancing hopefully in economic and social progress....
Asian regional organizations have come into being.... These offer great
promise that in the future Asians, working together, can increasingly
shape their own destiny. Japan, now the third industrial power in the
world, is evidently prepared to help others in the region.... China ...
is experimenting, at least, with the idea of normalizing its relations
with Asia and the rest of the world.*

*Without the U.S. effort in Southeast Asia, there would be no Ping-
Pong diplomacy and no presidential visit to Peking.*

From W. W. Rostow, ''Vietnam: Was It Worth It?'' *Look,* September 21, 1971.

*There may be a limit beyond which many Americans and much of the
world will not permit the United States to go. The picture of the
world's greatest superpower killing or seriously injuring 1,000 noncombatants a week, while trying to pound a tiny backward nation into
submission on an issue whose merits are hotly disputed, is not a pretty
one. It could conceivably produce a costly distortion in the American
national consciousness and in the world image of the United States—
especially if the damage to North Vietnam is complete enough to be
'successful.'*

From Secretary of Defense Robert S. McNamara, Memorandum to President Johnson,
May 19, 1967.

that the NLF be admitted ''to a share of power
and responsibility'' in a coalition government
as the only way to end the war. Vice President
Humphrey replied that this would be like putting ''a fox in the chicken coop; soon there
wouldn't be any chickens left''; and the debate sharpened. As dove senators, joined by
foreign-policy experts like Walter Lippmann,
George F. Kennan, and Hans Morgenthau,
enlarged the attack on the war, Johnson denounced the opposition as ''nervous Nellies''
ready to ''turn on their own leaders, and their
country, and on our fighting men.''

In the spring of 1967 Lippmann wrote that
the Indochina War had become ''the most
unpopular war in American history.'' Antiwar
protests exploded in major cities, culminating
on October 21, 1967, when 200,000 people

led by noted literary figures like Norman
Mailer and Robert Lowell marched on the
Pentagon. Martin Luther King, attributing the
waning of civil-rights enthusiasm to preoccupation with Vietnam, joined the peace movement. Though the campuses had generally
supported escalation, the restriction of educational deferments early in 1968 confronted
not only college students but their middle-
class parents with the reality of the war. Never
before in American history were so many
young men declaring conscientious objection,
burning draft cards, or fleeing abroad to avoid
military service. Many more, accepting what
they saw as their democratic obligation,
brought their antiwar convictions with them
into the army. Their parents, oblivious to the
war as long as it had swept up only poor

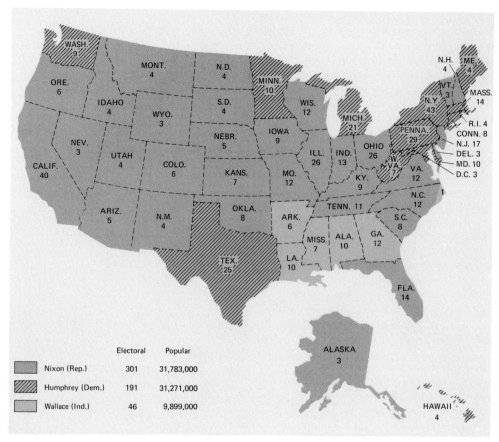

	Electoral	Popular
Nixon (Rep.)	301	31,783,000
Humphrey (Dem.)	191	31,271,000
Wallace (Ind.)	46	9,899,000

The election of 1968

Campus poster, 1967

whites and poor blacks, began to wonder whether Vietnam was worth the sacrifice of their own sons, and this widened the national opposition.

In the meantime, Vietnam had been affecting American life in other ways. Johnson's domestic policy was an early casualty. The Republican comeback in the 1966 elections lost him his working majority in the House of Representatives; and the mounting cost of the war—over $20 billion a year by 1967—argued against the expansion of domestic programs. He even stopped using the phrase Great Society. Moreover, Johnson's reluctance to tell his own Council of Economic Advisers the probable size of the war effort led to budgetary underestimates of military spending and miscalculations in fiscal policy. Had the cost of the war been foreseen, excise taxes would not have been cut in 1965 and taxes should have been increased in 1966. The failure to attempt a pay-as-you-go policy soon produced inflation at home—in 1968 the consumer price index, after a decade of

relative stability, rose by 4.2 percent—and balance-of-payments strains abroad.

The 1968 election. The Administration continued to profess optimism about the war and to discern light at the end of the tunnel. "I see progress as I travel all over Vietnam," said General Westmoreland in November 1967. ". . . The enemy's hopes are bankrupt." And on January 1, 1968: "We should expect our gains of 1967 to be increased manyfold in 1968." Four weeks later, during the Tet holiday, the lunar New Year, a massive enemy offensive took American and South Vietnamese forces by surprise, convulsed thirty provincial capitals, and even penetrated the American Embassy in Saigon. While the North Vietnamese failed to achieve their maximum objectives and suffered grievous losses in the process, the Tet offensive destroyed what remained of the Johnson Administration's credibility on Vietnam and gave potent support to the dove argument that escalation had failed.

Westmoreland's reaction was to escalate further; and his February request for 206,000 additional troops now produced a showdown within the Administration. Johnson, exasperated by McNamara's opposition to escalation, shifted him to the World Bank; but the new Secretary of Defense, Clark Clifford, though long a hawk, had begun to question the war when a mission he undertook in 1967 had disclosed to him that pro-American Asian states, though much nearer Indochina than the Americans, saw much less at stake in the Indochina War than Washington did. Now in the Pentagon and confronted by the Westmoreland request, Clifford concluded that further escalation was futile and disengagement the proper course.

The Tet offensive intensified domestic criticism of the war. ''Are we like the God of the Old Testament,'' Robert Kennedy asked, ''that can decide, in Washington, D.C., what cities, what towns, what hamlets in Vietnam are going to be destroyed?'' And the approach of the 1968 presidential election consolidated the protest within Johnson's own party. The antiwar activists, having failed to persuade Kennedy to oppose Johnson, turned to another senatorial dove, Eugene McCarthy of Minnesota. A man of enigmatic and mischievous intelligence, McCarthy, followed by a virtual ''children's crusade,'' campaigned effectively against Johnson and the war in the New Hampshire primary in March. The Tet offensive, McCarthy's success in New Hampshire, and Kennedy's entry into the contest for Democratic nomination increased the pressure on Johnson. In Washington not only Clifford and civilian officials in the Defense Department but Dean Acheson, McGeorge Bundy, and other former hawks urged him to abandon the war. On March 31, 1968, Johnson announced the cessation of bombing in North Vietnam except in the area below the twentieth parallel. Also, faced by defeat in the impending Wisconsin primary, he withdrew from the presidential contest. In a few weeks, negotiations began in Paris between the North Vietnamese and an American delegation led by Averell Harriman.

With Johnson's withdrawal Humphrey became the Administration candidate. Once a liberal leader, Humphrey was now identified with Johnson and the war and did nothing to diminish this identification. Kennedy and McCarthy, on the other hand, generated crusading enthusiasm among their followers—

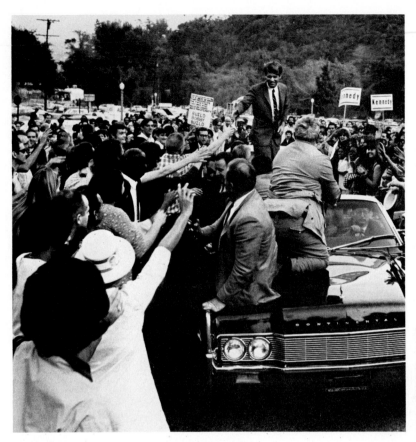

Robert F. Kennedy: enthusiasm in California, 1968

Kennedy among the poor, the blacks, the Mexican-Americans, McCarthy among suburbanites and independent voters, both among the young and the intellectuals. Their combined vote in a succession of primaries expressed a widespread repudiation of the Johnson Administration within his own party. However, on June 6, the night of his victory in the California primary, Kennedy was murdered by a Palestinian Arab who resented the senator's sympathy for Israel. The nation, appalled at the assassination of a second Kennedy within five years, mourned the death of a man many believed the most brilliant and radical among the national leaders.

After Kennedy's death Humphrey had no serious opposition. Protest against the war policy erupted, however, in shocking scenes at the Democratic convention in Chicago in August, when the local police in a frenzy of violence clubbed hundreds of antiwar agitators. Senator Edmund Muskie of Maine, who had defended the Administration plank on Vietnam at the convention, received the vice-

Chicago, August 1968: a frenzy of violence

*Richard M. Nixon, 1968:
an astonishing
political comeback*

presidential nomination. In the meantime, Richard M. Nixon, completing an astonishing political comeback, received the Republican nomination and picked Governor Spiro T. Agnew of Maryland, the first suburban politician to rise to national prominence, as his running mate.

The campaign itself was desultory and unenlightening. Nixon, who in past years had been more hawkish than the Administration, now pledged that "new leadership will end the war" and hinted that he had a secret plan to produce that result. Humphrey came out from under the shadow of the unpopular Johnson Presidency too slowly to rouse the enthusiasm of the Kennedy-McCarthy wing of the party. Among the vice-presidential candidates, Agnew attracted attention by careless comment about "fat Japs" and "Polacks" and by suggesting that "if you've seen one city slum you've seen them all." In contrast to the others, Muskie, by his dignity and candor of manner, alone emerged from the campaign with increased stature. The most picturesque candidate, running on the American Independent party ticket with General Curtis LeMay as his partner, was former Governor George Wallace of Alabama. Attacking "pointy-headed" intellectuals and invoking

local values against federally enforced equal rights, Wallace threatened for a time to run well not only in the South but among blue-collar workers in the North. In October, however, when organized labor threw itself into the contest, the working-class vote moved back to the Democrats. In the meantime, Nixon, through the vagueness of his campaigning, frittered away his commanding lead of September.

Much depended on the progress of negotiations in Paris. Hanoi wanted a total cessation of the bombing of North Vietnam and the presence of the National Liberation Front at the conference table. Washington wanted the Saigon government at the table as well as assurance that, if there was a full bombing halt, Hanoi would not violate the demilitarized zone between North and South Vietnam. As the negotiators approached agreement in late October, President Thieu, perhaps fearing that a total bombing halt might elect the Democrats and expecting more sympathy from a Republican administration, began to stall. After painful delay, Johnson decided to go ahead anyway. But the announcement on October 31 came too late to have much influence on the elections.

The vote cast—73.2 million—was the

largest in American history, but it included only 61 percent of the eligible electorate (as against 62 percent in 1964 and 63.8 in 1960). Nixon received 31.8 million votes as against 31.3 million for Humphrey and 9.9 million for Wallace. With only 43.4 percent of the total, he became a minority President. The margins were greater in the Electoral College: 301 for Nixon, 191 for Humphrey, and 46, all in the Deep South, for Wallace. The Democrats carried both houses of Congress, which made Nixon the first President since Zachary Taylor whose party on his election did not control at least one chamber.

Lyndon Johnson left the White House an unpopular and unlamented President. Yet history may see in the Great Society a serious effort to overcome the tensions and inequities produced by social and technological change. The irony of his Presidency was that he sacrificed domestic policy, a field in which his knowledge was great and his instinct sure, to foreign policy, where his knowledge was scant and his instinct simplistic.

A decade of violence

The social fabric unravels. The decade that had begun in exhilaration and hope was dissolving into bitterness and hate. "Before my term is ended," Kennedy had said in 1961, "we shall have to test anew whether a nation organized and governed such as ours can endure. The outcome is by no means certain." Convinced that the inequalities in American society were a source of danger to American life, Kennedy tried to get America moving toward his New Frontier, carrying the poor and nonwhites with him. He was murdered. After his death his brother Robert made himself the peculiar champion of the outcasts and victims of American life. He was murdered. Martin Luther King was the eloquent advocate of nonviolence in the pursuit of racial justice. In April 1968 an assassin killed him. Some Americans regarded these murders as isolated aberrations. Others began to lose faith in a society that destroyed the three men of the decade who seemed most to embody American idealism.

The panorama of American life, especially after 1963, became one of epithets, demonstrations, sit-ins, marches, burnings, riots, shootings, bombings. Frustrated minorities, feeling the "system" hopelessly rigged against them, turned to violence, if only because they could see no other way to get a hearing for just grievances. Political philosophers offered rationales for violent action. The experience of a generation of war doubtless habituated people to killing; and the war in Vietnam, by legitimizing violent methods in a dubious cause abroad, justified for some the use of violence in better causes at home. Television not only transmitted the techniques of protest but fostered a competition for visibility. In addition, by its immediacy, television encouraged the habit of instant reaction and the hope of instant results.

The black revolution turns left. The most influential models of protest arose out of the black community. Here the center of agitation was shifting from the South to the North. Dr. King, though still the preeminent leader, appealed particularly to Southern blacks responsive to religious traditions and accustomed to relations with whites. But, whereas in 1910 only 9 percent of blacks lived outside the South and only 27 percent in urban areas, by 1970, 47 percent lived outside the South and 70 percent in urban areas. Washington was now 71 percent nonwhite, Newark 54 percent, Detroit 44 percent; and the proportion in Northern cities tended to grow as the last wave of white immigrants, moving out to the suburbs, abandoned the decaying central city to the newcomers.

The civil-rights legislation of the sixties was addressed primarily to the removal of legal and political disabilities and therefore applied most particularly to the South. Even here progress was slow. In 1967, thirteen years after the Supreme Court decision, only 16 percent of the 3 million black students in the South were attending desegregated schools. Improvement in voter registration was more impressive; and race barriers fell in restaurants, hotels, and other places of public resort.

Northern blacks faced different problems. The rights provided by the new laws were those they nominally possessed already. Their concern was less with the abolition of legal and political barriers than with the achievement of equal social and economic opportunity, an objective that seemed to require radical social action and one that roused more

There has always existed in the Black colony of Afro-America a fundamental difference over which tactics from the broad spectrum of alternatives Black people should employ in their struggle for national liberation. One side of this difference contends that Black people ... must employ no tactic that will anger the oppressor whites. This view holds that Black people constitute a hopeless minority and that salvation for Black people lies in developing brotherly relations....

On the other side of the difference, we find that the point of departure is the principle that the oppressor has no rights that the oppressed is bound to respect. Kill the slavemaster, destroy him utterly, move against him with implacable fortitude. Break his oppressive power by any means necessary.... The heirs of Malcolm have picked up the gun and, taking first things first, are moving to expose the endorsed leaders for the Black masses to see them for what they are and always have been. The choice offered by the heirs of Malcolm is to repudiate the oppressor ... or face a merciless, speedy and most timely execution for treason.

From Huey P. Newton, "In Defense of Self Defense," *The Black Panther*, July 3, 1967.

---

white resistance. Black housing and black schools were inferior; black unemployment was greater; and the rise in politics of the "white backlash," astutely encouraged by racist politicians like George Wallace, increased the black sense of grievance and frustration. Northern blacks were less involved in the old-time religion and, shut off in ghettos, were more hostile toward whites. Despair thus grew in the ghettos and produced challenges to King's ideals of nonviolence and an integrated society.

A movement founded in 1930 under the name Nation of Islam and now known as the Black Muslims gathered strength. Its leader was Elijah Muhammad, its most eloquent voice Malcolm X, and its program one of black separatism, self-discipline, and self-defense. Breaking with the Muslims in 1964, Malcolm X traveled to Arabia and Africa and returned an advocate of "a working unity among all peoples, black as well as white." He had hardly embarked in new directions, however, before he was murdered in February 1965, apparently as an aftermath of the feud with the Muslims. His powerful *Autobiography* (1965) became a central document of black nationalism.

Events strengthened the nationalist mood. In August 1965 riots in Watts, California, eventually suppressed by the National Guard, resulted in thirty-four deaths and property damage of $35 million. In 1966 National Guardsmen put down riots in Chicago. In

The growing bitterness: Detroit, 1967

1967 riots swept through the black sections of Tampa, Cincinnati, Atlanta, and New Brunswick, New Jersey, and broke out with desperate force in Detroit and Newark. These developments both encouraged and expressed a growing radicalization of the urban black—a radicalization symbolized in the summer of 1966 when Stokely Carmichael of the Student Nonviolent Coordinating Committee and Floyd McKissick of the Congress of Racial Equality raised the standard of "black power."

Black power. The idea of black power could imply simply a demand for black regrouping and self-reliance as part of the transition to eventual integration on an equal basis; integration on any other basis, it was contended, would mean surrender to white values. In this sense black power was an affirmation of racial and cultural pride. Black became beautiful; blacks threw away hair-straighteners and rejoiced in the Afro hairdo; soul music and soul food became items not of shame but of identity. Black power, said Dr. King, was a "call to manhood."

But, as expounded by Carmichael, it went much further. It meant economic radicalism, permanent racial separation, even retaliatory vengeance against the "honky"; the blacks, Carmichael said in 1968, must become "the executioners of our executioners." In this more drastic mood, slogans of the King period—"We Shall Overcome" and "Freedom Now"—gave way to more bitter

Probably the most destructive feature of Black Power is its uncon-
scious and often conscious call for retaliatory violence.... The problem
with hatred and violence is that they intensify the fears of the white
majority, and leave them less ashamed of their prejudices toward
Negroes. In the guilt and confusion confronting our society, violence
only adds to the chaos. It deepens the brutality of the oppressor and
increases the bitterness of the oppressed. Violence is the antithesis
of creativity and wholeness. It destroys community and makes brother-
hood impossible....

The ultimate weakness of violence is that it is a descending spiral,
begetting the very thing it seeks to destroy. Instead of diminishing
evil, it multiplies it. Through violence you may murder the liar, but
you cannot murder the lie, nor establish the truth. Through violence
you may murder the hater, but you do not murder hate. In fact, violence
merely increases hate. So it goes. Returning violence for violence
multiplies violence, adding deeper darkness to a night already devoid
of stars. Darkness cannot drive out darkness; only light can do that.
Hate cannot drive out hate; only love can do that.

From Martin Luther King, Jr., *Where Do We Go from Here: Chaos or Community?*, 1967.

The case against violence

phrases—"Burn, Baby, Burn" and "Violence Is as American as Cherry Pie." The most militant black-power group, the Black Panther party, was organized on military lines in 1966 with Bobby Seale as chairman, Huey P. Newton as Minister of Defense, and Eldridge Cleaver as Minister of Information. Cleaver's *Soul on Ice* (1967), with its disturbing fusion of sensitivity and savagery, was a strong statement of the Black Panther ethos. In 1968 he ran for President as the candidate of the Peace and Freedom party. Though the Panthers diverged from the Carmichael group in their willingness to work with white revolutionaries, both groups shared contempt for "white liberals" and both believed that white America would respond only to force. The unprovoked murder by Chicago police of two Panthers in 1969 increased black resentment (though the theory of a national police campaign to kill Panthers turned out, on investigation, to be groundless).

Cleaver and Carmichael also agreed in rejecting the older black leadership—Roy Wilkins and the NAACP, Whitney Young, Jr., and the Urban League, even Dr. King and his Southern Christian Leadership Conference. These leaders for their part condemned separatism and violence as self-defeating. As King wrote of the new militancy, "In advocating violence it is imitating the worst, the most brutal, and the most uncivilized value of American life." He added, "There is no salvation for the Negro through isolation. . . . The

black man needs the white man and the white man needs the black man."

For white America the emergence of black power constituted an unmistakable warning that the national society would have to move with greater speed and effect if it was convincingly to redress the injustices it had so long perpetrated against its black citizens. In a moving speech at Howard University in 1965, Lyndon Johnson said, "We seek . . . not just equality as a right and a theory but equality as a fact and equality as a result." He pressed the fight for civil-rights legislation, securing the passage of an open-housing law in 1968. He appointed Thurgood Marshall as the first black Justice to the Supreme Court. During the riots of 1967 he set up under the chairmanship of Governor Otto Kerner of Illinois a Commission on Civil Disorders, which produced a strong and somber report:

> This is our basic conclusion: our nation is moving toward two societies, one black, one white—separate but unequal. . . . This deepening racial division is not inevitable. The movement apart can be reversed. Choice is still possible. Our principal task is to define that choice and to press for a national solution.

A few weeks after the Kerner Commission issued its report, Martin Luther King was assassinated in Memphis. As the nation underwent a spasm of shock and grief, riots exploded in ghetto after ghetto across the land, most spectacularly of all in the nation's capital

Malcolm X: eloquent Black Muslim

Black power: Eldridge Cleaver, 1968

itself. Riots in 172 cities resulted in 43 deaths, 3,500 injuries, and 27,000 arrests. The subsequent murder of Robert Kennedy, the one white leader in whom black Americans believed, intensified a mood of alienation and hopelessness. But this mood was still more a warning than a broad reality. Polls in 1969 showed that the majority of black Americans continued to feel that they could win equality without violence and to accept the ideal of a multiracial society.

Revolt on the campus. In the early sixties the New Frontier gospel of challenge and hope stirred the instincts of the young in more purposeful directions. The campuses, silent during the fifties, now erupted in political and intellectual activity. The Peace Corps, VISTA, and civil-rights projects like "Freedom Summer" in Mississippi in 1964 were only the most dramatic forms of the new idealism. Some of the moral energy Kennedy released moved rather quickly beyond him and against him, subjecting his own Administration to unsparing criticism. But the larger effect was to incite a remarkable outpouring of youthful self-definition. Then Kennedy's murder, by confirming the new generation's worst suspicions about the absurdity and evil of contemporary American society, accelerated the movement toward a drastic rejection of the existing order—and, with it, the older generation.

Tension between generations was nothing new; but in the sixties it seemed to assume unprecedentedly conscious and doctrinaire forms, as in the motto popularized in student demonstrations at the University of California in 1964: "You can't trust anyone over thirty." This new generational conflict sprang not only from familiar psychological causes but from novel social circumstance. Marshall McLuhan insisted that its peculiar force came from the fact that the youth of the sixties represented the first generation reared in an electronic culture. Others pointed out that these were the children of affluence, liberated from the economic pressures that had ruled their parents and therefore free to heed their consciences and follow their ideals. Certainly much of the new generation was in rebellion against a society that seemed determined to cast them in what they considered artificial and false roles. They dreaded in particular the power of large organizations to deprive them of choice and to "process" them for meaningless work

and meaningless lives. "Don't bend, fold, spindle, or mutilate!" was a favorite slogan. Inspired by the example of the blacks, they wanted to affirm their distinctive identity. Against the hypocrisy of adult society they advanced a politics of personal authenticity.

Since the university was the first large organization the young encountered, it became the first target of their revolt against the world of structures. What university presidents hailed as the "multiversity," their students regarded as a callously impersonal assembly line of higher education. Only a minority of students shared the mood of estrangement and hostility; but it was an alert and articulate minority, and its activism dominated the student life of the decade. Moreover, more young men and women were going to college than ever before; total enrollment more than doubled in the decade, rising from 3.8 million in 1960 to 8.5 million in 1970. The impact of students on society was therefore greater than in the past. And it often seemed that, the brighter the student and the better the institution, the greater the likelihood of revolt. Nor was this mood to be explained only in American terms—as a result of permissive child-rearing practices or of racial injustice or of the Vietnam War. It was part of a worldwide wave of student protest that swept through universities in Europe, Asia, Latin America, and on both sides of the Iron Curtain.

The first notable outbreak came at the University of California in December 1964, when university efforts to restrict student advocacy of off-campus action led to the formation of a Free Speech Movement, followed by angry demonstrations, sit-ins in campus buildings, mass arrests, and a student strike. As time passed new issues provided outlets for the basic feelings of alienation and resentment. The Americanization of the Vietnam War in 1965 led first to teach-ins and then to a student march in Washington, organized by Students for a Democratic Society.

SDS in its influential Port Huron Statement of 1962 had introduced "participatory democracy"—that is, active individual participation "in those social decisions determining the quality and direction of his life"—as the student's basic demand. In analyzing the past, SDS militants tended to be rigidly ideological and, in their insistence on simplistic economic determinism, sounded rather like the Trotskyites of the thirties. But, in assessing the future, they avoided ideology and program, opposing

Our work is guided by the sense that we may be the last generation in the experiment with living. But we are a minority—the vast majority of our people regard the temporary equilibrium of our society and world as eternally functional parts. In this is perhaps the outstanding paradox: we ourselves are imbued with urgency, yet the message of our society is that there is no viable alternative to the present....

Loneliness, estrangement, isolation describe the vast distance between man and man today.... We would replace power rooted in possession, privilege, or circumstance by power and uniqueness rooted in love, reflectiveness, reason, and creativity. As a social system we seek the establishment of a democracy of individual participation, governed by two central aims: that the individual share in those social decisions determining the quality and direction of his life; that society be organized to encourage independence in men and provide the media for their common participation.

From Students for a Democratic Society, The Port Huron Statement, June 1962.

Participatory democracy

leadership, élitism, centralization, dehumanizing bureaucracies, and the national state. Here they approached both Goldwater conservatism and intellectual anarchism in their stress on decentralization, voluntarism, self-determination, and small communities. Their methods were, in theory at least, humane. Against Vietnam they cried: ''Make love, not war.'' ''The student movement,'' one observed, ''is not a cause. . . . It is a collision between this one person and that one person. It is a *I am going to sit beside you. . . .* Love alone is radical.''

The New Left. But the war continued to escalate, and protests grew more drastic. In the mid-sixties radical students attacked, with increasing rage, various forms of collaboration by universities with the military effort—the Reserve Officers Training Corps; recruiting on campuses by CIA or by companies manufacturing tools of war like napalm; research financed by the Pentagon or the CIA. As changes in the draft reduced student immunity, the number of disaffected students multiplied. As undergraduate defiance and provocation increased, university authorities began to call in the local police. In 1968–69, four thousand students were arrested; and, as police violence went out of control—as at Columbia University and the Democratic convention in 1968 and at Harvard in 1969— student radicalization intensified.

As early as 1967, the SDS national secretary announced, ''We are working to build a guerrilla force in an urban environment. We are actively organizing sedition. . . . Che's message is applicable to urban America.'' Che Guevara, the Argentinian revolutionary who had worked with Castro and was to die in Bolivia, became for the militant young the ideal of the incorruptible revolutionary. The example of the Black Panthers was also influential, as was the analysis of the Algerian revolution by the black psychiatrist Frantz Fanon.

Soon a New Left ideology emerged to explain the rejection of American society and the necessity for violence. Liberals, who were charged with the sin of trying to improve things within the ''system,'' were particular targets of condemnation; ''cop-out'' was the mildest term employed. In his book *One Dimensional Man* (1964), the philosopher Herbert Marcuse joined insights from Marx and Freud to argue that contemporary industrial society had developed a nonterroristic totalitarianism and that, in particular, the welfare state had corrupted the working class, integrated it into capitalism, and disqualified it as an agency of revolutionary change. The hope for a transformation that would restore the wholeness of man lay, he said, in ''the substratum of the outcasts and outsiders, the exploited and persecuted of other races''; as campus discontent increased, Marcuse added students to the revolutionary vanguard. Though Marcuse was not himself a man of violence and doubted the possibility of revolution in the United States, he argued for the suppression of ideas he considered antisocial and affirmed ''a 'natural right' of resistance for oppressed and overpowered minorities to use extralegal means if the legal ones have

Tolerance cannot be indiscriminate and equal with respect to the contents of expression, neither in word nor in deed; it cannot protect false words and wrong deeds which demonstrate that they contradict and counteract the possibilities of liberation.... Here, certain things cannot be said, certain ideas cannot be expressed, certain policies cannot be proposed, certain behavior cannot be permitted without making tolerance an instrument for the continuation of servitude....

They would include the withdrawal of toleration of speech and assembly from groups and movements which promote aggressive policies, armament, chauvinism, discrimination on the grounds of race and religion, or which oppose the extension of public services, social security, medical care, etc. Moreover, the restoration of freedom of thought may necessitate new and rigid restrictions on teachings and practices in the educational institutions.

From Herbert Marcuse, "Repressive Tolerance," *A Critique of Pure Tolerance,* 1965.

proved to be inadequate. . . . If they use violence, they do not start a new chain of violence but try to break an established one. . . . No third person, and least of all the educator and intellectual, has the right to preach them abstention."

Other theorists of the New Left, like the linguist Noam Chomsky, shared Marcuse's general diagnosis but rejected violence and called instead for civil disobedience. But the gospel of violence won followers, especially in the SDS's Weatherman faction (so-called because of the Bob Dylan lyric, "You don't need a weatherman to know which way the wind is blowing"). Seeing American (or, as they preferred to put it, Amerikan) society as irretrievably corrupt, beyond all hope of salvation through liberal reform, they concluded that the only way to deal with an inherently destructive apparatus was to destroy it. In October 1969 Weathermen, wearing football helmets and steel-toed work boots and carrying bicycle chains, swarmed through the streets of Chicago attacking "pigs" (policemen). In the next months there were a series of bombings in cities and universities across the country. In 1970, when SDS broke up in factional feuds, the Weathermen went underground.

One function of violence in the New Left ideology was to "unmask" the "Establishment" by provoking it into acts of violent retaliation. Some of the time, however, the Establishment, whether because of bad conscience or Machiavellian ingenuity, employed the subtler tactic denounced by the militants as "cooptation"—the tactic of disarming dissent by absorbing it. Thus revolutionaries

appeared on television talk shows and commanded large lecture fees. But government also showed itself capable of more drastic action. Policemen beat up long-haired demonstrators, often on meager pretexts, and the Department of Justice made recurrent efforts to indict and imprison those associated with the New Left. This produced a series of celebrated trials: in 1968, the trial of Dr. Benjamin Spock and three others for conspiring to encourage draft resistants to violate the Selective Service Act; in 1969–70, the prolonged and often raucous trial of the Chicago Seven, including several New Left leaders, for crossing state lines with the intent to incite violence at the Democratic convention; and a number of trials of Black Panthers and other Negro militants, one of which, involving an escape attempt and a courtroom shoot-up, led to the subsequent arrest and trial of Angela Davis, a black teacher and communist, for allegedly supplying guns used in the episode.

The hippie scene. Not all those estranged by the high-technology society took the path of political activism. Some responded by dropping out of society rather than by trying to change it. These defectors followed trails marked out by the beatniks of the fifties. But the "hippies" of the sixties were generally less educated, less verbal, younger, and of lower social class. Where the beats were a literary movement, the hippies were, in the phrase of the decade, a "life-style." As the beat poet Gregory Corso put it, "The hippies are acting out what the beats wrote."

Disdaining ties, jackets, and socks, affecting long hair, beards, and beads, hating the adult

A dizzying variety of customs, creeds, and diets

world as "uptight" and "plastic," they congregated in the middle sixties in the Haight-Ashbury district of San Francisco or the Sunset Strip of Los Angeles or New York's East Village. They called themselves "flower children," in part because of their custom of offering flowers to cops and other persecutors, and celebrated their rites, not in the teach-ins or sit-ins of the activists, but in "be-ins" or "love-ins." "Flower power" implied a diffuse, semiliterate, spontaneous gentleness, concerned not with doing but with being: life not as a purpose but as a happening.

Soon hippies joined together in "communes" weirdly reminiscent of the communitarian enthusiasm in nineteenth-century America; and, as urban hippie centers became overcrowded or dangerous, an increasing number established communes in rural areas. Though the communes had a dizzying variety of customs, creeds, and diets, they were characteristically based on the idea of the "extended family," with collective property, love, and children. Living was often hard and sometimes squalid. By 1970 over two hundred communes scattered across the land involved perhaps forty thousand people, mostly under the age of thirty.

Do your own thing, drop out, turn on— these were the principles of the hippie ethos. Above all, the hippie mystique was founded on the use of drugs. During the nineteenth century in America, narcotics had been sold over the counter and without prescription; before the Pure Food and Drug Act of 1906 (see p. 524), popular patent medicines often had a narcotic base. In 1914 the Federal Narcotics Bureau estimated that one in every four hundred Americans was an addict. The Harrison Act of that year was the first of a series of federal laws and regulations designed to control the use of narcotics, one result of which was to transfer the narcotics traffic to the underworld.

By the thirties the use of drugs was pretty well confined to the nonwhite ghettos and to the jazz world. The increase in drug use after the Second World War produced a tough Narcotics Control Act in 1956. This act drew no distinction between soft and nonaddictive drugs like marijuana and hard drugs like heroin and imposed severe mandatory sentences for sale or possession. The law had little effect, however, and by the sixties the hippies, followed by college students and later by high-school students, were increasingly into drugs.

Dr. Norman Zinberg has divided drug-takers into two categories—the "oblivion-seekers" and the "experience-seekers." The oblivion-seekers, trying to deaden the hopelessness of life, used heroin. This became the typical ghetto addiction, though in time it began to spread among hippies and then into the middle class. For the experience-seekers, trying to blow their minds and open wide what Aldous Huxley called in an influential book *The Doors of Perception* (1954), marijuana ("pot" or "grass") was the most common drug. Some, wishing something more intense than the mild euphoria they enjoyed when "stoned" on pot, turned to stronger hallucinogens, notably lysergic acid diethylamide (LSD or "acid") and mescaline; others to amphetamines, especially methedrine ("pep pills" or "speed"). LSD "highs" sometimes produced "good trips," with extraordinary heightening

Woodstock, August 1969: even their elders were impressed

of perceptions of sound, color, and motion; they also very often produced "bad trips" and chemical changes leading to panic, prolonged depression, psychosis, and suicide. For some, notably Dr. Timothy Leary and his followers, LSD became a "sacrament" and psychedelic ecstasy a new form of religious revelation. By the conservative estimate of the director of the Institute of Mental Health, there were in 1969 more than 100,000 "active narcotic abusers" in the United States, and 8 to 12 million who had used marijuana at least once.

The height of the hippie movement came in August 1969 when four hundred thousand young people gathered at a three-day rock music festival in Woodstock, New York. Despite inclement weather, drugs, and food and water shortages, the tranquil and cooperative "sharing" of the Woodstock Nation impressed even their skeptical elders. In December 1969, however, another rock festival held at the Altamont Speedway in Livermore, California, broke up in violence and caused four deaths. The catastrophe produced by this assemblage of potheads, acidheads, and speed freaks led reflective hippies into intensive re-examination. "In 24 hours," one said, "we created all the problems of our society in one place: congestion, violence, dehumanization." "'Kill the pig,' seems to have become our rallying cry," said another. "We fail to con-

front the pig in ourselves, the childish, egotistical, selfish irresponsibility."

As the decade came to an end, the idyl—the Age of Aquarius—was turning sour. In the cities the flower people gave way to a new, tough breed, the "street people," priding themselves on "ripping off" (stealing), "trashing" (vandalism), "gang bangs" (mass rape), and promiscuous violence. Even worse were the roving motorcycle gangs, like the sadistic Hell's Angels in California. Throughout the scene were the pushers of hard drugs. In August 1969 the atrocious murder of the actress Sharon Tate and six others at the order of Charles Manson by three women members of Manson's hippie "family," though it was briefly glorified by the Weathermen and by some in the drug culture, forced many in the new generation to confront the destructiveness in themselves.

Most political activists mistrusted drugs, but a few saw in violence itself the means of uniting political and cultural revolution. In 1967 two New Left leaders who had discovered the drug scene, Abbie Hoffman and Jerry Rubin, formed the Youth International Party or Yippies dedicated to "the blending of pot and politics." The Yippie tactic was, in the title of Hoffman's book of 1968, *Revolution for the Hell of It*. "Confusion," wrote Hoffman, "is mightier than the sword." Rubin added,

"When in doubt, burn. Fire is the revolutionary's god. . . . Burn the flag. Burn churches. Burn, burn, burn." No doubt there was an element of put-on in this apocalyptic rhetoric. In any case, even most of the young knew that, if American politics became a contest in violence, it seemed unlikely that the Weathermen and Yippies could overcome the National Guard.

Rise of the counterculture. But the fusion between political radicalism and cultural alienation that the Yippies attempted in terms of violence could also be sought in terms of ideas. Out of the varieties of revolt, out of New Left activism, the hippie movement, the communes, the drug trips, the rock music, there emerged the outline of what came to be known from within as "the Movement" and from without as the "counterculture." It rejected the achievement society and aimed for the creation of a new human consciousness.

Music played a vital role in the formation of the counterculture. English groups, especially the Beatles and later the Rolling Stones, registered the trajectory of the young—from the communal "We All Live in a Yellow Submarine" through the psychedelic "Lucy in the Sky with Diamonds" to Mick Jagger's sinister "Sympathy for the Devil." Bob Dylan was the generation's American bard, singing his poignant and evocative songs—first social conscience and then folk rock—and offering open and honest talk about drugs, race, sex, life, and memory. As Hollywood, already against the wall economically, sought out a new market, films reflected the generation's moods, from the derisive satire of *The Graduate* through the romantic pessimism of *Easy Rider* and *Five Easy Pieces* to the celebration of violence in *Bonnie and Clyde* and *The Wild Bunch.*

If Marcuse was the approved ideologist for the political rebellion, Norman Mailer was, initially at least, the most eloquent exponent of the cultural rebellion. A gifted writer and bravura personality, Mailer had first won attention with his novel on the Second World War, *The Naked and the Dead* (1948). His 1957 essay "The White Negro" mythologized the "hipster" (from which the word "hippie" subsequently came) as an existential sub-hero, living in a death-haunted society and surviving only by severing his roots, setting out on "that uncharted journey with the rebellious impera-

tives of the self," and encouraging the psychopath within. Mailer foresaw the "underground revolution" of the sixties; but by the time it arrived and hipsters surfaced *en masse* in the form of the street people, Mailer himself had moved on to other things. Too many aspects of "straight" society, from the Kennedys to the Apollo project, fascinated him; and, as a man who relished audiences and publicity, he became almost a member of the Establishment himself.

Other prophets fell by the wayside. Next to Mailer, Paul Goodman best articulated the first impulses of the cultural rebellion. His *Growing Up Absurd* (1960) sharply defined the predicament of the young growing up in an irrational society. But the cultural revolt, as it gathered momentum, moved toward an irrationalism of its own that eventually left Goodman behind. Ideas gave way to feelings; and the goal became increasingly the achievement of a mystical consciousness that would transcend the mind-body dualism and end the alienation of self from the organic world around it. Allen Ginsberg, the only poet who survived from the beats as an influence among the hippies and whose *Howl* (1955) became a manifesto for the new generation, and Alan Watts propagated the gospel of Zen Buddhism as the means to transcendence. Timothy Leary and the novelist Ken Kesey (*One Flew Over the Cuckoo's Nest,* 1962) argued for drugs. Norman O. Brown in *Life Against Death* (1959) and *Love's Body* (1966) worked out an extreme version of Freudianism and promised liberation from repressive instincts through the creation of a "Dionysian ego."

The counterculture was more unified in mood than in ideas. Marcuse and Brown, its two most systematic thinkers, had severe disagreements as well as evident affinities. But the unity of mood seemed to portend the rise of a new consciousness—a consciousness that Charles Reich described in his briefly influential book *The Greening of America* (1970) as Consciousness III, superseding the entrepreneurial consciousness of the nineteenth century and the managerial consciousness of the earlier twentieth century. Consciousness III regarded the individual self as the only true reality; rejected the "Corporate State" and all structural and institutional solutions; mistrusted logic, analysis, and rationality; and affirmed the ideal of community, "the feeling of together, an organic relationship, a shared set of laws or values, and a shared quest for experience and wisdom." Consciousness III, Reich contended, was the basis of a coming American revolution. "It will originate with the individual and with culture, and it will change the political structure only as its final act. It will not require violence to succeed, and it cannot be successfully resisted by violence."

The hard New Leftists were unpersuaded by Reich's theory of a nonviolent movement into utopia; but *The Greening* at least gave older Americans a more sympathetic picture of their children. A French philosopher, Jean-François Revel, who visited America at the end of the decade, propounded a more sober statement of a similar thesis in *Without Marx or Jesus* (1970). Only in America, Revel wrote, was there the combination of technological plenty, cultural multiplicity, and intellectual dynamism to bring about the "revolution of the twentieth century." He concluded: "The American Left is probably the world's only hope for a revolution that will save it from destruction."

The meaning of the ferment of the sixties remained indecipherable—whether it signified vaudeville or change, vitality or disintegration, renewal or destruction. As usual, only the future could make clear the significance of the past.

Suggestions for reading

DOMESTIC POLICY

W. L. O'Neill, *Coming Apart: An Informal History of America in the 1960's* (1971), is lively but uneven. For the Kennedy Administration, A. M. Schlesinger, Jr., *A Thousand Days* (1965), and T. C. Sorensen, *Kennedy* (1965), are comprehensive accounts by participants; see also Pierre Salinger, *With Kennedy* (1966), and R. E. Neustadt, *Presidential Power** (rev. ed., 1969, with afterword on Kennedy). J. M. Burns, *John Kennedy* (1959), is an admirable biography written on the eve of the 1960 election. On economic questions, Seymour Harris, *The Economics of the Kennedy Years* (1964), and Walter Heller, *New Dimensions of Political Economy* (1966), are essential. For the Kennedy assassination, see the Warren Commission *Report* (1964) and a thoughtful critique by E. J. Epstein, *Inquest** (1966). William Manchester, *Death of a President* (1967), provides a sometimes powerful, sometimes lurid, account of the tragedy.

For the Johnson Administration, L. B. Johnson, *The Vantage Point* (1971), offers a somewhat formal account of things as Johnson saw them. Rowland Evans, Jr., and Robert Novak, *Lyndon B. Johnson: The Exercise of Power** (1966), provide an astute midterm assessment. George Reedy, *The Twilight of the Presidency** (1970), and Harry McPherson, *A Political Education* (1972), are illuminating works by Johnson staffers. E. F. Goldman, an historian who served briefly in the White House, has written about *The Tragedy of Lyndon Johnson** (1969). M. E. Gettleman and David Mermelstein, eds., provide a useful collection of documents in *The Great Society Reader** (1967). On the war against poverty, Michael Harrington, *The Other America** (1963), provided initial stimulus; H. P. Miller, *Rich Man, Poor Man** (1964), is a valuable statistical analysis; H. M. Caudill, *Night Comes to the Cumberlands** (1963), is a graphic portrayal of conditions in Appalachia; D. P. Moynihan, *Maximum Feasible Misunderstanding** (1969), is a thoughtful critique.

For the politics of the period, T. H. White's two volumes, *The Making of the President, 1964, 1968** (1965, 1969), recount the presidential elections in vivid style. Lewis Chester, *et al.*, *An American Melodrama** (1969), is a knowledgeable British account of the 1968 campaign. Norman Mailer, *Miami and the Siege of Chicago** (1968), evokes the atmosphere of the two conventions of that year. For the impact of Robert F. Kennedy, see Jack Newfield, *Robert Kennedy* (1969), David Halberstam, *The Unfinished Odyssey of Robert Kennedy* (1968), and George Plimpton and Jean Stein, *American Journey* (1970). Eugene McCarthy writes on the 1968 campaign in *Year of the People* (1969); see also Jeremy Larner, *Nobody Knows: Reflections on the McCarthy Campaign of 1968* (1970).

FOREIGN AND MILITARY POLICY

For the Kennedy Administration, in addition to the Schlesinger and Sorensen books, there is valuable material in Roger Hilsman, *To Move a Nation** (1967), and W. W. Rostow, *The Diffusion*

*Available in a paperback edition.

of Power (1972). Louise FitzSimons, *The Kennedy Doctrine* (1972), and R. J. Walton, *Cold War and Counter-Revolution* (1972), are revisionist critiques. On defense policy, see R. S. McNamara, *The Essence of Security* (1968); H. L. Trewhitt, *McNamara* (1971); J. M. Roherty, *Decisions of Robert S. McNamara* (1970); and A. C. Enthoven and K. W. Smith, *How Much Is Enough? Shaping the Defense Program, 1961–1969* (1971).

On the Bay of Pigs, see H. B. Johnson, *The Bay of Pigs* (1964). On the missile crisis, R. F. Kennedy, *Thirteen Days** (1971 ed., with an afterword by R. E. Neustadt and G. T. Allison), is an indispensable account by a participant; Elie Abel, *The Missile Crisis* (1966), an effective journalistic recapitulation; G. T. Allison, *Essence of Decision** (1971), a rigorous analysis; R. A. Divine, ed., *The Cuban Missile Crisis** (1971), a collection of essays from varying viewpoints. For the Alliance for Progress, see W. D. Rogers, *The Twilight Struggle* (1967), a useful account by a participant, and Jerome Levinson and Juan de Onis, *The Alliance That Lost Its Way* (1970).

On Soviet policy, in addition to the works of Adam Ulam cited in Chapter 30, see Michel Tatu, *Power in the Kremlin** (1969). Peter Ryan, *The Invasion of the Moon* (rev. ed., 1971), and J. M. Logsdon, *The Decision to Go to the Moon* (1970), describe the beginnings of space exploration.

For the Johnson foreign policy, P. L. Geyelin, *Lyndon B. Johnson and the World* (1966), is perceptive; Theodore Draper, *Abuse of Power** (1967), and J. W. Fulbright, *The Arrogance of Power** (1967), are sharply and convincingly critical. On the Dominican affair, see Jerome Slater, *Intervention and Negotiation* (1970), A. F. Lowenthal, *The Dominican Intervention* (1972), and, for a memoir by a participant, J. B. Martin, *Overtaken by Events* (1966).

On Vietnam, in addition to works cited in Chapters 30 and 31, see the following accounts by participants of the American policy debate: Townsend Hoopes, *The Limits of Intervention** (1969); Chester Cooper, *The Lost Crusade* (1970); Maxwell Taylor, *Swords and Ploughshares* (1972). Specific episodes are well described in E. G. Windchy, *Tonkin Gulf* (1971); Anthony Austin, *The President's War* (1971); and Don Oberdorfer, *Tet* (1971). For important journalistic portrayals from Vietnam, see David Halberstam, *The Making of a Quagmire* (1965); M. W. Browne, *The New Face of War* (1965); John Mecklin, *Mission in Torment* (1965); Ward Just, *To What End?* (1968); and Robert Shaplen, *Time Out of Hand** (1969). Aspects of domestic criticism are reflected in A. M. Schlesinger, Jr., *The Bitter Heritage** (1966); R. N. Goodwin, *Triumph or Tragedy?* (1966); Louis Menashe and Ronald Radosh, eds., *Teach-Ins: U.S.A.** (1967); Norman Mailer, *The Armies of the Night** (1968); and Noam Chomsky, *American Power and the New Mandarins** (1969). W. W. Rostow defends the war in *The Diffusion of Power*. In forthcoming works, David Halberstam and Leslie Gelb will provide critical accounts of the origins and history of the war.

A SOCIETY IN FERMENT

The course of the black revolution may be followed in these works by black leaders: James Baldwin, *The Fire Next Time** (1963); Malcolm X, *Autobiography** (1965); Eldridge Cleaver, *Soul on Ice** (1967); Stokely Carmichael and C. V. Hamilton, *Black Power** (1967); M. L. King, Jr., *Where Do We Go from Here: Chaos or Community?** (1967); Julius Lester, *Look Out, Whitey!** (1968); and H. P. Newton, *To Die for the People* (1972). C. E. Lincoln, ed., *Martin Luther King, Jr.** (1970), is a valuable collection of pieces. For black nationalism, see J. H. Bracey, Jr., et al., *Black Nationalism in America** (1969), and E. U. Essien-Udom, *Black Nationalism** (1962). J. W. Silver, *Mississippi: The Closed Society** (rev. ed., 1966), is an excellent portrayal by a white historian of conditions in the Deep South. C. E. Silberman, *Crisis in Black and White** (1964), is a sensitive contemporaneous report.

On the stirrings among the young, Alexander Klein, ed., *Natural Enemies: Youth and the Clash of Generations* (1970), is a useful collection of documents; Kenneth Keniston, *The Uncommitted** (1965), *Young Radicals** (1968), and *Youth and Dissent* (1971), contain perceptive and sympathetic diagnoses; and Margaret Mead, *Culture and Commitment** (1970), is a sagacious analysis.

*Available in a paperback edition.

For the New Left, Jack Newfield, *A Prophetic Minority** (new Introduction, 1970), and Paul Jacobs and Saul Landau, eds., *The New Radicals** (1966), are indispensable. Alan Adelson, *S.D.S.* (1971), describes the most militant student organization. Abbie Hoffman, *Revolution for the Hell of It** (1968), and Tom Hayden, *Trial** (1970), are declarations by New Left leaders. For ideology, see Herbert Marcuse, *One Dimensional Man** (1964), and Carl Oglesby, ed., *The New Left Reader** (1969); for critique, Irving Howe, ed., *Beyond the New Left* (1970), and Maurice Cranston, ed., *The New Left* (1971).

On the counterculture, Norman Mailer, *Advertisements for Myself** (1959) and *The Presidential Papers** (1963), and Paul Goodman, *Growing Up Absurd** (1960), are essential introductions. Theodore Roszak, *The Making of a Counter-Culture** (1969), is a helpful survey. The counter-culture testifies about itself in Henry Gross, *The Flower People** (1968); Jerry Hopkins, ed., *The Hippie Papers** (1968); Jonathan Eisen, ed., *Altamont: Death of Innocence in the Woodstock Nation** (1970); R. S. Gold, ed., *The Rebel Culture** (1970); the editors of *Rolling Stone, The Age of Paranoia: How the Sixties Ended* (1972); and, for a massive and invaluable collection of documents, Mitchell Goodman, ed., *The Movement Toward a New America* (1970). For drugs, see D. B. Louria, *The Drug Scene** (1968); Lester Grinspoon, *Marihuana Reconsidered** (1971); and N. E. Zinberg and J. A. Robertson, *Drugs and the Public* (1972). In Helen Perry, *The Human Be-In* (1970), an attempt is made to relate communes to earlier American communitarian experience; see also Keith Melville, *Communes in the Counter Culture* (1972).

C. A. Reich sets forth his thesis in *The Greening of America** (1970); for criticism, see Philip Nobile, ed., *The Con III Controversy* (1971). A more lucid statement of the character of the revolution is to be found in L. C. Stevens, *EST** (1970), and a foreign interpretation in Jean-François Revel, *Without Marx or Jesus* (1971).

On social disorder, the *Reports* of three presidential commissions are indispensable: the Kerner Commission on Civil Disorders* (1968); the Scranton Commission on Campus Unrest* (1970); and the Eisenhower Commission on the Causes and Prevention of Violence (1970). See also H. D. Graham and T. R. Gurr, *Violence in America** (1969); Thomas Rose, ed., *Violence in America** (1970); and R. H. Connery, ed., *Urban Riots** (1969).

*Available in a paperback edition.

33 Toward the bicentennial

The man who became President in January 1969 was the antithesis of the rebel mood of the sixties. Fifty-six years old on his inauguration, Richard Milhous Nixon came from a lower-middle-class Quaker family in California, where a frugal upbringing had instilled traditional virtues of work, discipline, and ambition. Receiving a law degree in 1937, he served in the navy during the Second World War and entered politics thereafter, gaining election to the House of Representatives in 1946 and to the Senate in 1950. His diligence as a member of a House investigating committee helped break the case of Alger Hiss, and anticommunism was the issue with which he was most identified in his early career. His alacrity in dispensing accusations of disloyalty outraged his political opponents, who denounced him as Tricky Dick, but Republicans admired him as an intelligent lawyer and a good party man.

Elected Vice President in 1952, Nixon did not enjoy easy relations with Eisenhower but served him faithfully. After being defeated by Kennedy in 1960, Nixon was defeated again in 1962 for the governorship of California; and his career was supposed over. But, with dogged perseverance, he rebuilt his position until he won nomination and election in 1968. Lonely and solemn as a young man, he was fluent and affable in middle age. Sympathizers saw him as the embodiment of middle-class values in a degenerate time; critics found him defensive, righteous, and shifty. Of conservative inclination but flexible temper, Nixon maintained an uneven balance between the rhetoric of the right and the realities of his time.

Return to Republicanism

From confrontation to negotiation. Foreign affairs were Nixon's consuming interest and, in his view of himself, his field of main expertise. His Secretary of State, William P. Rogers, was an old friend who had been Attorney General during the Eisenhower Administration; but his principal adviser was Henry A. Kissinger, a Harvard intellectual who had come to the United States from Germany as a boy in 1938 and was an accomplished diplomatic historian as well as an astute analyst of strategic problems. Serving as Nixon's Special Assistant for National Security, Kissinger carried to new lengths the process already well advanced in the Kennedy and Johnson Administrations of centralizing control over foreign policy in the White House.

Though Nixon himself had been a devoted cold warrior who had criticized Kennedy and Johnson as inadequately militant in their Cuba and Vietnam policies, he was also a realist who recognized, as he said in 1970, that ''the postwar period in international relations has ended.'' As the bipolar world was dissolving

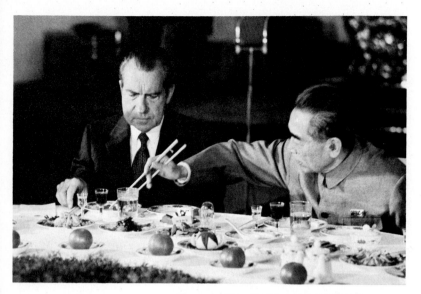

Nixon and Chou En-lai: a reversal of policy

munist states free to pursue national policies. It could no longer be assumed that the extension of communism would mean the automatic extension of Russian, or Chinese, power.

Nixon's task was to adjust American policy to changing international realities as well as to the mounting domestic revulsion against the war in Vietnam. His *beau idéal* of a statesman was de Gaulle, who had always supposed national interest more potent than ideology; Kissinger, the student of Metternich and Bismarck, reinforced this pragmatic view. As President, Nixon began to liberate himself from the ideological obsessions of the Dulles years. Security, as he saw it, demanded no longer the rollback of communism but rather the reestablishment of the classical balance of power. "It will be a safer world and a better world," he said in 1971, "if we have a strong, healthy United States, Europe, Soviet Union, China, Japan—each balancing the other, not playing one against the other, an even balance."

Rapprochement with communist powers.

In his faith in peace through the balancing of power, Nixon seemed to minimize the need for international institutions designed to accommodate the interests of the power centers and protect the interests of smaller states. No previous Administration had displayed such skepticism about the United Nations or such disdain about America's UN obligations. Nixon concentrated rather on developing and stabilizing American relationships with the other great powers.

His boldest step in the pursuit of the balance-of-power design was his reversal of American policy toward the Chinese People's Republic. After the Korean War domestic political pressures had frozen successive Administrations into a posture of grim nonrecognition of the Peking regime. The excesses of the Cultural Revolution of 1966–68 seemed to verify the theory that Maoism represented the ultimate in communist fanaticism. However, when Russia stationed nearly fifty divisions along its Chinese frontier, Mao Tse-tung and Chou En-lai evidently decided they must take steps to block a Soviet-American alliance against China. Washington was responsive, and a mission by Kissinger to Peking in July 1971 was followed by an extraordinary presidential trip to China in February–March 1972. Nixon stayed in China for nearly a week—a

into multipolarity, the relationship between America and Russia, Nixon said, was moving "from an era of confrontation to an era of negotiation."

The reign of the superpowers was indeed drawing to a close. For a decade after the Second World War, America and Russia, entering the vacuums of power left in the wake of war, had almost divided and dominated the planet. But in subsequent years, the resurgence of nationalism—in Europe, within the communist world, and in the Third World—was filling these vacuums from within. The reinvigoration of nationalism meant growing opposition to the United States in the western bloc, growing opposition to the Soviet Union in the communist bloc, and growing opposition to both in the Third World. The consequence was to place limits on the power of the two countries. Tocqueville's celebrated forecast—America and Russia, each "marked out by the will of Heaven to sway the destinies of half the globe''—had in the end an exceedingly short run.

In addition, the fragmentation of the communist world by nationalism altered the nature of the problem that communism presented to the United States. The intensifying quarrel between Russia and China meant the end of any single center of authority in the communist movement and hence the end of the unity of communist ideology and discipline. In the age of Stalin communist parties everywhere had responded to the directives of Moscow; the rise of "polycentrism" set comlonger state visit than any President had ever made to a foreign nation. On departure, he signed a declaration saying that Taiwan, where Chiang Kai-shek still ruled, was part of mainland China, that American forces would eventually withdraw from Taiwan, and that the island's future was to be settled by the Chinese themselves.

The new China policy came as a notable shock to both Japan and India, America's older friends in Asia and the prospective makeweights against Chinese domination. During the India-Pakistan War of December 1971 when Nixon, despite public protestations of neutrality, instructed his government secretly to "tilt" American power in favor of Pakistan, he confirmed India's inclination to strengthen ties to the Soviet Union. Some in Japan wished to do likewise. Critics wondered whether Nixon was putting too many Asian eggs in the Chinese basket and thereby undermining his own balance-of-power policy. But most Americans welcomed his courage in terminating the sterile pretense that Communist China did not exist.

As for the Soviet Union, the first necessity was an intensified effort to control the arms race. After the Cuban missile crisis, Russia had drastically enlarged its production of land-based intercontinental ballistic missiles (ICBMs). By 1972 it had about 1,600 missile-launchers as against 1,054 for the United States. On the other hand, the United States retained a great superiority in offensive nuclear warheads—about 5,700 against 2,500. And American security rested not only on ICBMs but on submarine-based missiles and the strategic bombing force—three independent strategic systems, each invulnerable to Soviet attack, each capable of inflicting deadly damage even after a Soviet first strike. With the Soviet Union now in a comparable stage of assured retaliatory capacity, it seemed increasingly foolish for the two powers, each with the ability to blow up the world, to continue piling overkill on overkill. Then in the late sixties both began the construction of anti-ballistic missile (ABM) systems, highly expensive and of dubious effectiveness; worse, if effective, such systems would upset the existing stalemate, give the nation with the more extensive ABM defense a new advantage, and set off an even more costly phase in the arms race.

Beset by budgetary difficulties, each government was prepared to explore measures for

Nixon at the Summit, Moscow, May 1972

arms control. Strategic Arms Limitation Talks (SALT), initiated in 1969, resulted in an agreement, concluded by Nixon at a summit meeting in Moscow in May 1972, to freeze the number of offensive strategic missiles and a treaty to restrict each nation to two ABM deployments. By these acts the United States acquiesced in Soviet superiority in ICBMs, submarine-based missiles, and total missile megatonnage while keeping its three to one advantage in numbers of warheads. The fact that the ceilings were quantitative opened the possibility that the arms race would now assume a qualitative form (for example, the Soviet Union, by increasing the number and accuracy of the warheads carried by each missile, could overcome its inferiority in warheads) and that each side would hasten to build up weapons systems not covered in the agreements. Nevertheless the agreements and the accompanying Nixon-Brezhnev declarations signaled, if not a finish to the Cold War, at least its modulation into a form less menacing to the future of mankind.

Progress was also made toward defining the status quo in Europe. The ratification in May 1972 of treaties by West Germany with Russia and Poland provided in effect the territorial settlement the wartime coalition had failed to conclude after the Second World War. A quadripartite agreement on the status of West Berlin gave promise of ending what had been for twenty-five years a situation of danger between the Soviet Union and the West. At Moscow Nixon accepted the Soviet

The Nixon Doctrine   *Our important interests and those of our friends are still threatened by those nations which would exploit change and which proclaim hostility to the United States as one of the fundamental tenets of their policies....*

—The United States will keep all its treaty commitments.

—We shall provide a shield if a nuclear power threatens the freedom of a nation allied with us, or of a nation whose survival we consider vital to our security and the security of the region as a whole.

—In cases involving other types of aggression we shall furnish military and economic assistance when requested and as appropriate. But we shall look to the nation directly threatened to assume the primary responsibility of providing the manpower for its defense.

This approach requires our commitment to helping our partners develop their own strength. In doing so, we must strike a careful balance. If we do too little to help them—and erode their belief in our commitments—they may lose the necessary will to conduct their own self-defense or become disheartened about prospects of development. Yet, if we do too much, and American forces do what local forces can and should be doing, we promote dependence rather than independence.

From Richard M. Nixon, Report to the Congress, February 18, 1970.

---

proposal that a European security conference be convened "without undue delay."

The Moscow summit failed, however, to resolve the clash of Russian and American objectives in the Middle East. Here Moscow sought to attain historic Russian goals by enlarging its Mediterranean fleet and sending arms to Arab states, notably Egypt. The United States retained its traditional commitment to the independence of Israel. The still irreconcilable conflict between Israel and the Arabs constantly threatened to draw Soviet and American policy into sharp collision. United Nations efforts to compose the situation proved unavailing.

In general, Nixon wrought his changes in American policy toward China and Russia with surprisingly little resistance at home. No doubt his own anticommunist credentials facilitated the process, and observers wryly noted the irony of the old Red-hunter exchanging genial toasts with Chou En-lai and Brezhnev. But even conservatives confined themselves to stoical warnings. Fundamentally the ideological intensities of the Cold War were now played out.

The Nixon Doctrine. The establishment of a working balance of power would presumably diminish the global involvements of the United States. This Nixon seemed to suggest when he promulgated, while in Guam in July 1969, what he thereafter termed the Nixon Doctrine. The "central thesis," Nixon said in 1970, was that "the United States will participate in the defense and development of allies and friends, but cannot—and will not—conceive *all* the plans, design *all* the programs, execute *all* the decisions and undertake *all* the defense of the free nations of the world. We will help where it will make a real difference and is considered in our interest." Even in such cases, he added, the nations directly threatened had the "primary responsibility" of providing the manpower for their own defense.

This presumed retreat from overseas activity reflected the national mood. Economic assistance, so long a basic part of American foreign policy, also lost its popularity and suffered severe reductions. Even liberal senators now argued that foreign aid encouraged American military intervention in other nations, enriched native oligarchies, and undercut the internal discipline necessary for economic development.

But Nixon soon rejected the view that his doctrine portended a general contraction of American overseas obligations. By 1971 he was warning against the "danger" of "under-involvement" and emphasizing that the Nixon Doctrine did not mean the "precipitate shrinking of the American role" or "the automatic reduction of the American presence everywhere." All this suggested that the doctrine meant a contraction not of American commitments but of the American military force available to meet those commitments, with the gap to be filled by local forces or, some feared, by the use of nuclear weapons.

The Nixon Doctrine seemed to apply primarily to Asia. In other parts of the world the Nixon policy moved in generally conservative directions. In Europe new friendship was expressed for a military dictatorship in Greece and right-wing regimes in Spain and Portugal. In Africa the Administration sought systematically to enlarge contacts with white governments—not only in South Africa and Rhodesia but with Portuguese governments in Angola and Mozambique. This course led to resentment in black Africa. In Latin America, Nixon, referring to the military dictatorship in Brazil, said, "As Brazil goes so will go the rest of that Latin American continent." In 1972 he announced that it would be United States policy to retaliate against governments that nationalized American companies without assuring adequate compensation. This would be done not only by ending American aid but by trying to veto aid from the World Bank and other multilateral institutions. Such solicitude for private business did not increase American popularity in the Western Hemisphere.

As for Asia, where Secretary Rogers defined the Nixon Doctrine in 1972 as one of "shared responsibilities" charting "a continuing and substantial U.S. role in East Asia in partnership with the Asians," it was not clear what it meant beyond the withdrawal of American ground forces from exposed places, especially from Vietnam.

The Indochina War

Still Vietnam. The Vietnam War remained the nation's most anguishing international problem. In November 1968 the North Vietnamese had begun to respond to the start of negotiations in Paris by withdrawing twenty-two of twenty-five regiments from the northern two provinces of South Vietnam; but Johnson, as lame-duck President, decided to keep up the military pressure, and the withdrawals ceased. President Thieu delayed for five weeks before sending representatives to Paris. When the Saigon delegates arrived, they stalled further by raising inane objections to the shape of the negotiating table. This momentous question was finally settled four days before Nixon's inauguration. Nixon promptly replaced Averell Harriman with

Henry Cabot Lodge as chief negotiator; private meetings that Harriman had initiated with the representatives of the National Liberation Front were suspended; and, though official meetings took place at regular intervals over the next years, they produced little except propaganda and recrimination.

The new Administration shared some of Johnson's preconceptions about the war. "Our defeat and humiliation in South Vietnam," Nixon said in November 1969, "without question would promote recklessness in the councils of those great powers who have not yet abandoned their goals of world conquest." The world's hope for the survival of freedom, he added, "will be determined by whether the American people have the moral

*The most intense college protests
in American history*

stamina and the courage to meet the challenge of free-world leadership." He also feared that "precipitous withdrawal" from Vietnam would produce a right-wing reaction within the United States.

Instead Nixon proposed to "wind down" the war through a policy of Vietnamization. Vietnamization meant the withdrawal of American troops and their replacement by South Vietnamese troops until South Vietnamese forces could "assume the full responsibility for the security of South Vietnam." The withdrawal policy was pursued with some steadiness, until the number of American ground troops in Vietnam had been reduced from the high point of 543,400 in April 1969 to 60,000 by September 1972. This withdrawal, accompanied by a cutback in American ground offensives, resulted in the lowering of American casualties. At the same time, the proportion of draftees in the American forces in Vietnam fell sharply. All this diminished the domestic political impact of the war and bought time for the Vietnamization policy to produce results, though it was not always clear whether the intended result of Vietnamization was negotiation or victory.

The serious negotiating effort was conducted in great secrecy by Kissinger, who made thirteen clandestine trips to France between 1969 and 1971 for this purpose. But the North Vietnamese and the Viet Cong were not interested in any compromise that would mean giving up goals for which they had fought for thirty years; they were still determined to dominate South Vietnam. The death of Ho Chi Minh in September 1969 may well have increased Hanoi's inflexibility. The American proposals, varying in detail, all insisted on a cease-fire in advance of a political settlement, and all involved a favored position for the Thieu regime in Saigon; indeed, at times they appeared subject to the veto of General Thieu.

Some observers concluded that Vietnamization and negotiation were incompatible. Successful negotiation required American renunciation of the Thieu regime; successful Vietnamization required American strengthening of that regime. Thus Nixon pronounced General Thieu one of the four or five great political leaders of the world. Washington supported Thieu in South Vietnam's presidential election of 1971, though with some embarrassment when his opponents, denouncing the contest as rigged, bowed out of the race.

Widening the war. With Hanoi unwilling to accept his terms, Nixon retained the hope that Vietnamization, if it would not produce negotiation, might produce victory. Victory meant the assured survival of a noncommunist regime in Saigon. To accomplish this at the same time that American troops were leaving Vietnam demanded, in Nixon's judgment, extraordinary measures to protect the Vietnamization process—measures long urged by the military, rejected by Johnson, and designed to destroy the North Vietnamese military buildup in the presumably neutral countries of Cambodia and Laos.

For nearly twenty years the wily Prince Sihanouk had managed through artful dodging to preserve the neutrality of Cambodia. In the middle sixties Hanoi had begun to place troops along Cambodia's frontier with South Vietnam and to set up staging areas for attacks on South Vietnam. In March 1970 Sihanouk was overthrown by a prowestern military coup headed by General Lon Nol. Soon thereafter North Vietnamese units moved into the interior of Cambodia. On April 30 Nixon, after twice seeing the stirring and bellicose movie *Patton,* announced an American incursion into Cambodia to "clean out major enemy sanctuaries." If, said Nixon, "the world's most powerful nation . . . acts like a pitiful, helpless giant . . . all other nations will be on notice that despite its overwhelming power the United States when a real crisis comes will be found wanting. . . . We will not be humiliated. We will not be defeated."

For much of 1969 the American antiwar movement had been in abeyance, its leaders wishing to give the new President a chance to end the war. Then on October 15 the Vietnam Moratorium Committee brought hundreds of thousands of citizens to Washington in an impressive demonstration against the war. Vice President Agnew promptly said that the protest had been "encouraged by an effete corps of impudent snobs who characterize themselves as intellectuals." Six months later, the invasion of Cambodia set off the most widespread and intense college protests in American history, involving 1.5 million students and half of America's twenty-five hundred campuses. On May 4, 1970, four students were killed and ten wounded by National Guardsmen at Kent State University in Ohio; Nixon, who a few days before had described student agitators as "bums," observed, "When dissent turns to violence, it invites tragedy." On May 14 police killed two black youths and wounded twelve at Jackson State College in Mississippi.

The Cambodian episode also produced strong reactions on Capitol Hill. For some time members of Congress had been growing restive over what seemed to some the loss to the executive of the constitutional power to declare war; the dispatch of American troops into Cambodia now raised the constitutional issue in acute form. Many found this an employment of presidential power without precedent in American history—a military invasion of another country undertaken without request from the government of that country, without statutory or treaty authorization, without consultation with the American Congress, without the excuse of emergency, the sanctuaries having been there for several years, or of the need to repel sudden attack. The Administration replied that the President was exercising authority to protect American troops inherent in his role as commander in chief—a principle which, critics felt, would not be persuasive if invoked by the Soviet Union as a justification for similar action by the Red Army. Congress, hoping to reclaim lost powers, now repealed the Tonkin Gulf resolution (see p. 774) and debated a variety of proposals designed to restrict the commitment of American troops to other countries and even

to cut off funds for further prosecution of the war in Vietnam.

American forces were out of Cambodia by the end of June 1970. The incursion had failed to have the decisive effect hoped for, and the Administration soon considered new actions to reduce the communist threat to the Saigon regime. Denied by Congress funds to finance the introduction of American ground troops into Laos, Nixon in February 1971 provided American air support for a South Vietnamese invasion of that country. The idea was to cut the Ho Chi Minh trails. "The South Vietnamese by themselves can hack it," Nixon said, but it turned out they couldn't. In a few weeks, badly battered, they withdrew. The war went on.

As American ground strength declined, Nixon increased the deployment and use of American air and naval power. By the end of 1971 his Administration had dropped 3.3 million tons of bombs on South Vietnam, Laos, Cambodia, and, toward the end, North Vietnam—more in three years than the Johnson Administration had dropped in five (and the bombing rate mounted in Nixon's fourth year). But aerial terror accomplished no more than it had in the past; and, when a strong North Vietnamese offensive in the spring of 1972 achieved tactical surprise and set back South Vietnamese forces, Nixon, fearing loss of "respect for the office of the President of the United States" on the eve of the Moscow summit, retaliated by ordering the air force to widen the bombing of North Vietnam and the navy to mine North Vietnamese harbors. This would be, he said, the "decisive military action to end the war"; and it was required because "an American defeat in Vietnam would encourage this kind of aggression all over the world . . . in the Mid-East, in Europe, and other areas." Some supposed that intensification of the war would cause the Russians to cancel the summit; but Moscow, afraid of strengthening the Chinese-American relationship, swallowed hard and digested the new escalation. The war went on.

Vietnam inquest. By 1972 the Vietnam War had lasted longer than any war in American history, had caused more American deaths in combat than any war except the Civil War and the two World Wars, and had cost more money than any war except the Second World War. Budgeted war costs amounted to $120 billion for the years 1965–71; with the addi-

Senator J. W. Fulbright: strong reactions on Capitol Hill

Appalled by the war

tion of associated costs, from economic assistance to veterans' benefits, and indirect costs, from inflation and high interest rates to balance-of-payment deficits, the figure would rise toward $400 billion. Moreover, the war had created the most widespread and bitter domestic resistance in American history—a condition dramatized by the trial in 1972 of Father Philip Berrigan and two Catholic nuns on the charge of plotting to kidnap Henry Kissinger.

Disgust with the war was seeping into the army itself. By 1970 soldiers in Vietnam were wearing peace symbols and refusing to go into combat. The use of marijuana was general; and, according to estimates, 10 to 15 percent of the troops were addicted to heroin. "Fragging"—the use of fragmentation grenades to kill unpopular officers—was not uncommon. In the United States underground newspapers and antiwar coffee houses ventilated G.I. discontent. Amnesty for draft dodgers and deserters became an increasingly popular issue. Military morale and discipline were probably worse than at any point in American history. The incipient demoralization of the army strengthened the spreading determination to get out of the war.

In Indochina the war had killed 1½ million Indochinese and had turned a third of the population into refugees. Saturation bombing had left the landscape scarred with craters.

Defoliation, undertaken to deprive the Viet Cong of forest cover, had affected one-third of the forest area of South Vietnam and had killed off perhaps half the country's mangrove forests. The indiscriminate use of chemical herbicides and giant bulldozers led to talk of "ecocide"—the crime of destroying the natural environment in which people live. President Marcos of the Philippines spoke for many Asians when he said in 1971, "Heaven forbid that the U.S. should duplicate what it has done in South Vietnam if the war should come to our country."

The subtler horror of the war burst on the American public in the spring of 1969 with the disclosure that American soldiers had massacred more than a hundred unarmed Vietnamese civilians at My Lai in March 1968. The subsequent arrest and conviction of Lieutenant William F. Calley, Jr., produced strong if confused reactions. Many defended Calley; the President even interceded sympathetically on his behalf. Many, not unreasonably, thought it unfair that Calley should be the only man convicted for the massacre. Many could not believe that My Lai was a unique episode. Some called for a war-crimes inquiry; some even demanded the prosecution of top military and civilian leaders as war criminals. Whatever else, My Lai forced many Americans suddenly to see the war from an appalled new perspective, to wonder whether the United

States had not brutalized itself in Vietnam, and to conclude that the means employed and the destruction wrought had grown out of all proportion to the interests involved and the goals sought. In 1971 public opinion polls reported that 65 percent of respondents believed it ''morally wrong'' for Americans to be fighting in Vietnam.

The Vietnam experience corroded the spirit of self-confidence that had characterized America in 1945. By the early seventies the American people were divided, the economy was in trouble, the armed forces were in discredit, national motives were in doubt, and liberal ideals themselves seemed implicated in the disaster. One result was an intensive examination of the bases of American foreign policy to account for the ghastly consequence.

American empire? Most Americans believed during the quarter-century after the Second World War that America had extended its power around the planet in order to protect free nations from communist aggression. But the shock of Vietnam put the situation in a chilling new light. In the course of these twenty-five years, it now seemed, America had established an empire of its own. It had military commitments to 47 nations; 375 major bases and 3,000 minor facilities in foreign lands; 1 million troops stationed abroad; 2.5 million more troops under arms at home. It had spent more than $1 trillion for its own military programs and $150 billion for foreign aid. American business also controlled more than half of all direct foreign private investment, produced more than half of the world's manufactured products, and consumed a disproportionate quantity of the world's raw materials.

How had this empire arisen? On the left a tendency arose to ascribe everything—not only the Indochina War but the Cold War and even American participation in the Second World War—to the quest of American capitalism for world hegemony. It was true that American overseas investments had grown strikingly in the postwar period—from $8.4 billion in 1945 to $78 billion in 1970. Though it was hard to argue that America went into Vietnam to gain markets or protect investments, more sophisticated exponents of the economic thesis contended that, because defeat in Vietnam would jeopardize American markets and investments throughout the Third World, economic interest compelled Washing-

ton to a course of ruthless counterrevolution. Close analysis of the figures showed, however, that the dependence of American capitalism on the underdeveloped world was limited. Two-thirds of American exports went to industrialized rather than to developing countries, and sales to the Third World amounted to about 3 percent of the annual national output. Investment in the Third World represented a declining fraction of total foreign investment—35 percent in 1960 and only 28 percent in 1970. Of Third World investment, 40 percent was in petroleum; with that excluded, only about one-sixth of American overseas investment was in the developing nations, and few American businessmen seemed interested in increasing that proportion. American business earned $5 billion on direct foreign investment in 1968 as against $89 billion on investment in the United States. In so far as American capitalism depended on the world outside, it depended on markets and investments in developed and not in underdeveloped countries. Nor had American business been, for example, notably eager for escalation in Vietnam.

If not American capitalism, what? No single explanation of the imperial impulse seemed satisfactory. A number of factors appear to have led Americans to suppose themselves entitled, as appointed custodians of freedom, to intervene freely and righteously around the planet. The American empire, such as it was, resulted from the distortion of decent beliefs: of the belief in the necessity of creating an international structure in which America would accept full global responsibility; of the belief in America's mission to uplift and save suffering mankind; of the belief in America's capacity to instruct and rebuild other nations. The perversion of these beliefs was strengthened by the national reaction to the quite ugly problem of Stalinist communism and then by the counterideology of anticommunism, persisting in rigid and absolutist form long after the circumstances giving it validity had begun to change.

The special pressure encouraging active intervention, above all in Vietnam, appeared to be the military establishment, emerging from the Second World War with new power and status, professionally persuaded that political problems had military solutions, professionally committed to multiplying appropriations and weapons, professionally adept at playing upon national desires to appear virile

A ghastly consequence

*Whether or not the very survival of American capitalism does depend
on its economic stake in the underdeveloped countries, there is no
question but that a tremendously powerful group of corporate concerns
have a great deal at stake in the American Empire. These corporations
exercise decisive influence on the policies of the American government.... The fact of corporate influence in the government, together
with the large corporate interest in an aggressive foreign policy to
maintain and expand the American Empire (imperialism), leads to some
clear conclusions.... The United States government opposes socialist
revolution all over the world, as it is an attempt to achieve independence from imperial domination. Such an attempt threatens present
and future economic interests in the country in question. Furthermore,
a successful socialist revolution would undermine the confidence of
American investors in other places, while encouraging revolutionaries
and oppressed peoples around the world to fight for liberation against
a colossus that has proven vulnerable. These are the bases for United
States opposition to socialist revolution in Vietnam.*

From Dan Gilbarg, "United States Imperialism," in William Slate, ed., *Power to the People!
New Left Writings,* 1970.

and patriotic. This was not Eisenhower's
"military-industrial complex." The military
establishment was rather an independent
force in its own right, operating according to
its institutional needs and imperatives and not
at the bidding of business, which by the late
sixties had turned predominantly against escalation in Vietnam.

A look at other nations confirmed the proposition that the imperial impulse was not
rooted in a specific economic structure or
system of ownership. Every great power,
whatever its ideology, had its military machine. Every military machine supposed that
national security required the domination of
"strategic" weaker states, if only to prevent
their domination by some rival power. If, for
example, what the Soviet Union did to Czechoslovakia was not imperialism, then the term
had no meaning; if it was imperialism, then
imperialism was not uniquely rooted in capitalism, nor would the abolition of capitalism
end it. It seemed likely that no change in the
system of ownership would reduce the power
of the professional military in a time of accelerating nuclear technology and chronic international crisis.

In any case, revulsion against the American
empire crystallized new conceptions of American foreign policy. While there was little inclination to revert to isolationism, Americans
began to conclude that not everything in the
world was of equal concern to the United
States; that there were strict limits on the

American capacity to decide the destiny of
other nations; that in an age of local savagery
and upheaval many terrible things would take
place that America lacked the power to prevent or the wisdom to cure; that the United
States could not be the permanent guarantor
of stability in a turbulent world; that military
force was not necessarily the most effective
form of national power; and that in the future
American influence abroad would derive less
from economic and military might than from
political and social example.

Modern Toryism. For Nixon domestic policy
was admittedly secondary to foreign policy.
"I've always thought this country could run
itself domestically without a President," he
said in 1968. "All you need is a competent
cabinet to run the country at home." His own
disposition was to mistrust the national government, to reduce federal spending and regulation, and to give free rein to business enterprise. He identified himself with the middle
class, the "great silent majority" of "forgotten
Americans," as against the importunings of
small and loud minorities. At the same time,
he had some desire to go down in history as
a reformer; and here he was responsive to
liberals who had turned against the bureaucratized liberalism of the last generation.

Daniel Patrick Moynihan, a Kennedy Democrat whom Nixon brought into the White
House and who used to remind the President
of Disraeli's success in dishing the Whigs

through Tory reform, urged a new approach to the troubling question of welfare. There had been a disturbing expansion of relief rolls during the sixties, especially in the category of Aid to Families with Dependent Children (AFDC). Between 1961 and 1970 the AFDC caseload rose from 921,000 to 2.2 million families, with an increase of almost 30 percent in 1970 alone. The federal welfare bill grew from $2.1 billion in 1960 to nearly $18 billion in 1972, while the number of persons on welfare rolls increased from 7.3 million in January 1961 to 9.9 million in January 1969 and 14.9 million three years later. Fifteen percent of the population of New York, a quarter of the population of Newark, and about 6 percent of all Americans were on welfare.

Though this welfare explosion was often attributed to the migration to Northern cities of black families forced by mechanization off Southern farms, in fact the rate of such migration did not increase during the sixties. What did increase was turmoil in the ghettos; historically, relief rolls have tended to expand in response to militancy among the poor. Moreover, the antipoverty officials of the Johnson Administration had taught the poor how to apply for relief and had presented welfare as a right. Then unemployment, induced by Nixon's anti-inflation program in 1969–71, decisively swelled the rolls. Of families on welfare, about 49 percent were white and 46 percent black. Of those receiving welfare in 1971, 55.5 percent were children, 15.6 percent old people, 9.4 percent blind and disabled. Another 18.6 percent were mothers of working age, of whom one-fifth were at work or in work training and two-fifths were unemployable. Less than 1 percent of welfare recipients were able-bodied unemployed males.

The existing welfare system buckled under the new burdens thrust upon it. It was widely condemned because it required employed fathers to leave the household in order that their families could qualify for public assistance, because its procedures were degrading, and because it helped only about a fourth of the poor. A presidential Commission on Income Maintenance, established by Johnson in 1964, recommended a minimum annual cash income of $2,400 for families of four. Nixon's own proposal of 1969 was less far-reaching. He called for the replacement of AFDC by a Family Assistance Plan that would provide a family-income payment floor (Nixon later said,

"I do not favor a guaranteed annual income") and would cover the working poor as well as current welfare recipients. Liberals criticized the plan because they considered its benefits unduly low and because its insistence on work requirements seemed to perpetuate the myth that most people on welfare were loafers or chiselers. At times, moreover, the Administration's own devotion to the plan was in question. Nonetheless, the Family Assistance Plan, whatever its final fate, at least provided a valuable new framework within which the nation could approach the welfare problem.

In his 1972 state-of-the-union message Nixon, returning to his reforming mood, proposed "a New American Revolution" designed to turn power "back to the people." The ingredients of the revolution, however, turned out to be less than inflammatory: welfare reform, revenue-sharing (that is, the transfer of $5 billion in federal revenues to the states), a pretentious reorganization of the executive branch, and health-care and anti-pollution programs. As the proposals stalled in the Democratic Congress, the Administration itself seemed to lose interest. The New American Revolution turned out to be one of the shortest revolutions on record.

The "great silent majority." A more consistent Administration theme was the defense of traditional middle-class values—a theme powerfully asserted by the Attorney General, John Mitchell, and by the Vice President, Spiro T. Agnew. In their view, the solid average American, harassed by government, crime, inflation, taxes, unrest, drugs, pornography, and uppity blacks, represented the heart of the Nixon constituency and the foundation of a future Republican majority. The great bulk of the electorate, it was noted, was unyoung, unpoor, and unblack. This approach was reinforced by Mitchell's "southern strategy," which involved the repayment to Southern Republicans of obligations incurred during Nixon's campaign for the nomination as well as an effort to make the South into a new Republican stronghold. "It is time for the preponderant majority, the responsible citizens of this country, to assert their rights," Agnew said in 1969. ". . . If, in challenging, we polarize the American people, I say it is time for a positive polarization."

Agnew concentrated much of his own challenge against television and the press, questioning the fairness of the mass media and

Spiro T. Agnew: ". . . time for a positive polarization"

demanding that they be "made more responsive to the views of the nation." Nixon, who during his campaign had blamed the Supreme Court for decisions that, in his view, had bred disorder and crime, now took advantage of vacancies to appoint justices more to his liking. The retirement of Earl Warren in 1968 enabled Nixon the next year to designate Warren Burger as the new Chief Justice. His next two appointments, both federal judges from the South, were turned down by the Senate, the first because of conflicts of interest, the second because of evident intellectual mediocrity. In a bitter statement Nixon attributed their rejection to "the fact that they had the misfortune of being born in the South." Subsequently, however, three less vulnerable but equally conservative nominees, one born in the South, were approved. By 1972 the Supreme Court had taken on a markedly more conservative complexion.

The antiwar demonstrations of 1969–70, and especially the outbursts following the Kent State shootings, encouraged Nixon to pursue a strategy of confrontation, confident that the majority of voters were fed up with protest and violence. This policy roused doubts among his own appointees: Secretary of the Interior Walter J. Hickel wrote Nixon that his Administration appeared "to lack appropriate concern for the attitude of a great mass of Americans—our young people." Nevertheless Nixon made lawlessness the central theme of the 1970 midterm election. In a concluding speech, he denounced "creeping permissiveness," called for "new and strong laws that will give the peace forces new muscle to deal with the criminal forces," and said that "appeasement" of "thugs and hoodlums" in American society must end. This appeal, quietly answered by Senator Muskie in an election-eve broadcast, failed. The Republicans lost nine seats in the House and eleven governorships but gained two seats in the Senate.

New directions in the economy. The condition of the economy contributed to Nixon's political difficulties. Inheriting the inflation generated by the Vietnam War, he at first supposed that a severe monetary policy would suffice to bring the problem under control. He consequently denounced the idea of "jawboning" (official admonitions against price increases) or of price-wage guidelines, extolled the virtues of a balanced budget, and

called for a policy of tight money and high interest rates.

The immediate effect of what he termed his "game plan" was to produce the first recession in a decade. Unemployment, which had been at 3.3 percent at the end of 1968, rose to 5.8 percent (4.6 million persons) in 1970; and the gross national product declined. Moreover, inflation did not stop. From January 1969 to August 1971 the cost of living increased by an astonishing 14.5 percent, and the purchasing power of the dollar shrank by 8.5 percent. Furthermore, inflation was overpricing American exports and weakening the dollar abroad. In 1971 the balance-of-payments deficit reached the record figure of $29.6 billion. There was, in addition, for the first time since 1893, a deficit in the balance of trade; imports exceeded exports by almost $3 billion.

By 1970 J. K. Galbraith and others were urging a policy of reviving the economy through fiscal stimulus along with the containment of inflationary pressures through an "incomes policy"—that is, the establishment of controls in industries where prices and wages, because of corporate concentration, did not respond to the play of market forces. Still confident his game plan would work, Nixon said in June 1970: "I will not take this nation down the road of wage and price controls, however politically expedient that may seem." But as "stagflation"—the combination of stagnation and inflation—persisted, Nixon finally was forced to jettison his game plan. Fortified by the appointment of a Texas Democrat, John B. Connally, as Secretary of the Treasury, Nixon declared himself a Keynesian in the summer of 1971 and on August 15 announced a startling reversal of economic course: a ninety-day price-wage freeze, during which time the government would establish machinery to achieve continuing price and wage stability; the suspension of the convertibility of dollars into gold, thereby freeing the dollar for devaluation against other currencies; a 10 percent surcharge on imports; and various tax proposals.

At home the new course represented a sharp break with traditional Republican policies of noninterference with the market. Some observers regarded the stabilization apparatus set up in Phase Two of the program as temporary; others felt that an incomes policy would be permanently needed to control inflation in a concentrated, full-employment economy. In any case the public role in economic management was entering a new period. At the same time, the Nixon Administration renounced budget-balancing and forecast a deficit of $38.8 billion in 1972, the largest in peacetime history, after a deficit of $30.2 billion the year before.

Abroad, the new course also meant the end of the international monetary system based on gold-dollar convertibility set up at Bretton Woods (see p. 708); and it led in December 1971 to the formal devaluation of the dollar. The form a new monetary system would take remained obscure. And, though the import surcharge was soon removed, it expressed a rising protectionist sentiment that, along with efforts to place quotas on imports, especially from Japan, threatened an abandonment of the long-standing American commitment to freer trade, expressed in the Kennedy round of tariff reductions in the sixties. Some now feared the resumption of the international trade wars of the thirties.

As the 1972 election approached, the war was intensifying in Vietnam, unemployment was still high, and the stabilization program was in precarious shape. The Twenty-sixth Amendment, ratified in June 1971, lowered the voting age to eighteen, thereby qualifying 11.5 million young men and women between eighteen and twenty-one to vote in 1972. In addition, 14.2 million who had become twenty-one after 1968 were eligible in 1972 to cast their first presidential votes, making a total of 25.7 million first voters, nearly one-fifth of the potential 1972 electorate. Some of Nixon's decisions—especially price controls and the visit to China—had roused opposition on the right; his lack of initiative in meeting the urban crisis and in pursuing racial justice led other Republicans, notably Mayor John V. Lindsay of New York, to shift to the Democratic party. Nevertheless Nixon remained in firm control, while the Democrats, confronting primaries in nearly half the states, went through a fatiguing spring.

Senator Muskie of Maine, the early front-runner, was quickly eliminated; and the contest settled down to a choice between Hubert Humphrey, the 1968 candidate, and Senator George McGovern of South Dakota. McGovern, a Second World War hero who had served in the Kennedy Administration and was a long-time opponent of the Vietnam War, addressed himself candidly and persuasively to questions of interventionism abroad and

inequality at home. Though discounted by professional politicians and the press, he succeeded in uniting the Robert Kennedy and Eugene McCarthy forces of 1968; and, benefiting by reforms in the delegate-selection process brought about by a Democratic party commission that he himself had chaired, he won first-ballot nomination at the Democratic convention in July. Senator Thomas Eagleton of Missouri, his first choice as running mate, retired from the ticket after failing to disclose to McGovern a history of psychiatric treatment. His replacement was Sargent Shriver of Maryland, former head of Kennedy's Peace Corps and Johnson's war on poverty and later ambassador to Paris. In August the Republicans renominated Nixon and Agnew.

Thrown badly off stride by the Eagleton affair, McGovern never recovered momentum. Disclosures of financial scandal in the Nixon Administration, even organized political espionage and sabotage implicating the White House itself, failed to impress the electorate. Nixon prudently kept his own campaigning to a minimum; and the "southern strategy" now paid off, especially when George Wallace, disabled in an assassination attempt, decided not to run. Nixon's views on busing, job quotas, Supreme Court appointments, and the permissive society, as well as his rhetoric on welfare and crime and attacks on McGovern's "radicalism," pricked cultural and racial nerves: the appeal was not only to the Wallace voters of 1968 but to elements in the old New Deal coalition, especially blue-collar workers who did not want equal rights for nonwhites at the expense of their children, their neighborhoods, or their jobs.

In addition, after concessions to Hanoi, the Administration shortly before the election announced progress toward an Indochina cease-fire. The war issue neutralized, Nixon sailed to an impressive victory, carrying every area except Massachusetts and the District of Columbia. In an election marked by ticket-splitting and voter indifference—the turnout of 55 percent was the lowest since 1948— Nixon polled 46 million votes against 28.5 million for McGovern, winning the largest proportion (60.8 percent) of the popular vote since 1964 and the largest margin in the Electoral College (521 to 17) since 1936. However, the Democrats added two to their Senate majority and retained control of the House. As in the 1950s, the voters balanced a Republican President with a Democratic Congress.

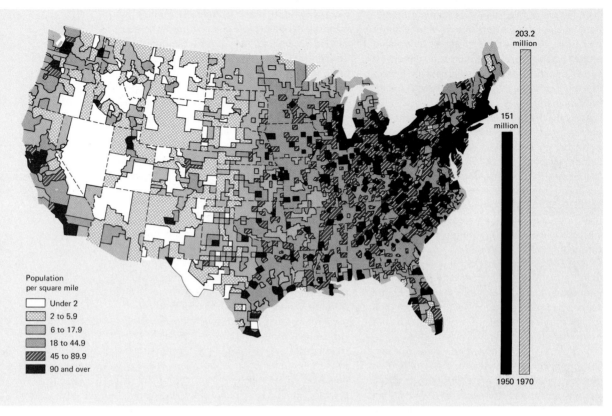

Population per square mile

- Under 2
- 2 to 5.9
- 6 to 17.9
- 18 to 44.9
- 45 to 89.9
- 90 and over

203.2 million

151 million

1950 1970

Population 1950

The quality of American society

Population trends. The census of 1970 showed that, once again, the American people were preparing to outwit the demographers. The total—203,184,772—represented almost a doubling of the population in the half-century since 1920 and an increase of 24 million, or 13.3 percent, since 1960. But, though this was the second-highest numerical increase in American history, it was also the second-lowest percentage increase; only the 7.3 percent growth rate of the depression decade, the 1930s, was lower.

The postwar baby boom, which began about 1947, came to an end about 1965. The number of births per 1,000 women of child-bearing age declined sharply from 118 in 1960 to 82.3 in 1971. In the 1950s women of child-bearing age averaged 3.35 children; the average had fallen to 2.45 by the late sixties and appeared in the early seventies to be sinking below the depression rate and toward the replacement rate of 2.11 percent. This, if sustained for half a century, would mean zero population growth. Demographers who

had forecast an American population of 300 million by the year 2000 decided on second thought it would be closer to 270 million.

The drop in fertility was doubtless encouraged by the use of the birth control pill, by the liberalization of state abortion laws, and by the economic recession. But it basically reflected new attitudes toward marriage and family. Women were marrying later (in 1960 one-third of women aged twenty-one were single; by 1970 almost one-half). More were pursuing their own careers. Above all, the large family of the fifties was now out of fashion, even among Roman Catholics. Some parents feared the impact of growing population on the environment; some were alarmed by the prospect of rearing children in an age of local and nuclear violence; some perhaps felt that the generational conflict was taking the fun out of family life.

The decline in population growth also meant that the generation born between 1947 and 1965, which in 1970 numbered 74 million persons and 36 percent of the population,

How many people will we have in 1985? How many in the year 2000?... Assuming that the young women who are beginning their childbearing after 1970 stay with the replacement average of 2110 children per thousand women, our population would be 237 million by 1985 and 266 million by the year 2000. If, however, we continue at the rates which have prevailed in recent years, the size of our population in 1985 would be 241 million and by the year 2000 we would have reached 281 million.... Perhaps the potential contributions of the young women now entering on childbearing could best be visualized if one assumes that they duplicate the rates which young women had in the late 1950's. If that were the case, the population by 1985 would number 256 million, and it would reach 321 million by the year 2000....

ZPG, Zero Population Growth, has become a slogan.... If fertility rates should drop to the replacement level and continue there, and if there were to be no net immigration, our numbers in the year 2000 would be about 250 million.... We would cease to grow about the year 2037. We would, of course, be a much older population. The median age would be 37.3, almost 10 years more than it is today. We would have only 20 per cent of our population under 15, which is substantially lower than the present 29 per cent. We would have half again as large a proportion of our population in the 65 and over group as we have today. Perhaps by then the age at which a person is no longer to be trusted would have to move up to 40.

From Conrad Taeuber, Associate Director, Bureau of the Census, ''The People of the United States at the Beginning of the 1970's,'' January 13, 1971.

would continue as a disproportionate bulge in the population curve. This group was the basis for the youthful unrest of the sixties; it might have quite a different impact when its members became middle-aged, even more different when they became a claimant group of old folks. In any case, for the foreseeable future the young would be a declining proportion of the total population.

Americans continued to be a wandering people; nearly one-fifth moved each year from one residence to another. The Western states grew in the sixties by almost a quarter, with California gaining 4.2 million during the decade and becoming the nation's most populous state. The South also gained heavily. For the first decade since the 1870s more people moved into the South than moved out. Immigration, continuing at a rate of four hundred thousand a year, accounted for about 20 percent of total growth in the sixties. The composition of these new arrivals, however, was altered by the Immigration Act of 1965, which abolished the national-quota system and for the first time permitted large-scale immigration from countries outside northern Europe. By 1970 Italy and the Philippines had dis-

placed Canada and Great Britain in the list of the top-three immigration sources. Nearly 14 percent of immigrants in the sixties were non-white, and this proportion would presumably increase in the future.

The corporate economy. The central unit of the American economy was more than ever the corporation. During the sixties the great corporations tightened their control over American industry; the top eighty-seven corporations, with assets of more than $1 billion, increased their share of the total assets of industrial corporations from 26 to 46 percent. Less than 1 percent of all manufacturing firms—the twenty-six hundred corporations with assets of more than $10 million—held 86 percent of the assets and received 88 percent of the profits.

Oligopoly or shared monopoly—control of a market by a small number of firms—characterized widening areas of the economy. The rise of the conglomerate—a single corporation extending its operations into many varied markets—enlarged the zones of concentration and domination. By 1970 the two hundred largest industrial corporations were active in

The authors pile up the evidence toward one searing conclusion—that corporate economic, product and environmental crimes ... are part of a raging corporate radicalism which generates technological violence, undermines the integrity of government, breaks laws, blocks needed reforms, and repudiates a quality-competitive system with substantial consumer sovereignty....

The central question, then, is what changes are necessary to direct corporate resources toward respecting the values and pleas that are beyond the balance sheet's morality? And what are the instruments to achieve these changes?... A deconcentration of corporate power in two principal ways—through antitrust action and the federal chartering of corporations to rewrite the contract between the corporations and its creator—the state.... The charter can make the grant of corporate status conditional on a responsiveness to well-defined public interests and a social accounting of corporate performance. The charter can establish structural receptiveness to official accountability, detailed disclosure, and rights of access by the various constituencies including victims.... But even solid structural changes have a way of concentrating old powers in new forms sooner or later unless there is a continual assertion and defense of individual rights and responsibilities within the corporate institution itself.... The entire range of legal sanctions against both the corporate structure and its officials has to be reconsidered ... beyond just simple civil-criminal fines toward a more flexible array of civil-criminal sanctions tailored to maximum deterrence.... Together with such internal changes, the emergence of full-time, independent corporate monitors, staffed by lawyers and other skilled professionals in Washington and state capitals, would have lasting effect.... The modern corporation is the engine of the world's largest production machine. If it is to be more than a mindless, parochial juggernaut, the hands of diverse human values and trusteeships for future generations must be exerted on the steering wheel.

From Ralph Nader, Introduction to *America, Inc.: Who Owns and Operates the United States?*, by Morton Mintz and Jerry S. Cohen, 1971.

---

more than ten times that number of product markets. The largest merger wave in American history took place in the late sixties, and four-fifths of all mergers resulted in conglomeration. Moreover, large corporations seemed to enjoy an undue influence in Washington. International Telephone and Telegraph was the largest of all conglomerates, and revelations of its special relationship to the Nixon Administration roused much concern in 1972.

In addition, great corporations were moving beyond industry to take advantage of the technological revolution in agriculture and to establish bridgeheads in the countryside. In the years after 1940, mechanization, by increasing man-hour productivity twice as fast on the farm as in industry, enabled the farm population to decline from 31 million (1940) to less than 10 million (1970) and the number of farms to decline from 6.4 million to 2.9

million while total output steadily increased. A single farm worker produced food for sixteen people in 1951 and for fifty-one two decades later. The American farmer not only heaped food on his own country's tables but produced a surplus that constituted about a fifth of all exports during the sixties.

At the same time the average size of farms increased from 167 to 387 acres; and the largest forty thousand farms—less than 2 percent of the total—accounted for one-third of all farm sales. Government subsidies of $4 billion a year went primarily to large- and medium-size agricultural enterprises. The corporate invasion of farming began as a result of investment in land for speculation and for tax shelters, but increasingly it aimed to establish profitable control over every stage of food production and distribution. The goal, as Tenneco (formerly Tennessee Gas and Trans-

The great corporation: here to stay

mission) put it, was "integration from the seedling to the supermarket." Corporate farming—"agribusiness"—made its first strides in the South and West; cattle, poultry, fruits, cotton, and lettuce were early conquests. By 1970 nearly half the agricultural land in California was owned by forty-five corporate farms. Enjoying the competitive advantages of vertical integration as well as superior access to capital, credit, and government subsidies, corporate farming intensified the pressure on small farmers. The family farm held its own mainly in the corn and wheat regions of the Middle West. Many observers doubted the economic advantages to the consumer of agribusiness—certainly the insistence on machine harvesting in corporate farms lowered the quality of food—and many more questioned the social costs as 20 million Americans, 4 million of them black, were forced off the land and into the cities in the years after 1940.

Corporate expansion overseas also entered into a new phase. The American-based multinational corporation carried increasing quantities of American capital, technology, plants, and jobs to foreign countries. In the decade after 1958 domestic manufacturing capacity increased 72 percent while the foreign capacity of American firms increased 471 percent. The sales of foreign subsidiaries of American companies were estimated in 1969 at $142 billion—larger than the gross national product of France or England. The rise of the multinational corporation strengthened protectionist sentiment, particularly among labor unions, and aroused much international concern, especially when it was revealed in 1972 that International Telephone and Telegraph had been trying to stir up revolt against the left-wing government of Chile.

The phenomenon of the great corporation continued to baffle its critics. Nationalization, the traditional solution of the Old Left, was not politically feasible; in any case, the example of the Soviet Union gave little hope that a change in the system of ownership would significantly alter the impact of economic organizations on society. The New Left had no solution at all, except the dismantlement of the corporate system and the consequent sharp reduction in living standards. Liberals continued to argue the old question of the inevitability of economic concentration—the argument that had divided the New Nationalism of Theodore Roosevelt and the New Freedom of Woodrow Wilson.

Some analysts, like Adolf Berle, J. K. Galbraith, and David Lilienthal, contended that sophisticated technology created needs for capital, research, development, and long-range planning that could only be met by the great corporation. And the great corporation could be made safe for democracy, they believed, through a combination of external pressure—the countervailing powers of government, labor, consumers, and other firms—with a growing sense of inner responsibility, produced by what Berle saw as the emergence of a corporate conscience. This sense would be strengthened, in Galbraith's view, by the rising purpose and power of the "techno-structure," those scientists, engineers, and economists without whom the great corporation could not survive, and of their colleagues in the "educational and scientific estate."

Others, including members of Congress most concerned with the question, inclined toward the classical antitrust theories of the Sherman Act. They explained economic concentration not as a natural growth but as the artificial creation of greedy entrepreneurs in alliance with high finance and, more recently, with government. They denied that concentration promoted efficiency or innovation, claimed it as the leading cause of stagflation, pointed to the undemocratic pressures and powers exerted by large corporations, and called for policies of "deconcentration"—the breakup of great enterprises into small and competitive units.

An influential spokesman for this view was Ralph Nader, a practitioner in the new field of "public service law." Under Nader's leadership, teams of lawyers and economists, known popularly as "Nader's Raiders," documented cases of corporate inefficiency and graft and of corporate domination of government regulatory commissions. Nader's own book *Unsafe at Any Speed* (1965) started the movement for auto safety and led in the course of the decade to the recall by manufacturers of thousands of defective cars. Subsequent Nader investigations uncovered conditions ranging from filth in meatpacking plants to air and water pollution to industrial price-fixing. Nader's example inspired a revival of the consumers' movement, moribund since New Deal days, resulting in truth-in-packaging, truth-in-lending, and auto-safety legislation; labeling of drugs by generic names; health warnings on cigarette packages; restrictions on cigarette advertising; and the establishment of the National Commission on Product Safety. Nader accompanied his brilliant guerrilla warfare against corporate iniquity with proposals for the democratization, decentralization, and federal chartering of corporations as well as "creative regulation" by strengthening the capacity of the "public citizen" to act against the corporation. In his insistence on high ethical standards and citizen responsibility as well as in his muckracking methods, Nader represented in some respects a throwback to the Progressive era at the start of the century; by embodying the notion of one man taking on the giant monopolies, he gave hope to many individuals in a new age dominated by the idea of powerlessness.

Automation. Manufacturing capacity grew by 165 percent in the twenty years after 1950, and output per man-hour increased 35 percent in the decade of the sixties alone. A significant contribution to this striking increase in productivity came from the development of the industrial techniques summed up in the word "automation." The basis of automation was the electronic computer. The first electric digital computer was built in 1946; and scientists and engineers rapidly explored the dazzling potentialities of what Norbert Wiener called "cybernetics," the science devoted to the study of communication and control mechanisms. The distinctive element in the industrial application of the computer was the introduction into the manufacturing sequence of self-regulating devices based on the "feedback" principle. The computer, once it had been programed, could absorb information that would enable it to continue, vary, or correct automatic operations. The computer promised to revolutionize every aspect of industry from research through production to marketing and to affect the methods of everyone from the engineer to the economist. In the short run it intensified problems of technological unemployment, but experts sharply disagreed on its longer-run impact.

Certainly one effect of automation was to direct employment toward the service sector of the economy. In the fifties white-collar workers began for the first time to outnumber blue-collar workers. By 1970 there were about 28 million workers employed in the production of goods as against over 46 million employed in the production of services (trade, transport, finance, education, health, government). Not all service workers were in fact removed from the blue-collar culture. Many had manual jobs (mail-carriers, janitors, garbage-collectors, supermarket clerks); some were wives of blue-collar workers. Nevertheless the fastest-growing occupational categories were professional and technical workers and managers, officials and proprietors. By 1970 these groups constituted a quarter of the labor force, and in 1971 the Labor Department estimated that by 1980 there would be as many professional and technical as blue-collar workers. Because organized labor could not keep up with the expansion of the service sector, membership in labor unions slowly declined as a proportion of nonfarm employment from 31.4 percent in 1960 to 27.9 percent (23 percent of the total labor force) in 1968.

The specialized requirements of the new technology contributed to the unprecedented expansion of the educational community. In 1970 more than 62 million Americans were students, teachers, or administrators as against about 48 million in 1960; educational costs increased in the same period from $27 billion to $70 billion a year. In 1940 only one-quarter of adults had a high-school education and only one-tenth attended college at all; by 1970, 55 percent were high-school graduates and 21 percent had completed some years of college. Among those from twenty-five to twenty-nine years old, 31 percent had gone to college as against 13 percent in 1940.

If such developments portended the enlargement of middle-class society, they showed little promise of lifting all Americans to the condition of middle-class beatitude. The slow but real tendency in the thirties and early forties toward a reduction in the inequality of income had come to a stop. After 1947 there were only slight changes in the distribution of income: the richest 1 percent continued to receive as much money as the poorest 20 percent; the richest 5 percent continued to receive as much as the poorest 40 percent. As the tax system became riddled with loopholes, taxation tapered off as a mechanism for serious redistribution. Public-sector spending, which some saw as the means of transferring income to the poor, did indeed save the very poor, but, on the whole, it built facilities used preponderantly by the middle class and financed predominantly by regressive taxes. The combination of high employment with antipoverty programs decreased the poverty

Communication and control

population by about 5 percent a year during the sixties; but in 1970 recession and inflation reversed the trend and actually increased the poverty population from 24.3 to 25.5 million. While this was a response to transient economic stringency, existing strategies had plainly failed to overcome the inflexibility of income distribution. Observers concluded that new measures of redistribution would be necessary if America was to make further progress toward an equalitarian society.

The ordeal of the city. Nearly all the 1969–70 increase in poverty was in urban areas; indeed, the disorders of industrial society were coming to a climax above all in the city. Poverty, racial tension, unequal and inadequate education, air and water pollution, the deterioration of municipal services, the choking of transportation, the collapse of the welfare system, the decay of public housing projects into slums, the ugly upsurge of crime, the spread of congestion, filth, drugs, alienation, and anger, the erosion of any lingering sense of community—all these made the city a central battlefield in the future of the nation.

In every major city white families fled such conditions for the suburbs. Metropolitan areas grew by about 15 percent during the sixties, but the suburbs gained 28 percent in population while the central cities gained only 1 percent. As late as 1940 only 27 million people had lived in suburbs. By 1970 more Americans lived in suburbs than in central cities— 75 million as against 62 million in the inner cities and 63 million in nonurban areas. Many suburbanites, blaming urban decay on the blacks, did their best to prevent black families from following their example, even burning down houses bought or rented by black newcomers. The myth of suburbia—ranch houses, green lawns, swimming pools, station wagons, lavish shopping centers—exerted a continuing appeal. But, with the pressure of migration, suburbs acquired their own forms of diversity and soon began to reproduce the problems of the inner city—pollution, blight, drugs, and crime.

As for the cities themselves, they became somewhat more black and brown in the sixties. Deserted by much of the middle class, populated more and more by the poor, they had fewer resources on which to draw at the very time that the need for ampler public facilities became more urgent. The property tax was both overburdened and regressive; municipal taxing powers were sometimes limited; the removal of business to the suburbs contracted the tax base; state legislatures, dominated by rural counties, were often indifferent. Education consumed 16 percent of municipal budgets and remained the most helpful means of social conciliation and improvement. But inner-city schools tended to be overcrowded and underequipped. The spread of *de facto* segregation and the chaotic family life in the ghettos undermined educational motivation. The drop-out rate was three times as high among black high-school students as among white. Many schools were demoralized by defeatism and paralyzed by drug addiction and random violence.

"Crime in the streets" became an issue in the 1964 presidential campaign; and, though many who invoked the phrase used it as a code word with which to incite emotion against blacks, no one could deny the sharp and disquieting rise in crime rates. By 1970 it was estimated that 10 million serious crimes were committed each year, of which 1.2 million were violent crimes. The homicide rate increased nearly 75 percent in the decade. More than 90 million firearms were in American households, of which 25 million were handguns, easily concealed in hip pockets. The United States comfortably outstripped all other modern democratic nations in its rates of homicide, assault, rape, and robbery. With 200 million people, America provided about fifty times as many gun murders every year as did England, Japan, and West Germany with their combined population of 214 million. Pressure for federal gun control, arising after the Kennedy assassination of 1963, resulted after the assassinations of Martin Luther King and Robert Kennedy in the passage of the Gun Control Act of 1968 restricting interstate and mail-order shipment of firearms to individuals. This law did little, however, to reduce the gun traffic; and, even though American states and

foreign nations with strict gun control laws had much lower gun murder rates, the Nixon Administration, for all its preoccupation with law and order, opposed stiffer national legislation.

The violent crime rate in the cities was eight times the rate on the countryside; the 26 cities with more than 500,000 inhabitants included only one-sixth of the nation's population but reported almost one-half the violent crimes. In 1960 violent crimes had been committed in cities of over 250,000 population at the rate of about 294 per 100,000 population; the rate increased to 773 per 100,000 by 1968. The crimes were characteristically committed by males between eighteen and twenty-four, generally poor, often drug addicts. The crime rate was naturally highest where poverty, drugs, discrimination, and unemployed youth converged: the ghetto. And, though some tried to suggest that violent crime was a form of race war committed by blacks against whites, the victims themselves, except in robberies, were typically male, young, poor, and black.

In 1969 the Commission on the Causes and Prevention of Violence predicted that, unless the nation awoke to the crisis of the cities, within a few years

> . . . central business districts . . . will be largely deserted except for police patrols during night-time hours. High rise apartment buildings and residential compounds protected by private guards and security devices will be fortified cells for upper-middle and high-income populations. . . . Ownership of guns will be almost universal in the suburbs; homes will be fortified by an array of devices from window grills to electronic surveillance equipment, armed citizen volunteers in cars will supplement inadequate police patrols. . . . Residential neighborhoods in the central city will be unsafe in differing degrees, and the ghetto slum neighborhoods will be places of terror with widespread crime, perhaps entirely out of police control during night-time hours.

In 1972 Stanley Kubrick's popular film *A Clockwork Orange* offered a horrific rendition of this vision of the urban future.

The troubles of Metropolis were compounded by the fact that it had begun to give way to Megalopolis. Cities wandered aimlessly into the surrounding countryside, generating suburbs and then exurbs, sprawling across

Ordeal of the city

municipal and even state frontiers, creating vast ungovernable urban regions, stretching from Boston to Washington, from Pittsburgh through Chicago to Milwaukee, from San Diego to San Francisco. With more than two out of every three Americans living in these regions, the government of cities had become the greatest challenge to the American political system.

Ninety years before, Bryce had pronounced municipal government to be "the one conspicuous failure of the United States." But after the Second World War municipal government had had a resurgence, attracting able men to city politics and administration. And, though the urban crisis was exceedingly grim, there were also grounds for hope. The establishment in Washington of the Department of Housing and Urban Development gave promise of increasing federal action. The Supreme Court decision on legislative apportionment in *Baker* v. *Carr* (1962) facilitated more equitable urban representation in state legislatures; and court decisions in 1972 requiring that educational costs be equalized throughout a state helped city schools. At the same time, the drop in the birthrate portended a drop in the number of school-children. With 70 percent of the blacks already in urban areas, migration from the countryside was nearing its end. The flight to the suburbs was reducing population density in urban areas—from 6,580 per square mile in 1920 to about 4,000 in 1970. Such developments created the possibility that in time the ordeal of the cities might undergo alleviation.

The permissive society. The ideological rebelliousness of the sixties seemed to have reached a point of exhaustion. After 1970 demonstrations were less frequent, the campuses quieted down, the great urban riots became a memory. The New Left itself declined in militancy, and even factions in the Weathermen and Black Panthers eschewed violence.

Several things brought about this change in mood. Some activists were undone by a sense of fatigue and futility; however often they demonstrated, the war still went on in Vietnam. Some were frightened by what the excursions into violence had revealed of their own potentiality for destructiveness. Some felt that the generation ahead had rejected too much: "How many things can you discard," a teacher observed in 1972, "before you have

a massive nervous breakdown? Which is just what we had in this country at the end of the decade." The fact that the draft was no longer a daily threat diminished concern about Vietnam, while the recession turned the worries of many of the young toward jobs. Moreover, the existence of a conservative national Administration discouraged protest, at least in the short run. When there was no receptivity to change, as in the fifties and the early seventies, only the highly committed continued to agitate for it; it required a time like the sixties, when the mood at the top favored change, for everyone to begin to clamor for it.

And, indeed, because the protest of the late sixties had had its measure of success, the seventies may have felt less need for further protest. After all, troops were coming back from Vietnam. Draft calls were diminishing. Blacks were gaining political and economic advancement. Colleges had democratized their procedures. In 1972 a presidential Commission on Marijuana and Drug Abuse, headed by a former Republican governor of Pennsylvania, even recommended the removal of criminal penalties for the private use of marijuana. Above all, the rebel mood had left its imprint in the increased tolerance of American society for a wide variety of idiosyncratic and unconventional behavior.

So far as people's dress, appearance, conduct, and life-style were concerned, there never had been a time when individual variations were more pronounced or individual choice was more unfettered. Men, so long the sober species, blossomed out in mustaches, beards, sideburns, and shoulder-length hair. Casting aside their traditional uniform, they wore anything from blue jeans and work shirts to cowboy boots and elaborately embroidered and ruffled jackets. Even business executives affected shirts of bold stripes and colors. For their part, women (and men too) reveled for a season in the miniskirt and, by rejecting the attempt of Paris designers in 1971 to order them into calf-length midiskirts, declared their independence of *haute couture*. Slacks, regrettably, became the casual wear of everyone from dowagers to hookers.

The same freedom extended to what had been historically the most sensitive of all problems for Americans—sex. The objective study of sexuality had gained new impetus from two works by the biologist Alfred Kinsey: *Sexual Behavior in the Human Male* (1948) and *Sexual Behavior of the Human Female*

(1953). The sexual act itself received unrelenting scrutiny from William Masters and Virginia Johnson in *Human Sexual Response* (1968). While sociologists doubted that even during the sixties there were great changes in American sexual practices, no one could doubt a vast change in public attitudes. The old inhibitions and reticences disappeared. Premarital relations, facilitated by the pill, were less concealed. "Shacking up" and other forms of trial marriage became not uncommon. By 1972 divorces granted per 1,000 marriages—had reached a new high of 455. Married couples sometimes indulged in "swinging"—that is, group intercourse with other couples. Homosexuals, male and female, came "out of the closet" to declare their identity.

The candid acceptance of sexuality as part of life transformed society's ideas of what was acceptable in books, on the stage, and on the screen. Joyce's *Ulysses,* though recognized as a classic, had actually been banned in the United States till 1933. Forty years later American novelists were routinely outdoing Joyce in uninhibitedness of situation and language, and a faithful film transcription of *Ulysses* was shown around the country almost without complaint. Pornographic favorites, like John Cleland's *Fanny Hill,* available for centuries only under the counter, were now freely distributed in paperback. Nudity burst out on the stage, and films displayed scenes of sex and violence in intense and sometimes obsessive detail. Hugh Hefner's popular magazine *Playboy* erected permissiveness into a cultural if not a moral principle, interspersing anatomical cartoons and photographs with crusading attacks on archaic sexual legislation.

The barriers of censorship crumbled away, at least in the large cities. Even the question of "hard-core" pornography, for which no artistic or social defense could be offered, remained in suspense as a result of an erratic series of Supreme Court decisions. A presidential Commission on Obscenity and Pornography, though its conclusions were sternly rejected by President Nixon, found little evidence that pornography was harmful to adults and recommended the repeal of laws that prohibited the distribution of pornographic materials to adults who wanted to receive them.

Some observers regarded the dissolution of old taboos as evidence of progress toward more healthy and authentic human rela-

tionships; others saw the "permissive society" as proof of moral collapse. Whatever the ultimate verdict, the United States had clearly become, in these matters at least, the freest country in the world—a fact hard to reconcile with the stereotype of America as a repressive and conformist society.

New impulses in religion. Religion also responded to the intellectual and social ferment. Here the "neo-orthodoxy" of Reinhold Niebuhr provided a strong vantage point from which to criticize the popular religiosity of the fifties. Where the Niebuhrians insisted on the independence of Christian faith from contemporary culture, the disciples of Norman Vincent Peale had identified faith with the values of contemporary society. Where one urged the church to reestablish transcendent norms, the other wanted faith to sanction the status quo. Niebuhr himself sharply criticized the notion that public avowals of religious concern constituted genuine religious belief. "The greatest corruption of all," he wrote, "is a corrupt religion." He agreed that religion could produce peace of soul, but not the peace of positive thoughts or of self-congratulation; true religion aimed rather at the "peace of God which passeth all understanding." "That peace passes understanding," added Niebuhr, "precisely because it is a peace with pain in it." The object of faith was to induce not contentment but contrition, not complacency but repentance.

Niebuhr and his Protestant associate Paul Tillich, along with the Catholic Jacques Maritain and the Jew Martin Buber, thus renewed the existential vision in religion. That is, they regarded the "human condition" as the starting point of theology and sought to base religion on the concreteness, uniqueness, and decisiveness of individual experience.

In this spirit a "new breed" of Christian clergymen plunged into the problems of American society, fighting for civil rights in Mississippi and Alabama, organizing welfare unions, tenants' councils, and rent strikes in the slums of Northern cities. Eugene Carson Blake, soon to become secretary general of the World Council of Churches, spoke for the new mood in Protestantism: "The Church must identify itself much more radically with the interests of the poor, the 'losers,' the outcasts and the alienated. . . . The mark of the presence of the awaited Messiah is still related to the poor having the Gospel preached to them and the captives being released."

Similar currents flowed through the Roman Catholic Church. The release of liberal energy brought about by Pope John XXIII and the Second Vatican Council wrought striking changes in what had long been a markedly conservative institution. Masses were of a sudden conducted in English; meat was eaten on Friday; nuns doffed their habits; priests questioned the rules on celibacy and birth control and left the priesthood in unprecedented numbers. The Catholic left, once embraced in Dorothy Day's doughty but tiny Catholic Worker Movement, now pervaded the Catholic community and, rallied by radical priests like Philip and Daniel Berrigan, challenged the state in resistance to the Indochina War. The Vatican Council also gave new impetus to ecumenism and, coming at a time when the American Church was in transition from an immigrant church to one fully accepted as part of American society, brought heartening collaboration among Catholics, Protestants, and Jews in the United States.

The new ferment had a deflating effect on the institutionalized religious boom of the fifties. A Gallup poll reported that only 23 percent of Americans in 1967 believed religion was increasing its influence in American life as against nearly 70 percent ten years earlier; and by 1972 only 40 percent of adults claimed church attendance in a typical week as against 49 percent in 1958. The religious spirit, more concerned now with religion as a means to experience than as a guide to morality, was taking new and sometimes disconcerting forms—from the "Jesus freaks" among the hippies through the Pentecostalists speaking in tongues to the witch covens and the satanists, not to mention the devotees of astrology, Zen Buddhism, and I Ching. All this indicated a flight from the religious orthodoxies of the fifties rather than a rejection of the religious impulse itself. Though much of this underground religious enthusiasm was anti-intellectual, there was also rigorous intellectual effort in the seminaries. The result might well be a more complex understanding of authentic religious experience—of peace with pain in it.

The quest for group identity: black America. The rebel mood of the sixties also left its imprint in the continued drive of submerged groups for justice and identity. More-over, despite the power of the great organizations, small groups and even individuals retained a capacity to throw monkey wrenches into the complex social machinery of modern life and bring it to a stop. In this respect, the skyjacker became a symbolic figure of the age. But far more important was the capacity of groups long denied full membership in American society to use the mass media, especially television, to convey and dramatize legitimate grievances.

The black population, whose rate of increase during the later sixties was about one-third higher than that of white Americans, amounted to 22 million in 1970, 11 percent of the national total. Median black family income increased 50 percent during the sixties but was still only three-fifths that of white families. Though the proportion of blacks living in poverty declined from one-half to one-third, the fact that five times as many whites as blacks escaped from poverty during the decade meant that blacks in 1972 constituted 32 percent of the nation's poor as against 26 percent in 1960. Moreover, the nonwhite unemployment rate in 1970 was almost twice that for whites, and black teenage unemployment in the ghettos was over 40 percent in 1971. The number of nonwhite families headed by women increased sharply to almost 30 percent of all nonwhite families by 1971.

On the other hand, more than half of young blacks had finished high school in 1970 as against just over a third in 1960; and education, combined with the growing white acknowledgment of black rights, brought about dramatic employment changes. Nonwhite professional and technical employment more than doubled, increasing at a much faster rate than white. In 1960 the median income of white male college graduates was 72 percent greater than that for comparably educated blacks; in 1970 the differential had almost disappeared for young graduates. Still, though gifted Negroes were in urgent demand in education, business, and government, the majority of black Americans had significantly less education, income, opportunity, and life expectancy than the average white American. And the growth in size and power of a black middle class was accompanied by a deepening gap between the educated and undereducated within the Negro community.

In the meantime, school desegregation in the South had made accelerating progress, partly because of court orders and partly because of powers conferred on the federal government by the Civil Rights Act of 1964 to institute suits against noncomplying school districts and to deny them federal funds. Though the Nixon Administration was a good deal less ardent in using these powers than its predecessor, the momentum of the changes meant that by 1971 the public schools of the South were more integrated than those of the North in the sense that a smaller proportion of black students were attending all-black schools and a larger proportion were in schools with a white majority.

The requirements of the "southern strategy," however, led the Nixon Administration not only to Southern white appointments to the Supreme Court but to a slowdown in the use of federal funds as a means of hastening desegregation. Nixon himself displayed particular resistance to busing as a means of achieving a measure of racial integration. Actually 19.6 million school-children—42 percent of all those in elementary or secondary schools—were bused to school throughout the country every day; it was the way most children outside cities got to school; and the proportion of children riding buses to school in the Deep South was less than 3 percent above the national average. Before 1954 black children were bused, often for long distances, in order to achieve racial segregation. And in April 1971 a unanimous Supreme Court speaking through Chief Justice Burger in the case of *Swann* v. *Charlotte-Mecklenburg Board of Education* upheld reasonable busing as a means of dismantling dual school systems. Nonetheless, in extreme cases busing raised real problems, especially when children were bused from good and safe school districts to inferior and hazardous schools.

Opposition to busing did not mean opposition to desegregated schools: even 58 percent of Southern whites, according to a Gallup poll in 1972, favored educational integration. The "white backlash" of anger against blacks, so long predicted as the consequence of the pressure for racial change, had not appeared. Nonetheless in many places busing was the only way by which integration could be achieved; and the bus' rising unpopularity, played upon by politicians like George Wallace of Alabama, became a weapon against integration itself. It soon led to a movement, carried forward with increasing determination by the Nixon Administration, to eliminate busing in the integration process. Enthusiasts

even sought a constitutional amendment for this purpose. Nixon's antibusing proposals in 1972 withdrew the Presidency, and sought to withdraw the courts, from the struggle against school segregation.

Busing became a symbolic issue as the nation pondered the decision whether to fulfill or to relax the commitment to desegregation. Evidence of a retreat to the supposedly repudiated "separate but equal" doctrine produced mixed reactions in the black community. Black separatists, like Roy Innes and the Congress of Racial Equality (CORE), joined the opposition to busing. But black nationalism was taking a more moderate form in the seventies. Major apostles of violence had left the scene—Stokely Carmichael to Ghana, Eldridge Cleaver to Algeria—and the Black Panthers were split into bitterly warring factions. Moreover, there were no major ghetto riots for some years after 1968, whether because it was apparent that blacks themselves were the main victims or because the unsympathetic attitude of the Nixon Administration reduced the payoffs for militancy. And, as Harold Cruse had written in *The Crisis of the Negro Intellectual,* "While the nationalist wing may criticize the integrationist aims in life, the integrationists at least have a program which (the impact of Malcolm X notwithstanding) the nationalists do not."

In the meantime, blacks had been making significant gains in conventional politics. In 1962 there were four in the House of Representatives; in 1970 there were thirteen, as well as the first black senator since Reconstruction, and two hundred five blacks in state legislatures, seventy-three in the South. Blacks served as mayors of Cleveland, Gary, Newark, and other cities, North and South. Moreover, black political action had a promising future not only in large Northern cities but in the South itself, where one hundred two counties had black majorities. The prospect of progress through politics brought together nationalists with political leaders in the National Black Political Convention at Gary, Indiana, in early 1972. Under the chairmanship of Imamu Baraka (LeRoi Jones) black leaders from Jesse Jackson of Chicago, the heir of Martin Luther King, to the Panther Bobby Seale called for an "independent black political movement" dedicated to "the creation of our own black life." Such separatist aspirations roused the concern of the NAACP, still the most influential black organization, and of

The official, announced position of the Black Political Convention favors a separate black nation or separate racial enclaves within the United States; the theory of Negro withdrawal from the American political process is implicit or explicit in every major Convention proposal. The NAACP, on the other hand, was organized to win for non-white citizens complete equality within the American system....

In instance after instance, the [National Black Political] Agenda spells out its separatist and nationalist intent by specific calls for black control of all the economic, social and political agencies, undertakings and institutions presently to be found in the black communities and neighborhoods. At almost no point does the Agenda also demand an equitable black share of control in institutions and agencies now controlled and dominated by whites. Yet these are the real repositories of American wealth and power. In foregoing a share of them, Negro Americans would sell themselves short; in focusing all its concern upon controlling the meager, poverty-ridden institutions of the ghetto, the Agenda would fetter black America forever into the poorest and least influential sectors of the national life.

From Roy Wilkins, Letter to the Three Cochairmen of the National Black Political Convention, May 3, 1972.

Black power: integration or separatism?

---

integrationist leaders. Still, if nationalism seemed for a time a dominant mood among Negro activists, most blacks evidently embraced it as a means to the achievement of a multiracial society, not as an alternative to such a society.

Chicanos, Puerto Ricans, and Indians.

The second-largest minority in the United States in 1970 consisted of Spanish-speaking peoples—9.2 million in all according to the census (some authorities believed this a considerable underestimate), including 5.1 million of Mexican origin, 1.4 million Puerto Ricans, and the rest mostly from Latin America and the Philippines. Of this population 61 percent lived in the five southwestern states. Spanish-speaking enclaves had survived in New Mexico for nearly five centuries, and for many decades Mexicans had entered the United States—often illegally, as "wetbacks" (so-called because they swam the Rio Grande to avoid immigration barriers)—to satisfy the need for cheap agricultural labor. But it was not till after the Second World War that the Mexican-Americans, who in the sixties called themselves proudly "Chicanos," began to act as a conscious minority.

Most lived below the poverty line, often in the "barrios" of cities like Los Angeles. Family income was about 70 percent of the national average, and schooling was both limited and,

for linguistic reasons, frustrating. Nevertheless pride in their history and traditions facilitated the quest for identity. In California, Cesar Chavez and his United Farm Workers improved the wages and working conditions of migrant farm-laborers. In New Mexico, Reies Lopez Tijerina tried to reclaim land grants that "Anglos" had long since wangled from the original owners. In Texas, Jose Angel Gutierrez formed a political party, *La Raza Unida*. John F. Kennedy was the first President to recognize the Chicanos, and his brother Robert, a friend of Chavez, received their impassioned support.

The Puerto Rican population on the mainland rose by 55 percent in the sixties, with more than three-fifths living in New York City. In 1970 New York elected its first Puerto Rican congressman, Herman Badillo. The brilliant musical show *West Side Story* (1957), adapting the Romeo and Juliet theme to "rumbles" between Puerto Rican street gangs, won a sympathetic hearing for that minority's problems in the larger community. Hardworking and religious, the Puerto Ricans showed considerable aptitude for assimilation, though Puerto Rican nationalists insisted on the identity of Boricua culture.

The oldest Americans, the Indians, no longer seemed the vanishing Americans. As a result of public health improvements, the Indian population was growing four times as fast as the population as a whole, more than

Cesar Chavez

We, the first Americans, come to the Congress of the United States that you give us the chance to try to solve what you call the Indian problem. You have had two hundred years and you have not succeeded by your standards. It is clear that you have not succeeded in ours.... We ask you, as the representatives of the people of the United States, to serve as our representatives too—to help us see that assurances do not become empty promises. And, if necessary, to enact legislation which will create such a process where Indians can really shape government policy and control their own lives and destinies....

The present [congressional] committees have pushed for termination, and have fostered on Congress seemingly neutral and technical legislation, under the guise of Indian expertise, which has taken away our land, our water rights, our mineral resources and handed them over to the white man. You have been duped—as we have been duped. These committees have created a monstrous bureaucracy insensitive to Indians which trembles and cringes before them.... We know you are highly conscious of your national obligations when you deliberate on such problems as the war in Viet Nam. We know that you have even taken those obligations seriously enough to go to Viet Nam in order to personally inform yourself on how the Executive carries out the commitments of the United States. We ask that you do no less at home—for the United States has made older and more sacred commitments to the people who have occupied these shores for twenty-five thousand years.... In essence, we ask the restoration of what you claimed at the founding of your nation—the inalienable right to pursue happiness.

From the American Indian Task Force, Statement to Congress, November 12, 1969.

---

doubling between 1950 to 1970. Of the eight hundred thousand Indians of the early seventies, half lived in the West and a quarter in the South. Slightly more than half lived on reservations; most of the rest lived in cities. Wherever they lived, they tended to be the poorest of the poor, at the end of the line in employment, income, education, and health. The suicide rate among Indians was one hundred times that among whites.

National policy toward the Indians continued to vacillate between the goals of assimilation and autonomy. The policy established under the New Deal by John Collier to encourage "a self-governing self-determination" and to revitalize tribal government was rejected by Congress after the Second World War. The new policy, crystallized in a congressional resolution of 1953, had the ultimate goal of "termination"—that is, liquidating the reservation system, dismantling the tribes, removing special federal protection and services, and hoping that Indians could somehow fend for themselves as individuals in white society. In the meantime, the Bureau of Indian Affairs in Washington continued to be

a white agency governing reservation Indians according to highly paternalistic principles.

The Kennedy Administration arrested the termination process and began to move tentatively toward self-determination. Under Johnson the Economic Opportunity Act gave Indians the right to propose and administer antipoverty programs on reservations—an experience that led Indian activists to demand comparable control of all federal programs on reservations. Inspired in part by the black example, Indians began to develop nationalist organizations. The National Congress of American Indians (NCAI), founded during the Second World War (in which twenty-five thousand Indians had served in the armed forces), became more militant; and the National Indian Youth Council, founded in 1961, organized demonstrations on behalf of Indian rights. Soon Indian activists were talking about "red power"; in November 1969 an Indian group dramatized their case by occupying Alcatraz Island, a former federal prison site in San Francisco Bay. A number of books—notably *Custer Died for Your Sins* (1969) by Vine Deloria, Jr., a Standing Rock Sioux and a former executive director of the NCAI, and Dee Brown's *Bury My Heart at Wounded Knee* (1971)—brought the Indian case to the larger public. By the end of the decade, in films like *Little Big Man* (1970), Indians began to appear as the victims rather than the villains of the West, often cruelly massacred by whites rather in the manner of My Lai.

Nevertheless neither the Kennedy nor the Johnson Administrations, in great part because of the resistance of the congressional committees dealing with Indian affairs, explicitly abandoned the ultimate goal of Indian assimilation. As late as 1970 only 1.5 percent of the Department of the Interior's Indian programs were under Indian control. But the Nixon Administration, in one of its notable achievements, set in motion the process of Indianizing the Indian Bureau, asked Congress to repeal the termination resolution of 1953, and proclaimed "self-determination without termination" as the new national policy. In 1970 the Zūnis of New Mexico became the first tribe to assume control of their own affairs.

Women's liberation. The black experience inspired not only other ethnic minorities but a diversity of social groups to revolt against the roles in which they felt American society had cast them, roles that, they believed, demeaned their status and falsified their identity. Students, blue-collar workers, convicts, homosexuals—all began to organize against what they conceived as the psychic aggression of the social order. Most powerful of all was the revolt of the only minority that, in fact, constituted a majority of Americans—women— who, outnumbered by men in 1940, exceeded the male population by nearly 5.5 million (mostly in the over-sixty category) thirty years later. As the original women's rights movement was a spinoff from abolitionism (see p. 450), so the women's liberation movement of the seventies was a spinoff from the movement for civil rights.

To American males this revolt came as a surprise. They had long been accustomed to hearing from foreigners that America was, in effect, a matriarchy. In comic strips Maggie was always chasing Jiggs with a rolling-pin. Philip Wylie's much-read and lively polemic *Generation of Vipers* (1942) had contended that from mother to teacher to wife to daughter the American male was systematically castrated by his women and that "momism" was the besetting sin of American life. In some sense this may have been true, but the power of the American woman was exercised by stealth and subterfuge from a position of weakness.

The earlier feminist agitations had gained women a measure of legal identity and, in due course, the right to vote. But all indexes showed them remaining in secure social and economic inferiority. Women were the weaker sex, their place was the home, their destiny to serve their husband and children. When they struck out on their own, most professions (except for elementary-school teaching, nursing, and librarianships) resisted them. Shirley Chisholm, the first black congresswoman, said she was subjected to more discrimination as a woman than as a black. Women constituted more than 51 percent of the population but 7.6 percent of the nation's doctors (and only 1 percent of the general surgeons); 1 percent of the members of the American Institute of Architects; and 9 percent of the full professors on university faculties. Of the 325,000 lawyers in the United States, 9,000—2.8 percent—were women in 1970; all but one of the 97 federal appeals court judges and all but four of the 402 federal district court judges were men. The average earnings of a woman college graduate were about the same as those of a man with an eighth-grade education. Only 7 percent of working-women earned more than $10,000, as against 40 percent of working-men.

And in some respects the position of women was getting worse. The feminist movement of the early twentieth century had stimulated many able women to seek careers. The example of Eleanor Roosevelt and Frances Perkins in the thirties, the participation of women in the Second World War as WACs and WAVEs and as workers in munitions plants—all this had strengthened the image of the self-reliant woman. But in the forties and fifties the tide had turned, as the tide turned against the Negro after Reconstruction. By 1960 women were receiving a smaller proportion of university degrees than in 1930; their median earnings relative to similarly employed men were declining; in 1971 the percentage of women in managerial and proprietorial jobs was lower than in 1960.

It was against this background that a Commission on the Status of Women, set up by Kennedy in 1961, began to document the discriminations and disabilities to which

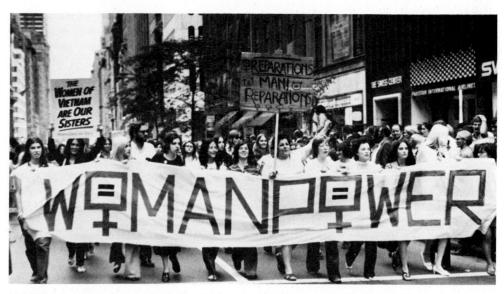

Majority rights

women were subjected. Then Betty Friedan in her influential book *The Feminine Mystique* (1963) called on women to recognize what society was doing to them and urged them to reclaim their identities. Finding even the civil-rights groups and the New Left dominated by "male chauvinism," Friedan and others established the National Organization for Women (NOW) in 1966. The chief recruiting instrument for women's liberation was the "consciousness-raising" group, where women in towns across the land met in "rap sessions" to reflect on their lives. This activity raised the consciousness of many men too, startled to discover the manifold ways in which male condescension and female subordination were built into the structure and language of society.

NOW, which became the NAACP of the women's movement, concentrated on economic and social issues: an equal-rights amendment; equal pay for equal work; the abolition of sexual discrimination in employment; child-care centers; equal access to education and the professions; and birth control and abortion. In 1972 the National Women's Political Caucus ("Women! Make policy not coffee") sought to enlarge female participation in politics. NOW and NWPC worked within the system, and their goals commanded support from most Americans. Men were increasingly prepared to take a larger share in child-rearing and household tasks; some, noting that "Mr." as a title did not reveal whether or not a man was married,

were even willing to acquiesce in "Ms." as a substitute for both "Miss" and "Mrs."

But women's liberation also generated various forms of revolutionary feminism based on the idea that through history men, as the master class, were propelled by *machismo* to war and tyranny, that racism and imperialism were the consequences of male supremacy, and that, as a consequence (in the words of Robin Morgan), "we women must seize control over our own lives and try, in the process, to salvage the planet from ecological disaster and nuclear threat created by male-oriented power nations." In this more drastic mood militants saw marriage as a condition where the husband was a rapist, the wife a prostitute, and family responsibility an enslavement. As an interim measure, they proposed "marriage contracts" spelling out household roles and obligations. Some moved on to attack the "nuclear family" itself, hoping to replace it by an extended family structure with the collective raising of children.

Some observers believed that revolutionary feminism was essentially an enthusiasm of young, educated, middle-class women and that its failure to find a convincing place for the rearing of children doomed it to futility. Most women continued to think that taking care of a home and family was more rewarding than having a job—by 71 to 16 percent in a Harris poll of 1970. But in its more moderate version women's liberation had indeed altered the consciousness of American society, had greatly increased male sensitivity to fe-

We, men and women who hereby constitute ourselves as the National Organization for Women, believe that the time has come for a new movement toward true equality for all women in America, and toward a fully equal partnership of the sexes, as part of the world-wide revolution of human rights now taking place within and beyond our national borders....

WE REJECT the current assumption that a man must carry the sole burden of supporting himself, his wife, and family, and that a woman is automatically entitled to lifelong support by a man upon her marriage, or that marriage, home and family are primarily woman's world and responsibility—hers, to dominate—his to support. We believe that a true partnership between the sexes demands a different concept of marriage, an equitable sharing of the responsibilities of home and children and of the economic burdens of their support....

IN THE INTERESTS OF THE HUMAN DIGNITY OF WOMEN, we will protest, and endeavor to change, the false image of women now prevalent in the mass media, and in the texts, ceremonies, laws, and practices of the major social institutions. Such images perpetuate contempt for women by society and by women for themselves.... WE BELIEVE THAT women will do most to create a new image of women by acting now, and by speaking out in behalf of their own equality, freedom, and human dignity—not in pleas for special privilege, nor in enmity toward men, who are also victims of the current, half-equality between the sexes —but in an active, self-respecting partnership with men.

From the National Organization for Women, Statement of Purpose, 1966.

Women on the march

---

male frustrations, and had encouraged in women themselves new purposes of self-reliance and personal responsibility.

By the early seventies barriers to female participation were falling throughout American society. Forty-three percent of all adult women, including a third of all married women, were in the labor force. The proportion of women in higher education and the professions was growing. In March 1972 the Senate approved the Equal Rights Amendment, completing an effort that had begun in 1923. This amendment—it would be the Twenty-seventh when ratified—wrote into the Constitution the rule that "equality of rights under the law shall not be denied or abridged by the United States or by any state on account of sex."

Literature and art. America of the seventies, a more highly educated society than ever before, read more books than ever before. Book sales of nearly $3 billion in 1970—$1.2 billion more than in 1963—included 400 million paperbacks, two for every person in the country. If many bought lurid best sellers by authors like Irving Wallace, Harold Rob-

bins, and Jacqueline Susann, serious writing was also finding unprecedented markets.

In the novel the quest for regional and ethnic self-definition in the unstable mass society was a pervading theme. The tradition of Southern writing, intensified and elaborated by Faulkner in the twenties and thirties, was continued by Robert Penn Warren of Tennessee, notably in *All the King's Men* (1946), his novel about Huey Long's Louisiana, and by writers of the next generation—William Styron of Virginia, whose *Confessions of Nat Turner* (1967) was the moving attempt of a Southern white to come to a reckoning with the historical fact of slavery; Walker Percy of Mississippi; and the exquisite women writers Eudora Welty of Mississippi and Flannery O'Connor of Georgia.

In the North the white Anglo-Saxon Protestant tradition of the novel of manners, exemplified in the older generation by the astute satire of J. P. Marquand and the sardonic realism of James Gould Cozzens, was also carried on by a new generation. But the age of Anglo-Saxon dominance was receding; the younger writers—John Cheever, especially in *The Wapshot Chronicle* (1957) and in probing short stories, John Updike in *Rabbit, Run* (1960), *Couples* (1968), and *Rabbit Redux* (1971), and, more in the older school, Louis Auchincloss—portrayed the WASP at bay in an increasingly heterogeneous and bewildering society. The stories and novels of Joyce Carol Oates caught with eerie intensity the hysteria under the surface of middle-class American life.

The newer ethnic groups found their own chroniclers. Edwin O'Connor, especially in his irresistible novel of Boston politics *The Last Hurrah* (1956) and in *All in the Family* (1966), and J. F. Powers in *Morte D'Urban* (1962) recorded the assimilation of the Irish into middle-class American life. Mario Puzo dealt with the Italian-Americans in *The Dark Arena* (1955) and in his best seller *The Godfather* (1969). Richard Wright's *Native Son* (1940) was a powerful rendition of the fate of the American black; and Ralph Ellison's *Invisible Man* (1952), one of the distinguished novels of the period, displayed in forceful terms the struggle of the Negro for visibility in American society. James Baldwin in a series of books played upon the agony of two minorities—blacks and homosexuals.

Most striking of all was the emergence of a gifted generation of Jewish novelists. Coming from a rich traditional culture, afflicted by historical and contemporary woes, the best writers in this school not only offered vivid annotations of Jewish-American life but spoke in some sense for all minorities in the quest for identity. Philip Roth in *Goodbye, Columbus* (1959) and *Portnoy's Complaint* (1969) combined a merciless novelist's eye with sharp comic and mimetic instincts. Bernard Malamud fabulized Jewish urban life in a series of piquant fantasies. J. D. Salinger's tales about the Glass family, especially in *Franny and Zooey* (1961), explored the possibilities of mysticism and sainthood in an affluent society.

In *The Catcher in the Rye* (1951) Salinger also portrayed an adolescent crisis of identity—Huck Finn at an Eastern prep school—in terms that spoke arrestingly to a whole generation. And two other Jewish writers, Saul Bellow and Norman Mailer, transcended their cultural base to deal in large terms with the incoherence and anguish of contemporary life as, indeed, did Styron, Welty, Mary McCarthy, and other novelists from different perspectives. Joyce Carol Oates formulated the common effort: "I have tried to give a shape to certain obsessions of mid-

century Americans—a confusion of love and money, of the categories of public and private experience, of a demonic urge I sense all around me, an urge to violence as the answer to all problems, an urge to self-annihilation as the ultimate experience and the ultimate surrender. The use of language is all we have to pit against death and silence."

No American novelist dealt more searchingly with contemporary man than Bellow in such novels as *The Adventures of Augie March* (1953), *Seize the Day* (1954), *Herzog* (1964), and *Mr. Sammler's Planet* (1970). A writer of enormous and diverse gifts, he was the artist of the dialectic between inner consciousness and external society—the predicament of "civilized people" of whom his character Herzog said, "What they love is an imaginary human situation invented by their own genius and which they believe is the only true and the only human reality." But, where Bellow looked on the ravages of modernity with increasing distaste, his younger and less finished contemporary Mailer plunged truculently into the swirl around him.

Novelist, poet, journalist, film director and actor, political aspirant, pugilist, male chauvinist, showman, public personality, the spoiled and symptomatic talent of his time, Mailer saw art as, above all, the precipitate of minority experience. "What characterizes the sensations of being a member of a minority group," he wrote,

> is that one's emotions are forever locked in the chains of ambivalence—the expression of an emotion forever releasing its opposite—the ego in perpetual transit from the tower to the dungeon and back again. By this definition nearly everyone in America is a member of a minority group, alienated from the self by a double sense of identity and so at the mercy of a self which demands action and more action to define the most rudimentary borders of identity.

Though by the sixties some critics believed Mailer more comfortable in his nonfiction, like *The Armies of the Night* (1968) and *Of a Fire on the Moon* (1970), his highly charged reporting was of a piece with the vision of the American experience conveyed brilliantly in his novel *Why Are We in Vietnam?* (1967) and less successfully in *An American Dream* (1965). The tension between rationality and irrationality, between the public act and the underground emotion, fascinated him; and though he himself wondered whether his "vision, for lack of some cultivation in the middle, was not too compulsively ready for the apocalyptic," no writer sought a more direct confrontation with the existential risks of American art.

More extreme novelists like William Burroughs, *The Naked Lunch* (1959), tried to force consciousness to its outermost limits of self-debasement and destruction. And the parallel development of "black humor" moved into a phase of exuberant if savage anarchism, well typified in Joseph Heller's war novel, *Catch-22* (1961), and concluded in nihilism with the sadistic "sick joke" and deliberate attempts, in the manner of Lennie Bruce, to become as wounding to as many people and groups as possible, exercises redeemed only by an evident component of self-loathing.

The cultural vibrations ran through poetry, where Robert Lowell in *Life Studies* (1959) and *For the Union Dead* (1964) registered the impact of an incoherent age on a Puritan sensibility, and where Sylvia Plath expressed the terror of women in a world of treacherous men. The best drama of the period, Eugene O'Neill's *A Long Day's Journey into Night*, was produced in 1956 but written fifteen years before. Arthur Miller revived the social drama in strong and somber plays like *Death of a Salesman* (1949); and such dramas as Tennessee Williams' *A Streetcar Named Desire* (1947) and Edward Albee's *Who's Afraid of Virginia Woolf?* (1962) concentrated with brilliant if cold effect on the pathology of modern life. In due course new currents struck the drama when the "theater of the absurd" of Ionesco and the "theater of cruelty" of Artaud came from Europe to stimulate American playwrights off Broadway, if not on.

Andy Warhol: "Campbell's Soup Can," 1965

Other arts were affected by the tendencies toward anarchy and nihilism. In painting, abstract expressionism superseded for a season the representational art of an earlier time. Jackson Pollock, who had died little known in 1956, was now taken up as the forerunner of an attempt to give the tensions of contemporary culture their objective correlative in color and design. In the sixties "pop art" sought to discover artistic significance in the commercial artifacts of contemporary civilization. Meantime John Cage and other composers explored the possibilities of various experimental forms of music.

The velocity of history

The electronic society. The artistic sensibility itself seemed to be in a stage of profound dissociation. The Canadian Marshall McLuhan, a professional literary critic and amateur anthropologist, ascribed this condition to the basic shift that, in his view, Western civilization was undergoing as it moved from a typographical to an electronic culture. Where Marx had located the motive force of history in changes in the means of production,

McLuhan located it in changes in the means of communication.

Thus the prevailing sensibility, he suggested, had been created by the print media, which gave experience a frame and viewed it in sequence and from a distance. Its distinctive qualities were logic, precision, specialization, individualism. But the modern world, and America first of all, was moving from the mechanical to the electronic age—the fantastic new epoch of electronic mechanisms of information, feedback and control, foreshadowed by television, the computer, and the space satellite. In the new age, McLuhan wrote, "Everything descends upon us from everywhere all at once. . . . The contained, the distinct, the separate—our western legacy—are being replaced by the flowing, the unified, the fused." The oncoming modes of communication, founded on instantaneity, simultaneity, and collectivity, promised to alter the very reflexes of psychological reaction and expectation. Where the print culture had programed the mind in a one-at-a-time, step-by-step way, the electronic culture undermined linear processes of thought, replacing one-at-a-time by all-at-once. Though the terms of McLuhan's argument were often extravagant, there remained the possibility that, beneath the hyperbole and the showmanship, he was onto a significant and fertile truth.

Certainly the movement into the electronic age accentuated the gap between generations. Those born after 1950 were the first generation to grow up in the electronic environment and therefore may well have differed more from their parents than the older generation differed from its great-grandparents; all previous generations in the United States had been conditioned by the same linear culture. Indeed, as the pace of change intensified, the experience of the parents became less and less relevant to the needs of the children, and parents therefore were decreasingly effective as models and authorities. Some observers even saw the old condemned by the whirl of history to become strangers in the land of the young.

The electronic age also contributed to the increasing instability of American politics. For a century a cluster of agencies—the political machine, the farm organization, the trade union, the chamber of commerce, the ethnic federation—had, in effect, mediated between the politician and the voter, interceding for each on behalf of the other and providing the links that held the party system together. Electronic innovations were now severing these links and bypassing the traditional political structure. Television presented the politicians directly to the voter; public opinion polls presented the voter directly to the politician; and neither felt the need to consult the power-brokers.

As voters increasingly made their own judgments on the basis of what they themselves saw on the tiny screen, party loyalties, once as sacred as religious affiliations, lost their grip. Beginning in the fifties, voters began to use both parties for their own purposes, thus balancing off a Republican President with a Democratic Congress. Ticket-splitting took place on less than one-fifth of the ballots in 1950; by 1970 tickets were split on more than one-half. In 1920 only 3.2 percent of congressional districts voted one party for President and another for the House of Representatives; by 1968 the figure had grown tenfold to 32.4 percent. The proportion of voters describing themselves as "independent" increased strikingly in the sixties to nearly one-third of the total electorate and nearly one-half among the young. The proportion of activists—those taking a direct part in campaign activities—also increased and more and more found its expression outside the party machinery. What the political analyst Samuel Lubell called the "struggle for political visibility" became a means by which an unprecedentedly demanding electorate enforced its demands. Lubell saw "a war of the voters against the party system." Some observers expected a trend toward multiple parties and minority victors; others even began to speculate about a "politics without parties." Whether or not the two-party system was in dissolution, no one could deny that it was in crisis.

The law of acceleration. The salient fact of the modern age was the increasing instability of the world dominated by the cumulative momentum of science and technology. Henry Adams had been the first American historian to note the transcendent significance of the ever-quickening acceleration in the velocity of history. "The world did not [just] double or treble its movement between 1800 and 1900," he wrote in "The Rule of Phase Applied to History" (1909), "but, measured by any standard known to science—by horsepower, calories, volts, mass in any shape—the tension and vibration and volume and so-called progression of society were fully a thousand times greater in 1900 than in 1800." And the pace of change, urged ever onward by the self-accelerating internal processes of scientific inquiry, increased exponentially in the twentieth century when, it was noted, of all the scientists who had ever lived in the history of the planet, 90 percent were alive and active. Annual expenditures for re-

I cannot say I believe that there is life out there. All I can say is that there are a number of reasons to think it is possible and that we have at our command the means of finding out. Those two things being the case, I would be very ashamed of my civilization if we did not try to find out.

From Professor Carl Sagan, Cornell University, quoted in *Time,* December 13, 1971.

Should we seek out life in space?

A thousand, or ten thousand, years of evolutionary difference is just nothing on cosmic scales; and the chances that we could come across another civilisation in the Universe at approximately the same level of development—and with which we could effect some kind of intellectual understanding—are, therefore, vanishingly small. And such being the case, what gain ... could we hope to derive from contacts with hypothetical civilisations which are likely to be removed, not thousands, but millions or hundred millions of years from our level? Certainly the risks entailed in such an encounter would vastly exceed any possible interest—let alone benefit; and could easily prove fatal. Therefore, should we ever hear that "space-phone" ringing in the form of observational evidence which may admit of no other explanation, for God's sake let us not answer; but rather make ourselves as inconspicuous as we can to avoid attracting attention.

From Professor Zdenek Kopal, University of Manchester, quoted in the London *Telegraph,* March 3, 1972.

---

search and development (R&D) rose from $6.3 billion in 1955 to $27.9 billion in 1971. During this period 50 to 60 percent of R&D funds came from the federal government (and during most of the period 40 to 55 percent of the outlays went to defense and space projects).

The most spectacular expression of the onward drive of science and technology came in man's leap into space. By the end of 1971, a short fifteen years after Sputnik, America and Russia had launched 1,425 space missions (of which 764 were American) and were sending out about three spacecraft per week. Kennedy's old idea of joint American-Russian orbital flights was ratified at the Moscow summit in 1972. The development of space-shuttle rocket-planes would soon make space-flights almost routine. The course of the seventies was further expected to produce "skylabs" and space stations and bring closer the world portrayed by Stanley Kubrick in his haunting film *2001, A Space Odyssey* (1968).

Already the exploration of the moon had produced new knowledge about the formation and evolution of the solar system 3 to 5 billion years ago; the radar mapping of the surfaces of Mars and Venus had begun; and an unmanned spacecraft had been launched toward Jupiter. As the space probes went forward, the question was ever more insistently raised whether earthlings were alone in the universe. Finding evidence that the chemical elements basic to life existed beyond the earth's solar system, scientists worked on means to communicate with other intelligences in the universe. In September 1971 American radio astronomers, physicists, and biologists joined colleagues from the Soviet Union and other nations at Byurakan Astrophysical Observatory in Soviet Armenia for the world's first Conference on Communication with Extra-Terrestrial Intelligence. With every passing year, scientists around the world watched ever more urgently for signals from the sky, wondering what nature of being might be on similar watch in remote and unknown planets, what forms of intelligence, perhaps immeasurably superior forms, might exist in the cold reaches of galactic space.

On earth, science was thrusting forward into the very bases of human life. The discovery in 1953 of the double-helical shape of deoxyribonucleic acid (DNA), for which the American James D. Watson and the Englishmen F. H. C. Crick and Maurice Wilkins received the Nobel Prize (1962), gave extraordinary new impetus to the field of molecular biology. The unveiling of the genetic code provided new insight into basic life processes and held out

*The case for
no growth*

The total rate by which men exploit the earth's ecosystem has some upper limit; if this rate is exceeded, the system will eventually be driven to collapse. Hence, all productive systems must eventually reach a no-growth condition—at least with respect to the accumulation of capital goods designed to exploit the ecosystem, and the products that these yield.... My own judgment, based on the evidence now at hand, is that the present course of environmental degradation, at least in industrialized countries, represents such a serious challenge to essential ecological systems that if it is continued it will destroy the ability of the environment to support a reasonably civilized human society. Some number of human beings might well survive such a catastrophe, for the collapse of civilization would reduce the pace of environmental degradation. What would then remain would be a kind of neobarbarism....

The world is being carried to the brink of ecological disaster not by a single fault, which some clever scheme could correct, but by a phalanx of powerful economic, technological, and social forces. What is required is nothing less than a change in the course of history.... Human beings have broken out of the circle of life, driven not by biological need but by the social organizations that they have devised to ''conquer'' nature. Once more, in order to survive, we must close the circle. We must learn to restore to nature the wealth we borrow from it.

From Barry Commoner, *The Closing Circle*, 1971.

---

possibilities not only for the cure of genetic diseases but for test-tube babies and for ''cloning''—that is, the production of genetically identical copies of individual human beings. In addition, scientists might soon develop the capacity through genetic surgery to alter man's genetic makeup. Scientists also saw the possibility of remolding not only man's body but his mind, if not through genetic engineering, then through drugs, psychosurgery (operation on the brain in order to modify behavior), electrochemical controls, or the system of behavioral conditioning and reinforcements set forth by the psychologist B. F. Skinner.

DNA molecule

Within a generation science had begun to devise the means to transform reproduction, consciousness, intellect, behavior, and the very genetic nature of man. These developments, opening frightening vistas of manipulation and control by white-coated Dr. Strangeloves, increased public suspicion of science; between 1966 and 1972, according to one poll, the proportion of Americans professing respect for the scientific community dropped from 56 to 32 percent. Scientists themselves recoiled from some of the consequences of their work. James D. Watson,

reflecting on his clarification of the genetic code, called in 1971 for an end to experimentation with human cell fusion and embryos: ''If we do not think about the matter now, the possibility of our having a free choice will one day suddenly be gone.'' Watson added that the idea science always moves forward ''represents a form of laissez-faire nonsense dismally reminiscent of the creed that American business, if left to itself, will solve everybody's problems.''

If science and technology could not be left to themselves, they had to be brought under forms of social and ethical control. Leading scientists now helped found the Institute of Society, Ethics and Life to consider the moral problems raised by scientific success, while in 1972 Congress moved toward the establishment of a National Advisory Commission on Health Science and Society as well as an Office of Technology Assessment.

The critique of growth. Nowhere was control more fervently advocated than by those determined to save and restore the natural environment. The accelerating rate of technological change, combined with population growth and the expanding demands of an

The case for growth

affluent society, produced by the late sixties an incipient ecological crisis. The fact that the ecological problem did not become acute until after the Second World War led some observers to lay particular stress on postwar changes in the character of goods produced—in particular, the replacement of organic products, which were "biodegradable" and thus assimilable in the ecological cycle, by synthetic products, which could not be thus decomposed: plastics and aluminum in place of lumber and steel; detergents in place of soap; synthetic fibers in place of cotton and wool; synthetic pesticides like DDT in place of older methods of insect control; nitrogen fertilizers in place of manure.

The alarming results were pollution of water and air, erosion of the soil, disturbance of the balance of nature, disruption of the self-replenishing cycles that for eons had sustained life on earth. America the Beautiful was now marked, not by alabaster cities and fruited plains, but by black oil slicks smearing the beaches of California; by the stink of Lake Erie, once a shining inland sea, now dying from sewage, factory wastes, phosphates and detergents; by cities enveloped in smog spewed forth by automobile exhausts, factory chimneys, and burning dumps; by the destruction of the relationship between plants, animals, and the natural environment through the use of pesticides.

The production of synthetics also intensified the drain on energy resources, sorely pressed in any case by the increase in aggregate demand. Between 1930 and 1968, while population grew by 63 percent, energy use grew by nearly 300 percent. Already consuming 35 percent of the world's energy resources and experiencing an annual increase of 5 percent in energy use, the United States became uneasily aware in the seventies of local shortages and rising prices in electric power, natural gas, petroleum, and coal. Moreover, mineral resources of energy were nonrenewable. The supply of natural gas and oil in the United States, geologists thought, would run out in another century. While coal reserves were more abundant, the increasing shift in the sixties from the more expensive and dangerous deep mining to strip mining (44 percent of coal production in 1970) was aggravating the ecological crisis. Ripping the surface off the soil produced landslides in the hills, sulphuric acid and sedimentation in the streams, and permanent damage to soil, foliage, and

San Francisco Bay: oil slicks smeared the beaches

wildlife. The long-term solution of the energy stringency seemed to lie in the enlarged use of nuclear power, which in 1970 supplied only 1.4 percent of the nation's electricity. But nuclear reactors were costly to build, hazardous because of radiation, and themselves mighty contributors to thermal pollution.

In the meantime, legislators tried to find statutory remedies in a series of laws designed, often over strong business opposition, to enforce federal standards against industrial practices that caused water and air pollution. The congressional rejection of the supersonic transport in 1971 seemed of symbolic importance as implying the proposition that, because something was technically feasible, this did not impose on Americans a moral duty to build it, especially if it would befoul the environment, deafen those in its path, and produce no compensating benefits.

Looking to the farther future, some observers began to question the very gospel of growth itself. This question emerged not only because of the impact of growth on the environment. Even more significant perhaps was the impact of incessant change on the individual psyche—the condition of stress and disorientation described by Alvin Toffler as "future shock," arising when more change was injected into society than the human organism could absorb. As Sir Geoffrey Vickers, the British social scientist, put it, "The rate of change increases at an accelerating speed, without a corresponding acceleration in the rate at which further responses can be made; and this brings us nearer the threshold beyond which control is lost."

The challenge to the idea of growth was fundamental. It went to the heart of the Western ethos, which had so long regarded change and expansion as the essence of life; it particularly ran counter to the creed of the American people, for whom the maximization of growth had been an abiding ideal. Moreover, growth had been in midcentury an explicit and almost sacred objective—growth to keep ahead of the Russians; growth to enlarge the economic pie without altering the size of the slices and thereby to achieve a painless resolution of social tensions. And the cessation of growth would indeed make many social problems harder to solve. It would require controls over technology, population, and the labor market; it would raise the question of the uses of leisure; it would force hard and politically explosive decisions on the distribution of in-

come and the allocation of resources. It would either have to create intrusive government machinery to enforce such controls and decisions or else (or also) increase unemployment, solidify poverty, and constrict economic opportunity and social mobility. Still, natural resources were not limitless nor could the human psyche withstand indefinitely the assaults of change; and persistence in uncontrolled growth might mean the eventual extinction of life on the planet. Whatever the outcome, the debate was on.

If growth slowed down, the problem of the allocation of resources would become especially acute. Even when growth had been the unchallenged goal, American society had tended to starve its public sector; and, if the gross national product stopped rising, the financing of essential public services could take place only at the expense of private consumption. At the same time, the technological revolution had induced a transformation from a low-expectation to a high-expectation society, where everyone demanded full membership and opportunity and where television gave all a glimpse of the abundant life.

The problem was that the need for public services at levels of high technological development increased at a far faster rate than the nation's willingness to accept the taxes necessary to pay for those services (though, in comparison with other industrial nations, Americans were not heavily taxed; total tax collections amounted to only 31 percent of gross national product as against 37 percent in Canada and 43 percent in Great Britain). By the early seventies it was hardly an exaggeration to say that much of the nonprofit sector of American society was on the edge of financial bankruptcy: state and local governments, universities and school boards, railroads and public transit, hospitals and welfare agencies, libraries, museums, and opera houses. And this was at a time when unmet national tasks—welfare, health care, education, urban disorders, law enforcement, the war against poverty, the control of pollution and erosion—called for marked increases in the allocation of resources to public purposes (as well as for social and administrative inventiveness to assure the productive use of such resources). If the way a nation spends its money is a test of its values, it seemed as if the velocity of history had created problems beyond the capacity of American society to solve within terms of its existing value system.

Could values change? Gunnar Myrdal, the Swedish social scientist, once remarked that a good thing about America's Calvinist tradition was the possibility of conversions: ''I know of no nation in the world that can change its fundamental attitudes so rapidly as Americans.'' Certainly in half a century America had undergone notable conversions: from economic laissez faire to government intervention and regulation; from commitment to white supremacy to commitment to a multiracial society; from isolationism to globalism and then back toward a more selective internationalism; from the puritanical to the permissive society; from the idea that national morality required the prohibition of alcoholic beverages to the idea that drinking is a private habit; most recently, from the exaltation to the questioning of economic growth. Such shifts displayed the national capacity to alter its value systems. In the seventies, as the existence of the counterculture demonstrated, American values were again in flux.

After two centuries. July 4, 1976, would be the two hundredth anniversary of the Declaration of Independence. America was still a youngish nation. If one counted American history by generations, eight would span the national experience; if by lifetimes, three would nearly do it. Justice Oliver Wendell Holmes, who died just before his ninety-fourth birthday in 1935, told his last secretary: ''Always remember that you have spoken to a man who once spoke to a veteran of the American Revolution.'' 423 widows of Civil War veterans were still alive on Memorial Day 1971.

As the republic faced its third century, many Americans found themselves in moods of unaccustomed pessimism. The feeling of immunity from world troubles, conferred at first by two great oceans, later by the brief monopoly of nuclear weapons, had slipped away. Americans now had a sense, new to their experience, of being on the defensive—of being shoved and harried by peremptory and hostile historical forces, at home as well as abroad. Public opinion polls reported an increase in a sense of alienation from American society, a decline of confidence in institutions and leadership, even a fear of a breakdown in the country. In 1971 President Nixon compared the American situation to the fate of great civilizations of the past: ''As they have become wealthy, as they have lost their will

to live, to improve, they then have become subject to the decadence that eventually destroys the civilization. The United States is now reaching that period.''

Still it was not necessary to accept the thesis of irreversible decline. No one could doubt that the nation had its troubles. But, if the American crisis seemed acute, it was perhaps not the result of the decline of moral standards or of a peculiar depravity in the economic system or the national character. It may well have been because the revolution wrought of science and technology had gone farther in America than anywhere else. The world was changing faster than ever before, and changing fastest of all in America. As the nation on the farthest frontier of technological development, America had been the first to experience the shattering impact of the acceleration in the velocity of history. The crises were not uniquely American: they were the crises of modernity. Every nation, whatever its system of ideology or ownership, would undergo comparable crises as it began to attain a comparable stage of technological development. The American turmoil might well be less the proof of decay than the price of progress.

As the processes of change gathered momentum, the immediate results had been— were almost bound to be—social and moral confusion, frustration, fear, violence. Yet the turmoil, the confusion, even the violence would be the birth pangs of a new epoch in the history of man. If Americans developed the intelligence, will, and leadership to control the law of acceleration, the United States could avoid the fate of internal demoralization and disintegration that the momentum of technology was holding out before them. As they did this, they could begin to restore their influence in the world by offering an example to other nations destined soon to struggle themselves with the problems created by the ever-quickening velocity of history.

So, on the brink of its third century, facing new trials and opportunities, Americans could refresh themselves in the spirit of Emerson: ''If there is any period one would desire to be born in—is it not the era of revolution when the old and the new stand side by side and admit of being compared; when all the energies of man are searched by fear and hope; when the historic glories of the old can be compensated by the rich possibilities of the new era? This time like all times is a very good one if one but knows what to do with it.''

Suggestions for reading

THE NIXON ADMINISTRATION

For Nixon, see the sympathetic biography by Earl Mazo and Stephen Hess, *Nixon, A Political Portrait* (1968), the able description of his political comeback by Jules Witcover, *The Resurrection of Richard Nixon* (1970), the critical analysis by Garry Wills, *Nixon Agonistes* (1970), and, for a "psychohistorical" approach, Bruce Mazlish, *In Search of Nixon* (1972). Rowland Evans, Jr., and R. D. Novak, *Nixon in the White House: A Critical Portrait* (1971), provide an excellent account of the Nixon Administration in midstream; and John Osborne, *The Nixon Watch* (1970), supplies perceptive glimpses of the Nixon White House in action. Leonard Silk, *Nixonomics* (1972), is an able study of the Nixon economic policies. Former Nixon associates give more or less disenchanted testimony in Walter Hickel, *Who Owns America?* (1971), Leon Panetta and Peter Gall, *Bring Us Together* (1971), and R. J. Whalen, *Catch the Falling Flag* (1972). Jules Witcover, *White Knight: The Rise of Spiro Agnew* (1972), is an effective portrait.

For Vietnam, Frances Fitzgerald, *Fire in the Lake* (1972), is a penetrating summation. Seymour Hersh, *My Lai Four* (1970) and *Cover Up* (1972), describes the My Lai massacre and its aftermath; R. A. Falk, Gabriel Kolko, and R. J. Lifton, eds., *Crimes of War** (1971), widen the inquiry into atrocities in Indochina; and Telford Taylor, *Nuremberg and Vietnam** (1970), is a trenchant analysis. Contrasting stories of the Kent State tragedy can be found in J. A. Michener, *Kent State: What Happened and Why* (1971), and I. F. Stone, *Killings at Kent State: How Murder Went Unpunished** (1971). For the influence of the military establishment, consult Adam Yarmolinsky, *The Military Establishment: Its Impacts on American Society* (1971); J. A. Donovan, *Militarism, U.S.A.** (1970); and J. W. Fulbright, *The Pentagon Propaganda Machine** (1970). R. J. Barnet, *Roots of War* (1972), offers a radical view of American foreign policy; and in *The Age of Imperialism** (1969), Harry Magdoff advances a Marxist interpretation. R. W. Tucker, *The Radical Left and American Foreign Policy** (1971), is a thoughtful commentary.

The domestic political situation is perceived as in a condition of crisis by Samuel Lubell, *The Hidden Crisis in American Politics** (1970), F. G. Dutton, *Changing Sources of Power* (1971), and David Broder, *The Party's Over* (1972). R. M. Scammon and B. J. Wattenberg take a more conventional view in *The Real Majority* (1970). H. E. Alexander, *Money in Politics* (1972), is the standard work on this troubling and pervasive question. Walter De Vries and V. L. Tarrance portray the decline of party loyalties in *The Ticket-Splitters* (1972). W. D. Burnham, *Critical Elections and the Mainsprings of American Politics* (1970), is a searching study by a political scientist. Jack Newfield and Jeff Greenfield, *The Populist Manifesto* (1972), call for radical political action. R. S. Anson, *McGovern* (1972), is a superior campaign biography.

SOCIAL AND ECONOMIC CONDITIONS

Current apprehensions about the city are well summed up in the Report of the Commission on the Cities in the '70s, F. R. Harris and J. V. Lindsay, cochairmen, *The State of the Cities* (1972). R. C. Wood, *The Necessary Majority: Middle America and the Urban Crisis* (1972), records the views of a former Secretary of Housing and Urban Development. Jean Gottman, *Megalopolis** (1961), remains a valuable study. F. F. Piven and R. A. Cloward, *Regulating the Poor: The Functions of Public Welfare* (1971), provide a provocative analysis of the welfare system. Ramsey Clark, *Crime in America** (1970), is a humane survey. V. R. Fuchs and I. F. Leveson, *The Service Economy** (1968), describe the shift of labor from goods to services. J. K. Galbraith, *The New Industrial State** (rev. ed., 1971), and David Lilienthal, *Big Business, A New Era* (1953) and *The Multinational Corporation* (1960), regard the great corporation as inevitable; Morton Mintz and J. S. Cohen, *America, Inc.* (1971), urge a return to trust-busting; and R. J. Barber, *The American Corporation** (1970), favors increased government regulation. See also R. F. Buckthorn, *Nader: The People's Lawyer* (1972), and J. M. Blair, *Economic Concentration* (1972).

Two useful introductions to the ecological crises are Garrett De Bell, ed., *The Environmental Handbook** (1970), and R. M. Linton, *Terracide** (1970). Barbara Ward and Rene Dubos place the problem in its world setting in *Only One Earth* (1972). Rachel Carson, *Silent Spring** (1962), helped awaken American concern over environmental problems. Barry Commoner, *The Closing*

*Available in a paperback edition.

Circle (1971), lays particular stress on the destructive impact of technology, while Paul Ehrlich, *The Population Bomb** (1968), focuses on population growth. Ben Kelley, *The Pavers and the Paved* (1970), discusses the role of automobiles and superhighways. Nancy Wood, *Clearcut: The Deforestation of America** (1971), deals with the assault on the woodlands.

J. D. Watson, *The Double Helix** (1968), is a spirited account of a scientific breakthrough. B. F. Skinner argues his case for behavioral engineering in *Walden Two** (1948) and *Beyond Freedom and Dignity* (1972); Leroy Augenstein dissents in *Come, Let Us PLay God* (1969). Norbert Wiener considers the impact of the electronic computer in *The Human Use of Human Beings: Cybernetics and Society** (1954); see also Martin Greenberger, ed., *Computers, Communications, and the Public Interest* (1972). Electronic invasion of privacy is discussed in Alan Westin, *Privacy and Freedom* (1967), and A. R. Miller, *The Assault on Privacy* (1971). The case for the existence of other beings in the universe is analyzed in Carl Sagan and I. S. Shklovsky, *Intelligent Life in the Universe** (1968).

THE STATE OF THE CULTURE

For general diagnoses of the national condition, see Arthur Schlesinger, Jr., *The Crisis of Confidence* (1969), and Andrew Hacker, *End of the American Era** (1970). Marshall McLuhan's eccentric but suggestive views can be traced in *The Gutenberg Galaxy** (1962), *Understanding Media** (1964), and *The Medium Is the Massage** (1967). V. C. Ferkiss, *Technological Man** (1969), and Alvin Toffler, *Future Shock** (1970), offer stimulating speculations about the consequences for man and society of the increased velocity of history.

For the women's liberation movement, see Betty Friedan, *The Feminine Mystique** (1963); Robin Morgan, ed., *Sisterhood Is Powerful** (1970), and Judith Hole and Ellen Levine, *Rebirth of Feminism* (1972), two useful anthologies; and two perceptive discussions, Elizabeth Janeway, *Man's World, Women's Place: A Study in Social Mythology* (1971), and Juliet Mitchell, *Women's Estate* (1972). Michael Gordon, ed., *The Nuclear Family in Crisis* (1972), provides diverse views on the future of the family.

Blue-collar workers and ethnic minorities of European origin are discussed in S. A. Levitan, ed., *Blue-Collar Workers* (1972), L. K. Howe, ed., *The White Majority** (1970), and Michael Novak, *The Rise of the Unmeltable Ethnics* (1972). For the Mexican-Americans, see M. S. Meier and Feliciano Rivera, *The Chicanos* (1972); Stan Steiner, *La Raza** (1970); Leo Grebler, J. W. Moore, and R. C. Guzman, *The Mexican American People* (1970); and Wayne Moquin, ed., *A Documentary History of the Mexican-Americans* (1971). For Puerto Ricans on the mainland, consult Clarence Senior, *The Puerto Rican in New York City* (1948). Valuable works on the Indian are A. M. Josephy, ed., *Red Power* (1971); Stuart Levine and N. O. Lurie, eds., *The American Indian Today** (rev. ed., 1968); Stan Steiner, *The New Indians** (1968); and S. A. Levitan and Barbara Hetrick, *Big Brother's Indian Programs* (1972).

Edmund Wilson, *Classics and Commercials** (1950) and *The Bit Between My Teeth** (1965), provides a distinguished critic's views on postwar literature; see also J. W. Aldridge, *After the Lost Generation* (1951) and *The Devil in the Fire* (1971). Charles Rembar, *The End of Obscenity** (1968), reviews the decline of censorship. For contemporary developments in religion, see A. M. Greeley, *Come Blow Your Mind with Me* (1971) and *Priests in the United States* (1972), and J. C. Cooper, *The New Mentality** (1969) and *Religion in the Age of Aquarius** (1971). Educational problems are considered in Charles Silberman, *Crisis in the Classroom* (1970); Jonathan Kozol, *Death at an Early Age* (1967); Paul Goodman, *Growing Up Absurd** (1960); Arthur Bestor, *The Restoration of Learning* (1955); Christopher Jencks and David Riesman, *The Academic Revolution** (2nd ed., 1969); and J. B. Conant's valuable series of studies, especially *Shaping Educational Policy** (1964).

*Available in a paperback edition.

Appendix

The Declaration of Independence*

THE UNANIMOUS DECLARATION of the thirteen united STATES OF AMERICA,

WHEN in the Course of human events it becomes necessary for one people to dissolve the political bands which have connected them with another, and to assume among the Powers of the earth, the separate and equal station to which the Laws of Nature and of Nature's God entitle them, a decent respect to the opinions of mankind requires that they should declare the causes which impel them to the separation.

We hold these truths to be self-evident, that all men are created equal, that they are endowed by their Creator with certain unalienable Rights, that among these are Life, Liberty and the pursuit of Happiness. That to secure these rights, Governments are instituted among Men, deriving their just Powers from the consent of the governed. That whenever any Form of Government becomes destructive of these ends, it is the Right of the People to alter or to abolish it, and to institute new Government, laying its foundation on such principles and organizing its Powers in such form, as to them shall seem most likely to effect their Safety and Happiness. Prudence, indeed, will dictate that Governments long established should not be changed for light and transient causes; and accordingly all experience hath shewn, that mankind are more disposed to suffer, while evils are sufferable, than to right themselves by abolishing the forms to which they are accustomed. But when a long train of abuses and usurpations, pursuing invariably the same Object evinces a design to reduce them under absolute Despotism, it is their right, it is their duty, to throw off such Government, and to provide new Guards for their future security. Such has been the patient sufferance of these Colonies; and such is now the necessity which constrains them to alter their former Systems of Government. The history of the present King of Great Britain is a history of repeated injuries and usurpations, all having in direct object the establishment of an absolute

Tyranny over these States. To prove this, let Facts be submitted to a candid world.

He has refused his Assent to Laws, the most wholesome and necessary for the public good.

He has forbidden his Governors to pass Laws of immediate and pressing importance, unless suspended in their operation till his Assent should be obtained; and when so suspended, he has utterly neglected to attend to them.

He has refused to pass other Laws for the accommodation of large districts of people, unless those people would relinquish the right of Representation in the Legislature, a right inestimable to them and formidable to tyrants only.

He has called together legislative bodies at places unusual, uncomfortable, and distant from the depository of their Public Records, for the sole Purpose of fatiguing them into compliance with his measures.

He has dissolved Representative Houses repeatedly, for opposing with manly firmness his invasions on the rights of the People.

He has refused for a long time, after such dissolutions, to cause others to be elected; whereby the Legislative Powers, incapable of Annihilation, have returned to the People at large for their exercise; the State remaining in the mean time exposed to all the dangers of invasion from without, and convulsions within.

He has endeavoured to prevent the Population of these States; for that purpose obstructing the Laws for Naturalization of Foreigners; refusing to pass others to encourage their migrations hither, and raising the conditions of new Appropriations of Lands.

He has obstructed the Administration of Justice, by refusing his Assent to Laws for establishing Judiciary Powers.

He has made Judges dependent on his Will alone, for the tenure of their offices, and the amount and payment of their salaries.

He has erected a multitude of New Offices, and sent

*Reprinted from the facsimile of the engrossed copy in the National Archives. The original spelling, capitalization, and punctuation have been retained. Paragraphing has been added.

hither swarms of Officers to harrass our People, and eat out their substance.

He has kept among us, in times of peace, Standing Armies without the Consent of our legislatures.

He has affected to render the Military independent of and superior to the Civil Power.

He has combined with others to subject us to a jurisdiction foreign to our constitution, and unacknowledged by our laws; giving his Assent to their Acts of pretended Legislation:

For Quartering large bodies of armed troops among us:

For protecting them, by a mock Trial, from Punishment for any Murders which they should commit on the Inhabitants of these States:

For cutting off our Trade with all parts of the world:

For imposing Taxes on us without our Consent:

For depriving us in many cases, of the benefits of Trial by Jury:

For transporting us beyond Seas to be tried for pretended offences:

For abolishing the free System of English Laws in a neighbouring Province, establishing therein an Arbitrary government, and enlarging its Boundaries so as to render it at once an example and fit instrument for introducing the same absolute rule into these Colonies:

For taking away our Charters, abolishing our most valuable Laws, and altering fundamentally the Forms of our Governments:

For suspending our own Legislatures, and declaring themselves invested with Power to legislate for us in all cases whatsoever.

He has abdicated Government here, by declaring us out of his Protection, and waging War against us.

He has plundered our seas, ravaged our Coasts, burnt our towns, and destroyed the lives of our people.

He is at this time transporting large Armies of foreign Mercenaries to compleat the works of death, desolation and tyranny, already begun with circumstances of Cruelty and perfidy scarcely paralleled in the most barbarous ages, and totally unworthy the Head of a civilized nation.

He has constrained our fellow Citizens taken Captive on the high Seas to bear Arms against their Country, to become the executioners of their friends and Brethren, or to fall themselves by their Hands.

He has excited domestic insurrections amongst us, and has endeavoured to bring on the inhabitants of our frontiers, the merciless Indian Savages, whose known rule of warfare, is an undistinguished destruction of all ages, sexes and conditions.

In every stage of these Oppressions We have Petitioned for Redress in the most humble terms: Our repeated Petitions have been answered only by repeated injury. A Prince, whose character is thus marked by every act which may define a Tyrant, is unfit to be the ruler of a free People.

Nor have We been wanting in attentions to our Brittish brethren. We have warned them from time to time of attempts by their legislature to extend an unwarrantable jurisdiction over us. We have reminded them of the circumstances of our emigration and settlement here. We have appealed to their native justice and magnanimity, and we have conjured them by the ties of our common kindred to disavow these usurpations, which, would inevitably interrupt our connections and correspondence. They too have been deaf to the voice of justice and of consanguinity. We must, therefore, acquiesce in the necessity, which denounces our Separation, and hold them, as we hold the rest of mankind, Enemies in War, in Peace Friends.

WE, THEREFORE, the Representatives of the UNITED STATES OF AMERICA, in General Congress, Assembled, appealing to the Supreme Judge of the world for the rectitude of our intentions, do, in the Name, and by Authority of the good People of these Colonies, solemnly publish and declare, That these United Colonies are, and of Right ought to be FREE AND INDEPENDENT STATES; that they are Absolved from all Allegiance to the British Crown, and that all political connection between them and the State of Great Britain, is and ought to be totally dissolved; and that, as Free and Independent States, they have full Power to levy War, conclude Peace, contract Alliances, establish Commerce, and to do all other Acts and Things which Independent States may of right do. And for the support of this Declaration, with a firm reliance on the protection of divine Providence, we mutually pledge to each other our Lives, our Fortunes and our sacred Honor.

The Constitution of the United States of America*

We the People of the United States, in Order to form a more perfect Union, establish Justice, insure domestic Tranquility, provide for the common defence, promote the general Welfare, and secure the Blessings of Liberty to ourselves and our Posterity, do ordain and establish this Constitution for the United States of America.

Article. I.

Section. 1. All legislative Powers herein granted shall be vested in a Congress of the United States, which shall consist of a Senate and House of Representatives.

Section. 2. The House of Representatives shall be composed of Members chosen every second Year by the People of the several States, and the Electors in each State shall have the Qualifications requisite for Electors of the most numerous Branch of the State Legislature.

No Person shall be a Representative who shall not have attained to the Age of twenty five Years, and been seven Years a Citizen of the United States, and who shall not, when elected, be an Inhabitant of that State in which he shall be chosen.

Representatives and direct Taxes† shall be apportioned among the several States which may be included within this Union, according to their respective Numbers, which shall be determined by adding to the whole Number of free Persons, including those bound to Service for a Term of Years, and excluding Indians not taxed, three fifths of all other Persons.‡ The actual Enumeration shall be made within three Years after the first Meeting of the Congress of the United States, and within every subsequent Term of ten Years, in such Manner as they shall by Law direct. The Number of Representatives shall not exceed one for every thirty Thousand, but each State shall have at Least one Representative; and until such enumeration shall be made, the State of New Hampshire shall be entitled to chuse three; Massachusetts eight; Rhode Island and Providence Plantations one; Connecticut five; New York six; New Jersey four; Pennsylvania eight; Delaware one; Maryland six; Virginia ten; North Carolina five; South Carolina five; and Georgia three.

When vacancies happen in the Representation from any State, the Executive Authority thereof shall issue Writs of Election to fill such Vacancies.

The House of Representatives shall chuse their Speaker and other Officers; and shall have the sole Power of Impeachment.

Section. 3. The Senate of the United States shall be composed of two Senators from each State, chosen by the Legislature thereof, for six Years; and each Senator shall have one Vote.*

Immediately after they shall be assembled in Consequence of the first Election, they shall be divided as equally as may be into three Classes. The Seats of the Senators of the first Class shall be vacated at the Expiration of the second Year, of the second Class at the Expiration of the fourth Year, and of the third Class at the Expiration of the sixth Year, so that one third may be chosen every second Year; and if Vacancies happen by Resignation, or otherwise, during the Recess of the Legislature of any State, the Executive thereof may make temporary Appointments until the next Meeting of the Legislature, which shall then fill such Vacancies.†

No Person shall be a Senator who shall not have attained to the Age of thirty Years, and been nine Years a Citizen of the United States, and who shall not, when elected, be an Inhabitant of that State for which he shall be chosen.

The Vice President of the United States shall be President of the Senate, but shall have no Vote, unless they be equally divided.

The Senate shall chuse their other Officers, and also a

---

*From the engrossed copy in the National Archives. Original spelling, capitalization, and punctuation have been retained.

† Modified by the Sixteenth Amendment.

‡ Replaced by the Fourteenth Amendment.

*Superseded by the Seventeenth Amendment.

† Modified by the Seventeenth Amendment.

President pro tempore, in the Absence of the Vice President, or when he shall exercise the Office of President of the United States.

The Senate shall have the sole Power to try all Impeachments. When sitting for that Purpose, they shall be on Oath or Affirmation. When the President of the United States is tried, the Chief Justice shall preside: And no Person shall be convicted without the Concurrence of two thirds of the Members present.

Judgment in Cases of Impeachment shall not extend further than to removal from Office, and disqualification to hold and enjoy any Office of honor, Trust or Profit under the United States: but the Party convicted shall nevertheless be liable and subject to Indictment, Trial, Judgment and Punishment, according to Law.

Section. 4. The Times, Places and Manner of holding Elections for Senators and Representatives, shall be prescribed in each State by the Legislature thereof, but the Congress may at any time by Law make or alter such Regulation, except as to the Places of chusing Senators.

The Congress shall assemble at least once in every Year, and such Meeting shall be on the first Monday in December, unless they shall by Law appoint a different Day.*

Section. 5. Each House shall be the Judge of the Elections, Returns and Qualifications of its own Members, and a Majority of each shall constitute a Quorum to do Business; but a smaller Number may adjourn from day to day, and may be authorized to compel the Attendance of absent Members, in such Manner, and under such Penalties as each House may provide.

Each House may determine the Rules of its Proceedings, punish its Members for disorderly Behaviour, and, with the Concurrence of two thirds, expel a Member.

Each House shall keep a Journal of its Proceedings, and from time to time publish the same, excepting such Parts as may in their Judgment require Secrecy; and the Yeas and Nays of the Members of either House on any question shall, at the Desire of one fifth of those Present, be entered on the Journal.

Neither House, during the Session of Congress, shall, without the Consent of the other, adjourn for more than three days, nor to any other Place than that in which the two Houses shall be sitting.

Section. 6. The Senators and Representatives shall receive a Compensation for their Services, to be ascertained by Law, and paid out of the Treasury of the United States. They shall in all Cases, except Treason, Felony and Breach of the Peace, be privileged from Arrest during their Attendance at the Session of their respective Houses, and in going to and returning from the same; and for any Speech or Debate in either House, they shall not be questioned in any other Place.

No Senator or Representative shall, during the Time for which he was elected, be appointed to any civil Office under the Authority of the United States, which shall have been created, or the Emoluments whereof shall have been encreased during such time; and no Person holding any Office under the United States, shall be a Member of either House during his Continuance in Office.

Section. 7. All Bills for raising Revenue shall originate in the House of Representatives; but the Senate may propose or concur with Amendments as on other Bills.

Every Bill which shall have passed the House of Representatives and the Senate shall, before it become a Law, be presented to the President of the United States, If he approve he shall sign it, but if not he shall return it, with his Objections to that House in which it shall have originated, who shall enter the Objections at large on their Journal, and proceed to reconsider it. If after such Reconsideration two thirds of that House shall agree to pass the Bill, it shall be sent, together with the Objections, to the other House, by which it shall likewise be reconsidered, and if approved by two thirds of that House, it shall become a Law. But in all such Cases the Votes of both Houses shall be determined by yeas and Nays, and the Names of the Persons voting for and against the Bill shall be entered on the Journal of each House respectively. If any Bill shall not be returned by the President within ten Days (Sundays excepted) after it shall have been presented to him, the Same shall be a Law, in like Manner as if he had signed it, unless the Congress by their Adjournment prevent its Return, in which Case it shall not be a Law.

Every Order, Resolution, or Vote to which the Concurrence of the Senate and House of Representatives may be necessary (except on a question of Adjournment) shall be presented to the President of the United States; and before the Same shall take Effect, shall be approved by him, or being disapproved by him shall be repassed by two thirds of the Senate and House of Representatives, according to the Rules and Limitations prescribed in the Case of a Bill.

Section. 8. The Congress shall have Power To lay and collect Taxes, Duties, Imposts and Excises, to pay the Debts and provide for the common Defence and general Welfare of the United States; but all Duties, Imposts and Excises shall be uniform throughout the United States;

To borrow Money on the credit of the United States;

To regulate Commerce with foreign Nations, and among the several States, and with the Indian Tribes;

To establish an uniform Rule of Naturalization, and uniform Laws on the subject of Bankruptcies throughout the United States;

To coin Money, regulate the Value thereof, and of foreign Coin, and fix the Standard of Weights and Measures;

To provide for the Punishment of counterfeiting the Securities and current Coin of the United States;

To establish Post Offices and post Roads;

To promote the Progress of Science and useful Arts, by securing for limited Times to Authors and Inventors the exclusive Right to their respective Writings and Discoveries;

*Superseded by the Twentieth Amendment.

To constitute Tribunals inferior to the supreme Court;

To define and punish Piracies and Felonies committed on the high Seas, and Offences against the Law of Nations;

To declare War, grant Letters of Marque and Reprisal, and make Rules concerning Captures on Land and Water;

To raise and support Armies, but no Appropriation of Money to that Use shall be for a longer Term than two Years;

To provide and maintain a Navy;

To make Rules for the Government and Regulation of the land and naval Forces;

To provide for calling forth the Militia to execute the Laws of the Union, suppress Insurrections and repel Invasions;

To provide for organizing, arming, and disciplining, the Militia, and for governing such Part of them as may be employed in the Service of the United States, reserving to the States respectively, the Appointment of the Officers, and the Authority of training the Militia according to the discipline prescribed by Congress;

To exercise exclusive Legislation in all Cases whatsoever, over such District (not exceeding ten Miles square) as may, by Cession of particular States, and the Acceptance of Congress, become the Seat of the Government of the United States, and to exercise like Authority over all Places purchased by the Consent of the Legislature of the State in which the Same shall be, for the Erection of Forts, Magazines, Arsenals, dock-Yards, and other needful Buildings;—And

To make all Laws which shall be necessary and proper for carrying into Execution the foregoing Powers, and all other Powers vested by this Constitution in the Government of the United States, or in any Department or Officer thereof.

Section. 9. The Migration or Importation of such Persons as any of the States now existing shall think proper to admit, shall not be prohibited by the Congress prior to the Year one thousand eight hundred and eight, but a Tax or duty may be imposed on such Importation, not exceeding ten dollars for each Person.

The Privilege of the Writ of Habeas Corpus shall not be suspended, unless when in Cases of Rebellion or Invasion the public Safety may require it.

No Bill of Attainder or ex post facto Law shall be passed.

No Capitation, or other direct, Tax shall be laid, unless in Proportion to the Census or Enumeration herein before directed to be taken.

No Tax or Duty shall be laid on Articles exported from any State.

No Preference shall be given by any Regulation of Commerce or Revenue to the Ports of one State over those of another: nor shall Vessels bound to, or from, one State, be obliged to enter, clear, or pay Duties in another.

No Money shall be drawn from the Treasury, but in Consequence of Appropriations made by Law, and a regular Statement and Account of the Receipts and Expenditures of all public Money shall be published from time to time.

No Title of Nobility shall be granted by the United States: And no Person holding any Office of Profit or Trust under them, shall, without the Consent of the Congress, accept of any present, Emolument, Office, or Title, of any kind whatever, from any King, Prince, or foreign State.

Section. 10. No State shall enter into any Treaty, Alliance, or Confederation; grant Letters of Marque and Reprisal; coin Money; emit Bills of Credit; make any Thing but gold and silver Coin a Tender in Payment of Debts; pass any Bill of Attainder, ex post facto Law, or Law impairing the Obligation of Contracts, or grant any Title of Nobility.

No State shall, without the Consent of the Congress, lay any Imposts or Duties on Imports or Exports, except what may be absolutely necessary for executing it's inspection Laws: and the net Produce of all Duties and Imposts, laid by any State on Imports or Exports, shall be for the Use of the Treasury of the United States; and all such Laws shall be subject to the Revision and Controul of the Congress.

No State shall, without the Consent of Congress, lay any Duty of Tonnage, keep Troops, or Ships of War in time of Peace, enter into any Agreement or Compact with another State, or with a foreign Power, or engage in War, unless actually invaded, or in such imminent Danger as will not admit of delay.

Article. II.

Section. 1. The executive Power shall be vested in a President of the United States of America. He shall hold his Office during the Term of four Years, and, together with the Vice President, chosen for the same Term, be elected, as follows

Each State shall appoint, in such Manner as the Legislature thereof may direct, a Number of Electors, equal to the whole Number of Senators and Representatives to which the State may be entitled in the Congress: but no Senator or Representative, or Person holding an Office of Trust or Profit under the United States, shall be appointed an Elector.

The Electors shall meet in their respective States, and vote by Ballot for two Persons, of whom one at least shall not be an Inhabitant of the same State with themselves. And they shall make a List of all the Persons voted for, and of the Number of Votes for each; which List they shall sign and certify, and transmit sealed to the Seat of the Government of the United States, directed to the President of the Senate. The President of the Senate shall, in the Presence of the Senate and House of Representatives, open all the Certificates, and the Votes shall then be counted. The Person having the greatest Number of Votes shall be the President, if such Number be a Majority of the whole Number of Electors appointed; and if there be more than one who have such Majority, and have an equal Number of Votes, then the House of Representatives shall immediately chuse by Ballot one of them for President; and if no Person have a Majority, then from the five highest on the List the said House shall in like Manner chuse the President. But in chusing the President, the Votes shall be taken by States, the Representation from each State having one Vote; A quorum for this Purpose shall consist of a Member or Members from two thirds of the States, and a Majority of all the States shall be necessary to a Choice. In every Case, after the Choice of the President, the Person having the greatest Number of Votes of the Electors shall be the Vice President. But if there should remain two or more who have equal Votes, the Senate shall chuse from them by Ballot the Vice President.*

The Congress may determine the Time of chusing the Electors, and the Day on which they shall give their Votes; which Day shall be the same throughout the United States.

No Person except a natural born Citizen, or a Citizen of the United States, at the time of the Adoption of this Constitution, shall be eligible to the Office of President, neither shall any Person be eligible to that Office who shall not have attained to the Age of thirty five Years, and been fourteen Years a Resident within the United States.

In Case of the Removal of the President from Office, or of his Death, Resignation, or Inability to discharge the Powers and Duties of the said Office, the Same shall devolve on the Vice President, and the Congress may by Law provide for the Case of Removal, Death, Resignation or Inability, both of the President and Vice President, declaring what Officer shall then act as President, and such Officer shall act accordingly, until the Disability be removed, or a President shall be elected.†

The President shall, at stated Times, receive for his Services, a Compensation, which shall neither be encreased nor diminished during the Period for which he shall have been elected, and he shall not receive within that Period any other Emolument from the United States, or any of them.

Before he enter on the Execution of his Office, he shall take the following Oath or Affirmation:—''I do solemnly swear (or affirm) that I will faithfully execute the Office of President of the United States, and will to the best of my Ability, preserve, protect and defend the Constitution of the United States.''

Section. 2. The President shall be Commander in Chief of the Army and Navy of the United States, and of the Militia of the several States, when called into the actual Service of the United States; he may require the Opinion, in writing, of the principal Officer in each of the executive Departments, upon any Subject relating to the Duties of their respective Offices, and he shall have Power to grant Reprieves and Pardons for Offences against the United States, except in Cases of Impeachment.

He shall have Power, by and with the Advice and Consent of the Senate, to make Treaties, provided two thirds of the Senators present concur; and he shall nominate, and by and with the Advice and Consent of the Senate, shall appoint Ambassadors, other public Ministers and Consuls, Judges of the supreme Court, and all other Officers of the United States, whose Appointments are not herein otherwise provided for, and which shall be established by Law; but the Congress may by Law vest the Appointment of such inferior Officers, as they think proper, in the President alone, in the Courts of Law, or in the Heads of Departments.

The President shall have Power to fill up all Vacancies that may happen during the Recess of the Senate, by granting Commissions which shall expire at the End of their next Session.

Section. 3. He shall from time to time give to the Congress Information of the State of the Union, and recommend to their Consideration such Measures as he shall judge necessary and expedient; he may, on extraordinary Occasions, convene both Houses, or either of them, and in Case of Disagreement between them, with Respect to the Time of Adjournment, he may adjourn them to such Time as he shall think proper; he shall receive Ambassadors and other public Ministers; he shall take Care that the Laws be faithfully executed, and shall Commission all the Officers of the United States.

Section. 4. The President, Vice President and all civil Officers of the United States, shall be removed from Office on Impeachment for, and Conviction of, Treason, Bribery, or other high Crimes and Misdemeanors.

Article. III.

Section. 1. The judicial Power of the United States, shall be vested in one supreme Court, and in such inferior Courts as the Congress may from time to time ordain and establish. The Judges, both of the supreme and inferior Courts, shall hold their Offices during good Behaviour, and shall, at stated Times, receive for their Services, a Compensation, which shall not be diminished during their Continuance in Office.

Section. 2. The judicial Power shall extend to all Cases, in Law and Equity, arising under this Constitution, the Laws of the United States, and Treaties made, or which shall be made, under their Authority;—to all Cases affecting Ambassadors, other public Ministers and Consuls;—to all Cases of admiralty and maritime Jurisdiction;—to Controversies to which the United States shall be a Party;—to Controversies between two or more States;—between a State and Citizens of another State;*—between Citizens of different States,—between Citizens of the same State

*Superseded by the Twelfth Amendment.
†Modified by the Twenty-fifth Amendment.

*Modified by the Eleventh Amendment.

claiming Lands under Grants of different States, and between a State, or the Citizens thereof, and foreign States, Citizens or Subjects.

In all Cases affecting Ambassadors, other public Ministers and Consuls, and those in which a State shall be Party, the supreme Court shall have original Jurisdiction. In all the other Cases before mentioned, the supreme Court shall have appellate Jurisdiction, both as to Law and Fact, with such Exceptions, and under such Regulations as the Congress shall make.

The Trial of all Crimes, except in Cases of Impeachment, shall be by Jury; and such Trial shall be held in the State where the said Crimes shall have been committed; but when not committed within any State, the Trial shall be at such Place or Places as the Congress may by Law have directed.

Section. 3. Treason against the United States, shall consist only in levying War against them, or in adhering to their Enemies, giving them Aid and Comfort. No Person shall be convicted of Treason unless on the Testimony of two Witnesses to the same overt Act, or on Confession in open Court.

The Congress shall have Power to declare the Punishment of Treason, but no Attainder of Treason shall work Corruption of Blood, or Forfeiture except during the Life of the Person attainted.

Article. IV.

Section. 1. Full Faith and Credit shall be given in each State to the public Acts, Records, and judicial Proceedings of every other State. And the Congress may by general Laws prescribe the Manner in which such Acts, Records and Proceedings shall be proved, and the Effect thereof.

Section. 2. The Citizens of each State shall be entitled to all Privileges and Immunities of Citizens in the several States.

A Person charged in any State with Treason, Felony, or other Crime, who shall flee from Justice, and be found in another State, shall on Demand of the executive Authority of the State from which he fled, be delivered up, to be removed to the State having Jurisdiction of the Crime.

No Person held to Service or Labour in one State, under the Laws thereof, escaping into another, shall, in Consequence of any Law or Regulation therein, be discharged from such Service or Labour, but shall be delivered up on Claim of the Party to whom such Service or Labour may be due.

Section. 3. New States may be admitted by the Congress into this Union; but no new State shall be formed or erected within the Jurisdiction of any other State, nor any State be formed by the Junction of two or more States, or Parts of States, without the Consent of the Legislatures of the States concerned as well as of the Congress.

The Congress shall have Power to dispose of and make all needful Rules and Regulations respecting the Territory or other Property belonging to the United States; and nothing in this Constitution shall be so construed as to Prejudice any Claims of the United States, or of any particular State.

Section. 4. The United States shall guarantee to every State in this Union a Republican Form of Government, and shall protect each of them against Invasion; and on Application of the Legislature, or of the Executive (when the Legislature cannot be convened) against domestic Violence.

Article. V.

The Congress, whenever two thirds of both Houses shall deem it necessary, shall propose Amendments to this Constitution, or, on the Application of the Legislatures of two thirds of the several States, shall call a Convention for proposing Amendments, which, in either Case, shall be valid to all Intents and Purposes, as Part of this Constitution, when ratified by the Legislatures of three fourths of the several States, or by Conventions in three fourths thereof, as the one or the other Mode of Ratification may be proposed by the Congress; Provided that no Amendment which may be made prior to the Year One thousand eight hundred and eight shall in any Manner affect the first and fourth Clauses in the Ninth Section of the first Article; and that no State, without its Consent, shall be deprived of it's equal Suffrage in the Senate.

Article. VI.

All Debts contracted and Engagements entered into, before the Adoption of this Constitution, shall be as valid against the United States under this Constitution, as under the Confederation.

This Constitution, and the Laws of the United States which shall be made in Pursuance thereof; and all Treaties made, or which shall be made, under the Authority of the United States, shall be the supreme Law of the Land; and the Judges in every State shall be bound thereby, any Thing in the Constitution or Laws of any State to the Contrary notwithstanding.

The Senators and Representatives before mentioned, and the Members of the several State Legislatures, and all executive and judicial Officers, both of the United States and of the several States, shall be bound by Oath or Affirmation, to support this Constitution; but no religious Test shall ever be required as a Qualification to any Office or public Trust under the United States.

Article. VII.

The Ratification of the Conventions of nine States, shall be sufficient for the Establishment of this Constitution between the States so ratifying the Same.

done in Convention by the Unanimous Consent of the States present the Seventeenth Day of September in the Year of our Lord one thousand seven hundred and Eighty seven and of the Independance of the United States of America the Twelfth. *In witness* whereof We have hereunto subscribed our Names,

Articles in Addition to, and Amendment of, the Constitution of the United States of America, Proposed by Congress, and Ratified by the Legislatures of the Several States, Pursuant to the Fifth Article of the Original Constitution.

Amendment I*

Congress shall make no law respecting an establishment of religion, or prohibiting the free exercise thereof; or abridging the freedom of speech, or of the press; or the right of the people peaceably to assemble, and to petition the Government for a redress of grievances.

Amendment II

A well regulated Militia, being necessary to the security of a free State, the right of the people to keep and bear Arms shall not be infringed.

Amendment III

No Soldier shall, in time of peace, be quartered in any house, without the consent of the Owner, nor in time of war, but in a manner to be prescribed by law.

Amendment IV

The right of the people to be secure in their persons, houses, papers, and effects, against unreasonable searches and seizures, shall not be violated, and no Warrants shall issue, but upon probable cause, supported by Oath or affirmation, and particularly describing the place to be searched, and the persons or things to be seized.

Amendment V

No person shall be held to answer for a capital or otherwise infamous crime, unless on a presentment or indictment of a Grand Jury, except in cases arising in the land or naval forces, or in the Militia, when in actual service in time of War or public danger; nor shall any person be subject for the same offence to be twice put in jeopardy of life or limb; nor shall be compelled in any criminal case to be a witness against himself, nor be deprived of life, liberty, or property, without due process of law; nor shall

private property be taken for public use, without just compensation.

Amendment VI

In all criminal prosecutions, the accused shall enjoy the right to a speedy and public trial, by an impartial jury of the State and district wherein the crime shall have been committed, which district shall have been previously ascertained by law, and to be informed of the nature and cause of the accusation; to be confronted with the witnesses against him; to have compulsory process for obtaining witnesses in his favor, and to have the Assistance of Counsel for his defence.

Amendment VII

In suits at common law, where the value in controversy shall exceed twenty dollars, the right of trial by jury shall be preserved, and no fact tried by a jury, shall be otherwise reexamined in any Court of the United States, than according to the rules of the common law.

Amendment VIII

Excessive bail shall not be required, nor excessive fines imposed, nor cruel and unusual punishments inflicted.

Amendment IX

The enumeration in the Constitution, of certain rights, shall not be construed to deny or disparage others retained by the people.

Amendment X

The powers not delegated to the United States by the Constitution; nor prohibited by it to the States, are reserved to the States respectively, or to the people.

Amendment XI*

The Judicial power of the United States shall not be construed to extend to any suit in law or equity, commenced or prosecuted against one of the United States by Citizens of another State, or by Citizens or Subjects of any Foreign State.

Amendment XII†

The Electors shall meet in their respective States and vote by ballot for President and Vice-President, one of whom, at least, shall not be an inhabitant of the same

---

*The first ten amendments were passed by Congress September 25, 1789. They were ratified by three-fourths of the states December 15, 1791.

*Passed March 4, 1794. Ratified January 23, 1795.
†Passed December 9, 1803. Ratified June 15, 1804.

State with themselves; they shall name in their ballots the person voted for as President, and in distinct ballots the person voted for as Vice-President, and they shall make distinct lists of all persons voted for as President, and of all persons voted for as Vice-President, and of the number of votes for each, which lists they shall sign and certify, and transmit sealed to the seat of the government of the United States, directed to the President of the Senate;—The President of the Senate shall, in the presence of the Senate and House of Representatives, open all the certificates and the votes shall then be counted;—The person having the greatest number of votes for President, shall be the President, if such number be a majority of the whole number of Electors appointed; and if no person have such majority, then from the persons having the highest numbers not exceeding three on the list of those voted for as President, the House of Representatives shall choose immediately, by ballot, the President. But in choosing the President, the votes shall be taken by states, the representation from each state having one vote; a quorum for this purpose shall consist of a member or members from two-thirds of the states, and a majority of all the states shall be necessary to a choice. And if the House of Representatives shall not choose a President whenever the right of choice shall devolve upon them, before the fourth day of March next following, then the Vice-President shall act as President, as in the case of the death or other constitutional disability of the President.—The person having the greatest number of votes as Vice-President, shall be the Vice-President, if such number be a majority of the whole number of Electors appointed, and if no person have a majority, then from the two highest numbers on the list, the Senate shall choose the Vice-President; a quorum for the purpose shall consist of two-thirds of the whole number of Senators, and a majority of the whole number shall be necessary to a choice. But no person constitutionally ineligible to the office of President shall be eligible to that of Vice-President of the United States.

Amendment XIII*

SECTION 1. Neither slavery nor involuntary servitude, except as a punishment for crime whereof the party shall have been duly convicted, shall exist within the United States, or any place subject to their jurisdiction.

SECTION 2. Congress shall have power to enforce this article by appropriate legislation.

Amendment XIV†

SECTION 1. All persons born or naturalized in the United States, and subject to the jurisdiction thereof, are citizens of the United States and of the State wherein they reside.

No State shall make or enforce any law which shall abridge the privileges or immunities of citizens of the United States; nor shall any State deprive any person of life, liberty, or property, without due process of law; nor deny to any person within its jurisdiction the equal protection of the laws.

SECTION 2. Representatives shall be apportioned among the several States according to their respective numbers, counting the whole number of persons in each State, excluding Indians not taxed. But when the right to vote at any election for the choice of electors for President and Vice-President of the United States, Representatives in Congress, the Executive and Judicial officers of a State, or the members of the Legislature thereof, is denied to any of the male inhabitants of such State, being twenty-one years of age, and citizens of the United States, or in any way abridged, except for participation in rebellion, or other crime, the basis of representation therein shall be reduced in the proportion which the number of such male citizens shall bear to the whole number of male citizens twenty-one years of age in such State.

SECTION 3. No person shall be a Senator or Representative in Congress, or elector of President and Vice-President, or hold any office, civil or military, under the United States, or under any State, who, having previously taken an oath, as a member of Congress, or as an officer of the United States, or as a member of any State legislature, or as an executive or judicial officer of any State, to support the Constitution of the United States, shall have engaged in insurrection or rebellion against the same, or given aid or comfort to the enemies thereof. But Congress may by a vote of two-thirds of each House, remove such disability.

SECTION 4. The validity of the public debt of the United States, authorized by law, including debts incurred for payment of pensions and bounties for services in suppressing insurrection or rebellion, shall not be questioned. But neither the United States nor any State shall assume or pay any debt or obligation incurred in aid of insurrection or rebellion against the United States, or any claim for the loss or emancipation of any slave; but all such debts, obligations, and claims shall be held illegal and void.

SECTION 5. The Congress shall have the power to enforce, by appropriate legislation, the provisions of this article.

Amendment XV*

SECTION 1. The right of citizens of the United States to vote shall not be denied or abridged by the United States or by any State on account of race, color, or previous condition of servitude—

SECTION 2. The Congress shall have power to enforce this article by appropriate legislation.

---

*Passed January 31, 1865. Ratified December 6, 1865.
†Passed June 13, 1866. Ratified July 9, 1868.

*Passed February 26, 1869. Ratified February 2, 1870.

Amendment XVI*

The Congress shall have power to lay and collect taxes on incomes, from whatever source derived, without apportionment among the several States, and without regard to any census or enumeration.

Amendment XVII†

The Senate of the United States shall be composed of two Senators from each State, elected by the people thereof, for six years; and each Senator shall have one vote. The electors in each State shall have the qualifications requisite for electors of the most numerous branch of the State legislatures.

When vacancies happen in the representation of any State in the Senate, the executive authority of such State shall issue writs of election to fill such vacancies: *Provided,* That the legislature of any State may empower the executive thereof to make temporary appointments until the people fill the vacancies by election as the legislature may direct.

This amendment shall not be so construed as to affect the election or term of any Senator chosen before it becomes valid as part of the Constitution.

Amendment XVIII‡

SECTION 1. After one year from the ratification of this article the manufacture, sale, or transportation of intoxicating liquors within, the importation thereof into, or the exportation thereof from the United States and all territory subject to the jurisdiction thereof for beverage purposes is hereby prohibited.

SECTION 2. The Congress and the several States shall have concurrent power to enforce this article by appropriate legislation.

SECTION 3. This article shall be inoperative unless it shall have been ratified as an amendment to the Constitution by the legislatures of the several States, as provided in the Constitution, within seven years from the date of the submission hereof to the States by the Congress.

Amendment XIX§

The right of citizens of the United States to vote shall not be denied or abridged by the United States or by any State on account of sex.

Congress shall have power to enforce this article by appropriate legislation.

*Passed July 12, 1909. Ratified February 3, 1913.
†Passed May 13, 1912. Ratified April 8, 1913.
‡Passed December 18, 1917. Ratified January, 16, 1919.
§ Passed June 4, 1919. Ratified August 18, 1920.

Amendment XX*

SECTION 1. The terms of the President and Vice-President shall end at noon on the 20th day of January, and the terms of Senators and Representatives at noon on the 3d day of January, of the years in which such terms would have ended if this article had not been ratified; and the terms of their successors shall then begin.

SECTION 2. The Congress shall assemble at least once in every year, and such meeting shall begin at noon on the 3d day of January, unless they shall by law appoint a different day.

SECTION 3. If, at the time fixed for the beginning of the term of the President, the President elect shall have died, the Vice-President elect shall become President. If a President shall not have been chosen before the time fixed for the beginning of his term, or if the President elect shall have failed to qualify, then the Vice-President elect shall act as President until a President shall have qualified; and the Congress may by law provide for the case wherein neither a President elect nor a Vice-President elect shall have qualified, declaring who shall then act as President, or the manner in which one who is to act shall be selected, and such person shall act accordingly until a President or Vice-President shall have qualified.

SECTION 4. The Congress may by law provide for the case of the death of any of the persons from whom the House of Representatives may choose a President whenever the right of choice shall have devolved upon them, and for the case of the death of any of the persons from whom the Senate may choose a Vice-President whenever the right of choice shall have devolved upon them.

SECTION 5. Sections 1 and 2 shall take effect on the 15th day of October following the ratification of this article.

SECTION 6. This article shall be inoperative unless it shall have been ratified as an amendment to the Constitution by the legislatures of three-fourths of the several States within seven years from the date of its submission.

Amendment XXI†

SECTION 1. The eighteenth article of amendment to the Constitution of the United States is hereby repealed.

SECTION 2. The transportation or importation into any State, Territory, or possession of the United States for delivery or use therein of intoxicating liquors, in violation of the laws thereof, is hereby prohibited.

SECTION 3. This article shall be inoperative unless it shall have been ratified as an amendment to the Constitution by conventions in the several States, as provided in the Constitution, within seven years from the date of the submission hereof to the States by the Congress.

*Passed March 2, 1932. Ratified January 23, 1933.
†Passed February 20, 1933. Ratified December 5, 1933.

Amendment XXII*

No person shall be elected to the office of the President more than twice, and no person who has held the office of President, or acted as President, for more than two years of a term to which some other person was elected President shall be elected to the office of the President more than once.

But this Article shall not apply to any person holding the office of President when this Article was proposed by the Congress, and shall not prevent any person who may be holding the office of President, or acting as President, during the term within which this Article becomes operative from holding the office of President or acting as President during the remainder of such term.

Amendment XXIII†

SECTION 1. The District constituting the seat of Government of the United States shall appoint in such manner as the Congress may direct:

A number of electors of President and Vice President equal to the whole number of Senators and Representatives in Congress to which the District would be entitled if it were a State, but in no event more than the least populous State; they shall be in addition to those appointed by the States, but they shall be considered, for the purposes of the election of President and Vice President, to be electors appointed by the State; and they shall meet in the District and perform such duties as provided by the twelfth article of amendment.

SECTION 2. The Congress shall have power to enforce this article by appropriate legislation.

Amendment XXIV‡

SECTION 1. The right of citizens of the United States to vote in any primary or other election for President or Vice President, or for Senator or Representative in Congress, shall not be denied or abridged by the United States or any State by reason of failure to pay any poll tax or other tax.

SECTION 2. The Congress shall have power to enforce this article by appropriate legislation.

Amendment XXV§

SECTION 1. In case of the removal of the President from office or of his death or resignation, the Vice President shall become President.

SECTION 2. Whenever there is a vacancy in the office of the Vice President, the President shall nominate a Vice President who shall take office upon confirmation by a majority vote of both Houses of Congress.

SECTION 3. Whenever the President transmits to the President pro tempore of the Senate and the Speaker of the House of Representatives his written declaration that he is unable to discharge the powers and duties of his office, and until he transmits to them a written declaration to the contrary, such powers and duties shall be discharged by the Vice President as Acting President.

SECTION 4. Whenever the Vice President and a majority of either the principal officers of the executive department or of such other body as Congress may by law provide, transmit to the President pro tempore of the Senate and the Speaker of the House of Representatives their written declaration that the President is unable to discharge the powers and duties of his office, the Vice President shall immediately assume the powers and duties of the office of Acting President.

Thereafter, when the President transmits to the President pro tempore of the Senate and the Speaker of the House of Representatives his written declaration that no inability exists, he shall resume the powers and duties of his office unless the Vice President and a majority of either the principal officers of the executive department or of such other body as Congress may by law provide, transmit within four days to the President pro tempore of the Senate and the Speaker of the House of Representatives their written declaration that the President is unable to discharge the powers and duties of his office. Thereupon Congress shall decide the issue, assembling within forty-eight hours for that purpose if not in session. If the Congress, within twenty-one days after receipt of the latter written declaration, or, if Congress is not in session, within twenty-one days after Congress is required to assemble, determines by two-thirds vote of both Houses that the President is unable to discharge the powers and duties of his office, the Vice President shall continue to discharge the same as Acting President; otherwise, the President shall resume the powers and duties of his office.

Amendment XXVI*

SECTION 1. The right of citizens of the United States, who are eighteen years of age or older, to vote shall not be denied or abridged by the United States or by any State on account of age.

SECTION 2. The Congress shall have power to enforce this article by appropriate legislation.

---

*Passed March 12, 1947. Ratified March 1, 1951.
† Passed June 16, 1960. Ratified April 3, 1961.
‡ Passed August 27, 1962. Ratified January 23, 1964.
§ Passed July 6, 1965. Ratified February 11, 1967.

*Passed March 23, 1971. Ratified July 5, 1971.

Presidential elections (1789–1840)

Year	Number of states	Candidates	Parties	Popular vote	Electoral vote	Percentage of popular vote
1789	11	GEORGE WASHINGTON	No party designations		69	
		John Adams			34	
		Minor Candidates			35	
1792	15	GEORGE WASHINGTON	No party designations		132	
		John Adams			77	
		George Clinton			50	
		Minor Candidates			5	
1796	16	JOHN ADAMS	Federalist		71	
		Thomas Jefferson	Democratic-Republican		68	
		Thomas Pinckney	Federalist		59	
		Aaron Burr	Democratic-Republican		30	
		Minor Candiates			48	
1800	16	THOMAS JEFFERSON	Democratic-Republican		73	
		Aaron Burr	Democratic-Republican		73	
		John Adams	Federalist		65	
		Charles C. Pinckney	Federalist		64	
		John Jay	Federalist		1	
1804	17	THOMAS JEFFERSON	Democratic-Republican		162	
		Charles C. Pinckney	Federalist		14	
1808	17	JAMES MADISON	Democratic-Republican		122	
		Charles C. Pinckney	Federalist		47	
		George Clinton	Democratic-Republican		6	
1812	18	JAMES MADISON	Democratic-Republican		128	
		DeWitt Clinton	Federalist		89	
1816	19	JAMES MONROE	Democratic-Republican		183	
		Rufus King	Federalist		34	
1820	24	JAMES MONROE	Democratic-Republican		231	
		John Quincy Adams	Independent Republican		1	
1824	24	JOHN QUINCY ADAMS	Democratic-Republican	108,740	84	30.5
		Andrew Jackson	Democratic-Republican	153,544	99	43.1
		William H. Crawford	Democratic-Republican	46,618	41	13.1
		Henry Clay	Democratic-Republican	47,136	37	13.2
1828	24	ANDREW JACKSON	Democratic	647,286	178	56.0
		John Quincy Adams	National Republican	508,064	83	44.0
1832	24	ANDREW JACKSON	Democratic	687,502	219	55.0
		Henry Clay	National Republican	530,189	49	42.4
		William Wirt	Anti-Masonic	33,108	7	2.6
		John Floyd	National Republican		11	
1836	26	MARTIN VAN BUREN	Democratic	765,483	170	50.9
		William H. Harrison	Whig	739,795	73	49.1
		Hugh L. White	Whig		26	
		Daniel Webster	Whig		14	
		W. P. Mangum	Whig		11	
1840	26	WILLIAM H. HARRISON	Whig	1,274,624	234	53.1
		Martin Van Buren	Democratic	1,127,781	60	46.9

Candidates receiving less than 1 percent of the popular vote have been omitted. For that reason the percentage of popular vote given for any election year may not total 100 percent.

Before the passage of the Twelfth Amendment in 1804, the Electoral College voted for two presidential candidates; the runner-up became Vice President. Figures are from *Historical Statistics of the United States, Colonial Times to 1957* (1961), pp. 682–83; and the U.S. Department of Justice.

Presidential elections (1844–1900)

Year	Number of states	Candidates	Parties	Popular vote	Electoral vote	Percentage of popular vote
1844	26	JAMES K. POLK	Democratic	1,338,464	170	49.6
		Henry Clay	Whig	1,300,097	105	48.1
		James G. Birney	Liberty	62,300		2.3
1848	30	ZACHARY TAYLOR	Whig	1,360,967	163	47.4
		Lewis Cass	Democratic	1,222,342	127	42.5
		Martin Van Buren	Free Soil	291,263		10.1
1852	31	FRANKLIN PIERCE	Democratic	1,601,117	254	50.9
		Winfield Scott	Whig	1,385,453	42	44.1
		John P. Hale	Free Soil	155,825		5.0
1856	31	JAMES BUCHANAN	Democratic	1,832,955	174	45.3
		John C. Frémont	Republican	1,339,932	114	33.1
		Millard Fillmore	American	871,731	8	21.6
1860	33	ABRAHAM LINCOLN	Republican	1,865,593	180	39.8
		Stephen A. Douglas	Democratic	1,382,713	12	29.5
		John C. Breckinridge	Democratic	848,356	72	18.1
		John Bell	Constitutional Union	592,906	39	12.6
1864	36	ABRAHAM LINCOLN	Republican	2,206,938	212	55.0
		George B. McClellan	Democratic	1,803,787	21	45.0
1868	37	ULYSSES S. GRANT	Republican	3,013,421	214	52.7
		Horatio Seymour	Democratic	2,706,829	80	47.3
1872	37	ULYSSES S. GRANT	Republican	3,596,745	286	55.6
		Horace Greeley	Democratic	2,843,446	*	43.9
1876	38	RUTHERFORD B. HAYES	Republican	4,036,572	185	48.0
		Samuel J. Tilden	Democratic	4,284,020	184	51.0
1880	38	JAMES A. GARFIELD	Republican	4,453,295	214	48.5
		Winfield S. Hancock	Democratic	4,414,082	155	48.1
		James B. Weaver	Greenback-Labor	308,578		3.4
1884	38	GROVER CLEVELAND	Democratic	4,879,507	219	48.5
		James G. Blaine	Republican	4,850,293	182	48.2
		Benjamin F. Butler	Greenback-Labor	175,370		1.8
		John P. St. John	Prohibition	150,369		1.5
1888	38	BENJAMIN HARRISON	Republican	5,477,129	233	47.9
		Grover Cleveland	Democratic	5,537,857	168	48.6
		Clinton B. Fisk	Prohibition	249,506		2.2
		Anson J. Streeter	Union Labor	146,935		1.3
1892	44	GROVER CLEVELAND	Democratic	5,555,426	277	46.1
		Benjamin Harrison	Republican	5,182,690	145	43.0
		James B. Weaver	People's	1,029,846	22	8.5
		John Bidwell	Prohibition	264,133		2.2
1896	45	WILLIAM McKINLEY	Republican	7,102,246	271	51.1
		William J. Bryan	Democratic	6,492,559	176	47.7
1900	45	WILLIAM McKINLEY	Republican	7,218,491	292	51.7
		William J. Bryan	Democratic; Populist	6,356,734	155	45.5
		John C. Wooley	Prohibition	208,914		1.5

*Greeley died shortly after the election; the electors supporting him then divided their votes among minor candidates.
Candidates receiving less than 1 percent of the popular vote have been omitted. For that reason the percentage of popular vote given for any election year may not total 100 percent.

Presidential elections (1904–1956)

Year	Number of states	Candidates	Parties	Popular vote	Electoral vote	Percentage of popular vote
1904	45	THEODORE ROOSEVELT	Republican	7,628,461	336	57.4
		Alton B. Parker	Democratic	5,084,223	140	37.6
		Eugene V. Debs	Socialist	402,283		3.0
		Silas C. Swallow	Prohibition	258,536		1.9
1908	46	WILLIAM H. TAFT	Republican	7,675,320	321	51.6
		William J. Bryan	Democratic	6,412,294	162	43.1
		Eugene V. Debs	Socialist	420,793		2.8
		Eugene W. Chafin	Prohibition	253,840		1.7
1912	48	WOODROW WILSON	Democratic	6,296,547	435	41.9
		Theodore Roosevelt	Progressive	4,118,571	88	27.4
		William H. Taft	Republican	3,486,720	8	23.2
		Eugene V. Debs	Socialist	900,672		6.0
		Eugene W. Chafin	Prohibition	206,275		1.4
1916	48	WOODROW WILSON	Democratic	9,127,695	277	49.4
		Charles E. Hughes	Republican	8,533,507	254	46.2
		A. L. Benson	Socialist	585,113		3.2
		J. Frank Hanly	Prohibition	220,506		1.2
1920	48	WARREN G. HARDING	Republican	16,143,407	404	60.4
		James N. Cox	Democratic	9,130,328	127	34.2
		Eugene V. Debs	Socialist	919,799		3.4
		P. P. Christensen	Farmer-Labor	265,411		1.0
1924	48	CALVIN COOLIDGE	Republican	15,718,211	382	54.0
		John W. Davis	Democratic	8,385,283	136	28.8
		Robert M. La Follette	Progressive	4,831,289	13	16.6
1928	48	HERBERT C. HOOVER	Republican	21,391,993	444	58.2
		Alfred E. Smith	Democratic	15,016,169	87	40.9
1932	48	FRANKLIN D. ROOSEVELT	Democratic	22,809,638	472	57.4
		Herbert C. Hoover	Republican	15,758,901	59	39.7
		Norman Thomas	Socialist	881,951		2.2
1936	48	FRANKLIN D. ROOSEVELT	Democratic	27,752,869	523	60.8
		Alfred M. Landon	Republican	16,674,665	8	36.5
		William Lemke	Union	882,479		1.9
1940	48	FRANKLIN D. ROOSEVELT	Democratic	27,307,819	449	54.8
		Wendell L. Willkie	Republican	22,321,018	82	44.8
1944	48	FRANKLIN D. ROOSEVELT	Democratic	25,606,585	432	53.5
		Thomas E. Dewey	Republican	22,014,745	99	46.0
1948	48	HARRY S. TRUMAN	Democratic	24,105,812	303	49.5
		Thomas E. Dewey	Republican	21,970,065	189	45.1
		J. Strom Thurmond	States' Rights	1,169,063	39	2.4
		Henry A. Wallace	Progressive	1,157,172		2.4
1952	48	DWIGHT D. EISENHOWER	Republican	33,936,234	442	55.1
		Adlai E. Stevenson	Democratic	27,314,992	89	44.4
1956	48	DWIGHT D. EISENHOWER	Republican	35,590,472	457	57.6
		Adlai E. Stevenson	Democratic	26,022,752	73	42.1

Candidates receiving less than 1 percent of the popular vote have been omitted. For that reason the percentage of popular vote given for any election year may not total 100 percent.

Presidential elections (1960–1972)

Year	Number of states	Candidates	Parties	Popular vote	Electoral vote	Percentage of popular vote
1960	50	JOHN F. KENNEDY	Democratic	34,227,096	303	49.9
		Richard M. Nixon	Republican	34,108,546	219	49.6
1964	50	LYNDON B. JOHNSON	Democratic	43,126,506	486	61.1
		Barry M. Goldwater	Republican	27,176,799	52	38.5
1968	50	RICHARD M. NIXON	Republican	31,785,480	301	43.4
		Hubert H. Humphrey	Democratic	31,275,165	191	42.7
		George C. Wallace	American Independent	9,906,473	46	13.5
1972*	50	RICHARD M. NIXON	Republican	45,767,218	521	60.8
		George S. McGovern	Democratic	28,357,668	17	37.7

Candidates receiving less than 1 percent of the popular vote have been omitted. For that reason the percentage of popular vote given for any election year may not total 100 percent.

*Figures (from the New York *Times,* November 9, 1972) do not represent final tally.

Admission of states

Order of admission	State	Date of admission	Order of admission	State	Date of admission
1	Delaware	December 7, 1787	26	Michigan	January 26, 1837
2	Pennsylvania	December 12, 1787	27	Florida	March 3, 1845
3	New Jersey	December 18, 1787	28	Texas	December 29, 1845
4	Georgia	January 2, 1788	29	Iowa	December 28, 1846
5	Connecticut	January 9, 1788	30	Wisconsin	May 29, 1848
6	Massachusetts	February 7, 1788	31	California	September 9, 1850
7	Maryland	April 28, 1788	32	Minnesota	May 11, 1858
8	South Carolina	May 23, 1788	33	Oregon	February 14, 1859
9	New Hampshire	June 21, 1788	34	Kansas	January 29, 1861
10	Virginia	June 25, 1788	35	West Virginia	June 30, 1863
11	New York	July 26, 1788	36	Nevada	October 31, 1864
12	North Carolina	November 21, 1789	37	Nebraska	March 1, 1867
13	Rhode Island	May 29, 1790	38	Colorado	August 1, 1876
14	Vermont	March 4, 1791	39	North Dakota	November 2, 1889
15	Kentucky	June 1, 1792	40	South Dakota	November 2, 1889
16	Tennessee	June 1, 1796	41	Montana	November 8, 1889
17	Ohio	March 1, 1803	42	Washington	November 11, 1889
18	Louisiana	April 30, 1812	43	Idaho	July 3, 1890
19	Indiana	December 11, 1816	44	Wyoming	July 10, 1890
20	Mississippi	December 10, 1817	45	Utah	January 4, 1896
21	Illinois	December 3, 1818	46	Oklahoma	November 16, 1907
22	Alabama	December 14, 1819	47	New Mexico	January 6, 1912
23	Maine	March 15, 1820	48	Arizona	February 14, 1912
24	Missouri	August 10, 1821	49	Alaska	January 3, 1959
25	Arkansas	June 15, 1836	50	Hawaii	August 21, 1959

Population of the United States (1790–1971)

Year	Total population (in thousands)	Number per square mile of land area (continental United States)	Year	Total population (in thousands)	Number per square mile of land area (continental United States)
1790	3,929	4.5	1835	15,003	
1791	4,056		1836	15,423	
1792	4,194		1837	15,843	
1793	4,332		1838	16,264	
1794	4,469		1839	16,684	
1795	4,607		1840	17,120	9.8
1796	4,745		1841	17,733	
1797	4,883		1842	18,345	
1798	5,021		1843	18,957	
1799	5,159		1844	19,569	
1800	5,297	6.1	1845	20,182	
1801	5,486		1846	20,794	
1802	5,679		1847	21,406	
1803	5,872		1848	22,018	
1804	5,065		1849	22,631	
1805	6,258		1850	23,261	7.9
1806	6,451		1851	24,086	
1807	6,644		1852	24,911	
1808	6,838		1853	25,736	
1809	7,031		1854	26,561	
1810	7,224	4.3	1855	27,386	
1811	7,460		1856	28,212	
1812	7,700		1857	29,037	
1813	7,939		1858	29,862	
1814	8,179		1859	30,687	
1815	8,419		1860	31,513	10.6
1816	8,659		1861	32,351	
1817	8,899		1862	33,188	
1818	9,139		1863	34,026	
1819	9,379		1864	34,863	
1820	9,618	5.6	1865	35,701	
1821	9,939		1866	36,538	
1822	10,268		1867	37,376	
1823	10,596		1868	38,213	
1824	10,924		1869	39,051	
1825	11,252		1870	39,905	13.4
1826	11,580		1871	40,938	
1827	11,909		1872	41,972	
1828	12,237		1873	43,006	
1829	12,565		1874	44,040	
1830	12,901	7.4	1875	45,073	
1831	13,321		1876	46,107	
1832	13,742		1877	47,141	
1833	14,162		1878	48,174	
1834	14,582		1879	49,208	

Figures are from *Historical Statistics of the United States, Colonial Times to 1957* (1961), pp. 7, 8; *Statistical Abstract of the United States: 1971*, p. 5.

Year	Total population (in thousands)	Number per square mile of land area (continental United States)	Year	Total population (in thousands)*	Number per square mile of land area (continental United States)
1880	50,262	16.9	1926	117,399	
1881	51,542		1927	119,038	
1882	52,821		1928	120,501	
1883	54,100		1929	121,770	
1884	55,379		1930	122,775	41.2
1885	56,658		1931	124,040	
1886	57,938		1932	124,840	
1887	59,217		1933	125,579	
1888	60,496		1934	126,374	
1889	61,775		1935	127,250	
1890	63,056	21.2	1936	128,053	
1891	64,361		1937	128,825	
1892	65,666		1938	129,825	
1893	66,970		1939	130,880	
1894	68,275		1940	131,669	44.2
1895	69,580		1941	133,894	
1896	70,885		1942	135,361	
1897	72,189		1943	137,250	
1898	73,494		1944	138,916	
1899	74,799		1945	140,468	
1900	76,094	25.6	1946	141,936	
1901	77,585		1947	144,698	
1902	79,160		1948	147,208	
1903	80,632		1949	149,767	
1904	82,165		1950	150,697	50.7
1905	83,820		1951	154,878	
1906	85,437		1952	157,553	
1907	87,000		1953	160,184	
1908	88,709		1954	163,026	
1909	90,492		1955	165,931	
1910	92,407	31.0	1956	168,903	
1911	93,868		1957	171,984	
1912	95,331		1958	174,882	
1913	97,227		1959	177,830	
1914	99,118		1960	178,464	60.1
1915	100,549		1961	183,672	
1916	101,966		1962	186,504	
1917	103,414		1963	189,197	
1918	104,550		1964	191,833	
1919	105,063		1965	194,237	
1920	106,466	35.6	1966	196,485	
1921	108,541		1967	198,629	
1922	110,055		1968	200,619	
1923	111,950		1969	202,599	
1924	114,113		1970	203,185	57.4†
1925	115,832		1971	206,676	

*Figures after 1940 represent total population including Armed Forces abroad, except in official census years.
†Figure includes Alaska and Hawaii.

Presidents, Vice Presidents, and Cabinet members (1789–1841)

President	Vice President	Secretary of State	Secretary of Treasury	Secretary of War
George Washington 1789–97	John Adams 1789–97	Thomas Jefferson 1789–94 Edmund Randolph 1794–95 Timothy Pickering 1795–97	Alexander Hamilton 1789–95 Oliver Wolcott 1795–97	Henry Knox 1789–95 Timothy Pickering 1795–96 James McHenry 1796–97
John Adams 1797–1801	Thomas Jefferson 1797–1801	Timothy Pickering 1797–1800 John Marshall 1800–01	Oliver Wolcott 1797–1801 Samuel Dexter 1801	James McHenry 1797–1800 John Marshall 1800 Samuel Dexter 1800–01 Roger Griswold 1801
Thomas Jefferson 1801–09	Aaron Burr 1801–05 George Clinton 1805–09	James Madison 1801–09	Samuel Dexter 1801 Albert Gallatin 1801–09	Henry Dearborn 1801–09
James Madison 1809–17	George Clinton 1809–13 Elbridge Gerry 1813–17	Robert Smith 1809–11 James Monroe 1811–17	Albert Gallatin 1809–14 George Campbell 1814 Alexander Dallas 1814–16 William Crawford 1816–17	William Eustis 1809–13 John Armstrong 1813–14 James Monroe 1814–15 William Crawford 1815–17
James Monroe 1817–25	Daniel D. Tompkins 1817–25	John Quincy Adams 1817–25	William Crawford 1817–25	Isaac Shelby 1817 George Graham 1817 John C. Calhoun 1817–25
John Quincy Adams 1825–29	John C. Calhoun 1825–29	Henry Clay 1825–29	Richard Rush 1825–29	James Barbour 1825–28 Peter B. Porter 1828–29
Andrew Jackson 1829–37	John C. Calhoun 1829–33 Martin Van Buren 1833–37	Martin Van Buren 1829–31 Edward Livingston 1831–33 Louis McLane 1833–34 John Forsyth 1834–37	Samuel Ingham 1829–31 Louis McLane 1831–33 William Duane 1833 Roger B. Taney 1833–34 Levi Woodbury 1834–37	John H. Eaton 1829–31 Lewis Cass 1831–37 Benjamin Butler 1837
Martin Van Buren 1837–41	Richard M. Johnson 1837–41	John Forsyth 1837–41	Levi Woodbury 1837–41	Joel R. Poinsett 1837–41
William H. Harrison 1841	John Tyler 1841	Daniel Webster 1841	Thomas Ewing 1841	John Bell 1841

Secretary of Navy	Postmaster General	Attorney General
	Samuel Osgood 1789–91 Timothy Pickering 1791–95 Joseph Habersham 1795–97	Edmund Randolph 1789–94 William Bradford 1794–95 Charles Lee 1795–97
Benjamin Stoddert 1798–1801	Joseph Habersham 1797–1801	Charles Lee 1797–1801 Theodore Parsons 1801
Benjamin Stoddert 1801 Robert Smith 1801–09	Joseph Habersham 1801 Gideon Granger 1801–09	Levi Lincoln 1801–05 Robert Smith 1805 John Breckinridge 1805-07 Caesar Rodney 1807–09
Paul Hamilton 1809–13 William Jones 1813–14 Benjamin Crowninshield 1814–17	Gideon Granger 1809–14 Return Meigs 1814–17	Caesar Rodney 1809–11 William Pinckney 1811–14 Richard Rush 1814–17
Benjamin Crowninshield 1817–18 Smith Thompson 1818–23 Samuel Southard 1823–25	Return Meigs 1817–23 John McLean 1823–25	Richard Rush 1817 William Wirt 1817–25
Samuel Southard 1825–29	John McLean 1825–29	William Wirt 1825–29
John Branch 1829–31 Levi Woodbury 1831–34 Mahlon Dickerson 1834–37	William Barry 1829–35 Amos Kendall 1835–37	John M. Berrien 1829–31 Roger B. Taney 1831–33 Benjamin Butler 1833–37
Mahlon Dickerson 1837–38 James K. Paulding 1838–41	Amos Kendall 1837–40 John M. Niles 1840–41	Benjamin Butler 1837–38 Felix Grundy 1838–40 Henry D. Gilpin 1840–41
George E. Badger 1841	Francis Granger 1841	John J. Crittenden 1841

Presidents, Vice Presidents, and Cabinet members (1841–81)

President	Vice President	Secretary of State	Secretary of Treasury	Secretary of War
John Tyler 1841–45		Daniel Webster 1841–43 Hugh S. Legaré 1843 Abel P. Upshur 1843–44 John C. Calhoun 1844–45	Thomas Ewing 1841 Walter Forward 1841–43 John C. Spencer 1843–44 George M. Bibb 1844–45	John Bell 1841 John McLean 1841 John C. Spencer 1841–43 James M. Porter 1843–44 William Wilkins 1844–45
James K. Polk 1845–49	George M. Dallas 1845–49	James Buchanan 1845–49	Robert J. Walker 1845–49	William L. Marcy 1845–49
Zachary Taylor 1849–50	Millard Fillmore 1849–50	John M. Clayton 1849–50	William M. Meredith 1849–50	George W. Crawford 1849–50
Millard Fillmore 1850–53		Daniel Webster 1850–52 Edward Everett 1852–53	Thomas Corwin 1850–53	Charles M. Conrad 1850–53
Franklin Pierce 1853–57	William R. King 1853–57	William L. Marcy 1853–57	James Guthrie 1853–57	Jefferson Davis 1853–57
James Buchanan 1857–61	John C. Breckinridge 1857–61	Lewis Cass 1857–60 Jeremiah S. Black 1860–61	Howell Cobb 1857–60 Philip F. Thomas 1860–61 John A. Dix 1861	John B. Floyd 1857–61 Joseph Holt 1861
Abraham Lincoln 1861–65	Hannibal Hamlin 1861–65 Andrew Johnson 1865	William H. Seward 1861–65	Salmon P. Chase 1861–64 William P. Fessenden 1864–65 Hugh McCulloch 1865	Simon Cameron 1861–62 Edwin M. Stanton 1862–65
Andrew Johnson 1865–69		William H. Seward 1865–69	Hugh McCulloch 1865–69	Edwin M. Stanton 1865–67 Ulysses S. Grant 1867–68 Lorenzo Thomas 1868 John M. Schofield 1868–69
Ulysses S. Grant 1869–77	Schuyler Colfax 1869–73 Henry Wilson 1873–77	Elihu B. Washburne 1869 Hamilton Fish 1869–77	George S. Boutwell 1869–73 William A. Richardson 1873–74 Benjamin H. Bristow 1874–76 Lot M. Morrill 1876–77	John A. Rawlins 1869 William T. Sherman 1869 William W. Belknap 1869–76 Alphonso Taft 1876 James D. Cameron 1876–77
Rutherford B. Hayes 1877–81	William A. Wheeler 1877–81	William M. Evarts 1877–81	John Sherman 1877–81	George W. McCrary 1877–79 Alexander Ramsey 1879–81

Secretary of Navy	Postmaster General	Attorney General	Secretary of Interior
George E. Badger 1841	Francis Granger 1841	John J. Crittenden 1841	
Abel P. Upshur 1841–43	Charles A. Wickliffe 1841–45	Hugh S. Legaré 1841–43	
David Henshaw 1843–44		John Nelson 1843–45	
Thomas Gilmer 1844			
John Y. Mason 1844–45			
George Bancroft 1845–46	Cave Johnson 1845–49	John Y. Mason 1845–46	
John Y. Mason 1846–49		Nathan Clifford 1846–48	
		Isaac Toucey 1848–49	
William B. Preston 1849–50	Jacob Collamer 1849–50	Reverdy Johnson 1849–50	Thomas Ewing 1849–50
William A. Graham 1850–52	Nathan K. Hall 1850–52	John J. Crittenden 1850–53	A. H. H. Stuart 1850–53
John P. Kennedy 1852–53	Sam D. Hubbard 1852–53		
James C. Dobbin 1853–57	James Campbell 1853–57	Caleb Cushing 1853–57	Robert McClelland 1853–57
Isaac Toucey 1857–61	Aaron V. Brown 1857–59	Jeremiah S. Black 1857–60	Jacob Thompson 1857–61
	Joseph Holt 1859–61	Edwin M. Stanton 1860–61	
Gideon Welles 1861–65	Horatio King 1861	Edward Bates 1861–63	Caleb B. Smith 1861–63
	Montgomery Blair 1861–64	Titian J. Coffey 1863–64	John P. Usher 1863–65
	William Dennison 1864–65	James Speed 1864–65	
Gideon Welles 1865–69	William Dennison 1865–66	James Speed 1865–66	John P. Usher 1865
	Alexander Randall 1866–69	Henry Stanbery 1866–68	James Harlan 1865–66
		William M. Evarts 1868–69	O. H. Browning 1866–69
Adolph E. Borie 1869	John A. J. Creswell 1869–74	Ebenezer R. Hoar 1869–70	Jacob D. Cox 1869–70
George M. Robeson 1869–77	James W. Marshall 1874	Amos T. Akerman 1870–71	Columbus Delano 1870–75
	Marshall Jewell 1874–76	G. H. Williams 1871–75	Zachary Chandler 1875–77
	James N. Tyner 1876–77	Edwards Pierrepont 1875–76	
		Alphonso Taft 1876–77	
R. W. Thompson 1877–81	David M. Key 1877–80	Charles Devens 1877–81	Carl Schurz 1877–81
Nathan Goff, Jr. 1881	Horace Maynard 1880–81		

Presidents, Vice Presidents, and Cabinet members (1881–1933)

President	Vice President	Secretary of State	Secretary of Treasury	Secretary of War	Secretary of Navy
James A. Garfield 1881	Chester A. Arthur 1881	James G. Blaine 1881	William Windom 1881	Robert T. Lincoln 1881	William H. Hunt 1881
Chester A. Arthur 1881–85		F. T. Frelinghuysen 1881–85	Charles J. Folger 1881–84 Walter Q. Gresham 1884 Hugh McCulloch 1884–85	Robert T. Lincoln 1881–85	William E. Chandler 1881–85
Grover Cleveland 1885–89	T. A. Hendricks 1885–89	Thomas F. Bayard 1885–89	Daniel Manning 1885–87 Charles S. Fairchild 1887–89	William C. Endicott 1885–89	William C. Whitney 1885–89
Benjamin Harrison 1889–93	Levi P. Morton 1889–93	James G. Blaine 1889–92 John W. Foster 1892–93	William Windom 1889–91 Charles Foster 1891–93	Redfield Procter 1889–91 Stephen B. Elkins 1891–93	Benjamin F. Tracy 1889–93
Grover Cleveland 1893–97	Adlai E. Stevenson 1893–97	Walter Q. Gresham 1893–95 Richard Olney 1895–97	John G. Carlisle 1893–97	Daniel S. Lamont 1893–97	Hilary A. Herbert 1893–97
William McKinley 1897–1901	Garret A. Hobart 1897–1901 Theodore Roosevelt 1901	John Sherman 1897–98 William R. Day 1898 John Hay 1898–1901	Lyman J. Gage 1897–1901	Russell A. Alger 1897–99 Elihu Root 1899–1901	John D. Long 1897–1901
Theodore Roosevelt 1901–09	Charles Fairbanks 1905–09	John Hay 1901–05 Elihu Root 1905–09 Robert Bacon 1909	Lyman J. Gage 1901–02 Leslie M. Shaw 1902–07 George B. Cortelyou 1907–09	Elihu Root 1901–04 William H. Taft 1904–08 Luke E. Wright 1908–09	John D. Long 1901–02 William H. Moody 1902–04 Paul Morton 1904–05 Charles J. Bonaparte 1905–07 Victor H. Metcalf 1907–08 T. H. Newberry 1908–09
William H. Taft 1909–13	James S. Sherman 1909–13	Philander C. Knox 1909–13	Franklin MacVeagh 1909–13	Jacob M. Dickinson 1909–11 Henry L. Stimson 1911–13	George von L. Meyer 1909–13
Woodrow Wilson 1913–21	Thomas R. Marshall 1913–21	William J. Bryan 1913–15 Robert Lansing 1915–20 Bainbridge Colby 1920–21	William G. McAdoo 1913–19 Carter Glass 1919–20 David F. Houston 1920–21	Lindley M. Garrison 1913–16 Newton D. Baker 1916–21	Josephus Daniels 1913–21
Warren G. Harding 1921–23	Calvin Coolidge 1921–23	Charles E. Hughes 1921–23	Andrew W. Mellon 1921–23	John W. Weeks 1921–23	Edwin Denby 1921–23
Calvin Coolidge 1923–29	Charles G. Dawes 1925–29	Charles E. Hughes 1923–25 Frank B. Kellogg 1925–29	Andrew W. Mellon 1923–29	John W. Weeks 1923–25 Dwight F. Davis 1925–29	Edwin Denby 1923–24 Curtis D. Wilbur 1924–29
Herbert C. Hoover 1929–33	Charles Curtis 1929–33	Henry L. Stimson 1929–33	Andrew W. Mellon 1929–32 Ogden L. Mills 1932–33	James W. Good 1929 Patrick J. Hurley 1929–33	Charles F. Adams 1929–33

Postmaster General	Attorney General	Secretary of Interior	Secretary of Agriculture	Secretary of Commerce and Labor	
Thomas L. James 1881	Wayne MacVeagh 1881	S. J. Kirkwood 1881			
Timothy O. Howe 1881–83 Walter Q. Gresham 1883–84 Frank Hatton 1884–85	B. H. Brewster 1881–85	Henry M. Teller 1881–85			
William F. Vilar 1885–88 Don M. Dickinson 1888–89	A. H. Garland 1885–89	L. Q. C. Lamar 1885–88 William F. Vilas 1888–89	Norman J. Colman 1889		
John Wanamaker 1889–93	W. H. H. Miller 1889–93	John W. Noble 1889–93	Jeremiah M. Rusk 1889–93		
Wilson S. Bissel 1893–95 William L. Wilson 1895–97	Richard Olney 1893–95 Judson Harmon 1895–97	Hoke Smith 1893–96 David R. Francis 1896–97	J. Sterling Morton 1893–97		
James A. Gary 1897–98 Charles E. Smith 1898–1901	Joseph McKenna 1897 John W. Griggs 1897–1901 Philander C. Knox 1901	Cornelius N. Bliss 1897–99 E. A. Hitchcock 1899–1901	James Wilson 1897–1901		
Charles E. Smith 1901–02 Henry C. Payne 1902–04 Robert J. Wynne 1904–05 George B. Cortelyou 1905–07 George von L. Meyer 1907–09	Philander C. Knox 1901–04 William H. Moody 1904–06 Charles J. Bonaparte 1906–09	E. A. Hitchcock 1901–07 James R. Garfield 1907–09	James Wilson 1901–09	George B. Cortelyou 1903–04 Victor H. Metcalf 1904–06 Oscar S. Straus 1906–09	

Postmaster General	Attorney General	Secretary of Interior	Secretary of Agriculture	Charles Nagel 1909–13	
Frank H. Hitchcock 1909–13	G. W. Wickersham 1909–13	R. A. Ballinger 1909–11 Walter L. Fisher 1911–13	James Wilson 1909–13	Secretary of Commerce	Secretary of Labor
Albert S. Burleson 1913–21	J. C. McReynolds 1913–14 T. W. Gregory 1914–19 A. Mitchell Palmer 1919–21	Franklin K. Lane 1913–20 John B. Payne 1920–21	David F. Houston 1913–20 E. T. Meredith 1920–21	W. C. Redfield 1913–19 J. W. Alexander 1919–21	William B. Wilson 1913–21
Will H. Hays 1921–22 Hubert Work 1922–23 Harry S. New 1923	H. M. Daugherty 1921–23	Albert B. Fall 1921–23 Hubert Work 1923	Henry C. Wallace 1921–23	Herbert C. Hoover 1921–23	James J. Davis 1921–23
Harry S. New 1923–29	H. M. Daugherty 1923–24 Harlan F. Stone 1924–25 John D. Sargent 1925–29	Hubert Work 1923–28 Roy O. West 1928–29	Henry C. Wallace 1923–24 Howard M. Gore 1924–25 W. M. Jardine 1925–29	Herbert C. Hoover 1923–25 William F. Whiting 1925–29	James J. Davis 1923–29
Walter F. Brown 1929–33	W. D. Mitchell 1929–33	Ray L. Wilbur 1929–33	Arthur M. Hyde 1929–33	Robert P. Lamont 1929–32 Roy D. Chapin 1932–33	William N. Doak 1930–33

Presidents, Vice Presidents, and Cabinet members (1933–)

President	Vice President	Secretary of State	Secretary of Treasury	Secretary of War	Secretary of Navy
Franklin Delano Roosevelt 1933–45	John Nance Garner 1933–41 Henry A. Wallace 1941–45 Harry S Truman 1945	Cordell Hull 1933–44 E. R. Stettinius, Jr. 1944–45	William H. Woodin 1933–34 Henry Morgenthau, Jr. 1934–45	George H. Dern 1933–36 Harry H. Woodring 1936–40 Henry L. Stimson 1940–45	Claude A. Swanson 1933–40 Charles Edison 1940 Frank Knox 1940–44 James V. Forrestal 1944–45
Harry S Truman 1945–53	Alben W. Barkley 1949–53	James F. Byrnes 1945–47 George C. Marshall 1947–49 Dean G. Acheson 1949–53	Fred M. Vinson 1945–46 John W. Snyder 1946–53	Robert H. Patterson 1945–47 Kenneth C. Royall 1947	James V. Forrestal 1945–47
				Secretary of Defense James V. Forrestal 1947–49 Louis A. Johnson 1949–50 George C. Marshall 1950–51 Robert A. Lovett 1951–53	
Dwight D. Eisenhower 1953–61	Richard M. Nixon 1953–61	John Foster Dulles 1953–59 Christian A. Herter 1959–61	George M. Humphrey 1953–57 Robert M. Anderson 1957–61	Charles E. Wilson 1953–57 Neil H. McElroy 1957–61	
John F. Kennedy 1961–63	Lyndon B. Johnson 1961–63	Dean Rusk 1961–63	C. Douglas Dillon 1961–63	Robert S. McNamara 1961–63	
Lyndon B. Johnson 1963–69	Hubert H. Humphrey 1965–69	Dean Rusk 1963–69	C. Douglas Dillon 1963–65 Henry H. Fowler 1965–68 Joseph W. Barr 1968–69	Robert S. McNamara 1963–68 Clark M. Clifford 1968–69	
Richard M. Nixon 1969–	Spiro T. Agnew 1969–	William P. Rogers 1969–	David M. Kennedy 1969–70 John B. Connally 1970–72 George P. Shultz 1972–	Melvin R. Laird 1969–	

Postmaster General	Attorney General	Secretary of Interior	Secretary of Agriculture	Secretary of Commerce	Secretary of Labor	Secretary of Health, Education and Welfare
James A. Farley 1933–40 Frank C. Walker 1940–45	H. S. Cummings 1933–39 Frank Murphy 1939–40 Robert Jackson 1940–41 Francis Biddle 1941–45	Harold L. Ickes 1933–45	Henry A. Wallace 1933–40 Claude R. Wickard 1940–45	Daniel C. Roper 1933–39 Harry L. Hopkins 1939–40 Jesse Jones 1940–45 Henry A. Wallace 1945	Frances Perkins 1933–45	
R. E. Hannegan 1945–47 Jesse L. Donaldson 1947–53	Tom C. Clark 1945–49 J. H. McGrath 1949–53	Harold L. Ickes 1945–46 Julius A. Krug 1946–49 Oscar L. Chapman 1949–53	C. P. Anderson 1945–48 C. F. Brannan 1948–53	W. A. Harriman 1946–48 Charles Sawyer 1948–53	L. B. Schwellenbach 1945–48 Maurice J. Tobin 1948–53	
A. E. Summerfield 1953–61	H. Brownell, Jr. 1953–57 William P. Rogers 1957–61	Douglas McKay 1953–56 Fred Seaton 1956–61	Ezra T. Benson 1953–61	Sinclair Weeks 1953–58 Lewis L. Strauss 1958–59 Frederick H. Mueller 1959–61	Martin P. Durkin 1953 James P. Mitchell 1953–61	Oveta Culp Hobby 1953–55 Marion B. Folsom 1955–58 Arthur S. Flemming 1958–61
J. Edward Day 1961–63 John A. Gronouski 1963	Robert F. Kennedy 1961–63	Stewart L. Udall 1961–63	Orville L. Freeman 1961–63	Luther H. Hodges 1961–63	Arthur J. Goldberg 1961–62 W. Willard Wirtz 1962–63	A. H. Ribicoff 1961–62 Anthony J. Celebrezze 1962–63
John A. Gronouski 1963–65 Lawrence F. O'Brien 1965–68 W. Marvin Watson 1968–69	Robert F. Kennedy 1963–65 N. deB. Katzenbach 1965–67 Ramsey Clark 1967–69	Stewart L. Udall 1963–69	Orville L. Freeman 1963–69	Luther H. Hodges 1963–64 John T. Connor 1964–67 Alexander B. Trowbridge 1967–68 C. R. Smith 1968–69	W. Willard Wirtz 1963–69	Anthony J. Celebrezze 1963–65 John W. Gardner 1965–68 Wilbur J. Cohen 1968–69
				Secretary of Housing and Urban Development		Secretary of Transportation
				Robert C. Weaver 1966–68 Robert C. Wood 1968–69		Alan S. Boyd 1966–69
Winston M. Blount 1969–71	John M. Mitchell 1969–72 Richard G. Kleindienst 1972–	Walter J. Hickel 1969–71 Rogers C. B. Morton 1971–	Clifford M. Hardin 1969–71 Earl L. Butz 1971–	Maurice H. Stans 1969–72 Peter G. Peterson 1972–	George P. Shultz 1969–70 James D. Hodgson 1970–	Robert H. Finch 1969–70 Elliot L. Richardson 1970–
				Secretary of Housing and Urban Development		Secretary of Transportation
				George W. Romney 1969–		John A. Volpe 1969–

Source of illustrations

Color insert

I: National Gallery of Art; Fogg Art Museum

II: Metropolitan Museum of Art

III: Corcoran Gallery of Art; National Gallery of Art; Art Institute of Chicago

IV: Ted Spiegel, from Rapho Guillumette; USDA (2); Library of Congress

V: USDA; Grant Heilman

VI: Bancroft Library, University of California, Berkeley; The Tenth Muse; Marathon Oil Company

VII: Ted Spiegel, from Rapho Guillumette; National Coal Association; Billy Davis

VIII: Smithsonian Institution; Museum of Fine Arts, Boston; Smithsonian Institution

IX: Susan McCartney, from Photo Researchers; Carl Purcell, from Photo Researchers; P. W. Grace, from Photo Researchers; Van Bucher, from Photo Researchers; Laurence Lowry, from Rapho Guillumette; Barnes Engineering Company

X: British Museum; Old Print Shop; American Museum of Natural History; Louisiana State Museum

XI: Library of Congress; Stokes Collection, New York Public Library; Collection of Stratford Lee Morton

XII: Paolo Koch, from Rapho Guillumette; Porterfield-Chickering, from Photo Researchers; Esther Henderson, from Rapho Guillumette

XIII: Van Bucher, from Photo Researchers; Harbrace Photo; Philadelphia Redevelopment Authority; Tom McHugh, from Photo Researchers

XIV: Model Products; Smithsonian Institution; Museum of the City of New York

XV: Farrell Grehan, from Photo Researchers; Helen Nathan; Farrell Grehan, from Photo Researchers; Jim Amos, from Photo Researchers

XVI: New York Public Library; Museum of Fine Arts, Boston; Robert Perron, from Photo Researchers

XVII: Leo Willette, from National Park Service; Laurence Pringle, from Photo Researchers; Harbrace Photo; Eugene Gordon

XVIII: Tom McHugh, from Photo Researchers; Farrell Grehan, from Photo Researchers; Paolo Koch, from Rapho Guillumette

XIX: Chuck Abbott, from Rapho Guillumette; Inger McCabe, from Rapho Guillumette; Van Bucher, from Photo Researchers; Esther Henderson, from Rapho Guillumette

XX: New York Public Library; National Park Service; John Stage, from Photo Researchers

XXI: Van Bucher, from Photo Researchers; Geroge E. Jones III, from Photo Researchers; John Stage, from Photo Researchers; Joe Bilbao, from Photo Researchers

XXII: Marilyn Cooper; Meryl Sussman; Weyerhaeuser Corporation; Westvaco Corporation

XXIII: Balthazar Korab; W. T. Davidson, from National Audubon Society; Van Bucher, from Photo Researchers

XXIV: Bureau of Reclamation; Joe Munroe, from Photo Researchers; Tomas D. Friedmann, from Photo Researchers; Russ Kinne, from Photo Researchers

XXV: Tennessee Valley Authority

XXVI: Bruce Roberts, from Rapho Guillumette; Helen Nathan; Esther Henderson, from Rapho Guillumette

XXVII: Charles Harbutt, from Magnum; Susan Haggerty; Harbrace Photo by Theologos; Esther Henderson, from Rapho Guillumette

XXVIII: Jack Fields, from Photo Researchers; U.S. Navy; Signal Corps (2)

XXIX: Library of Congress; Signal Corps

XXX: Philip Jones Griffiths, from Magnum

XXXI: Bruno Barbey, from Magnum

XXXII: NASA; Harbrace Photo by Weitz

Index

Index

Boldface numbers refer to maps, charts, or illustrations. When an entry is mentioned both in the text and in the artwork of a single page, the page number is set lightface.

American Sugar Refining Company, 428
American System, 184, 188, 190, 196, 215, 216, 223, 229, 234, 235
American Telephone and Telegraph Company, 430
American Tobacco Company, 395, 520, 538
Americanism, 61, 113, 552–53
Americans for Democratic Action, 719
Amerinds. *See* Indians, American
Ames, Fisher, 165
Ames, Oakes, 373
Amherst, Jeffrey, 79, 80, 83, 86
Amnesty Act (*1872*), 376
Amos Bad Heart Bull, 403
Anaconda Plan, 336, 351
Anderson, Robert, 322, 323, 324
Anderson, Sherwood, 606, 624
Andrew, John, 342, 345
Andros, Sir Edmund, 33, 43–44
Anglican Church, 38, 58, 62, 63, 93, 113. *See also* Church of England; Episcopal Church
Anglo-American Combined Chiefs of Staff, 694
Angola, 797
Antarctic Treaty, 775
Anthony, Susan B., 451
Antietam, Battle of, 343–44, 345
Anti-Imperialist League, 504
Anti-Masonic party, 229
Antislavery movement. *See* Abolitionism
Appalachia, 767
Appleton, Nathan, 206
Appomattox Court House, 354
Arab League, 738
Arab nationalism, 749, 796
Arapaho Indians, 401
Archaeological Institute of America, 455
Architecture, 457–58
Area Development Act (*1961*), 767
Argall, Samuel, 13
Argentia Conference, 674, 675
Argentina, 547, 548, 600, 618, 750
Arianism, 240
Aristocracy, American, 114, 124, 159
Arizona, statehood of, 536
Arkansas: statehood of, 193, 260, **268;** and desegregation, 744
"Arkies," 649
Armada, Spanish, 10
Armed Services Committee (Senate), 725, 776
Arminianism, 240
Armstrong, Neil A., 766
Army, American. *See* Army, U.S.; Continental Army
Army, U.S., 110, 150, 153, 160–61, 173–74, 184, 402, 553, 601, 706, 738; demobilization of, 712; and First World War, 558–60; and Korean War, 726; and McCarthy, 742; pre-Second World War rearmament of, 665–66; reorganization of, by Root, 526; and Second World War, 691. *See also* Vietnam War
Army Appropriations Act (*1867*), 366, 370
Army of Northern Virginia, 340, 346, 347, 348, 349, 352, 354
Army of the Potomac, 345, 346
Army War College, 526
Arnold, Benedict, 106, 108

Arnold, Thurman, 642
Art, 456, 459, 514, 821. *See also* Architecture; Literature
Artaud, Antonin, 823
Arthur, Chester A., 463, 469; Administration of, 470–71, 492
Articles of Confederation, 117, 118, 124; acceptance by states, 117, 118; cession of Western lands, 117–18; compared with Constitution, 126; Congress under, 117, 118–19; executive under, 119; revision of, 128; weaknesses of, 133
Ashburton, Lord, 236
Asia, 494, 530, 566, 569, 594, 618, 676, 758; new nations of, 721, 739
Association of Collegial Alumnae, 450
Association of Gentlemen, 244
Astor, John Jacob, 206, 263, 264
Atchison, David R., 306–07, 308
Atchison, Topeka, and Santa Fe Railway. *See* Santa Fe Railway
Atlanta Compromise (*1895*), 387–89
Atlantic Charter, 674–75, 694, 695
Atomic Energy Commission (AEC), 709
Attlee, Clement, 703
Auchincloss, Louis, 822
Austin, Stephen F., 262
Australia, 314, 488, 567, 690, 691
Austria, 565, 580, 665, 710, **752**
Austro-Hungarian Empire, 549, 565, 567
Automation, 810–11
Avery, Rachel Foster, 451
Azores, 2
Aztecs, 3

Babbitt, Irving, 607
Babcock, Orville E., 376
Bacon, Nathaniel, 51
Bacon's Rebellion, 52, 117
Badillo, Herman, 817
Badoglio, Pietro, 686
Baer, George F., 521
Baghdad Pact (*1955*), 737, 749. *See also* CENTO
Bagot, Charles, 180
Bahamas, 43
Bailey v. *Drexel Furniture Company,* 584, 585
Baker, Newton D., 553
Baker, Ray Stannard, 483, 515
Baker v. *Carr,* 813
Baldwin, James, 683, 769, 822
Ball, George W., 774
Ballinger, Richard A., 536
Baltic, 554, 695
Baltimore, Lord, 23, 38, 46
Baltimore and Ohio Railroad, 295, 296, 328, 421, 424, 437, 467
Baltimore Turnpike, **194,** 195
Bank of England, 543, 619
Bank of the United States, 140, 160, 174, 185, 186, 188, 208, 227–31, 235, 543
Banking, 377, 482; in depression of '29, 613, 614, 615, 619, 621; federal control over, 335; under Jackson, 227–31, 232–33; and New Deal, 629, 631; reform of, 543–44; and state banks, 231–32, 233. *See also* Federal Reserve Board
Banking Act (*1935*), 642

Bao Dai, 740
Baptists, 63, 243, 244, 257, 451, 452
Barbados, 34, 35
Barbary pirates, 167
Barenblatt case, 746
Barkley, Alben W., 672
Barlow, Arthur, **8,** 10
Barlow, Joel, 123
Barnburners, 275, 281
Barras, comte de, 111, 112
Barré, Isaac, 85
Barry, USS, 764
Barton, Bruce, 590
Baruch, Bernard, 561, 572, 631, 709
Bates, Edward, 332
Batista, Fulgencio, 750
Battery Wagner, Battle of, 345
Bay of Pigs, 761, 762, 766
Bayard, James A., 179
Beadle, J. H., 412
Bear Flag Revolt, 272
Beard, Charles A., 302, 607, 672
"Beat generation," 748, 786
Beatles, 789
Beatty, John, 350
Beaumarchais, Pierre, 108
Beauregard, P. G. T., 324, 336, 337, 338
Beck, John, 404
Beckley, John, 145
Beecher, Henry Ward, 308, 432, 451
Beef trust, 520
Belgian Relief Commission, 561
Belgium, 550, 552, 554, 565, 581, 600, 668, 688, 718
Belknap, William W., 376
Bell, Alexander Graham, 429–30, 444
Bell, John, 320, 321, 353
Bell Telephone Company, 429
Bellamy, Edward, 434, 487
Bellow, Saul, 822
Benjamin, Judah P., 330
Benton, Thomas Hart, 208, 217, 221, 227, 268, 271, 310
Benton, William, 728
Bering Sea incident, 492, 495*n*
Berkeley, Lord John, 33, 34, **36**
Berkeley, Sir William, 34, 51
Berle, Adolf A., Jr., 630, 810
Berlin Conference (*1884–85*), 492
Berlin crisis, 712, 717–18, 725, 753, 762–63, 795
Bermuda, 16
Bernard, Francis, 83, 86, 89
Berstein, Barton J., 650
Berrigan, Daniel, 815
Berrigan, Philip, 800, 815
Bessemer, Henry, 424
Beveridge, Albert, 503, 506, 536, 537
Bevin, Ernest, 712, 716–17, 718
Biddle, Francis, 682
Biddle, Nicholas, 227, 228, 229, 230, 231
Big Four, 695, 752
Big Three, 696, 697
Bigelow, Jacob, 206
Bikini, atomic bomb test on, **709**
Bill of Rights, U.S., 129, 134–35, 139, 159, 786
Birch Society. *See* John Birch Society
Birney, James G., 253
Birth control, 806, 814
Birth rate, 741, 806

Classes, social, 207, 212, 256, 257; and distribution of wealth, 811; divisions among, 207, 446; middle class, 446; mobility of, 68–69, 113–14, 212; and progressivism, 518, 519

Clay, Henry, 171, 173, 183, 185, 211, 221, 229, 230, 233, 234, 237; "American System" of, 184, 188, 190, 196, 215, 216, 223, 229, 234, 235; and Compromise of *1850*, 277–80; and compromise tariff, 226; and election of *1844*, 267; and Latin American revolutions, 190; and Missouri Compromise, 203; and National Republicans, 214–15, 229; and Treaty of Ghent, 179; and War of *1812*, 171

Clay, Lucius, 717

Clayton, John M., 289, 290

Clayton Act (*1914*), 544, 584, 585

Clayton-Bulwer Treaty (*1850*), 289

Cleaver, Eldridge, 783, 816

Clemenceau, Georges, 566, 569, 570

Clemens, Samuel L., 406, 459, 460, 504

Cleveland, Grover, 471, 504; Administration of, 412, 423, 438, 463, 472–74, 481–86, 487, 492, 493, 496, 498

Clifford, Clark, 718, 779

Clinton, De Witt, 173, 195

Clinton, George, 166

Clinton, Henry, 99, 106, 110, 111

Clipper ships, 291–92

Cloning, 826

Coal mining, 358, 521, 575, 584, 645, 681, 827

Coexistence, 715, 726, 736, 752–53, 759

Cohen, Benjamin, 640

Cohens v. *Virginia*, 188

Cohn, Roy, 741, 742

Colbert de Croissy, Charles, 71

Cold Harbor, Battle of, 352

Cold War, 706–30, 733, 736, 751, 795; absolutist policy of, 737, 738–39; beginnings of, 699, 709–10, 712–13; and Kennedy, 758–66; and Moscow Summit, 795, 799, 825; and nationalism, 749–51; and nuclear-test-ban treaty, 765; thaw in, 752, 775

Cole, Nathan, 64

Coleridge, Samuel Taylor, 241

Colfax, Schuyler, 371, 373

Collective bargaining, 437, 512, 633, 646

Colleges and universities, 66, 113, 206, 249, 450, 454–56, 714, 784; women on faculties of, 819. *See also* Campus revolt; Draft

Colleton, Sir John, 34–35

Collier, John, 403, 818

Colombia, 289, 529, 580

Colonial life: and education, 65–66; and government, 57, 61–62; on plantation and farm, 49–55, 57–59; and religion, 62–65; in towns and cities, 55–57, 59–61

Colonies, early American, 9–24; assemblies in, 62, 115; corporate, 46; county government in, 59, 62; and Declaration of Independence, 102, 104; earliest European settlements in, 5; East-West split in, 83–84; governors in, 47, 83, 96, 97; imperial authority over, 82–83;

life in, 49–61; political strife in, 39–47; post-Revolutionary governments of, 115; private property in, 114–15; proprietary, 23–24, 32, 47; religion as factor in proliferation of, 20–23; during Restoration, 32–39; royal, 33, 40; towns in, 55–57; unity of, 89, 100–02. *See also individual colonies*

Colorado, 401, 451; statehood of, **406**

Colored Farmers' National Alliance and Cooperative Union, 478

Columbia Broadcasting System, 747

Columbian Exposition (*1893*), 430, 458, 483

Columbus, Christopher, 2–4, 11

Comanche Indians, 400, 401

Comintern, 717

Commission on the Causes and Prevention of Violence, 812

Commission on Civil Disorders, 783

Commission on Income Maintenance, 803

Commission on Intergovernmental Relations, 743

Commission on Obscenity and Pornography, 814

Commission on the Status of Women, 819

Committee on Government Operations (Senate), 741

Committee on Public Information (CPI), 562–63

Committee on Social and Political Implications, 702

Committee on Un-American Activities, 647

Committee to Defend America by Aiding the Allies, 673

Committees of Correspondence, 95

Commodity Credit Corporation, 478n

Common law, 207n

Common Market, 717, 763

Commoner, Barry, 826

Commons, John R., 516, 597, 607, 608

Commonwealth v. *Hunt*, 301

Communes, 787

Communism, 576, 624, 648, 711, 727, 733, 746, 801; and capitalism, 695, 711, 752, 753; containment of vs. coexistence with, 715–16, 726, 736, 752–53, 759; and Red scare, 576–79, 727–28, 741–42; resistance to, 711, 712, 726, 736, 739; and uncommitted nations, 721; and Yalta Conference, 697–700. *See also* Cold War; Soviet Union

Communist Information Bureau, (Cominform), 717

Communist Labor party, 576

Communist party of America, 576, 597, 624, 627, 648, 660, 667, 727

Communist party congresses: Nineteenth, 739; Twentieth, 752

Communitarianism, 250–51, 787

Community Action program, 772

Compromise of *1850*, 277–80, 305, **306**, 307

Comstock, Henry, 405

Concord, 116; Battle of, 98, 113

Confederacy, 310, 321, 322, 332, 346; and amnesty, 360–61, 376; and border states, 326–29; Congress of, 331, 346; and conscription, 331; Constitution of, 330; and England, 340–41; preparation for war, 331–32; and readmission of

states, 353, 357, 361, 367; and secession, 277, 280, 318, 320, 321–22, 357; and surrender, 354. *See also* Civil War

Confederation of Industrial Organizations, 479

Conference on Communication with Extra-Terrestrial Intelligence, 825

Conference for Progressive Political Action, 597

Confiscation Act (*1862*), 343

Conglomerates, 807, 808

Congo, 492, 554

Congregationalists, 17, 18, 19, 62, 63, 93, 243, 265, 451

Congress, U.S., 118–19, 126, 127, 188, 274, 357–58, 359–60, 466, 718–19, 799

Congress of Industrial Organizations (CIO), 645–46, 649

Congress of Racial Equality (CORE), 782, 816

Conkling, Roscoe, 373, 381, 464, 466, 467, 469, 470

Connally, John B., 804

Connecticut, colony of, 22, 39, 41, 45, 46, 60, 77, 115, 117; charter of, 39; dispute with Pennsylvania, 93; in Dominion of New England, 43–45; settling of, 22

Connor, Eugene, 768

Conquistadors, 3–4

Conscience Whigs, 271, 275, 279, 307

Consciousness III, 789–90

Conscription Act: Confederate (*1862*), 331; Union (*1863*), 333–34

Conservation, 524, 536, 636

Conservatism: in government, 467–75, 498, 590, 718; and laissez-faire doctrine, 430–34; and New Deal, 652

Conservative party, Southern Democratic, 376, 385–87, 389–90, 394, 465

Constitution, English, 116

Constitution, state, 115–16; in post-Civil War South, 368, 389

Constitution, U.S., 115–16, 124–30, 132, 152, 305, 330; amending of, 128; and Congress, 126, 127; and executive, 127, 128; and federal and state powers, 128, 274; and judicial review, 187–88; liberal construction of, 188, 189, 746; opposition to, 129; ratification of, 128–30. *See also* Amendments, constitutional; Articles of Confederation; Bill of Rights

Constitutional Convention (*1787*), 116, 124–30, 133, 134, 135, 139, 188, 202

Constitutional Union party, 320

Consumers, 809, 810

Continental Army: enlistment of, 104; establishment of, 100; in Revolutionary War, 104–13

Continental Congress, First, 95–97, 100; final resolutions of, 96; moderates at, 96; radical contingency of, 96

Continental Congress, Second, 100–02, 107; and Continental Army, 100; and French alliance, 108–09, 112–13; and independence, 101; and peace negotiations, 112; in Revolution, 119; voting in, 126

Washington Conference, 580–82; and Western expansion in the U.S., 84, 231, 232, 261, 263

Great Northern Railway, 413, 419, 420–21, 520

Great Society, 770, 771, 772, 778, 781

Greater East Asia Co-Posterity Sphere, 690

Greece, 696, 697, 698, 712, 714, 715, 722, 797

Greeley, Horace, 239, 343, 344, 375, 376

Green, William, 648

Green Berets, 760, 762

Greenback Labor party, 468, 479

Greenback party, 391, 467, 468

Greenbacks, 334, 358, 371, 376–77

Greene, Nathanael, 111

Greenwood, John, 30

Gregg, William, 302

Grenville, George, 84–85, 88, 90, 142

Grenville, Sir Richard, 10

Grier, Robert C., 312

Griffith, John, 292

Grimké, Angelina and Sarah, 248

Griswold, Roger, 152

Grossilliers, Sieur de (Médart Chouart), 71

Growth, problems of, 826–29

Gruening, Ernest, 776

Grundy, Felix, 171, 172

Guadalcanal, 691

Guadeloupe, 82, 84

Guam, 503, 504, 527, 582, 690

Guatemala, 738, 755, 761

Guevara, Che, 785

Guffey Coal Act (1935), 641, 643

Guggenheim, David, 536

Guiteau, Charles J., 470

Gun Control Act (1968), 812

Gutierrez, Jose Angel, 817

Hague Conference (1907), 660, 736

Haiti, 491, 495, 547, 600, 618, 655, 656

Hakluyt, Richard, 10, 27, 28, 30

Hale, Eugene, 504

Hale, John P., 281

Half-Breeds, 381, 464, 469

Halleck, Henry W., 337, 338, 340, 351

Hals, Frans, 31

Hamilton, Alexander, 125, 132, 133, 134, 135, 142, 144, 145, 147, 154, 188, 205; and assumption of states' debts, 136–37, 160; and Burr, 155, 166; at Constitutional Convention, 124, 129; economic policy of, 137–38, 159, 160; and French Revolution, 141; funding plan of, 136, 160; and national bank, 137–38, 140, 160; on society, 138

Hamilton, M. A., 617

Hammer v. Dagenhart, 584–85

Hammett, Dashiell, 741

Hammond, George, 140, 142

Hammond, James H., 257, 329

Hampton, Wade, 385

Hancock, Cornelia, 352

Hancock, John, 129

Hancock, Winfield Scott, 402, 469

Hand, Learned, 742

Hanna, Marcus Alonzo, 466, 486, 487, 488, 508, 519, 521

Hanover, House of, 81, 86, 101

Hanson, Ole, 577

Harding, Warren G., 573, 579, 589; Administration of, 580–87, 649; and agriculture, 585; and business, 582–84; and imperialism, 580; and labor, 584–85; scandals of, 585–87; and tariff, 583; and taxation, 582, 583; and Washington Conference, 580–82; and World Court, 602

Hardwick, Thomas W., 577

Hariot, Thomas, 10, 11

Harlan, John Marshall, 386, 746

Harlem Renaissance, 606–07

Harmar, Josiah, 141, **142**

Harper's Ferry, 317, 318

Harriman, E. H., 520

Harriman, W. Averell, 696, 761, 762, 766, 779, 797

Harrington, James, 35, 86

Harrington, Michael, 767

Harris, Joel Chandler, 392

Harris, Townsend, 291

Harrison, Benjamin, 473, 481; Administration of, 463, 474–75, 492, 495, 497

Harrison, William Henry, **174,** 231, 233–34, 310, 473; and Indian war, 171–72, 175

Harrison Act (1914), 787

Hartford Convention, 178

Harvard, John, 66

Harvey, George, 579

Harvey, William H., 485

Hat Act (1732), 30

Haugen, Gilbert N., 608

Haupt, Herman, 347

Havana Conference (1928), 656

Hawaii, 491; and annexation, 288, 290, 496–97, 503, 527; bombing of, 677; and Second World War, 690, 691; statehood of, 755

Hawks, 776

Hawley-Smoot Tariff (1930), 613, 615

Hawthorne, Nathaniel, 241, 251, 287

Hay, John, 500, 503, 504, 506, 507

Hay-Pauncefote Treaty (1901), 528

Hayes, Rutherford B., 381, 382–83; Administration of, 384–85, 420, 463, 467–69, 470, 492; Cabinet of, 383, 384, 467; monetary policies of, 468; and segregation, 385; and Southern rehabilitation, 384

Haymarket riot, 437–38, 460, 486–87

Hayne, Robert Y., 225, 226

Hays, Arthur Garfield, 596

Hays, Will, 564

Head Start program, 772

Hearst, W. R., 454, 498

Hefner, Hugh, 814

Hegel, Georg W. F., 241, 726

Heller, Joseph, 823

Heller, Walter, 767

Hell's Angels, 788

Helper, Hinton Rowan, 318

Hemingway, Ernest, 606

Henderson, Leon, 681

Hendrick, Burton J., 515

Hendricks, Thomas A., 382, 471

Henning, W. W., 52, 53

Henri, Robert, 514

Henry VII (king of England), 6

Henry VIII (king of England), 6–8

Henry, Patrick, 87, 90, 94, 129, 132

Henry Street Settlement, 449

Hepburn Act, 524

Herbart, Johann Friedrich, 453

Herter, Christian A., 753

Hickel, Walter J., 804

Higginson, Thomas W., 449

Highway Beautification Act (1965), 771

Hill, Isaac, 217, 219

Hill, James J., 413, 420, **421,** 424, 520

Hillman, Sidney, 694

Hillsborough, Lord, 92, 93, 94

Himmler, Heinrich, 696

Hippies, 786–88, 789, 815

Hipsters, 748, 749

Hiroshima, 703

Hiss, Alger, 727, 729, 793

Hitchcock, Gilbert, 572, 573

Hitler, Adolf, 621, 654, 664, 665, 666, 673, 674, 683, 685, 688, 696, 701, 711, 775

Ho Chi Minh, 726, 739, 751, 761, 775, 798

Hoar, George F., 504, 505

Hobart, Garret A., 486

Hobbema, Meindert, 31

Hoffman, Abbie, 788

Hofstadter, Richard, 441

Holbrook, Josiah, 249

Holding companies, 428, 429, 520, 538, 544, 642

Holding Company Act, 644

Holland, 112; control of seas by, 31; exploration of New World by, 6; financial assistance from, 119; mercantilism of, 31; and settlement of New York, 32; war between England and, 32. See also Netherlands

Holmes, Oliver Wendell, Jr., 515, 577, 829

Holy See, 452

Home Owners' Loan Act, 635

Homer, Winslow, 459

Homestead Act (1862), 358, 410, 412

Homestead strike, 425, 438

Homosexuality, 814

Honduras, 537

Hooch, Pieter de, 31

Hood, John B., 352, 353, 354

Hooker, Joseph, 346, 347, 348, **349**

Hooker, Thomas, 22

Hoover, Herbert C., 561, 579, 582, 585, 593, 602n, 604, 608–09, 643, 667; Administration of, 612, 627, 631, 649, 656; and bank crisis, 613, 615, 617, 618, 621–22; and business, 612–13; and depression, 613–17, 621–25, 650; early career of, 593; and employment service, 616; and farmers, 612–13, 623–24; and Japanese aggression, 619–21; and moratorium on war debts, 618–19; and public works, 622–23

Hoover, J. Edgar, 681

Hopkins, Harry L., 635, 636, 646, 674, 710

Horseshoe Bend, Battle of, 175

House, Edward M., 542, 552, 564, 565, 566

House of Burgesses, 87, 90

House of Commons, 14, 61–62, 68, 81, 144

House of Lords, 68, 81

WHO. *See* World Health Organization
WLB. *See* War Labor Board
WLPB. *See* War Labor Policies Board
WPA. *See* Works Progress Administration
WPB. *See* War Production Board
Wabash, St. Louis, and Pacific Railway Co.
    v. *Illinois*, 423
WACS, 819
Wade, Benjamin, 310, 353, 362
Wade-Davis Bill, 353, 369
Wage-price guidelines, 767, 804
Wages and Hours Act. *See* Fair Labor
    Standards Act
Wagner, Robert, 616
Wagner Labor Relations Act (*1935*), 641,
    644, 645, 718
Waite, Davis H., 479
Waite, Morrison R., 385
Wald, Lillian, 449
Wales, 32
Walker, David, 252
Walker, Robert J., 267, 312
Walker, William, 289
Walker Tariff, 267, 273
Wall Street, 302, 520, 597, 635
Wallace, George, 768, 780, 782, 816
Wallace, Henry A., 631, 632, 633, 670,
    693, 714, 716, 719, 720
Wallace, Henry C., 582
Wallace, Irving, 821
Walsh, Frank P., 562
Walsh, Thomas J., 586
Wampanoag Indians, 70
Wanamaker, John, 474
War Finance Corporation (*1918*), 622, 631
War Food Administration (*1942*), 679
War Hawks, 171, 174
War Industries Board (*1917*), 561, 574,
    631, 633
War Investigating Committee (Senate), 683
War Labor Board (WLB), 681
War Labor Policies Board (WLPB), 562
War Manpower Commission (*1942*), 679
War of *1812*, 173–78, 235; American
    unpreparedness for, 173–78, 235; and
    English blockade, 176–77, 178; cam-
    paigns of, 174–77; causes of, 168–72;
    consequences of, 185, 205, 211, 250;
    Federalist opposition to, 170; and peace
    negotiations, 179–80; and postwar set-
    tlements, 180–81; support of, 170, 173;
    and War Hawks, 171
War of Jenkins' Ear, 74
War of the Austrian Succession. *See* King
    George's War
War of the League of Augsburg. *See* King
    William's War
War of the Spanish Succession. *See* Queen
    Anne's War
War Production Board (WPB), 679, 680
Ward, Lester Frank, 433–34
Ward, Samuel Ringgold, 252
Warhol, Andy, 823
Warmoth, Henry Clay, 374
Warren, Earl, 719, 744, 746, 770, 804
Warren, Joseph, 89
Warren, Robert Penn, 821
Warsaw invasion, **667**
Warwick, Earl of, 23
Washington, Augustine, 78
Washington, Booker T., 387–89, 513,
    522

Washington, George, 78, **79,** 90, 123,
    125, 150, 735, 755; Administration of,
    133–47; at Constitutional Convention,
    124, 129; and Continental Army, 100,
    104; domestic policy of, 135–37; elec-
    tion of, 132, 140; on Federal authority,
    146; and foreign policy, 134, 140–43;
    and Indians, 141, 143; and Republican
    protest, 146; and Revolutionary War,
    100, 104–13; and westward expansion,
    143
Washington, Lawrence, 78
Washington, statehood of, **406,** 482
Washington Conference (*1921*), 580–82,
    594
Washington Naval Treaty (*1922*), 581–82,
    659, 662
Watauga Compact (*1772*), 121
Water Power Act (*1920*), 574
Water Quality Act (*1965*), 771
Watertown settlement, 19
Watkins case, 746
Watson, James D., 825, 826
Watson, Thomas E., 477, 479, 487, 489,
    508
Watterson, Henry, 391, 503
Watts, Alan, 789
WAVES, 819
Wayland, Francis, 177
Wayne, Anthony, **111,** 112, 142, 143
Wayne, James, 311
Wealth, 299, 511, 682; distribution of,
    811; Gospel of, 430–34; inequalities of,
    510, 811; national, 396, 510–11
Weathermen, 786, 788, 789, 813
Weaver, James B., 468, 479
Weaver, Robert C., 771
Webb, Walter P., 399, 404, 407–08, 410
Webster, Daniel, 177, 193, 211, 225,
    226, 227, 229, 230, 234, 236; and
    Compromise of *1850,* 279–80; and
    Dartmouth College case, 190; on the
    Union, 225, 279
Webster, Noah, 123
Webster-Ashburton Treaty (*1842*), 236
Webster-Hayne debate, 225
Wedemeyer, A. C., 722
Weed, Thurlow, 309
Weimar Republic, 658
Welch, Robert, 765
Weld, Theodore Dwight, 244, 251, 254
Welfare, public, 635–36, 641, 803, 828
Welfare legislation, 512, 515, 516,
    517–18, 548, 584–85, 609; move-
    ment for, 449–50; under L. B. Johnson,
    770, 771–72, 803; under Kennedy,
    767–68; under F. D. Roosevelt, 641,
    648–49; under T. Roosevelt, 524;
    under Truman, 713, 718–19, 721;
    under Wilson, 545
Weller, Lemuel H., 479
Welles, Gideon, 332, 336, 338
Welles, Sumner, 656, 665
Wellington, Duke of, 179
Welty, Eudora, 821, 822
West Indies, 3, 16, 29, 49, 52, 53, 54,
    84
West Side Story, 817
West Virginia, statehood of, 328
Western Union Telegraph Company, 429,
    430
Westinghouse, George, 418, 430

Westmoreland, William C., 774, 776,
    778, 779
Westward movement. *See* Frontier; Immi-
    gration; Manifest Destiny
Wethersfield, Conn., **55**
Weyler, Valeriano, 497, 498
Whately, Thomas, 90
Wheeler, Burton K., 597, 672, 673
Wheeler, Earle, 762
Wheeler, William A., 381
Wheelwright, John, 22
Whig party, 211, 219, 221, 230, 233–34,
    236, 307, 309, 310, 311, 320; and
    American party, 295; and Conscience
    Whigs, 271, 275, 279, 307; and
    demise of, 280, 295; and election of
    1844, 267; and election of *1848,* 275;
    and election of *1852,* 280–81, 295; and
    Wilmot Proviso, 273. *See also* National
    Republican party; Republican party
Whiskey Rebellion, 145–46, 153
Whiskey Ring, 376
White, Andrew D., 447
White, Henry, 566
White, Hugh Lawson, 230
White, John, 10
White, Leonard D., 466
White, Stanford, 458
White, William Allen, 480, 586, 590,
    594, 621, 673
White Citizens' Councils, 744
Whitefield, George, 63, 64, 65
Whitman, Marcus, 265
Whitman, Walt, 287, 459; on American
    genius, 286
Whitney, Eli, 198, 205, 591
Whittier, John Greenleaf, 308
Whyte, William H., Jr., 748
Wide Awakes, 320
Wiener, Norbert, 810
Wigglesworth, Michael, 66
Wilderness, Battle of the, 352
Wilderness Road, **194**
Wiley, Harvey W., 524
Wilkins, Maurice, 825
Wilkins, Roy, 768, 783, 817
Wilkinson, James, 122, 166, 341
Willard, Emma, 248
William II (emperor of Germany), 530,
    552, 565
William III (king of England), 28, 44, 45,
    46, 47
William, Earl of Craven, 34
William of Orange. *See* William III
Williams, Roger, 21, 22
Williams, Tennessee, 823
Williams, William Appleman, 663
Williams v. *Mississippi,* 387
Willkie, Wendell L., 669–70, 671, 672,
    693
Wilmot, David, 273
Wilmot Proviso, 273–75, 276–77, 278
Wilson, Charles E., 741
Wilson, James, 96
Wilson, William L., 484
Wilson, Woodrow, 579, 585, 630, 733,
    758; Administration of, 542–55,
    557–74, 578, 579, 580, 597, 600,
    631; and banking reform, 543–44; early
    career of, 540; and First World War,
    555, 557–74; and foreign policy,
    545–47, 566; and Fourteen Points,

565, 567, 571; as governor, 517, 540; and labor strife, 561–62; and Mexico, 547–49; and neutrality, 549–55; and "New Freedom," 541, 542, 543, 544, 564, 631, 713, 809; and peace treaty, 566–73, 574; as a progressive, 541, 545; and Red scare, 576–79; and tariff, 542–43

Wilson-Gorman Tariff (*1894*), 484, 489

Winthrop, John, 19, 20, 21, 40

Wirt, William, 229, 230

Wisconsin, statehood of, 260, **268**

Witchcraft, 66

Wolcott, Oliver, Jr., 143, 148–49

Wolfe, James, **79**, 80, 83

Woman Suffrage Association, 451

Women's Rights Convention (*1848*), 247

Women's rights movement, 246–48, 450–51, 605, 819–21. *See also* Suffrage

Wood, Leonard, 501, 526, 558, 579

Woodin, William, 631

Woods, Arthur, 616

Woodstock festival, 788

Wool Act (*1699*), 30

Wordsworth, William, 241

Workingmen's parties, 407–08

Works Progress Administration (WPA), 635–36, 641, 646, 680; and state guidebooks, 651

World Antislavery Convention, 246

World Bank. *See* International Bank for Reconstruction and Development

World Council of Churches, 814

World Court. *See* Permanent Court of International Justice

World Disarmament Conference (*1932*), 621

World Health Organization (WHO), 708

World War I. *See* First World War

World War II. *See* Second World War

World's Christian Fundamental Association, 596

Wounded Knee, Battle of, **401,** 403

Wright, Frances, 248

Wright, Henry Clark, 250

Wright, Frank Lloyd, 458

Wright, Richard, 822

Wylie, Philip, 819

Wyoming, statehood of, **406,** 451, 482

XYZ Affair, 150, 151, 153

Yalta Conference (*1945*), 697–700, 709–10, 721, 736

Yamamoto, Isoroku, 691

Yamasee Indians, 73

Yancey, William L., 280, 305, 319, 321, 322

Yazoo Land Companies, 166, 189

Yorktown, Battle of, 112

Youmans, Edward L., 431

Young, Brigham, 266

Young, Owen D., 601

Young, Roy, 604

Young America, 285, 289

Youth International party (Yippies), 788–89

Yugoslavia, 570, 689, 695, 696, 715

Zen Buddhism, 748, 789, 815

Zimmermann, Arthur, 555

Zinberg, Norman, 787

Zūni Indians, 819

B 3
C 4
D 5
E 6
F 7
G 8
H 9
I 0
J 1